1993-94 BASKETBALL ALMANAC

Contributing Writers
Marty Strasen
Matt Marsom
Nick Rousso
Michael Bradley
Mike Sheridan
Pete Palmer
David Korus
Bruce Herman
Tom Owens

Marty Strasen is a freelance sports writer who has covered both pro and college basketball. He is a sports writer for the *Waterloo (Iowa) Courier* and has also written for several major newspapers, including the *Detroit Free Press*.

Matt Marsom is managing editor of *Basketball Weekly*, where he also serves as a writer of both pro and college basketball. Marsom is a contributing writer for *Street & Smith* magazines.

Nick Rousso is the editor of *Hubie Brown's Pro Basketball* and *Lee Corso's College Football*. He was a co-author of *Meet Shaquille O'Neal*.

Michael Bradley is a freelance writer whose work has appeared in *The Sporting News, The Philadelphia Inquirer,* and a variety of national sports publications.

Mike Sheridan is managing editor of both *Basketball Times* and *Eastern Basketball*.

Pete Palmer edited both *Total Baseball* and *The Hidden Game of Baseball* with John Thorn. He was the statistician for the *1993 Baseball Almanac* and *1993 Golf Almanac*. Palmer is a member of the Society for American Baseball Research (SABR).

David Korus is a freelance sports statistician who lives in Massachusetts.

Bruce Herman is a freelance writer who has contributed to *Sports Illustrated, Inside Sports,* and *USA TODAY Baseball Weekly*. He is also the managing editor of the *New York Mets Official Yearbook.*

Tom Owens is the author of *Greatest Baseball Players of All Time, Collecting Sports Autographs,* and the *1993 Official Baseball Card Price Guide*. He is a former editor of *Sports Collectors Digest.*

Statistics in the College Basketball Review section were provided by the National Collegiate Athletic Association.

CONTENTS

**NBA Veterans and
Rookies** 7

NBA Veterans 8
Alaa Abdelnaby 8
Michael Adams................9
Rafael Addison...............10
Mark Aguirre..................11
Danny Ainge...................12
Victor Alexander............13
Kenny Anderson.............14
Nick Anderson...............15
Ron Anderson 16
Willie Anderson 17
Greg Anthony 18
B.J. Armstrong...............19
Vincent Askew...............20
Keith Askins 21
Stacey Augmon...............22
Anthony Avent................23
Thurl Bailey 24
Charles Barkley..............25
Dana Barros 26
Jon Barry......................27
John Battle....................28
Benoit Benjamin 29
Tony Bennett..................30
David Benoit...................31
Rolando Blackman 32
Lance Blanks.................33
Mookie Blaylock 34
Muggsy Bogues..............35
Manute Bol 36
Walter Bond 37
Anthony Bonner 38
Anthony Bowie 39
Sam Bowie.....................40
Terrell Brandon..............41
Frank Brickowski 42
Kevin Brooks 43
Scott Brooks..................44
Chucky Brown 45
Dee Brown 46
Mike Brown 47
Randy Brown..................48
Mark Bryant...................49
Jud Buechler 50

Matt Bullard 51
Willie Burton 52
Michael Cage 53
Elden Campbell..............54
Tony Campbell...............55
Antoine Carr 56
Bill Cartwright 57
Terry Catledge 58
Duane Causwell 59
Cedric Ceballos..............60
Tom Chambers 61
Rex Chapman 62
Maurice Cheeks 63
Pete Chilcutt 64
Doug Christie 65
Derrick Coleman 66
Bimbo Coles 67
Duane Cooper 68
Tyrone Corbin 69
Terry Cummings.............70
Dell Curry 71
Lloyd Daniels.................72
Brad Daugherty..............73
Dale Davis 74
Hubert Davis 75
Terry Davis 76
Johnny Dawkins 77
Todd Day.......................78
Vinny Del Negro 79
Vlade Divac 80
Sherman Douglas 81
Clyde Drexler 82
Kevin Duckworth 83
Chris Dudley..................84
Joe Dumars...................85
Richard Dumas 86
Mark Eaton....................87
Blue Edwards 88
James Edwards..............89
Kevin Edwards 90
Craig Ehlo 91
Mario Elie 92
Sean Elliott 93
Dale Ellis 94
LaPhonso Ellis 95
Pervis Ellison 96
Patrick Ewing 97

Duane Ferrell 98
Danny Ferry 99
Vern Fleming 100
Sleepy Floyd 101
Greg Foster..................102
Rick Fox 103
Kevin Gamble...............104
Chris Gatling 105
Kenny Gattison 106
Matt Geiger..................107
Tate George 108
Kendall Gill 109
Armon Gilliam...............110
Gerald Glass 111
Snoopy Graham............112
Gary Grant...................113
Harvey Grant................114
Horace Grant................115
Jeff Grayer 116
A.C. Green 117
Litterial Green...............118
Sidney Green 119
Tom Gugliotta................120
Tom Hammonds............121
Tim Hardaway 122
Derek Harper................123
Ron Harper...................124
Scott Hastings 125
Hersey Hawkins 126
Steve Henson................127
Carl Herrera 128
Rod Higgins..................129
Tyrone Hill 130
Donald Hodge...............131
Jeff Hornacek 132
Robert Horry.................133
Byron Houston 134
Brian Howard................135
Jay Humphries 136
Mike Iuzzolino...............137
Chris Jackson...............138
Jim Jackson 139
Mark Jackson 140
Keith Jennings..............141
Avery Johnson 142
Buck Johnson...............143
Eddie Johnson 144

4 CONTENTS

Frank Johnson 145
Kevin Johnson...............146
Larry Johnson 147
Michael Jordan 148
Adam Keefe 149
Shawn Kemp................150
Steve Kerr 151
Jerome Kersey 152
Bernhard King 153
Stacey King 154
Greg Kite 155
Joe Kleine 156
Negele Knight...............157
Jon Koncak 158
Larry Krystkowiak 159
Christian Laettner 160
Bill Laimbeer 161
Andrew Lang................162
Jim Les 163
Lafayette Lever 164
Marcus Liberty..............165
Todd Lichti...................166
Brad Lohaus 167
Grant Long 168
Luc Longley 169
Don MacLean 170
Mark Macon 171
Rick Mahorn 172
Dan Majerle.................173
Jeff Malone..................174
Karl Malone.................175
Moses Malone..............176
Danny Manning 177
S. Marciulionis.............178
Anthony Mason 179
Vernon Maxwell............180
Lee Mayberry 181
Travis Mays..................182
Bob McCann 183
George McCloud..........184
Rodney McCray 185
Xavier McDaniel 186
Derrick McKey 187
Nate McMillan 188
Oliver Miller 189
Reggie Miller 190
Terry Mills...................191
Harold Miner................192
Sam Mitchell................193
Chris Morris 194

Alonzo Mourning 195
Chris Mullin 196
Eric Murdock 197
Tracy Murray 198
Jerrod Mustaf 199
Dikembe Mutombo 200
Larry Nance.................201
Johnny Newman 202
Ken Norman 203
Charles Oakley 204
Hakeem Olajuwon 205
Shaquille O'Neal 206
Doug Overton...............207
Billy Owens 208
Robert Pack 209
Robert Parish 210
John Paxson 211
Gary Payton.................212
Anthony Peeler.............213
Will Perdue..................214
Sam Perkins 215
Tim Perry....................216
Chuck Person..............217
Ricky Pierce 218
Ed Pinckney 219
Scottie Pippen.............220
Gary Plummer..............221
Olden Polynice 222
Terry Porter 223
Brent Price 224
Mark Price 225
Kurt Rambis 226
Blair Rasmussen...........227
J.R. Reid.....................228
Jerry Reynolds 229
Glen Rice 230
Pooh Richardson..........231
Mitch Richmond 232
Doc Rivers...................233
Stanley Roberts............234
Alvin Robertson............235
Cliff Robinson..............236
David Robinson.............237
Rumeal Robinson..........238
Dennis Rodman 239
Sean Rooks..................240
Donald Royal...............241
Delaney Rudd 242
John Salley...................243
Mike Sanders 244

Danny Schayes 245
Dwayne Schintzius.......246
Detlef Schrempf 247
Byron Scott..................248
Dennis Scott.................249
Malik Sealy..................250
Rony Seikaly 251
Brian Shaw...................252
Lionel Simmons.............253
Scott Skiles 254
Charles Smith...............255
Chris Smith..................256
Doug Smith..................257
Kenny Smith.................258
LaBradford Smith 259
Larry Smith 260
Steve Smith..................261
Tony Smith 262
Rik Smits.....................263
Elmore Spencer 264
Felton Spencer.............265
Latrell Sprewell.............266
John Starks 267
Larry Stewart 268
Bryant Stith..................269
John Stockton 270
Rod Strickland..............271
Isiah Thomas................272
LaSalle Thompson 273
Otis Thorpe 274
Sedale Threatt..............275
Wayman Tisdale 276
Tom Tolbert..................277
Trent Tucker.................278
Jeff Turner...................279
Kiki Vandeweghe 280
Loy Vaught...................281
Sam Vincent.................282
Darrell Walker...............283
C. Weatherspoon 284
Spud Webb...................285
Doug West 286
Mark West....................287
Randy White.................288
Morlon Wiley.................289
Dominique Wilkins.........290
Gerald Wilkins 291
Brian Williams 292
Buck Williams...............293
Corey Williams 294

CONTENTS   5

Herb Williams 295
John Williams 296
John Williams 297
Kenny Williams...............298
Micheal Williams...........299
Reggie Williams 300
Scott Williams...............301
Walt Williams................302
Kevin Willis...................303
David Wingate 304
Orlando Woolridge 305
James Worthy 306
Danny Young 307

1993 NBA Draft 308

Rookies: 1st-Rounders
.....................................309
Vin Baker......................309
Corie Blount 310
Shawn Bradley..............311
Scott Burrell.................312
Sam Cassell 313
Calbert Cheaney 314
Terry Dehere 315
Acie Earl......................316
Doug Edwards..............317
Greg Graham 318
Geert Hammink 319
Anfernee Hardaway 320
Scott Haskin..................321
Allan Houston...............322
Lindsey Hunter.............323
Bobby Hurley...............324
Ervin Johnson..............325
George Lynch...............326
Malcolm Mackey 327
Jamal Mashburn...........328
Chris Mills....................329
Isaiah Rider 330
James Robinson 331
Rodney Rogers 332
Rex Walters.................333
Chris Webber...............334
Luther Wright...............335

**Rookies: 2nd-
Rounders/Others.........336**
John Best 336
P.J. Brown....................336

Mark Buford..................337
Evers Burns..................337
Spencer Dunkley..........338
Jo Jo English................338
Alphonso Ford..............339
Josh Grant....................339
Lucious Harris 340
Thomas Hill 340
Alex Holcombe 341
Popeye Jones 341
Adonis Jordan 342
Toni Kukoc 342
Gerald Madkins............343
Rich Manning 343
Conrad McRae 344
Darnell Mee..................344
Sherron Mills................345
Gheorghe Muresan 345
Marcelo Nicola 346
Mike Peplowski 346
Richard Petruska..........347
Dino Radja...................347
Anthony Reed 348
Eric Riley......................348
Bryon Russell...............349
Ed Stokes.....................349
Kevin Thompson 350
Nick Van Exel..............350
Leonard White 351
Chris Whitney................351
Byron Wilson 352
Top Non-Drafted Players
.....................................352

NBA Team Overviews
.....................................353
Boston Celtics 354
Miami Heat...................357
New Jersey Nets 360
New York Knicks 363
Orlando Magic..............366
Philadelphia 76ers........369
Washington Bullets 372
Atlanta Hawks...............375
Charlotte Hornets 378
Chicago Bulls 381
Cleveland Cavaliers 384
Detroit Pistons..............387
Indiana Pacers 390
Milwaukee Bucks 393

Dallas Mavericks 396
Denver Nuggets 399
Houston Rockets..........402
Minnesota T'Wolves 405
San Antonio Spurs 408
Utah Jazz 411
Golden State Warriors..414
Los Angeles Clippers ...417
Los Angeles Lakers......420
Phoenix Suns 423
Portland Trail Blazers...426
Sacramento Kings........429
Seattle SuperSonics.....432

**NBA Awards and
Records.......................435**

**NBA Year-by-Year
Results 462**

1993-94 NBA Schedule
.....................................513

Basketball Hall of Fame
.....................................520

100 Top College Stars
.....................................544
Cory Alexander 545
Jerome Allen 545
Derrick Alston 546
Adrian Autry 546
Damon Bailey................547
Anthony Beane..............547
Travis Best 548
Bernard Blunt 548
Melvin Booker 549
Donnie Boyce 549
Jamie Brandon 550
Joey Brown 550
Junior Burrough............551
Randolph Childress......551
Charles Claxton............552
Jevon Crudup...............552
Bill Curley 553
Yinka Dare 553
Tyus Edney 554
David Edwards..............554
Steve Edwards.............555
Howard Eisley 555
Michael Finley..............556

6 CONTENTS

Travis Ford 556
James Forrest 557
Lawrence Funderburke 557
Brian Grant...................558
Rashard Griffith 558
Othella Harrington 559
Alan Henderson 559
Ronnie Henderson 560
Grant Hill.....................560
Juwan Howard 561
Askia Jones..................561
Dana Jones 562
Eddie Jones 562
Arturas Karnishovas.....563
Damon Key 563
Jason Kidd 564
Jimmy King 564
Tom Kleinschmidt..........565
Voshon Lenard..............565
Orlando Lightfoot..........566
Donyell Marshall...........566
Billy McCaffrey 567
Jerry McCullough 567
Aaron McKie.................568
Sam Mitchell.................568
Eric Montross 569
Harry Moore 569
Martice Moore 570
Dwayne Morton 570
Lawrence Moten...........571
Kenyon Murray 571
Lamond Murray 572
Ed O'Bannon 572
Cherokee Parks 573
Wesley Person 573
Derrick Phelps..............574
Eric Piatkowski.............574
Kevin Rankin 575
Brian Reese 575
Bryant Reeves..............576
Khalid Reeves 576
Terrence Rencher.........577
Shawn Respert.............577
Johnny Rhodes 578
Rodrick Rhodes............578
Glenn Robinson 579
Lou Roe.......................579
Carlos Rogers 580
Jalen Rose 580

Clifford Rozier 581
Jervaughn Scales........581
Richard Scott...............582
Orlando Smart..............582
Michael Smith..............583
Stevin Smith 583
Duane Spencer 584
Jerry Stackhouse.........584
Damon Stoudamire 585
Bob Sura 585
Shon Tarver 586
Dedan Thomas.............586
Deon Thomas...............587
Scotty Thurman............587
Tony Tolbert.................588
Kareem Townes............588
David Vaughn...............589
Rasheed Wallace 589
Charlie Ward 590
Kendrick Warren 590
Jeff Webster.................591
Tracy Webster..............591
Donald Williams 592
Monty Williams 592
Corliss Williamson.........593
Dontonio Wingfield.......593
Steve Woodberry 594
Sharone Wright 594

64 Top College Teams
......................................595
Alabama 595
Arizona 596
Arizona State...............597
Arkansas 598
Auburn.........................599
Boston College.............600
Brigham Young 601
California 602
Cincinnati 603
Connecticut 604
DePaul.........................605
Duke............................606
Florida.........................607
Florida State................608
Georgetown.................609
George Washington 610
Georgia........................611
Georgia Tech 612

Illinois 613
Indiana 614
Iowa.............................615
Iowa State 616
Kansas.........................617
Kansas State...............618
Kentucky 619
Louisiana State 620
Louisville 621
Marquette 622
Massachusetts 623
Memphis State.............624
Michigan.......................625
Michigan State 626
Minnesota....................627
Missouri 628
Nebraska......................629
Nevada-Las Vegas.......630
New Orleans 631
North Carolina 632
Ohio State 633
Oklahoma State 634
Old Dominion 635
Pennsylvania................636
Pepperdine..................637
Providence 638
Purdue.........................639
St. John's 640
St. Joseph's.................641
St. Louis 642
Santa Clara 643
Seton Hall....................644
Syracuse 645
Temple 646
Texas...........................647
Texas Tech 648
Toledo..........................649
Tulane..........................650
UCLA...........................651
Vanderbilt 652
Virginia 653
Virg. Commonwealth 654
Wake Forest.................655
West Virginia 656
Wisconsin 657
Xavier...........................658

College Basketball
Review..........................659

NBA Veterans and Rookies

In this section, you'll find scouting reports on 300 NBA veterans and 60 NBA rookies (plus a recap of the 1993 college draft on page 308). When you consider that the NBA will tip off the 1993-94 season with 324 players, this section is sure to include virtually every NBA player—and then some.

Each player's scouting report begins with his vital stats: team, position, height, weight, etc. Next comes a four-part evaluation of the player. "Background" reviews the player's career, starting with college and continuing up through the 1992-93 season. "Strengths" examines his best assets, including things like character and leadership.

"Weaknesses" assesses the player's significant flaws, including things like attitude and off-court behavior. And "analysis" tries to put the player's game into perspective. Is he on the way up or on the way down? How does he fit in with his team's system? What can be expected of him in 1993-94? These are some of the questions that are explored.

For a quick run-down on each player, you'll find a "player summary" box. The box also includes a "fantasy value" figure, which suggests a draft price for any of the fantasy basketball games that have mushroomed throughout the country. The price range is a guide based on $260 for a 15-player roster in a ten-team league. Some players are valued at $0, meaning they are not worth drafting. Finally, the box contains a "card value" figure, which is a suggested buying price for a mint 1993-94 basketball card of that player. The values do not reflect cards from premium sets, such as Fleer Ultra.

The scouting reports of the NBA veterans include their college and NBA statistics. The college stats include games (G), field goal percentage (FGP), free throw percentage (FTP), rebounds per game (RPG), and points per game (PPG). The veterans' NBA stats include the following:

- games (G)
- minutes (MIN)
- field goals made (FGs/FG)
- field goal percentage (FGs/PCT)
- 3-point field goals made (3-PT FGs/FG)
- 3-point field goal percentage (3-PT FGs/PCT)
- free throws made (FTs/FT)
- free throw percentage (FTs/PCT)
- offensive rebounds (Rebounds/OFF)
- total rebounds (Rebounds/TOT)
- assists (AST)
- steals (STL)
- blocked shots (BLK)
- points (PTS)
- points per game (PPG)

The 60 NBA rookies are divided into two categories. The 27 first-round draft picks receive one-page write-ups, while the 27 second-rounders—as well as a half-dozen top nondrafted players—receive half-page write-ups.

ALAA ABDELNABY

Team: Boston Celtics
Position: Forward
Height: 6'10" **Weight:** 240
Birthdate: June 24, 1968

NBA Experience: 3 years
College: Duke
Acquired: Traded from Bucks for draft rights to Jon Barry, 12/92

Background: Abdelnaby, who was born in Egypt and moved to the United States in 1971, led Duke to three Final Fours and established a school record for career field goal percentage (.599). His playing time as a Trail Blazer rookie was limited, but he doubled his scoring average with Portland in 1991-92. He was traded to Milwaukee, then dealt to Boston for rookie guard Jon Barry. Abdelnaby was an early disappointment as a Celtic starter before excelling as a role-player off the bench. As well, he improved his shooting percentage and scoring average last year.

Strengths: Abdelnaby will not lead a team in scoring but is capable of hitting double figures when called upon. He possesses good offensive skills around the basket and will not force bad shots. He is a solid rebounder and gets many of his points off the offensive glass. He has good hands and works hard. Abdelnaby is willing to play defense and do whatever else is asked of him.

Weaknesses: Abdelnaby's perimeter game has a long way to go, especially in the areas of passing and ball-handling. His defensive repertoire does not include blocking shots, despite his size. His confidence has improved, but he is still prone to becoming rattled when off to a slow start.

Analysis: Abdelnaby continues to grow as a player. Thought to be a bust after the trade to Boston, the Celtics found that he could be a very productive player off the bench. This allowed him to take a look at his assignment and apply his intellect rather than trying to do too much, as he did as a starter. His total game is still developing.

PLAYER SUMMARY	
Will	hustle
Can't	distribute
Expect	further improvement
Don't Expect	shot-blocking
Fantasy Value	$1-3
Card Value	5-8¢

COLLEGE STATISTICS

		G	FGP	FTP	RPG	PPG
86-87	DUKE	29	.580	.522	1.7	3.7
87-88	DUKE	34	.496	.698	2.0	4.9
88-89	DUKE	33	.634	.701	3.8	8.9
89-90	DUKE	38	.620	.775	6.6	15.1
Totals		134	.599	.728	3.7	8.5

NBA REGULAR-SEASON STATISTICS

		G	MIN	FG	PCT	FG	PCT	FT	PCT	OFF	TOT	AST	STL	BLK	PTS	PPG
90-91	POR	43	290	55	.474	0	.000	25	.568	27	89	12	4	12	135	3.1
91-92	POR	71	934	178	.493	0	.000	76	.752	81	260	30	25	16	432	6.1
92-93	MIL/BOS	75	1311	245	.518	0	.000	88	.759	126	337	27	25	26	578	7.7
Totals		189	2535	478	.503	0	.000	189	.724	234	686	69	54	54	1145	6.1

MICHAEL ADAMS

Team: Washington Bullets
Position: Guard
Height: 5'10" **Weight:** 175
Birthdate: January 19, 1963
NBA Experience: 8 years

College: Boston College
Acquired: Traded from Nuggets with a 1991 1st-round pick for a 1991 1st-round pick, 6/91

Background: Adams was named second-team All-Big East three straight years at Boston College. The former CBA Rookie of the Year (1986) holds or has held numerous NBA 3-point records. After becoming the NBA's all-time leader in 3-pointers made while playing with Denver, he was dealt to Washington, where he has run the point for two seasons. He played in the 1992 All-Star Game. The Bullets had waived him twice and traded him once previously.

Strengths: Adams has two primary weapons: his quickness and his 3-point shooting. He is, quite literally, a threat to score from anywhere on the court. He can penetrate almost at will and still races the ball to the offensive end. He is nearly automatic from the free throw line.

Weaknesses: Although he shoots 3-pointers like there's no tomorrow, he converts less than one-third of them. His field goal percentage is traditionally brutal, although last season was a mild improvement. He should be more of a defensive thief for as quick as he is. Naturally, he's a prime post-up target because of his stature.

Analysis: Adams has made some real strides in Washington. He no longer shoots less than 40 percent from the field, although this gunner will never be a high percentage man. He also shows greater control more often, which is both a positive and a negative. He has shown an ability to adjust for teammates.

PLAYER SUMMARY

Will...let shots fly
Can't ....shoot 50 percent
Expect...........playmaking, excitement
Don't Expect.....................a slow pace
Fantasy Value............................$12-15
Card Value.....................................5-10¢

COLLEGE STATISTICS

		G	FGP	FTP	APG	PPG
81-82	BC	26	.495	.590	1.5	5.3
82-83	BC	32	.481	.809	5.3	16.2
83-84	BC	30	.455	.756	3.5	17.3
84-85	BC	31	.467	.748	3.2	15.3
Totals		119	.470	.750	3.5	13.9

NBA REGULAR-SEASON STATISTICS

				FGs		3-PT FGs		FTs		Rebounds						
		G	MIN	FG	PCT	FG	PCT	FT	PCT	OFF	TOT	AST	STL	BLK	PTS	PPG
85-86	SAC	18	139	16	.364	0	.000	8	.667	2	6	22	9	1	40	2.2
86-87	WAS	63	1303	160	.407	28	.275	105	.847	38	123	244	85	6	453	7.2
87-88	DEN	82	2778	416	.449	139	.367	166	.834	40	223	503	168	16	1137	13.9
88-89	DEN	77	2787	468	.433	166	.356	322	.819	71	283	490	166	11	1424	18.5
89-90	DEN	79	2690	398	.402	158	.366	267	.850	49	225	495	121	3	1221	15.5
90-91	DEN	66	2346	560	.394	167	.296	465	.879	58	256	693	147	6	1752	26.5
91-92	WAS	78	2795	485	.393	125	.324	313	.869	58	310	594	145	9	1408	18.1
92-93	WAS	70	2499	365	.393	68	.321	237	.856	52	240	526	100	4	1035	14.8
Totals		533	17337	2868	.414	851	.335	1883	.853	368	1666	3567	941	56	8470	15.9

RAFAEL ADDISON

Team: New Jersey Nets
Position: Forward/Guard
Height: 6'7" **Weight:** 245
Birthdate: July 22, 1964

NBA Experience: 3 years
College: Syracuse
Acquired: Signed as a free agent, 9/91

Background: Addison was a first-team All-Big East selection as a junior at Syracuse, where his career scoring average was nearly 15 PPG. He switched from forward to guard as a senior and did not enjoy as solid a year, but he was selected 39th overall by Phoenix in 1986. He played 62 games for the Suns in 1986-87 before signing to play in Italy. He rejoined the NBA with New Jersey for the 1991-92 season and has been a two-year reserve. Last year was the first in which he has averaged more than six points per game.

Strengths: Addison is an impressive athlete. He can jump out of the gym and is tough to keep off the boards. He can slash, run the floor well, and finish on the break. He can be a disruptive defender when he sets his mind (and his athletic ability) to it, as coach Chuck Daly has discovered. Addison is a very good free throw shooter.

Weaknesses: Addison's struggles are largely position-related. Physically, he is in between a big guard and a small forward. He does not possess the accurate jump shot, range, or confidence to be an offensive standout at either position. Quicker guards pose big match-up problems, as do strong forwards. His assists, steals, and blocks numbers are low.

Analysis: A Jersey City native, Addison is playing in the right town. If only he could be playing in the right position. Problem is, no one seems to know what his position is. It's hard to figure his poor shooting in light of his free throw accuracy, other than lack of confidence. Addison will probably play more this year due to the tragic loss of Drazen Petrovic.

PLAYER SUMMARY	
Will	out-jump his man
Can't	provide steady offense
Expect	athletic finishes
Don't Expect	a go-to guy
Fantasy Value	$0
Card Value	5-8¢

COLLEGE STATISTICS

		G	FGP	FTP	RPG	PPG
82-83	SYR	31	.521	.651	3.2	8.4
83-84	SYR	32	.559	.836	6.0	17.7
84-85	SYR	31	.520	.727	5.8	18.4
85-86	SYR	32	.532	.793	5.6	15.0
Totals		126	.534	.763	5.2	14.9

NBA REGULAR-SEASON STATISTICS

				FGs		3-PT FGs		FTs		Rebounds						
		G	MIN	FG	PCT	FG	PCT	FT	PCT	OFF	TOT	AST	STL	BLK	PTS	PPG
86-87	PHO	62	711	146	.441	16	.320	51	.797	41	106	45	27	7	359	5.8
91-92	NJ	76	1175	187	.433	14	.286	56	.737	65	165	68	28	28	444	5.8
92-93	NJ	68	1164	182	.443	7	.206	57	.814	45	132	53	23	11	428	6.3
Totals		206	3050	515	.439	37	.278	164	.781	151	403	166	78	46	1231	6.0

MARK AGUIRRE

Team: Detroit Pistons
Position: Forward
Height: 6'6" **Weight:** 232
Birthdate: December 10, 1959
NBA Experience: 12 years

College: DePaul
Acquired: Traded from Mavericks for Adrian Dantley and a 1991 1st-round pick, 2/89

Background: Aguirre is credited with putting DePaul on the big-time NCAA basketball map. He made the 1980 U.S. Olympic team and, in 1981, was the *Sporting News'* college Player of the Year. Aguirre was the No. 1 pick in the 1981 draft and was a mainstay with the Mavericks for almost eight years. He joined the Pistons in 1989 and helped them win back-to-back championships. A strained arch sidelined him for several games late last season.

Strengths: Aguirre is a scorer, period. When he's hot, he's instant offense. He can hit 3-pointers and post up equally well. While doing the latter, he uses his backside as well as anyone in the league.

Weaknesses: Team play has never been his forte. He has always rubbed people the wrong way with his complaining. If it's not about playing time, it's about the offensive system, the game plan, etc. He doesn't play much defense.

Analysis: Despite all the talk about wanting to be elsewhere, Aguirre has stuck around with the post-championship Pistons. He sacrificed his numbers for two championship rings but would probably rather finish his career as a big-time scorer. That, he can still do.

PLAYER SUMMARY	
Will	back in and score
Can't	play defense
Expect	instant offense
Don't Expect	smiles
Fantasy Value	$1
Card Value	5-10¢

COLLEGE STATISTICS

		G	FGP	FTP	RPG	PPG
78-79	DeP	32	.520	.765	7.6	24.0
79-80	DeP	28	.540	.766	7.6	26.8
80-81	DeP	29	.582	.774	8.6	23.0
Totals		89	.546	.768	7.9	24.5

NBA REGULAR-SEASON STATISTICS

		G	MIN	FGs FG	FGs PCT	3-PT FGs FG	3-PT FGs PCT	FTs FT	FTs PCT	Rebounds OFF	Rebounds TOT	AST	STL	BLK	PTS	PPG
81-82	DAL	51	1468	381	.465	25	.352	168	.680	89	249	164	37	22	955	18.7
82-83	DAL	81	2784	767	.483	16	.211	429	.728	191	508	332	80	26	1979	24.4
83-84	DAL	79	2900	925	.524	15	.268	465	.749	161	469	358	80	22	2330	29.5
84-85	DAL	80	2699	794	.506	27	.318	440	.759	188	477	249	60	24	2055	25.7
85-86	DAL	74	2501	668	.503	16	.286	318	.705	177	445	339	62	14	1670	22.6
86-87	DAL	80	2663	787	.495	53	.353	429	.770	181	427	254	84	30	2056	25.7
87-88	DAL	77	2610	746	.475	52	.302	388	.770	182	434	278	70	57	1932	25.1
88-89	DAL/DET	80	2597	586	.461	51	.293	288	.733	146	386	278	45	36	1511	18.9
89-90	DET	78	2005	438	.480	31	.333	192	.756	117	305	145	34	19	1099	14.1
90-91	DET	78	2006	420	.462	24	.308	240	.757	134	374	139	47	20	1104	14.2
91-92	DET	75	1582	339	.431	15	.211	158	.687	67	236	126	51	11	851	11.3
92-93	DET	51	1056	187	.443	30	.361	99	.767	43	152	105	16	7	503	9.9
Totals		884	26871	7036	.485	355	.305	3614	.742	1676	4462	2767	666	288	18045	20.4

DANNY AINGE

Team: Phoenix Suns
Position: Guard
Height: 6'5" **Weight:** 185
Birthdate: March 17, 1959

NBA Experience: 12 years
College: Brigham Young
Acquired: Signed as a free agent, 7/92

Background: Ainge was a multi-sport star at Brigham Young and played two years of professional baseball with the Toronto Blue Jays, primarily as an infielder. He batted .220. He has enjoyed much greater success in the NBA, where he was an All-Star in 1988 and won two championship rings with the Boston Celtics. His highest scoring days came in Sacramento and he played a prominent reserve role with Portland. He signed with Phoenix before last season and helped the Suns become the league's hottest team.

Strengths: Ainge is one of the most accurate 3-point shooters in the league. He is also a fierce competitor with championship experience and tremendous leadership skills. When games are up for grabs, Ainge can win them with his shooting and know-how.

Weaknesses: Ainge is not a first-rate defender and he's not getting any quicker—though he is feisty. On offense, he is not much of a creator.

Analysis: Once a superbrat, Ainge has become a steadying influence. Much was said about the presence of Charles Barkley in Phoenix, but Ainge has had almost as much to do with the team's rise. He knows what it takes to win and gets it done.

PLAYER SUMMARY

Will	knock down treys
Can't	out-quick defenders
Expect	poise, leadership
Don't Expect	shyness
Fantasy Value	$2-4
Card Value	5-10¢

COLLEGE STATISTICS

		G	FGP	FTP	RPG	PPG
77-78	BYU	30	.514	.864	5.8	21.1
78-79	BYU	27	.548	.768	3.8	18.4
79-80	BYU	29	.533	.782	3.9	19.1
80-81	BYU	32	.518	.824	4.8	24.4
Totals		118	.526	.816	4.6	20.9

NBA REGULAR-SEASON STATISTICS

		G	MIN	FGs FG	FGs PCT	3-PT FGs FG	3-PT FGs PCT	FTs FT	FTs PCT	Rebounds OFF	Rebounds TOT	AST	STL	BLK	PTS	PPG
81-82	BOS	53	564	79	.357	5	.294	56	.862	25	56	87	37	3	219	4.1
82-83	BOS	80	2048	357	.496	5	.172	72	.742	83	214	251	109	6	791	9.9
83-84	BOS	71	1154	166	.460	6	.273	46	.821	29	116	162	41	4	384	5.4
84-85	BOS	75	2564	419	.529	15	.268	118	.868	76	268	399	122	6	971	12.9
85-86	BOS	80	2407	353	.504	26	.356	123	.904	47	235	405	94	7	855	10.7
86-87	BOS	71	2499	410	.486	85	.443	148	.897	49	242	400	101	14	1053	14.8
87-88	BOS	81	3018	482	.491	148	.415	158	.878	59	249	503	115	17	1270	15.7
88-89	BOS/SAC	73	2377	480	.457	116	.380	205	.854	71	255	402	93	8	1281	17.5
89-90	SAC	75	2727	506	.438	108	.374	222	.831	69	326	453	113	18	1342	17.9
90-91	POR	80	1710	337	.472	102	.406	114	.826	45	205	285	63	13	890	11.1
91-92	POR	81	1595	299	.442	78	.339	108	.824	40	148	202	73	13	784	9.7
92-93	PHO	80	2163	337	.462	150	.403	123	.848	49	214	260	69	8	947	11.8
Totals		900	24826	4225	.472	844	.385	1493	.850	642	2528	3809	1030	117	10787	12.0

VICTOR ALEXANDER

Team: Golden State Warriors
Position: Center/Forward
Height: 6'9" **Weight:** 265
Birthdate: August 31, 1969

NBA Experience: 2 years
College: Iowa St.
Acquired: 1st-round pick in 1991 draft (17th overall)

Background: Alexander played sparingly his freshman season at Iowa State. The Cyclones listed him at 265 pounds, but he often played at closer to 300. "Pasta" was a laughingstock as a freshman but exploded as a sophomore, finishing third in the Big Eight in scoring and rebounding. He had an outstanding senior season, was drafted in the first round, and has played a prominent role in his first two seasons with Golden State. Alexander's overall play has been better than most people expected, and most of his numbers improved last season when the Warriors suffered a rash of injuries.

Strengths: Alexander is a highly skilled offensive player. He has surprising mobility, good post-up skills, a soft shooting touch, and tremendous hands. He knows what to do with the ball near the basket and can amaze people with some of the shots he'll pull off in traffic. He even drills 3-pointers when left open.

Weaknesses: Defense has never been a high priority with Alexander, whose weight can also still be a problem. Commitment comes into play in both areas. He's also inconsistent. He needs to recognize double-teams earlier and find open men. He too often relies on offensive finesse rather than power. He's a below-average free throw shooter.

Analysis: Trim the fat jokes, especially if Alexander keeps in some kind of shape during the off-season. He did a better job of controlling his weight in his second pro season and became the Warriors' best inside scorer. All the skills are there. Alexander is a very polished offensive player—maybe too polished in some cases—who will become more of a force when he learns to use his body to his advantage.

PLAYER SUMMARY	
Will	get his shots inside
Can't	dominate on defense
Expect	polished skills
Don't Expect	a power game
Fantasy Value	$4-6
Card Value	8-12¢

COLLEGE STATISTICS

		G	FGP	FTP	RPG	PPG
87-88	ISU	23	.600	.500	1.4	1.7
88-89	ISU	29	.583	.651	8.8	19.9
89-90	ISU	28	.585	.578	8.7	19.7
90-91	ISU	31	.659	.677	9.0	23.4
Totals		111	.538	.635	7.3	17.0

NBA REGULAR-SEASON STATISTICS

			FGs		3-PT FGs		FTs		Rebounds						
	G	MIN	FG	PCT	FG	PCT	FT	PCT	OFF	TOT	AST	STL	BLK	PTS	PPG
91-92 GS	80	1350	243	.529	0	.000	103	.691	106	336	32	45	62	589	7.4
92-93 GS	72	1753	344	.516	10	.455	111	.685	132	420	93	34	53	809	11.2
Totals	152	3103	587	.521	10	.435	214	.688	238	756	125	79	115	1398	9.2

KENNY ANDERSON

Team: New Jersey Nets
Position: Guard
Height: 6'1" **Weight:** 170
Birthdate: October 9, 1970

NBA Experience: 2 years
College: Georgia Tech
Acquired: 1st-round pick in 1991 draft
(2nd overall)

Background: A legend at New York City's Archbishop Malloy High, Anderson was an instant hit at Georgia Tech. He led the ACC in assists as a freshman. When teammates Dennis Scott and Brian Oliver left for the NBA, Anderson was forced to carry Tech on his back. He appeared very tired by the end of his sophomore year, after which he turned pro. A contract holdout and a feud with then-coach Bill Fitch made for a disappointing rookie year. However, he thrived under Chuck Daly in his second season before a flagrant foul by John Starks in late February broke his left wrist and sidelined him for the rest of the year. He finished ninth in the league in APG.

Strengths: Anderson is a classic point guard with a scorer's mentality. He is a terrific ball-handler, passer, and penetrator with a special ability to see the floor. He can create plays and finish them and has decent range with his awkward-looking jumper—though not quite to the 3-point arc. Defensively, he relies on quick hands and superior anticipation. He has become a team leader.

Weaknesses: Anderson can play out of control at times and is still too scrawny to bang with the league's better post-up guards. He is not a consistent perimeter shooter, which begs defenders to sag.

Analysis: The 1992-93 season was Anderson's coming-out party. That is, until Starks took him out with a hard foul as Anderson was driving for a lay-up. The former prep and college All-American proved to be one of the most gifted young point guards in the pro game. He put to rest his rookie-year criticisms with much-improved leadership ability after being told to run the show. He is sure to do just that for years to come.

PLAYER SUMMARY	
Will	create scoring chances
Can't	post up
Expect	dazzling abilities
Don't Expect	more let-downs
Fantasy Value	$15-18
Card Value	20-35¢

COLLEGE STATISTICS

		G	FGP	FTP	APG	PPG
89-90	GT	35	.515	.733	5.3	20.6
90-91	GT	30	.437	.829	5.6	25.9
Totals		65	.473	.787	5.4	23.0

NBA REGULAR-SEASON STATISTICS

				FGs		3-PT FGs		FTs		Rebounds						
		G	MIN	FG	PCT	FG	PCT	FT	PCT	OFF	TOT	AST	STL	BLK	PTS	PPG
91-92	NJ	64	1086	187	.390	3	.231	73	.745	38	127	203	67	9	450	7.0
92-93	NJ	55	2010	370	.435	7	.280	180	.776	51	226	449	96	11	927	16.9
Totals		119	3096	557	.419	10	.263	253	.767	89	353	652	163	20	1377	11.6

NICK ANDERSON

Team: Orlando Magic
Position: Forward/Guard
Height: 6'6" **Weight:** 205
Birthdate: January 20, 1968

NBA Experience: 4 years
College: Illinois
Acquired: 1st-round pick in 1989 draft
(11th overall)

Background: Anderson was a starter on the "Flying Illini" Final Four team of 1988-89, and he was a unanimous All-Big Ten selection that year. In his rookie season with Orlando, he played in 81 games and reached double figures in scoring. He finished fourth on the club in that department in 1990-91 and became their top scorer in 1991-92, then yielded that role only to rookie sensation Shaquille O'Neal last season.

Strengths: Anderson can put the ball in the basket. Though not an exceptional shooter, he is able to get to the hoop with his tremendous quickness and leaping ability. At his offensive best when aggressive, he's strong enough to attack the hoop through traffic and draw fouls. As well, he works diligently on his game and has become a better passer, free throw shooter, 3-point shooter, and team player.

Weaknesses: Though shorter than the 6'6" at which he is listed, Anderson tends to play more like a small forward than a two guard at times. His most significant weakness is at the defensive end. His numbers declined in the middle of last season, when he went through contract haggles.

Analysis: Anderson is quickly becoming a standout player in the NBA. He became a big-time scorer two years ago, but last season improved to a level at which his overall abilities were also worthy of rave reviews. He honed virtually every aspect of his game—even defense, on occasion—and grew much more consistent in all phases. He can carry a team if he has to.

PLAYER SUMMARY	
Will	get to the hoop
Can't	overshadow Shaq
Expect	a future standout
Don't Expect	great defense
Fantasy Value	$27-30
Card Value	8-12¢

COLLEGE STATISTICS

		G	FGP	FTP	RPG	PPG
87-88	ILL	33	.572	.642	6.6	15.9
88-89	ILL	36	.538	.669	7.9	18.0
Totals		69	.553	.657	7.3	17.0

NBA REGULAR-SEASON STATISTICS

		G	MIN	FGs FG	FGs PCT	3-PT FGs FG	3-PT FGs PCT	FTs FT	FTs PCT	Rebounds OFF	Rebounds TOT	AST	STL	BLK	PTS	PPG
89-90	ORL	81	1785	372	.494	1	.059	186	.705	107	316	124	69	34	931	11.5
90-91	ORL	70	1971	400	.467	17	.293	173	.668	92	386	106	74	44	990	14.1
91-92	ORL	60	2203	482	.463	30	.353	202	.667	98	384	163	97	33	1196	19.9
92-93	ORL	79	2920	594	.449	88	.353	298	.741	122	477	265	128	56	1574	19.9
Totals		290	8879	1848	.465	136	.333	859	.700	419	1563	658	368	167	4691	16.2

RON ANDERSON

Team: Philadelphia 76ers
Position: Forward
Height: 6'7" **Weight:** 215
Birthdate: October 15, 1958
NBA Experience: 9 years

College: Santa Barbara City;
Fresno St.
Acquired: Traded from Pacers for
draft rights to Everette Stephens,
10/88

Background: Anderson did not play high school ball but was discovered on a playground. He was a supermarket stock manager at the time and was persuaded to play junior college ball. He advanced to Fresno State, where he led his team in scoring both years. He was the 76ers' top bench scorer over the last five years, but he was allowed to leave after last season.

Strengths: Anderson has made a living on his smooth jump shot. He moves well without the ball and can bury jumpers—even from 3-point range. He is also a solid free throw shooter and stays in great physical shape. He scores in spurts.

Weaknesses: Anderson remains a one-dimensional player. He shoots jump shots, period. He never met a shot he didn't like. When they're not falling, which has become more frequent, he belongs on the bench because he does little else to help his team. He's not a factor on the boards, and defense has never been his strong suit.

Analysis: Anderson remains a productive scorer off the bench but his reliability has declined. His shooting percentage in 1992-93 was his worst ever and, although the Sixers needed to pick up the scoring slack without Charles Barkley, he failed to reach double figures for the first time in five seasons.

PLAYER SUMMARY	
Will	take his shots
Can't	muscle inside
Expect	scoring binges
Don't Expect	rebounds
Fantasy Value	$0
Card Value	5-10¢

COLLEGE STATISTICS

		G	FGP	FTP	RPG	PPG
80-81	SBC	33	.502	.747	9.9	11.8
81-82	SBC	32	.652	.786	10.6	20.3
82-83	FSU	35	.549	.813	5.8	16.3
83-84	FSU	33	.570	.788	6.1	17.6
Totals		133	.573	.788	8.1	16.5

NBA REGULAR-SEASON STATISTICS

		G	MIN	FGs FG	FGs PCT	3-PT FGs FG	3-PT FGs PCT	FTs FT	FTs PCT	Rebounds OFF	Rebounds TOT	AST	STL	BLK	PTS	PPG
84-85	CLE	36	520	84	.431	1	.500	41	.820	39	88	34	9	7	210	5.8
85-86	CLE/IND	77	1676	310	.494	2	.222	85	.669	130	274	144	56	6	707	9.2
86-87	IND	63	721	139	.473	0	.000	85	.787	73	151	54	31	3	363	5.8
87-88	IND	74	1097	217	.498	0	.000	108	.766	89	216	78	41	6	542	7.3
88-89	PHI	82	2618	566	.491	2	.182	196	.856	167	406	139	71	23	1330	16.2
89-90	PHI	78	2089	379	.451	3	.143	165	.838	81	295	143	72	13	926	11.9
90-91	PHI	82	2340	512	.485	9	.209	165	.833	103	367	115	65	13	1198	14.6
91-92	PHI	82	2432	469	.465	42	.331	143	.877	96	278	135	86	11	1123	13.7
92-93	PHI	69	1263	225	.414	39	.325	72	.809	62	184	93	31	5	561	8.1
Totals		643	14756	2901	.471	98	.288	1060	.814	840	2259	935	462	87	6960	10.8

WILLIE ANDERSON

Team: San Antonio Spurs
Position: Guard/Forward
Height: 6'8" **Weight:** 200
Birthdate: January 8, 1967

NBA Experience: 5 years
College: Georgia
Acquired: 1st-round pick in 1988 draft
(10th overall)

Background: During his college days at Georgia, Anderson finished eighth on the all-time scoring list. He also found time to make a name for himself on the international level. He competed on the United States Olympic team in 1988 and played in the 1987 Pan-Am Games. After averaging 18.6 PPG as a rookie with San Antonio, his scoring average has declined in each of his four subsequent years. He suffered a stress fracture in his leg late in 1991-92 and missed most of 1992-93 after two surgeries.

Strengths: When healthy, Anderson is still one of the more versatile players around. He plays both the two and three spots. He can penetrate and is a good passer. Though lean in build, he is not afraid to challenge with drives to the hoop. He was once compared to former Spurs scoring great George Gervin, although that was years ago.

Weaknesses: Injuries have taken the punch out of Anderson, who was not an especially gifted jump-shooter in the first place. His scoring average has dropped every year, and his field goal percentage has also taken a plunge. His confidence seemed to be on the decline even before his injury problems began.

Analysis: The Spurs were happy to see Anderson back in the lineup late last season and he showed flashes of returning to his old self. However, he still has a lot to prove. A player who relies on his athletic skills, Anderson at anything less than 100 percent could quickly become a liability. If he can regain his health and subsequently his confidence, he could again become a big-time player.

PLAYER SUMMARY	
Will	play two positions
Can't	shoot consistently
Expect	athletic drives
Don't Expect	confidence of old
Fantasy Value	$3-5
Card Value	5-10¢

COLLEGE STATISTICS

		G	FGP	FTP	RPG	PPG
84-85	GA	13	.487	.625	1.5	3.3
85-86	GA	29	.503	.787	3.4	8.5
86-87	GA	30	.500	.794	4.1	15.9
87-88	GA	35	.500	.784	5.1	16.7
Totals		107	.500	.784	3.9	12.6

NBA REGULAR-SEASON STATISTICS

				FGs		3-PT FGs		FTs		Rebounds						
		G	MIN	FG	PCT	FG	PCT	FT	PCT	OFF	TOT	AST	STL	BLK	PTS	PPG
88-89	SA	81	2738	640	.498	4	.190	224	.775	152	417	372	150	62	1508	18.6
89-90	SA	82	2788	532	.492	7	.269	217	.748	115	372	364	111	58	1288	15.7
90-91	SA	75	2592	453	.457	7	.200	170	.798	68	351	358	79	46	1083	14.4
91-92	SA	57	1889	312	.455	13	.232	107	.775	62	300	302	54	51	744	13.1
92-93	SA	38	560	80	.430	1	.125	22	.786	7	57	79	14	6	183	4.8
Totals		333	10567	2017	.477	32	.219	740	.772	404	1497	1475	408	223	4806	14.4

GREG ANTHONY

Team: New York Knicks
Position: Guard
Height: 6'2" **Weight:** 185
Birthdate: November 15, 1967

NBA Experience: 2 years
College: Portland; Nevada-Las Vegas
Acquired: 1st-round pick in 1991 draft
(12th overall)

Background: Anthony spent his first college season at Portland, where he played shooting guard. Jerry Tarkanian moved him to point guard at UNLV, where Anthony eventually became one of the nation's best lead guards. He directed the Rebels to the national title in 1990 and to the Final Four in 1991. He showed glimpses of great play as a rookie with the Knicks but also made his share of mistakes. He asked for a trade early last year but rescinded the statement after becoming a key contributor. He was a lead figure in a controversial fight in Phoenix in March.

Strengths: Some may not appreciate his demeanor, but there is no arguing the fact that Anthony is a take-charge type. He loves to compete and is extremely confident, especially in his ball-handling. He is adept at the running game and can thread the needle with his passing. His decision-making has improved.

Weaknesses: Anthony isn't a good outside shooter—especially from 3-point range. In fact, it's a safe bet he'll be left wide open in favor of double-teams elsewhere. He tends to gamble too much on defense, a habit picked up during his college days, and he's an easy post-up victim for bigger guards. He is inexperienced and tends to be erratic.

Analysis: Anthony improved in several important areas as a second-year pro, but he has not yet displayed the ability to be a halfcourt scorer in the NBA. His control with the ball has improved exponentially. His worst decision was leaving the bench in street clothes to join a brawl with the Suns, an act that drew him a hefty fine and a five-game suspension.

PLAYER SUMMARY	
Will	challenge his man
Can't	shoot straight
Expect	enthusiasm
Don't Expect	consistency
Fantasy Value	$2-4
Card Value	7-12¢

COLLEGE STATISTICS

		G	FGP	FTP	APG	PPG
86-87	PORT	28	.398	.694	4.0	15.3
88-89	UNLV	36	.443	.699	6.6	12.9
89-90	UNLV	39	.457	.682	7.4	11.2
90-91	UNLV	35	.456	.775	8.9	11.6
Totals		138	.437	.707	6.9	12.6

NBA REGULAR-SEASON STATISTICS

				FGs		3-PT FGs		FTs		Rebounds						
		G	MIN	FG	PCT	FG	PCT	FT	PCT	OFF	TOT	AST	STL	BLK	PTS	PPG
91-92	NY	82	1510	161	.370	8	.145	117	.741	33	136	314	59	9	447	5.5
92-93	NY	70	1699	174	.415	4	.133	107	.673	42	170	398	113	12	459	6.6
Totals		152	3209	335	.392	12	.141	224	.707	75	306	712	172	21	906	6.0

B.J. ARMSTRONG

Team: Chicago Bulls
Position: Guard
Height: 6'2" **Weight:** 185
Birthdate: September 9, 1967

NBA Experience: 4 years
College: Iowa
Acquired: 1st-round pick in 1989 draft
(18th overall)

Background: After becoming Iowa's all-time leader in assists, Armstrong was plucked by the Bulls in the 1989 draft. Though he had the look of a 15-year-old, he played alongside Michael Jordan in his rookie year. He was Chicago's top bench player during the team's 1991 and 1992 NBA championship seasons and started regularly during the 1992-93 campaign. B.J. enjoyed his best pro year in 1992-93, leading the NBA in 3-point shooting.

Strengths: Armstrong has made himself one of the most dangerous, confident, and underrated jump-shooters in the game. Leave him open and he'll kill you, from both inside and behind the 3-point arc. He possesses the quickness to trigger Chicago's running game and defend quick point guards. He's bright, works hard, and does what is asked of him. When the Bulls needed scoring off the bench, he willingly relinquished his newfound starting role. He later won it back. He's also a steady free throw shooter.

Weaknesses: Armstrong's continued development leaves less and less to lump into this category. He will play out of control on occasion, although those times are becoming less frequent. His passing skills are perhaps not of the caliber of other point guards. He was third on his team in assists last year.

Analysis: Armstrong finally appears to be Chicago's starting point guard. He was the team's best point guard all last season, returning to the bench only because the Bulls needed his scoring and quickness with the second unit. He is supremely confident with his jump shot, and for good reason. Few are more reliable from outside. He has also displayed a willingness to attack the hoop.

PLAYER SUMMARY

Will.....................knock down jumpers
Can't............outshine Jordan, Pippen
Expect.....................many more starts
Don't Expect.....................selfishness
Fantasy Value...............................$7-9
Card Value.....................................8-15¢

COLLEGE STATISTICS

		G	FGP	FTP	APG	PPG
85-86	IOWA	29	.485	.905	1.4	2.9
86-87	IOWA	35	.519	.794	4.2	12.4
87-88	IOWA	34	.482	.849	4.6	17.4
88-89	IOWA	32	.484	.833	5.4	18.6
Totals		130	.492	.831	4.0	13.1

NBA REGULAR-SEASON STATISTICS

			FGs		3-PT FGs		FTs		Rebounds						
		G	MIN	FG	PCT	FG	PCT	FT	PCT	OFF	TOT	AST	STL	BLK	PTS	PPG
89-90	CHI	81	1291	190	.485	3	.500	69	.885	19	102	199	46	6	452	5.6
90-91	CHI	82	1731	304	.481	15	.500	97	.874	25	149	301	70	4	720	8.8
91-92	CHI	82	1875	335	.481	35	.402	104	.806	19	145	266	46	5	809	9.9
92-93	CHI	82	2492	408	.499	63	.453	130	.861	27	149	330	66	6	1009	12.3
Totals		327	7389	1237	.487	116	.443	400	.853	90	545	1096	228	21	2990	9.1

VINCENT ASKEW

Team: Seattle SuperSonics
Position: Guard
Height: 6'6" **Weight:** 226
Birthdate: February 28, 1966

NBA Experience: 4 years
College: Memphis St.
Acquired: Traded from Kings for a
1993 2nd-round pick, 11/92

Background: After a three-year career at Memphis State, Askew entered the NBA draft early and found the going rough. He was selected 39th overall by Philadelphia in 1987 but was waived after 14 games. He played in Italy and in the World Basketball League and was twice named MVP of the Continental Basketball Association, where he set the single-season scoring record in 1989-90 (26.5 PPG). Signed by Golden State in March 1991, Askew became a valuable reserve. He latched on with Seattle in November of 1992 and was used as a reserve there as well.

Strengths: Askew is a survivor who has paid his dues. He does not specialize in anything spectacular, but he'll give you quality minutes and shoot 50 percent. He has more than enough size to bang with big guards.

Weaknesses: His journeys through four pro leagues also indicate that his game is not suited for every team. Askew is not a great shooter and has yet to prove he can score bushels of points in the NBA. Like many who get stranded at the CBA level, Askew has the style of a small forward and the size of a big guard. His range is limited.

Analysis: It took him a while to find a place in the NBA, but Askew can play at that level. He saw more minutes with the Warriors two years ago than first-rounder Vic Alexander, and he averaged double-figure minutes with a Seattle team that became a Western Conference contender. Although he will never be a big-time scorer in the NBA, as he was in the "minor" leagues, Askew will stick around because of his toughness.

PLAYER SUMMARY	
Will	give you defense
Can't	eat up NBA defenders
Expect	reserve minutes
Don't Expect	big numbers
Fantasy Value	$1-3
Card Value	5-8¢

COLLEGE STATISTICS

		G	FGP	FTP	RPG	PPG
84-85	MSU	35	.511	.634	3.3	8.3
85-86	MSU	34	.490	.814	6.7	10.9
86-87	MSU	34	.483	.787	5.0	15.1
Totals		103	.492	.751	5.0	11.4

NBA REGULAR-SEASON STATISTICS

				FGs		3-PT FGs		FTs		Rebounds						
		G	MIN	FG	PCT	FG	PCT	FT	PCT	OFF	TOT	AST	STL	BLK	PTS	PPG
87-88	PHI	14	234	22	.297	0	.000	8	.727	6	22	33	10	6	52	3.7
90-91	GS	7	85	12	.480	0	.000	9	.818	7	11	13	2	0	33	4.7
91-92	GS	80	1496	193	.509	1	.100	111	.694	89	233	188	47	23	498	6.2
92-93	SAC/SEA	73	1129	152	.492	2	.333	105	.705	62	161	122	40	19	411	5.6
Totals		174	2944	379	.482	3	.188	233	.704	164	427	356	99	48	994	5.7

KEITH ASKINS

Team: Miami Heat
Position: Guard/Forward
Height: 6'8" **Weight:** 216
Birthdate: December 15, 1967

NBA Experience: 3 years
College: Alabama
Acquired: Signed as a free agent, 9/90

Background: Askins was a top player for coach Wimp Sanderson in his home state of Alabama, but he did not draw enough acclaim during his college career to get much of a look on draft day. Miami signed him as a free agent in the 1990 preseason. A stress fracture to his ankle kept him out for the first month of 1990-91 and he returned to play sparingly. He saw more action with the Heat in each of the last two seasons but averaged less than 4.0 PPG each year, as he was relegated to spot duty.

Strengths: One aspect of his game stands out above all others—his hard work. Askins knows it's his best chance to stay in the league. He'll play defense, set picks, crash the boards, and fill in wherever there's time to be found. He wants to get better and he's willing to put the effort into it. He has improved from the free throw and 3-point lines.

Weaknesses: Opposing teams love to see Askins shooting the ball when he's in the game, because his offensive game is poor. His field goal percentage hovers around 40, and almost one of every three shots he attempts is a trey. He is not a skilled passer and creates little for himself and others. He's weak with the dribble and draws a lot of fouls.

Analysis: The Heat re-signed Askins as a restricted free agent before the 1992-93 season because of his work ethic and defense. You don't want him in the game when you need scoring, but he can help preserve a lead while giving regulars a breather. Askins is a marginal NBA talent, but he has won jobs for three straight seasons.

PLAYER SUMMARY	
Will	put forth effort
Can't	contribute offensively
Expect	defense, hustle
Don't Expect	10 PPG
Fantasy Value	$0
Card Value	5-8¢

COLLEGE STATISTICS

		G	FGP	FTP	RPG	PPG
86-87	ALA	32	.475	.552	3.0	2.9
87-88	ALA	30	.417	.694	4.9	5.7
88-89	ALA	31	.497	.686	4.2	7.8
89-90	ALA	35	.437	.656	5.1	9.9
Totals		128	.453	.658	4.3	6.7

NBA REGULAR-SEASON STATISTICS

		G	MIN	FGs FG	FGs PCT	3-PT FGs FG	3-PT FGs PCT	FTs FT	FTs PCT	Rebounds OFF	Rebounds TOT	AST	STL	BLK	PTS	PPG
90-91	MIA	39	266	34	.420	6	.240	12	.480	30	68	19	16	13	86	2.2
91-92	MIA	59	843	84	.410	25	.342	26	.703	65	142	38	40	15	219	3.7
92-93	MIA	69	935	88	.413	22	.338	29	.725	74	198	31	31	29	227	3.3
Totals		167	2044	206	.413	53	.325	67	.657	169	408	88	87	57	532	3.2

STACEY AUGMON

Team: Atlanta Hawks
Position: Guard/Forward
Height: 6'8" **Weight:** 205
Birthdate: August 1, 1968

NBA Experience: 2 years
College: Nevada-Las Vegas
Acquired: 1st-round pick in 1991 draft
(9th overall)

Background: Augmon, who played four positions for UNLV, established a reputation as the nation's finest college defensive player. After his freshman season, that defensive prowess earned him a berth on the U.S. Olympic team. Augmon was a key player in UNLV's run to the national title in 1990 and Final Four appearance in 1991. His defensive reputation followed him to the NBA, where he was drafted No. 9 by Atlanta, became a starter, and made the NBA All-Rookie first team. He improved his numbers in virtually every category as a second-year starter.

Strengths: Known for his defense, Augmon has lived up to that billing while also proving to be a vastly underrated offensive player. He gets to the basket, runs the floor, and is a superb finisher. He has worked to improve his free throw and field goal percentages. His post-up game is strong. His defense is boosted by great instincts for the ball and benefits as well from his long wingspan and ability to get to the boards.

Weaknesses: Augmon's field goal percentage has risen because he gets to the hoop, not because he has a perimeter jumper you can take to the bank. His glaring offensive deficiencies are his outside shooting and ball-handling. He lacks range on offense and bulk on defense.

Analysis: Augmon, drafted for his defense, has turned out to be a wonderfully versatile player after only two years in the league. He can be unstoppable when slashing to the hoop, and he still shows the defensive tenacity that earned him fame as a collegian. A great athlete with a great attitude, Augmon has given the Hawks stability at the two-guard position.

PLAYER SUMMARY	
Will	thrive at both ends
Can't	shoot treys
Expect	defense, 10-plus PPG
Don't Expect	a gunner
Fantasy Value	$11-14
Card Value	8-12¢

COLLEGE STATISTICS

		G	FGP	FTP	RPG	PPG
87-88	UNLV	34	.574	.647	6.1	9.2
88-89	UNLV	37	.519	.663	7.4	9.5
89-90	UNLV	39	.553	.671	6.9	14.2
90-91	UNLV	35	.587	.727	7.3	16.5
Totals		145	.555	.677	6.9	13.7

NBA REGULAR-SEASON STATISTICS

				FGs		3-PT FGs		FTs		Rebounds						
		G	MIN	FG	PCT	FG	PCT	FT	PCT	OFF	TOT	AST	STL	BLK	PTS	PPG
91-92	ATL	82	2505	440	.489	1	.167	213	.666	191	420	201	124	27	1094	13.3
92-93	ATL	73	2112	397	.501	0	.000	227	.739	141	287	170	91	18	1021	14.0
Totals		155	4617	837	.495	1	.100	440	.702	332	707	371	215	45	2115	13.6

ANTHONY AVENT

Team: Milwaukee Bucks
Position: Forward
Height: 6'10" **Weight:** 235
Birthdate: October 18, 1969
NBA Experience: 1 year

College: Seton Hall
Acquired: Draft rights traded from Nuggets for draft rights to Kevin Brooks, a 1994 2nd-round pick, and other considerations, 7/91

Background: Avent was considered one of the best prep centers in the country while at Shabazz High School in Newark, New Jersey. He averaged 17.8 points and 9.9 points per game during his senior year at Seton Hall and became the highest draft choice ever out of that school when Atlanta selected him 15th overall in 1991. He came to Milwaukee as part of a three-way deal, but he spent his first pro season in Italy where he averaged 13 points and ten rebounds per game. He led the Bucks in rebounds as a solid 1992-93 rookie.

Strengths: Avent is a strong interior defender and rebounder with a good NBA body. He runs the floor, finishes breaks, and hustles on both ends. A natural on the offensive glass, Avent uses his instincts to get a lot of points on put-backs. The year spent in Italy helped and humbled Avent, who joined the NBA with a great attitude.

Weaknesses: Avent's offensive skills remain unpolished and somewhat mechanical. He thinks too much about his moves instead of using his strength to pull them off. He was demoted to a lesser league in Italy, where defense often goes unappreciated. He is not a good outside shooter, lacks consistency inside, and coughs up the ball too often.

Analysis: Milwaukee's inability to sign Avent out of college because of salary-cap restrictions may have been the best scenario for both parties. The year in Italy helped him mature to the point where he could contribute as an NBA rookie. He was the Bucks' best rebounder, especially on the offensive glass, and scored more than many expected. With a little offensive refinement, Avent should carve himself a nice pro career.

PLAYER SUMMARY
Will ....rebound
Can't............................handle the ball
Expect........................quality minutes
Don't Expect..........................high FGP
Fantasy Value.................................$1
Card Value...............................10-15¢

COLLEGE STATISTICS

		G	FGP	FTP	RPG	PPG
88-89	SH	38	.456	.653	3.0	4.4
89-90	SH	28	.488	.618	9.4	10.5
90-91	SH	34	.577	.750	9.9	17.8
Totals		100	.531	.701	7.1	10.7

NBA REGULAR-SEASON STATISTICS

			FGs		3-PT FGs		FTs		Rebounds						
	G	MIN	FG	PCT	FG	PCT	FT	PCT	OFF	TOT	AST	STL	BLK	PTS	PPG
92-93 MIL	82	2285	347	.433	0	.000	112	.651	180	512	91	57	73	806	9.8
Totals	82	2285	347	.433	0	.000	112	.651	180	512	91	57	73	806	9.8

THURL BAILEY

Team: Minnesota Timberwolves
Position: Forward
Height: 6'11" **Weight:** 232
Birthdate: April 7, 1961
NBA Experience: 10 years

College: North Carolina St.
Acquired: Traded from Jazz with a
1992 2nd-round pick for Tyrone
Corbin, 11/91

Background: Bailey starred for the 1983 N.C. State national championship team and hit the critical shot versus UNLV to send the Wolfpack to the Final Four. With Utah, he twice finished second in the voting for the NBA's Sixth Man Award. He was traded to Minnesota in 1991-92 and has not enjoyed as much success. Last season marked the first time since his rookie year that he did not average double figures in scoring.

Strengths: No one in the league has an unkind word to say about Bailey, a soft-spoken leader. He is a well-schooled low-post player and a quick turnaround shooter with decent range. He's a good free throw shooter and rebounder. He is also a record-cutting vocalist, trombone player, and avid charity worker.

Weaknesses: Bailey's skills have diminished over the last three years. His field goal percentage had dipped for four consecutive years before last season. His overall game is on the decline, as evidenced by his decreased scoring and shot-blocking effectiveness in 1992-93.

Analysis: Bailey was one of Minnesota's better inside scoring threats in 1992-93, which says more about the state of the Timberwolves than it does about Bailey. He is capable of contributing on both ends of the court, but not like he once could. He might be most valuable as a locker room presence.

PLAYER SUMMARY	
Will	hit the turnaround
Can't	carry a team
Expect	class, leadership
Don't Expect	starts
Fantasy Value	$0
Card Value	5-10¢

COLLEGE STATISTICS

		G	FGP	FTP	RPG	PPG
79-80	NCST	28	.436	.673	3.6	4.5
80-81	NCST	27	.525	.736	6.1	12.3
81-82	NCST	32	.548	.814	6.8	13.7
82-83	NCST	36	.501	.717	7.7	16.7
Totals		123	.513	.745	6.2	12.2

NBA REGULAR-SEASON STATISTICS

				FGs		3-PT FGs		FTs		Rebounds						
		G	MIN	FG	PCT	FG	PCT	FT	PCT	OFF	TOT	AST	STL	BLK	PTS	PPG
83-84	UTA	81	2009	302	.512	0	.000	88	.752	115	464	129	38	122	692	8.5
84-85	UTA	80	2481	507	.490	1	1.000	197	.842	153	525	138	51	105	1212	15.1
85-86	UTA	82	2358	483	.448	0	.000	230	.830	148	493	153	42	114	1196	14.6
86-87	UTA	81	2155	463	.447	0	.000	190	.805	145	432	102	38	88	1116	13.8
87-88	UTA	82	2804	633	.492	1	.333	337	.826	134	531	158	49	125	1604	19.6
88-89	UTA	82	2777	615	.483	2	.400	363	.825	115	447	138	48	91	1595	19.5
89-90	UTA	82	2583	470	.481	0	.000	222	.779	116	410	137	32	100	1162	14.2
90-91	UTA	82	2486	399	.458	0	.000	219	.808	101	407	124	53	91	1017	12.4
91-92	UTA/MIN	84	2104	368	.440	0	.000	215	.796	122	485	78	35	117	951	11.3
92-93	MIN	70	1276	203	.455	0	.000	119	.838	53	215	61	20	47	525	7.5
Totals		806	23033	4443	.471	4	.129	2180	.813	1202	4409	1218	406	1000	11070	13.7

CHARLES BARKLEY

Team: Phoenix Suns
Position: Forward
Height: 6'6" **Weight:** 252
Birthdate: February 20, 1963
NBA Experience: 9 years

College: Auburn
Acquired: Traded from 76ers for Jeff Hornacek, Tim Perry, and Andrew Lang, 6/92

Background: Barkley was known as the "Round Mound of Rebound" at Auburn, where he starred at nearly 270 pounds. He was named SEC Player of the Year as a junior and then entered the NBA draft. In just his second season, he developed into a 20-PPG, 12-RPG player. He has since played at a level few can match. In the 1992 off-season, he won Olympic gold and was traded to Phoenix. The good times continued as he led the Suns to the league's best record and was named the NBA's Most Valuable Player.

Strengths: Barkley's game features the complete package. He is among the top rebounders and scorers in the league. He scores, muscles inside against seven-footers, and gets to the line. His strength and demeanor make him intimidating at both ends. He's capable of dominating, yet he also showed great poise and leadership while on a contending team.

Weaknesses: Barkley's controversial past includes late-night bar fights and courtside spitting. He toned down his act last year but remains an outspoken figure. He is not a consistent 3-point shooter, yet still heaves them far too often.

Analysis: A true superstar, Barkley is clearly one of the best players in the game and certainly one of its most colorful. In Phoenix, he has also proved he is a winner who can be a great team player.

PLAYER SUMMARY

Will	do it all
Can't	keep quiet
Expect	more MVP contention
Don't Expect	selfishness
Fantasy Value	$85-90
Card Value	25-40¢

COLLEGE STATISTICS

		G	FGP	FTP	RPG	PPG
81-82	AUB	28	.595	.636	9.8	12.7
82-83	AUB	28	.644	.631	9.5	14.4
83-84	AUB	28	.638	.683	9.5	15.1
Totals		84	.626	.652	9.6	14.1

NBA REGULAR-SEASON STATISTICS

		G	MIN	FGs FG	FGs PCT	3-PT FGs FG	3-PT FGs PCT	FTs FT	FTs PCT	Rebounds OFF	Rebounds TOT	AST	STL	BLK	PTS	PPG
84-85	PHI	82	2347	427	.545	1	.167	293	.733	266	703	155	95	80	1148	14.0
85-86	PHI	80	2952	595	.572	17	.227	396	.685	354	1026	312	173	125	1603	20.0
86-87	PHI	68	2740	557	.594	21	.202	429	.761	390	994	331	119	104	1564	23.0
87-88	PHI	80	3170	753	.587	44	.280	714	.751	385	951	254	100	103	2264	28.3
88-89	PHI	79	3088	700	.579	35	.216	602	.753	403	986	325	126	67	2037	25.8
89-90	PHI	70	3085	706	.600	20	.217	557	.749	361	909	307	148	50	1989	28.4
90-91	PHI	67	2498	665	.570	44	.284	475	.722	258	680	284	110	33	1849	27.6
91-92	PHI	75	2881	622	.552	32	.234	454	.695	271	830	308	136	44	1730	23.1
92-93	PHO	76	2859	716	.520	67	.305	445	.765	237	928	385	119	74	1944	25.6
Totals		677	25620	5741	.569	281	.254	4365	.736	2925	8007	2661	1126	680	16128	23.8

DANA BARROS

Team: Seattle SuperSonics
Position: Guard
Height: 5'11" **Weight:** 165
Birthdate: April 13, 1967

NBA Experience: 4 years
College: Boston College
Acquired: 1st-round pick in 1989 draft
(16th overall)

Background: Barros, the all-time scoring leader at Boston College, became the first player in Big East history to lead the conference in scoring in back-to-back years. He started every game during his four seasons there. He has not been as fortunate as a pro despite starting 25 games as a rookie. In each of the last two seasons, he has come off the bench and averaged a steady eight points per game. His .446 3-point average in 1991-92 was tops in the NBA, and he again led the Sonics from behind the arc in 1992-93.

Strengths: The diminutive Barros was an explosive college scorer, largely because of his sheer quickness. He has proven he can score at the NBA level as well. He is a very good 3-point shooter and can get to the bucket when he decides to put it on the floor.

Weaknesses: The biggest concern was the drop in his 3-point percentage last year. Opponents don't give him a good look at the basket, and he is too willing to stay on the perimeter. Barros is not as polished a playmaker as most point guards, possessing the mentality of a two guard. He is also suspect on defense because of his size.

Analysis: Barros could be a high scorer if given a starter's minutes. Too bad Gary Payton is the Sonics' point guard of the future. Barros can't compare to Payton's playmaking and defense, but he remains a valuable player because of his stroke and range. If he can hoist his 3-point percentage to its standard of two years ago, he'll reach double figures in future years.

PLAYER SUMMARY

Will .... stick 3-pointers
Can't .... displace Gary Payton
Expect .... 8-10 PPG
Don't Expect .... playmaking
Fantasy Value $1
Card Value .... 8-12¢

COLLEGE STATISTICS

		G	FGP	FTP	APG	PPG
85-86	BC	28	.479	.791	3.5	13.7
86-87	BC	29	.458	.850	3.8	18.7
87-88	BC	33	.480	.850	4.1	21.9
88-89	BC	29	.475	.857	3.3	23.9
Totals		119	.473	.841	3.7	19.7

NBA REGULAR-SEASON STATISTICS

			FGs		3-PT FGs		FTs		Rebounds						
		G	MIN	FG	PCT	FG	PCT	FT	PCT	OFF	TOT	AST	STL	BLK	PTS	PPG
89-90	SEA	81	1630	299	.405	95	.399	89	.809	35	132	205	53	1	782	9.7
90-91	SEA	66	750	154	.495	32	.395	78	.918	17	71	111	23	1	418	6.3
91-92	SEA	75	1331	238	.483	83	.446	60	.759	17	81	125	51	4	619	8.3
92-93	SEA	69	1243	214	.451	64	.379	49	.831	18	107	151	63	3	541	7.8
Totals		291	4954	905	.449	274	.407	276	.829	87	391	592	190	9	2360	8.1

JON BARRY

Team: Milwaukee Bucks
Position: Guard
Height: 6'5" **Weight:** 195
Birthdate: July 25, 1969

NBA Experience: 1 year
College: Pacific; Paris; Georgia Tech
Acquired: Draft rights traded from
Celtics for Alaa Abdelnaby, 12/92

Background: One of four sons of Hall of Famer Rick Barry to play Division I basketball, the younger Barry began his college career at Pacific, sat out a year, and played a season at Paris (Texas) Junior College before settling down at Georgia Tech. He led the Yellow Jackets in 3-point field goals and ranks second to Dennis Scott on the school's all-time list of 3-pointers made. He was drafted 21st overall by Boston in 1992 and traded to Milwaukee in a deal that brought Alaa Abdelnaby to the Celtics. Barry struggled in limited action as a rookie, averaging less than five PPG and hitting less than 40 percent of his shots from the field.

Strengths: Barry knows the game, hustles, and displayed a tremendous court sense as a collegian. He is a splendid passer, perhaps from having to give up the ball while teamed with his father during pick-up games. He owns 3-point range with his jumper and will lead the break.

Weaknesses: If Barry played his rookie year over again, there would be plenty of things he would try to change. One is more playing time, although he still has to earn it. Rookies will have shooting troubles, but good shooters ought to top 40 percent. He did not approach it. His sub-70-percent free throw shooting also made Dad cringe. He struggled in almost every area.

Analysis: Don't give up on Barry. If there's one trait that characterizes him, it's his willingness to do whatever it takes to make it. His shooting will improve. The question is whether or not it will improve enough to earn him the minutes he needs to adjust the rest of his game to the pro level.

PLAYER SUMMARY	
Will	improve shooting
Can't	earn crunch-time minutes
Expect	gradual progress
Don't Expect	another Rick
Fantasy Value	$1
Card Value	8-12¢

COLLEGE STATISTICS

		G	FGP	FTP	RPG	PPG
87-88	PAC	29	.372	.746	2.6	9.5
90-91	GT	30	.444	.732	3.7	15.9
91-92	GT	35	.429	.697	4.3	17.2
Totals		94	.421	.717	3.6	14.4

NBA REGULAR-SEASON STATISTICS

			FGs		3-PT FGs		FTs		Rebounds						
	G	MIN	FG	PCT	FG	PCT	FT	PCT	OFF	TOT	AST	STL	BLK	PTS	PPG
92-93 MIL	47	552	76	.369	21	.333	33	.673	10	43	68	35	3	206	4.4
Totals	47	552	76	.369	21	.333	33	.673	10	43	68	35	3	206	4.4

JOHN BATTLE

Team: Cleveland Cavaliers
Position: Guard
Height: 6'2" **Weight:** 190
Birthdate: November 9, 1962

NBA Experience: 8 years
College: Rutgers
Acquired: Signed as a free agent, 7/91

Background: Battle led the Atlantic 10 in scoring in his last two years at Rutgers and came into the league known for his shooting and scoring ability. He demonstrated both in six years with Atlanta, where he averaged about ten PPG and his field goal percentage was always around 45 or 46. He signed as a free agent with Cleveland and enjoyed one of his better years in 1991-92 before slumping for much of last season.

Strengths: Battle is known as a shooter. He knocks down the mid-range jumper, gets his shot off in the paint, uses screens to get open, and is a strong leaper. He's solid from the free throw line and is well-liked by teammates.

Weaknesses: Battle struggled through the worst shooting year of his career last season and his worst scoring campaign since he was a rookie. He has never been a threat from beyond the 3-point line and he no longer offers much on defense. He is not a playmaker and is one of the least-effective rebounding guards in the league.

Analysis: Battle has been a solid reserve guard during his eight-year career. That was not the case last season, when he was lost in the shuffle on a contending Cleveland squad. He signed a six-year, multi-million-dollar contract with the Cavs in 1991 and has not performed to the expectations that accompanied it. If his jump shot returns, so will his minutes.

PLAYER SUMMARY	
Will	get open
Can't	shoot treys
Expect	reserve offense
Don't Expect	rebounds
Fantasy Value	$0
Card Value	5-10¢

COLLEGE STATISTICS

		G	FGP	FTP	APG	PPG
81-82	RUT	29	.433	.429	0.8	2.4
82-83	RUT	31	.489	.725	1.3	5.9
83-84	RUT	25	.493	.725	1.4	21.0
84-85	RUT	29	.491	.729	2.6	21.0
Totals		114	.488	.707	1.5	12.1

NBA REGULAR-SEASON STATISTICS

		G	MIN	FGs FG	FGs PCT	3-PT FGs FG	3-PT FGs PCT	FTs FT	FTs PCT	Rebounds OFF	Rebounds TOT	AST	STL	BLK	PTS	PPG
85-86	ATL	64	639	101	.455	0	.000	75	.728	12	62	74	23	3	277	4.3
86-87	ATL	64	804	144	.457	0	.000	93	.738	16	60	124	29	5	381	6.0
87-88	ATL	67	1227	278	.454	16	.390	141	.750	26	113	158	31	5	713	10.6
88-89	ATL	82	1672	287	.457	11	.324	194	.815	30	140	197	42	9	779	9.5
89-90	ATL	60	1477	275	.506	2	.154	102	.756	27	99	154	28	3	654	10.9
90-91	ATL	79	1863	397	.461	14	.286	270	.854	34	159	217	45	6	1078	13.6
91-92	CLE	76	1637	316	.480	2	.118	145	.848	19	112	159	36	5	779	10.3
92-93	CLE	41	497	83	.415	1	.167	56	.778	4	29	54	9	5	223	5.4
Totals		533	9816	1881	.465	46	.260	1076	.798	168	774	1137	243	41	4884	9.2

BENOIT BENJAMIN

Team: New Jersey Nets
Position: Center
Height: 7'0" **Weight:** 260
Birthdate: November 22, 1964
NBA Experience: 8 years

College: Creighton
Acquired: Traded from Lakers for Sam Bowie and a future 2nd-round pick, 6/93

Background: Benjamin played for Creighton and led the nation in blocked shots (5.1 BPG) as a junior. He gave up his final year of college eligibility to enter the NBA draft and played five-plus years with the Los Angeles Clippers. He recorded the highest rebounding average of his career during the 1990-91 season (with the Clippers and Sonics). His 1991-92 season was cut short because of a broken hand, and he was traded from the Sonics to the Lakers just before the 1992-93 trading deadline. After the season, he was shipped to New Jersey.

Strengths: Benjamin is a very good defensive rebounder and shot-blocker. He has a soft touch on offense and very refined passing skills for a big man. Some nights—albeit very few—he looks like one of the better centers in the league.

Weaknesses: The word "enigma" should be stitched on the back of Benjamin's extra-large jersey. For reasons mostly unknown, he has never displayed the desire or consistency to raise his game to the next level.

Analysis: Capable of huge nights in the scoring, rebounding, shot-blocking, and even the assists and steals columns, Benjamin has been too content to come off the bench and sleepwalk. He played some of his better games in Seattle but, due to his lack of enthusiasm, could not avoid the trading block. His numbers declined once back in L.A., where he first earned his underachiever's reputation.

PLAYER SUMMARY	
Will	have big games
Can't	shake reputation
Expect	too many nights off
Don't Expect	desire
Fantasy Value	$6-8
Card Value	5-10¢

COLLEGE STATISTICS

		G	FGP	FTP	RPG	PPG
82-83	CRE	27	.555	.655	9.6	14.8
83-84	CRE	30	.543	.743	9.8	16.2
84-85	CRE	32	.582	.738	14.1	21.5
Totals		89	.562	.720	11.3	17.7

NBA REGULAR-SEASON STATISTICS

				FGs		3-PT FGs		FTs		Rebounds						
		G	MIN	FG	PCT	FG	PCT	FT	PCT	OF	TOT	AST	STL	BLK	PTS	PPG
85-86	LAC	79	2088	324	.490	1	.333	229	.746	161	600	79	64	206	878	11.1
86-87	LAC	72	2230	320	.449	0	.000	188	.715	134	586	135	60	187	828	11.5
87-88	LAC	66	2171	340	.491	0	.000	180	.706	112	530	172	50	225	860	13.0
88-89	LAC	79	2585	491	.541	0	.000	317	.744	164	696	157	57	221	1299	16.4
89-90	LAC	71	2313	362	.526	0	.000	235	.732	156	657	159	59	187	959	13.5
90-91	LAC/SEA	70	2236	386	.496	0	.000	210	.712	157	723	119	54	145	982	14.0
91-92	SEA	63	1941	354	.478	0	.000	171	.687	130	513	76	39	118	879	14.0
92-93	SEA/LAL	59	754	133	.491	0	.000	69	.663	51	209	22	31	48	335	5.7
Totals		559	16318	2710	.497	1	.056	1599	.720	1065	4514	919	414	1337	7020	12.6

TONY BENNETT

Team: Charlotte Hornets
Position: Guard
Height: 6'0" **Weight:** 175
Birthdate: June 1, 1969

NBA Experience: 1 year
College: Wisconsin-Green Bay
Acquired: 2nd-round pick in 1992 draft (35th overall)

Background: Bennett finished his career at the University of Wisconsin-Green Bay as the Mid-Continent Conference's all-time scoring and assist leader as well as the NCAA's all-time leader in 3-point field goal percentage (.497). Named the top player under six feet after averaging 20.2 PPG and 5.1 APG during his senior year, he also broke or tied 22 school records at UWGB, where he was coached by his father, Dick. Bennett was drafted in the second round by Charlotte. He served as a back-up point guard and 3-point shooting threat as a rookie last year, averaging 11 minutes per game.

Strengths: Like many a coach's son, Bennett displays a keen understanding of the game. He plays within himself, sees the court well, distributes the ball to the right people, and handles pressure. He is a fine shooter with range beyond the NBA 3-point arc and has the makings of a productive long-distance scorer.

Weaknesses: Bennett is a step slower than most NBA point guards, a fact that emerged during pre-draft camps and dropped his stock a bit. He can overcome his lack of speed on the offensive end with sound decision-making but has trouble on defense, where he is forced to reach. He is more of a passer than a playmaker and needs to be more aggressive in penetrating on offense.

Analysis: Charlotte figured Bennett as a solid back-up for speedster Muggsy Bogues at the point. It could turn out that way, although opposing guards get the impression Bennett is standing still compared to his pint-sized teammate. As a rookie, Bennett showed he has pro 3-point range and a nice feel for the game. If he can mix in some drives to the bucket and better defense, he'll begin to earn more respect.

PLAYER SUMMARY

Will ....distribute
Can't.......................defend quickness
Expect ....3-point shooting
Don't Expect ....dunks
Fantasy Value..................................$0
Card Value ....5-10¢

COLLEGE STATISTICS

		G	FGP	FTP	APG	PPG
88-89	WGB	27	.522	.847	5.1	19.1
89-90	WGB	30	.504	.859	5.2	16.6
90-91	WGB	31	.547	.836	5.0	21.5
91-92	WGB	30	.534	.826	5.1	20.2
Totals		118	.528	.840	5.1	19.4

NBA REGULAR-SEASON STATISTICS

			FGs		3-PT FGs		FTs		Rebounds						
	G	MIN	FG	PCT	FG	PCT	FT	PCT	OFF	TOT	AST	STL	BLK	PTS	PPG
92-93 CHA	75	857	110	.423	26	.325	30	.732	12	63	136	30	0	276	3.7
Totals	75	857	110	.423	26	.325	30	.732	12	63	136	30	0	276	3.7

DAVID BENOIT

Team: Utah Jazz
Position: Forward
Height: 6'8" **Weight:** 225
Birthdate: May 9, 1968

NBA Experience: 2 years
College: Tyler; Alabama
Acquired: Signed as a free agent, 8/91

Background: Benoit started playing basketball in high school and began his college career at Tyler Junior College, averaging 19.3 PPG and 13.7 RPG. He transferred to Alabama, started in both of his years there, and led the Tide to two NCAA tourney berths. He was named All-SEC in 1990 and was the Rookie of the Year in the Spanish League in 1990-91 after averaging 22 PPG and ten RPG. He became a 1992 playoff starter for Utah as an NBA rookie and spent most of his second season backing up Tyrone Corbin.

Strengths: Benoit can provide offense in a number of ways. He runs the court, finishes on the break, and was Utah's second-best 3-point shooter last season. He also hustles on defense. Benoit can leap and has long arms, traits that combine to make him a fine shot-blocker and rebounder.

Weaknesses: Not a consistent player, Benoit has his problems handling the ball and passing. He turns the ball over about twice as often as he gets credit for an assist. He tends to play too fast for his own good. His jump shot abandoned him last year and contributed to a disappointing sophomore campaign. As well, he can be pushed around in the blocks. Although aggressive on defense, he's often caught out of position.

Analysis: Expected to take over the starting small-forward role after Utah traded Blue Edwards, Benoit did not rise to the challenge. While his scoring and 3-point shooting numbers increased, he never found much consistency in his jumper from inside the arc and was generally overshadowed by Corbin. Some of Benoit's troubles resulted from better respect among opposing defenders. He is still learning the game and could bounce back.

PLAYER SUMMARY

Will..............................fire 3-pointers
Can't..................create for teammates
Expect ....streak shooting
Don't Expect..................ball-handling
Fantasy Value..............................$1-3
Card Value ....5-10¢

COLLEGE STATISTICS

		G	FGP	FTP	RPG	PPG
88-89	ALA	31	.507	.738	8.0	10.8
89-90	ALA	35	.515	.767	6.1	10.5
Totals		66	.511	.752	7.0	10.6

NBA REGULAR-SEASON STATISTICS

		G	MIN	FGs FG	FGs PCT	3-PT FGs FG	FGs PCT	FTs FT	FTs PCT	Rebounds OFF	TOT	AST	STL	BLK	PTS	PPG
91-92	UTA	77	1161	175	.467	3	.214	81	.810	105	296	34	19	44	434	5.6
92-93	UTA	82	1712	258	.436	34	.347	114	.750	116	392	43	45	43	664	8.1
Totals		159	2873	433	.448	37	.330	195	.774	221	688	77	64	87	1098	6.9

ROLANDO BLACKMAN

Team: New York Knicks
Position: Guard
Height: 6'6" **Weight:** 206
Birthdate: February 26, 1959

NBA Experience: 12 years
College: Kansas St.
Acquired: Traded from Mavericks for a 1995 1st-round pick, 6/92

Background: Blackman earned All-America recognition at Kansas State and was named to the Big Eight All-Decade Team for the 1980s. His pro career has included four All-Star appearances. He was Dallas' all-time leader in points, field goals, and starts when he was traded to the New York Knicks in June 1992. Last year was the first of his 12 in which he failed to score 1,000 points.

Strengths: Blackman has long been known as a terrific spot-up shooter who has won countless games with his cool in the clutch. He has 3-point range and a quick release. He plays solid defense, provides veteran leadership, and remains among the best in the league from the free throw line.

Weaknesses: Blackman has lost a step over his 12 years, and his shooting percentage has slipped over the last two campaigns. He did not play well during the first half of last season and missed part of the second with a knee injury.

Analysis: For the first time in his career, Blackman was not asked to be a primary scorer last season. One of the classiest players in the league, he still gave the Knicks enough offense, defense, and leadership to help them win the Atlantic Division.

PLAYER SUMMARY	
Will	knock down jumpers
Can't	return to 20 PPG
Expect	classy leadership
Don't Expect	young legs
Fantasy Value	$1-3
Card Value	5-10¢

COLLEGE STATISTICS

		G	FGP	FTP	RPG	PPG
77-78	KSU	29	.472	.656	6.4	10.9
78-79	KSU	28	.510	.735	3.9	17.3
79-80	KSU	31	.539	.690	4.7	17.8
80-81	KSU	33	.532	.783	5.0	15.0
Totals		121	.517	.717	5.0	15.2

NBA REGULAR-SEASON STATISTICS

				FGs		3-PT FGs		FTs		Rebounds						
		G	MIN	FG	PCT	FG	PCT	FT	PCT	OFF	TOT	AST	STL	BLK	PTS	PPG
81-82	DAL	82	1979	439	.513	1	.250	212	.768	97	254	105	46	30	1091	13.3
82-83	DAL	75	2349	513	.492	3	.200	297	.780	108	293	185	37	29	1326	17.7
83-84	DAL	81	3025	721	.546	1	.091	372	.812	124	373	288	56	37	1815	22.4
84-85	DAL	81	2834	625	.508	6	.300	342	.828	107	300	289	16	16	1598	19.7
85-86	DAL	82	2787	677	.514	4	.138	404	.836	88	291	271	79	25	1762	21.5
86-87	DAL	80	2758	626	.495	5	.333	419	.884	96	278	266	64	21	1676	21.0
87-88	DAL	71	2580	497	.473	0	.000	331	.873	82	246	262	64	18	1325	18.7
88-89	DAL	78	2946	594	.476	30	.353	316	.854	70	273	288	65	20	1534	19.7
89-90	DAL	80	2934	626	.498	13	.302	287	.844	88	280	289	77	21	1552	19.4
90-91	DAL	80	2965	634	.482	40	.351	282	.865	63	256	301	69	19	1590	19.9
91-92	DAL	75	2527	535	.461	65	.385	239	.898	78	239	204	50	22	1374	18.3
92-93	NY	60	1434	239	.443	31	.425	71	.789	23	102	157	22	10	580	9.7
Totals		925	31118	6726	.495	199	.341	3572	.839	1024	3185	2905	645	268	17223	18.6

LANCE BLANKS

Team: Minnesota Timberwolves
Position: Guard
Height: 6'4" **Weight:** 195
Birthdate: September 9, 1966
NBA Experience: 3 years

College: Virginia; Texas
Acquired: Traded from Pistons with Brad Sellers and a 2000 2nd-round pick for Gerald Glass and Mark Randall, 11/92

Background: Blanks transferred from Virginia to Texas after his sophomore year and became part of the Longhorns' famed and feared outside-shooting, high-scoring attack. He's the son of ex-Oilers and Patriots running back Sid Blanks and the cousin of ex-Rangers infielder Larvell Blanks. Despite his first-round draft status, his first three seasons in the NBA have been disappointing. He rarely played in two years at Detroit before an early-season trade last year brought him to a different bench in Minnesota.

Strengths: Blanks possesses good quickness and good backcourt size and can be a dangerous long-range shooter when he gets on a roll. He was No. 3 on the Timberwolves in 3-pointers made despite his limited minutes. He hustles and can match up athletically.

Weaknesses: All facets of his game need work, including his shooting, which was supposedly his strong suit. At Texas, a few consecutive missed shots were no big deal. In the pros, they send him back to the bench. He is neither a capable ball-handler nor a skilled passer. Blanks was out of his league among Detroit's talented guard corps but has not found Minnesota much better.

Analysis: Blanks has stuck around the league because of his athletic ability and the hope that he will someday make a break for himself. But the facts are impossible to overlook. Shooters must do better than the low 40-percent range. And confident guards should not have the trouble he does with the ball. He saw more action last year than the previous two combined but still did not produce.

PLAYER SUMMARY	
Will	shoot from deep
Can't	get off the bench
Expect	athletic ability
Don't Expect	ball skills
Fantasy Value	$0
Card Value	5-10¢

COLLEGE STATISTICS

		G	FGP	FTP	RPG	PPG
85-86	VA	14	.438	.500	1.1	2.4
86-87	VA	24	.520	.286	0.8	1.2
88-89	TEX	34	.450	.684	5.6	19.7
89-90	TEX	32	.402	.797	4.3	20.3
Totals		104	.429	.729	3.5	13.3

NBA REGULAR-SEASON STATISTICS

			FGs		3-PT FGs		FTs		Rebounds						
	G	MIN	FG	PCT	FG	PCT	FT	PCT	OFF	TOT	AST	STL	BLK	PTS	PPG
90-91 DET	38	214	26	.426	2	.125	10	.714	4	20	26	9	2	64	1.7
91-92 DET	43	189	25	.455	6	.375	8	.727	9	22	19	14	1	64	1.5
92-93 MIN	61	642	65	.433	11	.256	20	.625	18	68	72	16	5	161	2.6
Totals	142	1045	116	.436	19	.253	38	.667	31	110	117	39	8	289	2.0

MOOKIE BLAYLOCK

Team: Atlanta Hawks
Position: Guard
Height: 6'1" **Weight:** 185
Birthdate: March 20, 1967

NBA Experience: 4 years
College: Midland; Oklahoma
Acquired: Traded from Nets with Roy Hinson for Rumeal Robinson, 11/92

Background: Mookie, born Daron Oshay Blaylock, earned All-America recognition in 1989 on a powerhouse Oklahoma team. He was the first NCAA player to collect 200 assists and 100 steals in back-to-back seasons. Blaylock was selected 12th by New Jersey in 1989 and became the Nets' starting point guard. He was acquired by Atlanta in a 1992 trade for Rumeal Robinson, averaged double figures in scoring for the fourth straight season, and posted career highs in most statistical categories during 1992-93.

Strengths: Blaylock is one of the best defensive point guards in the game. His quickness and instincts help him rank among the league leaders in steals annually. Offensively, he's a prototypical point guard with sharp passing skills who can score on drives through the lane and with his jumper, which last year became both accurate and productive from long range for the first time. He handles the ball capably against pressure and has become a team leader.

Weaknesses: Blaylock can still play out of control at times, although Atlanta likes the fact that he always looks to push the ball upcourt. He remains a streaky shooter, meaning there are times he should stick to driving and dishing instead of firing his improved 3-point bombs.

Analysis: The Blaylock-for-Robinson deal turned out to be a great one for both Blaylock and the Hawks. Not only did Atlanta get a point guard geared for a fast pace, but it got one who gave his new team the best campaign of his career. Blaylock continues to emerge as a complete player whose future will become even brighter if his jump shot keeps improving.

PLAYER SUMMARY	
Will	push the pace
Can't	be left open anymore
Expect	hounding defense
Don't Expect	high FGP
Fantasy Value	$14-17
Card Value	5-10¢

COLLEGE STATISTICS

		G	FGP	FTP	APG	PPG
85-86	MID	34	.566	.738	—	16.8
86-87	MID	33	.516	.723	—	19.6
87-88	OKLA	39	.460	.684	5.9	16.4
88-89	OKLA	35	.455	.650	6.7	20.0
Totals		141	.495	.696	6.3	18.1

NBA REGULAR-SEASON STATISTICS

			FGs		3-PT FGs		FTs		Rebounds						
		G	MIN	FG	PCT	FG	PCT	FT	PCT	OFF	TOT	AST	STL	BLK	PTS	PPG
89-90	NJ	50	1267	212	.371	18	.225	63	.778	42	140	210	82	14	505	10.1
90-91	NJ	72	2585	432	.416	14	.154	139	.790	67	249	441	169	40	1017	14.1
91-92	NJ	72	2548	429	.432	12	.222	126	.712	101	269	492	170	40	996	13.8
92-93	ATL	80	2820	414	.429	118	.375	123	.728	89	280	671	203	23	1069	13.4
Totals		274	9220	1487	.417	162	.300	451	.748	299	938	1814	624	117	3587	13.1

MUGGSY BOGUES

Team: Charlotte Hornets
Position: Guard
Height: 5'3" **Weight:** 144
Birthdate: January 9, 1965

NBA Experience: 6 years
College: Wake Forest
Acquired: Selected from Bullets in 1988 expansion draft

Background: Bogues learned the game at famed Dunbar High School in Baltimore, where he teamed with Reggie Lewis and Reggie Williams. At Wake Forest, he terrorized ACC guards with his intimidating quickness, and he set ACC career records for assists and steals. His pro career took off after Charlotte plucked him from the Bullets in the 1988 expansion draft. He has ranked among the league leaders in assists and steals each of the last two seasons.

Strengths: Bogues makes some of the league's so-called quick playmakers look as though they're standing still. Always moving, he's a pest on both ends of the floor. Few can stop him from driving past his man and dishing off on offense, and he's always a threat to swipe your dribble if your eyes wander for a second. He is a perennial league leader in assist-to-turnover ratio and an accurate free throw shooter.

Weaknesses: His most obvious drawback is his size. He can't shoot over anyone and even Spud Webb can post him up. His shooting has improved but remains suspect and he is not a threat to beat you from 3-point range. He still looks to pass before shooting.

Analysis: Charlotte searched for a starting point guard to displace Bogues, but no one could beat him out. In the meantime, the smallest player in the league has done nothing but grow in basketball stature. He enjoyed the best scoring year of his career last season while continuing to burn people with his speed and non-stop movement.

PLAYER SUMMARY	
Will	swipe your dribble
Can't	block shots
Expect	non-stop movement
Don't Expect	post-up offense
Fantasy Value	$6-8
Card Value	5-10¢

COLLEGE STATISTICS

		G	FGP	FTP	APG	PPG
83-84	WF	32	.304	.692	1.7	1.2
84-85	WF	29	.500	.682	7.1	6.6
85-86	WF	29	.455	.730	8.4	11.3
86-87	WF	29	.500	.806	9.5	14.8
Totals		119	.473	.749	6.6	8.3

NBA REGULAR-SEASON STATISTICS

				FGs		3-PT FGs		FTs		Rebounds						
		G	MIN	FG	PCT	FG	PCT	FT	PCT	OFF	TOT	AST	STL	BLK	PTS	PPG
87-88	WAS	79	1628	166	.390	3	.188	58	.784	35	136	404	127	3	393	5.0
88-89	CHA	79	1755	178	.426	1	.077	66	.750	53	165	620	111	7	423	5.4
89-90	CHA	81	2743	326	.491	5	.192	106	.791	48	207	867	166	3	763	9.4
90-91	CHA	81	2299	241	.460	0	.000	86	.796	58	216	669	137	3	568	7.0
91-92	CHA	82	2790	317	.472	2	.074	94	.783	58	235	743	170	6	730	8.9
92-93	CHA	81	2833	331	.453	6	.231	140	.833	51	298	711	161	5	808	10.0
Totals		483	14048	1559	.454	17	.142	550	.795	303	1257	4014	872	27	3685	7.6

MANUTE BOL

Team: Philadelphia 76ers
Position: Center
Height: 7'7" **Weight:** 225
Birthdate: October 16, 1962

NBA Experience: 8 years
College: Bridgeport
Acquired: Traded from Warriors for a 1991 1st-round pick, 8/90

Background: Bol might be the most fascinating player in a league full of characters. A member of the Dinka Tribe, he was discovered in the Sudan and imported to Bridgeport College, where he was more a novelty than anything. He speaks four languages and once killed a lion with a spear in an African tribal ritual. He scores fewer than three points per game but perennially ranks among the league leaders in blocked shots. After the Sixers signed 7'6" Shawn Bradley in July, they let Bol go.

Strengths: The tallest man in NBA history does one thing well—block shots. He led the league in that category in 1986 and '89 despite limited playing time. He was named to the second-team All-Defensive Team in 1986. He forces even the best leapers to alter their shots.

Weaknesses: Everything other than shot-blocking falls into this category. Bol can't shoot at all and has no post-up skills to speak of. He can't dribble, pass, or run the floor effectively. When he scores, it's accidental.

Analysis: Bol had one heck of a 1992-93 season. His wife won $486,000 from an Atlantic City slot machine, and the next game Bol was ejected for throwing a punch at the Knicks' Anthony Mason. In March, he made a staggering six treys against Phoenix despite making just two of 31 from long range over the previous three years. That output ought to hold him for a year or two.

PLAYER SUMMARY	
Will	swat shots
Can't	dribble
Expect	nightly laughs
Don't Expect	4 PPG
Fantasy Value	$0
Card Value	5-10¢

COLLEGE STATISTICS

		G	FGP	FTP	RPG	PPG
84-85	BPT	31	.611	.595	13.5	22.5
Totals		31	.611	.595	13.5	22.5

NBA REGULAR-SEASON STATISTICS

				FGs		3-PT FGs		FTs		Rebounds						
		G	MIN	FG	PCT	FG	PCT	FT	PCT	OFF	TOT	AST	STL	BLK	PTS	PPG
85-86	WAS	80	2090	128	.460	0	.000	42	.488	123	477	23	28	397	298	3.7
86-87	WAS	82	1552	103	.446	0	.000	45	.672	84	362	11	20	302	251	3.1
87-88	WAS	77	1136	75	.455	0	.000	26	.531	72	275	13	11	208	176	2.3
88-89	GS	80	1769	127	.369	20	.220	40	.606	116	462	27	11	345	314	3.9
89-90	GS	75	1310	56	.331	9	.188	25	.510	33	276	36	13	238	146	1.9
90-91	PHI	82	1522	65	.396	1	.071	24	.585	66	350	20	16	247	155	1.9
91-92	PHI	71	1267	49	.383	0	.000	12	.462	54	222	22	11	205	110	1.5
92-93	PHI	58	855	52	.409	10	.313	12	.632	44	193	18	14	119	126	2.2
Totals		605	11501	655	.408	40	.203	226	.561	592	2617	170	124	2061	1576	2.6

WALTER BOND

Team: Dallas Mavericks
Position: Guard
Height: 6'5" **Weight:** 200
Birthdate: February 1, 1969

NBA Experience: 1 year
College: Minnesota
Acquired: Signed as a free agent, 10/92

Background: After a standout career at Collins High School in south Chicago, Bond saw action in all 26 games as a freshman at the University of Minnesota. He averaged double figures in scoring as both a junior and a senior but his final year was cut nearly in half by a stress fracture in his right foot. Overlooked in the 1991 NBA draft, Bond wound up making the CBA All-Rookie Team with the Wichita Falls Texans. Dallas signed him before the 1992-93 season and he averaged 8.0 PPG in the Mavericks' backcourt.

Strengths: Bond does a little bit of everything. He is a solid rebounder for a guard and is willing to guard his man. He can also score points by posting up smaller defenders and by nailing an occasional jumper. He once hit nine 3-pointers in a CBA playoff game and shot .333 from long range in that league. He is well-liked by teammates.

Weaknesses: Bond is not very quick, which is probably the biggest reason he was passed up in the draft. It takes away options at the offensive end and causes him to draw a lot of whistles on defense. He has not displayed his aptitude for perimeter scoring in the big leagues. His field goal percentage hovered around .400 last year and he was particularly inept from long range. He makes poor decisions with the ball.

Analysis: All things considered, Bond turned out to be a good pickup for the dismal Mavericks. He started for much of the season, gave teammates free haircuts, and spent his share of games as a double-figure scorer. His poor shooting and decision-making, however, would have put him on the benches of a lot of other teams.

PLAYER SUMMARY

Will	hit the boards
Can't	find his stroke
Expect	post-up offense
Don't Expect	playmaking
Fantasy Value	$0
Card Value	5-10¢

COLLEGE STATISTICS

		G	FGP	FTP	RPG	PPG
87-88	MINN	26	.527	.500	1.4	2.4
88-89	MINN	30	.531	.556	3.7	6.0
89-90	MINN	32	.510	.678	4.2	10.5
90-91	MINN	15	.381	.657	4.5	11.6
Totals		103	.480	.635	3.4	7.3

NBA REGULAR-SEASON STATISTICS

			FGs		3-PT FGs		FTs		Rebounds						
	G	MIN	FG	PCT	FG	PCT	FT	PCT	OFF	TOT	AST	STL	BLK	PTS	PPG
92-93 DAL	74	1578	227	.402	7	.167	129	.772	52	196	122	75	18	590	8.0
Totals	74	1578	227	.402	7	.167	129	.772	52	196	122	75	18	590	8.0

ANTHONY BONNER

Team: Sacramento Kings
Position: Forward
Height: 6'8" **Weight:** 225
Birthdate: June 8, 1968

NBA Experience: 3 years
College: St. Louis
Acquired: 1st-round pick in 1990 draft
(23rd overall)

Background: Bonner led all Division I players in rebounding as a senior at St. Louis University. He finished his career there as the school's all-time leader in points, rebounds, steals, and games played. His rookie season in Sacramento saw him play in only 34 games, as he was injured with two separate stress fractures. He has been a valuable sixth man and part-time starter for the Kings over the last two seasons and enjoyed his best shooting year in 1992-93.

Strengths: Bonner is a bruising rebounder who is willing to sacrifice his body in match-ups with bigger players. He shows a great work ethic and is willing to mix it up at both ends of the floor. He's especially strong on defense, where he lacks power-forward size but can match up with them. He's fearless and shows good quickness.

Weaknesses: Though his range extends to about 15 feet and his shooting has improved, Bonner has no business putting up a lot of jumpers. Offense is not his game. He's a dismal free throw shooter. His dribbling, passing, and decision-making are sub-par, although the latter improved greatly last year. He still tends to play out of control.

Analysis: Bonner has refined his game, but he remains more valuable for his extra effort and physical presence than for his skills. He is a workhorse, especially on defense and on the glass, and he has demonstrated a willingness to play through pain. He broke into the Kings' starting five and contributes with defense and rebounding while scoring in transition and off the offensive boards. His offense is improving.

PLAYER SUMMARY	
Will	bang the boards
Can't	shoot FTs
Expect	defense, hustle
Don't Expect	treys
Fantasy Value	$1-3
Card Value	5-10¢

COLLEGE STATISTICS

		G	FGP	FTP	RPG	PPG
86-87	STL	35	.592	.661	9.6	10.3
87-88	STL	28	.537	.597	8.8	13.8
88-89	STL	37	.560	.582	10.4	15.5
89-90	STL	33	.500	.693	13.8	19.8
Totals		133	.539	.634	10.7	14.8

NBA REGULAR-SEASON STATISTICS

				FGs		3-PT FGs		FTs		Rebounds						
		G	MIN	FG	PCT	FG	PCT	FT	PCT	OFF	TOT	AST	STL	BLK	PTS	PPG
90-91	SAC	34	750	103	.448	0	.000	44	.579	59	161	49	39	5	250	7.4
91-92	SAC	79	2287	294	.447	1	.250	151	.627	192	485	125	94	26	740	9.4
92-93	SAC	70	1764	229	.461	0	.000	143	.593	188	455	96	86	17	601	8.6
Totals		183	4801	626	.452	1	.091	338	.606	439	1101	270	219	48	1591	8.7

ANTHONY BOWIE

Team: Orlando Magic
Position: Guard
Height: 6'6" **Weight:** 190
Birthdate: November 9, 1963

NBA Experience: 4 years
College: Seminole; Oklahoma
Acquired: Signed as a free agent,
12/91

Background: Bowie played college ball at run-and-gun Oklahoma, where he learned to play at a breakneck pace. He was drafted by Houston with the 66th overall pick in 1986, but he played his first NBA ball (18 games) with San Antonio in 1988-89. He was picked up by the Rockets in the summer of '89 and played 66 games in 1989-90 before becoming expendable the next year. Bowie has played some of his best ball since being picked up by Orlando from the CBA during the 1991-92 campaign. He has been a part-time starter the last two years.

Strengths: Bowie is a versatile player who can be used at up to three positions. He glides up and down the court and can shoot the lights out in streaks with a pull-up jumper. He can also get to the basket and he's a very good free throw shooter. He understands the game. Bowie plays hard off the bench and has shown he can start when called upon.

Weaknesses: Bowie is vulnerable against quicker guards and bigger forwards. He tends to play out of control at times—trying to do too much. He's not a great ball-handler. Although he's a good passer, he sometimes forces the ball. Bowie is at his best in transition and coming off screens rather than creating offense on his own.

Analysis: The Magic signed Bowie, a restricted free agent before the 1992-93 season, because they fell in love with his attitude, effort, and ability to fill in where needed. He became a starter for the injured Dennis Scott in January of last season and played well.

PLAYER SUMMARY	
Will	sink FTs
Can't	thrive as playmaker
Expect	versatility
Don't Expect	more CBA days
Fantasy Value	$0
Card Value	5-10¢

COLLEGE STATISTICS

		G	FGP	FTP	RPG	PPG
84-85	OKLA	37	.515	.773	5.8	13.4
85-86	OKLA	35	.502	.808	4.6	13.3
Totals		72	.509	.787	5.2	13.4

NBA REGULAR-SEASON STATISTICS

		G	MIN	FGs FG	FGs PCT	3-PT FGs FG	3-PT FGs PCT	FTs FT	FTs PCT	Rebounds OFF	Rebounds TOT	AST	STL	BLK	PTS	PPG
88-89	SA	18	438	72	.500	1	.200	10	.667	25	56	29	18	4	155	8.6
89-90	HOU	66	.918	119	.406	6	.286	40	.741	36	118	96	42	5	284	4.3
91-92	ORL	52	1721	312	.493	17	.386	117	.860	70	245	163	55	38	758	14.6
92-93	ORL	77	1761	268	.471	15	.313	67	.798	36	194	175	54	14	618	8.0
Totals		213	4838	771	.470	39	.331	234	.810	167	613	463	169	61	1815	8.5

SAM BOWIE

Team: Los Angeles Lakers
Position: Center
Height: 7'1" **Weight:** 263
Birthdate: March 17, 1961
NBA Experience: 8 years

College: Kentucky
Acquired: Traded from Nets with a future 2nd-round pick for Benoit Benjamin, 6/93

Background: Bowie and Ralph Sampson came out of high school in the same year as perhaps the most heralded tandem of big men ever. Bowie was on his way to becoming a dominant collegian at Kentucky when serious leg injuries forced him to sit out two seasons. Portland drafted him ahead of Michael Jordan and will never live that down. His career has been slowed by injuries. After a poor 1992-93 season with New Jersey, he was traded to the Lakers.

Strengths: Bowie has a soft touch and is a fine passer for a big man. His perimeter game is polished. He hits the 18-footer, sticks free throws, and does a decent job on the glass. Despite having leg injuries throughout his career, he still gets up to block shots.

Weaknesses: The word soft has been used to describe Bowie's overall game. A center should shoot better than 45 percent. He tends to fade away instead of going strong to the hoop. He could stand to use his size more effectively on defense too.

Analysis: Despite his skills and his draft status, Bowie is not considered one of the top centers in the league. Injuries have had something to do with that, but so has his inability to develop a power game on the pro level. He plays with finesse and contributes by blocking shots, hitting jumpers, and playing within the offense.

PLAYER SUMMARY	
Will	find cutters
Can't	live up to draft status
Expect	finesse
Don't Expect	power
Fantasy Value	$1-3
Card Value	5-10¢

COLLEGE STATISTICS

		G	FGP	FTP	RPG	PPG
79-80	KEN	34	.531	.764	8.1	12.9
80-81	KEN	28	.520	.720	9.1	17.4
83-84	KEN	34	.516	.722	9.2	10.5
Totals		96	.522	.735	8.8	13.4

NBA REGULAR-SEASON STATISTICS

				FGs		3-PT FGs		FTs		Rebounds						
		G	MIN	FG	PCT	FG	PCT	FT	PCT	OFF	TOT	AST	STL	BLK	PTS	PPG
84-85	POR	76	2216	299	.537	0	.000	160	.711	207	656	215	55	203	758	10.0
85-86	POR	38	1132	167	.484	0	.000	114	.708	93	327	99	21	96	448	11.8
86-87	POR	5	163	30	.455	0	.000	20	.667	14	33	9	1	10	80	16.0
88-89	POR	20	412	69	.451	5	.714	28	.571	36	106	36	7	33	171	8.6
89-90	NJ	68	2207	347	.416	10	.323	294	.776	206	690	91	38	121	998	14.7
90-91	NJ	62	1916	314	.434	4	.182	169	.732	176	480	147	43	90	801	12.9
91-92	NJ	71	2179	421	.445	8	.320	212	.757	203	578	186	41	120	1062	15.0
92-93	NJ	79	2092	287	.450	2	.333	141	.779	158	556	127	32	128	717	9.1
Totals		419	12317	1934	.454	29	.319	1138	.741	1093	3426	910	238	801	5035	12.0

TERRELL BRANDON

Team: Cleveland Cavaliers
Position: Guard
Height: 5'11" **Weight:** 180
Birthdate: May 20, 1970

NBA Experience: 2 years
College: Oregon
Acquired: 1st-round pick in 1991 draft
(11th overall)

Background: Brandon led Portland's Grant High to the 1988 Oregon state championship, and he also won the state title in the triple-jump. He sat out his freshman year at Oregon under Prop 40, then had two terrific seasons at point guard, leading the Pac-10 in scoring and steals as a junior. He entered the NBA draft a year early and was selected 11th overall by Cleveland. Brandon was a crucial performer as a rookie when Mark Price was injured and settled into a key reserve role as a second-year player on a good team.

Strengths: Brandon led all rookies in assists two years ago. He has good vision and court sense, is an excellent leaper, and is explosive with the ball. He was a terrific offensive player in college and has improved his shooting and scoring in each of his two years as a pro. He has a quick release and a pull-up jump shot. He gives the Cavs a spark with his energy off the bench.

Weaknesses: Defense is the main topic here. He did not play much of it in college and is still in the learning stages at the NBA level. He has the quickness and gets back in transition but needs to muscle up against his man in halfcourt play. He is also learning to refine his decision-making. The NBA 3-pointer is not his shot.

Analysis: Brandon gives the Cavaliers a reserve sparkplug. Last year, he overcame his rookie shooting woes, learned a little more about defense, and improved his decisions with the basketball. The question now is how long this up-and-comer will be content to fill in behind Price, one of the premier point guards in the game.

PLAYER SUMMARY

Will..............................provide a spark
Can't......................beat out Mark Price
Expect.......................scoring, assists
Don't Expect.............................muscle
Fantasy Value..............................$3-5
Card Value.....................................8-12¢

COLLEGE STATISTICS

		G	FGP	FTP	APG	PPG
89-90	ORE	29	.474	.752	6.0	17.9
90-91	ORE	28	.491	.850	5.0	26.6
Totals		57	.484	.810	5.5	22.2

NBA REGULAR-SEASON STATISTICS

			MIN	FGs		3-PT FGs		FTs		Rebounds						
		G	MIN	FG	PCT	FG	PCT	FT	PCT	OFF	TOT	AST	STL	BLK	PTS	PPG
91-92	CLE	82	1605	252	.419	1	.043	100	.806	49	162	316	81	22	605	7.4
92-93	CLE	82	1622	297	.478	13	.310	118	.825	37	179	302	79	27	725	8.8
Totals		164	3227	549	.449	14	.215	218	.816	86	341	618	160	49	1330	8.1

FRANK BRICKOWSKI

Team: Milwaukee Bucks
Position: Forward/Center
Height: 6'10" **Weight:** 248
Birthdate: August 14, 1959

NBA Experience: 9 years
College: Penn St.
Acquired: Traded from Spurs for Paul Pressey, 8/90

Background: Brickowski led Penn State in scoring his junior and senior years. After being drafted in the third round by the Knicks, he played overseas for three years in Italy, France, and Israel. Brickowski was part of the deal that brought Mychal Thompson to the Lakers from the Spurs. With Milwaukee, he has finished among the team's top five scorers and rebounders each of the last three campaigns. He enjoyed a career-high scoring season last year.

Strengths: After developing some surprisingly effective moves around the basket, Brickowski often surprises defenders with quickness that belies his big body. He is an effective shooter when open and can also power inside for points. He's strong on the defensive end.

Weaknesses: Brickowski is not as athletic as many of the power forwards around the league and has trouble keeping up with them in an open-court game. Nagging injuries the last two years have slowed him even further. He is not a good ball-handler or passer and draws a lot of whistles.

Analysis: Once a back-up and occasional on-court bodyguard for David Robinson in San Antonio, Brickowski has become a more offensive-minded player with the Bucks. He's a better overall player for it. However, he would probably not be a primary scorer on a more talented team.

PLAYER SUMMARY	
Will	get his points
Can't	thrive in transition
Expect	high FG pct.
Don't Expect	ball-handling
Fantasy Value	$15-18
Card Value	5-8¢

COLLEGE STATISTICS

		G	FGP	FTP	RPG	PPG
77-78	PSU	25	.457	.840	2.6	3.8
78-79	PSU	24	.495	.792	4.5	5.7
79-80	PSU	27	.521	.781	7.5	11.3
80-81	PSU	24	.601	.778	6.3	13.0
Totals		100	.537	.788	5.3	8.5

NBA REGULAR-SEASON STATISTICS

		G	MIN	FGs		3-PT FGs		FTs		Rebounds		AST	STL	BLK	PTS	PPG
				FG	PCT	FG	PCT	FT	PCT	OFF	TOT					
84-85	SEA	78	1115	150	.492	0	.000	85	.669	76	260	100	34	15	385	4.9
85-86	SEA	40	311	30	.517	0	.000	18	.667	16	54	21	11	7	78	2.0
86-87	LA/SA	44	487	63	.508	0	.000	50	.714	48	116	17	20	6	176	4.0
87-88	SA	70	2227	425	.528	1	.200	268	.766	167	483	266	74	36	1119	16.0
88-89	SA	64	1822	337	.515	0	.000	201	.715	148	406	131	102	35	875	13.7
89-90	SA	78	1438	211	.545	0	.000	95	.674	89	327	105	66	37	517	6.6
90-91	MIL	75	1912	372	.527	0	.000	198	.798	129	426	131	86	43	942	12.6
91-92	MIL	65	1556	306	.524	3	.500	125	.767	97	344	122	60	23	740	11.4
92-93	MIL	66	2075	456	.545	8	.308	195	.728	120	405	196	80	44	1115	16.9
Totals		580	12943	2350	.527	12	.235	1235	.738	890	2821	1089	533	246	5947	10.3

KEVIN BROOKS

Team: Denver Nuggets
Position: Forward
Height: 6'8" **Weight:** 200
Birthdate: October 29, 1969
NBA Experience: 2 years

College: S.W. Louisiana
Acquired: Draft rights traded from
Bucks with a future 2nd-round pick for
draft rights to Anthony Avent, 7/91

Background: Perhaps the most heralded recruit in Southwestern Louisiana history, Brooks, from nearby White Castle, Louisiana, was an immediate hit for the run-and-gun Ragin' Cajuns. He finished third among the nation's freshmen in scoring in 1988 and finished his career third behind Bo Lamar and Andrew Toney on USL's all-time scoring list. He was drafted 18th overall by Milwaukee in 1991 but his rights were traded to the Nuggets. He played in less than half of Denver's games as a rookie and continued to ride the pine in his second year.

Strengths: Brooks has been compared to George Gervin and Alex English for his offensive abilities. He can slash to the hoop, was a capable college ball-handler and passer, and can run the floor. Most thought he'd be a perfect fit for Denver's up-tempo offense. Brooks is versatile and is a very good free throw shooter.

Weaknesses: Brooks has been anything but reliable when he has seen action. He shoots around 40 percent from the field, turns the ball over, does not have 3-point range, and shows very little defensive interest. He is not strong enough to defend forwards and lacks the quickness to handle most guards. He has been "lost in the shuffle" among a group of young and talented Denver forwards.

Analysis: An unknown to most as a collegian, Brooks has remained an unknown in the NBA. Quite simply, he has to put the ball in the basket to earn his minutes and he has not done so with any regularity when given a chance. Until he shows he can, he will not play enough to pick up the nuances of NBA defense and sound decision-making.

PLAYER SUMMARY	
Will	struggle for minutes
Can't	shut down his man
Expect	offensive improvement
Don't Expect	consistency
Fantasy Value	$0
Card Value	5-10¢

COLLEGE STATISTICS

		G	FGP	FTP	RPG	PPG
87-88	SWL	27	.565	.761	6.3	16.8
88-89	SWL	29	.522	.753	5.4	20.7
89-90	SWL	29	.499	.816	7.0	20.1
90-91	SWL	31	.515	.778	6.0	21.2
Totals		116	.522	.774	6.2	19.8

NBA REGULAR-SEASON STATISTICS

			FGs		3-PT FGs		FTs		Rebounds						
		G	MIN	FG	PCT	FG	PCT	FT	PCT	OFF	TOT	AST	STL	BLK	PTS	PPG
91-92	DEN	37	270	43	.443	2	.182	17	.810	13	39	11	8	2	105	2.8
92-93	DEN	55	571	93	.399	6	.231	35	.875	22	81	34	10	2	227	4.1
Totals		92	841	136	.412	8	.216	52	.852	35	120	45	18	4	332	3.6

SCOTT BROOKS

Team: Houston Rockets
Position: Guard
Height: 5'11" **Weight:** 165
Birthdate: July 31, 1965
NBA Experience: 5 years

College: Texas Christian; San Joaquin
Delta; Cal.-Irvine
Acquired: Traded from Timberwolves
for a 1995 2nd-round pick, 9/92

Background: Brooks divided his college career among Texas Christian, San Joaquin Delta Junior College, and finally Cal.-Irvine, where he led the Pacific Coast Athletic Association in scoring, steals, and free throw percentage in 1986-87. Despite being passed up in the NBA draft, he emerged from the CBA and appeared in 154 games in two years with Philadelphia. Brooks missed just two games in his two seasons with Minnesota. He enjoyed his best overall season as a Houston reserve during the 1992-93 campaign.

Strengths: Brooks is a tireless worker who loves to pressure the ball from one end of the court to the other. His quickness, great hands, and ability to handle the ball make him the consummate point guard and a nice sparkplug off the bench. He's downright pesky, is a good penetrator, hits the 3, is a great free throw shooter, and has improved his scoring proficiency.

Weaknesses: Most of his offense comes when nothing else is available for Brooks, who is a passer first and scorer second. His size works against him on defense, where bigger guards shoot over him or post him up. He is a contributor rather than a good team's ideal starter.

Analysis: Brooks, a California surfer type, simply loves to play the game and has contributed everywhere he has unpacked his bags. He was a highly effective presence for Houston, usually on the floor in the fourth quarter. He posted career highs in virtually every statistical category last year and displayed the kind of leadership coaches love to see.

PLAYER SUMMARY

Will.............................run the offense
Can't.....................................post up
Expect..................hustle, leadership
Don't Expect ....slam dunks
Fantasy Value..............................$1
Card Value.............................8-12¢

COLLEGE STATISTICS

		G	FGP	FTP	APG	PPG
83-84	TCU	27	.529	.714	1.4	3.8
84-85	SJD	31	.525	.882	—	13.1
85-86	C-I	30	.448	.886	3.2	10.3
86-87	C-I	28	.478	.845	3.8	23.8
Totals		116	.489	.860	2.8	12.8

NBA REGULAR-SEASON STATISTICS

		G	MIN	FGs FG	FGs PCT	3-PT FGs FG	3-PT FGs PCT	FTs FT	FTs PCT	Rebounds OFF	Rebounds TOT	AST	STL	BLK	PTS	PPG
88-89	PHI	82	1372	156	.420	55	.359	61	.884	19	94	306	69	3	428	5.2
89-90	PHI	72	975	119	.431	31	.392	50	.877	15	64	207	47	0	319	4.4
90-91	MIN	80	980	159	.430	45	.333	61	.847	28	72	204	53	5	424	5.3
91-92	MIN	82	1082	167	.447	32	.356	51	.810	27	99	205	66	7	417	5.1
92-93	HOU	82	1516	183	.475	41	.414	112	.830	22	99	243	79	3	519	6.3
Totals		398	5925	784	.441	204	.367	335	.846	111	428	1165	314	18	2107	5.3

CHUCKY BROWN

Team: New Jersey Nets
Position: Forward
Height: 6'8" **Weight:** 215
Birthdate: February 29, 1968

NBA Experience: 4 years
College: North Carolina St.
Acquired: Signed as a free agent, 10/92

Background: Brown was an All-ACC first-team selection after his senior season at N.C. State, in which he averaged 16.4 PPG and 8.8 RPG. He finished second on the school's all-time field goal-percentage list. Although he was drafted 43rd overall in 1989, he was one of three rookies to make Cleveland's roster. After playing in 75 and 74 games with the Cavs in his first two years, he saw limited action as a Laker in 1991-92 before enjoying a better season with the Nets during the 1992-93 campaign.

Strengths: Brown fares well in an up-tempo game. He's a good athlete and has decent low-post moves, including a jump hook that he can shoot with either hand, but his best shot is the pull-up jumper. He works hard, loves to play the game, and is a favorite among teammates.

Weaknesses: Brown is not a good ball-handler, has trouble creating his own shot, and does not pass well. He'll cough up the basketball as often as he gets credit for an assist. He's not a consistent stand-still shooter and has limited range. Also, Brown is not as good a defender or rebounder as an athlete of his caliber should be.

Analysis: A personable young man who is willing to work, Brown bounced back from a frustrating stint with the Lakers and was a contributor off the New Jersey bench for most of last season. He even filled in as a starter for a handful of games. As long as he continues to shoot near 50 percent, his athletic ability and work ethic will keep him in the hunt for playing time.

PLAYER SUMMARY	
Will	get down the floor
Can't	create opportunities
Expect	a willing worker
Don't Expect	assists
Fantasy Value	$0
Card Value	5-10¢

COLLEGE STATISTICS

		G	FGP	FTP	RPG	PPG
85-86	NCST	31	.475	.618	2.2	3.1
86-87	NCST	34	.587	.762	4.3	6.6
87-88	NCST	32	.572	.636	6.0	16.6
88-89	NCST	31	.548	.648	8.8	16.4
Totals		128	.557	.667	5.3	10.6

NBA REGULAR-SEASON STATISTICS

				FGs		3-PT FGs		FTs		Rebounds						
		G	MIN	FG	PCT	FG	PCT	FT	PCT	OFF	TOT	AST	STL	BLK	PTS	PPG
89-90	CLE	75	1339	210	.470	0	.000	125	.762	83	231	50	33	26	545	7.3
90-91	CLE	74	1485	263	.524	0	.000	101	.701	78	213	80	26	24	627	8.5
91-92	CLE/LAL	42	431	60	.469	0	.000	30	.612	31	82	26	12	7	150	3.6
92-93	NJ	77	1186	160	.483	0	.000	71	.724	88	232	51	20	24	391	5.1
Totals		232	4060	638	.495	0	.000	302	.729	251	682	184	82	74	1578	6.8

DEE BROWN

Team: Boston Celtics
Position: Guard
Height: 6'1" **Weight:** 161
Birthdate: November 29, 1968

NBA Experience: 3 years
College: Jacksonville
Acquired: 1st-round pick in 1990 draft
(19th overall)

Background: Brown was Jacksonville's main man as a junior, leading the Dolphins in scoring, rebounding, and steals while splitting time between big guard and small forward. He set a school mark for career 3-pointers with 87. He helped solidify the Celtics' backcourt as a first-team All-Rookie performer, then missed more than half of the 1991-92 season following arthroscopic knee surgery required by a preseason injury. Brown bounced back last year and served as Boston's starting point guard for most of the season.

Strengths: Brown has a tremendous vertical leap that he displayed in winning the NBA's Slam Dunk Contest in Charlotte in 1991. He has lightning-quick speed and is especially dangerous on the fastbreak, where he can dish off or finish the play himself. Brown is one of the quickest players in the league. He's a good on-the-ball defender who can play above the rim despite his size. He has also become a 3-point threat.

Weaknesses: While he has made great strides in his shooting, defenders are still best advised to back off and let him put it up. His game takes a hit when you take away his drive to the hoop. He can play too rapidly for his own good at times, yet is not at his best in a halfcourt game.

Analysis: Though he lost his starting job to much-improved Sherman Douglas for part of the second half of last season, Brown provides too much spark to be sitting on the bench. He bounced back nicely from a knee injury that was of some concern and continues to improve his shooting and overall play.

PLAYER SUMMARY	
Will	get to the rim
Can't	rely on jump-shooting
Expect	great quickness
Don't Expect	a slow pace
Fantasy Value	$10-12
Card Value	8-12¢

COLLEGE STATISTICS

		G	FGP	FTP	APG	PPG
86-87	JACK	21	.431	.591	0.8	3.4
87-88	JACK	28	.452	.818	2.0	10.1
88-89	JACK	30	.490	.824	3.7	19.6
89-90	JACK	29	.496	.683	5.2	19.3
Totals		108	.482	.762	3.1	13.9

NBA REGULAR-SEASON STATISTICS

			FGs		3-PT FGs		FTs		Rebounds						
		G	MIN	FG	PCT	FG	PCT	FT	PCT	OFF	TOT	AST	STL	BLK	PTS	PPG
90-91	BOS	82	1945	284	.464	7	.206	137	.873	41	182	344	83	14	712	8.7
91-92	BOS	31	883	149	.426	5	.227	60	.769	15	79	164	33	7	363	11.7
92-93	BOS	80	2254	328	.468	26	.317	192	.793	45	246	461	138	32	874	10.9
Totals		193	5082	761	.458	38	.275	389	.816	101	507	969	254	53	1949	10.1

MIKE BROWN

Team: Minnesota Timberwolves
Position: Forward/Center
Height: 6'10" **Weight:** 260
Birthdate: July 19, 1963

NBA Experience: 7 years
College: George Washington
Acquired: Traded from Jazz for Felton Spencer, 6/93

Background: Brown went from being the Atlantic 10's Freshman of the Year to becoming George Washington University's second all-time leading scorer and rebounder, despite being hindered by a toe injury as a senior. He began his pro career in Italy before moving to Chicago and then Utah. He was a workhorse with the Jazz, appearing in all 82 games each of the last four years. On draft day, however, he was traded to Minnesota.

Strengths: Strength and size are Brown's biggest attributes. He's got enough power in his frame to push around even the strongest big men. He can play power forward or center. He's capable of scoring in spurts if you don't guard him. Brown is most valuable as a defender, where his physical style irritates opponents.

Weaknesses: Brown's bulk can work against him, as quicker players often beat him to the spot. Move him away from the basket and his game suffers. He has little touch from the perimeter and struggled from the field last season. He'll disappear at times and is not much of a shot-blocking threat for a center.

Analysis: Brown has been a reliable role-player. Not only will he make his fouls worth their while, but he'll grab some rebounds, score a few points, and keep the opposition from getting anything easy inside. He'll get a warm welcome from the Timberwolves, who have lacked consistency from their big men.

PLAYER SUMMARY

Will ....score when open
Can't ....thrive on perimeter
Expect ....consistent minutes
Don't Expect............................finesse
Fantasy Value................................$1-3
Card Value ....5-10¢

COLLEGE STATISTICS

		G	FGP	FTP	RPG	PPG
81-82	GW	27	.497	.518	8.5	15.6
82-83	GW	29	.520	.655	10.3	17.1
83-84	GW	29	.535	.730	12.1	19.6
84-85	GW	26	.480	.649	11.0	16.6
Totals		111	.509	.653	10.5	17.3

NBA REGULAR-SEASON STATISTICS

		G	MIN	FGs FG	PCT	3-PT FGs FG	PCT	FTs FT	PCT	Rebounds OFF	TOT	AST	STL	BLK	PTS	PPG
86-87	CHI	62	818	106	.527	0	.000	46	.639	71	214	24	20	7	258	4.2
87-88	CHI	46	591	78	.448	0	.000	41	.577	66	159	28	11	4	197	4.3
88-89	UTA	66	1051	104	.419	0	.000	92	.708	92	258	41	25	17	300	4.5
89-90	UTA	82	1397	177	.515	1	.500	157	.789	111	373	47	32	49	512	6.2
90-91	UTA	82	1391	129	.454	0	.000	132	.742	109	337	49	29	24	390	4.8
91-92	UTA	82	1783	221	.453	0	.000	190	.667	187	476	81	42	34	632	7.7
92-93	UTA	82	1551	176	.430	0	.000	113	.689	147	391	64	32	23	465	5.7
Totals		502	8582	991	.461	1	.200	771	.702	783	2208	334	191	137	2754	5.5

RANDY BROWN

Team: Sacramento Kings
Position: Guard
Height: 6'3" **Weight:** 190
Birthdate: May 22, 1968

NBA Experience: 2 years
College: Houston; New Mexico St.
Acquired: 2nd-round pick in 1991 draft (31st overall)

Background: Brown played at Collins High School in Chicago before beginning his college career at Houston, where he started 12 games as a freshman. After his sophomore season with the Cougars, he transferred to New Mexico State and became one of the top players in the Big West Conference. He set school records for assists and steals in a season, and steals in a career, while twice earning first-team all-conference honors. A second-round choice by Sacramento, Brown played in 56 games as a rookie and became a part-time starter last year, when he averaged better than seven PPG and broke the 100-steal barrier.

Strengths: Known as a defensive whiz at up-tempo New Mexico State, Brown has backed up his reputation as a pro. He's quick, is tough, has good hands, and is not afraid to challenge opponents. He also rebounds very well from the backcourt. His ball-handling, decision-making, and passing all improved during his second year.

Weaknesses: Brown is not considered a big-time scorer. His jump shot is sporadic, though he has nights when everything falls, and he's not a 3-point threat. As well, his playmaking does not put him in a class with the average NBA point guard. His assist-to-turnover ratio is less than two. Sometimes he can be too aggressive on the defensive end.

Analysis: An injury to Spud Webb early last season opened the door for Brown, who handled the team well and earned the right to play even in a healthy Kings lineup. He showed he could score a bit in addition to making his defensive contributions. He does not have the look of a 15-PPG man and his playmaking skills need work, but he does enough to earn his minutes.

PLAYER SUMMARY	
Will	swipe the ball
Can't	rack up assists
Expect	defense off the bench
Don't Expect	treys
Fantasy Value	$1-3
Card Value	5-10¢

COLLEGE STATISTICS

		G	FGP	FTP	APG	PPG
86-87	HOU	28	.506	.583	2.9	3.8
87-88	HOU	29	.451	.750	5.6	7.0
89-90	NMST	31	.446	.712	3.5	13.2
90-91	NMST	29	.399	.691	6.4	12.1
Totals		117	.436	.703	4.6	9.1

NBA REGULAR-SEASON STATISTICS

		G	MIN	FGs FG	FGs PCT	3-PT FGs FG	3-PT FGs PCT	FTs FT	FTs PCT	Rebounds OFF	Rebounds TOT	AST	STL	BLK	PTS	PPG
91-92	SAC	56	535	77	.456	0	.000	38	.655	26	69	59	35	12	192	3.4
92-93	SAC	75	1726	225	.463	2	.333	115	.732	75	212	196	108	34	567	7.6
Totals		131	2261	302	.461	2	.167	153	.712	101	281	255	143	46	759	5.8

MARK BRYANT

Team: Portland Trail Blazers
Position: Forward
Height: 6'9" **Weight:** 245
Birthdate: April 25, 1965

NBA Experience: 5 years
College: Seton Hall
Acquired: 1st-round pick in 1988 draft
(21st overall)

Background: As a senior, Bryant helped take Seton Hall to its first NCAA Tournament and was an All-Big East selection. He started 32 of his first 34 games as a pro but then encountered injury problems. His rookie year was cut short by more than a month when he fractured his thumb in a fight with Joe Kleine, and he missed 27 games the next year with a broken bone in his foot. Last year was his first in which he saw action in more than 60 games.

Strengths: Bryant is physically impressive and plays tough defense. He's willing to throw his weight around and battle inside with the league's power forwards. He's a good rebounder, runs the floor, and owns a decent short-range jumper.

Weaknesses: Bryant's offensive repertoire is limited and he is not a good ball-handler or passer. He doesn't specialize in any one thing, so he's easy to overlook. He's not the kind of bench player who comes into the game and ignites his team. Injuries have set him back. His range is limited and he does not excel from the free throw line.

Analysis: A valuable banger and role-player because of his size and strength, Bryant is not a power forward who will dazzle you with his skills. Last year was the healthiest and most productive of his career, yet he still averaged less than six PPG and was not among his team's top rebounders. He is probably not the heir apparent to Portland starter Buck Williams, although he helps his team in a reserve role.

PLAYER SUMMARY	
Will	play physical defense
Can't	take over offensively
Expect	size, strength
Don't Expect	10 PPG
Fantasy Value	$0
Card Value	5-10¢

COLLEGE STATISTICS

		G	FGP	FTP	RPG	PPG
84-85	SH	26	.475	.649	6.8	12.2
85-86	SH	30	.523	.678	7.5	14.0
86-87	SH	28	.496	.706	7.1	16.8
87-88	SH	34	.564	.748	9.1	20.5
Totals		118	.521	.705	7.7	16.2

NBA REGULAR-SEASON STATISTICS

			FGs		3-PT FGs		FTs		Rebounds						
		G	MIN	FG	PCT	FG	PCT	FT	PCT	OFF	TOT	AST	STL	BLK	PTS	PPG
88-89	POR	56	803	120	.486	0	.000	40	.580	65	179	33	20	7	280	5.0
89-90	POR	58	562	70	.458	0	.000	28	.560	54	146	13	18	9	168	2.9
90-91	POR	53	781	99	.488	0	.000	74	.733	65	190	27	15	12	272	5.1
91-92	POR	56	800	95	.480	0	.000	40	.667	87	201	41	26	8	230	4.1
92-93	POR	80	1396	186	.503	0	.000	104	.703	132	324	41	37	23	476	5.9
Totals		303	4342	570	.487	0	.000	286	.668	403	1040	155	116	59	1426	4.7

JUD BUECHLER

Team: Golden State Warriors
Position: Forward
Height: 6'6" **Weight:** 220
Birthdate: June 19, 1968

NBA Experience: 3 years
College: Arizona
Acquired: Signed as a free agent, 12/91

Background: Buechler was Arizona's scoring and rebounding leader as a senior and was always a top marksman, finishing his career with a blazing 54.7 shooting percentage. He was All-Pac-10 his senior year before being drafted in the second round by Seattle for New Jersey as part of a pre-draft deal. He played in 74 games as a rookie, but was released by the Nets two games into his second campaign. He was then picked up by San Antonio, waived after 11 games with the Spurs, and signed by Golden State in December 1991. He saw extensive action off the Warrior bench last season.

Strengths: The kind of player who doesn't mind doing the dirty work, Buechler will rebound, hustle, set picks, and play sound, physical defense. In short, he'll do whatever it takes to play. He'll also knock down the 3-point shot if you leave him unattended. He's unselfish, makes good passes, and won't do much to hurt the cause.

Weaknesses: Buechler is not the most gifted player in the league. He does not make a whole lot happen in the scoring column and usually defers to others at the offensive end. He also falls somewhere between a shooting guard and small forward. Quickness causes him trouble on defense.

Analysis: It's nice to be needed, and Buechler was last year. It was a season of injury after injury for Golden State, but Buechler was there night after night doing the things a coach loves to see. He would not have seen as much action under different circumstances and will never be a big scorer, but it was a healthy change over his second-year travels.

PLAYER SUMMARY	
Will	expend himself
Can't	create offensively
Expect	fundamentals, defense
Don't Expect	a natural
Fantasy Value	$0
Card Value	5-10¢

COLLEGE STATISTICS

		G	FGP	FTP	RPG	PPG
86-87	ARIZ	30	.486	.571	2.3	4.5
87-88	ARIZ	36	.516	.655	2.4	4.7
88-89	ARIZ	33	.607	.816	6.6	11.0
89-90	ARIZ	32	.538	.765	8.3	14.9
Totals		131	.547	.743	4.9	8.7

NBA REGULAR-SEASON STATISTICS

		G	MIN	FGs FG	FGs PCT	3-PT FGs FG	3-PT FGs PCT	FTs FT	FTs PCT	Rebounds OFF	Rebounds TOT	AST	STL	BLK	PTS	PPG
90-91	NJ	74	859	94	.416	1	.250	43	.652	61	141	51	33	15	232	3.1
91-92	NJ/SA/GS	28	290	29	.408	0	.000	12	.571	18	52	23	19	7	70	2.5
92-93	GS	70	1287	176	.437	20	.339	65	.747	81	195	94	47	19	437	6.2
Totals		172	2436	299	.427	21	.328	120	.690	160	388	168	99	41	739	4.3

MATT BULLARD

Team: Houston Rockets
Position: Forward
Height: 6'10" **Weight:** 235
Birthdate: June 5, 1967

NBA Experience: 3 years
College: Colorado; Iowa
Acquired: Signed as a free agent, 8/90

Background: Bullard played two years at Colorado, led the team in scoring as a sophomore, and then transferred to Iowa, where he once connected on six 3-pointers in a game. He was not drafted but played well enough in the Los Angeles summer league to earn a spot with the Rockets for the 1990-91 season. He saw action in just 18 games as a rookie (his left knee gave him trouble) before developing into a regular reserve the past two seasons. He had career highs in several categories last season.

Strengths: An excellent outside shooter, Bullard was second to Vernon Maxwell on the Rockets in 3-pointers made during 1991-92 and third a year ago. He converts about 38 percent of his treys and 78 percent of his free throws. He plays within himself and makes the right pass. His knee is no longer a concern.

Weaknesses: Bullard is not the kind of guy who will create with the dribble. He needs open jumpers or screens to be effective. He's not a good offensive rebounder, and low-post offense is not a solid part of his game. He lacks the quickness to defend small forwards. Bullard does not shoot a high percentage from inside the paint.

Analysis: Bullard has been a pleasant surprise for the Rockets the last two years. His game is one-dimensional, but he performs that dimension well enough to force the opposition to defend him. If teams forget about him, he'll drill 3-point buckets all night. He has improved his contributions in other areas but would really give his career a boost by learning to put the ball on the floor.

PLAYER SUMMARY

Will ....bury 3-pointers
Can't........................create on his own
Expect..........firepower, fundamentals
Don't Expect ....quickness
Fantasy Value...................................$1
Card Value...............................5-10¢

COLLEGE STATISTICS

		G	FGP	FTP	RPG	PPG
85-86	COLO	28	.604	.818	6.4	12.7
86-87	COLO	28	.521	.742	10.0	16.6
88-89	IOWA	20	.564	.800	6.2	9.1
89-90	IOWA	18	.434	.720	2.9	11.4
Totals		94	.533	.768	6.8	12.8

NBA REGULAR-SEASON STATISTICS

		G	MIN	FGs FG	FGs PCT	3-PT FGs FG	3-PT FGs PCT	FTs FT	FTs PCT	Rebounds OFF	Rebounds TOT	AST	STL	BLK	PTS	PPG
90-91	HOU	18	63	14	.452	0	.000	11	.647	6	14	2	3	0	39	2.2
91-92	HOU	80	1278	205	.459	64	.386	38	.760	73	223	75	26	21	512	6.4
92-93	HOU	79	1356	213	.431	91	.374	58	.784	66	222	110	30	11	575	7.3
Totals		177	2697	432	.444	155	.376	107	.759	145	459	187	59	32	1126	6.4

WILLIE BURTON

Team: Miami Heat
Position: Guard/Forward
Height: 6'8" **Weight:** 217
Birthdate: May 26, 1968

NBA Experience: 3 years
College: Minnesota
Acquired: 1st-round pick in 1990 draft
(9th overall)

Background: A four-sport athlete in high school, Burton became the University of Minnesota's No. 2 career scorer (behind Mychal Thompson). As a senior, he led the Gophers into the Southeast Regional finals and was named first-team All-Big Ten. Miami chose him ninth in the 1990 draft and he started the last 24 games of his rookie season. Recurring knee injuries and a late-season bout with depression slowed him in 1991-92. Surgery to repair major cartilage and ligament damage in his right wrist cost him most of the 1992-93 campaign, as he played in just 26 games.

Strengths: Burton has the versatility to play either big guard or small forward. He can hurt you in a variety of ways with his scorer's mentality. Slashing to the hoop is his bread and butter. He draws fouls and has good range with a hot-and-cold jumper.

Weaknesses: Burton has never been a good or willing passer. He wasn't asked to do much of it in college and he does not keep his eyes open for teammates as a pro either. He commits a lot of turnovers, does not put much energy into defense, and is horribly inconsistent from the perimeter.

Analysis: Burton seems to be over his bout with depression, which seemed to take some of the fire out of his game two years ago. Now he must overcome a season that was plagued by both a long stint on the injured list and his own up-and-down play. He thinks like a scorer, but to this point in his career he has yet to prove he can score a lot of points in the NBA.

PLAYER SUMMARY	
Will	slash to the hoop
Can't	stay healthy
Expect	a scorer's mindset
Don't Expect	2 APG
Fantasy Value	$2-4
Card Value	5-10¢

COLLEGE STATISTICS

		G	FGP	FTP	RPG	PPG
86-87	MINN	28	.455	.649	4.2	8.7
87-88	MINN	28	.516	.713	5.6	13.7
88-89	MINN	30	.529	.797	7.5	18.6
89-90	MINN	32	.519	.770	6.4	19.3
Totals		118	.511	.749	6.0	15.3

NBA REGULAR-SEASON STATISTICS

				FGs		3-PT FGs		FTs		Rebounds						
		G	MIN	FG	PCT	FG	PCT	FT	PCT	OFF	TOT	AST	STL	BLK	PTS	PPG
90-91	MIA	76	1928	341	.441	4	.133	229	.782	111	262	107	72	24	915	12.0
91-92	MIA	68	1585	280	.450	6	.400	196	.800	76	244	123	46	37	762	11.2
92-93	MIA	26	451	54	.383	5	.333	91	.717	22	70	16	13	16	204	7.8
Totals		170	3964	675	.439	15	.250	516	.776	209	576	246	131	77	1881	11.1

MICHAEL CAGE

Team: Seattle SuperSonics
Position: Forward/Center
Height: 6'9" **Weight:** 230
Birthdate: January 28, 1962
NBA Experience: 9 years

College: San Diego St.
Acquired: Traded from Clippers for draft rights to Gary Grant and a 1989 1st-round pick, 6/88

Background: Cage was voted Western Athletic Conference Player of the Year as a senior at San Diego State. He finished as the school's career leader in scoring, rebounding, and games played. With the Los Angeles Clippers in 1987-88, he won the NBA rebounding title by grabbing 30 boards on the final night of the season. He was second on Seattle in rebounding last year and has shot better than 50 percent in each of the last four seasons.

Strengths: The tough, muscular Cage has made his living off the backboard. While he is no longer a shoo-in among the league's top ten rebounders, he still gets the job done and has become a more complete player. He shoots a high percentage and plays defense.

Weaknesses: Cage is not known for his offense. His low-post moves are predictable, but he has spent a large portion of his career playing out of position at center. He's not much of a ball-handler or passer and is a lousy free throw shooter.

Analysis: Cage comes to work every day ready to rebound and mix it up. A team player, he does not think his starting role entitles him to a certain number of shots or points per game. He is content to do whatever job is required to win games.

PLAYER SUMMARY

Will ....get physical
Can't ....shoot FTs
Expect ....rebounds, defense
Don't Expect ....10 PPG
Fantasy Value $1
Card Value ....5-10¢

COLLEGE STATISTICS

		G	FGP	FTP	RPG	PPG
80-81	SDS	27	.558	.756	13.1	10.9
81-82	SDS	29	.488	.661	8.8	11.0
82-83	SDS	28	.570	.747	12.6	19.5
83-84	SDS	28	.562	.741	12.6	24.5
Totals		112	.548	.732	11.8	16.5

NBA REGULAR-SEASON STATISTICS

		G	MIN	FGs		3-PT FGs		FTs		Rebounds		AST	STL	BLK	PTS	PPG
				FG	PCT	FG	PCT	FT	PCT	OFF	TOT					
84-85	LAC	75	1610	216	.543	0	.000	101	.737	126	392	51	41	32	533	7.1
85-86	LAC	78	1566	204	.479	0	.000	113	.649	168	417	81	62	34	521	6.7
86-87	LAC	80	2922	457	.521	0	.000	341	.730	354	922	131	99	67	1255	15.7
87-88	LAC	72	2660	360	.470	0	.000	326	.688	371	938	110	91	58	1046	14.5
88-89	SEA	80	2536	314	.498	0	.000	197	.743	276	765	126	92	52	825	10.3
89-90	SEA	82	2595	325	.504	0	.000	148	.698	306	821	70	79	45	798	9.7
90-91	SEA	82	2141	226	.508	0	.000	70	.625	177	558	89	85	58	522	6.4
91-92	SEA	82	2461	307	.566	0	.000	106	.620	266	728	92	99	55	720	8.8
92-93	SEA	82	2156	219	.526	0	.000	61	.469	268	659	69	76	46	499	6.1
Totals		713	20647	2628	.511	0	.000	1463	.683	2312	6200	819	724	447	6719	9.4

ELDEN CAMPBELL

Team: Los Angeles Lakers
Position: Forward/Center
Height: 6'11" **Weight:** 235
Birthdate: July 23, 1968

NBA Experience: 3 years
College: Clemson
Acquired: 1st-round pick in 1990 draft
(27th overall)

Background: Campbell led the Atlantic Coast Conference in blocked shots three straight years and became Clemson's career scoring leader. As a rookie in 1990-91, he saw limited action in 52 regular-season games but played some key stretches during the playoffs. He scored 21 points in Game 5 of the Finals. He was the Lakers' starting power forward for most of 1991-92 because of an injury to Sam Perkins, and finished 13th in the league in blocks per game. He returned to a reserve role for most of the 1992-93 campaign but increased his per-minute scoring average.

Strengths: Best known for his shot-blocking and defensive intimidation, Campbell has great instincts for the ball, has a huge wingspan, and is a superb athlete and leaper. He gets up and down the floor, finishes with flair, and has become a better scorer.

Weaknesses: Campbell is very limited in what he can do in a halfcourt set. His fundamentals on both ends of the floor could stand some work. He does not shoot a high percentage from the field, even when he gets the ball on the blocks. He is a poor free throw shooter, does not spot open men, and commits too many turnovers.

Analysis: The clock is ticking on Campbell. He is a splendid athlete and has given indications that he can be an impact player at the pro level. But throw out a few fantastic games and you have an inconsistent player who has yet to take hold of an opportunity to solidify a spot in the starting lineup. The prevailing opinion is that Campbell possesses loads of untapped potential.

PLAYER SUMMARY

Will.............................block shots
Can't ....spot open men
Expect..................points in transition
Don't Expect...............halfcourt skills
Fantasy Value................................$1-3
Card Value ....8-12¢

COLLEGE STATISTICS

		G	FGP	FTP	RPG	PPG
86-87	CLEM	31	.554	.702	4.1	8.8
87-88	CLEM	28	.629	.619	7.4	18.8
88-89	CLEM	29	.550	.688	7.7	17.5
89-90	CLEM	35	.522	.599	8.0	16.4
Totals		123	.562	.641	6.8	15.3

NBA REGULAR-SEASON STATISTICS

			FGs		3-PT FGs		FTs		Rebounds							
		G	MIN	FG	PCT	FG	PCT	FT	PCT	OFF	TOT	AST	STL	BLK	PTS	PPG
90-91	LAL	52	380	56	.455	0	.000	32	.653	40	96	10	11	38	144	2.8
91-92	LAL	81	1876	220	.448	0	.000	138	.619	155	423	59	53	159	578	7.1
92-93	LAL	79	1551	238	.458	0	.000	130	.637	127	332	48	59	100	606	7.7
Totals		212	3807	514	.453	0	.000	300	.630	322	851	117	123	297	1328	6.3

TONY CAMPBELL

Team: New York Knicks
Position: Guard/Forward
Height: 6'7" **Weight:** 215
Birthdate: May 7, 1962

NBA Experience: 9 years
College: Ohio St.
Acquired: Traded from Timberwolves for a future 2nd-round pick, 9/92

Background: Campbell was selected Big Ten Player of the Year after leading Ohio State in four statistical categories as a senior. His pro career started on the Detroit bench and in the CBA, but he exploded onto the scene with the Lakers when Byron Scott and Magic Johnson suffered injuries in the 1989 playoffs. He was Minnesota's leading scorer in its first three years of existence before becoming a role-player with the Knicks last season.

Strengths: Putting the ball in the basket is Campbell's specialty. He gets to the hoop, draws fouls, and is not afraid to take the high-pressure shots. He is able to play both small forward and big guard. He works hard and has tons of confidence.

Weaknesses: There are those who say Campbell cares too much about his stat line. He has not been a willing passer. Campbell is also a below-average rebounder for his position, and much of his early struggles on the New York bench stemmed from his allergies to defense.

Analysis: Campbell is a scorer, period. He wanted out of Minnesota and got his wish, then found himself riding the pine with the Knicks until he became more willing to pass and defend. He will never do either of those things as well as he puts the ball in the basket.

PLAYER SUMMARY	
Will	create his shots
Can't	shut down his man
Expect	instant offense
Don't Expect	assists
Fantasy Value	$1
Card Value	5-10¢

COLLEGE STATISTICS

		G	FGP	FTP	RPG	PPG
80-81	OSU	14	.417	.500	0.6	1.6
81-82	OSU	31	.424	.798	5.0	12.8
82-83	OSU	30	.503	.799	8.3	19.0
83-84	OSU	29	.513	.807	7.4	18.6
Totals		104	.482	.798	6.0	14.7

NBA REGULAR-SEASON STATISTICS

		G	MIN	FGs FG	FGs PCT	3-PT FGs FG	3-PT FGs PCT	FTs FT	FTs PCT	Rebounds OFF	Rebounds TOT	AST	STL	BLK	PTS	PPG
84-85	DET	56	625	130	.496	0	.000	56	.800	41	89	24	28	3	316	5.6
85-86	DET	82	1292	294	.484	2	.222	58	.795	83	236	45	62	7	648	7.9
86-87	DET	40	332	57	.393	0	.000	24	.615	21	58	19	12	1	138	3.5
87-88	LAL	13	242	57	.564	1	.333	28	.718	8	27	15	11	2	143	11.0
88-89	LAL	63	787	158	.458	2	.095	70	.843	53	130	47	37	6	388	6.2
89-90	MIN	82	3164	723	.457	9	.167	448	.787	209	451	213	111	31	1903	23.2
90-91	MIN	77	2893	652	.434	16	.262	358	.803	161	346	214	121	48	1678	21.8
91-92	MIN	78	2441	527	.464	13	.351	240	.803	141	286	229	84	31	1307	16.8
92-93	NY	58	1062	194	.490	2	.400	59	.678	59	155	62	34	5	449	7.7
Totals		549	12838	2792	.459	45	.232	1341	.787	776	1778	868	500	134	6970	12.7

ANTOINE CARR

Team: San Antonio Spurs
Position: Forward
Height: 6'9" **Weight:** 255
Birthdate: July 23, 1961
NBA Experience: 9 years

College: Wichita St.
Acquired: Traded from Kings for Dwayne Schintzius and a 1994 2nd-round pick, 9/91

Background: Carr played with Cliff Levingston and Xavier McDaniel at Wichita State, where his No. 35 was retired after an All-America career. He played five-plus years in Atlanta with varying degrees of success before becoming a big scorer in Sacramento. He has served as both a starter and reserve in two years with San Antonio. He finished fourth on the team in scoring last season despite early shoulder and knee injuries.

Strengths: Carr can play both power forward and center because of his strong low-post game at both ends of the floor. He holds his position in the lane, loves to put his body on opposing players, and can put the ball in the hole. He's a fierce finisher, once shattering a backboard in warm-ups with the Hawks.

Weaknesses: When pushed away from the paint, Carr becomes largely ineffective. Most of his rebounding and scoring comes as a result of superior positioning rather than hustle. As a result, he gets called for a lot of fouls.

Analysis: Carr has been invaluable to the Spurs, especially when regular power forward Terry Cummings was sidelined for the 1992-93 season. Carr started for most of the year, increased both his scoring and field goal shooting from the year before, and helped the Spurs toughen up after a poor start.

PLAYER SUMMARY	
Will	throw his weight around
Can't	excel on perimeter
Expect	nice touch inside
Don't Expect	10 RPG
Fantasy Value	$6-8
Card Value	5-10¢

COLLEGE STATISTICS

		G	FGP	FTP	RPG	PPG
79-80	WSU	29	.501	.667	5.9	15.2
80-81	WSU	33	.586	.765	7.3	15.8
81-82	WSU	28	.566	.791	7.0	16.0
82-83	WSU	22	.575	.765	7.6	22.6
Totals		112	.557	.746	6.9	17.1

NBA REGULAR-SEASON STATISTICS

				FGs		3-PT FGs		FTs		Rebounds						
		G	MIN	FG	PCT	FG	PCT	FT	PCT	OFF	TOT	AST	STL	BLK	PTS	PPG
84-85	ATL	62	1195	198	.528	2	.333	101	.789	79	232	80	29	78	499	8.0
85-86	ATL	17	258	49	.527	0	.000	18	.667	16	52	14	7	15	116	6.8
86-87	ATL	65	695	134	.506	1	.333	73	.709	60	156	34	14	48	342	5.3
87-88	ATL	80	1483	281	.544	1	.250	142	.780	94	289	103	38	83	705	8.8
88-89	ATL	78	1488	226	.480	0	.000	130	.855	106	274	91	31	62	582	7.5
89-90	ATL/SAC	77	1727	356	.494	0	.000	237	.795	115	322	119	30	68	949	12.3
90-91	SAC	77	2527	628	.511	0	.000	295	.758	163	420	191	45	101	1551	20.1
91-92	SA	81	1867	359	.490	1	.200	162	.764	128	346	63	32	96	881	10.9
92-93	SA	71	1947	379	.490	0	.000	174	.777	107	388	97	35	87	932	13.1
Totals		608	13187	2610	.511	5	.147	1332	.777	868	2479	792	261	638	6557	10.8

BILL CARTWRIGHT

Team: Chicago Bulls
Position: Center
Height: 7'1" **Weight:** 245
Birthdate: July 30, 1957
NBA Experience: 13 years

College: San Francisco
Acquired: Traded from Knicks with 1988 1st- and 3rd-round picks for Charles Oakley and 1988 1st- and 3rd-round picks, 6/88

Background: Cartwright was an All-American at San Francisco, and the Knicks chose him third overall in the 1979 draft. He had an up-and-down career in New York, twice averaging 20-plus PPG but then languishing because of chronic knee, back, and foot problems. He caught his second wind in Chicago, where he has started on the Bulls' world championship teams. Off-season surgery and recurring knee problems contributed to a sub-par year in 1992-93.

Strengths: Cartwright is an old-fashioned low-post scorer who uses his size well on the blocks. His gangly, over-the-head shot somehow goes in often enough to make him an offensive threat away from the paint, and he still plays above-average defense against the league's top big men.

Weaknesses: Mr. Bill has a faulty pair of hands, has very little athletic ability, and is not a good rebounder. Age and injuries are wearing down his body.

Analysis: Cartwright quite literally is on his last leg. His time spent on the injured list last February and March does not bode well. Expect a limited role from Cartwright in 1993-94 and retirement soon after.

PLAYER SUMMARY	
Will	play sound defense
Can't	regain his legs
Expect	size on the blocks
Don't Expect	many more years
Fantasy Value	$0
Card Value	5-10¢

COLLEGE STATISTICS

		G	FGP	FTP	RPG	PPG
75-76	SF	30	.530	.735	6.9	12.5
76-77	SF	31	.566	.733	8.5	19.4
77-78	SF	21	.667	.733	10.1	20.6
78-79	SF	29	.605	.734	15.7	24.5
Totals		111	.589	.734	10.2	19.1

NBA REGULAR-SEASON STATISTICS

		G	MIN	FGs FG	FGs PCT	3-PT FGs FG	3-PT FGs PCT	FTs FT	FTs PCT	Rebounds OFF	Rebounds TOT	AST	STL	BLK	PTS	PPG
79-80	NY	82	3150	665	.547	0	.000	451	.797	194	726	165	48	101	1781	21.7
80-81	NY	82	2925	619	.554	0	.000	408	.788	161	613	111	48	83	1646	20.1
81-82	NY	72	2060	390	.562	0	.000	257	.763	116	421	87	48	65	1037	14.4
82-83	NY	82	2468	455	.566	0	.000	380	.744	185	590	136	41	127	1290	15.7
83-84	NY	77	2487	453	.561	0	.000	404	.805	195	649	107	44	97	1310	17.0
85-86	NY	2	36	3	.429	0	.000	6	.600	2	10	5	1	1	12	6.0
86-87	NY	58	1989	335	.531	0	.000	346	.790	132	445	96	40	26	1016	17.5
87-88	NY	82	1676	287	.544	0	.000	340	.798	127	384	85	43	43	914	11.1
88-89	CHI	78	2333	365	.475	0	.000	236	.766	152	521	90	21	41	966	12.4
89-90	CHI	71	2160	292	.468	0	.000	227	.811	137	465	145	38	34	811	11.4
90-91	CHI	79	2273	318	.490	0	.000	124	.697	167	486	126	32	15	760	9.6
91-92	CHI	64	1471	208	.467	0	.000	96	.604	93	324	87	22	14	512	8.0
92-93	CHI	63	1253	141	.411	0	.000	72	.735	83	233	83	20	10	354	5.6
Totals		892	26281	4531	.526	0	.000	3347	.773	1744	5867	1323	446	657	12409	13.9

TERRY CATLEDGE

Team: Orlando Magic
Position: Forward
Height: 6'8" **Weight:** 230
Birthdate: August 22, 1963

NBA Experience: 8 years
College: South Alabama
Acquired: Selected from Bullets in
1989 expansion draft

Background: Catledge led the nation in rebounding and finished fifth in scoring as a senior at South Alabama. After his rookie campaign with Philadelphia, he became a double-figure scorer in Washington and led Orlando in his first year there. After signing a six-year, big-money contract, Catledge had a sub-par 1990-91 showing. He led the Magic in minutes played and rebounds the following year but missed most of the 1992-93 season with a broken hand and tendinitis in his left knee.

Strengths: Catledge is a gifted post-up power forward with good back-to-the-basket moves. He's also a good offensive rebounder, although some say it's just another example of his infatuation with scoring. Much of his past success stems from his now-questionable athletic abilities.

Weaknesses: Other than scoring, the rest of Catledge's game is suspect. He demonstrates poor passing skills and poor judgment. He has never shown much interest in playing defense or in coming off the bench. He's not nearly as prolific a scorer when facing the basket. He's been called selfish.

Analysis: There are those who wonder how much Catledge would have played last season even if he were healthy. He would not have started for Orlando, and he has yet to prove he is willing or able to come off the bench as a contributing role-player. He seems to need a lot of minutes to perform well.

PLAYER SUMMARY

Will ....launch his shots
Can't...............................hit open men
Expect......................low-post offense
Don't Expect................wise decisions
Fantasy Value...........................$1-3
Card Value ....5-10¢

COLLEGE STATISTICS

		G	FGP	FTP	RPG	PPG
82-83	SALA	28	.558	.696	9.9	19.7
83-84	SALA	30	.590	.717	11.1	19.9
84-85	SALA	28	.532	.592	11.5	25.6
Totals		86	.556	.663	10.8	21.7

NBA REGULAR-SEASON STATISTICS

				FGs		3-PT FGs		FTs		Rebounds						
		G	MIN	FG	PCT	FG	PCT	FT	PCT	OFF	TOT	AST	STL	BLK	PTS	PPG
85-86	PHI	64	1092	202	.469	0	.000	90	.647	107	272	21	31	8	494	7.7
86-87	WAS	78	2149	413	.495	0	.000	199	.594	248	560	56	43	14	1025	13.1
87-88	WAS	70	1610	296	.506	0	.000	154	.655	180	397	63	33	9	746	10.7
88-89	WAS	79	2077	334	.490	1	.200	153	.602	230	572	75	46	25	822	10.4
89-90	ORL	74	2462	546	.474	2	.250	341	.702	271	563	72	36	17	1435	19.4
90-91	ORL	51	1459	292	.462	0	.000	161	.624	168	355	58	34	9	745	14.6
91-92	ORL	78	2430	457	.496	0	.000	240	.694	257	549	109	58	16	1154	14.8
92-93	ORL	21	262	36	.493	0	.000	27	.794	18	46	5	4	1	99	4.7
Totals		515	13541	2576	.485	3	.094	1365	.654	1479	3314	459	285	99	6520	12.7

DUANE CAUSWELL

Team: Sacramento Kings
Position: Center
Height: 7'0" **Weight:** 240
Birthdate: May 31, 1968

NBA Experience: 3 years
College: Temple
Acquired: 1st-round pick in 1990 draft
(18th overall)

Background: Causwell's college career at Temple was cut a semester short because of academic ineligibility, but he finished second in the nation in blocked shots as a junior (4.1 BPG). Projected as a back-up center by most observers, Causwell started 55 games as a rookie and finished 15th in the league in blocked shots. He improved his shot-swatting total during his second season but was slowed last year by a post-All-Star-break foot injury. He has led the Kings in field goal percentage each of the last two seasons.

Strengths: With his quick leaping ability and long wingspan, Causwell has become a big-time shot-blocker. He gets up and down the floor better than most of the league's centers and is a fine overall athlete. In addition, he does not take many bad shots.

Weaknesses: Causwell lacks toughness. He tends to leave the dirty work for others while he lunges to block every shot. He does not put his body on people at the defensive end. He could also stand to be a lot more physical on offense. He gets called for a lot of fouls, and passing the ball is not in his repertoire. He's a dismal outside shooter, as reflected in his free throw percentage, which is in the low 60s.

Analysis: Considered a project coming out of college, Causwell has raised his stock to that of a player with potential. He is a very talented shot-blocker who needs to refine the other aspects of his game. With him as the starting center, the Kings developed a reputation of being soft in the middle. Causwell needs to make himself a more physical player at both ends.

PLAYER SUMMARY	
Will	steer away shots
Can't	push people around
Expect	high FG pct.
Don't Expect	an enforcer
Fantasy Value	$2-4
Card Value	5-10¢

COLLEGE STATISTICS

		G	FGP	FTP	RPG	PPG
87-88	TEMP	33	.491	.433	2.6	2.0
88-89	TEMP	30	.514	.683	8.9	11.3
89-90	TEMP	12	.486	.596	8.3	11.3
Totals		75	.504	.624	6.0	7.2

NBA REGULAR-SEASON STATISTICS

			FGs		3-PT FGs		FTs		Rebounds						
	G	MIN	FG	PCT	FG	PCT	FT	PCT	OFF	TOT	AST	STL	BLK	PTS	PPG
90-91 SAC	76	1719	210	.508	0	.000	105	.636	141	391	69	49	148	525	6.9
91-92 SAC	80	2291	250	.549	0	.000	136	.613	196	580	59	47	215	636	7.9
92-93 SAC	55	1211	175	.545	0	.000	103	.624	112	303	35	32	87	453	8.2
Totals	211	5221	635	.534	0	.000	344	.623	449	1274	163	128	450	1614	7.6

CEDRIC CEBALLOS

Team: Phoenix Suns
Position: Forward
Height: 6'6" **Weight:** 220
Birthdate: August 2, 1969

NBA Experience: 3 years
College: Cal. St. Fullerton
Acquired: 2nd-round pick in 1990 draft (48th overall)

Background: Ceballos, a Maui, Hawaii, native, played just one year of varsity basketball in high school before going on to lead the Big West in scoring as a junior and senior at Cal. State Fullerton. He finished in the nation's top ten in rebounding as a senior. His rookie season in the NBA came as a pleasant surprise to the Suns, as he averaged a point every 1.4 minutes. His points and minutes decreased in his second year, then last season he shared starting small-forward duties with Richard Dumas. Ceballos led the NBA in field goal percentage, although an injury kept him out of the NBA Finals.

Strengths: The athletic Ceballos has wide shoulders and long arms, allowing him to gain inside position and play above the rim. His scoring instincts are sophisticated and he shoots a high percentage from the field. He runs the floor, loves working the baseline, and has great hands. He's a flashy dunker who won the NBA's Slam Dunk Contest in 1992 with a blindfolded jam. He more than doubled his rebounding average last season.

Weaknesses: The biggest flaw in his game, now that he has become a more consistent shooter, is his lack of defensive intensity. Ceballos often perceives stopping his man as a chore.

Analysis: If you think Ceballos enjoyed a coming-out year with the Suns, imagine what he would have done had Dumas not also exploded onto the scene. Ceballos always had flair; now he also has substance. He became a better shooter, scorer, and rebounder last season. If he could add better defense to the mix, he'd be a star in the making.

PLAYER SUMMARY

Will.........................patrol the baseline
Can't ....star on defense
Expect ....athletic drives, dunks
Don't Expect ....slow tempo
Fantasy Value.............................$7-10
Card Value ....8-15¢

COLLEGE STATISTICS

		G	FGP	FTP	RPG	PPG
88-89	CSF	29	.442	.672	8.8	21.2
89-90	CSF	29	.485	.670	12.5	23.1
Totals		58	.463	.671	10.7	22.1

NBA REGULAR-SEASON STATISTICS

		G	MIN	FGs FG	FGs PCT	3-PT FGs FG	3-PT FGs PCT	FTs FT	FTs PCT	Rebounds OFF	Rebounds TOT	AST	STL	BLK	PTS	PPG
90-91	PHO	63	730	204	.487	1	.167	110	.663	77	150	35	22	5	519	8.2
91-92	PHO	64	725	176	.482	1	.167	109	.736	60	152	50	16	11	462	7.2
92-93	PHO	74	1607	381	.576	0	.000	187	.725	172	408	77	54	28	949	12.8
Totals		201	3062	761	.526	2	.143	406	.710	309	710	162	92	44	1930	9.6

TOM CHAMBERS

Team: Utah Jazz
Position: Forward
Height: 6'10" **Weight:** 230
Birthdate: June 21, 1959

NBA Experience: 12 years
College: Utah
Acquired: Signed as a free agent, 8/93

Background: Chambers earned All-America recognition at the University of Utah before moving on to become one of the NBA's most productive scorers. He has played in four All-Star Games, winning the MVP Award in 1987. He came to the Suns in 1988 as the first unrestricted free agent in NBA history. The 1992-93 season was his fifth in Phoenix. He averaged a career low in scoring and missed nearly a month with a torn quadriceps muscle. Utah picked him up in August.

Strengths: Still capable of scoring from anywhere, Chambers can shoot from outside or go strong to the hoop with either hand. He provides stable leadership and has always been a very reliable free throw shooter.

Weaknesses: Chambers has lost a step and is therefore not the match-up problem he once was. He was never a top-notch defender and still isn't. His field goal percentage over the last three seasons has not been impressive.

Analysis: No, Chambers is not nearly the player he once was. However, his leadership was crucial as the Suns raised their game to the next level last season. Once one of the best scorers in the game, he is winding down his career as a veteran reserve.

PLAYER SUMMARY	
Will	score inside or out
Can't	regain stardom
Expect	veteran leadership
Don't Expect	starts
Fantasy Value	$1-3
Card Value	5-10¢

COLLEGE STATISTICS

		G	FGP	FTP	RPG	PPG
77-78	UTA	28	.496	.625	3.7	6.4
78-79	UTA	30	.544	.543	8.9	16.0
79-80	UTA	28	.543	.713	8.7	17.2
80-81	UTA	30	.594	.742	8.7	18.6
Totals		116	.553	.665	7.6	14.6

NBA REGULAR-SEASON STATISTICS

		G	MIN	FGs FG	FGs PCT	3-PT FGs FG	3-PT FGs PCT	FTs FT	FTs PCT	Rebounds OFF	Rebounds TOT	AST	STL	BLK	PTS	PPG
81-82	SD	81	2682	554	.525	0	.000	284	.620	211	561	146	58	46	1392	17.2
82-83	SD	79	2665	519	.472	0	.000	353	.723	218	519	192	79	57	1391	17.6
83-84	SEA	82	2570	554	.499	0	.000	375	.800	219	532	133	47	51	1483	18.1
84-85	SEA	81	2923	629	.483	6	.273	475	.832	164	579	209	70	57	1739	21.5
85-86	SEA	66	2019	432	.466	13	.271	346	.836	126	431	132	55	37	1223	18.5
86-87	SEA	82	3018	660	.456	54	.372	535	.849	163	545	245	81	50	1909	23.3
87-88	SEA	82	2680	611	.448	33	.303	419	.807	135	490	212	87	53	1674	20.4
88-89	PHO	81	3002	774	.471	28	.326	509	.851	143	684	231	87	55	2085	25.7
89-90	PHO	81	3046	810	.501	24	.279	557	.861	121	571	190	88	47	2201	27.2
90-91	PHO	76	2475	556	.437	20	.274	379	.826	104	490	194	65	52	1511	19.9
91-92	PHO	69	1948	426	.431	18	.367	258	.830	86	401	142	57	37	1128	16.3
92-93	PHO	73	1723	320	.447	11	.393	241	.837	96	345	101	43	23	892	12.2
Totals		933	30751	6845	.471	207	.310	4731	.808	1786	6148	2127	817	565	18628	20.0

REX CHAPMAN

Team: Washington Bullets
Position: Guard
Height: 6'4" **Weight:** 205
Birthdate: October 5, 1967

NBA Experience: 5 years
College: Kentucky
Acquired: Traded from Hornets for Tom Hammonds, 2/92

Background: At Kentucky, Chapman became the first freshman to lead the Wildcats in scoring. He also became only the third Kentucky player to score 1,000 points in his first two years, placing him in the company of Dan Issel and Cotton Nash. Chapman left school after his sophomore year and was a 15-plus PPG scorer for Charlotte in his first three pro years. He was acquired by Washington in 1991-92 but missed three-quarters of that season with a heel injury. He saw starting time with the Bullets last year but spent a significant stretch on the injured list with a wounded ankle.

Strengths: Chapman can sky. His vertical leap has been measured at 42 inches. Yet lay off him in fear of the drive and he can burn you from outside with 3-point range. He posted a career-high shooting percentage last year and is solid from the line.

Weaknesses: Chapman has always had a problem with his shot selection. He tends to look for the spectacular rather than making the sound, simple play. He fails to make teammates look better and is still a little shy on defense.

Analysis: Despite All-Star athletic ability, Chapman has yet to push the limits of that potential as a pro. Injuries have slowed him over the last two years, and he was benched as a Bullets starter in mid-January last season even when healthy. Poor defense and decision-making are the two biggest reasons he hasn't become a star.

PLAYER SUMMARY	
Will	take his shots
Can't	pass up the spectacular
Expect	some great games
Don't Expect	a defensive ace
Fantasy Value	$3-5
Card Value	5-10¢

COLLEGE STATISTICS

		G	FGP	FTP	RPG	PPG
86-87	KEN	29	.444	.735	2.3	16.0
87-88	KEN	32	.501	.794	2.9	19.0
Totals		61	.475	.771	2.6	17.6

NBA REGULAR-SEASON STATISTICS

		G	MIN	FGs FG	FGs PCT	3-PT FGs FG	3-PT FGs PCT	FTs FT	FTs PCT	Rebounds OFF	Rebounds TOT	AST	STL	BLK	PTS	PPG
88-89	CHA	75	2219	526	.414	60	.314	155	.795	74	187	176	70	25	1267	16.9
89-90	CHA	54	1762	377	.408	47	.331	144	.750	52	179	132	46	6	945	17.5
90-91	CHA	70	2100	410	.445	48	.324	234	.830	45	191	250	73	16	1102	15.7
91-92	CHA/WAS	22	567	113	.448	8	.276	36	.679	10	58	89	15	8	270	12.3
92-93	WAS	60	1300	287	.477	43	.371	132	.810	19	88	116	38	10	749	12.5
Totals		280	7926	1708	.431	206	.330	701	.792	199	699	760	241	65	4323	15.4

MAURICE CHEEKS

Team: New Jersey Nets
Position: Guard
Height: 6'1" **Weight:** 180
Birthdate: September 8, 1956

NBA Experience: 15 years
College: West Texas St.
Acquired: Signed as a free agent, 1/93

Background: Cheeks was a three-time all-conference choice at West Texas State and the point guard on all the talented Philadelphia teams of the early 1980s. In the last four years, he has played in San Antonio, New York, Atlanta, and most recently New Jersey. He is the NBA's all-time steals leader.

Strengths: Once the league's premier point guard, Cheeks remains a consummate professional who knows how to win. He can still pick your pocket and run an offense with precision. In addition, he can hit the perimeter shot if you leave him open.

Weaknesses: Age is the biggest weakness, as Cheeks has probably seen the last of his starting assignments. Also, he's never been a vocal leader; just a leader by example.

Analysis: Cheeks, nearing the end of a Hall of Fame-type career, will go down in NBA annals as one of the premier point guards of all time. In his prime, he was a clutch performer who led the Sixers to the 1983 championship. He's still capable of playing as a reserve.

PLAYER SUMMARY

Will .... pick your pocket
Can't .... play 48 minutes
Expect .... Hall of Fame status
Don't Expect .... many more years
Fantasy Value $0
Card Value .... 5-10¢

COLLEGE STATISTICS

		G	FGP	FTP	APG	PPG
74-75	WTS	26	.467	.585	1.1	3.9
75-76	WTS	23	.600	.619	3.7	11.1
76-77	WTS	30	.606	.704	7.1	13.9
77-78	WTS	27	.545	.714	5.7	16.8
Totals		106	.568	.678	4.5	11.6

NBA REGULAR-SEASON STATISTICS

				FGs		3-PT FGs		FTs		Rebounds						
		G	MIN	FG	PCT	FG	PCT	FT	PCT	OFF	TOT	AST	STL	BLK	PTS	PPG
78-79	PHI	82	2409	292	.510	0	.000	101	.721	63	254	431	174	12	685	8.4
79-80	PHI	79	2623	357	.540	4	.444	180	.779	75	274	556	183	32	898	11.4
80-81	PHI	81	2415	310	.534	3	.375	140	.787	67	245	560	193	39	763	9.4
81-82	PHI	79	2498	352	.521	6	.273	171	.777	51	248	667	209	33	881	11.2
82-83	PHI	79	2465	404	.542	1	.167	181	.754	53	209	543	184	31	990	12.5
83-84	PHI	75	2494	386	.550	8	.400	170	.733	44	205	478	171	20	950	12.7
84-85	PHI	78	2616	422	.570	6	.231	175	.879	54	217	497	169	24	1025	13.1
85-86	PHI	82	3270	490	.537	4	.235	282	.842	55	235	753	207	27	1266	15.4
86-87	PHI	68	2624	415	.527	4	.235	227	.777	47	215	538	180	15	1061	15.6
87-88	PHI	79	2871	428	.495	3	.136	227	.825	59	253	635	167	22	1086	13.7
88-89	PHI	71	2298	336	.483	1	.077	151	.774	39	183	554	105	17	824	11.6
89-90	SA/NY	81	2519	307	.504	4	.250	171	.847	50	240	453	124	10	789	9.7
90-91	NY	76	2147	241	.499	5	.250	105	.814	22	173	435	128	10	592	7.8
91-92	ATL	56	1086	115	.462	3	.500	26	.605	29	95	185	83	0	259	4.6
92-93	NJ	35	510	51	.548	0	.000	24	.889	5	42	107	33	2	126	3.6
Totals		1101	34845	4906	.523	52	.255	2331	.793	713	3088	7392	2310	294	12195	11.1

PETE CHILCUTT

Team: Sacramento Kings
Position: Forward/Center
Height: 6'10" **Weight:** 232
Birthdate: September 14, 1968

NBA Experience: 2 years
College: North Carolina
Acquired: 1st-round pick in 1991 draft
(27th overall)

Background: A solid complementary player for coach Dean Smith at North Carolina, Chilcutt was slow to reach his potential and was never named first- or second-team All-ACC. He played every game during his four years with the Tar Heels and upped his draft stock with his play in the postseason tournaments and camps. He also played well in a summer pro league. He saw limited action as a rookie with Sacramento during 1991-92, averaging less than four PPG. He raised his average by two points and drew an occasional start last year.

Strengths: Chilcutt has a very soft shooting touch for a big man, with range out to 18-20 feet. He has the potential to be a match-up problem for power forwards and centers. He's fundamentally sound and hits the boards, although he does nothing eye-catching. He works hard and shows a nice feel for the game.

Weaknesses: Chilcutt doesn't possess exceptional speed, quickness, jumping ability, or any other athletic skill. In fact, nothing about his game is awe-inspiring. He's not able to create his own shot or set up others, although he is a skilled high-post passer. He tends to play soft at both ends. Physical defense and post-up offense are not his style. He rarely gets to the free throw line and is no threat from 3-point range.

Analysis: Chilcutt is a better offensive basketball player than people give him credit for, but his game still lacks depth. He can shoot, but he can't go inside. He plays position defense, but he doesn't throw his weight around. He hustles, but he's still a little shy about getting involved. He has a lot of work to do, but he seems willing to do it.

PLAYER SUMMARY	
Will	toss in jumpers
Can't	get to the stripe
Expect	an eager learner
Don't Expect	physical play
Fantasy Value	$1-3
Card Value	8-12¢

COLLEGE STATISTICS

		G	FGP	FTP	RPG	PPG
87-88	NC	34	.564	.706	3.2	4.9
88-89	NC	37	.537	.623	5.4	6.9
89-90	NC	34	.514	.714	6.6	9.0
90-91	NC	35	.538	.765	6.6	12.0
Totals		140	.536	.710	5.5	8.2

NBA REGULAR-SEASON STATISTICS

				FGs		3-PT FGs		FTs		Rebounds						
		G	MIN	FG	PCT	FG	PCT	FT	PCT	OFF	TOT	AST	STL	BLK	PTS	PPG
91-92	SAC	69	817	113	.452	2	1.000	23	.821	78	187	38	32	17	251	3.6
92-93	SAC	59	834	165	.485	0	.000	32	.696	80	194	64	22	21	362	6.1
Totals		128	1651	278	.471	2	1.000	55	.743	158	381	102	54	38	613	4.8

DOUG CHRISTIE

Team: Los Angeles Lakers
Position: Guard/Forward
Height: 6'6" **Weight:** 205
Birthdate: May 9, 1970
NBA Experience: 1 year

College: Pepperdine
Acquired: Draft rights traded from SuperSonics with Benoit Benjamin for Sam Perkins, 2/93

Background: Christie sat out his freshman season at Pepperdine under Prop 48, but became the Waves' best player since Dennis Johnson. He led them to the NCAA Tournament in 1991 and 1992, though he missed the '91 game because of a knee injury that required surgery. He was MVP and slam-dunk champion at the NABC All-Star Game and was drafted 17th overall by the Sonics. Unable to sign him after a prolonged holdout, Seattle traded his rights and Benoit Benjamin to the Lakers for Sam Perkins. Christie wound up playing a quarter of a season as a Laker reserve.

Strengths: Christie, a great athlete, is versatile and super-smooth. He can play either guard spot or small forward. Despite his surgically repaired knee, he plays above the rim. He can slash to the hoop and is a gifted passer who never averaged less than four APG in college. He has been compared favorably to Scottie Pippen.

Weaknesses: Losing most of a rookie year over contract squabbles has set more than a few players back. There are other concerns as well, starting with his jump shot. He was horribly inconsistent from the field during his short rookie campaign. He has a lot to learn about NBA defense.

Analysis: How versatile is Christie? He's so versatile that the Lakers were talking about making him a point guard while others contend his future is at forward. At any position, he has shown he is capable of bringing a crowd to its feet with his high energy and athletic ability. However, poor shooting can turn fans against you in a hurry. Give him a full season to prove his wares.

PLAYER SUMMARY

Will......................play three positions
Can't................tear it up from outside
Expect ....dazzling drives
Don't Expect ....consistency
Fantasy Value...............................$1-3
Card Value.................................25-75¢

COLLEGE STATISTICS

		G	FGP	FTP	RPG	PPG
89-90	PEP	28	.503	.714	4.1	8.9
90-91	PEP	28	.469	.765	5.2	19.1
91-92	PEP	31	.466	.746	5.9	19.5
Totals		87	.473	.747	5.1	16.0

NBA REGULAR-SEASON STATISTICS

			FGs		3-PT FGs		FTs		Rebounds						
	G	MIN	FG	PCT	FG	PCT	FT	PCT	OFF	TOT	AST	STL	BLK	PTS	PPG
92-93 LAL	23	332	45	.425	2	.167	50	.758	24	51	53	22	5	142	6.2
Totals	23	332	45	.425	2	.167	50	.758	24	51	53	22	5	142	6.2

DERRICK COLEMAN

Team: New Jersey Nets
Position: Forward
Height: 6'10" **Weight:** 258
Birthdate: June 21, 1967

NBA Experience: 3 years
College: Syracuse
Acquired: 1st-round pick in 1990 draft (1st overall)

Background: Teamed with Billy Owens and Sherman Douglas, Coleman played on one of Syracuse's most talented squads ever. In his senior year, he averaged 17.9 PPG and 12.1 RPG and earned several college Player of the Year awards. New Jersey selected him as the No. 1 pick in the 1990 draft and he lived up to his billing immediately by winning the NBA Rookie of the Year Award. He has finished second on the Nets in scoring and has led the team in rebounding each of the past two years.

Strengths: Coleman scores from all over. He can kill you with his jump shot, his moves to the bucket, or his post-up repertoire. He's supremely confident, having learned the game on the Detroit playgrounds. He can either start or finish the break. He blocked 126 shots last season and is one of the better rebounding forwards in the league.

Weaknesses: Coleman's biggest flaw has been trying to do too much. He is near the top of the league's turnover chart and also has a sub-par shooting percentage. He can be too cocky and has earned himself a spot in more than one coach's doghouse.

Analysis: Coleman was a little upset about being overlooked for the All-Star Game last season—and with some justification. He'll likely be selected for that honor within the next couple years. He's got athletic talent, a huge repertoire of moves to the hoop, a nose for the ball off the glass, and some untapped potential at the defensive end. With a little more control, he'll be one of the best players in the game.

PLAYER SUMMARY

Will	score from everywhere
Can't	avoid turnovers
Expect	an All-Star invite
Don't Expect	humility
Fantasy Value	$45-50
Card Value	15-25¢

COLLEGE STATISTICS

		G	FGP	FTP	RPG	PPG
86-87	SYR	38	.560	.686	8.8	11.9
87-88	SYR	35	.587	.630	11.0	13.5
88-89	SYR	37	.575	.692	11.4	16.9
89-90	SYR	33	.551	.715	12.1	17.9
Totals		143	.568	.684	10.7	15.0

NBA REGULAR-SEASON STATISTICS

				FGs		3-PT FGs		FTs		Rebounds						
	G	MIN	FG	PCT	FG	PCT	FT	PCT	OFF	TOT	AST	STL	BLK	PTS	PPG
90-91 NJ	74	2602	514	.467	13	.342	323	.731	269	759	163	71	99	1364	18.4
91-92 NJ	65	2207	483	.504	23	.303	300	.763	203	618	205	54	98	1289	19.8
92-93 NJ	76	2759	564	.460	23	.232	421	.808	247	852	276	92	126	1572	20.7
Totals	215	7568	1561	.475	59	.277	1044	.770	719	2229	644	217	323	4225	19.7

BIMBO COLES

Team: Miami Heat
Position: Guard
Height: 6'2" **Weight:** 185
Birthdate: April 22, 1968

NBA Experience: 3 years
College: Virginia Tech
Acquired: Draft rights traded from Kings for Rory Sparrow, 6/90

Background: Coles left Virginia Tech as the all-time leading scorer in the Metro Conference, and he became the first player to lead the league in scoring three straight years. He also set the Virginia Tech record for assists and was a member of the 1988 United States Olympic team. As a rookie with Miami, he played in all 82 games and averaged just under five PPG. He has averaged more than ten PPG in his second and third seasons, seeing action as a part-time starter.

Strengths: Coles is extremely quick and can get to the hoop against virtually anyone. After shooting 40 percent as a college senior and 41 percent as an NBA rookie, he has hit better than 45 percent in each of his last two seasons. Defense has never been a problem, thanks to his fleet feet. Coles is a solid free throw shooter who is still improving his overall game.

Weaknesses: His perimeter shooting is still inconsistent, and Coles should not be launching as many NBA 3-pointers as he does. He makes less than a third of them. His over-aggressiveness on defense often gets him into foul trouble and he sometimes tries to do too much on offense.

Analysis: Coles has been called a shooting guard in the body of a point guard, and in many respects that description fits. But he enjoyed another solid year as a lead guard in 1992-93, filling in admirably for injured starter Steve Smith. He improved his assist-to-turnover ratio by a considerable margin while remaining a double-figure scorer in his best campaign yet.

PLAYER SUMMARY

Will............................get to the hoop
Can't..............make a living with treys
Expect ....cat-like quickness
Don't Expect...........conservative play
Fantasy Value...............................$3-5
Card Value.....................................5-8¢

COLLEGE STATISTICS

		G	FGP	FTP	APG	PPG
86-87	VT	28	.412	.716	4.0	10.0
87-88	VT	29	.443	.741	5.9	24.2
88-89	VT	27	.455	.785	5.2	26.6
89-90	VT	31	.404	.738	3.9	25.3
Totals		115	.429	.748	4.8	21.6

NBA REGULAR-SEASON STATISTICS

				FGs		3-PT FGs		FTs		Rebounds						
		G	MIN	FG	PCT	FG	PCT	FT	PCT	OFF	TOT	AST	STL	BLK	PTS	PPG
90-91	MIA	82	1355	162	.412	6	.176	71	.747	56	153	232	65	12	401	4.9
91-92	MIA	81	1976	295	.455	10	.192	216	.824	69	189	366	73	13	816	10.1
92-93	MIA	81	2232	318	.464	42	.307	177	.805	58	166	373	80	11	855	10.6
Totals		244	5563	775	.448	58	.260	464	.804	183	508	971	218	36	2072	8.5

DUANE COOPER

Team: Los Angeles Lakers
Position: Guard
Height: 6'1" **Weight:** 185
Birthdate: June 25, 1969

NBA Experience: 1 year
College: Southern California
Acquired: 2nd-round pick in 1992 draft (36th overall)

Background: Cooper played in the shadow of Robert Pack and Harold Miner at Southern Cal but was voted the Most Valuable Trojan by his teammates after a senior year in which he averaged 12.2 PPG and 5.4 APG. He led USC to its first top-ten ranking since 1975 and was a first-team All-Pac-10 selection. He missed the 1989-90 season with a broken right foot. Cooper was chosen in the second round (36th overall) of the '92 draft by the Lakers, who acquired the pick from Milwaukee as compensation for allowing head coach Mike Dunleavy out of his contract to join the Bucks. He saw limited action as a rookie reserve.

Strengths: Combining strength and quickness, Cooper is willing to use his athletic ability on the defensive end. He plays bigger than his actual size. He is a good passer and ball-handler who looks to create opportunities for teammates. He is especially adept at transition passing and loves to run.

Weaknesses: Cooper, a capable outside shooter in college, did not show much consistency from the pro perimeter. The NBA 3-point shot seems a couple feet out of his range, and his accuracy from inside the arc was also sub-par. He has also struggled in the playmaking department, with an assist-to-turnover ratio just slightly better than two-to-one. He will not be a big-time pro scorer. Also, his defensive repertoire is short on steals.

Analysis: Although known as a defensive standout and good shooter, this Cooper has not made Laker backers forget Michael Cooper, who once excelled on both counts in the Forum. L.A. took a chance on this local product, and they got a reserve point guard who struggled as a rookie. He'll need to improve his outside shooting to secure a spot in the NBA.

PLAYER SUMMARY	
Will	run the floor
Can't	dazzle with playmaking
Expect	defense
Don't Expect	10 PPG
Fantasy Value	$0
Card Value	5-10¢

COLLEGE STATISTICS

		G	FGP	FTP	APG	PPG
87-88	USC	27	.313	.667	0.6	1.1
88-89	USC	32	.421	.465	2.7	4.1
90-91	USC	29	.451	.633	4.6	7.1
91-92	USC	30	.496	.644	5.4	12.2
Totals		118	.456	.604	3.4	6.2

NBA REGULAR-SEASON STATISTICS

				FGs		3-PT FGs		FTs		Rebounds						
		G	MIN	FG	PCT	FG	PCT	FT	PCT	OFF	TOT	AST	STL	BLK	PTS	PPG
92-93	LAL	65	645	62	.392	7	.233	25	.714	13	50	150	18	2	156	2.4
Totals		65	645	62	.392	7	.233	25	.714	13	50	150	18	2	156	2.4

TYRONE CORBIN

Team: Utah Jazz
Position: Forward
Height: 6'6" **Weight:** 222
Birthdate: December 31, 1962
NBA Experience: 8 years

College: DePaul
Acquired: Traded from Timberwolves for Thurl Bailey and a 1991 2nd-round pick, 11/91

Background: After leading DePaul in both scoring and rebounding as a junior and senior, Corbin made his NBA debut with San Antonio. He played for Cleveland, Phoenix, and Minnesota before the Timberwolves traded him to Utah in 1991-92. Corbin was a valuable reserve in his first season with the Jazz and became the starting small forward for most of last year.

Strengths: Corbin has rightfully earned his reputation as a hard worker and physical player. He fights for rebounds, gets good inside position, comes up with steals and loose balls, and plays strong defense on men his size or bigger. Corbin is able to stick the 15- to 18-footer pretty consistently and is a very accurate free throw shooter. He's a workaholic and a class act.

Weaknesses: The bumping and grinding inside are necessary because Corbin does not own the silky smooth game that many of the league's premier small forwards possess. He does not create much off the dribble for either himself or his teammates. He commits a lot of fouls and does not own 3-point range.

Analysis: Corbin is the kind of player a coach loves. On a Minnesota team that needed scoring, he was a scorer. On a Utah team that needs his grit, he provides it. He works hard and will do whatever is asked of him, either starting or off the bench. Defenders hate to guard him because he never stops working.

PLAYER SUMMARY	
Will	do whatever is asked
Can't	stop working
Expect	hustle, defense
Don't Expect	3-point shooting
Fantasy Value	$8-10
Card Value	5-10¢

COLLEGE STATISTICS

		G	FGP	FTP	RPG	PPG
81-82	DeP	28	.417	.718	6.1	5.1
82-83	DeP	33	.471	.773	7.9	10.6
83-84	DeP	30	.525	.744	7.4	14.2
84-85	DeP	29	.534	.814	8.1	15.9
Totals		120	.504	.764	7.4	11.5

NBA REGULAR-SEASON STATISTICS

		G	MIN	FGs FG	FGs PCT	3-PT FGs FG	3-PT FGs PCT	FTs FT	FTs PCT	Rebounds OFF	Rebounds TOT	AST	STL	BLK	PTS	PPG
85-86	SA	16	174	27	.422	0	.000	10	.714	11	25	11	11	2	64	4.0
86-87	SA/CLE	63	1170	156	.409	1	.250	91	.734	88	215	97	55	5	404	6.4
87-88	CLE/PHO	84	1739	257	.490	1	.167	110	.797	127	350	115	72	18	625	7.4
88-89	PHO	77	1655	245	.540	0	.000	141	.788	176	398	118	82	13	631	8.2
89-90	MIN	82	3011	521	.481	0	.000	161	.770	219	604	216	175	41	1203	14.7
90-91	MIN	82	3196	587	.448	2	.200	296	.798	185	589	347	162	53	1472	18.0
91-92	MIN/UTA	80	2207	303	.481	0	.000	174	.866	163	472	140	82	20	780	9.8
92-93	UTA	82	2555	385	.503	0	.000	180	.826	194	519	173	108	32	950	11.6
Totals		497	13844	2235	.473	4	.100	1033	.791	1024	2769	1110	677	170	5507	11.1

TERRY CUMMINGS

Team: San Antonio Spurs
Position: Forward
Height: 6'9" **Weight:** 245
Birthdate: March 15, 1961

NBA Experience: 11 years
College: DePaul
Acquired: Traded from Bucks for Alvin Robertson and Greg Anderson, 5/89

Background: Cummings led DePaul in rebounding in each of his three seasons before heading into the draft a year early. He was drafted second overall by San Diego in 1982 and became the first rookie since Kareem Abdul-Jabbar to rank in the top ten in scoring and rebounding. Cummings played in two All-Star Games while with Milwaukee and has excelled with San Antonio. He tore ligaments in his right knee in July 1992 and was expected to miss all of last season, but he returned with two weeks left in the regular season.

Strengths: When healthy, Cummings can score and rebound with the best forwards in the game. He has a large array of post-up moves and can drill the jumper with consistency. Few can match his smarts. He is still capable of taking charge of a game.

Weaknesses: Defense has always been the knock on Cummings, but that seems to go with the territory when you're that good on offense. The knee injury has slowed him.

Analysis: Cummings plays the game like he's been called to war. His earlier-than-expected return to the lineup is a testament to his work ethic, and you can bet he'll make a strong comeback bid this year. His name must be mentioned among the top power forwards in league history.

PLAYER SUMMARY	
Will	score, rebound
Can't	regain young legs
Expect	veteran leadership
Don't Expect	the days of old
Fantasy Value	$9-11
Card Value	5-10¢

COLLEGE STATISTICS

		G	FGP	FTP	RPG	PPG
79-80	DeP	28	.508	.832	9.4	14.2
80-81	DeP	29	.498	.750	9.0	13.0
81-82	DeP	28	.567	.756	11.9	22.3
Totals		85	.530	.775	10.1	16.4

NBA REGULAR-SEASON STATISTICS

				FGs		3-PT FGs		FTs		Rebounds						
		G	MIN	FG	PCT	FG	PCT	FT	PCT	OFF	TOT	AST	STL	BLK	PTS	PPG
82-83	SD	70	2531	684	.523	0	.000	292	.709	303	744	177	129	62	1660	23.7
83-84	SD	81	2907	737	.494	0	.000	380	.720	323	777	139	92	57	1854	22.9
84-85	MIL	79	2722	759	.495	0	.000	343	.741	244	716	228	117	67	1861	23.6
85-86	MIL	82	2669	681	.474	0	.000	265	.656	222	694	193	121	51	1627	19.8
86-87	MIL	82	2770	729	.511	0	.000	249	.662	214	700	229	129	81	1707	20.8
87-88	MIL	76	2629	675	.485	1	.333	270	.665	184	553	181	78	46	1621	21.3
88-89	MIL	80	2824	730	.467	7	.467	362	.787	281	650	198	106	72	1829	22.9
89-90	SA	81	2821	728	.475	19	.322	343	.780	226	677	219	110	52	1818	22.4
90-91	SA	67	2195	503	.484	7	.212	164	.693	194	521	157	61	30	1177	17.6
91-92	SA	70	2149	514	.488	5	.385	177	.711	247	631	102	58	34	1210	17.3
92-93	SA	8	76	11	.379	0	.000	5	.500	6	19	4	1	1	27	3.4
Totals		776	26293	5751	.489	39	.293	2850	.715	2444	6682	1827	1002	553	16391	21.1

DELL CURRY

Team: Charlotte Hornets
Position: Guard
Height: 6'5" **Weight:** 208
Birthdate: June 25, 1964

NBA Experience: 7 years
College: Virginia Tech
Acquired: Selected from Cavaliers in 1988 expansion draft

Background: Curry, the Metro Conference's Player of the Year as a senior, became the league's second-leading career scorer behind Keith Lee. He was a successful pitcher in college and was drafted by the Baltimore Orioles in the 14th round. Curry was drafted by the Utah Jazz, traded to Cleveland, and picked up by Charlotte in the expansion draft. He has averaged double figures in each of the last six years and was one of the league's most productive sixth men last season.

Strengths: Curry has the ability to light up the scoreboard in a hurry with a dangerous outside shot, particularly from 3-point land. He ranks among the most accurate 3-point and free throw shooters in the game. Former Timberwolves coach Bill Musselman once described him as one of the five best pure shooters in the NBA.

Weaknesses: Perhaps too congenial in his approach, Curry is not a willing or able defender. He's not physical with players his size or larger and lacks the quickness and desire to keep up with smaller ones. Curry is not a gifted passer and would rather shoot anyway.

Analysis: When Curry is hot, you want the ball to touch his hands every time down the floor. When he's not, he'll keep gunning until he gets there. Few can match his perimeter prowess and range. The other attribute Curry offers is a willingness to do his job in a reserve role.

PLAYER SUMMARY

Will ....knock down treys
Can't ....shut down his man
Expect...........................instant offense
Don't Expect ....10 APG
Fantasy Value................................$4-6
Card Value ....5-12¢

COLLEGE STATISTICS

		G	FGP	FTP	RPG	PPG
82-83	VT	32	.475	.850	3.0	14.5
83-84	VT	35	.522	.759	4.1	19.3
84-85	VT	29	.482	.758	5.8	18.2
85-86	VT	30	.529	.789	6.8	24.1
Totals		126	.505	.785	4.8	19.0

NBA REGULAR-SEASON STATISTICS

				FGs		3-PT FGs		FTs		Rebounds						
		G	MIN	FG	PCT	FG	PCT	FT	PCT	OFF	TOT	AST	STL	BLK	PTS	PPG
86-87	UTA	67	636	139	.426	17	.283	30	.789	30	78	58	27	4	325	4.9
87-88	CLE	79	1499	340	.458	28	.346	79	.782	43	166	149	94	22	787	10.0
88-89	CHA	48	813	256	.491	19	.345	40	.870	26	104	50	42	4	571	11.9
89-90	CHA	67	1860	461	.466	52	.354	96	.923	31	168	159	98	26	1070	16.0
90-91	CHA	76	1515	337	.471	32	.372	96	.842	47	199	166	75	25	802	10.6
91-92	CHA	77	2020	504	.486	74	.404	127	.836	57	259	177	93	20	1209	15.7
92-93	CHA	80	2094	498	.452	95	.401	136	.866	51	286	180	87	23	1227	15.3
Totals		494	10437	2535	.467	317	.373	604	.848	285	1260	939	516	124	5991	12.1

LLOYD DANIELS

Team: San Antonio Spurs
Position: Guard
Height: 6'7" **Weight:** 210
Birthdate: September 4, 1967

NBA Experience: 1 year
College: None
Acquired: Signed as a free agent, 7/92

Background: A New York City playground legend, Daniels dropped out of three high schools. He never played college basketball after his recruitment to UNLV resulted in an NCAA investigation. He was also arrested on drug charges. He has been a ballplayer in the CBA, GBA, USBL, and New Zealand. He enrolled at the John Lucas Treatment and Recovery Center and credits Lucas for helping him overcome drug and alcohol problems. Daniels finally reached the NBA last season with San Antonio, where he finished second on the Spurs in 3-pointers made and approached double figures in scoring.

Strengths: Once considered the top prep player in the nation, Daniels still brings a lot of natural ability to the floor. He owns a dangerous jump shot with great range, fine offensive post-up moves, and a nice feel for the game. His passing skills have always drawn rave reviews and he can play either shooting guard or point guard.

Weaknesses: Daniels is not much help on defense, due both to a lack of interest and a lack of quickness. He can match up with big guards but quicker point guards give him trouble. His shooting is streaky and prone to bitter cold spells. His biggest weaknesses in the past have been off the court.

Analysis: The world finally got to see "Swee' Pea," a rare player who made a name for himself without ever playing college basketball. He is not the NBA legend some might have expected. He made a handful of starts, but his floor time decreased after Jerry Tarkanian was fired and Lucas took over as Spurs coach. Daniels has the look of a sixth man who can light it up. The fact that he kept clean for a full NBA season is a great sign.

PLAYER SUMMARY	
Will	fire from long range
Can't	excel on defense
Expect	streak shooting
Don't Expect	legendary feats
Fantasy Value	$2-4
Card Value	10-20¢

COLLEGE STATISTICS
—DID NOT PLAY—

NBA REGULAR-SEASON STATISTICS

			FGs		3-PT FGs		FTs		Rebounds						
	G	MIN	FG	PCT	FG	PCT	FT	PCT	OFF	TOT	AST	STL	BLK	PTS	PPG
92-93 SA	77	1573	285	.443	59	.333	72	.727	86	216	148	38	30	701	9.1
Totals	77	1573	285	.443	59	.333	72	.727	86	216	148	38	30	701	9.1

BRAD DAUGHERTY

Team: Cleveland Cavaliers
Position: Center
Height: 7'0" **Weight:** 263
Birthdate: October 19, 1965

NBA Experience: 7 years
College: North Carolina
Acquired: 1st-round pick in 1986 draft
(1st overall)

Background: Ahead of his time, Daugherty was performing in the McDonald's High School All-Star Game as a 16-year-old senior. At North Carolina, he led the Atlantic Coast Conference in rebounding as a junior and led the country in field goal percentage as a senior. He has appeared in the NBA All-Star Game in five of the last six years. He led the league in field goal percentage for most of last season and once again finished high in both scoring and rebounding.

Strengths: Daugherty can hurt you inside or out. He has the power to muscle underneath for baskets and also has the touch to make precision passes from the high post. Rivals have called him the best passing center in the league. Of his many offensive weapons, the best is a jump hook. His high shooting percentage speaks volumes.

Weaknesses: Daugherty won't block as many shots as you'd like—less than one per game. He was also criticized early in his career, and still is by some, for playing soft underneath.

Analysis: Among the best centers in the league, Daugherty takes a back seat in the publicity department to Patrick Ewing, Hakeem Olajuwon, David Robinson, and now Shaquille O'Neal. He is a complete player with one of the best attitudes you'll find among pro athletes. He is the kind of center with whom a team can win a championship.

PLAYER SUMMARY

Will ....keep All-Star status
Can't ....be shut down inside
Expect.......................20 PPG, 10 RPG
Don't Expect......mega-endorsements
Fantasy Value............................$55-60
Card Value ....10-15¢

COLLEGE STATISTICS

		G	FGP	FTP	RPG	PPG
82-83	NC	35	.558	.663	5.2	8.2
03-04	NC	30	.610	.670	5.6	10.5
84-85	NC	36	.625	.742	9.7	17.3
85-86	NC	34	.648	.684	9.0	20.2
Totals		135	.620	.700	7.4	14.2

NBA REGULAR-SEASON STATISTICS

		G	MIN	FGs FG	FGs PCT	3-PT FGs FG	3-PT FGs PCT	FTs FT	FTs PCT	Rebounds OFF	Rebounds TOT	AST	STL	BLK	PTS	PPG
86-87	CLE	80	2695	487	.538	0	.000	279	.696	152	647	304	49	63	1253	15.7
87-88	CLE	79	2957	551	.510	0	.000	378	.716	151	665	333	48	56	1480	18.7
88-89	CLE	78	2821	544	.538	1	.333	386	.737	167	718	285	63	40	1475	18.9
89-90	CLE	41	1438	244	.479	0	.000	202	.704	77	373	130	29	22	690	16.8
90-91	CLE	76	2946	605	.524	0	.000	435	.751	177	830	253	74	46	1645	21.6
91-92	CLE	73	2643	576	.570	0	.000	414	.777	191	760	262	65	78	1566	21.5
92-93	CLE	71	2691	520	.571	1	.500	391	.795	164	726	312	53	56	1432	20.2
Totals		498	18191	3527	.536	2	.143	2485	.743	1079	4719	1879	381	361	9541	19.2

DALE DAVIS

Team: Indiana Pacers
Position: Forward
Height: 6'11" **Weight:** 230
Birthdate: March 25, 1969

NBA Experience: 2 years
College: Clemson
Acquired: 1st-round pick in 1991 draft
(13th overall)

Background: At Clemson, Davis teamed with Elden Campbell for three seasons to form the "Duo of Doom." They led the 1989-90 Tigers to a 26-9 record and their first ACC title. As a senior, he led the ACC in rebounding for the third consecutive season and joined Mike Gminski and Ralph Sampson as the only ACC players with more than 1,500 points, 1,200 rebounds, and 200 blocked shots. He enjoyed a fine rookie year with the Pacers after a contract holdout, finishing second on the team in blocked shots and rebounding. He led the team in blocks last year as the starting power forward.

Strengths: Davis is the aggressive, hard-working type who loves a challenge. His long arms and great athletic ability make him a force as a rebounder and shot-blocker. A fan favorite in Indianapolis, he maintains a high percentage from the field because he does not put up many ill-advised shots. He runs the floor as well, and he picks up quite a few fastbreak points.

Weaknesses: Davis's offensive skills are not polished. His range is limited and his low-post moves are predictable. However, he knows his limitations on the offensive end and doesn't care how many points he scores. Most of his non-transition chances follow offensive rebounds. He's a dismal free throw shooter and passer.

Analysis: Coaches and fans alike love Davis for his effort, aggressiveness, and willingness to do the dirty work. But his contributions hardly stop there. He is already an intimidating shot-blocker and strong rebounder who will get his points without hurting the team. He quietly enjoyed a fine second season and will make some noise in years to come.

PLAYER SUMMARY	
Will	swat shots
Can't	shoot FTs
Expect	relentless effort
Don't Expect	outside shooting
Fantasy Value	$4-6
Card Value	7-12¢

COLLEGE STATISTICS

		G	FGP	FTP	RPG	PPG
87-88	CLEM	29	.532	.506	7.7	7.8
88-89	CLEM	29	.670	.646	8.9	13.3
89-90	CLEM	35	.625	.596	11.3	15.3
90-91	CLEM	28	.532	.580	12.1	17.9
Totals		121	.588	.589	10.0	13.6

NBA REGULAR-SEASON STATISTICS

			FGs		3-PT FGs		FTs		Rebounds						
		G	MIN	FG	PCT	FG	PCT	FT	PCT	OFF	TOT	AST	STL	BLK	PTS	PPG
91-92	IND	64	1301	154	.552	0	.000	87	.572	158	410	30	27	74	395	6.2
92-93	IND	82	2264	304	.568	0	.000	119	.529	291	723	69	63	148	727	8.9
Totals		146	3565	458	.563	0	.000	206	.546	449	1133	99	90	222	1122	7.7

HUBERT DAVIS

Team: New York Knicks
Position: Guard
Height: 6'5" **Weight:** 183
Birthdate: May 17, 1970

NBA Experience: 1 year
College: North Carolina
Acquired: 1st-round pick in 1992 draft (20th overall)

Background: A nephew of former North Carolina and NBA great Walter Davis, Hubert Davis reportedly was signed by UNC as a favor to his uncle. He gradually developed into a star, leading the Atlantic Coast Conference in 3-point field goal percentage as a junior and helping the Tar Heels to the Final Four. He led North Carolina in scoring as a senior and was taken by the Knicks with the 20th pick in 1992. His play as a rookie drew praise but not much playing time with the Atlantic Division champions.

Strengths: Walter Davis was one of the greatest shooters in NBA history, and his nephew has a sweet stroke as well. Hubert has range beyond the 3-point line, boasts an accurate pull-up jumper, and can be deadly when he squares up to the basket. He moves well without the ball and uses screens to get open. He runs the floor, makes sound choices, and is a better passer than most notice. He's also a deadly free throw shooter.

Weaknesses: Davis is slight in build and can be shoved around by bigger guards. His lack of muscle hurts him on the defensive end, where he can be backed into the post. He also lacks the raw quickness and athletic ability required to keep his man from getting past him. Offensively, there are concerns about his ability to create his own shots and put the ball on the floor.

Analysis: Davis could not crack the regular lineup as a rookie on a Knicks team loaded with backcourt talent. When he did see action, people were impressed with his shooting ability and smarts. Early on, fans were calling for him to play more. Davis, like his uncle, comes to work with a good attitude. He wants to improve and will get his chance.

PLAYER SUMMARY	
Will	spot up for jumpers
Can't	push people around
Expect	pure shooting
Don't Expect	a stopper
Fantasy Value	$1-3
Card Value	10-20¢

COLLEGE STATISTICS

		G	FGP	FTP	RPG	PPG
88-89	NC	35	.512	.774	0.8	3.3
89-90	NC	34	.446	.797	1.8	9.6
90-91	NC	35	.521	.835	2.4	13.3
91-92	NC	33	.508	.828	2.3	21.4
Totals		137	.498	.819	1.8	11.8

NBA REGULAR-SEASON STATISTICS

			FGs		3-PT FGs		FTs		Rebounds						
	G	MIN	FG	PCT	FG	PCT	FT	PCT	OFF	TOT	AST	STL	BLK	PTS	PPG
92-93 NY	50	815	110	.438	6	.316	43	.796	13	56	83	22	4	269	5.4
Totals	50	815	110	.438	6	.316	43	.796	13	56	83	22	4	269	5.4

TERRY DAVIS

Team: Dallas Mavericks
Position: Forward/Center
Height: 6'10" **Weight:** 250
Birthdate: June 17, 1967

NBA Experience: 4 years
College: Virginia Union
Acquired: Signed as a free agent,
8/91

Background: From tiny Virginia Union, Davis made headlines as a two-time Central Intercollegiate Athletic Association Player of the Year. Though he wasn't drafted, he signed with Miami as a free agent in 1989. He was a bench player with the Heat for two years before signing with Dallas in August 1991. He has enjoyed his two most productive seasons with the Mavericks. He averaged 10.2 PPG and a team-high 9.9 RPG in 1991-92 and boosted his scoring average by 2.5 points a game in 1992-93. Last spring, Davis was involved in a gruesome car accident in which he shattered his elbow.

Strengths: One of the lone bright spots for Dallas over the past two years, Davis emerged as a full-time starter, big-time board man, and tough defender. He played with fire in his eyes and provided a good combination of strength and agility. He could play both forward and center.

Weaknesses: Prior to the accident, Davis had a modest offensive game. His offensive rebounding made the scoring and shooting numbers look better than they should have. He did not possess good ball-handling or passing skills and did not make wise decisions with the ball. He was a horrible free throw shooter.

Analysis: The elbow injury was terribly serious, as it was shattered into 15 pieces. Davis, who underwent reconstructive surgery after the accident, was just hoping to move his arm again. It's uncertain when or if he'll return to competitive basketball. A friend of his was killed in the accident, and Davis felt fortunate just to be alive. His attitude remained positive, which should help him on his long road back.

PLAYER SUMMARY	
Will	spend his days in rehab
Can't	afford to slack off
Expect	a tough road back
Don't Expect	to see him soon
Fantasy Value	$0
Card Value	5-10¢

COLLEGE STATISTICS

		G	FGP	FTP	RPG	PPG
85-86	VU	27	.462	.605	4.3	4.1
86-87	VU	32	.521	.690	11.3	11.5
87-88	VU	31	.566	.715	10.9	22.7
88-89	VU	31	.615	.682	11.9	22.3
Totals		121	.567	.692	9.8	15.5

NBA REGULAR-SEASON STATISTICS

				FGs		3-PT FGs		FTs		Rebounds						
		G	MIN	FG	PCT	FG	PCT	FT	PCT	OFF	TOT	AST	STL	BLK	PTS	PPG
89-90	MIA	63	884	122	.466	0	.000	54	.621	93	229	25	25	28	298	4.7
90-91	MIA	55	996	115	.487	1	.500	69	.556	107	266	39	18	28	300	5.5
91-92	DAL	68	2149	256	.482	0	.000	181	.635	228	672	57	26	29	693	10.2
92-93	DAL	75	2462	393	.455	2	.250	167	.594	259	701	68	36	28	955	12.7
Totals		261	6491	886	.468	3	.188	471	.606	687	1868	189	105	113	2246	8.6

JOHNNY DAWKINS

Team: Philadelphia 76ers
Position: Guard
Height: 6'2" **Weight:** 170
Birthdate: September 28, 1963
NBA Experience: 7 years

College: Duke
Acquired: Traded from Spurs with Jay Vincent for Maurice Cheeks, Chris Welp, and David Wingate, 8/89

Background: Dawkins finished his college career No. 1 on Duke's all-time scoring list and No. 2 in the ACC. He was the first ACC player to collect 2,000 points, 500 assists, and 500 rebounds. San Antonio selected him with the No. 10 pick in the first round of the 1987 draft. He missed most of 1988-89 with a leg injury and was then traded to Philadelphia. He sat out 1990-91 because of a torn anterior cruciate ligament. He returned to lead the Sixers in assists the next season but lost his starting job to Jeff Hornacek in 1992-93.

Strengths: A slasher who can get to the basket, Dawkins can also drive and dish. He generally makes wise choices with the ball, especially in transition, and has become a better handler since his rookie season. He is a reliable free throw shooter, although his percentage dipped last season with fewer attempts.

Weaknesses: The knee injury seems to have made Dawkins more tentative about taking the ball to the bucket. His field goal percentage is low, as he is too content to settle for 3-pointers or outside jumpers. Bigger guards give him problems on the defensive end.

Analysis: Dawkins once looked like a future star point guard. His knee injury, however, seems to have taken away some of his fearlessness, and last season he found himself a back-up on a non-playoff team. Dawkins can still be a legitimate NBA starter.

PLAYER SUMMARY

Will ....drive and dish
Can't ....regain fearlessness
Expect..............assists, ball-handling
Don't Expect ....15 PPG
Fantasy Value................................$2-4
Card Value....................................5-10¢

COLLEGE STATISTICS

		G	FGP	FTP	APG	PPG
82-83	DUKE	28	.500	.682	4.8	18.1
83-84	DUKE	34	.481	.831	4.1	19.4
84-85	DUKE	31	.495	.795	5.0	18.8
85-86	DUKE	40	.549	.812	3.2	20.2
Totals		133	.508	.790	4.2	19.2

NBA REGULAR-SEASON STATISTICS

		G	MIN	FGs FG	FGs PCT	3-PT FGs FG	3-PT FGs PCT	FTs FT	FTs PCT	Rebounds OFF	Rebounds TOT	AST	STL	BLK	PTS	PPG
86-87	SA	81	1682	334	.437	14	.298	153	.801	56	169	290	67	3	835	10.3
87-88	SA	65	2179	405	.485	19	.311	198	.896	66	204	480	88	2	1027	15.8
88-89	SA	32	1083	177	.443	0	.000	100	.893	32	101	224	55	0	454	14.2
89-90	PHI	81	2865	465	.489	22	.333	210	.861	48	247	601	121	9	1162	14.3
90-91	PHI	4	124	26	.634	1	.250	10	.909	0	16	28	3	0	63	15.8
91-92	PHI	82	2815	394	.437	36	.356	164	.882	42	227	567	89	5	988	12.0
92-93	PHI	74	1598	258	.437	26	.310	113	.796	33	136	339	80	4	655	8.9
Totals		419	12346	2059	.459	118	.322	948	.856	277	1100	2529	503	23	5184	12.4

TODD DAY

Team: Milwaukee Bucks
Position: Guard
Height: 6'8" **Weight:** 200
Birthdate: January 7, 1970

NBA Experience: 1 year
College: Arkansas
Acquired: 1st-round pick in 1992 draft
(8th overall)

Background: The 1988 prep Player of the Year in Memphis, Day signed with Arkansas and teamed in the backcourt with fellow frosh Lee Mayberry. Day had a brilliant college career on the court, leading Arkansas to a 115-24 record in four seasons and earning several All-America honors as a junior and senior. Off the court, he had problems. He was suspended for the first 12 games of his senior year for his alleged involvement in the sexual assault of a woman. Day was drafted eighth by Milwaukee and finished fourth on the team in scoring as a rookie last year.

Strengths: Day is a great athlete with all the tools to be a standout at the NBA level. He shoots with range, can put the ball on the floor, gets up and down the court quickly, and is a fine finisher. His quick feet, long arms, and ability to leap out of the gym make him a potentially dominant defensive player. The feisty Day will not back down from a challenge.

Weaknesses: Day is a streaky player in almost all respects. That goes for his shooting, his control of the basketball, and especially his defense. His head is not always in the game at both ends and he picks up his share of fouls. A scorer, he'll continue launching ill-advised shots even when ice-cold. His 3-point percentage was poor.

Analysis: Milwaukee desperately needed an infusion of young athletes and Day is certainly that. He'll run up and down the floor all day and do some good things while out there. He is capable of scoring in bunches and of igniting a team with big plays. However, he is also capable of playing out of control. He needs to become more consistent.

PLAYER SUMMARY	
Will	get up and down
Can't	gain consistency
Expect	an athletic sparkplug
Don't Expect	error-free play
Fantasy Value	$8-10
Card Value	20-50¢

COLLEGE STATISTICS

		G	FGP	FTP	RPG	PPG
88-89	ARK	32	.451	.715	4.0	13.3
89-90	ARK	35	.491	.760	5.4	19.5
90-91	ARK	38	.473	.747	5.3	20.7
91-92	ARK	22	.499	.764	7.0	22.7
Totals		127	.479	.747	5.3	18.9

NBA REGULAR-SEASON STATISTICS

			FGs		3-PT FGs		FTs		Rebounds						
		G	MIN	FG	PCT	FG	PCT	FT	PCT	OFF	TOT	AST	STL	BLK	PTS	PPG
92-93	MIL	71	1931	358	.432	54	.293	213	.717	144	291	117	75	48	983	13.8
Totals		71	1931	358	.432	54	.293	213	.717	144	291	117	75	48	983	13.8

VINNY DEL NEGRO

Team: San Antonio Spurs
Position: Guard
Height: 6'4" **Weight:** 200
Birthdate: August 9, 1966

NBA Experience: 3 years
College: North Carolina St.
Acquired: Signed as a free agent, 7/92

Background: Sinking nearly 45 percent of his 3-point shots as a collegian at North Carolina State, Del Negro was an All-ACC pick as a senior. He finished his career as one of the top assist men in school history. He averaged 8.4 PPG in his first two pro seasons with Sacramento before putting in a two-year stint in Italy. He led his team to the Italian A League title in 1992 and was named league MVP after averaging 26.0 PPG. He shot 61 percent from the field and 91 percent from the free throw line. He returned to the NBA last season as a part-time starter for San Antonio.

Strengths: Del Negro is sound in most aspects of the game. He is a very accurate jump-shooter from 20 feet and in, can get his own shots, handles the ball expertly, and makes the right passes. He rarely misses a free throw. He's a fine defensive rebounder for a guard thanks to superior positioning.

Weaknesses: What Del Negro offers in fundamentals he lacks in sheer explosiveness. He is not quick enough to create havoc off the dribble or to enjoy much success defensively against speedy point guards, although he is a better athlete than his body indicates. Though a very fine outside shooter, he doesn't quite have 3-point range.

Analysis: Del Negro does not pretend to be among the best point guards in the league, but he certainly ranks as a good one. He's not flashy but does just about everything pretty well. He was MVP of an Italian league that featured the much talked-about Toni Kukoc. That says something.

PLAYER SUMMARY

Will ....shoot a high percentage
Can't ....explode to the goal
Expect ....a steady hand
Don't Expect ....slam dunks
Fantasy Value................................$2-4
Card Value ....5-8¢

COLLEGE STATISTICS

		G	FGP	FTP	RPG	PPG
84-85	NCST	19	.571	.652	0.7	2.1
85-86	NCST	17	.367	.636	0.8	1.7
86-87	NCST	35	.494	.887	3.3	10.4
87-88	NCST	32	.515	.839	4.9	15.9
Totals		103	.502	.825	2.9	9.1

NBA REGULAR-SEASON STATISTICS

				FGs		3-PT FGs		FTs		Rebounds						
		G	MIN	FG	PCT	FG	PCT	FT	PCT	OFF	TOT	AST	STL	BLK	PTS	PPG
88-89	SAC	80	1556	239	.475	6	.300	85	.850	48	123	206	65	14	569	7.1
89-90	SAC	76	1858	643	.462	10	.313	135	.871	39	198	250	64	10	739	9.7
92-93	SA	73	1526	218	.507	6	.250	101	.863	19	163	291	44	1	543	7.4
Totals		229	4940	754	.478	22	.289	321	.863	106	532	747	173	25	1851	8.1

VLADE DIVAC

Team: Los Angeles Lakers
Position: Center
Height: 7'1" **Weight:** 260
Birthdate: February 3, 1968

NBA Experience: 4 years
College: None
Acquired: 1st-round pick in 1989 draft
(26th overall)

Background: Divac was a national sports hero in Yugoslavia before being drafted by the Lakers in 1989. In fact, his wedding was televised nationally. He led Partizan to the European club championship in 1988, and he averaged approximately 20 points and 11 rebounds in his three years there. He was named to the 1990 NBA All-Rookie Team and started 81 of 82 games in 1990-91. A herniated disk caused him to miss 46 games of the 1991-92 campaign, but he bounced back with a full season last year.

Strengths: A gifted passer and ball-handler for a big man, Divac is especially dangerous when dishing off from the high post. His low-post offense, while not physical, has improved and he has always been a good outside shooter with range. Divac provides shot-blocking and rebounding, and he runs the floor well for a big man.

Weaknesses: The biggest knock on Divac, and it's a big one, is his inconsistency. When he plays aggressively, he can be a force. He just doesn't play at that level on a nightly basis. Divac can rely too much on finesse when he has the ball in the paint and too often settles for jump shots. His shooting percentage reflects it.

Analysis: At his best, Divac provides scoring, passing, shot-blocking, and rebounding while providing another ball-handler to help beat pressure. Other nights, he slips quietly into the background and the Lakers usually struggle. Divac carries the skills to be an above-average starting center. Until he asserts himself more consistently, however, he will not be among the better ones.

PLAYER SUMMARY	
Will	force defenders outside
Can't	play well consistently
Expect	lots of finesse
Don't Expect	a bruiser
Fantasy Value	$24-27
Card Value	10-15¢

COLLEGE STATISTICS

—DID NOT PLAY—

NBA REGULAR-SEASON STATISTICS

			FGs		3-PT FGs		FTs		Rebounds						
		G	MIN	FG	PCT	FG	PCT	FT	PCT	OFF	TOT	AST	STL	BLK	PTS	PPG
89-90	LAL	82	1611	274	.499	0	.000	153	.708	167	512	75	79	114	701	8.5
90-91	LAL	82	2310	360	.565	5	.357	196	.703	205	666	92	106	127	921	11.2
91-92	LAL	36	979	157	.495	5	.263	86	.768	87	247	60	55	35	405	11.3
92-93	LAL	82	2525	397	.485	21	.280	235	.689	220	729	232	128	140	1050	12.8
Totals		282	7425	1188	.512	31	.274	670	.707	679	2154	459	368	416	3077	10.9

SHERMAN DOUGLAS

Team: Boston Celtics
Position: Guard
Height: 6'0" **Weight:** 180
Birthdate: September 15, 1966

NBA Experience: 4 years
College: Syracuse
Acquired: Traded from Heat for Brian Shaw, 1/92

Background: Douglas was the catalyst in Syracuse's "Clockwork Orange" triumvirate that included Billy Owens and Derrick Coleman. As a senior, he became the NCAA career assists leader and a first-team All-American. Despite being drafted in the second round, he made the NBA All-Rookie Team with Miami in 1989-90. Douglas held out for the first half of 1991-92 until the Heat engineered a trade with Boston. He took a short leave to settle personal problems early last season, then returned to the Celtics and won the starting point-guard spot after the All-Star break with the best play of his career.

Strengths: A nifty ball-handler with deceptive moves to the hoop, Douglas is a tremendous penetrator and shows strong leadership skills. He takes care of the ball and knows where to dish it. He is an above-average scorer from the point-guard position. In 1990-91, he led the Heat in scoring.

Weaknesses: Defense and Douglas still need to become better acquainted. He does not come up with a lot of steals, largely because of his tendency to sag. He is not a pure shooter from the perimeter and has big trouble from the foul line. He has gone through periods where he has lost interest.

Analysis: Douglas struggled after joining Boston in midseason two years ago and things looked even worse when he up and left town (with permission) for a few days last season. Lo and behold, he returned to the Celtics a new man. His leadership and playmaking were enough to displace Dee Brown as the starter during the season's second half.

PLAYER SUMMARY	
Will	penetrate
Can't	bury his FTs
Expect	scoring, assists
Don't Expect	steals
Fantasy Value	$5-7
Card Value	5-10¢

COLLEGE STATISTICS

		G	FGP	FTP	APG	PPG
85-86	SYR	27	.613	.727	2.1	5.4
86-87	SYR	38	.531	.744	7.6	17.3
87-88	SYR	35	.519	.693	8.2	16.1
88-89	SYR	38	.546	.632	8.6	18.2
Totals		138	.538	.695	7.0	14.9

NBA REGULAR-SEASON STATISTICS

			FGs		3-PT FGs		FTs		Rebounds						
	G	MIN	FG	PCT	FG	PCT	FT	PCT	OFF	TOT	AST	STL	BLK	PTS	PPG
89-90 MIA	81	2470	463	.494	5	.161	224	.687	70	206	619	145	10	1155	14.3
90-91 MIA	73	2562	532	.504	4	.129	284	.686	78	209	624	121	5	1352	18.5
91-92 MIA/BOS	42	752	117	.462	1	.100	73	.682	13	63	172	25	9	308	7.3
92-93 BOS	79	1932	264	.498	6	.207	84	.560	65	162	508	49	10	618	7.8
Totals	275	7716	1376	.496	16	.158	665	.667	226	640	1923	340	34	3433	12.5

CLYDE DREXLER

Team: Portland Trail Blazers
Position: Guard
Height: 6'7" **Weight:** 222
Birthdate: June 22, 1962

NBA Experience: 10 years
College: Houston
Acquired: 1st-round pick in 1983 draft
(14th overall)

Background: Drexler gained notoriety at the University of Houston (where he played in two Final Fours) for his breathtaking dunks. He has maintained that reputation as a pro and has led Portland in scoring average each of the past six years. Drexler is the Blazers' all-time leader in games, minutes, scoring, offensive rebounds, and steals. The seven-time All-Star had one of his most frustrating seasons in 1992-93. Knee surgery in September 1992 caused him to start slowly, and he later wound up missing more than 20 games with a hamstring injury.

Strengths: Phenomenal leaping ability and hang time have helped "Clyde the Glide" establish himself as a superstar. Few can make things happen in the open court or finish a break like he can. Drexler is a reliable shooter with 3-point range. His post-up moves give small guards fits. He rebounds well and has become a team leader.

Weaknesses: His recent injury problems are the biggest concern. Before last year, Drexler had never missed more than nine games in any season. As well, Drexler is not a candidate for the All-Defensive Team.

Analysis: Drexler has done just about everything in his pro career, except win an NBA title. Once considered a highlight-reel type, he has demonstrated an overall game that ranks him among the best big guards in the league.

PLAYER SUMMARY

Will......................score inside and out
Can't............be stopped in transition
Expect..............All-Star performances
Don't Expect................timid shooting
Fantasy Value..............................$30-35
Card Value....................................15-25¢

COLLEGE STATISTICS

		G	FGP	FTP	RPG	PPG
80-81	HOU	30	.505	.588	10.5	11.9
81-82	HOU	32	.569	.608	10.5	15.2
82-83	HOU	34	.536	.737	8.8	15.9
Totals		96	.538	.643	9.9	14.4

NBA REGULAR-SEASON STATISTICS

				FGs		3-PT FGs		FTs		Rebounds						
		G	MIN	FG	PCT	FG	PCT	FT	PCT	OFF	TOT	AST	STL	BLK	PTS	PPG
83-84	POR	82	1408	252	.451	1	.250	123	.728	112	235	153	107	29	628	7.7
84-85	POR	80	2555	573	.494	8	.216	223	.759	217	476	441	177	68	1377	17.2
85-86	POR	75	2576	542	.475	12	.200	293	.769	171	421	600	197	46	1389	18.5
86-87	POR	82	3114	707	.502	11	.234	357	.760	227	518	566	204	71	1782	21.7
87-88	POR	81	3060	849	.506	11	.212	476	.811	261	533	467	203	52	2185	27.0
88-89	POR	78	3064	829	.496	27	.260	438	.799	289	615	450	213	54	2123	27.2
89-90	POR	73	2683	670	.494	30	.283	333	.774	208	507	432	145	51	1703	23.3
90-91	POR	82	2852	645	.482	61	.319	416	.794	212	546	493	144	60	1767	21.5
91-92	POR	76	2751	694	.470	114	.337	401	.794	166	500	512	138	70	1903	25.0
92-93	POR	49	1671	350	.429	31	.233	245	.839	126	309	278	95	37	976	19.9
Totals		758	25734	6111	.485	306	.285	3305	.787	1989	4660	4392	1623	538	15833	20.9

KEVIN DUCKWORTH

Team: Washington Bullets
Position: Center
Height: 7'0" **Weight:** 280
Birthdate: April 1, 1964

NBA Experience: 7 years
College: Eastern Illinois
Acquired: Traded from Trail Blazers
for Harvey Grant, 6/93

Background: Duckworth established a career rebounding record at Eastern Illinois, where his .631 field goal percentage as a senior placed him sixth in the nation. His pro career started slowly in San Antonio. However, he was voted the NBA's Most Improved Player for 1987-88 with Portland, where he upped his scoring to 15.8 PPG. He played in the 1988-89 All-Star Game, but his shooting and scoring marks have taken a plunge over the last two years. In June, he was swapped to the Bullets.

Strengths: Duckworth is agile and possesses a soft touch for a man of his size. His low-post game can be potent and polished, featuring accurate hooks and turnaround jumpers. In addition, his range is pretty good for a big man and he is capable of huge scoring nights.

Weaknesses: The past two seasons have been forgettable for Duckworth. Weight and foul problems have always followed him, but his problems have now stretched to all aspects of his game. He's never been a great rebounder, shot-blocker, or defender, and now he seems to have lost his touch on offense.

Analysis: Duckworth can hardly be considered one of the top centers in the game, although he appeared to be heading in that direction earlier in his career. Several would contend that his demeanor and attitude have had a lot to do with his declining play. Perhaps the change of scenery will do him good.

PLAYER SUMMARY

Will ....convert on the blocks
Can't ....regain shooting touch
Expect ....hooks, turnarounds
Don't Expect ....great confidence
Fantasy Value.............................$1-3
Card Value ....5-10¢

COLLEGE STATISTICS

		G	FGP	FTP	RPG	PPG
82-83	EILL	30	.528	.674	6.0	9.6
83-84	EILL	28	.597	.685	6.8	11.6
84-85	EILL	28	.516	.657	7.5	19.0
85-86	EILL	32	.631	.762	9.1	19.5
Totals		118	.577	.705	7.4	15.0

NBA REGULAR-SEASON STATISTICS

		G	MIN	FGs FG	FGs PCT	3-PT FGs FG	3-PT FGs PCT	FTs FT	FTs PCT	Rebounds OFF	Rebounds TOT	AST	STL	BLK	PTS	PPG
86-87	SA/POR	65	875	130	.476	0	.000	92	.687	76	223	29	21	21	352	5.4
87-88	POR	78	2223	450	.496	0	.000	331	.770	224	576	66	31	32	1231	15.8
88-89	POR	79	2662	554	.477	0	.000	324	.757	246	635	60	56	49	1432	18.1
89-90	POR	82	2462	548	.478	0	.000	231	.740	184	509	91	36	34	1327	16.2
90-91	POR	81	2511	521	.481	0	.000	240	.772	177	531	89	33	34	1282	15.8
91-92	POR	82	2222	362	.461	0	.000	156	.690	151	497	99	38	37	880	10.7
92-93	POR	74	1762	301	.438	0	.000	127	.730	118	387	70	45	39	729	9.9
Totals		541	14717	2866	.474	0	.000	1501	.745	1176	3358	504	260	246	7233	13.4

CHRIS DUDLEY

Team: Portland Trail Blazers
Position: Center
Height: 6'11" **Weight:** 240
Birthdate: February 22, 1965

NBA Experience: 6 years
College: Yale
Acquired: Signed as a free agent, 8/93

Background: A Yale graduate, Dudley is one of the rare Ivy Leaguers to make it to the NBA. The three-time all-conference big man was second in the nation in rebounding as a senior. Cleveland drafted him in 1987, but the Cavs banished him to New Jersey in 1989-90. In 1990-91, Dudley came off the bench to average a career-high 7.1 PPG. Although his scoring has dipped since then, he has improved most of his other numbers. He was awarded for his efforts over the summer, when he signed a multi-million-dollar contract with Portland.

Strengths: Dudley attacks the glass and opposing players with equal abandon. He knows how to use his large frame inside to wall off opponents from the backboards. He has an aggressive, forceful approach to everything he does. Dudley is a smart, tough defender who blocks a lot of shots.

Weaknesses: Dudley has proven that brains have nothing to do with free throw shooting. Four years ago, he hit just .319 from the line. He has toyed with the 50-percent mark ever since. In fact, his offensive game in general, including his field goal shooting and passing, is very weak. He also commits a lot of fouls.

Analysis: Dudley continues to amaze. Anyone who shoots like he does has no right playing in the NBA, yet Dudley does just that—and does it pretty well. Not many pro players are content to pound the daylights out of people and chase every rebound, but he is. He makes the most of his six fouls and intimidates opponents.

PLAYER SUMMARY	
Will	rebound, block shots
Can't	shoot straight
Expect	bumps and bruises
Don't Expect	touch
Fantasy Value	$1-3
Card Value	5-10¢

COLLEGE STATISTICS

		G	FGP	FTP	RPG	PPG
83-84	YALE	26	.464	.467	5.1	4.5
84-85	YALE	26	.446	.533	10.2	12.6
85-86	YALE	26	.539	.482	9.8	16.2
86-87	YALE	24	.569	.542	13.3	17.8
Totals		102	.513	.512	9.5	12.7

NBA REGULAR-SEASON STATISTICS

		G	MIN	FGs FG	FGs PCT	3-PT FGs FG	3-PT FGs PCT	FTs FT	FTs PCT	Rebounds OFF	Rebounds TOT	AST	STL	BLK	PTS	PPG
87-88	CLE	55	513	65	.474	0	.000	40	.563	74	144	23	13	19	170	3.1
88-89	CLE	61	544	73	.435	0	.000	39	.364	72	157	21	9	23	185	3.0
89-90	CLE/NJ	64	1356	146	.411	0	.000	58	.319	174	423	39	41	72	350	5.5
90-91	NJ	61	1560	170	.408	0	.000	94	.534	229	511	37	39	153	434	7.1
91-92	NJ	82	1902	190	.403	0	.000	80	.468	343	739	58	38	179	460	5.6
92-93	NJ	71	1398	94	.353	0	.000	57	.518	215	513	16	17	103	245	3.5
Totals		394	7273	738	.407	0	.000	368	.450	1107	2487	194	157	549	1844	4.7

JOE DUMARS

Team: Detroit Pistons
Position: Guard
Height: 6'3" **Weight:** 195
Birthdate: May 23, 1963

NBA Experience: 8 years
College: McNeese St.
Acquired: 1st-round pick in 1985 draft (18th overall)

Background: At McNeese State, Dumars led the Southland Conference in scoring three times and averaged 26.4 PPG his junior year. He left the school ranked among the NCAA's top 20 all-time leading scorers. In Detroit, he got pegged early as all-defense, no-offense. He has increased his scoring steadily, however, and now scores a team-leading 20-plus PPG. He was named MVP of the 1989 NBA Finals, remains an all-defensive performer, and has played in four straight All-Star Games.

Strengths: Michael Jordan will vouch for the one-on-one defensive prowess of Joe D. He is a modest, unassuming leader who is also a deadly shooter. Moreover, he can penetrate and pass like a point guard when asked to fill that role. He's one of the premier clutch shooters in the league. He's a complete player and also one of the class players in the game.

Weaknesses: Dumars is not a strong rebounder at all, especially on the defensive end. He was slowed somewhat last season by sore knees and recurring stomach ulcers.

Analysis: Once an unheralded player, Dumars now commands respect throughout the league. He doesn't do it verbally, but he will quietly beat you both offensively and defensively. There are very few big guards in the league you'd take over this guy. He's a warrior, having battled through knee and stomach problems last season for the best scoring year of his career.

PLAYER SUMMARY

Will .... shut down his man
Can't .... hoard rebounds
Expect .... leadership, 20 PPG
Don't Expect .... soft defense
Fantasy Value $16-19
Card Value .... 10-15¢

COLLEGE STATISTICS

		G	FGP	FTP	RPG	PPG
81-82	MSU	29	.444	.719	2.2	18.2
82-83	MSU	29	.435	.711	4.4	19.6
83-84	MSU	31	.471	.824	5.3	26.4
84-85	MSU	27	.495	.852	4.9	25.8
Totals		116	.462	.788	4.2	22.5

NBA REGULAR-SEASON STATISTICS

		G	MIN	FGs FG	FGs PCT	3-PT FGs FG	3-PT FGs PCT	FTs FT	FTs PCT	Rebounds OFF	Rebounds TOT	AST	STL	BLK	PTS	PPG
85-86	DET	82	1957	287	.481	5	.313	190	.798	60	119	390	66	11	769	9.4
86-87	DET	79	2439	369	.493	9	.409	184	.748	50	167	352	83	5	931	11.8
87-88	DET	82	2732	453	.472	4	.211	251	.815	63	200	387	87	15	1161	14.2
88-89	DET	69	2408	456	.505	14	.483	260	.850	57	172	390	63	5	1186	17.2
89-90	DET	75	2578	508	.480	22	.400	297	.900	60	212	368	63	2	1335	17.8
90-91	DET	80	3046	622	.481	14	.311	371	.890	62	187	443	89	7	1629	20.4
91-92	DET	82	3192	587	.448	49	.408	412	.867	82	188	375	71	12	1635	19.9
92-93	DET	77	3094	677	.466	112	.375	343	.864	63	148	308	78	7	1809	23.5
Totals		626	21446	3959	.476	229	.379	2308	.849	497	1393	3013	600	64	10455	16.7

RICHARD DUMAS

Team: Phoenix Suns
Position: Forward
Height: 6'7" **Weight:** 204
Birthdate: May 19, 1969

NBA Experience: 1 year
College: Oklahoma St.
Acquired: 2nd-round pick in 1991 draft (46th overall)

Background: Dumas made an instant splash at Oklahoma State, making the All-Big Eight second team as a freshman and leading the Cowboys in scoring as a sophomore. Chased by academic and alcohol troubles, however, Dumas was forced to take his career to Israel for a season. He was drafted in the second round by the Suns in 1991 but was suspended before the 1991-92 season began for failing a random drug test. He played for Miami of the USBL and Oklahoma City of the CBA and completed a drug treatment program. Dumas then exploded onto the NBA scene with Phoenix in 1992-93, scoring 16 points in his December debut and finishing fourth on the team in scoring average.

Strengths: Dumas is a flashy, exciting, and tremendously talented player. He slashes to the hoop as well as anyone in the league and is a splendid finisher. He thrives in the open court but also has a steady mid-range jumper. He also knows how to put the ball in the hole and can hold his own defensively, despite the fact he had never defended NBA-caliber players before last year. Dumas is good off the dribble with both hands.

Weaknesses: There is obviously a checkered history with Dumas, but if his rookie year is any indication, there is not much to worry about. He is not as strong a passer as the Suns had anticipated. He tallied more turnovers than he did assists, and he does not have 3-point range.

Analysis: Spurs coach John Lucas, who helped him rehabilitate from his drug problem, says Dumas has "Dr. J.-type ability." Phoenix coach Paul Westphal calls his small forward a potential Dream Team player. Though hampered by an ankle injury late in the year, Dumas was a potent weapon in the NBA Finals.

PLAYER SUMMARY	
Will	slash to the hoop
Can't	afford to slip up
Expect	exciting finishes
Don't Expect	3 APG
Fantasy Value	$20-23
Card Value	50¢-$2.00

COLLEGE STATISTICS

		G	FGP	FTP	RPG	PPG
87-88	OSU	30	.548	.747	6.4	17.4
88-89	OSU	28	.448	.617	7.0	15.7
Totals		58	.494	.694	6.7	16.6

NBA REGULAR-SEASON STATISTICS

	G	MIN	FGs FG	FGs PCT	3-PT FGs FG	3-PT FGs PCT	FTs FT	FTs PCT	Rebounds OFF	Rebounds TOT	AST	STL	BLK	PTS	PPG
92-93 PHO	48	1320	302	.524	1	.333	152	.707	100	223	60	85	39	757	15.8
Totals	48	1320	302	.524	1	.333	152	.707	100	223	60	85	39	757	15.8

MARK EATON

Team: Utah Jazz
Position: Center
Height: 7'4" **Weight:** 290
Birthdate: January 24, 1957

NBA Experience: 11 years
College: Cypress; UCLA
Acquired: 4th-round pick in 1982 draft (72nd overall)

Background: Eaton was 22 years old and fixing cars when he was found by an assistant coach at Cypress Junior College in California. After two years at Cypress, he jumped to UCLA, where he played just 196 minutes in two seasons. In his first ten pro campaigns, Eaton never finished lower than seventh in blocked shots and set a league record with 456 in 1984-85. He was the league's Defensive Player of the Year in both 1985 and 1989. Last season was the first in which he failed to block 100 shots.

Strengths: Eaton will go down as one of the most intimidating shot-blockers in history. When healthy, he is still capable of steering opponents away from the middle with his size and shot-altering skills.

Weaknesses: Everything but shot-blocking can be considered a weakness for Eaton, especially at this late stage of his career. Eaton is as slow as they come, which limits his ability when pulled away from the hoop. He does not rebound well and he is no threat on offense.

Analysis: Knee and back injuries, combined with Eaton's lack of athletic ability even when healthy, have slowed this one-time defensive force considerably. There is no reason to believe he can return to his old form.

PLAYER SUMMARY

Will ....still block shots
Can't ....do much else
Expect ....size, immobility
Don't Expect........................durability
Fantasy Value.....................................$0
Card Value ....5-10¢

COLLEGE STATISTICS

		G	FGP	FTP	RPG	PPG
78-79	CYP	35	.633	.667	10.9	13.8
79-80	CYP	25	.578	.482	8.7	15.0
80-81	UCLA	19	.459	.294	2.6	2.1
81-82	UCLA	11	.417	.800	2.0	1.3
Totals		90	.595	.572	7.4	10.1

NBA REGULAR-SEASON STATISTICS

		G	MIN	FG	FGs PCT	3-PT FGs FG	PCT	FT	FTs PCT	Rebounds OFF	TOT	AST	STL	BLK	PTS	PPG
82-83	UTA	81	1528	146	.414	0	.000	59	.656	86	462	112	24	275	351	4.3
83-84	UTA	82	2139	194	.466	0	.000	73	.593	148	595	113	25	351	461	5.6
84-85	UTA	82	2813	302	.449	0	.000	190	.712	207	927	124	36	456	794	9.7
85-86	UTA	80	2551	277	.470	0	.000	122	.604	172	675	101	33	369	676	8.4
86-87	UTA	79	2505	234	.400	0	.000	140	.657	211	697	105	43	321	608	7.7
87-88	UTA	82	2731	226	.418	0	.000	119	.623	230	717	55	41	304	571	7.0
88-89	UTA	82	2914	188	.462	0	.000	132	.660	227	843	83	40	315	508	6.2
89-90	UTA	82	2281	158	.527	0	.000	79	.669	171	601	39	33	201	395	4.8
90-91	UTA	80	2580	169	.579	0	.000	71	.634	182	667	51	39	188	409	5.1
91-92	UTA	81	2023	107	.446	0	.000	52	.598	150	491	40	36	205	266	3.3
92-93	UTA	64	1104	71	.546	0	.000	35	.700	73	264	17	18	79	177	2.8
Totals		875	25169	2072	.458	0	.000	1072	.649	1857	6939	840	368	3064	5216	6.0

BLUE EDWARDS

Team: Milwaukee Bucks
Position: Forward/Guard
Height: 6'5" **Weight:** 200
Birthdate: October 31, 1965
NBA Experience: 4 years

College: Louisburg; East Carolina
Acquired: Traded from Jazz with Eric
Murdock and a 1992 1st-round pick for
Jay Humphries and Larry Krystkowiak,
6/92

Background: Edwards was a junior college All-American before his two-year career at East Carolina. As a senior, he led the Pirates in scoring, rebounds, steals, assists, blocked shots, 3-point percentage, and field goals. He has improved steadily as a pro, becoming Utah's starting small forward over his last two seasons there. He was traded to Milwaukee before the 1992-93 season and nearly led the Bucks in scoring at 16.9 PPG.

Strengths: One of the best young athletes and leapers in the league, Edwards presents an All-Star combination of speed and strength. He's a tremendous finisher on the break, can post up, and is blessed with a nice outside jumper with 3-point range. Edwards has increased his scoring average every year in the league. He also passes well and his field goal percentage has never been below .500. He can play both big guard and small forward.

Weaknesses: Edwards has improved his outside shooting and passing, but his perimeter ability still does not include a confident handle on the ball—he turns it over too often. Edwards gets broken down off the dribble by guards yet lacks the size to defend forwards well. He's prone to fouls and is still learning to box out.

Analysis: Milwaukee revamped its roster last season with an eye on athletes, and the versatile Edwards was the best of the bunch. He started his career as a reserve role-player, advanced to starter, and now has established himself as a primary NBA scorer. He's not a superstar, but further improvement could put him close to that class. He clearly fills a huge need for the Bucks.

PLAYER SUMMARY	
Will	finish breaks
Can't	dribble like a guard
Expect	15-plus PPG
Don't Expect	bench time
Fantasy Value	$24-27
Card Value	5-10¢

COLLEGE STATISTICS

		G	FGP	FTP	RPG	PPG
84-85	LOU	29	.636	.645	6.1	17.8
85-86	LOU	31	.700	.658	6.0	22.3
86-87	ECAR	28	.561	.739	5.6	14.4
88-89	ECAR	29	.551	.755	6.9	26.7
Totals		117	.612	.701	6.2	20.4

NBA REGULAR-SEASON STATISTICS

		G	MIN	FGs FG	FGs PCT	3-PT FGs FG	3-PT FGs PCT	FTs FT	FTs PCT	Rebounds OFF	Rebounds TOT	AST	STL	BLK	PTS	PPG
89-90	UTA	82	1889	286	.507	9	.300	146	.719	69	251	145	76	36	727	8.9
90-91	UTA	62	1611	244	.526	6	.250	82	.701	51	201	108	57	29	576	9.3
91-92	UTA	81	2283	433	.522	39	.379	113	.774	86	298	137	81	46	1018	12.6
92-93	MIL	82	2729	554	.512	37	.349	237	.790	123	382	214	129	45	1382	16.9
Totals		307	8512	1517	.516	91	.346	578	.755	329	1132	604	343	156	3703	12.1

JAMES EDWARDS

Team: Los Angeles Lakers
Position: Center
Height: 7'1" **Weight:** 252
Birthdate: November 22, 1955

NBA Experience: 16 years
College: Washington
Acquired: Signed as a free agent, 8/92

Background: "Buddha" was All-Pac-10 at Washington, finishing as the school's No. 2 all-time scorer. Edwards was drafted by the Lakers and played for Indiana, Cleveland, Phoenix, Detroit, and the Clippers before returning to the Lakers as a free agent last year. Last season, he scored at a career-low pace while coming off the Laker bench sparingly.

Strengths: Edwards can still score in the low post with his dangerous fadeaway jumper. He has a soft touch for a big man, though he rarely makes power moves.

Weaknesses: His rebounding and shot-blocking are nowhere near what they should be for a man his size. Age is his biggest weakness. His best and healthiest days have passed him by.

Analysis: As long as Edwards can plant himself in the post and knock down those fadeaway jumpers, there should be a market for him as a reserve. However, he tends to wear down over the course of a season and does not have many seasons left.

PLAYER SUMMARY	
Will	hit the fadeaway
Can't	log starter's minutes
Expect	declining effectiveness
Don't Expect	two more years
Fantasy Value	$0
Card Value	5-10¢

COLLEGE STATISTICS

		G	FGP	FTP	RPG	PPG
73-74	WASH	25	.425	.548	4.6	6.8
74-75	WASH	26	.473	.543	7.6	12.3
75-76	WASH	28	.523	.606	7.1	17.6
76-77	WASH	27	.552	.647	10.4	20.9
Totals		106	.509	.598	7.5	14.6

NBA REGULAR-SEASON STATISTICS

		G	MIN	FGs		3-PT FGs		FTs		Rebounds		AST	STL	BLK	PTS	PPG
				FG	PCT	FG	PCT	FT	PCT	OFF	TOT					
77-78	LAL/IND	83	2405	495	.453	0	.000	272	.646	197	615	85	53	78	1262	15.2
78-79	IND	82	2546	534	.501	0	.000	298	.676	179	693	92	60	109	1366	16.7
79-80	IND	82	2314	528	.512	0	.000	231	.681	179	578	127	55	104	1287	15.7
80-81	IND	81	2375	511	.509	0	.000	244	.703	191	571	212	32	128	1266	15.6
81-82	CLE	77	2539	528	.511	0	.000	232	.684	189	581	123	24	117	1288	16.7
82-83	CLE/PHO	31	667	128	.487	0	.000	69	.639	56	155	40	12	19	325	10.5
83-84	PHO	72	1897	438	.536	0	.000	183	.720	108	348	184	23	30	1059	14.7
84-85	PHO	70	1787	384	.501	0	.000	276	.746	95	387	153	26	52	1044	14.9
85-86	PHO	52	1314	318	.542	0	.000	212	.702	79	301	74	23	29	848	16.3
86-87	PHO	14	304	57	.518	0	.000	54	.771	20	60	19	6	7	168	12.0
87-88	PHO/DET	69	1705	302	.470	0	.000	210	.654	119	412	78	16	37	814	11.8
88-89	DET	76	1254	211	.500	0	.000	133	.686	68	231	49	11	31	555	7.3
89-90	DET	82	2283	462	.498	0	.000	265	.749	112	345	63	23	37	1189	14.5
90-91	DET	72	1903	383	.484	1	.500	215	.729	91	277	65	12	30	982	13.6
91-92	LAC	72	1437	250	.465	0	.000	198	.731	55	202	53	24	33	698	9.7
92-93	LAL	52	617	122	.452	0	.000	84	.712	30	100	41	10	7	328	6.3
Totals		1067	27347	5651	.497	1	.048	3176	.699	1768	5856	1458	410	848	14479	13.6

KEVIN EDWARDS

Team: New Jersey Nets
Position: Guard
Height: 6'3" **Weight:** 202
Birthdate: October 30, 1965

NBA Experience: 5 years
College: Lakewood; DePaul
Acquired: Signed as a free agent, 7/93

Background: One of the bright stars who was supposed to return DePaul to its glory years, Edwards finished his two-year career with the best shooting percentage (.534) ever by a DePaul guard and became known as a high-flying dunker. In his first four years with the Heat, he played in nearly every game, averaging in double figures each year. Edwards started last season on that same pace and once again averaged double figures. But, as Miami's fifth guard, he rarely got in a game after the All-Star break. The Nets picked him up in July.

Strengths: Edwards has a quick first step to the basket and isn't bashful about putting it up on his drives. He is capable of posting big-time scoring numbers. He puts out a good effort on the defensive end and comes up with a lot of steals. He's a very good foul shooter.

Weaknesses: Edwards is there one night, gone the next. Because of his inconsistency, he was out of the Heat's rotation for more than half of the 1992-93 season. His jump shot is streaky and he is not reliable from behind the 3-point stripe. Edwards is not a reliable playmaker and he's had a history of being turnover-prone.

Analysis: As many expected would happen, Edwards found himself lost in the shuffle behind four other Miami guards. He was a regular starter when the Heat encountered injury problems in the season's first half and played well at times. When the team got healthy, Edwards was not steady enough to maintain his minutes. He may get the starting nod in New Jersey because of the death of Drazen Petrovic, but he's not an ideal starter.

PLAYER SUMMARY	
Will	drive the lane
Can't	find consistency
Expect	high FT pct.
Don't Expect	great playmaking
Fantasy Value	$10-13
Card Value	5-10¢

COLLEGE STATISTICS

		G	FGP	FTP	RPG	PPG
84-85	LAKE	33	.589	.715	5.4	18.6
85-86	LAKE	32	.626	.761	7.5	24.1
86-87	DeP	31	.536	.808	5.0	14.4
87-88	DeP	30	.533	.783	5.3	18.3
Totals		126	.576	.760	5.8	18.9

NBA REGULAR-SEASON STATISTICS

		G	MIN	FGs FG	FGs PCT	3-PT FGs FG	3-PT FGs PCT	FTs FT	FTs PCT	Rebounds OFF	Rebounds TOT	AST	STL	BLK	PTS	PPG
88-89	MIA	79	2349	470	.425	10	.270	144	.746	85	262	349	139	27	1094	13.8
89-90	MIA	78	2211	395	.412	9	.300	139	.760	77	282	252	125	33	938	12.0
90-91	MIA	79	2000	380	.410	24	.286	171	.803	80	205	240	130	46	955	12.1
91-92	MIA	81	1840	325	.454	7	.219	162	.848	56	211	170	99	20	819	10.1
92-93	MIA	40	1134	216	.468	5	.294	119	.844	48	121	120	68	12	556	13.9
Totals		357	9534	1786	.428	55	.275	735	.798	346	1081	1131	561	138	4362	12.2

CRAIG EHLO

Team: Atlanta Hawks
Position: Guard/Forward
Height: 6'7" **Weight:** 205
Birthdate: August 11, 1961

NBA Experience: 10 years
College: Odessa; Washington St.
Acquired: Signed as a free agent, 7/93

Background: As a senior, Ehlo set a Pac-10 record for assists at Washington State. He was a reserve for Houston before spending some time in the CBA. He played in all 82 games for Cleveland in two of the last three seasons as both a starter and reserve. He started most of the 1992-93 season and averaged double figures in scoring for the fourth straight time. In July, he signed a free-agent deal with the Atlanta Hawks.

Strengths: Ehlo is a versatile player with solid skills in most phases of the game. He is a tough defender who throws his body around for the team. He is an underrated scorer and shooter with 3-point range. In fact, he's one of the most reliable in the league from long range. His traits were overlooked with a star like Mark Price in the lineup.

Weaknesses: "A step slow" is the knock on Ehlo. He does not possess the quickness or athletic ability to stick with faster players one-on-one. As well, he does not create much on offense, but rather feeds off teammates.

Analysis: Ehlo is a fine complementary player on a good team, whether he's starting or providing a lift off the bench. He can hurt you if you leave him open and he rarely does anything to hurt his own team. Ehlo fills a need for the Hawks, who were lacking a shooter at two guard.

PLAYER SUMMARY	
Will	bury 3-pointers
Can't	blow past defenders
Expect	a gritty player
Don't Expect	headlines
Fantasy Value	$6-8
Card Value	5-10¢

COLLEGE STATISTICS

		G	FGP	FTP	RPG	PPG
79-80	ODES	28	.487	.714	5.1	12.6
80-81	ODES	30	.500	.772	6.8	20.7
81-82	WSU	30	.479	.600	2.2	5.1
82-83	WSU	30	.547	.633	3.2	12.0
Totals		118	.505	.701	4.3	12.6

NBA REGULAR-SEASON STATISTICS

		G	MIN	FGs FG	FGs PCT	3-PT FGs FG	3-PT FGs PCT	FTs FT	FTs PCT	Rebounds OFF	Rebounds TOT	AST	STL	BLK	PTS	PPG
83-84	HOU	7	63	11	.407	0	.000	1	1.000	4	9	6	3	0	23	3.3
84-85	HOU	45	189	34	.493	0	.000	19	.633	8	25	26	11	3	87	1.9
85-86	HOU	36	199	36	.429	3	.333	23	.793	17	46	29	11	4	98	2.7
86-87	CLE	44	890	99	.414	5	.172	70	.707	55	161	92	40	30	273	6.2
87-88	CLE	79	1709	226	.466	22	.344	89	.674	86	274	206	82	30	563	7.1
88-89	CLE	82	1867	249	.475	39	.390	71	.607	100	295	266	110	19	608	7.4
89-90	CLE	81	2894	436	.464	104	.419	126	.681	147	439	371	126	23	1102	13.6
90-91	CLE	82	2766	344	.445	49	.329	95	.879	142	388	376	121	34	832	10.1
91-92	CLE	63	2016	310	.453	69	.413	87	.707	94	307	238	78	22	776	12.3
92-93	CLE	82	2559	385	.490	93	.381	86	.717	113	403	254	104	22	949	11.6
Totals		601	15152	2130	.462	384	.379	667	.683	766	2347	1864	686	187	5311	8.8

MARIO ELIE

Team: Houston Rockets
Position: Guard
Height: 6'5" **Weight:** 210
Birthdate: November 26, 1963

NBA Experience: 3 years
College: American International
Acquired: Traded from Trail Blazers for a 1995 2nd-round pick, 8/93

Background: A world traveler, Elie played in Portugal, Argentina, Ireland, and Miami (of the USBL) after his college career at American International. He speaks four languages. He was drafted by Milwaukee in 1985 but was released before the season. He joined Albany of the CBA during 1989-90 and saw his first NBA action in 1990-91 with Philadelphia (three games). The Warriors picked him up in February of 1991 and he became a key contributor. Portland signed him away from the Warriors and he played in every game last year. Over the summer, he was traded to Houston.

Strengths: Elie is one of the most underrated defensive stalwarts in the league. He holds his own against big scorers on a nightly basis. He can play just about any position except center. Offensively, Elie shoots his unorthodox jump shot with 3-point range. He is a very good ball-handler and passer and one of the more accurate free throw shooters in the game.

Weaknesses: Quick guards cause problems for Elie, who is not a dominant athlete and is not overpowering in any one area. He's just a solid overall player. His jumper is not as consistent as the Portland brass would have liked it to be. He shot much better two years ago.

Analysis: The fact that Elie took such advantage of his NBA chance when it finally came says loads about his character. He is willing and able to do whatever is asked of him. Portland thought enough of him to pursue him in the free-agent market and he responded with another solid year. Role-players who specialize in defense don't get much notoriety, but Elie deserves some.

PLAYER SUMMARY

Will ....thrive on defense
Can't ....dominate offensively
Expect ....plenty of heart
Don't Expect ....raw speed
Fantasy Value.............................$1-3
Card Value ....5-12¢

COLLEGE STATISTICS

		G	FGP	FTP	RPG	PPG
81-82	AI	25	.586	.742	8.3	15.4
82-83	AI	31	.527	.739	7.7	15.9
83-84	AI	31	.565	.794	8.6	18.9
84-85	AI	33	.549	.777	9.0	20.1
Totals		120	.555	.767	8.4	17.7

NBA REGULAR-SEASON STATISTICS

				FGs		3-PT FGs		FTs		Rebounds						
		G	MIN	FG	PCT	FG	PCT	FT	PCT	OFF	TOT	AST	STL	BLK	PTS	PPG
90-91	Phi/GS	33	644	79	.497	4	.400	75	.843	46	110	45	19	10	237	7.2
91-92	GS	79	1677	221	.521	23	.329	155	.852	69	227	174	68	15	620	7.8
92-93	POR	82	1757	240	.458	45	.349	183	.855	59	216	177	74	20	708	8.6
Totals		194	4078	540	.488	72	.344	413	.852	174	553	396	161	45	1565	8.1

SEAN ELLIOTT

Team: San Antonio Spurs
Position: Forward
Height: 6'8" **Weight:** 215
Birthdate: February 2, 1968

NBA Experience: 4 years
College: Arizona
Acquired: 1st-round pick in 1989 draft (3rd overall)

Background: Elliott was college basketball's 1989 Player of the Year at Arizona, where he broke Lew Alcindor's Pac-10 record with 2,555 career points. He started 69 of 81 games as a rookie for San Antonio and followed that up with 82 consecutive starts in each of the next two years, when he emerged as a shooter, scorer, and rebounder. He has improved his scoring average every year, topped by a 17.2 PPG season in 1992-93.

Strengths: Elliott loves roaming the baseline, and his offensive arsenal is virtually unlimited. He can shoot from the perimeter, drive to the hoop, handle the ball, and make crisp passes. Despite his lack of bulk, he is a better-than-expected rebounder and a standout defender. His versatility allows him to play big guard in addition to small forward. He can flat-out score against anyone in the league.

Weaknesses: There are not many flaws in Elliott's game. He is not overly physical in his approach, but he makes up for that deficiency with his quickness. He has been overshadowed somewhat by superstar teammate David Robinson. He is not quite as effective in a halfcourt game as he is in transition.

Analysis: There were questions about his knee when San Antonio drafted Elliott third overall. Now, only one question remains: When will Elliott be an All-Star? He's been called a notch below Scottie Pippen—a versatile forward who can score from inside and out, create for himself, and leave a crowd dazzled. Elliott truly came into his own after John Lucas replaced Jerry Tarkanian last year as coach of the Spurs.

PLAYER SUMMARY	
Will	score inside and out
Can't	overshadow Mr. Robinson
Expect	a future All-Star
Don't Expect	a bruiser
Fantasy Value	$29-32
Card Value	8-15¢

COLLEGE STATISTICS

		G	FGP	FTP	RPG	PPG
85-86	ARIZ	32	.486	.749	5.3	15.6
86-87	ARIZ	30	.510	.770	6.0	19.3
87-88	ARIZ	38	.570	.793	5.8	19.6
88-89	ARIZ	33	.480	.841	7.2	22.3
Totals		133	.512	.793	6.1	19.2

NBA REGULAR-SEASON STATISTICS

			FGs		3-PT FGs		FTs		Rebounds						
	G	MIN	FG	PCT	FG	PCT	FT	PCT	OFF	TOT	AST	STL	BLK	PTS	PPG
89-90 SA	81	2032	311	481	1	.111	187	.866	127	297	154	45	14	810	10.0
90-91 SA	82	3044	478	.490	20	.313	325	.808	142	456	238	69	33	1301	15.9
91-92 SA	82	3120	514	.494	25	.305	285	.861	143	439	214	84	29	1338	16.3
92-93 SA	70	2604	451	.491	37	.356	268	.795	85	322	265	68	28	1207	17.2
Totals	315	10800	1754	.490	83	.320	1065	.828	497	1514	871	266	104	4656	14.8

DALE ELLIS

Team: San Antonio Spurs
Position: Guard/Forward
Height: 6'7"　**Weight:** 215
Birthdate: August 8, 1960
NBA Experience: 10 years

College: Tennessee
Acquired: Traded from Bucks via the
Trail Blazers; Blazers sent Alaa
Abdelnaby to Bucks, and Spurs sent
rights to Tracy Murray to Blazers, 7/92

Background: Ellis was an All-American at Tennessee, where his shooting accuracy enabled him to average 22.6 PPG his senior year. He was a faceless reserve for Dallas for three years, but the infamous trade for Al Wood brought him to Seattle and NBA stardom. Ellis was dealt to Milwaukee in 1990-91 and led the team in scoring. The Bucks traded him to San Antonio in July 1992, and last season he hit 100-plus 3-point field goals for the fourth time in his career.

Strengths: Ellis has one of the prettiest—and one of the deadliest—jumpers in the league. He is particularly effective coming off screens and shooting from 3-point land. He was once one of the game's greatest offensive weapons, and he can still fill it up from anywhere with great accuracy.

Weaknesses: The biggest flaws have come off the court, including a fight with ex-teammate Xavier McDaniel, a drunk-driving conviction, and other problems. Ellis doesn't dedicate himself to defense, rebounding, or ball-handling.

Analysis: The Spurs needed some 3-point punch and they got it in Ellis, one of the greatest long-distance shooters in league history. He still has his 3-point stroke and has stayed out of trouble in recent years. If you want points in a hurry, Ellis is your man.

PLAYER SUMMARY

Will	hit from long range
Can't	star on defense
Expect	100 treys a year
Don't Expect	playmaking
Fantasy Value	$9-11
Card Value	5-10¢

COLLEGE STATISTICS

		G	FGP	FTP	RPG	PPG
79-80	TENN	27	.445	.775	3.6	7.1
80-81	TENN	29	.597	.748	6.4	17.7
81-82	TENN	30	.654	.796	6.3	21.2
82-83	TENN	21	.601	.751	10.0	22.6
Totals		107	.595	.765	6.3	19.3

NBA REGULAR-SEASON STATISTICS

				FGs		3-PT FGs		FTs		Rebounds						
		G	MIN	FG	PCT	FG	PCT	FT	PCT	OFF	TOT	AST	STL	BLK	PTS	PPG
83-84	DAL	67	1059	225	.456	12	.414	97	.719	106	250	56	41	9	549	8.2
84-85	DAL	72	1314	274	.454	42	.385	77	.740	100	238	56	46	7	667	9.3
85-86	DAL	72	1086	193	.411	63	.364	59	.720	86	168	37	40	9	508	7.1
86-87	SEA	82	3073	785	.516	86	.358	385	.787	187	447	238	104	32	2041	24.9
87-88	SEA	75	2790	764	.503	107	.413	303	.767	167	340	197	74	11	1938	25.8
88-89	SEA	82	3190	857	.501	162	.478	377	.816	156	342	164	108	22	2253	27.5
89-90	SEA	55	2033	502	.497	96	.375	193	.818	90	238	110	59	7	1293	23.5
90-91	SEA/MIL	51	1424	340	.474	57	.363	120	.723	66	173	95	49	8	857	16.8
91-92	MIL	81	2191	485	.469	138	.419	164	.774	92	253	104	57	18	1272	15.7
92-93	SA	82	2731	545	.499	119	.401	157	.797	81	312	107	78	18	1366	16.7
Totals		719	20891	4970	.489	882	.403	1922	.780	1131	2761	1164	656	141	12744	17.7

LaPHONSO ELLIS

Team: Denver Nuggets
Position: Forward
Height: 6'8" **Weight:** 240
Birthdate: May 5, 1970

NBA Experience: 1 year
College: Notre Dame
Acquired: 1st-round pick in 1992 draft (5th overall)

Background: Ellis finished his college career as one of only four Notre Dame players to score 1,000 points and grab 1,000 rebounds. He is the all-time Fighting Irish leader in blocked shots despite missing parts of his sophomore and junior seasons because of academics. He was drafted fifth overall by Denver and enjoyed a fine rookie season with the Nuggets. He finished among the 1992-93 rookie leaders in blocked shots, rebounding, and scoring and was third on the Nuggets with 14.7 PPG.

Strengths: Ellis combined with Denver center Dikembe Mutombo to form one of the best shot-blocking tandems in the league last season. He has great natural instincts and is an outstanding athlete who plays above the rim. He also gave the Nuggets another big-time rebounder and produced on the offensive end. Ellis possesses a nice shooting touch both facing the basket and in the post.

Weaknesses: While Ellis gets by with his refined skills and shooting, he could stand to become more forceful offensively and try to draw more fouls. He is not nearly as polished on the defensive end as he is offensively. He tends to rely too much on the blocked shot as a weapon instead of muscling his man away from the hoop.

Analysis: The Nuggets have to be pleased with the performance of Ellis, who has the look of a potential star player. There is virtually no limit to what he can do as a rebounder and shot-blocker, and his scoring output should grow even further when he adds a little more power to his moves. Ellis is extremely confident in his ability. "I feel I'm a great talent," he has said. Those who have seen him play are not arguing.

PLAYER SUMMARY

Will	rebound, block shots
Can't	shoot 3-pointers
Expect	15 PPG, 10 RPG
Don't Expect	sheer power
Fantasy Value	$18-21
Card Value	25-75¢

COLLEGE STATISTICS

		G	FGP	FTP	RPG	PPG
88-89	ND	27	.563	.684	9.4	13.5
89-90	ND	22	.511	.675	12.6	14.0
90-91	ND	15	.573	.716	10.5	16.4
91-92	ND	33	.631	.655	11.7	17.7
Totals		97	.577	.675	11.1	15.5

NBA REGULAR-SEASON STATISTICS

			FGs		3-PT FGs		FTs		Rebounds						
	G	MIN	FG	PCT	FG	PCT	FT	PCT	OFF	TOT	AST	STL	BLK	PTS	PPG
92-93 DEN	82	2749	483	.504	2	.154	237	.748	274	744	151	72	111	1205	14.7
Totals	82	2749	483	.504	2	.154	237	.748	274	744	151	72	111	1205	14.7

PERVIS ELLISON

Team: Washington Bullets
Position: Forward/Center
Height: 6'10" **Weight:** 225
Birthdate: April 3, 1967
NBA Experience: 4 years

College: Louisville
Acquired: Traded from Kings via the Jazz; Jazz sent Eric Leckner and Bobby Hansen to Kings, and Bullets sent Jeff Malone to Jazz, 6/90

Background: As a freshman, Ellison was the MVP of the 1986 NCAA Tournament after his 25 points and 11 rebounds lifted Louisville past Duke for the title. He recorded 2,000 points and 1,000 rebounds in college and is among the Division I's all-time leaders in blocked shots. The No. 1 pick in the 1989 draft by Sacramento, he struggled with the Kings for a season and was traded to Washington. He won the Most Improved Player Award in 1991-92, scoring a team-leading 20.0 PPG. His 1992-93 season was cut short when he sprained a ligament in his left knee in early March.

Strengths: Ellison has long arms and good athletic skills and gets airborne quickly. That makes him an effective shot-blocker and rebounder. In fact, he led the team in blocks last year despite missing 30-plus games. He possesses potent moves around the basket, is good with both hands, and shoots a high percentage. He moves well for a big man and has become more assertive.

Weaknesses: Injuries played a key role in Ellison's slow NBA start and have continued to hinder him. Although he has become reliable as an NBA center, he is not one of the more physical.

Analysis: Ellison has truly made a name for himself after many NBA followers had written him off as a big-time bust. While he has often panned out as a player, he has also made a living on the injured list. Ellison would gain much more respect throughout the league if he could string a few healthy and successful seasons together.

PLAYER SUMMARY	
Will	steer away shots
Can't	stay healthy
Expect	intimidation
Don't Expect	muscle
Fantasy Value	$35-40
Card Value	10-20¢

COLLEGE STATISTICS

		G	FGP	FTP	RPG	PPG
85-86	LOU	39	.554	.682	8.2	13.1
86-87	LOU	31	.533	.719	8.7	15.2
87-88	LOU	35	.601	.692	8.3	17.6
88-89	LOU	31	.615	.652	8.7	17.6
Totals		136	.577	.687	8.4	15.8

NBA REGULAR-SEASON STATISTICS

				FGs		3-PT FGs		FTs		Rebounds						
		G	MIN	FG	PCT	FG	PCT	FT	PCT	OFF	TOT	AST	STL	BLK	PTS	PPG
89-90	SAC	34	866	111	.442	0	.000	49	.628	64	196	65	16	57	271	8.0
90-91	WAS	76	1942	326	.513	0	.000	139	.650	224	585	102	49	157	791	10.4
91-92	WAS	66	2511	547	.539	1	.333	227	.728	217	740	190	62	177	1322	20.0
92-93	WAS	49	1701	341	.521	0	.000	170	.702	138	433	117	45	108	852	17.4
Totals		225	7020	1325	.518	1	.067	585	.691	643	1954	474	172	499	3236	14.4

PATRICK EWING

Team: New York Knicks
Position: Center
Height: 7'0" **Weight:** 240
Birthdate: August 5, 1962

NBA Experience: 8 years
College: Georgetown
Acquired: 1st-round pick in 1985 draft (1st overall)

Background: Ewing led Georgetown to three NCAA finals, including the championship in 1984, and was the consensus Player of the Year as a senior while setting records across the board. He is one of the greatest defensive players in NCAA history, and he starred on the 1984 and 1992 gold-medal-winning Olympic teams. He was named NBA Rookie of the Year with the Knicks in 1986 and has been a perennial All-Star. He led the Knicks to the 1992-93 Atlantic Division championship in what may have been his best season yet.

Strengths: A franchise player, Ewing is quite simply the complete package in the pivot. He intimidates on defense, swats shots, hoards boards, and is virtually unstoppable one-on-one when he gets the ball in the post. He has developed a dangerous jump shot that no one can challenge, and he gets his points despite double- and triple-teams. He's the team leader.

Weaknesses: There is very little Ewing can't do outside of shooting 3-pointers. He commits a lot of turnovers, but that goes with the territory when you're surrounded at all times.

Analysis: Ewing has been considered one of the premier centers in the league for several years, and his play in 1992-93 was more than worthy of MVP consideration. Ironically, it was a year in which fans voted Shaquille O'Neal as the All-Star starter over Ewing. O'Neal has yet to approach Ewing's level.

PLAYER SUMMARY	
Will	dominate
Can't	get MVP nod
Expect	an All-Star regular
Don't Expect	single coverage
Fantasy Value	$65-70
Card Value	20-35¢

COLLEGE STATISTICS

		G	FGP	FTP	RPG	PPG
81-82	GEOR	37	.631	.617	7.5	12.7
82-83	GEOR	32	.570	.629	10.2	17.7
83-84	GEOR	37	.658	.656	10.0	16.4
84-85	GEOR	37	.625	.637	9.2	14.6
Totals		143	.620	.635	9.2	15.3

NBA REGULAR-SEASON STATISTICS

			FGs		3-PT FGs		FTs		Rebounds						
	G	MIN	FG	PCT	FG	PCT	FT	PCT	OFF	TOT	AST	STL	BLK	PTS	PPG
85-86 NY	50	1771	386	.474	0	.000	226	.739	124	451	102	54	103	998	20.0
86-87 NY	63	2206	530	.503	0	.000	296	.713	157	555	104	89	147	1356	21.5
87-88 NY	82	2546	656	.555	0	.000	341	.716	245	676	125	104	245	1653	20.2
88-89 NY	80	2896	727	.567	0	.000	361	.746	213	740	188	117	281	1815	22.7
89-90 NY	82	3165	922	.551	1	.250	502	.775	235	893	182	78	327	2347	28.6
90-91 NY	81	3104	845	.514	0	.000	464	.745	194	905	244	80	258	2154	26.6
91-92 NY	82	3150	796	.522	1	.167	377	.738	228	921	156	88	245	1970	24.0
92-93 NY	81	3003	779	.503	1	.143	400	.719	191	980	151	74	161	1959	24.2
Totals	601	21841	5641	.526	3	.068	2967	.738	1587	6121	1252	684	1767	14252	23.7

DUANE FERRELL

Team: Atlanta Hawks
Position: Forward
Height: 6'7" **Weight:** 209
Birthdate: February 28, 1965

NBA Experience: 5 years
College: Georgia Tech
Acquired: Signed as a free agent, 11/90

Background: At Georgia Tech, Ferrell pumped in more than 1,800 points in his four years. Although he averaged 18.6 PPG his senior year, he wasn't drafted by an NBA team. He signed with the Hawks as a free agent, was cut after one year, and then re-signed with them four months later. Ferrell has averaged double figures in scoring his last two seasons with Atlanta. Last season, he filled in and fared well as a starter when Dominique Wilkins was injured.

Strengths: Ferrell's greatest asset might be his attitude. He appreciates his job and shows it with all-out effort. He's got a quick first step and gets to the hoop with scoring in mind. He has become a better passer and his defense is solid if unspectacular. In addition, he has developed a decent mid-range jumper.

Weaknesses: Outside shooting has always been the weakest part of Ferrell's offense, although he has improved. His shooting percentage went down last season after a career-best effort in 1991-92. Teams are best advised to give him the 3-point shot. He does not create much for teammates and he's not a big help on the boards.

Analysis: Ferrell is one of those guys who takes nothing for granted, especially his job. His CBA days have taught him that much. He played some of his best ball when Wilkins was out last year, and he has shown great improvement in his game over the past two seasons. He plays with a scorer's mentality and has great desire.

PLAYER SUMMARY

Will ....give his all
Can't.......................replace Dominique
Expect............................scoring drives
Don't Expect ....strong rebounding
Fantasy Value...............................$1-3
Card Value ....5-10¢

COLLEGE STATISTICS

		G	FGP	FTP	RPG	PPG
84-85	GT	32	.504	.571	4.1	9.1
85-86	GT	34	.595	.758	4.9	12.1
86-87	GT	29	.519	.812	5.9	17.9
87-88	GT	32	.532	.749	6.6	18.6
Totals		127	.537	.733	5.4	14.3

NBA REGULAR-SEASON STATISTICS

		G	MIN	FG	PCT	FG	PCT	FT	PCT	OFF	TOT	AST	STL	BLK	PTS	PPG
				FGs		3-PT FGs		FTs		Rebounds						
88-89	ATL	41	231	35	.422	0	.000	30	.682	19	41	10	7	6	100	2.4
89-90	ATL	14	29	5	.357	0	.000	2	.333	3	7	2	1	0	12	0.9
90-91	ATL	78	1165	174	.489	2	.667	125	.801	97	179	55	33	27	475	6.1
91-92	ATL	66	1598	331	.524	11	.333	166	.761	105	210	92	49	17	839	12.7
92-93	ATL	82	1736	327	.470	9	.250	176	.779	97	191	132	59	17	839	10.2
Totals		281	4759	872	.490	22	.301	499	.768	321	628	291	149	67	2265	8.1

DANNY FERRY

Team: Cleveland Cavaliers
Position: Forward
Height: 6'10" **Weight:** 245
Birthdate: October 17, 1966
NBA Experience: 3 years
College: Duke

Acquired: Draft rights traded from Clippers with Reggie Williams for Ron Harper, 1990 and 1992 1st-round picks, and a 1991 2nd-round pick, 11/89

Background: After an illustrious career at Duke, in which he was named the nation's Player of the Year as a senior, Ferry snubbed the NBA and spent a year in Italy to avoid playing with the moribund L.A. Clippers. When his rights were traded to Cleveland for Ron Harper, he came home and was a big disappointment. He has come off the bench for three years with the Cavs and his best NBA scoring output was 8.6 PPG in 1990-91. He averaged 7.5 points per outing last season.

Strengths: Ferry has a good long-range shooting stroke, and he's at his best on the perimeter despite his 6'10" size. He knows where to spot up and can hit from 3-point land. Having grown up the son of former NBA player Bob Ferry, Danny has shown decent instincts. He is a precise passer and you won't find many who shoot free throws more accurately.

Weaknesses: It looks like Ferry will never translate his college potential into NBA success. He is slow and can't work for his own shot. He feeds off others instead of making things happen. He's not much help on defense, where small forwards blow by him. Ferry has tried very hard—perhaps too hard—to achieve.

Analysis: Ferry is a dangerous 3-point threat off the bench and finally seems to have regained some of the confidence that made him a college star. But the former college Player of the Year is far from being the kind of multi-talented player he was expected to be. He's a role-player who is not liable to make many starts with the talented Cavs.

PLAYER SUMMARY

Will	convert from long range
Can't	return to stardom
Expect	a reserve shooter
Don't Expect	overachieving
Fantasy Value	$2-4
Card Value	5-12¢

COLLEGE STATISTICS

		G	FGP	FTP	RPG	PPG
85-86	DUKE	40	.460	.628	5.5	5.9
86-87	DUKE	33	.449	.844	7.8	14.0
87-88	DUKE	35	.476	.828	7.6	19.1
88-89	DUKE	35	.522	.756	7.4	22.6
Totals		143	.484	.775	7.0	15.1

NBA REGULAR-SEASON STATISTICS

			FGs		3-PT FGs		FTs		Rebounds						
	G	MIN	FG	PCT	FG	PCT	FT	PCT	OFF	TOT	AST	STL	BLK	PTS	PPG
90-91 CLE	81	1661	275	.428	23	.299	124	.816	99	286	142	43	25	697	8.6
91-92 CLE	68	937	134	.409	17	.354	61	.836	53	213	75	22	15	346	5.1
92-93 CLE	76	1461	220	.479	34	.415	99	.876	81	279	137	29	49	573	7.5
Totals	225	4059	629	.440	74	.357	284	.840	233	778	354	94	89	1616	7.2

VERN FLEMING

Team: Indiana Pacers
Position: Guard
Height: 6'5" **Weight:** 185
Birthdate: February 4, 1962

NBA Experience: 9 years
College: Georgia
Acquired: 1st-round pick in 1984 draft
(18th overall)

Background: Fleming teamed with Dominique Wilkins at Georgia and, as a senior, led the SEC in scoring. He played on the 1984 Olympic team and was credited by Michael Jordan as providing his toughest defense in practices. The last two seasons were the only ones in his nine with the Pacers in which he did not average double figures in scoring. He backed up Micheal Williams two years ago, then Pooh Richardson last year.

Strengths: Fleming is a savvy player who can play either shooting or point guard. He has a height advantage over most playmakers. Fleming is the Pacers' all-time assists leader. He plays defense and makes very few mistakes. He can still get to the hoop and he looks to finish what he starts.

Weaknesses: The reason the Pacers searched for several years to find a better point guard than Fleming is his sub-par creative ability. Indiana feels his scorer's mentality is better suited to a spot on the second unit. Fleming does not possess great quickness and is a terrible 3-point shooter.

Analysis: Barring an injury, it looks like Fleming will never again be Indiana's starting point guard. Still, he can be very valuable as a back-up point man because he can give you minutes of leadership off the bench without making mistakes. He is well-respected around the league.

PLAYER SUMMARY	
Will	penetrate
Can't	regain starting job
Expect	veteran leadership
Don't Expect	treys
Fantasy Value	$1-3
Card Value	5-10¢

COLLEGE STATISTICS

		G	FGP	FTP	RPG	PPG
80-81	GEOR	30	.480	.697	2.7	10.0
81-82	GEOR	31	.496	.640	3.9	9.9
82-83	GEOR	34	.535	.716	4.6	16.9
83-84	GEOR	30	.503	.754	4.0	19.8
Totals		125	.508	.705	3.8	14.2

NBA REGULAR-SEASON STATISTICS

		G	MIN	FG	FGs PCT	FG	3-PT FGs PCT	FT	FTs PCT	OFF	Rebounds TOT	AST	STL	BLK	PTS	PPG
84-85	IND	80	2486	433	.470	0	.000	260	.767	148	323	247	99	8	1126	14.1
85-86	IND	80	2870	436	.506	1	.167	263	.745	102	386	505	131	5	1136	14.2
86-87	IND	82	2549	370	.509	2	.200	238	.788	109	334	473	109	18	980	12.0
87-88	IND	80	2733	442	.523	0	.000	227	.802	106	364	568	115	11	1111	13.9
88-89	IND	76	2552	419	.515	3	.130	243	.799	85	310	494	77	12	1084	14.3
89-90	IND	82	2876	467	.508	12	.353	230	.782	118	322	610	92	10	1176	14.3
90-91	IND	69	1929	356	.531	4	.222	161	.729	83	214	369	76	13	877	12.7
91-92	IND	82	1737	294	.482	6	.222	132	.737	69	209	266	56	7	726	8.9
92-93	IND	75	1503	280	.505	7	.194	143	.726	63	169	224	63	9	710	9.5
Totals		706	21235	3497	.505	35	.205	1897	.767	883	2631	3756	818	93	8926	12.6

SLEEPY FLOYD

Team: San Antonio Spurs
Position: Guard
Height: 6'3" **Weight:** 183
Birthdate: March 6, 1960

NBA Experience: 11 years
College: Georgetown
Acquired: Signed as a free agent, 8/93

Background: Floyd was an All-American at Georgetown, leading the Hoyas to the NCAA championship game in 1982 and in scoring all four years. He was an All-Star in 1986-87, when he set a Golden State season assists record with 848. He played in all 82 games for Houston for four straight years before last season, when his playing time tailed off. The Rockets waived Floyd over the summer but he was picked up by San Antonio.

Strengths: Floyd still makes things happen by attacking the bucket. A streak shooter, he has 3-point range and excels on the fastbreak. He's always been a good straight-up defender.

Weaknesses: Plain and simple, Floyd is no longer reliable offensively. He has shot in the 41-percent range over the last three years yet he'll keep firing away as long as he's in the game. He has never been the kind of player who makes those around him better.

Analysis: Everything finally came together for Houston during the second half of last season, and the veteran Floyd did not have much to do with it. The decline in his game in recent years forced the Rockets to look elsewhere and they were a better team for it. Floyd has never been happy when he's not getting a lot of minutes, but he doesn't deserve many anymore.

PLAYER SUMMARY

Will	keep shooting
Can't	convert consistently
Expect	sound defense
Don't Expect	starts
Fantasy Value	$0
Card Value	5-10¢

COLLEGE STATISTICS

		G	FGP	FTP	APG	PPG
78-79	GEOR	29	.456	.813	2.7	16.6
79-80	GEOR	32	.554	.757	3.0	18.7
80-81	GEOR	32	.467	.806	2.6	19.0
81-82	GEOR	37	.504	.720	2.7	16.7
Totals		130	.496	.774	2.7	17.7

NBA REGULAR-SEASON STATISTICS

			FGs		3-PT FGs		FTs		Rebounds						
	G	MIN	FG	PCT	FG	PCT	FT	PCT	OFF	TOT	AST	STL	BLK	PTS	PPG
82-83 NJ/GS	76	1248	226	.429	10	.400	150	.833	56	137	138	58	17	612	8.1
83-84 GS	77	2555	484	.463	8	.178	315	.816	87	271	269	103	31	1291	16.8
84-85 GS	82	2873	610	.445	42	.294	336	.810	62	202	406	134	41	1598	19.5
85-86 GS	82	2764	510	.506	39	.328	351	.796	77	297	746	157	16	1410	17.2
86-87 GS	82	3064	503	.488	73	.384	462	.860	56	268	848	146	18	1541	18.8
87-88 GS/HOU	77	2514	420	.433	14	.194	301	.850	77	296	544	95	12	1155	15.0
88-89 HOU	82	2788	396	.443	109	.373	261	.845	48	306	709	124	11	1162	14.2
89-90 HOU	82	2630	362	.451	89	.380	187	.806	46	198	600	94	11	1000	12.2
90-91 HOU	82	1850	386	.411	48	.273	185	.752	52	159	317	95	17	1005	12.3
91-92 HOU	82	1662	286	.406	37	.301	135	.794	34	150	239	57	21	744	9.1
92-93 HOU	52	867	124	.407	16	.286	81	.794	14	86	132	32	6	345	6.6
Totals	856	24815	4307	.449	485	.329	2764	.820	608	2370	4948	1095	201	11863	13.9

GREG FOSTER

Team: Atlanta Hawks
Position: Forward/Center
Height: 6'11" **Weight:** 240
Birthdate: September 3, 1968

NBA Experience: 3 years
College: UCLA; Texas-El Paso
Acquired: Signed as a free agent, 12/92

Background: Foster was the big man for the University of Texas-El Paso, helping the Miners to two consecutive NCAA Tournament appearances. As a senior, he was named the MVP of the Western Athletic Conference Tournament. A second-round pick in 1990, he earned a job with the Bullets but was used sparingly in his two-plus seasons in Washington. He has yet to top his 54 games played as a rookie, and a move to Atlanta early last season did not help his cause.

Strengths: Foster's biggest plus is his 6'11", 240-pound body. The hope is that one day he will develop into an NBA banger. He runs the floor and has a soft outside touch for a big man.

Weaknesses: He came out of college a project, and Foster remains just that. He's slow, has no low-post moves, and sometimes appears as if he'd rather play on the perimeter. If he's going to emerge as a banger, he hasn't shown many signs of it. His shooting percentage is poor for an inside player, but then he has never been much of a scorer. He did not get along with Bullets coach Wes Unseld.

Analysis: Have body, will stick around. Perhaps he will turn his career around now that he's out of a bad situation in Washington, but so far Foster has not played like a guy who will emerge in the NBA. He has the shot, but it's not of much use to him in a non-scoring role. He needs to apply his body on defense and the backboards if he hopes to become a contributing player.

PLAYER SUMMARY	
Will	run the floor
Can't	get off the bench
Expect	good size
Don't Expect	physical play
Fantasy Value	$0
Card Value	5-8¢

COLLEGE STATISTICS

		G	FGP	FTP	RPG	PPG
86-87	UCLA	31	.500	.500	2.5	3.3
87-88	UCLA	11	.527	.432	5.5	8.5
88-89	UTEP	26	.483	.651	7.3	11.1
89-90	UTEP	32	.465	.811	6.2	10.6
Totals		100	.483	.661	5.2	8.2

NBA REGULAR-SEASON STATISTICS

		G	MIN	FGs FG	FGs PCT	3-PT FGs FG	3-PT FGs PCT	FTs FT	FTs PCT	Rebounds OFF	Rebounds TOT	AST	STL	BLK	PTS	PPG
90-91	WAS	54	606	97	.460	0	.000	42	.689	52	151	37	12	22	236	4.4
91-92	WAS	49	548	89	.461	0	.000	35	.714	43	145	35	6	12	213	4.3
92-93	WAS/ATL	43	298	55	.458	0	.000	15	.714	32	83	21	3	14	125	2.9
Totals		146	1452	241	.460	0	.000	92	.702	127	379	93	21	48	574	3.9

RICK FOX

Team: Boston Celtics
Position: Forward/Guard
Height: 6'7" **Weight:** 231
Birthdate: July 24, 1969

NBA Experience: 2 years
College: North Carolina
Acquired: 1st-round pick in 1991 draft
(24th overall)

Background: Born in Canada, Fox moved to the Bahamas when he was two years old. He had a very limited basketball background before playing high school ball in Warsaw, Indiana. Though he was never a marquee player at North Carolina, he was consistent and had a knack for late-game heroics. He was drafted late in the first round by the Celtics and proved to be a wise choice. He saw action in all but one game as a rookie and averaged 8.0 PPG. He started more than a dozen games in 1992-93, but his scoring average sank by a bucket per outing.

Strengths: Fox is a very good athlete, a well-rounded player with good skills in most phases of the game and a great feel for what to do with the ball. He owns a strong body and is not afraid to challenge. He's an excellent passer and a solid defender. He has 3-point range, although he struggled from that distance last year. He works hard.

Weaknesses: The biggest flaw that has kept Fox from being a primary threat with the Celtics is the inconsistency of his perimeter shooting. Opponents have learned to cut off his drive to the bucket and force him to shoot from 15 feet and beyond. Fox is not a big factor on the boards.

Analysis: Fox was virtually an overnight hit with the Celtics early in his rookie season but he has since leveled off. He replaced Kevin Gamble at small forward last December but spent most of the season providing a spark off the bench. His defense, athletic ability, and work ethic promise a bright future, especially if he can become a better shooter.

PLAYER SUMMARY	
Will	go after the ball
Can't	hoard rebounds
Expect	defense, instincts
Don't Expect	a gunner
Fantasy Value	$5-7
Card Value	8-15¢

COLLEGE STATISTICS

		G	FGP	FTP	RPG	PPG
87-88	NC	34	.628	.500	1.9	4.0
88-89	NC	37	.583	.790	3.8	11.5
89-90	NC	34	.522	.735	4.6	16.2
90-91	NC	35	.453	.804	6.6	16.9
Totals		140	.518	.757	4.2	12.2

NBA REGULAR-SEASON STATISTICS

				FGs		3-PT FGs		FTs		Rebounds						
		G	MIN	FG	PCT	FG	PCT	FT	PCT	OFF	TOT	AST	STL	BLK	PTS	PPG
91-92	BOS	81	1535	241	.459	23	.329	139	.755	73	220	126	78	30	644	8.0
92-93	BOS	71	1082	184	.484	4	.174	81	.802	55	159	113	61	21	453	6.4
Totals		152	2617	425	.470	27	.290	220	.772	128	379	239	139	51	1097	7.2

KEVIN GAMBLE

Team: Boston Celtics
Position: Guard/Forward
Height: 6'5" **Weight:** 210
Birthdate: November 13, 1965

NBA Experience: 6 years
College: Lincoln; Iowa
Acquired: Signed as a free agent, 12/88

Background: After an unspectacular college career at Lincoln College and Iowa, Gamble was drafted by Portland in the third round. He didn't make it with the Trail Blazers and he wound up playing in the CBA and the Philippines. Gamble was given one last NBA chance in 1988-89 with a rebuilding Celtics team. He made the most of it, becoming the team's top shooter from the perimeter. He took over a full-time starting role in 1992-93 and was third on the team in scoring.

Strengths: Gamble is proving to be Mr. Dependable, having played in every game over the last three seasons. He is also a remarkably reliable outside shooter who has connected at better than 50 percent from the field in four of his five Celtic years. He is a 3-point and free throw ace who also gets out on the break and finishes with either hand. He is a scrappy, hungry ballplayer who appreciates where he is and how he got there.

Weaknesses: Gamble, a former big guard, has problems defensively against the better small forwards in the league. He also struggles with the quick guards. Due to his size, he is not a great rebounding forward.

Analysis: Gamble has become not only a legitimate NBA starter, but a pretty darn good one. Where would the Celtics have been without his dead-eye marksmanship? He has made himself one of the most accurate non-All-Star jump-shooters in the league. Better defense and rebounding are the ingredients that would make Gamble a complete player.

PLAYER SUMMARY

Will.........................bury wing jumpers
Can't ....dominate the glass
Expect ....high percentages
Don't Expect ....20 PPG
Fantasy Value..............................$9-11
Card Value ....5-10¢

COLLEGE STATISTICS

		G	FGP	FTP	RPG	PPG
83-84	LINC	30	.559	.777	9.2	21.3
84-85	LINC	31	.579	.817	9.7	20.5
85-86	IOWA	30	.474	.700	1.7	2.6
86-87	IOWA	35	.544	.697	4.5	11.9
Totals		126	.558	.768	6.2	14.1

NBA REGULAR-SEASON STATISTICS

		G	MIN	FGs FG	FGs PCT	3-PT FGs FG	3-PT FGs PCT	FTs FT	FTs PCT	Rebounds OFF	Rebounds TOT	AST	STL	BLK	PTS	PPG
87-88	POR	9	19	0	.000	0	.000	0	.000	2	3	1	2	0	0	0.0
88-89	BOS	44	375	75	.551	2	.182	35	.636	11	42	34	14	3	187	4.3
89-90	BOS	71	990	137	.455	3	.167	85	.794	42	112	119	28	8	362	5.1
90-91	BOS	82	2706	548	.587	0	.000	185	.815	85	267	256	100	34	1281	15.6
91-92	BOS	82	2496	480	.529	9	.290	139	.885	80	286	219	75	37	1108	13.5
92-93	BOS	82	2541	459	.507	52	.374	123	.826	46	246	226	86	37	1093	13.3
Totals		370	9127	1699	.533	66	.319	567	.816	266	956	855	305	119	4031	10.9

CHRIS GATLING

Team: Golden State Warriors
Position: Forward
Height: 6'10" **Weight:** 220
Birthdate: September 3, 1967

NBA Experience: 2 years
College: Old Dominion
Acquired: 1st-round pick in 1991 draft
(16th overall)

Background: Gatling did not play during his first two years in college. He originally signed with Pittsburgh but sat out the 1986-87 season because of Prop 48 restrictions. He then transferred to Old Dominion, where NCAA rules required him to sit out the 1987-88 season. Though ODU was a disappointing 43-45 during his tenure, Gatling was a two-time Sun Belt Conference Player of the Year. His rookie year with the Warriors started modestly, but he came on during the regular-season stretch. Gatling averaged better than nine PPG during his second season and made a handful of starts for the injury-depleted Warriors.

Strengths: Gatling is an explosive leaper who blocks shots and gets to the offensive and defensive glass. He possesses very good agility and runs the floor like a guard. He is quick to the basket with a soft touch, good hands, and fine ball-handling ability. He shoots well over 50 percent from the field and has displayed the confidence and ability to be an NBA scorer.

Weaknesses: Gatling was a post player in college and is still polishing his moves while facing the basket. He does not dominate physically but rather with his leaping ability and long arms. He's been called soft, especially on defense. His outside shooting is streaky and his range is limited to 15-18 feet.

Analysis: Gatling began turning his potential into tangible results in the final two weeks of his rookie season. He carried that momentum into last year and wound up being a fine player for a Golden State team that truly needed a lift during a long season. Gatling is more than just an impressive athlete. He's a promising and up-and-coming talent who thrives in an up-tempo game.

PLAYER SUMMARY

Will ....block shots, rebound
Can't.................................shoot treys
Expect.................50-percent shooting
Don't Expect.........................a banger
Fantasy Value................................$4-6
Card Value ....8-15¢

COLLEGE STATISTICS

		G	FGP	FTP	RPG	PPG
88-89	OD	27	.616	.704	9.0	22.4
89-90	OD	26	.580	.670	10.0	20.5
90-91	OD	32	.620	.692	11.1	21.0
Totals		85	.606	.689	10.1	21.3

NBA REGULAR-SEASON STATISTICS

			FGs		3-PT FGs		FTs		Rebounds						
	G	MIN	FG	PCT	FG	PCT	FT	PCT	OFF	TOT	AST	STL	BLK	PTS	PPG
91-92 GS	54	612	117	.568	0	.000	72	.661	75	182	16	31	36	306	5.7
92-93 GS	70	1248	249	.539	0	.000	150	.725	129	320	40	44	53	648	9.3
Totals	124	1860	366	.548	0	.000	222	.703	204	502	56	75	89	954	7.7

KENNY GATTISON

Team: Charlotte Hornets
Position: Forward/Center
Height: 6'8" **Weight:** 246
Birthdate: May 23, 1964

NBA Experience: 6 years
College: Old Dominion
Acquired: Signed as a free agent, 12/89

Background: The Sun Belt Conference Player of the Year in 1986, Gattison finished his career as the league's all-time leading rebounder. He also garnered All-America consideration as a senior at Old Dominion, where he ranked third nationally in field goal percentage with a mark of .637. Gattison played with Phoenix for a year before tearing the anterior cruciate ligament in his left knee. He played part of 1988-89 in Italy and signed with Charlotte in 1989-90. He was the starting center in 1991-92, but saw his playing time and numbers decrease last year with the addition of rookie Alonzo Mourning.

Strengths: Gattison is super-intense, the kind of player who will do whatever is asked, no matter the consequences. He sets screens, blocks out, and bangs the boards. He is versatile and can perform a number of functions, including strong inside scoring. He plays both center and power forward.

Weaknesses: Gattison has virtually no touch from beyond 12 feet and his free throw shooting needs serious improvement. His reckless, physical style of play often puts him in foul trouble. He is just too small to guard centers effectively despite all the time he has spent trying to do so.

Analysis: Gattison fits in well as a reserve role-player, and the addition of Mourning by the Hornets allowed him to fill that role instead of starting. He'll come in and snare rebounds and even do some inside scoring with his high-percentage shooting. His versatility and work ethic will keep him in a team's regular rotation.

PLAYER SUMMARY	
Will	rebound
Can't	defend 7-footers
Expect	versatility
Don't Expect	outside shooting
Fantasy Value	$1-3
Card Value	5-8¢

COLLEGE STATISTICS

		G	FGP	FTP	RPG	PPG
82-83	OD	29	.503	.705	7.5	8.4
83-84	OD	31	.494	.650	7.1	11.1
84-85	OD	31	.538	.610	9.2	16.1
85-86	OD	31	.637	.673	7.8	17.4
Totals		122	.552	.650	7.9	13.3

NBA REGULAR-SEASON STATISTICS

				FGs		3-PT FGs		FTs		Rebounds						
		G	MIN	FG	PCT	FG	PCT	FT	PCT	OFF	TOT	AST	STL	BLK	PTS	PPG
86-87	PHO	77	1104	148	.476	0	.000	108	.632	87	270	36	24	33	404	5.2
88-89	PHO	2	9	0	.000	0	.000	1	.500	0	1	0	0	0	1	0.5
89-90	CHA	63	941	148	.550	1	1.000	75	.682	75	197	39	35	31	372	5.9
90-91	CHA	72	1552	243	.532	0	.000	164	.661	136	379	44	48	67	650	9.0
91-92	CHA	82	2223	423	.529	0	.000	196	.686	177	580	131	59	69	1042	12.7
92-93	CHA	75	1475	203	.529	0	.000	102	.604	108	353	68	48	55	508	6.8
Totals		371	7304	1165	.525	1	.091	646	.656	583	1780	318	214	255	2977	8.0

MATT GEIGER

Team: Miami Heat
Position: Center
Height: 7'0" **Weight:** 245
Birthdate: September 10, 1969

NBA Experience: 1 year
College: Auburn; Georgia Tech
Acquired: 2nd-round pick in 1992 draft (42nd overall)

Background: Geiger made the SEC All-Freshman team and started all 28 games as a sophomore at Auburn. He then transferred to Georgia Tech, where his 65 blocked shots as a senior ranked second to John Salley in the school history books. Once considered a lottery-type talent, Geiger did not develop as much as some expected and he slipped to the 42nd overall choice in the 1992 draft. He saw very little action as a rookie with Miami but did score 18 points in a game once. He played high school ball in Clearwater, Florida.

Strengths: Geiger got his chance in the NBA because of his seven-foot, 245-pound body. He shoots the ball well for a big man and has the ability to put it on the floor when the situation calls for such action. He was impressive in summer-league play for his willingness to bang. His size allows him to block shots, although he didn't swat many last year.

Weaknesses: When Geiger steps on the floor, officials prepare to blow the whistle. He picked up more fouls than he did rebounds last season—a dubious accomplishment for a player who's seven feet tall. Another feat was fouling out of five games despite his limited playing time. He simply does not have great control over his massive body. Geiger does not pass well or shoot free throws with any accuracy.

Analysis: Geiger is a definite NBA project. He shot a high percentage from the field but he does not make much happen offensively. On defense, he makes more bad things than good happen for his team. His future in the league, if there is one, is as a shot-blocker, rebounder, and physical defender. Geiger has a long way to go.

PLAYER SUMMARY

Will	draw fouls
Can't	play with finesse
Expect	much tutoring
Don't Expect	an NBA force
Fantasy Value	$0
Card Value	5-10¢

COLLEGE STATISTICS

		G	FGP	FTP	RPG	PPG
87-88	AUB	30	.513	.660	4.1	6.4
88-89	AUB	28	.504	.688	6.6	15.9
90-91	GT	27	.549	.671	6.4	11.4
91-92	GT	35	.611	.706	7.3	11.8
Totals		120	.545	.687	6.1	11.4

NBA REGULAR-SEASON STATISTICS

			FGs		3-PT FGs		FTs		Rebounds						
	G	MIN	FG	PCT	FG	PCT	FT	PCT	OFF	TOT	AST	STL	BLK	PTS	PPG
92-93 MIA	48	554	76	.524	0	.000	62	.674	46	120	14	15	18	214	4.5
Totals	48	554	76	.524	0	.000	62	.674	46	120	14	15	18	214	4.5

TATE GEORGE

Team: New Jersey Nets
Position: Guard
Height: 6'5" **Weight:** 208
Birthdate: May 29, 1968

NBA Experience: 3 years
College: Connecticut
Acquired: 1st-round pick in 1990 draft
(22nd overall)

Background: At Connecticut, George was the school's all-time leader in assists and steals. In the 1990 NCAA Tournament, he hit a dramatic game-winning shot at the buzzer to beat Clemson 71-70 in the third round. George became the first Connecticut player to be selected in the first round when the Nets took him 22nd overall in 1990. He was used sparingly as a rookie, saw nearly twice as much action in 1991-92 and averaged 6.0 PPG, then saw his playing time plummet again last season.

Strengths: George has the size and ability to play both guard spots. His 6'5" frame allows him to see the floor well and match up with bigger men on defense. He has good leadership and playmaking skills, and he handles the ball with confidence. He's a very good free throw shooter.

Weaknesses: Not a good enough shooter to stay on the floor, George is more in his element as a point guard rather than a shooting guard. However, the Nets have not had room for him at the point. Mookie Blaylock, Mo Cheeks, and future star Kenny Anderson have all played ahead of him during his three years. He shot worse than 40 percent from the field last year and did not make much happen.

Analysis: George is a better player than his career numbers would indicate. He is not much help as a big guard, however, unless he can start getting his shots to fall at a respectable clip. The best aspect of his game right now is defense, but there are plenty of questions to be answered about the rest of his game.

PLAYER SUMMARY

Will ....play two positions
Can't ....find steady minutes
Expect ....high FT pct.
Don't Expect ....many starts
Fantasy Value $0
Card Value ....5-10¢

COLLEGE STATISTICS

		G	FGP	FTP	RPG	PPG
86-87	CONN	26	.368	.775	3.6	10.0
87-88	CONN	34	.500	.831	2.9	9.9
88-89	CONN	31	.433	.758	3.4	7.3
89-90	CONN	37	.479	.727	3.5	11.5
Totals		128	.448	.773	3.3	9.7

NBA REGULAR-SEASON STATISTICS

			FGs		3-PT FGs		FTs		Rebounds						
	G	MIN	FG	PCT	FG	PCT	FT	PCT	OFF	TOT	AST	STL	BLK	PTS	PPG
90-91 NJ	56	594	80	.415	0	.000	32	.800	19	47	104	25	5	192	3.4
91-92 NJ	70	1037	165	.427	1	.167	87	.821	36	105	162	41	3	418	6.0
92-93 NJ	48	380	51	.378	0	.000	20	.833	9	27	59	10	3	122	2.5
Totals	174	2011	296	.415	1	.077	139	.818	64	179	325	76	11	732	4.2

KENDALL GILL

Team: Charlotte Hornets
Position: Guard
Height: 6'5" **Weight:** 210
Birthdate: May 25, 1968

NBA Experience: 3 years
College: Illinois
Acquired: 1st-round pick in 1990 draft (5th overall)

Background: At Illinois, Gill was considered one of the top guards in the country. As a junior, he canned 38-of-83 3-point attempts and helped his team to the Final Four. As a senior, he was a first-team All-Big Ten selection and a UPI first-team All-American. He became the first Illini to lead the Big Ten in scoring since 1943. Gill played in all 82 games as a Charlotte rookie, then led the Hornets in scoring with 20.5 PPG during his second season. He fell to third on the team last season but helped drive Charlotte to its first-ever playoff berth.

Strengths: Gill's versatility allows him to play both guard positions, although a large reason for his success was his move from point guard to off guard two years ago. He is a great leaper, and that allows him to play bigger than his 6'5" height. Gill is not afraid to take the clutch jumpers. He's a well-rounded athlete who plays defense and crashes the boards.

Weaknesses: Gill has grown more confident in his 3-point shooting but does not connect regularly enough to make opponents respect him from that range. He needs to avoid future shooting seasons like last year's 45-percent effort.

Analysis: Last year, Gill fell into a little funk after becoming the team's third option, behind young guns Larry Johnson and Alonzo Mourning. Despite being on a rising, exciting team, Gill said he wanted to leave Charlotte. He still wanted out even after the Hornets excelled in the playoffs, where they knocked off Boston. If he commits himself to Charlotte, both he and the Hornets will be successful for years to come.

PLAYER SUMMARY

Will	play above the rim
Can't	make living on treys
Expect	a little of everything
Don't Expect	him to leave
Fantasy Value	$20-23
Card Value	10-15¢

COLLEGE STATISTICS

		G	FGP	FTP	RPG	PPG
86-87	ILL	31	.482	.642	1.4	3.7
87-88	ILL	33	.471	.753	2.2	10.4
88-89	ILL	24	.542	.793	2.9	15.4
89-90	ILL	29	.500	.777	4.9	20.0
Totals		117	.501	.755	2.8	12.0

NBA REGULAR-SEASON STATISTICS

			FGs		3-PT FGs		FTs		Rebounds						
	G	MIN	FG	PCT	FG	PCT	FT	PCT	OFF	TOT	AST	STL	BLK	PTS	PPG
90-91	CHA	82	1944	376	.450	2	.143	152	.835	105	263	303	104	39	906	11.0
91-92	CHA	79	2906	666	.467	6	.240	284	.745	165	402	329	154	46	1622	20.5
92-93	CHA	69	2430	463	.449	17	.274	224	.772	120	340	268	98	36	1167	16.9
Totals		230	7280	1505	.457	25	.248	660	.774	390	1005	900	356	121	3695	16.1

ARMON GILLIAM

Team: New Jersey Nets
Position: Forward/Center
Height: 6'9" **Weight:** 245
Birthdate: May 28, 1964

NBA Experience: 6 years
College: Independence; UNLV
Acquired: Signed as a free agent,
8/93

Background: As a college senior, Gilliam was a consensus second-team All-American while leading UNLV to a Final Four appearance. That year, he averaged 23.2 points and 9.3 rebounds per game. Phoenix selected him No. 2 in the 1987 draft, and he responded by making the All-Rookie Team. He was traded to Charlotte and then Philadelphia, where he spent his first full season and enjoyed a career year in 1991-92. After Gilliam's poor 1992-93 season, Philadelphia let him go and New Jersey picked him up.

Strengths: A versatile player, Gilliam can play both center and power forward. Nicknamed "The Hammer" for his physical style, he can be unstoppable when he gets the ball in the low post, where he beats opponents with accurate hook shots and turnaround jumpers. He has stretched his shooting range.

Weaknesses: Gilliam is a scorer first and everything else second. Despite his size and strength, he is not a good defender. The knock has always been his lack of interest in that phase of the game. He's a poor ball-handler and no better as a passer. In concentrating on perimeter shooting, his inside offense and consistency seem to have suffered.

Analysis: Gilliam followed what was probably his best pro season with what was certainly his worst. One theory is that the absence of Charles Barkley last season forced him to try to do too much on his own. Barkley certainly helped him, but Gilliam has more natural ability than he showed last season. He's an above-average talent.

PLAYER SUMMARY

Will	look at the hoop
Can't	play strong defense
Expect	double-figure scoring
Don't Expect	assists
Fantasy Value	$2-4
Card Value	5-10¢

COLLEGE STATISTICS

		G	FGP	FTP	RPG	PPG
82-83	IND	38	.621	.632	8.3	16.9
84-85	UNLV	31	.621	.653	6.8	11.9
85-86	UNLV	37	.529	.737	8.5	15.7
86-87	UNLV	39	.600	.728	9.3	23.2
Totals		145	.590	.693	8.3	17.2

NBA REGULAR-SEASON STATISTICS

			FGs		3-PT FGs		FTs		Rebounds						
		G	MIN	FG	PCT	FG	PCT	FT	PCT	OFF	TOT	AST	STL	BLK	PTS	PPG
87-88	PHO	55	1807	342	.475	0	.000	131	.679	134	434	72	58	29	815	14.8
88-89	PHO	74	2120	468	.503	0	.000	165	.743	165	541	52	54	27	1176	15.9
89-90	PHO/CHA	76	2426	484	.515	0	.000	303	.723	211	599	99	69	51	1271	16.7
90-91	CHA/PHI	75	2644	487	.487	0	.000	268	.815	220	598	105	69	53	1242	16.6
91-92	PHI	81	2771	512	.511	0	.000	343	.807	234	660	118	51	85	1367	16.9
92-93	PHI	80	1742	359	.464	0	.000	274	.843	136	472	116	37	54	992	12.4
Totals		441	13510	2652	.494	0	.000	1559	.774	1100	3304	562	338	299	6863	15.6

GERALD GLASS

Team: Detroit Pistons
Position: Guard/Forward
Height: 6'6" **Weight:** 231
Birthdate: November 12, 1967
NBA Experience: 3 years

College: Delta St.; Mississippi
Acquired: Traded from Timberwolves with Mark Randall for Brad Sellers, Lance Blanks, and a 2000 2nd-round pick, 11/92

Background: Glass began his college career at Division II Delta State before transferring to Ole Miss and becoming the school's No. 6 career scorer in just two seasons. As an NBA rookie in 1990-91, he scored 32 points against the Lakers and led Minnesota in scoring in three straight games on a December road trip, averaging 27.7 points during that stretch. His playing time diminished at the end of the year. Glass started exactly half of the Timberwolves' games in 1991-92 and was traded to Detroit early last season. He played sparingly for the Pistons and posted career lows in several categories.

Strengths: A scorer first and foremost, Glass can get to the hoop, convert in transition, or back defenders in and hit fadeaway jumpers. He uses his behind on post-up moves, a la Mark Aguirre. Glass is a decent passer who keeps his eyes open for teammates.

Weaknesses: Glass has a glaring deficiency on defense. At times, he looks like he is going through the motions. He does not possess great quickness and has had a history of trouble with his weight. Glass is a dismal free throw shooter and his field goal and 3-point averages are also sub-par.

Analysis: For a player of his reputation, Glass has not turned out to be the kind of scorer most expected. The Pistons need offensive help and, while he can provide it in spurts, he has not been able to do so consistently. Toss in his defensive troubles and it looks as though Glass will have to settle for a limited role off the bench.

PLAYER SUMMARY	
Will	back into the post
Can't	hit shots consistently
Expect	a scorer's mentality
Don't Expect	defensive help
Fantasy Value	$1
Card Value	8-12¢

COLLEGE STATISTICS

		G	FGP	FTP	RPG	PPG
85-86	DELT	31	.554	.722	6.5	12.5
86-87	DELT	33	.605	.702	12.5	26.1
88-89	MISS	30	.532	.736	8.5	28.0
89-90	MISS	30	.490	.736	7.6	24.1
Totals		124	.544	.724	8.9	22.7

NBA REGULAR-SEASON STATISTICS

			FGs		3-PT FGs		FTs		Rebounds						
	G	MIN	FG	PCT	FG	PCT	FT	PCT	OFF	TOT	AST	STL	BLK	PTS	PPG
90-91 MIN	51	606	149	.438	2	.118	52	.684	54	102	42	28	9	352	6.9
91-92 MIN	75	1822	383	.440	16	.296	77	.616	107	260	175	66	30	859	11.5
92-93 MIN/DET	60	848	142	.419	7	.212	25	.641	61	142	77	33	18	316	5.3
Totals	186	3276	674	.435	25	.240	154	.642	222	504	294	127	57	1527	8.2

SNOOPY GRAHAM

Team: Atlanta Hawks
Position: Forward
Height: 6'6" **Weight:** 200
Birthdate: November 28, 1967

NBA Experience: 2 years
College: Ohio
Acquired: Signed as a free agent, 11/91

Background: Paul "Snoopy" Graham led Ohio University in scoring with 22.2 PPG during his final year with the Bobcats. Before the 1991-92 season, he played for the Philadelphia Spirit of the United States Basketball League, averaging 18.2 PPG and 3.6 RPG. He was voted MVP of the USBL All-Star Game. He has also played in Australia and the CBA. Atlanta signed him in November 1991 and Graham wound up playing in 78 games and scoring in double figures. His average dropped two points last season but he was again among the team's top six scorers.

Strengths: Graham is somewhat unorthodox but knows how to put the ball in the hole. He is a gifted outside shooter with 3-point range and can also get to the basket for easier conversions. Graham owns a nice post-up repertoire, since he learned to play with his back to the bucket in college. He's also a nifty passer who sees the floor well.

Weaknesses: Graham is a below-average defender who tends to use his hands more than his feet. His wheels simply aren't up to the task of handling the quicker guards. He is a below-average rebounder, and pressure defense can cause him problems when he handles the ball. Graham does not rank among the better athletes in the league.

Analysis: Graham was waived by the Hawks on Halloween of 1991 only to re-sign a week later. Since then, he has started 20-plus games and been a reliable, full-time NBA player. He does not have star potential, but he is a survivor who knows the game and how to score. Graham always believed in his ability and fought through the minor circuits for a big-league career.

PLAYER SUMMARY	
Will	find open men
Can't	outquick opponents
Expect	about 8-10 PPG
Don't Expect	great defense
Fantasy Value	$1
Card Value	5-10¢

COLLEGE STATISTICS

		G	FGP	FTP	RPG	PPG
85-86	OHIO	29	.480	.773	4.7	15.9
86-87	OHIO	22	.478	.743	5.4	21.1
87-88	OHIO	30	.550	.770	5.1	20.0
88-89	OHIO	29	.520	.811	7.0	22.2
Totals		110	.508	.780	5.5	19.7

NBA REGULAR-SEASON STATISTICS

			FGs		3-PT FGs		FTs		Rebounds						
	G	MIN	FG	PCT	FG	PCT	FT	PCT	OFF	TOT	AST	STL	BLK	PTS	PPG
91-92 ATL	78	1718	305	.447	55	.390	126	.741	72	231	175	96	21	791	10.1
92-93 ATL	80	1508	256	.457	42	.298	96	.733	61	190	164	86	6	650	8.1
Totals	158	3226	561	.452	97	.344	222	.738	133	421	339	182	27	1441	9.1

GARY GRANT

Team: Los Angeles Clippers
Position: Guard
Height: 6'3" **Weight:** 195
Birthdate: April 21, 1965
NBA Experience: 5 years

College: Michigan
Acquired: Draft rights traded from SuperSonics with a 1989 1st-round pick for Michael Cage, 6/88

Background: A consensus All-American at Michigan, Grant concluded his career as the school's all-time leader in assists and earned Big Ten Defensive Player of the Year honors as a junior. He led all NBA rookies in steals and assists before spending two years in and out of a starting job with the Clippers. His scoring has dipped in each of the last three seasons. Grant spent much of the 1992-93 campaign as a back-up to Mark Jackson at point guard.

Strengths: Grant is known as a solid on-the-ball defender with good quickness and instincts. He overcame ankle surgery in 1990 and knee surgery in 1991with his athletic skills intact. He also has good size, handles the ball well, and is effective in transition.

Weaknesses: Grant's decision-making has long been questioned. He might have set a league record for turnovers in 1989-90 if a broken ankle had not forced him to abandon the "quest." Offensively, he does not do enough. He doesn't penetrate often enough, rarely gets to the line, and is not a good enough shooter to justify staying on the perimeter. Also, his 3-point percentage is poor.

Analysis: Grant had been making better decisions, but the Clippers felt they needed help at the point and Jackson enjoyed a fine first season in L.A. Meanwhile, Grant fell into some of his old habits while trying to impress. His defense is consistent but the rest of his game has not progressed much. He can be a solid back-up.

PLAYER SUMMARY

Will	gamble for steals
Can't	regain starting job
Expect	solid defense
Don't Expect	consistency
Fantasy Value	$1
Card Value	5-10¢

COLLEGE STATISTICS

		G	FGP	FTP	APG	PPG
84-85	MICH	30	.550	.817	4.7	12.9
85-86	MICH	33	.494	.744	5.6	12.2
86-87	MICH	32	.537	.782	5.4	22.4
87-88	MICH	34	.530	.808	6.9	21.1
Totals		129	.528	.790	5.7	17.2

NBA REGULAR-SEASON STATISTICS

		G	MIN	FGs FG	FGs PCT	3-PT FGs FG	3-PT FGs PCT	FTs FT	FTs PCT	Rebounds OFF	Rebounds TOT	AST	STL	BLK	PTS	PPG
88-89	LAC	71	1924	361	.435	5	.227	119	.735	80	238	506	144	9	846	11.9
89-90	LAC	44	1529	241	.466	5	.238	88	.779	59	195	442	108	5	575	13.1
90-91	LAC	68	2105	265	.451	9	.231	51	.689	69	209	587	103	12	590	8.7
91-92	LAC	78	2049	275	.462	15	.294	44	.815	34	184	538	138	14	609	7.8
92-93	LAC	74	1624	210	.441	11	.262	55	.743	27	139	353	106	9	486	6.6
Totals		335	9231	1352	.450	45	.257	357	.748	269	965	2426	599	49	3106	9.3

HARVEY GRANT

Team: Portland Trail Blazers
Position: Forward
Height: 6'9" **Weight:** 235
Birthdate: July 4, 1965
NBA Experience: 5 years

College: Clemson; Independence; Oklahoma
Acquired: Traded from Bullets for Kevin Duckworth, 6/93

Background: Harvey is the identical twin brother of the Bulls' Horace Grant. The tandem enrolled together at Clemson, but when it became apparent that they were competing for the same spot, Harvey transferred to Oklahoma. There, he led the Sooners to the NCAA title game in 1988 and was the tournament's top rebounder. He was a disappointment with Washington in his first two seasons, but he totaled 18-plus PPG in each of the last three years while becoming the Bullets' leader. Surprisingly, he was dealt to Portland in June.

Strengths: Grant is one of the hardest-working and most coachable players you'll encounter. He possesses a good outside shot with range up to 20 feet, and his lean, wiry body is perfect for running the court. He's a fine passer from his forward slot. Grant has good lateral quickness on defense and works hard at that end of the floor.

Weaknesses: Harvey is not as muscular as Horace and not as effective in the paint. His low-post offense is not nearly as refined. He has been accused of playing soft and staying away from the boards. His rebounding numbers are below average for his position.

Analysis: Harvey has not received the notoriety of his brother. He has, however, become a big-time player with the ability to score on anyone with his catch-and-shoot jumper. He improved his shooting percentage last year and should become even more effective with the up-tempo Blazers.

PLAYER SUMMARY

Will	catch and shoot
Can't	get brother's notoriety
Expect	18 PPG
Don't Expect	10 RPG
Fantasy Value	$12-15
Card Value	10-15¢

COLLEGE STATISTICS

		G	FGP	FTP	RPG	PPG
84-85	CLEM	28	.496	.585	4.5	5.1
85-86	IND	33	.586	.707	11.8	22.4
86-87	OKLA	34	.534	.730	9.9	16.9
87-88	OKLA	39	.547	.729	9.4	20.9
Totals		134	.553	.712	9.1	17.0

NBA REGULAR-SEASON STATISTICS

			FGs		3-PT FGs		FTs		Rebounds							
		G	MIN	FG	PCT	FG	PCT	FT	PCT	OFF	TOT	AST	STL	BLK	PTS	PPG
88-89	WAS	71	1193	181	.464	0	.000	34	.596	75	163	79	35	29	396	5.6
89-90	WAS	81	1846	284	.473	0	.000	96	.701	138	342	131	52	43	664	8.2
90-91	WAS	77	2842	609	.498	2	.133	185	.743	179	557	204	91	61	1405	18.2
91-92	WAS	64	2388	489	.478	1	.125	176	.800	157	432	170	74	27	1155	18.0
92-93	WAS	72	2667	560	.487	1	.100	218	.727	133	412	205	72	44	1339	18.6
Totals		365	10936	2123	.484	4	.095	709	.736	682	1906	789	324	204	4959	13.6

HORACE GRANT

Team: Chicago Bulls
Position: Forward
Height: 6'10" **Weight:** 235
Birthdate: July 4, 1965

NBA Experience: 6 years
College: Clemson
Acquired: 1st-round pick in 1987 draft
(10th overall)

Background: In his senior season at Clemson, Grant was the ACC Player of the Year after averaging 21.0 PPG. The Bulls were fortunate in getting Scottie Pippen (fifth) and Grant (tenth) in the 1987 draft. Grant has played a key role on Chicago's back-to-back-to-back NBA championship teams, finishing third in the league in field goal percentage in 1991-92. His shooting and scoring dropped a bit last season, but he again led the Bulls in rebounding.

Strengths: Grant ranks among the most talented and athletic power forwards in the game. He's a quick leaper who can outrun most power forwards while still holding his own in the strength department. He's in his element in the open court, and he has become a fine post scorer and passer. He's adored by teammates and fans for his work ethic. He's a stellar defender who will block shots.

Weaknesses: Grant has often questioned his role in Chicago's offense, and sometimes his discontent seems to affect his play. He was not shooting as well near the end of last season as he was at the start. Grant's range is limited and he is a poor free throw shooter.

Analysis: The things Grant does for his team are as valuable as the high-flying dunks of Michael Jordan and the acrobatics of Scottie Pippen. Grant simply busts his gut at both ends of the floor, cleans the glass, intimidates, and helps win ballgames. He would contribute more offensively if he saw the ball down low more often.

PLAYER SUMMARY	
Will	rebound, defend
Can't	outshine Jordan, Pippen
Expect	10 RPG
Don't Expect	20 PPG
Fantasy Value	$15-18
Card Value	10-15¢

COLLEGE STATISTICS

		G	FGP	FTP	RPG	PPG
83-84	CLEM	28	.533	.744	4.6	5.7
84-85	CLEM	29	.555	.637	6.8	11.3
85-86	CLEM	34	.584	.725	10.5	16.4
86-87	CLEM	31	.656	.708	9.6	21.0
Totals		122	.598	.704	8.0	13.9

NBA REGULAR-SEASON STATISTICS

		G	MIN	FGs FG	FGs PCT	3-PT FGs FG	3-PT FGs PCT	FTs FT	FTs PCT	Rebounds OFF	Rebounds TOT	AST	STL	BLK	PTS	PPG
87-88	CHI	81	1827	254	.501	0	.000	114	.626	155	447	89	51	53	622	7.7
88-89	CHI	79	2809	405	.519	0	.000	140	.704	240	681	168	86	62	950	12.0
89-90	CHI	80	2753	446	.523	0	.000	179	.699	236	629	227	92	84	1071	13.4
90-91	CHI	78	2641	401	.547	1	.167	197	.711	266	659	178	95	69	1000	12.8
91-92	CHI	81	2859	457	.578	0	.000	235	.741	344	807	217	100	131	1149	14.2
92-93	CHI	77	2745	421	.508	1	.200	174	.619	341	729	201	89	96	1017	13.2
Totals		476	15634	2384	.531	2	.100	1039	.687	1582	3952	1080	513	495	5809	12.2

JEFF GRAYER

Team: Golden State Warriors
Position: Guard/Forward
Height: 6'5"　**Weight:** 210
Birthdate: December 17, 1965

NBA Experience: 5 years
College: Iowa St.
Acquired: Signed as a free agent, 7/92

Background: This second-team All-American led Iowa State into the NCAA Tournament his senior year. He wound up his career as the Cyclones' all-time leading scorer, and he played on the 1988 U.S. Olympic team. Milwaukee drafted Grayer in the first round in 1988, but he missed most of his first year with a knee injury and never averaged double figures in scoring for the Bucks. Golden State signed him as an unrestricted free agent on July 1, 1992. He averaged 8.8 PPG in 48 games before his 1992-93 season was cut short because of surgery to remove bone spurs in his left knee.

Strengths: Grayer brings good defensive ability, athletic skills, and versatility to the court. He knows how to shake free and go to the hoop with a variety of moves. He's also a decent ball-handler and can rack up points posting up.

Weaknesses: Inconsistent perimeter shooting has plagued Grayer throughout his career. His jumper is awkward-looking and he has never reached 47 percent from the field with it. His free throw shooting is also sub-par and he's no threat from 3-point range. Grayer penetrates but will not be mistaken for a point guard because of his passing.

Analysis: Grayer is a role-player who is ideally suited to coming off the bench, although he did get a dozen starts with Golden State last year and would have drawn more if not for his season-ending injury. If he could ever get his jump shot to fall consistently, he would not be considered a below-average first-rounder.

PLAYER SUMMARY	
Will	play defense
Can't	get jumper to drop
Expect	a role-player
Don't Expect	high percentages
Fantasy Value	$1
Card Value	5-8¢

COLLEGE STATISTICS

		G	FGP	FTP	RPG	PPG
84-85	ISU	33	.529	.653	6.5	12.2
85-86	ISU	33	.547	.629	6.3	20.7
86-87	ISU	27	.504	.740	7.0	22.4
87-88	ISU	32	.523	.711	9.4	25.3
Totals		125	.526	.686	7.3	20.0

NBA REGULAR-SEASON STATISTICS

		G	MIN	FGs FG	FGs PCT	3-PT FGs FG	3-PT FGs PCT	FTs FT	FTs PCT	Rebounds OFF	Rebounds TOT	AST	STL	BLK	PTS	PPG
88-89	MIL	11	200	32	.438	0	.000	17	.850	14	35	22	10	1	81	7.4
89-90	MIL	71	1427	224	.460	1	.125	99	.651	94	217	107	48	10	548	7.7
90-91	MIL	82	1422	210	.433	0	.000	101	.687	111	246	123	48	9	521	6.4
91-92	MIL	82	1659	309	.448	19	.288	102	.667	129	257	150	64	13	739	9.0
92-93	GS	48	1025	165	.467	2	.143	91	.669	71	157	70	31	8	423	8.8
Totals		294	5733	940	.450	22	.237	410	.674	419	912	472	201	41	2312	7.9

A.C. GREEN

Team: Los Angeles Lakers
Position: Forward
Height: 6'9" **Weight:** 225
Birthdate: October 4, 1963

NBA Experience: 8 years
College: Oregon St.
Acquired: 1st-round pick in 1985 draft (23rd overall)

Background: Green was named Pac-10 Player of the Year as a junior at Oregon State and wound up his career as the school's second-leading rebounder and third-leading scorer. He led the Lakers in rebounding four straight years from 1986-90, and he was voted a starter in the 1989-90 All-Star Game. The 1990-91 campaign was a down year for Green, but he moved back into a key role in 1991-92 when the Lakers were ravaged by injuries. After a strong 1992-93 season, he became an unrestricted free agent.

Strengths: A hard-working player, Green rebounds, scores, gets to the line, and can play both forward spots and some big guard at 6'9". He has become a fine outside shooter and is not afraid to go inside. He's an aggressive defender, runs the floor, and provides great durability. He has played all 82 games in seven of his eight seasons.

Weaknesses: Green is not as strong on the defensive glass as he is on the offensive boards. A lot of his points come on put-backs and "garbage" buckets. He's not much of a creator.

Analysis: Whenever and wherever the Lakers needed A.C. Green, he was there. He played himself into the starting lineup early last season but is just as content and effective coming off the bench. One All-Star Game was all he'll take part in, but his contributions don't go unnoticed.

PLAYER SUMMARY	
Will	crash the boards
Can't	stick to one position
Expect	shooting skills
Don't Expect	creativity
Fantasy Value	$9-12
Card Value	5-12¢

COLLEGE STATISTICS

		G	FGP	FTP	RPG	PPG
81-82	OSU	30	.615	.610	5.3	8.6
82-83	OSU	31	.559	.689	7.6	14.0
83-84	OSU	23	.657	.770	8.7	17.8
84-85	OSU	31	.599	.680	9.2	19.1
Totals		115	.602	.696	7.7	14.7

NBA REGULAR-SEASON STATISTICS

		G	MIN	FGs FG	FGs PCT	3-PT FGs FG	3-PT FGs PCT	FTs FT	FTs PCT	Rebounds OFF	Rebounds TOT	AST	STL	BLK	PTS	PPG
85-86	LAL	82	1542	209	.539	1	.167	102	.611	160	381	54	49	49	521	6.4
86-87	LAL	79	2240	316	.538	0	.000	220	.780	210	615	84	70	80	852	10.8
87-88	LAL	82	2636	322	.503	0	.000	293	.773	245	710	93	87	45	937	11.4
88-89	LAL	82	2510	401	.529	4	.235	282	.786	258	739	103	94	55	1088	13.3
89-90	LAL	82	2709	385	.478	13	.283	278	.751	262	712	90	66	50	1061	12.9
90-91	LAL	82	2164	258	.476	11	.200	223	.738	201	516	71	59	23	750	9.1
91-92	LAL	82	2902	382	.476	12	.214	340	.744	306	762	117	91	36	1116	13.6
92-93	LAL	82	2819	379	.537	16	.348	277	.739	287	711	116	88	39	1051	12.8
Totals		653	19522	2652	.507	57	.245	2015	.749	1929	5146	728	604	377	7376	11.3

LITTERIAL GREEN

Team: Orlando Magic
Position: Guard
Height: 6'1" **Weight:** 185
Birthdate: March 7, 1970

NBA Experience: 1 year
College: Georgia
Acquired: Draft rights traded from
Bulls for a 1993 2nd-round pick, 7/92

Background: Green has always played in someone's shadow. As a prep in Mississippi, his rival was Chris Jackson. Then at Georgia, he led the Bulldogs in scoring, assists, and 3-pointers as a senior and finished his career as the school's all-time leader in points and assists. Nevertheless, he did not receive the publicity garnered by Kenny Anderson of Georgia Tech. Green was selected 39th overall by Chicago and traded to Orlando a couple weeks after the draft. He saw limited action as a rookie with the Magic, averaging less than five PPG but handing out 100-plus assists.

Strengths: Green boasts a quick first step and is a splendid athlete. He jumps out of the gym, handles the ball well, and can come off the bench at either guard position. The Magic fans took to him early, wanting him to start in place of Scott Skiles. Per minute, Green's assist average was quite respectable, and he can also do some scoring.

Weaknesses: Green has been called a shooting guard in a point guard's body. Problem is, he does not shoot the ball consistently enough to be a full-time shooting guard and he has not yet demonstrated that he can run a team as well as Skiles or other point guards. He does not have 3-point range, is not of much help on the boards, and needs to boost his below-average free throw percentage.

Analysis: The biggest question mark as Green entered the NBA involved his ability to play point guard at that level. He showed he could, at least in a reserve role, with some better-than-expected playmaking and passing skills. Still, Green did not play consistently enough to see action on a nightly basis.

PLAYER SUMMARY	
Will	impress athletically
Can't	shoots FTs
Expect	reserve minutes
Don't Expect	consistency
Fantasy Value	$0
Card Value	10-20¢

COLLEGE STATISTICS

		G	FGP	FTP	APG	PPG
88-89	GEOR	31	.404	.775	4.3	15.5
89-90	GEOR	28	.417	.708	4.3	17.5
90-91	GEOR	28	.442	.777	3.5	20.6
91-92	GEOR	29	.408	.687	4.0	19.4
Totals		116	.418	.737	4.0	18.2

NBA REGULAR-SEASON STATISTICS

	G	MIN	FGs FG	PCT	3-PT FGs FG	PCT	FTs FT	PCT	Rebounds OFF	TOT	AST	STL	BLK	PTS	PPG
92-93 ORL	52	626	87	.439	1	.100	60	.625	11	34	116	23	4	235	4.5
Totals	52	626	87	.439	1	.100	60	.625	11	34	116	23	4	235	4.5

SIDNEY GREEN

Team: Charlotte Hornets
Position: Forward
Height: 6'9" **Weight:** 250
Birthdate: January 4, 1961
NBA Experience: 10 years

College: UNLV
Acquired: Traded from Spurs with conditional draft picks for J.R. Reid, 12/92

Background: At UNLV, Green finished as the top rebounder and second-leading scorer in that school's history. He established himself as a productive board-crasher in Chicago, Detroit, New York, Orlando, and San Antonio. He saw limited action with the Spurs and Hornets in 1992-93 and never reached as many as ten points in a single game. He averaged less than three.

Strengths: Green's calling card is rebounding, especially on the offensive boards. His muscular frame and willingness to fight for position causes pain for the opposition and often disrupts their offensive gameplan. His low-post defense is aided by his physical nature. He has never been afraid to mix it up.

Weaknesses: Though he tries to be a scorer, Green is not and never will be. He converted less than 40 percent of his shots last season and coughed up the ball nearly as often as he passed it. He has no perimeter skills to speak of and thus becomes much less effective when pushed away from the post.

Analysis: Green has never achieved what he was expected to in the NBA and is not about to start living up to what was once great potential. At this point, he is a seldom-used reserve who provides a physical presence and little else. That accounts for his frequent cross-country travels.

PLAYER SUMMARY	
Will	mix it up
Can't	find permanent home
Expect	a physical presence
Don't Expect	much else
Fantasy Value	$0
Card Value	5-10¢

COLLEGE STATISTICS

		G	FGP	FTP	RPG	PPG
79-80	UNLV	32	.518	.727	11.1	15.6
80-81	UNLV	26	.515	.708	10.9	15.0
81-82	UNLV	30	.535	.769	9.0	16.7
82-83	UNLV	31	.548	.700	11.9	22.1
Totals		119	.531	.723	10.7	17.4

NBA REGULAR-SEASON STATISTICS

				FGs		3-PT FGs		FTs		Rebounds						
		G	MIN	FG	PCT	FG	PCT	FT	PCT	OFF	TOT	AST	STL	BLK	PTS	PPG
83-84	CHI	49	667	100	.439	0	.000	55	.714	58	174	25	18	17	255	5.2
84-85	CHI	48	740	108	.432	0	.000	79	.806	72	246	29	11	11	295	6.1
85-86	CHI	80	2307	407	.465	0	.000	262	.782	208	658	139	70	37	1076	13.4
86-87	DET	80	1792	256	.472	0	.000	119	.672	196	653	62	41	50	631	7.9
87-88	NY	82	2049	258	.441	0	.000	126	.663	221	642	93	65	32	642	7.8
88-89	NY	82	1277	194	.460	0	.000	129	.759	157	394	76	47	18	517	6.3
89-90	ORL	73	1860	312	.468	1	.333	136	.663	166	588	99	50	26	761	10.4
90-91	SA	66	1099	177	.461	0	.000	89	.848	98	313	52	32	13	443	6.7
91-92	SA	80	1127	147	.427	0	.000	73	.820	92	342	36	29	11	367	4.6
92-93	SA/CHA	39	329	34	.382	0	.000	25	.806	32	118	24	6	5	93	2.4
Totals		679	13247	1993	.454	1	.037	1093	.738	1300	4128	635	369	220	5080	7.5

TOM GUGLIOTTA

Team: Washington Bullets
Position: Forward
Height: 6'10" **Weight:** 240
Birthdate: December 19, 1969

NBA Experience: 1 year
College: North Carolina St.
Acquired: 1st-round pick in 1992 draft
(6th overall)

Background: One of the finest all-around players in the Atlantic Coast Conference,"Googs" started 92 games during his North Carolina State career and became only the third Wolfpack player to record 1,500 points and 800 rebounds in a career. He led the ACC in rebounding and 3-pointers per game as a senior. His father was a high school coach and two of his brothers played professionally in Europe. There was some groaning when the Bullets drafted him sixth overall, but he proved to be one of the top NBA rookies in 1992-93 by averaging 14-plus PPG and nearly ten RPG.

Strengths: Gugliotta has been compared to Larry Bird by none other than Michael Jordan and Pat Riley. That's because he does a little bit of everything. He shoots with range, finds open men, rebounds, handles the ball, plays tough defense, and runs the floor. He started at guard, forward, and center as a rookie. Gugliotta was also Washington's most durable player. He missed only one game, that because of the flu.

Weaknesses: Gugliotta does not have a great arsenal of inside moves, especially when asked to play center and power forward. His skills are better suited to the role of small forward. He needs to develop a power game and hoist his field goal and free throw percentages.

Analysis: No one expected Gugliotta to enjoy the rookie season he did. He led all rookies in assists and was among the top three in rebounding and the top ten in scoring. He was also one of the better defensive and most durable players in the rookie class. The Bird comparisons are premature, but the Bullets have a future franchise-type player in this hard-working youngster.

PLAYER SUMMARY	
Will	play multiple positions
Can't	dominate as a center
Expect	points, boards, assists
Don't Expect	many mistakes
Fantasy Value	$17-20
Card Value	40-75¢

COLLEGE STATISTICS

		G	FGP	FTP	RPG	PPG
88-89	NCST	21	.429	.655	1.7	2.7
89-90	NCST	30	.504	.672	7.0	11.1
90-91	NCST	31	.500	.644	9.1	15.2
91-92	NCST	30	.449	.685	9.8	22.5
Totals		112	.476	.668	7.3	13.7

NBA REGULAR-SEASON STATISTICS

				FGs		3-PT FGs		FTs		Rebounds						
		G	MIN	FG	PCT	FG	PCT	FT	PCT	OFF	TOT	AST	STL	BLK	PTS	PPG
92-93	WAS	81	2795	484	.426	38	.281	181	.644	219	781	306	134	35	1187	14.7
Totals		81	2795	484	.426	38	.281	181	.644	219	781	306	134	35	1187	14.7

TOM HAMMONDS

Team: Denver Nuggets
Position: Forward
Height: 6'9" **Weight:** 225
Birthdate: March 27, 1967

NBA Experience: 4 years
College: Georgia Tech
Acquired: Signed as a free agent, 2/93

Background: Hammonds was a third-team All-American as a senior at Georgia Tech and was described by rival Duke coach Mike Krzyzewski as "one of the best players to come out during my nine years in the league (ACC). I love Tom Hammonds." Though drafted No. 9 in the 1989 draft, Hammonds has played sparingly in his four NBA years. He was traded by the Bullets to Charlotte for Rex Chapman in February 1992, but he missed the final 30 games of the 1991-92 season with a groin pull. He signed with Denver in February 1993 and missed the last week of the season with a stress fracture in his right foot.

Strengths: Hammonds has a weight room-sculpted, NBA body. He showed flashes of scoring and rebounding ability early in 1991-92, when he finally seemed to be coming into his own as an NBA player, averaging 11.9 PPG before the groin injury. He hits the defensive glass.

Weaknesses: Hammonds is not wide or strong enough to thrive at power forward, yet his skills facing the basket are not where they need to be for the three spot. In addition, he has not shown an ability to put the ball on the floor, nor does he pass the ball well. He's often a victim of match-up problems on defense. Hammonds has also been prone to injury.

Analysis: His most recent stress fracture did not require surgery and Hammonds is expected to be at full strength when training camp opens. His task will be to try to regain the form he displayed early in 1991-92. He needs to develop better perimeter skills if he hopes to make a mark.

PLAYER SUMMARY

Will ....rebound
Can't ....stay healthy
Expect.......................reserve minutes
Don't Expect ....sleek drives
Fantasy Value..................................$0
Card Value......................................5-8¢

COLLEGE STATISTICS

		G	FGP	FTP	RPG	PPG
85-86	GT	34	.609	.816	6.4	12.2
86-87	GT	29	.569	.797	7.2	16.2
87-88	GT	30	.568	.826	7.2	18.9
88-89	GT	30	.538	.773	8.1	20.9
Totals		123	.566	.801	7.2	16.9

NBA REGULAR-SEASON STATISTICS

				FGs		3-PT FGs		FTs		Rebounds						
		G	MIN	FG	PCT	FG	PCT	FT	PCT	OFF	TOT	AST	STL	BLK	PTS	PPG
89-90	WAS	61	805	129	.437	0	.000	63	.643	61	168	51	11	14	321	5.3
90-91	WAS	70	1023	155	.461	0	.000	57	.722	58	206	43	15	7	367	5.2
91-92	WAS/CHA	37	984	195	.488	0	.000	50	.610	49	185	36	22	13	440	11.9
92-93	CHA/DEN	54	713	105	.475	0	.000	38	.613	38	127	24	18	12	248	4.6
Totals		222	3525	584	.466	0	.000	208	.648	206	686	154	66	46	1376	6.2

TIM HARDAWAY

Team: Golden State Warriors
Position: Guard
Height: 6'0" **Weight:** 195
Birthdate: September 12, 1966

NBA Experience: 4 years
College: Texas-El Paso
Acquired: 1st-round pick in 1989 draft
(14th overall)

Background: Hardaway surpassed Nate Archibald as the all-time scoring leader at the University of Texas-El Paso. In 1989-90, he led all rookies in assists and steals while directing the high-powered Golden State offense. Hardaway has since appeared in three straight All-Star Games and established himself as one of the league's premier point men. Per game, he was second in the league in assists during the 1992-93 season, although he missed more than a month of play after the All-Star break with an injury to his right knee.

Strengths: Few can handle the ball like Hardaway. His between-the-legs crossover dribble, dubbed the "UTEP two-step," mesmerizes even the best of defenders and usually opens a clear lane to the basket. His long-range shot is unorthodox but he shoots it with 3-point range. Hardaway is a quick, effective floor leader who gets the ball into the right hands, which are often his own. He is also solid on defense as a ball hounder.

Weaknesses: Hardaway's small frame makes him vulnerable against bigger guards, especially on defense. His shooting percentage has gone down in each of the past two years and was under 45 percent for the first time last season. He takes a few too many chances defensively.

Analysis: No question about it, Hardaway is a bona fide superstar. The king of the crossover dribble certainly ranks among the best and most explosive point guards in the game. The ball is attached to his hand. Having Hardaway out for better than a month was one of the most devastating of the injuries that crushed Golden State last season.

PLAYER SUMMARY	
Will	blow past defenders
Can't	post up
Expect	a perennial All-Star
Don't Expect	power
Fantasy Value	$45-50
Card Value	15-25¢

COLLEGE STATISTICS

		G	FGP	FTP	APG	PPG
85-86	UTEP	28	.521	.651	1.9	4.1
86-87	UTEP	31	.490	.663	4.8	10.0
87-88	UTEP	32	.449	.754	5.7	13.6
88-89	UTEP	33	.501	.741	5.4	22.0
Totals		124	.484	.718	4.5	12.8

NBA REGULAR-SEASON STATISTICS

			FGs		3-PT FGs		FTs		Rebounds						
		G	MIN	FG	PCT	FG	PCT	FT	PCT	OFF	TOT	AST	STL	BLK	PTS	PPG
89-90	GS	79	2663	464	.471	23	.274	211	.764	57	310	689	165	12	1162	14.7
90-91	GS	82	3215	739	.476	97	.385	306	.803	87	332	793	214	12	1881	22.9
91-92	GS	81	3332	734	.461	127	.338	298	.766	81	310	807	164	13	1893	23.4
92-93	GS	66	2609	522	.447	102	.330	273	.744	60	263	699	116	12	1419	21.5
Totals		308	11819	2459	.464	349	.342	1088	.770	285	1215	2988	659	49	6355	20.6

DEREK HARPER

Team: Dallas Mavericks
Position: Guard
Height: 6'4" **Weight:** 206
Birthdate: October 13, 1961

NBA Experience: 10 years
College: Illinois
Acquired: 1st-round pick in 1983 draft
(11th overall)

Background: Harper led the Big Ten in steals for two straight years, then declared for the NBA draft after his junior season. He was the first player in league history to improve his scoring average in each of his first eight years and is the Mavs' all-time leader in steals. Forced to carry the hapless Mavs in 1992-93, he missed several games with groin and hamstring injuries while easily leading the team in scoring.

Strengths: A respected all-around talent, Harper has good quickness and great reach and is willing to play belly-up defense against anyone. He can penetrate for shots close to the bucket while ranking among NBA leaders in 3-point shooting percentage as well. Harper is a veteran leader who gives all he's got every night.

Weaknesses: The decline of the Mavs has frustrated Harper. His shooting has suffered for it over the last two years and the load he has carried has worn him down. Harper, originally a two guard, will not amass staggering assist totals.

Analysis: Harper is a great all-purpose talent, and his leadership and savvy could help the right team contend for a title. No one should be subject to what he has gone through in the last two years with Dallas. Surrounded by marginal players, he has carried a huge mental and physical load.

PLAYER SUMMARY	
Will	bury wing jumpers
Can't	win games by himself
Expect	high percentages
Don't Expect	20 PPG
Fantasy Value	$17-20
Card Value	8-15¢

COLLEGE STATISTICS

		G	FGP	FTP	APG	PPG
80-81	ILL	29	.413	.717	5.4	8.3
81-82	ILL	29	.457	.756	5.0	8.4
82-83	ILL	32	.537	.675	3.7	15.4
Totals		90	.478	.701	4.7	10.9

NBA REGULAR-SEASON STATISTICS

				FGs		3-PT FGs		FTs		Rebounds						
		G	MIN	FG	PCT	FG	PCT	FT	PCT	OFF	TOT	AST	STL	BLK	PTS	PPG
83-84	DAL	82	1712	200	.443	3	.115	66	.673	53	172	239	95	21	469	5.7
84-85	DAL	82	2218	329	.520	21	.344	111	.721	47	199	360	144	37	790	9.6
85-86	DAL	79	2150	390	.534	12	.235	171	.747	75	226	416	153	23	963	12.2
86-87	DAL	77	2556	497	.501	76	.358	160	.684	51	199	609	167	25	1230	16.0
87-88	DAL	82	3032	536	.459	60	.313	261	.759	71	246	634	168	35	1393	17.0
88-89	DAL	81	2968	538	.477	99	.356	229	.806	46	228	570	172	41	1404	17.3
89-90	DAL	82	3007	567	.488	89	.371	250	.794	54	244	609	187	26	1473	18.0
90-91	DAL	77	2879	572	.467	89	.362	286	.731	59	233	548	147	14	1519	19.7
91-92	DAL	65	2252	448	.443	58	.312	198	.759	49	170	373	101	17	1152	17.7
92-93	DAL	62	2108	393	.419	101	.393	239	.756	42	123	334	80	16	1126	18.2
Totals		769	24882	4470	.474	608	.348	1971	.751	547	2040	4692	1414	255	11519	15.0

RON HARPER

Team: Los Angeles Clippers
Position: Guard
Height: 6'6" **Weight:** 198
Birthdate: January 20, 1964
NBA Experience: 7 years
College: Miami (OH)

Acquired: Traded from Cavaliers with 1990 and 1992 1st-round picks and a 1991 2nd-round pick for Reggie Williams and draft rights to Danny Ferry, 11/89

Background: Harper left Miami of Ohio with the all-time Mid-American Conference scoring record. He quickly established himself as a marquee player in Cleveland, finishing second in Rookie of the Year voting. He was traded to the Clippers in November 1989, but his first campaign there was cut short when he tore the anterior cruciate ligament in his right knee. Harper returned for the final 39 games of the 1990-91 season and the next year helped the Clippers to their first playoff berth in L.A. He was second on the team in scoring during the 1992-93 campaign.

Strengths: Harper is a dominant open-court player with slashing moves to the hoop and tremendous finishing ability. He's a nifty passer and a natural leader with supreme confidence. He rebounds and even blocks shots.

Weaknesses: Poor shot selection has been a knock on Harper, who does not shoot for a high percentage. He is more a scorer than a shooter. Harper was unhappy in L.A. last season and let it be known.

Analysis: One of the best open-court players and one-on-one scorers in the game, Harper said in January that he was hoping the Clippers did not pick up his contract at the end of the season. If L.A. goes that route, however, the team would give up one of the main reasons for its back-to-back playoff trips.

PLAYER SUMMARY	
Will	slash to the hoop
Can't	shoot 50 percent
Expect	18-plus PPG
Don't Expect	L.A. contentment
Fantasy Value	$30-35
Card Value	5-12¢

COLLEGE STATISTICS

		G	FGP	FTP	RPG	PPG
82-83	MIA	28	.497	.674	7.0	12.9
83-84	MIA	30	.537	.570	7.6	14.9
84-85	MIA	31	.541	.661	10.7	24.9
85-86	MIA	31	.545	.665	11.7	24.4
Totals		120	.534	.642	9.3	19.5

NBA REGULAR-SEASON STATISTICS

		G	MIN	FGs FG	FGs PCT	3-PT FGs FG	3-PT FGs PCT	FTs FT	FTs PCT	Rebounds OFF	Rebounds TOT	AST	STL	BLK	PTS	PPG
86-87	CLE	82	3064	734	.455	20	.213	386	.684	169	392	394	209	84	1874	22.9
87-88	CLE	57	1830	340	.464	3	.150	196	.705	64	223	281	122	52	879	15.4
88-89	CLE	82	2851	587	.511	29	.250	323	.751	122	409	434	185	74	1526	18.6
89-90	CLE/LAC	35	1367	301	.473	14	.275	182	.788	74	206	182	81	41	798	22.8
90-91	LAC	39	1383	285	.391	48	.324	145	.668	58	188	209	66	35	763	19.6
91-92	LAC	82	3144	569	.440	64	.303	293	.736	120	447	417	152	72	1495	18.2
92-93	LAC	80	2970	542	.451	52	.280	307	.769	117	425	360	177	73	1443	18.0
Totals		457	16609	3358	.456	230	.278	1832	.728	724	2290	2277	992	431	8778	19.2

SCOTT HASTINGS

Team: Denver Nuggets
Position: Forward/Center
Height: 6'11" **Weight:** 245
Birthdate: June 3, 1960
NBA Experience: 11 years

College: Arkansas
Acquired: Traded from Pistons with a 1992 2nd-round pick for Orlando Woolridge, 8/91

Background: Hard to believe, but Hastings was once the second-leading career scorer at Arkansas behind Sidney Moncrief. In 11 NBA seasons—with New York, Atlanta, Miami, Detroit, and Denver—he has never averaged more than 5.1 PPG. He usually scores closer to a bucket a game, an average he maintained as a first-year Nugget in 1992-93.

Strengths: Hastings bangs on defense, knows his limitations, and keeps a great sense of humor. He can also get to the boards and is a decent free throw shooter. Mostly, Hastings is used when you need someone to give a few fouls and move a few people around.

Weaknesses: Scoring NBA points is something Hastings has never shown an ability to do, even though he has been considered an above-average outside shooter for a big man. He simply does not get many shots and he rarely looks for them. He has few ball skills and is not a great athlete.

Analysis: Hastings is an NBA novelty. He appeared on *Late Night with David Letterman* as an example of a marginal pro player and has racked up more laughs with his jokes than he has career points. Coaches and teammates love him, but not because of any great basketball skills.

PLAYER SUMMARY	
Will	hustle
Can't	light the scoreboard
Expect	loads of laughs
Don't Expect	loads of talent
Fantasy Value	$0
Card Value	5-10¢

COLLEGE STATISTICS

		G	FGP	FTP	RPG	PPG
78-79	ARK	30	.508	.730	4.6	8.3
79-80	ARK	29	.534	.781	6.7	16.2
80-81	ARK	32	.563	.735	5.4	16.3
81-82	ARK	29	.553	.740	6.0	18.6
Totals		120	.544	.748	5.7	14.8

NBA REGULAR-SEASON STATISTICS

		G	MIN	FGs FG	FGs PCT	3-PT FGs FG	3-PT FGs PCT	FTs FT	FTs PCT	Rebounds OFF	Rebounds TOT	AST	STL	BLK	PTS	PPG
82-83	NY/ATL	31	140	13	.342	0	.000	11	.550	15	41	3	6	1	37	1.2
83-84	ATL	68	1135	111	.468	1	.250	82	.788	96	270	46	40	36	305	4.5
84-85	ATL	64	825	89	.473	0	.000	63	.778	59	159	46	24	23	241	3.8
85-86	ATL	62	650	65	.409	3	.750	60	.857	44	124	26	14	8	193	3.1
86-87	ATL	40	256	23	.338	2	.167	23	.793	16	70	13	10	7	71	1.8
87-88	ATL	55	403	40	.488	5	.417	25	.926	27	97	16	8	10	110	2.0
88-89	MIA	75	1206	143	.436	9	.321	91	.850	72	231	59	32	42	386	5.1
89-90	DET	40	166	10	.303	3	.250	19	.864	7	32	8	3	3	42	1.0
90-91	DET	27	113	16	.571	3	.750	13	1.00	14	28	7	0	0	48	1.8
91-92	DEN	40	421	17	.340	0	.000	24	.857	30	98	26	10	15	58	1.5
92-93	DEN	76	670	57	.509	2	.250	40	.727	44	137	34	12	8	156	2.1
Totals		578	5985	584	.441	28	.292	451	.811	424	1287	284	159	153	1647	2.8

HERSEY HAWKINS

Team: Philadelphia 76ers
Position: Guard
Height: 6'3" **Weight:** 190
Birthdate: September 29, 1966
NBA Experience: 5 years

College: Bradley
Acquired: Draft rights traded from Clippers with a 1989 1st-round pick for draft rights to Charles Smith, 6/88

Background: Hawkins went from being a 6'3", all-city center at Westinghouse High School in Chicago to an outside gunner at Bradley. As a senior, he led the nation in scoring and was named a consensus All-American and the nation's Player of the Year. He left college as the fourth-leading scorer in NCAA history. He has finished among the NBA's top 25 in scoring in each of the last three years, has played in the All-Star Game, and is Philadelphia's all-time leader in 3-pointers made.

Strengths: Hawkins is one of the more dangerous 3-point shooters in the league. He can dishearten the opposition by landing his bombs in rapid succession and now gets to the hoop more often. He is close to automatic from the free throw line. Hawkins does not slack off on defense.

Weaknesses: Hawkins became Philadelphia's team leader when Charles Barkley was traded to Phoenix before the 1992-93 campaign. However, he is not the vocal type who can take charge of a locker room. There is not much wrong with his game on the floor, although he did not chalk up his usual number of steals last season.

Analysis: A silent killer, Hawkins was one of very few bright spots in a dismal post-Barkley season in Philadelphia last year. He lacks the charisma to fill Barkley's shoes, but he is well-liked for his ability to put the ball in the basket from virtually anywhere and his willingness to play hard.

PLAYER SUMMARY	
Will	knock down treys
Can't	replace Barkley
Expect	20 PPG
Don't Expect	a mean streak
Fantasy Value	$40-45
Card Value	10-15¢

COLLEGE STATISTICS

		G	FGP	FTP	RPG	PPG
84-85	BRAD	30	.581	.771	6.1	14.6
85-86	BRAD	35	.542	.768	5.7	18.7
86-87	BRAD	29	.533	.793	6.7	27.2
87-88	BRAD	31	.524	.848	7.8	36.3
Totals		125	.539	.806	6.5	24.1

NBA REGULAR-SEASON STATISTICS

				FGs		3-PT FGs		FTs		Rebounds						
		G	MIN	FG	PCT	FG	PCT	FT	PCT	OFF	TOT	AST	STL	BLK	PTS	PPG
88-89	PHI	79	2577	442	.455	71	.428	241	.831	51	225	239	120	37	1196	15.1
89-90	PHI	82	2856	522	.460	84	.420	387	.888	85	304	261	130	28	1515	18.5
90-91	PHI	80	3110	590	.472	108	.400	479	.871	48	310	299	178	39	1767	22.1
91-92	PHI	81	3013	521	.462	91	.397	403	.874	53	271	248	157	43	1536	19.0
92-93	PHI	81	2977	551	.470	122	.397	419	.860	91	346	317	137	30	1643	20.3
Totals		403	14533	2626	.464	476	.406	1929	.867	328	1456	1364	722	177	7657	19.0

STEVE HENSON

Team: Atlanta Hawks
Position: Guard
Height: 6'1" **Weight:** 180
Birthdate: February 2, 1968

NBA Experience: 3 years
College: Kansas St.
Acquired: Signed as a free agent, 12/92

Background: Henson left Kansas State as the only player to lead the Wildcats in scoring and assists two straight seasons. As a senior, he became the only Big Eight player to rank among the top ten in six different statistical categories. Though taken late in the 1990 draft, he made the Milwaukee roster and played in all but 14 games. He saw action in 50 games in his second year with the Bucks before putting in a similar stint with Atlanta last season. He made two starts for the Hawks and averaged about two buckets and three assists a game throughout the season.

Strengths: Absolutely fearless, Henson is willing to throw himself in the way of players twice his size. He'll body up to his man on defense and never stop hustling. He is a very good ball-handler and passer, with an assist-to-turnover ratio of better than 3-to-1. Henson is an accurate shooter with fine free throw and 3-point percentages.

Weaknesses: Henson is undersized, which would not be a huge drawback if he offered more speed. He is simply not quick enough to thrive on either end of the court against speedy point guards. He offers very little offensively inside the arc. In fact, about half of his field goals last season were 3-pointers.

Analysis: Henson appears to have a future as a back-up point guard. He does not currently have the all-around ability to make a living as a starter, but as a specialty player he can shoot from long range and provide heads-up defense. What will keep him in the league, however, is his never-back-down approach.

PLAYER SUMMARY

Will	handle the ball
Can't	race past defenders
Expect	tenacity
Don't Expect	scoring
Fantasy Value	$0
Card Value	5-8¢

COLLEGE STATISTICS

		G	FGP	FTP	APG	PPG
86-87	KSU	31	.395	.826	3.7	7.5
87-88	KSU	34	.429	.925	5.5	9.1
88-89	KSU	30	.465	.920	4.7	18.5
89-90	KSU	32	.446	.902	4.4	17.4
Totals		127	.442	.900	4.6	13.0

NBA REGULAR-SEASON STATISTICS

			FGs		3-PT FGs		FTs		Rebounds						
	G	MIN	FG	PCT	FG	PCT	FT	PCT	OFF	TOT	AST	STL	BLK	PTS	PPG
90-91 MIL	68	690	79	.418	18	.333	38	.905	14	51	131	32	0	214	3.1
91-92 MIL	50	386	52	.361	23	.479	23	.793	17	41	82	15	1	150	3.0
92-93 ATL	53	719	71	.390	37	.463	34	.850	12	55	155	30	1	213	4.0
Totals	171	1795	202	.392	78	.429	95	.856	43	147	368	77	2	577	3.4

CARL HERRERA

Team: Houston Rockets
Position: Forward
Height: 6'9" **Weight:** 220
Birthdate: December 14, 1966
NBA Experience: 2 years

College: Jacksonville; Houston
Acquired: Draft rights traded from Heat with draft rights to Dave Jamerson for draft rights to Alec Kessler, 6/90

Background: Born in Trinidad and raised in Venezuela, Herrera did not play basketball until the age of 13. He was noticed by colleges for his play as a 16-year-old point guard on the Venezuelan national team in the Pan-Am Games. He spent two years at Jacksonville (Texas) Junior College and then one at the University of Houston. He was drafted by Miami and had his rights traded to Houston, but he decided to play in Spain instead. The Rockets bought out his Spanish League contract and he saw NBA action in 43 games in 1991-92. He became a full-time player in 1992-93, earning an occasional start and scoring more than seven PPG.

Strengths: Herrera is a magnificent athlete who was a volleyball star as a teenager. It's not difficult to see what made him a standout in that sport—tremendous leaping ability. He also possesses a great pair of hands and above-average ball-handling skills. He can play both forward spots, gets up and down the floor like a guard, and converts a high percentage of his shots.

Weaknesses: Herrera played power forward overseas but has the body of an NBA small forward. His offensive range is not good, although he rarely ventures out of it for a shot. He is also a poor free throw shooter. You'll too often find him out of position on the defensive end.

Analysis: Herrera is still learning the game, but you have to be impressed with the progress he's made so far. His stints overseas and with the 1992 Venezuelan Olympic team have helped him refine his inside arsenal. More confidence on the perimeter would push him up a notch as an NBA player.

PLAYER SUMMARY

Will ....run the court
Can't...........................shoot 3-pointers
Expect ....a spark off the bench
Don't Expect.............perimeter punch
Fantasy Value.....................................$1
Card Value ....10-15¢

COLLEGE STATISTICS

		G	FGP	FTP	RPG	PPG
89-90	HOU	33	.565	.804	9.2	16.7
Totals		33	.565	.804	9.2	16.7

NBA REGULAR-SEASON STATISTICS

				FGs		3-PT FGs		FTs		Rebounds						
		G	MIN	FG	PCT	FG	PCT	FT	PCT	OFF	TOT	AST	STL	BLK	PTS	PPG
91-92	HOU	43	566	83	.516	0	.000	25	.568	33	99	27	16	25	191	4.4
92-93	HOU	81	1800	240	.541	0	.000	125	.710	148	454	61	47	35	605	7.5
Totals		124	2366	323	.534	0	.000	150	.682	181	553	88	63	60	796	6.4

ROD HIGGINS

Team: Sacramento Kings
Position: Forward
Height: 6'7" **Weight:** 210
Birthdate: January 31, 1960

NBA Experience: 11 years
College: Fresno St.
Acquired: Signed as a free agent, 11/92

Background: Higgins led Fresno State to consecutive conference championships, pacing the team in scoring in each of his final three years. He overcame his journeyman label in the NBA (he was with four different teams in 1985-86) by playing for six years with Golden State, but he missed all but 25 games of the 1991-92 campaign with a broken wrist and the Warriors let him go after the season. Sacramento picked him up and he averaged better than eight PPG during the 1992-93 season.

Strengths: Though he plays both forward spots and even filled in at center for Golden State, Higgins is at his best from 3-point land. He is second to Chris Mullin on the Warriors' career list of 3-pointers made. He's also a very good free throw shooter.

Weaknesses: Higgins prefers to catch and shoot; he is not a great threat off the dribble. He is also no defensive threat when matched up with power forwards and centers.

Analysis: Higgins is a consummate pro. Team first, Higgins second. His 3-point shooting can turn games around, and he will not hurt his club defensively unless he is dwarfed by his match-up. His versatility also makes him valuable.

PLAYER SUMMARY	
Will	play three positions
Can't	create
Expect	a great attitude
Don't Expect	rebounds
Fantasy Value	$1
Card Value	5-10¢

COLLEGE STATISTICS

		G	FGP	FTP	RPG	PPG
78-79	FSU	22	.516	.742	5.8	9.4
79-80	FSU	24	.506	.837	5.7	12.9
80-81	FSU	29	.558	.852	5.4	15.4
81-82	FSU	29	.531	.771	6.3	15.1
Totals		104	.532	.805	5.8	13.5

NBA REGULAR-SEASON STATISTICS

			FGs		3-PT FGs		FTs		Rebounds						
	G	MIN	FG	PCT	FG	PCT	FT	PCT	OFF	TOT	AST	STL	BLK	PTS	PPG
82-83 CHI	82	2196	313	.448	13	.317	209	.792	159	366	175	66	65	848	10.3
83-84 CHI	78	1577	193	.447	1	.045	113	.724	87	206	116	49	29	500	6.4
84-85 CHI	68	942	119	.441	10	.270	60	.667	55	147	73	21	13	308	4.5
85-86 SEA/SA/NJ/CHI	30	332	39	.368	1	.111	19	.704	14	51	24	9	11	98	3.3
86-87 GS	73	1497	214	.519	3	.176	200	.833	72	237	96	40	21	631	8.6
87-88 GS	68	2188	381	.526	19	.487	273	.848	94	293	188	70	31	1054	15.5
88-89 GS	81	1887	301	.476	66	.393	188	.821	111	376	160	39	42	856	10.6
89-90 GS	82	1993	304	.481	67	.347	234	.821	120	422	129	47	53	909	11.1
90-91 GS	82	2024	259	.463	73	.332	185	.819	109	354	113	52	37	776	9.5
91-92 GS	25	535	87	.412	33	.347	48	.814	30	85	22	15	13	255	10.2
92-93 SAC	69	1425	199	.412	43	.323	130	.861	66	193	119	51	29	571	8.3
Totals	738	16596	2409	.467	329	.338	1659	.810	917	2730	1215	459	344	6806	9.2

TYRONE HILL

Team: Cleveland Cavaliers
Position: Forward
Height: 6'9" **Weight:** 243
Birthdate: March 17, 1968

NBA Experience: 3 years
College: Xavier (OH)
Acquired: Signed as a free agent, 7/93

Background: Hill joined an exclusive group of 62 college players to score 2,000 points and grab 1,000 rebounds in a career. He ranked third in the NCAA in rebounding as a senior at Xavier and second as a junior. He led Golden State in offensive rebounds as a rookie, in defensive boards during his second year, and in both categories last year. He finished among the top 20 rebounders in the league during the 1992-93 campaign. After the season, he signed as a free agent with Cleveland.

Strengths: Rebounding has always been Hill's forte, and he has shown he can dominate the glass at the NBA level. He has a muscular body and uses it to get inside position. You don't grab ten boards a game without great instincts, leaping ability, and hard work. Hill is an improving defender and can score on the low blocks. He also picks up points running the floor.

Weaknesses: Hill will never be a huge offensive player with the low-post arsenal he owns now. His repertoire of moves is a combination between the mechanical and predictable. He's most effective on put-backs. Hill is a poor outside shooter and is particularly ineffective from the free throw line. He led the league in fouls two years ago and was among the leaders last year as well. He averaged a whistle every 6½ minutes.

Analysis: Hill can be favorably compared to Dennis Rodman and Larry Smith. Like those two veterans, he plays physical, can dominate games with his rebounding, and is of little help on the offensive end. Hill is not the defender Rodman and Smith are, but he does have that potential.

PLAYER SUMMARY	
Will	clean the glass
Can't	shoot FTs
Expect	workmanlike approach
Don't Expect	perimeter points
Fantasy Value	$2-4
Card Value	8-15¢

COLLEGE STATISTICS

		G	FGP	FTP	RPG	PPG
86-87	XAV	31	.552	.672	8.4	8.8
87-88	XAV	30	.557	.745	10.5	15.3
88-89	XAV	33	.606	.701	12.2	18.9
89-90	XAV	32	.581	.658	12.6	20.2
Totals		126	.579	.692	11.0	15.9

NBA REGULAR-SEASON STATISTICS

				FGs		3-PT FGs		FTs		Rebounds						
		G	MIN	FG	PCT	FG	PCT	FT	PCT	OFF	TOT	AST	STL	BLK	PTS	PPG
90-91	GS	74	1192	147	.492	0	.000	96	.632	157	383	19	33	30	390	5.3
91-92	GS	82	1886	254	.522	0	.000	163	.694	182	593	47	73	43	671	8.2
92-93	GS	74	2070	251	.508	0	.000	138	.624	255	754	68	41	40	640	8.6
Totals		230	5148	652	.509	0	.000	397	.653	594	1730	134	147	113	1701	7.4

DONALD HODGE

Team: Dallas Mavericks
Position: Center
Height: 7'0" **Weight:** 240
Birthdate: February 25, 1969

NBA Experience: 2 years
College: Temple
Acquired: 2nd-round pick in 1991 draft (33rd overall)

Background: Hodge had a brief college career at Temple. He sat out his freshman year because of Prop 48 restrictions and forfeited his senior year to enter the NBA draft. As a sophomore, he led the Owls in rebounding and field goal percentage, and he scored 31 points against eventual NCAA champion UNLV. He had a sub-par junior year before being chosen by Dallas in the second round. Hodge played in each of the final 41 games as a rookie and in more games than any other Maverick last season.

Strengths: Hodge has excellent size and, some say, the kind of skills required to be an effective NBA post player. He has great hands, a soft touch around the basket, and a nice feel for the game. His range is better than expected—good enough to surprise some of the better pivots in the league as a rookie. He passes and runs the floor well for a big man.

Weaknesses: There is virtually no power in Hodge's game. He's a finesse player in all respects. He lacks the bulk to be considered a potentially dominant rebounder, although he has shown flashes of promise on the offensive glass. Defensively, he has a long way to go. After a strong rookie year from the field, his shooting was atrocious in 1992-93. He's a poor free throw shooter too.

Analysis: Hodge had a surprising finish to his rookie year, but last season he seemed to revert to the form that got him labeled a project coming into the league. What he really needs is a stronger body that he can use to challenge his opponents rather than trying to get too cute with the ball. He does have some talent and will be given the chance to manifest it.

PLAYER SUMMARY

Will	display touch
Can't	play tough defense
Expect	too much finesse
Don't Expect	power
Fantasy Value	$1
Card Value	8-15¢

COLLEGE STATISTICS

		G	FGP	FTP	RPG	PPG
89-90	TEMP	31	.541	.713	8.2	15.1
90-91	TEMP	34	.535	.716	6.9	11.6
Totals		65	.538	.714	7.5	13.3

NBA REGULAR-SEASON STATISTICS

		G	MIN	FG	PCT	FG	PCT	FT	PCT	OFF	TOT	AST	STL	BLK	PTS	PPG
91-92	DAL	51	1058	163	.497	0	.000	100	.667	118	275	39	25	23	426	8.4
92-93	DAL	79	1267	161	.403	0	.000	71	.683	93	294	75	33	37	393	5.0
Totals		130	2325	324	.445	0	.000	171	.673	211	569	114	58	60	819	6.3

JEFF HORNACEK

Team: Philadelphia 76ers
Position: Guard
Height: 6'4" **Weight:** 190
Birthdate: May 3, 1963
NBA Experience: 7 years

College: Iowa St.
Acquired: Traded from Suns with Tim Perry and Andrew Lang for Charles Barkley, 6/92

Background: Hornacek walked on at Iowa State, earned a scholarship, and wound up setting a Big Eight career assist record with 665. His pro career has evolved in a similar pattern—from unheralded to highly respected. He increased his scoring average each year through 1989-90, and he led the Suns in 1991-92 with 20.1 PPG. He earned a spot in the 1992 All-Star Game. Hornacek was traded to the 76ers before the 1992-93 campaign and he did not fare as well with his new team. His shooting percentage was the worst since his rookie year.

Strengths: A dead-eye gunner, Hornacek will kill you if you leave him open from anywhere on the court—inside or outside the 3-point line. He makes few mistakes, is good with both hands, and approaches the game with a great work ethic. He can handle both guard spots.

Weaknesses: The fact that Hornacek is not a great athlete has not stopped him from achieving at every level. As mentioned, he did not shoot as well last year as in previous seasons.

Analysis: A coach's son, Hornacek has a thorough understanding of the game and plays it at a very high level. That's why he will not settle for years like last season, when he fell out of the league's top ten in 3-point shooting and could not carry the 76ers to many wins. It would have been a nice year for a lot of players, but Hornacek expects better.

PLAYER SUMMARY

Will ....knock down treys
Can't ....carry 76ers alone
Expect ....return to form
Don't Expect ....dunks
Fantasy Value.........................$35-40
Card Value...................................5-12¢

COLLEGE STATISTICS

		G	FGP	FTP	RPG	PPG
82-83	ISU	27	.422	.711	2.3	5.4
83-84	ISU	29	.500	.790	3.5	10.0
84-85	ISU	34	.521	.844	3.6	12.5
85-86	ISU	33	.478	.776	3.8	13.7
Totals		123	.489	.790	3.3	10.7

NBA REGULAR-SEASON STATISTICS

				FGs		3-PT FGs		FTs		Rebounds						
		G	MIN	FG	PCT	FG	PCT	FT	PCT	OFF	TOT	AST	STL	BLK	PTS	PPG
86-87	PHO	80	1561	159	.454	12	.279	94	.777	41	184	361	70	5	424	5.3
87-88	PHO	82	2243	306	.506	17	.293	152	.822	71	262	540	107	10	781	9.5
88-89	PHO	78	2487	440	.495	27	.333	147	.826	75	266	465	129	8	1054	13.5
89-90	PHO	67	2278	483	.536	40	.408	173	.856	86	313	337	117	14	1179	17.6
90-91	PHO	80	2733	544	.518	61	.418	201	.897	74	321	409	111	16	1350	16.9
91-92	PHO	81	3078	635	.512	83	.439	279	.886	106	407	411	158	31	1632	20.1
92-93	PHI	79	2860	582	.470	97	.390	250	.865	84	342	548	131	21	1511	19.1
Totals		547	17240	3149	.502	337	.390	1296	.856	537	2095	3071	823	105	7931	14.5

ROBERT HORRY

Team: Houston Rockets
Position: Forward
Height: 6'9" **Weight:** 220
Birthdate: August 25, 1970

NBA Experience: 1 year
College: Alabama
Acquired: 1st-round pick in 1992 draft
(11th overall)

Background: Named Alabama prep Player of the Year at Andalusia High, Horry stayed at home to play his college ball with the Crimson Tide. He helped the Tide to the final 16 of the NCAA Tournament in 1990 and 1991 and finished his career as the all-time school leader in blocked shots. He was also among the top ten scorers and rebounders. Horry, the 11th pick overall in the 1992 draft, signed a five-year contract with Houston and started 79 games as a rookie. He finished among the top first-year players with 10.1 PPG and 83 blocked shots.

Strengths: Horry is a splendid athlete who loves to challenge shots. In addition to being All-SEC in college, he also made the all-league defensive team and has brought his nose for the ball and strong rebounding to the pros. He's also an accomplished scorer who creates his own shots and has a quick first step. His rookie field goal percentage was above average and he even dropped in a dozen 3-pointers. He oozes confidence.

Weaknesses: Horry turns the ball over about twice a game, not a great average for a small forward. His ball-handling in the open court could stand some shoring up and the Rockets will work on making him a more consistent player. Tendinitis in his right knee slowed him at times.

Analysis: How talented is Horry? Talented enough to be the starting small forward from Day One on a team that won the Midwest and set a franchise record for victories. It has been said that with better ball-handling, Horry can become another Scottie Pippen. That might not be far from the mark, as there are no other glaring deficiencies in his game.

PLAYER SUMMARY	
Will	challenge shots
Can't	handle like Pippen
Expect	rave reviews
Don't Expect	bench time
Fantasy Value	$10-13
Card Value	25-75¢

COLLEGE STATISTICS

		G	FGP	FTP	RPG	PPG
88-89	ALA	31	.427	.644	5.0	6.5
89-90	ALA	35	.467	.760	6.2	13.1
90-91	ALA	32	.449	.804	8.1	11.9
91-92	ALA	35	.470	.727	8.5	15.8
Totals		133	.458	.742	7.0	12.0

NBA REGULAR-SEASON STATISTICS

	G	MIN	FGs FG	PCT	3-PT FGs FG	PCT	FTs FT	PCT	Rebounds OFF	TOT	AST	STL	BLK	PTS	PPG
92-93 HOU	79	2330	323	.474	12	.255	143	.715	113	392	191	80	83	801	10.1
Totals	79	2330	323	.474	12	.255	143	.715	113	392	191	80	83	801	10.1

BYRON HOUSTON

Team: Golden State Warriors
Position: Forward
Height: 6'5" **Weight:** 250
Birthdate: November 22, 1969
NBA Experience: 1 year
College: Oklahoma St.

Acquired: Traded from Bulls in three-team deal; Warriors sent a conditional 1993 1st-round pick to Mavericks, and Mavericks sent Rodney McCray to Bulls, 9/92

Background: Houston was a force at Oklahoma State, finishing his career as the school's all-time leader in nine statistical categories, including scoring, rebounding, and blocked shots. The All-America forward joined Danny Manning and Wayman Tisdale as the only Big Eight players to total over 2,000 points, 1,000 rebounds, and 200 blocked shots in a career. He was plucked 27th overall in the 1992 draft by Chicago, then traded to Golden State in a three-way deal that sent Rodney McCray to the Bulls. He played in all but three games as a rookie and was the Warriors' No. 2 rebounder.

Strengths: Owner of a body that's been sculpted in the weight room, Houston is extremely strong. He is not afraid to bump and bruise and usually comes out on the better end of such physical play. Houston also possesses good quickness and is a great rebounder considering his height. In that sense, he has been compared to Charles Barkley.

Weaknesses: That whistle you hear is a referee nailing Houston for yet another personal foul. He was among the most guilty foulers in the league in his first season, getting disqualified from a whopping 12 games. He needs to learn about getting position with his feet rather than his frame. Houston is not nearly the scorer he was at the college level. He needs to develop a reliable jump shot.

Analysis: Houston has a long way to go before he can be compared to Barkley or Larry Johnson. Yes, he's physical. No, he does not possess their ability to score. Still, Houston was of big help to a Golden State team decimated by injuries last season. Better control will help keep the refs off his back.

PLAYER SUMMARY	
Will	throw weight around
Can't	avoid whistles
Expect	rebounding
Don't Expect	lots of scoring
Fantasy Value	$1
Card Value	10-20¢

COLLEGE STATISTICS

		G	FGP	FTP	RPG	PPG
88-89	OSU	30	.583	.745	8.4	13.0
89-90	OSU	31	.528	.731	10.0	18.5
90-91	OSU	32	.573	.743	10.5	22.7
91-92	OSU	34	.533	.700	8.6	20.2
Totals		127	.552	.729	9.4	18.7

NBA REGULAR-SEASON STATISTICS

			FGs		3-PT FGs		FTs		Rebounds					
	G	MIN	FG	PCT	FG	PCT	FT	PCT	OFF	TOT	AST	STL	BLK	PTS	PPG
92-93 GS	79	1274	145	.446	2	.286	129	.665	119	315	69	44	43	421	5.3
Totals	79	1274	145	.446	2	.286	129	.665	119	315	69	44	43	421	5.3

BRIAN HOWARD

Team: Dallas Mavericks
Position: Forward
Height: 6'6" **Weight:** 204
Birthdate: October 19, 1967

NBA Experience: 2 years
College: North Carolina St.
Acquired: Signed as a free agent, 2/92

Background: Howard was overshadowed by the likes of Rodney Monroe, Chris Corchiani, and Tom Gugliotta as a three-year starter at North Carolina State, averaging a career-best 13.0 PPG with 5.1 RPG as a senior. Undrafted, he began his pro career with Omaha of the CBA. He played for the Racers for a year and a half, averaging 20.8 PPG and 6.8 RPG during 1990-91. Dallas signed him in February 1992 and Howard averaged 4.9 PPG in 27 NBA games. He scored at a 6.5-PPG pace in 68 games in 1992-93, his first full season with the Mavericks.

Strengths: With Howard, the Mavericks gain versatility, defense, and basketball smarts. He plays small forward but can fill in at big guard in a pinch. He'll knock down jumpers if you leave him open. He rebounds and works hard at the defensive end. He plays within his limitations.

Weaknesses: Howard does nothing well enough to stand out at the NBA level. He's inconsistent from the perimeter and too small to muscle for points inside. His ball-handling and passing are way below average. He turns the ball over more often than he gets an assist. Howard also draws a lot of whistles. He fouled out eight times in 68 games last season.

Analysis: Howard is another example of a borderline NBA/CBA player, the type that found playing time in Dallas last season. He even made 22 starts before a strained calf muscle put him on the injured list for most of March. The Mavs first signed him when Fat Lever went on the injured list and they simply have not had enough talent since then to let him go.

PLAYER SUMMARY	
Will	play within himself
Can't	avoid fouling
Expect	defense
Don't Expect	much scoring
Fantasy Value	$0
Card Value	8-15¢

COLLEGE STATISTICS

		G	FGP	FTP	RPG	PPG
86-87	NCST	18	.357	.750	0.5	0.7
87-88	NCST	32	.492	.768	3.4	7.6
88-89	NCST	31	.523	.716	5.4	12.5
89-90	NCST	30	.461	.714	5.1	13.0
Totals		111	.489	.732	4.0	9.3

NBA REGULAR-SEASON STATISTICS

				FGs		3-PT FGs		FTs		Rebounds					
		G	MIN	FG	PCT	FG	PCT	FT	PCT	OFF	TOT	AST	STL	BLK	PTS	PPG
91-92	DAL	27	318	54	.519	1	.500	22	.710	17	51	14	11	8	131	4.9
92-93	DAL	68	1295	183	.442	1	.143	72	.766	66	212	67	55	34	439	6.5
Totals		95	1613	237	.458	2	.222	94	.752	83	263	81	66	42	570	6.0

JAY HUMPHRIES

Team: Utah Jazz
Position: Guard
Height: 6'3" **Weight:** 195
Birthdate: October 17, 1962
NBA Experience: 9 years

College: Colorado
Acquired: Traded from Bucks with
Larry Krystkowiak for Blue Edwards,
Eric Murdock, and a 1992 1st-round
pick, 6/92

Background: An All-Big Eight selection as a senior at Colorado, Humphries set
16 school records, including career assists, steals, and games played. He was
originally drafted by Phoenix, where he started all 82 games in his second and
third seasons. A 1988 trade brought him to Milwaukee, and he led the Bucks in
assists in his last three seasons there. He was dealt to Utah before the 1992-93
campaign and spent most of the year as a third guard.

Strengths: Humphries brought versatility to the Jazz in that he could back up
both John Stockton at the point and Jeff Malone at shooting guard. His all-around
abilities include scoring, handling the ball, solid passing, and above-average
defense. He's good with both hands. He was once Milwaukee's captain.

Weaknesses: Humphries lacks the creativity of the league's more spectacular
playmakers and does not shoot consistently enough to be a top-tier shooting
guard. He tends to play conservatively and is no threat from 3-point range.

Analysis: Last year was the first since his rookie season in which Humphries
scored less than ten PPG. However, it was also the first in a while in which he did
not start regularly. The Jazz expected Humphries to help push them over the top.
The plan didn't quite work out.

PLAYER SUMMARY	
Will	find open men
Can't	do the spectacular
Expect	versatility
Don't Expect	risk-taking
Fantasy Value	$1-3
Card Value	5-10¢

COLLEGE STATISTICS

		G	FGP	FTP	APG	PPG
80-81	COLO	28	.517	.660	3.5	6.4
81-82	COLO	27	.467	.639	4.3	10.3
82-83	COLO	28	.501	.632	6.2	14.3
83-84	COLO	29	.509	.788	6.0	15.4
Totals		112	.498	.696	5.0	11.7

NBA REGULAR-SEASON STATISTICS

				FGs		3-PT FGs		FTs		Rebounds						
		G	MIN	FG	PCT	FG	PCT	FT	PCT	OFF	TOT	AST	STL	BLK	PTS	PPG
84-85	PHO	80	2062	279	.446	4	.200	141	.829	32	164	350	107	8	703	8.8
85-86	PHO	82	2733	352	.479	4	.138	197	.767	56	260	526	132	9	905	11.0
86-87	PHO	82	2579	359	.477	5	.185	200	.769	62	260	632	112	9	923	11.3
87-88	PHO/MIL	68	1809	284	.528	3	.167	112	.732	49	174	395	81	5	683	10.0
88-89	MIL	73	2220	345	.483	25	.266	129	.816	70	189	405	142	5	844	11.6
89-90	MIL	81	2818	496	.494	21	.300	224	.786	80	269	472	156	11	1237	15.3
90-91	MIL	80	2726	482	.502	60	.373	191	.799	57	220	538	129	7	1215	15.2
91-92	MIL	71	2261	377	.469	42	.292	195	.783	44	184	466	119	13	991	14.0
92-93	UTA	78	2034	287	.436	15	.200	101	.777	40	143	317	101	11	690	8.8
Totals		695	21242	3261	.480	179	.281	1490	.784	490	1863	4101	1079	78	8191	11.8

MIKE IUZZOLINO

Team: Dallas Mavericks
Position: Guard
Height: 5'11" **Weight:** 176
Birthdate: January 22, 1968

NBA Experience: 2 years
College: Penn St.; St. Francis (PA)
Acquired: 2nd-round pick in 1991 draft (35th overall)

Background: Iuzzolino transferred from Penn State to St. Francis and became a star. As a senior, he finished in the top six nationally in free throw shooting and 3-point field goal percentage and led the Red Flash to the NCAA Tournament. A second-round draft choice, he worked his way into the Mavericks' rotation as a rookie. During each of his two pro seasons, he has started more than 20 games and finished among the team's top two in assist average and top three in 3-pointers made.

Strengths: Iuzzolino has been described as a "thinking man's guard" and a "coach's player," but he has been a lot more to a dismal Dallas club. He is a very good spot-up shooter, has great range, is steady from the stripe, and will find open men off penetration. He's what many call a pure point guard. His reputation as a court-smart, hard-nosed player has been well earned.

Weaknesses: Anything in the category of "natural athletic skills" falls in here. Iuzzolino is slow and short, with average quickness at best. He's not the kind of point guard who's going to take Tim Hardaway or Kevin Johnson to school. While he makes nice passes and chalks up assists, he is also prone to turning the ball over when pressured.

Analysis: Some thought Iuzzolino wouldn't make it in the NBA, but he has ended up being a valuable reserve and part-time starter on a club severely lacking in talent. He performed admirably as a starter last year while Derek Harper was injured. No, Iuzzolino would not play nearly as many minutes with a better team; however, he has done quite well with the time given to him.

PLAYER SUMMARY

Will......................spot up for 3's
Can't................save the Mavericks
Expect........................fine passing
Don't Expect......................quickness
Fantasy Value...............................$1
Card Value............................5-10¢

COLLEGE STATISTICS

		G	FGP	FTP	APG	PPG
86-87	PSU	27	.283	.854	1.1	2.4
87-88	PSU	26	.473	.895	1.2	3.2
89-90	STF	27	.552	.871	4.8	21.3
90-91	STF	32	.542	.885	4.0	24.1
Totals		112	.527	.877	2.8	13.3

NBA REGULAR-SEASON STATISTICS

		G	MIN	FGs FG	FGs PCT	3-PT FGs FG	3-PT FGs PCT	FTs FT	FTs PCT	Rebounds OFF	Rebounds TOT	AST	STL	BLK	PTS	PPG
91-92	DAL	52	1280	160	.451	59	.434	107	.836	27	98	194	33	1	486	9.3
92-93	DAL	70	1769	221	.462	54	.375	114	.765	31	140	328	49	6	610	8.7
Totals		122	3049	381	.457	113	.404	221	.798	58	238	522	82	7	1096	9.0

CHRIS JACKSON

Team: Denver Nuggets
Position: Guard
Height: 6'1" **Weight:** 168
Birthdate: March 9, 1969

NBA Experience: 3 years
College: Louisiana St.
Acquired: 1st-round pick in 1990 draft
(3rd overall)

Background: In two seasons at LSU, Jackson accomplished things most four-year players will never approach. He broke three NCAA freshman records: most points in a game against a Division I opponent (55), most in a season (965), and highest scoring average (30.2 PPG). Jackson's first pro season was cut short by foot surgery, and his second saw him used primarily in a reserve role. In 1992-93, he became an NBA star by leading the Nuggets in scoring and assists and finishing second in the league in free throw percentage. Over the summer, he announced he would officially change his name—to Mahmoud Abdul Rauf—in time for this season.

Strengths: A great athlete who is extremely quick, Jackson is blessed with big-time talent. He can score by getting to the hoop, with his long-range shooting, or in the open court. He does not use strings, but somehow the ball is attached to Jackson's hand. He has a nifty crossover dribble and an extremely quick release on his shot, which he creates on his own. Only Mark Price shot better from the line last year.

Weaknesses: The knock on Jackson is that he's a two guard in a point guard's body. He does not get teammates involved like the great point guards in the league. Jackson has never made a living on the defensive end.

Analysis: Jackson, who has a neurological disorder called Tourette's Syndrome, won the NBA's Most Improved Player Award last season. He displayed a much higher level of dedication, which helped him shake some of his many detractors. After two shaky seasons, Jackson has indeed converted his high-scoring college talents to the professional ranks.

PLAYER SUMMARY

Will ....create his shots
Can't ....star on defense
Expect ....open-court scoring
Don't Expect ....10 APG
Fantasy Value...........................$11-14
Card Value ....15-25¢

COLLEGE STATISTICS

		G	FGP	FTP	APG	PPG
88-89	LSU	32	.486	.815	4.1	30.2
89-90	LSU	32	.461	.910	3.2	27.8
Totals		64	.474	.863	3.6	29.0

NBA REGULAR-SEASON STATISTICS

		G	MIN	FGs FG	FGs PCT	3-PT FGs FG	3-PT FGs PCT	FTs FT	FTs PCT	Rebounds OFF	Rebounds TOT	AST	STL	BLK	PTS	PPG
90-91	DEN	67	1505	417	.413	24	.240	84	.857	34	121	206	55	4	942	14.1
91-92	DEN	81	1538	356	.421	31	.330	94	.870	22	114	192	44	4	837	10.3
92-93	DEN	81	2710	633	.450	70	.355	217	.935	51	225	344	84	8	1553	19.2
Totals		229	5753	1406	.431	125	.320	395	.902	107	460	742	183	16	3332	14.6

JIM JACKSON

Team: Dallas Mavericks
Position: Guard
Height: 6'6" **Weight:** 220
Birthdate: October 14, 1970

NBA Experience: 1 year
College: Ohio St.
Acquired: 1st-round pick in 1992 draft
(4th overall)

Background: A rare two-time Mr. Basketball in Ohio, Jackson led Toledo Macomber to a state championship as a senior. He started all 93 games the Buckeyes played in his three years at Ohio State. Jackson was named Big Ten Freshman of the Year and was a consensus All-American as a junior. He finished his career fifth on the all-time Buckeye scoring list despite bypassing his senior season. The fourth player taken in the 1992 draft, he went through a bitter contract holdout with Dallas before finally signing in early March. He made an instant impact, averaging 16.3 PPG while starting all 28 games.

Strengths: Jackson is a tremendous talent. He has big-time scoring potential with the ability to post up, drive to the hoop, or hit from the perimeter. He's also the kind of player who can make those around him look better, which is quite a feat with the Mavericks. His passing skills are highly advanced. Jackson's a gym rat who keeps himself in first-rate condition. The prolonged holdout did not dampen his impact.

Weaknesses: Jackson often tried to do too much with the ball during his shortened rookie season. He managed to turn it over a staggering 115 times in 28 games. He also encountered Rookie Shooting Syndrome, finishing below the 40-percent mark from the field.

Analysis: Jackson would have been a shoo-in for the All-Rookie Team had he played a full season. However, holding out for more than half the year did not hurt him as much as it would have hurt other rookies, thanks to his conditioning and the current state of the lowly Mavericks. He's a future star and already a franchise player.

PLAYER SUMMARY	
Will	lead the Mavs
Can't	do it all himself
Expect	a franchise player
Don't Expect	a quick title
Fantasy Value	$18-21
Card Value	50¢-$2.00

COLLEGE STATISTICS

		G	FGP	FTP	RPG	PPG
89-90	OSU	30	.499	.785	5.5	16.1
90-91	OSU	31	.517	.752	5.5	18.9
91-92	OSU	32	.493	.811	6.8	22.4
Totals		93	.503	.784	5.9	19.2

NBA REGULAR-SEASON STATISTICS

		G	MIN	FGs FG	FGs PCT	3-PT FGs FG	3-PT FGs PCT	FTs FT	FTs PCT	Rebounds OFF	Rebounds TOT	AST	STL	BLK	PTS	PPG
92-93	DAL	28	938	184	.395	21	.288	68	.739	42	122	131	40	11	457	16.3
Totals		28	938	184	.395	21	.288	68	.739	42	122	131	40	11	457	16.3

MARK JACKSON

Team: Los Angeles Clippers
Position: Guard
Height: 6'3" **Weight:** 185
Birthdate: April 1, 1965
NBA Experience: 6 years

College: St. John's
Acquired: Traded from Knicks in three-team deal, 9/92 (see page 543 for details)

Background: Jackson was a second-team All-American as a senior at St. John's and finished his career with the school's all-time assists record. He earned the unanimous vote for NBA Rookie of the Year in 1987-88 and won a trip to the All-Star Game the following season. With a dismal effort in 1989-90, however, he lost his starting job. Knicks coach Pat Riley placed the controls back in Jackson's hands in 1991-92 and he was sixth in the league in assist average. The Clippers traded for him and Jackson finished fourth in the league with 8.8 APG in 1992-93.

Strengths: Jackson is an explosive playmaker with big-time penetrating ability. He cuts through the lane and can either find the open man or make acrobatic shots. His court vision is superb. He's a good outside shooter and is capable of dropping in 3-pointers. Jackson thrives in transition, and he is also a fine free throw shooter.

Weaknesses: During his roller-coaster NBA history, the down times have been largely mental. His play deteriorated when fans in New York got on him and he was once suspended by the Knicks for constant criticism of the organization. On the court, defense is clearly Jackson's biggest weakness.

Analysis: The one-time "point guard of the future" for the Knicks is now the point guard of the present and near future in L.A. The Clippers were so impressed, they signed him to a five-year contract extension last season. Jackson was an effective leader and the only Clipper who saw action in all 82 games.

PLAYER SUMMARY	
Will	slice through traffic
Can't	be a stopper
Expect	assists, scoring
Don't Expect	much bench time
Fantasy Value	$20-23
Card Value	5-12¢

COLLEGE STATISTICS

		G	FGP	FTP	APG	PPG
83-84	STJ	30	.575	.688	3.6	5.8
84-85	STJ	35	.564	.725	3.1	5.1
85-86	STJ	36	.478	.739	9.1	11.3
86-87	STJ	30	.504	.806	6.4	18.9
Totals		131	.510	.751	5.6	10.1

NBA REGULAR-SEASON STATISTICS

		G	MIN	FGs FG	FGs PCT	3-PT FGs FG	3-PT FGs PCT	FTs FT	FTs PCT	Rebounds OFF	Rebounds TOT	AST	STL	BLK	PTS	PPG
87-88	NY	82	3249	438	.432	32	.254	206	.774	120	396	868	205	6	1114	13.6
88-89	NY	72	2477	479	.467	81	.338	180	.698	106	341	619	139	7	1219	16.9
89-90	NY	82	2428	327	.437	35	.267	120	.727	106	318	604	109	4	809	9.9
90-91	NY	72	1595	250	.492	13	.255	117	.731	62	197	452	60	9	630	8.8
91-92	NY	81	2461	367	.491	11	.256	171	.770	95	305	694	112	13	916	11.3
92-93	LAC	82	3117	459	.486	22	.268	241	.803	129	388	724	136	12	1181	14.4
Totals		471	15327	2320	.465	194	.288	1035	.755	618	1945	3961	761	51	5869	12.5

KEITH JENNINGS

Team: Golden State Warriors
Position: Guard
Height: 5'7" **Weight:** 160
Birthdate: November 2, 1968

NBA Experience: 1 year
College: East Tennessee St.
Acquired: Signed as a free agent, 7/92

Background: Nicknamed "Mister," Jennings was well-known during his college career for more than his 5'7" height. He was named Southern Conference Most Valuable Player as a junior and senior at East Tennessee State. Jennings finished his career as the all-time NCAA leader in 3-point percentage (.493) and finished second in career assists. Despite being voted the best college player in the country under six feet, he went undrafted and spent the 1991-92 season playing in Germany. Golden State signed him as a free agent but major surgery on his right knee after just eight games ended his rookie campaign.

Strengths: Jennings is quick as lightning and the ball is attached to his hand. He's creative with his passing and can also get through the trees himself. He brings a scoring mentality to the point-guard position. In just eight NBA games, he has already posted a 22-point outing. Jennings is a fantastic college shooter and has NBA 3-point range. He's also an accurate free throw shooter, finishing fourth in the country as a senior.

Weaknesses: Size is the obvious drawback, and it's the main reason Jennings was bypassed by everyone in the 1991 draft. Opponents can post him up and shoot over him at will. He's not a high-flying, dunker type like Spud Webb. For all his quickness, Jennings is more of a scorer than a disruptive defender.

Analysis: Jennings played only eight NBA games, but in them he showed the potential to be the league's newest talented little man. He averaged 8.6 PPG, made five of his nine 3-point attempts, and shot nearly 60 percent from the field in his first taste of the big leagues. Assuming his knee is fully healed, he has the look of a contributing reserve.

PLAYER SUMMARY

Will.............................shoot with range
Can't..................................block shots
Expect........................great quickness
Don't Expect ....dunks
Fantasy Value.................................$1
Card Value.............................8-15¢

COLLEGE STATISTICS

		G	FGP	FTP	APG	PPG
87-88	ETST	29	.489	.826	6.3	12.9
88-89	ETST	31	.510	.847	6.5	14.5
89-90	ETST	34	.575	.877	8.7	14.8
90-91	ETST	33	.596	.895	9.1	20.1
Totals		127	.549	.861	7.7	15.7

NBA REGULAR-SEASON STATISTICS

		G	MIN	FG	PCT	FG	PCT	FT	PCT	OFF	TOT	AST	STL	BLK	PTS	PPG
92-93	GS	8	136	25	.595	5	.556	14	.778	2	11	23	4	0	69	8.6
Totals		8	136	25	.595	5	.556	14	.778	2	11	23	4	0	69	8.6

AVERY JOHNSON

Team: San Antonio Spurs
Position: Guard
Height: 5'11" **Weight:** 175
Birthdate: March 25, 1965

NBA Experience: 5 years
College: Cameron; Southern
Acquired: Signed as a free agent, 11/92

Background: Johnson led the nation in assists as a junior and senior at Southern University, where he was a two-time Southwestern Athletic Conference Player of the Year. He was not drafted, but he latched on in Seattle as a free agent and played two years there. In 1990-91, he played for both Denver and San Antonio, and in 1991-92 he suited up with San Antonio and Houston. The Spurs signed him back early last season and he wound up starting more than half of their games. Avery is the younger brother of Vinnie Johnson.

Strengths: A pure point guard, Johnson covers the court like a pinball. His quickness allows him to penetrate and show off his crafty passing skills. A willing distributor, he has a knack for finding the open man and he sees the court better than most. For his small stature, Johnson displays the toughness and leadership coaches love.

Weaknesses: The younger Johnson is not the scoring and shooting machine his older brother once was for the Pistons. Avery prefers creating to finishing, although he averaged a career-high 8.7 PPG in 1992-93 and shot better than 50 percent for the first time. While his fullcourt defense can be disruptive, he's not a defensive stopper.

Analysis: For a guy who's been cut as often as Johnson, he sure proved to be a difference-maker last year in San Antonio. David Robinson reportedly convinced coach Jerry Tarkanian to sign him, and Johnson wound up being the catalyst when the Spurs made a remarkable turnaround after John Lucas took over.

PLAYER SUMMARY	
Will	distribute
Can't	score like Vinnie
Expect	fine playmaking
Don't Expect	10 PPG
Fantasy Value	$3-5
Card Value	5-10¢

COLLEGE STATISTICS

		G	FGP	FTP	APG	PPG
84-85	CAM	33	.509	.618	3.2	4.3
86-87	SU	31	.439	.615	10.7	7.1
87-88	SU	30	.537	.688	13.3	11.4
Totals		94	.497	.641	8.9	7.5

NBA REGULAR-SEASON STATISTICS

		G	MIN	FGs FG	FGs PCT	3-PT FGs FG	3-PT FGs PCT	FTs FT	FTs PCT	Rebounds OFF	Rebounds TOT	AST	STL	BLK	PTS	PPG
88-89	SEA	43	291	29	.349	1	.111	9	.563	11	24	73	21	3	68	1.6
89-90	SEA	53	575	55	.387	1	.250	29	.725	21	43	162	26	1	140	2.6
90-91	DEN/SA	68	959	130	.469	1	.111	59	.678	22	77	230	47	4	320	4.7
91-92	SA/HOU	69	1235	158	.479	4	.267	66	.653	13	80	266	61	9	386	5.6
92-93	SA	75	2030	256	.502	0	.000	144	.791	20	146	561	85	16	656	8.7
Totals		308	5090	628	.468	7	.156	307	.721	87	370	1292	240	33	1570	5.1

BUCK JOHNSON

Team: Washington Bullets
Position: Forward
Height: 6'7" **Weight:** 190
Birthdate: January 3, 1964

NBA Experience: 7 years
College: Alabama
Acquired: Signed as a free agent, 9/92

Background: Although he plays small forward in the NBA, Johnson was once a center at Alabama, where he paced the Crimson Tide in scoring and rebounding as a junior and senior. He spent his first six NBA seasons with Houston. Johnson was a double-digit scorer with the Rockets for two years before dropping to 8.6 PPG in 1991-92, after which the Rockets did not re-sign him. Washington inked him to a contract for the 1992-93 season and Johnson averaged 6.5 PPG, mostly in a reserve role.

Strengths: Johnson is an impressive athlete whose best offensive skill is finishing. He loves dunking and runs the floor well enough to do it quite a bit. Johnson is capable of being a decent scorer in an up-tempo system. He plays solid if unspectacular defense.

Weaknesses: Johnson is a poor passer and ball-handler, and for those reasons is not on the same level as the better small forwards in the game. Remember, he played with his back to the basket in college. He is also a shaky outside shooter and could do a better job on the boards.

Analysis: Johnson is much better in a reserve role than as a starting small forward. He simply does not possess the offensive expertise for the latter job, which in part explains Houston's decision to let him go. When his head's in the game, Johnson can contribute on defense and in transition.

PLAYER SUMMARY

Will	finish with dunks
Can't	dribble, pass
Expect	a willing defender
Don't Expect	5 RPG
Fantasy Value	$0
Card Value	5-10¢

COLLEGE STATISTICS

		G	FGP	FTP	RPG	PPG
82-83	ALA	32	.479	.636	4.5	8.3
83-84	ALA	28	.514	.730	8.5	17.0
84-85	ALA	33	.560	.712	9.4	16.0
85-86	ALA	29	.577	.832	8.3	20.7
Totals		122	.540	.739	7.6	15.3

NBA REGULAR-SEASON STATISTICS

		G	MIN	FGs FG	FGs PCT	3-PT FGs FG	3-PT FGs PCT	FTs FT	FTs PCT	Rebounds OFF	Rebounds TOT	AST	STL	BLK	PTS	PPG
86-87	HOU	60	520	94	.468	0	.000	40	.690	38	88	40	17	15	228	3.8
87-88	HOU	70	879	155	.520	1	.125	67	.736	49	168	49	30	26	378	5.4
88-89	HOU	67	1850	270	.524	1	.111	101	.754	114	286	126	64	35	642	9.6
89-90	HOU	82	2832	504	.495	2	.118	205	.759	113	381	252	104	62	1215	14.8
90-91	HOU	73	2279	416	.477	2	.133	157	.727	108	330	142	81	47	991	13.6
91-92	HOU	80	2202	290	.458	1	.111	104	.727	95	312	158	72	49	685	8.6
92-93	WAS	73	1287	193	.479	0	.000	92	.730	78	195	89	36	18	478	6.5
Totals		505	11849	1922	.488	7	.113	766	.738	623	1760	856	404	252	4617	9.1

EDDIE JOHNSON

Team: Seattle SuperSonics
Position: Forward/Guard
Height: 6'7" **Weight:** 215
Birthdate: May 1, 1959
NBA Experience: 12 years

College: Illinois
Acquired: Traded from Suns with
1991 and 1993 1st-round picks for
Xavier McDaniel, 12/90

Background: In college, Johnson set Illinois career records for scoring, rebounding, and field goals. He still ranks among the leaders in a number of categories for Kansas City/Sacramento, where he starred before taking a reserve role with Phoenix. He won the NBA's Sixth Man Award in 1988-89. Johnson was traded to Seattle in 1990-91 and remains one of the best sixth men around.

Strengths: One of the best off-the-bench shooters and team leaders in the league, Johnson releases the ball quickly and possesses great range. He was third on the Sonics in scoring last season. Johnson also is a deadly free throw shooter, finishing above 90 percent last year for the second time in his career.

Weaknesses: Johnson struggles when his jump shot is taken away. He does not go to the hoop with confidence and is not known for his passing. Defense is not a forte either.

Analysis: The veteran Johnson is still one of the best at what he does—shoot quick jumpers from long distance and provide leadership off the bench. He has played a big part in helping the Sonics become winners and will continue to contend for the Sixth Man Award.

PLAYER SUMMARY

Will.............................heat up off bench
Can't ....shut down his man
Expect ....superb leadership
Don't Expect ....flashy drives
Fantasy Value..............................$2-4
Card Value ....5-10¢

COLLEGE STATISTICS

		G	FGP	FTP	RPG	PPG
77-78	ILL	27	.427	.741	3.1	8.1
78-79	ILL	30	.415	.531	5.7	12.1
79-80	ILL	35	.462	.655	8.9	17.4
80-81	ILL	29	.494	.756	9.2	17.2
Totals		121	.454	.671	6.9	14.0

NBA REGULAR-SEASON STATISTICS

		G	MIN	FGs FG	FGs PCT	3-PT FGs FG	3-PT FGs PCT	FTs FT	FTs PCT	Rebounds OFF	Rebounds TOT	AST	STL	BLK	PTS	PPG
81-82	KC	74	1517	295	.459	1	.091	99	.664	128	322	109	50	14	690	9.3
82-83	KC	82	2933	677	.494	20	.282	247	.779	191	501	216	70	20	1621	19.8
83-84	KC	82	2920	753	.485	20	.313	268	.810	165	455	296	76	21	1794	21.9
84-85	KC	82	3029	769	.491	13	.241	325	.871	151	407	273	83	22	1876	22.9
85-86	SAC	82	2514	623	.475	4	.200	280	.816	173	419	214	54	17	1530	18.7
86-87	SAC	81	2457	606	.463	37	.314	267	.829	146	353	251	42	19	1516	18.7
87-88	PHO	73	1533	480	.480	24	.255	204	.850	121	318	180	33	9	1294	17.7
88-89	PHO	70	2043	608	.497	71	.413	217	.868	91	306	162	47	7	1504	21.5
89-90	PHO	64	1811	411	.453	70	.380	188	.917	69	246	107	32	10	1080	16.9
90-91	PHO/SEA	81	2085	543	.484	39	.325	229	.891	107	271	111	58	9	1354	16.7
91-92	SEA	81	2366	534	.459	27	.252	291	.861	118	292	161	55	11	1386	17.1
92-93	SEA	82	1869	463	.467	17	.304	234	.911	124	272	135	36	4	1177	14.4
Total		934	27721	6815	.478	343	.320	2849	.842	1584	4162	2215	636	163	16822	18.0

FRANK JOHNSON

Team: Phoenix Suns
Position: Guard
Height: 6'1" **Weight:** 180
Birthdate: November 23, 1958

NBA Experience: 9 years
College: Wake Forest
Acquired: Signed as a free agent, 10/92

Background: The brother of Eddie Johnson (a former All-Star guard with Atlanta), Frank Johnson was a former first-round pick of Washington out of Wake Forest. He spent seven relatively quiet years with the Bullets and one with Houston before playing three years in the Italian League. Phoenix cut him during 1992's training camp but called him back early in the season when Kevin Johnson injured a leg. Frank came off the bench in 77 games last year.

Strengths: Johnson provides veteran leadership to a second unit. He is very strong for his 180-pound frame and is an aggressive, fearless defender. He makes the right play at the right time and does not try to exceed his bounds. Johnson isn't one to squawk about playing time.

Weaknesses: The Suns tried to get Johnson to shoot more, but he is not a particularly offensive-minded player. He is not likely to return to his second-year numbers, when he averaged 12.5 PPG and 8.1 APG. He won't dazzle anyone with his creativity.

Analysis: The Suns were looking for a veteran guard and they found their man almost by accident. Johnson was probably about the tenth-best player on the team, but he produced when called upon and was extremely valuable when K.J. was sidelined.

PLAYER SUMMARY

Will	provide leadership
Can't	compare with K.J.
Expect	smarts, savvy
Don't Expect	much shooting
Fantasy Value	$0
Card Value	5-10¢

COLLEGE STATISTICS

		G	FGP	FTP	RPG	PPG
76-77	WF	30	.457	.696	2.8	11.6
77-78	WF	29	.492	.689	3.1	16.2
78-79	WF	27	.477	.768	2.3	16.1
79-80	WF	5	.281	1.00	1.8	5.6
80-81	WF	29	.521	.819	2.1	16.2
Totals		120	.483	.753	2.6	14.6

NBA REGULAR-SEASON STATISTICS

		G	MIN	FGs FG	FGs PCT	3-PT FGs FG	3-PT FGs PCT	FTs FT	FTs PCT	Rebounds OFF	Rebounds TOT	AST	STL	BLK	PTS	PPG
81-82	WAS	79	2027	336	.414	17	.215	153	.750	34	147	380	76	7	842	10.7
82-83	WAS	68	2324	321	.408	14	.230	196	.751	46	178	549	110	6	852	12.5
83-84	WAS	82	2686	392	.467	11	.256	187	.742	58	184	567	96	6	982	12.0
84-85	WAS	46	925	175	.489	6	.353	72	.750	23	63	143	43	3	428	9.3
85-86	WAS	14	402	69	.448	0	.000	38	.704	7	28	76	11	1	176	12.6
86-87	WAS	18	399	59	.461	0	.000	35	.714	10	30	58	21	0	153	8.5
87-88	WAS	75	1258	216	.434	1	.111	121	.812	39	121	188	70	4	554	7.4
88-89	HOU	67	879	109	.443	1	.167	75	.806	22	79	181	42	0	294	4.4
92-93	PHO	77	1122	136	.436	1	.083	59	.776	41	113	186	60	7	332	4.3
Totals		526	12022	1813	.439	51	.221	936	.759	280	943	2328	529	34	4613	8.8

KEVIN JOHNSON

Team: Phoenix Suns
Position: Guard
Height: 6'1" **Weight:** 190
Birthdate: March 4, 1966
NBA Experience: 6 years
College: California

Acquired: Traded from Cavaliers with Mark West, Tyrone Corbin, 1988 1st- and 2nd-round picks, and a 1989 2nd-round pick for Larry Nance, Mike Sanders, and a 1988 1st-round pick, 2/88

Background: Johnson concluded his college career as California's all-time leader in scoring, assists, and steals. He recorded the first triple-double in Pac-10 history. Johnson averaged more than 21 points and 11 assists per game in his first four full seasons with Phoenix. He won the league's Most Improved Player Award in 1988-89 and has played in two All-Star Games. Groin, hamstring, and knee injuries limited him to just 49 games last season.

Strengths: One frightening gift runs through everything Johnson does—unbelievable quickness. Because of it, there is virtually no one capable of stopping his one-on-one penetration. Leave him open from outside and he will bury jumpers up to 20 feet. His passing skills are made more devastating because he draws multiple defenders when he goes to the hoop. In addition, he comes up with a lot of steals.

Weaknesses: Injuries have become the primary area of concern. He was out of the lineup for nearly half of last season and the start of the playoffs. Johnson does not possess 3-point range, but he has never been asked to fill that role.

Analysis: Johnson, clearly one of the premier point guards in the league, had a bittersweet 1992-93 season. While his team amassed the best record in basketball, much of its success came with him on the injured list. When he's healthy, however, the fleet-footed Johnson can make a great team even better.

PLAYER SUMMARY

Will	drive and dish
Can't	shake injury bug
Expect	about 10 APG
Don't Expect	treys
Fantasy Value	$35-40
Card Value	12-20¢

COLLEGE STATISTICS

		G	FGP	FTP	APG	PPG
83-84	CAL	28	.510	.721	2.3	9.7
84-85	CAL	27	.450	.662	4.1	12.9
85-86	CAL	29	.490	.815	6.0	15.6
86-87	CAL	34	.471	.819	5.0	17.2
Totals		118	.477	.757	4.4	14.0

NBA REGULAR-SEASON STATISTICS

		G	MIN	FGs FG	FGs PCT	3-PT FGs FG	3-PT FGs PCT	FTs FT	FTs PCT	Rebounds OFF	Rebounds TOT	AST	STL	BLK	PTS	PPG
87-88	CLE/PHO	80	1917	275	.461	5	.208	177	.839	36	191	437	103	24	732	9.1
88-89	PHO	81	3179	570	.505	2	.091	508	.882	46	340	991	135	24	1650	20.4
89-90	PHO	74	2782	578	.499	8	.195	501	.838	42	270	846	95	14	1665	22.5
90-91	PHO	77	2772	591	.516	9	.205	519	.843	54	271	781	163	11	1710	22.2
91-92	PHO	78	2899	539	.479	10	.217	448	.807	61	292	836	116	23	1536	19.7
92-93	PHO	49	1643	282	.499	1	.125	226	.819	30	104	384	85	20	791	16.1
Totals		439	15192	2835	.496	35	.189	2379	.840	269	1468	4275	697	116	8084	18.4

LARRY JOHNSON

Team: Charlotte Hornets
Position: Forward
Height: 6'7" **Weight:** 250
Birthdate: March 14, 1969

NBA Experience: 2 years
College: Odessa; UNLV
Acquired: 1st-round pick in 1991 draft
(1st overall)

Background: The indomitable L.J. originally signed with Southern Methodist, but he ended up at Odessa (Texas) Junior College after SMU officials questioned his score on a retake of the SAT. UNLV won the national title in Johnson's first season (1989-90) and he was the nation's consensus Player of the Year in 1990-91. He was selected No. 1 overall by Charlotte in the 1991 draft and earned Rookie of the Year honors after leading his team in rebounding and all rookies in scoring. He made his first All-Star appearance last season and finished 12th in the league in scoring at 22.1 PPG.

Strengths: Johnson possesses incredible strength that carries over into virtually every aspect of the game. He can't be moved once he gets position on the low blocks. He has advanced post-up scoring skills, is a superb passer, rebounds with a vengeance, and is a tough defensive player. He can score from inside and out. He is also a fine free throw shooter. He's one of the most electrifying finishers in the game.

Weaknesses: Johnson came from a school that preached defense but he is not considered an NBA stopper. He does have that potential, however. Johnson blocked only 27 shots last season and does not come up with a lot of steals.

Analysis: Johnson picked up last year right where he left off as a rookie—dominating virtually everyone in his path. He is a force on the glass and owns the talent and determination to score seemingly at will. He is tremendously durable, playing in all 82 games each year and leading the league in total minutes last season. Johnson underwent back surgery over the summer, but he was expected to be fully healed by the start of the season.

PLAYER SUMMARY

Will	dominate inside
Can't	block shots
Expect	20 PPG, 10 RPG
Don't Expect	soft play
Fantasy Value	$50-55
Card Value	50-75¢

COLLEGE STATISTICS

		G	FGP	FTP	RPG	PPG
87-88	ODE	35	.649	.794	12.3	22.3
88-89	ODE	35	.653	.760	10.9	29.8
89-90	UNLV	40	.624	.767	11.4	20.6
90-91	UNLV	35	.662	.818	10.9	22.7
Totals		145	.648	.780	11.4	23.7

NBA REGULAR-SEASON STATISTICS

			FGs		3-PT FGs		FTs		Rebounds						
	G	MIN	FG	PCT	FG	PCT	FT	PCT	OFF	TOT	AST	STL	BLK	PTS	PPG
91-92 CHA	82	3047	616	.490	5	.227	339	.829	323	899	292	81	51	1576	19.2
92-93 CHA	82	3323	728	.526	18	.254	336	.767	281	864	353	53	27	1810	22.1
Totals	164	6370	1344	.509	23	.247	675	.797	604	1763	645	134	78	3386	20.6

MICHAEL JORDAN

Team: Chicago Bulls
Position: Guard
Height: 6'6" **Weight:** 198
Birthdate: February 17, 1963

NBA Experience: 9 years
College: North Carolina
Acquired: 1st-round pick in 1984 draft
(3rd overall)

Background: At North Carolina, Jordan hit the winning basket as a freshman in the 1982 NCAA championship game and went on to earn consensus All-America recognition. He earned NBA Rookie of the Year honors in 1984-85 and has been voted an All-Star starter in each of his nine seasons. Jordan owns three league MVP Awards, three NBA championship rings, three NBA Finals MVP honors, and Olympic gold medals from 1984 and 1992. He claimed his seventh straight scoring title in 1992-93, matching Wilt Chamberlain's record string. He has also made the NBA's All-Defensive first team each of the last seven years.

Strengths: Jordan plays every aspect of the game at its highest level. Sometimes overshadowed by his gravity-defying jams and huge scoring outbursts are his passing, ball-handling, rebounding, and remarkable defensive talents. Jordan's will to win might be unparalleled.

Weaknesses: Though flawless on the court, Jordan has had to carry the mental burden of being America's biggest superstar. Moreover, he must now cope with the loss of his father, James Jordan, who was murdered in August.

Analysis: Jordan may well be the most gifted player ever to pick up a basketball. His career scoring average is the highest in ABA/NBA history, he has three titles to his credit, and he excels in every aspect of the game. In a newspaper poll last year, his league mates voted him the greatest player of all time.

PLAYER SUMMARY

Will ....dominate games
Can't......................................be shut down
Expect......................more MVP Awards
Don't Expect............less than 30 PPG
Fantasy Value............................$85-90
Card Value ....50¢-$1.50

COLLEGE STATISTICS

		G	FGP	FTP	RPG	PPG
81-82	NC	34	.534	.722	4.4	13.5
82-83	NC	36	.345	.737	5.5	20.0
83-84	NC	31	.551	.779	5.3	19.6
Totals		101	.465	.748	5.0	17.7

NBA REGULAR-SEASON STATISTICS

				FGs		3-PT FGs		FTs		Rebounds						
		G	MIN	FG	PCT	FG	PCT	FT	PCT	OFF	TOT	AST	STL	BLK	PTS	PPG
84-85	CHI	82	3144	837	.515	9	.173	630	.845	167	534	481	196	69	2313	28.2
85-86	CHI	18	451	150	.457	3	.167	105	.840	23	64	53	37	21	408	22.7
86-87	CHI	82	3281	1098	.482	12	.182	833	.857	166	430	377	236	125	3041	37.1
87-88	CHI	82	3311	1069	.535	7	.132	723	.841	139	449	485	259	131	2868	35.0
88-89	CHI	81	3255	966	.538	27	.276	674	.850	149	652	650	234	65	2633	32.5
89-90	CHI	82	3197	1034	.526	92	.376	593	.848	143	565	519	227	54	2753	33.6
90-91	CHI	82	3034	990	.539	29	.312	571	.851	118	492	453	223	83	2580	31.5
91-92	CHI	80	3102	943	.519	27	.270	491	.832	91	511	489	182	75	2404	30.0
92-93	CHI	78	3067	992	.495	81	.352	476	.837	135	522	428	221	61	2541	32.6
Totals		667	25842	8079	.516	287	.301	5096	.846	1131	4219	3935	1815	684	21541	32.3

ADAM KEEFE

Team: Atlanta Hawks
Position: Forward
Height: 6'9" **Weight:** 240
Birthdate: February 22, 1970

NBA Experience: 1 year
College: Stanford
Acquired: 1st-round pick in 1992 draft (10th overall)

Background: Keefe was Stanford's rock in the middle, a three-time Pac-10 rebounding champion who led the Cardinal in one or more seasons in scoring, steals, field goal percentage, free throws, minutes, and blocked shots. The MVP of the NIT as a junior, Keefe was also a world-class volleyball player who had to de-emphasize the sport because of his basketball commitment. He was the tenth pick in the 1992 draft and played in all 82 games for Atlanta as a rookie. Keefe averaged 6.6 PPG and 5.3 RPG.

Strengths: Keefe is big, strong, and smart. He plays within himself and is unselfish, almost to a fault. He bangs the boards aggressively, is not afraid of contact, and gets to the free throw line. He is also a pretty good face-up shooter within his limited range. He's still improving, is extremely coachable, and is a team player all the way.

Weaknesses: Most of Keefe's skills are in the unpolished stage. He is very limited in his back-to-the-basket moves and is a step slow when he goes to the hoop. He often struggles to convert in traffic and is not much of a finisher. Keefe is a willing passer, but he needs to develop a sense of where and when to deliver the ball.

Analysis: The big redhead does not deserve mention among the premier rookies in the league. In fact, all nine players drafted ahead of him and several taken after him made greater impacts on their teams during the 1992-93 season. However, Keefe improved steadily after a horrible start and should continue to develop into a decent inside player. If he doesn't develop, lack of effort will not be the reason.

PLAYER SUMMARY	
Will	bang the boards
Can't	dazzle with finishes
Expect	continued improvement
Don't Expect	triple-doubles
Fantasy Value	$1-3
Card Value	12-20¢

COLLEGE STATISTICS

		G	FGP	FTP	RPG	PPG
88-89	STAN	33	.633	.689	5.4	8.4
89-90	STAN	30	.627	.725	9.1	20.0
90-91	STAN	33	.609	.760	9.5	21.5
91-92	STAN	29	.564	.746	12.2	25.3
Totals		125	.600	.736	9.0	18.6

NBA REGULAR-SEASON STATISTICS

			FGs		3-PT FGs		FTs		Rebounds						
	G	MIN	FG	PCT	FG	PCT	FT	PCT	OFF	TOT	AST	STL	BLK	PTS	PPG
92-93 ATL	82	1549	188	.500	0	.000	166	.700	171	432	80	57	16	542	6.6
Totals	82	1549	188	.500	0	.000	166	.700	171	432	80	57	16	542	6.6

SHAWN KEMP

Team: Seattle SuperSonics
Position: Forward
Height: 6'10" **Weight:** 245
Birthdate: November 26, 1969

NBA Experience: 4 years
College: None
Acquired: 1st-round pick in 1989 draft
(17th overall)

Background: Kemp never played a minute of college basketball before entering the NBA draft. He was a Proposition 48 casualty at Kentucky, transferred to Trinity Junior College amid scrutiny, then opted for the draft. His athletic dunks caught immediate attention during his rookie year, and he became a starter for the Sonics in his second year (1990-91) when Xavier McDaniel was traded. He averaged career highs of 17.8 PPG and 10.7 RPG last season and was chosen for his first All-Star Game.

Strengths: Witness one Kemp dunk and you'll realize that this phenom is blessed with dominating physical ability. He is strong, has a great vertical leap, and knows his way around the court. His quickness to the hoop and powerful finishes are awe-inspiring. Kemp also plays physical defense and blocks shots with the best of forwards. His work habits are impressive and he has helped the Sonics make a swift climb in the standings.

Weaknesses: Kemp still has a ways to go in the area of consistency. He favors making the phenomenal play rather than the obvious one. Coach George Karl took him out of the starting lineup late in last year's regular season and Kemp responded by fouling out of four of the last five games. He is not a reliable outside shooter.

Analysis: Kemp was a crowd-pleaser from the moment he stepped onto the NBA hardwood. You can almost always see him dunking on the nightly TV highlight shows and he is invaluable to his team as a scorer, rebounder, and shot-blocker. It's a good bet that last year's All-Star showing was not his last.

PLAYER SUMMARY	
Will	make highlight reels
Can't	shoot with range
Expect	more All-Star trips
Don't Expect	much bench time
Fantasy Value	$45-50
Card Value	40-75¢

COLLEGE STATISTICS

—DID NOT PLAY—

NBA REGULAR-SEASON STATISTICS

			FGs		3-PT FGs		FTs		Rebounds						
		G	MIN	FG	PCT	FG	PCT	FT	PCT	OFF	TOT	AST	STL	BLK	PTS	PPG
89-90	SEA	81	1120	203	.479	2	.167	117	.736	146	346	26	47	70	525	6.5
90-91	SEA	81	2442	462	.508	2	.167	288	.661	267	679	144	77	123	1214	15.0
91-92	SEA	64	1808	362	.504	0	.000	270	.748	264	665	86	70	124	994	15.5
92-93	SEA	78	2582	515	.492	0	.000	358	.712	287	833	155	119	146	1388	17.8
Totals		304	7952	1542	.498	4	.129	1033	.708	964	2523	411	313	463	4121	13.6

STEVE KERR

Team: Orlando Magic
Position: Guard
Height: 6'3" **Weight:** 180
Birthdate: September 27, 1965

NBA Experience: 5 years
College: Arizona
Acquired: Traded from Cavaliers for a 1996 2nd-round pick, 12/92

Background: Kerr was a second-team All-American as a senior at Arizona, where he set a Pac-10 record in 1987-88 by shooting .573 from 3-point range. He is the NBA's all-time leader in 3-point field goal percentage at .455, although he has served mostly in a reserve role with Phoenix, Cleveland, and Orlando. He was traded from the Cavaliers to the Magic early last season and averaged just 2.6 PPG, his lowest output since his rookie year.

Strengths: From just about anywhere, Kerr can flat-out shoot the ball. In 1989-90, he became one of two players in NBA history to shoot better than 50 percent from 3-point range over a season (Jon Sundvold's record is .522). Kerr is also a great free throw shooter. He works hard and plays with smarts.

Weaknesses: Kerr does very little off the dribble, largely because he is a step slower than the average NBA guard. He does not create much off the dribble for himself or his teammates. He hustles defensively but again is limited by his lack of speed. His shooting percentages were down last season, but limited playing time played a large role in the decline.

Analysis: No one has hit long-range jumpers at a better rate than Kerr during his career. The Magic, however, did not see that as enough reason to squeeze him into the rotation. "When they said they'd give me time, I didn't think they meant time to work on my golf game," Kerr quipped of the Magic. Several teams could use a reserve marksman with his eye.

PLAYER SUMMARY

Will ....bury 3-pointers
Can't...................crack Magic rotation
Expect ....record-setting accuracy
Don't Expect ....creativity
Fantasy Value...............................$0
Card Value...................................5-10¢

COLLEGE STATISTICS

		G	FGP	FTP	RPG	PPG
83-84	ARIZ	28	.516	.692	1.2	7.1
84-85	ARIZ	31	.568	.803	2.4	10.0
85-86	ARIZ	32	.540	.899	3.2	14.4
87-88	ARIZ	38	.559	.824	2.0	12.6
Totals		129	.548	.815	2.2	11.2

NBA REGULAR-SEASON STATISTICS

				FGs		3-PT FGs		FTs		Rebounds						
		G	MIN	FG	PCT	FG	PCT	FT	PCT	OFF	TOT	AST	STL	BLK	PTS	PPG
88-89	PHO	26	157	20	.435	8	.471	6	.667	3	17	24	7	0	54	2.1
89-90	CLE	78	1664	192	.444	73	.507	63	.863	12	98	248	45	7	520	6.7
90-91	CLE	57	905	99	.444	28	.452	45	.849	5	37	131	29	4	271	4.8
91-92	CLE	48	847	121	.511	32	.432	45	.833	14	78	110	27	10	319	6.6
92-93	CLE/ORL	52	481	53	.434	6	.231	22	.917	5	45	70	10	1	134	2.6
Totals		261	4054	485	.458	147	.455	181	.850	39	241	583	118	22	1298	5.0

JEROME KERSEY

Team: Portland Trail Blazers
Position: Forward
Height: 6'7" **Weight:** 225
Birthdate: June 26, 1962

NBA Experience: 9 years
College: Longwood College
Acquired: 2nd-round pick in 1984
draft (46th overall)

Background: Kersey rewrote the record books at NAIA Longwood College, where he became the all-time leader in points, rebounds, steals, and blocked shots. He started his pro career modestly before receiving consideration for the league's Most Improved Player Award in 1987-88, when he averaged 19.2 PPG. Since then, however, his scoring average has dipped in five consecutive years. A knee injury cost him 13 games last December.

Strengths: Kersey runs the floor and punctuates the fastbreak for many of his points. He owns great athletic ability and mixes it with hustle. He is an above-average rebounder for a small forward and loves to challenge opponents' lay-ups on the break.

Weaknesses: Kersey once took some of the worst shots available, and he still falls into that habit occasionally. Last year was the worst shooting season of his career. He has become more inconsistent over the past two years and he's below average from the free throw line.

Analysis: Kersey was once expected to develop into a dominant player, but no such expectations exist anymore. He seems to decline season by season. Last year, reserve Cliff Robinson stole the headlines and eventually a starting spot. Kersey is far from washed up as an NBA player, but his decreasing effectiveness and consistency are certainly cause for concern.

PLAYER SUMMARY	
Will	run the floor
Can't	achieve stardom
Expect	athletic finishes
Don't Expect	hot shooting
Fantasy Value	$3-5
Card Value	8-12¢

COLLEGE STATISTICS

		G	FGP	FTP	RPG	PPG
80-81	LONG	28	.629	.586	8.9	16.9
81-82	LONG	23	.585	.633	11.3	17.0
82-83	LONG	25	.560	.608	10.8	14.6
83-84	LONG	27	.521	.606	14.2	19.6
Totals		103	.570	.607	11.3	17.0

NBA REGULAR-SEASON STATISTICS

		G	MIN	FGs		3-PT FGs		FTs		Rebounds		AST	STL	BLK	PTS	PPG
				FG	PCT	FG	PCT	FT	PCT	OFF	TOT					
84-85	POR	77	958	178	.478	0	.000	117	.646	95	206	63	49	29	473	6.1
85-86	POR	79	1217	258	.549	0	.000	156	.681	137	293	83	85	32	672	8.5
86-87	POR	82	2088	373	.509	1	.043	262	.720	201	496	194	122	77	1009	12.3
87-88	POR	79	2888	611	.499	3	.200	291	.735	211	657	243	127	65	1516	19.2
88-89	POR	76	2716	533	.469	6	.286	258	.694	246	629	243	137	84	1330	17.5
89-90	POR	82	2843	519	.478	3	.150	269	.690	251	690	188	121	63	1310	16.0
90-91	POR	73	2359	424	.478	4	.308	232	.709	169	481	227	101	76	1084	14.8
91-92	POR	77	2553	398	.467	1	.125	174	.664	241	633	243	114	71	971	12.6
92-93	POR	65	1719	281	.438	8	.286	116	.634	126	406	121	80	41	686	10.6
Totals		690	19341	3575	.483	26	.190	1875	.693	1677	4491	1605	936	538	9051	13.1

BERNARD KING

Team: New Jersey Nets
Position: Forward
Height: 6'7" **Weight:** 205
Birthdate: December 4, 1956

NBA Experience: 14 years
College: Tennessee
Acquired: Signed as a free agent, 2/93

Background: King was a consensus All-American at Tennessee before leaving after his junior year for the NBA. He won the NBA scoring title with the Knicks in 1984-85 and led the team in scoring for three years. A career-threatening knee injury in 1985 kept King out the entire 1985-86 season and most of 1986-87 before he made his return with Washington in 1987-88. He made his fourth All-Star appearance in 1991. A second surgery on his right knee in September 1991 sidelined him for the 1991-92 season. He was signed by New Jersey in February 1993 and made another comeback, averaging 7.0 PPG in 32 games.

Strengths: King is a pure scorer with effective post-up moves, a lethal spinning jumper, and more tricks than most will ever know. He is nearing 20,000 career points. His two comebacks say much about his work ethic.

Weaknesses: King's right knee and his age are his main weaknesses. He never was a great defender, and now he's lost another step or two.

Analysis: King's second comeback wasn't nearly as impressive as his first one was. His ability to score, however, makes him dangerous in limited minutes.

PLAYER SUMMARY

Will ....outsmart defenders
Can't ....regain young knees
Expect ....points off the bench
Don't Expect ....durability
Fantasy Value $1
Card Value ....8-15¢

COLLEGE STATISTICS

		G	FGP	FTP	RPG	PPG
74-75	TENN	25	.622	.782	12.3	26.4
75-76	TENN	25	.573	.669	13.0	25.2
76-77	TENN	26	.578	.712	14.3	25.8
Totals		76	.590	.719	13.2	25.8

NBA REGULAR-SEASON STATISTICS

				FGs		3-PT FGs		FTs		Rebounds							
		G	MIN	FG	PCT	FG	PCT	FT	PCT	OFF	TOT	AST	STL	BLK	PTS	PPG	
77-78	NJ	79	3092	798	.479	0	.000	313	.677	265	751	193	122	36	1909	24.2
78-79	NJ	82	2859	710	.522	0	.000	349	.564	251	669	295	118	39	1769	21.6
79-80	UTA	19	419	71	.518	0	.000	34	.540	24	88	52	7	4	176	9.3
80-81	GS	87	2914	731	.588	2	.333	307	.703	178	551	287	72	34	1771	20.4
81-82	GS	79	2861	740	.566	1	.200	352	.705	140	469	282	78	23	1833	23.2
82-83	NY	68	2207	603	.528	0	.000	280	.722	99	326	195	90	13	1486	21.9
83-84	NY	77	2667	795	.572	0	.000	437	.779	123	394	164	75	17	2027	26.3
84-85	NY	55	2063	691	.530	1	.100	426	.772	114	317	204	71	15	1809	32.9
86-87	NY	6	214	52	.495	0	.000	32	.744	13	32	19	2	0	136	22.7
87-88	WAS	69	2044	470	.501	1	.167	247	.762	86	280	192	49	10	1188	17.2
88-89	WAS	81	2559	654	.477	5	.167	361	.819	133	384	294	64	13	1674	20.7
89-90	WAS	82	2687	711	.487	3	.130	412	.803	129	404	376	51	7	1837	22.4
90-91	WAS	64	2401	713	.472	8	.216	383	.790	114	319	292	56	16	1817	28.4
92-93	NJ	32	430	91	.514	2	.286	39	.684	35	76	18	11	3	223	7.0
Totals		880	29417	7830	.518	23	.172	3972	.730	1704	5060	2863	866	230	19655	22.3

STACEY KING

Team: Chicago Bulls
Position: Forward/Center
Height: 6'11" **Weight:** 230
Birthdate: January 29, 1967

NBA Experience: 4 years
College: Oklahoma
Acquired: 1st-round pick in 1989 draft (6th overall)

Background: King earned All-America and Big Eight Player of the Year accolades as a senior at Oklahoma, where he led the conference in scoring and rebounding as a senior. He was named second-team All-Rookie with Chicago in 1989-90, as he steadily improved through the season. Since then, his play has been up-and-down. His second season saw his productivity falter and he once walked out of a practice, but he returned to favor with the club during its second straight championship season in 1991-92. Last year, he averaged a career-worst 5.4 PPG.

Strengths: King runs the floor well for a big man and has shown some promise offensively. He was a scoring machine in college and he still looks to score whenever he touches the ball. He possesses a decent hook shot and can convert his turnaround jumper in the post. While not a banger, King does a decent job pressuring the ball in the Bulls' trapping defense.

Weaknesses: King's scoring mentality has not been what the Bulls would ideally like to see from him. They want rebounds and aggressive post play, and King is not the man for that kind of game. He gets murdered on the glass and does not shove people around on defense. His glaring weakness has simply been his inconsistency.

Analysis: King has gone from promising rookie to doghouse occupant to specialized reserve. He was one of several to fill in last year when Bill Cartwright was injured, but the Bulls used him primarily when they needed scoring from the middle. That was not as often as King would have liked.

PLAYER SUMMARY	
Will	look to score inside
Can't	earn regular starts
Expect	hooks, turnarounds
Don't Expect	intimidation
Fantasy Value	$1
Card Value	8-12¢

COLLEGE STATISTICS

		G	FGP	FTP	RPG	PPG
85-86	OKLA	14	.388	.744	3.8	6.0
86-87	OKLA	28	.438	.621	3.9	7.0
87-88	OKLA	39	.543	.675	8.5	22.3
88-89	OKLA	33	.524	.718	10.1	26.0
Totals		114	.516	.690	7.2	17.6

NBA REGULAR-SEASON STATISTICS

			FGs		3-PT FGs		FTs		Rebounds						
		G	MIN	FG	PCT	FG	PCT	FT	PCT	OFF	TOT	AST	STL	BLK	PTS	PPG
89-90	CHI	82	1777	267	.504	0	.000	194	.727	169	384	87	38	58	728	8.9
90-91	CHI	76	1198	156	.467	0	.000	107	.704	72	208	65	24	42	419	5.5
91-92	CHI	79	1268	215	.506	2	.400	119	.753	87	205	77	21	25	551	7.0
92-93	CHI	76	1059	160	.471	2	.333	86	.705	105	207	71	26	20	408	5.4
Totals		313	5302	798	.490	4	.286	506	.724	433	1004	300	109	145	2106	6.7

GREG KITE

Team: Orlando Magic
Position: Center
Height: 6'11" **Weight:** 260
Birthdate: August 5, 1961

NBA Experience: 10 years
College: Brigham Young
Acquired: Signed as a free agent, 8/90

Background: Kite helped Danny Ainge rally BYU into the 1981 NCAA East Regional finals. He finished his career ranked third on the school's rebounding charts. He was mostly a reserve center with Boston, the L.A. Clippers, and Charlotte before Sacramento picked him up in 1989-90. Kite started 47 games for the Kings that year, all 82 for Orlando in 1990-91, and 44 for the Magic in 1991-92. He was relegated to the bench last season after Orlando landed Shaquille O'Neal.

Strengths: Kite is a physical defender who gets under the skin of other centers. Some call him dirty. He bangs the body defensively, takes hard fouls, and knows his limitations on offense. His hard work has been rewarded with playing time on poor teams.

Weaknesses: Kite could not be an offensive force in an empty gym. He averaged less than a bucket per game last year and has a career mark below three PPG. He cannot capably dribble the ball, find open men, or hit free throws.

Analysis: The addition of O'Neal moved Kite to the position he ought to be in—reserve center. He averaged ten minutes per game last season and Orlando was a vastly improved team. Kite tries hard and deserves credit for making an NBA living, but he's not the best guy to have on the floor.

PLAYER SUMMARY

Will	irritate opponents
Can't	beat out Shaq
Expect	garbage minutes
Don't Expect	scoring
Fantasy Value	$0
Card Value	5-10¢

COLLEGE STATISTICS

		G	FGP	FTP	RPG	PPG
79-80	BYU	21	.292	.480	4.1	1.9
80-81	BYU	32	.489	.495	8.5	8.3
81-82	BYU	30	.467	.446	7.8	6.2
82-83	BYU	29	.437	.571	8.8	7.7
Totals		112	.452	.504	7.6	6.4

NBA REGULAR-SEASON STATISTICS

		G	MIN	FGs FG	FGs PCT	3-PT FGs FG	3-PT FGs PCT	FTs FT	FTs PCT	Rebounds OFF	Rebounds TOT	AST	STL	BLK	PTS	PPG
83-84	BOS	35	197	30	.455	0	.000	5	.313	27	62	7	1	5	65	1.9
84-85	BOS	55	424	33	.375	0	.000	22	.688	38	89	17	3	10	88	1.6
85-86	BOS	64	464	34	.374	0	.000	15	.385	35	128	17	3	28	83	1.3
86-87	BOS	74	745	47	.427	0	.000	29	.382	61	169	27	17	46	123	1.7
87-88	BOS/LAC	53	1063	92	.449	0	.000	40	.506	85	264	47	19	58	224	4.2
88-89	LAC/CHA	70	942	65	.430	0	.000	20	.488	81	243	36	27	54	150	2.1
89-90	SAC	71	1515	101	.432	1	1.000	27	.500	131	377	76	31	51	230	3.2
90-91	ORL	82	2225	166	.491	0	.000	63	.512	189	588	59	25	81	395	4.8
91-92	ORL	72	1479	94	.437	0	.000	40	.588	156	402	44	30	57	228	3.2
92-93	ORL	64	640	38	.452	0	.000	13	.542	66	193	10	13	12	89	1.4
Totals		640	9694	700	.442	1	.167	274	.496	869	2515	340	169	402	1675	2.6

JOE KLEINE

Team: Phoenix Suns
Position: Center
Height: 7'0" **Weight:** 271
Birthdate: January 4, 1962

NBA Experience: 8 years
College: Notre Dame; Arkansas
Acquired: Signed as a free agent, 8/93

Background: Kleine, who transferred to Arkansas after a year at Notre Dame, led the Razorbacks in scoring as a junior and senior and was a member of the gold-medal-winning 1984 U.S. Olympic team. He started 60 games and averaged nearly ten PPG with Sacramento in 1987-88, his best statistical year. He served as back-up center to Robert Parish in his four full seasons with the Celtics, but in August he signed with Phoenix.

Strengths: Opponents cringe when Kleine checks into the game. He uses his huge body to put the hurt on people. He rebounds, sets hard picks, and plays a style of defense that could get him arrested for assault. His fouls result in bruises. His work ethic is exemplary, making him a fan favorite.

Weaknesses: Finesse has no place in Kleine's game. He possesses poor hands, should be forbidden to dribble the ball, and is a below-average passer. His only real role in the offense is as a screen-setter and rebounder. Foul trouble would be a problem if he saw more minutes.

Analysis: As a back-up center who doesn't play a lot of minutes at a time, Kleine does all that is asked of him. He rebounds, plays defense, throws his weight around, and gets the most out of his fouls. He'll check into Suns games when coach Paul Westphal needs physical presence. Kleine's offensive skills have a long way to go before he could ever be a starter.

PLAYER SUMMARY	
Will	make fouls count
Can't	threaten offensively
Expect	hard picks, rebounds
Don't Expect	many starts
Fantasy Value	$0
Card Value	5-8¢

COLLEGE STATISTICS

		G	FGP	FTP	RPG	PPG
80-81	ND	29	.640	.750	2.4	2.6
82-83	ARK	30	.537	.633	7.3	13.3
83-84	ARK	32	.595	.773	9.2	18.2
84-85	ARK	35	.607	.720	8.4	22.1
Totals		126	.587	.723	7.0	14.5

NBA REGULAR-SEASON STATISTICS

		G	MIN	FGs FG	FGs PCT	3-PT FGs FG	3-PT FGs PCT	FTs FT	FTs PCT	Rebounds OFF	Rebounds TOT	AST	STL	BLK	PTS	PPG
85-86	SAC	80	1180	160	.465	0	.000	94	.723	113	373	46	24	34	414	5.2
86-87	SAC	79	1658	256	.471	0	.000	110	.786	173	483	71	35	30	622	7.9
87-88	SAC	82	1999	324	.472	0	.000	153	.814	179	579	93	28	59	801	9.8
88-89	SAC/BOS	75	1411	175	.405	0	.000	134	.882	124	378	67	33	23	484	6.5
89-90	BOS	81	1365	176	.480	0	.000	83	.830	117	355	46	15	27	435	5.4
90-91	BOS	72	850	102	.468	0	.000	54	.783	71	244	21	15	14	258	3.6
91-92	BOS	70	991	144	.491	4	.500	34	.708	94	296	32	23	14	326	4.7
92-93	BOS	78	1129	108	.404	0	.000	41	.707	113	346	39	17	17	257	3.3
Totals		617	10583	1445	.459	4	.174	703	.794	984	3054	415	190	218	3597	5.8

NEGELE KNIGHT

Team: Phoenix Suns
Position: Guard
Height: 6'1" **Weight:** 182
Birthdate: March 6, 1967

NBA Experience: 3 years
College: Dayton
Acquired: 2nd-round pick in 1990 draft (31st overall)

Background: Knight left Dayton as the school's all-time assists leader and finished sixth on Dayton's career scoring list. As a rookie, he emerged as a reliable back-up to Kevin Johnson at the point. His second season was sliced in half when a sprained neck muscle forced him to the injured list in February. Knight started more than 30 games when Johnson was injured last season and was a dependable reserve when the Suns were healthy. However, he saw zero playing time in the NBA Finals.

Strengths: Penetration and passing come naturally to Knight. He pushes the ball up-court quickly and makes good decisions at high speed. He is extremely confident with the ball and is a hard-nosed defender who will not back down. He accepts his reserve role and performs well in it, yet he has proven to be a capable starter as well. His teammates have confidence in him.

Weaknesses: Knight was a big-time scorer in college but has not displayed that potential as a pro. He received more starts and more minutes last year than in either of his previous two, yet his field goal percentage fell below the .400 mark. He is no threat from 3-point range.

Analysis: Knight was one of several players who stepped up his game during K.J.'s injury-plagued season. He and first-year Sun Frank Johnson were invaluable back-up point guards who ran the club capably and helped Phoenix compile the best record in the league. Still considered a second-round steal, Knight's poor shooting would be a big concern to anyone interested in making him a full-time starter.

PLAYER SUMMARY

Will	direct the offense
Can't	be a primary scorer
Expect	a reliable back-up
Don't Expect	another K.J.
Fantasy Value	$1-3
Card Value	5-12¢

COLLEGE STATISTICS

		G	FGP	FTP	APG	PPG
85-86	DAY	30	.379	.670	4.3	7.1
87-88	DAY	31	.472	.713	4.9	14.8
88-89	DAY	29	.366	.735	5.8	13.9
89-90	DAY	32	.503	.800	6.8	22.8
Totals		122	.440	.746	5.4	14.8

NBA REGULAR-SEASON STATISTICS

		G	MIN	FGs FG	FGs PCT	3-PT FGs FG	3-PT FGs PCT	FTs FT	FTs PCT	Rebounds OFF	Rebounds TOT	AST	STL	BLK	PTS	PPG
90-91	PHO	64	792	131	.425	6	.240	71	.602	20	71	191	20	7	339	5.3
91-92	PHO	42	631	103	.475	4	.308	33	.688	16	46	112	24	3	243	5.8
92-93	PHO	52	888	124	.391	0	.000	67	.779	28	64	145	23	4	315	6.1
Totals		158	2311	358	.425	10	.222	171	.679	64	181	448	67	14	897	5.7

JON KONCAK

Team: Atlanta Hawks
Position: Center
Height: 7'0"　**Weight:** 250
Birthdate: May 17, 1963

NBA Experience: 8 years
College: Southern Methodist
Acquired: 1st-round pick in 1985 draft
(5th overall)

Background: Koncak concluded his career at Southern Methodist as the school's all-time leader in rebounds, blocked shots, and field goal percentage. He played for the gold-medal-winning U.S. Olympic team in 1984. Most of his eight seasons with Atlanta have been spent as a reserve. Before the 1989-90 season, he signed a highly publicized, six-year, $13.2 million contract. He started a career-high 65 games in 1992-93, averaged 3.5 PPG, and led the team in blocked shots.

Strengths: The reason the Hawks were forced to match Detroit's huge contract offer four years ago was Koncak's value at the defensive end of the court. He bangs, plays sound position defense, and blocks shots. He brings good size to the middle.

Weaknesses: Koncak offers next to nothing offensively, which is why Atlanta fans see him as a big-league bust. He hasn't averaged more than six PPG since his rookie year, and two seasons ago he shot less than 40 percent from the field. He's a horrible shooter, ball-handler, and passer.

Analysis: Koncak will stick around as a defensive role-player, but he does nothing else to help a team other than set a pick or two. He has asked for a trade but the Hawks have yet to find a team that wants him. Last year was actually one of his better seasons, yet he didn't come close to earning his paycheck.

PLAYER SUMMARY	
Will	bang on defense
Can't	earn his money
Expect	frequent boos
Don't Expect	offense
Fantasy Value	$1
Card Value	5-8¢

COLLEGE STATISTICS

		G	FGP	FTP	RPG	PPG
81-82	SMU	27	.461	.620	5.7	10.0
82-83	SMU	30	.527	.691	9.4	14.6
83-84	SMU	33	.621	.607	11.5	15.5
84-85	SMU	33	.592	.667	10.7	17.2
Totals		123	.559	.649	9.5	14.5

NBA REGULAR-SEASON STATISTICS

		G	MIN	FGs FG	FGs PCT	3-PT FGs FG	3-PT FGs PCT	FTs FT	FTs PCT	Rebounds OFF	Rebounds TOT	AST	STL	BLK	PTS	PPG
85-86	ATL	82	1695	263	.507	0	.000	156	.607	171	467	55	37	69	682	8.3
86-87	ATL	82	1684	169	.480	0	.000	125	.654	153	493	31	52	76	463	5.6
87-88	ATL	49	1073	98	.483	0	.000	83	.610	103	333	19	36	56	279	5.7
88-89	ATL	74	1531	141	.524	0	.000	63	.553	147	453	56	54	98	345	4.7
89-90	ATL	54	977	78	.614	0	.000	42	.532	58	226	23	38	34	198	3.7
90-91	ATL	77	1931	140	.436	1	.125	32	.593	101	375	124	74	76	313	4.1
91-92	ATL	77	1489	111	.391	0	.000	19	.655	62	261	132	50	67	241	3.1
92-93	ATL	78	1975	124	.464	3	.375	24	.480	100	427	140	75	100	275	3.5
Totals		573	12355	1124	.480	4	.111	544	.598	895	3035	580	416	576	2796	4.9

LARRY KRYSTKOWIAK

Team: Utah Jazz
Position: Forward
Height: 6'10" **Weight:** 245
Birthdate: September 23, 1964
NBA Experience: 7 years

College: Montana
Acquired: Traded from Bucks with Jay Humphries for Blue Edwards, Eric Murdock, and a 1992 1st-round pick, 6/92

Background: At Montana, Krystkowiak was named Big Sky Conference MVP three times and Academic All-American twice, finishing his career as the school's all-time scoring leader. He played his rookie year with San Antonio and became a starter in his second year with Milwaukee, but a knee injury in the 1989 playoffs slowed his progress. After ten months of rehab, he played 16 of the last 20 games of 1989-90, then missed all of the 1990-91 regular season after reconstructive surgery. After his return in 1991-92, he was traded to Utah. He came off the Jazz bench to average 7.2 PPG last year.

Strengths: Krystkowiak knows his limits. His game is founded on heart and hustle and he is not afraid to sacrifice his body. His work ethic during his grueling rehab mirrored his style on the court. He can be a decent medium-range shooter.

Weaknesses: "Krysto" admits that his injured knee has taken something from his game, and he missed time late last season with a partially torn arch. He doesn't have much range on his jumper. His slow-footedness hurts him most on the defensive end.

Analysis: Krystkowiak showed what he's made of by recovering from a serious knee injury—the now-famous torn anterior cruciate ligament. Hard work is second nature to him. If he can ever stay healthy for a full season, he's capable of doing the things that help a good team get better.

PLAYER SUMMARY

Will ....dive for loose balls
Can't ....stay healthy
Expect............................reserve minutes
Don't Expect ....quickness
Fantasy Value...................................$0
Card Value...................................5-8¢

COLLEGE STATISTICS

		G	FGP	FTP	RPG	PPG
82-83	MONT	28	.433	.688	4.3	4.9
83-84	MONT	30	.547	.805	10.5	18.0
84-85	MONT	30	.585	.840	10.2	21.1
85-86	MONT	32	.578	.760	11.4	22.2
Totals		120	.561	.790	9.2	16.8

NBA REGULAR-SEASON STATISTICS

			FGs		3-PT FGs		FTs		Rebounds						
		G	MIN	FG	PCT	FG	PCT	FT	PCT	OFF	TOT	AST	STL	BLK	PTS	PPG
86-87	SA	68	1004	170	.456	1	.083	110	.743	77	239	85	22	12	451	6.6
87-88	MIL	50	1050	128	.481	0	.000	103	.811	88	231	50	18	8	359	7.2
88-89	MIL	80	2472	362	.473	4	.333	289	.823	198	610	107	93	9	1017	12.7
89-90	MIL	16	381	43	.364	0	.000	26	.788	16	76	25	10	2	112	7.0
91-92	MIL	79	1848	293	.444	0	.000	128	.757	131	429	114	54	12	714	9.0
92-93	UTA	71	1362	198	.466	0	.000	117	.796	74	279	68	42	13	513	7.2
Totals		364	8117	1194	.458	5	.143	773	.793	584	1864	449	239	56	3166	8.7

CHRISTIAN LAETTNER

Team: Minnesota Timberwolves
Position: Forward
Height: 6'11" **Weight:** 235
Birthdate: August 17, 1969

NBA Experience: 1 year
College: Duke
Acquired: 1st-round pick in 1992 draft
(3rd overall)

Background: The only collegiate player on the 1992 Olympic Dream Team, Laettner was named national Player of the Year as a senior and was the catalyst behind Duke's back-to-back national championships in 1991 and 1992. He remains the only player in history to start in four Final Fours. He became only the third Duke player to record 2,000 points and 1,000 rebounds. The third choice overall in the 1992 draft, he led the Timberwolves in both rebounds and blocked shots last year. Among rookies, he was third in scoring, fourth in assists, and fifth in rebounding.

Strengths: Laettner can score from inside and out. He has good range with his jumper yet is strong enough to muscle inside for short bank shots and dunks. He is solid fundamentally. Mentally tough, Laettner has never been afraid to take clutch shots and likes to have the ball in his hands. He's a very good free throw shooter and a strong rebounder.

Weaknesses: Abrasive. Selfish. Cocky. All have been used to describe Laettner, a difficult personality to size up. Teammates, Chuck Person in particular, spoke rather openly about Laettner's selfishness with the ball. While he did rack up a high assist total, he turned it over even more often. He brings a small forward's mentality to the power-forward position.

Analysis: Minnesota G.M. Jack McCloskey may have hit the nail on the head when he offered of Laettner: "He's going to become the player he already thinks he is." Indeed, Laettner's cocksure approach has alienated some. However, it also helped him make the transition to the NBA without losing his role as a major player. Say what you will about him, but Laettner is a big-league talent.

PLAYER SUMMARY	
Will	score, rebound
Can't	avoid conflict
Expect	loads of attention
Don't Expect	a shy shooter
Fantasy Value	$35-40
Card Value	50¢-$1.25

COLLEGE STATISTICS

		G	FGP	FTP	RPG	PPG
88-89	DUKE	36	.723	.717	4.7	8.9
89-90	DUKE	38	.511	.836	9.6	16.3
90-91	DUKE	39	.575	.802	8.7	19.8
91-92	DUKE	35	.575	.815	7.9	21.5
Totals		148	.574	.806	7.8	16.6

NBA REGULAR-SEASON STATISTICS

			FGs		3-PT FGs		FTs		Rebounds						
	G	MIN	FG	PCT	FG	PCT	FT	PCT	OFF	TOT	AST	STL	BLK	PTS	PPG
92-93 MIN	81	2823	503	.474	4	.100	462	.835	171	708	223	105	83	1472	18.2
Totals	81	2823	503	.474	4	.100	462	.835	171	708	223	105	83	1472	18.2

BILL LAIMBEER

Team: Detroit Pistons
Position: Center
Height: 6'11" **Weight:** 260
Birthdate: May 19, 1957
NBA Experience: 13 years

College: Notre Dame
Acquired: Traded from Cavaliers with Kenny Carr for Phil Hubbard, Paul Mokeski, and 1982 1st- and 2nd-round picks, 2/82

Background: Laimbeer helped Notre Dame to the school's only Final Four appearance in 1977-78. He spent his first pro season in Italy before spending a year and a half with Cleveland. Since joining Detroit, he has made four All-Star appearances and won two NBA championships. Laimbeer led the league in rebounding in 1985-86. He averaged a career-low 8.7 PPG last season.

Strengths: Laimbeer is a proven winner. He works hard and demands the same from teammates. He plays smart (some say dirty) defense, draws charges (often with "flops"), and pounds the boards. He's Detroit's all-time rebounding leader. He's still one of the top outside-shooting big men.

Weaknesses: Always among the league leaders in fines, Laimbeer owed more than $20,000 for three incidents last season. He lacks all the athletic skills. He has never been an offensive force in the paint, and he's not as steady from long range as he once was.

Analysis: Laimbeer continues to hint of retirement, but he continually returns to get under the skin of opponents. Will the NBA's most hated player really call it quits? If so, he'll force fans to find another villain.

PLAYER SUMMARY	
Will	irritate opponents
Can't	score like he used to
Expect	a few more fines
Don't Expect	fan clubs
Fantasy Value	$1-3
Card Value	5-12¢

COLLEGE STATISTICS

		G	FGP	FTP	RPG	PPG
75-76	ND	10	.492	.783	7.9	8.2
77-78	ND	29	.554	.677	6.6	8.1
78-79	ND	30	.538	.700	5.5	6.4
Totals		69	.538	.704	6.3	7.4

NBA REGULAR-SEASON STATISTICS

				FGs		3-PT FGs		FTs		Rebounds						
		G	MIN	FG	PCT	FG	PCT	FT	PCT	OFF	TOT	AST	STL	BLK	PTS	PPG
80-81	CLE	81	2460	337	.503	0	.000	117	.765	266	693	216	56	78	791	9.8
81-82	CLE/DET	80	1829	265	.494	4	.308	184	.793	234	617	100	39	64	718	9.0
82-83	DET	82	2871	436	.497	2	.154	245	.790	282	993	263	51	118	1119	13.6
83-84	DET	82	2864	553	.530	0	.000	316	.866	329	1003	149	49	84	1422	17.3
84-85	DET	82	2892	595	.506	4	.222	244	.797	295	1013	154	69	71	1438	17.5
85-86	DET	82	2891	545	.492	4	.286	266	.834	305	1075	146	59	65	1360	16.6
86-87	DET	82	2854	506	.501	6	.286	245	.894	243	955	151	72	69	1263	15.4
87-88	DET	82	2897	455	.493	13	.333	187	.874	165	832	199	66	78	1110	13.5
88-89	DET	81	2640	449	.499	30	.349	178	.840	138	776	177	51	100	1106	13.7
89-90	DET	81	2675	380	.484	57	.361	164	.854	166	780	171	57	84	981	12.1
90-91	DET	82	2668	372	.478	37	.296	123	.837	173	737	157	38	56	904	11.0
91-92	DET	81	2234	342	.470	32	.376	67	.893	104	451	160	51	54	783	9.7
92-93	DET	79	1933	292	.509	10	.370	93	.894	110	419	127	46	40	687	8.7
Totals		1057	33708	5527	.498	199	.326	2429	.837	2810	10344	2170	704	961	13682	12.9

ANDREW LANG

Team: Philadelphia 76ers
Position: Center
Height: 6'11" **Weight:** 250
Birthdate: June 28, 1966
NBA Experience: 5 years

College: Arkansas
Acquired: Traded from Suns with Jeff Hornacek and Tim Perry for Charles Barkley, 6/92

Background: Lang completed his collegiate career at Arkansas as the school's all-time leader in blocked shots and its fourth-leading rebounder. His playing time increased in each of his four years with Phoenix. Lang has emerged as a dominating shot-blocker, topping the 200 mark (201) and finishing tenth in the league in 1991-92. He was the league's 11th-best shot-swatter last season, his first in Philadelphia after the trade that sent Charles Barkley to Phoenix.

Strengths: When it comes to defensive middle men, Lang is one of the better ones. He blocks shots like few others and is capable of holding his own on the glass. He's blessed with great lateral quickness for his size. His instincts are first-rate and he runs the floor well for a center. He has dramatically improved his free throw touch since his first few years in the league.

Weaknesses: Lang's offensive skills are well behind those of most starting post players. Most of his points come from within a few feet of the hoop. After four years of shooting better than 50 percent, his accuracy dropped to a dismal .425 with the Sixers last season. In addition, he does not handle the ball well, even in the pivot, and he does not own a vast array of moves.

Analysis: Lang was certainly the best center Philadelphia had last year, which does not say a whole lot. Defensively, he can play with anyone in the league because of his quickness and shot-blocking. Offensively, Philadelphia did not find its answer. He'll share duties with Shawn Bradley this year.

PLAYER SUMMARY	
Will	defend the pivot
Can't	score in double figures
Expect	blocked shots
Don't Expect	offense
Fantasy Value	$1
Card Value	5-10¢

COLLEGE STATISTICS

		G	FGP	FTP	RPG	PPG
84-85	ARK	33	.405	.563	2.0	2.6
85-86	ARK	26	.466	.607	6.5	8.2
86-87	ARK	32	.500	.644	7.5	8.1
87-88	ARK	30	.527	.450	7.3	9.3
Totals		121	.489	.575	5.7	6.9

NBA REGULAR-SEASON STATISTICS

				FGs		3-PT FGs		FTs		Rebounds						
		G	MIN	FG	PCT	FG	PCT	FT	PCT	OFF	TOT	AST	STL	BLK	PTS	PPG
88-89	PHO	62	526	60	.513	0	.000	39	.650	54	147	9	17	48	159	2.6
89-90	PHO	74	1011	97	.557	0	.000	64	.653	83	271	21	22	133	258	3.5
90-91	PHO	63	1152	109	.577	0	.000	93	.715	113	303	27	17	127	311	4.9
91-92	PHO	81	1965	248	.522	0	.000	126	.768	170	546	43	48	201	622	7.7
92-93	PHI	73	1861	149	.425	1	.200	87	.763	136	436	79	46	141	386	5.3
Totals		353	6515	663	.508	1	.143	409	.723	556	1703	179	150	650	1736	4.9

JIM LES

Team: Sacramento Kings
Position: Guard
Height: 5'11" **Weight:** 175
Birthdate: August 18, 1963

NBA Experience: 5 years
College: Cleveland St.; Bradley
Acquired: Signed as a free agent, 12/90

Background: Les played with Hersey Hawkins at Bradley and finished as the school's all-time assists leader. After being cut by Atlanta and Philadelphia (twice), he switched to the CBA to play his first pro ball. Les finally landed an NBA job in 1988-89, playing all 82 games as back-up to John Stockton in Utah. He spent the 1989-90 season with the Jazz, with the Clippers, and back in the CBA. He was snared by Sacramento in 1990-91 and led the NBA in 3-point shooting (.461). He has not played nearly as much over the last two seasons.

Strengths: The 3-point shot became Les's ticket to the show, although he had converted only one NBA trey before 1990-91. Though he has not seen as much playing time as he did three years ago, he still lights it up from long range. His percentage (.429) was fifth in the league last year. Les makes few mistakes, hits his free throws, and handles the ball well.

Weaknesses: Les does not possess great speed and struggles to contain quicker point men. Bigger guards exploit him too by working the ball down low and posting him up. Les is too small to shoot over people as an off guard and does not create much as a point guard.

Analysis: Les came out of nowhere with the Kings in 1990-91 but spends more time on the bench now that the team has drafted more talent. He remains valuable, however, because few in the league can come off the bench cold and get as hot as Les can.

PLAYER SUMMARY

Will ....heat up quickly
Can't.........................create for others
Expect......................3-point accuracy
Don't Expect ....starts
Fantasy Value.....................................$0
Card Value ....5-8¢

COLLEGE STATISTICS

		G	FGP	FTP	APG	PPG
81-82	CSU	27	.467	.773	5.9	7.1
83-84	BRAD	22	.412	.707	7.2	6.3
84-85	BRAD	30	.498	.855	8.8	9.5
85-86	BRAD	35	.485	.756	7.9	14.2
Totals		114	.475	.775	7.5	9.8

NBA REGULAR-SEASON STATISTICS

		G	MIN	FGs		3-PT FGs		FTs		Rebounds		AST	STL	BLK	PTS	PPG
				FG	PCT	FG	PCT	FT	PCT	OFF	TOT					
88-89	UTA	82	781	40	.301	1	.071	57	.781	23	87	215	27	5	138	1.7
89-90	UTA/LAC	7	92	5	.357	0	.000	13	.765	3	7	21	3	0	23	3.3
90-91	SAC	55	1399	119	.444	71	.461	86	.835	18	111	299	57	4	395	7.2
91-92	SAC	62	712	74	.385	45	.344	38	.809	11	63	143	31	3	231	3.7
92-93	SAC	73	881	110	.425	66	.429	42	.840	20	89	169	40	7	328	4.5
Totals		279	3865	348	.402	183	.403	236	.814	75	357	847	158	19	1115	4.0

LAFAYETTE LEVER

Team: Dallas Mavericks
Position: Guard
Height: 6'3" **Weight:** 175
Birthdate: August 18, 1960

NBA Experience: 10 years
College: Arizona St.
Acquired: Traded from Nuggets for
1990 and 1991 1st-round picks, 6/90

Background: Lever led Arizona State in scoring, assists, and steals as a senior and once totaled 38 points, 13 rebounds, six assists, and seven steals in a game. He emerged as one of the top rebounding guards in NBA history, grabbing a staggering 734 boards in 1989-90. The two-time All-Star underwent arthroscopic surgery on his right knee four games into the 1990-91 campaign, his first with Dallas, and was out the remainder of the year. Similar surgery on his left knee followed, and he has not played since the middle of the 1991-92 season.

Strengths: When he was healthy, Lever established himself as one of the league's best and most complete guards. He could rebound, score, handle the ball, and play hard-nosed defense. Impressively versatile, Lever could play the point in addition to his natural off-guard slot.

Weaknesses: The biggest question mark regarding Lever is his health, as he's played only 35 games over the last three seasons. Can he pick up where he left off on two surgically repaired knees? He was never a great shooter to begin with.

Analysis: His chronic knee problems make one wonder whether Lever will ever return to play the kind of ball he once did, assuming he returns at all. If he can, it would be one of the most remarkable comebacks in recent years.

PLAYER SUMMARY	
Will	score, rebound
Can't	trade in his knees
Expect	a comeback bid
Don't Expect	an All-Star return
Fantasy Value	$2-4
Card Value	5-10¢

COLLEGE STATISTICS

		G	FGP	FTP	RPG	PPG
78-79	ASU	29	.413	.737	1.5	3.6
79-80	ASU	29	.445	.699	4.3	9.2
80-81	ASU	28	.463	.724	4.9	11.6
81-82	ASU	27	.454	.818	5.4	16.3
Totals		113	.450	.753	4.0	10.1

NBA REGULAR-SEASON STATISTICS

				FGs		3-PT FGs		FTs		Rebounds						
		G	MIN	FG	PCT	FG	PCT	FT	PCT	OFF	TOT	AST	STL	BLK	PTS	PPG
82-83	POR	81	2020	256	.431	5	.333	116	.730	85	225	426	153	15	633	7.8
83-84	POR	81	2010	313	.447	3	.200	159	.743	96	218	372	135	31	788	9.7
84-85	DEN	82	2559	424	.430	6	.250	197	.770	147	411	613	202	15	1051	12.8
85-86	DEN	78	2616	468	.441	12	.316	132	.725	136	420	584	178	15	1080	13.8
86-87	DEN	82	3054	643	.469	22	.239	244	.782	216	729	654	201	34	1552	18.9
87-88	DEN	82	3061	643	.473	12	.211	248	.785	203	665	639	223	21	1546	18.9
88-89	DEN	71	2745	558	.457	23	.348	270	.785	187	662	559	195	20	1409	19.8
89-90	DEN	79	2832	568	.443	36	.414	271	.804	230	734	517	168	13	1443	18.3
90-91	DAL	4	86	9	.391	0	.000	11	.796	3	15	12	6	3	29	7.3
91-92	DAL	31	884	135	.387	17	.327	60	.750	56	161	107	46	12	347	11.2
Totals		671	21867	4017	.449	136	.303	1708	.771	1359	4240	4483	1507	194	9878	14.7

MARCUS LIBERTY

Team: Denver Nuggets
Position: Forward
Height: 6'8" **Weight:** 208
Birthdate: October 27, 1968

NBA Experience: 3 years
College: Illinois
Acquired: 2nd-round pick in 1990 draft (42nd overall)

Background: High school basketball's most coveted recruit in 1987, Liberty sat out his freshman year at Illinois under Proposition 48 and did not live up to his lofty reputation until his junior year. He then entered the draft as an underclassman and played in a team-high 76 games as a Denver rookie. His next season was his best, as he averaged 9.3 PPG and started late in the year. He struggled through much of the 1992-93 campaign despite making 32 starts.

Strengths: A talented athlete, Liberty excels in the open court thanks to his boundless leaping and finishing ability. He is a natural scorer and promising rebounder who can put the ball on the floor and work for his own shots. The 3-pointer is within his range and he is versatile enough to play any of three positions.

Weaknesses: Liberty's carefree approach has earned him a label as an underachiever. Coaches will tell you that he needs to show more focus. The other big knock on Liberty is his inconsistent perimeter shooting. He played primarily in the paint in college and, though he'll make a few 3-pointers, his jumpers simply don't find the mark with enough regularity.

Analysis: Liberty probably left college too early and has been inconsistent as a pro. He's shown glimpses of big-time ability and there is no denying his athleticism, but he was handed Denver's starting small-forward role early last season and was not able to hang onto it. He shot a career-low 40.6 percent from the field, just one example of his lack of overall consistency. He has the raw ability to emerge.

PLAYER SUMMARY	
Will	get his shots off
Can't	stay in starting five
Expect	athletic finishes
Don't Expect	consistency
Fantasy Value	$1
Card Value	8-12¢

COLLEGE STATISTICS

		G	FGP	FTP	RPG	PPG
88-89	ILL	36	.476	.781	3.9	8.4
89-90	ILL	29	.507	.763	7.1	17.8
Totals		65	.495	.769	5.3	12.6

NBA REGULAR-SEASON STATISTICS

		G	MIN	FGs		3-PT FGs		FTs		Rebounds		AST	STL	BLK	PTS	PPG
				FG	PCT	FG	PCT	FT	PCT	OFF	TOT					
90-91	DEN	76	1171	216	.421	17	.298	58	.630	117	221	64	48	19	507	6.7
91-92	DEN	75	1527	275	.443	17	.340	131	.728	144	308	58	66	29	698	9.3
92-93	DEN	78	1585	252	.406	22	.373	102	.654	131	335	105	64	21	628	8.1
Totals		229	4283	743	.424	56	.337	291	.680	392	864	227	178	69	1833	8.0

TODD LICHTI

Team: Orlando Magic
Position: Guard
Height: 6'4" **Weight:** 205
Birthdate: January 8, 1967
NBA Experience: 4 years

College: Stanford
Acquired: Traded from Nuggets with Anthony Cook and a 1994 2nd-round pick for Brian Williams, 8/93

Background: At Stanford, Lichti was named All-Pac-10 four consecutive seasons. He left as the school's career leader in points, games, and minutes. Drafted by Denver in 1989, he missed most of the 1990-91 season after undergoing arthroscopic surgery on his left knee. Then, Lichti tore a ligament in his right knee during the 1991-92 preseason and missed most of November. He played in 48 games during the 1992-93 campaign before requiring surgery to repair a torn anterior cruciate ligament in his left knee. In August, he was dealt to Orlando.

Strengths: At his best, Lichti is a fearless penetrator with great finishing ability. He is strong with either hand and can convert in traffic. He backs down from no one and thrives in the open court. Lichti is a hustling defender with good athletic skills and a nice touch from the line.

Weaknesses: Injuries continue to plague Lichti, who might never reach his potential on surgically repaired knees. He is not known as a jump-shooter, which leads defenders to play off him and take away the drive to the basket. His play has been up-and-down.

Analysis: Lichti was coming into his own before the preseason injury two years ago took him out of a starting spot. His third knee injury prevented him from winning the job back last year, as Mark Macon also spent time on the injured list. Even if healthy, he probably won't be able to crack Orlando's starting lineup.

PLAYER SUMMARY	
Will	use both hands
Can't	keep knees healthy
Expect	quick penetration
Don't Expect	pure shooting
Fantasy Value	$1
Card Value	5-10¢

COLLEGE STATISTICS

		G	FGP	FTP	RPG	PPG
85-86	STAN	30	.533	.814	4.7	17.2
86-87	STAN	28	.517	.809	5.7	17.6
87-88	STAN	33	.547	.879	5.6	20.1
88-89	STAN	33	.549	.850	5.0	20.1
Totals		124	.538	.840	5.3	18.8

NBA REGULAR-SEASON STATISTICS

				FGs		3-PT FGs		FTs		Rebounds						
		G	MIN	FG	PCT	FG	PCT	FT	PCT	OFF	TOT	AST	STL	BLK	PTS	PPG
89-90	DEN	79	1326	250	.486	0	.000	130	.747	49	151	116	55	13	630	8.0
90-91	DEN	29	860	166	.439	14	.298	59	.855	49	112	72	46	8	405	14.0
91-92	DEN	68	1176	173	.460	1	.111	99	.839	36	118	74	43	12	446	6.6
92-93	DEN	48	752	124	.449	2	.333	81	.794	35	102	52	28	11	331	6.9
Totals		224	4114	713	.462	17	.224	369	.797	169	483	314	172	44	1812	8.1

BRAD LOHAUS

Team: Milwaukee Bucks
Position: Forward/Center
Height: 7'0" **Weight:** 235
Birthdate: September 29, 1964
NBA Experience: 6 years

College: Iowa
Acquired: Traded from Timberwolves for Randy Breuer and a conditional exchange of 1991 or 1992 2nd-round picks, 1/90

Background: In his senior year at Iowa, Lohaus increased his scoring average by nearly eight points per game and shot 54 percent from the field. He has played with four NBA teams in six years, his best numbers coming with expansion Minnesota in 1989. Lohaus was traded to Milwaukee in the middle of 1989-90. He matched his career high in scoring last season, averaging 9.1 PPG in 80 games for the Bucks.

Strengths: Lohaus is loaded with perimeter punch. He shoots with unlimited range and has a quick release. He ranked 11th in the league in 3-point percentage two years ago at nearly 40 percent and made a career-high 85 treys last season. Lohaus made down the floor as quickly as any seven-footer. He led the Bucks in blocked shots last year.

Weaknesses: If ever there was a guard in a center's body, Lohaus is the man. Despite his height, he possesses virtually no inside game. His back-to-the-basket skills are forgettable. He is also prone to cold spells from the outside and does not create his own shots with the dribble as well as he catches and fires. He plays soft.

Analysis: Lohaus is the definition of a match-up problem. What seven-footer wants to defend beyond the 3-point line? With Lohaus, you have to. On the flip side, Lohaus does not stack up with opposing big men in the paint on either end of the court. In fact, he doesn't offer much outside of shooting and shot-blocking.

PLAYER SUMMARY

Will ....shoot from downtown
Can't............................match up inside
Expect ....treys, blocked shots
Don't Expect ....much else
Fantasy Value $1
Card Value ....5-8¢

COLLEGE STATISTICS

		G	FGP	FTP	RPG	PPG
82-83	IOWA	20	.310	.538	0.6	1.3
83-84	IOWA	28	.404	.673	5.2	6.8
85-86	IOWA	32	.431	.794	3.2	3.6
86-87	IOWA	35	.540	.692	7.7	11.3
Totals		115	.467	.695	4.6	6.3

NBA REGULAR-SEASON STATISTICS

				FGs		3-PT FGs		FTs		Rebounds						
		G	MIN	FG	PCT	FG	PCT	FT	PCT	OFF	TOT	AST	STL	BLK	PTS	PPG
87-88	BOS	70	718	122	.496	3	.231	50	.806	46	138	49	20	41	297	4.2
88-89	BOS/SAC	77	1214	210	.432	1	.091	81	.786	84	256	66	30	56	502	6.5
89-90	MIN/MIL	80	1943	305	.460	47	.343	75	.728	98	398	168	58	88	732	9.1
90-91	MIL	81	1219	179	.431	33	.277	37	.685	59	217	75	50	74	428	5.3
91-92	MIL	70	1081	162	.450	57	.396	27	.659	65	249	74	40	71	408	5.8
92-93	MIL	80	1766	283	.461	85	.370	73	.723	59	276	127	47	74	724	9.1
Totals		458	7941	1261	.453	226	.346	343	.739	411	1534	559	245	404	3091	6.7

GRANT LONG

Team: Miami Heat
Position: Forward
Height: 6'8" **Weight:** 230
Birthdate: March 12, 1966

NBA Experience: 5 years
College: Eastern Michigan
Acquired: 2nd-round pick in 1988 draft (33rd overall)

Background: As a senior at Eastern Michigan, Long was named Mid-American Conference Player of the Year and MVP of the MAC Tournament. In his first two years as a pro, he approached the NBA lead in disqualifications (13 and 11). He became a full-time Miami starter in December 1990 and was one of the league's most improved players during the 1991-92 campaign. He was a contract holdout until a week into the regular season last year, then averaged 14 PPG for the second consecutive campaign.

Strengths: Long is a hard-working player who attacks the boards, runs the floor, plays go-get-'em defense, and can also score. Coaches love his attitude and his willingness to give 100 percent every night. He has made himself a good shooter from medium range. He ranks among the league's top thefts from the power-forward position.

Weaknesses: Some of the finesse aspects are missing from Long's game. He's not a smooth driver and his skills with the ball are nothing to boast about. He still hacks too often, fouling out of eight games last season. Last year also saw his field goal percentage drop by 25 points.

Analysis: Long continues to be one of the more underrated power forwards in the league. He will never be a superstar, but his work ethic and durability have made him invaluable to the Miami ballclub, especially over the last two years. On a more talented team, the well-liked Long would probably best fit in as a role-playing reserve.

PLAYER SUMMARY	
Will	work non-stop
Can't	attain stardom
Expect	defense, rebounds
Don't Expect	finesse
Fantasy Value	$13-16
Card Value	5-10¢

COLLEGE STATISTICS

		G	FGP	FTP	RPG	PPG
84-85	EMU	28	.564	.609	4.0	4.1
85-86	EMU	27	.526	.644	6.6	8.6
86-87	EMU	29	.549	.725	9.0	14.9
87-88	EMU	30	.555	.765	10.4	23.0
Totals		114	.549	.725	7.6	12.9

NBA REGULAR-SEASON STATISTICS

		G	MIN	FGs FG	FGs PCT	3-PT FGs FG	3-PT FGs PCT	FTs FT	FTs PCT	Rebounds OFF	Rebounds TOT	AST	STL	BLK	PTS	PPG
88-89	MIA	82	2435	336	.486	0	.000	304	.749	240	546	149	122	48	976	11.9
89-90	MIA	81	1856	257	.483	0	.000	172	.714	156	402	96	91	38	686	8.5
90-91	MIA	80	2514	276	.492	1	.167	181	.787	225	568	176	119	43	734	9.2
91-92	MIA	82	3063	440	.494	6	.273	326	.807	259	691	225	139	40	1212	14.8
92-93	MIA	76	2728	397	.469	6	.231	261	.765	197	568	182	104	31	1061	14.0
Totals		401	12596	1706	.484	13	.210	1244	.767	1077	2775	828	575	200	4669	11.6

LUC LONGLEY

Team: Minnesota Timberwolves
Position: Center
Height: 7'2" **Weight:** 265
Birthdate: January 19, 1969

NBA Experience: 2 years
College: New Mexico
Acquired: 1st-round pick in 1991 draft (7th overall)

Background: Originally from Perth, Australia, Longley was coveted by pro scouts from the day he set foot on the New Mexico campus. He progressed slowly for the Lobos, never really emerging as a consistent force. He became the school's all-time leading scorer and rebounder, but it was said that Longley could play like Bill Walton one night and John Boy Walton the next. He looked more like the latter as a Minnesota rookie, averaging 4.3 PPG and 3.9 RPG. He improved to 5.8 PPG and 4.4 RPG last season before a sprained foot in late March ended his season after 55 games and 25 starts.

Strengths: Longley has some refined skills for a big man. He is a very good passer, moves pretty well, and can occasionally score in the paint. His primary weapon, of course, is his size. But along with it, Longley owns a nice touch. He also rebounds and blocks shots. The latter has been probably his biggest asset as a professional.

Weaknesses: The big Aussie has always struggled to find consistency. If people thought he lacked it as a collegian (and he did), his first two pro seasons did nothing to dispel the rap. There are doubts about his intensity, desire, and ability to take the game seriously. Longley is not a banger on defense, preferring to lay off and go for the block.

Analysis: Not long ago, the consensus among NBA scouts was that Longley was a natural who would some day become a big-time pro center. One wonders whether anyone still believes that. Longley has done almost nothing to indicate he will emerge as anything but a mediocre, inconsistent back-up. As a lottery pick, he's been a major bust.

PLAYER SUMMARY	
Will	block shots
Can't	shoot 50 percent
Expect	inconsistency
Don't Expect	10 PPG
Fantasy Value	$1
Card Value	8-15¢

COLLEGE STATISTICS

		G	FGP	FTP	RPG	PPG
87-88	NM	35	.500	.392	2.7	4.0
88-89	NM	33	.578	.769	6.8	13.0
89-90	NM	34	.559	.821	9.7	18.4
90-91	NM	30	.656	.716	9.2	19.1
Totals		132	.586	.735	7.0	13.4

NBA REGULAR-SEASON STATISTICS

		G	MIN	FGs FG	FGs PCT	3-PT FGs FG	3-PT FGs PCT	FTs FT	FTs PCT	Rebounds OFF	Rebounds TOT	AST	STL	BLK	PTS	PPG
91-92	MIN	66	991	114	.458	0	.000	53	.663	67	257	53	35	64	281	4.3
92-93	MIN	55	1045	133	.455	0	.000	53	.715	71	240	51	47	77	319	5.8
Totals		121	2036	247	.457	0	.000	106	.688	138	497	104	82	141	600	5.0

DON MacLEAN

Team: Washington Bullets
Position: Forward
Height: 6'10" **Weight:** 235
Birthdate: January 16, 1970
NBA Experience: 1 year

College: UCLA
Acquired: Traded from Clippers with William Bedford for John Williams, 10/92

Background: MacLean finished his UCLA career as the leading scorer in school and Pac-10 history, a tremendous accomplishment. He led all Division I players in free throw percentage as a senior and was a first-team all-conference selection three years in a row. He was universally hated by opposing fans for incidents such as shoving Shaun Vandiver at U.S. national team tryouts in 1990 and throwing a ball at Brian Williams in a 1991 game. Detroit drafted MacLean 19th overall and traded him to the Clippers, but he wound up in Washington via another deal. He averaged 6.6 PPG in 62 rookie outings.

Strengths: MacLean is a deadly perimeter marksman with a quick release. He can make the NBA 3-pointer although his "comfortable" range extends only to about 18 feet. As his college numbers indicate, he knows how to put the ball in the hole. He is also a fine free throw shooter. MacLean possesses leadership qualities and seems to have matured.

Weaknesses: Spotting up, MacLean gets the job done. But get in his face and force him to use the dribble and he is not nearly as effective. He never shot below 50 percent from the field in college but connected on just 43.5 percent in his first pro season. MacLean turns the ball over more frequently than he records an assist. He is not a defensive stalwart.

Analysis: MacLean has the makings of a double-figure scorer even though he struggles to create his own shot. He is a good enough marksman to get by as a spot-up shooter who will come off a pick or pull up on the break. He is also a tenacious competitor, which leaves hope for his rebounding and defense.

PLAYER SUMMARY	
Will	stick jumpers
Can't	create off dribble
Expect	high FT pct.
Don't Expect	a distributor
Fantasy Value	$1
Card Value	12-35¢

COLLEGE STATISTICS

		G	FGP	FTP	RPG	PPG
88-89	UCLA	31	.555	.816	7.5	18.6
89-90	UCLA	33	.516	.848	8.7	19.9
90-91	UCLA	31	.551	.846	7.3	23.0
91-92	UCLA	32	.504	.921	7.8	20.7
Totals		127	.531	.860	7.8	20.5

NBA REGULAR-SEASON STATISTICS

				FGs		3-PT FGs		FTs		Rebounds						
		G	MIN	FG	PCT	FG	PCT	FT	PCT	OFF	TOT	AST	STL	BLK	PTS	PPG
92-93	WAS	62	674	157	.435	3	.500	90	.811	33	122	39	11	4	407	6.6
Totals		62	674	157	.435	3	.500	90	.811	33	122	39	11	4	407	6.6

MARK MACON

Team: Denver Nuggets
Position: Guard
Height: 6'5" **Weight:** 185
Birthdate: April 14, 1969

NBA Experience: 2 years
College: Temple
Acquired: 1st-round pick in 1991 draft (8th overall)

Background: Macon was a superstar from Day One at Temple, which eventually came back to haunt him. Among freshmen, he was the nation's leading scorer and led the Owls to a 32-2 record. After that, his shooting percentage plummeted. He still finished as the school's career scoring leader and struck for 31 points against North Carolina in his final college game. As a rookie with Denver in 1991-92, his field goal percentage of 37.5 was the lowest of any starter in the league. His second season was limited by injuries, including a sprained wrist that cost him several games late in the year.

Strengths: Macon was considered the best defensive guard in the 1991 draft, and he has backed it up with intense combativeness. He has excellent lateral quickness and is a good leaper. His size allows him to outrebound opposing guards and he comes up with a lot of steals. He averaged 10.6 PPG as a rookie, so there is evidence he can score.

Weaknesses: Macon simply cannot shoot the basketball with any consistency. He followed his poor rookie showing on offense with 41.5-percent shooting last year. He has no 3-point ability, he takes poor shots, and he turns the ball over far too often. Some thought he could play the point, but his poor assist-to-turnover ratio says otherwise.

Analysis: Bernie Bickerstaff says of Macon: "Here's a guy you want to be in a foxhole with." That is, unless the way to get out is having to make an outside jump shot. Macon's shooting is frighteningly low for an NBA starter. On defense, Macon is everything he was cracked up to be. That's clearly what Bickerstaff was referring to, and it's the reason Macon will continue to get his chance.

PLAYER SUMMARY	
Will	play defense
Can't	shoot straight
Expect	combativeness
Don't Expect	high FG pct.
Fantasy Value	$1
Card Value	10-20¢

COLLEGE STATISTICS

		G	FGP	FTP	RPG	PPG
87-88	TEMP	34	.454	.771	5.6	20.6
88-89	TEMP	30	.407	.776	5.6	18.3
89-90	TEMP	31	.389	.798	6.0	21.9
90-91	TEMP	31	.440	.766	4.9	22.0
Totals		126	.423	.780	5.6	20.7

NBA REGULAR-SEASON STATISTICS

			FGs		3-PT FGs		FTs		Rebounds						
		G	MIN	FG	PCT	FG	PCT	FT	PCT	OFF	TOT	AST	STL	BLK	PTS	PPG
91-92	DEN	76	2304	333	.375	4	.133	135	.730	80	220	168	154	14	805	10.6
92-93	DEN	48	1141	158	.415	0	.000	42	.700	33	103	126	69	3	358	7.5
Totals		124	3445	491	.387	4	.111	177	.722	113	323	294	223	17	1163	9.4

RICK MAHORN

Team: New Jersey Nets
Position: Forward/Center
Height: 6'10" **Weight:** 255
Birthdate: September 21, 1958

NBA Experience: 12 years
College: Hampton Institute
Acquired: Signed as a free agent, 11/92

Background: Ricky Mahorn was a small-college star at Hampton Institute. He spent his early pro days with Washington, and his 358 personal fouls during the 1983-84 campaign are the ninth most ever recorded in a season. Mahorn won an NBA championship ring with the Pistons in 1988-89 but was not protected by Detroit the following year. He played two years in Philadelphia and one year overseas before returning last season with the Nets, for whom he averaged 3.9 points per game.

Strengths: Mahorn is as physical as they come. He throws his weight around in the paint, applies his frame on the boards, and is known as a tough defender. He uses his backside to post up on offense.

Weaknesses: Offense has never been a big part of Mahorn's game. His range is limited and he is more effective with his back to the basket than as a face-up player. Officials don't like him.

Analysis: Any team with Mahorn on its roster by definition becomes more physical. Intimidation is a big part of his game and is the reason he was adored by Detroit fans as their favorite "Bad Boy." He filled in admirably as starting center for the injury-riddled Nets during last year's playoffs.

PLAYER SUMMARY	
Will	apply his physique
Can't	shoot with range
Expect	intimidation
Don't Expect	finesse
Fantasy Value	$0
Card Value	5-10¢

COLLEGE STATISTICS

		G	FGP	FTP	RPG	PPG
76-77	HAMP	28	.409	.659	6.0	5.7
77-78	HAMP	30	.511	.678	12.6	24.0
78-79	HAMP	30	.560	.685	14.3	22.8
79-80	HAMP	31	.567	.686	15.8	27.6
Totals		119	.534	.682	12.3	20.3

NBA REGULAR-SEASON STATISTICS

				FGs		3-PT FGs		FTs		Rebounds						
		G	MIN	FG	PCT	FG	PCT	FT	PCT	OFF	TOT	AST	STL	BLK	PTS	PPG
80-81	WAS	52	696	111	.507	0	.000	27	.675	67	215	25	21	44	249	4.8
81-82	WAS	80	2664	414	.507	0	.000	148	.632	149	704	150	57	138	976	12.2
82-83	WAS	82	3023	376	.490	0	.000	146	.575	171	779	115	86	148	898	11.0
83-84	WAS	82	2701	307	.507	0	.000	125	.651	169	738	131	62	123	739	9.0
84-85	WAS	77	2072	206	.499	0	.000	71	.683	150	608	121	59	104	483	6.3
85-86	DET	80	1442	157	.455	0	.000	81	.681	121	412	64	40	61	395	4.9
86-87	DET	63	1278	144	.447	0	.000	96	.821	93	375	38	32	50	384	6.1
87-88	DET	67	1963	276	.574	1	.500	164	.756	159	565	60	43	42	717	10.7
88-89	DET	72	1795	203	.517	0	.000	116	.748	141	496	59	40	66	522	7.3
89-90	PHI	75	2271	313	.497	2	.222	183	.715	167	568	98	44	103	811	10.8
90-91	PHI	80	2439	261	.467	0	.000	189	.788	151	621	118	79	56	711	8.9
92-93	NJ	74	1077	101	.472	1	.333	88	.800	93	279	33	19	31	291	3.9
Totals		884	23421	2869	.496	4	.125	1434	.704	1631	6360	1012	582	966	7176	8.1

DAN MAJERLE

Team: Phoenix Suns
Position: Guard/Forward
Height: 6'6" **Weight:** 220
Birthdate: September 9, 1965

NBA Experience: 5 years
College: Central Michigan
Acquired: 1st-round pick in 1988 draft
(14th overall)

Background: Majerle was a three-time All-Mid-American Conference selection at Central Michigan, where he ranked second on the all-time scoring, steals, and field goal-percentage lists. He totaled 27 points and six steals in his pro debut and has since emerged as one of the NBA's premier all-around players. Majerle made his first appearance in the All-Star Game in 1991-92 and his second consecutive trip last year. He tied Reggie Miller for the league lead in 3-pointers made last season and led the league in 3-point attempts.

Strengths: Majerle is one of the most versatile stars in the game. He handles the ball with confidence, rebounds well, plays relentless defense, and scores from both inside and outside. "Thunder Dan" possesses tremendous leaping ability and uses it to his full advantage, yet he also has become a dangerous 3-point shooter (he hit six during an NBA Finals game). His work ethic, all-out hustle, and physical style are contagious. Majerle plays guard and forward with equal success. He is a team player who hates to lose.

Weaknesses: Now that Majerle is an accomplished long-distance shooter, he must avoid the temptation to make a living on the perimeter. His best asset is still his ability to get the ball to the hoop off the dribble.

Analysis: Formerly recognized as one of the league's outstanding reserves, Majerle is now clearly one of the league's truly outstanding starters. Whatever his team needs—offense, defense, speed, leadership—Majerle provides. His 3-point numbers don't begin to describe his all-around ability.

PLAYER SUMMARY

Will	score inside and out
Can't	give less than his all
Expect	two treys per game
Don't Expect	limitations
Fantasy Value	$24-27
Card Value	15-25¢

COLLEGE STATISTICS

		G	FGP	FTP	RPG	PPG
84-85	CMU	12	.568	.582	6.7	18.6
85-86	CMU	27	.527	.718	7.9	21.4
86-87	CMU	23	.555	.552	8.5	21.1
87-88	CMU	32	.521	.645	10.8	23.7
Totals		94	.536	.631	8.9	21.8

NBA REGULAR-SEASON STATISTICS

				FGs		3-PT FGs		FTs		Rebounds						
		G	MIN	FG	PCT	FG	PCT	FT	PCT	OFF	TOT	AST	STL	BLK	PTS	PPG
88-89	PHO	54	1354	181	.419	27	.329	78	.614	62	209	130	63	14	467	8.6
89-90	PHO	73	2244	296	.424	19	.237	198	.762	144	430	188	100	32	809	11.1
90-91	PHO	77	2281	397	.484	30	.349	227	.762	168	418	216	106	40	1051	13.6
91-92	PHO	82	2853	551	.478	87	.382	229	.756	148	483	274	131	43	1418	17.3
92-93	PHO	82	3199	509	.464	167	.381	203	.778	120	383	311	138	33	1388	16.9
Totals		368	11931	1934	.460	330	.361	935	.749	642	1923	1119	538	162	5133	13.9

JEFF MALONE

Team: Utah Jazz
Position: Guard
Height: 6'4"　**Weight:** 205
Birthdate: June 28, 1961
NBA Experience: 10 years

College: Mississippi St.
Acquired: Traded from Bullets via the Kings; Jazz sent Eric Leckner and Bobby Hansen to Kings, and Kings sent Pervis Ellison to Bullets, 6/90

Background: Malone broke Bailey Howell's career scoring record as a four-year starter at Mississippi State and finished fifth on the all-time SEC scoring list. He spent his first seven NBA seasons with the Washington Bullets, played in two All-Star Games, and remains Washington's all-time leader in free throw percentage at 86.9. Malone has continued as one of the league's best pure shooters in his three years with Utah.

Strengths: You'll have to search to find a better pure shooter than Malone, who annually hovers around 50 percent from the perimeter and rarely misses from the line. Whether off the dribble or coming off a screen, Malone can fill the basket from anywhere inside the 3-point arc.

Weaknesses: Amazingly, Malone does not possess 3-point range. He's 7-of-52 from behind the arc over the last five seasons. Malone does not run the floor well for a guard, nor does he create. He will not provide assists, steals, rebounds, or blocked shots.

Analysis: Though he's destined to remain the "other" Malone in Utah, Jeff is one of a kind when it comes to shooting. His 18.1 PPG last year was his lowest scoring output since he was a rookie, yet that's nothing to complain about on a team that features a pair of All-Stars in Karl Malone and John Stockton.

PLAYER SUMMARY

Will	hit spinning jumpers
Can't	shoot beyond arc
Expect	high FT pct.
Don't Expect	rebounds
Fantasy Value	$6-8
Card Value	5-10¢

COLLEGE STATISTICS

		G	FGP	FTP	RPG	PPG
79-80	MSU	27	.459	.824	3.3	11.9
80-81	MSU	27	.490	.820	4.2	20.1
81-82	MSU	27	.549	.743	4.1	18.6
82-83	MSU	29	.531	.824	3.7	26.8
Totals		110	.512	.809	3.8	19.5

NBA REGULAR-SEASON STATISTICS

		G	MIN	FGs FG	FGs PCT	3-PT FGs FG	3-PT FGs PCT	FTs FT	FTs PCT	Rebounds OFF	Rebounds TOT	AST	STL	BLK	PTS	PPG
83-84	WAS	81	1976	408	.444	24	.324	142	.826	57	155	151	23	13	982	12.1
84-85	WAS	76	2613	605	.499	15	.208	211	.844	60	206	184	52	9	1436	18.9
85-86	WAS	80	2992	735	.483	3	.176	322	.868	66	288	191	70	12	1795	22.4
86-87	WAS	80	2763	689	.457	4	.154	376	.885	50	218	298	75	13	1758	22.0
87-88	WAS	80	2655	648	.476	10	.417	335	.882	44	206	237	51	13	1641	20.5
88-89	WAS	76	2418	677	.480	1	.053	296	.871	55	179	219	39	14	1651	21.7
89-90	WAS	75	2567	781	.491	1	.167	257	.877	54	206	243	48	6	1820	24.3
90-91	UTA	69	2466	525	.508	1	.167	231	.917	36	206	143	50	6	1282	18.6
91-92	UTA	81	2922	691	.511	1	.083	256	.898	49	233	180	56	5	1639	20.2
92-93	UTA	79	2558	595	.494	3	.333	236	.852	31	173	128	42	4	1429	18.1
Totals		777	25930	6354	.484	63	.238	2662	.874	502	2070	1974	506	95	15433	19.9

KARL MALONE

Team: Utah Jazz
Position: Forward
Height: 6'9" **Weight:** 256
Birthdate: July 24, 1963

NBA Experience: 8 years
College: Louisiana Tech
Acquired: 1st-round pick in 1985 draft
(13th overall)

Background: Malone finished his college career third on the all-time scoring list and sixth in career rebounding at Louisiana Tech—despite declaring for the NBA draft after his junior year. In eight years with Utah, he has missed only four games. Malone finished third in the voting for 1986 Rookie of the Year and has appeared in six All-Star Games, winning MVP honors in 1989 and 1993. He finished second to Michael Jordan in scoring four straight seasons before ranking third last year, and was a teammate of Jordan's in the 1992 Olympics.

Strengths: Nicknamed "The Mailman" because he delivers, Malone is virtually impossible for one man to stop. He is big, quick, and incredibly strong. If he fails to score, he almost always draws a foul. He has gone to the line more than anyone in the NBA for five straight years. He plays defense, runs the floor, and owns the boards.

Weaknesses: Malone commits a lot of turnovers, largely because defenders swarm him almost every time he touches the ball. He has not been able to bring the Jazz much playoff success.

Analysis: The Mailman has established himself as one of the premier forwards basketball has seen in recent years. Get him the ball in the post, and no one in the game is going to stop him from scoring or getting to the line. He's a tremendous offensive weapon who also excels in other aspects.

PLAYER SUMMARY	
Will	get to the line
Can't	be stopped by one man
Expect	25 PPG, 10 RPG
Don't Expect	soft play
Fantasy Value	$80-85
Card Value	20-35¢

COLLEGE STATISTICS

		G	FGP	FTP	RPG	PPG
82-83	LAT	28	.582	.623	10.3	20.9
83-84	LAT	32	.576	.682	8.8	18.8
84-85	LAT	32	.541	.571	9.0	16.5
Totals		92	.566	.631	9.3	18.7

NBA REGULAR-SEASON STATISTICS

		G	MIN	FGs FG	FGs PCT	3-PT FGs FG	3-PT FGs PCT	FTs FT	FTs PCT	Rebounds OFF	Rebounds TOT	AST	STL	BLK	PTS	PPG
85-86	UTA	81	2475	504	.496	0	.000	195	.481	174	718	236	105	44	1203	14.9
86-87	UTA	82	2857	728	.512	0	.000	323	.598	278	855	158	104	60	1779	21.7
87-88	UTA	82	3198	858	.520	0	.000	552	.700	277	986	199	117	50	2268	27.7
88-89	UTA	80	3126	809	.519	5	.313	703	.766	259	853	219	144	70	2326	29.1
89-90	UTA	82	3122	914	.562	16	.372	696	.762	232	911	226	121	50	2540	31.0
90-91	UTA	82	3302	847	.527	4	.286	684	.770	236	967	270	89	79	2382	29.0
91-92	UTA	81	3054	798	.526	3	.176	673	.778	225	909	241	108	51	2272	28.0
92-93	UTA	82	3099	797	.552	4	.200	619	.740	227	919	308	124	85	2217	27.0
Totals		652	24233	6255	.528	32	.258	4445	.722	1908	7118	1857	912	489	16987	26.1

MOSES MALONE

Team: Philadelphia 76ers
Position: Center
Height: 6'10" **Weight:** 255
Birthdate: March 23, 1955

NBA Experience: 17 years
College: None
Acquired: Signed as a free agent, 8/93

Background: Malone, who jumped straight from high school to the ABA, was voted the NBA's MVP in 1979 and 1982 with Houston, and again in 1983 with Philadelphia. He led the 76ers to the 1982-83 NBA title and played in 12 consecutive All-Star Games from 1978-89. With Atlanta in 1990-91, he surpassed the 25,000-point and 15,000-rebound plateaus. After a fine first year in Milwaukee, Malone missed most of last season with a herniated disc. Philadelphia picked him up over the summer.

Strengths: Malone is one of the greatest rebounders and low-post scorers in history. His businesslike approach has helped him set the NBA's career records for offensive caroms and free throws made.

Weaknesses: Malone is 38 years old and has a bad back. He wasn't quick before his injury problems limited him to 11 games last year.

Analysis: Though his 17th season was by far his least productive, Malone played enough to take over fifth place on the all-time games played list. It's safe to say that he doesn't have many NBA games left.

PLAYER SUMMARY	
Will	go for rebounds
Can't	dominate anymore
Expect	Hall of Fame induction
Don't Expect	many more games
Fantasy Value	$0
Card Value	10-15¢

COLLEGE STATISTICS

—DID NOT PLAY—

NBA REGULAR-SEASON STATISTICS

			FGs		3-PT FGs		FTs		Rebounds						
		G	MIN	FG	PCT	FG	PCT	FT	PCT	OFF	TOT	AST	STL	BLK	PTS	PPG
76-77	BUF/HOU	82	2506	389	.480	0	.000	305	.693	437	1072	89	67	181	1083	13.2
77-78	HOU	59	2107	413	.499	0	.000	318	.718	380	886	31	48	76	1144	19.4
78-79	HOU	82	3390	716	.540	0	.000	599	.739	587	1444	147	79	119	2031	24.8
79-80	HOU	82	3140	778	.502	0	.000	563	.719	573	1190	147	80	107	2119	25.8
80-81	HOU	80	3245	806	.522	1	.333	609	.757	474	1180	141	83	150	2222	27.8
81-82	HOU	81	3398	945	.519	0	.000	630	.762	558	1188	142	76	125	2520	31.1
82-83	PHI	78	2922	654	.501	0	.000	600	.761	445	1194	101	89	157	1908	24.5
83-84	PHI	71	2613	532	.483	0	.000	545	.750	352	950	96	71	110	1609	22.7
84-85	PHI	79	2957	602	.469	0	.000	737	.815	385	1031	130	67	123	1941	24.6
85-86	PHI	74	2706	571	.458	0	.000	617	.787	339	872	90	67	71	1759	23.8
86-87	WAS	73	2488	595	.454	0	.000	570	.824	340	824	120	59	92	1760	24.1
87-88	WAS	79	2692	531	.487	2	.286	543	.788	372	884	112	59	72	1607	20.3
88-89	ATL	81	2878	538	.491	0	.000	561	.789	386	956	112	79	100	1637	20.2
89-90	ATL	81	2735	517	.480	1	.111	493	.781	364	812	130	47	84	1528	18.9
90-91	ATL	82	1912	280	.468	0	.000	309	.831	271	667	68	30	74	869	10.6
91-92	MIL	82	2511	440	.474	3	.375	396	.786	320	744	93	74	64	1279	15.6
92-93	MIL	11	104	13	.310	0	.000	24	.774	22	46	7	1	8	50	4.5
Totals		1257	44304	9320	.492	7	.091	8419	.769	6605	15940	1756	1076	1713	27066	21.5

DANNY MANNING

Team: Los Angeles Clippers
Position: Forward
Height: 6'10" **Weight:** 235
Birthdate: May 17, 1966

NBA Experience: 5 years
College: Kansas
Acquired: 1st-round pick in 1988 draft
(1st overall)

Background: Manning was voted college Player of the Year in 1988, when he led Kansas to the NCAA championship. He ended his college career with more than three dozen school, conference, and NCAA records. His early NBA years were slowed by a tear of the anterior cruciate in his right knee in January 1989, which caused him to miss most of his rookie year and the early part of 1989-90. He has led the Clippers to the playoffs as the team's leading scorer each of the past two seasons and made an All-Star appearance in 1993.

Strengths: Manning is a big-time scorer. He drills his quick-release jumper and he owns a deadly half-hook that he throws in from all angles. He moves well without the ball. He has been called a point guard in the body of a forward—a tribute to his passing skills. He makes those around him better and is superb with the ball in his hands.

Weaknesses: Manning commits a lot of fouls and defense has never been a strength. He is an average rebounding forward. Manning encountered some off-court problems last year, at one point asking for a trade.

Analysis: It's ironic that just as Manning became an All-Star, he seemed unhappy. "It's time for me to get away from Larry Brown," he said in January of the man who coached him at Kansas and with the Clippers. Ironically, Brown quit the Clippers last spring. We'll have to wait and see if the coaching change affects Manning.

PLAYER SUMMARY	
Will	shoot for percentage
Can't	control the boards
Expect	more All-Star trips
Don't Expect	stellar defense
Fantasy Value	$50-55
Card Value	12-20¢

COLLEGE STATISTICS

		G	FGP	FTP	RPG	PPG
84-85	KAN	34	.566	.765	7.6	14.6
85-86	KAN	39	.600	.748	6.3	16.7
86-87	KAN	36	.617	.730	9.5	23.9
87-88	KAN	38	.583	.734	9.0	24.8
Totals		147	.593	.740	8.1	20.1

NBA REGULAR-SEASON STATISTICS

		G	MIN	FGs FG	FGs PCT	3-PT FGs FG	3-PT FGs PCT	FTs FT	FTs PCT	Rebounds OFF	Rebounds TOT	AST	STL	BLK	PTS	PPG
88-89	LAC	26	950	177	.494	1	.200	79	.767	70	171	81	44	25	434	16.7
89-90	LAC	71	2269	440	.533	0	.000	274	.741	142	422	187	91	39	1154	16.3
90-91	LAC	73	2197	470	.519	0	.000	219	.716	169	426	196	117	62	1159	15.9
91-92	LAC	82	2904	650	.542	0	.000	279	.725	229	564	285	135	122	1579	19.3
92-93	LAC	79	2761	702	.509	8	.267	388	.802	198	520	207	108	101	1800	22.8
Totals		331	11081	2439	.523	9	.188	1239	.752	808	2103	956	495	349	6126	18.5

SARUNAS MARCIULIONIS

Team: Golden State Warriors
Position: Guard
Height: 6'5" **Weight:** 215
Birthdate: June 13, 1964

NBA Experience: 4 years
College: Vilnius St.
Acquired: Signed as a free agent, 6/89

Background: The Lithuanian Marciulionis was the leading scorer on the Soviet Union's 1988 Olympic gold-medal-winning team in Seoul, South Korea, and played for Lithuania in the 1992 Games. He became the first Soviet player to play in the NBA when he signed in 1989, and he finished sixth among all rookies in scoring in 1989-90. After a knee injury slowed him in 1990-91, he led all non-starters in scoring (18.9 PPG) and all guards in field goal percentage (.538) during the 1991-92 campaign. Leg and ankle injuries limited him to a career-low 30 games last season.

Strengths: Although he plays left-handed, Marciulionis is ambidextrous. Anyone unconvinced should watch him handle the ball. He has a nice jumper but prefers driving inside, where he uses his strength. Many defenders simply opt to clear out of his path. When they don't, he's capable of scoring anyway, getting an assist, or going to the free throw line. His work habits are exceptional.

Weaknesses: Injuries are a big concern. His leg problems already border on the chronic stage. Marciulionis does not have as much confidence in his jumper as he has in his ability to get to the basket. He struggles from beyond the 3-point line. He is not nearly as effective on defense and is not much help on the boards.

Analysis: When healthy, Marciulionis is extremely valuable. He scores, handles the ball, distributes, and gets to the line with his uncanny penetration. Entering the second season of a five-year contract with Golden State, look for him to challenge for a starting spot if he can stay off the injured list.

PLAYER SUMMARY	
Will	drive to the hoop
Can't	stay healthy
Expect	trips to the line
Don't Expect	great defense
Fantasy Value	$14-17
Card Value	10-20¢

COLLEGE STATISTICS

—DID NOT PLAY—

NBA REGULAR-SEASON STATISTICS

			FGs		3-PT FGs		FTs		Rebounds						
		G	MIN	FG	PCT	FG	PCT	FT	PCT	OFF	TOT	AST	STL	BLK	PTS	PPG
89-90	GS	75	1695	289	.519	10	.256	317	.787	84	221	121	94	7	905	12.1
90-91	GS	50	987	183	.501	1	.167	178	.724	51	118	85	62	4	545	10.9
91-92	GS	72	2117	491	.538	3	.300	376	.788	68	208	243	116	10	1361	18.9
92-93	GS	30	836	178	.543	3	.200	162	.761	40	97	105	51	2	521	17.4
Totals		227	5635	1141	.528	17	.243	1033	.771	243	644	554	323	23	3332	14.7

ANTHONY MASON

Team: New York Knicks
Position: Forward
Height: 6'7" **Weight:** 250
Birthdate: December 14, 1966

NBA Experience: 4 years
College: Tennessee St.
Acquired: Signed as a free agent, 7/91

Background: Mason finished his career at Tennessee State with more than 2,000 career points. He was drafted by Portland in the third round in 1988 but spent his first pro season in Turkey. He was signed by New Jersey and played 21 games for the Nets in 1989-90. He spent the 1990-91 campaign mostly as a big scorer in the CBA, though he played three games with Denver while on ten-day contracts. Mason became a key free-agent signee with the Knicks in 1991-92, coming off the bench in all 82 games and averaging 7.0 RPG. He played in 81 games last year and averaged 7.9 RPG.

Strengths: Mason is a menace to opponents who have the misfortune of running into him. He owns a bruising body and uses it to help establish a physical presence. He bangs, plays defense, is a tremendous per-minute rebounder, and runs the court. He handles the ball quite well and can bring it up the floor to beat pressure. He works hard and is determined to make it.

Weaknesses: Mason, a former 20-PPG scorer in the CBA, does not have that potential as an NBA player despite his double-figure average last year. He's not a pure outside shooter, he struggles from the free throw line, and his lack of height puts him at a disadvantage as a post-up scorer.

Analysis: Mason lives up to his name in that he's built like a brick wall. It's no wonder that he has been a perfect fit with the defensive-minded Knicks. Mason was a key ingredient last year as the Knicks made themselves one of the top teams in the league with a physical approach.

PLAYER SUMMARY	
Will	rebound, defend
Can't	shoot FTs
Expect	physical play
Don't Expect	3-point attempts
Fantasy Value	$5-7
Card Value	10-20¢

COLLEGE STATISTICS

		G	FGP	FTP	RPG	PPG
84-85	TSU	28	.469	.648	5.3	10.0
85-86	TSU	28	.482	.715	6.9	18.0
86-87	TSU	27	.448	.659	9.7	18.8
87-88	TSU	28	.454	.773	10.4	28.0
Totals		111	.461	.713	8.1	18.7

NBA REGULAR-SEASON STATISTICS

			FGs		3-PT FGs		FTs		Rebounds						
		G	MIN	FG	PCT	FG	PCT	FT	PCT	OFF	TOT	AST	STL	BLK	PTS	PPG
89-90	NJ	21	108	14	.350	0	.000	9	.600	11	34	7	2	2	37	1.8
90-91	DEN	3	21	2	.500	0	.000	6	.750	3	5	0	1	0	10	3.3
91-92	NY	82	2198	203	.509	0	.000	167	.642	216	573	106	46	20	573	7.0
92-93	NY	81	2482	316	.502	0	.000	199	.682	231	640	170	43	19	831	10.3
Totals		187	4809	535	.499	0	.000	381	.663	461	1252	283	92	41	1451	7.8

VERNON MAXWELL

Team: Houston Rockets
Position: Guard
Height: 6'5" **Weight:** 190
Birthdate: September 12, 1965

NBA Experience: 5 years
College: Florida
Acquired: Acquired from Spurs for cash, 2/90

Background: Maxwell's past is cluttered with accomplishment and controversy. He broke Florida's all-time scoring record and finished as the SEC's No. 2 career scorer behind Pete Maravich. But Maxwell later admitted to using cocaine and accepting cash payments. He has been in and out of trouble as a pro as well, but since San Antonio sold his rights to Houston, he has made more news on the court than off. He led the league in 3-pointers made for two straight years before last season.

Strengths: Maxwell has always thrown his weight around on defense and he backs down from no one. He can match up effectively with big guards and smaller point men. He is a long-range force on offense but can also get to the hoop with his athletic ability and acrobatics. He plays the game with exuberance.

Weaknesses: Although Maxwell is annually among the most frequent 3-point shooters in the league, he has never been among the most accurate. Overall, he has not shot better than 41.3 percent from the field in any of his last three seasons. Too often, he favors long bombs instead of going strong to the basket.

Analysis: Maxwell has become a full-time starter because of his competitiveness and ability to be a defensive stopper. He can also be dangerous from 3-point range and has been among the Rockets' leading scorers the past three seasons. He broke his left wrist with a week left in the regular season, which kept him out early in the 1993 playoffs.

PLAYER SUMMARY	
Will	fire 3-pointers
Can't	shoot 50 percent
Expect	defense, exuberance
Don't Expect	great control
Fantasy Value	$8-10
Card Value	8-15¢

COLLEGE STATISTICS

		G	FGP	FTP	RPG	PPG
84-85	FLA	30	.445	.686	2.4	13.3
85-86	FLA	33	.463	.701	4.5	19.6
86-87	FLA	34	.485	.742	3.7	21.7
87-88	FLA	33	.447	.715	4.2	20.2
Totals		130	.462	.715	3.7	18.8

NBA REGULAR-SEASON STATISTICS

		G	MIN	FGs FG	FGs PCT	3-PT FGs FG	3-PT FGs PCT	FTs FT	FTs PCT	Rebounds OFF	Rebounds TOT	AST	STL	BLK	PTS	PPG
88-89	SA	79	2065	357	.432	32	.248	181	.745	49	202	301	86	8	927	11.7
89-90	SA/HOU	79	1987	275	.439	28	.267	136	.645	50	228	296	84	10	714	9.0
90-91	HOU	82	2870	504	.404	172	.337	217	.733	41	238	303	127	15	1397	17.0
91-92	HOU	80	2700	502	.413	162	.342	206	.772	37	243	326	104	28	1372	17.1
92-93	HOU	71	2251	349	.407	120	.332	164	.719	29	221	297	86	8	982	13.8
Totals		391	11873	1987	.416	514	.326	904	.726	206	1132	1523	487	69	5392	13.8

LEE MAYBERRY

Team: Milwaukee Bucks
Position: Guard
Height: 6'2" **Weight:** 175
Birthdate: June 12, 1970

NBA Experience: 1 year
College: Arkansas
Acquired: 1st-round pick in 1992 draft
(23rd overall)

Background: Mayberry grew up in Tulsa, where Nolan Richardson coached before coming to Arkansas, and often shot baskets in Richardson's driveway. Mayberry eventually played for Richardson at Arkansas. He led the Razorbacks to nine NCAA Tournament wins in four years and finished as the school's career leader in assists, steals, and 3-point field goal percentage. A first-round draft choice of the Bucks, he played in all 82 games as a rookie, averaging 3.3 APG and 5.2 PPG.

Strengths: Mayberry is a point guard who can shoot, forcing defenses to account for him. He hit 39 percent of his 3-point tries and shot 45.6 percent from the field—very good numbers for a rookie guard. He has fine leadership qualities, is durable, takes care of the ball, and runs the offense. His assist-to-turnover ratio is commendable and he loves the transition game.

Weaknesses: The biggest concern of scouts, and probably the reason Mayberry slipped to 23rd overall in the draft, is his slight build. He gets posted up on the defensive end and struggles when screened. Mayberry also lacks the lightning quickness to make up for his size. His rookie free throw shooting was terrible (57.4) after a 72-percent career mark in college.

Analysis: Mayberry came from a college program where defense started everything. As a pro, however, it appears his future is as an offensive-minded lead guard. He can get to the hoop or score from long range and makes pretty solid decisions with the ball. His on-the-ball defense could stand some shoring up. He backed up Eric Murdock in his first year, but look for Mayberry to push for a starting spot in the near future. He's a promising talent.

PLAYER SUMMARY	
Will	run the offense
Can't	muscle his man
Expect	a scoring mentality
Don't Expect	tough defense
Fantasy Value	$1-3
Card Value	12-35¢

COLLEGE STATISTICS

		G	FGP	FTP	APG	PPG
88-89	ARK	32	.500	.736	4.2	12.9
89-90	ARK	35	.507	.792	5.2	14.5
90-91	ARK	38	.484	.634	5.5	13.2
91-92	ARK	34	.492	.744	5.9	15.2
Totals		139	.495	.724	5.2	14.0

NBA REGULAR-SEASON STATISTICS

			FGs		3-PT FGs		FTs		Rebounds						
	G	MIN	FG	PCT	FG	PCT	FT	PCT	OFF	TOT	AST	STL	BLK	PTS	PPG
92-93 MIL	82	1503	171	.456	43	.391	39	.574	26	118	273	59	7	424	5.2
Totals	82	1503	171	.456	43	.391	39	.574	26	118	273	59	7	424	5.2

TRAVIS MAYS

Team: Atlanta Hawks
Position: Guard
Height: 6'2" **Weight:** 190
Birthdate: June 19, 1968

NBA Experience: 3 years
College: Texas
Acquired: Traded from Kings for Spud Webb and a 1994 2nd-round pick, 7/91

Background: While at Texas, Mays surpassed Terry Teagle as the top scorer in Southwest Conference history. He was named SWC Player of the Year as a junior and senior and set conference records for 3-pointers made and attempted. Mays was fourth among rookie scorers with Sacramento in 1990-91. He was traded to Atlanta and played in just two games in 1991-92, missing the rest of the year because of surgery to repair torn tendons in his right ankle. A strained rotator cuff and inconsistent play limited him to 49 games last season, and his scoring average dropped to 7.0 PPG. Atlanta let him go after the season.

Strengths: Mays is a perimeter scorer with great range and a fast trigger. His quick move to the hoop keeps defenders honest. He is not shy about taking big shots and he connected on more than a third of his treys last year. Mays, a collegiate stopper, plays smart, aggressive defense in the pros as well.

Weaknesses: Injuries have plagued Mays in each of his three years in the NBA. He is small for an off guard and lacks the distributing skills to be effective at the point. He is not overly willing or adept at creating for others, preferring to get his own shots. Poor shot selection has been the main reason for his dismal field goal percentage. He shot 66 percent from the free throw line last year.

Analysis: Mays seems to have run the injury gamut in his three pro seasons. His various ailments have cost him over 100 games during that time, after a college career beset with no such problems. Mays is the kind of player who needs some extended playing time to develop confidence and consistency.

PLAYER SUMMARY

Will	pull the trigger
Can't	stay healthy
Expect	perimeter scoring
Don't Expect	playmaking
Fantasy Value	$0
Card Value	8-15¢

COLLEGE STATISTICS

		G	FGP	FTP	APG	PPG
86-87	TEX	30	.423	.595	2.1	8.6
87-88	TEX	28	.459	.771	3.1	18.1
88-89	TEX	34	.449	.710	1.7	21.9
89-90	TEX	32	.433	.811	2.3	24.1
Totals		124	.442	.746	2.3	18.4

NBA REGULAR-SEASON STATISTICS

				FGs		3-PT FGs		FTs		Rebounds						
		G	MIN	FG	PCT	FG	PCT	FT	PCT	OFF	TOT	AST	STL	BLK	PTS	PPG
90-91	SAC	64	2145	294	.406	72	.365	255	.770	54	178	253	81	11	915	14.3
91-92	ATL	2	32	6	.429	3	.500	2	1.000	1	2	1	0	0	17	8.5
92-93	ATL	49	787	129	.417	29	.345	54	.659	20	53	72	21	3	341	7.0
Totals		115	2964	429	.410	104	.362	311	.749	75	233	326	102	14	1273	11.1

BOB McCANN

Team: Minnesota Timberwolves
Position: Forward
Height: 6'7" **Weight:** 248
Birthdate: April 22, 1964

NBA Experience: 3 years
College: Upsala; Morehead St.
Acquired: Signed as a free agent, 8/92

Background: After spending his freshman year at Division III Upsala, McCann transferred to Morehead State. As a senior in 1986-87, he led MSU with 18.6 PPG and 11.3 RPG, ranked sixth nationally in rebounding, and was named Ohio Valley Conference Player of the Year. A second-round pick of the Bucks in 1987, he played his first NBA ball in 1989-90 with Dallas. He caught on for 26 games with Detroit in 1991-92 and saw his first full season of action last year in Minnesota, where he averaged 20 minutes a game. McCann has played in the USBL, in Spain, and for two CBA teams.

Strengths: McCann can fill in at either forward spot because he's capable of playing in the post or facing the basket. His best asset is his defense, as he uses his huge upper body to push people away from the hoop. He also has decent ball-handling skills for a big man and has a great attitude.

Weaknesses: Offense in general can be considered a weakness for McCann. He does not shoot a steady jumper, has very limited range, and his low-post game is nothing you want young big men studying. His game is power forward, yet he's dwarfed by the players defending him. He has very little touch and does not pass the ball well.

Analysis: McCann can best be described as a survivor. He has yet to play two seasons with the same NBA team and his other pro basketball experience has included even more stops on the road map. His work ethic also shows up in the weight room. He finally landed on a team, the Timberwolves, that could give him some minutes.

PLAYER SUMMARY

Will.............................play defense
Can't........................unpack his bags
Expect.............................hard work
Don't Expect...................many starts
Fantasy Value...............................$1
Card Value...............................8-15¢

COLLEGE STATISTICS

		G	FGP	FTP	RPG	PPG
82-83	UPS	26	.475	.531	8.0	9.9
84-85	MSU	27	.491	.559	9.7	17.1
85-86	MSU	27	.534	.653	10.4	16.9
86-87	MSU	28	.548	.629	11.3	18.6
Totals		108	.515	.606	9.9	15.7

NBA REGULAR-SEASON STATISTICS

		G	MIN	FGs FG	FGs PCT	3-PT FGs FG	3-PT FGs PCT	FTs FT	FTs PCT	Rebounds OFF	Rebounds TOT	AST	STL	BLK	PTS	PPG
89-90	DAL	10	62	7	.333	0	.000	12	.857	4	12	6	2	2	26	2.6
91-92	DET	26	129	13	.394	0	.000	4	.308	12	30	6	6	4	30	1.2
92-93	MIN	79	1536	200	.488	0	.000	95	.625	92	282	68	51	58	495	6.3
Totals		115	1727	220	.474	0	.000	111	.620	108	324	80	59	64	551	4.8

GEORGE McCLOUD

Team: Indiana Pacers
Position: Guard
Height: 6'8" **Weight:** 215
Birthdate: May 27, 1967

NBA Experience: 4 years
College: Florida St.
Acquired: 1st-round pick in 1989 draft
(7th overall)

Background: McCloud was named Metro Conference Player of the Year as a senior at Florida State, where he finished his career ranked third on the career scoring list. He played in just 44 games in a disappointing rookie year with Indiana, and his numbers were again sub-par in 1990-91. After missing the first 24 games of the 1991-92 campaign because of thumb surgery, he enjoyed his first extended run of success, averaging 7.8 PPG over the last two months of that season. He scored at a career-high 7.2-PPG clip and made 21 starts last year.

Strengths: McCloud was drafted seventh overall for his perimeter shooting and 3-point range. He was second on the team to Reggie Miller in 3-pointers and 3-point attempts last season. He has a quick release and doesn't need much time to line it up. McCloud is also a sharp passer and does not back away on defense. He'll go to battle.

Weaknesses: Poor shooting percentage continues to plague McCloud, causing him to be considered an overall disappointment. His poor 41.1-percent field goal accuracy last year was a career high. McCloud does not accomplish much at all off the dribble. He's more the catch-and-shoot type than an offensive creator.

Analysis: Pooh Richardson, Tim Hardaway, Nick Anderson, and B.J. Armstrong were drafted with later picks than McCloud in 1989. Three separate operations since turning pro have contributed to his troubles, but inconsistent shooting has been by far the biggest problem. He does several things well and cannot be considered a bust just yet, but the shooting McCloud has been noted for has been missing too often.

PLAYER SUMMARY	
Will	shoot 3-pointers
Can't	hoist his percentage
Expect	tough defense
Don't Expect	consistency
Fantasy Value	$0
Card Value	8-15¢

COLLEGE STATISTICS

		G	FGP	FTP	RPG	PPG
85-86	FSU	27	.483	.633	1.8	4.3
86-87	FSU	30	.442	.618	4.2	7.7
87-88	FSU	30	.479	.786	3.7	18.2
88-89	FSU	30	.448	.875	3.6	22.8
Totals		117	.460	.778	3.4	13.5

NBA REGULAR-SEASON STATISTICS

			FGs		3-PT FGs		FTs		Rebounds						
		G	MIN	FG	PCT	FG	PCT	FT	PCT	OFF	TOT	AST	STL	BLK	PTS	PPG
89-90	IND	44	413	45	.313	13	.325	15	.789	12	42	45	19	3	118	2.7
90-91	IND	74	1070	131	.373	43	.347	38	.776	35	118	150	40	11	343	4.6
91-92	IND	51	892	128	.409	32	.340	50	.781	45	132	116	26	11	338	6.6
92-93	IND	78	1500	216	.411	58	.320	75	.735	60	205	192	53	11	565	7.2
Totals		247	3875	520	.390	146	.333	178	.761	152	497	503	138	36	1364	5.5

RODNEY McCRAY

Team: Chicago Bulls
Position: Forward
Height: 6'8" **Weight:** 248
Birthdate: August 29, 1961
NBA Experience: 10 years
College: Louisville

Acquired: Traded from Mavericks in three-team deal; Bulls sent Byron Houston to Warriors, and Warriors sent a conditional 1993 1st-round pick to Mavericks, 9/92

Background: McCray helped Louisville to the 1980 NCAA title and played in three Final Fours during his college career. As a pro, he made the All-Defensive Team with Houston in 1987-88 and led the league in minutes with Sacramento in 1989-90. McCray finished second on the Mavericks in rebounding in each of his two years in Dallas. The Bulls picked him up before last season.

Strengths: McCray is versatile and runs the floor with deceiving speed. He has earned his reputation as a solid rebounder and defender. A natural small forward, McCray can play on the perimeter or in the post. He is a very good passing forward and an unselfish team player in every respect.

Weaknesses: McCray disappears in a halfcourt offense. He looks to pass too often and is not a good jump-shooter. He really pulled a disappearing act with the Bulls, never contributing enough to fulfill the promise with which he arrived.

Analysis: Frustrated in Dallas, McCray was happy to pack his bags for a contender. However, Chicago did not turn out to be the answer. He helped the Bulls at times with his defense but offensively did nothing to relieve the scoring burden off the second-unit players. Instead, he slipped into the background.

PLAYER SUMMARY	
Will	find open men
Can't	take over on offense
Expect	reserve minutes
Don't Expect	10 PPG
Fantasy Value	$0
Card Value	5-10¢

COLLEGE STATISTICS

		G	FGP	FTP	RPG	PPG
79-80	LOU	36	.543	.647	7.5	7.8
80-81	LOU	30	.588	.667	7.4	9.6
81-82	LOU	33	.571	.702	7.1	8.6
82-83	LOU	36	.587	.742	8.4	11.0
Totals		135	.573	.693	7.6	9.2

NBA REGULAR-SEASON STATISTICS

				FGs		3-PT FGs		FTs		Rebounds						
		G	MIN	FG	PCT	FG	PCT	FT	PCT	OFF	TOT	AST	STL	BLK	PTS	PPG
83-84	HOU	79	2081	335	.499	1	.250	182	.731	173	450	176	53	54	853	10.8
84-85	HOU	82	3001	476	.535	0	.000	231	.738	201	539	355	90	75	1183	14.4
85-86	HOU	82	2610	338	.537	0	.000	171	.770	159	520	292	50	58	847	10.3
86-87	HOU	81	3136	432	.552	0	.000	306	.779	190	578	434	88	53	1170	14.4
87-88	HOU	81	2689	359	.481	0	.000	268	.785	232	631	264	57	51	1006	12.4
88-89	SAC	68	2435	340	.466	5	.227	169	.722	143	514	293	57	36	854	12.6
89-90	SAC	82	3238	537	.515	11	.262	273	.784	192	669	377	60	70	1358	16.6
90-91	DAL	74	2561	336	.495	13	.333	159	.803	153	560	259	70	51	844	11.4
91-92	DAL	75	2106	271	.436	25	.294	110	.719	149	468	219	48	30	677	9.0
92-93	CHI	64	1019	92	.451	2	.400	36	.692	53	158	81	12	15	222	3.5
Totals		768	24876	3516	.503	57	.260	1925	.761	1645	5087	2750	585	493	9014	11.7

XAVIER McDANIEL

Team: Boston Celtics
Position: Forward
Height: 6'7" **Weight:** 205
Birthdate: June 4, 1963

NBA Experience: 8 years
College: Wichita St.
Acquired: Signed as a free agent, 9/92

Background: McDaniel led Wichita State in scoring, rebounding, and field goal percentage as a junior and senior and was an All-American in 1985. He earned All-Rookie honors with Seattle and went on to score more than 20 PPG in each of his next four years, making the All-Star Game in 1988. He was traded to Phoenix 15 games into the 1990-91 season and to New York before the 1991-92 campaign. Boston signed him as a free agent before the 1992-93 season and McDaniel finished second on the Celtics in scoring.

Strengths: At his best, McDaniel is everything you look for in a small forward. He puts points on the board with a turnaround jump shot and is a fine finisher. He also rebounds and can play physical defense when he puts his heart into it. McDaniel backs down from no one. He's known as a big-game player.

Weaknesses: McDaniel does not come to work every night. He seems to go through frequent lapses. He is at his best when backing in rather than shooting jumpers. He is not a polished or willing passer.

Analysis: The "X-Man" has played for four teams in the last three years, with mixed reviews. He started slowly with Boston before a move to the bench seemed to bring the best out of him. When he's on his game, McDaniel can be one of the more explosive forwards in the league.

PLAYER SUMMARY	
Will	show up in big games
Can't	dominate consistently
Expect	a physical presence
Don't Expect	an All-Star
Fantasy Value	$6-8
Card Value	5-12¢

COLLEGE STATISTICS

		G	FGP	FTP	RPG	PPG
81-82	WSU	28	.504	.628	3.7	5.8
82-83	WSU	28	.593	.541	14.4	18.8
83-84	WSU	30	.564	.680	13.1	20.6
84-85	WSU	31	.559	.634	14.8	27.2
Totals		117	.564	.624	11.6	18.4

NBA REGULAR-SEASON STATISTICS

				FGs		3-PT FGs		FTs		Rebounds						
		G	MIN	FG	PCT	FG	PCT	FT	PCT	OFF	TOT	AST	STL	BLK	PTS	PPG
85-86	SEA	82	2706	576	.490	2	.200	250	.687	307	655	193	101	37	1404	17.1
86-87	SEA	82	3031	806	.509	3	.214	275	.696	338	705	207	115	52	1890	23.0
87-88	SEA	78	2803	687	.488	14	.280	281	.715	206	518	263	96	52	1669	21.4
88-89	SEA	82	2385	677	.489	11	.306	312	.732	177	433	134	84	40	1677	20.5
89-90	SEA	69	2432	611	.496	5	.294	244	.733	165	447	171	73	36	1471	21.3
90-91	SEA/PHO	81	2634	590	.497	0	.000	193	.723	173	557	187	76	46	1373	17.0
91-92	NY	82	2344	488	.478	12	.308	137	.714	176	460	149	57	24	1125	13.7
92-93	BOS	82	2215	457	.495	6	.273	191	.793	168	489	163	72	51	1111	13.5
Totals		638	20550	4892	.493	53	.270	1883	.721	1710	4264	1467	674	338	11720	18.4

DERRICK McKEY

Team: Seattle SuperSonics
Position: Forward
Height: 6'10" **Weight:** 220
Birthdate: October 10, 1966

NBA Experience: 6 years
College: Alabama
Acquired: 1st-round pick in 1987 draft
(9th overall)

Background: McKey earned Southeastern Conference Player of the Year accolades after leading Alabama to a conference title as a junior. He entered the draft a year early, was named to the 1987-88 All-Rookie Team, and became a starter the next year. McKey has averaged between 13 and 16 PPG every season since. He averaged 13.4 PPG during the 1992-93 season—his lowest mark since his rookie campaign.

Strengths: All the athletic skills are at McKey's disposal. His leaping ability makes him a great finisher, and he handles the ball like a big guard. He drives to the hoop for scores, passes well, and uses both hands effectively. He's a pure scorer who shoots well, has 3-point range, and also plays defense. He's quick and has a nice feel for the game.

Weaknesses: The knock on McKey since his first two years has been his inability to remain focused and play with intensity on a nightly basis. He'll score 20 points one night and take four shots the next. He tends to play passively on offense, is slight in build, and is an average rebounder at best. He seems too content with a supporting role.

Analysis: McKey's biggest mistake may have been establishing himself as one of the NBA's budding superstars after his first two years. Those All-Star visions have never materialized, though he is capable of playing some great basketball and is not short on talent. "I don't know which buttons to push," Sonics coach George Karl has said. No one does but McKey.

PLAYER SUMMARY

Will	score in spurts
Can't	become dominant
Expect	about 15 PPG
Don't Expect	intensity
Fantasy Value	$14-17
Card Value	8-15¢

COLLEGE STATISTICS

		G	FGP	FTP	RPG	PPG
84-85	ALA	33	.477	.606	4.1	5.1
85-86	ALA	33	.636	.786	7.9	13.6
86-87	ALA	33	.581	.862	7.5	18.6
Totals		99	.580	.797	6.5	12.4

NBA REGULAR-SEASON STATISTICS

		G	MIN	FGs FG	FGs PCT	3-PT FGs FG	3-PT FGs PCT	FTs FT	FTs PCT	Rebounds OFF	Rebounds TOT	AST	STL	BLK	PTS	PPG
87-88	SEA	82	1706	255	.491	11	.367	173	.772	115	328	107	70	63	694	8.5
88-89	SEA	82	2804	487	.502	30	.337	301	.803	167	464	219	105	70	1305	15.9
89-90	SEA	80	2748	468	.493	3	.130	315	.782	170	489	187	87	81	1254	15.7
90-91	SEA	73	2503	438	.517	4	.211	235	.845	172	423	169	91	56	1115	15.3
91-92	SEA	52	1757	285	.472	19	.380	188	.847	95	268	120	61	47	777	14.9
92-93	SEA	77	2439	387	.496	40	.357	220	.741	121	327	197	105	58	1034	13.4
Totals		446	13957	2320	.497	107	.331	1432	.796	840	2299	999	519	375	6179	13.9

NATE McMILLAN

Team: Seattle SuperSonics
Position: Guard/Forward
Height: 6'5" **Weight:** 190
Birthdate: August 3, 1964

NBA Experience: 7 years
College: Chowan; North Carolina St.
Acquired: 2nd-round pick in 1986 draft (30th overall)

Background: McMillan was a junior college All-American before transferring to North Carolina State and averaging nearly seven assists per game as a senior. As a pro, he finished among the NBA's top ten in assists in each of his first three years. He has never averaged more than eight points a game, but he has been a reliable assists man and a strong rebounding guard. McMillan is Seattle's career assists leader and was second on the Sonics in that category last season.

Strengths: McMillan is known for his defense, rebounding, and passing. His good size, deceiving quickness, and relentless effort help him shut down opponents ranging from point guards to small forwards. McMillan is a steady ball-handler and an unselfish leader. He has made 52 3-pointers over the last two years, matching his total from the previous five.

Weaknesses: McMillan has never been much of a scorer despite his ability to penetrate. The last time he averaged double figures in scoring was his second year of junior college. Shooting no longer falls into this category, although McMillan is still not reliable from the free throw line.

Analysis: McMillan has enjoyed a productive career in the NBA despite doing less glamorous things than scoring. His defense, versatility, and unselfish leadership have been greatly appreciated by the Seattle fans and front office people. His 3-point shooting adds another dimension to his game.

PLAYER SUMMARY

Will	shine on defense
Can't	score in bushels
Expect	steady leadership
Don't Expect	selfishness
Fantasy Value	$5-$7
Card Value	5-10¢

COLLEGE STATISTICS

		G	FGP	FTP	RPG	PPG
82-83	CHOW	27	.580	.696	5.0	9.9
83-84	CHOW	35	.544	.769	9.8	13.1
84-85	NCST	33	.454	.674	5.7	7.6
85-86	NCST	34	.485	.733	4.6	9.4
Totals		129	.515	.722	6.4	10.1

NBA REGULAR-SEASON STATISTICS

		G	MIN	FGs FG	FGs PCT	3-PT FGs FG	3-PT FGs PCT	FTs FT	FTs PCT	Rebounds OFF	Rebounds TOT	AST	STL	BLK	PTS	PPG
86-87	SEA	71	1972	143	.475	0	.000	87	.617	101	331	583	125	45	373	5.3
87-88	SEA	82	2453	235	.474	9	.375	145	.707	117	338	702	169	47	624	7.6
88-89	SEA	75	2341	199	.410	15	.214	119	.630	143	388	696	156	42	532	7.1
89-90	SEA	82	2338	207	.473	11	.355	98	.641	127	403	598	140	37	523	6.4
90-91	SEA	78	1434	132	.433	17	.354	57	.613	71	251	371	104	20	338	4.3
91-92	SEA	72	1652	177	.437	27	.276	54	.643	92	252	359	129	29	435	6.0
92-93	SEA	73	1977	213	.431	25	.385	95	.709	84	306	384	173	33	546	7.5
Totals		533	14167	1306	.452	104	.303	655	.656	735	2269	3693	996	253	3371	6.3

OLIVER MILLER

Team: Phoenix Suns
Position: Center
Height: 6'9" **Weight:** 285
Birthdate: April 6, 1970

NBA Experience: 1 year
College: Arkansas
Acquired: 1st-round pick in 1992 draft
(22nd overall)

Background: Miller never gained as much national attention as Arkansas teammates Todd Day and Lee Mayberry, yet he finished as the school's career leader in blocked shots (345) and field goal percentage (.636) while ranking second in career rebounds (886). Most of the attention received by Miller surrounded his 300-plus pounds. A late first-round choice by Phoenix in 1992, Miller spent time on the injured list because his weight was causing him aches and pains in his legs and feet. He shed some 45 pounds and returned as a key contributor late in the season and during the playoffs.

Strengths: Forget his frame; Miller is a tremendous all-around talent. He is a phenomenal outlet passer, owns a great pair of hands, and is very agile for a man his size. His touch with the basketball is extraordinary. Miller knows how to score on the interior, is a good short-range shooter, and blocks shots at the defensive end.

Weaknesses: Though his weight was no longer an issue near the end of his rookie season, it will always have to be monitored. Miller was slowed during his senior season by a stress fracture in his foot and his legs seem to give out when he balloons to over 300 pounds. He has trouble guarding centers who are quick and agile.

Analysis: The Suns took a gamble with Miller and it did not look to be a good one early on. The big man missed more than 20 games while on the injured list, but the lift he gave them when he returned has sparked enthusiasm from the Phoenix front office. If Miller keeps his weight under control, he has all the tools required to be a productive starter.

PLAYER SUMMARY

Will......................................block shots
Can't....................return to junk food
Expect..........................polished skills
Don't Expect..............a chiseled frame
Fantasy Value................................$4-6
Card Value..............................25-50¢

COLLEGE STATISTICS

		G	FGP	FTP	RPG	PPG
88-89	ARK	30	.547	.641	3.7	7.7
89-90	ARK	35	.639	.652	6.3	11.1
90-91	ARK	38	.704	.644	7.7	15.7
91-92	ARK	34	.602	.647	7.7	13.5
Totals		137	.636	.646	6.5	12.2

NBA REGULAR-SEASON STATISTICS

			FGs		3-PT FGs		FTs		Rebounds						
	G	MIN	FG	PCT	FG	PCT	FT	PCT	OFF	TOT	AST	STL	BLK	PTS	PPG
92-93 PHO	56	1069	121	.475	0	.000	71	.710	70	275	118	38	100	313	5.6
Totals	56	1069	121	.475	0	.000	71	.710	70	275	118	38	100	313	5.6

REGGIE MILLER

Team: Indiana Pacers
Position: Guard
Height: 6'7" **Weight:** 185
Birthdate: August 24, 1965

NBA Experience: 6 years
College: UCLA
Acquired: 1st-round pick in 1987 draft
(11th overall)

Background: Miller was an All-Pac-10 selection as a senior and left UCLA ranked second to Lew Alcindor on the school's career scoring list. He established himself as a 3-point shooter during his first two years with Indiana, then improved his all-around game and earned a trip to the All-Star Game in 1989-90. Miller's 91.8-percent free throw accuracy led the NBA in 1990-91. He tied for the league lead in 3-pointers last season and was 13th in long-range accuracy.

Strengths: Miller is not only one of the league's premier shooters, but also one of its best offensive players. He's virtually automatic from the line and deadly from long range. He has elevated his play to the star level, as there is no longer doubt about his ability to create his own shots and get to the basket. He works hard and moves extremely well without the ball. Miller is also an accomplished trash talker who is capable of distracting his opponent.

Weaknesses: Miller is rail thin and unable to play physical defense. He's not always the most willing defender anyway, and he has the potential to be a much better rebounder and shot-blocker.

Analysis: Miller became the Pacers' career scoring leader last season and has led the team in that category in each of the last four years. You won't find a more hard-working or durable player in the NBA. His 339 consecutive starts is the longest such streak in the league. Miller is a franchise player who longs for some playoff success.

PLAYER SUMMARY	
Will	hit from long range
Can't	star on defense
Expect	20-plus PPG
Don't Expect	silence
Fantasy Value	$40-45
Card Value	10-20¢

COLLEGE STATISTICS

		G	FGP	FTP	RPG	PPG
83-84	UCLA	28	.509	.643	1.5	4.6
84-85	UCLA	33	.553	.804	4.3	15.2
85-86	UCLA	29	.556	.882	5.3	25.9
86-87	UCLA	32	.543	.832	5.4	22.3
Totals		122	.547	.836	4.2	17.2

NBA REGULAR-SEASON STATISTICS

				FGs		3-PT FGs		FTs		Rebounds						
		G	MIN	FG	PCT	FG	PCT	FT	PCT	OFF	TOT	AST	STL	BLK	PTS	PPG
87-88	IND	82	1840	306	.488	61	.355	149	.801	95	190	132	53	19	822	10.0
88-89	IND	74	2536	398	.479	98	.402	287	.844	73	292	227	93	29	1181	16.0
89-90	IND	82	3192	661	.514	150	.414	544	.868	95	295	311	110	18	2016	24.6
90-91	IND	82	2972	596	.512	112	.348	551	.918	81	281	331	109	13	1855	22.6
91-92	IND	82	3120	562	.501	129	.378	442	.858	82	318	314	105	26	1695	20.7
92-93	IND	82	2954	571	.479	167	.399	427	.880	67	258	262	120	26	1736	21.2
Totals		484	16614	3094	.497	717	.385	2400	.872	493	1634	1577	590	131	9305	19.2

TERRY MILLS

Team: Detroit Pistons
Position: Forward
Height: 6'10" **Weight:** 250
Birthdate: December 21, 1967

NBA Experience: 3 years
College: Michigan
Acquired: Signed as a free agent, 9/92

Background: Mills helped lead Michigan to the 1989 NCAA championship as a junior, then earned honorable-mention All-America status as a senior, when he was the Wolverines' second-leading scorer and rebounder. He was drafted by Milwaukee, traded, and spent his rookie year with Denver and New Jersey. He saw action in all 82 games for the Nets in 1991-92. Detroit signed him as a free agent before the 1992-93 campaign and Mills had his most productive year, making 46 starts and averaging 14.8 PPG.

Strengths: Mills possesses loads of offensive talent. For a big man, he has extraordinary touch and very good range on his jumper. He loves the turnaround and keeps his defender away with his backside. He's a good rebounder, especially on the offensive glass. Mills knows how to play the game and seems to have overcome a weight problem.

Weaknesses: Ever since he came out of high school with a huge reputation, the underachiever tag has been pinned on Mills. Many of his early troubles stemmed from a weight problem that may or may not be behind him. Last year, foul trouble was a greater concern despite the fact he was not a physical defender. He won't get many assists despite fine passing skills.

Analysis: If Terry Mills continues to play like he did last season for his "hometown" Pistons, he might finally shake the critics who were convinced he would never reach his potential. He is a tremendously skilled offensive player who can score from inside and out. He scored 41 points in a game last season. Mills has cut a lot of the fat; now he could use a little muscle.

PLAYER SUMMARY	
Will	score inside and out
Can't	shake foul trouble
Expect	a soft touch
Don't Expect	assists
Fantasy Value	$6-8
Card Value	5-10¢

COLLEGE STATISTICS

		G	FGP	FTP	RPG	PPG
87-88	MICH	34	.531	.729	6.4	12.1
88-89	MICH	37	.564	.769	5.9	11.6
89-90	MICH	31	.585	.759	8.0	18.1
Totals		102	.562	.755	6.7	13.8

NBA REGULAR-SEASON STATISTICS

		G	MIN	FGs FG	FGs PCT	3-PT FGs FG	3-PT FGs PCT	FTs FT	FTs PCT	Rebounds OFF	Rebounds TOT	AST	STL	BLK	PTS	PPG
90-91	DEN/NJ	55	819	134	.465	0	.000	47	.712	82	229	33	35	29	315	5.7
91-92	NJ	82	1714	310	.463	8	.348	114	.750	187	453	84	48	41	742	9.0
92-93	DET	81	2183	494	.461	10	.278	201	.791	176	472	111	44	50	1199	14.8
Totals		218	4716	938	.462	18	.286	362	.767	445	1154	228	127	120	2256	10.3

HAROLD MINER

Team: Miami Heat
Position: Guard
Height: 6'4" **Weight:** 220
Birthdate: May 5, 1971

NBA Experience: 1 year
College: Southern California
Acquired: 1st-round pick in 1992 draft
(12th overall)

Background: A prized recruit of George Raveling at Southern Cal., Miner led the previously woeful Trojans to the NCAA Tournament in 1991 and 1992. He joined Lew Alcindor as the only players in Pac-10 history to score more than 2,000 points in three seasons. Miner, a left-hander, is nicknamed "Baby Jordan" for his similarities to Michael both in appearance and playing style. Miami took him 12th overall in the 1992 draft and he averaged 10.3 PPG as a rookie. Miner also won the NBA's Slam Dunk Contest on All-Star weekend.

Strengths: Miner has charisma. His great hang time and explosive dunks often send crowds into a frenzy, and he is very creative with the ball. A remarkable athlete, he is capable of going either around people or over them as he attacks the basket. He can get his shot whenever he wants it and will seldom lose a game of one-on-one.

Weaknesses: There were several legitimate concerns that allowed Miner to slip in the draft. One was his reluctance to pass the ball. Another was his poor college shooting percentage, especially during his senior year. In addition, Miner does not qualify for comparisons to Jordan when it comes to defense. All were reasons he did not play much early in his rookie season. He turned the ball over more often than he got an assist.

Analysis: Suffice it to say, the Jordan comparisons—at least on offense—are not all that far-fetched. Miner is an enormous talent. "The guy's unstoppable," teammate Rony Seikaly said. "He dribbles, hesitates, and jumps three stories." If Miner begins to approach Jordan in the areas of passing, shooting, and defense, he'll be a superstar. He has that potential.

PLAYER SUMMARY

Will ....make highlight reels
Can't......................................distribute
Expect......................acrobatic moves
Don't Expect.................great defense
Fantasy Value..............................$9-11
Card Value ....50¢-$1.50

COLLEGE STATISTICS

		G	FGP	FTP	RPG	PPG
89-90	USC	28	.473	.841	3.6	20.8
90-91	USC	29	.453	.800	5.5	23.5
91-92	USC	30	.438	.811	7.0	26.3
Totals		87	.453	.814	5.4	23.6

NBA REGULAR-SEASON STATISTICS

				FGs		3-PT FGs		FTs		Rebounds						
		G	MIN	FG	PCT	FG	PCT	FT	PCT	OFF	TOT	AST	STL	BLK	PTS	PPG
92-93	MIA	73	1383	292	.475	3	.333	163	.762	74	147	73	34	8	750	10.3
Totals		73	1383	292	.475	3	.333	163	.762	74	147	73	34	8	750	10.3

SAM MITCHELL

Team: Indiana Pacers
Position: Forward
Height: 6'7" **Weight:** 210
Birthdate: September 2, 1963
NBA Experience: 4 years

College: Mercer
Acquired: Traded from Timberwolves with Pooh Richardson for Chuck Person and Micheal Williams, 9/92

Background: Mitchell, the all-time leading scorer at Mercer, got a late start as a pro. After being drafted and cut by Houston in 1985, he began a teaching career. His hoop comeback took him to the USBL, to the CBA, and on a two-year stint in France before he became the NBA's oldest rookie (at 26) in 1989-90. Mitchell was a double-figure scorer for three seasons in Minnesota before a 1992 trade sent him, along with Pooh Richardson, to Indiana for Chuck Person and Micheal Williams. Mitchell averaged a career-low 7.2 PPG in 81 games last year.

Strengths: Mitchell is versatile, plays with intensity, and knows how to force an opponent to his weakness. He is tough, both mentally and physically, and has a great work ethic. On offense, Mitchell is best at driving and getting to the line. He canned 81 percent of his free throws last season.

Weaknesses: Mitchell is an inconsistent outside shooter who tries to do too much when the ball's in his hands. A 2-for-29 career 3-point shooter coming in, he still launched 23 last year. He made four. He sends opponents to the line too often. He led the league with 338 fouls three seasons ago. Mitchell is a below-average ball-handler and passer.

Analysis: As many expected during his Minnesota days, Mitchell is not a double-figure scorer on a decent team. That became apparent last year in Indiana, although Mitchell did play well enough defensively and in transition to see action in all but one game. Durable, he has missed only three games in his four-year NBA career.

PLAYER SUMMARY	
Will	play defense
Can't	hit his treys
Expect	a versatile reserve
Don't Expect	hot shooting
Fantasy Value	$0
Card Value	8-15¢

COLLEGE STATISTICS

		G	FGP	FTP	RPG	PPG
81-82	MER	27	.497	.717	3.7	7.1
82-83	MER	28	.519	.784	5.9	16.5
83-84	MER	26	.507	.781	7.1	21.5
84-85	MER	31	.516	.750	8.2	25.0
Totals		112	.512	.763	6.3	17.7

NBA REGULAR-SEASON STATISTICS

			FGs		3-PT FGs		FTs		Rebounds						
		G	MIN	FG	PCT	FG	PCT	FT	PCT	OFF	TOT	AST	STL	BLK	PTS	PPG
89-90	MIN	80	2414	372	.446	0	.000	268	.768	180	462	89	66	54	1012	12.6
90-91	MIN	82	3121	445	.441	0	.000	307	.775	188	520	133	66	57	1197	14.6
91-92	MIN	82	2151	307	.423	2	.182	209	.786	158	473	94	53	39	825	10.1
92-93	IND	81	1402	215	.445	4	.174	150	.811	93	248	76	23	10	584	7.2
Totals		325	9088	1339	.439	6	.115	934	.781	619	1703	392	208	160	3618	11.1

CHRIS MORRIS

Team: New Jersey Nets
Position: Forward
Height: 6'8" **Weight:** 220
Birthdate: January 20, 1966

NBA Experience: 5 years
College: Auburn
Acquired: 1st-round pick in 1988 draft
(4th overall)

Background: Following in the footsteps of past Auburn greats Charles Barkley and Chuck Person, Morris was the fourth player selected in the 1988 NBA draft. After season No. 1, the Nets looked like geniuses for taking him when they did. Morris, an All-Rookie second-team selection, was New Jersey's top all-around performer. Two straight years of 42-percent shooting dampened their hopes, but he improved to around 48 percent in each of the last two seasons.

Strengths: Morris is as athletic as any small forward in the NBA. He runs the floor, can handle the ball, drives to the hoop, and can even hit the 3-pointer now and then. In short, he's a pretty decent scorer in a position known for big scorers. He's also a solid defender and rebounder who loves a challenge.

Weaknesses: Morris has gained a reputation as a troublemaker. Two years ago, he refused to re-enter a game after then-coach Bill Fitch had pulled him. Inconsistency and poor shot selection have also plagued him. Morris shoots less than 30 percent from 3-point range yet has launched 186 long bombs over the last two years. The focus is not always there.

Analysis: For the most part, Morris was on his best behavior for first-year Nets coach Chuck Daly last year. The enigmatic forward played hard and averaged more than 14 points per game for the first time in three years. Daly likes Morris for the way he runs the floor and plays defense. The result was 57 starts and a pretty good season.

PLAYER SUMMARY

Will ....run the floor
Can't ....pass up bad shots
Expect ....12-14 PPG
Don't Expect ....leadership
Fantasy Value...........................$13-16
Card Value ....8-15¢

COLLEGE STATISTICS

		G	FGP	FTP	RPG	PPG
84-85	AUB	34	.477	.620	5.0	10.4
85-86	AUB	33	.500	.670	5.2	9.8
86-87	AUB	31	.559	.711	7.3	13.5
87-88	AUB	30	.481	.795	9.8	20.7
Totals		128	.501	.712	6.7	13.4

NBA REGULAR-SEASON STATISTICS

				FGs		3-PT FGs		FTs		Rebounds							
		G	MIN	FG	PCT	FG	PCT	FT	PCT	OFF	TOT	AST	STL	BLK	PTS	PPG
88-89	NJ	76	2096	414	.457	64	.366	182	.717	188	397	119	102	60	1074	14.1
89-90	NJ	80	2449	449	.422	61	.316	228	.722	194	422	143	130	79	1187	14.8
90-91	NJ	79	2553	409	.425	45	.251	179	.734	210	521	220	138	96	1042	13.2
91-92	NJ	77	2394	346	.477	22	.200	165	.714	199	494	197	129	81	879	11.4
92-93	NJ	77	2302	436	.481	17	.224	197	.794	227	454	106	144	52	1086	14.1
Totals		389	11794	2054	.450	209	.285	951	.735	1018	2288	785	643	368	5268	13.5

ALONZO MOURNING

Team: Charlotte Hornets
Position: Center
Height: 6'10" **Weight:** 240
Birthdate: February 8, 1970

NBA Experience: 1 year
College: Georgetown
Acquired: 1st-round pick in 1992 draft
(2nd overall)

Background: From Chesapeake, Virginia, Mourning was one of the country's best high school players ever, rating ahead of Shawn Kemp, Chris Jackson, and Billy Owens in the Class of 1988. He played both forward and center at Georgetown, where he teamed with Dikembe Mutombo and led the country in blocked shots as a freshman. As a senior, Mourning became the first player to be named outright Big East Player of the Year and Defensive Player of the Year in the same season. Though a holdout, he made a quick impact with Charlotte when he finally signed. He averaged 21.0 PPG and 10.3 RPG and hit a last-second jumper in the playoffs to eliminate Boston.

Strengths: Mourning is already a dominant NBA big man. He scores, rebounds, blocks shots, and is a ferocious competitor who loves contact and hates to lose. Mourning is more polished than Shaq at the offensive end, possessing a vast array of low-post moves and the ability to score from the perimeter. He gets to the line often. Mourning helped Charlotte to its first-ever playoff berth.

Weaknesses: Mourning often seems to go it alone. He made 236 turnovers and dished out only 76 assists (less than one per game). In his very first NBA game, he either shot or committed a turnover the first 12 times he touched the ball. Combative, Mourning was fined $5,000 for a run-in with Bill Laimbeer and once ordered a female reporter out of the locker room while he dressed.

Analysis: Like Mutombo and Patrick Ewing before him, Mourning is yet another dominant Georgetown center. While it is too early to predict whether he will match Ewing's pro career, Mourning is well on his way. Some feel he became a better overall player than O'Neal among the rookie class.

PLAYER SUMMARY	
Will	control the middle
Can't	find open men
Expect	20 PPG, 10 RPG
Don't Expect	passive defense
Fantasy Value	$50-55
Card Value	$1.50-5.00

COLLEGE STATISTICS

		G	FGP	FTP	RPG	PPG
88-89	GEOR	34	.603	.667	7.3	13.1
89-90	GEOR	31	.525	.783	8.5	16.5
90-91	GEOR	23	.522	.793	7.7	15.8
91-92	GEOR	32	.595	.758	10.7	21.3
Totals		120	.566	.754	8.6	16.7

NBA REGULAR-SEASON STATISTICS

				FGs		3-PT FGs		FTs		Rebounds						
		G	MIN	FG	PCT	FG	PCT	FT	PCT	OFF	TOT	AST	STL	BLK	PTS	PPG
92-93	CHA	78	2644	572	.511	0	.000	495	.781	263	805	76	27	271	1639	21.0
Totals		78	2644	572	.511	0	.000	495	.781	263	805	76	27	271	1639	21.0

CHRIS MULLIN

Team: Golden State Warriors
Position: Forward
Height: 6'7" **Weight:** 215
Birthdate: July 30, 1963

NBA Experience: 8 years
College: St. John's
Acquired: 1st-round pick in 1985 draft (7th overall)

Background: Mullin's college career at St. John's was highly celebrated, as he made every All-America team as a senior and virtually every one as a junior. He graduated as the Big East's all-time scoring leader. His pro career began with two good seasons, but ever since he voluntarily entered an alcohol rehab program in 1987-88, he has only gotten better. He has played in four All-Star Games, earned a spot on the 1992 Olympic team, and hasn't averaged below 20 PPG. After leading the league in minutes for two straight years, Mullin tore a ligament in his right thumb last February and missed the remainder of the 1992-93 season.

Strengths: Mullin shoots with great touch and 3-point range, and he can kill you even with a hand in his face. He is a superb passer, is an above-average rebounder, and plays heads-up defense. He's among the best free throw shooters in NBA history. Mullin is a leader with a great feel for the game.

Weaknesses: Mullin will never win any awards for his athletic ability, though he is actually quicker than he looks.

Analysis: Mullin was likened to Larry Bird coming out of college, and after a so-so start he has more than lived up to such a high billing. He is not just one of the premier scorers in the NBA, but one of its premier players as well. He has overcome far more than thumb injuries.

PLAYER SUMMARY

Will .... scorch the nets
Can't .... win dunk contest
Expect .... consistent leadership
Don't Expect .... less than 20 PPG
Fantasy Value $70-75
Card Value .... 15-25¢

COLLEGE STATISTICS

		G	FGP	FTP	RPG	PPG
81-82	STJ	30	.534	.791	3.2	16.6
82-83	STJ	33	.577	.878	3.7	19.1
83-84	STJ	27	.571	.904	4.4	22.9
84-85	STJ	35	.521	.824	4.8	19.8
Totals		125	.550	.848	4.1	19.5

NBA REGULAR-SEASON STATISTICS

				FGs		3-PT FGs		FTs		Rebounds						
		G	MIN	FG	PCT	FG	PCT	FT	PCT	OFF	TOT	AST	STL	BLK	PTS	PPG
85-86	GS	55	1391	287	.463	5	.185	169	.896	42	115	105	70	23	768	14.0
86-87	GS	82	2377	477	.514	19	.302	269	.825	39	181	261	98	36	1242	15.1
87-88	GS	60	2033	470	.508	34	.351	239	.885	58	205	290	113	32	1213	20.2
88-89	GS	82	3093	830	.509	23	.230	493	.892	152	483	415	176	39	2176	26.5
89-90	GS	78	2830	682	.536	87	.372	505	.389	130	463	319	123	45	1956	25.1
90-91	GS	82	3315	777	.536	40	.301	513	.884	141	443	329	173	63	2107	25.7
91-92	GS	81	3346	830	.524	64	.366	350	.833	127	450	286	173	62	2074	25.6
92-93	GS	46	1902	474	.510	60	.451	183	.810	42	232	166	68	41	1191	25.9
Totals		566	20287	4827	.517	332	.345	2741	.869	731	2572	2171	994	341	12727	22.5

ERIC MURDOCK

Team: Milwaukee Bucks
Position: Guard
Height: 6'2" **Weight:** 190
Birthdate: June 14, 1968
NBA Experience: 2 years

College: Providence
Acquired: Traded from Jazz with Blue
Edwards and a 1992 1st-round pick for
Jay Humphries and Larry Krystkowiak,
6/92

Background: As a junior at Providence, Murdock suffered a stress fracture in his leg and was hospitalized with an irregular heartbeat. He followed it up with a terrific senior season in which he set career scoring highs in four consecutive games. He also set an NCAA record with 376 career steals. He played in 50 games as a rookie with Utah, averaging over ten minutes per contest. He was traded to Milwaukee and emerged as one of the most improved players in the league in 1992-93. He started all but four games, averaged 14.4 PPG, and finished seventh in the NBA in steals and 12th in assists.

Strengths: The versatile Murdock proved to the league last year that he can fare quite well as an NBA point guard. He is quick to the hoop and can either finish the play himself or dish to open teammates after drawing traffic. He boosted his field goal percentage by more than 50 points with a more reliable jump shot. His quick hands make him an expert thief and fine overall defender.

Weaknesses: Murdock wiped out several of the elements in this category with his play last year. He is still not what you'd call a pure shooter and could stand to pass up the 3-pointers in favor of more drives. He hits less than 30 percent from long range. He is still prone to the turnover against pressure.

Analysis: If Murdock was not the most improved player in basketball last season, he was certainly among the top few in that category. Getting out of Utah allowed him to escape John Stockton's shadow and develop his game at the pro level. Murdock played so well that highly touted rookie Lee Mayberry settled for reserve minutes.

PLAYER SUMMARY	
Will	swipe the ball
Can't	thrive from long range
Expect	drives to the hoop
Don't Expect	rookie minutes
Fantasy Value	$15-18
Card Value	8-15¢

COLLEGE STATISTICS

		G	FGP	FTP	APG	PPG
87-88	PROV	28	.413	.738	3.8	10.7
88-89	PROV	29	.457	.762	4.9	16.2
89-90	PROV	28	.419	.762	3.3	15.4
90-91	PROV	32	.445	.812	4.6	25.6
Totals		117	.436	.783	4.2	17.3

NBA REGULAR-SEASON STATISTICS

		G	MIN	FG	PCT	FG	PCT	FT	PCT	OFF	TOT	AST	STL	BLK	PTS	PPG
91-92	UTA	50	478	76	.415	5	.192	46	.754	21	54	92	30	7	203	4.1
92-93	MIL	79	2437	438	.468	31	.261	231	.780	95	284	603	174	7	1138	14.4
Totals		129	2915	514	.459	36	.248	277	.776	116	338	695	204	14	1341	10.4

TRACY MURRAY

Team: Portland Trail Blazers
Position: Forward
Height: 6'8" **Weight:** 228
Birthdate: July 25, 1971
NBA Experience: 1 year

College: UCLA
Acquired: Draft rights traded from Spurs via the Bucks; Blazers sent Alaa Abdelnaby to Bucks, and Bucks sent Dale Ellis to Spurs, 7/92

Background: Murray was the highest scoring player in California prep history when he signed to play at UCLA. While sharing the ball with Don MacLean, Murray finished his college career second in Pac-10 history in 3-point field goals (197) and hit them at a 50-percent clip as a junior. He was among the conference's top ten in seven statistical categories as a junior. He left UCLA a year early and was drafted 18th by San Antonio. A three-way deal involving Milwaukee sent him to Portland, where he saw action in 48 games and averaged 5.7 PPG.

Strengths: Murray was a first-round draft choice for one simple reason—he can shoot the ball. He has NBA 3-point range and a quick release. Murray creates match-up problems because big men are forced to play him outside the arc. He also showed some ability in the post and is a fine passer. Murray has good instincts and smarts. He's automatic from the free throw line.

Weaknesses: Murray faces his own match-up problems on defense. When he plays guard, his opponents are too quick for him. When he's at forward, they're too tough. He does not have a body made for physical play. While he can shoot the lights out when open, he does not do much off the dribble. His rookie percentages from the field and 3-point line were sub-standard.

Analysis: Murray's shooting percentages will rise, especially from 3-point distance. However, he needs to improve his defense and become more versatile offensively. He made a dozen starts for the Blazers but will probably settle into the role of a shooter off the bench.

PLAYER SUMMARY	
Will	shoot from deep
Can't	star on defense
Expect	improved percentages
Don't Expect	creativity
Fantasy Value	$1
Card Value	10-20¢

COLLEGE STATISTICS

		G	FGP	FTP	RPG	PPG
89-90	UCLA	33	.442	.767	5.5	12.3
90-91	UCLA	32	.503	.794	6.7	21.2
91-92	UCLA	33	.538	.800	7.0	21.4
Totals		98	.500	.791	6.4	18.3

NBA REGULAR-SEASON STATISTICS

			FGs		3-PT FGs		FTs		Rebounds						
	G	MIN	FG	PCT	FG	PCT	FT	PCT	OFF	TOT	AST	STL	BLK	PTS	PPG
92-93 POR	48	495	108	.415	21	.300	35	.875	40	83	11	8	5	272	5.7
Totals	48	495	108	.415	21	.300	35	.875	40	83	11	8	5	272	5.7

JERROD MUSTAF

Team: Phoenix Suns
Position: Forward
Height: 6'10" **Weight:** 245
Birthdate: October 28, 1969
NBA Experience: 3 years

College: Maryland
Acquired: Traded from Knicks with
Trent Tucker and two 2nd-round picks
for Xavier McDaniel, 10/91

Background: Mustaf played high school ball at famed DeMatha High in
Washington D.C. After being criticized by some for leaving the University of
Maryland after only two seasons, Mustaf proved to be a key contributor as a
Knicks rookie until tendinitis in his knee sidelined him for almost a month. He was
traded to Phoenix before the 1991-92 campaign and appeared in 52 contests,
finishing near the bottom of the Suns' scoring list. He spent much of last season
on the injured list, saw action in 32 games, and averaged just 4.6 PPG.

Strengths: Mustaf has good size, can put the ball on the floor, and has a nice
offensive repertoire. He can shoot from the wing, can score inside, and has a
great pair of hands. He passes the ball well and has a nice feel for the game.
Mustaf is versatile and runs the floor.

Weaknesses: Mustaf plays soft despite his size. His weight doesn't include a lot
of muscle, and what muscle he does have he's not always willing to use. Though
considered a scorer, he has yet to average five PPG in three seasons. His
defense has a long way to go and he is not a good free throw shooter.

Analysis: The 1992-93 season was a nightmare for Mustaf. He missed the first
eight games of the year with a bruised shin, sat out 13 games with a broken
finger after jamming it in a car door in January, and sat out late in the year
because of a deep thigh bruise. What Mustaf needs is a healthy season and
some playing time so that he can learn the game. He would probably fit in better
with a young, rebuilding team.

PLAYER SUMMARY	
Will	run the floor
Can't	stay healthy
Expect	deft passing
Don't Expect	physical play
Fantasy Value	$0
Card Value	8-12¢

COLLEGE STATISTICS

		G	FGP	FTP	RPG	PPG
88-89	MD	26	.520	.716	7.8	14.3
89-90	MD	33	.529	.774	7.7	18.5
Totals		59	.525	.756	7.7	16.6

NBA REGULAR-SEASON STATISTICS

				FGs		3-PT FGs		FTs		Rebounds						
		G	MIN	FG	PCT	FG	PCT	FT	PCT	OFF	TOT	AST	STL	BLK	PTS	PPG
90-91	NY	62	825	106	.465	0	.000	56	.644	51	169	36	15	14	268	4.3
91-92	PHO	52	545	92	.477	0	.000	49	.690	45	145	45	21	16	233	4.5
92-93	PHO	32	336	57	.438	0	.000	33	.623	29	83	10	14	11	147	4.6
Totals		146	1706	255	.463	0	.000	138	.654	125	397	91	50	41	648	4.4

DIKEMBE MUTOMBO

Team: Denver Nuggets
Position: Center
Height: 7'2" **Weight:** 245
Birthdate: June 25, 1966

NBA Experience: 2 years
College: Georgetown
Acquired: 1st-round pick in 1991 draft
(4th overall)

Background: Mutombo was raised in Zaire, a French-speaking African nation, and was forced to sit out his freshman season at Georgetown because the SAT was not offered in French. His college scoring numbers were modest but his shot-blocking helped earn him Big East Defensive Player of the Year honors in 1990 and 1991. He was an instant success as a rookie with Denver and the only first-year player to appear in the All-Star Game, but a torn ulnar collateral ligament in his thumb sidelined him for the month of April. Last season, he finished third in the league in both rebounds and blocked shots.

Strengths: Great size, a giant wingspan, and underrated quickness make Mutombo a force to be reckoned with. He blocked 12 shots in a game against the Clippers in April, the top single-game mark in the league last season. Considered a below-average offensive player coming out of college, Mutombo has silenced his critics with accurate hook shots and inside conversions.

Weaknesses: Mutombo does not have the shooting range of a Patrick Ewing, David Robinson, or Hakeem Olajuwon. He also lags behind those post men in terms of knowledge of the game, especially where and when to deliver his passes. He does not handle double-teams well.

Analysis: Mutombo is one of the most dominant defensive centers in the game and is much better offensively than most expected. Last year, he became the first Denver player in NBA or ABA history to reach 1,000 rebounds in a season. An international spokesman for CARE, his No. 1 off-season priority is visiting and helping the poverty-stricken people of his homeland.

PLAYER SUMMARY	
Will	dominate defensively
Can't	score from outside
Expect	rebounds, blocks
Don't Expect	expert passing
Fantasy Value	$30-35
Card Value	15-25¢

COLLEGE STATISTICS

		G	FGP	FTP	RPG	PPG
88-89	GEOR	33	.707	.479	3.3	3.9
89-90	GEOR	31	.709	.598	10.5	10.7
90-91	GEOR	32	.586	.703	12.2	15.2
Totals		96	.644	.641	8.6	9.9

NBA REGULAR-SEASON STATISTICS

			FGs		3-PT FGs		FTs		Rebounds						
	G	MIN	FG	PCT	FG	PCT	FT	PCT	OFF	TOT	AST	STL	BLK	PTS	PPG
91-92 DEN	71	2716	428	.493	0	.000	321	.642	316	870	156	43	210	1177	16.6
92-93 DEN	82	3029	399	.510	0	.000	335	.681	344	1070	147	43	287	1131	13.8
Totals	153	5745	826	.501	0	.000	656	.661	660	1940	303	86	497	2308	15.1

LARRY NANCE

Team: Cleveland Cavaliers
Position: Forward
Height: 6'10" **Weight:** 235
Birthdate: February 12, 1959
NBA Experience: 12 years
College: Clemson

Acquired: Traded from Suns with Mike Sanders and a 1988 1st-round pick for Tyrone Corbin, Kevin Johnson, Mark West, 1988 1st- and 2nd-round picks, and a 1989 2nd-round pick, 2/88

Background: Nance, Clemson's leading rebounder for three consecutive seasons, joined the Suns 12 years ago. Between 1982-83 and 1986-87, he paced Phoenix in scoring with nearly 20 PPG. His trade to the Cavs for Kevin Johnson and others was, at the time, the biggest in Suns history. Nance was named to the NBA All-Defensive Team in 1989. He made his third trip to the All-Star Game in 1993 and finished sixth in the league in blocked shots.

Strengths: Nance is still the best shot-blocking forward in the league. He is capable of turning games around on the defensive end. He's also a good passer who scores on a wide variety of moves. He is crafty, still has spring in his legs, and hits a high percentage from the field and the line.

Weaknesses: Nance does not have 3-point range and he led the Cavs in personal fouls last year. Those can hardly be considered big knocks.

Analysis: Nance is a consummate pro. He does not garner big endorsement deals or applaud his own merits in the papers. He goes about his job in workmanlike fashion and has the respect of everyone in the league.

PLAYER SUMMARY

Will ....reject shots
Can't...........................be left open
Expect............leadership by example
Don't Expect ....selfishness
Fantasy Value...........................$25-28
Card Value ....5-10¢

COLLEGE STATISTICS

		G	FGP	FTP	RPG	PPG
77-78	CLEM	25	.467	.471	3.1	3.1
78-79	CLEM	29	.519	.636	7.2	11.1
79-80	CLEM	32	.515	.598	8.1	13.9
80-81	CLEM	31	.575	.690	7.6	15.9
Totals		117	.533	.628	6.7	11.5

NBA REGULAR-SEASON STATISTICS

		G	MIN	FGs FG	FGs PCT	3-PT FGs FG	3-PT FGs PCT	FTs FT	FTs PCT	Rebounds OFF	Rebounds TOT	AST	STL	BLK	PTS	PPG
81-82	PHO	80	1186	227	.521	0	.000	75	.641	95	256	82	42	71	529	6.6
82-83	PHO	82	2914	588	.550	1	.333	193	.672	239	710	197	99	217	1370	16.7
83-84	PHO	82	2899	601	.576	0	.000	249	.707	227	678	214	86	174	1451	17.7
84-85	PHO	61	2202	515	.587	1	.500	180	.709	195	536	159	88	104	1211	19.9
85-86	PHO	73	2484	582	.581	0	.000	310	.698	169	618	240	70	130	1474	20.2
86-87	PHO	69	2569	585	.551	1	.200	381	.773	188	599	233	86	148	1552	22.5
87-88	PHO/CLE	67	2383	487	.529	2	.333	304	.779	193	607	207	63	159	1280	19.1
88-89	CLE	73	2526	496	.539	0	.000	267	.799	156	581	159	57	206	1259	17.2
89-90	CLE	62	2065	412	.511	1	1.000	186	.778	162	516	161	54	122	1011	16.3
90-91	CLE	80	2927	635	.524	2	.250	265	.803	201	686	237	66	200	1537	19.2
91-92	CLE	81	2880	556	.539	0	.000	263	.822	213	670	232	80	243	1375	17.0
92-93	CLE	77	2753	533	.549	0	.000	202	.818	184	668	223	54	198	1268	16.5
Totals		887	29788	6217	.548	8	.145	2875	.755	2222	7125	2344	845	1972	15317	17.3

JOHNNY NEWMAN

Team: Charlotte Hornets
Position: Forward
Height: 6'7" **Weight:** 205
Birthdate: November 28, 1963

NBA Experience: 7 years
College: Richmond
Acquired: Signed as a free agent, 7/90

Background: Newman, who set a career scoring record at Richmond, spent one season with the Cavs before being waived. The Knicks picked him up and moved him from big guard to small forward. Signed by the Hornets as a restricted free agent three summers ago, Newman enjoyed his best pro season in Charlotte in 1990-91. He came off the bench for much of the 1992-93 season before regaining a starting spot late in the year.

Strengths: Newman is the definition of a slasher. He'll get to the hoop and either finish or get to the line. He has scored in double figures every season except his first. He is an impressive athlete and is not afraid to challenge. He shot a career-high 52.2 percent from the field last year and 80.8 percent from the line.

Weaknesses: Newman is streaky and prone to dismal nights. He does a poor job on the defensive boards. Moreover, he is not overly willing or able when it comes to passing and defense. He has been accused of caring too much about the stat sheet.

Analysis: An All-Star one night, a dog the next. That has been the book on Newman, although he played more consistently last year. He found himself sharing small-forward minutes with David Wingate, but it was Newman who was in the starting lineup when the Hornets made their run to the playoffs and beat Boston in the first round.

PLAYER SUMMARY	
Will	slash to the hoop
Can't	play defense
Expect	double-figure scoring
Don't Expect	rebounds
Fantasy Value	$6-8
Card Value	5-10¢

COLLEGE STATISTICS

		G	FGP	FTP	RPG	PPG
82-83	RICH	28	.529	.719	3.1	12.3
83-84	RICH	32	.435	.787	6.1	21.9
84-85	RICH	32	.551	.773	5.2	21.3
85-86	RICH	30	.517	.890	7.3	22.0
Totals		122	.532	.800	5.5	19.5

NBA REGULAR-SEASON STATISTICS

		G	MIN	FGs FG	FG PCT	3-PT FGs FG	FG PCT	FTs FT	FT PCT	Rebounds OFF	TOT	AST	STL	BLK	PTS	PPG
86-87	CLE	59	630	113	.411	1	.045	66	.868	36	70	27	20	7	293	5.0
87-88	NY	77	1589	270	.435	26	.280	207	.841	87	159	62	72	11	773	10.0
88-89	NY	81	2336	455	.475	97	.338	286	.815	93	206	162	111	23	1293	16.0
89-90	NY	80	2277	374	.476	45	.317	239	.799	60	191	180	95	22	1032	12.9
90-91	CHA	81	2477	478	.470	30	.357	385	.809	94	254	188	100	17	1371	16.9
91-92	CHA	55	1651	295	.477	13	.283	236	.766	71	179	146	70	14	839	15.3
92-93	CHA	64	1471	279	.522	12	.267	194	.808	72	143	117	45	19	764	11.9
Totals		497	12431	2264	.471	224	.312	1613	.808	513	1202	882	513	113	6365	12.8

KEN NORMAN

Team: Milwaukee Bucks
Position: Forward
Height: 6'8" **Weight:** 223
Birthdate: September 5, 1964

NBA Experience: 6 years
College: Wabash Valley; Illinois
Acquired: Signed as a free agent, 7/93

Background: Norman was a two-time All-Big Ten selection at Illinois, where he set a school record for field goal percentage and finished his three-year career seventh on the all-time scoring list. He became a starter for the Clippers late in his rookie season, then increased his scoring average by nearly ten points in 1988-89. He has not improved on that season since. Norman led L.A. in rebounds last year, then signed as a free agent with Milwaukee after the season.

Strengths: Norman always guards an opposing team's best forward, regardless of size or strength. He considers himself a banger and loves to rebound. He can score points in bunches. He thrives in the open court, where his finishing ability can ignite a team. Norman also owns a reliable mid-range jump shot, can post up, and attacks the basket.

Weaknesses: The glaring weakness in Norman's game is his horrendous free throw shooting, which stands at less than 60 percent for his career. It's perplexing because he's a fine shooter from 15 feet. Norman is not the kind of forward who can break down defenders with his dribble.

Analysis: Teammates, coaches, and opponents alike respect Norman for his toughness. He comes to battle and does the grunt work required to help his team win. He is also a dangerous offensive player when he gets on a roll. Norman will likely win a starting spot with the Milwaukee Bucks, who are in serious need of talent on the front line.

PLAYER SUMMARY

Will	defend top forwards
Can't	drain his FTs
Expect	tough rebounding
Don't Expect	fancy dribbling
Fantasy Value	$14-17
Card Value	8-12¢

COLLEGE STATISTICS

		G	FGP	FTP	RPG	PPG
82-83	WAB	35	.605	.673	10.3	20.4
84-85	ILL	29	.632	.663	3.7	7.8
85-86	ILL	32	.641	.802	7.1	16.4
86-87	ILL	31	.578	.727	9.8	20.7
Totals		127	.608	.717	7.9	16.6

NBA REGULAR-SEASON STATISTICS

				FGs		3-PT FGs		FTs		Rebounds						
		G	MIN	FG	PCT	FG	PCT	FT	PCT	OFF	TOT	AST	STL	BLK	PTS	PPG
87-88	LAC	66	1435	241	.482	0	.000	87	.512	100	263	78	44	34	569	8.6
88-89	LAC	80	3020	638	.502	4	.190	170	.630	245	667	277	106	66	1450	18.1
89-90	LAC	70	2334	484	.510	7	.438	153	.632	143	470	160	78	59	1128	16.1
90-91	LAC	70	2309	520	.501	6	.188	173	.629	177	497	159	63	63	1219	17.4
91-92	LAC	77	2009	402	.490	4	.143	121	.535	158	448	125	53	66	929	12.1
92-93	LAC	76	2477	498	.511	10	.263	131	.595	209	571	165	59	58	1137	15.0
Totals		439	13584	2783	.501	31	.214	835	.595	1032	2916	964	403	346	6432	14.7

CHARLES OAKLEY

Team: New York Knicks
Position: Forward
Height: 6'9" **Weight:** 245
Birthdate: December 18, 1963
NBA Experience: 8 years

College: Virginia Union
Acquired: Traded from Bulls with 1988 1st- and 3rd-round picks for Bill Cartwright and 1988 1st- and 3rd-round picks, 6/88

Background: The top Division II rebounder in the country in 1984-85, Oakley grabbed more than 17 per game at tiny Virginia Union. He made the NBA All-Rookie Team with Chicago the following season. A chronic complainer, he was shipped to New York in 1988 in exchange for Bill Cartwright. Oakley was second in the league in rebounding in 1986-87 and 1987-88 and third in 1990-91. He started all 82 games last season and averaged 6.9 PPG.

Strengths: Oakley rebounds and plays punishing defense. He has been a key tone-setter as the Knicks have risen to the top of the Eastern Conference standings. Once the NBA's "Chairman of the Boards," Oakley still uses his wide body and can dominate the glass on any given night. It requires great courage to drive toward him.

Weaknesses: Oakley's scoring has been way down over the past two years. He thinks he's a better offensive player than he really is, and he's prone to launching bad shots from the perimeter. He doesn't jump well, relying more on brute strength. He is not the most popular guy in the league.

Analysis: Oakley is an enforcer and a rock-solid complement to Patrick Ewing. Pat Riley has built his team around physical defense and rebounding, and Oakley is a proven star in those categories. He is probably the biggest reason the Knicks have earned their reputation as the toughest team in the league.

PLAYER SUMMARY	
Will	intimidate physically
Can't	return to double figures
Expect	rebounds, defense
Don't Expect	blocked shots
Fantasy Value	$1-3
Card Value	8-12¢

COLLEGE STATISTICS

		G	FGP	FTP	RPG	PPG
81-82	VU	28	.620	.610	12.5	15.9
82-83	VU	28	.582	.588	13.0	19.3
83-84	VU	30	.612	.621	13.1	21.7
84-85	VU	31	.625	.669	17.3	24.0
Totals		117	.611	.626	14.0	20.3

NBA REGULAR-SEASON STATISTICS

				FGs		3-PT FGs		FTs		Rebounds						
		G	MIN	FG	PCT	FG	PCT	FT	PCT	OFF	TOT	AST	STL	BLK	PTS	PPG
85-86	CHI	77	1772	281	.519	0	.000	178	.662	255	664	133	68	30	740	9.6
86-87	CHI	82	2980	468	.445	11	.367	245	.686	299	1074	296	85	36	1192	14.5
87-88	CHI	82	2816	375	.483	3	.250	261	.727	326	1066	248	68	28	1014	12.4
88-89	NY	82	2604	426	.510	12	.250	197	.773	343	861	187	104	14	1061	12.9
89-90	NY	61	2196	336	.524	0	.000	217	.761	258	727	146	64	16	889	14.6
90-91	NY	76	2739	307	.516	0	.000	239	.784	305	920	204	62	17	853	11.2
91-92	NY	82	2309	210	.522	0	.000	86	.735	256	700	133	67	15	506	6.2
92-93	NY	82	2230	219	.508	0	.000	127	.722	288	708	126	85	15	565	6.9
Totals		624	19646	2622	.497	26	.255	1550	.730	2330	6720	1473	603	171	6820	10.9

HAKEEM OLAJUWON

Team: Houston Rockets
Position: Center
Height: 7'0" **Weight:** 255
Birthdate: January 21, 1963

NBA Experience: 9 years
College: Houston
Acquired: 1st-round pick in 1984 draft
(1st overall)

Background: Olajuwon led Houston to the NCAA Final Four three consecutive years, and he led the nation in rebounding and field goal accuracy as a senior. He was selected Southwest Conference Player of the 1980s by media and coaches. The former soccer goalie in Nigeria has made eight All-Star trips in his nine pro seasons and has won three shot-blocking and two rebounding titles. The 1992-93 season was his best yet, as he led the league in blocks and finished fourth in scoring and rebounding. He also became a U.S. citizen.

Strengths: Olajuwon is one of the most versatile centers ever. He is the best shot-blocker in the game and he scores and rebounds as well as any center in the league. He has an amazing touch for a center, is an excellent passer, and is a team leader. Few play with his intensity.

Weaknesses: He has had his share of squabbles with Houston management, but it appears the hard feelings are a thing of the past. He signed a contract extension last year.

Analysis: Many considered Olajuwon the most dominant player in the game last season, as he could not be stopped at either end of the court. He ended up second in league MVP voting behind Charles Barkley. Though surrounded by mediocre talent in Houston, Olajuwon led the Rockets to 55 victories.

PLAYER SUMMARY

Will..dominate
Can't..............be stopped by one man
Expect........................MVP contention
Don't Expect..............more bitterness
Fantasy Value............................$85-90
Card Value....................................20-35¢

COLLEGE STATISTICS

		G	FGP	FTP	RPG	PPG
81-82	HOU	29	.607	.563	6.2	8.3
82-83	HOU	34	.611	.595	11.4	13.9
83-84	HOU	37	.675	.526	13.5	16.8
Totals		100	.639	.555	10.7	13.3

NBA REGULAR-SEASON STATISTICS

				FGs		3-PT FGs		FTs		Rebounds							
		G	MIN	FG	PCT	FG	PCT	FT	PCT	OFF	TOT	AST	STL	BLK	PTS	PPG
84-85	HOU	82	2914	677	.538	0	.000	338	.613	440	974	111	99	220	1692	20.6
85-86	HOU	68	2467	625	.526	0	.000	347	.645	333	781	137	134	231	1597	23.5
86-87	HOU	75	2760	677	.508	1	.200	400	.702	315	858	220	140	254	1755	23.4
87-88	HOU	79	2825	712	.514	0	.000	381	.695	302	959	163	162	214	1805	22.8
88-89	HOU	82	3024	790	.508	0	.000	454	.696	338	1105	149	213	282	2034	24.8
89-90	HOU	82	3124	806	.501	1	.167	382	.713	299	1149	234	174	376	1995	24.3
90-91	HOU	56	2062	487	.508	0	.000	213	.769	219	770	131	121	221	1187	21.2
91-92	HOU	70	2636	591	.502	0	.000	328	.766	246	845	157	127	304	1510	21.6
92-93	HOU	82	3242	848	.529	0	.000	444	.779	283	1068	291	150	342	2140	26.1
Totals		676	25054	6213	.515	2	.053	3287	.704	2775	8509	1593	1320	2444	15715	23.2

SHAQUILLE O'NEAL

Team: Orlando Magic
Position: Center
Height: 7'1" **Weight:** 303
Birthdate: March 6, 1972

NBA Experience: 1 year
College: Louisiana St.
Acquired: 1st-round pick in 1992 draft
(1st overall)

Background: Shaq was a two-time consensus All-American in his three years at Louisiana State and earned a handful of Player of the Year honors after his sophomore campaign. He finished his three-year career as the all-time SEC leader in blocked shots. Few players have ever made as big an impact as an NBA rookie. Shaq was the only player in the league to finish in the top ten in scoring, rebounding, field goal percentage, and blocked shots. He was the first rookie to start an All-Star Game since Michael Jordan, and he finished seventh in the voting for league MVP.

Strengths: O'Neal is as powerful as any player in the game. He tore down two backboards on slam dunks—an unprecedented feat—and is virtually unstoppable when he gets the ball in the paint and heads for the hoop. As the numbers indicate, he scores, rebounds, and swats shots with the best of them. O'Neal was also a smash at the box office, turning the Magic into the second-largest draw (after Chicago) on the road.

Weaknesses: Believe it or not, O'Neal is still learning the game. Critics say he does not have a go-to move other than the monster dunk. O'Neal does not own a reliable mid-range jumper and is a horrible free throw shooter. He turned the ball over 307 times and fouled out of eight games.

Analysis: What more can be said about the man-child who took the NBA by storm at the tender age of 20? He ran away with Rookie of the Year honors, receiving all but two of the 98 votes. He led Orlando to 20 more wins than it had the previous season, turning out to be worth every penny of the $40 million the team will pay him over his first seven years.

PLAYER SUMMARY	
Will	dominate inside
Can't	shoot FTs
Expect	superstardom
Don't Expect	soft play
Fantasy Value	$70-75
Card Value	$4.00-12.00

COLLEGE STATISTICS

		G	FGP	FTP	RPG	PPG
89-90	LSU	32	.573	.556	12.0	13.9
90-91	LSU	28	.628	.638	14.7	27.6
91-92	LSU	30	.615	.528	14.0	24.1
Totals		90	.610	.575	13.5	21.6

NBA REGULAR-SEASON STATISTICS

			FGs		3-PT FGs		FTs		Rebounds						
	G	MIN	FG	PCT	FG	PCT	FT	PCT	OFF	TOT	AST	STL	BLK	PTS	PPG
92-93 ORL	81	3071	733	.562	0	.000	427	.592	342	1122	152	60	286	1893	23.4
Totals	81	3071	733	.562	0	.000	427	.592	342	1122	152	60	286	1893	23.4

DOUG OVERTON

Team: Washington Bullets
Position: Guard
Height: 6'3" **Weight:** 190
Birthdate: August 3, 1969

NBA Experience: 1 year
College: La Salle
Acquired: Signed as a free agent, 10/92

Background: Overton, a high school teammate of Hank Gathers and Bo Kimble at Philadelphia's Dobbins Tech, spent most of his college career at La Salle as a point guard. He was a solid complementary player to Lionel Simmons from 1987-90 but struggled to take up the scoring slack after Simmons joined the NBA. Overton was drafted in the second round by Detroit in 1991-92 but was released by the Pistons without playing a game. He made his debut with Washington in 1992-93, averaging 8.1 PPG in 45 games and making 13 starts.

Strengths: Overton is a pretty steady outside shooter who also handles the ball well. He can play both guard positions and is capable of high-scoring nights, yet he will also feed the ball to the right people. His Philadelphia years taught him about toughness, and Overton will compete with anyone.

Weaknesses: There were questions about Overton's playmaking ability when he entered the league and many of those questions remain. Is he a natural point guard? He possesses only average quickness and does not penetrate as easily or as often as coaches would like. Though a good shooter, he has not proven himself from long range. While he challenges at the defensive end, he won't come up with a lot of steals or rebounds.

Analysis: Overton is a street-wise player who has a future in the NBA. He is versatile as a back-up, hits jumpers when left open, and does not shy away from a challenge. He has overcome the death of Gathers, a very close friend, and last year battled back from thumb surgery and played pretty well at times. Some feel he has the potential to be a 3-point specialist, though he made only three from that range last year.

PLAYER SUMMARY	
Will	play two positions
Can't	race by defenders
Expect	reserve minutes
Don't Expect	loads of steals
Fantasy Value	$1
Card Value	12-20¢

COLLEGE STATISTICS

		G	FGP	FTP	APG	PPG
87-88	LaS	34	.498	.841	2.7	7.8
88-89	LaS	32	.494	.787	7.6	13.2
89-90	LaS	32	.519	.798	6.6	17.2
90-91	LaS	25	.445	.818	5.0	22.3
Totals		123	.486	.814	5.5	14.6

NBA REGULAR-SEASON STATISTICS

			FGs		3-PT FGs		FTs		Rebounds						
	G	MIN	FG	PCT	FG	PCT	FT	PCT	OFF	TOT	AST	STL	BLK	PTS	PPG
92-93 WAS	45	990	152	.471	3	.231	59	.728	25	106	157	31	6	366	8.1
Totals	45	990	152	.471	3	.231	59	.728	25	106	157	31	6	366	8.1

BILLY OWENS

Team: Golden State Warriors
Position: Forward/Guard
Height: 6'9" **Weight:** 220
Birthdate: May 1, 1969
NBA Experience: 2 years

College: Syracuse
Acquired: Draft rights traded from
Kings for Mitch Richmond, Les
Jepsen, and a 1995 2nd-round pick,
11/91

Background: Owens, the 1988 A.P. High School Player of the Year at Carlisle (Pennsylvania) High, was Syracuse's prize recruit. He did not disappoint, finishing his three years ranked among the school's top seven in career scoring, rebounds, blocked shots, steals, and assists. He started all 103 games in his college career and became the first player to average 20 PPG under Jim Boeheim. With Golden State, Owens was third among rookies in scoring and rebounding in 1991-92 and No. 1 in field goal percentage. He missed 45 games last season because of an operation on his left knee to repair torn cartilage, then underwent surgery on his right knee over the summer.

Strengths: Owens brings tremendous versatility to the court. He can play every position but center, passes the ball well, runs the floor, and has great quickness. He's a strong finisher in the paint, can break his man down off the dribble, and can also score with wing jumpers. He's a scorer but will also play some defense.

Weaknesses: Warriors coach Don Nelson was not pleased with Owens's conditioning from the start of last year and now there are injury concerns on top of it. Owens must do a better job of off-season preparation. He also must avoid the temptation to stay outside and rely on his jump shot. He's too good off the dribble. He's a poor 3-point and free throw shooter.

Analysis: The 1993-94 season could be a critical one for Owens. He'll have to prove that his knees are healthy, that he can keep in top shape, and that he can pick up where he left off as a rookie two years ago. Don't count stardom out of his future.

PLAYER SUMMARY	
Will	score inside and out
Can't	bury his FTs
Expect	more off-season work
Don't Expect	shy shooting
Fantasy Value	$25-28
Card Value	25-50¢

COLLEGE STATISTICS

		G	FGP	FTP	RPG	PPG
88-89	SYR	38	.521	.648	6.9	13.0
89-90	SYR	33	.486	.722	8.4	18.2
90-91	SYR	32	.509	.674	11.6	23.3
Totals		103	.505	.682	8.8	17.7

NBA REGULAR-SEASON STATISTICS

				FGs		3-PT FGs		FTs		Rebounds						
		G	MIN	FG	PCT	FG	PCT	FT	PCT	OFF	TOT	AST	STL	BLK	PTS	PPG
91-92	GS	80	2510	468	.525	1	.111	204	.654	243	639	188	90	65	1141	14.3
92-93	GS	37	1201	247	.501	1	.091	117	.639	108	264	144	35	28	612	16.5
Totals		117	3711	715	.517	2	.100	321	.648	351	903	332	125	93	1753	15.0

ROBERT PACK

Team: Denver Nuggets
Position: Guard
Height: 6'2" **Weight:** 180
Birthdate: February 3, 1969

NBA Experience: 2 years
College: Tyler; Southern Cal.
Acquired: Traded from Trail Blazers
for a 1993 2nd-round pick, 10/92

Background: Pack totaled 319 assists in just two years at Southern Cal., finishing fourth on the Trojans' all-time list. He joined former USC stars Gus Williams, Jacque Hill, and Larry Friend when he recorded back-to-back years of 100 or more assists. He underwent arthroscopic surgery on his right shoulder after his junior year. Pack was not drafted, but he signed as a free agent with Portland and dished out nearly two APG in 72 contests in 1991-92. He was a valuable pick-up for the Nuggets last season, finishing a close second to Chris Jackson in assists.

Strengths: Pack has proven to be more than capable as a back-up point guard and can also play the two spot. He is an accomplished distributor who can score on drives to the basket or with the occasional jump shot. He averaged 10.5 PPG in just 21 minutes per outing last season. He has very good quickness, strength, and leaping ability and applies himself at the defensive end.

Weaknesses: Pack is not regarded as a pure shooter and his range is limited. As a pro, he has made just one of his 18 attempts from 3-point land. Pack's play is hot-and-cold and he is not well-schooled in fundamentals. He takes a few too many chances defensively and will get out of control at times.

Analysis: Pack deserves a lot of credit for making a very good Portland team as an undrafted rookie and then making an impact with Denver in his second year. Out of nowhere, he has become a double-figure scorer and a valuable distributor who should continue to earn his share of playing time. Better control and a more dangerous jump shot would gain him more respect.

PLAYER SUMMARY

Will ....distribute
Can't ....make 3-pointers
Expect ....strong drives
Don't Expect.............................control
Fantasy Value...............................$2-4
Card Value ....10-20¢

COLLEGE STATISTICS

		G	FGP	FTP	APG	PPG
1989-90	USC	28	.472	.677	5.9	12.1
1990-91	USC	29	.480	.794	5.3	14.7
Totals		57	.476	.742	5.6	13.4

NBA REGULAR-SEASON STATISTICS

		G	MIN	FGs FG	FGs PCT	3-PT FGs FG	3-PT FGs PCT	FTs FT	FTs PCT	Rebounds OFF	Rebounds TOT	AST	STL	BLK	PTS	PPG
91-92	POR	72	894	115	.423	0	.000	102	.803	32	97	140	40	4	332	4.6
92-93	DEN	77	1579	285	.470	1	.125	239	.766	52	160	335	81	10	810	10.5
Totals		149	2473	400	.456	1	.056	341	.779	84	257	475	121	14	1142	7.7

ROBERT PARISH

Team: Boston Celtics
Position: Center
Height: 7'0" **Weight:** 230
Birthdate: August 30, 1953
NBA Experience: 17 years

College: Centenary
Acquired: Traded from Warriors with
a 1980 1st-round pick for two 1980
1st-round picks, 6/80

Background: The best player in Centenary history, "Chief" enjoyed four solid seasons with Golden State before his career really blossomed in Boston. He played on championship Celtic teams in 1981, '84, and '86. He continues to lead the Celtics in rebounding and figure prominently into their scoring.

Strengths: Parish is a superb leader who still rebounds, scores, and blocks shots. His high-arching jumper still finds the net. Only he and Kareem Abdul-Jabbar have 20,000 career points, 12,000 rebounds, 1,200 games, and 2,000 blocks. Parish is second to Abdul-Jabbar in games played.

Weaknesses: Parish, the league's oldest player, needs more breathers than he used to. Last season, he was arrested on a marijuana charge.

Analysis: Parish is headed for the Hall of Fame the first year he's eligible. He will probably play just one more season, and he will probably again lead the Celtics in rebounding at the age of 40.

PLAYER SUMMARY	
Will	score, rebound
Can't	run like he used to
Expect	Hall of Fame induction
Don't Expect	two more years
Fantasy Value	$7-9
Card Value	10-15¢

COLLEGE STATISTICS

		G	FGP	FTP	RPG	PPG
72-73	CENT	27	.579	.610	18.7	23.0
73-74	CENT	25	.523	.628	15.3	19.9
74-75	CENT	29	.560	.661	15.4	18.9
75-76	CENT	27	.589	.694	18.0	24.8
Totals		108	.564	.655	16.9	21.6

NBA REGULAR-SEASON STATISTICS

				FGs		3-PT FGs		FTs		Rebounds						
		G	MIN	FG	PCT	FG	PCT	FT	PCT	OFF	TOT	AST	STL	BLK	PTS	PPG
76-77	GS	77	1384	288	.503	0	.000	121	.708	201	543	74	55	94	697	9.1
77-78	GS	82	1969	430	.472	0	.000	165	.625	211	679	95	79	123	1025	12.5
78-79	GS	76	2411	554	.499	0	.000	196	.698	265	916	115	100	217	1304	17.2
79-80	GS	72	2119	510	.507	0	.000	203	.715	257	793	122	58	115	1223	17.0
80-81	BOS	82	2298	635	.545	0	.000	282	.710	245	777	144	81	214	1552	18.9
81-82	BOS	80	2534	669	.542	0	.000	252	.710	288	866	140	68	192	1590	19.9
82-83	BOS	78	2459	619	.550	0	.000	271	.698	260	827	141	79	148	1509	19.3
83-84	BOS	80	2867	623	.542	0	.000	274	.745	243	857	139	55	116	1520	19.0
84-85	BOS	79	2850	551	.542	0	.000	292	.743	263	840	125	56	101	1394	17.6
85-86	BOS	81	2567	530	.549	0	.000	245	.731	246	770	145	65	116	1305	16.1
86-87	BOS	80	2995	588	.556	0	.000	227	.735	254	851	173	64	144	1403	17.5
87-88	BOS	74	2312	442	.589	0	.000	177	.734	173	628	115	55	84	1061	14.3
88-89	BOS	80	2840	596	.570	0	.000	294	.719	342	996	175	79	116	1486	18.6
89-90	BOS	79	2396	505	.580	0	.000	233	.747	259	796	103	38	69	1243	15.7
90-91	BOS	81	2441	485	.598	0	.000	237	.767	271	856	66	66	103	1207	14.9
91-92	BOS	79	2285	468	.535	0	.000	179	.772	219	705	70	68	97	1115	14.1
92-93	BOS	79	2146	416	.535	0	.000	162	.689	246	740	61	57	107	994	12.6
Totals		1339	40873	8909	.542	0	.000	3810	.721	4243	13440	2003	1123	2156	21628	16.2

JOHN PAXSON

Team: Chicago Bulls
Position: Guard
Height: 6'2" **Weight:** 185
Birthdate: September 29, 1960

NBA Experience: 10 years
College: Notre Dame
Acquired: Signed as a free agent, 10/85

Background: Drafted out of Notre Dame by San Antonio in 1983, Paxson was nothing more than a fringe player until he hooked up with Michael Jordan in Chicago. His 55-percent field goal accuracy in 1990-91 ranked No. 1 among NBA guards. He was the starting point guard and a playoff hero as the Bulls won back-to-back championships in 1991 and 1992. Paxson underwent knee surgery before the 1992-93 campaign and missed 23 games, but he clinched Chicago's third world title with a last-second 3-pointer in Game 6 of the NBA Finals.

Strengths: Paxson still spots up and nails the open jumper. If he hits his first couple of shots, he's usually in for a big night. Paxson is a team player who compensates for his lack of athletic ability with loads of court smarts and savvy. He is a steady passer and ball-handler.

Weaknesses: Paxson can be a little too unselfish at times, as he tries to get everyone involved at the expense of passing up good shots. Hardly a bona fide point guard, he is conservative with the ball. Quick guards can give him fits.

Analysis: Jordan could not have asked for a better complement in his championship runs. While the greatest player in the game drew all the attention, Paxson stepped into the openings and made the big shots. He was not the same player last season, but he still came up big when it mattered.

PLAYER SUMMARY	
Will	spot up for jumpers
Can't	trade in left knee
Expect	steady leadership
Don't Expect	10 PPG
Fantasy Value	$0
Card Value	5-12¢

COLLEGE STATISTICS

		G	FGP	FTP	APG	PPG
79-80	ND	27	.483	.745	2.3	4.6
80-81	ND	29	.518	.685	4.8	9.9
81-82	ND	27	.535	.774	3.7	16.4
82-83	ND	29	.533	.740	3.9	17.7
Totals		112	.526	.736	3.6	12.2

NBA REGULAR-SEASON STATISTICS

		G	MIN	FGs FG	FGs PCT	3-PT FGs FG	3-PT FGs PCT	FTs FT	FTs PCT	Rebounds OFF	Rebounds TOT	AST	STL	BLK	PTS	PPG
83-84	SA	49	458	61	.445	4	.182	16	.615	4	33	149	10	2	142	2.9
84-85	SA	78	1259	196	.509	10	.294	84	.840	19	68	215	45	3	486	6.2
85-86	CHI	75	1570	153	.466	15	.294	74	.804	18	94	274	55	2	395	5.3
86-87	CHI	82	2689	386	.487	52	.371	106	.809	22	139	467	66	8	930	11.3
87-88	CHI	81	1888	287	.493	33	.347	33	.733	16	104	303	49	1	640	7.9
88-89	CHI	78	1738	246	.480	44	.331	31	.861	13	94	308	53	6	567	7.3
89-90	CHI	82	2365	365	.516	33	.359	56	.824	27	119	335	83	6	819	10.0
90-91	CHI	82	1971	317	.548	42	.438	34	.829	15	91	297	62	3	710	8.7
91-92	CHI	79	1946	257	.528	12	.273	29	.784	21	96	241	49	9	555	7.0
92-93	CHI	59	1030	105	.451	19	.463	17	.850	9	48	136	38	2	246	4.2
Totals		745	16914	2373	.500	264	.353	480	.805	164	886	2725	510	42	5490	7.4

GARY PAYTON

Team: Seattle SuperSonics
Position: Guard
Height: 6'4" **Weight:** 190
Birthdate: July 23, 1968

NBA Experience: 3 years
College: Oregon St.
Acquired: 1st-round pick in 1990 draft
(2nd overall)

Background: Payton was an All-American as a senior at Oregon State, where he set a school scoring record, ended his career second on the NCAA assists list, and set a Pac-10 record with 100 steals in his final season. He has started all but seven games of his first three seasons and has led Seattle in steals and assists each year. Last season was his best yet. He tied for fourth in the league in total steals.

Strengths: Payton has lived up to his defensive reputation and is now considered one of the premier defensive guards in the game. He hounds the ball and makes his opponent work for everything he gets. He stands tall at the point, where he handles the ball expertly in the open court, gets good penetration, and is a fine finisher. He loves to run and makes things happen.

Weaknesses: Although he has become a much better leader, Payton is still capable of playing over his head at times. A noted trash talker, he tends to make opponents want to cram the ball down his throat. Payton is not that great at sticking jumpers off the dribble. His shooting range does not extend past the NBA 3-point line.

Analysis: Payton talks a big game but he also plays one. He's a natural point guard who penetrates, hits open teammates, handles the ball, and shuts down his man on defense. Last year, he added double-figure scoring and better shooting to the package. A talk with coach George Karl before last year prompted months of hard off-season work. It paid off.

PLAYER SUMMARY	
Will	hound his man
Can't	keep quiet
Expect	transition offense
Don't Expect	treys
Fantasy Value	$13-16
Card Value	12-25¢

COLLEGE STATISTICS

		G	FGP	FTP	APG	PPG
86-87	OSU	30	.459	.671	7.6	12.5
87-88	OSU	31	.489	.699	7.4	14.5
88-89	OSU	30	.475	.677	8.1	20.1
89-90	OSU	29	.504	.690	8.1	25.7
Totals		120	.485	.684	7.8	18.1

NBA REGULAR-SEASON STATISTICS

		G	MIN	FGs FG	FGs PCT	3-PT FGs FG	3-PT FGs PCT	FTs FT	FTs PCT	Rebounds OFF	Rebounds TOT	AST	STL	BLK	PTS	PPG
90-91	SEA	82	2244	259	.450	1	.077	69	.711	108	243	528	165	15	588	7.2
91-92	SEA	81	2549	331	.451	3	.130	99	.669	123	295	506	147	21	764	9.4
92-93	SEA	82	2548	476	.494	7	.206	151	.770	95	281	399	177	21	1110	13.5
Totals		245	7341	1066	.469	11	.157	319	.723	326	819	1433	489	57	2462	10.0

ANTHONY PEELER

Team: Los Angeles Lakers
Position: Guard
Height: 6'4" **Weight:** 212
Birthdate: November 25, 1969

NBA Experience: 1 year
College: Missouri
Acquired: 1st-round pick in 1992 draft
(15th overall)

Background: Perhaps the most heralded recruit in Missouri history, Peeler lived up to expectations despite an inability to stay out of trouble. He was named Big Eight Player of the Year after averaging 23.4 PPG, 5.5 RPG, and 3.9 APG as a senior. He dished out more than 100 assists every season, despite being suspended for a semester due to poor grades as a junior. His checkered off-court record includes a conviction on a felony weapons charge. Peeler's troubles dropped him to the 15th spot in the 1992 NBA draft. He made 11 starts as a rookie and was one of seven Lakers to average double figures in scoring.

Strengths: A tremendous athlete, Peeler was drafted by the Texas Rangers in 1988 as a left-handed pitcher/outfielder. He can play both guard positions and is capable of getting to the basket or pulling up for perimeter jumpers. Peeler led the Lakers in 3-pointers last season, and he also hit for a high percentage. He competes, has a great feel for the game, and gets his teammates involved with above-average passing skills.

Weaknesses: His off-court troubles have been the main setbacks in his basketball career to date. On the hardwood, he could stand to apply himself more on defense and on the boards. There are indications, however, that he can be a very good defensive player. Like many rookies, his play was up-and-down.

Analysis: Assuming Peeler continues to stay out of trouble, as he did as a rookie, the Lakers got a steal with their highest draft choice since No. 1 pick James Worthy in 1982. Peeler made an immediate impact with his quickness, his jumper, and his surprising on-court maturity. He knows the difference between good and bad shots and has star potential.

PLAYER SUMMARY	
Will	fill the nets
Can't	erase checkered past
Expect	star potential
Don't Expect	limited minutes
Fantasy Value	$9-12
Card Value	25-75¢

COLLEGE STATISTICS

		G	FGP	FTP	RPG	PPG
88-89	MO	36	.504	.754	3.7	10.1
89-90	MO	31	.446	.769	5.4	16.8
90-91	MO	21	.475	.768	6.2	19.4
91-92	MO	29	.459	.806	5.5	23.4
Totals		117	.466	.779	5.1	16.8

NBA REGULAR-SEASON STATISTICS

			FGs		3-PT FGs		FTs		Rebounds						
	G	MIN	FG	PCT	FG	PCT	FT	PCT	OFF	TOT	AST	STL	BLK	PTS	PPG
92-93 LAL	77	1656	297	.458	46	.390	162	.786	64	179	166	60	14	802	10.4
Totals	77	1656	297	.458	46	.390	162	.786	64	179	166	60	14	802	10.4

WILL PERDUE

Team: Chicago Bulls
Position: Center
Height: 7'0" **Weight:** 240
Birthdate: August 29, 1965

NBA Experience: 5 years
College: Vanderbilt
Acquired: 1st-round pick in 1988 draft
(11th overall)

Background: As a senior at Vanderbilt, Perdue led the league in rebounding and was named Southeastern Conference Player of the Year. Drafted by the Bulls in 1988, he played less than any other first-round pick as a rookie. His scoring average has improved each year since but is still not at five PPG. Perdue has served primarily as a back-up to Bill Cartwright in the middle for ten to 15 minutes a game over the last three seasons. He started 16 times last year while Cartwright was injured.

Strengths: Perdue has advanced to the point where Phil Jackson can use him at crucial times without worrying too much. Although he's a mediocre shooter, Perdue is now active offensively and gets to the boards. He's a better passer than Cartwright, plays physical defense, and will block a few shots.

Weaknesses: A gifted athlete he is not. Perdue doesn't jump well at all and he's even worse at anticipating the ball. He's more scorer than shooter, but he's not much of either. His best shot is the "Per-dunk." He added more than 100 points to his free throw percentage last year but was still awful.

Analysis: Perdue is popular among Chicago fans, even though his physical limitations will probably prevent him from ever being more than a back-up NBA pivot man. The Bulls missed Cartwright when the veteran was out of the lineup last season. Perdue is valuable as a role-player for his good attitude and willingness to bang and play defense.

PLAYER SUMMARY	
Will	defend, rebound
Can't	score in bunches
Expect	a physical reserve
Don't Expect	much touch
Fantasy Value	$1
Card Value	8-12¢

COLLEGE STATISTICS

		G	FGP	FTP	RPG	PPG
83-84	VAND	17	.467	.444	2.2	2.7
85-86	VAND	22	.585	.438	2.8	3.5
86-87	VAND	34	.599	.618	8.7	17.4
87-88	VAND	31	.634	.673	10.1	18.3
Totals		104	.606	.620	6.8	12.3

NBA REGULAR-SEASON STATISTICS

		G	MIN	FGs FG	FGs PCT	3-PT FGs FG	3-PT FGs PCT	FTs FT	FTs PCT	Rebounds OFF	Rebounds TOT	AST	STL	BLK	PTS	PPG
88-89	CHI	30	190	29	.403	0	.000	8	.571	18	45	11	4	6	66	2.2
89-90	CHI	77	884	111	.414	0	.000	72	.692	88	214	46	19	26	294	3.8
90-91	CHI	74	972	116	.494	0	.000	75	.670	122	336	47	23	57	307	4.1
91-92	CHI	77	1007	152	.547	1	.500	45	.495	108	312	80	16	43	350	4.5
92-93	CHI	72	998	137	.557	0	.000	67	.604	103	287	74	22	47	341	4.7
Totals		330	4051	545	.496	1	.091	267	.618	439	1194	258	84	179	1358	4.1

SAM PERKINS

Team: Seattle SuperSonics
Position: Forward/Center
Height: 6'9" **Weight:** 250
Birthdate: June 14, 1961
NBA Experience: 9 years

College: North Carolina
Acquired: Traded from Lakers for Benoit Benjamin and draft rights to Doug Christie, 2/93

Background: Perkins was a three-time All-American at North Carolina, where he earned an NCAA title in 1982, reached the finals in 1981, and won the Lapchick Award as the nation's outstanding senior in 1984. In six years with Dallas, he became the club's all-time leader in rebounds and ranked third in blocked shots, fifth in assists, and fifth in scoring. He was signed by the Lakers before the 1990-91 season and played two and a half years in L.A. Perkins was traded to Seattle for Doug Christie and Benoit Benjamin midway through last season.

Strengths: Perkins provides veteran leadership and versatility on the front line. He scores from both the post and the perimeter. He's a good free throw shooter and even hits 3-pointers. He plays defense, rebounds, and plays an intelligent brand of ball.

Weaknesses: For some reason, Perkins was slapped with an underachiever's label in L.A., although many forwards would have loved to put up his numbers. He has shot better than 50 percent just once in his career, but consider his range. He could be more assertive.

Analysis: Seattle felt it needed more leadership and some low-post offense off the bench, and the Sonics got those things and more when they got Perkins. He averaged 12.1 PPG in 30 outings with Seattle and excelled in the playoffs.

PLAYER SUMMARY	
Will	score inside and out
Can't	emerge as a superstar
Expect	versatility, smarts
Don't Expect	20 PPG
Fantasy Value	$9-12
Card Value	10-20¢

COLLEGE STATISTICS

		G	FGP	FTP	RPG	PPG
80-81	NC	37	.626	.741	7.8	14.9
81-82	NC	32	.578	.768	7.8	14.3
82-83	NC	35	.527	.819	9.4	16.9
83-84	NC	31	.589	.856	9.6	17.6
Totals		135	.576	.796	8.6	15.9

NBA REGULAR-SEASON STATISTICS

		G	MIN	FGs FG	FGs PCT	3-PT FGs FG	3-PT FGs PCT	FTs FT	FTs PCT	Rebounds OFF	Rebounds TOT	AST	STL	BLK	PTS	PPG
84-85	DAL	82	2317	347	.471	9	.250	200	.820	189	605	135	63	63	903	11.0
85-86	DAL	80	2626	458	.503	11	.333	307	.814	195	685	153	75	94	1234	15.4
86-87	DAL	80	2687	461	.482	19	.352	245	.828	197	616	146	109	77	1186	14.8
87-88	DAL	75	2499	394	.450	5	.167	273	.822	201	601	118	74	54	1066	14.2
88-89	DAL	78	2860	445	.464	7	.184	274	.833	235	688	127	76	92	1171	15.0
89-90	DAL	76	2668	435	.493	6	.214	330	.778	209	572	175	88	64	1206	15.9
90-91	LAL	73	2504	368	.495	18	.281	229	.821	167	538	108	64	78	983	13.5
91-92	LAL	63	2332	361	.450	15	.217	304	.817	192	556	141	64	62	1041	16.5
92-93	LAL/SEA	79	2351	381	.477	24	.338	250	.820	163	524	156	60	82	1036	13.1
Totals		686	22844	3650	.476	114	.270	2412	.815	1748	5385	1259	673	666	9826	14.3

TIM PERRY

Team: Philadelphia 76ers
Position: Forward
Height: 6'9" **Weight:** 220
Birthdate: June 4, 1965
NBA Experience: 5 years

College: Temple
Acquired: Traded from Suns with Jeff Hornacek and Andrew Lang for Charles Barkley, 6/92

Background: Perry was named Atlantic 10 Player of the Year as a senior at Temple, where he led the Owls to a top ranking for much of the season and finished as the school's career leader in blocked shots. Although he was the seventh player taken in the 1988 draft, he spent his first three pro seasons coming off the Phoenix bench. He started for most of the 1991-92 campaign and responded with his best year. He was traded to the 76ers in the Charles Barkley deal and started 51 games last season.

Strengths: Defense and rebounding are the best aspects of Perry's game. He skies over opponents, blocks shots, has good instincts for the ball, and works hard around the basket. He is at his best offensively in a transition game and on put-backs, although he has developed an accurate jump hook.

Weaknesses: Perry will never rank among the top scoring big men in the league. He does not shoot the ball well, has limited range, and his field goal percentage dropped below 50 last season despite his many dunks. Perry is not a skilled ball-handler or passer.

Analysis: Perry rebounds and plays defense, but he did not have the season Philadelphia expected from him last year. He seemed to have trouble finding his niche from the start. The former lottery pick does not perform consistently enough and does not do enough offensively to be called an above-average player. The Sixers want more in the years to come.

PLAYER SUMMARY	
Will	defend star forwards
Can't	star on offense
Expect	quickness, rebounds
Don't Expect	consistency
Fantasy Value	$4-6
Card Value	5-10¢

COLLEGE STATISTICS

		G	FGP	FTP	RPG	PPG
84-85	TEMP	30	.414	.500	3.9	2.3
85-86	TEMP	31	.566	.575	9.5	11.6
86-87	TEMP	36	.514	.620	8.6	12.9
87-88	TEMP	33	.585	.637	8.0	14.5
Totals		130	.544	.605	7.6	10.5

NBA REGULAR-SEASON STATISTICS

		G	MIN	FGs FG	FGs PCT	3-PT FGs FG	3-PT FGs PCT	FTs FT	FTs PCT	Rebounds OFF	Rebounds TOT	AST	STL	BLK	PTS	PPG
88-89	PHO	62	614	108	.537	1	.250	40	.615	61	132	18	19	32	257	4.1
89-90	PHO	60	612	100	.513	1	1.000	53	.589	79	152	17	21	22	254	4.2
90-91	PHO	46	587	75	.521	0	.000	43	.614	53	126	27	23	43	193	4.2
91-92	PHO	80	2483	413	.523	3	.375	153	.712	204	551	134	44	116	982	12.3
92-93	PHI	81	2104	287	.468	10	.204	147	.710	154	409	126	40	91	731	9.0
Totals		329	6400	983	.506	15	.224	436	.674	551	1370	322	147	304	2417	7.3

CHUCK PERSON

Team: Minnesota Timberwolves
Position: Forward
Height: 6'8" **Weight:** 225
Birthdate: June 27, 1964
NBA Experience: 7 years

College: Auburn
Acquired: Traded from Pacers with Micheal Williams for Pooh Richardson and Sam Mitchell, 9/92

Background: The all-time leading scorer in Auburn history when he graduated from college, Person immediately made his mark on the NBA with a Rookie of the Year season in 1986-87. In six seasons, he became Indiana's all-time leading NBA scorer. He set a league record for 3-pointers in a playoff game with seven in 1991. Dealt to Minnesota before the 1992-93 season, he surpassed the 10,000-career point plateau but scored a career-low 16.8 PPG.

Strengths: Person is one of those rare players who can take over games by himself. When his team needs a bucket, he craves the ball. He's both an excellent shooter and scorer who can put the ball in the hole from the post or from behind the 3-point line. He handles the ball and distributes.

Weaknesses: Person often tries to do too much by himself and has a history of getting down on teammates. Last year, he called Minnesota rookie Christian Laettner selfish, a description some would apply to Person. When his man scores, Person almost always tries to out-do him on the other end. He is not a good foul shooter.

Analysis: Person has the talent to be an All-Star, but his chances of reaching that level have been hurt by his tendency to want to do everything. At his best, Person is a dominant all-around player who can win ballgames with his shooting, passing, and even his defense.

PLAYER SUMMARY	
Will	hit 3-pointers
Can't	withhold opinions
Expect	clutch baskets
Don't Expect	high FT pct.
Fantasy Value	$10-13
Card Value	8-12¢

COLLEGE STATISTICS

		G	FGP	FTP	RPG	PPG
82-83	AUB	28	.541	.758	4.6	9.3
83-84	AUB	31	.543	.728	8.0	19.1
84-85	AUB	34	.544	.738	8.9	22.0
85-86	AUB	33	.519	.804	7.9	21.5
Totals		126	.536	.757	7.5	18.3

NBA REGULAR-SEASON STATISTICS

				FGs		3-PT FGs		FTs		Rebounds						
		G	MIN	FG	PCT	FG	PCT	FT	PCT	OFF	TOT	AST	STL	BLK	PTS	PPG
86-87	IND	82	2956	635	.468	49	.355	222	.747	168	677	295	90	16	1541	18.8
87-88	IND	79	2807	575	.459	59	.333	132	.670	171	536	309	73	8	1341	17.0
88-89	IND	80	3012	711	.489	63	.307	243	.792	144	516	289	83	18	1728	21.6
89-90	IND	77	2714	605	.487	94	.372	211	.781	126	445	230	53	20	1515	19.7
90-91	IND	80	2566	620	.504	69	.340	165	.721	121	417	238	56	17	1474	18.4
91-92	IND	81	2923	616	.480	132	.373	133	.675	114	426	382	68	18	1497	18.5
92-93	MIN	78	2985	541	.433	118	.355	109	.649	98	433	343	67	30	1309	16.8
Totals		557	19963	4303	.475	584	.351	1215	.730	942	3450	2086	490	127	10405	18.7

RICKY PIERCE

Team: Seattle SuperSonics
Position: Guard
Height: 6'4" **Weight:** 215
Birthdate: August 19, 1959

NBA Experience: 11 years
College: Rice
Acquired: Traded from Bucks for Dale Ellis, 2/91

Background: Pierce led Rice in scoring and rebounding for three straight years. He played single seasons in Detroit and San Diego, then became one of the NBA's most celebrated bench players in Milwaukee. He won the Sixth Man Award in 1986-87 and 1989-90. Pierce served the same reserve role in Seattle after a trade in 1990-91, and he played in his first All-Star Game that year. He became a starter in 1991-92 and has led the Sonics in scoring ever since.

Strengths: Pierce remains one of the best shooters in the NBA. His strong upper body helps him draw fouls on his way to the hoop, and he can recover to hit the shots. He's one of the league's all-time clutch scorers and was sixth in the league from the free throw line last year.

Weaknesses: Most talk of holes in Pierce's game starts and ends with defense. He lacks the lateral quickness and often the interest required to be a stopper. He does come up with the occassional steal, however.

Analysis: Pierce has thrived as a starter just as he did when coming off the bench. Was there any doubt? Pierce ruins defensive game plans with his one-on-one ability. He still ranks among the premier scorers in the game, and he ranks sixth all time in free throw shooting.

PLAYER SUMMARY

Will ....score in bushels
Can't.................................be a stopper
Expect ....great shooting
Don't Expect ....reserve minutes
Fantasy Value............................$15-18
Card Value....................................5-12¢

COLLEGE STATISTICS

		G	FGP	FTP	RPG	PPG
79-80	RICE	26	.480	.718	8.2	19.2
80-81	RICE	26	.518	.706	7.0	20.9
81-82	RICE	30	.511	.794	7.5	26.8
Totals		**82**	**.504**	**.751**	**7.6**	**22.5**

NBA REGULAR-SEASON STATISTICS

				FGs		3-PT FGs		FTs		Rebounds						
		G	MIN	FG	PCT	FG	PCT	FT	PCT	OFF	TOT	AST	STL	BLK	PTS	PPG
82-83	DET	39	265	33	.375	1	.143	18	.563	15	35	14	8	4	85	2.2
83-84	SD	69	1280	268	.470	0	.000	149	.861	59	135	60	27	13	685	9.9
84-85	MIL	44	882	165	.537	1	.250	102	.823	49	117	94	34	5	433	9.8
85-86	MIL	81	2147	429	.538	3	.130	266	.858	94	231	177	83	6	1127	13.9
86-87	MIL	79	2505	575	.534	3	.107	387	.880	117	266	144	64	24	1540	19.5
87-88	MIL	37	965	248	.510	3	.214	107	.877	30	83	73	21	7	606	16.4
88-89	MIL	75	2078	527	.518	8	.222	255	.859	82	197	156	77	19	1317	17.6
89-90	MIL	59	1709	503	.510	46	.390	307	.839	64	167	133	50	7	1359	23.0
90-91	MIL/SEA	78	2167	561	.485	46	.397	430	.913	67	191	168	60	13	1598	20.5
91-92	SEA	78	2658	620	.475	33	.268	417	.916	93	233	241	86	20	1690	21.7
92-93	SEA	77	2218	524	.489	42	.372	313	.889	58	192	220	100	7	1403	18.2
Totals		**716**	**18874**	**4453**	**.502**	**186**	**.307**	**2751**	**.876**	**728**	**1847**	**1480**	**610**	**125**	**11843**	**16.5**

ED PINCKNEY

Team: Boston Celtics
Position: Forward
Height: 6'9" **Weight:** 215
Birthdate: March 27, 1963
NBA Experience: 8 years

College: Villanova
Acquired: Traded from Kings with Joe Kleine for Danny Ainge and Brad Lohaus, 2/89

Background: The highlight of Pinckney's basketball career was leading Villanova to a national title in 1985 and being named tourney MVP. Pinckney shot 60 percent from the field during his four-year Wildcat career. He spent two years with Phoenix and a year and a half with Sacramento before Boston acquired him in 1989. He became a starter for the Celtics during the latter half of 1991-92. Arthroscopic surgery on his left knee limited his 1992-93 season to seven games.

Strengths: Pinckney provides strong rebounding on both ends, good defense, and some occasional offense when called upon. He's a nice finisher on the fastbreak and can also rise over his defender for mid-range jumpers. He possesses a soft touch. He shoots high percentages from the field and the line.

Weaknesses: Pinckney is no Kevin McHale in Boston's halfcourt set. "Easy Ed" has never really mastered the kind of low-post moves that would serve him well in a slow-down game. He relies on offensive boards for many of his points. Health has become a concern.

Analysis: Pinckney does a lot of things that don't show up in the boxscore, along with a few that do. His healthy return will be very important for the Celtics, who have lost McHale to retirement and need some help on the front line. If Pinckney can return to his form of late 1991-92, he can provide it.

PLAYER SUMMARY

Will	crash the boards
Can't	score like McHale
Expect	50-percent shooting
Don't Expect	15 PPG
Fantasy Value	$1-3
Card Value	5-8¢

COLLEGE STATISTICS

		G	FGP	FTP	RPG	PPG
81-82	VILL	32	.640	.714	7.8	14.2
82-83	VILL	31	.568	.760	9.7	12.5
83-84	VILL	31	.604	.694	7.9	15.4
84-85	VILL	35	.600	.730	8.9	15.6
Totals		129	.604	.723	8.6	14.5

NBA REGULAR-SEASON STATISTICS

				FGs		3-PT FGs		FTs		Rebounds							
		G	MIN	FG	PCT	FG	PCT	FT	PCT	OFF	TOT	AST	STL	BLK	PTS	PPG
85-86	PHO	80	1602	255	.558	0	.000	171	.673	95	308	90	71	37	681	8.5
86-87	PHO	80	2250	290	.584	0	.000	257	.739	179	580	116	86	54	837	10.5
87-88	SAC	79	1177	179	.522	0	.000	133	.747	94	230	66	39	32	491	6.2
88-89	SAC/BOS	80	2012	319	.513	0	.000	280	.800	166	449	118	83	66	918	11.5
89-90	BOS	77	1082	135	.542	0	.000	92	.773	93	225	68	34	42	362	4.7
90-91	BOS	70	1165	131	.539	0	.000	104	.897	155	341	45	61	43	366	5.2
91-92	BOS	81	1917	203	.537	0	.000	207	.812	252	564	62	70	56	613	7.6
92-93	BOS	7	151	10	.417	0	.000	12	.923	14	43	1	4	7	32	4.6
Totals		554	11356	1522	.541	0	.000	1256	.769	1048	2740	566	448	337	4300	7.8

SCOTTIE PIPPEN

Team: Chicago Bulls
Position: Forward
Height: 6'7" **Weight:** 225
Birthdate: September 25, 1965
NBA Experience: 6 years
College: Central Arkansas

Acquired: Draft rights traded from SuperSonics for draft rights to Olden Polynice, a 1988 or 1989 2nd-round pick, and the option to exchange 1988 or 1989 1st-round picks, 6/87

Background: An NAIA All-American as a senior at Central Arkansas, Pippen arrived in Chicago in the 1987 draft. He improved his all-around game every year and starred in the Bulls' 1991-93 NBA championships. He is Chicago's second-leading scorer, behind only Michael Jordan, and he has led all NBA forwards in assists over the last two years. Pippen has three All-Star Games under his belt and played on the 1992 U.S. Olympic team.

Strengths: The acrobatic Pippen has countless moves to the basket and is an electrifying finisher. He is a fine perimeter shooter with 3-point range. His long arms and quick hands regularly rank him among the league leaders in steals. Pippen thrives in a transition game, both offensively and defensively, and is the best passing forward in the game.

Weaknesses: Pippen gained a reputation as a big-game disappearing act when the Bulls were struggling to overcome the Pistons in the 1989 and 1990 playoffs, although he has pretty much answered that rap. He is not good from the line.

Analysis: It is some kind of tribute to Pippen that he has become a bona fide superstar on a team that already has the biggest star in the game. On a lot of other teams, the versatile Pippen would be the franchise. He was bothered all last season by tendinitis in his right ankle but played through the pain. He made the NBA All-Defensive first team.

PLAYER SUMMARY	
Will	get to the hoop
Can't	be stopped in transition
Expect	points, assists, steals
Don't Expect	All-Star snubs
Fantasy Value	$60-65
Card Value	20-35¢

COLLEGE STATISTICS

		G	FGP	FTP	RPG	PPG
83-84	CARK	20	.456	.684	3.0	4.3
84-85	CARK	19	.564	.676	9.2	18.5
85-86	CARK	29	.556	.686	9.2	19.8
86-87	CARK	25	.592	.719	10.0	23.6
Totals		93	.563	.695	8.1	17.2

NBA REGULAR-SEASON STATISTICS

		G	MIN	FGs FG	FGs PCT	3-PT FGs FG	3-PT FGs PCT	FTs FT	FTs PCT	Rebounds OFF	Rebounds TOT	AST	STL	BLK	PTS	PPG
87-88	CHI	79	1650	261	.463	4	.174	99	.576	115	298	169	91	52	625	7.9
88-89	CHI	73	2413	413	.476	21	.273	201	.668	138	445	256	139	61	1048	14.4
89-90	CHI	82	3148	562	.489	28	.250	199	.675	150	547	444	211	101	1351	16.5
90-91	CHI	82	3014	600	.520	21	.309	240	.706	163	595	511	193	93	1461	17.8
91-92	CHI	82	3164	687	.506	16	.200	330	.760	185	630	572	155	93	1720	21.0
92-93	CHI	81	3123	628	.473	22	.237	232	.663	203	621	507	173	73	1510	18.6
Totals		479	16512	3151	.491	112	.247	1301	.688	954	3136	2459	962	473	7715	16.1

GARY PLUMMER

Team: Denver Nuggets
Position: Forward
Height: 6'9" **Weight:** 255
Birthdate: February 21, 1962

NBA Experience: 2 years
College: Boston U.
Acquired: Signed as a free agent, 10/92

Background: After a solid but unspectacular career at Boston University, Plummer signed with Golden State before the 1984-85 NBA season. He saw action in 66 games as a rookie with the Warriors, averaging 3.8 points and two rebounds in a little over ten minutes per game. He was not re-signed for the next season and found a home in Europe, where he played pro basketball for the next seven years. Plummer returned to the NBA with the Nuggets in 1992-93, and averaged 4.7 points and 2.9 boards in 12.3 minutes per outing.

Strengths: Plummer is a well-liked, free-spirited forward who does not mind doing the grunt work. He plays belly-up defense, crashes the boards, sets picks, and gets up and down the court. He loves the game and it shows in his nightly effort. He's not the kind of player who gets caught up in stats or playing time.

Weaknesses: Plummer is a marginal NBA talent, and by no means a scorer. He does not shoot the ball with much range or consistency and his post-up game is not difficult to defend. He does not have great instincts for what to do with the ball. He'll turn it over more often than he'll get credit for an assist. Plummer draws a lot of whistles.

Analysis: Plummer's story is an interesting one. He says he enjoyed his years overseas and was in the Nuggets' camp before the 1992-93 campaign with the idea that training at high altitude would help build stamina for another European season. When Anthony Cook had to undergo major knee surgery, the 30-year-old Plummer found himself back in the NBA for the first time in eight years. A return overseas is a possibility.

PLAYER SUMMARY

Will	play defense
Can't	start in NBA
Expect	hard work
Don't Expect	big contracts
Fantasy Value	$0
Card Value	5-10¢

COLLEGE STATISTICS

		G	FGP	FTP	RPG	PPG
80-81	BOST	26	.493	.732	1.8	4.0
81-82	BOST	10	.519	.536	6.1	12.5
82-83	BOST	27	.464	.824	7.9	16.3
83-84	BOST	27	.500	.766	10.4	17.0
Totals		90	.487	.761	6.7	12.5

NBA REGULAR-SEASON STATISTICS

			FGs		3-PT FGs		FTs		Rebounds						
	G	MIN	FG	PCT	FG	PCT	FT	PCT	OFF	TOT	AST	STL	BLK	PTS	PPG
84-85 GS	66	702	92	.397	1	.250	65	.707	54	134	26	15	14	250	3.8
92-93 DEN	60	737	106	.465	0	.000	69	.726	53	173	40	14	11	281	4.7
Totals	126	1439	198	.430	1	.143	134	.717	107	307	66	29	25	531	4.2

OLDEN POLYNICE

Team: Detroit Pistons
Position: Center
Height: 7'0" **Weight:** 250
Birthdate: November 21, 1964
NBA Experience: 6 years

College: Virginia
Acquired: Traded from Clippers with 1996 and 1997 2nd-round picks for William Bedford and draft rights to Don MacLean, 6/92

Background: Polynice led Virginia in scoring and rebounding for two seasons and was a three-year leader in field goal accuracy. He was a back-up center with the Sonics until a trade with the L.A. Clippers in 1990-91 allowed him to start. He was a starter for the first four months of 1991-92, until Larry Brown took over as Clipper coach and made him a reserve again. After a June 1992 trade to Detroit, he averaged 7.3 PPG last season with the Pistons.

Strengths: Enthusiasm, defense, and hard work have earned Polynice respect. He can bang with big men yet is quick enough to get out and harass smaller players on the perimeter. He knows his offensive limitations and plays within them. He does not mind setting hard picks and crashing the boards.

Weaknesses: Polynice is not an offensive force by any stretch of the imagination. In fact, his repertoire is limited to mini-hook shots and a couple of low-post moves that force defenders to at least remember he's there. He is a poor ball-handler and perimeter shooter. His free throw shooting is atrocious.

Analysis: Unless the Pistons acquire another center, Polynice is the heir apparent as starter when Bill Laimbeer hangs up his sneakers. A team can do worse than Polynice, who does a lot of the physical things you want out of a center. He missed about a month of last season with a broken finger. He also announced a brief hunger strike for starving people in his native Haiti.

PLAYER SUMMARY	
Will	crash the boards
Can't	stick jumpers
Expect	great enthusiasm
Don't Expect	10 PPG
Fantasy Value	$1-3
Card Value	5-12¢

COLLEGE STATISTICS

		G	FGP	FTP	RPG	PPG
83-84	VA	33	.551	.588	5.6	7.7
84-85	VA	32	.603	.599	7.6	13.0
85-86	VA	30	.572	.637	8.0	16.1
Totals		95	.578	.612	7.0	12.1

NBA REGULAR-SEASON STATISTICS

				FGs		3-PT FGs		FTs		Rebounds						
		G	MIN	FG	PCT	FG	PCT	FT	PCT	OFF	TOT	AST	STL	BLK	PTS	PPG
87-88	SEA	82	1080	118	.465	0	.000	101	.639	122	330	33	32	26	337	4.1
88-89	SEA	80	835	91	.506	0	.000	51	.593	98	206	21	37	30	233	2.9
89-90	SEA	79	1085	156	.540	1	.500	47	.475	128	300	15	25	21	360	4.6
90-91	SEA/LAC	79	2092	316	.560	0	.000	146	.579	220	553	42	43	32	778	9.8
91-92	LAC	76	1834	244	.519	0	.000	125	.622	195	536	46	45	20	613	8.1
92-93	DET	67	1299	210	.490	0	.000	66	.465	181	418	29	31	21	486	7.3
Totals		463	8225	1135	.519	1	.111	536	.571	944	2343	186	213	150	2807	6.1

TERRY PORTER

Team: Portland Trail Blazers
Position: Guard
Height: 6'3" **Weight:** 195
Birthdate: April 8, 1963

NBA Experience: 8 years
College: Wisconsin-Stevens Point
Acquired: 1st-round pick in 1985 draft
(24th overall)

Background: Porter was an NAIA All-American as a junior and senior at Wisconsin-Stevens Point, where his shooting accuracy was remarkable for a guard. He improved his scoring average in each of his pro seasons before peaking in 1989-90, when he led the Trail Blazers to the NBA Finals. Portland's all-time assists king, Porter has never missed more than three games in a season. He's the team's annual leader in 3-pointers and played in his second All-Star Game last season.

Strengths: Porter boasts deadly shooting skills and unlimited range. He loves taking the big shot and he can stick it off the dribble. He is good with both hands and he uses his strength well on penetration moves and defense. Porter can play both guard positions and is a steady leader with the ball in his hands.

Weaknesses: Porter does not possess blinding speed and is not among the most creative guards in the league. In fact, he is not the best playmaker on his team now that Rod Strickland is on board. He has trouble defending some of the league's quick guards.

Analysis: Porter is a player, period. He's not your prototypical lead guard or the game's top shooting guard, but he gets the job done at both positions. His 3-point shooting can turn games around in a hurry. He was second in the Long Distance Shootout during last year's All-Star weekend.

PLAYER SUMMARY	
Will	play two positions
Can't	dazzle with creativity
Expect	100-plus 3-pointers
Don't Expect	10 APG
Fantasy Value	$16-19
Card Value	8-15¢

COLLEGE STATISTICS

		G	FGP	FTP	APG	PPG
81-82	WSP	25	.368	.692	0.8	2.0
82-83	WSP	30	.611	.697	5.2	11.4
83-84	WSP	32	.622	.830	4.2	18.8
84-85	WSP	30	.575	.834	4.3	19.7
Totals		117	.589	.796	3.8	13.5

NBA REGULAR-SEASON STATISTICS

				FGs		3-PT FGs		FTs		Rebounds						
		G	MIN	FG	PCT	FG	PCT	FT	PCT	OFF	TOT	AST	STL	BLK	PTS	PPG
85-86	POR	79	1214	212	.474	13	.310	125	.806	35	117	198	81	1	562	7.1
86-87	POR	80	2714	376	.488	13	.217	280	.838	70	337	715	159	9	1045	13.1
87-88	POR	82	2991	462	.519	24	.348	274	.846	65	378	831	150	16	1222	14.9
88-89	POR	81	3102	540	.471	79	.361	272	.840	85	367	770	146	8	1431	17.7
89-90	POR	80	2781	448	.462	89	.374	421	.892	59	272	726	151	4	1406	17.6
90-91	POR	81	2665	486	.515	130	.415	279	.823	52	282	649	158	12	1381	17.0
91-92	POR	82	2784	521	.461	128	.395	315	.856	51	255	477	127	12	1485	18.1
92-93	POR	81	2883	503	.454	143	.414	327	.843	58	316	419	101	10	1476	18.2
Totals		646	21134	3548	.479	619	.384	2293	.848	475	2324	4785	1073	72	10008	15.5

BRENT PRICE

Team: Washington Bullets
Position: Guard
Height: 6'1" **Weight:** 175
Birthdate: December 9, 1968

NBA Experience: 1 year
College: South Carolina; Oklahoma
Acquired: 2nd-round pick in 1992
draft (32nd overall)

Background: The younger brother of Cleveland guard Mark Price, Brent became a first-team All-Big Eight selection as a senior at Oklahoma after starting his career at South Carolina. He paced the Sooners in steals, assists, and 3-pointers in his final college season and also was the conference leader in the latter two categories. He scored 56 points against Loyola Marymount as a junior. A second-round selection of Washington, Price played in 68 games and started nine times as a rookie, averaging 3.9 PPG and 2.3 APG.

Strengths: Although not nearly on the same level as his big brother, Brent Price owns some of the same skills. He handles the ball well, finds open men, works extremely hard, and has a quick release on his jumper. He can shoot from 3-point distance, will become a reliable NBA free throw shooter, and is determined to make it at this level.

Weaknesses: Brent shot 35.8 percent from the field as a rookie, numbers that will hardly encourage defenders to respect him. For every 3-pointer he made, Price missed five. He's a good passer but is not an accomplished drive-and-dish player who makes things happen. Recall that he played mostly shooting guard in college. He'll go for steals but does not have stopper potential on defense.

Analysis: Brent Price will not soon become the best basketball player in his family. While he resembles his big brother on a few counts, he is not nearly as comfortable creating offense from the point-guard position and has a long way to go before he approaches Mark's shooting. In his favor is a gift for passing. He averaged 8.6 assists per 48 minutes as a rookie.

PLAYER SUMMARY	
Will	find open men
Can't	shoot for percentage
Expect	lots of hustle
Don't Expect	another Mark
Fantasy Value	$1
Card Value	8-15¢

COLLEGE STATISTICS

		G	FGP	FTP	APG	PPG
87-88	SC	29	.460	.857	2.7	10.7
88-89	SC	30	.490	.844	4.3	14.4
90-91	OKLA	35	.416	.838	5.5	17.5
91-92	OKLA	30	.465	.798	6.2	18.7
Totals		124	.454	.828	4.7	15.5

NBA REGULAR-SEASON STATISTICS

			FGs		3-PT FGs		FTs		Rebounds						
	G	MIN	FG	PCT	FG	PCT	FT	PCT	OFF	TOT	AST	STL	BLK	PTS	PPG
92-93 WAS	68	859	100	.358	8	.167	54	.794	28	103	154	56	3	262	3.9
Totals	68	859	100	.358	8	.167	54	.794	28	103	154	56	3	262	3.9

MARK PRICE

Team: Cleveland Cavaliers
Position: Guard
Height: 6'0" **Weight:** 178
Birthdate: February 16, 1964
NBA Experience: 7 years

College: Georgia Tech
Acquired: Draft rights traded from Mavericks for a 1989 2nd-round pick and cash, 6/86

Background: Price, Georgia Tech's second all-time leading scorer when he graduated in 1986, was drafted by Dallas and immediately traded to the Cavs. An emergency appendectomy cut short his rookie season, but he went on to become an NBA All-Star two years later. He tore the anterior cruciate ligament in his knee in 1990-91 but has played in the All-Star Game in both years since. He made 77 free throws in a row last season, the third-longest string in history, and his .948 percentage from the line was the second-best ever.

Strengths: Price is one of the most dangerous shooters in the game, ranking among the all-time leaders from 3-point range. Only Calvin Murphy has posted a better year from the stripe. Price is deceivingly quick, which allows him to create his own shots or get to the hoop. He's a splendid passer, is an underrated defender, and oozes with leadership qualities.

Weaknesses: Price does not have good size, and is therefore not much of a rebounder. Bigger guards can shoot over him.

Analysis: Price just might be the best point guard in the NBA right now. He was virtually unstoppable in the All-Star Game last season, setting a game record with six 3-pointers (in nine attempts) after winning the Long Distance Shootout title the previous night. He passed Rick Barry as the all-time leader in free throw percentage.

PLAYER SUMMARY

Will...........................hit 3's like lay-ups
Can't...................................block shots
Expect..........................All-Star starts
Don't Expect ....missed FTs
Fantasy Value...........................$30-35
Card Value...............................10-15¢

COLLEGE STATISTICS

		G	FGP	FTP	APG	PPG
82-83	GT	28	.435	.877	3.3	20.3
83-84	GT	29	.509	.824	4.2	15.6
84-85	GT	35	.483	.840	4.3	16.7
85-86	GT	34	.528	.855	4.4	17.4
Totals		**126**	**.487**	**.850**	**4.0**	**17.4**

NBA REGULAR-SEASON STATISTICS

			MIN	FGs		3-PT FGs		FTs		Rebounds						
		G	MIN	FG	PCT	FG	PCT	FT	PCT	OFF	TOT	AST	STL	BLK	PTS	PPG
86-87	CLE	67	1217	173	.408	23	.329	95	.833	33	117	202	43	4	464	6.9
87-88	CLE	80	2626	493	.506	72	.486	221	.877	54	180	480	99	12	1279	16.0
88-89	CLE	75	2728	529	.526	93	.441	263	.901	48	226	631	115	7	1414	18.9
89-90	CLE	73	2706	489	.459	152	.406	300	.888	66	251	666	114	5	1430	19.6
90-91	CLE	16	571	97	.497	18	.340	59	.952	8	45	166	42	2	271	16.9
91-92	CLE	72	2138	438	.488	101	.387	270	.947	38	173	535	94	12	1247	17.3
92-93	CLE	75	2380	477	.484	122	.416	289	.948	37	201	602	89	11	1365	18.2
Totals		**458**	**14366**	**2696**	**.486**	**581**	**.412**	**1497**	**.908**	**284**	**1193**	**3282**	**596**	**53**	**7470**	**16.3**

KURT RAMBIS

Team: Sacramento Kings
Position: Forward
Height: 6'8" **Weight:** 215
Birthdate: February 25, 1958

NBA Experience: 12 years
College: Santa Clara
Acquired: Signed as a free agent, 11/92

Background: Rambis was named West Coast Athletic Conference Player of the Year as a senior at Santa Clara before being drafted and waived by the Knicks in 1980. After a short stint in Greece, he signed with the Lakers and played on four championship teams. With Charlotte in 1988-89, Rambis averaged double-figure points for the only time in his career. He made 17 starts for Phoenix in 1990-91, but he saw action in just 28 games the next year and five early last season. In November, he signed with Sacramento and scored a career-low 2.5 PPG.

Strengths: Rambis is the ultimate hard worker who does not mind a job of setting picks, diving for loose balls, pounding the boards, and playing defense. He has gained a cult following for his dedication to getting his hands dirty.

Weaknesses: If you need a power forward who scores points, do not look for the one wearing glasses. His offensive game is certainly nothing to speak of. He is not fast, athletic, or anything close to graceful, and nagging injuries have caught up with him.

Analysis: Rambis approaches the game in workman-like fashion. He does everything he can to free up his teammates and doesn't expect to have the ball in his hands. Few players with his talent have enjoyed so much success.

PLAYER SUMMARY	
Will	dive for loose balls
Can't	light up scoreboards
Expect	defense, role-playing
Don't Expect	starts
Fantasy Value	$0
Card Value	5-10¢

COLLEGE STATISTICS

		G	FGP	FTP	RPG	PPG
76-77	SC	27	.527	.560	11.6	15.0
77-78	SC	27	.507	.692	8.6	13.7
78-79	SC	27	.512	.716	8.4	15.6
79-80	SC	27	.534	.637	9.9	19.6
Totals		108	.521	.650	9.6	16.0

NBA REGULAR-SEASON STATISTICS

				FGs		3-PT FGs		FTs		Rebounds						
		G	MIN	FG	PCT	FG	PCT	FT	PCT	OFF	TOT	AST	STL	BLK	PTS	PPG
81-82	LAL	64	1131	118	.518	0	.000	59	.504	116	348	56	60	76	295	4.6
82-83	LAL	78	1806	235	.569	0	.000	114	.687	164	531	90	105	63	584	7.5
83-84	LAL	47	743	63	.558	0	.000	42	.636	82	266	34	30	14	168	3.6
84-85	LAL	82	1617	181	.554	0	.000	68	.660	164	528	69	82	47	430	5.2
85-86	LAL	74	1573	160	.595	0	.000	88	.721	156	517	69	66	33	408	5.5
86-87	LAL	78	1514	163	.521	0	.000	120	.764	159	453	63	74	41	446	5.7
87-88	LAL	70	845	102	.548	0	.000	73	.785	103	268	54	39	13	277	4.0
88-89	CHA	75	2233	325	.518	0	.000	182	.734	269	703	159	100	57	832	11.1
89-90	CHA/PHO	74	1904	190	.509	0	.000	82	.646	156	525	135	100	37	462	6.2
90-91	PHO	62	900	83	.497	0	.000	60	.706	77	266	64	25	11	226	3.6
91-92	PHO	28	381	38	.463	0	.000	14	.778	23	106	37	12	14	90	3.2
92-93	PHO/SAC	72	822	67	.519	0	.000	43	.662	77	227	53	43	18	177	2.5
Totals		804	15469	1725	.535	0	.000	945	.691	1546	4738	883	736	424	4395	5.5

BLAIR RASMUSSEN

Team: Atlanta Hawks
Position: Center
Height: 7'0" **Weight:** 250
Birthdate: November 13, 1962

NBA Experience: 8 years
College: Oregon
Acquired: Traded from Nuggets for
draft rights to Anthony Avent, 7/91

Background: Rasmussen started all 114 games in which he played at Oregon, and he finished fourth on the school's all-time scoring list. His highest scoring year as a pro came in 1987-88, when he helped Denver to a Midwest Division title. Rasmussen led the Nuggets in rebounding and blocked shots in 1990-91, ranking in the NBA's top 20 in both categories. A trade brought him to Atlanta, where he started 61 games in 1991-92. His 1992-93 season was sliced to 22 games because of back injuries.

Strengths: Rasmussen has great range and a soft touch for a big man. He chases the ball off the board and he challenges shots on defense. His improvement in those areas is a testament to his work ethic. He is a good passer and is as unselfish as they come.

Weaknesses: The slow-footed Rasmussen is not a great athlete and now he has back problems. There are players much smaller in build that play more physically than Rasmussen. While he buries jumpers when open, Rasmussen cannot put the ball on the floor and get to the hoop. His field goal percentage took a nosedive last season.

Analysis: Rasmussen will never be considered one of the better pivots in the league, even if he overcomes his bad back. That's not to say he doesn't make some significant contributions. He can pull the opposition away from the hoop and can be a useful complementary player.

PLAYER SUMMARY	
Will	pull defenders outside
Can't	put it on the floor
Expect	limited playing time
Don't Expect	quickness
Fantasy Value	$1
Card Value	5-12¢

COLLEGE STATISTICS

		G	FGP	FTP	RPG	PPG
81-82	ORE	27	.475	.736	4.8	6.4
82-83	ORE	27	.541	.690	5.4	14.8
83-84	ORE	29	.520	.804	6.1	16.6
84-85	ORE	31	.512	.722	7.2	16.1
Totals		114	.517	.736	5.9	13.6

NBA REGULAR-SEASON STATISTICS

				FGs		3-PT FGs		FTs		Rebounds						
		G	MIN	FG	PCT	FG	PCT	FT	PCT	OFF	TOT	AST	STL	BLK	PTS	PPG
85-86	DEN	48	330	61	.407	0	.000	31	.795	37	97	16	3	10	153	3.2
86-87	DEN	74	1421	268	.470	0	.000	169	.732	183	465	60	24	58	705	9.5
87-88	DEN	79	1779	435	.492	0	.000	132	.776	130	437	78	22	81	1002	12.7
88-89	DEN	77	1308	257	.445	0	.000	69	.852	105	287	49	29	41	583	7.6
89-90	DEN	81	1995	445	.497	0	.000	111	.828	174	594	82	40	104	1001	12.4
90-91	DEN	70	2325	405	.458	2	.400	63	.677	170	678	70	52	132	875	12.5
91-92	ATL	81	1968	347	.478	5	.217	30	.750	94	393	107	35	48	729	9.0
92-93	ATL	22	283	30	.375	2	.333	9	.692	20	55	5	5	10	71	3.2
Totals		532	11409	2248	.472	9	.257	614	.767	913	3006	467	210	484	5119	9.6

J.R. REID

Team: San Antonio Spurs
Position: Forward
Height: 6'9" **Weight:** 260
Birthdate: March 31, 1968
NBA Experience: 4 years

College: North Carolina
Acquired: Traded from Hornets for Sidney Green and conditional draft picks, 12/92

Background: Coming out of high school in 1986, Reid was the No. 1-ranked player in America. A 1988 U.S. Olympian, he was a consensus All-American as a sophomore at North Carolina. He was forced to play out of position at center in all 82 games as a Charlotte rookie and was named second-team All-Rookie. Reid moved to forward halfway through the 1990-91 campaign and continued to average about 11 PPG in his second and third seasons. He was dealt to the Spurs 17 games into last season and averaged 9.9 PPG in San Antonio.

Strengths: Reid possesses a nice shooting touch from 12-15 feet and a nice offensive game when facing the bucket. He can use his size, strength, and speed to beat opposing forwards off the dribble and get to the hoop. He's a pretty good low-post defender who attacks the boards much better than he once did.

Weaknesses: Reid still struggles in the low post because of his limited offensive repertoire. He tends to rely too much on the jumper and not enough on aggressive moves. Many feel that he hasn't reached his potential because he hasn't put in the effort. His dribbling is below average and he rarely passes once he gets the ball.

Analysis: This one-time can't-miss superstar was a big disappointment in Charlotte. He played well with the Spurs, mostly in a reserve role, but still is not the player he was expected to be. Reid simply does not possess the complete game required to be a star. He's probably best suited as a sixth or seventh man who can help at both ends.

PLAYER SUMMARY	
Will	hit from 12-15 feet
Can't	fulfill expectations
Expect	solid defense
Don't Expect	stardom
Fantasy Value	$2-4
Card Value	8-15¢

COLLEGE STATISTICS

		G	FGP	FTP	RPG	PPG
86-87	NC	36	.584	.653	7.4	14.7
87-88	NC	33	.607	.680	8.9	18.0
88-89	NC	27	.614	.669	6.3	15.9
Totals		96	.601	.668	7.6	16.2

NBA REGULAR-SEASON STATISTICS

		G	MIN	FGs FG	FGs PCT	3-PT FGs FG	3-PT FGs PCT	FTs FT	FTs PCT	Rebounds OFF	Rebounds TOT	AST	STL	BLK	PTS	PPG
89-90	CHA	82	2757	358	.440	0	.000	192	.664	199	691	101	92	54	908	11.1
90-91	CHA	80	2467	360	.465	0	.000	182	.703	154	502	89	87	47	902	11.3
91-92	CHA	51	1257	213	.490	0	.000	134	.705	96	317	81	49	23	560	11.0
92-93	CHA/SA	83	1887	283	.476	0	.000	214	.764	120	456	80	47	31	780	9.4
Totals		296	8368	1214	.464	0	0	722	.709	569	1966	351	275	155	3150	10.6

JERRY REYNOLDS

Team: Orlando Magic
Position: Forward/Guard
Height: 6'8" **Weight:** 206
Birthdate: December 23, 1962

NBA Experience: 7 years
College: Louisiana St.
Acquired: Selected from SuperSonics in 1989 expansion draft

Background: Reynolds played four positions at LSU, where he was the ninth player in school history to total more than 1,000 points and 500 rebounds. He entered the draft after his junior season and was a reserve in Milwaukee and Seattle. Orlando plucked him in the 1989 expansion draft and he started 40 games in 1989-90. He has been used mostly off the bench since then. Reynolds has not played since March of the 1991-92 season because of a cervical strain.

Strengths: Reynolds thrives in the open court and his exciting finishes bring crowds to their feet. He can create shots in traffic and get to the line, where he is a reliable foul shooter. His anticipation allows him to come up with steals. "Ice" is cool in the clutch.

Weaknesses: Though he's not a good outside shooter, that has never stopped him from firing away. He connected on just 38 percent of his shots in 1991-92. Reynolds has never been an accurate 3-point shooter and he tends to force things with defenders all over him. He turns the ball over when pressured.

Analysis: Reynolds is a playground-type player who either lights it up with defenders in his face or looks bad trying. His inconsistency is directly related to his shot selection. Reynolds brings a level of excitement to the court and coaches love his effort. His neck injury was more serious than expected but he is expected to play in 1993-94.

PLAYER SUMMARY	
Will	score in spurts
Can't	stick to good shots
Expect	flashy finishes
Don't Expect	high FG pct.
Fantasy Value	$0
Card Value	5-10¢

COLLEGE STATISTICS

		G	FGP	FTP	RPG	PPG
82-83	LSU	32	.534	.620	6.2	10.6
83-84	LSU	29	.528	.538	8.2	14.1
84-85	LSU	29	.502	.598	6.1	11.0
Totals		90	.521	.582	6.8	11.9

NBA REGULAR-SEASON STATISTICS

				FGs		3-PT FGs		FTs		Rebounds						
		G	MIN	FG	PCT	FG	PCT	FT	PCT	OFF	TOT	AST	STL	BLK	PTS	PPG
85-86	MIL	55	508	72	.444	1	.500	58	.558	37	80	86	43	19	203	3.7
86-87	MIL	58	963	140	.393	6	.333	118	.641	72	173	106	50	30	404	7.0
87-88	MIL	62	1161	188	.449	3	.429	119	.773	70	160	104	74	32	498	8.0
88-89	SEA	56	737	149	.417	3	.200	127	.760	49	100	62	53	26	428	7.6
89-90	ORL	67	1817	309	.417	1	.071	239	.742	91	323	180	93	64	858	12.8
90-91	ORL	80	1843	344	.434	10	.294	336	.802	88	299	203	95	56	1034	12.9
91-92	ORL	46	1159	197	.380	3	.125	158	.836	47	149	151	63	17	555	12.1
Totals		424	8188	1399	.418	27	.237	1155	.750	454	1284	892	471	244	3980	9.4

GLEN RICE

Team: Miami Heat
Position: Forward/Guard
Height: 6'7" **Weight:** 220
Birthdate: May 28, 1967

NBA Experience: 4 years
College: Michigan
Acquired: 1st-round pick in 1989 draft
(4th overall)

Background: Rice led Michigan to a national title in 1989 while averaging nearly 31 PPG in NCAA tourney play. He finished his college career as the leading scorer in Big Ten history. After being chosen second-team All-Rookie in 1989-90, he improved his scoring, rebounding, field goal percentage, and 3-point percentage in each of the next two years. He was tenth in the league in scoring (22.3 PPG) in 1991-92 and has made more than 300 3-pointers over the last two seasons.

Strengths: Rice has become one of the top shooters and scorers in the game. He can play small forward or big guard, although he is most comfortable from behind the 3-point arc. Rice has also learned to take the ball to the bucket, and he now complements his perimeter prowess with effective drives. He has made a commitment to getting to the free throw line and is accurate when he gets there. Rice has become a leader.

Weaknesses: Rice dribbles more like a forward than a guard. His assist-to-turnover ratio is far closer to even than it should be, and he is better off giving it up under pressure. Quick players cause him problems on defense. He shot 44 percent last season, the worst mark since his rookie year.

Analysis: After a miserable rookie season that saw him out of shape and overweight, Rice appears to be a step away from All-Star caliber. Playing in an All-Star Game is a lifelong dream of his, and it could be fulfilled in the near future. His shooting and scoring speak for themselves; his work ethic and leadership have improved.

PLAYER SUMMARY	
Will	pour in treys
Can't	play the point
Expect	about 20 PPG
Don't Expect	fancy dribbling
Fantasy Value	$16-19
Card Value	10-15¢

COLLEGE STATISTICS

		G	FGP	FTP	RPG	PPG
85-86	MICH	32	.550	.600	3.0	7.0
86-87	MICH	32	.562	.787	9.2	16.9
87-88	MICH	33	.571	.806	7.2	22.1
88-89	MICH	37	.577	.832	6.3	25.6
Totals		134	.569	.797	6.4	18.2

NBA REGULAR-SEASON STATISTICS

		G	MIN	FGs FG	FGs PCT	3-PT FGs FG	3-PT FGs PCT	FTs FT	FTs PCT	Rebounds OFF	Rebounds TOT	AST	STL	BLK	PTS	PPG
89-90	MIA	77	2311	470	.439	17	.246	91	.734	100	352	138	67	27	1048	13.6
90-91	MIA	77	2646	550	.461	71	.386	171	.818	85	381	189	101	26	1342	17.4
91-92	MIA	79	3007	672	.469	155	.391	266	.836	84	394	184	90	35	1765	22.3
92-93	MIA	82	3082	582	.440	148	.383	242	.820	92	424	180	92	25	1554	19.0
Totals		315	11046	2274	.453	391	.378	770	.814	361	1551	691	350	113	5709	18.1

POOH RICHARDSON

Team: Indiana Pacers
Position: Guard
Height: 6'1" **Weight:** 180
Birthdate: May 14, 1966
NBA Experience: 4 years

College: UCLA
Acquired: Traded from Timberwolves with Sam Mitchell for Chuck Person and Micheal Williams, 9/92

Background: Richardson was a four-year starter and three-time All-Pac-10 star at UCLA, where he set a conference record for assists. His pro career with Minnesota was marred by inconsistent playing time and demands to be traded, but he started every game in his last two years with the Timberwolves and was seventh in the league with 8.4 APG during the 1991-92 season. Richardson got the trade he wanted when he and Sam Mitchell went to the Pacers before last season for Chuck Person and Micheal Williams. Richardson averaged 7.7 APG in his first year in Indiana.

Strengths: Richardson is a pure point guard who involves his teammates and runs the offense. He penetrates, handles the ball, and hits open men with crisp passes. His assist-to-turnover ratio is solid. Richardson is splendid in transition, is a good shooter with range, and can score points in bunches.

Weaknesses: Richardson was a chronic complainer in Minnesota and pretty much had to be dealt. He did not show great leadership with the Pacers either, and he lost minutes to Vern Fleming when his injured calf bothered him in the 1993 playoffs. Richardson made just three of 29 3-point tries last year.

Analysis: Talent-wise, Richardson has to be considered one of the NBA's better point guards. On the court, with the exception perhaps of his late-season play two years ago, he has not performed at a consistently high level. The Indiana brass hopes his second season with the Pacers brings him to the front of the point-guard class.

PLAYER SUMMARY	
Will	distribute the ball
Can't	shoot 50 percent
Expect	8 APG
Don't Expect	great leadership
Fantasy Value	$9-11
Card Value	10-20¢

COLLEGE STATISTICS

		G	FGP	FTP	APG	PPG
85-86	UCLA	29	.492	.689	6.2	10.6
86-87	UCLA	32	.527	.582	6.5	10.5
87-88	UCLA	30	.470	.667	7.0	11.6
88-89	UCLA	31	.555	.562	7.6	15.2
Totals		122	.513	.624	6.8	12.0

NBA REGULAR-SEASON STATISTICS

				FGs		3-PT FGs		FTs		Rebounds						
		G	MIN	FG	PCT	FG	PCT	FT	PCT	OFF	TOT	AST	STL	BLK	PTS	PPG
89-90	MIN	82	2581	426	.461	23	.277	63	.589	55	217	554	133	25	938	11.4
90-91	MIN	82	3154	635	.470	42	.328	89	.539	82	286	734	131	13	1401	17.1
91-92	MIN	82	2922	587	.466	53	.342	123	.691	91	301	685	119	25	1350	16.5
92-93	IND	74	2396	337	.479	3	.103	92	.742	63	267	573	94	12	769	10.4
Totals		320	11053	1985	.468	121	.306	367	.639	291	1071	2546	477	75	4458	13.9

MITCH RICHMOND

Team: Sacramento Kings
Position: Guard
Height: 6'5" **Weight:** 215
Birthdate: June 30, 1965
NBA Experience: 5 years

College: Moberly Area; Kansas St.
Acquired: Traded from Warriors with Les Jepsen and a 1995 2nd-round pick for draft rights to Billy Owens, 11/91

Background: Richmond was a junior college All-American before he spent two years at Kansas State, where he set a single-season record for points as a senior. He was a near-unanimous choice for Rookie of the Year in 1989, when he became the third Golden State rookie to average more than 20 points. He improved his scoring over the next two years, then was traded to Sacramento on the eve of the 1991-92 season opener. Richmond finished ninth in the league in scoring in his first year as a King and made his first All-Star Game last season. However, he missed the game and the rest of the season when he broke his right thumb in February.

Strengths: Look up "pure scorer" in the dictionary and it should mention Richmond. He nails jumpers with men all over him, hits 3-pointers, and drives through traffic without fear. When he sets his muscular frame in the post, he is almost impossible for smaller defenders to stop. He runs the floor and goes to the glass. He is a good passer who involves his teammates.

Weaknesses: Richmond commits a fair amount of turnovers and does not possess blinding speed. There is nothing spectacular about his defense.

Analysis: Richmond, Michael Jordan, and David Robinson are the only active players in the league who have averaged over 22 PPG in each of their first four years. Richmond's fifth year could have been his best thanks to a much-awaited All-Star invitation, but the broken thumb that required surgery spoiled it.

PLAYER SUMMARY	
Will	score 20 PPG
Can't	be stopped by one man
Expect	an All-Star trip
Don't Expect	blinding speed
Fantasy Value	$35-40
Card Value	10-20¢

COLLEGE STATISTICS

		G	FGP	FTP	RPG	PPG
84-85	MA	40	.480	.647	4.6	10.4
85-86	MA	38	.478	.689	6.6	16.0
86-87	KSU	30	.447	.761	5.7	18.6
87-88	KSU	34	.514	.775	6.3	22.6
Totals		142	.481	.732	5.8	16.5

NBA REGULAR-SEASON STATISTICS

				FGs		3-PT FGs		FTs		Rebounds						
		G	MIN	FG	PCT	FG	PCT	FT	PCT	OFF	TOT	AST	STL	BLK	PTS	PPG
88-89	GS	79	2717	649	.468	33	.367	410	.810	158	468	334	82	13	1741	22.0
89-90	GS	78	2799	640	.497	34	.358	406	.866	98	360	223	98	24	1720	22.1
90-91	GS	77	3027	703	.494	40	.348	394	.847	147	452	238	126	34	1840	23.9
91-92	SAC	80	3095	685	.468	103	.384	330	.813	62	319	411	92	34	1803	22.5
92-93	SAC	45	1728	371	.474	48	.369	197	.845	18	154	221	53	9	987	21.9
Totals		359	13366	3048	.480	258	.370	1737	.835	483	1753	1427	451	114	8091	22.5

DOC RIVERS

Team: New York Knicks
Position: Guard
Height: 6'4" **Weight:** 185
Birthdate: October 13, 1961
NBA Experience: 10 years

College: Marquette
Acquired: Traded from Clippers in three-team deal, 9/92 (see page 543 for details)

Background: A Marquette product, Rivers spent eight years with Atlanta before being traded to the Clippers on draft day, 1991. He was an All-Star in 1988-89, though a herniated disc caused him to miss 34 games in 1989-90. It was the first time in his career that he did not lead the Hawks in assists or steals. He struggled through his worst shooting season two years ago and was then dealt to the Knicks before last season. Rivers averaged 5.3 APG and 7.8 PPG while helping New York to the best record in the Eastern Conference.

Strengths: Rivers does nothing flashy; he just gets the job done. He's a world-class citizen who plays defense, delivers the ball, scores with drives and jumpers, and provides great leadership. Rivers knocks down his free throws and can hit from 3-point range.

Weaknesses: Rivers is not a pure shooter and his percentage has dropped. He does not score like he once did and injuries have limited him.

Analysis: Rivers is the guy you want on your side in a tough battle. Among other things last year, he had a broken nose, sprained wrist, sore back, cut chin requiring stitches, strained knee, and busted teeth. He still managed to play in 77 games and was a huge reason for the Knicks' success.

PLAYER SUMMARY

Will ....distribute
Can't ....stay healthy
Expect ....veteran leadership
Don't Expect ....backing down
Fantasy Value..............................$2-4
Card Value ....5-10¢

COLLEGE STATISTICS

		G	FGP	FTP	APG	PPG
80-81	MARQ	31	.553	.588	3.6	14.0
81-82	MARQ	29	.453	.648	5.9	14.3
82-83	MARQ	29	.437	.611	4.3	13.2
Totals		89	.478	.615	4.6	13.9

NBA REGULAR-SEASON STATISTICS

		G	MIN	FGs FG	FGs PCT	3-PT FGs FG	3-PT FGs PCT	FTs FT	FTs PCT	Rebounds OFF	Rebounds TOT	AST	STL	BLK	PTS	PPG
83-84	ATL	81	1938	250	.462	2	.167	255	.785	72	220	314	127	30	757	9.3
84-85	ATL	69	2126	334	.476	15	.417	291	.770	66	214	410	163	53	974	14.1
85-86	ATL	53	1571	220	.474	0	.000	172	.608	49	162	443	120	13	612	11.5
86-87	ATL	82	2590	342	.451	4	.190	365	.828	83	299	823	171	30	1053	12.8
87-88	ATL	80	2502	403	.453	9	.273	319	.758	83	366	747	140	41	1134	14.2
88-89	ATL	76	2462	371	.455	43	.347	247	.861	89	286	525	181	40	1032	13.6
89-90	ATL	48	1526	218	.454	24	.364	138	.812	47	200	264	116	22	598	12.5
90-91	ATL	79	2586	444	.435	88	.336	221	.844	47	253	340	148	47	1197	15.2
91-92	LAC	59	1657	226	.424	26	.283	163	.832	23	147	233	111	19	641	10.9
92-93	NY	77	1886	216	.437	39	.317	133	.821	26	192	405	123	9	604	7.8
Totals		704	20844	3024	.452	250	.318	2304	.788	585	2339	4504	1400	304	8602	12.2

STANLEY ROBERTS

Team: Los Angeles Clippers
Position: Center
Height: 7'0" **Weight:** 305
Birthdate: February 7, 1970
NBA Experience: 2 years

College: Louisiana St.
Acquired: Traded from Magic in three-team deal, 9/92 (see page 543 for details)

Background: After sitting out his freshman season at LSU because of academic reasons, Roberts teamed with Shaquille O'Neal for the 1989-90 season. Roberts had 14 double-doubles in his 32-game college career, but he also fouled out eight times. He was declared academically ineligible in August 1990 and signed with a professional team in Spain. Though his rookie year with Orlando began with jokes about his weight, he ended up averaging 10.4 PPG and making 34 starts. He signed with the Clippers before the 1992-93 campaign, was their starting center, and averaged 11.3 PPG and 6.2 RPG.

Strengths: Roberts is built like your average five-story building, only a lot softer. He can be an offensive force around the basket. He has a decent turnaround jumper, is virtually impossible to budge once he gets position on the interior, and owns a very soft inside shooting touch despite his bulk. Roberts finished 13th in the league in blocked shots last year and was effective on the boards.

Weaknesses: Weight and foul trouble have long been the biggest problems for Roberts. Fat jokes follow him. Roberts led the league in personal fouls (332) and disqualifications (15) last season. He does not run the floor well, he's a terrible free throw shooter, and his passing couldn't be worse.

Analysis: At his best, Roberts can be dominant offensively. Working against him, however, are his weight, his inconsistency, and his time spent on the bench because of foul trouble. He reported for training camp at 320 pounds last year, was down to 293 at one point, and finished the season at about 305. The Clippers project big things for Roberts if he can weigh in closer to 295.

PLAYER SUMMARY	
Will	score inside
Can't	pass up a meal
Expect	lots of whistles
Don't Expect	consistency
Fantasy Value	$5-7
Card Value	8-12¢

COLLEGE STATISTICS

		G	FGP	FTP	RPG	PPG
89-90	LSU	32	.576	.460	9.8	14.1
Totals		32	.576	.460	9.8	14.1

NBA REGULAR-SEASON STATISTICS

			FGs		3-PT FGs		FTs		Rebounds						
	G	MIN	FG	PCT	FG	PCT	FT	PCT	OFF	TOT	AST	STL	BLK	PTS	PPG
91-92 ORL	55	1118	236	.529	0	.000	101	.515	113	336	39	22	83	573	10.4
92-93 LAC	77	1816	375	.527	0	.000	120	.488	181	478	59	34	141	870	11.3
Totals	132	2934	611	.528	0	.000	221	.500	294	814	98	56	224	1443	10.9

ALVIN ROBERTSON

Team: Detroit Pistons
Position: Guard
Height: 6'4" **Weight:** 208
Birthdate: July 22, 1962

NBA Experience: 9 years
College: Crowder; Arkansas
Acquired: Traded from Bucks for Orlando Woolridge, 2/93

Background: Following a memorable career at Arkansas, Robertson was a member of the 1984 U.S. Olympic team. A four-time NBA All-Star, Robertson was named NBA Defensive Player of the Year in 1986. He spent five seasons with San Antonio before being traded to the Bucks in 1989. He led all guards in offensive rebounds in 1989-90 and has led the league in steals three times. Robertson was acquired by Detroit last year in a midseason trade for Orlando Woolridge and started 22 of his 30 games with the Pistons.

Strengths: Robertson creates offense with his tough defense. His on-the-ball defense and quick hands have earned him a reputation as a professional thief. Strong and competitive, he slashes his way inside for a lot of his points and rebounds. He has 3-point range.

Weaknesses: Robertson is an inconsistent perimeter jump-shooter. Opposing guards would rather leave him open than allow him to drive. He is not as quick as he used to be.

Analysis: A lot of the things Robertson does go unnoticed by the average fan. He is capable of disrupting opposing offenses by shutting down guards of all speeds and sizes. He gave the Pistons leadership both on and off the court and satisfied their need for a quality third guard.

PLAYER SUMMARY	
Will	play tough defense
Can't	rely on jumper
Expect	relentless effort
Don't Expect	young legs
Fantasy Value	$4-6
Card Value	5-10¢

COLLEGE STATISTICS

		G	FGP	FTP	RPG	PPG
80-81	CJC	34	.572	.652	8.4	18.0
81-82	ARK	28	.528	.603	2.2	7.3
82-83	ARK	28	.548	.661	4.9	14.2
83-84	ARK	32	.499	.670	5.5	15.5
Totals		122	.540	.655	5.4	14.0

NBA REGULAR-SEASON STATISTICS

		G	MIN	FGs FG	FGs PCT	3-PT FGs FG	3-PT FGs PCT	FTs FT	FTs PCT	Rebounds OFF	Rebounds TOT	AST	STL	BLK	PTS	PPG
84-85	SA	79	1685	299	.498	4	.364	124	.734	116	265	275	127	24	726	9.2
85-86	SA	82	2878	562	.514	8	.276	260	.795	184	516	448	301	40	1392	17.0
86-87	SA	81	2697	589	.466	13	.271	244	.753	186	424	421	260	35	1435	17.7
87-88	SA	82	2978	655	.465	27	.284	273	.748	165	498	557	243	69	1610	19.6
88-89	SA	65	2287	465	.483	9	.200	183	.723	157	384	393	197	36	1122	17.3
89-90	MIL	81	2599	476	.503	4	.154	197	.741	230	559	445	207	17	1153	14.2
90-91	MIL	81	2598	438	.485	23	.365	199	.757	191	459	444	246	16	1098	13.6
91-92	MIL	82	2463	396	.458	67	.319	151	.763	175	350	360	210	32	1010	12.3
92-93	MIL/DET	69	2006	247	.458	40	.328	84	.656	107	269	263	155	18	618	9.0
Totals		702	22191	4127	.478	195	.300	1715	.748	1511	3724	3606	1946	287	10164	14.5

CLIFF ROBINSON

Team: Portland Trail Blazers
Position: Forward
Height: 6'10" **Weight:** 225
Birthdate: December 16, 1966

NBA Experience: 4 years
College: Connecticut
Acquired: 2nd-round pick in 1989
draft (36th overall)

Background: Robinson led Connecticut in scoring for three consecutive seasons and was third in the Big East as a senior. Bypassed until the second round of the 1989 draft, he played all 82 games of his rookie year and provided solid minutes in the 1990 playoffs. He has been Portland's top scorer off the bench in each of the last three seasons and has not missed a game in his pro career. Last season, he easily captured the league's Sixth Man Award after averaging a career-high 19.1 PPG.

Strengths: Explosive athletic ability, versatility, and the ability to light up the scoreboard make Robinson an invaluable player. He can play just about any position but the point, although he is at his best when facing the basket and has improved his perimeter shooting. He is an elusive driver who can put the ball on the floor and get to the hoop for dazzling finishes. Robinson is a tremendous open-court player and intimidating defender who blocked nearly two shots per game last year.

Weaknesses: Robinson is better at recording turnovers than assists and is still prone to spells of cold shooting. He was ice cold in the 1993 playoffs. He has had some off-court incidents, including speeding tickets over the last two seasons for driving 110 and 89 mph.

Analysis: Robinson was by far the best reserve in the NBA last year and will likely become a starter in the future. He also received support for the Most Improved Player honor, as he raised his scoring average by nearly seven PPG and became a highly feared player on both ends of the court.

PLAYER SUMMARY	
Will	provide a spark
Can't	be kept on bench
Expect	fantastic finishes
Don't Expect	poor defense
Fantasy Value	$25-30
Card Value	8-15¢

COLLEGE STATISTICS

		G	FGP	FTP	RPG	PPG
85-86	CONN	28	.366	.610	3.1	5.6
86-87	CONN	16	.420	.570	7.4	18.1
87-88	CONN	34	.479	.655	6.9	17.6
88-89	CONN	31	.470	.684	7.4	20.0
Totals		109	.452	.644	6.1	15.3

NBA REGULAR-SEASON STATISTICS

				FGs		3-PT FGs		FTs		Rebounds						
		G	MIN	FG	PCT	FG	PCT	FT	PCT	OFF	TOT	AST	STL	BLK	PTS	PPG
89-90	POR	82	1565	298	.397	12	.273	138	.550	110	308	72	53	53	746	9.1
90-91	POR	82	1940	373	.463	6	.316	205	.653	123	349	151	78	76	957	11.7
91-92	POR	82	2124	398	.466	1	.091	219	.664	140	416	137	85	107	1016	12.4
92-93	POR	82	2575	632	.473	19	.247	287	.690	165	542	182	98	163	1570	19.1
Totals		328	8204	1701	.454	38	.252	849	.648	538	1615	542	314	399	4289	13.1

DAVID ROBINSON

Team: San Antonio Spurs
Position: Center
Height: 7'1" **Weight:** 235
Birthdate: August 6, 1965

NBA Experience: 4 years
College: Navy
Acquired: 1st-round pick in 1987 draft (1st overall)

Background: As a senior at Navy, Robinson led the nation in blocked shots and was college basketball's consensus Player of the Year. He set NCAA records for blocks in a game and a season. After a two-year stint in the Navy, he exploded onto the pro scene in 1989-90, winning Rookie of the Year honors by a unanimous vote. He has continued his All-Star play over the last three seasons. He led the league with 4.49 BPG in 1991-92 and was named Defensive Player of the Year. He is consistently in the top ten in blocks, scoring, and rebounding and played on the 1992 U.S. Olympic team.

Strengths: Robinson is simply dominant in most aspects of the game. His quickness allows him to explode to the hoop with unstoppable low-post spin moves. He can stick jumpers or swing the ball back outside. He clears the boards, runs the break as well as any center, and dominates on defense. He was the only big man among the top five in steals two years ago. Last year, he was second to Karl Malone in trips to the free throw line.

Weaknesses: Unlike, say, Patrick Ewing, Robinson is not a vocal leader who demands greatness from his teammates. He'd rather let his play do the talking. His field goal shooting dropped to mere-mortal level last year.

Analysis: Mr. Robinson is gifted with a physique few big men can dream of, and he has used it to become a force in the NBA. He clearly ranks among the elite players in the game—one of the top half-dozen—and it looks like he'll stay at that level for years to come.

PLAYER SUMMARY	
Will	dominate inside
Can't	be stopped near hoop
Expect	an All-Star regular
Don't Expect	selfishness
Fantasy Value	$80-85
Card Value	50¢-$1.00

COLLEGE STATISTICS

		G	FGP	FTP	RPG	PPG
83-84	NAVY	28	.623	.575	4.0	7.6
84-85	NAVY	32	.644	.626	11.6	23.6
85-86	NAVY	35	.607	.628	13.0	22.7
86-87	NAVY	32	.591	.637	11.8	28.2
Totals		127	.613	.627	10.3	21.0

NBA REGULAR-SEASON STATISTICS

				FGs		3-PT FGs		FTs		Rebounds						
		G	MIN	FG	PCT	FG	PCT	FT	PCT	OFF	TOT	AST	STL	BLK	PTS	PPG
89-90	SA	82	3002	690	.531	0	.000	613	.732	303	983	164	138	319	1993	24.3
90-91	SA	82	3095	754	.552	1	.143	592	.762	335	1063	208	127	320	2101	25.6
91-92	SA	68	2564	592	.551	1	.125	393	.701	261	829	181	158	305	1578	23.2
92-93	SA	82	3211	676	.501	3	.176	561	.732	229	956	301	127	264	1916	23.4
Totals		314	11872	2712	.533	5	.147	2159	.734	1128	3831	854	550	1208	7588	24.2

RUMEAL ROBINSON

Team: New Jersey Nets
Position: Guard
Height: 6'2" **Weight:** 195
Birthdate: November 13, 1966
NBA Experience: 3 years

College: Michigan
Acquired: Traded from Hawks for Mookie Blaylock and Roy Hinson, 11/92

Background: The hero of Michigan's 1989 NCAA championship as a junior, Robinson made a forgettable NBA debut in Atlanta. He was replaced as a starter during a nine-game November losing streak and missed 22 games due to coach's decision. He was reinstated as the starter for most of the 1991-92 campaign and led the team in assists. Robinson was traded to New Jersey before the 1992-93 season and became the starting point guard after Kenny Anderson was injured in February.

Strengths: Robinson has an NBA body and is willing to use it. He's strong, physical, and not afraid to challenge larger players on his way to the bucket for lay-ins. His confidence overflows and he has an offensive mind-set. He's a fierce competitor who comes to play every night. Robinson hustles, is dangerous in the open court, and has improved his defense and playmaking.

Weaknesses: Becoming a more traditional-style point guard is something Robinson has struggled with during his early pro days. He still looks to finish his own plays before looking to set up teammates, although he has made strides. He is not a great outside shooter, which leaves his defenders free to double-team. Seton Hall might argue otherwise, but he's horrible from the free throw line.

Analysis: Robinson has come a long way since his rookie season and was invaluable to the Nets after Anderson was lost for the season. In fact, Robinson was named NBA Player of the Week after his first few games as a New Jersey starter. Look for him to be a solid reserve who will continue to improve.

PLAYER SUMMARY	
Will	look to score
Can't	make his FTs
Expect	competitiveness
Don't Expect	10 APG
Fantasy Value	$3-5
Card Value	8-12¢

COLLEGE STATISTICS

		G	FGP	FTP	APG	PPG
87-88	MICH	33	.553	.667	4.8	9.7
88-89	MICH	37	.557	.656	6.3	14.9
89-90	MICH	30	.490	.676	6.1	19.2
Totals		100	.528	.666	5.8	14.5

NBA REGULAR-SEASON STATISTICS

			FGs		3-PT FGs		FTs		Rebounds						
	G	MIN	FG	PCT	FG	PCT	FT	PCT	OFF	TOT	AST	STL	BLK	PTS	PPG
90-91 ATL	47	674	108	.446	2	.182	47	.587	20	71	132	32	8	265	5.6
91-92 ATL	81	2220	423	.456	34	.327	175	.636	64	219	446	105	24	1055	13.0
92-93 NJ	80	1585	270	.423	20	.357	112	.574	49	159	323	96	12	672	8.4
Totals	208	4479	801	.443	56	.327	334	.607	133	449	901	233	44	1992	9.6

DENNIS RODMAN

Team: Detroit Pistons
Position: Forward
Height: 6'8" **Weight:** 210
Birthdate: May 13, 1961
NBA Experience: 7 years

College: Cooke County; S.E. Oklahoma St.
Acquired: 2nd-round pick in 1986 draft (27th overall)

Background: Standing only 5'11" as a high school senior, Rodman went to work for a few years as an airport laborer. An incredible nine-inch growth spurt finally convinced Rodman to give basketball a try. He was a three-time NAIA All-American at S.E. Oklahoma State and a second-round pick by Detroit. Rodman has played in two NBA All-Star Games and was the Defensive Player of the Year in 1989-90 and 1990-91. His 18.7 RPG in 1991-92 was the highest average since Wilt Chamberlain's 19.2 in 1971-72. He easily led the league at 18.3 RPG last season despite missing 20 games.

Strengths: No forward in recent history has been as dominant defensively and on the boards as Rodman. He's so versatile, he can cover centers or point guards. "Worm" smothers opponents with quickness, speed, and strength.

Weaknesses: Rodman is not in the NBA for his scoring. Although he can stick an occasional 3-pointer, his sub-60-percent free throw shooting illustrates his lack of touch. He has been a public-relations nightmare off the court.

Analysis: Rodman might be the hardest-working player in the NBA, yet he skipped team practices and functions last season and talked of retirement and wanting a trade. He fell out of favor with management, was suspended by the team early on, and was involved in a bizarre weapons incident. He performs on game nights, however, and Detroit was 4-16 without him last year.

PLAYER SUMMARY

Will	own the boards
Can't	win citizenship awards
Expect	defense, 18 RPG
Don't Expect	predictability
Fantasy Value	$10-13
Card Value	10-20¢

COLLEGE STATISTICS

		G	FGP	FTP	RPG	PPG
82-83	CCJ	16	.616	.582	13.3	17.6
83-84	SOS	30	.618	.655	13.1	26.0
84-85	SOS	32	.648	.648	15.9	26.8
85-86	SOS	34	.645	.655	17.8	24.4
Totals		112	.635	.620	15.3	24.5

NBA REGULAR-SEASON STATISTICS

		G	MIN	FGs FG	FGs PCT	3-PT FGs FG	3-PT FGs PCT	FTs FT	FTs PCT	Rebounds OFF	Rebounds TOT	AST	STL	BLK	PTS	PPG
86-87	DET	77	1155	213	.545	0	.000	74	.587	163	332	56	38	48	500	6.5
87-88	DET	82	2147	398	.561	5	.294	152	.535	318	715	110	75	45	953	11.6
88-89	DET	82	2208	316	.595	6	.231	97	.626	327	772	99	55	76	735	9.0
89-90	DET	82	2377	288	.581	1	.111	142	.654	336	792	72	52	60	719	8.8
90-91	DET	82	2747	276	.493	6	.200	111	.631	361	1026	85	65	55	669	8.2
91-92	DET	82	3301	342	.539	32	.317	84	.600	523	1530	191	68	70	800	9.8
92-93	DET	62	2410	183	.427	15	.205	87	.534	367	1132	102	48	45	468	7.5
Totals		549	16345	2016	.537	65	.253	747	.592	2395	6299	715	401	399	4844	8.8

SEAN ROOKS

Team: Dallas Mavericks
Position: Center/Forward
Height: 6'10" **Weight:** 260
Birthdate: September 9, 1969

NBA Experience: 1 year
College: Arizona
Acquired: 2nd-round pick in 1992
draft (30th overall)

Background: After joining Brian Williams and Ed Stokes on the "Tucson Skyline," Rooks led Arizona in scoring and was second in rebounding as a senior. He was a first-team All-Pac-10 selection and finished his career fifth on the Wildcats' career scoring list. A second-round choice of Dallas, Rooks played well in a summer league and became an instant rookie starter at center. He finished third on the Mavericks in scoring and second in rebounding during his first campaign.

Strengths: Rooks has good size and some skills to match. He has a wide body and has demonstrated a pretty good low-post repertoire, yet he also has the touch to slide out of the lane and knock down mid-range jumpers. Rooks owns good hands and a nice feel for the game. He'll block shots. Coaches have been impressed with his willingness to work and desire to prove himself.

Weaknesses: Originally projected as a first-rounder, Rooks slipped to the second round largely because of his inconsistency from one night to the next. He has a tendency to disappear when his head's not in the game. Although he helped the Mavericks on the boards, Rooks should be a more dominant rebounder and a better defender considering his size. He's a very poor free throw shooter and not much of a passer.

Analysis: "Wookie," nicknamed after the *Star Wars* character, did pretty well in his first year for a second-round pick with a dismal team. He's not the kind of player who can revive the floundering Mavericks, but he held his own against more talented players and demonstrated a promising offensive game. He seems to be taking advantage of a big opportunity.

PLAYER SUMMARY	
Will	score inside
Can't	revive Mavericks
Expect	further improvement
Don't Expect	assists
Fantasy Value	$6-8
Card Value	10-20¢

COLLEGE STATISTICS

		G	FGP	FTP	RPG	PPG
88-89	ARIZ	32	.598	.615	2.8	5.6
89-90	ARIZ	31	.532	.708	4.9	12.7
90-91	ARIZ	35	.562	.658	5.7	11.9
91-92	ARIZ	31	.560	.651	6.9	16.3
Totals		129	.558	.664	5.0	11.6

NBA REGULAR-SEASON STATISTICS

		G	MIN	FGs FG	FGs PCT	3-PT FGs FG	3-PT FGs PCT	FTs FT	FTs PCT	Rebounds OFF	Rebounds TOT	AST	STL	BLK	PTS	PPG
92-93	DAL	72	2087	368	.493	0	.000	234	.602	196	536	95	38	81	970	13.5
Totals		72	2087	368	.493	0	.000	234	.602	196	536	95	38	81	970	13.5

DONALD ROYAL

Team: Orlando Magic
Position: Forward
Height: 6'8" **Weight:** 210
Birthdate: May 2, 1966

NBA Experience: 3 years
College: Notre Dame
Acquired: Signed as a free agent, 8/92

Background: Royal averaged 15.8 PPG and 7.0 RPG during his senior year at Notre Dame, after which he was a third-round draft choice of Cleveland in 1987. He spent his first two pro seasons in the CBA, then played his first NBA ball with Minnesota in 1989-90. Royal left the Timberwolves for Israel the next year and averaged 20 PPG and eight RPG for Macabbi Tel Aviv. He played with San Antonio for a year and in Orlando last season. He enjoyed his best statistical year in the NBA in 1992-93, averaging 9.2 PPG.

Strengths: Royal makes a living with the drive. He is a slashing penetrator who knows no fear when it comes to taking the ball to the hole. He can finish his own plays and he makes numerous trips to the free throw line, where he improved to better than 80 percent last season. Royal is a good defensive player who runs the floor and plays with enthusiasm.

Weaknesses: Royal's drives would be even more effective if he could make defenders respect his jump shot. It's flat and Royal does not shoot it with much range. He has attempted only four 3-pointers in his NBA career. Other than penetrating, his offensive game has a number of holes. He is no better than average as a ball-handler and passer.

Analysis: Most players hate defending a driver like Royal because they know he'll make them work. He saw a lot of playing time down the stretch in close games because of his ability to get to the bucket or the line. That, along with his defense, has helped him improve his NBA stock.

PLAYER SUMMARY

Will ....drive the lane
Can't ....shoot pretty jumpers
Expect..................aggressive defense
Don't Expect ....playmaking
Fantasy Value....................................$1
Card Value ....5-10¢

COLLEGE STATISTICS

		G	FGP	FTP	RPG	PPG
83-84	ND	31	.594	.622	2.3	3.4
84-85	ND	30	.497	.782	5.5	9.1
85-86	ND	28	.583	.766	4.9	10.6
86-87	ND	28	.576	.820	7.0	15.8
Totals		117	.560	.780	4.9	9.5

NBA REGULAR-SEASON STATISTICS

			FGs		3-PT FGs		FTs		Rebounds						
	G	MIN	FG	PCT	FG	PCT	FT	PCT	OFF	TOT	AST	STL	BLK	PTS	PPG
89-90 MIN	66	746	117	.459	0	.000	153	.777	69	137	43	32	8	387	5.9
91-92 SA	60	718	80	.449	0	.000	92	.692	65	124	34	25	7	252	4.2
92-93 ORL	77	1636	194	.496	0	.000	318	.815	116	295	80	36	25	706	9.2
Totals	203	3100	391	.475	0	.000	563	.782	250	556	157	93	40	1345	6.6

DELANEY RUDD

Team: Portland Trail Blazers
Position: Guard
Height: 6'2" **Weight:** 195
Birthdate: November 8, 1962

NBA Experience: 4 years
College: Wake Forest
Acquired: Signed as a free agent, 1/93

Background: Rudd played with fellow NBA players Muggsy Bogues and Danny Young at Wake Forest, where he finished as the school's 12th-leading career scorer. After a brief stint in the CBA and two seasons in Greece, he served primarily as a back-up to John Stockton for three seasons with Utah. He fell to third on the depth chart and averaged just 3.0 PPG during the 1991-92 campaign, after which the Jazz let him go. Rudd was signed by Portland and played just 95 minutes last season. He spent much of the year on the injured list.

Strengths: Rudd, who played shooting guard in college but mostly the point as a pro, has a scorer's mentality. He can hit from 3-point range, is not shy with the jump shot, and can pass off his penetration moves. He plays defense and uses his strength well on both ends.

Weaknesses: While Rudd loves to launch his jumper, he has shot about 41 percent for his career. In his few minutes last year, he made one of 11 from 3-point range. His lack of quickness makes his point-guard skills pale in comparison to those of players like Stockton and Rod Strickland. He does little to make those around him look better.

Analysis: Rudd won't get much of a chance unless he improves his shooting. He does not help a team enough to warrant quality minutes unless his shot's on the mark. Rudd was the player who went to the injured list each time Clyde Drexler came off it last season. He would fit in best on a developing team that could use a little backcourt depth.

PLAYER SUMMARY	
Will	launch jumpers
Can't	earn minutes
Expect	inconsistent shooting
Don't Expect	quickness
Fantasy Value	$0
Card Value	8-12¢

COLLEGE STATISTICS

		G	FGP	FTP	APG	PPG
81-82	WF	22	.333	.500	1.0	1.1
82-83	WF	32	.528	.768	3.1	12.8
83-84	WF	31	.518	.859	2.6	13.3
84-85	WF	29	.465	.818	2.8	16.7
Totals		114	.495	.805	2.5	11.7

NBA REGULAR-SEASON STATISTICS

		G	MIN	FGs FG	FGs PCT	3-PT FGs FG	3-PT FGs PCT	FTs FT	FTs PCT	Rebounds OFF	Rebounds TOT	AST	STL	BLK	PTS	PPG
89-90	UTA	77	850	111	.429	16	.286	35	.660	12	55	177	22	1	273	3.5
90-91	UTA	82	874	124	.435	17	.279	59	.831	14	66	216	36	2	324	4.0
91-92	UTA	65	538	75	.399	11	.234	32	.762	15	54	109	15	1	193	3.0
92-93	POR	15	95	7	.194	1	.091	11	.786	4	9	17	1	0	26	1.7
Totals		239	2357	317	.413	45	.257	137	.761	45	184	519	74	4	816	3.4

JOHN SALLEY

Team: Miami Heat
Position: Forward/Center
Height: 6'11" **Weight:** 240
Birthdate: May 16, 1964
NBA Experience: 7 years

College: Georgia Tech
Acquired: Traded from Pistons for draft rights to Isaiah Morris and a 1993 1st-round pick, 9/92

Background: "Spider" was Georgia Tech's all-time leader in blocked shots before being selected by the Pistons (along with Dennis Rodman) in the 1986 draft. He's been talented but inconsistent for much of his career, though he came up big in the playoffs with Detroit, where he won two NBA championship rings. Salley scored a career-high 9.5 PPG in 1991-92, his final year with the Pistons, before signing with Miami. He made 34 starts with the Heat but missed nearly half of last season with a stress fracture in his left foot.

Strengths: Salley is one of the premier shot-blocking forwards in the league, as his size and quick feet make him tough to shoot around. His post-up game features a nifty hook shot along with his favorite, the spin move. He gets down-court on the break.

Weaknesses: Salley has been known to think more about his contract than his game. Offensively, he remains as inconsistent as any big forward in the league. Sometimes he's just not there. He has never been a great shooter. Salley picks up a lot of fouls and should be a better rebounder.

Analysis: Many thought a change of scenery would be perfect for Salley, an aspiring comedian who has had trouble staying focused on basketball. Instead of becoming a star, however, he spent the year battling Grant Long to start before his foot injury cost him virtually the entire second half.

PLAYER SUMMARY	
Will	swat shots
Can't	stay focused
Expect	funny one-liners
Don't Expect	stardom
Fantasy Value	$4-6
Card Value	5-10¢

COLLEGE STATISTICS

		G	FGP	FTP	RPG	PPG
82-83	GT	27	.502	.637	5.7	11.5
83-84	GT	29	.589	.674	5.8	11.8
84-85	GT	35	.627	.636	7.1	14.0
85-86	GT	34	.606	.594	6.7	13.1
Totals		125	.587	.633	6.4	12.7

NBA REGULAR-SEASON STATISTICS

				FGs		3-PT FGs		FTs		Rebounds						
		G	MIN	FG	PCT	FG	PCT	FT	PCT	OFF	TOT	AST	STL	BLK	PTS	PPG
86-87	DET	82	1463	163	.562	0	.000	105	.614	108	296	54	44	125	431	5.3
87-88	DET	82	2003	258	.566	0	.000	185	.709	166	402	113	53	137	701	8.5
88-89	DET	67	1458	166	.498	0	.000	135	.692	134	335	75	40	72	467	7.0
89-90	DET	82	1914	209	.512	1	.250	174	.713	154	439	67	51	153	593	7.2
90-91	DET	74	1649	179	.475	0	.000	186	.727	137	327	70	52	112	544	7.4
91-92	DET	72	1774	249	.512	0	.000	186	.715	106	296	116	49	110	684	9.5
92-93	MIA	51	1422	154	.502	0	.000	115	.799	113	313	83	32	70	423	8.3
Totals		510	11683	1378	.519	1	.091	1086	.709	918	2408	578	321	779	3843	7.5

MIKE SANDERS

Team: Cleveland Cavaliers
Position: Forward
Height: 6'6" **Weight:** 215
Birthdate: May 7, 1960

NBA Experience: 11 years
College: UCLA
Acquired: Signed as a free agent, 3/92

Background: Sanders was an All-Pac-10 selection at UCLA before being drafted in the fourth round by Kansas City. After being waived by the Kings and the Spurs and playing in the CBA, his career blossomed during his four-plus years in Phoenix. He was traded to Cleveland in 1988 and signed with Indiana prior to the 1989-90 season. He was waived by the Pacers early in 1991-92 and signed again with Cleveland. He has started 71 of the 74 regular-season games he has played for the Cavs.

Strengths: Sanders, a bona fide defensive stopper, has enjoyed great success against the big scorers in the league. He keeps his man in front of him. Sanders is selfless, hustles, and never complains. He won't take bad shots.

Weaknesses: Sanders does not look to score, and he does not offer much outside the paint on offense. With the Cavs, however, he has averaged close to double figures in scoring. He doesn't rebound real well.

Analysis: Sanders is not your typical small forward. While others of his position concentrate on scoring, he spends his time and energy playing defense and doing some of the little things required to win ballgames. Surgery to repair torn knee cartilage cost him several games last year.

PLAYER SUMMARY	
Will	chase loose balls
Can't	stick treys
Expect	defensive hustle
Don't Expect	slick moves
Fantasy Value	$1-3
Card Value	5-8¢

COLLEGE STATISTICS

		G	FGP	FTP	RPG	PPG
78-79	UCLA	23	.421	.688	1.5	1.9
79-80	UCLA	32	.573	.792	5.9	11.3
80-81	UCLA	27	.561	.766	6.6	15.4
81-82	UCLA	27	.502	.776	6.4	14.4
Totals		109	.538	.773	5.3	11.1

NBA REGULAR-SEASON STATISTICS

				FGs		3-PT FGs		FTs		Rebounds						
		G	MIN	FG	PCT	FG	PCT	FT	PCT	OFF	TOT	AST	STL	BLK	PTS	PPG
82-83	SA	26	393	76	.484	0	.000	31	.721	31	94	19	18	6	183	7.0
83-84	PHO	50	586	97	.478	0	.000	29	.690	40	103	44	23	12	223	4.5
84-85	PHO	21	418	85	.486	3	.200	45	.763	38	89	29	23	4	215	10.2
85-86	PHO	82	1644	347	.513	0	.000	208	.809	104	273	150	76	31	905	11.0
86-87	PHO	82	1655	357	.494	2	.118	143	.781	101	271	126	61	23	859	10.5
87-88	PHO/CLE	59	883	153	.505	0	.000	59	.776	38	109	56	31	9	365	6.2
88-89	CLE	82	2102	332	.453	3	.300	97	.719	98	307	133	89	32	764	9.3
89-90	IND	82	1531	225	.470	5	.357	55	.733	78	230	89	43	23	510	6.2
90-91	IND	80	1357	206	.417	4	.200	47	.825	73	185	106	37	26	463	5.8
91-92	IND/CLE	31	633	92	.571	1	.333	36	.766	27	96	53	24	10	221	7.1
92-93	CLE	53	1189	197	.497	1	.250	59	.756	52	170	75	39	30	454	8.6
Totals		648	12391	2167	.482	19	.221	809	.769	680	1927	880	464	206	5162	8.0

DANNY SCHAYES

Team: Milwaukee Bucks
Position: Center
Height: 6'11" **Weight:** 275
Birthdate: May 10, 1959

NBA Experience: 12 years
College: Syracuse
Acquired: Traded from Nuggets for draft rights to Terry Mills, 8/90

Background: The son of Hall of Famer Dolph Schayes, Danny was a late bloomer at Syracuse and didn't even start until his senior season. He was drafted by Utah but moved to Denver the following year. Schayes spent seven-plus seasons with the Nuggets before joining the Bucks in 1990. He led Denver in field goal percentage three times in the late 1980s. Schayes underwent arthroscopic surgery on his left knee that cost him half of the 1991-92 season. He returned last year to play in 70 games.

Strengths: Schayes has picked up a lot of tricks in his 12 seasons in the pivot. He knows what he can and can't get away with. He's willing to bang, play defense, and go to the defensive glass.

Weaknesses: Schayes has never been among the league's most athletic centers, even before the knee injury. He doesn't have good hands and he couldn't beat Bill Laimbeer in a jumping contest. Quick centers give him fits and his shooting has tailed off.

Analysis: Schayes appears to be on the last leg (knee, ankle, etc.) of a productive career. He has never been a superstar, but what he has lacked in gifts he's made up for with smarts, hard work, and consistency.

PLAYER SUMMARY	
Will	play smart
Can't	regain touch
Expect	veteran leadership
Don't Expect	the spectacular
Fantasy Value	$0
Card Value	5-8¢

COLLEGE STATISTICS

		G	FGP	FTP	RPG	PPG
77-78	SYR	24	.565	.756	4.0	4.7
78-79	SYR	29	.530	.833	4.2	6.2
79-80	SYR	30	.509	.769	4.5	5.9
80-81	SYR	34	.579	.822	8.4	14.6
Totals		117	.554	.806	5.4	8.2

NBA REGULAR-SEASON STATISTICS

		G	MIN	FGs FG	FGs PCT	3-PT FGs FG	3-PT FGs PCT	FTs FT	FTs PCT	Rebounds OFF	Rebounds TOT	AST	STL	BLK	PTS	PPG
81-82	UTA	82	1623	252	.481	0	.000	140	.757	131	427	146	46	72	644	7.9
82-83	UTA/DEN	82	2284	342	.457	0	.000	228	.773	200	635	205	54	98	912	11.1
83-84	DEN	82	1420	183	.493	0	.000	215	.790	145	433	91	32	60	581	7.1
84-85	DEN	56	542	60	.465	0	.000	79	.814	48	144	38	20	25	199	3.6
85-86	DEN	80	1654	221	.502	0	.000	216	.777	154	439	79	42	63	658	8.2
86-87	DEN	76	1556	210	.519	0	.000	229	.779	120	380	85	20	74	649	8.5
87-88	DEN	81	2166	361	.540	0	.000	407	.836	200	662	106	62	92	1129	13.9
88-89	DEN	76	1918	317	.522	3	.333	332	.826	142	500	105	42	81	969	12.8
89-90	DEN	53	1194	163	.494	0	.000	225	.852	117	342	61	41	45	551	10.4
90-91	MIL	82	2228	298	.499	0	.000	274	.835	174	535	98	55	61	870	10.6
91-92	MIL	43	726	83	.417	0	.000	74	.771	58	168	34	19	19	240	5.6
92-93	MIL	70	1124	105	.399	0	.000	112	.818	72	249	78	36	36	322	4.6
Totals		863	18435	2595	.491	3	.107	2531	.807	1561	4914	1126	469	726	7724	9.0

DWAYNE SCHINTZIUS

Team: New Jersey Nets
Position: Center
Height: 7'2" **Weight:** 260
Birthdate: October 14, 1968

NBA Experience: 3 years
College: Florida
Acquired: Signed as a free agent,
10/92

Background: Schintzius renounced his scholarship 11 games into his senior year at Florida because of a disagreement with coach Don DeVoe. Despite his All-Southeastern Conference play as a junior, pro scouts were leery because he reported to pre-draft camps out of shape. He played in 42 games as a rookie with San Antonio in 1990-91, but he injured his back late in the season and was traded to Sacramento. A herniated disc in his lower back cost him half of his second season and Sacramento let him go. His bad back limited him to five regular-season games with New Jersey last season, but he saw more than 21 minutes per outing during the playoffs.

Strengths: Schintzius has good passing skills, sees the whole court, and owns a nice touch for a man his size. His bulk helps him establish rebounding position and he has done a decent job on the glass.

Weaknesses: A bad back is a bad sign for someone with Schintzius's limited athletic ability. Certain skills like running and jumping seem tedious when performed by even a healthy Schintzius. He does not run the floor well and has not shot for a high percentage. He is not consistently focused and has yet to put in a full season.

Analysis: Schintzius was expected to miss all of last season, but to his credit, he bounced back to average six PPG and five RPG as New Jersey's back-up center in the playoffs. This far exceeded his contributions during the regular season. If Schintzius can overcome his bad back—a big if—then he should be able to make it as a back-up center.

PLAYER SUMMARY	
Will	rebound
Can't	stay healthy
Expect	bulk with finesse
Don't Expect	consistent focus
Fantasy Value	$0
Card Value	5-8¢

COLLEGE STATISTICS

		G	FGP	FTP	RPG	PPG
86-87	FLA	34	.440	.738	6.1	10.9
87-88	FLA	35	.491	.730	6.5	14.4
88-89	FLA	30	.521	.707	9.7	18.0
89-90	FLA	11	.552	.789	9.5	19.1
Totals		110	.494	.729	7.5	14.8

NBA REGULAR-SEASON STATISTICS

				FGs		3-PT FGs		FTs		Rebounds						
		G	MIN	FG	PCT	FG	PCT	FT	PCT	OFF	TOT	AST	STL	BLK	PTS	PPG
90-91	SA	42	398	68	.439	0	.000	22	.550	28	121	17	2	29	158	3.8
91-92	SAC	33	400	50	.427	0	.000	10	.833	43	118	20	6	28	110	3.3
92-93	NJ	5	35	2	.286	0	.000	3	1.00	2	8	2	2	2	7	1.4
Totals		80	833	120	.430	0	.000	35	.636	73	176	39	10	59	275	3.4

DETLEF SCHREMPF

Team: Indiana Pacers
Position: Forward
Height: 6'10" **Weight:** 230
Birthdate: January 21, 1963
NBA Experience: 8 years

College: Washington
Acquired: Traded from Mavericks with a future 2nd-round pick for Herb Williams, 2/89

Background: A graduate of the University of Washington, Schrempf spent the first three-plus years of his NBA career in Dallas. In 1989, he was traded to Indiana, where his game began to flourish. He won the NBA Sixth Man Award in 1991 and 1992 after finishing second in the voting after the 1989-90 season. Last year, he became the first European player to take part in the All-Star Game. His 60 starts made him ineligible for the Sixth Man Award.

Strengths: Schrempf is one of the league's most complete and versatile players. He's a superb ball-handler, shooter, and passer, and he can drive the lane or shoot from the outside. Either way, he scores. He's also great on the break, with the ability to start and/or finish plays. He plays strong defense and has finished in the league's top 20 in rebounding each of the last two seasons.

Weaknesses: Perhaps the one weakness in Schrempf's game is his tendency to spend too much time pleading his case to the refs. He shot poorly from 3-point range last year.

Analysis: Schrempf can do it all, a fact that was recognized last year when he received a much-deserved All-Star invitation. In his first year as a Pacer starter, he surpassed his previous top scoring average by nearly two points per game, led the team in rebounds, and was second in assists. He's a star.

PLAYER SUMMARY

Will	score, pass, rebound
Can't	be kept on bench
Expect	amazing versatility
Don't Expect	selfishness
Fantasy Value	$45-50
Card Value	8-12¢

COLLEGE STATISTICS

		G	FGP	FTP	RPG	PPG
81-82	WASH	28	.452	.553	2.0	3.3
82-83	WASH	31	.466	.717	6.8	10.6
83-84	WASH	31	.539	.736	7.4	16.8
84-85	WASH	32	.558	.714	8.0	15.8
Totals		122	.521	.708	6.2	11.9

NBA REGULAR-SEASON STATISTICS

				FGs		3-PT FGs		FTs		Rebounds						
		G	MIN	FG	PCT	FG	PCT	FT	PCT	OFF	TOT	AST	STL	BLK	PTS	PPG
85-86	DAL	64	969	142	.451	3	.429	110	.724	70	198	88	23	10	397	6.2
86-87	DAL	81	1711	265	.472	33	.478	193	.742	87	303	161	50	16	756	9.3
87-88	DAL	82	1587	246	.456	5	.156	201	.756	102	279	159	42	32	698	8.5
88-89	DAL/IND	69	1850	274	.474	7	.200	273	.780	126	395	179	53	19	828	12.0
89-90	IND	78	2573	424	.516	17	.354	402	.820	149	620	247	59	16	1267	16.2
90-91	IND	82	2632	432	.520	15	.375	441	.818	178	660	301	58	22	1320	16.1
91-92	IND	80	2605	496	.536	23	.324	365	.828	202	770	312	62	37	1380	17.3
92-93	IND	82	3098	517	.476	8	.154	525	.804	210	780	493	79	27	1567	19.1
Totals		618	17025	2796	.494	111	.314	2510	.797	1124	4005	1940	426	179	8213	13.3

BYRON SCOTT

Team: Los Angeles Lakers
Position: Guard
Height: 6'4" **Weight:** 200
Birthdate: March 28, 1961
NBA Experience: 10 years

College: Arizona St.
Acquired: Traded from Clippers with Swen Nater for Norm Nixon, Eddie Jordan, and 1986 and 1987 2nd-round picks, 10/83

Background: In just three years, Scott became Arizona State's career scoring leader and was an All-Pac-10 selection as a senior. He worked his way into the Lakers' starting lineup as a rookie and has broken Michael Cooper's team record for career 3-pointers. Scott helped guide the Lakers to three NBA championships in the 1980s. He missed 24 games last year with a foot injury and posted his lowest scoring average since his rookie year.

Strengths: Scott is a classic spot-up shooter who is deadly when he gets his feet together. He has great range, is almost automatic from the line, and does not mind taking the pressure shot. He has made plenty of them during his Laker career. He proved to be a fine leader after Magic Johnson retired.

Weaknesses: Scott's shooting percentage has declined over the last five years, dipping to a career-low .449 in 1992-93. He is not as adept at creating his own shot as he is at coming off a screen or finding an open seam. He's average, at best, with the dribble.

Analysis: Scott played the 1992-93 season with the idea that it was his last in a Laker uniform. He became a free agent at season's end. His playoff experience and long-range stroke will make him a significant player wherever he winds up.

PLAYER SUMMARY

Will ....hit from downtown
Can't................dazzle with his dribble
Expect ....clutch shooting
Don't Expect ....creativity
Fantasy Value................................$3-5
Card Value ....8-15¢

COLLEGE STATISTICS

		G	FGP	FTP	RPG	PPG
79-80	ASU	29	.500	.733	2.7	13.6
80-81	ASU	28	.505	.693	3.8	16.6
82-83	ASU	33	.513	.782	5.4	21.6
Totals		90	.507	.747	4.0	17.5

NBA REGULAR-SEASON STATISTICS

		G	MIN	FGs FG	FGs PCT	3-PT FGs FG	3-PT FGs PCT	FTs FT	FTs PCT	Rebounds OFF	Rebounds TOT	AST	STL	BLK	PTS	PPG
83-84	LAL	74	1637	334	.484	8	.235	112	.806	50	164	177	81	19	788	10.6
84-85	LAL	81	2305	541	.539	26	.433	187	.820	57	210	244	100	17	1295	16.0
85-86	LAL	76	2190	507	.513	22	.361	138	.784	55	189	164	85	15	1174	15.4
86-87	LAL	82	2729	554	.489	65	.436	224	.892	63	286	281	125	18	1397	17.0
87-88	LAL	81	3048	710	.527	62	.346	272	.858	76	333	335	155	27	1754	21.7
88-89	LAL	74	2605	588	.491	77	.399	195	.863	72	302	231	114	27	1448	19.6
89-90	LAL	77	2593	472	.470	93	.423	160	.766	51	242	274	77	31	1197	15.5
90-91	LAL	82	2630	501	.477	71	.324	118	.797	54	246	177	95	21	1191	14.5
91-92	LAL	82	2679	460	.458	54	.344	244	.838	74	310	226	105	28	1218	14.9
92-93	LAL	58	1677	296	.449	44	.326	156	.848	27	134	157	55	13	792	13.7
Totals		767	24093	4963	.492	522	.371	1806	.833	579	2416	2266	992	216	12254	16.0

DENNIS SCOTT

Team: Orlando Magic
Position: Forward
Height: 6'8" **Weight:** 250
Birthdate: September 5, 1968

NBA Experience: 3 years
College: Georgia Tech
Acquired: 1st-round pick in 1990 draft (4th overall)

Background: Scott led Georgia Tech to the NCAA Final Four as a senior. That year, he recorded the highest single-season point total in Atlantic Coast Conference history, was named ACC Player of the Year, and topped the 30-point mark 18 times. He earned All-Rookie honors in 1990-91, posting the third-highest scoring average among first-year players and setting an NBA rookie record for 3-pointers. He underwent surgery to relieve inflammation in his right knee 18 games into his second season. He returned last year and was ninth in the league in 3-point percentage, although Achilles tendinitis and a strained calf limited him to 54 games.

Strengths: Scott has range even beyond the 3-point line and boasts one of the sweetest strokes in the game. He hit nine treys in a game against Milwaukee last season. His size serves him well on the perimeter and in the post. He is also a solid passer and ball-handler.

Weaknesses: Injuries have become a concern for Scott, who bounced back from his knee surgery only to encounter more leg problems. Even when healthy, he does not possess great quickness. Scott has the potential to be a better rebounder. He too often stays glued to the perimeter.

Analysis: Scott has the look of an annual contender for the league's 3-point shooting crown, not to mention trips to the All-Star Game. All he needs to do is stay healthy for a full season. If he can, the Magic will have one of the best inside-outside combos in the game with Scott and Shaquille O'Neal. Scott, a leader, took Shaq under his wing last year.

PLAYER SUMMARY

Will ....knock down treys
Can't ....keep legs healthy
Expect................huge scoring nights
Don't Expect ....raw speed
Fantasy Value................................$6-8
Card Value ....12-25¢

COLLEGE STATISTICS

		G	FGP	FTP	RPG	PPG
87-88	GT	32	.440	.655	5.0	15.5
88-89	GT	32	.443	.814	4.1	20.3
89-90	GT	35	.465	.793	6.6	27.7
Totals		99	.452	.777	5.3	21.4

NBA REGULAR-SEASON STATISTICS

		G	MIN	FGs FG	FGs PCT	3-PT FGs FG	3-PT FGs PCT	FTs FT	FTs PCT	Rebounds OFF	Rebounds TOT	AST	STL	BLK	PTS	PPG
90-91	ORL	82	2336	503	.425	125	.374	153	.750	62	235	134	62	25	1284	15.7
91-92	ORL	18	608	133	.402	29	.326	64	.901	14	66	35	20	9	359	19.9
92-93	ORL	54	1759	329	.431	108	.403	92	.786	38	186	136	57	18	858	15.9
Totals		154	4703	965	.424	262	.379	309	.788	114	487	305	139	52	2501	16.2

MALIK SEALY

Team: Indiana Pacers
Position: Forward/Guard
Height: 6'8" **Weight:** 185
Birthdate: February 1, 1970

NBA Experience: 1 year
College: St. John's
Acquired: 1st-round pick in 1992 draft
(14th overall)

Background: Sealy starred at Tolentine High in the Bronx before making a national name for himself at hometown St. John's University. He led all Big East players in scoring as a senior (22.6 PPG) while earning his second straight spot on the all-conference first team. He finished his college career as the all-time St. John's steals leader and wound up second to Chris Mullin in scoring. The 14th overall pick in the 1992 draft, Sealy averaged 5.7 PPG in 58 games for Indiana during his rookie season.

Strengths: Sealy brings unlimited energy to the floor. He thrives in a running game, can play both big guard and small forward, and is tougher than he appears. Blessed with great quickness, Sealy has the potential to be a disruptive defensive player in a fullcourt attack. He also looks to score, moves well without the basketball, and does not shy away from pressure shots. He hit plenty of them in college.

Weaknesses: His slight build scared some NBA scouts away from Sealy and it hurts him in halfcourt defensive match-ups. Sealy has never been a pure shooter, although by the end of last season he looked much more comfortable and even showed 3-point range. He is a below-average passer and ball-handler who must learn to become more involved in the offense.

Analysis: Most of Sealy's rookie year can be called a big disappointment. He even lost his playbook on a playoff trip to New York and a radio station broadcast some of the scouting capsules out of it. By that time, however, Sealy appeared to be coming around with his performance on the court. He scored 23 points in 41 minutes over the last two regular-season games.

PLAYER SUMMARY	
Will	run the floor
Can't	dominate physically
Expect	quickness, energy
Don't Expect	halfcourt defense
Fantasy Value	$2-4
Card Value	10-20¢

COLLEGE STATISTICS

		G	FGP	FTP	RPG	PPG
88-89	STJ	31	.489	.558	6.4	12.9
89-90	STJ	34	.525	.746	6.9	18.1
90-91	STJ	32	.492	.743	7.7	22.1
91-92	STJ	30	.472	.793	6.8	22.6
Totals		127	.494	.729	6.9	18.9

NBA REGULAR-SEASON STATISTICS

			FGs		3-PT FGs		FTs		Rebounds						
	G	MIN	FG	PCT	FG	PCT	FT	PCT	OFF	TOT	AST	STL	BLK	PTS	PPG
92-93 IND	58	672	136	.426	7	.226	51	.689	60	112	47	36	7	330	5.7
Totals	58	672	136	.426	7	.226	51	.689	60	112	47	36	7	330	5.7

RONY SEIKALY

Team: Miami Heat
Position: Center
Height: 6'11" **Weight:** 252
Birthdate: May 10, 1965

NBA Experience: 5 years
College: Syracuse
Acquired: 1st-round pick in 1988 draft (9th overall)

Background: A native of Greece, Seikaly was one of Syracuse's all-time great big men. He was inconsistent as a rookie with Miami in 1988-89 but was chosen as the NBA's Most Improved Player in 1989-90. Seikaly was sidelined for more than a month of the 1990-91 campaign with a sprained ligament in his right knee, but he has bounced back for his two finest seasons. He has ranked in the league's top eight in rebounding the last two years and averaged a career-high 17.1 PPG in 1992-93.

Strengths: Seikaly is one of the most talented and productive rebounders in the league. He grabbed 34 in a game against Washington last March, more than the Bullets nabbed as a team. He has good quickness, speed, jumping ability, and confidence. He combines finesse with physical play and gets to the line frequently. He's a fine shot-blocker and low-post defender.

Weaknesses: Seikaly is not one of the league's better passing big men, and his turnover total (more than 200 each of the past two years) results largely from putting the ball on the floor too often. He coughs it up twice as often as he gets credit for an assist.

Analysis: Seikaly is a cornerstone of a Miami team that, two years ago, became the first recent expansion team to reach the playoffs. When he sets his mind to dominating the boards, he is completely capable of doing so. He is not one of the prime-time pivots in the NBA, but he is certainly one of the better ones.

PLAYER SUMMARY	
Will	clean the glass
Can't	avoid turnovers
Expect	17 PPG, 11 RPG
Don't Expect	good passing
Fantasy Value	$20-25
Card Value	10-20¢

COLLEGE STATISTICS

		G	FGP	FTP	RPG	PPG
84-85	SYR	31	.542	.558	6.4	8.1
85-86	SYR	32	.547	.563	7.8	10.1
86-87	SYR	38	.568	.600	8.2	15.1
87-88	SYR	35	.566	.568	9.6	16.3
Totals		136	.560	.576	8.0	12.6

NBA REGULAR-SEASON STATISTICS

		G	MIN	FGs FG	FGs PCT	3-PT FGs FG	3-PT FGs PCT	FTs FT	FTs PCT	Rebounds OFF	Rebounds TOT	AST	STL	BLK	PTS	PPG
88-89	MIA	78	1962	333	.448	1	.250	181	.511	204	549	55	46	96	848	10.9
89-90	MIA	74	2409	486	.502	0	.000	256	.594	253	766	78	78	124	1228	16.6
90-91	MIA	64	2171	395	.481	2	.333	258	.619	207	709	95	51	86	1050	16.4
91-92	MIA	79	2800	463	.489	0	.000	370	.733	307	934	109	40	121	1296	16.4
92-93	MIA	72	2456	417	.480	1	.125	397	.735	259	846	100	38	83	1232	17.1
Totals		367	11798	2094	.481	4	.182	1462	.651	1230	3804	437	253	510	5654	15.4

BRIAN SHAW

Team: Miami Heat
Position: Guard
Height: 6'6" **Weight:** 194
Birthdate: March 22, 1966
NBA Experience: 4 years

College: St. Mary's (CA); Cal.-Santa Barbara
Acquired: Traded from Celtics for Sherman Douglas, 1/92

Background: Shaw, the Pacific Coast Athletic Association Player of the Year as a senior at Cal.-Santa Barbara, was a second-team All-Rookie performer with the Celtics in 1988-89. He spent the 1989-90 season in the Italian League. He returned to Boston in 1990-91 and ranked 14th in the NBA in assists that year. After missing the first month of 1991-92 with a hamstring injury, he was traded to Miami for Sherman Douglas and started exactly half of his 46 games with the Heat. Last year, he slumped to career lows in shooting and scoring.

Strengths: Shaw brings good size and rebounding to the backcourt and has the versatility to play both point guard and off guard. He played forward in college and can post up smaller defenders. He's at his best in transition, has some quick moves to the hoop, and can handle and pass the ball. Last year, for the first time, he showed an ability to hit the 3-point shot.

Weaknesses: Sorely lacking the defensive skills the Celtics wanted from him, Shaw is often unwilling and not very able at that end. Offensively, his value plunges when you put him in a halfcourt offense. He is not a consistent shooter, will not score a lot, and is not among the more creative guards.

Analysis: Shaw stunned the league last April when he made an NBA-record ten 3-pointers (in 15 attempts) against the Bucks. In his first three seasons, he had made only eight 3's total. His shooting still has a long way to go, but Miami hopes the added dimension is a sign that Shaw will make strides in other areas.

PLAYER SUMMARY	
Will	handle the ball
Can't	shoot 50 percent
Expect	transition buckets
Don't Expect	great defense
Fantasy Value	$2-4
Card Value	8-15¢

COLLEGE STATISTICS

		G	FGP	FTP	RPG	PPG
83-84	SM	14	.361	.737	0.9	2.9
84-85	SM	27	.402	.724	5.3	9.4
86-87	CSB	29	.434	.712	7.7	10.9
87-88	CSB	30	.466	.740	8.7	13.3
Totals		100	.434	.728	6.4	10.1

NBA REGULAR-SEASON STATISTICS

		G	MIN	FGs FG	FGs PCT	3-PT FGs FG	3-PT FGs PCT	FTs FT	FTs PCT	Rebounds OFF	Rebounds TOT	AST	STL	BLK	PTS	PPG
88-89	BOS	82	2301	297	.433	0	.000	109	.826	119	376	472	78	27	703	8.6
90-91	BOS	79	2772	442	.469	3	.111	204	.819	104	370	602	105	34	1091	13.8
91-92	BOS/MIA	63	1423	209	.407	5	.217	72	.791	50	204	250	57	22	495	7.9
92-93	MIA	68	1603	197	.393	43	.331	61	.782	70	257	235	48	19	498	7.3
Totals		292	8099	1145	.433	51	.264	446	.811	343	1207	1559	288	102	2787	9.5

LIONEL SIMMONS

Team: Sacramento Kings
Position: Forward
Height: 6'7" **Weight:** 210
Birthdate: November 14, 1968

NBA Experience: 3 years
College: La Salle
Acquired: 1st-round pick in 1990 draft
(7th overall)

Background: Simmons, who won the Wooden Award in 1990 as college basketball's Player of the Year, finished his career at La Salle third on the all-time NCAA scoring list. He became the first player in college history to amass more than 3,000 points and 1,100 rebounds. He finished second to Derrick Coleman in the 1990-91 Rookie of the Year balloting after a torrid second half of the season. Simmons has finished second on the Kings in scoring each of the last two years, averaging 17.9 PPG last season. A bruised thigh cost him several games late last year.

Strengths: Simmons is an amazingly versatile player. He scores, rebounds, plays defense, and is a smooth passer from the wing. He understands the game and makes his teammates better. He possesses an enormous quantity of athletic ability, but his great work ethic and willingness to leave it all on the floor have just as much to do with his success.

Weaknesses: While Simmons is a scorer, he is not a shooter. His mid-range jump shot is unreliable and he does not have 3-point range (he has made five treys in three seasons). His field goal percentage is low. Other than that, there are very few holes in his game.

Analysis: There were several who thought Simmons would struggle to convert his college success to the pros. Where are the skeptics now? Simmons has the total package. He scores, rebounds, passes, blocks shots, plays defense, and leads by example. You'd have a hard time finding a player who is more valuable to his team. He's likely an improved jump shot away from an All-Star invite.

PLAYER SUMMARY	
Will	score, rebound, pass
Can't	rely on jump shot
Expect	leadership by example
Don't Expect	passive play
Fantasy Value	$17-20
Card Value	10-15¢

COLLEGE STATISTICS

		G	FGP	FTP	RPG	PPG
86-87	LaS	33	.526	.763	9.8	20.3
87-88	LaS	34	.485	.757	11.4	23.3
88-89	LaS	32	.487	.711	11.4	28.4
89-90	LaS	32	.513	.661	11.1	26.5
Totals		131	.501	.722	10.9	24.6

NBA REGULAR-SEASON STATISTICS

			FGs		3-PT FGs		FTs		Rebounds						
		G	MIN	FG	PCT	FG	PCT	FT	PCT	OFF	TOT	AST	STL	BLK	PTS	PPG
90-91	SAC	79	2978	549	.422	3	.273	320	.736	193	697	315	113	85	1421	18.0
91-92	SAC	78	2895	527	.454	1	.200	281	.770	149	634	337	135	132	1336	17.1
92-93	SAC	69	2502	468	.444	1	.091	298	.819	156	495	312	95	38	1235	17.9
Totals		226	8375	1544	.439	5	.185	899	.772	498	1826	964	343	255	3992	17.7

SCOTT SKILES

Team: Orlando Magic
Position: Guard
Height: 6'1" **Weight:** 180
Birthdate: March 5, 1964

NBA Experience: 7 years
College: Michigan St.
Acquired: Selected from Indiana in 1989 expansion draft

Background: Skiles was an All-America performer as a senior at Michigan State, finishing second in the nation in scoring, and setting school records for points, assists, steals, and free throw accuracy. However, he also earned a reputation for off-court trouble and spent time in jail. He was an NBA back-up for four years before coming into his own with Orlando in 1990-91, increasing his scoring average by 9.5 PPG and setting a league record with 30 assists in a game. He has started and averaged at least 14 PPG in the two years since.

Strengths: They do not come any more competitive than Skiles, who simply despises losing. He knows how to run an offense and find open men. He penetrates and passes with precision, shoots the 3-pointer, and is almost automatic from the free throw line.

Weaknesses: Skiles is not quick enough to keep opposing point guards from driving and is not big enough to keep from being posted up. He's not able to pressure the ball fullcourt and does not rank among the ball-handling wizards of the game.

Analysis: Skiles is as tough as nails and brings that competitive nature to the arena with him every night. He is the consummate playmaker, ranking third in the league in assists last year while still scoring his share of points. The Magic acquired superstar guard Anfernee Hardaway on draft day, but he'll have to fight to steal the starting job away from Skiles.

PLAYER SUMMARY	
Will	drive and dish
Can't	excel on defense
Expect	competitive fire
Don't Expect	raw speed
Fantasy Value	$12-15
Card Value	8-12¢

COLLEGE STATISTICS

		G	FGP	FTP	APG	PPG
82-83	MSU	30	.493	.831	4.9	12.5
83-84	MSU	28	.480	.832	4.6	14.5
84-85	MSU	29	.505	.789	5.8	17.7
85-86	MSU	31	.554	.900	6.3	27.4
Totals		118	.516	.850	5.4	18.2

NBA REGULAR-SEASON STATISTICS

		G	MIN	FGs FG	FGs PCT	3-PT FGs FG	3-PT FGs PCT	FTs FT	FTs PCT	Rebounds OFF	Rebounds TOT	AST	STL	BLK	PTS	PPG
86-87	MIL	13	205	18	.290	3	.214	10	.833	6	26	45	5	1	49	3.8
87-88	IND	51	760	86	.411	6	.300	45	.833	11	66	180	22	3	223	4.4
88-89	IND	80	1571	198	.448	20	.267	130	.903	21	149	390	64	2	546	6.8
89-90	ORL	70	1460	190	.409	52	.394	104	.874	23	159	334	36	4	536	7.7
90-91	ORL	79	2714	462	.445	93	.408	340	.902	57	270	660	89	4	1357	17.2
91-92	ORL	75	2377	359	.414	91	.364	248	.895	36	202	544	74	5	1057	14.1
92-93	ORL	78	3086	416	.467	80	.340	289	.892	52	290	735	86	2	1201	15.4
Totals		446	12173	1729	.435	345	.362	1166	.892	206	1162	2888	376	21	4969	11.1

CHARLES SMITH

Team: New York Knicks
Position: Forward/Center
Height: 6'10" **Weight:** 244
Birthdate: July 16, 1965
NBA Experience: 5 years

College: Pittsburgh
Acquired: Traded from Clippers in three-team deal, 9/92 (see page 543 for details)

Background: Smith, the Big East Player of the Year as a senior, left Pitt with the school's career records for points and blocked shots. He earned All-Rookie honors with the Clippers in 1988-89 and ranked among the league leaders in scoring, rebounding, and blocked shots over the next two years. A right knee injury kept him out of 33 games in 1991-92, after which he was traded to the Knicks. He struggled early last year but came on late, finishing third on his new team in scoring at 12.4 PPG and second in blocks with 96.

Strengths: Smith is an all-around talent who can play all three frontcourt positions. He plays bigger than his size, yet he runs the floor and can handle the ball like a smaller man. He is a combination of power and finesse on offense, with range beyond 18 feet. Smith's great reach helps him play solid defense.

Weaknesses: Smith's field goal percentage has dipped into the 46-percent range after topping out at 52 percent in his second season. He too often settles for outside shots and does not pass well out of double-teams. Some have questioned his feel for the game. He could be a better rebounder.

Analysis: Smith floundered in his early days as a Knick. A big part of his problem was foul trouble, but once he became comfortable in the Pat Riley system he played very well. He averaged 18 PPG over the last eight regular-season outings. Smith has all the skills you look for—scoring, rebounding, defense, etc.

PLAYER SUMMARY	
Will	play three positions
Can't	outscore Ewing
Expect	solid defense
Don't Expect	8 RPG
Fantasy Value	$7-9
Card Value	10-15¢

COLLEGE STATISTICS

		G	FGP	FTP	RPG	PPG
84-85	PITT	29	.502	.706	8.0	15.0
85-86	PITT	29	.404	.762	8.1	15.9
86-87	PITT	33	.550	.735	8.5	17.0
87-88	PITT	31	.558	.764	7.7	18.9
Totals		122	.500	.753	8.1	16.8

NBA REGULAR-SEASON STATISTICS

				FGs		3-PT FGs		FTs		Rebounds						
		G	MIN	FG	PCT	FG	PCT	FT	PCT	OFF	TOT	AST	STL	BLK	PTS	PPG
88-89	LAC	71	2161	435	.495	0	.000	285	.725	173	465	103	68	89	1155	16.3
89-90	LAC	78	2732	595	.520	1	.083	454	.794	177	524	114	86	119	1645	21.1
90-91	LAC	74	2703	548	.469	0	.000	384	.793	216	608	134	81	145	1480	20.0
91-92	LAC	49	1310	251	.466	0	.000	212	.785	95	301	56	41	98	714	14.6
92-93	NY	81	2172	358	.469	0	.000	287	.782	170	432	142	48	96	1003	12.4
Totals		353	11078	2187	.487	1	.033	1622	.778	831	2330	549	324	547	5997	17.0

CHRIS SMITH

Team: Minnesota Timberwolves
Position: Guard
Height: 6'3" **Weight:** 191
Birthdate: May 17, 1970

NBA Experience: 1 year
College: Connecticut
Acquired: 2nd-round pick in 1992 draft (34th overall)

Background: Smith became the first player in University of Connecticut history to surpass the 2,000-career point barrier. He also finished his career as the Huskies' all-time leader in 3-pointers made and attempted. Smith was a first-team All-Big East selection as a senior after leading the league in scoring at 21.2 PPG. He was selected in the second round of the 1992 draft by Minnesota and saw action in all but two games as a rookie. Smith averaged 4.3 PPG and made six starts for the Timberwolves.

Strengths: Smith is a splendid athlete with great quickness. He handles the ball well, can penetrate, and brings a scorer's mentality to the point-guard post. Smith has a nifty crossover dribble than he can use to get his own shots. He also did a better job of running the offense than most thought he could and is willing to expend energy on defense. He has the makings of a fine 3-point and free throw shooter.

Weaknesses: He has been called a shooting guard in a point guard's body, and for the most part the description fits. He did not spend his college career setting records for assists and is just learning to be a distributor. He does not always make the right pass. Smith is not much help on the boards and is not the thief he was expected to be.

Analysis: All in all, Smith's rookie year was promising. He did not completely silence those who said he's not a pro-style point guard, but there are a lot worse ball-handlers and penetrators playing the position in the NBA. Above all, Smith is a hard worker who wants to make a name for himself. He's fortunate to be on a team like Minnesota, which can afford to give him P.T.

PLAYER SUMMARY	
Will	handle the ball
Can't	score like in college
Expect	enthusiasm
Don't Expect	rebounds
Fantasy Value	$1
Card Value	8-15¢

COLLEGE STATISTICS

		G	FGP	FTP	RPG	PPG
88-89	CONN	29	.405	.565	2.8	9.9
89-90	CONN	37	.417	.811	2.5	17.2
90-91	CONN	31	.439	.719	2.9	18.9
91-92	CONN	30	.415	.800	3.3	21.2
Totals		127	.421	.761	2.9	16.9

NBA REGULAR-SEASON STATISTICS

			FGs		3-PT FGs		FTs		Rebounds						
	G	MIN	FG	PCT	FG	PCT	FT	PCT	OFF	TOT	AST	STL	BLK	PTS	PPG
92-93 MIN	80	1266	125	.433	2	.143	95	.792	32	96	196	48	16	347	4.3
Totals	80	1266	125	.433	2	.143	95	.792	32	96	196	48	16	347	4.3

DOUG SMITH

Team: Dallas Mavericks
Position: Forward
Height: 6'10" **Weight:** 240
Birthdate: September 17, 1969

NBA Experience: 2 years
College: Missouri
Acquired: 1st-round pick in 1991 draft (6th overall)

Background: Smith went from Detroit's MacKenzie High to immediate stardom at Missouri. He was named first-team Freshman All-American in 1988, and the Tigers went 94-35 in his four seasons. He was drafted sixth overall by Dallas, then missed all of training camp and the first regular-season game because of a contract holdout. He started 32 times, averaged 8.8 PPG, and was among the rookie leaders with 5.1 RPG. He raised his scoring average to 10.4 PPG last season but missed 21 games because of arch and eye injuries.

Strengths: Smith runs the floor as well as any player his size and dunks with authority. He is a good ball-handler and passer for a big man, with above-average awareness and instincts. He has the makings of a solid defensive rebounder who can turn his efforts on the glass into quick buckets on the other end of the floor.

Weaknesses: Smith does not have the low-post game to be a big-time player in the NBA. He needs a lot of work in terms of moves around the basket, and his shooting percentage is frighteningly low for a big man. He reported to the Mavericks overweight as a rookie and has not been in peak condition since. Smith is a defensive liability who fouled out 12 times last year.

Analysis: Smith's disappointing rookie year could be chalked up to his missed training camp and poor conditioning. After last season, however, one has to wonder whether Smith will ever be able to live up to his status as a No. 6 overall draft choice. He can be a very exciting player in the open court and has some natural ability, but he is not the scorer and rebounder the Mavericks expected him to be.

PLAYER SUMMARY	
Will	run the floor
Can't	dominate in post
Expect	rebounding
Don't Expect	stardom
Fantasy Value	$1
Card Value	10-15¢

COLLEGE STATISTICS

		G	FGP	FTP	RPG	PPG
87-88	MO	30	.504	.640	6.6	11.3
88-89	MO	36	.477	.736	6.9	13.9
89-90	MO	32	.563	.714	9.2	19.8
90-91	MO	30	.497	.821	10.4	23.6
Totals		128	.510	.747	8.2	17.1

NBA REGULAR-SEASON STATISTICS

			FGs		3-PT FGs		FTs		Rebounds						
	G	MIN	FG	PCT	FG	PCT	FT	PCT	OFF	TOT	AST	STL	BLK	PTS	PPG
91-92 DAL	76	1707	291	.415	0	.000	89	.736	129	391	129	62	34	671	8.8
92-93 DAL	61	1524	299	.434	0	.000	56	.757	96	328	104	48	52	634	10.4
Totals	137	3231	580	.424	0	.000	145	.744	225	719	233	110	86	1305	9.5

KENNY SMITH

Team: Houston Rockets
Position: Guard
Height: 6'3" **Weight:** 170
Birthdate: March 8, 1965
NBA Experience: 6 years

College: North Carolina
Acquired: Traded from Hawks with Roy Marble for Tim McCormick and John Lucas, 9/90

Background: Smith established all-time school records for assists and steals at North Carolina, where he was named All-Atlantic Coast Conference as a senior. He averaged double figures in scoring in his first three NBA seasons with Sacramento and Atlanta, but he did not truly shine until a trade brought him to Houston for the 1990-91 campaign. He shot 52 percent that year. Smith has led the Rockets in assists during each of the last three seasons and led all NBA guards in field goal percentage last year.

Strengths: Smith answered a lot of doubters after joining the Rockets. Foremost, he proved he was a point guard—a cat-quick penetrator who could get the ball into the right hands while scoring double figures himself. He has displayed consistency with his jumper, even from 3-point range. Smith is a very good free throw shooter, a leader, and a class act.

Weaknesses: Smith is not a great defensive player and does not come up with many steals. He seems to put more effort and focus into his offensive game. There are far more spectacular lead guards around.

Analysis: Smith will not post one of the best assist-to-turnover ratios in the league and will not likely play in the All-Star Game before his career is finished. But his game is more complete than most gave him credit for in his pre-Houston days. He started all 82 games for the first time last season and helped Houston to the Midwest Division title.

PLAYER SUMMARY	
Will	hit FTs, treys
Can't	dazzle with moves
Expect	a steady hand
Don't Expect	great defense
Fantasy Value	$11-14
Card Value	8-12¢

COLLEGE STATISTICS

		G	FGP	FTP	APG	PPG
83-84	NC	23	.519	.800	5.0	9.1
84-85	NC	36	.518	.860	6.5	12.3
85-86	NC	34	.516	.808	6.2	12.0
86-87	NC	34	.502	.807	6.1	16.9
Totals		127	.512	.823	6.0	12.9

NBA REGULAR-SEASON STATISTICS

			FGs		3-PT FGs		FTs		Rebounds						
	G	MIN	FG	PCT	FG	PCT	FT	PCT	OFF	TOT	AST	STL	BLK	PTS	PPG
87-88 SAC	61	2170	331	.477	12	.308	167	.819	40	138	434	92	8	841	13.8
88-89 SAC	81	3145	547	.462	46	.359	263	.737	49	226	621	102	7	1403	17.3
89-90 SAC/ATL	79	2421	378	.466	26	.313	161	.321	18	157	445	79	8	943	11.9
90-91 HOU	78	2699	522	.520	49	.363	287	.844	36	163	554	106	11	1380	17.7
91-92 HOU	81	2735	432	.475	54	.394	219	.866	34	177	562	104	7	1137	14.0
92-93 HOU	82	2422	387	.520	96	.438	195	.878	28	160	446	80	7	1065	13.0
Totals	462	15592	2597	.486	283	.382	1292	.822	205	1021	3062	563	48	6769	14.7

LaBRADFORD SMITH

Team: Washington Bullets
Position: Guard
Height: 6'3" **Weight:** 200
Birthdate: April 3, 1969

NBA Experience: 2 years
College: Louisville
Acquired: 1st-round pick in 1991 draft
(19th overall)

Background: Smith was expected to be the next Darrell Griffith at Louisville, and while he never lived up to those expectations, he had a solid, sometimes spectacular, four years with the Cardinals. He set an all-time school record for assists and was one of the top free throw shooters in college basketball history. He was drafted 19th overall by Washington and played in 48 games as a rookie, starting five and averaging 5.1 PPG. He boosted his average to 9.3 PPG and made 33 starts last season.

Strengths: Smith's greatest asset is his marvelous athletic ability. He has high-jumped 6'10" and was drafted by the Toronto Blue Jays as a pitching prospect. Combined with his good size, his leaping ability allows him to challenge (and dunk over) bigger people. He can penetrate, play both guard spots, and score from both inside and outside. He's a great free throw shooter and has much defensive potential.

Weaknesses: While he can fill both guard positions, his ball-handling and playmaking skills do not match up with those of the league's better point guards. Moreover, he has not shown steady enough shooting ability to tear it up at two guard. Smith will not light it up from 3-point range. He has carried a little extra weight during his first two years and has not shown much consistency.

Analysis: It has been said that Smith is more athlete than basketball player, and that might be true despite the fact he is more than capable of doing well in the NBA. He'll have a huge game one night (he scored 37 points once last year) and scramble for a bucket the next. The feeling is he'll continue to improve with more games under his belt.

PLAYER SUMMARY	
Will	dunk over people
Can't	star at the point
Expect	athletic ability
Don't Expect	consistency
Fantasy Value	$1-3
Card Value	10-20¢

COLLEGE STATISTICS

		G	FGP	FTP	RPG	PPG
87-88	LOU	35	.477	.905	2.5	12.7
88-89	LOU	33	.465	.868	2.3	11.9
89-90	LOU	35	.497	.860	3.3	13.5
90-91	LOU	30	.482	.825	3.7	16.6
Totals		133	.481	.866	2.9	13.6

NBA REGULAR-SEASON STATISTICS

		G	MIN	FGs FG	FGs PCT	3-PT FGs FG	3-PT FGs PCT	FTs FT	FTs PCT	Rebounds OFF	Rebounds TOT	AST	STL	BLK	PTS	PPG
91-92	WAS	48	708	100	.407	2	.095	45	.804	30	81	99	44	1	247	5.1
92-93	WAS	69	1546	261	.458	8	.348	109	.858	26	106	186	58	9	639	9.3
Totals		117	2254	361	.442	10	.227	154	.842	56	187	285	102	10	886	7.6

LARRY SMITH

Team: San Antonio Spurs
Position: Forward
Height: 6'8" **Weight:** 250
Birthdate: January 18, 1958

NBA Experience: 13 years
College: Alcorn St.
Acquired: Signed as a free agent, 8/92

Background: Smith won the 1979-80 Division I rebounding crown at Alcorn State. He played nine seasons in Golden State, where he was an All-Rookie selection and became the Warriors' third-leading career rebounder. He once grabbed 31 boards in a game. In his second year with Houston in 1990-91, he finished 18th in the league in rebounding. Knee surgery cut his 1991-92 season short. Smith signed with San Antonio before last season and started 13 games.

Strengths: Smith does two things well—rebound and play defense. His commitment to those aspects of the game is what made him a starter during his years with the Warriors. He boxes out, plays physically, and shoves people out of the post.

Weaknesses: Offensively, Smith is a factor only on the glass. Only once in his career has he averaged double figures in scoring. You would be hard-pressed to find a more dismal free throw shooter than Smith.

Analysis: Nicknamed "Mr. Mean," Smith can be just that as a rebounder and defensive presence. He won't have another year like 1990-91, when 20-rebound games were routine. He averaged a career-low 1.3 PPG last season.

PLAYER SUMMARY	
Will	bump and bruise
Can't	shoot the ball
Expect	rebounds, defense
Don't Expect	a bucket a game
Fantasy Value	$0
Card Value	5-8¢

COLLEGE STATISTICS

		G	FGP	FTP	RPG	PPG
76-77	ASU	34	.527	.597	6.5	14.6
77-78	ASU	22	.593	.608	10.1	14.5
78-79	ASU	29	.600	.570	13.7	17.7
79-80	ASU	26	.579	.692	15.1	20.1
Totals		111	.572	.625	11.1	16.7

NBA REGULAR-SEASON STATISTICS

				FGs		3-PT FGs		FTs		Rebounds						
		G	MIN	FG	PCT	FG	PCT	FT	PCT	OFF	TOT	AST	STL	BLK	PTS	PPG
80-81	GS	82	2578	304	.512	0	.000	177	.588	433	994	93	70	63	785	9.6
81-82	GS	74	2213	220	.534	0	.000	88	.553	279	813	83	65	54	528	7.1
82-83	GS	49	1433	180	.588	0	.000	53	.535	209	485	46	36	20	413	8.4
83-84	GS	75	2091	244	.560	0	.000	94	.560	282	672	72	61	22	582	7.8
84-85	GS	80	2497	366	.530	0	.000	155	.605	405	869	96	78	54	887	11.1
85-86	GS	77	2441	314	.536	0	.000	112	.493	384	856	95	62	50	740	9.6
86-87	GS	80	2374	297	.546	0	.000	113	.574	366	917	95	71	56	707	8.8
87-88	GS	20	499	58	.472	0	.000	11	.407	79	182	25	12	11	127	6.3
88-89	GS	80	1897	219	.552	0	.000	18	.310	272	652	118	61	54	456	5.7
89-90	HOU	74	1300	101	.474	0	.000	20	.364	180	452	69	56	28	222	3.0
90-91	HOU	81	1923	128	.487	0	.000	12	.240	302	709	88	83	22	268	3.3
91-92	HOU	45	800	50	.543	0	.000	4	.364	107	256	33	21	7	104	2.3
92-93	SA	66	833	38	.437	0	.000	9	.409	103	268	28	23	16	85	1.3
Totals		883	22879	2519	.531	0	.000	866	.531	3401	8125	941	699	457	5904	6.7

STEVE SMITH

Team: Miami Heat
Position: Guard
Height: 6'7" **Weight:** 208
Birthdate: March 31, 1969

NBA Experience: 2 years
College: Michigan St.
Acquired: 1st-round pick in 1991 draft
(5th overall)

Background: Smith, a Detroit product, surpassed Scott Skiles as Michigan State's all-time leading scorer. He led the Big Ten in scoring as a junior and senior and set a conference record by hitting 45 consecutive free throws. He got off to a quick start with Miami before tearing cartilage in his right knee in January 1992. Although injuries cost him 15 games, Smith made the All-Rookie Team. He missed the first couple months of the 1992-93 season while recovering from a second arthroscopic surgery on his right knee. He averaged 16.0 PPG and 5.6 APG and finished tenth in the league in 3-point percentage after his return.

Strengths: Not unlike another Spartan product named Magic Johnson, Smith brings great size and court sense to the point-guard spot. In fact, he has been the tallest starting point guard in the league. He owns extraordinary passing ability and always spots the open man. Smith is an athletic rebounder from the backcourt, has great leaping ability, and hits jumpers with 3-point range. He is one of the game's best post-up guards.

Weaknesses: Smith is a below-average defensive player, just as he was in college. He's slight in build and can be out-quicked by opposing point guards. He likes to talk trash on the court. At times, that's a strength. His right knee will continue to be a concern.

Analysis: Smith does most everything with an air of confidence, and he does most everything well. Whether it's scoring, shooting, passing, or rebounding, he can take over games. He has great size, composure, and leadership, and loves taking big shots. The Heat was 10-24 without him last season. Smith is probably a healthy season away from the first of many All-Star trips.

PLAYER SUMMARY	
Will	take big shots
Can't	trade in right knee
Expect	an All-Star future
Don't Expect	tough defense
Fantasy Value	$16-19
Card Value	15-25¢

COLLEGE STATISTICS

		G	FGP	FTP	APG	PPG
87-88	MSU	28	.466	.758	4.0	10.7
88-89	MSU	33	.478	.763	6.9	17.7
89-90	MSU	31	.526	.695	7.0	20.2
90-91	MSU	30	.474	.802	6.1	25.1
Totals		122	.487	.756	6.1	18.5

NBA REGULAR-SEASON STATISTICS

				FGs		3-PT FGs		FTs		Rebounds						
		G	MIN	FG	PCT	FG	PCT	FT	PCT	OFF	TOT	AST	STL	BLK	PTS	PPG
91-92	MIA	61	1806	297	.454	40	.320	95	.748	81	188	278	59	19	729	12.0
92-93	MIA	48	1610	279	.451	53	.402	155	.787	56	197	267	50	16	766	16.0
Totals		109	3416	576	.452	93	.362	250	.772	137	385	545	109	35	1495	13.7

TONY SMITH

Team: Los Angeles Lakers
Position: Guard
Height: 6'4" **Weight:** 205
Birthdate: June 14, 1968

NBA Experience: 3 years
College: Marquette
Acquired: 2nd-round pick in 1990 draft (51st overall)

Background: As a senior, Smith set Marquette single-season records for points and scoring average, earning All-Midwestern Collegiate Conference honors. He climbed to second on the all-time school assists list and finished third in scoring. He has spent his first three pro seasons as a back-up point guard to the likes of Magic Johnson and Sedale Threatt with the Lakers. In 1992-93, he made nine starts but averaged just 1.1 APG in 55 games.

Strengths: A big scorer in college, Smith has become somewhat of a defensive specialist with the Lakers. He first proved himself at that end against Michael Jordan in the 1991 NBA Finals. He has good size, speed, and quickness to stick with his man, whether he's guarding a one or a two. Smith looks to score in addition to his passing. He can play both guard spots.

Weaknesses: While his defense has been a pleasant surprise to the Lakers, Smith has not helped his team much offensively. He's not a natural point guard in the first place, and he is not nearly the playmaker a team likes to have running the show. He has made only two 3-pointers in 29 career attempts.

Analysis: If someone would have predicted during Smith's college career that he would wind up as a defensive specialist who would struggle on offense in the NBA, it would have been written off as a joke. But the former Marquette scoring whiz is just that. He did hoist his field goal percentage last year—to a very respectable mark of .484—but he lost playing time due to the presence of rookie guard Anthony Peeler.

PLAYER SUMMARY	
Will	look to score
Can't	convert treys
Expect	defensive punch
Don't Expect	playmaking
Fantasy Value	$1
Card Value	5-10¢

COLLEGE STATISTICS

		G	FGP	FTP	APG	PPG
86-87	MARQ	29	.534	.753	2.1	8.1
87-88	MARQ	28	.523	.739	2.9	13.1
88-89	MARQ	28	.556	.730	5.6	14.2
89-90	MARQ	29	.495	.856	5.8	23.8
Totals		114	.521	.785	4.1	14.8

NBA REGULAR-SEASON STATISTICS

			FGs		3-PT FGs		FTs		Rebounds						
	G	MIN	FG	PCT	FG	PCT	FT	PCT	OFF	TOT	AST	STL	BLK	PTS	PPG
90-91 LAL	64	695	97	.441	0	.000	40	.702	24	71	135	28	12	234	3.7
91-92 LAL	63	820	113	.399	0	.000	49	.653	31	76	109	39	8	275	4.4
92-93 LAL	55	752	133	.484	2	.182	62	.756	46	87	63	50	7	330	6.0
Totals	182	2267	343	.441	2	.069	151	.706	101	234	307	117	27	839	4.6

RIK SMITS

Team: Indiana Pacers
Position: Center
Height: 7'4" **Weight:** 265
Birthdate: August 23, 1966

NBA Experience: 5 years
College: Marist
Acquired: 1st-round pick in 1988 draft (2nd overall)

Background: Smits, a two-time East Coast Athletic Conference Player of the Year at Marist, was the second overall selection in the 1988 draft. He was named to the NBA All-Rookie Team. He led the NBA in disqualifications his first two years but ranked among the leaders in field goal percentage as well. In 1992-93, he averaged 14.3 PPG in 81 starts but failed to block 100 shots for the first time in his career.

Strengths: At 7'4", Smits amazingly has the coordination, mobility, and soft touch of a small forward. He can shoot from 15 feet and in, go right or left, and is confident with either hand on hook shots in the lane. Smits has the height and anticipation to reject a lot of shots, though his BPG total is on the decline.

Weaknesses: Smits is not always assertive, and he has not become a great center because of it. He lacks the upper-body strength to keep from being pushed around inside. His rebounding totals remain an embarrassment for a player with his height (just 5.3 RPG last year), and no one 7'4" should be blocking less than a shot per outing. He commits a lot of fouls and has been slowed by tendinitis in both knees.

Analysis: Smits has many gifts you would not expect from someone his size, but he has yet to build on the success he enjoyed in his second season. His injured knees have been a big part of the problem, but his lack of consistent aggressiveness is just as much to blame.

PLAYER SUMMARY	
Will	get his points
Can't	hoard rebounds
Expect	great size, touch
Don't Expect	dominance
Fantasy Value	$7-9
Card Value	5-12¢

COLLEGE STATISTICS

		G	FGP	FTP	RPG	PPG
84-85	MAR	29	.567	.577	5.6	11.2
85-86	MAR	30	.622	.681	8.1	17.7
86-87	MAR	21	.609	.722	8.1	20.1
87-88	MAR	27	.623	.735	8.7	24.7
Totals		107	.609	.693	7.6	18.2

NBA REGULAR-SEASON STATISTICS

			FGs		3-PT FGs		FTs		Rebounds						
	G	MIN	FG	PCT	FG	PCT	FT	PCT	OFF	TOT	AST	STL	BLK	PTS	PPG
88-89 IND	82	2041	386	.517	0	.000	184	.722	185	500	70	37	151	956	11.7
89-90 IND	82	2404	515	.533	0	.000	241	.811	135	512	142	45	169	1271	15.5
90-91 IND	76	1690	342	.485	0	.000	144	.762	116	357	84	24	111	828	10.9
91-92 IND	74	1772	436	.510	0	.000	152	.789	124	417	116	29	100	1024	13.8
92-93 IND	81	2072	494	.486	0	.000	167	.732	126	432	121	27	75	1155	14.3
Totals	395	9979	2173	.507	0	.000	888	.764	686	2218	533	162	606	5234	13.3

ELMORE SPENCER

Team: Los Angeles Clippers
Position: Center
Height: 7'0" **Weight:** 270
Birthdate: December 6, 1969
NBA Experience: 1 year

College: Georgia; Connors St.;
Nevada-Las Vegas
Acquired: 1st-round pick in 1992 draft
(25th overall)

Background: Spencer starred at Booker T. Washington High School in Atlanta and averaged 12.0 PPG as a redshirt freshman at Georgia before breaking his foot 11 games into the season. He spent the next year as the nation's hottest junior college prospect while leading Connors State (Oklahoma) to the national junior college title. In just two years at Nevada-Las Vegas, Spencer set a school record for career blocked shots with 146. He was drafted 25th overall by the Clippers in the 1992 draft but saw less than seven minutes of action per game as a rookie last year.

Strengths: Spencer offers great size and a nice feel for the game. He has a soft touch inside, moves well for a big man, and is regarded as an above-average passer. He plays hard and with enthusiasm. Spencer does not try to do more than he is capable of on offense and he has loads of defensive potential. He has been an accomplished shot-blocker and will bang in the post.

Weaknesses: What the Clippers found out last year is that Spencer is not much of an offensive player. His high field goal percentage results from dunks and put-backs, not from a vast repertoire of inside moves. Spencer will make only about half of his free throws and does little from the perimeter. Last season, he was not nearly the rebounder, defender, or shot-blocker he was expected to be.

Analysis: Rookie years can be rocky, and Spencer's was just that. He rode the bench of an up-and-coming Clipper team and did not get a chance to develop his game on the pro level. He needs the work. Spencer needs to drop a few pounds and report to training camp ready to make an impact.

PLAYER SUMMARY	
Will	bang inside
Can't	shoot FTs
Expect	better days ahead
Don't Expect	a scoring machine
Fantasy Value	$1
Card Value	10-20¢

COLLEGE STATISTICS

		G	FGP	FTP	RPG	PPG
88-89	GEOR	11	.641	.500	5.3	12.0
90-91	UNLV	31	.522	.471	4.0	6.4
91-92	UNLV	28	.637	.546	8.1	14.8
Totals		70	.603	.516	5.9	10.6

NBA REGULAR-SEASON STATISTICS

		G	MIN	FGs FG	FGs PCT	3-PT FGs FG	3-PT FGs PCT	FTs FT	FTs PCT	Rebounds OFF	Rebounds TOT	AST	STL	BLK	PTS	PPG
92-93	LAC	44	280	44	.537	0	.000	16	.500	17	62	8	8	18	104	2.4
Totals		44	280	44	.537	0	.000	16	.500	17	62	8	8	18	104	2.4

FELTON SPENCER

Team: Utah Jazz
Position: Center
Height: 7'0" **Weight:** 265
Birthdate: January 5, 1968

NBA Experience: 3 years
College: Louisville
Acquired: Traded from Timberwolves for Mike Brown, 6/93

Background: Spencer ended his career at Louisville as the school's all-time leader in field goal percentage and ranked third in the nation in that category in 1989-90. He moved into the starting lineup as a senior and was one of college basketball's most improved players. Spencer earned second-team NBA All-Rookie honors in 1990-91 with Minnesota after setting club records for rebounds and blocks. His scoring average dropped in each of his two subsequent seasons despite the fact that he started 48 games last season. Over the summer, he was traded to Utah for Mike Brown.

Strengths: Spencer loves contact, has good size, and works hard. He is very strong, is solid on the boards (as a rookie, he was seventh in the league in offensive rebounds), and is a better-than-expected defender who can block shots. He plays within himself on offense.

Weaknesses: Spencer is not the kind of player who can carry a team. His range is limited to the paint, and he converts field goals at a very poor rate for a big man. He needs to develop some low-post moves and learn to find open teammates when nothing is there. He is slow on his feet and fouled out of ten games last season. Free throws are an adventure.

Analysis: Spencer is a hard worker who will give you hard-nosed, physical defense but not much else. He raised his field goal percentage by nearly 40 points last season but still fell well short of where he should be. He also failed to block at least one shot per game for the first time. Utah needs someone to replace Mark Eaton at center, but Spencer isn't the answer.

PLAYER SUMMARY

Will.............................use his strength
Can't.......................outscore his man
Expect.......................defensive effort
Don't Expect......................a standout
Fantasy Value.............................$1-3
Card Value................................10-20¢

COLLEGE STATISTICS

		G	FGP	FTP	RPG	PPG
86-87	LOU	31	.551	.492	2.7	3.8
87-88	LOU	35	.592	.640	4.2	7.4
88-89	LOU	33	.607	.733	5.1	8.2
89-90	LOU	35	.681	.716	8.5	14.9
Totals		134	.628	.676	5.2	8.7

NBA REGULAR-SEASON STATISTICS

			FGs		3-PT FGs		FTs		Rebounds						
		G	MIN	FG	PCT	FG	PCT	FT	PCT	OFF	TOT	AST	STL	BLK	PTS	PPG
90-91	MIN	81	2099	195	.512	0	.000	182	.722	272	641	25	48	121	572	7.1
91-92	MIN	61	1481	141	.426	0	.000	123	.691	167	435	53	27	79	405	6.6
92-93	MIN	71	1296	105	.465	0	.000	83	.654	134	324	17	23	66	293	4.1
Totals		213	4876	441	.470	0	.000	388	.697	573	1400	95	98	266	1270	6.0

LATRELL SPREWELL

Team: Golden State Warriors
Position: Guard/Forward
Height: 6'5" **Weight:** 190
Birthdate: September 8, 1970

NBA Experience: 1 year
College: Three Rivers; Alabama
Acquired: 1st-round pick in 1992 draft
(24th overall)

Background: Though not recruited by a Division I school, Sprewell was a first-team All-SEC selection and also made the league's all-defensive team as a senior at Alabama, when he averaged 17.8 points, 5.2 rebounds, and 1.8 steals per contest. He broke Derrick McKey's school record for minutes in a season and set another school mark by hitting seven 3-pointers in a row. He was drafted 24th overall by Golden State and made 69 starts as a rookie last year. He led the Warriors in steals, averaged 15.4 PPG, and earned a spot on the All-Rookie second team.

Strengths: Sprewell is a legitimate stopper who has long arms to go along with great quickness and instincts. He can run and jump with virtually anyone in the league and matches up at three positions. He is also a much better offensive player than anticipated. He is a good outside shooter with 3-point range, can spot up or work for his own shots, and led all rookies with 3.8 APG. His attitude and toughness are admirable.

Weaknesses: Sprewell is not a great ball-handler or distributor despite the assist numbers, although he is clearly capable. He turned the ball over more than 200 times last season. He's an explosive player; now he needs to become a little more consistent.

Analysis: Sprewell did not play organized basketball until his senior year of high school, but he has come a long way since. He makes an impact on both ends of the court. Don Nelson liked him so much that he put the rookie in the opening-day starting lineup, where he remained most of the year. If Sprewell continues to develop, there's no reason to believe he will not become a star.

PLAYER SUMMARY	
Will	challenge his man
Can't	be left open
Expect	explosive play
Don't Expect	poor shooting
Fantasy Value	$14-17
Card Value	25-50¢

COLLEGE STATISTICS

		G	FGP	FTP	RPG	PPG
90-91	ALA	33	.511	.690	5.0	8.9
91-92	ALA	35	.493	.771	5.2	17.8
Totals		68	.499	.740	5.1	13.5

NBA REGULAR-SEASON STATISTICS

			FGs		3-PT FGs		FTs		Rebounds						
	G	MIN	FG	PCT	FG	PCT	FT	PCT	OFF	TOT	AST	STL	BLK	PTS	PPG
92-93 GS	77	2741	449	.464	73	.369	211	.746	79	271	295	126	52	1182	15.4
Totals	77	2741	449	.464	73	.369	211	.746	79	271	295	126	52	1182	15.4

JOHN STARKS

Team: New York Knicks
Position: Guard
Height: 6'5" **Weight:** 185
Birthdate: August 10, 1965
NBA Experience: 4 years

College: Northern Oklahoma;
Oklahoma St.
Acquired: Signed as a free agent,
10/90

Background: Starks is a product of four colleges in four years, including Oklahoma State as a senior (1987-88). He signed on with Golden State as a free agent but a back injury ended his rookie season prematurely. After the Warriors cut him loose, he became a CBA All-Star with Cedar Rapids. He also played for Memphis in the WBL before reporting to the Knicks' camp in 1990. Starks was a reserve in his first year in New York before breaking through during the 1991-92 season. Last year, he led the team in 3-pointers and was second in scoring.

Strengths: Starks jump-starts the Knicks with his competitive fire, long-range shooting, and outstanding defense. He has made 202 3-pointers over the last two years. He finds open men and is also strong enough and quick enough to penetrate. He wreaks havoc defensively with his supreme quickness and get-out-of-my-face attitude.

Weaknesses: Starks can play out of control and is prone to launching wild shots. He commits nearly as many fouls as his team's bruising big men. He has earned a reputation as a hot head. Three times last year he was fined at least $5,000, including once for head-butting Reggie Miller in the playoffs.

Analysis: Starks, who worked at a grocery store before gaining success in pro basketball, has been a sparkplug for the Knicks. He has been in and out of Pat Riley's doghouse for his combativeness, but there is no denying the impact he makes with his shooting, defense, and will to win. He's the kind of player you want on your side.

PLAYER SUMMARY	
Will	bury clutch shots
Can't	control emotions
Expect	disruptive defense
Don't Expect	backing down
Fantasy Value	$10-13
Card Value	12-20¢

COLLEGE STATISTICS

		G	FGP	FTP	RPG	PPG
84-85	NOK	14	.463	.774	2.4	11.1
87-88	OSU	30	.497	.838	4.7	15.4
Totals		44	.487	.820	4.0	14.0

NBA REGULAR-SEASON STATISTICS

				FGs		3-PT FGs		FTs		Rebounds						
		G	MIN	FG	PCT	FG	PCT	FT	PCT	OFF	TOT	AST	STL	BLK	PTS	PPG
88-89	GS	36	316	51	.408	10	.385	34	.654	15	41	27	23	3	146	4.1
90-91	NY	61	1173	180	.439	27	.290	79	.752	30	131	204	59	17	466	7.6
91-92	NY	82	2118	405	.449	94	.348	235	.778	45	191	276	103	18	1139	13.9
92-93	NY	80	2477	513	.428	108	.321	263	.795	54	204	404	91	12	1397	17.5
Totals		259	6084	1149	.436	239	.330	611	.773	144	567	911	276	50	3148	12.2

LARRY STEWART

Team: Washington Bullets
Position: Forward
Height: 6'8" **Weight:** 220
Birthdate: September 21, 1968

NBA Experience: 2 years
College: Coppin St.
Acquired: Signed as a free agent, 9/91

Background: Stewart attended Dobbins Tech, the same Philadelphia high school that produced Lionel Simmons, Hank Gathers, and Bo Kimble. He starred for three years at Coppin State and won the 1991 McClendon Trophy, presented to the top player at an historically black college or university. He was a two-time Mid-Eastern Athletic Conference Player of the Year and finished his career as Coppin State's all-time rebounding king. Although he was not drafted in 1991, Stewart earned second-team All-Rookie honors with the Bullets. He played in 81 games last year, averaging 9.8 PPG and 4.7 RPG.

Strengths: Stewart is a great athlete who supplements his natural ability with tremendous desire. He's not afraid to battle in the paint against much bigger players. He is especially productive on the offensive glass and in transition. He doesn't take bad shots and shows nice touch around the bucket. He finished ninth in field goal percentage last year with his 54.3-percent shooting.

Weaknesses: A little undersized to be playing in the paint, Stewart is not able to overpower players like he did in college. He does not shoot with enough range or handle the ball well enough to make a living on the perimeter. In fact, he turns it over more often than he gets an assist. Stewart is no better than average as a rebounder.

Analysis: Stewart will not be a star, but his first two seasons have caused many to wonder why he was not drafted. His work ethic is contagious and has made him a favorite of coach Wes Unseld. He accepts his role and thrives in it. His numbers declined slightly in his second season and he could stand to develop more confidence away from the basket.

PLAYER SUMMARY	
Will	battle inside
Can't	shoot with range
Expect	high FG pct.
Don't Expect	15 PPG
Fantasy Value	$2-4
Card Value	8-15¢

COLLEGE STATISTICS

		G	FGP	FTP	RPG	PPG
88-89	CSC	28	.659	.691	10.0	17.6
89-90	CSC	33	.645	.701	11.2	18.7
90-91	CSC	30	.635	.785	13.4	23.9
Totals		91	.646	.737	11.6	20.0

NBA REGULAR-SEASON STATISTICS

			FGs		3-PT FGs		FTs		Rebounds						
		G	MIN	FG	PCT	FG	PCT	FT	PCT	OFF	TOT	AST	STL	BLK	PTS	PPG
91-92	WAS	76	2229	303	.514	0	.000	188	.807	186	449	120	51	44	794	10.4
92-93	WAS	81	1823	306	.543	0	.000	184	.727	154	383	146	47	29	796	9.8
Totals		157	4052	609	.528	0	.000	372	.765	340	832	266	98	73	1590	10.1

BRYANT STITH

Team: Denver Nuggets
Position: Guard
Height: 6'5" **Weight:** 210
Birthdate: December 10, 1970

NBA Experience: 1 year
College: Virginia
Acquired: 1st-round pick in 1992 draft (13th overall)

Background: Without much national fanfare, Stith was named All-ACC three consecutive seasons and led Virginia to the 1992 NIT championship as tournament MVP. He finished his career as the Cavaliers' all-time leader in scoring, minutes, and free throws made. The MVP of the 1992 pre-draft Orlando Classic, he was taken 13th overall by Denver. A broken foot and broken hand limited his rookie season to 39 games. He started 12 of those contests and averaged 8.9 PPG.

Strengths: Stith is a streak shooter who can get on a roll. He was deadly from all over the court in college and loves taking the big shot. He hit more than his share at Virginia. Coaches also love the intangibles he brings to the floor. He offers smarts and toughness, moves well without the ball, and is a winner. Stith will run the court and work hard at the defensive end.

Weaknesses: While Stith seems to present the total package, he does not stand out in any one aspect of his game. He will not startle NBA defenders with his ball-handling, passing, or quickness. The same goes for his defense. He'll get mired in his share of shooting slumps and does not seem to have NBA 3-point range. Nothing about his game is flashy.

Analysis: Consider the first half of the upcoming season the conclusion of Stith's rookie year. He broke his right foot early last season when he landed on teammate Dikembe Mutombo's foot and then ended the year early when he broke his hand April 4. While active, however, Stith showed he can put the ball in the basket like he did in college. Look for him to become a solid double-figure scorer with the Nuggets.

PLAYER SUMMARY

Will ....play with smarts
Can't ....star in one area
Expect ....double-figure points
Don't Expect................anything fancy
Fantasy Value..................................$5-7
Card Value ....10-20¢

COLLEGE STATISTICS

		G	FGP	FTP	RPG	PPG
88-89	VA	33	.548	.769	6.5	15.5
89-90	VA	32	.481	.777	6.9	20.8
90-91	VA	33	.471	.791	6.2	19.8
91-92	VA	33	.452	.815	6.6	20.7
Totals		131	.483	.789	6.6	19.2

NBA REGULAR-SEASON STATISTICS

			FGs		3-PT FGs		FTs		Rebounds						
	G	MIN	FG	PCT	FG	PCT	FT	PCT	OFF	TOT	AST	STL	BLK	PTS	PPG
92-93 DEN	39	865	124	.446	0	.000	99	.832	39	124	49	24	5	347	8.9
Totals	39	865	124	.446	0	.000	99	.832	39	124	49	24	5	347	8.9

JOHN STOCKTON

Team: Utah Jazz
Position: Guard
Height: 6'1" **Weight:** 175
Birthdate: March 26, 1962

NBA Experience: 9 years
College: Gonzaga
Acquired: 1st-round pick in 1984 draft
(16th overall)

Background: Stockton led the West Coast Athletic Conference in points as a senior at Gonzaga, and in assists and steals as a sophomore, junior, and senior. He broke into Utah's starting lineup in 1986-87 and began shattering NBA assist records. He is the first player in history to record five straight seasons of 1,000 or more assists. He holds the single-season record and has led the league six straight times. He has played in five consecutive All-Star Games and was a 1992 Olympic gold-medalist.

Strengths: Stockton is the best playmaker in basketball. He is quick and masterful with the ball, with an uncanny ability to take it to the hole and create easy shots for teammates. He gets into the lane for his own scores as well. He is also a great shooter. He hits the 3-pointer, plays defense, and makes few mistakes.

Weaknesses: About the only thing Stockton does not do is crash the boards, but he's not asked to. Larger opponents can shoot over him.

Analysis: Stockton is one of the premier guards in the league—and certainly its best distributor. He makes everyone on his team look better and he has made himself look pretty good along the way. Last year, he became the fourth player to record 8,000 career assists and the third to reach 1,800 steals.

PLAYER SUMMARY

Will....................set career assist mark
Can't.................................be left open
Expect ....masterful playmaking
Don't Expect.................All-Star snubs
Fantasy Value............................$45-50
Card Value ....20-35¢

COLLEGE STATISTICS

		G	FGP	FTP	APG	PPG
80-81	GONZ	25	.578	.743	1.4	3.1
81-82	GONZ	27	.576	.676	5.0	11.2
82-83	GONZ	27	.518	.791	6.8	13.9
83-84	GONZ	28	.577	.692	7.2	20.9
Totals		107	.559	.719	5.2	12.5

NBA REGULAR-SEASON STATISTICS

		G	MIN	FGs FG	FGs PCT	3-PT FGs FG	3-PT FGs PCT	FTs FT	FTs PCT	Rebounds OFF	Rebounds TOT	AST	STL	BLK	PTS	PPG
84-85	UTA	82	1490	157	.471	2	.182	142	.736	26	105	415	109	11	458	5.6
85-86	UTA	82	1935	228	.489	2	.133	172	.839	33	179	610	157	10	630	7.7
86-87	UTA	82	1858	231	.499	7	.184	179	.782	32	151	670	177	14	648	7.9
87-88	UTA	82	2842	454	.574	24	.358	272	.840	54	237	1128	242	16	1204	14.7
88-89	UTA	82	3171	497	.538	16	.242	390	.863	83	248	1118	263	14	1400	17.1
89-90	UTA	78	2915	472	.514	47	.416	354	.819	57	206	1134	207	18	1345	17.2
90-91	UTA	82	3103	496	.507	58	.345	363	.836	46	237	1164	234	16	1413	17.2
91-92	UTA	82	3002	453	.482	83	.407	308	.842	68	270	1126	244	22	1297	15.8
92-93	UTA	82	2863	437	.486	72	.385	293	.798	64	237	987	199	21	1239	15.1
Totals		734	23179	3425	.510	311	.358	2473	.824	463	1870	8352	1832	142	9634	13.1

ROD STRICKLAND

Team: Portland Trail Blazers
Position: Guard
Height: 6'3" **Weight:** 185
Birthdate: July 11, 1966

NBA Experience: 5 years
College: DePaul
Acquired: Signed as a free agent, 7/92

Background: Strickland left DePaul for the pros a year early, but not before he led the Blue Demons in scoring, assists, and steals as a junior and climbed among the school's career leaders in each category. He was a back-up point guard with New York as a rookie before a trade for Maurice Cheeks made him a starter in San Antonio. He led the Spurs in assists in 1990-91 and 1991-92 before signing as a free agent with Portland. He started 35 games last year, leading the Blazers in assists and finishing fourth in scoring.

Strengths: Few players penetrate with the ease and frequency of Strickland, whose nifty ball-handling and great quickness allow him to get past even the best defenders. He hits acrobatic shots off his drives and is a fine passer on the move. Strickland is outstanding in transition and is a good on-the-ball defender when he wants to be.

Weaknesses: Strickland has had some off-court slip-ups and earned a reputation as a troublemaker in New York and San Antonio. He still is not completely confident in his perimeter jumper and is not an accurate 3-point or free throw shooter.

Analysis: Strickland was a great pick-up for Portland. He admits to having made mistakes in the past, and he shed his label as a troublemaker while giving the team a spark off the bench for most of last season. His scoring and passing skills complement one another and his quickness gives Portland an extra dimension.

PLAYER SUMMARY

Will	drive and dish
Can't	rely on jumper
Expect	great quickness
Don't Expect	high FT pct.
Fantasy Value	$19-22
Card Value	8-12¢

COLLEGE STATISTICS

		G	FGP	FTP	APG	PPG
85-86	DeP	31	.497	.675	5.1	14.1
86-87	DeP	30	.582	.606	6.5	16.3
87-88	DeP	26	.528	.606	7.8	20.0
Totals		87	.534	.626	6.4	16.6

NBA REGULAR-SEASON STATISTICS

		G	MIN	FGs		3-PT FGs		FTs		Rebounds						
				FG	PCT	FG	PCT	FT	PCT	OFF	TOT	AST	STL	BLK	PTS	PPG
88-89	NY	81	1358	265	.467	19	.322	172	.745	51	160	319	98	3	721	8.9
89-90	NY/SA	82	2140	343	.454	8	.267	174	.626	90	259	468	127	14	868	10.6
90-91	SA	58	2076	314	.482	11	.333	161	.763	57	219	463	117	11	800	13.8
91-92	SA	57	2053	300	.455	5	.333	182	.687	92	265	491	118	17	787	13.8
92-93	POR	78	2474	396	.485	4	.133	273	.717	120	337	559	131	24	1069	13.7
Totals		356	10101	1618	.469	47	.281	962	.704	410	1240	2300	591	69	4245	11.9

ISIAH THOMAS

Team: Detroit Pistons
Position: Guard
Height: 6'1" **Weight:** 185
Birthdate: April 30, 1961

NBA Experience: 12 years
College: Indiana
Acquired: 1st-round pick in 1981 draft (2nd overall)

Background: Thomas was the leader of Indiana's 1981 national championship team as a sophomore. He declared for the draft as an underclassman and was selected by Detroit with the second overall pick. An All-Star every year he's been in the league, Isiah captured All-Star MVP honors in 1984 and '86. He guided the Pistons to back-to-back world championships in 1989 and '90, and he ranks among the league's all-time leaders in assists and steals.

Strengths: Thomas has been called the best little man in NBA history. There's not another 6'1" player in basketball who has been able to take over games like Zeke. A superb ball-handler and passer, Thomas still drives and dishes with the best of them and can score in traffic. He hits jumpers with 3-point range.

Weaknesses: Thomas is often among the league leaders in turnovers and he's been known to take ill-advised shots. His shooting is streaky. Last season was his worst shooting year as a pro.

Analysis: A can't-miss Hall of Famer, Thomas is one of the greatest guards in NBA history. His best days are behind him, but that won't stop Thomas from trying to return the Pistons to the playoffs. He's a winner.

PLAYER SUMMARY	
Will	enter Hall of Fame
Can't	regain peak form
Expect	clutch scoring
Don't Expect	another title
Fantasy Value	$9-11
Card Value	10-15¢

COLLEGE STATISTICS

		G	FGP	FTP	APG	PPG
79-80	IND	29	.510	.772	5.5	14.6
80-81	IND	34	.554	.742	5.8	16.0
Totals		63	.534	.756	5.7	15.4

NBA REGULAR-SEASON STATISTICS

		G	MIN	FGs FG	PCT	3-PT FGs FG	PCT	FTs FT	PCT	Rebounds OFF	TOT	AST	STL	BLK	PTS	PPG
81-82	DET	72	2433	453	.424	17	.288	302	.704	57	209	565	150	17	1225	17.0
82-83	DET	81	3093	725	.472	36	.288	368	.710	105	328	634	199	29	1854	22.9
83-84	DET	82	3007	669	.462	22	.338	388	.733	103	327	914	204	33	1748	21.3
84-85	DET	81	3089	646	.458	29	.257	399	.809	114	361	1123	187	25	1720	21.2
85-86	DET	77	2790	609	.488	26	.310	365	.790	83	277	830	171	20	1609	20.9
86-87	DET	81	3013	626	.463	19	.194	400	.768	82	319	813	153	20	1671	20.6
87-88	DET	81	2927	621	.463	30	.309	305	.774	64	278	678	141	17	1577	19.5
88-89	DET	80	2924	569	.464	33	.273	287	.818	49	273	663	133	20	1458	18.2
89-90	DET	81	2993	579	.438	42	.309	292	.775	74	308	765	139	19	1492	18.4
90-91	DET	48	1657	289	.435	19	.292	179	.782	35	160	446	75	10	776	16.2
91-92	DET	78	2918	564	.446	25	.291	292	.772	68	247	560	118	15	1445	18.5
92-93	DET	79	2922	526	.418	61	.308	278	.737	71	232	671	123	18	1391	17.6
Totals		921	33766	6876	.454	359	.288	3855	.762	905	3319	8662	1793	243	17966	19.5

LaSALLE THOMPSON

Team: Indiana Pacers
Position: Forward
Height: 6'10" **Weight:** 260
Birthdate: June 23, 1961
NBA Experience: 11 years

College: Texas
Acquired: Traded from Kings with Randy Wittman for Wayman Tisdale and a future 2nd-round pick, 2/89

Background: Thompson left Texas after his junior year and was drafted No. 5 overall by Kansas City in 1982. He spent more than six seasons with the Kings in K.C. and Sacramento. He ranked among the franchise's all-time leaders in games, rebounds, blocked shots, and field goal percentage. In 1989, he was shipped to Indiana in the Wayman Tisdale deal. He was the Pacers' second-leading rebounder for two straight years before the last two seasons, during which his playing time and numbers declined.

Strengths: Thompson's primary strength is crashing the boards. The former NCAA rebounding champ has a massive frame, huge hands, and good timing. Thompson is a strong low-post defender who can play power forward or center.

Weaknesses: Thompson doesn't often look for scoring opportunities. He also commits a lot of fouls and lacks quickness. The biggest knock on him throughout his career has been his inconsistency. He does not always show up.

Analysis: Thompson has made a decent NBA living with his rebounding, interior defense, and ability to fill in at two positions. He has never been an integral part of the Indiana offense and does not look to be a major player as he enters his final years.

PLAYER SUMMARY	
Will	play defense
Can't	burn up the nets
Expect	limited minutes
Don't Expect	consistency
Fantasy Value	$0
Card Value	5-10¢

COLLEGE STATISTICS

		G	FGP	FTP	RPG	PPG
79-80	TEX	30	.558	.748	9.7	12.8
80-81	TEX	30	.572	.728	12.3	19.2
81-82	TEX	27	.528	.677	13.5	18.6
Totals		87	.553	.713	11.8	16.8

NBA REGULAR-SEASON STATISTICS

			FGs		3-PT FGs		FTs		Rebounds						
		G	MIN	FG	PCT	FG	PCT	FT	PCT	OFF	TOT	AST	STL	BLK	PTS	PPG
82-83	KC	71	987	147	.512	0	.000	89	.650	133	375	33	40	61	383	5.4
83-84	KC	80	1915	333	.523	0	.000	160	.717	260	709	86	71	145	826	10.3
84-85	KC	82	2458	369	.531	0	.000	227	.721	274	854	130	98	128	965	11.8
85-86	SAC	80	2377	411	.518	0	.000	202	.732	252	770	168	71	109	1024	12.8
86-87	SAC	82	2166	362	.481	0	.000	188	.737	237	687	122	69	126	912	11.1
87-88	SAC	69	1257	238	.471	2	.400	118	.720	138	427	68	54	73	550	8.0
88-89	SAC/IND	76	2329	416	.489	0	.000	227	.808	224	718	81	79	94	1059	13.9
89-90	IND	82	2126	223	.473	1	.200	107	.799	175	630	106	65	71	554	6.8
90-91	IND	82	1946	276	.488	1	.200	72	.692	154	563	147	63	63	625	7.6
91-92	IND	80	1299	168	.463	0	.000	58	.817	98	381	102	52	34	394	4.9
92-93	IND	63	730	104	.488	0	.000	29	.744	55	178	34	29	24	237	3.8
Totals		847	19590	3024	.497	4	.154	1477	.739	2000	6292	1077	691	928	7529	8.9

OTIS THORPE

Team: Houston Rockets
Position: Forward
Height: 6'10" **Weight:** 245
Birthdate: August 5, 1962
NBA Experience: 9 years

College: Providence
Acquired: Traded from Kings for Rodney McCray and Jim Petersen, 10/88

Background: Thorpe left Providence with the all-time Big East record for rebounds and was a consensus all-conference selection as a senior. He started his pro career with the Kings, where he began a streak of starts that did not end until last season, his fourth in Houston. He played in the 1992 All-Star Game. Thorpe was second in the NBA in field goal accuracy two years ago and fifth last season. His 12.8 PPG in 1992-93 was his lowest average since his second year.

Strengths: Thorpe gives a team steady rebounding and is especially productive on the offensive glass. He uses his muscular frame to bang in the post. The same goes for his interior defense. Thorpe runs the floor, handles the ball, dunks, and does not take unwise shots.

Weaknesses: Thorpe is not among the most polished low-post players in the league. He gets his points off the pick-and-roll and by going to the offensive boards. He also commits a lot of fouls and is a horrible free throw shooter.

Analysis: You know what you'll get from Thorpe on a nightly basis. He'll score in double figures, ignite the transition game, and battle on the boards for eight to ten rebounds an outing. You can also count on good defense and a great attitude. He's one of the better power forwards in the league.

PLAYER SUMMARY	
Will	dunk in transition
Can't	make FTs
Expect	defense, rebounds
Don't Expect	outside shots
Fantasy Value	$8-10
Card Value	8-12¢

COLLEGE STATISTICS

		G	FGP	FTP	RPG	PPG
80-81	PROV	26	.515	.658	5.3	9.6
81-82	PROV	27	.541	.643	8.0	14.1
82-83	PROV	31	.636	.659	8.0	16.1
83-84	PROV	29	.580	.653	10.3	17.1
Totals		113	.575	.653	8.0	14.4

NBA REGULAR-SEASON STATISTICS

				FGs		3-PT FGs		FTs		Rebounds						
		G	MIN	FG	PCT	FG	PCT	FT	PCT	OFF	TOT	AST	STL	BLK	PTS	PPG
84-85	KC	82	1918	411	.600	0	.000	230	.620	187	556	111	34	37	1052	12.8
85-86	SAC	75	1675	289	.587	0	.000	164	.661	137	420	84	35	34	742	9.9
86-87	SAC	82	2956	567	.540	0	.000	413	.761	259	819	201	46	60	1547	18.9
87-88	SAC	82	3072	622	.507	0	.000	460	.755	279	837	266	62	56	1704	20.8
88-89	HOU	82	3135	521	.542	0	.000	328	.729	272	787	202	82	37	1370	16.7
89-90	HOU	82	2947	547	.548	0	.000	307	.688	258	734	261	66	24	1401	17.1
90-91	HOU	82	3039	549	.556	3	.429	334	.696	287	846	197	73	20	1435	17.5
91-92	HOU	82	3056	558	.592	0	.000	304	.657	285	862	250	52	37	1420	17.3
92-93	HOU	72	2357	385	.558	0	.000	153	.598	219	589	181	43	19	923	12.8
Totals		721	24155	4449	.554	3	.077	2693	.697	2183	6450	1753	493	324	11594	16.1

SEDALE THREATT

Team: Los Angeles Lakers
Position: Guard
Height: 6'2" **Weight:** 185
Birthdate: September 10, 1961
NBA Experience: 10 years

College: West Virginia Tech
Acquired: Traded from SuperSonics for 2nd-round picks in 1994, 1995, and 1996, 10/91

Background: Threatt was an NAIA All-American at West Virginia Tech, where he finished his career as the school's all-time scoring leader. Threatt, originally a sixth-round draft pick by Philadelphia, played seven NBA seasons before becoming a double-digit scorer with Seattle. He was acquired by the Lakers for three draft picks in October 1991 as a back-up for Magic Johnson, but he ended up becoming the team's floor leader after Johnson's retirement. He averaged 15.1 PPG for the second consecutive season in 1992-93.

Strengths: Threatt is one of the league's purest shooters. He is at his best when spotting up off the break. He developed into a solid floor leader after being thrust into that role in L.A. Threatt has been among the league's top 20 in steals and assists in both years with the Lakers. He can defend virtually any guard.

Weaknesses: Threatt does not dribble and shoot as well as he catches and shoots. He's still more natural at off guard than at the point.

Analysis: Threatt has had the unenviable task of trying to replace Magic, and he has done it as well as anyone could have expected. He will never be among the premier point guards in the game, but he has arguably been the Lakers' best player since arriving.

PLAYER SUMMARY	
Will	spot up for jumpers
Can't	create like Magic
Expect	quickness, 15 PPG
Don't Expect	slack defense
Fantasy Value	$10-13
Card Value	5-12¢

COLLEGE STATISTICS

		G	FGP	FTP	APG	PPG
79-80	WVAT	28	.481	.714	3.9	17.8
80-81	WVAT	31	.452	.712	5.7	17.7
81-82	WVAT	34	.500	.729	5.9	22.2
82-83	WVAT	27	.557	.732	6.7	25.5
Totals		120	.498	.724	5.5	20.7

NBA REGULAR-SEASON STATISTICS

		G	MIN	FG	PCT	FG	PCT	FT	PCT	OFF	TOT	AST	STL	BLK	PTS	PPG
83-84	PHI	45	464	62	.419	1	.125	23	.821	17	40	41	13	2	148	3.3
84-85	PHI	82	1304	188	.452	4	.182	66	.733	21	99	175	80	16	446	5.4
85-86	PHI	70	1754	310	.453	1	.042	75	.833	21	121	193	93	5	696	9.9
86-87	PHI/CHI	68	1446	239	.448	7	.219	95	.798	26	108	259	74	13	580	8.5
87-88	CHI/SEA	71	1055	216	.508	3	.111	57	.803	23	88	160	60	8	492	6.9
88-89	SEA	63	1220	235	.494	11	.367	63	.818	31	117	238	83	4	544	8.6
89-90	SEA	65	1481	303	.506	8	.250	130	.828	43	115	216	65	8	744	11.4
90-91	SEA	80	2066	433	.519	10	.286	137	.792	25	99	273	113	8	1013	12.7
91-92	LAL	82	3070	509	.489	20	.323	202	.831	43	253	593	168	16	1240	15.1
92-93	LAL	82	2893	522	.508	14	.264	177	.823	47	273	564	142	11	1235	15.1
Totals		708	16753	3017	.488	79	.243	1025	.812	297	1313	2712	891	91	7138	10.1

WAYMAN TISDALE

Team: Sacramento Kings
Position: Forward
Height: 6'9" **Weight:** 260
Birthdate: June 9, 1964
NBA Experience: 8 years

College: Oklahoma
Acquired: Traded from Pacers with a 1990 2nd-round pick for LaSalle Thompson and Randy Wittman, 2/89

Background: At Oklahoma, Tisdale became the first player in college basketball history to be named first-team All-America in his first three seasons. He led the 1984 gold-medal-winning U.S. Olympic team in rebounds and finished his college career with 17 school records and nine Big Eight marks. He was an All-Rookie selection with Indiana before coming into his own as Sacramento's top scorer. He started 75 games last season, his most in three years, and led the Kings in total rebounds.

Strengths: Tisdale is an accomplished low-post scorer who gets his shots off despite his relatively small size. His offensive arsenal includes a variety of twisting moves in the lane and a consistent short-range jumper.

Weaknesses: Defense is not in Tisdale's vocabulary. His size does not serve him well on that end of the court and he expends a lot of energy on offense. He does not pass well out of double-teams and does not have great range on his shot. He fouled out of eight games last year.

Analysis: Tisdale is a solid scorer and decent rebounder who has been immensely valuable to the Kings, but the All-Star future some had planned for him does not appear to be in the cards. He is no longer Sacramento's top attraction. Tisdale will get his points inside and will shoot for a high percentage.

PLAYER SUMMARY	
Will	score inside
Can't	attain stardom
Expect	15-plus PPG
Don't Expect	spirited defense
Fantasy Value	$10-13
Card Value	8-12¢

COLLEGE STATISTICS

		G	FGP	FTP	RPG	PPG
82-83	OKLA	33	.580	.635	10.3	24.5
83-84	OKLA	34	.577	.640	9.7	27.0
84-85	OKLA	37	.578	.703	10.2	25.2
Totals		104	.578	.661	10.1	25.6

NBA REGULAR-SEASON STATISTICS

				FGs		3-PT FGs		FTs		Rebounds						
		G	MIN	FG	PCT	FG	PCT	FT	PCT	OFF	TOT	AST	STL	BLK	PTS	PPG
85-86	IND	81	2277	516	.515	0	.000	160	.684	191	584	79	32	44	1192	14.7
86-87	IND	81	2159	458	.513	0	.000	258	.709	217	475	117	50	26	1174	14.5
87-88	IND	79	2378	511	.512	0	.000	246	.783	168	491	103	54	34	1268	16.1
88-89	IND/SAC	79	2434	532	.514	0	.000	317	.773	187	609	128	55	52	1381	17.5
89-90	SAC	79	2937	726	.525	0	.000	306	.783	185	595	108	54	54	1758	22.3
90-91	SAC	33	1116	262	.483	0	.000	136	.800	75	253	66	23	28	660	20.0
91-92	SAC	72	2521	522	.500	0	.000	151	.763	135	469	106	55	79	1195	16.6
92-93	SAC	76	2283	544	.509	0	.000	175	.758	127	500	108	52	47	1263	16.6
Totals		580	18105	4071	.511	0	.000	1749	.756	1285	3976	815	375	364	9891	17.1

TOM TOLBERT

Team: Orlando Magic
Position: Forward
Height: 6'8" **Weight:** 240
Birthdate: October 16, 1965

NBA Experience: 5 years
College: Cal.-Irvine; Cerritos; Arizona
Acquired: Signed as a free agent, 11/92

Background: Tolbert played college basketball at Cal.-Irvine (ten games), Cerritos College, and finally the University of Arizona, where he teamed with fellow NBA players Sean Elliott, Steve Kerr, and Jud Buechler on a Final Four squad. He played 14 games with Charlotte as a rookie before spending the rest of 1988-89 playing in the Canary Islands. He landed with the Warriors in 1989-90 and became a key role-player. He was injured for much of the 1991-92 season but bounced back last year in Orlando, where he made 61 starts and averaged 8.1 PPG.

Strengths: Tolbert is aggressive on the boards and owns a decent perimeter game, although he is not on the roster for his offense. He is not afraid to go after the ball or set hard picks, and he plays physical defense against bigger men. Tolbert plays both forward spots, handles the ball well, and can hit the 3-pointer.

Weaknesses: Judging by athletic ability, you would never imagine Tolbert making it in the NBA. He is not quick, does not jump to the moon, and is undersized for a power forward at this level. He does not own a low-post game and he is not much of a passer.

Analysis: Tolbert is not your prototypical power forward, but the man has continued to find playing time despite his physical limitations. The Magic signed him early last year as a back-up when Brian Williams and Terry Catledge were sidelined, but his hard work kept him in the starting five for most of the year.

PLAYER SUMMARY

Will	bang the boards
Can't	outjump his man
Expect	inspired defense
Don't Expect	a primary scorer
Fantasy Value	$1
Card Value	5-12¢

COLLEGE STATISTICS

		G	FGP	FTP	RPG	PPG
83-84	C-I	4	.750	.000	0.3	1.5
84-85	C-I	6	.316	.800	2.0	2.7
85-86	CERR	32	.613	.680	7.8	16.2
86-87	ARIZ	30	.511	.705	6.2	13.9
87-88	ARIZ	38	.547	.812	5.8	14.1
Totals		110	.556	.743	6.1	13.6

NBA REGULAR-SEASON STATISTICS

		G	MIN	FGs FG	FGs PCT	3-PT FGs FG	3-PT FGs PCT	FTs FT	FTs PCT	Rebounds OFF	Rebounds TOT	AST	STL	BLK	PTS	PPG
88-89	CHA	14	117	17	.459	0	.000	6	.500	7	21	7	2	4	40	2.9
89-90	GS	70	1347	218	.493	5	.278	175	.726	122	363	58	23	25	616	8.8
90-91	GS	62	1371	183	.423	7	.333	127	.738	87	275	76	35	38	500	8.1
91-92	GS	35	310	33	.384	2	.250	22	.550	14	55	21	10	6	90	2.6
92-93	ORL	72	1838	226	.498	9	.321	122	.726	133	412	91	33	21	583	8.1
Totals		253	4983	677	.466	23	.295	452	.714	363	1126	253	103	94	1829	7.2

TRENT TUCKER

Team: Chicago Bulls
Position: Guard
Height: 6'5" **Weight:** 195
Birthdate: December 20, 1959

NBA Experience: 11 years
College: Minnesota
Acquired: Signed as a free agent, 10/92

Background: Tucker teamed with Kevin McHale for two seasons as a standout at the University of Minnesota. He was taken sixth by the Knicks in the 1982 draft and played nine seasons in New York. His most productive year was in 1986-87, when he averaged 11.4 PPG. He made more than 500 3-pointers for the Knicks before playing 24 games with San Antonio in 1991-92 and then signing with Chicago last year. Tucker was third on the Bulls with 52 treys.

Strengths: Few in the league have been as reliable as Tucker at knocking down open 3-pointers. He finished 15th in the league in 3-point percentage (.397) in limited minutes last season. Tucker is smart, plays sound position defense, doesn't turn the ball over, and knows his role on the team.

Weaknesses: The spot-up jumper is about the only shot left in Tucker's arsenal. He does not drive to the hoop and is not much help in the areas of passing, playmaking, etc. He won't get many rebounds.

Analysis: Tucker has enjoyed a solid but unheralded NBA career as an accurate marksman. You never want to leave him open because he can still bury those long-range jumpers, but his best scoring days are behind him.

PLAYER SUMMARY	
Will	hit open treys
Can't	get his own shots
Expect	role-playing, smarts
Don't Expect	a starting job
Fantasy Value	$0
Card Value	5-10¢

COLLEGE STATISTICS

		G	FGP	FTP	RPG	PPG
78-79	MINN	25	.477	.594	3.4	9.9
79-80	MINN	32	.490	.739	3.2	10.6
80-81	MINN	29	.517	.812	3.5	14.8
81-82	MINN	29	.504	.822	3.6	14.8
Totals		115	.499	.772	3.4	12.6

NBA REGULAR-SEASON STATISTICS

		G	MIN	FGs FG	FGs PCT	3-PT FGs FG	3-PT FGs PCT	FTs FT	FTs PCT	Rebounds OFF	Rebounds TOT	AST	STL	BLK	PTS	PPG
82-83	NY	78	1830	299	.462	14	.467	43	.672	75	216	195	56	6	655	8.4
83-84	NY	63	1228	225	.500	6	.375	25	.758	43	130	138	63	8	481	7.6
84-85	NY	77	1819	293	.483	29	.403	38	.792	74	188	199	75	15	653	8.5
85-86	NY	77	1788	349	.472	41	.451	79	.790	70	192	65	8	818	10.6
86-87	NY	70	1691	325	.470	68	.422	77	.762	49	135	166	116	13	795	11.4
87-88	NY	71	1248	193	.424	69	.413	51	.718	32	119	117	53	6	506	7.1
88-89	NY	81	1824	263	.454	118	.399	43	.782	55	176	132	88	6	687	8.5
89-90	NY	81	1725	253	.417	95	.388	66	.767	57	174	173	74	8	667	8.2
90-91	NY	65	1194	191	.440	64	.418	17	.630	33	105	111	44	9	463	7.1
91-92	SA	24	415	60	.465	19	.396	16	.800	8	37	27	21	3	155	6.5
92-93	CHI	69	909	143	.485	52	.397	18	.818	16	71	82	24	6	356	5.2
Totals		756	15671	2594	.461	575	.408	473	.754	512	1520	1532	679	88	6236	8.2

JEFF TURNER

Team: Orlando Magic
Position: Forward
Height: 6'9" **Weight:** 240
Birthdate: April 9, 1962

NBA Experience: 7 years
College: Vanderbilt
Acquired: Signed as a free agent, 7/89

Background: Turner was a two-time SEC All-Academic selection at Vanderbilt and played for the 1984 gold-medal-winning U.S. Olympic team. Turner saw limited action with New Jersey in his first three pro seasons before opting to play in Europe for two years. He returned to the NBA with Orlando, where he was primarily a back-up in 1989-90 but started for more than half of the 1990-91 and 1991-92 seasons. He started 20 games last year and averaged seven PPG, his lowest output in three years.

Strengths: A perimeter-oriented forward, Turner has a soft touch with his lefty jump shot and can stroke it with good range. He uses his head, is usually in the right spot, and does not try to do more than he is capable of offensively.

Weaknesses: Turner can do little offensively other than shoot. He cannot put the ball on the floor and does not possess an inside game to bail him out. He lacks quickness for the perimeter and muscle for the paint. The same dilemma haunts him on defense, where he often resorts to fouling both quicker and bigger guards.

Analysis: Turner has done his share of starting, but he is better suited to a reserve role. He is the kind of player who won't hurt his team and is capable of knocking down jumpers when left open. He never takes a shot he can't make and hit ten of 17 3-point attempts last season.

PLAYER SUMMARY

Will	hit open jumpers
Can't	do much off dribble
Expect	smart decisions
Don't Expect	sleek moves
Fantasy Value	$1
Card Value	5-8¢

COLLEGE STATISTICS

		G	FGP	FTP	RPG	PPG
80-81	VAND	28	.417	.645	3.0	3.6
81-82	VAND	27	.524	.732	5.4	9.3
82-83	VAND	33	.492	.765	5.5	13.2
83-84	VAND	29	.533	.843	7.3	16.8
Totals		117	.506	.772	5.3	10.9

NBA REGULAR-SEASON STATISTICS

			FGs		3-PT FGs		FTs		Rebounds						
	G	MIN	FG	PCT	FG	PCT	FT	PCT	OFF	TOT	AST	STL	BLK	PTS	PPG
84-85 NJ	72	1429	171	.454	0	.000	79	.859	88	218	108	29	7	421	5.8
85-86 NJ	53	650	84	.491	0	.000	58	.744	45	137	14	21	3	226	4.3
86-87 NJ	76	1003	151	.465	0	.000	76	.731	80	197	60	33	13	378	5.0
89-90 ORL	60	1105	132	.429	2	.200	42	.778	52	227	53	23	12	308	5.1
90-91 ORL	71	1683	259	.487	6	.400	85	.759	108	363	97	29	10	609	8.6
91-92 ORL	75	1591	225	.451	1	.125	79	.693	62	246	92	24	16	530	7.1
92-93 ORL	75	1479	231	.529	10	.588	56	.800	74	252	107	19	9	528	7.0
Totals	482	8940	1253	.473	19	.345	475	.761	509	1640	531	178	70	3000	6.2

KIKI VANDEWEGHE

Team: Los Angeles Clippers
Position: Forward
Height: 6'8" **Weight:** 220
Birthdate: August 1, 1958

NBA Experience: 13 years
College: UCLA
Acquired: Signed as a free agent, 10/92

Background: Vandeweghe led UCLA to the NCAA title game vs. Louisville in 1980. Unable to come to terms with Dallas that same year, he was sent to Denver for draft choices. After four years with the Nuggets, including two All-Star Game invites, he went to Portland in a multi-player trade. The Blazers shipped him to New York in 1989 for a first-round draft choice. Between 1981-82 and 1987-88, he averaged more than 20 PPG. He has served as a reserve in recent years, including a 41-game stint with the Clippers in 1992-93.

Strengths: Vandeweghe has made a career out of his ability to put the ball in the basket. He shoots with 3-point range and has been one of the best foul shooters in the league.

Weaknesses: Defensively, the slow-footed Vandeweghe is not much help. There's not a small forward in the league who can't beat him off the dribble. He's a lousy rebounder.

Analysis: Vandeweghe is nearing the end of a high-scoring, hot-shooting career. He's still of value to a team that needs scoring off the bench. He is 20 points away from 16,000 for his career.

<table>
<tr><th colspan="2">PLAYER SUMMARY</th></tr>
<tr><td>Will</td><td>score off the bench</td></tr>
<tr><td>Can't</td><td>help on defense</td></tr>
<tr><td>Expect</td><td>16,000 career points</td></tr>
<tr><td>Don't Expect</td><td>starts</td></tr>
<tr><td>Fantasy Value</td><td>$0</td></tr>
<tr><td>Card Value</td><td>5-8¢</td></tr>
</table>

COLLEGE STATISTICS

		G	FGP	FTP	RPG	PPG
76-77	UCLA	23	.500	.706	1.8	3.6
77-78	UCLA	28	.549	.687	4.4	8.9
78-79	UCLA	30	.622	.812	6.3	14.2
79-80	UCLA	32	.557	.791	6.8	19.5
Totals		113	.570	.776	5.0	12.2

NBA REGULAR-SEASON STATISTICS

		G	MIN	FGs FG	FGs PCT	3-PT FGs FG	3-PT FGs PCT	FTs FT	FTs PCT	Rebounds OFF	Rebounds TOT	AST	STL	BLK	PTS	PPG
80-81	DEN	51	1376	229	.426	0	.000	130	.818	86	270	94	29	24	588	11.5
81-82	DEN	82	2775	706	.560	1	.077	347	.857	149	461	247	52	29	1760	21.5
82-83	DEN	82	2909	841	.547	15	.294	489	.875	124	437	203	66	38	2186	26.7
83-84	DEN	78	2734	895	.558	11	.367	494	.852	84	373	238	53	50	2295	29.4
84-85	POR	72	2502	618	.534	11	.333	369	.896	74	228	106	37	22	1616	22.4
85-86	POR	79	2791	719	.540	1	.125	523	.869	92	216	187	54	17	1962	24.8
86-87	POR	79	3029	808	.523	39	.481	467	.886	86	251	220	52	17	2122	26.9
87-88	POR	37	1038	283	.508	22	.379	159	.878	36	109	71	21	7	747	20.2
88-89	POR/NY	45	934	200	.469	19	.396	80	.899	26	71	69	19	11	499	11.1
89-90	NY	22	563	102	.442	10	.526	44	.917	15	53	41	15	3	258	11.7
90-91	NY	75	2420	458	.494	51	.362	259	.899	78	180	110	42	10	1226	16.3
91-92	NY	67	956	188	.491	26	.394	65	.802	31	88	57	15	8	467	7.0
92-93	LAC	41	494	92	.453	12	.324	58	.879	12	48	25	13	7	254	6.2
Totals		810	24521	6139	.525	218	.368	3484	.872	893	2785	1668	468	243	15980	19.7

LOY VAUGHT

Team: Los Angeles Clippers
Position: Forward
Height: 6'9" **Weight:** 240
Birthdate: February 27, 1967

NBA Experience: 3 years
College: Michigan
Acquired: 1st-round pick in 1990 draft (13th overall)

Background: Vaught led the Big Ten in field goal percentage as a junior and senior and was the first Michigan player since Roy Tarpley to average double-figure points and rebounds. He also paced the conference in rebounding as a senior. He saw action in 73 games as a rookie with the Clippers, made 38 starts the next year, and enjoyed his best campaign as a reserve last season. He averaged 9.4 PPG and shot better than 50 percent from the field for the first time in his career.

Strengths: Vaught approaches basketball in workman-like fashion. Coaches love his desire to hit the boards at both ends. Equally impressive is his muscular frame. He gets up and down the floor, finishes plays, and hits the jumper from medium range with regularity. He rarely puts up a bad shot. He's comfortable as a starter or a reserve and is a more active scorer than initially expected.

Weaknesses: Low-post offense is not Vaught's forte. Most of his points come off rebounds, off fastbreaks, or from the perimeter. He does not pass or handle the ball well, amassing a higher number of turnovers than assists over his three-year pro career. He is not a shut-down defender or intimidating shot-blocker.

Analysis: Vaught says he admires players who do the dirty work but do not get a lot of credit, and that is exactly how he plays. He was expected to be a strong NBA rebounder and has not disappointed in that area, averaging 14 per 48 minutes in his career. He has also come a long way with his offensive game and is on the verge of becoming a double-figure scorer.

PLAYER SUMMARY	
Will	crash the boards
Can't	hit open men
Expect	relentless effort
Don't Expect	ball-handling
Fantasy Value	$7-9
Card Value	5-10¢

COLLEGE STATISTICS

		G	FGP	FTP	RPG	PPG
86-87	MICH	32	.557	.500	3.9	4.6
87-88	MICH	34	.621	.724	4.4	10.5
88-89	MICH	37	.661	.778	8.0	12.6
89-90	MICH	31	.595	.804	11.2	15.5
Totals		134	.617	.752	6.8	10.8

NBA REGULAR-SEASON STATISTICS

		G	MIN	FGs FG	FGs PCT	3-PT FGs FG	3-PT FGs PCT	FTs FT	FTs PCT	Rebounds OFF	Rebounds TOT	AST	STL	BLK	PTS	PPG
90-91	LAC	73	1178	175	.487	0	.000	49	.662	124	349	40	20	23	399	5.5
91-92	LAC	79	1687	271	.492	4	.800	55	.797	160	512	71	37	31	601	7.6
92-93	LAC	79	1653	313	.508	1	.250	116	.748	164	492	54	55	39	743	9.4
Totals		231	4518	759	.497	5	.455	220	.738	448	1353	165	112	93	1743	7.5

SAM VINCENT

Team: Milwaukee Bucks
Position: Guard
Height: 6'2" **Weight:** 185
Birthdate: May 18, 1963
NBA Experience: 7 years

College: Michigan St.
Acquired: Traded from Magic with a 1994 2nd-round pick for Lester Conner, 8/92

Background: Vincent led the Big Ten in scoring as a senior at Michigan State, where he combined with brother Jay to form the highest-scoring brother duo in conference history. He also played college ball with Scott Skiles. Vincent was the lone rookie on Boston's 1985-86 championship team. He played in Seattle and Chicago before becoming a starter for 45 games for the Magic in 1989-90. That spot was taken by Skiles in 1990-91, and Vincent became a reserve again. He was traded to Milwaukee but missed all of his first season with the Bucks because of a ruptured Achilles tendon.

Strengths: Vincent is a very good athlete with blazing speed. He races the ball up-court on the break and can penetrate through the lane. He handles the ball well with both hands and gets his shots off the dribble. Vincent is also a very good free throw shooter.

Weaknesses: Vincent is a point guard who looks to score first and pass second. He takes ill-advised shots and doesn't convert at a respectable rate. He's not the drive-and-dish type and he plays virtually no defense.

Analysis: Vincent possesses the body of a point guard but the approach of a two guard. He is too selfish on offense and of no help defensively to warrant many minutes. He has not performed well in a back-up role, although some feel he is suited for it.

PLAYER SUMMARY	
Will	race up-court
Can't	stay in control
Expect	reserve minutes
Don't Expect	distribution
Fantasy Value	$0
Card Value	8-12¢

COLLEGE STATISTICS

		G	FGP	FTP	APG	PPG
81-82	MSU	28	.461	.747	2.0	11.7
82-83	MSU	30	.449	.773	2.2	16.6
83-84	MSU	23	.498	.811	3.0	15.6
84-85	MSU	29	.544	.846	4.0	23.0
Totals		110	.491	.803	2.8	16.8

NBA REGULAR-SEASON STATISTICS

				FGs		3-PT FGs		FTs		Rebounds					
		G	MIN	FG	PCT	FG	PCT	FT	PCT	OFF	TOT	AST	STL	BLK	PTS	PPG
85-86	BOS	57	432	59	.364	1	.250	65	.929	11	48	69	17	4	184	3.2
86-87	BOS	46	374	60	.441	0	.000	51	.927	5	27	59	13	1	171	3.7
87-88	SEA/CHI	72	1501	210	.456	8	.381	145	.868	35	152	381	55	16	573	8.0
88-89	CHI	70	1703	274	.484	2	.118	106	.822	34	190	335	53	10	656	9.4
89-90	ORL	63	1657	258	.457	1	.071	188	.879	37	194	354	65	20	705	11.2
90-91	ORL	49	975	152	.431	3	.158	99	.825	17	107	197	30	5	406	8.3
91-92	ORL	39	885	150	.430	1	.077	110	.846	19	101	148	35	4	411	10.5
Totals		396	7527	1163	.449	16	.182	764	.863	158	819	1543	268	60	3106	7.8

DARRELL WALKER

Team: Chicago Bulls
Position: Guard
Height: 6'4" **Weight:** 180
Birthdate: March 9, 1961

NBA Experience: 10 years
College: Westark; Arkansas
Acquired: Signed as a free agent, 1/93

Background: Following his college days at Arkansas, Walker made the NBA All-Rookie Team in 1984 as a member of the Knicks. He missed only one game with New York in three seasons. Walker was traded to Denver for a No. 1 draft choice in 1986. After one year with the Nuggets, he was dealt along with Mark Alarie to the Bullets. Walker was Washington's leading rebounder in 1989-90 and its top assists man in 1990-91. Detroit picked him up for 1991-92 but released him early last season. Chicago signed him in January and he played 28 games for the Bulls, averaging 2.6 PPG.

Strengths: Walker remains a standout defender. He stays in front of his man, does not shy away from contact, and backs down from no one. He has always been a terrific rebounder from the backcourt.

Weaknesses: Walker is not an offensive contributor. His jumper is erratic, he can't shoot treys, and his marksmanship from the line is an embarrassment. He shot a career-low 35.4 percent from the field last year. He was also bothered by a back injury.

Analysis: Walker has enjoyed a fine career as a jack-of-all-trades, a utility-infielder type. He can still help even the toughest of teams defensively, but it appears his days as a major contributor are in the past. He has lost a step or two.

PLAYER SUMMARY	
Will	get in your face
Can't	contribute offensively
Expect	tough defense
Don't Expect	starts
Fantasy Value	$0
Card Value	8-12¢

COLLEGE STATISTICS

		G	FGP	FTP	RPG	PPG
79-80	WEST	37	.540	.657	7.0	16.9
80-81	ARK	31	.509	.600	4.5	11.3
81-82	ARK	29	.513	.658	5.2	14.8
82-83	ARK	30	.527	.639	5.7	18.2
Totals		127	.525	.641	5.7	15.4

NBA REGULAR-SEASON STATISTICS

		G	MIN	FGs FG	FGs PCT	3-PT FGs FG	3-PT FGs PCT	FTs FT	FTs PCT	Rebounds OFF	Rebounds TOT	AST	STL	BLK	PTS	PPG
83-84	NY	82	1324	216	.417	4	.267	208	.791	74	167	284	127	15	644	7.9
84-85	NY	82	2489	430	.435	0	.000	243	.700	128	278	408	167	21	1103	13.5
85-86	NY	81	2023	324	.430	0	.000	190	.686	100	220	337	146	36	838	10.3
86-87	DEN	81	2020	358	.482	0	.000	272	.745	157	327	282	129	37	988	12.2
87-88	WAS	52	940	114	.392	0	.000	82	.781	43	127	100	62	10	310	6.0
88-89	WAS	79	2565	286	.420	0	.000	142	.772	135	507	496	155	23	714	9.0
89-90	WAS	81	2883	318	.454	2	.095	138	.687	173	714	652	139	30	772	9.5
90-91	WAS	71	2305	230	.430	0	.000	93	.604	140	498	459	78	33	553	7.8
91-92	DET	74	1541	161	.423	0	.000	65	.619	85	238	205	63	18	387	5.2
92-93	DET/CHI	37	511	34	.354	0	.000	12	.462	22	58	53	33	2	80	2.2
Totals		720	18601	2469	.435	6	.059	1445	.713	1057	3134	3276	1099	225	6389	8.9

CLARENCE WEATHERSPOON

Team: Philadelphia 76ers
Position: Forward
Height: 6'6" **Weight:** 245
Birthdate: September 8, 1970

NBA Experience: 1 year
College: Southern Mississippi
Acquired: 1st-round pick in 1992 draft
(9th overall)

Background: Weatherspoon attended Motley High in Crawford, Mississippi, the same school that produced NFL star Jerry Rice. "Spoon" was an instant force at Southern Mississippi, finishing 13th in the nation in rebounding as a freshman. He finished his college career as the all-time school leader in scoring, rebounding, and blocked shots, and joined football star Ray Guy when his USM jersey was retired. Weatherspoon was drafted ninth and was a second-team All-Rookie choice for Philadelphia in 1992-93. He started all 82 games, led the 76ers in rebounds, and was fourth among first-year scorers at 15.6 PPG.

Strengths: Weatherspoon has been compared to Charles Barkley, and not without foundation. He has the same powerful build and leaping ability, plays hard at both ends, and can dominate the backboards. Weatherspoon can face the basket and shoot or post up his man, and he set an all-time Sixer rookie scoring record. He is unassuming and plays within a team concept. Weatherspoon is agile, runs well, and finishes with a flourish.

Weaknesses: Spoon is no Sir Charles when it comes to breaking down defenders off the dribble. He needs to improve his ball-handling ability as well as his consistency with the mid-range jumper. Weatherspoon will bang in the paint and block a few shots, but he is not a great perimeter defender.

Analysis: While Weatherspoon was by no means able to replace Barkley (and who could?) after the Sixers traded the latter to Phoenix, the rookie proved to be the biggest bright spot in an otherwise frustrating year in Philadelphia. He scores, rebounds, plays a little defense, and works his tail off. Sixer brass likes his attitude much more than it did Barkley's.

PLAYER SUMMARY

Will ....explode off the floor
Can't ....drive like Barkley
Expect ....points, rebounds
Don't Expect ....a big ego
Fantasy Value............................$14-17
Card Value ....25-75¢

COLLEGE STATISTICS

		G	FGP	FTP	RPG	PPG
88-89	SMU	27	.545	.590	10.7	14.7
89-90	SMU	32	.605	.691	11.6	17.8
90-91	SMU	29	.589	.745	12.2	17.8
91-92	SMU	29	.563	.675	10.5	22.3
Totals		117	.576	.677	11.3	18.7

NBA REGULAR-SEASON STATISTICS

			FGs		3-PT FGs		FTs		Rebounds						
	G	MIN	FG	PCT	FG	PCT	FT	PCT	OFF	TOT	AST	STL	BLK	PTS	PPG
92-93 PHI	82	2654	494	.469	1	.250	291	.713	179	589	147	85	67	1280	15.6
Totals	82	2654	494	.469	1	.250	291	.713	179	589	147	85	67	1280	15.6

SPUD WEBB

Team: Sacramento Kings
Position: Guard
Height: 5'7" **Weight:** 135
Birthdate: July 13, 1963
NBA Experience: 8 years

College: Midland; North Carolina St.
Acquired: Traded from Hawks with a 1994 2nd-round pick for Travis Mays, 7/91

Background: After pacing North Carolina State in assists for two straight seasons, Webb was drafted by Detroit in 1985 and signed as a free agent with Atlanta three months later. As a Hawks rookie, he won the NBA's Slam Dunk Contest. Webb led Atlanta in assists in 1990-91, then was traded to Sacramento for Travis Mays. He has averaged about seven APG in each of his first two years with the Kings.

Strengths: Webb overcomes his small stature by playing big. Almost everything he does starts with his incredible quickness. When teams double down in the paint, he is capable of making jumpers with 3-point range. He's a great leaper who finishes breaks with slams. Webb has led the Kings in assists the last two years and is also a reliable free throw shooter.

Weaknesses: For obvious reasons, Webb is always going to be susceptible to being posted up and shot over. He's also no Magic Johnson when it comes to seeing the court. He's a better spot-up shooter than he is off the dribble and he hit a career-low 43.3 percent last year.

Analysis: Webb is no All-Star point guard, but he makes good things happen. With regular minutes in Sacramento the last two seasons, he has demonstrated an ability to score while still running a precise offense. A hand injury sidelined him early last year, and he'll lose P.T. to rookie Bobby Hurley this season.

PLAYER SUMMARY	
Will	run the show
Can't	shoot 50 percent
Expect	7 APG
Don't Expect	a slow pace
Fantasy Value	$9-11
Card Value	8-15¢

COLLEGE STATISTICS

		G	FGP	FTP	APG	PPG
81-82	MID	38	.515	.781	—	20.8
82-83	MID	35	.445	.774	—	14.6
83-84	NCST	33	.459	.761	6.0	9.8
84-85	NCST	33	.481	.761	5.3	11.1
Totals		139	.479	.773	5.7	14.3

NBA REGULAR-SEASON STATISTICS

				FGs		3-PT FGs		FTs		Rebounds						
		G	MIN	FG	PCT	FG	PCT	FT	PCT	OFF	TOT	AST	STL	BLK	PTS	PPG
85-86	ATL	79	1229	199	.483	2	.182	216	.785	27	123	337	82	5	616	7.8
86-87	ATL	33	532	71	.438	1	.167	80	.762	6	60	167	34	2	223	6.8
87-88	ATL	82	1347	191	.475	1	.053	107	.817	16	146	337	63	11	490	6.0
88-89	ATL	81	1219	133	.459	1	.045	52	.867	21	123	284	70	6	319	3.9
89-90	ATL	82	2184	294	.477	1	.053	162	.871	38	201	477	105	12	751	9.2
90-91	ATL	75	2197	359	.447	54	.321	231	.868	41	174	417	118	6	1003	13.4
91-92	SAC	77	2724	448	.445	73	.367	262	.859	30	223	547	125	24	1231	16.0
92-93	SAC	69	2335	342	.433	37	.274	279	.851	44	193	481	104	6	1000	14.5
Totals		578	13767	2037	.455	170	.294	1389	.839	223	1243	3047	701	72	5633	9.7

DOUG WEST

Team: Minnesota Timberwolves
Position: Guard
Height: 6'6" **Weight:** 200
Birthdate: May 27, 1967

NBA Experience: 4 years
College: Villanova
Acquired: 2nd-round pick in 1989
draft (38th overall)

Background: West was a four-year starter at Villanova, finishing his career third on the school's all-time scoring list and seventh in steals. He served as a reserve for Minnesota in each of his first two NBA seasons before being promoted to the starting lineup in 1991-92. He led the Timberwolves in scoring during the 1992-93 season, raising his average for the third consecutive year to 19.3 PPG. He finished last year as the lone holdover from Minnesota's inaugural 1989-90 campaign.

Strengths: West is an explosive player with a sweet jumper and good size for the big-guard spot. He finished third among NBA guards last year in shooting percentage (.517). The athletic West is a fabulous finisher who can take it in traffic for jams. He owns excellent court sense and knows where to deliver the ball. His defense and free throw shooting are solid.

Weaknesses: West will occasionally launch jump shots that are out of his range. He has made just six of his 46 3-point attempts in the last two years. What he gives you in ball-handling and passing he could be giving you on the boards. In other words, he has the makings of a good rebounder if he puts his mind to it.

Analysis: West has worked hard to improve his game and the results speak for themselves. He has gone from a reserve on a bad team to its most valuable performer. About the only thing he has not been able to do is carry the Timberwolves to respectability. With his shooting, scoring, defense, and crowd-pleasing, West is doing all he can toward that end.

PLAYER SUMMARY	
Will	dunk over people
Can't	hit 3-pointers
Expect	sweet shooting
Don't Expect	many wins
Fantasy Value	$8-10
Card Value	8-12¢

COLLEGE STATISTICS

		G	FGP	FTP	RPG	PPG
85-86	VILL	37	.515	.682	3.7	10.2
86-87	VILL	31	.479	.729	4.9	15.2
87-88	VILL	37	.497	.724	4.9	15.8
88-89	VILL	33	.463	.720	4.9	18.4
Totals		138	.486	.716	4.6	14.8

NBA REGULAR-SEASON STATISTICS

			FGs		3-PT FGs		FTs		Rebounds					
		G	MIN	FG	PCT	FG	PCT	FT	PCT	OFF	TOT	AST	STL	BLK	PTS	PPG
89-90	MIN	52	378	53	.393	3	.273	26	.813	24	70	18	10	6	135	2.6
90-91	MIN	75	824	118	.480	0	.000	58	.690	56	136	48	35	23	294	3.9
91-92	MIN	80	2540	463	.518	4	.174	186	.805	107	257	281	66	26	1116	13.9
92-93	MIN	80	3104	646	.517	2	.087	249	.841	89	247	235	85	21	1543	19.3
Totals		287	6846	1280	.507	9	.155	519	.807	276	710	582	196	76	3088	10.8

MARK WEST

Team: Phoenix Suns
Position: Center
Height: 6'10" **Weight:** 246
Birthdate: November 5, 1960
NBA Experience: 10 years
College: Old Dominion

Acquired: Traded from Cavaliers with Kevin Johnson, Tyrone Corbin, 1988 1st- and 2nd-round picks, and a 1989 2nd-round pick for Larry Nance, Mike Sanders, and a 1988 1st-round pick, 2/88

Background: West ended his college career at Old Dominion as the third-leading shot-blocker in NCAA history. He was cast off by Dallas and Milwaukee in his first two seasons before landing with Cleveland in 1984-85. A 1988 trade to Phoenix gave him a chance to start. West led the league in field goal accuracy in 1989-90 and led the Suns in rebounding and blocked shots for two straight years. He started all 82 games last season.

Strengths: West is a workhorse, a capable shot-blocker, and a strong interior defender. He attacks both boards and rarely takes a bad shot. He has shot better than 60 percent from the floor in each of the past five years and has not missed a game over the last six.

Weaknesses: Foul trouble follows West. He becomes ineffective offensively when outside the paint and he is not a force around the basket either. West can't dribble or pass and he's a poor free throw shooter.

Analysis: West is an old pro who helps his team with defense and comes to play every night. Offensively, however, he was one of Phoenix's few weak links last season. He'll likely be replaced in the starting lineup before long by Oliver Miller.

PLAYER SUMMARY	
Will	defend, rebound
Can't	stick jumpers
Expect	82 games
Don't Expect	much scoring
Fantasy Value	$0
Card Value	5-8¢

COLLEGE STATISTICS

		G	FGP	FTP	RPG	PPG
79-80	OD	30	.475	.370	7.1	4.8
80-81	OD	28	.527	.578	10.3	10.9
81-82	OD	30	.610	.531	10.0	15.7
82-83	OD	29	.569	.491	10.8	14.4
Totals		117	.559	.514	9.5	11.4

NBA REGULAR-SEASON STATISTICS

		G	MIN	FGs FG	FGs PCT	3-PT FGs FG	3-PT FGs PCT	FTs FT	FTs PCT	Rebounds OFF	Rebounds TOT	AST	STL	BLK	PTS	PPG
83-84	DAL	34	202	15	.357	0	.000	7	.318	19	46	13	1	15	37	1.1
84-85	MIL/CLE	66	888	106	.545	0	.000	43	.494	90	251	15	13	49	255	3.9
85-86	CLE	67	1172	113	.541	0	.000	54	.524	97	322	20	27	62	280	4.2
86-87	CLE	78	1333	209	.543	0	.000	89	.514	126	339	41	22	81	507	6.5
87-88	CLE/PHO	83	2098	316	.551	0	.000	170	.596	165	523	74	47	147	802	9.7
88-89	PHO	82	2019	243	.653	0	.000	108	.535	167	551	39	35	187	594	7.2
89-90	PHO	82	2399	331	.625	0	.000	199	.691	212	728	45	36	184	861	10.5
90-91	PHO	82	1957	247	.647	0	.000	135	.655	171	564	37	32	161	629	7.7
91-92	PHO	82	1436	196	.632	0	.000	109	.637	134	372	22	14	81	501	6.1
92-93	PHO	82	1558	175	.614	0	.000	86	.518	153	458	29	16	103	436	5.3
Totals		738	15062	1951	.594	0	.000	1000	.587	1334	4154	335	243	1070	4902	6.6

RANDY WHITE

Team: Dallas Mavericks
Position: Forward
Height: 6'8" **Weight:** 238
Birthdate: November 4, 1967

NBA Experience: 4 years
College: Louisiana Tech
Acquired: 1st-round pick in 1989 draft
(8th overall)

Background: White was named American South Player of the Year as a senior at Louisiana Tech, where he drew comparisons to former Bulldog standout Karl Malone. Those comparisons began to cease in White's rookie year with Dallas, as he struggled to a .369 shooting campaign in which he did not get off the bench for 26 of the last 55 games. He has made 61 starts over the last three years, and he averaged a career-high 9.7 PPG during the 1992-93 season.

Strengths: White is strong, athletic, and a good rebounder. A former college center, he is willing to bang inside with the big guys. He runs the floor aggressively, scores off the offensive glass, and finishes on the break. He has improved his shooting and displayed shot-blocking potential. He has struggled, but not for lack of a work ethic.

Weaknesses: It hasn't gone as planned for Dallas with this former inside player. White has shot below 40 percent in three of his four seasons, yet he thinks he is a good outside shooter. In truth, he is a center in a small forward's body. Defensively, White is not quick enough to guard the NBA's explosive forwards. He does not show a good feel for the game and is a sub-par dribbler and passer.

Analysis: White has to be considered a bust. He played with his back to the basket in college and has done little as a pro to prove he can be an effective face-up player. To make matters worse, he underwent arthroscopic surgery on both knees after last season because of torn cartilage in one and a calcium deposit in the other.

PLAYER SUMMARY	
Will	run the court
Can't	thrive on perimeter
Expect	a first-round let-down
Don't Expect	Karl Malone
Fantasy Value	$1
Card Value	5-12¢

COLLEGE STATISTICS

		G	FGP	FTP	RPG	PPG
85-86	LAT	34	.520	.667	4.6	9.2
86-87	LAT	30	.575	.677	6.5	12.6
87-88	LAT	31	.638	.640	11.6	18.6
88-89	LAT	32	.600	.747	10.5	21.2
Totals		127	.592	.689	8.3	15.3

NBA REGULAR-SEASON STATISTICS

				FGs		3-PT FGs		FTs		Rebounds						
		G	MIN	FG	PCT	FG	PCT	FT	PCT	OFF	TOT	AST	STL	BLK	PTS	PPG
89-90	DAL	55	707	93	.369	1	.071	50	.562	78	173	21	24	6	237	4.3
90-91	DAL	79	1901	265	.396	6	.162	159	.707	173	504	63	81	44	695	8.8
91-92	DAL	65	1021	145	.380	4	.148	124	.765	96	236	31	31	22	418	6.4
92-93	DAL	64	1433	235	.435	10	.238	138	.750	154	370	49	63	45	618	9.7
Totals		263	5062	738	.401	21	.175	471	.714	501	1283	164	199	117	1968	7.5

MORLON WILEY

Team: Dallas Mavericks
Position: Guard
Height: 6'4" **Weight:** 192
Birthdate: September 24, 1966

NBA Experience: 5 years
College: Long Beach St.
Acquired: Signed as a free agent, 2/93

Background: Wiley was a first-team All-Big West selection as a senior at Long Beach State, when he averaged 19.9 PPG and helped the 49ers break a string of six consecutive losing seasons. He was drafted late in the second round by Dallas and played his first pro season with the Mavericks. Orlando picked him up in the 1989 expansion draft and he spent two-plus years with the Magic. He started off 1991-92 in Orlando, stopped in San Antonio, and finished the year in Atlanta. Wiley began last season with the Hawks and wound up back in Dallas, where he made 13 starts.

Strengths: Wiley has good size and quickness for the backcourt and uses those strengths most effectively on defense. He can stick with his man all over the court and is not easy to shoot over. He's a solid 3-point shooter and a pretty good passer.

Weaknesses: While Wiley can stick the long-range jumper when he has time to set himself, he will not shoot for a high percentage from either the field or the free throw line. He does not have the offensive artillery to thrive at the shooting-guard spot and he lacks the playmaking bent to make a big impact as a lead guard.

Analysis: You have to admire Wiley for his patience. This journeyman has made five stops in as many years, including two in Dallas. Though he played in only 58 games, last season was one of his better ones statistically. He will stick around because of his fine defensive skills.

PLAYER SUMMARY	
Will	stick with his man
Can't	score in bunches
Expect	a team player
Don't Expect	10 PPG
Fantasy Value	$0
Card Value	5-10¢

COLLEGE STATISTICS

		G	FGP	FTP	RPG	PPG
84-85	LBS	27	.382	.750	1.9	5.8
85-86	LBS	29	.458	.794	2.6	11.7
86-87	LBS	28	.386	.800	2.9	12.8
87-88	LBS	29	.513	.766	4.0	19.9
Totals		113	.448	.780	2.8	12.7

NBA REGULAR-SEASON STATISTICS

				FGs		3-PT FGs		FTs		Rebounds						
		G	MIN	FG	PCT	FG	PCT	FT	PCT	OFF	TOT	AST	STL	BLK	PTS	PPG
88-89	DAL	51	408	46	.404	6	.250	13	.813	13	47	76	25	6	111	2.2
89-90	ORL	40	638	92	.442	17	.370	28	.737	13	52	114	45	3	229	5.7
90-91	ORL	34	350	45	.417	6	.500	17	.680	4	17	73	24	0	113	3.3
91-92	ORL/SA/ATL	53	870	83	.430	14	.333	24	.686	24	81	180	47	3	204	3.8
92-93	ATL/DAL	58	995	96	.378	54	.351	17	.654	29	91	181	65	3	263	4.5
Totals		236	3261	362	.413	97	.349	99	.707	83	288	624	206	15	920	3.9

DOMINIQUE WILKINS

Team: Atlanta Hawks
Position: Forward
Height: 6'8" **Weight:** 218
Birthdate: January 12, 1960
NBA Experience: 11 years

College: Georgia
Acquired: Draft rights traded from
Jazz for John Drew, Freeman
Williams, and cash, 9/82

Background: Born in France while his father was stationed in the Air Force, Wilkins went on to become a first-team All-American at Georgia in 1982. He left college following his junior year. Wilkins led the NBA in scoring in 1985-86 and has been named to the All-Star Game eight times. 'Nique received MVP consideration for the first time in 1990-91, but his 1991-92 season was cut nearly in half by a ruptured Achilles tendon. He bounced back last year and was second to Michael Jordan in scoring.

Strengths: The 11th NBA player to reach 22,000 career points, Wilkins has the ability to take over games. He has made himself a great outside shooter with 3-point range. "The Human Highlight Film" can still dunk with as much authority as anyone. He's a fine rebounder and an underrated team player.

Weaknesses: Wilkins has a weak left hand. 'Nique has never been a great defensive player even though he has had the athletic skills to reach such heights.

Analysis: Wilkins gained notoriety as a tremendous one-on-one player and has since added to his repertoire. He passed Bob Pettit as the Hawks' all-time scoring leader last season and set an NBA game record by making 23 of 23 free throw attempts against the Bulls.

PLAYER SUMMARY	
Will	score on anyone
Can't	be left open
Expect	more All-Star trips
Don't Expect	a title
Fantasy Value	$30-35
Card Value	15-25¢

COLLEGE STATISTICS

		G	FGP	FTP	RPG	PPG
79-80	GA	16	.525	.730	6.5	18.6
80-81	GA	31	.533	.752	7.5	23.6
81-82	GA	31	.529	.644	8.1	21.3
Totals		78	.530	.699	7.5	21.6

NBA REGULAR-SEASON STATISTICS

		G	MIN	FG	FG PCT	3-PT FG	3-PT PCT	FT	FT PCT	OFF	TOT	AST	STL	BLK	PTS	PPG
82-83	ATL	82	2697	601	.493	2	.182	230	.682	226	478	129	84	63	1434	17.5
83-84	ATL	81	2961	684	.479	0	.000	382	.770	254	582	126	117	87	1750	21.6
84-85	ATL	81	3023	853	.451	25	.309	486	.806	226	557	200	135	54	2217	27.4
85-86	ATL	78	3049	888	.468	13	.186	577	.818	261	618	206	138	49	2366	30.3
86-87	ATL	79	2969	828	.463	31	.292	607	.818	210	494	261	117	51	2294	29.0
87-88	ATL	78	2948	909	.464	38	.295	541	.826	211	502	224	103	47	2397	30.7
88-89	ATL	80	2997	814	.464	29	.276	442	.844	256	553	211	117	52	2099	26.2
89-90	ATL	80	2888	810	.484	59	.322	459	.807	217	521	200	126	47	2138	26.7
90-91	ATL	81	3078	770	.470	85	.341	476	.829	261	732	265	123	65	2101	25.9
91-92	ATL	42	1601	424	.464	37	.289	294	.835	103	295	158	52	24	1179	28.1
92-93	ATL	71	2647	741	.468	120	.380	519	.828	187	482	227	70	27	2121	29.9
Totals		833	30858	8322	.469	439	.316	5013	.811	2412	5814	2207	1182	566	22096	26.5

GERALD WILKINS

Team: Cleveland Cavaliers
Position: Guard
Height: 6'6" **Weight:** 210
Birthdate: September 11, 1963
NBA Experience: 8 years

College: Moberly Area; Tennessee-Chattanooga
Acquired: Signed as a free agent, 10/92

Background: Dominique's little brother, Gerald slam-dunked his way to three outstanding collegiate seasons at Tennessee-Chattanooga. A durable veteran, he has logged 80 or more games in seven of his eight pro campaigns. He spent his first seven seasons with the Knicks before Cleveland picked him up last year. Wilkins averaged a career-low 11.1 PPG with the Cavs.

Strengths: Wilkins is a fine defensive player because of his quickness, strength, leaping ability, and long arms. Few defend Michael Jordan better. He has some of his big brother's offensive explosiveness, although Gerald is not nearly as consistent as Dominique. He drives the entire lane with a single stride and has 3-point range. His ball skills and passing have improved.

Weaknesses: Wilkins is a streaky shooter. He'll shoot the lights out one night and go 1-for-12 the next. The halfcourt game is not his specialty. He has always shown a flair for the dramatic rather than making sound decisions with the ball. As mentioned, he is inconsistent offensively.

Analysis: Cleveland was thinking of Jordan and the Bulls when they went after Wilkins, one of the top defensive guards in basketball. So what happens? Jordan eliminates the Cavs from another playoff series with a jumper over Wilkins. Gerald played very well over the last half of 1992-93 after a hot-and-cold start and has earned league-wide respect as a stopper.

PLAYER SUMMARY

Will.......................play tough defense
Can't...................outscore his brother
Expect.....................aggressive drives
Don't Expect ....solid shooting
Fantasy Value...........................$2-4
Card Value...................................8-15¢

COLLEGE STATISTICS

		G	FGP	FTP	RPG	PPG
81-82	MA	39	.551	.770	5.9	18.5
82-83	T-C	30	.483	.661	3.8	12.6
83-84	T-C	23	.542	.695	4.0	17.3
84-85	T-C	32	.519	.632	4.6	21.0
Totals		124	.526	.685	4.7	17.5

NBA REGULAR-SEASON STATISTICS

				FGs		3-PT FGs		FTs		Rebounds						
		G	MIN	FG	PCT	FG	PCT	FT	PCT	OFF	TOT	AST	STL	BLK	PTS	PPG
85-86	NY	81	2025	437	.468	7	.280	132	.557	92	208	161	68	9	1013	12.5
86-87	NY	80	2758	633	.486	26	.351	235	.701	120	294	354	88	18	1527	19.1
87-88	NY	81	2703	591	.446	39	.302	191	.786	106	270	326	90	22	1412	17.4
88-89	NY	81	2414	462	.451	51	.297	186	.756	95	244	274	115	22	1161	14.3
89-90	NY	82	2609	472	.457	39	.312	208	.803	133	371	330	95	21	1191	14.5
90-91	NY	68	2164	380	.473	9	.209	169	.820	78	207	275	82	23	938	13.8
1-92	NY	82	2344	431	.447	38	.352	116	.730	74	206	219	76	17	1016	12.4
92-93	CLE	80	2079	361	.453	16	.276	152	.840	74	214	183	78	18	890	11.1
Totals		635	19096	3767	.460	225	.307	1389	.744	772	2014	2122	692	150	9148	14.4

BRIAN WILLIAMS

Team: Denver Nuggets
Position: Forward/Center
Height: 6'11" **Weight:** 242
Birthdate: April 6, 1969
NBA Experience: 2 years

College: Maryland; Arizona
Acquired: Traded from Magic for
Todd Lichti, Anthony Cook, and a 1994
2nd-round pick, 8/93

Background: Williams, who played at three different high schools, had a terrific freshman season at Maryland but then transferred to Arizona. The Wildcats went 53-14 in his two seasons there. After being drafted tenth overall by Orlando, Williams missed training camp because of a holdout, then averaged 9.1 PPG and 5.7 RPG in 48 outings in 1991-92. He sat out until February of last season during a bout with clinical depression, returned for 21 games, then missed the rest of the year with a broken hand. In August, he was traded to Denver.

Strengths: Williams has an abundance of physical gifts. He is quick, jumps well, and runs the floor like a small forward. He's a promising, explosive shot-blocker with good fundamentals in his low-post defense. He's a fine inside scorer with a soft touch in the paint and the ability to hit the 15-foot jumper. Williams can be a force on the boards. He has huge hands.

Weaknesses: Several concerns have surfaced regarding Williams. It turns out that his inconsistency might be a symptom of a larger emotional problem. Even in college, when he should have been dominant, Williams just didn't show up for certain games. He is not a good passer and rarely gives up the ball once he touches it. He is not a steady shooter and he is often on the verge of fouling out.

Analysis: Orlando fans treated Williams to great support after he returned from his battle with depression. He showed only flashes of promise, however, before the hand injury wiped out the rest of his 1992-93 campaign. Next season will have to be considered a rookie year in the sense that Williams has not had an extended chance to develop.

PLAYER SUMMARY	
Will	run the floor
Can't	distribute
Expect	low-post defense
Don't Expect	consistency
Fantasy Value	$1-3
Card Value	12-25¢

COLLEGE STATISTICS

		G	FGP	FTP	RPG	PPG
87-88	MD	29	.600	.671	6.1	12.5
89-90	ARIZ	32	.553	.727	5.7	10.6
90-91	ARIZ	35	.619	.673	7.8	14.0
Totals		96	.594	.691	6.6	12.4

NBA REGULAR-SEASON STATISTICS

		G	MIN	FGs FG	FGs PCT	3-PT FGs FG	3-PT FGs PCT	FTs FT	FTs PCT	Rebounds OFF	Rebounds TOT	AST	STL	BLK	PTS	PPG
91-92	ORL	48	905	171	.528	0	.000	95	.669	115	272	33	41	53	437	9.1
92-93	ORL	21	240	40	.513	0	.000	16	.800	24	56	5	14	17	96	4.6
Totals		69	1145	211	.525	0	.000	111	.685	139	328	38	55	70	533	7.7

BUCK WILLIAMS

Team: Portland Trail Blazers
Position: Forward
Height: 6'8" **Weight:** 225
Birthdate: March 8, 1960

NBA Experience: 12 years
College: Maryland
Acquired: Traded from Nets for Sam Bowie and a 1989 1st-round pick, 6/89

Background: Williams turned pro after his junior season at Maryland, where he ended his career ranked second on the school's all-time rebounding chart. He was named 1982 NBA Rookie of the Year and played in three All-Star Games as a Net. Williams helped lead Portland to the championship series after the 1989-90 and 1991-92 seasons. He won the NBA's field goal-percentage crown in 1990-91 and 1991-92. He was the only Blazer to start all 82 games last season.

Strengths: Williams's calling card is rebounding, and he also ranks among the best low-post defenders. Offensively, he converts short jumpers and hooks and never takes a bad shot. He has never shot less than 51 percent from the field. Williams brings a great attitude to work.

Weaknesses: Williams is a below-average passer and does not handle the ball well in the open court. He scored a career-low 8.3 PPG last year and is a poor free throw shooter.

Analysis: Williams, one of the hardest-working men the game has known, continues to lead by example. His businesslike approach is contagious. Not by coincidence, Portland made the NBA Finals the year he arrived. He surpassed 14,000 career points and 10,000 career rebounds last season.

PLAYER SUMMARY	
Will	rebound, defend
Can't	lead the break
Expect	blue-collar effort
Don't Expect	bad shots
Fantasy Value	$2-4
Card Value	5-12¢

COLLEGE STATISTICS

		G	FGP	FTP	RPG	PPG
78-79	MD	30	.583	.550	10.8	10.0
79-80	MD	24	.606	.664	10.1	15.5
80-81	MD	31	.647	.637	11.7	15.5
Totals		85	.615	.623	10.9	13.6

NBA REGULAR-SEASON STATISTICS

		G	MIN	FGs FG	FGs PCT	3-PT FGs FG	3-PT FGs PCT	FTs FT	FTs PCT	Rebounds OFF	Rebounds TOT	AST	STL	BLK	PTS	PPG
81-82	NJ	82	2825	513	.582	0	.000	242	.624	347	1005	107	84	84	1268	15.5
82-83	NJ	82	2961	536	.588	0	.000	324	.620	365	1027	125	91	110	1396	17.0
83-84	NJ	81	3003	495	.535	0	.000	284	.570	355	1000	130	81	125	1274	15.7
84-85	NJ	82	3182	577	.530	1	.250	336	.625	323	1005	167	63	110	1491	18.2
85-86	NJ	82	3070	500	.523	0	.000	301	.676	329	986	131	73	96	1301	15.9
86-87	NJ	82	2976	521	.557	0	.000	430	.731	322	1023	129	78	91	1472	18.0
87-88	NJ	70	2637	466	.560	1	1.000	346	.668	298	834	109	68	44	1279	18.3
88-89	NJ	74	2446	373	.531	0	.000	213	.666	249	696	78	61	36	959	13.0
89-90	POR	82	2801	413	.548	0	.000	288	.706	250	800	116	69	39	1114	13.6
90-91	POR	80	2582	358	.602	0	.000	217	.705	227	751	97	47	47	933	11.7
91-92	POR	80	2519	340	.604	0	.000	221	.754	260	704	108	62	41	901	11.3
92-93	POR	82	2498	270	.511	0	.000	138	.645	232	690	75	81	61	678	8.3
Totals		959	33500	5362	.554	2	.087	3340	.663	3557	10521	1372	858	884	14066	14.7

COREY WILLIAMS

Team: Chicago Bulls
Position: Guard
Height: 6'2" **Weight:** 190
Birthdate: April 24, 1970

NBA Experience: 1 year
College: Oklahoma St.
Acquired: 2nd-round pick in 1992 draft (33rd overall)

Background: Williams was a basketball and baseball star at Northeast High School in Macon, Georgia, before enjoying a productive but unheralded career at Oklahoma State. A two-time Big Eight All-Defensive player, he earned all-league honorable-mention honors as a senior and finished his career as the all-time Cowboy leader in games played and 3-point attempts. He was drafted in the second round by the Bulls in 1992 and played sparingly in 35 games as a rookie in 1992-93. A strained abdominal muscle sent him to the injured list late last season.

Strengths: Williams, known in college as "The Blur" for his quickness and "The Terminator" for his defensive ability, was drafted by the Bulls for those two reasons. Draft guru Marty Blake called him the fastest guard among the class of 1992. Williams is capable of hounding his man the length of the court. He can ignite the fastbreak.

Weaknesses: Williams might be too fast for his own good. He plays out of control and has been guilty of trying to do too much. Offensively, he has a long way to go. He shot 36.5 percent from the field last season. He is not confident in his outside stroke and the 3-pointer might be a little out of his range. For a defensive whiz, his total of four steals is discouraging.

Analysis: For athletic ability, speed, and quickness, Williams fits the bill. He was drafted in the 12th round by the Kansas City Chiefs despite not having played football since junior high school, and he has been clocked at 4.4 seconds in the 40-yard dash. But speed alone will not cut it in the NBA. Right now, he's more athlete than basketball player.

PLAYER SUMMARY	
Will	race up the court
Can't	earn steady minutes
Expect	defensive prowess
Don't Expect	much control
Fantasy Value	$0
Card Value	10-20¢

COLLEGE STATISTICS

		G	FGP	FTP	APG	PPG
88-89	OSU	30	.443	.688	3.3	12.4
89-90	OSU	31	.427	.755	2.7	9.4
90-91	OSU	32	.529	.697	2.3	8.3
91-92	OSU	35	.418	.770	2.6	11.2
Totals		128	.447	.729	2.7	10.3

NBA REGULAR-SEASON STATISTICS

			FGs		3-PT FGs		FTs		Rebounds						
	G	MIN	FG	PCT	FG	PCT	FT	PCT	OFF	TOT	AST	STL	BLK	PTS	PPG
92-93 CHI	35	242	31	.365	1	.333	18	.818	19	31	23	4	2	81	2.3
Totals	35	242	31	.365	1	.333	18	.818	19	31	23	4	2	81	2.3

HERB WILLIAMS

Team: New York Knicks
Position: Forward/Center
Height: 6'11" **Weight:** 260
Birthdate: February 16, 1958

NBA Experience: 12 years
College: Ohio St.
Acquired: Signed as a free agent, 11/92

Background: Williams left Ohio State as the school's all-time scoring leader. He spent his first seven-plus NBA seasons with Indiana, where he was a double-figure scorer every season. When he joined Dallas in 1988-89, he left as the Pacers' career leader in 12 categories, including points, rebounds, minutes, and blocked shots. He led the Mavericks in blocks during two of his last three seasons there. The Knicks signed him last year but he rarely left the bench.

Strengths: Williams's main weapon is his defense, although he has averaged double figures in scoring every year but two. He remains active on the interior, can play both center and power forward, and is capable of swatting teams out of their game plans.

Weaknesses: Despite a decent jump hook and turnaround jumper, Williams has floundered through some horrendous shooting seasons. He forces bad shots and doesn't spot open men when doubled. He is no better than a spot player on a team that has frontcourt talent.

Analysis: Williams is a fine defender, an accomplished shot-blocker, and a solid role-player. However, his days as a major contributor appear to be behind him. He does not have too many good years left in his legs.

PLAYER SUMMARY

Will	play defense
Can't	find open men
Expect	limited minutes
Don't Expect	much offense
Fantasy Value	$0
Card Value	5-8¢

COLLEGE STATISTICS

		G	FGP	FTP	RPG	PPG
77-78	OSU	27	.482	.659	11.4	16.7
78-79	OSU	31	.524	.669	10.5	19.9
79-80	OSU	29	.496	.660	9.1	17.6
80-81	OSU	27	.486	.688	8.0	16.0
Totals		114	.499	.669	9.7	17.6

NBA REGULAR-SEASON STATISTICS

		G	MIN	FGs FG	FGs PCT	3-PT FGs FG	3-PT FGs PCT	FTs FT	FTs PCT	Rebounds OFF	Rebounds TOT	AST	STL	BLK	PTS	PPG
81-82	IND	82	2277	407	.477	2	.286	126	.670	175	605	139	53	178	942	11.5
82-83	IND	78	2513	580	.499	0	.000	155	.705	151	583	262	54	171	1315	16.9
83-84	IND	69	2279	411	.478	0	.000	207	.702	154	554	215	60	108	1029	14.9
84-85	IND	75	2557	575	.475	1	.111	224	.657	154	634	252	54	134	1375	18.3
85-86	IND	78	2770	627	.492	1	.083	294	.730	172	710	174	50	184	1549	19.9
86-87	IND	74	2526	451	.480	0	.000	199	.740	143	543	174	59	93	1101	14.9
87-88	IND	75	1966	311	.425	0	.000	126	.737	116	469	98	37	146	748	10.0
88-89	IND/DAL	76	2470	322	.436	2	.222	133	.686	135	593	124	46	134	777	10.2
89-90	DAL	81	2199	295	.444	2	.000	108	.679	108	391	119	51	106	700	8.6
90-91	DAL	60	1832	332	.507	0	.000	83	.638	86	357	95	30	88	747	12.4
91-92	DAL	67	2040	367	.431	1	.167	124	.725	106	454	94	35	98	859	11.5
92-93	NY	55	571	72	.411	0	.000	14	.667	44	146	19	21	28	158	2.9
Totals		878	26000	4750	.469	7	.090	1793	.700	1512	6039	1765	550	1468	11300	12.9

JOHN WILLIAMS

Team: Cleveland Cavaliers
Position: Forward/Center
Height: 6'11" **Weight:** 245
Birthdate: August 9, 1962

NBA Experience: 7 years
College: Tulane
Acquired: 2nd-round pick in 1985 draft (45th overall)

Background: Williams's involvement in an alleged point-fixing scandal at Tulane rocked the college basketball world in the mid-1980s. He paced the Green Wave in scoring three of his four seasons. Williams was named to the NBA All-Rookie Team in 1987. A stress fracture in his foot shelved him for nearly half of the 1990-91 season, but he has returned as one of the top sixth men in the NBA over the last two years.

Strengths: Williams can shoot, go hard to the basket, draw fouls, block shots, crash the boards, and muscle people off the ball. His ability to play shut-down defense at multiple positions may be his greatest asset. Williams would start for most teams, but you won't hear him complain about his role. He gives his team a lift with his aggressive, unselfish play.

Weaknesses: Passing and ball-handling aren't his best skills, and his left hand is a little shaky. "Hot Rod" also picks up his share of fouls. He is one of his team's poorest free throw shooters.

Analysis: Williams does his best to earn his big bucks (almost $4 million a year). He is a force in the paint on both ends, runs the floor, and can stick 15-footers in streaks. He works hard, knows his role, and is quite consistent coming off the bench. He has averaged between 11 and 12 PPG each of the last three years. Williams and Larry Nance form a dynamite shot-blocking tandem.

PLAYER SUMMARY	
Will	provide a spark
Can't	be taken lightly
Expect	11-12 PPG
Don't Expect	bankruptcy
Fantasy Value	$10-13
Card Value	8-12¢

COLLEGE STATISTICS

		G	FGP	FTP	RPG	PPG
81-82	TUL	28	.584	.662	7.2	14.8
82-83	TUL	31	.476	.703	5.4	12.4
83-84	TUL	28	.569	.761	7.9	19.4
84-85	TUL	28	.566	.774	7.8	17.8
Totals		115	.549	.731	7.0	16.0

NBA REGULAR-SEASON STATISTICS

				FGs		3-PT FGs		FTs		Rebounds						
		G	MIN	FG	PCT	FG	PCT	FT	PCT	OFF	TOT	AST	STL	BLK	PTS	PPG
86-87	CLE	80	2714	435	.485	0	.000	298	.745	222	629	154	58	167	1168	14.6
87-88	CLE	77	2106	316	.477	0	.000	211	.756	159	506	103	61	145	843	10.9
88-89	CLE	82	2125	356	.509	1	.250	235	.748	173	477	108	77	134	948	11.6
89-90	CLE	82	2776	528	.493	0	.000	325	.739	220	663	168	86	167	1381	16.8
90-91	CLE	43	1293	199	.463	0	.000	107	.652	111	290	100	36	69	505	11.7
91-92	CLE	80	2432	341	.503	0	.000	270	.752	228	607	196	60	182	952	11.9
92-93	CLE	67	2055	263	.470	0	.000	212	.716	127	415	152	48	105	738	11.0
Totals		511	15501	2438	.488	1	.091	1658	.736	1240	3587	981	426	969	6535	12.8

JOHN WILLIAMS

Team: Los Angeles Clippers
Position: Forward
Height: 6'9" **Weight:** 300
Birthdate: October 26, 1966

NBA Experience: 6 years
College: Louisiana St.
Acquired: Traded from Bullets for Don MacLean and William Bedford, 10/92

Background: A product of the streets of Los Angeles, Williams played only two years of college ball at LSU. He was the SEC's top freshman in 1984-85 and a unanimous All-SEC pick in 1985-86. Eighteen games into the 1989-90 campaign, Williams severely injured his right knee and hasn't been the same since. He appeared in only 33 games in 1990-91 and spent the 1991-92 season on the Bullets' suspended list after he reported to camp weighing 305 pounds. His weight was again a factor last season, when he played in 74 games for the Clippers and averaged a career-low 6.6 PPG.

Strengths: Williams remains a bundle of potential, albeit an enormous bundle. He can handle the ball, runs the floor, goes to the glass hard, and shoots a smooth mid-range jumper. His big, quick hands can make him deceivingly tough defensively. At his best, he's a rare mix of finesse and power.

Weaknesses: Enigma. Head case. Pain in the rear. Williams wore out his welcome in Washington and did not bounce back with a smooth year in his hometown. Williams has yet to show a willingness to work at keeping his weight below the 300 mark. He has been horribly inconsistent throughout his career. He shot less than 55 percent from the line last year.

Analysis: Somewhere inside the body of Williams is a player with the skills of a star. Don't count on that player ever emerging, however, because "Hot Plate" seems to have buried himself under a thick layer of flesh and inconsistency.

PLAYER SUMMARY	
Will	handle the ball
Can't	pass up a meal
Expect	inconsistency
Don't Expect	dedication
Fantasy Value	$1-3
Card Value	8-12¢

COLLEGE STATISTICS

		G	FGP	FTP	RPG	PPG
84-85	LSU	29	.534	.765	6.6	13.4
85-86	LSU	37	.498	.774	8.5	17.8
Totals		66	.511	.771	7.6	15.8

NBA REGULAR-SEASON STATISTICS

				FGs		3-PT FGs		FTs		Rebounds						
		G	MIN	FG	PCT	FG	PCT	FT	PCT	OFF	TOT	AST	STL	BLK	PTS	PPG
86-87	WAS	78	1773	283	.454	8	.222	144	.646	130	366	191	129	30	718	9.2
87-88	WAS	82	2428	427	.469	5	.132	188	.734	127	444	232	117	34	1047	12.8
88-89	WAS	82	2413	438	.466	19	.268	225	.776	158	573	356	142	70	1120	13.7
89-90	WAS	18	632	130	.474	2	.111	65	.774	27	136	84	21	9	327	18.2
90-91	WAS	33	941	164	.417	10	.244	73	.753	42	177	133	39	6	411	12.5
92-93	LAC	74	1638	205	.430	12	.226	70	.543	88	316	142	83	23	492	6.6
Totals		367	9825	1647	.455	56	.218	765	.709	572	2012	1138	531	172	4115	11.2

KENNY WILLIAMS

Team: Indiana Pacers
Position: Forward
Height: 6'9" **Weight:** 205
Birthdate: June 9, 1969

NBA Experience: 3 years
College: Barton County
Acquired: 2nd-round pick in 1990
draft (46th overall)

Background: Recognized as one of the top five high school players in America in 1988, Williams was recruited by North Carolina but never enrolled due to poor grades. He played one year of junior college ball at Barton County Community College in Kansas. The Pacers were impressed enough with his Chicago pre-draft camp performance to select him in 1990. He has ranked third on the team in blocked shots each of the past three years, despite limited playing time. He has yet to reach 850 minutes in a season.

Strengths: Williams plays above the rim. He's an excellent athlete who can run the floor all day long, has a quick first step, and knows how to get to the hoop. Williams passes and jumps exceptionally well and he's pretty solid defensively. He has big-time potential as a shot-blocker and pulls down a lot of rebounds, especially on offense.

Weaknesses: Williams is a big forward playing in a small forward's body. He is more effective as an inside player than on the perimeter but lacks the size to dominate in the paint. His field goal percentage is boosted by "garbage buckets." Although he shows an occasional glimmer of brilliance, Williams does not have a great feel for the game.

Analysis: Williams played a little more last season, but he still lacks the organized basketball background and solid fundamentals to be consistently effective. He's a hard worker who will electrify a crowd from time to time with a dazzling dunk in transition, but the rest of his game lacks a layer or two of polish. He's still a raw talent.

PLAYER SUMMARY	
Will	dunk in transition
Can't	score consistently
Expect	athleticism
Don't Expect	fundamentals
Fantasy Value	$1-3
Card Value	8-12¢

COLLEGE STATISTICS

		G	FGP	FTP	RPG	PPG
88-89	BC	31	—	—	9.0	20.5
Totals		31	—	—	9.0	20.5

NBA REGULAR-SEASON STATISTICS

		G	MIN	FGs FG	FG PCT	3-PT FGs FG	FG PCT	FTs FT	FT PCT	Rebounds OFF	TOT	AST	STL	BLK	PTS	PPG
90-91	IND	75	527	93	.520	0	.000	34	.680	56	131	31	11	31	220	2.9
91-92	IND	60	565	113	.518	0	.000	26	.605	64	129	40	20	41	252	4.2
92-93	IND	57	844	150	.532	0	.000	48	.706	102	228	38	21	45	348	6.1
Totals		192	1936	356	.524	0	.000	108	.671	222	488	109	52	117	820	4.3

MICHEAL WILLIAMS

Team: Minnesota Timberwolves
Position: Guard
Height: 6'2" **Weight:** 175
Birthdate: July 23, 1966
NBA Experience: 5 years

College: Baylor
Acquired: Traded from Pacers with Chuck Person for Pooh Richardson and Sam Mitchell, 9/92

Background: Williams, a two-time all-league selection at Baylor, has played for a slew of pro teams. A member of Detroit's championship team in 1988-89, he spent the following season with Phoenix, Dallas, Charlotte, and the CBA's Rapid City Thrillers. He was signed as a free agent by Indiana, became the Pacers' starting point guard in 1990-91, and has ranked among the league's steals leaders ever since. He was traded along with Chuck Person to Minnesota before the 1992-93 campaign and broke Calvin Murphy's record by making his final 84 free throw attempts of the season.

Strengths: Williams has emerged in the NBA with his blistering speed, quick hands, and much-improved playmaking. He possesses a lightning-quick first step and an above-average pull-up jumper. His anticipation for steals is exceptional. Last year, he finished eighth in the league in steals, sixth in assists, and fourth in free throw shooting.

Weaknesses: Williams is not the defensive player his numbers say he is. He gets beaten routinely by his man and comes up with steals because he takes too many gambles. While Williams racks up the assists, he also racks up the turnovers. He's not a steady 3-point shooter.

Analysis: This former journeyman might not be a star, but he has clearly emerged as a legitimate starting point guard who scores, distributes, and thrives at a fast pace. He can dart to the hoop and you'd better not foul him, because he is automatic from the free throw line.

PLAYER SUMMARY	
Will	pick your pocket
Can't	stop penetration
Expect	great quickness
Don't Expect	missed FTs
Fantasy Value	$17-20
Card Value	8-12¢

COLLEGE STATISTICS

		G	FGP	FTP	APG	PPG
84-85	BAY	28	.487	.793	2.4	14.6
85-86	BAY	22	.462	.806	2.7	13.0
86-87	BAY	31	.475	.714	5.1	17.2
87-88	BAY	34	.505	.697	5.4	18.4
Totals		115	.485	.738	4.0	16.1

NBA REGULAR-SEASON STATISTICS

				FGs	3-PT FGs		FTs		Rebounds						
		G	MIN	FG	PCT	FG	PCT	FT	PCT	OFF	TOT	AST	STL	BLK	PTS	PPG
88-89	DET	49	358	47	.364	2	.222	31	.660	9	27	70	13	3	127	2.6
89-90	PHO/CHA	28	329	60	.504	0	.000	36	.783	12	32	81	22	1	156	5.6
90-91	IND	73	1706	261	.499	1	.143	290	.879	49	176	348	150	17	813	11.1
91-92	IND	79	2750	404	.490	8	.242	372	.871	73	282	647	233	22	1188	15.0
92-93	MIN	76	2661	353	.446	26	.243	419	.907	84	273	661	165	23	1151	15.1
Totals		305	7804	1125	.472	37	.233	1148	.875	227	790	1807	583	66	3435	11.3

REGGIE WILLIAMS

Team: Denver Nuggets
Position: Forward/Guard
Height: 6'7" **Weight:** 195
Birthdate: March 5, 1964

NBA Experience: 6 years
College: Georgetown
Acquired: Signed as a free agent, 1/91

Background: As a senior at Georgetown, Williams was a consensus All-American and Big East Player of the Year. He was named NCAA Tournament MVP when the Hoyas won the title in 1984. He was a letdown with the Clippers, Cleveland, and San Antonio and was released by the Spurs in 1990-91. After being signed by Denver two weeks later, Williams came to life. He finished fourth in the voting for the NBA's Most Improved Player Award in 1991-92 and has enjoyed his two best seasons with the Nuggets.

Strengths: Williams has made a name for himself as a shooter over the last three years, although the first three teams he played with never would have believed it. He knocks down jumpers with 3-point range and has a scorer's mentality. He runs the floor, has become a willing passer, and has a quick first step to the hoop. He is now a go-to guy.

Weaknesses: Williams has never been accused of indulging in defense. The interest is simply not there, although he will come up with steals. He is a below-average ball-handler and his 3-point percentage took a big drop last year.

Analysis: Williams's career has been a great roller-coaster ride. Projected as a star coming out of college, he was a first-rate flop for three-plus years before finding new life in the Rockies. He has been on a personal high for two years, scoring in the high teens. It seems like his biggest struggles are over.

PLAYER SUMMARY

Will ....fire away
Can't................dazzle with the dribble
Expect.....................................17 PPG
Don't Expect ....defense
Fantasy Value.........................$15-18
Card Value ....5-10¢

COLLEGE STATISTICS

		G	FGP	FTP	RPG	PPG
83-84	GEOR	37	.433	.768	3.5	9.1
84-85	GEOR	35	.506	.755	5.7	11.9
85-86	GEOR	32	.528	.732	8.2	17.6
86-87	GEOR	34	.482	.804	8.6	23.6
Totals		138	.490	.768	6.4	15.3

NBA REGULAR-SEASON STATISTICS

				FGs		3-PT FGs		FTs		Rebounds						
		G	MIN	FG	PCT	FG	PCT	FT	PCT	OFF	TOT	AST	STL	BLK	PTS	PPG
87-88	LAC	35	857	152	.356	13	.224	48	.727	55	118	58	29	21	365	10.4
88-89	LAC	63	1303	260	.438	30	.288	92	.754	70	179	103	81	29	642	10.2
89-90	LAC/CLE/SA															
		47	743	131	.388	6	.162	52	.765	28	83	53	32	14	320	6.8
90-91	SA/DEN	73	1896	384	.449	57	.363	166	.843	133	306	133	113	41	991	13.6
91-92	DEN	81	2623	601	.471	56	.359	215	.803	145	405	235	148	68	1474	18.2
92-93	DEN	79	2722	535	.458	33	.270	238	.804	132	428	295	126	76	1341	17.0
Totals		378	10144	2063	.443	195	.308	812	.798	563	1519	877	529	249	5133	13.6

SCOTT WILLIAMS

Team: Chicago Bulls
Position: Center
Height: 6'10" **Weight:** 230
Birthdate: March 21, 1968

NBA Experience: 3 years
College: North Carolina
Acquired: Signed as a free agent, 7/90

Background: Williams was Dean Smith's first West Coast recruit. Though great personal tragedy affected his early development at UNC, Williams paced Carolina in rebounding and blocked shots as a senior. After being bypassed in the 1990 NBA draft, Williams was signed by the Bulls as a free agent. He was the only rookie on the 1991 NBA championship squad and helped produce another Chicago title in 1992. He averaged 5.9 PPG last season yet finished fifth on the Bulls in scoring.

Strengths: Williams gives the Bulls size, rebounding, shot-blocking ability, and gutty low-post defense. He is quick for his size, agile, and possesses a nice touch within 12 feet of the bucket, although he is at his offensive best on put-backs. He has big, strong hands and an above-average feel for the game. He's rarely caught out of position, plays hard, and won't do anything to hurt his team.

Weaknesses: Williams is not much of a scorer, and he will not become one unless he develops more effective post moves and boosts his confidence in attacking the hoop. His range is limited and he is not reliable from the free throw line. He has been plagued by shoulder problems and was out with tendinitis in his right knee early last year.

Analysis: What Williams does, he does pretty well. He has been part of a four-headed center situation in Chicago, and it says a great deal that Williams saw more minutes last season than Stacey King, Will Perdue, and injury-plagued starter Bill Cartwright. He asked for a trade early last season, but Chicago likes the progress he has made.

PLAYER SUMMARY

Will ....challenge shots
Can't ....shoot with range
Expect ....a spark off the bench
Don't Expect.............a primary scorer
Fantasy Value...............................$2-4
Card Value ....8-12¢

COLLEGE STATISTICS

		G	FGP	FTP	RPG	PPG
86-87	NC	36	.497	.558	4.2	5.5
87-88	NC	34	.572	.673	6.4	12.8
88-89	NC	35	.556	.654	7.3	11.4
89-90	NC	33	.554	.615	7.3	14.5
Totals		138	.551	.636	6.2	10.9

NBA REGULAR-SEASON STATISTICS

				FGs		3-PT FGs		FTs		Rebounds						
		G	MIN	FG	PCT	FG	PCT	FT	PCT	OFF	TOT	AST	STL	BLK	PTS	PPG
90-91	CHI	51	337	53	.510	1	.500	20	.714	42	98	16	12	13	127	2.5
91-92	CHI	63	690	83	.463	0	.000	48	.649	90	247	50	13	36	214	3.4
92-93	CHI	71	1369	166	.466	0	.000	90	.714	168	451	68	55	66	422	5.9
Totals		185	2396	302	.478	1	.083	158	.693	300	796	134	80	115	763	4.1

WALT WILLIAMS

Team: Sacramento Kings
Position: Guard/Forward
Height: 6'8" **Weight:** 230
Birthdate: April 16, 1970

NBA Experience: 1 year
College: Maryland
Acquired: 1st-round pick in 1992 draft
(7th overall)

Background: Williams, the Washington, D.C.-area prep Player of the Year in 1988, made an early impact at Maryland. He started 12 games as a freshman and went on to break Len Bias's school record for points in a season as a senior. He averaged 26.8 points, 5.6 rebounds, 3.6 assists, and 2.1 steals per outing in his final season, then was drafted seventh overall by Sacramento. Williams earned second-team NBA All-Rookie honors last year after averaging 17.0 points per game. He was limited to 59 games because he broke a finger on his shooting hand in January.

Strengths: Williams has already earned a reputation as one of the most versatile players in the game. By late December of his rookie season, he had seen action at all five positions. He is an accomplished scorer with creative moves, a quick release, 3-point range, and a post-up game. There is very little Williams is unable to do offensively. He is both productive and exciting.

Weaknesses: There are doubts about the shooting touch of Williams, who converted just 43.5 percent of his field goals as a rookie. He was not among the better pure athletes in the first-year class. He plays defense like a lot of scorers, which is to say his interests and abilities are elsewhere. Williams fouled out six times in 59 games last season.

Analysis: During one calendar year, the multi-talented Williams overcame a training-camp holdout, a broken finger, and the death of his father to cancer. Considering all that, his rookie year in the NBA was even more amazing. He wears his socks at his knees a la his idol, George Gervin. Williams, nicknamed "The Wizard," has star potential.

PLAYER SUMMARY	
Will	score from anywhere
Can't	star on defense
Expect	great versatility
Don't Expect	high percentages
Fantasy Value	$18-21
Card Value	40¢-$1.00

COLLEGE STATISTICS

		G	FGP	FTP	RPG	PPG
88-89	MD	26	.441	.623	3.5	7.3
89-90	MD	33	.483	.776	4.2	12.7
90-91	MD	17	.449	.837	5.1	18.7
91-92	MD	29	.472	.758	5.6	26.8
Totals		105	.466	.762	4.6	16.2

NBA REGULAR-SEASON STATISTICS

				FGs		3-PT FGs		FTs		Rebounds						
		G	MIN	FG	PCT	FG	PCT	FT	PCT	OFF	TOT	AST	STL	BLK	PTS	PPG
92-93	SAC	59	1673	358	.435	61	.319	224	.742	115	265	178	66	29	1001	17.0
Totals		59	1673	358	.435	61	.319	224	.742	115	265	178	66	29	1001	17.0

KEVIN WILLIS

Team: Atlanta Hawks
Position: Forward/Center
Height: 7'0" **Weight:** 235
Birthdate: September 6, 1962

NBA Experience: 8 years
College: Michigan St.
Acquired: 1st-round pick in 1984 draft
(11th overall)

Background: Willis was tops in the Big Ten in rebounding and field goal percentage as a junior at Michigan State, where he received all-league mention as a senior. He sat out the 1988-89 season with a broken left foot. Willis was second on his own team in rebounds three years ago before dedicating his 1991-92 campaign to board work. He finished second to Dennis Rodman with 15.5 RPG, scored a career-high 18.3 PPG, and played in his first NBA All-Star Game. He dropped slightly to 17.9 PPG and 12.9 RPG last season.

Strengths: Willis is, above all, a strong rebounder. Two years ago, even his teammates were clearing out of the way. He has also picked up his offensive game and is his team's second-best scorer after Dominique Wilkins. He runs the floor well for a seven-footer, is a sweet jump-shooter, and owns a nifty hook shot.

Weaknesses: Willis still puts up bad shots more often than he should, although his decision-making has improved. He is a poor passer and ball-handler, and his dismal free throw shooting returned last year.

Analysis: Willis, among the most improved players in the league two years ago, fell back to some of his inconsistent habits last season. He went into a midseason slump that some attributed to back problems. He remains a talented offensive player and rebounder who has over 30 career 20-20 games.

PLAYER SUMMARY	
Will	own the boards
Can't	pass with precision
Expect	20-20 games
Don't Expect	consistency
Fantasy Value	$21-24
Card Value	5-10¢

COLLEGE STATISTICS

		G	FGP	FTP	RPG	PPG
81-82	MSU	27	.474	.567	4.2	6.0
82-83	MSU	27	.596	.514	9.6	13.3
83-84	MSU	25	.492	.661	7.7	11.0
Totals		79	.530	.579	7.1	10.1

NBA REGULAR-SEASON STATISTICS

				FGs		3-PT FGs		FTs		Rebounds						
		G	MIN	FG	PCT	FG	PCT	FT	PCT	OFF	TOT	AST	STL	BLK	PTS	PPG
84-85	ATL	82	1785	322	.467	2	.222	119	.657	177	522	36	31	49	765	9.3
85-86	ATL	82	2300	419	.517	0	.000	172	.654	243	704	45	66	44	1010	12.3
86-87	ATL	81	2626	538	.536	1	.250	227	.709	321	849	62	65	61	1304	16.1
87-88	ATL	75	2091	356	.518	0	.000	159	.649	235	547	28	68	42	871	11.6
89-90	ATL	81	2273	418	.519	2	.286	168	.683	253	645	57	63	47	1006	12.4
90-91	ATL	80	2373	444	.504	4	.400	159	.668	259	704	99	60	40	1051	13.1
91-92	ATL	81	2962	591	.483	6	.162	292	.804	418	1258	173	72	54	1480	18.3
92-93	ATL	80	2878	616	.506	7	.241	196	.653	335	1028	165	68	41	1435	17.9
Totals		642	19288	3704	.506	22	.212	1492	.692	2241	6257	665	493	378	8922	13.9

DAVID WINGATE

Team: Charlotte Hornets
Position: Guard/Forward
Height: 6'5" **Weight:** 185
Birthdate: December 15, 1963

NBA Experience: 7 years
College: Georgetown
Acquired: Signed as a free agent, 11/92

Background: Wingate was a member of the great Georgetown teams of the mid-1980s. He was drafted by Philadelphia in the second round and played three seasons with the Sixers. He also spent two years in San Antonio, including a period in which the Spurs placed him on the suspended list following two off-court legal incidents. The charges were eventually dropped, but the Spurs waived him. Wingate started for Washington in 1991-92 and shared starting duties with Johnny Newman in Charlotte last year.

Strengths: Wingate is a certified stopper. He is quick, stays in front of his man, and goes after the ball. He can defend ones and twos effectively. He has improved his outside shooting vastly and is a reliable ball-handler and passer. He also rebounds pretty well from the backcourt and is a strong finisher. He shot a career-high 53.6 percent last season.

Weaknesses: Wingate is not a confident scorer, which makes him unique for a starting off guard. Many of his points come in transition. Very few of them come from 3-point range (five treys over the last five years).

Analysis: Wingate has enjoyed pretty solid seasons with Washington and Charlotte. He can be effective as a starter or a reserve. He won't wear out the scoring column like most shooting guards, but he'll make sure his man doesn't burn the nets either. A knee injury bothered him late last year.

PLAYER SUMMARY	
Will	shut down his man
Can't	score in double figures
Expect	a defensive specialist
Don't Expect	a go-to guy
Fantasy Value	$0
Card Value	5-10¢

COLLEGE STATISTICS

		G	FGP	FTP	RPG	PPG
82-83	GEOR	32	.445	.702	3.0	12.0
83-84	GEOR	37	.435	.721	3.6	11.2
84-85	GEOR	38	.484	.689	3.6	12.4
85-86	GEOR	32	.497	.755	4.0	15.9
Totals		139	.467	.719	3.6	12.8

NBA REGULAR-SEASON STATISTICS

			FGs		3-PT FGs		FTs		Rebounds						
	G	MIN	FG	PCT	FG	PCT	FT	PCT	OFF	TOT	AST	STL	BLK	PTS	PPG
86-87 PHI	77	1612	259	.430	13	.250	149	.741	70	156	155	93	19	680	8.8
87-88 PHI	61	1419	218	.400	10	.250	99	.750	44	101	119	47	22	545	8.9
88-89 PHI	33	372	54	.470	2	.333	27	.794	12	37	73	9	2	137	4.2
89-90 SA	78	1856	220	.448	0	.000	87	.777	62	195	208	89	18	527	6.8
90-91 SA	25	563	53	.384	1	.111	29	.707	24	75	46	19	5	136	5.4
91-92 WAS	81	2127	266	.465	1	.056	105	.719	80	269	247	123	21	638	7.9
92-93 CHA	72	1471	180	.536	1	.167	79	.738	49	174	183	66	9	440	6.1
Totals	427	9420	1250	.447	28	.194	575	.744	341	1007	1031	446	96	3103	7.3

ORLANDO WOOLRIDGE

Team: Milwaukee Bucks
Position: Forward
Height: 6'9" **Weight:** 215
Birthdate: December 16, 1959

NBA Experience: 12 years
College: Notre Dame
Acquired: Traded from Pistons for Alvin Robertson, 2/93

Background: Woolridge ranked third in the nation in field goal percentage during his senior year at Notre Dame. In the NBA, he averaged more than 20 PPG for three straight years with Chicago and New Jersey. Woolridge entered a drug treatment center in February 1988, and he returned with the Lakers to become a big scorer off the bench in 1989-90. He was in the hunt for the 1991 scoring crown with Denver. He played more than a year in Detroit before a midseason deal brought him to Milwaukee last season. A broken right hand limited him to eight games with the Bucks.

Strengths: Woolridge remains an explosive scorer; he has more than 12,000 points to his credit. Few are willing to stand in front of his muscular frame. He is a tremendous finisher who runs the floor well and has developed his jump shot.

Weaknesses: Throughout his career, points have been more important to him than wins. Not surprisingly, he gets out on the break instead of rebounding.

Analysis: Woolridge is a natural scorer who has beaten countless defenders off the dribble. However, every new team he has joined in his career fared worse than it did the season before. That's six teams and counting.

PLAYER SUMMARY

Will ....get his points
Can't ....control the boards
Expect......................powerful finishes
Don't Expect ....team play
Fantasy Value.................................$1
Card Value ....5-12¢

COLLEGE STATISTICS

		G	FGP	FTP	RPG	PPG
77-78	ND	24	.526	.485	2.1	4.1
78-79	ND	30	.573	.732	4.8	11.0
79-80	ND	27	.585	.692	6.9	12.2
80-81	ND	28	.650	.667	6.0	14.4
Totals		109	.595	.669	5.0	10.6

NBA REGULAR-SEASON STATISTICS

		G	MIN	FGs FG	FGs PCT	3-PT FGs FG	3-PT FGs PCT	FTs FT	FTs PCT	Rebounds OFF	Rebounds TOT	AST	STL	BLK	PTS	PPG
81-82	CHI	75	1188	202	.513	0	.000	144	.699	82	227	81	23	24	548	7.3
82-83	CHI	57	1627	361	.580	0	.000	217	.638	122	298	97	38	44	939	16.5
83-84	CHI	75	2544	570	.525	1	.500	303	.715	130	369	136	71	60	1444	19.3
84-85	CHI	77	2816	679	.554	0	.000	409	.785	158	435	135	58	38	1767	22.9
85-86	CHI	70	2248	540	.495	4	.174	364	.788	150	350	213	49	47	1448	20.7
86-87	NJ	75	2638	556	.521	1	.125	438	.777	118	367	261	54	86	1551	20.7
87-88	NJ	19	622	110	.445	0	.000	92	.708	31	91	71	13	20	312	16.4
88-89	LAL	74	1491	231	.468	0	.000	253	.738	81	270	58	30	65	715	9.7
89-90	LAL	62	1421	306	.506	0	.000	176	.733	49	185	96	39	46	788	12.7
90-91	DEN	53	1823	490	.498	0	.000	350	.797	141	361	119	69	23	1330	25.1
91-92	DET	82	2113	452	.498	1	.111	241	.683	100	280	88	41	33	1146	14.0
92-93	DET/MIL	58	1555	289	.482	0	.000	120	.678	87	185	115	27	27	698	12.0
Totals		777	22086	4786	.517	7	.095	3107	.740	1258	3398	1470	512	513	12686	16.3

JAMES WORTHY

Team: Los Angeles Lakers
Position: Forward
Height: 6'9" **Weight:** 225
Birthdate: February 27, 1961

NBA Experience: 11 years
College: North Carolina
Acquired: 1st-round pick in 1982 draft (1st overall)

Background: Worthy passed up his senior year at North Carolina after leading the Tar Heels to the 1982 NCAA title. He was named MVP of the Final Four after his All-America junior campaign. The top overall draft choice in 1982, Worthy shot above 53 percent in his first eight pro seasons. He won NBA titles with the Lakers in 1985, 1987, and 1988, and was named MVP of the 1988 Finals. He played in his seventh All-Star Game in 1992 before knee surgery cut his season short. He averaged 14.9 PPG last year, third lowest of his career.

Strengths: Worthy can still put the ball in the hoop, as he showed during last year's playoffs. His baseline spin move is still effective and usually ends with a patented one-handed dunk. Worthy passes well and is a leader.

Weaknesses: Worthy's knees have caused him to lose a step and have made him almost completely ineffective as a rebounder. Muggsy Bogues averages more boards per game than Worthy's three.

Analysis: It was quite a shock to Worthy when he was reduced to a bench player last April, but he understands he is not the player he once was. "Big Game James" can still light up the scoreboard when healthy.

PLAYER SUMMARY	
Will	spin to the hoop
Can't	regain young legs
Expect	veteran leadership
Don't Expect	rebounds
Fantasy Value	$5-7
Card Value	10-15¢

COLLEGE STATISTICS

		G	FGP	FTP	RPG	PPG
79-80	NC	14	.587	.600	7.4	12.5
80-81	NC	36	.500	.640	8.4	14.2
81-82	NC	34	.573	.674	6.3	15.6
Totals		84	.541	.652	7.4	14.5

NBA REGULAR-SEASON STATISTICS

				FGs		3-PT FGs		FTs		Rebounds						
		G	MIN	FG	PCT	FG	PCT	FT	PCT	OFF	TOT	AST	STL	BLK	PTS	PPG
82-83	LAL	77	1970	447	.579	1	.250	138	.624	157	399	132	91	64	1033	13.4
83-84	LAL	82	2415	495	.556	0	.000	195	.759	157	515	207	77	70	1185	14.5
84-85	LAL	80	2696	610	.572	0	.000	190	.776	169	511	201	87	67	1410	17.6
85-86	LAL	75	2454	629	.579	0	.000	242	.771	136	387	201	82	77	1500	20.0
86-87	LAL	82	2819	651	.539	0	.000	292	.751	158	466	226	108	83	1594	19.4
87-88	LAL	75	2655	617	.531	2	.125	242	.796	129	374	289	72	55	1478	19.7
88-89	LAL	81	2960	702	.548	2	.087	251	.782	169	489	288	108	56	1657	20.5
89-90	LAL	80	2960	711	.548	15	.306	248	.782	160	478	288	99	49	1685	21.1
90-91	LAL	78	3008	716	.492	26	.289	212	.797	107	356	275	104	35	1670	21.4
91-92	LAL	54	2108	450	.447	9	.209	166	.814	98	305	252	76	23	1075	19.9
92-93	LAL	82	2359	510	.447	30	.270	171	.810	73	247	278	92	27	1221	14.9
Totals		846	28404	6538	.529	85	.227	2347	.770	1513	4527	2637	996	606	15508	18.3

DANNY YOUNG

Team: Detroit Pistons
Position: Guard
Height: 6'4" **Weight:** 175
Birthdate: July 26, 1962

NBA Experience: 9 years
College: Wake Forest
Acquired: Signed as a free agent, 12/92

Background: Young graduated as Wake Forest's career leader in games played and was third on the all-time assists list. He was waived twice in his four-year stint in Seattle and spent time in the CBA during the 1984-85 season. He served primarily as a back-up point guard in his three-plus years with Portland, and has since served reserve stints with the Clippers and Pistons. He averaged less than three PPG with Detroit last year.

Strengths: Young is reliable with the ball and doesn't force plays when nothing is there. His assist-to-turnover ratio approaches four-to-one. He is a decent 3-point shooter and an excellent free throw shooter (never less than .850 in the last three years). Young plays within his limitations.

Weaknesses: Once a decent shooter, Young's percentage has fallen off a cliff. Hence, so has his job security. While he is a steady passer and ball-handler, Young does not possess the quickness to create much offense on his own. He goes with what's there and no more.

Analysis: Young is a capable back-up guard who does not hurt his team and will stick an occasional long-range jumper. His sagging shooting percentage and inability to create, however, have limited his contributions and playing time over the last few years.

PLAYER SUMMARY	
Will	make his FTs
Can't	hoist FG pct.
Expect	control of the ball
Don't Expect	creativity
Fantasy Value	$0
Card Value	5-10¢

COLLEGE STATISTICS

		G	FGP	FTP	RPG	PPG
80-81	WF	29	.496	.688	1.3	5.1
81-82	WF	30	.508	.714	2.5	10.6
82-83	WF	31	.457	.713	2.1	12.8
83-84	WF	32	.456	.707	1.8	9.6
Totals		122	.475	.708	1.9	9.6

NBA REGULAR-SEASON STATISTICS

		G	MIN	FGs FG	FGs PCT	3-PT FGs FG	3-PT FGs PCT	FTs FT	FTs PCT	Rebounds OFF	Rebounds TOT	AST	STL	BLK	PTS	PPG
84-85	SEA	3	26	2	.200	0	.000	0	.000	0	3	2	3	0	4	1.3
85-86	SEA	82	1901	227	.506	24	.324	90	.849	29	120	303	110	9	568	6.9
86-87	SEA	73	1482	132	.458	29	.367	59	.831	23	113	353	74	3	352	4.8
87-88	SEA	77	949	89	.408	22	.286	43	.811	18	75	218	52	2	243	3.2
88-89	POR	48	952	115	.460	17	.340	50	.781	17	74	123	55	3	297	6.2
89-90	POR	82	1393	138	.421	16	.271	91	.813	29	122	231	82	4	383	4.7
90-91	POR	75	897	103	.380	36	.346	41	.911	22	75	141	50	7	283	3.8
91-92	POR/LAC	62	1023	100	.392	23	.329	57	.851	16	75	172	46	4	280	4.5
92-93	DET	65	836	69	.413	22	.324	13	.875	13	47	119	31	5	188	2.9
Totals		567	9459	975	.436	189	.325	459	.835	167	704	1662	503	37	2598	4.6

1993 NBA DRAFT

FIRST ROUND

	Player	College	Team
1)	Chris Webber	Michigan	Orlando
2)	Shawn Bradley	Brigham Young	Philadelphia
3)	Anfernee Hardaway	Memphis St.	Golden State
4)	Jamal Mashburn	Kentucky	Dallas
5)	Isaiah (J.R.) Rider	UNLV	Minnesota
6)	Calbert Cheaney	Indiana	Washington
7)	Bobby Hurley	Duke	Sacramento
8)	Vin Baker	Hartford	Milwaukee
9)	Rodney Rogers	Wake Forest	Denver
10)	Lindsey Hunter	Jackson St.	Detroit
11)	Allan Houston	Tennessee	Detroit
12)	George Lynch	North Carolina	L.A. Lakers
13)	Terry Dehere	Seton Hall	L.A. Clippers
14)	Scott Haskin	Oregon St.	Indiana
15)	Doug Edwards	Florida St.	Atlanta
16)	Rex Walters	Kansas	New Jersey
17)	Greg Graham	Indiana	Charlotte
18)	Luther Wright	Seton Hall	Utah
19)	Acie Earl	Iowa	Boston
20)	Scott Burrell	Connecticut	Charlotte
21)	James Robinson	Alabama	Portland
22)	Chris Mills	Arizona	Cleveland
23)	Ervin Johnson	New Orleans	Seattle
24)	Sam Cassell	Florida St.	Houston
25)	Corie Blount	Cincinnati	Chicago
26)	Geert Hammink	Louisiana St.	Orlando
27)	Malcolm Mackey	Georgia Tech	Phoenix

SECOND ROUND

	Player	College	Team
28)	Lucious Harris	Long Beach St.	Dallas
29)	Sherron Mills	Virginia Commonwealth	Minnesota
30)	Gheorghe Muresan	Romania	Washington
31)	Evers Burns	Maryland	Sacramento
32)	Alphonso Ford	Miss. Valley St.	Philadelphia
33)	Eric Riley	Michigan	Dallas
34)	Darnell Mee	Western Kentucky	Golden State
35)	Ed Stokes	Arizona	Miami
36)	John Best	Tennessee Tech	New Jersey
37)	Nick Van Exel	Cincinnati	L.A. Lakers
38)	Conrad McRae	Syracuse	Washington
39)	Thomas Hill	Duke	Indiana
40)	Richard Manning	Washington	Atlanta
41)	Anthony Reed	Tulane	Chicago
42)	Adonis Jordan	Kansas	Seattle
43)	Josh Grant	Utah	Denver
44)	Alex Holcombe	Baylor	Sacramento
45)	Bryon Russell	Long Beach St.	Utah
46)	Richard Petruska	UCLA	Houston
47)	Chris Whitney	Clemson	San Antonio
48)	Kevin Thompson	North Carolina St.	Portland
49)	Mark Buford	Miss. Valley St.	Phoenix
50)	Marcelo Nicola	Argentina	Houston
51)	Spencer Dunkley	Delaware	Indiana
52)	Mike Peplowski	Michigan St.	Sacramento
53)	Leonard White	Southern	L.A. Clippers
54)	Byron Wilson	Utah	Phoenix

VIN BAKER

Team: Milwaukee Bucks
Position: Forward
Height: 6'11"
Weight: 232

Birthdate: November 23, 1971
College: Hartford
Acquired: 1st-round pick in 1993 draft
(8th overall)

Background: Baker toiled in obscurity for Hartford, a member of the lowly North Atlantic Conference. However, he caught the eye of NBA scouts when he finished second in scoring in Division I as a junior. Baker became a media darling during his senior season, when he ranked fourth in the nation in scoring and 17th in rebounding. Moreover, he set school records in career scoring, field goals, free throws, and blocked shots. A do-it-all center at Hartford, he is expected to play small forward in the NBA.

Strengths: Baker is big but has the skills for a finesse game. Likened to Danny Manning by several general managers, Baker has range to about 20 feet and quick post-up moves inside. He's a very good ball-handler for his size and runs the court smoothly. There's a lot of room for growth in his game.

Weaknesses: Baker is making a big jump in competition and thus must be more intense and consistent than he was at Hartford. His passing and man-to-man defense also need work. Because he'll eventually play small forward, he must polish his facing-the-basket game.

Analysis: The Bucks shopped their draft position before the draft but couldn't find a deal they liked. They needed a big man to play inside, but they had to settle for a big man who plays small. Baker will need a while to acclimate himself to the NBA—as well as a new position—after playing against inferior competition in the NAC. The Bucks can afford to wait because they have good young forwards—Anthony Avent, Blue Edwards, and Ken Norman—already in place.

PLAYER SUMMARY

Will ....run the floor
Can't ....wrestle inside
Expect............................a quality pro
Don't Expect.................a power game
Fantasy Value....................................$1
Card Value ....25-40¢

COLLEGE HIGHLIGHTS

- A.P. honorable-mention All-American, 1992 and 1993
- ECAC Division I Player of the Year, 1993
- North Atlantic Player of the Year, 1993

COLLEGE STATISTICS

		G	FGs FG	FGs PCT	3-PT FGs FG	3-PT FGs PCT	FTs FT	FTs PCT	REB	AST	STL	BLK	PTS	PPG
89-90	HART	28	58	.617	0	.000	16	.390	82	7	7	47	132	4.7
90-91	HART	29	216	.491	0	.000	137	.678	302	18	31	58	569	19.6
91-92	HART	27	281	.440	41	.331	142	.657	267	36	35	100	745	27.6
92-93	HART	28	305	.477	32	.269	150	.625	300	54	39	74	792	28.3
Totals		112	860	.475	73	.300	445	.637	951	115	112	279	2238	20.0

CORIE BLOUNT

Team: Chicago Bulls
Position: Forward/Center
Height: 6'10"
Weight: 242

Birthdate: January 4, 1969
College: Rancho Santiago; Cincinnati
Acquired: 1st-round pick in 1993 draft
(25th overall)

Background: Standing 6'5" when he finished high school, Blount enrolled at Rancho Santiago C.C. in his home state of California. He missed his first season because of a broken foot but, in his third season, was named Junior College Player of the Year by *Basketball Times.* Blount then transferred to Cincinnati, where he became an immediate starter in 1991-92 and helped the Bearcats to the Final Four. Last year, he sat out the first 11 games while waiting for the NCAA to recognize his redshirt season at Rancho Santiago. He was finally reinstated on January 16 and helped Cincinnati to three wins in the NCAAs.

Strengths: Blount is an athletic big man with a tremendous upside, especially for defense. He's wiry-strong, runs the court, and blocks shots instinctively. He's an average rebounder and can get better. Scouts liken him to John Salley, but Blount has more zest for the game than Salley.

Weaknesses: Blount could stand to bulk up a bit for the NBA grind. Though he can score with garbage around the basket, he isn't a good shooter and has very limited range. He has never made a 3-pointer. He's also a lousy free throw shooter, averaging 56 percent at Cincinnati.

Analysis: The champs took what they could get at the bottom of the first round in a weak draft. Blount has potential, and the Bulls can afford to be patient with him. He'll never be a starter as long as Horace Grant is around, but he could become a pretty good reserve power forward. And on this team, he won't have to score to be effective.

PLAYER SUMMARY

Will .... hit the boards
Can't .... hit his FTs
Expect .... long-term results
Don't Expect .... a starter
Fantasy Value $0
Card Value .... 15-30¢

COLLEGE HIGHLIGHTS

- *Basketball Times* Juco Player of the Year, 1991
- California Juco Player of the Year, 1991
- Juco All-American, 1991

COLLEGE STATISTICS

		G	FGs FG	FGs PCT	3-PT FGs FG	3-PT FGs PCT	FTs FT	FTs PCT	REB	AST	STL	BLK	PTS	PPG
89-90	RS	34	200	.536	0	.000	72	.585	279	56	—	—	472	13.9
90-91	RS	37	301	.589	0	.000	121	.665	333	108	—	—	723	19.5
91-92	CINC	34	114	.479	0	.000	50	.556	213	69	39	52	278	8.2
92-93	CINC	21	104	.550	0	.000	30	.566	170	47	37	33	238	11.3
Cinc. Totals		55	218	.511	0	.000	80	.559	383	116	76	85	516	9.4

SHAWN BRADLEY

Team: Philadelphia 76ers
Position: Center
Height: 7'6"
Weight: 245

Birthdate: March 22, 1972
College: Brigham Young
Acquired: 1st-round pick in 1993 draft (2nd overall)

Background: From tiny Castle Dale, Utah, Bradley stayed close to home as a collegian. He played just one season at Brigham Young (as a freshman in 1990-91) and became the talk of the college basketball world. He blocked 177 shots that year—the second-highest figure in NCAA history—and once swatted 14 in a game. He spent the last two years in Australia on a Mormon mission, which is required for all BYU students. Expected to return to school this season, he instead entered the draft. A rail-thin 205 pounds when he enrolled at BYU, Bradley gained 40 pounds while overseas.

Strengths: Bradley grades highly when compared with fellow giants Manute Bol and Mark Eaton. He runs better than those two, is quicker, sees the floor better, and has better timing for blocking shots. He has an array of offensive moves, including a jump shot. Unlike other giants, Bradley has real athletic skills: He was actually a star baseball player in high school. Add in moxie and solid work habits (he put in 16-hour days on his Mormon mission), and you have the ingredients for greatness.

Weaknesses: Two big negatives: a body that could stand another 50 pounds, and two years of inactivity. Said Philly general manager Jimmy Lynam: "You don't worry about his skills eroding during those two years away, but you do worry that they didn't develop."

Analysis: The Sixers love Bradley, but some people question whether he can withstand the nightly pounding in the NBA. Most likely, he'll take a couple years to mature physically and adjust to the competition. After that, there are no limits. Even as a rookie, he'll upgrade Philly's center play. Manute Bol and Charles Shackleford were dumped in the off-season.

PLAYER SUMMARY

Will......................................block shots
Can't.....................................muscle up
Expect.................NBA growing pains
Don't Expect ....lack of effort
Fantasy Value............................$10-12
Card Value $2.00-4.50

COLLEGE HIGHLIGHTS

- A.P. honorable-mention All-American, 1991
- WAC Player of the Year, 1991
- All-WAC Tournament team, 1991
- WAC All-Defensive team, 1991

COLLEGE STATISTICS

		G	FGs		3-PT FGs		FTs		REB	AST	STL	BLK	PTS	PPG
			FG	PCT	FG	PCT	FT	PCT						
90-91	BYU	34	187	.518	1	1.00	128	.692	262	41	23	177	503	14.8
Totals		34	187	.518	1	1.00	128	.692	262	41	23	177	503	14.8

SCOTT BURRELL

Team: Charlotte Hornets
Position: Forward
Height: 6'7"
Weight: 218

Birthdate: January 12, 1971
College: Connecticut
Acquired: 1st-round pick in 1993 draft
(20th overall)

Background: A terrific athlete, Burrell doubled as a baseball pitcher in the Toronto Blue Jays' farm system for three seasons, although he has given up baseball to play in the NBA. Defense was his strength at Connecticut, where as a sophomore he finished second in Division I in steals. He's the only player in Division I history to have 1,500 points, 750 rebounds, 300 steals, and 275 assists. He was named second-team All-Big East after his junior season.

Strengths: Scouts predict a strong upside for Burrell now that he has given up baseball and will concentrate year-round on hoops. A very good defender, he anticipates his opponent's actions and has quick hands for steals. He runs well and is a good offensive player in a push game. He rebounds well for his size. His college totals prove his ability to do a little bit of everything—score, rebound, pass, and play defense.

Weaknesses: Though he improved his offense each year at Connecticut, Burrell remains erratic. He could hit five shots in a row and then miss eight. His career field goal percentage of .426—and .411 as a senior—is a bad sign. Though a solid all-around player, he's not great in any area.

Analysis: Charlotte used the last of its two first-round picks to grab Burrell, who should be right at home in the Hornets' high-octane offense. David Wingate and Johnny Newman shared the small-forward spot last season, and neither is a lock to beat out Burrell for the job this year. If Burrell can curb his taste for bad shots, he could be one of the biggest rookie surprises.

PLAYER SUMMARY	
Will	run and shoot
Can't	hit consistently
Expect	a valuable reserve
Don't Expect	lack of effort
Fantasy Value	$1-3
Card Value	35-50¢

COLLEGE HIGHLIGHTS

• Second-team All-Big East, 1992
• Third-team All-Big East, 1991
• Big East All-Rookie team, 1990

COLLEGE STATISTICS

			FGs		3-PT FGs		FTs							
		G	FG	PCT	FG	PCT	FT	PCT	REB	AST	STL	BLK	PTS	PPG
89-90	CONN	32	88	.386	20	.313	66	.623	177	57	60	30	262	8.2
90-91	CONN	31	136	.440	37	.343	84	.592	234	95	112	40	393	12.7
91-92	CONN	30	175	.453	61	.396	77	.611	183	87	75	31	488	16.3
92-93	CONN	26	145	.411	50	.345	79	.780	156	54	63	28	419	16.1
Totals		119	544	.426	168	.356	306	.640	750	293	310	129	1562	13.1

SAM CASSELL

Team: Houston Rockets
Position: Guard
Height: 6'3"
Weight: 195

Birthdate: November 18, 1969
College: San Jacinto; Florida St.
Acquired: 1st-round pick in 1993 draft
(24th overall)

Background: From legendary Dunbar High School in Baltimore, Cassell signed with DePaul but was diverted to a junior college because of academic shortcomings. After two sensational seasons at San Jacinto J.C. in Texas, in which he averaged 22 points and six assists per game, Cassell transferred to Florida State. He prospered with the Seminoles, which was not an easy task on a club that included Doug Edwards, Rodney Dobard, Bob Sura, and Charlie Ward. Last season, Cassell led the Atlantic Coast Conference in steals and scored 30 or more points four times. He was named second-team All-ACC for the second consecutive year.

Strengths: Sedale Threatt is the player to whom Cassell is often compared. Cassell has the same kind of quickness, agility, and hands as Threatt, yet Sam is better at taking the ball to the basket and finishing with a flourish. He shoots with range, pushes the ball in transition, and can play both guard spots. He can be outstanding defensively when he wants to be.

Weaknesses: While a solid man-to-man defender, Cassell gets lost in traps and rotations. Concentration often is lacking from his game, and he gets wild with the ball. He can't be trusted to make the right decision in pressure situations.

Analysis: A perfect pick for the Rockets, Cassell should be a better option than Scott Brooks and Winston Garland as a back-up guard. He's a lock to make the team, as Sleepy Floyd was waived and Garland left as a free agent. Cassell is best suited for two guard, and that is where he should see most of his minutes.

PLAYER SUMMARY
Will...............................make the team
Can't.........................control the tempo
Expect.........................a bench boost
Don't Expect..........................a starter
Fantasy Value.................................$0
Card Value..............................10-20¢

COLLEGE HIGHLIGHTS
- Second-team All-ACC, 1992 and 1993
- Juco All-American, 1991
- Honorable-mention Juco All-American, 1990

COLLEGE STATISTICS

		G	FGs FG	FGs PCT	3-PT FGs FG	3-PT FGs PCT	FTs FT	FTs PCT	REB	AST	STL	BLK	PTS	PPG
89-90	SJ	38	296	.495	82	.446	136	.800	208	200	—	—	810	21.3
90-91	SJ	31	233	.495	63	.394	198	.805	157	237	—	—	727	23.5
91-92	FSU	31	206	.454	58	.354	100	.704	141	119	56	8	570	18.4
92-93	FSU	35	234	.502	50	.382	123	.759	152	170	97	10	641	18.3
FSU Totals		66	440	.478	105	.356	223	.733	293	289	153	18	1211	18.3

CALBERT CHEANEY

Team: Washington Bullets
Position: Forward
Height: 6'7"
Weight: 209

Birthdate: July 17, 1971
College: Indiana
Acquired: 1st-round pick in 1993 draft
(6th overall)

Background: Though not highly recruited out of high school in Evansville, Indiana, Cheaney received a scholarship from Bob Knight and developed into one of the best players in Hoosiers history. He set a Big Ten record for total points with 2,613, breaking Glen Rice's mark of 2,442, and scored in double figures in 58 of his final 59 games. The John Wooden and James Naismith Awards, both recognizing the national Player of the Year, were among the honors Cheaney earned last season.

Strengths: The best pure shooter in the draft, Cheaney rarely misses when given an opening on the perimeter. He's quick and agile and effective in transition. Moreover, he can work the baseline with spin moves and other tricks. Said one general manager: "He's the whole package—an athlete who can shoot, pass, run, and knows how to play." Also, scouts love his competitive makeup.

Weaknesses: Cheaney can swing between small forward and shooting guard, but he needs to expand his range to play the latter. Some people say he won't improve in the NBA because Knight already has maximized his talents.

Analysis: The drafting of Cheaney completed an overhaul of the Bullets' front line. Kevin Duckworth is the new center, Pervis Ellison is moving to power forward, and Tom Gugliotta and Cheaney are the small forwards. Suddenly, the Bullets aren't undersized anymore; they should be a better defensive team than they were a year ago. Cheaney can swing to shooting guard too, though Rex Chapman and LaBradford Smith have first call at that position.

PLAYER SUMMARY

Will ....work the baseline
Can't............................hit the 3-pointer
Expect ....a smooth scorer
Don't Expect ....a savior
Fantasy Value..............................$8-10
Card Value ....25-40¢

COLLEGE HIGHLIGHTS

- John Wooden Award winner, 1993
- A.P. national Player of the Year, 1993
- *Sports Illustrated* national Player of the Year, 1993
- All-Big Ten, 1991, 1992, and 1993

COLLEGE STATISTICS

			FGs		3-PT FGs		FTs		REB	AST	STL	BLK	PTS	PPG
		G	FG	PCT	FG	PCT	FT	PCT						
89-90	IND	29	199	.572	25	.490	72	.750	133	48	24	16	495	17.1
90-91	IND	34	289	.596	43	.473	113	.801	188	47	24	13	734	21.6
91-92	IND	34	227	.522	33	.384	112	.800	166	48	36	6	599	17.6
92-93	IND	35	303	.549	47	.427	132	.795	223	84	33	10	785	22.4
Totals		132	1018	.559	148	.438	429	.790	710	227	117	45	2613	19.8

TERRY DEHERE

Team: Los Angeles Clippers
Position: Guard
Height: 6'2"
Weight: 190

Birthdate: September 12, 1971
College: Seton Hall
Acquired: 1st-round pick in 1993 draft
(13th overall)

Background: A prep teammate of Bobby Hurley, Dehere was slow to develop in high school but became a star in his first season as a collegian, leading Seton Hall in scoring and steals. He was the Pirates' primary offensive weapon for four years, during which he surpassed Chris Mullin to become the Big East's all-time leading scorer. He was named first-team All-Big East three times, and last year he was voted his conference's Player of the Year. Dehere was listed at 6'4" in college but measured just over 6'2" at the NBA's pre-draft camp in Chicago.

Strengths: Dehere's a winner. NBA people give him high marks for character and intelligence. Known primarily for his offense, he can get his own shot in halfcourt situations and is dangerous in transition. Though only adequate defensively, he works hard and doesn't back down. Dehere has proven durable, starting all of Seton Hall's 128 games over the last four years.

Weaknesses: Dehere may take a year or two to become a legitimate player. He's a bit small for shooting guard and, though constantly improving, needs more work handling the ball. He has faulty rotation on his shot, which makes him susceptible to bad nights.

Analysis: The Clippers have no discernible plan, and on draft day they still didn't have a coach, but they did the right thing when they took Dehere. He should be a quality back-up for shooting guard Ron Harper. With Dehere, Harper, and Mark Jackson, the Clips are set at guard and now can focus on finding front-line replacements for Ken Norman and, next year, Danny Manning.

PLAYER SUMMARY

Will..........................shoot on the move
Can't ....defend bigger guards
Expect..........................some bad shots
Don't Expect ....a big role this year
Fantasy Value....................................$1
Card Value ....20-35¢

COLLEGE HIGHLIGHTS

• A.P. second-team All-American, 1993
• Big East Player of the Year, 1993
• All-Big East, 1991, 1992, and 1993
• Big East Tournament MVP, 1993

COLLEGE STATISTICS

		G	FGs FG	FGs PCT	3-PT FGs FG	3-PT FGs PCT	FTs FT	FTs PCT	REB	AST	STL	BLK	PTS	PPG
89-90	SH	28	134	402	73	.390	110	.797	94	60	26	13	451	16.1
90-91	SH	34	213	.463	105	.429	141	.839	101	76	48	14	672	19.8
91-92	SH	31	196	.427	53	.321	156	.830	115	85	38	9	601	19.4
92-93	SH	35	242	.461	84	.396	202	.818	105	93	40	8	770	22.0
Totals		128	785	.442	315	.389	609	.822	415	314	152	44	2494	19.5

ACIE EARL

Team: Boston Celtics
Position: Center/Forward
Height: 6'11"
Weight: 240

Birthdate: June 23, 1970
College: Iowa
Acquired: 1st-round pick in 1993 draft
(19th overall)

Background: Though slow to develop a well-rounded game, Earl always has been a good shot-blocker. After redshirting his first year at Iowa, he led the Big Ten in blocks as a freshman and finished his career with 365 swats—seventh-best in NCAA annals. He ranks in the top five in Hawkeye history in points, rebounds, and blocks. His scoring and shot-blocking numbers dipped a bit during his senior season, yet he was selected as a finalist for the Wooden Award. Listed at 6'10" in college, Earl measured over 6'11" at the Chicago pre-draft camp.

Strengths: Earl's greatest asset is his big body, and his No. 1 skill is blocking shots. He does so with good timing. Offensively, he catches the basketball well and has been able to put the ball in the hole, although he has looked awkward doing so. He has pretty good touch from outside and is able to can the medium-range jumper.

Weaknesses: Earl won't be able to block as many shots in the pros as he did in college because he's not a good jumper. Rebounding will be a problem too because he's slow-footed and lacks quickness to the ball. He needs to develop a low-post repertoire, and he would be best advised to learn a hook shot.

Analysis: The Celtics finally addressed their need for a big man after passing on Oliver Miller and Sean Rooks in 1992. Earl will be tutored by Robert Parish, one of the great centers, and better be a quick learner because Parish is 40 and ready for pasture. Though he doesn't run well, Earl may be a good fit with Boston, which has become mostly a halfcourt team.

PLAYER SUMMARY

Will	reject shots
Can't	face and shoot
Expect	a role-player
Don't Expect	The Chief II
Fantasy Value	$1
Card Value	25-40¢

COLLEGE HIGHLIGHTS

- John Wooden Award finalist, 1993
- All-Big Ten, 1992
- Second-team All-Big Ten, 1991 and 1993
- Big Ten Defensive Player of the Year, 1992

COLLEGE STATISTICS

		G	FGs FG	FGs PCT	3-PT FGs FG	3-PT FGs PCT	FTs FT	FTs PCT	REB	AST	STL	BLK	PTS	PPG
89-90	IOWA	22	48	.440	1	.333	34	.739	78	24	11	50	131	6.0
90-91	IOWA	32	179	.503	1	1.00	161	.665	213	48	29	106	520	16.3
91-92	IOWA	30	212	.533	0	.000	162	.667	234	27	30	121	586	19.5
92-93	IOWA	32	203	.505	0	.000	136	.701	286	40	41	88	542	16.9
Totals		116	642	.508	2	.286	493	.680	811	139	111	365	1779	15.3

DOUG EDWARDS

Team: Atlanta Hawks
Position: Forward
Height: 6'7"
Weight: 220

Birthdate: January 21, 1971
College: Florida St.
Acquired: 1st-round pick in 1993 draft
(15th overall)

Background: One of the nation's top recruits in 1989, Edwards is considered the best player in Florida high school history. Forced to sit out his freshman season because of Proposition 48, he arrived with a bang as a sophomore, torching Syracuse for 31 points. He didn't improve much as a junior and senior but was still a quality player. Last year, he recorded 16 double-doubles and was among the ACC's top ten in six categories. Though listed at 6'9" in college, he measured 6'7" at the Chicago pre-draft camp. His younger brother Steve is an up-and-coming star at Miami of Florida.

Strengths: Edwards is a good all-around player but not great in any area. He shoots well facing the basket, has improved his passing skills, and grabs his share of rebounds. Having starred in the ACC, he has proven he can handle good competition. Said one general manager: "He's very tough and very talented."

Weaknesses: A limited athlete, Edwards lacks quickness and end-to-end speed. He needs to work on his low-post offensive game. Defensively, he figures to struggle stopping anyone 6'8" or taller. He lacks the explosiveness to be a starting small forward, and at 6'7" he's too short to start at the power spot.

Analysis: The Hawks wanted Scott Haskin but he went to Indiana a pick earlier, so they took a flyer on Edwards. The only way he'll play much is if Dominique Wilkins or Kevin Willis is traded. The Hawks seem committed to back-up forwards Duane Ferrell and Adam Keefe, meaning Edwards will struggle for playing time. Some NBA people insist Edwards is vastly overrated.

PLAYER SUMMARY	
Will	share the ball
Can't	get excited
Expect	an all-around talent
Don't Expect	marquee talent
Fantasy Value	$0
Card Value	15-25¢

COLLEGE HIGHLIGHTS
- John Wooden Award finalist, 1993
- Second-team All-ACC, 1992, 1993
- Second-team All-Metro, 1991

COLLEGE STATISTICS

			FGs		3-PT FGs		FTs							
		G	FG	PCT	FG	PCT	FT	PCT	REB	AST	STL	BLK	PTS	PPG
90-91	FSU	32	200	.519	12	.333	112	.709	227	61	32	36	524	16.4
91-92	FSU	30	197	.512	12	.226	106	.747	271	80	48	41	512	17.1
92-93	FSU	31	224	.526	6	.240	114	.722	290	91	43	44	568	18.3
Totals		93	621	.520	30	.263	332	.725	788	232	123	121	1604	17.2

GREG GRAHAM

Team: Charlotte Hornets
Position: Guard
Height: 6'4"
Weight: 183

Birthdate: November 26, 1970
College: Indiana
Acquired: 1st-round pick in 1993 draft
(17th overall)

Background: A high-profile recruit for Bob Knight, Graham took a couple years to become a dependable player. He was an effective sixth man as a junior, when the Hoosiers went to the Final Four, and a force as a senior, when he shot the lights out from all over the court. Graham shot 55 percent from the floor, 82 percent from the line, and an amazing 51 percent from 3-point land (57 of 111). His stock shot up with good postseason showings in the NABC All-Star Game and the Phoenix Desert Classic.

Strengths: Stout defensively, Graham can trap and press with the best guards and is tough to shake one-on-one. He has a good feel for offense too. He has the quickness to get open for shots and, as mentioned, buries a high percentage of his attempts. He's still learning and has room for improvement.

Weaknesses: Graham might get pushed around in the NBA since he's very small for a shooting guard. Scouts say he's closer to 6'3" and 175 pounds than his listed dimensions. He must learn how to run a team and set up people so that he can play more at the point. Though he can score, he's not a pure jump-shooter. He was more of a stand-up shooter in college.

Analysis: The Hornets have a good guard rotation (Kendall Gill, Muggsy Bogues, and Dell Curry), but Gill wants out and will leave as a free agent after this season if he isn't traded first. That makes Graham a valuable insurance policy. Graham probably won't play a lot as a rookie. However, if he can refine his offensive game, he'll have a long, solid career in the NBA.

PLAYER SUMMARY	
Will	play both ends
Can't	create his own shot
Expect	a quality back-up
Don't Expect	an attitude
Fantasy Value	$1
Card Value	15-30¢

COLLEGE HIGHLIGHTS
• Big Ten Defensive Player of the Year, 1993
• All-Big Ten, 1993
• Third-team All-Big Ten, 1992
• Phoenix Desert Classic MVP, 1993

COLLEGE STATISTICS

			FGs		3-PT FGs		FTs							
		G	FG	PCT	FG	PCT	FT	PCT	REB	AST	STL	BLK	PTS	PPG
89-90	IND	29	89	.471	12	.387	91	.778	76	59	23	13	281	9.7
90-91	IND	34	106	.510	7	.241	77	.694	87	53	35	6	296	8.7
91-92	IND	34	132	.502	32	.427	140	.741	137	90	46	9	436	12.8
92-93	IND	35	180	.551	57	.514	160	.825	112	102	47	8	577	16.5
Totals		132	507	.514	108	.439	468	.766	412	304	151	36	1590	12.0

GEERT HAMMINK

Team: Orlando Magic
Position: Center
Height: 7'0"
Weight: 262

Birthdate: July 12, 1969
College: Louisiana St.
Acquired: 1st-round pick in 1993 draft
(26th overall)

Background: This guy can't seem to escape the lengthy shadow of Shaquille O'Neal. Born and raised in the Netherlands, Hammink in 1988 went to LSU, where he played sparingly as a freshman and took a redshirt the next season. During his next two years—1990-91 and 1991-92—he backed up the Shaq and again played few minutes. Hammink finally entered the starting lineup as a senior and he responded big time, leading the SEC in rebounding and finishing in the top ten in both field goal and free throw accuracy. If he sticks with the Magic this year, he'll again serve as a back-up to O'Neal.

Strengths: Offensively, Hammink is little more than a jump-shooter, but he's a good one. He also scores on put-backs and tips and is decent from the line for a big man. Hammink plays hard and is improving.

Weaknesses: Many felt Hammink wouldn't be selected until deep in the second round. Slow and lacking athletically, he seldom blocks shots and projects as a below-average rebounder. He'll have trouble getting off shots in the NBA because he lacks a good back-to-the-basket game. Passing is another area that needs work. He's a project.

Analysis: The Magic grabbed what they hoped would be a low-priced back-up for O'Neal. Veteran Greg Kite filled the back-up role last season, but he makes more than $1 million per year and Orlando would love to trade him. Because the Magic have few options, Hammink has a good chance to make the team. If he doesn't make it, he could play a year or two in his native Europe.

PLAYER SUMMARY
Will...............................score in close
Can't............................face and shoot
Expect...........................a fringe player
Don't Expect....................a roadrunner
Fantasy Value.............................$0
Card Value................................15-25¢

COLLEGE HIGHLIGHTS
- All-SEC, 1993
- All-SEC Tournament team, 1993
- European junior national team, 1988
- All-Maui Invitational team, 1992

COLLEGE STATISTICS

			FGs		3-PT FGs		FTs							
		G	FG	PCT	FG	PCT	FT	PCT	REB	AST	STL	BLK	PTS	PPG
89-90	LSU	25	19	.463	0	.000	11	.407	54	4	4	3	49	2.0
90-91	LSU	27	44	.423	0	.000	36	.818	78	11	7	2	124	4.6
91-92	LSU	29	27	.403	0	.000	15	.517	79	12	7	6	69	2.4
92-93	LSU	32	190	.497	0	.000	108	.730	325	61	30	30	488	15.3
Totals		113	280	.471	0	.000	170	.685	536	88	48	41	730	6.5

ANFERNEE HARDAWAY

Team: Orlando Magic
Position: Guard
Height: 6'7"
Weight: 195
Birthdate: July 18, 1972

College: Memphis St.
Acquired: Draft rights traded from Warriors with 1996, 1998, and 2000 1st-round picks for draft rights to Chris Webber, 6/93

Background: Hardaway was *Parade's* 1989-90 national High School Player of the Year, after averaging nearly 37 PPG at Memphis Treadwell High. However, he sat out his freshman year at Memphis State after failing to meet Prop 48 requirements, then suffered a gunshot wound in his right foot in the summer of 1991. He recovered fully and became his conference's Player of the Year in 1991-92 and 1992-93. Hardaway was spectacular in scrimmages against the U.S. Olympic team in the summer of 1992. He was drafted No. 3 overall by Golden State but was immediately dealt to Orlando.

Strengths: Hardaway has all the skills a team would want from its point guard, plus he stands 6'7". That enables him to see over opposing point guards, as well as post them up whenever he wants. He directs a fastbreak with authority, handles the ball deftly, and knows how to get off his shot in traffic. Many scouts rated him the best all-around player in the draft.

Weaknesses: There's little not to like. He could stand to add meat to his bones and become more consistent with his shooting, which is the weakest part of his game. Though solid defensively, he occasionally becomes lax at that end.

Analysis: The Magic's draft-day deal netted a potential superstar, plus three draft picks, but didn't address its crying need for a power forward. G.M. Pat Williams figured Hardaway, drafted No. 3, would be easier to sign than Chris Webber at No. 1. Some think that Hardaway and Shaquille O'Neal will give Orlando many of the attributes the Lakers had with Magic Johnson and Kareem Abdul-Jabbar.

PLAYER SUMMARY	
Will	get to the rim
Can't	miss as a pro
Expect	an instant starter
Don't Expect	a power game
Fantasy Value	$11-14
Card Value	$2.00-4.00

COLLEGE HIGHLIGHTS
- Great Midwest Player of the Year, 1992 and 1993
- A.P. All-American, 1993
- Member of USA Basketball developmental team, 1992
- John Wooden Award finalist, 1993

COLLEGE STATISTICS

			FGs		3-PT FGs		FTs							
		G	FG	PCT	FG	PCT	FT	PCT	REB	AST	STL	BLK	PTS	PPG
91-92	MSU	34	209	.433	69	.363	103	.652	237	188	86	45	590	17.4
92-93	MSU	32	249	.477	73	.332	158	.767	273	204	76	39	729	22.8
Totals		66	458	.456	142	.346	261	.717	510	392	162	84	1319	20.0

SCOTT HASKIN

Team: Indiana Pacers
Position: Center/Forward
Height: 6'11"
Weight: 250

Birthdate: September 19, 1970
College: Oregon St.
Acquired: 1st-round pick in 1993 draft (14th overall)

Background: Stashed in Corvallis, Oregon, Haskin enjoyed a nice college career without any fanfare. He wasn't much as a freshman or sophomore, and he missed the 1990-91 season because of a back injury that required surgery. However, he came on strongly the past two seasons, making the ten-man All-Pac-10 team both years. NBA scouts warmed to Haskin last season, when he topped the conference in blocked shots for the second straight campaign. Though unheralded, he was the first senior center selected in the draft. A strong showing at the Phoenix Desert Classic raised his stock.

Strengths: One G.M. called Haskin a poor man's Kevin McHale. He is an agile athlete who can help a team on both ends. He can face the basket and score or back in and hook with either hand. Quick feet and good timing serve him well as a shot-blocker, and he runs the court efficiently. Said one scout: "He's tough and aggressive and doesn't back down. He takes his game at people."

Weaknesses: Haskin needs to add weight and strength in order to play back-up center. Some scouts doubt whether he can score consistently with the bump in competition—the Pac-10 itself wasn't even a strong college conference. However, other scouts love Haskin's offensive potential.

Analysis: The Pacers have been good enough to avoid the lottery the past two seasons, and that's why they seem to be running in place. Last year's pick, Malik Sealy, didn't help, and it's doubtful Haskin will make a sudden impact. Look for him to average ten to 15 minutes backing up Dale Davis at power forward.

PLAYER SUMMARY	
Will	go toe-to-toe
Can't	hit the trey
Expect	good mobility
Don't Expect	style points
Fantasy Value	$1
Card Value	15-25¢

COLLEGE HIGHLIGHTS
- All-Pac-10, 1992 and 1993
- Oregon State MVP, 1992 and 1993
- Oregon State Most Improved Player, 1990
- Two-time Pac-10 Player of the Week, 1993

COLLEGE STATISTICS

		G	FGs FG	FGs PCT	3-PT FGs FG	3-PT FGs PCT	FTs FT	FTs PCT	REB	AST	STL	BLK	PTS	PPG
88-89	OSU	24	29	.492	0	.000	16	.571	59	4	5	11	74	3.1
89-90	OSU	29	93	.497	0	.000	51	.785	140	19	10	42	237	8.2
91-92	OSU	31	226	.613	0	.000	106	.779	201	35	9	68	558	18.0
92-93	OSU	27	176	.521	0	.000	98	.645	220	19	15	51	450	16.7
Totals		111	524	.550	0	.000	271	.711	620	77	39	172	1319	11.9

ALLAN HOUSTON

Team: Detroit Pistons
Position: Guard
Height: 6'6"
Weight: 200

Birthdate: April 4, 1971
College: Tennessee
Acquired: 1st-round pick in 1993 draft
(11th overall)

Background: Kentucky's "Mr. Basketball" as a prepster, Houston was headed to the University of Louisville, where his father, Wade, was one of Denny Crum's assistants. Plans changed, however, when the elder Houston was offered the head-coaching job at Tennessee. Allowed to follow Dad to Knoxville, Allan had a bang-up career, amassing 2,801 points. In Southeastern Conference history, only Pete Maravich scored more. Houston was named first-team all-conference all four years and never averaged below 20 PPG.

Strengths: A pure shooter, Houston has excellent mechanics. He can score pulling up off the dribble or spotting up behind a screen. He piles up points without taking a lot of shots: He made 346 3-pointers in college—the sixth-highest total in NCAA history—and connected on 42 percent of his 3-point attempts. He also makes good on his free throws opportunities. The son of a coach, he knows the game inside and out and seems to do everything easily.

Weaknesses: Scouts would like to see more intensity from Houston, who could dominate if he had a bit of mean streak and demanded the ball more often. His defense needs work. "He's a little soft," said one general manager.

Analysis: Joe Dumars is an old 30, having played an ironman's role over the past few seasons. Houston is good enough to take some of Dumars's minutes this year. The Pistons have a glut of guards and may use one of them as trade bait for a big man. Houston and fellow draft pick Lindsey Hunter were coveted by other teams and could be dealt.

PLAYER SUMMARY	
Will	catch and shoot
Can't	guard the jets
Expect	a steady pro
Don't Expect	outward intensity
Fantasy Value	$1
Card Value	20-35¢

COLLEGE HIGHLIGHTS
- All-SEC, 1990, 1991, 1992, and 1993
- Member of USA Basketball developmental team, 1992
- Member of U.S. junior national team, 1990

COLLEGE STATISTICS

			FGs		3-PT FGs		FTs							
		G	FG	PCT	FG	PCT	FT	PCT	REB	AST	STL	BLK	PTS	PPG
89-90	TENN	30	203	.437	83	.432	120	.805	88	127	36	11	609	20.3
90-91	TENN	34	265	.482	99	.429	177	.863	104	131	37	16	806	23.7
91-92	TENN	34	223	.453	82	.418	189	.840	180	110	32	15	717	21.1
92-93	TENN	30	211	.465	82	.414	165	.878	145	92	28	8	669	22.3
Totals		128	902	.460	346	.424	651	.849	517	460	133	50	2801	21.9

LINDSEY HUNTER

Team: Detroit Pistons
Position: Guard
Height: 6'2"
Weight: 170

Birthdate: December 3, 1970
College: Alcorn St.; Jackson St.
Acquired: 1st-round pick in 1993 draft
(10th overall)

Background: After playing high school ball in Jackson, Mississippi, Hunter played a year at Alcorn State but then transferred to Jackson State for the 1990-91 season. He was an immediate success at JSU, reaching double figures in 29 of 30 games during his first year there. Last season, Hunter proved his mettle against good competition, lighting up Illinois for 43 points and Kansas for 48. He stole the show at the NBA's pre-draft camp in Chicago, sealing his status as a lottery pick.

Strengths: A top-drawer athlete, Hunter is lethal in the open court and explosive taking the ball to the rim. He's not tall, but he gets off his shot against taller players because he has a quick release and jumps very well. He has excellent range, nailing 112 3-pointers last year. He has the tools to grow into a good defensive player.

Weaknesses: Scouts want to see how he adjusts to the bump in competition and the move from off guard—his position at Jackson State—to point guard. His playmaking skills need a lot of work, as do his shot selection and decision-making. He has room for growth as a defensive player.

Analysis: The aging Pistons acquired their backcourt of the future with the tenth and 11th picks in the draft. Hunter will be the understudy to Isiah Thomas (whom Hunter calls his idol) for the next year or two, while Allan Houston will back up Joe Dumars. Or, the Pistons could trade one of their guards (they also have Alvin Robertson) for a big man. Hunter should develop into a solid starter, but his first couple years will be rocky.

PLAYER SUMMARY
Will................................stick in Detroit
Can't..........................resist temptation
Expect ....running and gunning
Don't Expect ....many rebounds
Fantasy Value.................................$1
Card Value ....20-40¢

COLLEGE HIGHLIGHTS
• SWAC Player of the Year, 1993
• McClendon Award winner (black college Player of the Year), 1993
• SWAC Freshman of the Year, 1989
• A.P. honorable-mention All-American, 1993

COLLEGE STATISTICS

		G	FGs FG	FGs PCT	3-PT FGs FG	3-PT FGs PCT	FTs FT	FTs PCT	REB	AST	STL	BLK	PTS	PPG
88-89	ASU	28	70	.393	4	.333	23	.719	67	99	39	—	167	6.0
90-91	JSU	30	229	.409	86	.366	82	.695	100	105	69	9	626	20.9
91-92	JSU	28	249	.412	95	.370	100	.637	96	121	60	5	693	24.8
92-93	JSU	34	320	.412	112	.341	155	.771	115	115	89	14	907	26.7
Totals		120	868	.409	297	.357	360	.709	378	440	257	—	2393	19.9

BOBBY HURLEY

Team: Sacramento Kings
Position: Guard
Height: 6'0"
Weight: 165

Birthdate: June 28, 1971
College: Duke
Acquired: 1st-round pick in 1993 draft
(7th overall)

Background: One of many quality players from St. Anthony's, a prep powerhouse in New Jersey, Hurley came to Duke and did nothing but win. The Blue Devils went to three Final Fours and won two national championships (1991 and 1992), as Hurley led them to an 18-2 record in NCAA action. Moreover, Hurley set the NCAA career assists record (1,076) and set a Duke standard for career 3-pointers (264). Doubts about his pro potential persisted until the summer of 1992, when he sparkled in scrimmages against the U.S. Olympic Dream Team.

Strengths: The prototypical point guard, Hurley runs a team adroitly and with panache. He's quick, anticipates well in transition, and can break down a defense with his dribble. He has expanded his shooting range and consistency the past two seasons, and he isn't afraid to take the big shot. Defensively, he plays the passing lanes well and has a nose for steals.

Weaknesses: Lack of size is Hurley's biggest liability. He'll be at a disadvantage defensively against most NBA point guards, while on offense it's questionable whether he can penetrate against the giants. Also, his jump shot might be less effective in the pros because defenders will be taller and quicker.

Analysis: Sacramento G.M. Jerry Reynolds said long before the draft that Hurley was the player he wanted. In Hurley, some see Bob Cousy-type characteristics, while others compare him to John Stockton. Spud Webb may retain his starting spot for awhile, but Hurley figures to take it before the season's over. He's a lock to lead all rookies in assists.

PLAYER SUMMARY	
Will	draw and dish
Can't	bang inside
Expect	steady progress
Don't Expect	Bob Cousy
Fantasy Value	$6-8
Card Value	25-50¢

COLLEGE HIGHLIGHTS
• Final Four MVP, 1992
• John Wooden Award finalist, 1993
• Consensus All-American, 1993
• All-ACC, 1992 and 1993

COLLEGE STATISTICS

			FGs		3-PT FGs		FTs							
		G	FG	PCT	FG	PCT	FT	PCT	REB	AST	STL	BLK	PTS	PPG
89-90	DUKE	38	92	.351	41	.357	110	.769	68	288	67	1	335	8.8
90-91	DUKE	39	141	.423	76	.404	83	.728	93	289	51	3	441	11.3
91-92	DUKE	31	123	.433	59	.421	105	.789	61	237	35	1	410	13.2
92-93	DUKE	32	157	.421	88	.421	143	.803	84	262	49	1	545	17.0
Totals		140	513	.410	264	.405	441	.776	306	1076	202	6	1731	12.4

ERVIN JOHNSON

Team: Seattle SuperSonics
Position: Center
Height: 6'11"
Weight: 242

Birthdate: December 21, 1967
College: New Orleans
Acquired: 1st-round pick in 1993 draft (23rd overall)

Background: Johnson didn't play high school ball and nearly passed on college too. He bagged groceries in a Baton Rouge, Louisiana, store for nearly three years before soliciting a scholarship from New Orleans coach Tim Floyd. Last season, Johnson ranked in the nation's top 20 in rebounding, blocked shots, and field goal percentage. He had 21 points, ten rebounds, and six blocks in the Privateers' NCAA Tournament loss to Xavier. Johnson ranks as New Orleans' all-time leader in rebounds, blocked shots, and field goal percentage and ranks second in career scoring.

Strengths: Johnson is from Block High School, and blocks are what he does best. E.J. is a defensive specialist who also excels on the glass. He gives maximum effort and won't hesitate to use his nightly allotment of six fouls. He satisfies Seattle's need for more size and fits the Sonics' style because he runs the floor easily.

Weaknesses: Johnson is very limited offensively, capable of scoring only on tips and simple plays. One problem is his hands; they're small and stiff and prevent him from catching the ball surely. Some people consider his age—26 in December—a negative.

Analysis: The Sonics hoped Scott Burrell or James Robinson would drop to them in the draft, but they were pleased to land Johnson. He doesn't figure to play anytime soon, though, what with Sam Perkins, Michael Cage, Rich King, and Shawn Kemp on hand to play center. Johnson's only hope is that someone is traded or, in King's case, released.

PLAYER SUMMARY	
Will	block shots
Can't	hit FTs
Expect	a project
Don't Expect	a sudden impact
Fantasy Value	$0
Card Value	15-25¢

COLLEGE HIGHLIGHTS
- UPI third-team All-American, 1993
- Sun Belt Player of the Year, 1993
- All-Sun Belt, 1992 and 1993
- NABC All-Star Game MVP, 1993

COLLEGE STATISTICS

		G	FGs FG	FGs PCT	3-PT FGs FG	3-PT FGs PCT	FTs FT	FTs PCT	REB	AST	STL	BLK	PTS	PPG
89-90	NO	32	84	.579	0	.000	32	.561	218	29	29	62	200	6.3
90-91	NO	30	162	.572	0	.000	58	.537	367	34	22	74	382	12.7
91-92	NO	32	185	.584	0	.000	122	.714	356	56	31	81	492	15.4
92-93	NO	29	208	.619	0	.000	118	.674	346	16	27	77	534	18.4
Totals		123	639	.591	0	.000	330	.646	1287	135	109	294	1608	13.1

GEORGE LYNCH

Team: Los Angeles Lakers
Position: Forward
Height: 6'8"
Weight: 218

Birthdate: September 3, 1970
College: North Carolina
Acquired: 1st-round pick in 1993 draft
(12th overall)

Background: Lynch never became the superstar that some thought he would be, but he found a niche and flourished in Dean Smith's system. He's the second-leading rebounder in Tar Heels history, and his 241 career steals set a North Carolina record. Moreover, Lynch and Christian Laettner are the only players in ACC history to have at least 1,500 points, 200 steals, 200 assists, and 1,000 rebounds. Lynch was a key factor in North Carolina's run to the national championship this past season.

Strengths: NBA people love his makeup. "He's so gutsy, he could play small or big forward," said one general manager. Like most North Carolina players, Lynch is well-schooled fundamentally and knows how to win. He steals the ball often and is an above-average offensive rebounder.

Weaknesses: Poor ball-handling and perimeter-shooting skills kept Lynch from being a lottery pick. Mainly a power forward in college, he's not big enough to play that position in the NBA. Although he draws fouls and gets to the line, he converts at a low rate when he gets there. The key to his career will be his ability to develop a consistent shooting stroke.

Analysis: The Lakers pulled the first surprise of the draft, as most savants thought Lynch would go around No. 20 in the first round. The Lakers have had success with other Tar Heels, including James Worthy and Sam Perkins, and they have a UNC alum, Mitch Kupchak, in the front office, which may have colored their thinking. Lynch could be a valuable addition because A.C. Green left via free agency.

PLAYER SUMMARY	
Will	rebound
Can't	hit the bomb
Expect	a quality sub
Don't Expect	Sam Perkins
Fantasy Value	$1
Card Value	20-35¢

COLLEGE HIGHLIGHTS
- All-ACC, 1993
- Third-team All-ACC, 1992
- All-ACC Tournament, 1992
- Final Four All-Tournament team, 1993

COLLEGE STATISTICS

			FGs		3-PT FGs		FTs							
		G	FG	PCT	FG	PCT	FT	PCT	REB	AST	STL	BLK	PTS	PPG
89-90	NC	34	112	.521	1	.333	67	.663	183	34	37	14	292	8.6
90-91	NC	35	172	.523	7	.700	85	.630	258	41	49	15	436	12.5
91-92	NC	33	192	.539	1	.125	74	.649	291	86	66	10	459	13.9
92-93	NC	38	235	.501	2	.182	88	.667	365	72	89	21	560	14.7
Totals		140	711	.519	11	.344	314	.651	1097	233	241	60	1747	12.5

MALCOLM MACKEY

Team: Phoenix Suns
Position: Forward/Center
Height: 6'11"
Weight: 248

Birthdate: July 11, 1970
College: Georgia Tech
Acquired: 1st-round pick in 1993 draft
(27th overall)

Background: Malcolm Malik Mackey started as a freshman and helped the Yellow Jackets to the Final Four. He appeared to be headed for stardom; however, Tech never made it back to the Final Four and Mackey's game leveled off after his sophomore season. He was named second-team All-ACC as a sophomore and third-team all-conference as a junior, but he didn't make either team as a senior. Still, Mackey is Tech's all-time leader in games played and rebounds, and he ranks second to John Salley in blocked shots. He compiled 33 double-doubles during his last two seasons.

Strengths: Mackey has the prototypical body for an NBA power forward, plus he's big enough to back up at center. He has a soft scoring touch around the basket, usually with a little hook shot or a jumper. Said one general manager: "(He has) a great attitude and is a great listener."

Weaknesses: Mackey doesn't show up night in and night out, and he's too soft to handle players like Karl Malone and Shawn Kemp. He was a good rebounder in college but will be average at best in the pros because he's not a leaper and not really a good athlete.

Analysis: Mackey was projected to go as high as 14th in the draft, yet he nearly slipped out of the first round. Phoenix has needed more muscle up front and Mackey can provide it, though he's no cinch to make the team. In August, the Suns signed free agent Joe Kleine, a seven-footer who might push Mackey out of the picture. Mackey will land with some club, however.

PLAYER SUMMARY	
Will	run the floor
Can't	muscle inside
Expect	a back-up
Don't Expect	leadership
Fantasy Value	$0
Card Value	15-25¢

COLLEGE HIGHLIGHTS
- Second-team All-ACC, 1991
- Third-team All-ACC, 1992
- Phoenix Desert Classic All-Tournament team, 1993

COLLEGE STATISTICS

			FGs		3-PT FGs		FTs							
		G	FG	PCT	FG	PCT	FT	PCT	REB	AST	STL	BLK	PTS	PPG
89-90	GT	35	113	.559	0	.000	26	.441	262	16	13	41	252	7.2
90-91	GT	30	190	.551	0	.000	80	.597	321	30	16	54	460	15.3
91-92	GT	35	212	.546	0	.000	129	.683	316	54	17	43	553	15.8
92-93	GT	30	193	.530	0	.000	83	.638	306	41	14	61	469	15.6
Totals		130	708	.545	0	.000	318	.621	1205	141	60	199	1734	13.3

JAMAL MASHBURN

Team: Dallas Mavericks
Position: Forward
Height: 6'8"
Weight: 240

Birthdate: November 29, 1972
College: Kentucky
Acquired: 1st-round pick in 1993 draft (4th overall)

Background: Dan Issel, Kenny Walker, and Jack Givens are the only Kentucky players to score more points than Mashburn, who started every game in his three years in Lexington. This past season, Mashburn led the Wildcats to the Final Four—where they lost to Michigan in the semifinals—and finished second to Indiana's Calbert Cheaney in balloting for the John Wooden Award as national Player of the Year. He also finished second in the SEC in scoring in 1992-93 with 21.0 PPG. He forfeited a year's eligibility to enter the draft.

Strengths: A can't-miss pro, Mashburn can muscle in the paint or stretch a defense with his perimeter shooting. He canned 66 3-pointers last year. His actions are graceful and liquid, and he plays with great exuberance. Fans love his "Monster Mash" dunks. He works hard defensively and has the athleticism to clamp most small forwards. Versatile, he can swing to power forward if need be. He played in a running, teamwork-oriented system at Kentucky that prepared him well for the NBA.

Weaknesses: Mash is a good but not great rebounder and doesn't swat many shots, but there's not much to dislike about his game. He was probably the most well-rounded player in the draft.

Analysis: The Mavs were in a no-lose situation, guaranteed to get Chris Webber, Anfernee Hardaway, or Mashburn in the draft. Some scouts think Mashburn will be the Rookie of the Year because he'll be a primary offensive option with the Mavericks. He upgrades a poor front line that was further weakened when Terry Davis was injured in a car wreck. The Mavs can say "so long" to Randy White, who has been a major disappointment.

PLAYER SUMMARY	
Will	score inside and out
Can't	miss as a pro
Expect	an instant starter
Don't Expect	a shot-blocker
Fantasy Value	$14-17
Card Value	$1.50-3.00

COLLEGE HIGHLIGHTS
- Consensus All-American, 1993
- SEC Player of the Year, 1993
- All-SEC, 1992 and 1993
- Member of USA Basketball developmental team, 1992
- John Wooden Award runner-up, 1993

COLLEGE STATISTICS

			FGs		3-PT FGs		FTs							
		G	FG	PCT	FG	PCT	FT	PCT	REB	AST	STL	BLK	PTS	PPG
90-91	KEN	28	137	.474	24	.293	64	.727	195	42	37	15	362	12.9
91-92	KEN	36	279	.567	58	.439	151	.709	281	52	65	23	767	21.3
92-93	KEN	34	259	.492	66	.367	130	.670	284	124	51	15	714	21.0
Totals		98	675	.516	148	.376	345	.697	760	218	153	53	1843	18.8

CHRIS MILLS

Team: Cleveland Cavaliers
Position: Forward/Guard
Height: 6'6"
Weight: 216

Birthdate: January 25, 1970
College: Kentucky; Arizona
Acquired: 1st-round pick in 1993 draft (22nd overall)

Background: Though he started every college game he played and won Pac-10 Player of the Year honors as a senior, Mills had a star-crossed career. He played one year at Kentucky but was forced to leave because of an illegal-payments scandal. Allegedly, a package containing $1,000 in cash was shipped from the Kentucky basketball office to Mills's home. Mills transferred to Arizona, where he was labeled an underachiever despite two strong seasons and one outstanding season. He was projected to be a lottery pick, but his stock dipped badly in the weeks preceding the draft.

Strengths: The best part of Mills's game, by far, is his perimeter shooting. He has outstanding mechanics and range and can fill it up in a hurry. He canned 48.3 percent of his 3-pointers last year. Mills can finish on the break too, and he rates highly when it comes to basketball smarts. He's an adequate defender at shooting guard, though not at small forward.

Weaknesses: Is he a shooting guard or is he a small forward? There's no consensus, so Mills will have to play both, at least for a while. He doesn't handle the ball well enough for guard, and he can't rebound, defend, or run with NBA small forwards. Lacking explosiveness, he can't take his man off the dribble.

Analysis: Some NBA gurus think the Cavs got the steal of the draft in Mills, who has the ability to be a starter. He takes Craig Ehlo's guard spot and will also see time at small forward, Cleveland's weakest position. With a new coach, Mike Fratello, Mills will get every opportunity.

PLAYER SUMMARY

Will.................................drain the "J"
Can't.....................muscle the forwards
Expect...............................a good pro
Don't Expect ....a showboat
Fantasy Value...............................$1
Card Value ....15-25¢

COLLEGE HIGHLIGHTS

• Pac-10 Player of the Year, 1993
• All-Pac-10, 1992 and 1993
• SEC All-Freshman team, 1989
• Four-time Pac-10 Player of the Week, 1993

COLLEGE STATISTICS

		G	FGs FG	FGs PCT	3-PT FGs FG	3-PT FGs PCT	FTs FT	FTs PCT	REB	AST	STL	BLK	PTS	PPG
88-89	KEN	32	180	.484	17	.315	82	.713	277	92	46	26	459	14.3
90-91	ARIZ	35	206	.519	42	.344	91	.746	216	66	29	17	545	15.6
91-92	ARIZ	31	198	.506	28	.315	80	.777	244	73	36	8	504	16.3
92-93	ARIZ	28	211	.520	56	.483	92	.836	222	53	30	14	570	20.4
Totals		126	795	.508	143	.375	345	.767	959	284	141	65	2078	16.5

ISAIAH RIDER

Team: Minnesota Timberwolves
Position: Guard
Height: 6'5"
Weight: 215

Birthdate: March 12, 1971
College: Nevada-Las Vegas
Acquired: 1st-round pick in 1993 draft
(5th overall)

Background: Upon graduating from an Alameda high school in California, Rider committed to Kansas State because his idol was Wildcats star Mitch Richmond. Failing to qualify academically, Rider transferred to a junior college in Kansas, then to a junior college in California, then to UNLV for Jerry Tarkanian's last season. Rider ranked second nationally in scoring last season with 29.1 PPG. However, he received more notoriety when he was suspended by the team late in the year for allegedly cheating on classwork. He was known as J.R. Rider in college but, over the summer, announced his preference for Isaiah.

Strengths: Rider is an explosive athlete who plays with uncommon intensity. Said one G.M.: "He's versatile—he can score a number of ways. He can put it on the floor or post people up. He also has great confidence." Rider gets to the rim and finishes better than any other guard in the draft: He even won a national slam-dunk contest after the season. Rider makes his free throws and rebounds very well for his size.

Weaknesses: Teams were concerned about his off-court problems, but they found little fault with his game. Like most young players, Rider needs to fine-tune the more subtle skills, such as passing and ball-handling.

Analysis: The last marquee talent available in the draft, Rider was a no-brainer choice for the Timberwolves, whose plan was to trade small forward Chuck Person, move guard Doug West to Person's spot, and insert Rider at shooting guard. The T'Wolves still are a long way from respectability, but Rider and Christian Laettner are players they can build around. Rider could become a 20-PPG scorer in the NBA.

PLAYER SUMMARY	
Will	light it up
Can't	give it up
Expect	Rookie of the Year bid
Don't Expect	much defense
Fantasy Value	$7-9
Card Value	50-75¢

COLLEGE HIGHLIGHTS
• Big West Player of the Year, 1993
• A.P. second-team All-American, 1993
• All-Big West, 1992 and 1993

COLLEGE STATISTICS

			FGs		3-PT FGs		FTs							
		G	FG	PCT	FG	PCT	FT	PCT	REB	AST	STL	BLK	PTS	PPG
91-92	UNLV	27	206	.490	81	.401	65	.747	141	87	19	11	558	20.7
92-93	UNLV	28	282	.515	55	.401	195	.826	250	71	41	18	814	29.1
Totals		55	488	.505	136	.401	260	.805	391	158	60	29	1372	24.9

JAMES ROBINSON

Team: Portland Trail Blazers
Position: Guard
Height: 6'2"
Weight: 180

Birthdate: August 31, 1970
College: Alabama
Acquired: 1st-round pick in 1993 draft
(21st overall)

Background: Robinson was a prolific scorer as a schoolboy, pouring in 40 PPG as a senior at Murrah High School in Mississippi. He was a marquee recruit for Alabama but sat on the sidelines his first year because of a questionable ACT score. He eventually was given four full years of eligibility. In 1990-91, Robinson became the first freshman to lead the Tide in scoring since 1953. In three seasons, he scored 20 or more points 45 times, including a run of 12 straight games. He forfeited his last year of eligibility to enter the NBA draft.

Strengths: A top-flight athlete, Robinson explodes to the basket in transition, finishes with gusto, and is too much for most defenders to handle one-on-one. To illustrate his athletic skills, Robinson set a Mississippi high school record in the 300-meter hurdles and also won the slam-dunk competition at the McDonald's All-America Game. Robinson shoots with good range and knows how to get open. His athleticism allows him to be a strong defender when he wants to be.

Weaknesses: Robinson is a man without a position. He will never be a point guard because he makes bad decisions, and he's too small to dominate at shooting guard. He plays out of control at times and lets a substantial ego obscure the team concept.

Analysis: A shake-up has begun in Portland. Kevin Duckworth was traded prior to the draft, and the selection of Robinson gives the team a glut of guards. Terry Porter and/or Clyde Drexler could be dealt to make way for youngsters such as Robinson and Dave Johnson, a first-round pick in 1992. Whatever happens, Robinson should stick.

PLAYER SUMMARY	
Will	score
Can't	resist temptation
Expect	growing pains
Don't Expect	much P.T. in 1993-94
Fantasy Value	$0
Card Value	15-25¢

COLLEGE HIGHLIGHTS
- A.P. honorable-mention All-American, 1991 and 1993
- All-SEC, 1993
- SEC All-Freshman team, 1991
- SEC All-Tournament team, 1991 and 1992

COLLEGE STATISTICS

			FGs		3-PT FGs		FTs							
		G	FG	PCT	FG	PCT	FT	PCT	REB	AST	STL	BLK	PTS	PPG
90-91	ALA	33	194	.470	64	.418	102	.699	130	40	35	15	554	16.8
91-92	ALA	34	237	.445	83	.358	104	.712	138	74	38	10	661	19.4
92-93	ALA	29	202	.420	78	.351	116	.682	130	68	47	21	598	20.6
Totals		96	633	.444	225	.371	322	.695	398	182	120	46	1813	18.9

RODNEY ROGERS

Team: Denver Nuggets
Position: Forward
Height: 6'7"
Weight: 250

Birthdate: June 20, 1971
College: Wake Forest
Acquired: 1st-round pick in 1993 draft (9th overall)

Background: Rogers quickly established himself as a force in the ACC, earning second-team all-conference honors as a freshman while going head-to-head with the likes of Christian Laettner, Pete Chilcutt, Dale Davis, and Malcolm Mackey. At his best in big games, Rogers scored a career-high 35 points at Duke this past season, then 33 against Iowa in the NCAA Tournament. He was named 1992-93 Player of the Year in the ACC, the country's premier conference. An early entrant into the NBA draft, Rogers slipped to the ninth pick because of concerns about his ever-expanding girth. Listed in college at 235 pounds, he weighed about 260 on draft day.

Strengths: Rogers is a strong rebounder and inside player who doesn't back down from contact. He occasionally will pop out and hit a jump shot, and he can shoot them with range—he made 36 percent of his 3-pointers last year. Rogers rates average or above as a ball-handler and passer, and he's versatile enough to swing from power forward to small forward.

Weaknesses: His height and weight are concerns. Rogers is not tall enough to score in close against the league's bigger players, and on draft day he was too heavy to play extended minutes. He tends to lose concentration on defense.

Analysis: Many bird dogs think the Nuggets got the steal of the draft, as there's no doubt Rogers would have gone higher had his weight not become an issue. He'll be a good fit along a youthful front line that needs only maturity and a little more muscle. Look for Rogers to get most of his minutes as the back-up to power forward LaPhonso Ellis, a first-round pick in 1992.

PLAYER SUMMARY	
Will	strongarm opponents
Can't	stay in shape
Expect	an enforcer
Don't Expect	an instant star
Fantasy Value	$1-3
Card Value	25-50¢

COLLEGE HIGHLIGHTS
• ACC Player of the Year, 1993
• ACC Freshman of the Year, 1991
• Member of USA Basketball developmental team, 1992
• A.P. second-team All-American, 1993

COLLEGE STATISTICS

			FGs		3-PT FGs		FTs							
		G	FG	PCT	FG	PCT	FT	PCT	REB	AST	STL	BLK	PTS	PPG
90-91	WF	30	199	.570	10	.286	81	.669	237	46	53	19	489	16.3
91-92	WF	29	245	.614	19	.380	86	.683	247	81	39	27	595	20.5
92-93	WF	30	239	.555	24	.358	134	.717	221	68	54	28	636	21.2
Totals		89	683	.579	53	.349	301	.694	705	195	146	74	1720	19.3

REX WALTERS

Team: New Jersey Nets
Position: Guard
Height: 6'4"
Weight: 190

Birthdate: March 12, 1970
College: Northwestern; Kansas
Acquired: 1st-round pick in 1993 draft
(16th overall)

Background: Walters was ignored by Kansas University as a high school senior, but he transferred to Kansas after a strong sophomore season at Northwestern. After sitting out the 1990-91 campaign, he became an immediate success in 1991-92, teaming with Adonis Jordan to form a dynamic backcourt. Walters garnered first-team all-conference honors that season and was selected as *Basketball Weekly's* Transfer of the Year. Last year, he and Jordan helped lead the Jayhawks into the Final Four. Again, Walters was named All-Big Eight.

Strengths: Walters brings a spirit to the game that the Nets need badly. He's competitive and feisty, an aggressive defender, and a better ball-handler than scouts thought until they saw him in the Phoenix Desert Classic. Though not yet a threat from NBA 3-point range, he's a dependable shooter from 20 feet and has a lot of tricks close to the basket. He's left-handed, which makes him difficult to guard for most players. He has been compared favorably to Sarunas Marciulionis.

Weaknesses: Not particularly big for a shooting guard, Walters must learn to dish the ball in traffic because he won't be able to finish drives as well as he did in college. Some scouts question his lateral mobility.

Analysis: The Nets, in desperate need of a shooting guard after Drazen Petrovic was killed in a car crash, figured Walters was a better option than Greg Graham, who was available with the 16th pick. In July, the Nets signed Kevin Edwards as a free agent and planned to use him as a starter. However, Walters will still get significant minutes off the bench.

PLAYER SUMMARY	
Will	light it up
Can't	outquick good guards
Expect	lots of minutes
Don't Expect	Drazen Petrovic
Fantasy Value	$1
Card Value	25-40¢

COLLEGE HIGHLIGHTS
- All-Big Eight, 1992 and 1993
- Big Eight Newcomer of the Year, 1992
- Honorable-mention All-Big Ten, 1990
- Desert Classic All-Tournament team, 1993

COLLEGE STATISTICS

		G	FGs FG	FGs PCT	3-PT FGs FG	3-PT FGs PCT	FTs FT	FTs PCT	REB	AST	STL	BLK	PTS	PPG
88-89	NW	24	17	.378	5	.278	11	.917	17	33	4	0	50	2.1
89-90	NW	28	181	.503	53	.473	77	.794	75	125	34	7	492	17.6
91-92	KAN	32	165	.525	68	.405	115	.827	105	124	53	10	513	16.0
92-93	KAN	36	179	.490	83	.430	110	.873	96	154	40	7	551	15.3
Totals		120	542	.500	209	.426	313	.837	293	436	131	24	1606	13.4

CHRIS WEBBER

Team: Golden State Warriors
Position: Forward/Center
Height: 6'9"
Weight: 245
Birthdate: March 1, 1973

College: Michigan
Acquired: Draft rights traded from Magic for draft rights to Anfernee Hardaway and 1996, 1998, and 2000 1st-round picks, 6/93

Background: The cornerstone of Michigan's Fab Five 1991 recruiting class, Webber led his team to back-to-back appearances in the NCAA championship game. The Wolverines lost to Duke in 1992 and North Carolina in '93, but Webber became the first player selected to the Final Four All-Tournament team as both a freshman and sophomore. He made a fatal blunder in the waning moments of last year's championship game, calling a timeout when his team didn't have any and being assessed a technical. In the draft, Webber was selected No. 1 overall by Orlando but was traded minutes later for Anfernee Hardaway and three future No. 1 picks.

Strengths: Strong and quick, Webber has a physical edge against most power forwards and some centers. Superb in transition, he runs the floor easily, handles the ball well, and has soft—yet very strong—hands. Jump-hooks and dunks are his offensive signatures, though he can knock down 15-footers when left alone. He rebounds aggressively and blocks shots. He knows how to win.

Weaknesses: Though he was perhaps the best raw talent in the draft, Webber is far from a finished product, having played only two years of college ball. His low-post fundamentals need work, as does his free throw shooting. He is not a refined outside shooter.

Analysis: Webber, the enforcer the Warriors have lacked for many years, is a natural fit in the middle of a lineup that includes scorers Chris Mullin, Tim Hardaway, and (when healthy) Billy Owens. The Warriors paid dearly for Webber—some say too dearly—but had to exit the draft with a big man. That done, they should challenge Phoenix for supremacy in the West.

PLAYER SUMMARY	
Will	intimidate
Can't	sink his FTs
Expect	an impact player
Don't Expect	a polished pro
Fantasy Value	$10-13
Card Value	$3.00-6.00

COLLEGE HIGHLIGHTS
• Consensus All-American, 1993
• Member of USA Basketball developmental team, 1992
• Final Four All-Tournament team, 1992 and 1993
• John Wooden Award finalist, 1993

COLLEGE STATISTICS

			FGs		3-PT FGs		FTs							
		G	FG	PCT	FG	PCT	FT	PCT	REB	AST	STL	BLK	PTS	PPG
91-92	MICH	34	229	.556	14	.259	56	.496	340	76	54	84	528	15.5
92-93	MICH	36	281	.619	27	.338	101	.552	362	90	49	91	690	19.2
Totals		70	510	.589	41	.306	157	.530	702	166	103	175	1218	17.4

LUTHER WRIGHT

Team: Utah Jazz
Position: Center
Height: 7'2"
Weight: 300

Birthdate: September 22, 1971
College: Seton Hall
Acquired: 1st-round pick in 1993 draft
(18th overall)

Background: Wright starred at Elizabeth High School in New Jersey, where he averaged 19 points, 12 rebounds, and six blocks per game as a senior. He was a much-ballyhooed recruit but his college career was brief and disappointing. Wright had to sit out his freshman year for academic reasons, then did little to distinguish himself in two subsequent seasons. He was overweight most of the time and quarreled with Seton Hall coach P.J. Carlesimo. Wright entered the draft two years early, citing family concerns.

Strengths: Wright is a huge man with impressive basketball skills and vast potential. He catches the ball easily and knows what to do with it, whether it's lofting a soft hook or turnaround jumper, or passing to an open teammate. He's unselfish, almost to a fault. He did make great strides last season after a dismal 1991-92 campaign.

Weaknesses: Wright is a project. He didn't play much in college, and when he did play; he rarely was asked to show his skills. He averaged in single digits in scoring both years. The Jazz will have to work with him and be patient, and they must also make sure that he keeps his weight under control. He can run when he's in shape (290 pounds would be ideal), but he's not fast.

Analysis: The big, slow Jazz became bigger and slower on draft day, trading for seven-foot Felton Spencer and drafting Wright. They figure to back up Mark Eaton (giving the team three lumbering centers), although Eaton has fallen out of favor in Utah and may be traded. In that case, Spencer would be the stop-gap starter until Wright is ready, probably in a couple years. Most scouts think Wright was worth the gamble.

PLAYER SUMMARY	
Will	eat space
Can't	stay svelte
Expect	a three-year project
Don't Expect	deft passing
Fantasy Value	$0
Card Value	15-25¢

COLLEGE HIGHLIGHTS
• Member of Big East championship team, 1993

COLLEGE STATISTICS

			FGs		3-PT FGs		FTs							
		G	FG	PCT	FG	PCT	FT	PCT	REB	AST	STL	BLK	PTS	PPG
91-92	SH	30	60	.517	0	.000	25	.625	85	8	8	42	145	4.8
92-93	SH	34	128	.525	0	.000	51	.654	255	26	36	76	307	9.0
Totals		64	188	.522	0	.000	76	.644	340	34	44	118	452	7.1

JOHN BEST

Team: New Jersey Nets
Position: Forward
Height: 6'8" **Weight:** 215
Birthdate: March 27, 1971
College: Tennessee Tech
Acquired: 2nd-round pick in 1993 draft
(36th overall)

PLAYER SUMMARY	
Will	get his points
Can't	face and shoot
Expect	a long shot
Don't Expect	a finished product
Fantasy	$0 Card	10-20¢

Background: Best lit up the Ohio Valley Conference as a senior, finishing third nationally in scoring. The two-time All-OVC selection topped 30 points a dozen times last season. He impressed scouts at the postseason Portsmouth Invitational.

Strengths: More of a scorer than a shooter, Best has a knack for getting to the basket in traffic and being in the right place at the right time. He runs well and mixes it up under the boards.

Weaknesses: Most of his points are the result of work in the paint, which could be a problem in the NBA, where he will be undersized. He needs to develop some semblance of a perimeter game.

Analysis: The Nets acquired the 36th pick from the Bullets and used it to draft Best. They hope he can develop into a competent back-up small forward. He could stick this year, though the Nets probably would prefer that he go to Europe for a season so he can learn while playing, rather than sitting on the bench.

COLLEGE STATISTICS

		G	FGP	FTP	RPG	APG	PPG
89-90	TT	15	.429	.708	1.7	0.1	3.1
90-91	TT	25	.547	.754	5.3	0.2	13.9
91-92	TT	29	.568	.710	7.0	1.0	20.0
92-93	TT	28	.553	.749	8.4	2.6	28.5
Totals		97	.553	.736	6.1	1.1	18.3

P.J. BROWN

Team: New Jersey Nets
Position: Forward/Center
Height: 6'11" **Weight:** 240
Birthdate: October 14, 1969
College: Louisiana Tech
Acquired: 2nd-round pick in 1992 draft
(29th overall)

PLAYER SUMMARY	
Will	reject shots
Can't	catch and shoot
Expect	a 12th man
Don't Expect	much P.T. now
Fantasy	$0 Card	15-25¢

Background: Drafted a year ago, Brown made contract demands that the Nets weren't prepared to meet, so he spent the season playing for a pro team in Greece. Brown was a solid role-player in college, helping Louisiana Tech to a 23-8 record in 1991-92.

Strengths: Brown can play power forward or back up at center. He's agile and runs the court well for a big man. His long arms and good timing allow him to block shots.

Weaknesses: Brown needs to add meat to his frame, especially if he's going to back up at center. His offensive game is raw, though it improved last year in Greece. Still, he has nothing to offer from the perimeter. Scouts have questioned his intensity.

Analysis: The Nets, who retained Brown's NBA rights while he played in Europe, signed him as an insurance policy against the loss of free agent center Chris Dudley, who did indeed leave. The Nets have no depth to speak of, so Brown should make the team.

COLLEGE STATISTICS

		G	FGP	FTP	RPG	APG	PPG
88-89	LT	32	.415	.568	5.6	1.1	4.7
89-90	LT	27	.461	.593	8.5	1.1	8.9
90-91	LT	31	.540	.653	9.7	1.9	14.4
91-92	LT	31	.489	.730	9.9	1.7	12.7
Totals		121	.488	.654	8.4	1.5	10.1

MARK BUFORD

Team: Phoenix Suns
Position: Center/Forward
Height: 6'11" **Weight:** 255
Birthdate: October 8, 1970
College: Mississippi Valley St.
Acquired: 2nd-round pick in 1993 draft (49th overall)

PLAYER SUMMARY	
Will	move the pile
Can't	maintain focus
Expect	growing pains
Don't Expect	great instincts
Fantasy	$0 Card ..... 10-20¢

Background: Buford played center for Mississippi Valley State, which also featured Alphonso Ford, a second-round pick of Philadelphia. NBA savants were shocked when the Suns drafted Buford because scouts knew little or nothing about him. Buford had to sit out his freshman year and didn't blossom until his senior season.

Strengths: Buford is built like a football player. He has decent mobility and footwork and catches the ball well in the post. He bounces people around underneath and is a competent rebounder.

Weaknesses: Buford's concentration tends to waver when he's on the court. And when he's on the bench, said one scout, "he prefers making eye contact with the cheerleaders."

Analysis: Phoenix, eyeing Buford long before the draft, was happy that he was available. However, he has little chance to stick, especially since the Suns signed center Joe Kleine. First-rounder Malcolm Mackey, also 6'11", may edge Buford out of the picture.

COLLEGE STATISTICS

		G	FGP	FTP	RPG	APG	PPG
90-91	MVS	18	.408	.200	2.3	—	2.3
91-92	MVS	30	.453	.618	5.8	0.2	4.9
92-93	MVS	28	.453	.551	7.5	0.1	13.0
Totals		76	.478	.478	5.6	0.1	7.2

EVERS BURNS

Team: Sacramento Kings
Position: Forward
Height: 6'8" **Weight:** 260
Birthdate: August 24, 1971
College: Maryland
Acquired: 2nd-round pick in 1993 draft (31st overall)

PLAYER SUMMARY	
Will	bump and grind
Can't	score from the post
Expect	a 12th man
Don't Expect	a shot-blocker
Fantasy	$0 Card ..... 10-20¢

Background: As his stats attest, Burns improved each season at Maryland. Last year, he finished in the ACC's top ten in scoring, rebounding, and steals. He cemented his draft status with good showings at the Portsmouth Invitational and the Phoenix Desert Classic.

Strengths: Scouts like his toughness and physical approach to the game. Burns runs well, plays hard, and rebounds effectively at both ends. He works the baseline well offensively and will occasionally stick a jump shot from the corner.

Weaknesses: Though bull-strong, Burns lacks a dependable back-to-the-basket game. He positions himself well for rebounds but doesn't jump very high. He's also a poor free throw shooter.

Analysis: A center in college, Burns will have to play power forward in the NBA. He's one of three power players drafted this year by the Kings, who are reuniting Burns with his college teammate, Walt Williams. Burns should make the grade.

COLLEGE STATISTICS

		G	FGP	FTP	RPG	APG	PPG
89-90	MD	28	.543	.227	2.7	0.3	4.3
90-91	MD	28	.431	.568	3.7	0.6	7.7
91-92	MD	29	.516	.643	7.1	1.2	15.9
92-93	MD	28	.506	.671	8.9	1.5	18.5
Totals		113	.499	.614	5.6	0.9	11.6

SPENCER DUNKLEY

Team: Indiana Pacers
Position: Forward/Center
Height: 6'11" **Weight:** 238
Birthdate: September 5, 1969
College: Delaware
Acquired: 2nd-round pick in 1993 draft
(51st overall)

PLAYER SUMMARY	
Will	send it back
Can't	dribble drive
Expect	a three-year project
Don't Expect	anything now
Fantasy	$0 Card ..... 20-30¢

Background: From England, Dunkley came to the U.S. as a high school exchange student. He attended Delaware, where he became the Blue Hens' all-time leader in rebounds and blocked shots. He was a member of Great Britain's 1992 Olympic team. In the weeks before the draft, Dunkley starred in the USBL.

Strengths: Dunkley projects as a finesse-type power forward who can outrun opposing players and block shots. He didn't take up basketball until his late teens, yet he has good timing and anticipation.

Weaknesses: Dunkley is a long way from being a polished player, especially offensively. He must learn how to face the basket, feed the post, put the ball on the floor, and create shots. He needs to add bulk.

Analysis: Dunkley already was under contract to a pro team in Israel when the Pacers drafted him. He'll come to Indiana's rookie camp but will play overseas this year. The Pacers retain his rights. They hope he can become a suitable back-up for Dale Davis.

COLLEGE STATISTICS

		G	FGP	FTP	RPG	APG	PPG
89-90	DELA	26	.412	.469	2.8	0.3	2.7
90-91	DELA	23	.444	.571	8.9	0.5	7.6
91-92	DELA	31	.550	.594	8.8	0.9	10.7
92-93	DELA	30	.515	.758	12.2	0.9	19.2
Totals		110	.502	.671	8.3	0.7	10.5

JO JO ENGLISH

Team: Unsigned
Position: Guard
Height: 6'4" **Weight:** 195
Birthdate: February 4, 1970
College: South Carolina

PLAYER SUMMARY	
Will	penetrate
Can't	cooperate
Expect	a fringe guy
Don't Expect	Alex English
Fantasy	$0 Card ..... 10-20¢

Background: Though he led South Carolina in scoring and 3-pointers for three consecutive seasons, English was ignored in the 1992 NBA draft. He played well in Houston's summer camp but lost a numbers game and went to the CBA, where he averaged 14.5 points for the Tri-City Chinook. He also had a 31-minute cup of coffee with the Chicago Bulls.

Strengths: Despite a low field goal percentage, English is a good offensive player. Very quick, he can pull up and score with a jump shot or take the ball all the way for a dunk. He's a good enough athlete to defend most guards when the mood strikes.

Weaknesses: English developed a bad reputation in college. He's too selfish with the ball, so he must prove he's a team player to stick in the NBA. He needs more consistency at the foul line and on defense.

Analysis: Jo Jo is good enough to play in the big leagues, particularly as a back-up shooting guard. He was invited to the NBA's pre-draft camp in Chicago in June. Several teams were interested in bringing him to training camp.

COLLEGE STATISTICS

		G	FGP	FTP	RPG	APG	PPG
88-89	SC	28	.422	.586	1.1	1.2	3.8
89-90	SC	27	.489	.626	4.8	2.9	15.3
90-91	SC	33	.462	.736	3.3	2.9	15.0
91-92	SC	27	.430	.620	3.6	1.9	15.8
Totals		115	.452	.659	3.1	2.2	12.5

ALPHONSO FORD

Team: Philadelphia 76ers
Position: Guard
Height: 6'2" **Weight:** 190
Birthdate: October 31, 1971
College: Mississippi Valley St.
Acquired: 2nd-round pick in 1993 draft (32nd overall)

PLAYER SUMMARY	
Will	drill it
Can't	defend big guards
Expect	a rookie surprise
Don't Expect	a shy guy
Fantasy	$0 Card	10-20¢

Background: One of the most prolific shooters in college history, Ford set ten school records and was first-team all-league four times in the offensive-minded Southwestern Athletic Conference. He launched 985 3-pointers, making 37.5 percent.

Strengths: Though he shoots a lot, Ford is unselfish and a good passer. Strong and quick, he usually can create a shot for himself off the dribble. He changes gears smoothly and handles the ball very well. He has good shooting range.

Weaknesses: Scouts say Ford has no clue how to maximize his talents. He warms up poorly and is prone to faulty shooting in the first half of games. At 6'2", he's too small to play a lot at shooting guard.

Analysis: The Sixers dumped a lot of players in the off-season and were talking trade. Nothing will be settled until training camp, but Ford has a good chance to make the team. He needs coaching, though, and Philly boss Fred Carter is not considered a teacher.

COLLEGE STATISTICS

		G	FGP	FTP	RPG	APG	PPG
89-90	MVS	27	.450	.734	4.9	3.3	29.9
90-91	MVS	28	.480	.765	6.0	1.4	32.6
91-92	MVS	26	.450	.757	5.6	3.7	27.5
92-93	MVS	28	.436	.791	5.3	3.9	26.0
Totals		109	.454	.763	5.4	3.0	29.0

JOSH GRANT

Team: Golden State Warriors
Position: Forward
Height: 6'9" **Weight:** 223
Birthdate: August 7, 1967
College: Utah
Acquired: Draft rights traded from Nuggets with a 1994 2nd-round pick for draft rights to Darnell Mee, 6/93

PLAYER SUMMARY	
Will	use his head
Can't	attack the middle
Expect	Mr. Smooth
Don't Expect	a rim-buster
Fantasy	$0 Card	15-25¢

Background: Grant delayed college for two years while serving a church mission in England, then took five years to play four because of a knee injury in 1991-92. A two-time WAC Player of the Year, he is Utah's second all-time leading scorer and rebounder. He was drafted 43rd overall.

Strengths: Grant knows the game, plays unselfishly, and moves well without the ball. He's a first-rate passer and a good shooter when given time to set himself.

Weaknesses: Grant has a bad body and is a marginal athlete. He has tricks along the baseline but lacks the quickness to get his shot consistently. His surgically repaired knee is a concern.

Analysis: Utah coach Rick Majerus is one of Warriors coach Don Nelson's closest friends, which might explain the deal. Grant fits well into Golden State's perimeter- and passing-oriented game. He has a chance to make the team.

COLLEGE STATISTICS

		G	FGP	FTP	RPG	APG	PPG
88-89	UTAH	33	.461	.754	7.2	3.5	10.4
89-90	UTAH	30	.511	.783	7.0	2.8	16.5
90-91	UTAH	34	.475	.825	8.0	2.7	17.5
91-92	UTAH	3	.375	.778	5.0	3.0	9.3
92-93	UTAH	31	.530	.920	10.7	2.8	17.3
Totals		131	.492	.827	8.1	3.0	15.2

LUCIOUS HARRIS

Team: Dallas Mavericks
Position: Guard
Height: 6'5" **Weight:** 190
Birthdate: December 18, 1970
College: Long Beach St.
Acquired: 2nd-round pick in 1993 draft (28th overall)

PLAYER SUMMARY	
Will	score
Can't	draw and dish
Expect	a legit player
Don't Expect	a starter
Fantasy	$0 Card ......15-25¢

Background: The leading scorer in Big West history, Harris earned all-league honors each of the past two seasons and was rated by some scouts as the best all-around senior player on the West Coast. His teammate, Bryon Russell, also went in the draft's second round.

Strengths: An accomplished marksman, Harris can produce for the Mavs if they run plays for him. They can pop him off screens along the baseline, where's he's excellent at catching and shooting. He has good range, hitting 73 3-pointers last season.

Weaknesses: Harris needs to work on all areas of the game other than shooting. He cannot create shots for others or get his own shot off the dribble. He lacks the explosiveness, quickness, and end-to-end speed of many of the league's better off guards.

Analysis: Harris should have no trouble making the team and could develop into an outstanding third guard. Some scouts liken him to Rolando Blackman for his ability to consistently drain mid-range jump shots.

COLLEGE STATISTICS

		G	FGP	FTP	RPG	APG	PPG
89-90	LBS	32	.430	.694	4.8	1.6	14.3
90-91	LBS	28	.396	.700	4.7	2.5	19.7
91-92	LBS	30	.471	.734	4.3	3.2	18.8
92-93	LBS	32	.525	.774	5.3	2.5	23.1
Totals		122	.458	.727	4.8	2.4	19.0

THOMAS HILL

Team: Indiana Pacers
Position: Guard
Height: 6'5" **Weight:** 200
Birthdate: August 31, 1971
College: Duke
Acquired: 2nd-round pick in 1993 draft (39th overall)

PLAYER SUMMARY	
Will	excel on defense
Can't	create offensively
Expect	a bench player
Don't Expect	a hot dog
Fantasy	$0 Card ......20-35¢

Background: Though never a star, Hill was a key contributor to Duke's national championships in 1991 and 1992. In the 1992 title game against Michigan, he had 16 points and seven rebounds. His father, Thomas Sr., won a bronze medal in the 1972 Olympics (110-meter hurdles).

Strengths: Scouts love the intangibles—competitiveness, intelligence—that Hill brings to the table. He has a head start on most rookies because he played in a demanding program. He defends aggressively, has good end-to-end speed, and has improved his shooting stroke.

Weaknesses: Hill still needs to improve his perimeter and free throw shooting. He rarely handled the ball at Duke, so he needs work in that area. "He needs a more well-rounded offensive game," said one scout.

Analysis: The Pacers are trying to upgrade at shooting guard. They're happy with starter Reggie Miller but aren't pleased with last year's back-up, George McCloud. Hill should make the team.

COLLEGE STATISTICS

		G	FGP	FTP	RPG	APG	PPG
89-90	DUKE	34	.517	.629	2.2	0.7	3.4
90-91	DUKE	39	.552	.743	3.6	1.3	11.5
91-92	DUKE	36	.534	.768	3.4	1.5	14.6
92-93	DUKE	32	.479	.680	4.7	1.5	15.7
Totals		141	.519	.720	3.5	0.8	11.3

ALEX HOLCOMBE

Team: Sacramento Kings
Position: Forward
Height: 6'9" **Weight:** 244
Birthdate: November 22, 1969
College: Baylor
Acquired: 2nd-round pick in 1993 draft (44th overall)

PLAYER SUMMARY	
Will	bang inside
Can't	do much else
Expect	shooting woes
Don't Expect	a roster spot
Fantasy	$0 Card ......10-20¢

Background: Holcombe sat out a year as a redshirt, did almost nothing for three seasons, then was drafted on the basis of one good campaign. As a senior, he nearly tripled his scoring output and doubled his rebounds. He was also named to the Southwest Conference All-Defensive team.

Strengths: Rebounding is what Holcombe does best, thanks to his good size and strength. He tries hard defensively. The rest of his game rates below average.

Weaknesses: Holcombe is not particularly athletic, which hurts him when it comes to shot-blocking and man-to-man defense. He has a lot of holes in his offensive game. He tallied only 62 assists in college, never made a 3-pointer, and had a lower free throw percentage than field goal percentage.

Analysis: The Kings, desperate for interior muscle, drafted several big men. Second-round picks Evers Burns and Mike Peplowski have a better chance to stick than Holcombe, who one scout described as "a big, strong body for training camp."

COLLEGE STATISTICS

		G	FGP	FTP	RPG	APG	PPG
89-90	BAY	24	.566	.548	3.6	0.6	4.9
90-91	BAY	26	.578	.391	3.5	0.3	4.7
91-92	BAY	27	.600	.583	4.6	0.4	7.6
92-93	BAY	27	.624	.578	9.4	1.1	19.2
Totals		104	.605	.546	5.3	0.6	9.3

POPEYE JONES

Team: Dallas Mavericks
Position: Forward
Height: 6'8" **Weight:** 270
Birthdate: June 17, 1970
College: Murray St.
Acquired: Draft rights traded from Rockets for rights to Eric Riley, 6/93

PLAYER SUMMARY	
Will	use his rear end
Can't	rough it up
Expect	a role-player
Don't Expect	a sprinter
Fantasy	$0 Card ......15-25¢

Background: A two-time Ohio Valley Conference Player of the Year, Jones was drafted by Houston in the second round in 1992. He played last season in the Italian A2 League, averaging 21.1 points and 13.3 rebounds a game. His rights were traded to Dallas on draft day of 1993.

Strengths: Popeye has the skills to stick in the NBA. His footwork and back-to-the-basket game are fundamentally sound. Also, he shoots with a soft touch and is an outstanding passer. He uses his big rear end to back into the paint, and he has a nice little jump hook.

Weaknesses: Weight problems have held Jones back. When he's too heavy, he can't run or jump well enough to keep up with good players.

Analysis: Dallas made a good move, as Jones has better potential than Eric Riley. Jones is capable at both power forward and small forward and should stick as a backup. However, he must stay in shape if he's to last in the NBA.

COLLEGE STATISTICS

		G	FGP	FTP	RPG	APG	PPG
88-89	MSU	30	.489	.754	4.6	0.7	5.8
89-90	MSU	30	.500	.757	11.2	2.0	19.5
90-91	MSU	33	.493	.711	14.2	2.1	20.2
91-92	MSU	30	.488	.778	14.4	2.4	21.1
Totals		123	.493	.751	11.2	1.8	16.7

ADONIS JORDAN

Team: Seattle SuperSonics
Position: Guard
Height: 5'11" **Weight:** 170
Birthdate: August 21, 1970
College: Kansas
Acquired: 2nd-round pick in 1993 draft
(42nd overall)

PLAYER SUMMARY	
Will	draw and dish
Can't	see over the trees
Expect	a gamer
Don't Expect	a roster spot
Fantasy	$0 Card 15-25¢

Background: Jordan and Rex Walters (first round, New Jersey) formed the best backcourt in college basketball last year. Jordan led the Jayhawks to the Final Four in 1991 and 1993. He is third in K.U. history in assists and steals.

Strengths: One of the best pure point guards in the draft, Jordan knows how to run a team and set up his mates for good shots. He sticks the outside shot when left alone. A clever defender, he steals the ball often and is quick enough to apply fullcourt pressure.

Weaknesses: Jordan has two strikes against him: He's undersized at 5'11" and he has very bad knees. He tested poorly in the pre-draft Chicago camp. There are no glaring weaknesses in his game.

Analysis: The Sonics have two quality point guards (Gary Payton, Nate McMillan) and probably don't need a third. However, Jordan is good enough to play in the league and probably will eventually. He may have to pay his dues in the CBA.

COLLEGE STATISTICS

	G	FGP	FTP	RPG	APG	PPG
89-90 KANS	35	.340	.694	1.2	3.1	3.0
90-91 KANS	34	.507	.765	3.0	4.5	12.5
91-92 KANS	32	.464	.735	3.3	4.4	12.8
92-93 KANS	36	.462	.789	2.3	4.5	12.1
Totals	137	.463	.755	2.5	4.1	10.0

TONI KUKOC

Team: Chicago Bulls
Position: Forward/Guard
Height: 6'10" **Weight:** 230
Birthdate: September 18, 1968
College: None
Acquired: 2nd-round pick in 1990 draft
(29th overall)

PLAYER SUMMARY	
Will	draw and dish
Can't	bang inside
Expect	a thoroughbred
Don't Expect	a bust
Fantasy	$2-4 Card 60¢-$1.50

Background: Kukoc was one of the greatest players in Europe, playing the past two seasons for Benetton Treviso of the Italian 1A League. Last year, he averaged 19 points, six rebounds, and five assists a game. His NBA rights have belonged to the Bulls since 1990, when they drafted him in the second round.

Strengths: Kukoc is a tremendous all-around player whose best assets are his court vision and unselfishness. One scout called him "the ideal complementary player." He's big and quick, able to dribble the ball and block shots. He finishes plays effectively.

Weaknesses: Kukoc is not strong, so he must bulk up to withstand the 82-game grind. His man-to-man defense needs work, as is the case with most European players since they're accustomed to playing zones.

Analysis: If Kukoc had been eligible for the 1993 draft, he would have been a high first-round pick. Though he's primarily a small forward, look for the Bulls to play Kukoc, Scottie Pippen, and Michael Jordan at the same time often. Kukoc eventually will be a star in the NBA.

COLLEGE STATISTICS
—DID NOT PLAY—

GERALD MADKINS

Team: Cleveland Cavaliers
Position: Guard
Height: 6'3" **Weight:** 205
Birthdate: April 18, 1969
College: UCLA
Acquired: Signed as a free agent, 6/93

PLAYER SUMMARY	
Will	defend aggressively
Can't	find a position
Expect	a solid sub
Don't Expect	a big scorer
Fantasy	$0 Card	15-25¢

Background: Madkins, who captained UCLA as a senior in 1992, ranks fourth in school history in steals and fifth in assists. His career nearly ended in 1988 when he was badly injured in a motorbike accident. Undrafted in '92, he played for the Grand Rapids Hoops and won the CBA Rookie of the Year Award.

Strengths: An aggressive defender, Madkins plays tough and can stop point guards and shooting guards alike. He has long arms, good lateral mobility, and good anticipation. He's an asset in transition because he runs the floor easily and is unselfish.

Weaknesses: Offensively, he's a "tweener." Madkins doesn't shoot well enough to play long minutes at big guard, and he lacks the playmaking skills needed at the point.

Analysis: The Cavs moved quickly to sign Madkins, snatching him before other teams could evaluate him at the NBA's Chicago pre-draft camp. That figures to be a good move for Cleveland, which can use Madkins as a back-up at both point guard and shooting guard.

COLLEGE STATISTICS

	G	FGP	FTP	RPG	APG	PPG
87-88 UCLA	30	.595	.829	1.3	1.5	5.8
89-90 UCLA	33	.491	.688	2.4	3.7	7.2
90-91 UCLA	32	.515	.756	2.6	3.9	9.2
91-92 UCLA	28	.503	.671	2.4	4.0	8.2
Totals	123	.520	.725	2.2	3.3	7.6

RICH MANNING

Team: Atlanta Hawks
Position: Center
Height: 6'11" **Weight:** 251
Birthdate: June 23, 1970
College: Syracuse; Washington
Acquired: 2nd-round pick in 1993 draft (40th overall)

PLAYER SUMMARY	
Will	hustle
Can't	rebound consistently
Expect	a plugger
Don't Expect	a thoroughbred
Fantasy	$0 Card	10-20¢

Background: Manning began his college career at Syracuse, but after playing very little for two seasons, he transferred to Washington. He scored in double figures in 51 of 54 games for the Huskies and is their all-time leader in field goal accuracy.

Strengths: Manning shoots softly when facing the basket and has range to about 15 feet. He's steady from the free throw line and is developing a jump hook. He's smart and plays under control.

Weaknesses: Scouts cite sub-par strength and quickness as areas that will hold Manning back. He probably can't run the floor with most NBA power forwards and will be overpowered in man-to-man defense. He rarely blocks shots.

Analysis: Blair Rasmussen's career may be over because of a back injury, so the Hawks need a center to back up John Koncak. Manning, who some scouts say is a power forward, could stick. More likely, he will play in Europe for a year or two before giving the NBA another try.

COLLEGE STATISTICS

	G	FGP	FTP	RPG	APG	PPG
88-89 SYR	36	.511	.763	1.8	0.2	3.4
89-90 SYR	31	.430	.739	2.1	0.3	3.1
91-92 WASH	29	.568	.673	6.1	0.8	16.8
92-93 WASH	25	.575	.800	8.4	1.4	17.9
Totals	121	.550	.738	4.3	0.6	9.5

CONRAD McRAE

Team: Minnesota Timberwolves
Position: Center/Forward
Height: 6'10" **Weight:** 222
Birthdate: January 11, 1971
College: Syracuse
Acquired: Traded from Bullets for Tim Burroughs, 8/93

PLAYER SUMMARY	
Will	reject shots
Can't	bury his FTs
Expect	a leaper
Don't Expect	to see him soon
Fantasy	$0 Card ......15-25¢

Background: McRae was a role-player at Syracuse but finished fourth on the school's blocked-shots list. He also led the Orange in field goal percentage three straight years. McRae was drafted 38th overall by Washington but his rights were traded to Minnesota. He'll play in Turkey in 1993-94.

Strengths: McRae is a great athlete, especially when it comes to jumping. He's strong, plays physical defense, blocks shots, and runs the floor smoothly.

Weaknesses: McRae has no offensive game to speak of. As one scout said, "Dunks are his life; they're all he's interested in." McRae didn't progress in college and he needs a lot of work on his passing, dribbling, and shooting. "He's just out there jumping around," said a scout.

Analysis: McRae would have preferred the NBA to Turkey, but he just wasn't ready for the big leagues. He needs to substantially upgrade his offensive game before NBA teams come calling.

COLLEGE STATISTICS

		G	FGP	FTP	RPG	APG	PPG
89-90	SYR	16	.471	.625	2.0	0.3	1.9
90-91	SYR	32	.543	.622	4.2	0.4	5.0
91-92	SYR	28	.540	.570	6.2	0.9	8.7
92-93	SYR	28	.560	.606	6.9	0.5	12.3
Totals		104	.548	.598	5.1	0.5	7.5

DARNELL MEE

Team: Denver Nuggets
Position: Guard
Height: 6'5" **Weight:** 177
Birthdate: February 11, 1971
College: Western Kentucky
Acquired: Draft rights traded from Warriors for draft rights to Josh Grant and a 1994 2nd-round pick, 6/93

PLAYER SUMMARY	
Will	stroke the "J"
Can't	muscle up
Expect	quick hands
Don't Expect	sudden impact
Fantasy	$0 Card ......15-25¢

Background: Mee was a big factor in Western Kentucky's run to the Sweet 16 last season. He set a Sun Belt record with 100 steals last year, which placed him fourth nationally. Mee earned honorable-mention All-America honors from the Associated Press. He was drafted 34th overall.

Strengths: Scouts like Mee's ability to shoot consistently from long range, as he can hit from near the NBA 3-point line. Defensively, he gets a lot of steals by anticipating plays and leaking into the passing lanes.

Weaknesses: Mee played alongside a good point guard in college, so he rarely handled the ball. He'll have to prove that he can create shots for himself and his teammates, and he needs to get to the basket more often and draw fouls. He could stand to add a little muscle.

Analysis: Denver may be the wrong team for Mee. The Nuggets have a surplus of guards, especially at the shooting spot, so Mee probably will be the victim of a numbers game. His likely destination is the CBA.

COLLEGE STATISTICS

		G	FGP	FTP	RPG	APG	PPG
90-91	WKU	27	.457	.797	5.1	2.3	10.7
91-92	WKU	32	.402	.644	4.5	3.3	11.2
92-93	WKU	32	.434	.707	6.0	3.3	18.9
Totals		91	.429	.712	5.2	3.0	13.8

SHERRON MILLS

Team: Minnesota Timberwolves
Position: Forward/Center
Height: 6'9" **Weight:** 220
Birthdate: July 29, 1971
College: Virginia Commonwealth
Acquired: 2nd-round pick in 1993 draft (29th overall)

PLAYER SUMMARY	
Will	run and jump
Can't	nail the trey
Expect	a roster spot
Don't Expect	a stiff
Fantasy	$0 Card 10-15¢

Background: After a brief detour to a junior college, Mills played three years at VCU, but he didn't develop into a prospect until late in his senior season. He came on strongly after VCU's best player, Kendrick Warren, was lost because of an injury. In his best game, Mills tallied 19 points and 19 rebounds against Tulane.

Strengths: A fine athlete with above-average quickness and agility, Mills runs the court easily and jumps very well. He has a decent offensive game within ten feet of the basket, and he knows how to work the offensive boards. He plays hard.

Weaknesses: There are no glaring weaknesses in Mills's game, though he could stand to add about 20 pounds and expand his offensive game to the perimeter. He probably can't play center in the NBA.

Analysis: A strong showing at the Portsmouth Invitational boosted Mills's stock. Minnesota, which has been trying to solidify its front line, should have room for Mills. Sherron would help back up Christian Laettner at power forward.

COLLEGE STATISTICS

	G	FGP	FTP	RPG	APG	PPG
90-91 VCU	24	.570	.727	3.9	0.5	5.4
91-92 VCU	29	.503	.699	7.4	1.7	12.9
92-93 VCU	30	.563	.700	8.4	1.7	15.4
Totals	83	.540	.703	6.8	1.3	11.6

GHEORGHE MURESAN

Team: Washington Bullets
Position: Center
Height: 7'7" **Weight:** 315
Birthdate: February 14, 1971
College: Cluj University
Acquired: 2nd-round pick in 1993 draft (30th overall)

PLAYER SUMMARY	
Will	work diligently
Can't	run worth a lick
Expect	a fringe player
Don't Expect	a shot-blocker
Fantasy	$0 Card 25-40¢

Background: Muresan is a 22-year-old giant who is taller than Shawn Bradley and much heavier than either Bradley or Manute Bol. Muresan played well last season for Pau Orthez, a professional team in France, averaging 18.7 points and 10.3 rebounds per game. He has failed several physical exams because of leg injuries.

Strengths: Size is Muresan's greatest asset, though he has skills and is fundamentally sound. Soft hands enable him to catch the ball in traffic, and he shoots with good touch. Scouts say Muresan has an NBA-caliber post game.

Weaknesses: Muresan is limited athletically and has suffered numerous ankle and knee injuries, which will prevent him from playing and practicing throughout an entire NBA season. Though effective in halfcourt situations, Muresan runs very slowly and can't jump at all.

Analysis: Coach Wes Unseld will have to treat Muresan with kid gloves if he hopes to get anything out of him. He was a worthwhile gamble for the Bullets, who need size badly. If Washington carries three centers, Muresan should stick.

COLLEGE STATISTICS
—DID NOT PLAY—

MARCELO NICOLA

Team: Houston Rockets
Position: Forward/Center
Height: 6'10" **Weight:** 240
Birthdate: May 21, 1971
College: None
Acquired: 2nd-round pick in 1993 draft
(50th overall)

PLAYER SUMMARY	
Will ....convert in the paint
Can't............................stay healthy
Expect ....a future player
Don't Expect..............anything now
Fantasy ....$0   Card .....15-25¢

Background: A native of Argentina, Nicola has played the past couple seasons for Taugres, a Spanish pro team that was coached by Larry Brown's brother, Herb. This past summer, Nicola was MVP in the qualifying round for the World 22-and-Under Championships. He led his team to victory against the United States. Nicola played briefly in the USBL in 1991.

Strengths: Nicola is a fine power-forward prospect. He runs well, catches the ball softly, and makes a high percentage of his shots. He has good size for power forward and can play spot duty at center. Scouts say he has a good all-around game.

Weaknesses: Nicola's only key weakness is the health of his ankles, which are brittle and could cause big problems when he's asked to play a full NBA season.

Analysis: The Rockets regularly scout the Spanish League, which enabled them to keep tabs on Nicola. Though he has a long-term contract in Spain, Nicola can buy out the deal soon. He probably won't play with the Rockets this year, but look for him in 1994-95.

COLLEGE STATISTICS
—DID NOT PLAY—

MIKE PEPLOWSKI

Team: Sacramento Kings
Position: Center
Height: 6'11" **Weight:** 270
Birthdate: October 15, 1970
College: Michigan St.
Acquired: 2nd-round pick in 1993 draft
(52nd overall)

PLAYER SUMMARY	
Will ....lay it on the line
Can't............................run and jump
Expect...............................a bruiser
Don't Expect.................style points
Fantasy ....$0   Card .....10-20¢

Background: Peplowski overcame serious knee surgery to form a good college career. He represented the U.S. in the Pan Am Games in 1991 and was named All-Big Ten in 1992. He has the second-highest field goal percentage in school history.

Strengths: A big, strong plugger, Peplowski does the dirty work, whether it's setting forceful picks, grabbing rebounds, or giving hard fouls. He's effective around the basket and rarely takes a bad shot. Scouts love his work ethic and determination.

Weaknesses: Leg problems, including ankle woes his senior year, kept Peplowski out of shape for long periods. Even when healthy, he's a plodder in transition and lacks explosiveness. His perimeter defense is weak.

Analysis: The Kings need rebounders. Peplowski, Evers Burns, and Alex Holcombe—all second-round draft picks—will compete for roster spots. Said one scout: "The more I look at their roster, the more I think Peplowski can make the team."

COLLEGE STATISTICS

		G	FGP	FTP	RPG	APG	PPG
89-90	MSU	28	.546	.628	5.8	0.7	5.3
90-91	MSU	30	.627	.680	6.9	0.5	7.7
91-92	MSU	30	.632	.688	8.6	1.1	13.3
92-93	MSU	28	.639	.667	10.0	1.4	14.5
Totals		116	.620	.670	7.8	0.9	10.2

RICHARD PETRUSKA

Team: Houston Rockets
Position: Center
Height: 6'10" **Weight:** 260
Birthdate: January 25, 1969
College: Loyola Marymount; UCLA
Acquired: 2nd-round pick in 1993 draft
(46th overall)

PLAYER SUMMARY	
Will	stick the foul-line "J"
Can't	run and jump
Expect	a big body
Don't Expect	a roster spot
Fantasy	$0 Card	15-25¢

Background: The 24-year-old Petruska attended college in Czechoslovakia for two years before enrolling at Loyola Marymount. He played there one season and led the Lions in rebounding and blocked shots. He then transferred to UCLA for his senior season. He cracked the Bruins' starting lineup but was not a go-to guy.

Strengths: Petruska is a big man but plays more of a finesse game. A left-hander, he shoots with a soft touch from 15 feet while getting most of his interior points on putbacks and tips. He has a nose for offensive rebounds.

Weaknesses: Like many foreign players, Petruska roams too far outside—despite his large body. He hasn't worked enough to develop a low-post game and is limited athletically. Jumping, running, and lateral movement are weak spots.

Analysis: The Rockets traded for second-round pick Eric Riley and drafted Petruska, hoping one of them will make the grade as Hakeem Olajuwon's back-up. That player will most likely be Riley, with Petruska heading overseas to play in Europe.

COLLEGE STATISTICS

	G	FGP	FTP	RPG	APG	PPG
90-91 LOY	28	.589	.683	7.6	0.4	16.4
92-93 UCLA	33	.499	.598	6.2	0.9	11.8
Totals	61	.543	.644	6.9	0.7	13.9

DINO RADJA

Team: Boston Celtics
Position: Forward
Height: 6'11" **Weight:** 225
Birthdate: April 24, 1967
College: None
Acquired: 2nd-round pick in 1989 draft
(40th overall)

PLAYER SUMMARY	
Will	find ways to score
Can't	stop anybody
Expect	a softy
Don't Expect	Mr. Personality
Fantasy	$1 Card	15-25¢

Background: The Celtics have had to wait four years for Radja, who has been playing basketball in Europe. Last season, he averaged 21.5 points and 10.2 rebounds per game for Virtus Roma of the Italian 1A League. He has been considered a legitimate NBA prospect.

Strengths: Radja is a better offensive player than many power forwards. He can get out and score in transition and knock down jump shots from the deep corner or the top of the key. He's a good pick-and-roll player and gets his share of rebounds.

Weaknesses: Said one scout: "He can't contribute a lot because he's so poor defensively. He guards no one." Radja is reputed to be spoiled, selfish, and egotistical and may not fit in. He's too soft for his size and lacks a quality post-up game.

Analysis: Kevin McHale is gone, so the Celtics have a hole at power forward. Scouts say Radja is better than Alaa Abdelnaby, last year's starter. If he dedicates himself to defense, Radja could move into the lineup by the middle of the season.

COLLEGE STATISTICS
—DID NOT PLAY—

ANTHONY REED

Team: Chicago Bulls
Position: Forward
Height: 6'9" **Weight:** 220
Birthdate: January 3, 1971
College: Tulane
Acquired: 2nd-round pick in 1993 draft (41st overall)

PLAYER SUMMARY	
Will	rebound
Can't	post and score
Expect	a struggle to stick
Don't Expect	Willis Reed
Fantasy	$0 Card .....10-20¢

Background: Reed had a fruitful career at Tulane, starting all 118 games and finishing as the school's all-time leading scorer. He also ranks second in steals and fourth in rebounds, and he was twice named first-team All-Metro. He expanded his game as a senior, making 33 3-pointers after making none his first three seasons.

Strengths: Reed has a dependable stand-still jump shot from 15 feet and in. He crashes the boards at both ends and plays hard all the time.

Weaknesses: Reed is too small for power forward and lacks the quickness and ball-handling skills to play small forward. He hasn't displayed a consistent back-to-the-basket game, and he has weak legs. His free throw shooting needs work.

Analysis: Scouts say Reed is a good player without a position. However, he could stick in Chicago because the Bulls have holes up front after some off-season house cleaning. Most likely, Reed will try Europe if the Bulls can make suitable arrangements.

COLLEGE STATISTICS

		G	FGP	FTP	RPG	APG	PPG
89-90	TUL	28	.533	.658	8.4	0.8	18.4
90-91	TUL	28	.489	.546	7.9	1.2	16.0
91-92	TUL	31	.477	.624	6.5	1.0	14.4
92-93	TUL	31	.459	.630	6.8	1.0	15.7
Totals		118	.488	.617	7.4	1.0	16.1

ERIC RILEY

Team: Houston Rockets
Position: Center
Height: 7'0" **Weight:** 245
Birthdate: June 2, 1970
College: Michigan
Acquired: Draft rights traded from Mavericks for draft rights to Popeye Jones, 6/93

PLAYER SUMMARY	
Will	run the floor
Can't	wrestle inside
Expect	a battle to stick
Don't Expect	an NBA center
Fantasy	$0 Card .....10-20¢

Background: Riley started 26 games his sophomore season at Michigan, finishing second in the Big Ten in rebounding and blocked shots, but became a reserve when the Fab Five arrived. Riley is third on Michigan's career blocked-shots list. He was drafted 33rd overall.

Strengths: Riley is big and a good athlete, capable of running the floor smoothly. Scouts like the fact that he hails from a winning program and practiced every day against Chris Webber and Juwan Howard. He has good offensive potential.

Weaknesses: Riley needs to add meat to his bones or he will be driven out of the league by stronger players. His low-post offense leaves a lot to be desired, and he's not much better facing the basket.

Analysis: The Rockets have an open spot for Riley because Tree Rollins isn't expected to return. However, scouts aren't sure Riley is good enough to take it. He's just too frail and soft to make it in the big leagues.

COLLEGE STATISTICS

		G	FGP	FTP	RPG	APG	PPG
89-90	MICH	31	.607	.457	3.3	0.5	2.7
90-91	MICH	28	.447	.704	8.6	1.0	10.6
91-92	MICH	32	.590	.578	4.3	0.7	6.3
92-93	MICH	35	.586	.736	4.8	0.4	5.6
Totals		126	.531	.648	5.2	0.6	6.1

BRYON RUSSELL

Team: Utah Jazz
Position: Forward
Height: 6'7" **Weight:** 225
Birthdate: December 31, 1970
College: Long Beach St.
Acquired: 2nd-round pick in 1993 draft
(45th overall)

PLAYER SUMMARY	
Will	give the effort
Can't	shake and bake
Expect	a long shot
Don't Expect	Cazzie Russell
Fantasy	$0 Card .....10-20¢

Background: Though he was a good player at Long Beach State, Russell was considered a surprise draft pick. He sat out a year to become academically eligible, then steadily progressed the next three seasons while teaming with fellow second-round pick Lucious Harris (Dallas). Russell led the 49ers in rebounding and blocked shots last season.

Strengths: A small forward, Russell is active, does the dirty work defensively and on the boards, and has intangibles that scouts like. He's tough, physical, and isn't afraid to wrestle with bigger players. Fifteen-foot jump shots are well within his range.

Weaknesses: Lack of an in-between game could keep Russell out of the NBA. He can't put the ball on the floor and make something happen, whether it's driving to the rim or pulling up for a shot or pass.

Analysis: Barring a trade, Utah will go with Tyrone Corbin and David Benoit at small forward, leaving little room for Russell. Russell is tough and will fight in training camp, but the CBA is his likely destination.

COLLEGE STATISTICS

		G	FGP	FTP	RPG	APG	PPG
90-91	LBS	28	.430	.652	5.8	1.5	7.9
91-92	LBS	26	.555	.656	7.4	1.2	13.9
92-93	LBS	32	.537	.727	6.7	2.1	13.2
Totals		86	.513	.683	6.6	1.6	11.7

ED STOKES

Team: Miami Heat
Position: Center
Height: 7'0" **Weight:** 264
Birthdate: September 3, 1971
College: Arizona
Acquired: 2nd-round pick in 1993 draft
(35th overall)

PLAYER SUMMARY	
Will	flash skills
Can't	stay focused
Expect	some time in Europe
Don't Expect	a long career
Fantasy	$0 Card .....15-25¢

Background: A highly rated recruit for Lute Olson, Stokes moved into Arizona's starting lineup as a freshman but regressed the next three seasons. He was bothered by Achilles, hamstring, and ankle injuries. He'll play this season for Panionios in Greece.

Strengths: Stokes has a big body, and that's enough to warrant a look-see in the NBA. Stokes is a good, strong athlete who runs well and can jump. "He has the size and toughness to play in the NBA," said one G.M. He has good hands and passes well.

Weaknesses: The biggest problem with Stokes is that he doesn't play hard. He has physical strength but doesn't use it to his best advantage. He rarely blocks shots or scores on anything other than garbage around the hoop. He struggles at the line.

Analysis: Stokes wasn't ready to play in the NBA, so the seasoning in Greece will do him good. He could make the Heat in 1994-95 season as a back-up to Rony Seikaly.

COLLEGE STATISTICS

		G	FGP	FTP	RPG	APG	PPG
89-90	ARIZ	29	.599	.564	4.6	0.2	8.0
90-91	ARIZ	34	.470	.538	4.3	0.4	5.9
91-92	ARIZ	30	.517	.613	5.1	0.5	7.6
92-93	ARIZ	28	.489	.715	7.4	0.7	11.5
Totals		121	.515	.597	5.3	0.5	8.0

KEVIN THOMPSON

Team: Portland Trail Blazers
Position: Forward
Height: 6'10" **Weight:** 260
Birthdate: February 7, 1971
College: North Carolina St.
Acquired: 2nd-round pick in 1993 draft (48th overall)

PLAYER SUMMARY	
Will	hit the hook
Can't	convert his FTs
Expect	a struggle to stick
Don't Expect	P.T. as a rookie
Fantasy	$0 Card ..... 10-20¢

Background: Thompson bumped up his game a notch as a sophomore and again as a junior, but he leveled off as a senior. Thompson is the Wolfpack's all-time leader in career field goal accuracy.

Strengths: Scouts say Thompson could develop into a quality power forward. He has a good body, runs the court easily, and blocks shots. He scores inside with an assortment of hooks and jumpers, and he's quick to pursue rebounds.

Weaknesses: Which is the real Thompson—the one who showed vast promise two years ago, or the one who disappeared at times last season? Thompson has no glaring weaknesses other than free throw shooting, but he needs to refine his all-around game.

Analysis: The Trail Blazers lack size after trading Kevin Duckworth, so Thompson could make the team. To do so, he'll probably have to beat out 1992 draft pick Reggie Smith, which won't be easy. Even if he sticks, Thompson won't play much.

COLLEGE STATISTICS

		G	FGP	FTP	RPG	APG	PPG
89-90	NCS	30	.592	.381	2.8	0.4	3.3
90-91	NCS	31	.605	.571	7.7	1.3	8.6
91-92	NCS	30	.624	.572	8.2	1.9	15.6
92-93	NCS	27	.543	.579	9.1	2.0	15.5
Totals		118	.588	.575	6.9	1.4	10.6

NICK VAN EXEL

Team: Los Angeles Lakers
Position: Guard
Height: 6'1" **Weight:** 171
Birthdate: November 27, 1971
College: Cincinnati
Acquired: 2nd-round pick in 1993 draft (37th overall)

PLAYER SUMMARY	
Will	press the pace
Can't	control his ego
Expect	a back-up
Don't Expect	a coach's pet
Fantasy	$0 Card ..... 15-30¢

Background: Van Exel was the ringleader of a Cincinnati team that advanced to the Final Four in 1992 and the round of eight in 1993. He was expected to be a first-round pick but fell out of favor with scouts, who questioned his attitude. He displayed top-notch point-guard skills in two seasons with the Bearcats after playing his first two years at a junior college.

Strengths: Van Exel is extremely quick both defensively and with the ball. Capable at both guard spots, he's best suited for the point because he's only 6'1". He can turn on his offense, hitting seven or eight baskets in a row. He handles the ball very well.

Weaknesses: Van Exel scores, but he sometimes takes too many shots. He can be streaky and a bit selfish. "He has alienated a lot of people," said one scout. He's also small by NBA standards.

Analysis: The Lakers are rebuilding and were fortunate that Van Exel slipped to them in the second round. He's good enough to make the team and could be an integral part of L.A.'s backcourt of the future, which includes Anthony Peeler and Doug Christie.

COLLEGE STATISTICS

		G	FGP	FTP	RPG	APG	PPG
91-92	CINC	34	.446	.673	2.6	2.9	12.3
92-93	CINC	31	.386	.725	2.4	4.5	18.3
Totals		65	.409	.701	2.5	3.6	15.2

LEONARD WHITE

Team: Los Angeles Clippers
Position: Forward
Height: 6'7" **Weight:** 218
Birthdate: February 21, 1971
College: Southern
Acquired: 2nd-round pick in 1993 draft
(53rd overall)

PLAYER SUMMARY	
Will	shoot with range
Can't	guard anybody
Expect	a slick athlete
Don't Expect	consistency
Fantasy	$0 Card	10-20¢

Background: White was the leading scorer on the Southern team that upset Georgia Tech in the first round of the 1993 NCAA Tournament. He played two seasons at a junior college before transferring to Southern, where he twice was named first-team All-Southwestern Athletic Conference.

Strengths: White has a body that's built for the NBA, and he's an outstanding athlete. He has no problem hitting jump shots from 20 feet out. In fact, he converted 45.7 percent of his 3-point attempts last season. He was a good rebounder in college.

Weaknesses: Scouts question White's intensity and want to know why he's not more consistent. He'll have to stay outside in the NBA, so he needs to work on his ball-handling skills and beating defenders with his dribble. His defense is sub-standard.

Analysis: Who knows what will happen with the Clippers? They didn't name a coach until late July, so it's difficult to speculate whether White will make the team. It's a good bet he'll spend time in the CBA, which is filled with inconsistent scorers who struggle on defense.

COLLEGE STATISTICS

	G	FGP	FTP	RPG	APG	PPG
91-92 SOU	30	.481	.724	12.5	1.9	22.4
92-93 SOU	30	.450	.697	10.1	1.8	20.6
Totals	60	.466	.712	11.3	1.9	21.5

CHRIS WHITNEY

Team: San Antonio Spurs
Position: Guard
Height: 6'0" **Weight:** 171
Birthdate: October 5, 1971
College: Clemson
Acquired: 2nd-round pick in 1993 draft
(47th overall)

PLAYER SUMMARY	
Will	shoot with range
Can't	body-up on defense
Expect	a fringe guy
Don't Expect	a finisher
Fantasy	$0 Card	10-20¢

Background: A relatively obscure player (he played two years at a junior college) until his senior season at Clemson, Whitney rapidly emerged as a prospect. Last year, he was the only ACC player to finish in the top five in five statistical categories. He made the grade in assists, 3-point baskets and accuracy, steals, and free throw percentage.

Strengths: A legitimate point guard, Whitney has good quickness and, at times, a good jump shot. He made eight 3-pointers in a game against North Carolina last year. He passes the ball crisply, makes things happen off the dribble, and is durable.

Weaknesses: Lack of size hurts Whitney's chances on the pro level, especially when it comes to defense. Scouts like his overall game, though they say he's not great in any particular area.

Analysis: The Spurs, without a first-round pick, had to settle for Whitney as their only fruit from this year's draft. San Antonio would like to replace Avery Johnson at point guard, but Whitney isn't good enough to do so. If he makes the team, he'll play few minutes.

COLLEGE STATISTICS

	G	FGP	FTP	RPG	APG	PPG
91-92 CLEM	28	.410	.767	3.3	5.8	13.4
92-93 CLEM	30	.441	.802	4.1	6.4	15.7
Totals	58	.428	.788	3.7	6.1	14.6

BYRON WILSON

Team: Phoenix Suns
Position: Guard
Height: 6'2" **Weight:** 215
Birthdate: September 1, 1971
College: Utah
Acquired: 2nd-round pick in 1993 draft
(54th overall)

PLAYER SUMMARY	
Will	give his all
Can't	run a team
Expect	a CBA stop-over
Don't Expect	a sudden impact
Fantasy	$0 Card	10-20¢

Background: A prep star in Indiana, Wilson was lured to Utah by coach Rick Majerus but had to sit out the 1989-90 season as an academic non-qualifier. He developed into one of the WAC's best swing men, twice leading the Utes into the NCAA Tournament. He earned first-team all-conference honors as a senior.

Strengths: Wilson has no special skills, but he plays hard at both ends, penetrates aggressively, and is a very good rebounder for a guard. He takes a tough, physical approach to defense. Scouts like his work habits and athleticism. He's built for an up-tempo game.

Weaknesses: Wilson is a bit undersized for shooting guard and lacks shooting consistency. Otherwise, he has no critical weaknesses.

Analysis: Both Wilson and Mark Buford were surprise second-round picks by Phoenix. Wilson is a long shot to make the team, though the Suns may carry him as the 12th man, hoping he can grow into the eventual replacement for Danny Ainge.

COLLEGE STATISTICS

	G	FGP	FTP	RPG	APG	PPG
90-91 UTAH	32	.429	.663	3.0	1.5	8.7
91-92 UTAH	35	.440	.780	5.1	1.8	12.1
92-93 UTAH	31	.474	.759	5.7	2.8	12.5
Totals	98	.449	.745	4.6	2.0	11.1

TOP NONDRAFTED PLAYERS

Sam Crawford

New Mexico St., 5'8", 155

An outstanding little point guard, Crawford led the nation in assists with 9.1 per game last year. He's a good playmaker and shooter, but he probably lacks the special quickness and speed that small players need to thrive in the NBA.

Warren Kidd

Middle Tennessee St., 6'9", 235

A big, strong, physical player, Kidd led the nation in rebounding last season (14.8 per game) while averaging 15 PPG. A potential NBA power forward, he has good mobility and gets good position for rebounds. Most of his points come off garbage around the hoop.

Justus Thigpen

Iowa St., 6'2", 195

Thigpen ranks second on ISU's all-time steals list behind Jeff Hornacek, and he led the Cyclones in scoring the past two seasons. Thigpen is a bull-strong shooting guard who needs to learn point-guard skills. He tends to carry too much weight and is a poor free throw shooter.

Rodney Dobard

Florida St., 6'6", 210

Dobard ranked seventh nationally in blocked shots last season (3.2 BPG) and was expected to go in the second round. However, he measured only 6'6" at the Chicago pre-draft camp (he was listed at 6'9" in college) and fell out of the draft. He's active at both ends, jumps extremely well, and has great timing for blocking shots.

Lance Miller

Villanova, 6'5", 200

Miller is a cousin of Eric Murdock, and he has a similar game. He gets after people defensively, runs very well, and won the 3-point shooting contest at the Portsmouth Invitational. He wasn't drafted, partly because he had a sub-par senior season.

NBA Team Overviews

This section evaluates all 27 NBA teams, sectioning them off by their divisions. For each team, you'll find:

- the club's address and phone number
- arena information
- a listing of the team's owner, general manager (or equivalent thereof), and coaches
- the head coach's record (lifetime and with team)
- a review of the team's history
- team finishes over the last seven years
- a review of the team's 1992-93 season
- the club's 1993-94 roster
- a preview of the 1993-94 season

The team rosters include players who were drafted in June. The rosters list each player's 1992-93 statistics. Stats include games (G), points per game (PPG), rebounds per game (RPG), and assists per game (APG). The category "Exp." (experience) indicates the number of years the player has played in the NBA.

Each 1993-94 season preview tips off with an "opening line," which looks at the players the team lost and those that are coming in. The preview then examines the team at each position, including guard, forward, center, and coaching. "Analysis" evaluates the team's strengths and weaknesses and puts it all into perspective. The preview ends with a prediction, stating where the club will finish within its division.

BOSTON CELTICS

Home: Boston Garden
Capacity: 14,890
Year Built: 1928

Address
151 Merrimac St.
Boston, MA 02114
(617) 523-6050

Chairman of the Board: Don F. Gaston
General Manager: Jan Volk
Head Coach: Chris Ford
Assistant Coach: Don Casey
Assistant Coach: Jon Jennings
Assistant Coach: Dennis Johnson

Coach Chris Ford			
	W	L	Pct.
NBA Record	155	91	.630
W/Celtics	155	91	.630
1992-93 Record	48	34	.585

Celtics History

The history of the Boston Celtics drips with tradition. The Celtics have won 16 world championships and must be listed with baseball's Yankees, football's Packers, and hockey's Canadiens among the greatest teams in sports history.

Boston began as a member of the old BAA in 1946-47 and joined the NBA at its inception. Red Auerbach took over as coach of the team in 1950-51 and began assembling the pieces of the Celtic machine. He started with guard Bob Cousy (perhaps the best ever on the fastbreak), added Bill Sharman, and in 1956 bagged the big one—Bill Russell.

Boston won its first championship in 1956-57, then won every title from 1958-59 through 1965-66, thoroughly dominating pro basketball. Russell, famous for his battles with Wilt Chamberlain, redefined post defense. His supporting cast included Sam and K.C. Jones, Tom Heinsohn, Frank Ramsey, and John Havlicek.

Auerbach moved to the front office in 1966 and Russell took over as player/coach, but the Celtics didn't falter, winning championships in 1968 and '69. Heinsohn assumed control of the bench in 1969 and won titles in 1974 and '76 with stars like Havlicek, center Dave Cowens, and guard Jo Jo White.

The Celtics' modern era dawned in 1979, when the team drafted forward Larry Bird. Behind Bird and frontcourt partners Robert Parish and Kevin McHale, Boston shared the 1980s spotlight with the Los Angeles Lakers, taking world championships in 1981, '84, and '86.

Last Seven Years

Season	W	L	Pct.	Place	Playoffs	Coach
1986-87	59	23	.720	First	L-NBA Finals	K.C. Jones
1987-88	57	25	.695	First	L-East Finals	K.C. Jones
1988-89	42	40	.512	Third	L-Round 1	Jimmy Rodgers
1989-90	52	30	.634	Second	L-Round 1	Jimmy Rodgers
1990-91	56	26	.683	First	L-East Semis	Chris Ford
1991-92	51	31	.622	First	L-East Semis	Chris Ford
1992-93	48	34	.585	Second	L-Round 1	Chris Ford

1992-93 Review

The Boston Celtics' 1992-93 season ended painfully in May, when Charlotte's Alonzo Mourning nailed a last-second jumper to eliminate Boston from the first round of the playoffs. But that difficult loss wasn't nearly as painful as the tragic death of Celtics star Reggie Lewis, who died of a heart attack on July 27, 1993, at the age of 27.

Ironically, Lewis had collapsed on the court early in the Charlotte series and did not play the remaining games. Two teams of doctors examined Lewis, the first saying he had a heart condition similar to that of Hank Gathers, who died on the court in 1990. The second group of doctors, led by Dr. Gilbert Mudge, said Lewis's problem was treatable and that he would be able to play NBA ball again. Lewis chose to follow Dr. Mudge's advice, which was a tragic mistake. Lewis suffered his heart attack during a light workout at Brandeis University. He was simply shooting baskets.

Lewis's death followed a joyless Celtic season. Boston had to endure its first campaign without Larry Bird, while Kevin McHale announced in midseason that he would retire when the year was out. The ancient Robert Parish, the oldest man in the league, soldiered on at age 39. The Celtics posted a surprising 48-34 record, but they never did challenge New York for first place in the Atlantic.

During the season, coach Chris Ford never quite found a set lineup. Lewis, McHale, and Parish—all former All-Stars—were the soul of the ballclub, with Lewis leading the team in scoring (20.8 PPG) and Parish leading the club in rebounding (9.4 RPG). Ford turned to a host of others to help bandage the season together.

Small forwards Kevin Gamble and Xavier McDaniel each poured in 13 PPG. Big forward Alaa Abdelnaby was rather unproductive in his 52 starts, while Joe Kleine provided boards, bumps, and bruises as a back-up to Parish. Guards Sherman Douglas and Dee Brown—both of whom were known as talented underachievers—shared the point-guard duties and did an adequate job.

1993-94 Roster

No.	Player	Pos.	Ht.	Wt.	Exp.	College	G	PPG	RPG	APG
4	Alaa Abdelnaby	F	6'10"	240	3	Duke	75	7.7	4.5	0.4
5	John Bagley	G	6'0"	205	10	Boston College	10	2.3	0.7	2.0
7	Dee Brown	G	6'1"	161	3	Jacksonville	80	10.9	3.1	5.8
20	Sherman Douglas	G	6'0"	180	4	Syracuse	79	7.8	2.1	6.4
—	Acie Earl	C/F	6'11"	240	R	Iowa	—	—	—	—
44	Rick Fox	F/G	6'7"	231	2	North Carolina	71	6.4	2.2	1.6
34	Kevin Gamble	G/F	6'5"	210	6	Iowa	82	13.3	3.0	2.8
31	Xavier McDaniel	F	6'7"	205	8	Wichita St.	82	13.5	6.0	2.0
00	Robert Parish	C	7'0"	230	17	Centenary	79	12.6	9.4	0.8
54	Ed Pinckney	F	6'9"	215	8	Villanova	7	4.6	6.1	0.1
—	Dino Radja	F	6'11"	225	R	None	—	—	—	—
43	Lorenzo Williams	F/C	6'9"	200	1	Stetson	27	1.3	2.0	0.2

Boston Celtics
1993-94 Season Preview

Opening Line: These are not good times for the NBA's most storied franchise. Retirement, injury, age, and, of course, the tragic death of Reggie Lewis have devastated the Celtics. Last season's playoff appearance could be Boston's last postseason action for quite a while. Besides the painful loss of Lewis, Kevin McHale has retired and Joe Kleine left as a free agent. European import Dino Radja (6'11") and shot-blocking rookie Acie Earl are little consolation.

Guard: The loss of Lewis obviously decimates the backcourt. All that's left are point guards Dee Brown (6'1") and Sherman Douglas (6'0"). Though talented, both players have been inconsistent, with Brown often out of control and Douglas sometimes petulant. Douglas, who scored 18.5 PPG with Miami in 1990-91, could get the start at two guard; however, that would leave Boston with an extremely small starting backcourt. Swing man Kevin Gamble, a sweet outside shooter, may end up starting at big guard. Rick Fox is another swing man who could see more time at the two spot.

Forward: McHale's retirement represents a further crumbling of Boston's front line. Xavier McDaniel proved to be a valuable acquisition last year, finishing second on the team in scoring and adding a needed physical presence up front. He doesn't show up every night, however. Gamble can fill it up as a small forward, but at 6'5" he's too short for the position. Youngster Alaa Abdelnaby still has a lot to learn underneath. Boston could use a healthy return of power forward Ed Pinckney, who missed most of last year with a knee injury. Radja, a power forward who can run the floor and shoot, could be a pleasant surprise.

Center: All hail the Chief—for the last time. Old double zero makes a last trip around the NBA in the green and white, and though Parish's stamina is down, his strength and knowledge of the game still make him a formidable pivot man. However, if the old man breaks down, the Celtics could be in serious trouble. Earl offers little besides his shot-blocking skills.

Coaching: Chris Ford remains a good player's coach, thanks to his NBA experience. And though he doesn't show much emotion, he is certainly in control of the Celtics. Unless the talent level improves, though, he may be a casualty of a youth movement. After all, they've fired guys with more championships than he has. Dennis Johnson joins Don Casey and Jon Jennings as an assistant.

Analysis: After years of championship glory, the Celtics have fallen into the depths of despair. Boston has drafted two great talents in the past eight years, Len Bias (1986) and Lewis (1987), but both have passed on. Add to that the retirements of Larry Bird and McHale—and the upcoming retirement of Parish— and you get a franchise that has been virtually wiped out. This will be one of the toughest seasons in Celtic history.

Prediction: Fifth place, Atlantic

MIAMI HEAT

Home: Miami Arena
Capacity: 15,008
Year Built: 1988

Address
Miami Arena
Miami, FL 33136
(305) 577-4328

Partners: Ted Arison, Zev Bufman, Billy Cunningham, Lewis Schaffel
Managing Partner: Lewis Schaffel
Head Coach: Kevin Loughery
Assistant Coach: Alvin Gentry
Assistant Coach: Bob Staak

Coach Kevin Loughery			
	W	L	Pct.
NBA Record	415	593	.412
W/Heat	74	90	.451
1992-93 Record	36	46	.439

Heat History

In its first three years of existence, Miami won 57 games—combined. But the Heat finally rose in 1991-92, becoming the first of the league's recent expansion teams to make the playoffs.

The city was awarded a franchise in April 1987 and entered the league in 1988-89 under the direction of coach Ron Rothstein. The team had few recognizable players at its inception (Clinton Wheeler? Craig Neal?), but it certainly had some ownership clout in the form of Billy Cunningham, the coach of the 1982-83 champion Philadelphia 76ers.

The Heat stumbled to a 15-67 record in its inaugural campaign, relying on rookies Rony Seikaly and Kevin Edwards and a collection of NBA castaways. One of the definite highlights of the first year was the sharp shooting of guard Jon Sundvold, who led the league in 3-point shooting with a remarkable 52-percent average.

The following year brought rookies Glen Rice and Sherman Douglas to the Heat, but only three more wins. Miami fans got to vent their frustrations on a new rival—the expansion Orlando Magic; and the arrival of the 1990 All-Star Game in Miami helped perk up the season. However, the team struggled through another bad campaign in 1990-91, going 24-58. In May 1991, Rothstein resigned under pressure.

New coach Kevin Loughery arrived in 1991-92 and all of a sudden the Heat came alive. With the help of rookie guard Steve Smith, Seikaly in the middle, and an improved Rice, Miami snuck into the playoffs. Once there, however, they were quickly swept by the world champion Chicago Bulls.

Last Five Years

Season	W	L	Pct.	Place	Playoffs	Coach
1988-89	15	67	.183	Sixth	DNQ	Ron Rothstein
1989-90	18	64	.220	Fifth	DNQ	Ron Rothstein
1990-91	24	58	.293	Sixth	DNQ	Ron Rothstein
1991-92	38	44	.463	Fourth	L-Round 1	Kevin Loughery
1992-93	36	46	.439	Fifth	DNQ	Kevin Loughery

1992-93 Review

It was beautiful, albeit short-lived. For one year, Miami was the king of all expansion teams, beating all of its foundling brethren to the postseason and appearing to be the Young Franchise on the Rise.

Yes, sir, 1991-92 was a great year. Then came the draft. When the Shaq landed in Orlando and Alonzo Mourning joined Charlotte, trouble started in Miami. It didn't end until midway through the 1992-93 season, and by then it was too late to recoup any of the previous season's momentum. Miami finished 36-46 for the season, ahead of only pitiful Minnesota in the Expansion Derby.

There were extenuating circumstances, and certainly guard Steve Smith's knee injury was a killer. When the talented 6'7" second-year point guard returned to the lineup, the Heat improved greatly. But he played only 48 games.

That was unfortunate, but the Heat's decision to dish a 1993 first-round pick to Detroit for the extremely limited power forward John Salley was completely self-inflicted. The Spider missed more than a month with a stress fracture in his left foot, and when he did play his numbers were disappointing.

Frontcourt gunner Glen Rice again led the team in scoring, but his average dropped, largely due to his 44-percent shooting from the field—a product of his astronomical 386 3-point attempts. Center Rony Seikaly was again solid in the middle. Though undersized, Seikaly pulled down 34 rebounds March 3 against the Bullets. Grant Long remained a strong power forward, but Brian Shaw was a giant disappointment at two guard, shooting 39.3 percent from the field and making the Celtics look like geniuses for getting rid of him.

Rookie Harold Miner had a curious season. When he played, he scored, but the former USC prodigy scraped for minutes, apparently unwilling to play coach Kevin Loughery's aggressive defense. Swing man Willie Burton (wrist) joined Smith and Salley on the injury list for nearly half of the season, while Bimbo Coles proved an adequate back-up at the point-guard spot.

1993-94 Roster

| | | | | | | | —1992-93— | | |
No.	Player	Pos.	Ht.	Wt.	Exp.	College	G	PPG	RPG	APG
2	Keith Askins	G/F	6'8"	215	3	Alabama	69	3.3	2.9	0.4
34	Willie Burton	G/F	6'7"	219	3	Minnesota	26	7.8	2.7	0.6
12	Bimbo Coles	G	6'1"	182	3	Virginia Tech	81	10.6	2.0	4.6
52	Matt Geiger	C	7'1"	250	1	Georgia Tech	48	4.5	2.5	0.3
33	Alec Kessler	F/C	6'11"	240	3	Georgia	40	3.9	2.3	0.4
43	Grant Long	F	6'8"	230	5	E. Michigan	76	14.0	7.5	2.4
32	Harold Miner	G	6'4"	220	1	Southern Cal.	73	10.3	2.0	1.0
41	Glen Rice	G/F	6'7"	220	4	Michigan	82	19.0	5.2	2.2
22	John Salley	F/C	6'11"	244	7	Georgia Tech	51	8.3	6.1	1.6
4	Rony Seikaly	C	6'11"	252	5	Syracuse	72	17.1	11.8	1.4
20	Brian Shaw	G	6'6"	195	4	Cal.-Santa Bar.	68	7.3	3.8	3.5
3	Steve Smith	G	6'7"	205	2	Michigan St.	48	16.0	4.1	5.6

Miami Heat
1993-94 Season Preview

Opening Line: Wasn't it just a year ago that the Heat appeared poised to leave their expansion brethren behind? You remember. Miami had become the first of the newcomers to qualify for the playoffs, and its young cast needed just a couple strategic additions to make some big noise. As 1993-94 dawns, Miami is no longer the big dog among the expansion teams. In fact, it's third. The club was stung by injuries last season, but even a healthy cast doesn't guarantee success. Moreover, last year's deal for underachieving John Salley robbed the club of a 1993 first-round pick. Miami has some young talent, but a lot of teams have that these days.

Guard: If Steve Smith's cranky knee stays healthy, he'll become one of the league's top point guards. He has size (6'7"), strength, and the ability to score in bunches. His backcourt mate is a bit of a mystery. Brian Shaw also has good size for a guard, but he has trouble scoring and is also lax defensively. That could mean that sophomore Harold Miner will take the job. Miner impressed NBA fans last year with his brilliant one-on-one moves and ability to light it up. He resembles Michael Jordan offensively, although he's light-years behind M.J. on defense. Bimbo Coles is a solid back-up at the point. He can handle it well and has 3-point range.

Forward: Glen Rice shot only 44 percent from the floor last year, but that can be expected when you launch 386 treys. Rice is a classic gunner with little taste for the rough stuff. Power forward Grant Long had another good year and is one of the league's more underrated performers at the position. He's not smooth, but he tries hard. "Spider" Salley missed a good portion of last year with a stress fracture in his left foot. Even when healthy, he didn't live up to his own advance billing. Back-up swing man Willie Burton has skills but needs to overcome injuries and personal problems.

Center: Rony Seikaly continues to post big numbers in the pivot. He works hard, has a variety of effective offensive moves, and rebounds with ferocity. If he could be paired with a little more size inside, he would be even more effective. Back-ups Matt Geiger and Alec Kessler are slow and lacking in talent.

Coaching: Kevin Loughery has made the Heat somewhat competitive in the East, but with Orlando and Charlotte advancing, he'll now face more pressure to produce. He doesn't rant as much as he did during his early coaching days, and that's a plus. He's assisted by Bob Staak and Alvin Gentry.

Analysis: The Heat staggered early last year, largely due to Smith's injury. A healthy roster will help considerably this season, yet the team remains ill-equipped to play the physical style of ball needed to win. Moreover, a starting backcourt of Smith and Miner—though very talented—is also very young. The Heat might make the playoffs this year, but it's extremely doubtful that they'll make it past the first round.

Prediction: Fourth place, Atlantic

NEW JERSEY NETS

Home: Meadowlands Arena
Capacity: 20,049
Year Built: 1981

Chairman of the Board: Alan L. Aufzien
Executive V.P./General Manager:
Willis Reed
Head Coach: Chuck Daly
Assistant Coach: Brendan Suhr
Assistant Coach: Paul Silas
Assistant Coach: Rick Carlisle

Address
Meadowlands Arena
East Rutherford, NJ 07073
(201) 935-8888

Coach Chuck Daly			
	W	L	Pct.
NBA Record	519	342	.603
W/Nets	43	39	.524
1992-93 Record	43	39	.524

Nets History

Basketball fans can choose from two images of the Nets. The first comes from the mid-1970s, back in the days of the ABA, when the club was still based on Long Island. Back then, the team featured skywalking forward Julius Erving, the man who carried the Nets to the 1976 league title. The second image is that of the late '80s/early '90s club, one that posted six straight depressing seasons in the New Jersey Meadowlands.

The franchise was born in 1967 as the New Jersey Americans, a charter member of the ABA. The team moved to Long Island the next year, became the New York Nets, and acquired high-scoring Rick Barry for the 1970-71 season. The Nets made it to the ABA Finals the next year, but they lost Barry to the NBA. Erving came aboard in 1973-74 and led the team to the league title in 1975-76. When the Nets became one of four teams to merge with the NBA, they appeared to be in great shape.

Then the problems started. Erving had a contract dispute with owner Roy Boe, who sold him to Philly. The Nets made the playoffs six of the next ten years but won only one series, beating Philadelphia in 1983-84. That team featured an impressive frontcourt of Buck Williams, Albert King, and Darryl Dawkins.

The years 1986-91 were dismal, as management made some poor draft decisions. The Nets have improved in the last two years, thanks to forward Derrick Coleman and coach Chuck Daly, but haven't done much better than .500.

Last Seven Years

Season	W	L	Pct.	Place	Playoffs	Coach
1986-87	24	58	.293	Fourth	DNQ	Dave Wohl
1987-88	19	63	.232	Fifth	DNQ	D. Wohl/
						B. MacKinnon/W. Reed
1988-89	26	56	.317	Fifth	DNQ	Willis Reed
1989-90	17	65	.207	Sixth	DNQ	Bill Fitch
1990-91	26	56	.317	Fifth	DNQ	Bill Fitch
1991-92	40	42	.488	Third	L-Round 1	Bill Fitch
1992-93	43	39	.524	Third	L-Round 1	Chuck Daly

1992-93 Review

Just weeks after the New Jersey Nets were eliminated from the 1993 playoffs, the team was hit with tragic news. Drazen Petrovic, their superb shooting guard who had averaged 22.3 PPG during the season, had been killed in an auto accident in Europe. The news numbed basketball fans, especially those overseas. Petrovic, from Yugoslavia, was considered the greatest player ever produced in Europe.

Petrovic had helped guide the Nets to the '93 playoffs, where they lost in the first round to Cleveland, falling in Game 5 99-89. The season didn't go as planned for new coach Chuck Daly, although there were a few bright spots.

Topping the plus side was the play of power forward Derrick Coleman, who shed his problem-child image to become one of the game's elite players. Second-year point guard Kenny Anderson was also a revelation, as he proved he could shine in the NBA. However, his season was cut to 55 games by a broken wrist. And Chris Morris, one of the league's moodier players, played with hustle and heart in Daly's defensive-oriented system.

There were some pleasant surprises. The Nets actually played defense by year's end and held the Cavs under 100 points in four of the five playoff games. And Rumeal Robinson, acquired early in the season for Mookie Blaylock, played well while filling in for the injured Anderson. Sam Bowie was again a capable NBA center, although his point production dropped.

The Nets' bench had similar problems. Rafael Addison, Chucky Brown, and late-season signee Bernard King provided minimal spark at forward. Chris Dudley rebounded well but shot only 35 percent from the floor. Aging Rick Mahorn was a solid clubhouse presence but no longer a Bad Boy, while Maurice Cheeks filled in as well as could be expected for a 36-year-old point guard.

1993-94 Roster

No.	Player	Pos.	Ht.	Wt.	Exp.	College	G	PPG	RPG	APG
21	Rafael Addison	F/G	6'7"	245	3	Syracuse	68	6.3	1.9	0.8
7	Kenny Anderson	G	6'1"	166	2	Georgia Tech	55	16.9	4.1	8.1
00	Benoit Benjamin	C	7'0"	265	8	Creighton	59	5.7	3.5	0.4
—	John Best	F	6'8"	215	R	Tenn. Tech	—	—	—	—
52	Chucky Brown	F	6'8"	214	4	N. Carolina St.	77	5.1	3.0	0.7
—	P.J. Brown	F/C	6'11"	240	R	Louisiana Tech	—	—	—	—
10	Maurice Cheeks	G	6'1"	180	15	W. Texas St.	35	3.6	1.2	3.1
44	Derrick Coleman	F	6'10"	258	3	Syracuse	76	20.7	11.2	3.6
—	Kevin Edwards	G	6'3"	210	5	DePaul	40	13.9	3.0	3.0
12	Tate George	G	6'5"	208	5	Connecticut	48	2.5	0.6	1.2
—	Armon Gilliam	F	6'9"	245	6	UNLV	80	12.4	5.9	1.5
30	Bernard King	F	6'7"	205	14	Tennessee	32	7.0	2.4	0.6
4	Rick Mahorn	F/C	6'10"	260	12	Hampton Inst.	74	3.9	3.8	0.4
34	Chris Morris	F	6'8"	220	5	Auburn	77	14.1	5.9	1.4
20	Rumeal Robinson	G	6'2"	200	3	Michigan	80	8.4	2.0	4.0
33	Dwayne Schintzius	C	7'2"	285	3	Florida	5	1.4	1.6	0.4
—	Rex Walters	G	6'4"	190	R	Kansas	—	—	—	—

New Jersey Nets
1993-94 Season Preview

Opening Line: A year ago, the dawning of the Chuck Daly Era injected a sense of enthusiasm rarely felt in New Jersey. The Nets played some exciting basketball, made the playoffs, and even scared Cleveland before succumbing in the first round. Now what? The tragic off-season death of shooting guard Drazen Petrovic and the questionable swap of center Sam Bowie for enigmatic malingerer Benoit Benjamin leaves New Jersey with more questions than hopes. The Nets picked up scoring forward Armon Gilliam but lost bruising forward Chris Dudley. Guards Rex Walters (draft pick) and Kevin Edwards (free-agent signee) will try to help out.

Guard: Before he broke his wrist last season, Kenny Anderson displayed the jet-quick, exciting play that led New Jersey to select him second overall in the 1991 draft. Anderson may be pencil-thin and not much of a defender, but he is a scintillating offensive catalyst who can score. The loss of Petrovic leaves a colossal void at the two spot, one Rumeal Robinson may have to fill. Robinson played admirably in Anderson's absence last year, but he isn't a true scorer—nor a full-fledged point, for that matter. Edwards has starting experience, but he's too streaky to be trusted. Though a little slow, Walters is an excellent shooter with plenty of moxie. Unhappy Tate George has the skills to contribute a little at both guard spots.

Forward: Derrick Coleman has cut down on the immature outbursts and stands on the threshold of becoming the game's top power forward. He scores. He rebounds. If he doesn't pout, he's the man. Chris Morris kept the crying to a minimum last year and was rewarded with a solid season. He can be dazzling offensively. Armon Gilliam, an offensive talent with no interest in defense, gives the Nets another talented but enigmatic forward. Rafael Addison and Chucky Brown love to run the floor, while Rick Mahorn does the dirty work inside.

Center: What were the Nets thinking when they dealt Bowie, a solid center, for Benjamin, one of the league's biggest disappointments? Benjamin has the physical tools but lacks the drive Daly demands. One positive at the spot is Dwayne Schintzius, who played well in the playoffs. Gilliam and Mahorn can also fill in at center, though they're undersized.

Coaching: The tumultuous off-season nearly caused Daly to take a spot in the NBC broadcast booth. But the Dream Team guy is back, preaching defense, patterned offense, and a commitment to the game. Paul Silas, Brendan Suhr, and Rick Carlisle assist him.

Analysis: The Nets appeared headed in the right direction until the death of Petrovic. With two new starters and a retooled bench, it's difficult to see the team picking up where it left off last season. If they stay focused, Coleman and Anderson could win a few games by themselves; but then again, Benjamin could lose a few by himself as well. In all likelihood, the Nets will struggle to reach .500.

Prediction: Third place, Atlantic

NEW YORK KNICKS

Home: Madison Square Garden
Capacity: 19,941
Year Built: 1968

Governor: Stanley R. Jaffe
President: Dave Checketts
Head Coach: Pat Riley
Assistant Coach: Dick Harter
Assistant Coach: Jeff Van Gundy

Address
Two Pennsylvania Plaza
New York, NY 10121
(212) 465-6499

Coach Pat Riley			
	W	L	Pct.
NBA Record	644	247	.723
W/Knicks	111	53	.677
1992-93 Record	60	22	.732

Knicks History

Despite playing in the nation's media capital, the Knicks have spent much of their existence in the shadow of their rival to the north—Boston.

Soon after the franchise's inception as a BAA member, the Knicks made trips to the NBA Finals—in 1951, '52, and '53. Hall of Fame coach Joe Lapchick melded forward Carl Braun with Harry Gallatin, Dick McGuire, and Nat "Sweetwater" Clifton and reached the playoffs nine consecutive years (1947-55).

The following ten years were not so kind. The Knicks wandered through six coaches and made the playoffs only once—1958-59. But fortunes changed quickly when Red Holzman took over in 1967-68. The Knicks built a powerhouse on the backs of center Willis Reed, forwards Bill Bradley and Dave DeBusschere, and guards Walt "Clyde" Frazier and Dick Barnett. In 1969-70, they defeated the Lakers in seven games for the title.

Jerry Lucas replaced Reed in the middle, and flashy Earl Monroe joined Frazier to form one of the game's best-ever backcourts. Together, they won the NBA championship in 1973.

The subsequent 20 seasons have featured only modest success. High-scoring Bernard King provided some thrills in the mid-1980s, and star center Patrick Ewing sparked the team to the Atlantic Division title in 1988-89. New coach Pat Riley has taken the Knicks to new heights over the last two seasons, although they've been knocked out of the playoffs both years by Chicago.

Last Seven Years

Season	W	L	Pct.	Place	Playoffs	Coach
1986-87	24	58	.293	Fourth	DNQ	Hubie Brown/Bob Hill
1987-88	38	44	.463	Second	L-Round 1	Rick Pitino
1988-89	52	30	.634	First	L-East Semis	Rick Pitino
1989-90	45	37	.549	Third	L-East Semis	Stu Jackson
1990-91	39	43	.476	Third	L-Round 1	Stu Jackson/J. MacLeod
1991-92	51	31	.622	First	L-East Semis	Pat Riley
1992-93	60	22	.732	First	L-East Finals	Pat Riley

1992-93 Review

An off-season filled with wheeling and dealing was supposed to give the Knicks everything they needed to overtake the Chicago Bulls in 1992-93. Instead, the revamped squad advanced one round further in the playoffs before succumbing to the Bulls, this time in the Eastern finals.

For much of the year, the Knicks' rugged, physical brand of ball appeared unstoppable, particularly at home in Madison Square Garden, where New York forged a 27-game winning streak that extended into the playoffs. But after taking the first two games against the Bulls—following playoff routs of Indiana and Charlotte—the Knicks dropped four straight.

Despite 60 regular-season wins and an Atlantic Division title, there was a sense of profound disappointment in the Big Apple. Coach Pat Riley had been hired in 1991 to duplicate the four world titles he won with the Lakers, and he had failed for the second straight year. Depth was his biggest problem. By the time of the Bulls series, Riley was playing primarily a seven-man rotation, one that lacked scoring punch off the bench.

No one could fault center Patrick Ewing, who had a tremendous year and quieted many of his critics. Ewing's outside counterpart was shooting guard John Starks, whose controversial and hot-headed antics could not overshadow his superb talent and gunslinger's arrogance. Veteran Doc Rivers filled the point-guard role well, but he didn't score very much and shot only 43.7 percent.

Up front, the Knicks boasted size, strength, and little scoring. Charles Smith had his moments on offense, but he was soft inside. On the other hand, blacksmiths Charles Oakley and Anthony Mason were fearsome inside players with little talent away from the hoop. Herb Williams gave Ewing a little rest, while Tony Campbell was a shooter who didn't fit into Riley's defensive philosophy.

Back-up point guard Greg Anthony made more headlines for a midseason fight in Phoenix than for his on-court play, and shooter Rolando Blackman spent much of the year fighting off a knee injury.

1993-94 Roster

No.	Player	Pos.	Ht.	Wt.	Exp.	College	G	1992-93 PPG	RPG	APG
42	Eric Anderson	F	6'9"	230	1	Indiana	16	1.3	0.9	0.2
50	Greg Anthony	G	6'2"	185	2	UNLV	70	6.6	2.4	5.7
20	Rolando Blackman	G	6'6"	206	12	Kansas St.	60	9.7	1.7	2.6
9	Tony Campbell	G/F	6'7"	215	9	Ohio St.	58	7.7	2.7	1.1
44	Hubert Davis	G	6'5"	185	1	North Carolina	50	5.4	1.1	1.7
33	Patrick Ewing	C	7'0"	240	8	Georgetown	81	24.2	12.1	1.9
16	Bo Kimble	G	6'4"	190	3	Loyola Mary	9	3.7	1.2	0.6
14	Anthony Mason	F	6'7"	250	4	Tennessee St.	81	10.3	7.9	2.1
40	Tim McCormick	C	7'0"	240	8	Michigan	—	—	—	—
34	Charles Oakley	F	6'9"	245	8	Virginia Union	82	6.9	8.6	1.5
25	Doc Rivers	G	6'4"	185	10	Marquette	77	7.8	2.5	5.3
54	Charles Smith	F/C	6'10"	244	5	Pittsburgh	81	12.4	5.3	1.8
3	John Starks	G	6'5"	185	4	Oklahoma St.	80	17.5	2.6	5.1
32	Herb Williams	C/F	6'11"	260	12	Ohio St.	55	2.9	2.7	0.3

New York Knicks
1993-94 Season Preview

Opening Line: If everything follows a nice, orderly pattern, this will finally be the season the Knicks dispose of the Chicago Bulls in the NBA playoffs. Two years ago, the Bulls bounced New York in the Eastern semis. Last season, Chicago did it in the conference finals. It's about time, don't you think? Don't look for any young, new faces, though. The Knicks did not select a soul in the 1993 draft.

Guard: John Starks came up big time with an amazing left-handed facial on Horace Grant and Michael Jordan in Game 2 of the conference finals. Starks is a terrific scorer with the confidence and skills to play nasty defense as well. Starks is joined in the backcourt by the oft-injured Doc Rivers. Doc enters his 11th NBA season as a steady point guard, but his best years were spent in an Atlanta uniform. Veteran Rolando Blackman remembers the good old days in Dallas, where he averaged 19 PPG. However, he suffered through injuries last season and then underwent back surgery. Back-up Greg Anthony has a different set of problems, most notably a poor shot, a bad attitude, and a propensity for turnovers. Bo Kimble looks great on the bench in those flashy suits, but his game isn't so attractive.

Forward: Won't somebody here please step up and become a complete player? Charles Smith can score some, but he's softer than a mashed-potato sandwich underneath. Charles Oakley and Anthony Mason could do barbell commercials, but neither is a big-time offensive threat more than two feet away from the basket. Riley is stuck with this talented, but limited, triumvirate as his main men. Don't look for help from Tony Campbell. He's a softer version of Smith.

Center: It's time for all those Patrick Ewing critics to shut up. Ewing's mammoth 1992-93 season and strong playoff performance proved what every sensible basketball analyst has known for a while: The man can play. He is a potent offensive weapon in the Knicks' halfcourt sets and is an even mightier presence at the defensive end. He needs some reserve help, though, since aging Herb Williams was able to provide little in a reserve role.

Coaching: What can you say about a guy whose coaching guide is *The Art of War* by Sun Tzu? Pat Riley has put together a defensive juggernaut in New York, proving that he was much more than just the guy who rolled out the red carpet for Showtime in L.A. Riley is exacting, autocratic, and brilliant. He is assisted by Dick Harter and Jeff Van Gundy.

Analysis: New York plays the best defense around—that's a given. But the Knicks have to score some more points this year if they want to win the NBA title. Ewing and Starks are solid inside-outside options, but another reliable offensive source needs to be cultivated. Smith signed a fat contract and should contribute more offensively. If he does, it could mean a title. The worst New York will do is a return trip to the Eastern finals. In the Big Apple, that may not be enough.

Prediction: First place, Atlantic

ORLANDO MAGIC

Home: Orlando Arena
Capacity: 15,077
Year Built: 1989

Address
Orlando Arena
One Magic Place
Orlando, FL 32801
(407) 649-3200

Chairman: Rich DeVos
President/General Manager:
Pat Williams
Head Coach: Brian Hill

Coach Brian Hill			
	W	L	Pct.
NBA Record	0	0	.000
W/Magic	0	0	.000
1992-93 Record	0	0	.000

Magic History

It's surprising that the Magic is not owned by a consortium of Mickey Mouse, Donald Duck, and Pluto. After all, the team has worked hard to tie itself to the Disney World image of Orlando. When the team presented its franchise application check to David Stern on July 2, 1986, it also handed the NBA commissioner a set of Mickey Mouse ears.

Magic fans have ridden a roller-coaster of emotions over the last four years. After a predictably dreadful 18-64 debut in 1989-90, the Magic improved to 31-51 in 1990-91. Injuries ruined the 1991-92 season, but center Shaquille O'Neal brought glittering new magic to Orlando in 1992-93.

Orlando's inaugural season was noteworthy for style, if not substance. The Magic unveiled their pinstriped uniforms, and Orlando Arena's playing surface paid parquet homage to venerable Boston Garden. But the play on that hardwood was not reminiscent of the old Celtics. Coach Matt Guokas blended expansion pick-ups Reggie Theus, Sam Vincent, Otis Smith, and Scott Skiles with rookie Nick Anderson into a team that was exciting, though not very good.

Things perked up in 1990-91. Orlando drafted sharp-shooter Dennis Scott, and Skiles developed into one of the league's top point guards. Orlando played .500 ball after the All-Star break and had a 24-17 home record. However, Skiles fizzled out in 1991-92 and Scott missed most of the year with an injury. With little other talent, Orlando finished the year as the East's worst team.

With the No. 1 pick in the 1992 draft, the Magic grabbed O'Neal, a mega-superstar who improved the club by 20 games in 1992-93. Orlando missed the 1993 playoffs by a tie-breaker but amazingly won the pre-draft lottery again, giving the team a chance to draft another shining star.

Last Four Years

Season	W	L	Pct.	Place	Playoffs	Coach
1989-90	18	64	.220	Seventh	DNQ	Matt Guokas
1990-91	31	51	.378	Fourth	DNQ	Matt Guokas
1991-92	21	61	.256	Seventh	DNQ	Matt Guokas
1992-93	41	41	.500	Fourth	DNQ	Matt Guokas

1992-93 Review

Shaq Mania hit the NBA in a big way in 1992-93 with the league's newest endorsement machine. When Magic prodigy Shaquille O'Neal broke backboard supports with his 7'1", 303-pound frame, league officials laughed, fans cheered, and opponents ran for cover. The man who claimed to have three smiles—"one million dollars, two million dollars, and three million dollars"—was everything the Magic hoped he would be. Except for a quick ticket to the playoffs.

Despite O'Neal's outrageous first season in Disney World, he was only one man—granted, one big man—in a five-man game. The Magic did add 20 wins to the previous year's record, but the team fell one game short of the playoffs.

Orlando's biggest problem was a lack of quality forward-line support for Shaq, who was left to inhale every rebound and was the team's only low-post option. The collective talent of Tom Tolbert, Jeff Turner, and Greg Kite couldn't fill Shaq's sneakers. Had Terry Catledge's bum knee allowed him to play more than just 21 games, and Brian Williams's blackouts and heart problems not prohibited him from participating in the same number, things might have been different.

One thing the Magic did get was a lot of outside production. When healthy, Dennis Scott gunned his way to big numbers, while swing man Nick Anderson enjoyed good health and another fine scoring year. Point man Scott Skiles had his best year as a pro, his assist total boosted considerably by O'Neal's finishing powers. Of course, somebody's numbers had to suffer, and that somebody was small forward Anthony Bowie, whose scoring dropped more than six PPG.

Though Orlando just missed making the playoffs, the near-miss turned out to be a blessing in disguise. Eligible for the draft lottery, the team hit the jackpot again. The Magic snatched the No. 1 pick and had the chance to add a front-line star to complement the Shaq.

1993-94 Roster

No.	Player	Pos.	Ht.	Wt.	Exp.	College	G	PPG	RPG	APG
25	Nick Anderson	G/F	6'6"	205	4	Illinois	79	19.9	6.0	3.4
14	Anthony Bowie	G	6'6"	190	4	Oklahoma	77	8.0	2.5	2.3
33	Terry Catledge	F	6'8"	230	8	South Alabama	21	4.7	2.2	0.2
—	Anthony Cook	F/C	6'9"	215	2	Arizona	—	—	—	—
11	Litterial Green	G	6'1"	185	1	Georgia	52	4.5	0.7	2.2
—	Geert Hammink	C	7'0"	262	R	Louisiana St.	—	—	—	—
—	Anfernee Hardaway	G	6'7"	195	R	Memphis St.	—	—	—	—
2	Steve Kerr	G	6'3"	180	5	Arizona	52	2.6	0.9	1.3
34	Greg Kite	C	6'11"	260	10	Brigham Young	64	1.4	3.0	0.2
—	Todd Lichti	G	6'4"	205	4	Stanford	48	6.9	2.1	1.1
32	Shaquille O'Neal	C	7'1"	300	1	Louisiana St.	81	23.4	13.9	1.9
35	Jerry Reynolds	G/F	6'8"	206	8	Louisiana St.	—	—	—	—
5	Donald Royal	F	6'8"	210	3	Notre Dame	77	9.2	3.8	1.0
3	Dennis Scott	G/F	6'8"	229	3	Georgia Tech	54	15.9	3.4	2.5
4	Scott Skiles	G	6'1"	180	7	Michigan St.	78	15.4	3.7	9.4
40	Tom Tolbert	F	6'8"	240	5	Arizona	72	8.1	5.7	1.3
31	Jeff Turner	F	6'9"	240	7	Vanderbilt	75	7.0	3.4	1.4
42	Howard Wright	F	6'9"	240	2	Stanford	4	2.0	0.5	0.0

Orlando Magic
1993-94 Season Preview

Opening Line: With two consecutive lottery wins to his credit, Orlando G.M. Williams has to be one of the luckiest men alive. Williams used this year's No. 1 pick to draft Chris Webber, but he traded him minutes later to Golden State for the rights to super-guard Anfernee Hardaway and three future No. 1's. The Magic also drafted seven-footer Geert Hammink and bumped coach Matt Guokas upstairs, replacing him with assistant Brian Hill. Later in the summer, they traded high-priced Brian Williams to Denver for Todd Lichti and Anthony Cook.

Guard: Hardaway is a 6'7" Magic Johnson clone who is tremendous on the break or in the halfcourt. He runs. He jumps. He shoots. He passes. Orlando wins. He'll replace pugnacious Scott Skiles, a fine NBA point guard with a few weaknesses—lack of height, limited quickness, below-average shooting. Skiles is a scrapper and a good passer who got the ball to Shaquille O'Neal plenty last year. Shooting guard Dennis Scott is a pudgy, oft-injured, high-priced, one-dimensional gunner who can shoot a team into and out of a game, depending on his stroke. Donald Royal is an adequate scorer off the bench and can play either the two or three spot. Don't expect much from Lichti; his knees are shot.

Forward: Undersized three man Nick Anderson is a slashing scorer who averaged nearly 20 PPG last year. Though once known only for his scoring, Anderson significantly improved the rest of his game last year. The rest of the forwards have some kind of limitations. Jeff Turner has a nice baseline jumper and little else, sleek Anthony Bowie fills it up but is streaky, and bulky Terry Catledge can bang some, provided his knee is healthy. Tom Tolbert has won P.T. thanks to his hard work, not his talent.

Center: Everybody expected O'Neal to detonate in his rookie year, but who could have predicted a nuclear explosion? O'Neal started fast and sustained his high level of play. His bulk, mobility, and quickness make him nearly impossible to guard. Journeyman Greg Kite can give O'Neal a couple minutes rest every night. And Hammink, Shaq's replacement at LSU last season, is a mobile guy with good range.

Coaching: Hill takes over the head-coaching job after serving three years as an assistant to Guokas. His only previous top-dog experience came at Lehigh University from 1975-83. Though knowledgeable and well-organized, Hill seems to lack charisma.

Analysis: The addition of Hardaway makes Orlando an instant playoff contender and a frightening specter in years to come. It may take the new guy a little while to mesh with O'Neal, but the two should work smoothly by midseason. Combine their talents with the scoring skills of Scott and Anderson and you've got a potentially powerful offense. The team is a power forward away from achieving greatness.

Prediction: Second place, Atlantic

PHILADELPHIA 76ERS

Home: The Spectrum
Capacity: 18,168
Year Built: 1967

Address
Veterans Stadium
P.O. Box 25040
Philadelphia, PA 19148
(215) 339-7600

Owner: Harold Katz
General Manager: Jim Lynam
Head Coach: Fred Carter
Assistant Coach: Tony DiLeo
Assistant Coach: Jeff Ruland

Coach Fred Carter			
	W	L	Pct.
NBA Record	7	19	.269
W/76ers	7	19	.269
1992-93 Record	7	19	.269

Sixers History

The 76ers own the distinction of having the Alpha and Omega of NBA basketball history. The 1966-67 Sixers thrashed the league with a 68-13 record and a world title. On the other hand, the 1972-73 Sixers stumbled to the worst-ever mark of 9-73.

The Sixers began in 1949-50 as the Syracuse Nationals and reached the first NBA Finals series, losing in six games to Minneapolis. Hall of Fame center Dolph Schayes was the big gun on both that team and the 1953-54 squad that fell again in the NBA Finals, this time to the Lakers.

The team moved to Philadelphia in 1963-64 and acquired Wilt Chamberlain in a trade in early 1965. They moved onto a level with the dominating Boston Celtics and began to challenge them for league supremacy. In fact, the Nationals/Sixers have met the Celtics in 17 playoff series, winning seven. Philadelphia beat Boston in the 1967 East finals on the way to the NBA title.

The Sixers nosedived in the early 1970s, but the arrival of coach Gene Shue and ABA imports George McGinnis and Julius Erving signaled a renaissance. Philadelphia advanced to the NBA Finals in 1976-77 but lost to Portland. Similar excursions were made in 1979-80 and 1981-82, thanks to Erving, Bobby Jones, Maurice Cheeks, and Andrew Toney.

Moses Malone arrived for the 1982-83 season, and the Sixers blitzed to another NBA title. In 1984, Philly drafted super-forward Charles Barkley, who led the team to the 1989-90 Atlantic Division title.

Last Seven Years

Season	W	L	Pct.	Place	Playoffs	Coach
1986-87	45	37	.549	Second	L-Round 1	Matt Guokas
1987-88	36	46	.439	Fourth	DNQ	Matt Guokas/Jim Lynam
1988-89	46	36	.561	Second	L-Round 1	Jim Lynam
1989-90	53	29	.646	First	L-East Semis	Jim Lynam
1990-91	44	38	.537	Second	L-East Semis	Jim Lynam
1991-92	35	47	.427	Fifth	DNQ	Jim Lynam
1992-93	26	56	.317	Sixth	DNQ	Doug Moe/Fred Carter

1992-93 Review

It made so much sense in June of 1992. Trade unhappy Charles Barkley for three younger guys, plug them into Doug Moe's dragstrip offense, and watch the ugly memories of 1991-92 disappear in a cloud of high-test exhaust.

So much for logic. The Sixers' much-heralded retooling was a season-long mistake, costing the team any toehold it might have had among Eastern Conference contenders. G.M. Jimmy Lynam axed Moe after 56 games, replacing him with long-time assistant Fred Carter, who also had little success with a miserable collection of talent. Philadelphia's 26-56 record was the second poorest in the conference. The Sixers made their second consecutive trip to the draft lottery.

The rest of the story is even uglier. Barkley, given a new start away from years of controversy in Philadelphia, helped lead Phoenix to the Western Conference's best record. Philadelphia's 1992-93 "highlights" film could easily be entitled, "Held Up Without a Gun."

Among the three players acquired for Sir Charles, only guard Jeff Hornacek performed well enough to justify his inclusion in the deal. Hornacek shrugged off his early anger at being traded to team with Hersey Hawkins in a potent backcourt. They joined talented rookie forward Clarence Weatherspoon as the only real offensive threats on the team.

Since none of those players was taller than 6'6", the team's season-long weakness was obvious. The Sixers lacked any inside offensive presence, and their interior defense—save 7'7" totem pole Manute Bol—was equally atrocious. Center Andrew Lang and forward Tim Perry, who joined Hornacek as payment for Barkley, were inconsistent and overmatched, while veteran Armon Gilliam was content to trade baskets with whomever guarded him.

Veteran backcourt men Johnny Dawkins and Ron Anderson provided some pop off the bench, but they were hardly the answer to Philadelphia's season-long problems inside. Neither was Bol, whose contract expired mercifully at season's end after two years of fly-swatting and little else.

1993-94 Roster

							—1992-93—			
No.	Player	Pos.	Ht.	Wt.	Exp.	College	G	PPG	RPG	APG
—	Shawn Bradley	C	7'6"	245	R	Brigham Young	—	—	—	—
12	Johnny Dawkins	G	6'2"	170	7	Duke	74	8.9	1.8	4.6
—	Alphonso Ford	G	6'2"	190	R	Miss. Vall. St.	—	—	—	—
33	Hersey Hawkins	G	6'3"	190	5	Bradley	81	20.3	4.3	3.9
14	Jeff Hornacek	G	6'4"	190	7	Iowa St.	79	19.1	4.3	6.9
55	Thomas Jordan	F	6'10"	220	1	Oklahoma St.	4	11.0	4.8	0.8
28	Andrew Lang	C	6'11"	250	5	Arkansas	73	5.3	6.0	1.1
—	Moses Malone	C	6'10"	255	17	None	11	4.5	4.2	0.6
23	Tim Perry	F	6'9"	220	5	Temple	81	9.0	5.1	1.6
30	C. Weatherspoon	F	6'6"	240	1	S. Mississippi	82	15.6	7.2	1.8

Philadelphia 76ers
1993-94 Season Preview

Opening Line: Following one of the worst seasons in franchise history, there is actually hope and excitement in Philadelphia this season. The arrival of 7'6" center Shawn Bradley gives the Sixers a marketing tool and, they hope, a dominating big man for the next 15 years. Hours after they signed Bradley, Sixers brass announced they had waived one player (Armon Gilliam) and renounced their rights to six others—Manute Bol, Charles Shackleford, Ron Anderson, Greg Grant, Mitchell Wiggins, and Eddie Lee Wilkins. Weeks later, they signed the legendary Moses Malone.

Guard: Last year, guards Hersey Hawkins and Jeff Hornacek finished one-two on the team in scoring. Hawkins hasn't yet become the dominating two man Sixers brass hoped he would, but he is a good 3-point shooter who can go to the basket. Hornacek, who made a living as a spot-up jump-shooter in Phoenix, demonstrated an ability to handle the ball and create, though he remains largely a two man as well. Johnny Dawkins has not returned to the quicksilver form that keyed the Sixer attack before his knee injury, but he is an above-average point guard off the bench. Rookie Alphonso Ford is a lead guard with big-time scoring skills and a great body, but he'll need to play some defense to get time under coach Carter.

Forward: Sophomore Clarence Weatherspoon may only be 6'6", but he is a prolific scorer and a fair rebounder at the three spot. One of the few bright spots on last year's team, Weatherspoon must improve his outside shooting in order to star in the league. Tim Perry disappointed everyone last year, looking like a befuddled collegian rather than the fluid three/four man he was in Phoenix in 1991-92. If he doesn't improve this year, he'll be out of work.

Center: Bradley hasn't played basketball in two years because of his Mormon mission in Australia. But the former BYU prodigy has remarkable athletic ability for his size and could become a deadly high-low weapon for the Sixers—although it will take time. Andrew Lang provides strong defense inside, but is of little help offensively. It will be surprising if the ancient Malone lasts the season.

Coaching: After several assistant-coaching stints, Fred Carter gets to handle his own team. As a player, "Mad Dog" was known for his defense and hard work, and that's what he'll try to instill in the Sixers, one of the league's poorest rebounding and defensive clubs last year. He'll be assisted by Jeff Ruland and Tony DiLeo.

Analysis: Philly fans are elated to have Bradley, but more pieces must be found before the Sixers can realistically challenge for the playoffs. Hornacek and Hawkins are a serviceable backcourt, and Weatherspoon has talent at small forward. But the Sixers are woefully weak in the power game, and Bradley isn't exactly Shaquille O'Neal. The optimism is deserved, but a trip to the playoffs shouldn't be expected.

Prediction: Sixth place, Atlantic

WASHINGTON BULLETS

Home: Capital Centre
Capacity: 18,756
Year Built: 1973

Address
One Harry S. Truman Dr.
Landover, MD 20785
(301) 773-2255

Chairman of the Board: Abe Pollin
V.P./General Manager: John Nash
Head Coach: Wes Unseld
Assistant Coach: Jeff Bzdelik

Coach Wes Unseld			
	W	L	Pct.
NBA Record	178	287	.383
W/Bullets	178	287	.383
1992-93 Record	22	60	.268

Bullets History

The Bullets' greatest years came in the 1970s, but the franchise rolled off the assembly line in 1961-62 as the Chicago Packers. In 1963, it blew the Windy City, moved to Baltimore, and adopted its current nickname.

In 1964-65, the Bullets advanced to the Western finals behind center Walt Bellamy and forward Bailey Howell. Prior to the 1968-69 season, Baltimore drafted huge Wes Unseld, and he went on to win the MVP Award in his first season. Unseld teamed with bruising Gus Johnson and slick Earl "The Pearl" Monroe to help the Bullets win the Eastern Division.

The Bullets made their first trip to the NBA Finals in 1970-71, but they were dispatched in four games by Milwaukee. They made it back in 1974-75, this time as Washington, but Golden State swept them 4-0. Dick Motta took over the Bullets in 1976-77 and led them to the Finals the following year. This time, Unseld, Elvin Hayes, Bob Dandridge, and company whipped Seattle in seven games. The Sonics got revenge in the Finals the next year, winning in five games and closing out the Bullets' big decade.

The 1980s featured some talented players (Jeff Ruland, Rick Mahorn, Greg Ballard, Jeff Malone) but few highlights. The Bullets won just one playoff series during the whole decade, and by its end they were a lottery team. Unseld took over as coach in 1987-88 but—outside of Bernard King and then Pervis Ellison—has had little to work with. Injuries and thin talent have stymied his efforts.

Last Seven Years

Season	W	L	Pct.	Place	Playoffs	Coach
1986-87	42	40	.512	Third	L-Round 1	Kevin Loughery
1987-88	38	44	.463	Second	L-Round 1	K. Loughery/Wes Unseld
1988-89	40	42	.488	Fourth	DNQ	Wes Unseld
1989-90	31	51	.378	Fourth	DNQ	Wes Unseld
1990-91	30	52	.366	Fourth	DNQ	Wes Unseld
1991-92	25	57	.305	Sixth	DNQ	Wes Unseld
1992-93	22	60	.268	Seventh	DNQ	Wes Unseld

1992-93 Review

It was a bad year in Washington for just about everybody. George Bush was tossed out of the White House, along with half of Congress. The Redskins and Capitals took early leaves from their respective playoff tourneys, and the Bullets settled comfortably into the Atlantic Division dungeon—once again.

Few excuses apply here. Sure, center Pervis Ellison missed a third of the season with a cranky left knee, but the Bullets were already toast by the time he checked out for good in early March. This was just a bad team, and it's a wonder that coach Wes Unseld survived another season in the Beltway with the team in free-fall. Not that it was Unseld's fault, mind you. Red Auerbach couldn't have won with last season's Bullets. It's just easier to can the coach than dump all the players.

As the season began, Bullets fans had high hopes. The addition of rookie forward Tom Gugliotta and a full season from guard Rex Chapman were supposed to take care of many problems. Well, Gugliotta delivered while Chapman was his usual inconsistent self. Although Gugliotta wore down as the season progressed, he was a multi-talented scorer/rebounder/passer and should have a bright future in the league. He teamed with Harvey Grant, happy with his new mega-buck contract but not with his environs, in a fairly potent front line.

Ellison, however, was not so inspiring, even when his knee held up. His numbers sagged, proving once again that he is a power forward and not a center. Speedy point guard Michael Adams was his usual waterbug self, but he and Chapman had little help in the backcourt. Early-season pick-up Doug Overton played adequately before succumbing to thumb problems, but LaBradford Smith was too inconsistent.

Steady Larry Stewart provided solid frontcourt support, but soft rookie Don MacLean had problems scoring against the big fellas. Small forward Buck Johnson, a former starter with Houston, was terribly unproductive, and Charles Jones was his usual good-field, no-hit self as a back-up pivot man.

1993-94 Roster

No.	Player	Pos.	Ht.	Wt.	Exp.	College	G	PPG	RPG	APG
							1992-93			
10	Michael Adams	G	5'10"	175	8	Boston College	70	14.8	3.4	7.5
3	Rex Chapman	G	6'4"	205	5	Kentucky	60	12.5	1.5	1.9
40	Calbert Cheaney	F	6'7"	209	R	Indiana	—	—	—	—
00	Kevin Duckworth	C	7'0"	280	7	Eastern Illinois	74	9.9	5.2	0.9
43	Pervis Ellison	F/C	6'10"	225	4	Louisville	49	17.4	8.8	2.4
24	Tom Gugliotta	F	6'10"	240	1	N. Carolina St.	81	14.7	9.6	3.8
2	Buck Johnson	F	6'7"	190	7	Alabama	73	6.5	2.7	1.2
34	Don MacLean	F	6'10"	235	1	UCLA	62	6.6	2.0	0.6
—	Gheorghe Muresan	C	7'7"	315	R	Cluj	—	—	—	—
14	Doug Overton	G	6'3"	190	1	La Salle	45	8.1	2.4	3.5
20	Brent Price	G	6'1"	175	1	Oklahoma	68	3.9	1.5	2.3
22	LaBradford Smith	G	6'3"	200	2	Louisville	69	9.3	1.5	2.7
33	Larry Stewart	F	6'8"	220	2	Coppin St.	81	9.8	4.7	1.8

Washington Bullets
1993-94 Season Preview

Opening Line: Over the summer, the Bullets traded starting forward Harvey Grant to Portland for Kevin Duckworth, a brooding center who will fit in well with the gloom-and-doom Bullets. Coach Wes Unseld has one year—maybe—to see what he can do with Washington's weak lineup. Despite the arrival of Indiana star Calbert Cheaney, the Bullets need plenty more to bid adieu to lottery life.

Guard: Life certainly seems to speed up to 78 rpm when Michael Adams has the ball. The 5'10" bundle of energy scurries around the court, launching shots from everywhere and connecting every so often. His mate, Rex Chapman, personifies inconsistency. He's a great leaper with 3-point range, but his decision-making needs major improvement. LaBradford Smith is another great leaper who's just as erratic as Chapman. Brent Price needs to improve his .358 shooting percentage if he wants to be compared to his brother Mark. Doug Overton held his own at both guard positions last year before suffering a thumb injury.

Forward: After four seasons playing out of place in the pivot, Pervis Ellison gets to move a couple steps away from the basket, courtesy of Duckworth's presence. If he stays healthy (hardly a guarantee), Ellison should again produce big offensive numbers and grab a bunch of rebounds. Second-year forward Tom Gugliotta brings a solid all-around game to the three spot. An excellent passer and active rebounder, Gugliotta must work on his shooting and conditioning. He wore down last season. If Duckworth doesn't do it in the middle, Cheaney may move to the three, pushing Googs to power forward. Cheaney can score inside and out and plays solid defense. Hard-working Larry Stewart is an accomplished inside scorer and a decent rebounder. He could teach a few things to pouty outside gunner Don MacLean.

Center: Don't get too excited, Bullets fans. Duckworth may have a soft touch, but his production has shrunk each of the last four years. Duckworth prefers life away from the basket, which doesn't make him the best rebounder. His doughy frame makes him an easy mark on defense.

Coaching: For the fifth straight year, the Bullet loss total increased under Unseld, whose stoic sideline demeanor just isn't working. Unless this team surprises everyone, expect the big guy to be working elsewhere next season. He's assisted by Jeff Bzdelik.

Analysis: For the first time in a while, the Bullets field a team with everyone playing their true position. That's the good news. The downside comes when the lineup is introduced. Ellison and Gugliotta are solid, and Adams plays well in spurts, but Duckworth is trouble and Chapman has yet to make good on the potential he flashed in high school. Cheaney will be a valuable weapon off the bench and could be starting by midseason—particularly if Duckworth stumbles. But don't expect more than 30 wins this year, and even that will take some luck.

Prediction: Seventh place, Atlantic

ATLANTA HAWKS

Home: The Omni
Capacity: 16,371
Year Built: 1972

Address
One CNN Center
Suite 405, South Tower
Atlanta, GA 30303
(404) 827-3800

Owner: Ted Turner
V.P./General Manager: Pete Babcock
Head Coach: Lenny Wilkens
Assistant Coach: Dick Helm
Assistant Coach: Brian Winters

Coach Lenny Wilkens			
	W	L	Pct.
NBA Record	869	892	.493
W/Hawks	0	0	.000
1992-93 Record	54	28	.659

Hawks History

Few teams have had as many different addresses as the Hawks. Before settling in Georgia, the franchise roamed the Midwest, calling Moline, Rock Island, Davenport, Milwaukee, and St. Louis home.

An original member of the NBA, the franchise was first known as the Tri-City (Moline, Rock Island, and Davenport) Blackhawks. Two years later, it moved to Milwaukee and shortened its nickname to its current form. Though active off the court, it wasn't until the team drafted Bob Pettit in 1954 that it started to show some life on it.

The Hawks moved to St. Louis in 1955, won consecutive Western Conference championships from 1957-61, and defeated Boston in 1958 for the franchise's lone NBA title. Pettit, Cliff Hagan, Ed Macauley, Charlie Share, and Slater Martin formed the nucleus of those teams. In the title win over Boston, Pettit played with his broken left wrist in a cast, and Share played with his busted jaw wired shut.

The 1960s featured talented players like Lou Hudson, Joe Caldwell, and Zelmo Beatty, but the Hawks could not get back to the NBA Finals. The team moved to Atlanta for the 1968-69 season and staggered through the next decade as a .500 team.

Things started to change in 1982, when Atlanta drafted exciting forward Dominique Wilkins. The Hawks won the NBA Central Division title in 1986-87 and recorded a franchise-record 57 wins. Despite the improvement, the Hawks never advanced past the Eastern Conference semifinals.

Last Seven Years

Season	W	L	Pct.	Place	Playoffs	Coach
1986-87	57	25	.695	First	L-East Semis	Mike Fratello
1987-88	50	32	.610	Second	L-East Semis	Mike Fratello
1988-89	52	30	.634	Third	L-Round 1	Mike Fratello
1989-90	41	41	.500	Sixth	DNQ	Mike Fratello
1990-91	43	39	.524	Fourth	L-Round 1	Bob Weiss
1991-92	38	44	.463	Fifth	DNQ	Bob Weiss
1992-93	43	39	.524	Fourth	L-Round 1	Bob Weiss

1992-93 Review

Although Atlanta rebounded nicely from a disastrous 1991-92 season, it would be inaccurate to describe the team as doing anything more than treading water. Atlanta increased its win total by five, finishing fourth in the Central Division with a 43-38 record, then lost in three games to Chicago in the first round of the playoffs. That kind of mediocrity earned coach Bob Weiss a pink slip.

The return of Dominique "Human Highlight Film" Wilkins from his torn Achilles tendon helped the Hawks' scoring considerably, and his season-long battle with Michael Jordan for the scoring crown (Wilkins lost) was an interesting one. But while Wilkins scored in bunches, his teammates struggled to hold their own.

A thin front line and poor team defense made it difficult for Atlanta to compete in the rugged Central Division. Hawk foes shot 49.6 percent from the field, and Atlanta gave up nearly a point more than it scored—a curious statistic for a team with a winning record.

Power forward Kevin Willis had another big year, shooting 50.6 percent from the field and finishing fifth in the league in rebounding with 12.9 per game. Stacey Augmon improved his shooting numbers from the field and the line but was still unsure with the ball and easy to guard on the perimeter. And what can you say about Jon Koncak? The Worst Contract Ever continued to be among the league's worst starting centers, posting minimal numbers in maximum minutes while still raking in nearly as much money as Michael Jordan.

The Hawks did upgrade at point guard, grabbing Mookie Blaylock from New Jersey early in the season for shaky Rumeal Robinson. Blaylock then proved that he was indeed a starting NBA point guard. Another solid year from forward Duane Ferrell highlighted an average bench performance. Forward Snoopy Graham was inconsistent, as was guard Travis Mays. Rookie forward Adam Keefe was soft inside, and back-up point man Steve Henson was steady but hardly spectacular.

1993-94 Roster

No.	Player	Pos.	Ht.	Wt.	Exp.	College	G	PPG	RPG	APG
								—1992-93—		
2	Stacey Augmon	G/F	6'8"	206	2	UNLV	73	14.0	3.9	2.3
10	Mookie Blaylock	G	6'1"	185	4	Oklahoma	80	13.4	3.5	8.4
—	Doug Edwards	F	6'7"	220	R	Florida St.	—	—	—	—
3	Craig Ehlo	G/F	6'7"	205	10	Washington St.	82	11.6	4.9	3.1
33	Duane Ferrell	F	6'7"	215	5	Georgia Tech	82	10.2	2.3	1.6
44	Greg Foster	F/C	6'11"	240	3	Texas-El Paso	43	2.9	1.9	0.5
25	Snoopy Graham	F	6'6"	200	2	Ohio	80	8.1	2.4	2.1
12	Steve Henson	G	6'1"	180	3	Kansas St.	53	4.0	1.0	2.9
6	Roy Hinson	F	6'9"	215	8	Rutgers	—	—	—	—
31	Adam Keefe	F	6'9"	240	1	Stanford	82	6.6	5.3	1.0
32	Jon Koncak	C	7'0"	250	8	Southern Meth.	78	3.5	5.5	1.8
—	Rich Manning	C	6'11"	251	R	Washington	—	—	—	—
41	Blair Rasmussen	C	7'0"	260	8	Oregon	22	3.2	2.5	0.2
21	Dominique Wilkins	F	6'8"	215	11	Georgia	71	29.9	6.8	3.2
42	Kevin Willis	F/C	7'0"	240	8	Michigan St.	80	17.9	12.9	2.1

Atlanta Hawks
1993-94 Season Preview

Opening Line: After all the trouble Lenny Wilkens had with Chicago during his Cleveland coaching tenure, one would think he'd have taken a job in Outer Mongolia before re-upping in the NBA Central Division. Wrong. Wilkens will try to resurrect the stumbling Hawks. Atlanta has struggled through injuries and a general malaise, but there remains some talent on the roster—particularly on offense. Wilkens hopes importing Craig Ehlo from Cleveland and drafting forward Doug Edwards from Florida State will help.

Guard: Mookie Blaylock is the pure point guard that Atlanta has been seeking for years. Mook is an outstanding passer, tenacious defender, and a pretty good scorer. Stacey Augmon may be more suited to small forward, but the Hawks need him and Dominique Wilkins on the floor at the same time. Augmon is a superb finisher on the break and an active defender, and his shooting improved considerably last season. Ehlo nails the 3-pointer, hustles every night, and gives the Hawks major-league depth at guard. Swing man Snoopy Graham is a stone scorer with little predisposition toward defense or rebounding, and Steve Henson is an adequate back-up point guard.

Forward: One year after suffering a potentially career-ending Achilles tendon tear, Wilkins enjoyed a remarkable season. 'Nique was his old, spectacular self, as he scored in bunches and even unveiled a new 3-point stroke. Power forward Kevin Willis is a wonderful complement to Dominique. Willis will grab ten to 12 boards a game and score around the basket. Duane Ferrell works hard enough as a reserve three man, but his poor outside shooting holds him back. Adam Keefe hopes to improve upon a so-so rookie season, during which he showed a propensity to bang some. Edwards, who measured only 6'7" at the pre-draft camps, is a giant question mark.

Center: Now we come to the team's weak link, Jon Koncak, who's still reaping the rewards of a fat, multi-year contract. Koncak can neither score nor rebound, but the Hawks must play him because they can't unload him. Blair Rasmussen and his cranky back will compete for back-up minutes with rookie Richard Manning, whose inside play is as soft as his shot.

Coaching: Wilkens should make an immediate impact on the Hawks. He'll find a strong eight-man rotation and stick with it, and he'll have the patience to handle the tough times. Wilkens is just 69 victories short of tying Red Auerbach for the most wins in NBA history. He brings his assistant coaches, Dick Helm and Brian Winters, over from Cleveland.

Analysis: The Hawks will continue to score points in bushels, but Wilkens's challenge is to get the team to play at the other end too. Dominique will score around 30 per game again, but he may actually belly-up on an opponent once in a while also. Wilkens's toughest job, though, may be overcoming the presence of Koncak. That task may be insurmountable.

Prediction: Sixth place, Central

CHARLOTTE HORNETS

Home: Charlotte Coliseum
Capacity: 23,901
Year Built: 1988

Address
Hive Drive
Charlotte, NC 28217
(704) 357-0252

Owner: George Shinn
Director of Player Personnel:
Dave Twardzik
Head Coach: Allan Bristow
Assistant Coach: Bill Hanzlik
Assistant Coach: T.R. Dunn

Coach Allan Bristow			
	W	L	Pct.
NBA Record	75	89	.457
W/Hornets	75	89	.457
1992-93 Record	44	38	.537

Hornets History

They've always loved college basketball down on Tobacco Road, so it was a natural for the NBA to try and tap into that market. Huge crowds have filled Charlotte Coliseum to back the Hornets since their inception. In the first three years, the level of play was below the high expectations of spoiled Carolina fans. However, the club has improved significantly over the last two seasons.

The city was awarded a franchise in April 1987, and it created an immediate stir by commissioning renowned clothing designer Alexander Julian to create the uniforms. The Hornets may have looked sharp in their teal-and-blue pinstriped duds, but their 20-62 record in 1988-89, their initial season, wasn't as fashionable. Among the highlights of that first season was the play of veteran Kelly Tripucka and exciting guards Muggsy Bogues and Rex Chapman.

Charlotte took a step backward in 1989-90, winning only 19 games, and coach Dick Harter was replaced by Gene Littles. Rookie J.R. Reid, a star at North Carolina, was a crowd favorite, though his 6'9" frame seemed too small for the center spot.

Littles boosted the team's production to 26 wins in 1990-91, as rookie guard Kendall Gill showed flashes of a brilliant future. In 1991-92, Allan Bristow took over as coach and the team added thunder-dunking rookie Larry Johnson, who helped improve the team by five games. With the addition of yet another stellar rookie—tenacious center Alonzo Mourning—Charlotte took a monster step in 1992-93, knocking off Boston in the first round of the playoffs.

Last Five Years

Season	W	L	Pct.	Place	Playoffs	Coach
1988-89	20	62	.244	Sixth	DNQ	Dick Harter
1989-90	19	63	.232	Seventh	DNQ	Dick Harter/Gene Littles
1990-91	26	56	.317	Seventh	DNQ	Gene Littles
1991-92	31	51	.378	Sixth	DNQ	Allan Bristow
1992-93	44	38	.537	Third	L-East Semis	Allan Bristow

1992-93 Review

Subtitle Charlotte's 1992-93 season, "NBA, The Next Generation." The young Hornets look ready for greatness after a breakthrough 1992-93 campaign.

The optimism isn't just based on a strong regular season—although the Hornets did finish with the fifth-best overall record in the Eastern Conference (11th in the NBA) to qualify for their first-ever playoff berth. Charlotte's postseason disposal of Boston and subsequent strong showing in a five-game semifinal loss to New York offer more evidence of a bright future.

Perhaps the most important day in the entire season came in May 1992, when the Hornets drew the second slot in the NBA draft lottery, assuring them the services of talented Georgetown center Alonzo Mourning. Though 'Zo didn't make training camp and even sat out a pair of regular-season tilts—thanks to protracted contract negotiations—he was well worth the wait. His growling countenance was perfect in the Charlotte middle, and his big numbers warranted him serious Rookie of the Year consideration.

Of course, the Hornets' team leader was second-year forward Larry Johnson, a second-team All-NBA selection and one mean Grandma-ma. In just his second year, Johnson led the team in both scoring and rebounding. Veterans Johnny Newman, Kenny Gattison, and David Wingate rotated in the other forward spot, providing adequate support but hardly rivaling the play of their more heralded frontcourt mates.

Two guard Kendall Gill's numbers slipped some, and he was none too happy about that; but with Mourning around, there were simply fewer shots and fewer points for the backcourt. Gill may have shot only 45 percent, but he remained a tremendous weapon for the Hornets. He and veteran speedster Muggsy Bogues combined in a talented guard lineup, with the 5'3" Bogues finishing fifth in the league in assists. Veteran bomber Dell Curry was his usual dangerous self off the bench, shooting 40.1 percent from 3-point land, while rookie Tony Bennett was a valuable point-guard reserve.

1993-94 Roster

No.	Player	Pos.	Ht.	Wt.	Exp.	College	G	PPG	RPG	APG
25	Tony Bennett	G	6'0"	175	1	Wis.-Green Bay	75	3.7	0.8	1.8
1	Muggsy Bogues	G	5'3"	140	6	Wake Forest	81	10.0	3.7	8.8
—	Scott Burrell	F	6'7"	218	R	Connecticut	—	—	—	—
30	Dell Curry	G	6'5"	200	7	Virginia Tech	80	15.3	3.4	2.3
44	Kenny Gattison	F	6'8"	252	6	Old Dominion	75	6.8	4.7	0.9
13	Kendall Gill	G	6'5"	200	3	Illinois	69	16.9	4.9	3.9
42	Mike Gminski	C	6'11"	260	13	Duke	34	2.7	2.5	0.2
—	Greg Graham	G	6'4"	183	R	Indiana	—	—	—	—
21	Sidney Green	F	6'9"	250	10	UNLV	39	2.4	3.0	0.6
2	Larry Johnson	F	6'7"	250	2	UNLV	82	22.1	10.5	4.3
9	Kevin Lynch	G/F	6'5"	200	2	Minnesota	40	2.2	0.9	0.6
33	Alonzo Mourning	C	6'10"	240	1	Georgetown	78	21.0	10.3	1.0
22	Johnny Newman	F	6'7"	190	7	Richmond	64	11.9	2.2	1.8
55	David Wingate	G/F	6'5"	185	7	Georgetown	72	6.1	2.4	2.5

Charlotte Hornets
1993-94 Season Preview

Opening Line: Anyone interested in buying NBA basketball futures had better throw some cash down on the Charlotte Hornets. Last year's postseason appearance was thrilling, yet it's easy to envision so much more for this blossoming franchise. The Hornets have a solid nucleus of young stars and have the opportunity to thrive immediately in the Central Division morass below Chicago. The draft-day additions of gunner Greg Graham and athletic forward Scott Burrell should bolster a shaky bench.

Guard: Kendall Gill continues to grouse about his diminished offensive role, but he would be wise to shut up and keep playing hard. Gill is still the team's main man at two guard, and launching fewer shots for a contender is better than gunning it up for an also-ran. Dell Curry continues to be a valuable downtown bomber, making nearly 41 percent of his 3-pointers last year. Tiny Muggsy Bogues is a high-energy catalyst for Charlotte, but at 5'3", he continues to have trouble getting off his shot and is a liability down low on defense. Expect a big contribution from Graham, an outstanding defender with a long-range jumper and growing playmaking skills. He should take time away from second-year man Tony Bennett, who can shoot but is slow.

Forward: In just his second season, Larry Johnson made the second-team All-NBA squad. The talented, athletic L.J. is Charlotte's main man underneath, despite the considerable presence of sophomore center Alonzo Mourning. Johnson can score from inside or out and rebounds like a pivot man. There's trouble at the other spot, where David Wingate and Johnny Newman split time last year. Wingate is a one-dimensional defensive specialist, while Newman is a scorer without the skills (or desire) to play defense or rebound. Burrell, who has been a pitcher in the Toronto Blue Jays organization, can shoot well and has solid ball-handling skills.

Center: Already, Mourning is one of the better middle men in the NBA. He's a scowling, intimidating force on defense with a much more substantial offensive repertoire than anyone imagined. Back-up Kenny Gattison is a workhorse, willing to bang and work with little statistical reward.

Coaching: The Hornets scared the heck out of the Knicks in last year's Eastern semis, and all anyone in Charlotte could talk about was the lousy job Allan Bristow was doing. Figure that one out. Bristow has helped nurture the young Hornets into the playoffs but now must take the team from young curiosity to established contender. Bill Hanzlik and T.R. Dunn assist him.

Analysis: The Hornets are on the threshold of NBA contention, and last year's playoff loss to the Knicks was a valuable lesson about what must be done to go even farther. Charlotte appears more than ready to challenge Cleveland for second in the Central Division and seems just a couple years away from (gasp) supplanting Chicago atop the division.

Prediction: Third place, Central

CHICAGO BULLS

Home: Chicago Stadium
Capacity: 17,339
Year Built: 1929

Address
980 N. Michigan Ave, Suite 1600
Chicago, IL 60611
(312) 943-5800

Chairman: Jerry Reinsdorf
V.P./Basketball Operations: Jerry Krause
Head Coach: Phil Jackson
Assistant Coach: John Bach
Assistant Coach: Jim Cleamons
Assistant Coach: Tex Winter

Coach Phil Jackson			
	W	L	Pct.
NBA Record	240	88	.732
W/Bulls	240	88	.732
1992-93 Record	57	25	.695

Bulls History

The Bulls are defined today by the atmospheric antics of all-world Michael Jordan, but the team's 27-year history has not always been so spectacular. Until 1991, Chicago never advanced to the NBA Finals.

Chicago joined the league in 1966 as a lone expansion club. After four losing seasons, the Bulls enjoyed regular-season success during their next five. Coach Dick Motta pulled together Chet Walker, Bob Love, Jerry Sloan, and Norm Van Lier to form a quick team that advanced to the West finals in 1973-74, losing in four games to Milwaukee. The following year, the Bulls acquired Nate Thurmond from Golden State and won the Midwest Division, only to drop a disappointing 4-3 decision to the Warriors in the West finals.

Chicago managed only two winning seasons during the next 12 and won just one playoff series, but the Bulls' fortunes changed radically in 1984 when they selected Jordan with the third pick in the draft. Almost instantly, Jordan became an ambassador for basketball everywhere.

By 1987, the results matched the enthusiasm. Chicago surrounded Jordan with young talents like Scottie Pippen, John Paxson, and Horace Grant and advanced to the Eastern Conference finals in 1988-89 and 1989-90, losing both times to Detroit. The Bulls matured in 1990-91 and knocked off the L.A. Lakers in the NBA Finals. In 1991-92, Chicago defeated Portland for its second world crown, then, in 1992-93, three-peated with a win over Phoenix.

Last Seven Years

Season	W	L	Pct.	Place	Playoffs	Coach
1986-87	40	42	.488	Fifth	L-Round 1	Doug Collins
1987-88	50	32	.610	Second	L-East Semis	Doug Collins
1988-89	47	35	.573	Fifth	L-East Finals	Doug Collins
1989-90	55	27	.671	Second	L-East Finals	Phil Jackson
1990-91	61	21	.744	First	NBA Champs	Phil Jackson
1991-92	67	15	.817	First	NBA Champs	Phil Jackson
1992-93	57	25	.695	First	NBA Champs	Phil Jackson

1992-93 Review

Knicks coach Pat Riley may have copyrighted the term "three-peat," but the Bulls were the ones who pulled it off. Despite a slip during the regular season and a surprising underdog status during the playoffs, Chicago became the first team since the Boston Celtics (1959-66) to win back-to-back-to-back NBA titles.

After sweeping Atlanta in the first round of the playoffs, the Bulls mastered three difficult opponents en route to their three-feat. They dusted off Cleveland in four games in the Eastern Conference semis, outslugged New York in six games in the Eastern finals (after dropping the first two), and then subdued Sir Charles and the Suns in six to win it all.

Michael Jordan was the undeniable catalyst—again. He led the NBA in scoring and proved that his Dream Team participation was little more than an off-season conditioning regimen. His 54-point outburst against the Knicks in Game 4 of the Eastern finals and 55 spot against Phoenix in Game 4 of the Finals were remarkable demonstrations of his basketball primacy.

The Bulls' other superstar, Scottie Pippen, came up big in the playoffs to quiet the remaining critics who maintained he was still soft. Pippen teamed with warrior Horace Grant to form one of the league's best forward tandems.

Chicago's four-headed pivot monster was again adequate. Prehistoric starter Bill Cartwright squeezed another season out of his big body, while young colt Scott Williams continued to improve. Stacey King and Will Perdue had their moments, though neither was particularly impressive.

B.J. Armstrong finally got his chance to start at point guard, thanks to veteran John Paxson's troubled knee, and Armstrong responded. He was the league's top 3-point shooter (.453) and played with a competitiveness belied by his baby face. Though Paxson played a limited role throughout the year, his last-second 3-pointer in Game 6 against Phoenix clinched the title.

1993-94 Roster

No.	Player	Pos.	Ht.	Wt.	Exp.	College	G	PPG	RPG	APG
10	B.J. Armstrong	G	6'2"	185	4	Iowa	82	12.3	1.8	4.0
—	Corie Blount	F/C	6'10"	242	R	Cincinnati	—	—	—	—
24	Bill Cartwright	C	7'1"	245	13	San Francisco	63	5.6	3.7	1.3
54	Horace Grant	F	6'10"	235	6	Clemson	77	13.2	9.5	2.6
23	Michael Jordan	G	6'6"	198	9	North Carolina	78	32.6	6.7	5.5
21	Stacey King	F/C	6'11"	230	4	Oklahoma	76	5.4	2.7	0.9
—	Toni Kukoc	F/G	6'10"	230	R	None	—	—	—	—
22	Rodney McCray	F	6'8"	248	10	Louisville	64	3.5	2.5	1.3
45	Ed Nealy	F	6'7"	240	10	Kansas St.	41	1.7	1.6	0.4
5	John Paxson	G	6'2"	185	10	Notre Dame	59	4.2	0.8	2.3
32	Will Perdue	C	7'0"	240	5	Vanderbilt	72	4.7	4.0	1.0
33	Scottie Pippen	F	6'7"	225	6	Cent. Arkansas	81	18.6	7.7	6.3
—	Anthony Reed	F	6'9"	220	R	Tulane	—	—	—	—
6	Trent Tucker	G	6'5"	200	11	Minnesota	69	5.2	1.0	1.2
20	Darrell Walker	G	6'4"	180	10	Arkansas	37	2.2	1.6	1.4
12	Corey Williams	G	6'2"	190	1	Oklahoma St.	35	2.3	0.9	0.7
42	Scott Williams	C	6'10"	230	3	North Carolina	71	5.9	6.4	1.0

Chicago Bulls
1993-94 Season Preview

Opening Line: Enough already! The Bulls won their third straight title in 1993, assuring themselves a place in NBA history. Great. Now move aside, guys, and let someone else have a chance. That's how the rest of the league feels, but the Bulls themselves aren't about to ease off. Management has brought in Croatian superstar Toni Kukoc, a versatile talent who's the equivalent of a lottery pick. Chicago also nabbed 6'10" Corie Blount late in the first round. Most of last year's veteran pick-ups will not be re-signed.

Guard: All hail Michael Jordan. No matter how many controversies swirl around him off the court, the seven-time NBA scoring champ reigns supreme on it. His ability to come up big in important games was proved continually last season. Lost amidst the continued hosannas for Jordan last season was the development of B.J. Armstrong as a legitimate NBA point guard. Beej led the league in 3-point percentage last year, played sticky defense, and had a tremendous assist-to-turnover ratio. The reserves are a problem. Veteran John Paxson nailed the big shot to subdue Phoenix, but his creaky knees limit his abilities considerably.

Forward: Scottie Pippen's enormous contributions to the Bulls' three-peat re-established him as one of the game's best. Pippen's extraordinary athletic skills make him too quick for most small forwards to corral. He's also a first-team All-Defensive performer. Power forward Horace Grant gets little credit, but his substantial contributions inside make up for the team's weakness in the pivot. It will be interesting to see how the 6'10" Kukoc blends in. Like Pippen and Jordan, he can play two or three positions with considerable success. Blount is a banger who will see little playing time.

Center: Wasn't that Bill Cartwright making a cameo appearance in *Jurassic Park?* The 14-year vet continues to bang down low, but his tank is just about empty. Ever-improving Scott Williams could be starting by season's end. Back-up Stacey King is more concerned with scoring than fitting in as a team player, and Will Perdue continues to be merely a warm body. Make that a tall warm body.

Coaching: Phil Jackson hardly fits the mold of a typical NBA coach, what with his off-the-wall quotes, liberal political agenda, and gangly physique. But give the guy credit. Few men could have kept a team fresh enough to win three straight titles. Maybe being atypical isn't so bad after all. He is assisted by John Bach, Tex Winter, and Jim Cleamons.

Analysis: The Bulls have a better chance to four-peat than they did to three-peat. After all, Jordan and Pippen enter this season well-rested (after Dream Teaming it in 1992), and the addition of Kukoc should make things easier for everybody. No other team in the East has improved enough to overtake the Bulls, and nobody else has Michael Jordan. Pencil in the Bulls as Eastern Conference champions, and consider them the favorites in the NBA Finals.

Prediction: First place, Central

CLEVELAND CAVALIERS

Home: The Coliseum
Capacity: 20,273
Year Built: 1974

Address
The Coliseum
2923 Streetsboro Rd.
Richfield, OH 44286
(216) 659-9100

Chairman of the Board: Gordon Gund
Executive V.P./General Manager:
Wayne Embry
Head Coach: Mike Fratello
Assistant Coach: Richie Adubato
Assistant Coach: Ron Rothstein
Assistant Coach: Jim Boylan

Coach Mike Fratello			
	W	L	Pct.
NBA Record	324	250	.564
W/Cavaliers	0	0	.000
1992-93 Record	0	0	.000

Cavaliers History

Since their debut in 1970, the Cavaliers have been one of the NBA's most disappointing teams, winning only one playoff series in their first 21 years. In their early years, the Cavs didn't have many marquee players—the result of some poor drafting and questionable trades during the 1970s. Things changed in the late 1980s thanks to smarter drafting and the stewardship of coach Lenny Wilkens.

The early years were tough, as Cleveland spent its first four seasons in the Central basement. In 1975-76, coach Bill Fitch was rewarded for his patience with a division title, as well as the team's first playoff series win. They beat Washington in seven games in the Eastern Conference semis.

Center Jim Chones, forwards Campy Russell and Jim Brewer, and guard Bobby "Bingo" Smith were the main performers on that team, but the good times ended soon thereafter. Cleveland qualified for the playoffs the next two seasons but made it back only once (1984-85) in the ensuing nine years.

In 1986, the Cavs began their renaissance by drafting center Brad Daugherty. Daugherty, guards Ron Harper and Mark Price, and forward Larry Nance led the Cavs to a 42-40 record in 1987-88 and a 57-25 mark the next year. After two disappointing seasons, Cleveland put it together again in 1991-92. The Cavaliers went 57-25 and roared to the conference finals, where they lost to Chicago in six games. They again lost to the Bulls in the 1993 playoffs.

Last Seven Years

Season	W	L	Pct.	Place	Playoffs	Coach
1986-87	31	51	.378	Sixth	DNQ	Lenny Wilkens
1987-88	42	40	.512	Fourth	L-Round 1	Lenny Wilkens
1988-89	57	25	.695	Second	L-Round 1	Lenny Wilkens
1989-90	42	40	.512	Fourth	L-Round 1	Lenny Wilkens
1990-91	33	49	.402	Sixth	DNQ	Lenny Wilkens
1991-92	57	25	.695	Second	L-East Finals	Lenny Wilkens
1992-93	54	28	.659	Second	L-East Semis	Lenny Wilkens

1992-93 Review

If Cleveland owner Gordon Gund was looking to save a little money following the 1992-93 season, he could have cut back on the Cavaliers' promotional video. Just take a few clips from the previous five or six seasons, splice them together, and you basically have the Cavs' year.

Of course, if he wanted to spend some bucks, he could have moved the team west, far, far away from the Chicago Bulls.

Yes, it happened again. For the fourth time in six years, Da Bulls eliminated Cleveland from the NBA playoffs. This year's exit came in the Eastern semifinals. It took just four games, and Michael Jordan stuck in the final dagger with a turnaround jumper at the buzzer. Afterward, coach Lenny Wilkens resigned following seven years of near-misses and maddening unfulfilled potential.

The rest of the year was typically Cavalier. Cleveland stayed close to Chicago in the Central Division, winning 54 games and entering the postseason with its usual hope and good spirits. But Cleveland was again a little too soft to succeed in the playoffs' tense setting, perhaps a reflection of Wilkens's stoic presence or the players' laid-back personalities.

The usual cast of characters—plus off-season import Gerald Wilkins—maintained the status quo. Center Brad Daugherty was again a quiet stalwart and an NBA All-Star, while the forward rotation of veteran Larry Nance, John "Hot Rod" Williams, and Mike Sanders was strong, although the trio's numbers did slip some.

Mark Price had another outstanding year at the point, and Wilkins teamed with Craig Ehlo to upgrade Cleveland's two-guard spot. The flamboyant Wilkins was particularly effective on the defensive end, a spot where Cleveland needed help.

Though the Cavs' top seven was solid, the rest of the reserves were shaky. Terrell Brandon showed some promise at the point, and his production did increase from his rookie year. But Danny Ferry continued to stumble around the frontcourt and John Battle struggled through his worst season as a pro.

1993-94 Roster

No. Player	Pos.	Ht.	Wt.	Exp.	College	G	PPG	RPG	APG
							—1992-93—		
10 John Battle	G	6'2"	190	8	Rutgers	41	5.4	0.7	1.3
11 Terrell Brandon	G	6'0"	180	2	Oregon	82	8.8	2.2	3.7
43 Brad Daugherty	C	7'0"	263	7	North Carolina	71	20.2	10.2	4.4
35 Danny Ferry	F	6'10"	245	3	Duke	76	7.5	3.7	1.8
54 Jay Guidinger	C	6'10"	255	1	Minn.-Duluth	32	1.6	2.0	0.5
— Tyrone Hill	F	6'9"	243	3	Xavier	74	8.6	10.2	0.9
30 Jerome Lane	F	6'6"	230	5	Pittsburgh	21	2.8	2.5	0.8
12 Gerald Madkins	G	6'3"	205	R	UCLA	—	—	—	—
— Chris Mills	F/G	6'6"	216	R	Arizona	—	—	—	—
22 Larry Nance	F/C	6'10"	235	12	Clemson	77	16.5	8.7	2.9
14 Bobby Phills	G	6'5"	217	2	Southern	31	3.0	0.5	0.3
25 Mark Price	G	6'0"	178	7	Georgia Tech	75	18.2	2.7	8.0
33 Mike Sanders	F	6'6"	215	11	UCLA	53	8.6	3.2	1.4
21 Gerald Wilkins	G	6'6"	210	8	Tenn.-Chattan.	80	11.1	2.7	2.3
18 John Williams	F/C	6'11"	245	7	Tulane	67	11.0	6.2	2.3

Cleveland Cavaliers
1993-94 Season Preview

Opening Line: Let's see what Mike Fratello can do against the Chicago Bulls. After the Cavs fell to the Jordanaires in the playoffs for the umpteenth time last year, Cleveland management forced out coaching great Lenny Wilkens and brought in the czar of the NBC Telestrator. Fratello will try to instill a little of his passion into the Cavs, who have a reputation of being mentally soft. Free-agent pick-up Tyrone Hill will also toughen things up. Rookie Chris Mills will try to replace free-agent deserter Craig Ehlo.

Guard: Two years removed from major knee surgery, point guard Mark Price had one of his best seasons last year. He remains among the elite NBA point guards, combining tremendous ball-handling and passing skills with an excellent shot—particularly from 3-point range. Back-up Terrell Brandon improved considerably in his second pro season. His quickness and defensive abilities are welcomed on the slow-footed Cavs. Big guard Gerald Wilkins can be exciting on offense, dogged on defense, and maddeningly inconsistent—all at the same time. Mills, who played four positions at Arizona and scored well everywhere, will share time with Wilkins.

Forward: One of these days, Larry Nance's play will recede as badly as his hairline. Until then, expect continued excellence from the acrobatic forward, who scores, rebounds, and swats numerous shots. Sixth man John "Hot Rod" Williams is another demon around the basket. Williams, like Nance, can play any of the frontcourt positions and excel offensively or defensively. The addition of Hill gives the Cavaliers a fearsome front line. As a starter with Golden State last year, Hill ripped down ten boards per game. Mike Sanders, a defensive specialist, will likely lose his starting job. Danny Ferry remains an NBA bust, too slow to play outside and too soft to play inside. The Cavs, though, are stuck with his fat contract.

Center: The arrival of Shaquille O'Neal last season pushed talented Cav center Brad Daugherty down another notch on the pivot food chain. Not that Daugherty is worse than Shaq. It's just that his calm, easygoing demeanor is no match in the image war. All you get with Daugherty are 20 points, 11 boards, and five assists—every night.

Coaching: Fratello brings a temper and a high profile to the Cavs, something Lenny Wilkens didn't. But remember: Though Fratello's Hawks won 50-plus games four years in a row, they never escaped the Eastern semis. He's assisted by former head coaches Ron Rothstein and Richie Adubato, plus Jim Boylan.

Analysis: There is talent in Cleveland, as there has been for about five years. But another year of burning up the regular season and then flaming out in the playoffs will not be accepted. Fratello was paid big money to rile up his troops. That he'll do, but it's still questionable—even doubtful—that he'll push the Cavs past the Bulls in next spring's playoffs.

Prediction: Second place, Central

DETROIT PISTONS

Home: The Palace
Capacity: 21,454
Year Built: 1988

Address
The Palace
Two Championship Dr.
Auburn Hills, MI 48326
(313) 377-0100

Managing Partner: William Davidson
Director of Player Personnel:
Billy McKinney
Head Coach: Don Chaney
Assistant Coach: Brendan Malone

Coach Don Chaney			
	W	L	Pct.
NBA Record	191	240	.443
W/Pistons	0	0	.000
1992-93 Record	0	0	.000

Pistons History

Any discussion of Pistons history is bound to be a little heavy on the "Bad Boy" years. After three fruitless decades, the Pistons won back-to-back NBA titles in 1988-89 and 1989-90.

The franchise was established in Fort Wayne, Indiana, in 1941 as a member of the old National Basketball League. It joined the BAA in 1948 and became a charter NBA club in 1949. The Fort Wayne Pistons, led by high-scoring George Yardley, advanced to the NBA Finals twice during the 1950s, losing to Syracuse in 1954-55 and Philadelphia in 1955-56.

The Pistons moved to Detroit in 1957 but began to falter, finishing below .500 for the next 13 seasons. Detroit made some news during the period, naming 24-year-old Dave DeBusschere player/coach in 1964 and drafting hot-shot guard Dave Bing in 1966. Things got a little better in the mid-1970s. Detroit posted a 52-30 record in 1973-74, due largely to the play of Bing and center Bob Lanier. But the Pistons were eliminated in the Western semis and had to wait another nine seasons for a strong team.

That came in 1983-84 when Chuck Daly took over as coach. Daly, building his team around point guard Isiah Thomas, won the Central Division title in 1987-88. They advanced to the NBA Finals that season, losing to Los Angeles in seven games. Thomas, Bill Laimbeer, Dennis Rodman, and Joe Dumars were not denied the next two years, sweeping the Lakers in 1988-89 and whipping Portland in 1989-90.

Last Seven Years

Season	W	L	Pct.	Place	Playoffs	Coach
1986-87	52	30	.634	Second	L-East Finals	Chuck Daly
1987-88	54	28	.650	First	L-NBA Finals	Chuck Daly
1988-89	63	19	.768	First	NBA Champs	Chuck Daly
1989-90	59	23	.720	First	NBA Champs	Chuck Daly
1990-91	50	32	.610	Second	L-East Finals	Chuck Daly
1991-92	48	34	.585	Third	L-Round 1	Chuck Daly
1992-93	40	42	.488	Sixth	DNQ	Ron Rothstein

1992-93 Review

As the 1992-93 season wore on, the once-ballyhooed Motor City Bad Boys proved to the NBA that they were no longer so "bad." In fact, they were just plain bad. Bad, as in missing the playoffs for the first time in ten years. Bad, as in scoring a measly 100.6 PPG.

It all added up to a 40-42 record for the Pistons, good for sixth in the Central Division. In a classic case of "we can't fire 12 players, but we can fire one coach," Detroit president Tom Wilson and player personnel director Billy McKinney canned coach Ron Rothstein after just one season. Hey, it took Chuck Daly a couple years to get things rolling. Evidently, Wilson and McKinney were not students of history.

Rothstein's biggest problem—other than an aging, gap-filled roster—was forward Dennis "The Worm" Rodman, whose league-leading rebounding and statement-making hairdos wore thin when compared to his other childish antics. Rodman missed training camp, skipped a West Coast road trip, blew off practices, and demanded to be traded. And that was the normal stuff. How do you explain being found in the gym at 6 a.m. shooting around? You don't.

As always, the veteran backcourt of Isiah Thomas and Joe Dumars performed well—Dumars especially. Joe D. proved he was the best two guard in the league not named Michael Jordan. Power forward Terry Mills, stolen from the Nets prior to the season, was a pleasant surprise up front, even though he was forced to play the pivot most of the year. Mills showed some consistency that he had lacked while a Net.

The rest of the gang was marginal at best. Mark Aguirre's minutes and production slipped considerably, and Bill Laimbeer, once the spirit of the Bad Boys, was reduced to cartoon-character status by age and decaying ability. Olden Polynice had some moments at center but made more news for a brief hunger strike in protest of developments in Haiti. Alvin Robertson—acquired in a midseason trade for Orlando Woolridge—did give Detroit a solid third guard.

1993-94 Roster

							—1992-93—			
No.	Player	Pos.	Ht.	Wt.	Exp.	College	G	PPG	RPG	APG
23	Mark Aguirre	F	6'6"	232	12	DePaul	51	9.9	3.0	2.1
4	Joe Dumars	G	6'3"	195	8	McNeese St.	77	23.5	1.9	4.0
25	Gerald Glass	G/F	6'6"	221	3	Mississippi	60	5.3	2.4	1.3
—	Allan Houston	G	6'6"	200	R	Tennessee	—	—	—	—
1	Lindsey Hunter	G	6'2"	170	R	Jackson St.	—	—	—	—
40	Bill Laimbeer	C	6'11"	260	13	Notre Dame	79	8.7	5.3	1.6
6	Terry Mills	F	6'10"	250	3	Michigan	81	14.8	5.8	1.4
35	Isaiah Morris	F	6'8"	228	1	Arkansas	25	2.2	0.5	0.2
23	Melvin Newbern	G	6'4"	200	1	Minnesota	33	3.6	1.1	1.7
34	Olden Polynice	C	7'0"	250	6	Virginia	67	7.3	6.2	0.4
42	Mark Randall	F	6'9"	235	2	Kansas	37	2.6	1.5	0.3
3	Alvin Robertson	G	6'4"	208	9	Arkansas	69	9.0	2.3	3.8
10	Dennis Rodman	F	6'8"	210	7	S.E. Okla. St.	62	7.5	18.3	1.6
11	Isiah Thomas	G	6'1"	182	12	Indiana	79	17.6	2.9	8.5
20	Danny Young	G	6'4"	175	9	Wake Forest	65	2.9	0.7	1.8

Detroit Pistons
1993-94 Season Preview

Opening Line: All of a sudden, the Pistons are looking like Golden State East. By using their two first-round picks to snatch two high-scoring guards, Detroit solved its point-production problem of a year ago but did little to bolster its front line. Oh, well. New coach Don Chaney was an NBA guard, so maybe he wanted a team full of players to whom he can relate. Rookies Lindsey Hunter and Allan Houston will form an excellent back-up duo for the Pistons, and the 6'6" Houston may even find himself swinging to the three position on occasion. But Detroit may lack the muscle and size to hang in the East.

Guard: The backcourt is suddenly overflowing with talent. Isiah Thomas may be on the downside of a great career, but he remains a first-rate point guard. He's aggressive and fearless and has the ability to score and distribute the ball. Joe Dumars just keeps scoring and scoring. He does it off the dribble, from beyond the 3-point line, and in transition. Expect Houston to do a little of the same, with an emphasis on long-range bombing. The guy can shoot. Hunter is a 6'2" combo guard with a scorer's mentality and plenty of physical tools. Veteran Alvin Robertson remains one of the game's top defensive guards—as does Dumars.

Forward: Here's where the trouble starts. Dennis Rodman—the all-world rebounder, defender, and problem child—can lift a team with his enthusiasm and aggressive play or bury it with his antics. Should Chaney be able to keep him happy, the Pistons will be a playoff team. Mark Aguirre continues to score on anyone in the low post, although injuries did limit him last year. Aguirre doesn't help much off the glass, nor is he willing defensively. Soft-shooting power forward Terry Mills surprised plenty of people with his high level of play last season. If Mills can keep the fat off his frame, he'll be a good one.

Center: Veteran Olden Polynice, one of the league's top bangers, is not your ideal starter. He works hard underneath and grabs rebounds, but he's lacking offensively. It's been a nice career for 13-year veteran Bill Laimbeer, but the sands are slipping out of the hourglass. His elbows—and jumper—remain sharp, but his stamina is waning.

Coaching: Chaney had an ill-fated, 3½-year stint in Houston, where he failed to win a playoff series and had the bad luck of having to endure Hakeem Olajuwon's feud with management. He'll bring the ever-popular "player's approach" to the bench and should get along well with Piston veterans. He's assisted by Brendan Malone.

Analysis: The Pistons played pretty good defense last year, but they were largely impotent on offense. The selections of Houston and Hunter should change that, although it will make Detroit even more reliant on its backcourt—not such a good thing these days in the East. The Pistons will likely battle Indiana and Atlanta for fourth place in the Central Division.

Prediction: Fifth place, Central

INDIANA PACERS

Home: Market Square Arena
Capacity: 16,530
Year Built: 1974

Owners: Melvin Simon, Herbert Simon
President: Don Walsh
Head Coach: Larry Brown
Assistant Coach: Gar Heard
Assistant Coach: Bill Blair

Address
300 E. Market St.
Indianapolis, IN 46204
(317) 263-2100

Coach Larry Brown			
	W	L	Pct.
NBA Record	434	342	.559
W/Pacers	0	0	.000
1992-93 Record	41	41	.500

Pacers History

If there could be such a thing as the "Boston Celtics of the ABA," it definitely would have been the Indiana Pacers. The Pacers won three ABA titles and finished second twice between 1968-69 and 1974-75.

But the Pacers were sorry to see the old league die. Since joining the NBA, the Pacers have been nearly moribund, reaching the playoffs only six times during their 17 years in the league. Despite playing in a basketball-crazed state, the Pacers have never won an NBA playoff series.

But the old days were something in Indianapolis. Led by Mel Daniels, a 6'9" bull of a center, the early Pacers featured a lineup that was equal to many NBA teams. Guard Freddie Lewis and forward Roger Brown were deadly scorers, and power forward Bob Netolicky was a bruiser. In 1971, Indiana signed forward George McGinnis from Indiana University. It later added guard Bill Keller and forward Billy Knight to a potent rotation.

Yet the same penchant for accumulating talented personnel did not carry over to Indiana's years in the NBA. The Pacers have had only two winning seasons since the merger, and in recent years they've become known for they're perennial mediocrity. Indiana has had the offense in recent seasons—from long-range bombers Chuck Person and Reggie Miller to do-everything forward Detlef Schrempf—but it has lacked the strong defense, team chemistry, and mental toughness to excel in the playoffs.

Last Seven Years

Season	W	L	Pct.	Place	Playoffs	Coach
1986-87	41	41	.500	Fourth	L-Round 1	Jack Ramsay
1987-88	38	44	.463	Sixth	DNQ	Jack Ramsay
1988-89	28	54	.341	Sixth	DNQ	J. Ramsay/G. Irvine/ D. Versace
1989-90	42	40	.512	Fourth	L-Round 1	Dick Versace
1990-91	41	41	.500	Fifth	L-Round 1	Dick Versace/Bob Hill
1991-92	40	42	.488	Fourth	L-Round 1	Bob Hill
1992-93	41	41	.500	Fifth	L-Round 1	Bob Hill

1992-93 Review

The Pacers are nothing if not consistent. For the fourth consecutive year, they hovered around the .500 mark, hitting the number exactly—41-41—and earning the right to be first-round playoff fodder for the New York Knicks.

An attempted preseason shake-up that sent Micheal Williams and Chuck Person to Minnesota for Pooh Richardson and Sam Mitchell did little—for either team. Richardson was inconsistent, Mitchell nearly nonexistent, and Williams and Person were not really missed.

About the only big news in Indiana was the giant four-year contract signed by center Rik Smits, once again proving the lack of talented pivot men in the league. Though the 7'4" Dutchman was a consistent scorer, he was soft on the backboards and blocked only 75 shots.

Smits didn't have too much help up front. Second-year man Dale Davis rebounded well and shot 56.8 percent from the field, but his shooting range was limited primarily to offensive putbacks. Aging LaSalle Thompson was an inadequate back-up, and reserve power forward Kenny Williams didn't add much.

The Pacers did score some points, as their 107.8 PPG—second in the conference—indicated. Gunning, trash-talking off guard Reggie Miller shot nearly 48 percent, despite launching a league-leading 419 3's. And Detlef Schrempf was his usual, outstanding all-around self. He rebounded, passed, and scored well, again proving to be one of the league's more valuable players.

Richardson had his moments at the point—particularly on the break—but he struggled when opponents forced the Pacers into halfcourt sets. Vern Fleming was a steady back-up, but reserve two guard George McCloud shot only 41.1 percent, and rookie forward Malik Sealy made more news for losing his playbook during the playoffs than for his play. Mitchell, who scored well for the expansion T'Wolves, was a streaky reserve.

1993-94 Roster

| No. | Player | Pos. | Ht. | Wt. | Exp. | College | 1992-93 | | |
							G	PPG	RPG	APG
32	Dale Davis	F	6'11"	230	2	Clemson	82	8.9	8.8	0.8
54	Greg Dreiling	C	7'1"	250	7	Kansas	43	1.1	1.5	0.2
—	Spencer Dunkley	F/C	6'11"	238	R	Delaware	—	—	—	—
10	Vern Fleming	G	6'5"	185	9	Georgia	75	9.5	2.3	3.0
23	Sean Green	G	6'5"	210	2	Iona	13	4.8	0.7	0.5
43	Scott Haskin	C/F	6'11"	250	R	Oregon St.	—	—	—	—
—	Thomas Hill	G	6'5"	200	R	Duke	—	—	—	—
20	George McCloud	G/F	6'8"	215	4	Florida St.	78	7.2	2.6	2.5
31	Reggie Miller	G	6'7"	185	6	UCLA	82	21.2	3.1	3.2
5	Sam Mitchell	F	6'7"	210	4	Mercer	81	7.2	3.1	0.9
24	Pooh Richardson	G	6'1"	180	4	UCLA	74	10.4	3.6	7.7
11	Detlef Schrempf	F	6'10"	230	8	Washington	82	19.1	9.5	6.0
21	Malik Sealy	F	6'8"	192	1	St. John's	58	5.7	1.9	0.8
45	Rik Smits	C	7'4"	265	5	Marist	81	14.3	5.3	1.5
41	LaSalle Thompson	F/C	6'10"	260	11	Texas	63	3.8	2.8	0.5
44	Kenny Williams	F	6'9"	205	3	Elizabeth City	57	6.1	4.0	0.7

Indiana Pacers
1993-94 Season Preview

Opening Line: Coaching nomad Larry Brown makes a stop in the Hoosier state, taking on his latest challenge and making no promises about how long he'll be in town. You can bet Brown will stir things up some in Indianapolis, but whether that spoon will be big enough to propel the Pacers past the .500 level is another question. There's some talent on the roster but not much depth, though first-round draft choice Scott Haskin (6'11") will probably help up front. Brown would be advised to rent, not buy, a home. Then again, he always does.

Guard: Pooh Richardson brings a mixed bag to the point. He'll score a little, particularly in transition, but don't expect him to get to the free throw line too often. He can distribute the ball but—like most of his teammates—isn't the stickiest defender. Count on shooting (and we mean shooting) guard Reggie Miller for 400-plus 3-point attempts, at least one temper tantrum, and very little physical play. Back-up point man Vern Fleming gets the Good Soldier Award for playing behind first Micheal Williams and now Richardson. Fleming contributes steady ball-handling and veteran leadership.

Forward: In his first season as a full-time starter, Detlef Schrempf made the NBA All-Star Game last year, thus becoming the first European player to do so. Schrempf's tremendous all-around skills make him one of the NBA's best forwards. He'll give Brown what Danny Manning gave him last year. Dale Davis continues to improve and could become a top-flight power forward by the end of this year. Sure, his range is limited, but he shoots 57 percent. And the guy can rebound. Unfortunately, the trio of George McCloud, Sam Mitchell, and Malik Sealy can neither rebound nor shoot straight. Skinny Kenny Williams gets after it underneath despite limited skills.

Center: What an agent Rik Smits must have! How else do you explain the five-year, $17-million deal he signed before last season? Smits has a nice touch around the basket, but he's the shortest 7'4" guy you've ever seen. Smits blocked all of 75 shots in 81 games last year, most by accident. Haskin is the antithesis of Smits—aggressive and fearless. But he lacks muscle and is not too productive on offense. Back-up veterans LaSalle Thompson and Greg Dreiling bring little to the dance.

Coaching: Brown is intense, fiery, smart, and capable—when he's around. Any team that hires him is looking decidedly short-term, and the Pacers fit the bill. They need to win something now, and team president Donnie Walsh must figure his old friend is a good quick-fix. Brown will be assisted by Garfield Heard and Bill Blair.

Analysis: Brown has some talent with which to work, but the Pacers need an increased defensive presence—particularly underneath—and more from the bench if they're going to win anything of consequence. Maybe the Pacers will win their first-ever NBA playoff series this year. However, they won't win two.

Prediction: Fourth place, Central

MILWAUKEE BUCKS

Home: Bradley Center
Capacity: 18,633
Year Built: 1988

Address
Bradley Center
1001 N. Fourth St.
Milwaukee, WI 53203
(414) 227-0500

Owner: Herb Kohl
V.P./Player Personnel: Lee Rose
Head Coach: Mike Dunleavy
Assistant Coach: Frank Hamblen
Assistant Coach: Jim Eyen
Assistant Coach: Butch Carter

Coach Mike Dunleavy			
	W	L	Pct.
NBA Record	129	117	.524
W/Bucks	28	54	.341
1992-93 Record	28	54	.341

Bucks History

In their first 23 years of existence (through 1990-91), the Bucks missed out on postseason play only four times. But despite that gleaming record, the franchise's glory period is long past.

Milwaukee stumbled through its rookie season in 1968-69, but the Bucks won the coin toss with Phoenix for the rights to UCLA star Lew Alcindor. The Bucks signed the big rookie and embarked on a five-year run of success. In 1969-70, Milwaukee reached the Eastern finals, and the arrival of guard Oscar Robertson during the off-season was the final piece in coach Larry Costello's puzzle. In 1970-71, Alcindor, Robertson, Bob Dandridge, Greg Smith, and Jon McGlocklin led the Bucks to a 66-16 record and the NBA championship.

Alcindor changed his name to Kareem Abdul-Jabbar, and in 1973-74 the Bucks made it back to the title series. However, they lost to Boston in seven games. Jabbar was dealt to Los Angeles for four players following the 1974-75 season, and the Bucks floundered for the next four years, finishing over the .500 mark just once.

Don Nelson took over as coach in 1976-77 and directed the team back into the playoffs on a regular basis. But although the nucleus of Sidney Moncrief, Junior Bridgeman, Marques Johnson, and Terry Cummings was strong enough to win 50-plus games each year from 1980-81 to 1986-87, the Bucks couldn't get back to the NBA Finals. The club had grown too old by the early 1990s and began a rebuilding program.

Last Seven Years

Season	W	L	Pct.	Place	Playoffs	Coach
1986-87	50	32	.610	Third	L-East Semis	Don Nelson
1987-88	42	40	.512	Fourth	L-Round 1	Del Harris
1988-89	49	33	.598	Fourth	L-East Semis	Del Harris
1989-90	44	38	.537	Third	L-Round 1	Del Harris
1990-91	48	34	.585	Third	L-Round 1	Del Harris
1991-92	31	51	.378	Sixth	DNQ	Del Harris/Frank Hamblen
1992-93	28	54	.341	Seventh	DNQ	Mike Dunleavy

1992-93 Review

That 10-3 start in Cheesetown last year was a complete illusion. There was no way coach Mike Dunleavy would cobble together a quality team out of a few remaining vets, a couple of imports, and rookies galore. In fact, by the time it was over, the Bucks didn't even challenge the sixth-place Pistons. It's a good thing Dunleavy has a big, fat, long-term contract. He's going to need it.

The new-look Bucks sagged to 28-54, three wins fewer than the 1991-92 season, which precipitated all the upheaval in the first place. Dunleavy struggled all season to find a rotation that worked, and ten Bucks logged more than 1,000 minutes each. Hey, sometimes you have to go backward to go forward.

A pair of veteran frontcourters led the way. Frank Brickowski and former Utah Jazz reserve Blue Edwards each averaged 16.9 PPG, but they were the closest things to big-time scorers in Milwaukee. The Bucks averaged only 102.3 PPG, sixth worst in the league. Since they allowed 106.1 and permitted opponents to shoot 48.3 percent from the field, you can see where their troubles lay.

Veteran forward Orlando Woolridge missed time with a broken hand after coming over in a midseason trade for Alvin Robertson, and Anthony Avent was erratic in his first try at NBA life after a season in Italy.

Part of the problem was that Milwaukee lacked a legitimate center. Ancient Moses Malone played just 11 games because of back problems, leaving Brad Lohaus, Danny Schayes, and undersized Fred Roberts as the primary pivot men. Not good.

The new-look backcourt played to mixed reviews. Speedy Eric Murdock, freed from bench life in Utah, was a solid point man, and rookie Todd Day was promising at the two spot, despite some poor shooting (43.2 percent). Even so, the Bucks missed Sam Vincent (out for the year with a blown Achilles tendon). Rookie Lee Mayberry, a backcourt mate of Day at Arkansas, did not enjoy the same rookie success as his collegiate partner. He backed up Murdock adequately but had problems on defense.

1993-94 Roster

No.	Player	Pos.	Ht.	Wt.	Exp.	College	G	PPG	RPG	APG
							\multicolumn{4}{c}{—1992-93—}
00	Anthony Avent	F	6'10"	235	1	Seton Hall	82	9.8	6.2	1.1
42	Vin Baker	F	6'11"	232	R	Hartford	—	—	—	—
17	Jon Barry	G	6'5"	195	1	Georgia Tech	47	4.4	0.9	1.4
40	Frank Brickowski	F/C	6'10"	248	9	Penn St.	66	16.9	6.1	3.0
10	Todd Day	G/F	6'8"	200	1	Arkansas	71	13.8	4.1	1.6
30	Blue Edwards	F	6'5"	200	4	East Carolina	82	16.9	4.7	2.6
54	Brad Lohaus	F/C	6'11"	238	6	Iowa	80	9.1	3.5	1.6
11	Lee Mayberry	G	6'2"	175	1	Arkansas	82	5.2	1.4	3.3
5	Eric Murdock	G	6'2"	189	2	Providence	79	14.4	3.6	7.6
3	Ken Norman	F	6'8"	223	6	Illinois	76	15.0	7.5	2.2
24	Dan Schayes	C	6'11"	275	12	Syracuse	70	4.6	3.6	1.1
20	Derek Strong	F	6'8"	220	2	Xavier	23	6.8	5.0	0.6
7	Sam Vincent	G	6'2"	194	7	Michigan St.	—	—	—	—
6	Orlando Woolridge	F	6'9"	215	12	Notre Dame	58	12.0	3.2	2.0

Milwaukee Bucks
1993-94 Season Preview

Opening Line: It's a good thing Mike Dunleavy signed an eight-year contract in Brew Town, because he's going to need plenty of time to convert the young Bucks from Central Division stragglers to playoff contenders. First-round draft choice Vin Baker of Hartford should contribute, as should free-agent signee Ken Norman. Still, Dunleavy has a roster full of young, raw talent. Few expect them to escape the Central Division basement this year.

Guard: Given an opportunity to run his own team last season, Eric Murdock responded with a big year. He may not be the smoothest shooter around, but Murdock is quick, handles the ball well, and is a dervish on defense. Second-year mate Todd Day epitomizes the Bucks' raw talent. He has great size and speed and can hit the long jumper, but he's inconsistent in all phases of the game. His former Arkansas teammate, back-up point guard Lee Mayberry, distributes it well and has some 3-point range. If he returns from last season's knee surgery, out-of-control Sam Vincent will add experience, though not stability, to the backcourt rotation.

Forward: Norman will add leadership, rebounding, and double-digit scoring to the Bucks. He'll likely start opposite Blue Edwards, a smallish small forward who compensates with impressive athletic skills and exciting finishes. Norman will replace Anthony Avent, who somehow found his way into the starting lineup last year. While the second-year man has a big-time body and some rebounding skills, he is wooden on offense and easily beaten by the league's better inside scorers. The 6'11" Baker has been called a "bigger Scottie Pippen" for his outside touch and fastbreak skills. But he didn't face top competition at Hartford and could be "the next Brad Sellers." If healthy, aging Orlando Woolridge can be counted on for scoring and little else. Reserve Fred Roberts opted to play this year in Spain.

Center: Moses Malone's back troubles, Brad Lohaus's incompetence, and Danny Schayes's decaying skills left a hole in the middle last year. Frank Brickowski, not a true center, managed to lead the team in scoring. He works hard on both ends and is a good veteran example for the Milwaukee youngsters.

Coaching: Dunleavy expected a tough first year and he got it. Though he was successful with the Lakers, that team was packed with veterans—a luxury not present in Milwaukee. Still, Dunleavy's laid-back approach will work well with the young Bucks. He's assisted by Jim Eyen, Butch Carter, and Frank Hamblen.

Analysis: Ken Norman will definitely help the Bucks' pathetic front line, but the frontcourt still lacks both talent and size. The backcourt, meanwhile, has promising talent but lacks experience. There's not much Dunleavy can do except teach the game to the youngsters and wait for a couple lottery picks to arrive. Milwaukee has no chance of contending in 1993-94.

Prediction: Seventh place, Central

DALLAS MAVERICKS

Home: Reunion Arena
Capacity: 17,502
Year Built: 1980

Address
777 Sports St.
Dallas, TX 75207
(214) 748-1808

Owner: Donald Carter
General Manager: Norm Sonju
Head Coach: Quinn Buckner
Assistant Coach: Tom Newell
Assistant Coach: Randy Wittman

Coach Quinn Buckner			
	W	L	Pct.
NBA Record	0	0	.000
W/Mavericks	0	0	.000
1992-93 Record	0	0	.000

Mavericks History

Most NBA franchises start out bad and then get better. The Mavericks started out surprisingly well but have since gone down the tubes.

Dallas entered the league in 1980 and soon made its mark. In the 1981 draft, the Mavs selected Mark Aguirre, Rolando Blackman, and Jay Vincent. In 1983, they brought in standout guards Dale Ellis and Derek Harper. That high-scoring nucleus, coached by Dick Motta, won 43 games in 1983-84, finishing second in the Midwest and advancing to the West semifinals.

Dallas won the Midwest in 1986-87, buoyed by the addition of mammoth center James Donaldson and rookie forward Roy Tarpley, but the Mavs bowed out in the first round of the playoffs. The excitement really ran high the next season. Motta was replaced by former Phoenix coach John MacLeod, and Dallas stretched eventual champion Los Angeles to seven games in the Western finals.

Things started to sour in 1988-89. Aguirre was traded in midseason to Detroit for the mercurial Adrian Dantley, and Tarpley played only 19 games due to alcohol-abuse problems. The Mavericks fell to 38-44 in 1988-89, and though they rebounded to 47-35 the next season, MacLeod was fired and Dallas lost in the first round of the 1990 playoffs.

The last three seasons have been disastrous. The downfall was triggered by a lifetime ban on Tarpley, but injuries, bad trades, and dissension have also crippled the Mavericks. In 1992-93, they fielded one of the poorest teams in NBA history, going 11-71.

Last Seven Years

Season	W	L	Pct.	Place	Playoffs	Coach
1986-87	55	27	.671	First	L-Round 1	Dick Motta
1987-88	53	29	.646	Second	L-West Finals	John MacLeod
1988-89	38	44	.463	Fourth	DNQ	John MacLeod
1989-90	47	35	.573	Third	L-Round 1	John Macleod/R. Adubato
1990-91	28	54	.341	Sixth	DNQ	Richie Adubato
1991-92	22	60	.268	Fifth	DNQ	Richie Adubato
1992-93	11	71	.134	Sixth	DNQ	R. Adubato/Gar Heard

1992-93 Review

Champagne corks were popping all over Dallas April 23 when the Mavs knocked off Minnesota 103-100. The win guaranteed that Dallas would not duplicate the sad 9-73 record of the 1972-73 76ers, and prevented the once-proud Mavericks from attaining basketball infamy.

While the win—and another the next night over Houston—prevented an entry in the record books, it couldn't rescue Dallas from becoming the league's laughingstock. The Mavericks may not have been the worst ever, but they've probably retired the trophy for the 1990s.

As aggravating as the team's 11-71 record was, its off-court antics were even more ridiculous. Carter and G.M. Norm Sonju staged an eight-month staring contest with first-round draft choice Jimmy Jackson, balking at the talented guard's substantial salary demands. They finally signed Jackson on March 4, the same day Dallas announced that Quinn Buckner would jump from his NBC broadcasting chair to the head-coaching spot for the 1993-94 season. Buckner replaces Gar Heard, who stepped in for Richie Adubato—fired after 29 games.

Buckner must have incredible self-confidence, because the team he inherits had the worst talent in the league last year. Other than classy veteran point guard Derek Harper and Jackson, who should be a star in the league, the Mavs were dreadful. They scored the second-fewest points in the league (99.3 PPG), allowed the most (114.5 PPG), and shot a miserable 43.5 percent from the field.

Among the few promising players Buckner inherits are power forward Terry Davis, who suffered a serious elbow injury in an automobile accident one week after the regular season's close, soft second-year center Sean Rooks, and frenetic back-up point guard Mike Iuzzolino. None could boast about his 1992-93 antics, but they were the best of a putrid lot.

1993-94 Roster

No.	Player	Pos.	Ht.	Wt.	Exp.	College	G	PPG	RPG	APG
40	Walter Bond	G	6'5"	213	1	Minnesota	74	8.0	2.6	1.6
30	Dexter Cambridge	F	6'7"	225	1	Texas	53	7.0	3.2	1.1
43	Terry Davis	F/C	6'10"	250	4	Virginia Union	75	12.7	9.3	0.9
12	Derek Harper	G	6'4"	206	10	Illinois	62	18.2	2.0	5.4
—	Lucious Harris	G	6'5"	190	R	Long Beach St.	—	—	—	—
35	Donald Hodge	C	7'0"	240	2	Temple	79	5.0	3.7	0.9
41	Brian Howard	F	6'6"	204	2	N. Carolina St.	68	6.5	3.1	1.0
13	Mike Iuzzolino	G	5'11"	172	2	St. Francis (PA)	70	8.7	2.0	4.7
24	Jimmy Jackson	G	6'6"	220	1	Ohio St.	28	16.3	4.4	4.7
—	Popeye Jones	F	6'8"	270	R	Murray St.	—	—	—	—
23	Tim Legler	G	6'4"	200	3	La Salle	33	8.8	1.8	1.4
21	Lafayette Lever	G	6'3"	180	10	Arizona St.	—	—	—	—
32	Jamal Mashburn	F	6'8"	240	R	Kentucky	—	—	—	—
45	Sean Rooks	C/F	6'10"	260	1	Arizona	72	13.5	7.4	1.3
34	Doug Smith	F	6'10"	238	2	Missouri	61	10.4	5.4	1.7
52	Randy White	F	6'8"	238	4	Louisiana Tech	64	9.7	5.8	0.8
20	Morlon Wiley	G	6'4"	192	5	Long Beach St.	58	4.5	1.6	3.1

Dallas Mavericks
1993-94 Season Preview

Opening Line: Soon after last season's 11-71 debacle, the Mavericks received more bad news: Forward Terry Davis shattered his elbow in an automobile accident and will likely miss the season. New coach Quinn Buckner does have some reason for optimism, however. Jim Jackson, who held out most of last season, will be around all year. The addition of Jamal Mashburn, the fourth pick in this year's draft, means the Mavs have a pair of young, marquee talents. Also, second-round pick Lucious Harris is a big-time scorer.

Guard: Jackson entered the Maverick lineup in March and began firing immediately. He has good range on his shot and is physical enough to go inside. He needs to cut down on his turnovers and boost his field goal percentage. Veteran Derek Harper deserves better than the Mavs, but you won't hear too much grousing from him. What he will do is produce points and get the ball to folks like Jackson and Mashburn in good position. Back-up Mike Iuzzolino may be short—he's 5'11"—but he chalks up assists and has good range on his shot. Morlon Wiley, acquired in midseason from Atlanta, is almost exclusively a 3-point specialist. Harris, a 2,000-plus point scorer at Long Beach State, can shoot it from Fort Worth or take it to the hole.

Forward: The loss of Davis substantially hurts the Mavs' front line, but the addition of Mashburn helps considerably. "Monster Mash" is a 6'8" blend of outside marksmanship and inside power. He'll be an NBA All-Star some day. Buckner must choose another starter from Randy White, Doug Smith, and Brian Howard—hardly a strong collection. White, who was once heralded as the next Mailman, has now been demoted to postal clerk. He is slow, foul-prone, and a poor shooter. Smith is another example of poor Maverick drafting. He too is a weak shooter and a big-time hack. Howard plays within his limitations, but his limitations are considerable.

Center: Second-year man Sean Rooks had a pretty good rookie campaign, leading the team in shooting percentage and showing some willingness to hit the boards. He could develop into a serviceable NBA center. Back-up Donald Hodge, on the other hand, remains timid on defense and raw offensively.

Coaching: Buckner moves from the cushy NBC studios to Dante's seventh level of basketball hell. Expect him to try to instill some of the winning attitude he possessed as a member of the Celtics in the mid-1980s, while showing the patience needed to bring a young club to respectability. He'll be assisted by Tom Newell and Randy Wittman.

Analysis: With last year's nightmare over, Dallas can concentrate on moving slowly toward contention. The road back will be long and hard, but Buckner should have the team playing competitive basketball before long. His nucleus of Jackson, Harper, and Mashburn is a good start, although considerable help is needed up front. Harper could, and probably should, be traded.

Prediction: Sixth place, Midwest

DENVER NUGGETS

Home: McNichols Sports Arena
Capacity: 17,022
Year Built: 1975

Owner: COMSAT Denver, Inc.
General Manager: Bernie Bickerstaff
Head Coach: Dan Issel
Assistant Coach: Gene Littles
Assistant Coach: Mike Evans

Address
1635 Clay St.
Denver, CO 80204
(303) 893-6700

Coach Dan Issel			
	W	L	Pct.
NBA Record	36	46	.439
W/Nuggets	36	46	.439
1992-93 Record	36	46	.439

Nuggets History

The Nuggets were one of the rarities of the old ABA—a team that stayed in the same place throughout the league's tumultuous nine-year history. A charter ABA member, the Denver Rockets were one of the league's strongest franchises, though they never won a championship.

Early on, Rocket fans were thrilled by the high-flying exploits of forward Spencer Haywood, who led Denver to the Western Conference finals in 1969-70, where it lost to Los Angeles. But Haywood soon left and the franchise's fortunes dimmed until 1974, when G.M. Carl Scheer and coach Larry Brown came to the Rockies from the Carolina Cougars.

Scheer immediately changed the team nickname to the Nuggets. Denver won 65 games in 1974-75 but lost in the Western finals to Indiana. The next season, the Nuggets acquired star guard David Thompson and made it to the league championship series.

The Nuggets were one of four ABA teams to merge with the NBA in 1976, and they won the Midwest Division in their first two seasons. Denver won Midwest titles in 1984-85 and 1987-88 under Doug Moe and made it to the Western finals in 1985, but they failed in their bid for the elusive NBA championship.

Following the 1989-90 season, Denver fired Moe and hired Paul Westhead. Westhead's high-octane running game didn't bring too many results, as Denver registered the league's worst record in 1990-91. A modified system and rookie center Dikembe Mutombo led to a few more wins in 1991-92.

Last Seven Years

Season	W	L	Pct.	Place	Playoffs	Coach
1986-87	37	45	.451	Fourth	L-Round 1	Doug Moe
1987-88	54	28	.659	First	L-West Semis	Doug Moe
1988-89	44	38	.537	Third	L-Round 1	Doug Moe
1989-90	43	39	.524	Fourth	L-Round 1	Doug Moe
1990-91	20	62	.244	Seventh	DNQ	Paul Westhead
1991-92	24	58	.293	Fourth	DNQ	Paul Westhead
1992-93	36	46	.439	Fourth	DNQ	Dan Issel

1992-93 Review

No parades were scheduled, but there was reason for optimism in Mile High Country throughout 1992-93. In the inaugural post-Paul Westhead campaign, coach Dan Issel's team gave the home folks plenty to cheer about.

The Nuggets improved their wretched 24-58 record of the season before by 12 games and actually looked like a team heading in the right direction. Although the Nuggets were porous defensively, Issel's up-tempo philosophy created plenty of points—especially at home. The young team went 28-13 in the mountains.

Perhaps the biggest reason for Denver's turnaround was the play of guard Chris Jackson. Jackson trimmed substantial weight off his previously portly frame and ran the Nugget offense with confidence and effectiveness. He registered a career-high scoring average (19.2) and brought a much-needed steady hand to a Nugget backcourt that floundered two seasons ago.

Jackson could have used some help. Other than lightning-quick point-guard reserve Robert Pack, Denver's guards were below average. Todd Lichti missed most of the season with a knee injury—again, as did second-year man Mark Macon (wrist), who has yet to prove he can score in the NBA. Rookie Bryant Stith showed some promise, but he too was slowed by injury.

Denver's strength was its frontcourt. Adding athletic rookie LaPhonso Ellis to second-year center Dikembe Mutombo and scoring machine Reggie Williams gave the Nuggets a good, young nucleus up front. Though Mutombo's scoring numbers dropped a little, his rebounding stats were out of sight.

There was quite a drop-off after those three, however. Marcus Liberty shot 40.6 percent from the field while Anthony Cook never even played a game, thanks to major knee surgery in the off-season. Still, it was a pretty good year for the Nuggets, who shed the laughingstock image created during Westhead's tenure and appeared but a player away from future playoff contention.

1993-94 Roster

No.	Player	Pos.	Ht.	Wt.	Exp.	College	G	PPG	RPG	APG
43	Kevin Brooks	F	6'8"	200	2	S.W. Louisiana	55	4.1	1.5	0.6
20	LaPhonso Ellis	F	6'8"	240	1	Notre Dame	82	14.7	9.1	1.8
21	Tom Hammonds	F	6'9"	225	4	Georgia Tech	54	4.6	2.4	0.4
10	Scott Hastings	F/C	6'11"	245	11	Arkansas	76	2.1	1.8	0.4
3	Chris Jackson	G	6'1"	168	3	Louisiana St.	81	19.2	2.8	4.2
30	Marcus Liberty	F	6'8"	205	3	Illinois	78	8.1	4.3	1.3
12	Mark Macon	G	6'5"	185	2	Temple	48	7.5	2.1	2.6
4	Darnell Mee	G	6'5"	177	R	W. Kentucky	—	—	—	—
55	Dikembe Mutombo	C	7'2"	245	2	Georgetown	82	13.8	13.0	1.8
14	Robert Pack	G	6'2"	180	2	Southern Cal.	77	10.5	2.1	4.4
45	Gary Plummer	F	6'9"	255	2	Boston Univ.	60	4.7	2.9	0.7
54	Rodney Rogers	F	6'7"	250	R	Wake Forest	—	—	—	—
23	Bryant Stith	G	6'5"	208	1	Virginia	39	8.9	3.2	1.3
28	Robert Werdann	C	6'11"	250	1	St. John's	28	1.9	1.9	0.3
8	Brian Williams	F	6'11"	242	2	Arizona	21	4.6	2.7	0.2
34	Reggie Williams	F/G	6'7"	195	6	Georgetown	79	17.0	5.4	3.7

Denver Nuggets
1993-94 Season Preview

Opening Line: The Nuggets may soon have a team as impressive as the uniforms they wear. Denver is slowly, steadily improving by adding one or two young players every year and creating a team that will soon be a playoff contender. Coach Dan Issel's second season should be an improvement on his first, thanks primarily to his young team's maturity and the addition of Wake Forest small forward Rodney Rogers, the ninth pick in June's draft. Power forward Brian Williams, acquired from Orlando for Todd Lichti and Anthony Cook, also might contribute.

Guard: Denver said good-bye to Chris Jackson after a tremendous comeback year—and said hi to Mahmoud Abdul-Rauf, Jackson's new Islamic moniker. No matter what the name, expect some big results from the talented lead guard, who can score in droves and thrill in the open court. He's backed up by speedy Robert Pack, a productive distributor and excellent fastbreak leader. The two-guard spot is not so settled. Mark Macon still can't shoot the ball straight and second-year man Bryant Stith didn't see enough time last year to prove he was the answer. Second-round rookie Darnell Mee has a good long-range stroke.

Forward: The Nuggets boast a fine starting combo, at least offensively. Three man Reggie Williams won't ever stop firing, much to the detriment of his shooting percentage. Williams is pretty strong on the backboards but has never been mistaken for a defensive specialist. Second-year pro LaPhonso Ellis is an aggressive inside player, active rebounder, and strong finisher on the break. As he matures, he'll become more of a defensive presence against the league's strong men. Expect Rogers to contribute enough to push Williams to the two-guard spot, provided he sheds the extra pounds he carried into the pre-draft camp. When in shape, he can rebound and score inside or out. Back-up Marcus Liberty continues to shoot the ball atrociously but excels in the open court. Brian Williams needs to overcome injuries and personal problems.

Center: After approaching mythical proportions as an NBA rookie, Dikembe Mutombo leveled off last year and has become a solid NBA center. He rebounds with fervor, blocks plenty of shots, and shoots at a 50-percent clip. He'll be backed up by veteran Scott Hastings, whose one-liners are as funny as his play.

Coaching: The Nuggets still score, but they're actually trying to play some defense too. Credit Issel with that. Credit him also with showing extreme patience with a young, oft-erratic team. He and the Nuggets should grow together. Gene Littles and Mike Evans assist him.

Analysis: With Utah sliding a little and Dallas and Minnesota headed for the glue factory, Denver has a chance to make some headway in the Midwest Division. The addition of Rogers to a strong, young nucleus should help, as could healthy seasons from Stith and Brian Williams. The Nuggets aren't headed for the playoffs, but they definitely will flirt with .500. That's not too bad. For now.

Prediction: Fourth place, Midwest

HOUSTON ROCKETS

Home: The Summit
Capacity: 16,279
Year Built: 1975

Address
10 Greenway Plaza East
P.O. Box 272349
Houston, TX 77277
(713) 627-0600

Owner: Les Alexander
General Manager: Steve Patterson
Head Coach: Rudy Tomjanovich
Assistant Coach: Bill Berry
Assistant Coach: Carroll Dawson

Coach Rudy Tomjanovich			
	W	L	Pct.
NBA Record	71	41	.634
W/Rockets	71	41	.634
1992-93 Record	55	27	.671

Rockets History

Throughout their 26 seasons in San Diego and Houston, the Rockets have featured some of the NBA's finest big men. The tradition began during the team's second year when it drafted Elvin Hayes. Behind Hayes, the league's leading scorer and Rookie of the Year, San Diego advanced to the 1968-69 Western Conference semis, losing to Atlanta.

The Rockets moved to Houston in 1971, but Hayes spent only one season there before being dealt to Baltimore. Houston then built its team around considerably shorter players like 5'11" guard Calvin Murphy and forwards Mike Newlin and Rudy Tomjanovich.

Star center No. 2 came in 1976, when Moses Malone moved over from the defunct ABA. Houston won the Central Division crown in 1976-77 and advanced to the NBA Finals in 1980-81, losing in six games to Boston. In 1983, the Rockets drafted 7'4" Ralph Sampson from Virginia; one year later, they selected the dominating Akeem Olajuwon. In 1985-86, Houston made it back to the NBA Finals behind its "Twin Towers," only to lose to Boston in six.

Trouble hit the next season when guards Lewis Lloyd and Mitchell Wiggins were banned for two years for violating the league's drug-abuse policy. Injuries crippled Sampson's career and coach Bill Fitch was fired following the 1987-88 season. Don Chaney took over in 1988-89, and though the Rockets showed some spunk in 1990-91, they again fizzled in the playoffs. Houston won its division under Tomjanovich in 1992-93, but it lost in the West semis.

Last Seven Years

Season	W	L	Pct.	Place	Playoffs	Coach
1986-87	42	40	.512	Third	L-West Semis	Bill Fitch
1987-88	46	36	.561	Fourth	L-Round 1	Bill Fitch
1988-89	45	37	.549	Second	L-Round 1	Don Chaney
1989-90	41	41	.500	Fifth	L-Round 1	Don Chaney
1990-91	52	30	.634	Third	L-Round 1	Don Chaney
1991-92	42	40	.512	Third	DNQ	D. Chaney/R. Tomjanovich
1992-93	55	27	.671	First	L-West Semis	Rudy Tomjanovich

1992-93 Review

Talk about your transformations. Following the 1991-92 season, the Rockets were drifting aimlessly in outer space, unsure of their place in the Midwest Division arms race and adjusting to new coach Rudy Tomjanovich's direction. One year later, the Rockets detonated, winning 15 in a row in the season's second half and capturing the Midwest crown.

The Rockets' 55 wins were a franchise record. And although the team's seven-game loss to Seattle in the Western semis was a heartbreaker, it was still the club's first trip beyond the first round of the playoffs since 1987.

There are several reasons for the big turnaround, but one looms larger than any other. Center Hakeem Olajuwon had a mammoth season, largely due to his newfound happiness. No longer sparring with Rocket management, Olajuwon rejoined the league's elite performers, winning the NBA's Defensive Player of the Year honor and finishing second in the MVP voting. His dazzling array of offensive moves yielded a career-high scoring average of 26.1.

While Olajuwon was marvelous, his supporting cast stepped up. Guards Kenny Smith and Vernon Maxwell helped Houston finish second in 3-pointers made, and Smith's 52-percent shooting led all NBA guards. Though Maxwell (40.7 percent) continued to be an erratic shooter, he proved his toughness and desire by shrugging off a late-season wrist injury to play in the postseason.

Although his numbers fell, veteran Otis Thorpe was again a rock-solid presence at power forward. Horry, one of the unheralded members of the 1992-93 rookie class, was a big surprise, starting at small forward and giving the Rockets some needed offensive punch. Second-year forward Carl Herrera improved as the season wore on, while 6'10" Matt Bullard provided outside pop.

The backcourt reserves were led by frenetic, 5'11" Scott Brooks, who backed up Smith admirably and kept the Rocket offense moving. Veteran Sleepy Floyd backed up Maxwell but was erratic.

1993-94 Roster

No.	Player	Pos.	Ht.	Wt.	Exp.	College	G	PPG	RPG	APG
1	Scott Brooks	G	5'11"	165	5	Cal.-Irvine	82	6.3	1.2	3.0
50	Matt Bullard	F	6'10"	235	3	Iowa	79	7.3	2.8	1.4
10	Sam Cassell	G	6'3"	195	R	Florida St.	—	—	—	—
17	Mario Elie	G	6'5"	210	3	American Inter.	82	8.6	2.6	2.2
7	Carl Herrera	F	6'9"	225	2	Houston	81	7.5	5.6	0.8
25	Robert Horry	F	6'9"	220	1	Alabama	79	10.1	5.0	2.4
32	Dave Jamerson	G	6'5"	192	3	Ohio	—	—	—	—
11	Vernon Maxwell	G	6'4"	190	5	Florida	71	13.8	3.1	4.2
17	Tod Murphy	F/C	6'9"	235	4	Cal.-Irvine	—	—	—	—
—	Marcelo Nicola	F/C	6'10"	240	R	None	—	—	—	—
34	Hakeem Olajuwon	C	7'0"	255	9	Houston	82	26.1	13.0	3.5
—	Richard Petruska	C	6'10"	260	R	UCLA	—	—	—	—
42	Eric Riley	C	7'0"	245	R	Michigan	—	—	—	—
15	Tree Rollins	C	7'1"	255	16	Clemson	42	0.7	1.4	0.2
30	Kenny Smith	G	6'3"	170	6	North Carolina	82	13.0	2.0	5.4
33	Otis Thorpe	F	6'10"	246	9	Providence	72	12.8	8.2	2.5

Houston Rockets
1993-94 Season Preview

Opening Line: Every preseason forecast of the Rockets should begin with a quick look at Hakeem Olajuwon's face. Is the big guy smiling? Good. That means six months of good times ahead for the Rockets. He was happy last year, and the Rockets won a franchise-record 55 games and came within a game of advancing to the Western Conference finals. In the off-season, Houston waived guard Sleepy Floyd and then lost guard Winston Garland to free agency. They compensated by drafting point guard Sam Cassell and trading a draft pick to Portland for Mario Elie.

Guard: Kenny Smith's mid-career development continues. Though his numbers sagged somewhat in 1992-93, his leadership skills and solid ball distribution— i.e., get it to Hakeem—were enhanced. His backcourt mate, Vernon Maxwell, teams with Smith to give the Rockets a pair of dangerous 3-point threats. Back-up point guard Scott Brooks brings a high level of energy and a deep jumper to the proceedings. Elie, a solid all-around player, is a taller version of Garland. Cassell, a scorer who can play the point, is a younger version of Floyd.

Forward: Rockets fans may have booed when Houston made Robert Horry the 11th pick in last year's draft, but Horry heard no such catcalls by season's end. The athletic three man started all 79 games he played last year and was an outstanding inside/outside complement to rugged power forward Otis Thorpe. Horry can shoot it and isn't afraid to go after the boards. Thorpe, on the other hand, is the classic four man, bringing solid defense and rebounding to the Houston mix. Carl Herrera is a solid third forward. He's a quality rebounder who can also score around the basket. Back-up Matt Bullard may look like a bruiser, but he prefers to send it up from the outside.

Center: Though Houston has added some substantial pieces to its puzzle, the team still belongs to Olajuwon. And how! Olajuwon combines an athletic, get-up-and-down-the-court style with extraordinary skills on the low blocks. His fallaway jumper is undefensible, and his rebounding skills and desire are considerable. Moreover, he was the league's Defensive Player of the Year last season thanks to his 342 blocked shots. Second-rounder Eric Riley is the closest thing Houston has to a back-up center.

Coaching: There were plenty of questions about Rudy Tomjanovich when he took over late in the 1991-92 season, but he provided all the answers last year. A player's coach with the patience to develop youngsters, Rudy T. is a good fit for the Rockets. He is assisted by Bill Berry and Carroll Dawson.

Analysis: With Utah fading in the Midwest, Houston will battle San Antonio for the division's top spot. A healthy, happy year from Olajuwon is a must. What the Rockets could really use, however, is more quality talent off the bench. Back-ups like Elie, Herrera, Bullard, and Brooks—though solid—lack real firepower.

Prediction: Second place, Midwest

MINNESOTA TIMBERWOLVES

Home: Target Center
Capacity: 19,006
Year Built: 1990

Address
Target Center
600 First Ave. North
Minneapolis, MN 55403
(612) 673-1600

Owners: Harvey Ratner, Marv Wolfenson
General Manager: Jack McCloskey
Head Coach: Sidney Lowe
Assistant Coach: Jim Brewer
Assistant Coach: Chuck Davisson
Assistant Coach: Bob Weinhauer

Coach Sidney Lowe			
	W	L	Pct.
NBA Record	13	40	.245
W/Wolves	13	40	.245
1992-93 Record	13	40	.245

Timberwolves History

After four years in the NBA, Minnesota finds itself right where it started—at the bottom rung of the ladder.

The Timberwolves first took to the court in 1989-90, and the initial year's results were predictable—22-60. Ironically, the poor record did nothing to stem the enthusiasm of the Twin Cities faithful, who packed the Metrodome with 26,000-plus fans per night, establishing a season attendance record of more than one-million patrons.

The team featured some bright spots that first year. Forward Tony Campbell emerged as a top scoring threat, and rookie guard Pooh Richardson was an adroit playmaker and scorer. Under defensive-minded coach Bill Musselman, the T'Wolves were one of the league's best at maintaining tempo and stopping opponents from scoring.

For 1990-91, Minnesota added 7'0" center Felton Spencer and forward Gerald Glass, and they moved into the brand new Target Center in downtown Minneapolis. The team improved to 29-53, good for fifth in the Midwest Division. But despite the six-game improvement, Musselman got the axe and was replaced by Jimmy Rodgers.

The change did nothing to help the team, as the 1991-92 T'Wolves finished with the league's worst record. After the season, Minnesota drafted Christian Laettner and landed standouts Chuck Person and Micheal Williams in a trade for Richardson and Sam Mitchell. Nevertheless, the 1992-93 club still lacked the talent to win 20 games. In midseason, Rodgers was replaced by the young Sidney Lowe.

Last Four Years

Season	W	L	Pct.	Place	Playoffs	Coach
1989-90	22	60	.268	Sixth	DNQ	Bill Musselman
1990-91	29	53	.354	Fifth	DNQ	Bill Musselman
1991-92	15	67	.183	Sixth	DNQ	Jimmy Rodgers
1992-93	19	63	.232	Fifth	DNQ	J. Rodgers/Sidney Lowe

1992-93 Review

Thank God for Dallas. That was the refrain heard in the Land of 10,000 Lakes throughout the 1992-93 season. If the Mavwrecks hadn't been so awful, the distinction of being the NBA's worst team would have fallen on the Timberwolves, who finished a poor fifth in the Midwest Division.

Four years after its birth, Minnesota is the only recent NBA expansion team still acting like an expansion team. Minnesota "improved" to 19-63 in 1992-93, a four-game jump from the previous year's wretched performance. At this rate, the Wolves may make the playoffs before the next century—maybe.

The T'Wolves scored only 98.1 PPG, the worst mark in the league, and allowed opponents to shoot 48.8 percent, fourth worst in the NBA. And no team rebounded more poorly than the T'Dogs. Don't blame coach Sidney Lowe, who replaced Jimmy Rodgers in midseason and should have received combat pay.

Heralded first-round draft pick Christian Laettner posted respectable enough statistics but was soft inside. He also grabbed the league's Spoiled Brat Award for his temper tantrums, practice no-shows, and arrogant remarks.

Leading scorer Doug West scored in bushels, shooting 51.7 percent on his way to a career-high 19.3 PPG. Chuck Person was not too happy in the snow belt, and his 43.3-percent shooting and a career-low scoring average reflected that. Point guard Micheal Williams was solid, and his season-ending string of 84 free throws in a row broke Calvin Murphy's NBA record.

The big trouble—once again—was in the middle, where career disappointments Luc Longley and Felton Spencer took up space and did little else. Another frustration was forward Thurl Bailey, who was largely unproductive in a reserve role. Post man Bob McCann was a pleasant surprise, giving the Wolves some production in the middle, and 1992 second-round pick Marlon Maxey had his moments at forward. However, those bright spots were hardly enough to overcome another season-long circus in the Twin Cities.

1993-94 Roster

No.	Player	Pos.	Ht.	Wt.	Exp.	College	G	PPG	RPG	APG
41	Thurl Bailey	F	6'11"	232	10	N. Carolina St.	70	7.5	3.1	0.9
21	Lance Blanks	G	6'4"	195	3	Texas	61	2.6	1.1	1.2
—	Mike Brown	F/C	6'10"	260	7	G. Washington	82	5.7	4.8	0.8
32	Christian Laettner	F	6'11"	235	1	Duke	81	18.2	8.7	2.8
13	Luc Longley	C	7'2"	265	2	New Mexico	55	5.8	4.4	0.9
25	Marlon Maxey	F	6'8"	250	1	Texas-El Paso	43	5.4	3.8	0.3
30	Bob McCann	F	6'7"	248	3	Morehead St.	79	6.3	3.6	0.9
—	Sherron Mills	F/C	6'9"	220	R	Virginia Comm.	—	—	—	—
45	Chuck Person	F	6'8"	225	7	Auburn	78	16.8	5.6	4.4
—	Isaiah Rider	G	6'5"	215	R	UNLV	—	—	—	—
4	Brad Sellers	F	7'0"	227	6	Ohio St.	54	2.5	1.5	0.9
3	Chris Smith	G	6'3"	190	1	Connecticut	80	4.3	1.2	2.5
2	Gundars Vetra	G/F	6'6"	196	1	Latvia	13	3.5	0.6	0.5
5	Doug West	G	6'6"	200	4	Villanova	80	19.3	3.1	2.9
24	Micheal Williams	G	6'2"	175	5	Baylor	76	15.1	3.6	8.7

Minnesota Timberwolves
1993-94 Season Preview

Opening Line: While the other three recent expansion clubs zoom toward postseason play and contention, Minnesota remains a mess. The club's poor drafting history, questionable trades, and overall inability to land a superstar have left it well behind its expansion brethren. Sure, first-round pick Isaiah Rider will probably help this year, and the acquisition of Mike Brown might improve the front line. But no matter how cold it gets in Minneapolis during this long NBA winter, opponents will always find a warm reception at the Target Center.

Guard: In gunner Doug West, the Timberwolves have a no-conscience scorer who has an undeniably accurate stroke (51.7-percent shooting in 1992-93) and the ability to score inside or out. Don't expect any passing, rebounding, or defense, however. Expect the same from Rider, a prime-time scorer who can do it inside, outside, or on the break. He just might lead all rookies in scoring this year. Point guard Micheal Williams will again challenge for the league lead in assists, steals, and free throw percentage, although he'll also turn the ball over and get beaten defensively. Sophomore Chris Smith showed promise as a back-up point guard last year.

Forward: Anyone who thought Christian Laettner was a spoiled problem child in college was vindicated by his prima donna performance as an NBA rookie—missed practices, squabbles with teammates, etc. Though the former Blue Devil contributes much-needed scoring and rebounding to the T'Wolves' front line, he's a little soft and has an overly inflated opinion of himself. Trash-talker Chuck Person is a scorer, from anywhere, but isn't too fond of defense or rebounding. Thurl Bailey, once a heralded sixth man, has slipped considerably over the last couple years. Sherron Mills, a second-round pick, is a good athlete but probably won't see much P.T. Journeyman Bob McCann specializes in low-post defense.

Center: Ouch. Despite trying to draft for the position, Minnesota has not succeeded. Consequently, the Timberwolves have one of the worst pivot situations in the league. Brown should start here and will bring solid defense and rebounding, though he's slow and can't shoot. Luc Longley is slow and soft and would be playing back in Australia if he weren't seven feet tall.

Coaching: Sidney Lowe took over midway through last season for Jimmy Rodgers, proving some guys will do anything to coach in the NBA. Expect Lowe to bring the increasingly popular "player's perspective" to the bench, but he had better pair it with liberal doses of patience and optimism—not to mention antacid. He's assisted by Jim Brewer, Chuck Davisson, and Bob Weinhauer.

Analysis: Expect the Timberwolves and the Dallas Mavericks to stage a knock-down, drag-out fight for fifth place in the Midwest Division this year. The T'Wolves have too many personnel mistakes on their roster to improve quickly, so they'll have to rely on better judgment in ensuing lotteries to reshape their team. It will take some time.

Prediction: Fifth place, Midwest

SAN ANTONIO SPURS

Home: HemisFair Arena
Capacity: 16,057
Year Built: 1968

Address
600 E. Market, Suite 102
San Antonio, TX 78205
(210) 554-7787

Chief Executive Officer: Bob Coleman
V.P./Basketball Operations: Bob Bass
Head Coach: John Lucas
Assistant Coach: Ron Adams
Assistant Coach: Rex Hughes
Assistant Coach: George Gervin
Assistant Coach: Tom Thibodeau

Coach John Lucas			
	W	L	Pct.
NBA Record	40	22	.645
W/Spurs	40	22	.645
1992-93 Record	40	22	.645

Spurs History

This Texas franchise was born in Dallas in 1967 as a charter member of the ABA. Its name? The Dallas Chaparrals. The stay in Dallas was a haphazard one, featuring six coaches in six years, low attendance, and little playoff success.

Angelo Drossos moved the club to the home of the Alamo in 1973, and the team was renamed the Spurs. It was an exciting squad that fans embraced immediately. The Spurs had 50-plus-win seasons in 1974-75 and 1975-76 and moved into the NBA at full gallop.

Led by unstoppable guard George Gervin, mammoth center Artis Gilmore, and a talented supporting cast that included Johnny Moore, Larry Kenon, and James Silas, the Spurs won two Central and three Midwest Division championships in six years. Gervin was the NBA scoring champ four times. However, San Antonio could not make it to the NBA Finals, as it fell in the conference finals three times.

The Spurs' nucleus began to age in the mid-1980s, and the team fell from its lofty status. But the collapse did lead to something worthwhile. In 1987, the Spurs drafted David Robinson of Navy. The team continued to sag in the next two seasons while Robinson completed his military obligation, but he joined the Spurs in 1989-90.

Robinson immediately emerged as one of the NBA's best centers. He teamed with Terry Cummings and Sean Elliott to help San Antonio win the Midwest title in both 1989-90 and 1990-91. Despite fine records over the last four years, the Spurs haven't been able to reach the conference finals.

Last Seven Years

Season	W	L	Pct.	Place	Playoffs	Coach
1986-87	28	54	.341	Sixth	DNQ	Bob Weiss
1987-88	31	51	.378	Fifth	L-Round 1	Bob Weiss
1988-89	21	61	.256	Fifth	DNQ	Larry Brown
1989-90	56	26	.683	First	L-West Semis	Larry Brown
1990-91	55	27	.671	First	L-Round 1	Larry Brown
1991-92	47	35	.573	Second	L-Round 1	Larry Brown/Bob Bass
1992-93	49	33	.598	Second	L-West Semis	J. Tarkanian/John Lucas

1992-93 Review

In a storage room somewhere deep in the recesses of San Antonio's HemisFair Arena, there lay boxes and boxes of Shark Attack promotional materials. Their value plummeted last December when the Spurs dumped former UNLV coach Jerry Tarkanian as their bench jockey. Tark the Shark had amassed a weak 9-11 record during his short tenure in San Antonio, not quite justification for the quick hook. However, his complete lack of knowledge of the pro game and apparent inability to learn quickly were.

San Antonio owner Red McCombs made the quick coaching change. Tark was out. John Lucas, a recovering alcohol and drug addict, was in. The Spurs ignited under Lucas's leadership, winning 24 of their next 27 games and becoming significant players in the Midwest Division. San Antonio won 49 games, beat Portland in the playoffs, and lost to Phoenix in a hard-fought, six-game Western Conference semifinal series.

Lucas's sudden success was amazing considering the personnel problems San Antonio encountered. Sure, David Robinson was again a supreme presence in the middle, doing it all, and sleek Sean Elliott had another fine year at small forward. But that was about it for the constants.

Veteran power forward Terry Cummings played in only eight games after suffering a knee injury during a pick-up game in the summer of '92. Gunslinging guard Willie Anderson missed most of the year while rehabilitating from surgery on both legs. And point guard Rod Strickland was no longer around, as he had bolted for Portland before the season.

So, the Spurs scrambled. Midseason acquisition J.R. Reid and grizzled vet Antoine Carr held down Cummings's four spot, each making significant contributions. Dale Ellis had his best year in the last three at shooting guard. And the troika of nomad Avery Johnson, former Italian League star Vinny Del Negro, and renowned problem child Lloyd Daniels got it done at the point.

1993-94 Roster

No.	Player	Pos.	Ht.	Wt.	Exp.	College	G	PPG	RPG	APG
40	Willie Anderson	G/F	6'8"	200	5	Georgia	38	4.8	1.5	2.1
35	Antoine Carr	F	6'9"	255	9	Wichita St.	71	13.1	5.5	1.4
34	Terry Cummings	F	6'9"	245	11	DePaul	8	3.4	2.4	0.5
24	Lloyd Daniels	G	6'7"	205	1	None	77	9.1	2.8	1.9
15	Vinny Del Negro	G	6'6"	200	3	N. Carolina St.	73	7.4	2.2	4.0
32	Sean Elliott	F	6'8"	215	4	Arizona	70	17.2	4.6	3.8
3	Dale Ellis	G	6'7"	215	10	Tennessee	82	16.7	3.8	1.3
—	Sleepy Floyd	G	6'3"	183	11	Georgetown	52	6.6	1.7	2.5
6	Avery Johnson	G	5'11"	175	5	Southern	75	8.7	1.9	7.5
5	Sam Mack	F	6'7"	220	1	Houston	40	3.6	1.2	0.4
7	J.R. Reid	F/C	6'9"	265	4	North Carolina	83	9.4	5.5	1.0
50	David Robinson	C	7'1"	235	4	Navy	82	23.4	11.7	3.7
2	Larry Smith	F/C	6'8"	250	13	Alcorn St.	66	1.3	4.1	0.4
—	Chris Whitney	G	6'0"	171	R	Clemson	—	—	—	—
10	David Wood	F	6'9"	230	3	Nevada-Reno	64	2.4	1.5	0.5

San Antonio Spurs
1993-94 Season Preview

Opening Line: Finally, things can return to normal at the NBA's South Texas outpost. The injuries are healed, the coaching spot is secured, and everyone can talk about basketball. This year, the Spurs will try to continue the momentum that extended Phoenix to six games in the Western semis. They do so with a deep lineup, plenty of scoring pop, and one of the league's great superstars—David Robinson—in the middle.

Guard: Between Avery Johnson, Vinny Del Negro, and Lloyd "Sweet Pea" Daniels, San Antonio has a complete lead guard, each of the men adding something different to the mix. Johnson is a steady performer with good court sense and an improved jump shot. Del Negro is a little flashier, bolder in the open court, and more likely to look for his own shot. Daniels is streaky and lax on defense but is brilliant at times on offense. Two guard Dale Ellis seems to be on good behavior in San Antonio, and he is a potent weapon—especially when he shoots like he did last year (50 percent). Sleek Willie Anderson may not be the best shooter, but he can score—particularly if his legs are completely recovered from surgery that robbed him of most of last year. The Spurs also signed Sleepy Floyd, but his best days are behind him.

Forward: Sean Elliott is still not the most rugged forward around, but he can score from most anywhere and has a deft passing touch. He moaned a little about persistent trade rumors last season but he's a multi-talented star-in-the-making. Veteran Terry Cummings should return to form at power forward, provided his reconstructed knee obliges. He has a myriad of low-post offensive moves and is a solid rebounding complement to the Admiral. J.R. Reid is still not the superstar folks thought he would be when he came into the league, but he's a wide body who can bang and score some. Grizzled vet Antoine Carr brings much of the same up front, enhancing San Antonio's physical presence.

Center: Four years into his NBA life, Robinson is one of the elite NBA centers. He scores just about any way you want, is ferocious on the boards, and blocks shots by the handful. And—surprise—he was second on the team in assists last year. His game is flawless.

Coaching: In less than a year, John Lucas has established himself as one of the top player's coaches around. Now, the challenge is for him to do it again. Over the summer, Lucas coached his Miami Tropics team in the USBL, so he'll have to guard against burnout. He is assisted by Rex Hughes, Ron Adams, George Gervin, and Tom Thibodeau.

Analysis: Last year at this time, the Spurs were the thinnest team in the league. Now, with everyone reasonably healthy, they're one of the deepest. San Antonio can bang, run, or play solid halfcourt ball and should overcome Houston for the top spot in the Midwest Division. If Cummings and Anderson regain their old magic, this could be a dynamite team.

Prediction: First place, Midwest

UTAH JAZZ

Home: Delta Center
Capacity: 19,500
Year Built: 1991

Address
Delta Center
301 W. South Temple
Salt Lake City, UT 84101
(801) 325-2500

Owner: Larry H. Miller
General Manager: Tim Howells
Head Coach: Jerry Sloan
Assistant Coach: Phil Johnson
Assistant Coach: Gordon Chiesa
Assistant Coach: David Fredman

Coach Jerry Sloan			
	W	L	Pct.
NBA Record	345	263	.567
W/Jazz	251	142	.639
1992-93 Record	47	35	.573

Jazz History

About the last city you'd expect to find a team named the Jazz would be in puritan Salt Lake City, Utah. However, the name comes with an easy explanation. When the franchise was born back in 1974, its hometown was New Orleans, a jazzy place if ever there was one. When it moved west in 1979, it decided to hold onto the name.

The early days did have their moments. In the mid-1970s, Louisiana native "Pistol" Pete Maravich lit up the Bayou, scoring baskets in bushels and once torching the Knicks for 68. Maravich's knee went out in 1977-78 and, despite the emergence of all-world rebounder Leonard "Truck" Robinson, the Jazz limped along for several years.

Coach Frank Layden was hired in 1981-82 and immediately became popular for his sense of humor and regular-guy charm. The Jazz captured the Midwest Division crown in 1983-84 and advanced to the conference semifinals, relying on league scoring leader Adrian Dantley, quick backcourt men Darrell Griffith and Ricky Green, and mammoth, 7'4" center Mark Eaton.

The Jazz selected power forward Karl Malone in the 1985 draft, and he was an immediate sensation, teaming with assist machine John Stockton to form a solid nucleus. Utah won the 1988-89 Midwest title under new coach Jerry Sloan but fell in the first round of the playoffs. Utah advanced to the conference semis in 1990-91, and in 1991-92 the Jazz fell to Portland in the West finals.

Last Seven Years

Season	W	L	Pct.	Place	Playoffs	Coach
1986-87	44	38	.537	Second	L-Round 1	Frank Layden
1987-88	47	35	.573	Third	L-West Semis	Frank Layden
1988-89	51	31	.622	First	L-Round 1	Frank Layden/Jerry Sloan
1989-90	55	27	.671	Second	L-Round 1	Jerry Sloan
1990-91	54	28	.659	Second	L-West Semis	Jerry Sloan
1991-92	55	27	.671	First	L-West Finals	Jerry Sloan
1992-93	47	35	.573	Third	L-Round 1	Jerry Sloan

1992-93 Review

After reaching the "next level" in 1991-92—the Western Conference finals—the Jazz plunged back to their old ways in 1992-93 and looked dangerously like a team with a past brighter than its future. Utah failed to win 50 games for the first time since 1987-88, and the Jazz were dismissed in the first round of the playoffs by Seattle in an ugly five-game series, during which Utah did not top 92 points in any one game.

The slump produced a season-long chorus of calls for coach Jerry Sloan's scalp, but he couldn't be faulted for injuries that kept gigantic center Mark Eaton out of 18 games and a roster that had severe limitations.

In 1992-93, Karl Malone, Jeff Malone, and John Stockton were Utah's focal points—again. But last year, three-man basketball didn't quite do it in the Midwest Division. The Jazz had trouble with team-oriented Houston and San Antonio and fell behind each in the standings.

The powerful Karl Malone showed no effects of post-Olympic fatigue, posting his usual high numbers in scoring and rebounding and once again leading the league in free throw attempts. But Stockton's assist numbers fell and his minutes played were the lowest in five seasons. Still, few point guards were better, and it would be wrong to blame Stockton for the Jazz's fall.

Jeff Malone had another solid year, shooting well, scoring plenty, and generally avoiding the lane and effort on defense. Forward Tyrone Corbin had a big year starting in place of Blue Edwards, who was traded to Milwaukee, but that was about it for Utah's offensive output.

Eaton was again a mammoth presence in the middle, but his rebounding and shot-blocking numbers were well below his usual output, and—of course—his offense was awful. Former Buck Jay Humphries spelled Stockton at the point but wasn't a huge scoring threat. Neither was David Benoit or Larry Krystkowiak, another Milwaukee refugee. Mike Brown enjoyed banging underneath, but his limited game precluded him from being anything more than a back-up center.

1993-94 Roster

| No. | Player | Pos. | Ht. | Wt. | Exp. | College | 1992-93 | | |
							G	PPG	RPG	APG
50	Isaac Austin	C	6'10"	290	2	Arizona St.	46	2.8	1.7	0.1
21	David Benoit	F	6'8"	220	2	Alabama	82	8.1	4.8	0.5
—	Tom Chambers	F	6'10"	230	12	Utah	73	12.2	4.7	1.4
23	Tyrone Corbin	F	6'6"	222	8	DePaul	82	11.6	6.3	2.1
25	John Crotty	G	6'1"	185	1	Virginia	40	2.6	0.4	1.4
54	James Donaldson	C	7'2	278	13	Washington St.	6	3.5	4.8	0.2
53	Mark Eaton	C	7'4"	286	11	UCLA	64	2.8	4.1	0.3
6	Jay Humphries	G	6'3"	185	9	Colorado	78	8.8	1.8	4.1
42	Larry Krystkowiak	F	6'10"	240	7	Montana	71	7.2	3.9	1.0
24	Jeff Malone	G	6'4"	205	10	Mississippi St.	79	18.1	2.2	1.6
32	Karl Malone	F	6'9"	256	8	Louisiana Tech	82	27.0	11.1	3.8
—	Bryon Russell	F	6'7"	225	R	Long Beach St.	—	—	—	—
—	Felton Spencer	C	7'0"	265	3	Louisville	71	4.1	4.6	0.2
12	John Stockton	G	6'1"	175	9	Gonzaga	82	15.1	2.9	12.0
—	Luther Wright	C	7'2"	300	R	Seton Hall	—	—	—	—

Utah Jazz
1993-94 Season Preview

Opening Line: Just who were those guys zipping past Utah in the Midwest Division last year, and how in the world can the Jazz catch up? Like many of the teams that have enjoyed consistent success over the last decade, the Jazz are at a crossroads. The current nucleus is too good to smash apart but not good enough to challenge for the NBA title. The Jazz revamped their center position over the summer, trading Mike Brown for 7'0" Felton Spencer and drafting 7'2" project Luther Wright. Utah also signed 6'10" shooter Tom Chambers.

Guard: Okay, so maybe John Stockton's numbers at the point were down a little last year. He still remains the league's premier assist machine, and his scoring is still above average for his position. If Jay Humphries hadn't arrived last year to give him a little rest, Stockton would have had his 1,000-plus assists. The Jazz are glad to have Humphries around. He can back up at both guard spots and he brings quickness to a pretty slow team. Shooter Jeff Malone remains a successful hired gun from inside 20 feet, but he brings nothing else to the proceedings.

Forward: The Mailman continues to deliver on schedule. Karl Malone rebounds with a vengeance, shoots for a high percentage, scores on the fastbreak, and gets to the line more than anyone in the NBA. Year after year, he reigns as the game's best power forward. There's a big drop-off at the three spot, however. Tyrone Corbin will score and rebound, but be prepared for a truckload of fouls. Benoit runs the court and can hit the 3-pointer, but he's streaky and lacking on defense. Chambers plays soft, but he'll provide needed offense off the bench. Larry Krystkowiak is a solid back-up at both positions.

Center: Let's get this straight. Utah didn't win anything of consequence with mammoth Mark Eaton plugging up the middle, so it went out and got 14 more feet of hulking pivot projects. Let's hope the Delta Center's foundation is solid. Eaton is slow, but at least he's imposing on defense. Spencer is slower and often lost. And Wright could be three years away from contributing anything.

Coaching: Jerry Sloan needed a bulletproof vest to handle all the flak directed at him last year. Hey, is it his fault the Jazz front office hasn't been able to provide him with the talent to go to the next level? No way. But remember who's the first to go when there's trouble. Keep the resume fresh, Jerry. He's assisted by Gordon Chiesa, David Fredman, and Phil Johnson.

Analysis: This is a crucial year for the Utah franchise. A return to Midwest Division primacy and a couple playoff series wins will keep the folks happy. Another slide into the middle of the pack and a quick postseason exit will probably lead to a big shake-up. Bet on the latter. The Jazz will struggle to stay close to Houston and San Antonio, and they won't have enough to stay with any of the Pacific heavies—except on the scales.

Prediction: Third place, Midwest

GOLDEN STATE WARRIORS

Home: Oakland Coliseum Arena
Capacity: 15,025
Year Built: 1966

Chairman: Jim Fitzgerald
General Manager: Don Nelson
Head Coach: Don Nelson
Assistant Coach: Donn Nelson
Assistant Coach: Gregg Popovich
Assistant Coach: Paul Pressey

Address
Oakland Coliseum Arena
Oakland, CA 94621
(510) 638-6300

Coach Don Nelson			
	W	L	Pct.
NBA Record	753	541	.582
W/Warriors	213	197	.520
1992-93 Record	34	48	.415

Warriors History

Present-day Warrior fans may find it difficult to identify with the team's East Coast roots. For 16 seasons, the Philadelphia Warriors enjoyed success in the old BAA and as a charter member of the NBA. Philadelphia won the first BAA championship in 1946-47 behind scoring machine Joe Fulks.

The Warriors advanced to the BAA finals in 1948, losing to Baltimore. But they defeated Fort Wayne in 1956 to win the NBA title behind Paul Arizin, Neil Johnston, and Tom Gola. In 1959, Wilt Chamberlain joined the team and was an immediate sensation, winning the MVP Award in his rookie season. The team moved to San Francisco in 1962 and lost to Boston in the NBA Finals in 1963-64. The Warriors traded Chamberlain to the new Philadelphia 76ers in 1964-65, then lost to the Sixers in the NBA Finals two years later.

The Warriors changed their name to Golden State in 1971 and moved across the bay to Oakland, where the championship drought continued until 1974-75. That year, coach Al Attles incorporated a ten-man rotation around Rick Barry and took the Warriors to the NBA title.

The Warriors didn't rebound again until 1988, when Don Nelson took over as coach. Using a small lineup built around Chris Mullin and Mitch Richmond, the Warriors made it to the Western semis in 1988-89. Point guard Tim Hardaway was added for the 1989-90 season, and in 1990-91 Golden State again advanced to the West semis, losing to Los Angeles.

Last Seven Years

Season	W	L	Pct.	Place	Playoffs	Coach
1986-87	42	40	.512	Third	L-West Semis	George Karl
1987-88	20	62	.244	Fifth	DNQ	George Karl/Ed Gregory
1988-89	43	39	.524	Fourth	L-West Semis	Don Nelson
1989-90	37	45	.451	Fifth	DNQ	Don Nelson
1990-91	44	38	.537	Fourth	L-West Semis	Don Nelson
1991-92	55	27	.671	Second	L-Round 1	Don Nelson
1992-93	34	48	.415	Sixth	DNQ	Don Nelson

1992-93 Review

In the past, treatises on the Warriors' failures always began with some clever metaphor for lack of height. Had Golden State remained injury-free last season, that procedure would have been repeated here. As it was, a slew of physical miseries never even gave Don Nelson's gang a chance.

This wasn't your usual run of bad luck that hits a starter or a few reserves. Hardly anyone was spared. Star forward Chris Mullin played only 46 games before tearing a ligament in his right thumb and requiring surgery. Sarunas Marciulionis missed all but 30 games with a broken leg and bad ankle. Tim Hardaway's cranky knee cost him 16 games, Billy Owens made only 37 contests, and a variety of problems limited aging center Alton Lister to just 20 appearances. Mullin, Marciulionis, Hardaway, and Owens appeared on the court together a total of two minutes, 37 seconds in 1992-93.

The resulting 34-48 record and sixth-place Pacific Division finish were entirely predictable, given that M*A*S*H scenario. The only good news was that Golden State finally got a lottery pick to spend on a big man. And they needed one because—even without injuries—Chris Gatling, Victor Alexander, Tyrone Hill, and Jud Buechler weren't enough up front.

When healthy, Hardaway was his usual lightning-quick self, becoming the only man in the league to reach 20 PPG and ten APG. Mullin was on his way to another all-world season when the thumb went, and Marciulionis and Owens would have filled in the other parts of the World's Greatest Offense had they been healthy.

The big surprise by the Bay was rookie Latrell Sprewell, a supposed defensive specialist who turned into one of the team's MVPs. He scored, he ran the team, and he played killer "D." Of course, he was only 6'4". To their credit, Alexander and Gatling tried hard in the middle, but neither is an NBA center. Hill did his part on the glass, tallying 10.1 caroms per game.

1993-94 Roster

No.	Player	Pos.	Ht.	Wt.	Exp.	College	G	PPG	RPG	APG
								1992-93		
52	Victor Alexander	C/F	6'9"	265	2	Iowa St.	72	11.2	5.8	1.3
35	Jud Buechler	F/G	6'6"	220	3	Arizona	70	6.2	2.8	1.3
45	Joe Courtney	F	6'8"	240	1	S. Mississippi	12	2.8	1.6	0.3
25	Chris Gatling	F/C	6'10"	225	2	Old Dominion	70	9.3	4.6	0.6
—	Josh Grant	F	6'9"	223	R	Utah	—	—	—	—
44	Jeff Grayer	G/F	6'5"	210	5	Iowa St.	48	8.8	3.3	1.5
10	Tim Hardaway	G	6'0"	195	4	Texas-El Paso	66	21.5	4.0	10.6
3	Sean Higgins	G/F	6'9"	210	3	Michigan	29	8.3	2.3	2.3
21	Byron Houston	F	6'5"	250	1	Oklahoma St.	79	5.3	4.0	0.9
2	Keith Jennings	G	5'7"	160	1	E. Tenn. St.	8	8.6	1.4	2.9
13	S. Marciulionis	G	6'5"	215	4	Lithuania	30	17.4	3.2	3.5
17	Chris Mullin	F	6'7"	215	8	St. John's	46	25.9	5.0	3.6
30	Billy Owens	F/G	6'9"	220	2	Syracuse	37	16.5	7.1	3.9
12	Andre Spencer	F	6'6"	210	1	N. Arizona	20	9.4	4.1	1.2
15	Latrell Sprewell	G	6'5"	190	1	Alabama	77	15.4	3.5	3.8
4	Chris Webber	F/C	6'9"	245	R	Michigan	—	—	—	—

Golden State Warriors
1993-94 Season Preview

Opening Line: Future? Heck, the future is now. Don Nelson said as much when he dished three first-round draft choices, as well as 1993 draft pick Anfernee Hardaway, to Orlando for rookie stud Chris Webber. Webber should provide instant presence down low, something Golden State has lacked for years. He'll replace Tyrone Hill, who left as a free agent. Nelson still must hope that Chris Mullin, Billy Owens, Tim Hardaway, and Sarunas Marciulionis—all injured last year—are healthy again.

Guard: Hardaway continues to be one of the league's top point men. He'll dazzle with his crossover dribble, score more than 20 PPG, and challenge for the league lead in assists. Marciulionis, who missed most of last year with leg problems, can score with the best in the league. If either guy falters, expect second-year man Latrell Sprewell to shine. Sprewell got a chance to play because of injuries last season and excelled on both ends of the floor. Jeff Grayer, another of the team's walking wounded last season, is a versatile two or three man. Keith Jennings had major knee surgery last year and may not return to his lightning-quick self.

Forward: Until he injured his thumb, Chris Mullin was cruising toward another big-number campaign. If healthy, Mullin will murder teams with his bull's-eye shooting and special "point forward" skills. Owens, who had off-season arthroscopic knee surgery, is now a medical question mark—as well as a potential attitude problem. When he wants to play, Owens can set up at four different positions and be effective. Byron Houston, a 6'5" bruiser, is best described as a poor man's Charles Barkley. Second-round pick Josh Grant, age 26, might hang on as a fill-in.

Center: He may be better suited as a power forward, but Webber will open the season as the starting center. Webber's hands are large and strong, and he'll rip rebounds right out of the hands of his opponents. He can handle the ball but needs work shooting it. Portly Victor Alexander is a solid scorer but soft on defense. The same can be said for Chris Gatling.

Coaching: It's no secret. Nelson needs to win—now. His fun days of playing five small guys yielded a little excitement but few results. With Webber in the middle, Golden State may not be the prototypical NBA team, but Nelson finally has a big man. He's assisted by his son Donn, Gregg Popovich, and Paul Pressey.

Analysis: The addition of Webber should make an enormous difference for the Warriors, but the team's health is just as important. If all the big guns stay injury-free all year, expect Golden State to be tough—particularly by season's end. Webber won't have to score to be effective, since Mullin, Hardaway, Marciulionis, and/or Owens will handle that responsibility. He just needs to battle inside and rip down boards, which he will. The Warriors will be one of the most talented, exciting, and interesting teams in the league this year.

Prediction: Third place, Pacific

LOS ANGELES CLIPPERS

Home: L.A. Memorial Sports Arena
Capacity: 16,150
Year Built: 1959

Address
3939 S. Figueroa St.
Los Angeles, CA 90037
(213) 748-8000

Owner: Donald T. Sterling
General Manager: Elgin Baylor
Head Coach: Bob Weiss
Assistant Coach: Dave Wohl
Assistant Coach: Johnny Davis

Coach Bob Weiss	W	L	Pct.
NBA Record	183	227	.446
W/Clippers	0	0	.000
1992-93 Record	43	39	.524

Clippers History

Despite brief success in the mid-1970s, and playoff appearances the last two years, the Clippers have been one of the league's weakest and most poorly managed teams.

Born the Buffalo Braves in 1970, the team flourished briefly under the direction of Jack Ramsay. The Braves crept above the .500 mark (42-40) in 1973-74, behind NBA scoring leader Bob McAdoo and slick playmaker Ernie DiGregorio. The Braves improved to 49-33 the next season with MVP McAdoo again leading the way. Washington bounced the Braves from the 1975 Eastern semifinals, but the Braves persevered and whipped Philadelphia in the first round of the 1976 playoffs, before succumbing to Boston in the semis.

Thus ended the good times for Braves/Clippers fans. Prior to the 1978-79 season, Braves owner John Y. Brown traded the team to Irving Levin in return for control of the Celtics. Levin moved the club to San Diego, renamed it the Clippers, and watched it register an abysmal 17-65 mark in 1981-82. The Clippers moved north to L.A. for the 1984-85 season and were an immediate poor cousin to the flourishing Lakers.

Though it won 30-plus games in 1984-85 and 1985-86, L.A. embarked on three straight miserable seasons, with the lowlight being a 12-70 mark in 1986-87. Despite young and talented players like Charles Smith, Ron Harper, and Danny Manning, the Clippers failed to rise above mediocrity in the late '80s and early '90s.

Last Seven Years

Season	W	L	Pct.	Place	Playoffs	Coach
1986-87	12	70	.146	Sixth	DNQ	Don Chaney
1987-88	17	65	.207	Sixth	DNQ	Gene Shue
1988-89	21	61	.256	Seventh	DNQ	Gene Shue/Don Casey
1989-90	30	52	.366	Sixth	DNQ	Don Casey
1990-91	31	51	.378	Sixth	DNQ	Mike Schuler
1991-92	45	37	.549	Fifth	L-Round 1	Mike Schuler/Mack Calvin/Larry Brown
1992-93	41	41	.500	Fourth	L-Round 1	Larry Brown

1992-93 Review

Admit it, Los Angelenos. For a while there, you were hiding your purple-and-gold Laker paraphernalia and joining the rush for that red-white-and-blue Clipper gear. In 1991-92, Larry Brown's exciting team won 45 games, crashed the playoff party, and gave L.A. hope that while Showtime was over, Cliptime was on the horizon.

Forget it. The high hopes that preceded the 1992-93 season were soon diminished, as the Clippers sagged into their usual morass of uneven play, contract disputes, and backbiting. Sure, they finished the 1992-93 season at 41-41 (ahead of the Lakers) and even extended Houston to a fifth game in the playoffs' first round before losing. But throughout the year, the feeling that trouble—big trouble—loomed was apparent.

By year's end, a few things were givens. Solid forward Ken Norman, a reliable scorer and rebounder, was headed for the free-agent waters. His frontcourt mate talented but petulant Danny Manning, had made it clear that he was staying in L.A. for one more year and then bolting to a team that would satisfy his gargantuan contract demands. And injury-prone Ron Harper concluded the year with an option season remaining on his $4 million-a-year contract, leaving the Clips with a tough choice. After the season, Brown decided to resign and try his luck somewhere else.

Manning had another strong year—tallying points, rebounds, and assists—and Harper was his usual versatile self. Off-season acquisition Mark Jackson avoided controversy and had a steady year at the point, and reliable Loy Vaught posted high rebounding numbers per minutes played.

L.A.'s curious fat frontcourt tandem of center Stanley Roberts and power forward John "Hot Plate" Williams was maddeningly inconsistent, and rookie center Elmore Spencer was overmatched. Gary Grant took his demotion from the starting point-guard spot without much squawking and performed adequately, but rookie guard Randy Woods—last year's first-round pick—was erratic and played just 174 minutes.

1993-94 Roster

No.	Player	Pos.	Ht.	Wt.	Exp.	College	G	PPG	RPG	APG
7	Lester Conner	G	6'4"	180	10	Oregon St.	31	2.4	1.6	2.1
—	Terry Dehere	G	6'2"	190	R	Seton Hall	—	—	—	—
23	Gary Grant	G	6'3"	195	5	Michigan	74	6.6	1.9	4.8
4	Ron Harper	G	6'6"	198	7	Miami (OH)	80	18.0	5.3	4.5
8	Jaren Jackson	F	6'6"	200	3	Georgetown	34	3.9	1.1	1.0
13	Mark Jackson	G	6'3"	192	6	St. John's	82	14.4	4.7	8.8
—	Henry James	F	6'9"	220	3	St. Mary's (TX)	8	7.5	1.3	0.1
5	Danny Manning	F	6'10"	234	5	Kansas	79	22.8	6.6	2.6
53	Stanley Roberts	C	7'0"	290	2	Louisiana St.	77	11.3	6.2	0.8
27	Elmore Spencer	C	7'0"	270	1	UNLV	44	2.4	1.4	0.2
55	Kiki Vandeweghe	F	6'8"	220	13	UCLA	41	6.2	1.2	0.6
35	Loy Vaught	C	6'9"	240	3	Michigan	79	9.4	6.2	0.7
34	John Williams	F	6'9"	300	6	Louisiana St.	74	6.6	4.3	1.9
14	Randy Woods	G	6'0"	190	1	La Salle	41	1.7	0.3	1.0

Los Angeles Clippers
1993-94 Season Preview

Opening Line: What a shock. Larry Brown, the NBA's traveling coaching show, lasted a season and a half in Cliptown before heading to Indiana. Sure, Brown injected a little excitement into the dormant Clippers for a while, but by the time he abandoned the team, it was headed straight back toward its old laughingstock status. The 1993-94 roster boasts some talent but also features big doses of unhappiness, big egos, and big bellies. Forward Ken Norman has already departed as a free agent. Danny Manning should leave after this season and Ron Harper will probably follow him. Draft pick Terry Dehere of Seton Hall will try to ease the pain.

Guard: The Clippers exercised their right to keep Ron Harper in town for another year, meaning they'll get 82 more exciting games from the versatile 6'6" two man. Harper can score (although his shooting isn't the greatest), hit the boards, and excel on the fastbreak. He teams nicely with Mark Jackson, a former malcontent who has emerged as a team leader. Jackson distributes it well, loves the open court, and can even get up on the boards at times. Dehere can light it up in bunches and he handles the ball pretty well. Though a bit streaky, Dehere still likes to take the big shot. Deposed point man Gary Grant continues to be inconsistent, shooting poorly and committing plenty of turnovers. Randy Woods, taken with the 16th pick in last year's draft, turned out to be a bust.

Forward: When he wasn't fighting with Brown in hotels, Manning had another productive season last year, further solidifying his status as one of the game's top all-around talents. Pity he has only one more year in Los Angeles. Pudgy John Williams has many of the same all-around skills as Manning but little of the desire or work ethic. Loy Vaught, on the other hand, understands his role as designated banger quite well. He's good for ten points and six boards a night.

Center: If Williams is fat, Stanley Roberts is downright obese. Roberts can block shots and score around the basket, but he's the only player in the league whose weight and personal fouls are both over the 300 mark. Second-year pro Elmore Spencer is another plodding big man. He needs a lot of work.

Coaching: No one seemed to want the Clippers' head-coaching job, and it took the team until the end of July to find a taker. They came to terms with Bob Weiss, the former Atlanta Hawks coach. Though certainly not one of the league's marquee coaches, Weiss prefers an up-tempo, wide-open offense, which will fit the Clips' style. He's assisted by Dave Wohl and Johnny Davis.

Analysis: The good times are over in Clipperland. (Did they ever really start?) Weiss must keep this sinking ship afloat, but it won't be easy. Williams and Roberts are weighing the boat down, while Manning and others are looking to jump ship. Don't be surprised if Weiss becomes the team's 15th coaching casualty since 1976.

Prediction: Sixth place, Pacific

LOS ANGELES LAKERS

Home: The Great Western Forum
Capacity: 17,505
Year Built: 1967

Address
3900 W. Manchester Blvd.
P.O. Box 10
Inglewood, CA 90306
(310) 419-3100

Owner: Dr. Jerry Buss
General Manager: Jerry West
Head Coach: Randy Pfund
Assistant Coach: Bill Bertka
Assistant Coach: Larry Drew
Assistant Coach: Chet Kammerer

Coach Randy Pfund			
	W	L	Pct.
NBA Record	39	43	.476
W/Lakers	39	43	.476
1992-93 Record	39	43	.476

Lakers History

No team has equaled the tradition and success of the Boston Celtics, but the Lakers have come close. During the franchise's 45 years of existence, it has put a dazzling array of talent onto NBA courts. Along the way, it has won 11 world championships.

The Laker magic began in Minneapolis and was built around 6'10" center George Mikan, clearly the premier player of his day. With Mikan, Bob Pollard, Vern Mikkelsen, and Slater Martin, the Minneapolis Lakers won five titles in six years from 1949-54. In 1960, the team moved to Los Angeles, keeping its Minnesota-style nickname. But the early years in L.A. led to heartbreak, as the Lakers lost in the NBA Finals to the Celtics six times, despite the heroics of guard Jerry West and forward Elgin Baylor.

Even the arrival of Wilt Chamberlain in 1968-69 couldn't stop the string of runner-up finishes. The Lakers dropped the 1968-69 series to the Celtics and the 1969-70 title series to the Knicks. The Lakers gained revenge two years later by going 69-13 (including a 33-game winning streak) and beating New York 4-1 in the Finals.

Kareem Abdul-Jabbar continued the tradition of Hall of Fame pivot men for the Lakers when he was acquired from Milwaukee in 1975. But it wasn't until Magic Johnson was drafted in 1979 that the Lakers truly began to shine. The team won five titles in the 1980s, including two over Boston, and assumed the "Showtime" image that predominated its home city.

Last Seven Years

Season	W	L	Pct.	Place	Playoffs	Coach
1986-87	65	17	.793	First	NBA Champs	Pat Riley
1987-88	62	20	.756	First	NBA Champs	Pat Riley
1988-89	57	25	.695	First	L-NBA Finals	Pat Riley
1989-90	63	19	.768	First	L-West Semis	Pat Riley
1990-91	58	24	.707	Second	L-NBA Finals	Mike Dunleavy
1991-92	43	39	.524	Sixth	L-Round 1	Mike Dunleavy
1992-93	39	43	.476	Fifth	L-Round 1	Randy Pfund

1992-93 Review

For two games, the entire Laker season suddenly had a purpose. Here was Los Angeles, a long way removed from the glorious Showtime days of the 1980s, holding a 2-0 first-round playoff lead over the best-record-in-the-NBA Phoenix Suns. Could L.A. pull off the biggest upset in playoff history?

Not quite. After winning a pair on enemy turf, the Lakers reverted to form and lost the next three. Though L.A. took the Suns to O.T. in Game 5, it wasn't enough to erase an unsavory season. The team's lackluster performance raised questions about first-year coach Randy Pfund's leadership abilities.

The season began when Magic Johnson, fresh off a superior performance in the Barcelona Dream Team Follies, re-retired amidst a growing storm of protest from fellow NBA players about Johnson's HIV-positive condition. Although veteran Sedale Threatt was a fine stand-in (and even led the team in scoring), he was no Magic, and the Lakers suffered.

The aging holdovers from Pat Riley's championship teams lacked their old luster. Shooting guard Byron Scott shot only 44.9 percent from the field and left the team at the end of the season to pursue free agency. Forward James Worthy performed with grit and vigor in the playoffs after a difficult regular season. Veteran front-line banger A.C. Green was his usual, reliable self but not nearly enough on an inconsistent forward wall.

L.A. shocked many by dishing center Sam Perkins to Seattle for perennial underachieving pivot man Benoit Benjamin and the rights to unsigned rookie guard Doug Christie. The move set up the Lakers' future backcourt by pairing the athletic and versatile Christie with fellow rookie gunner Anthony Peeler, who showed flashes of NBA competence.

With Perkins gone, Vlade Divac again became the focus in the middle, and again the big Serb import showed a periodic aversion to physical play, although his cranky back did hold up throughout the season. Elden Campbell continued to frustrate, mixing fine outings with disinterested performances.

1993-94 Roster

No.	Player	Pos.	Ht.	Wt.	Exp.	College	G	PPG	RPG	APG
							\-\-\-1992-93\-\-\-			
30	Alex Blackwell	F	6'6"	257	1	Monmouth	27	1.3	0.9	0.3
31	Sam Bowie	C	7'1"	263	8	Kentucky	79	9.1	7.0	1.6
41	Elden Campbell	F/C	6'11"	230	3	Clemson	79	7.7	4.2	0.6
8	Doug Christie	G/F	6'6"	205	R	Pepperdine	23	6.2	2.2	2.3
5	Duane Cooper	G	6'1"	185	1	Southern Cal.	65	2.4	0.8	2.3
12	Vlade Divac	C	7'1"	260	4	Yugoslavia	82	12.8	8.9	2.8
53	James Edwards	C	7'1"	252	16	Washington	52	6.3	1.9	0.8
45	A.C. Green	F	6'9"	224	8	Oregon St.	82	12.8	8.7	1.4
54	Jack Haley	F/C	6'10"	250	4	UCLA	—	—	—	—
—	George Lynch	F	6'8"	218	R	North Carolina	—	—	—	—
1	Anthony Peeler	G	6'4"	212	1	Missouri	77	10.4	2.3	2.2
34	Tony Smith	G	6'4"	205	3	Marquette	55	6.0	1.6	1.1
3	Sedale Threatt	G	6'2"	185	10	W. Virg. Tech	82	15.1	3.3	6.9
—	Nick Van Exel	G	6'1"	171	R	Cincinnati	—	—	—	—
42	James Worthy	F	6'9"	225	11	North Carolina	82	14.9	3.0	3.4

Los Angeles Lakers
1993-94 Season Preview

Opening Line: If the Lakers are going to even approach contention, Jerry West will have to reclaim his reputation as one of the league's shrewdest general managers. Acquiring Sam Bowie for deadwood Benoit Benjamin was a good first step, and getting rid of moody Byron Scott was another positive move. But the Lakers need the young backcourt of Doug Christie and Anthony Peeler to develop and must get consistent play from Elden Campbell. Rookie George Lynch might have to replace A.C. Green, a probable free-agent deserter.

Guard: He's certainly not Magic, but veteran Sedale Threatt is a capable NBA point guard. He takes care of the ball, shoots it judiciously, and even led the Lakers in scoring last year. With Scott gone, Peeler becomes the starting two guard. Peeler is athletic and possesses pretty good range, but he needs to become more consistent. Christie played very little last season, his first, due to a protracted holdout that ultimately forced his trade (with Benjamin for Sam Perkins) from Seattle to L.A. He's a 6'6" combination guard with all the athletic tools. Tony Smith, a defensive specialist, backs up Threatt at the point. Second-round pick Nick Van Exel, 6'1", can shoot a team into or out of a game.

Forward: Though his remaining days are few, and his swooping forays to the hoop have been replaced largely by a variety of low-post moves, James Worthy remains a very tangible reminder of the Lakers' Showtime era. Worthy is still dangerous on offense, although his consistency is lagging. It's time for Elden Campbell to make good on his potential—or risk being swept away by a youth movement. Campbell's annoying inconsistency has been well-documented, and it won't be tolerated much longer. Lynch is a strong rebounder and tenacious defender, though he can't shoot worth a lick.

Center: The acquisition of Bowie gives the Lakers a pair of mobile combination pivot men with histories of injury. Bowie will play some pretty good defense and can grab rebounds, although don't expect Ewing-like numbers. Vlade Divac rebounded from back surgery nicely last year but remains the prototypical European big man, preferring to stay outside than to mix it up around the hoop.

Coaching: Randy Pfund's job was in jeopardy late in his rookie year, but a strong showing against the Suns in the first round of the playoffs might have saved him. However, he won't last long if the Lakers remain stagnant, no matter how much he looks like Pat Riley. He's assisted by Bill Bertka, Larry Drew, and Chet Kammerer.

Analysis: The Lakers are in transition, and things aren't going to get better too quickly. The frontcourt is crumbling, the backcourt is young, and no one has the star quality of the old days. L.A. may sneak into the playoffs, but it will not advance past the first round. Until the guards mature and some capable forwards are found, the Lakers will wallow in mediocrity.

Prediction: Fifth place, Pacific

PHOENIX SUNS

Home: America West Arena
Capacity: 19,000
Year Built: 1992

Address
P.O. Box 1369
Phoenix, AZ 85001
(602) 379-7900

Chief Executive Officer:
Jerry Colangelo
V.P./Player Personnel:
Dick Van Arsdale
Head Coach: Paul Westphal
Assistant Coach: Scotty Robertson
Assistant Coach: Lionel Hollins

Coach Paul Westphal			
	W	L	Pct.
NBA Record	62	20	.756
W/Suns	62	20	.756
1992-93 Record	62	20	.756

Suns History

If there is one team in the NBA synonymous with the term "near miss," it is the Suns. Throughout its 25-year history, Phoenix has missed out on superstars and championships by the narrowest of margins.

The team's destiny was shaped by a coin toss following the 1968-69 season, when the Suns lost the draft rights to Lew Alcindor to the Milwaukee Bucks. Instead, the Suns chose journeyman-to-be Neal Walk and continued a seven-year run of mediocrity. Players like Connie Hawkins and Dick Van Arsdale made things exciting, but the Suns could only make the playoffs once during the period.

The next close call came during the 1976 playoffs, when underdog Phoenix advanced to the NBA Finals against Boston. With the series tied 2-2, the Suns lost Game 5 in a triple-overtime heart-stopper, 128-126. In 1978-79, center Alvan Adams, forward Truck Robinson, and superb guard Paul Westphal formed a solid nucleus that again fell just short, losing to Seattle in a seven-game Western Conference finals.

The Suns enjoyed some success in the early 1980s and won the Pacific Division in 1980-81. They dropped off in the middle of the decade but picked up the slack again in the late 1980s. Tom Chambers, Kevin Johnson, and Dan Majerle led Phoenix to four straight 50-plus-win seasons. The addition of Charles Barkley pushed Phoenix past the 60-win plateau in 1992-93, and they made it all the way to the NBA Finals before losing to Chicago.

Last Seven Years

Season	W	L	Pct.	Place	Playoffs	Coach
1986-87	36	46	.439	Fifth	DNQ	John MacLeod/
						Dick Van Arsdale
1987-88	28	54	.341	Fourth	DNQ	John Wetzel
1988-89	55	27	.671	Second	L-West Finals	Cotton Fitzsimmons
1989-90	54	28	.659	Third	L-West Finals	Cotton Fitzsimmons
1990-91	55	27	.671	Third	L-Round 1	Cotton Fitzsimmons
1991-92	53	29	.646	Third	L-West Semis	Cotton Fitzsimmons
1992-93	62	20	.756	First	L-NBA Finals	Paul Westphal

1992-93 Review

The year dawned with a host of changes in Phoenix. There was a new arena, new uniforms, and—most of all—a new anticipation, thanks to the arrival of Charles Barkley, the colorful, blunt, controversial forward. Sure, the Suns had to surrender three players—Jeff Hornacek, Tim Perry, and Andrew Lang—to get the bald Nike salesman, but Barkley delivered. He led the Suns to an NBA-best 62 wins and earned his first-ever MVP trophy.

Though the Suns almost choked against the Lakers in Round 1 of the playoffs (dropping the first two at home), they came back to whip L.A. in five and then San Antonio in six. After surviving a seven-game stomach-churner with Seattle—winning Game 7 123-110—Phoenix fell to the tougher, more experienced Bulls in the NBA Finals. Despite a triple-overtime win in Game 3 and a ten-point triumph in Game 5, the Suns bowed out after losing 99-98 in Game 6.

Still, Phoenix was the league's best team throughout the season, thanks to Barkley's awesome power game and a wonderfully talented supporting cast. Multi-talented All-Star Dan Majerle poured in two 3-pointers per contest. Backcourt mate Kevin Johnson was again dogged by injuries for much of the year, but he was a fastbreaking dervish during the playoffs.

Rookie small forward Richard Dumas wowed Phoenix fans with his wicked moves to the hoop. He and Cedric Ceballos, who suffered a stress fracture in the Western finals, gave the Suns stability at the three spot. Danny Ainge did the same thing at the off-guard position, providing leadership, fire, and 150 3-pointers. He, veteran Frank Johnson, and talented youngster Negele Knight gave coach Paul Westphal plenty of backcourt options while K.J. was injured.

And rookie center Oliver Miller provided excitement. Though a back-up to dependable starter Mark West, Miller dropped 40 pounds early in the season and became a force underneath by the playoffs. Forward/center Tom Chambers offered leadership and shooting off the bench.

1993-94 Roster

No.	Player	Pos.	Ht.	Wt.	Exp.	College	G	PPG	RPG	APG
22	Danny Ainge	G	6'5"	185	12	Brigham Young	80	11.8	2.7	3.3
34	Charles Barkley	F	6'6"	250	9	Auburn	76	25.6	12.2	5.1
—	Mark Buford	C/F	6'11"	255	R	Miss. Valley St.	—	—	—	—
23	Cedric Ceballos	F	6'6"	220	3	Cal. St. Fuller.	74	12.8	5.5	1.0
21	Richard Dumas	F	6'7"	204	1	Oklahoma St.	48	15.8	4.6	1.3
3	Frank Johnson	G	6'1"	185	9	Wake Forest	77	4.3	1.5	2.4
7	Kevin Johnson	G	6'1"	190	6	California	49	16.1	2.1	7.8
8	Tim Kempton	C	6'10"	255	4	Notre Dame	30	1.9	1.3	0.6
—	Joe Kleine	C	7'0"	271	8	Arkansas	78	3.3	4.4	0.5
32	Negele Knight	G	6'1"	182	3	Dayton	52	6.1	1.2	2.8
—	Malcolm Mackey	F/C	6'11"	248	R	Georgia Tech	—	—	—	—
9	Dan Majerle	G/F	6'6"	220	5	Cent. Michigan	82	16.9	4.7	3.8
25	Oliver Miller	C/F	6'9"	285	1	Arkansas	56	5.6	4.9	2.1
0	Jerrod Mustaf	F	6'10"	244	3	Maryland	32	4.6	2.6	0.3
41	Mark West	C	6'10"	246	10	Old Dominion	82	5.3	5.6	0.4
—	Byron Wilson	G	6'2"	215	R	Utah	—	—	—	—

Phoenix Suns
1993-94 Season Preview

Opening Line: Okay now, how do the Suns avoid becoming the Portland Trail Blazers? Like the Blazers of a couple years ago, the Suns boast championship talent and players who are in their prime, but they must find what it takes to take the final step. The missing ingredients are defense and halfcourt scoring. Newcomers include rookie Malcolm Mackey (27th pick) and free-agent center Joe Kleine. Aging vet Tom Chambers was not re-signed.

Guard: His poor play in the first two Finals games notwithstanding, Kevin Johnson remains a quicksilver catalyst for Phoenix. He's a flashy penetrator and a solid shooter who ignites Phoenix's fast-paced offense. Guard Dan Majerle offers incredible shooting range, stifling defense, and substantial heart and desire. Veteran Danny Ainge is more than just another bomber. His experience and leadership are vital to the Suns, as is his versatility. Veteran Frank Johnson and Negele Knight are adequate reserves for K.J., who misses at least one long stretch a year with injuries.

Forward: Charles Barkley came to Phoenix to win a title, and he got pretty close last season. The 1993 MVP brings a variety of pluses (and a few minuses) to the court, most notably his insatiable rebounding, immense strength around the basket, and boundless desire. All that outweighs his big mouth, off-court antics, and various other personality quirks. Richard Dumas, dubbed "Julius Erving with a jump shot" by Spurs coach John Lucas, is a big-time NBA scorer with little predisposition toward defense. He and Cedric Ceballos give coach Paul Westphal a pair of potent small-forward options. Mackey, 6'11", can play either the four or five spot. He's a strong rebounder who can also run the floor.

Center: Veteran banger Mark West gives the Suns a wide body, six fouls, and little else—and that's basically what the bruising Kleine will provide. Unless second-year man Oliver Miller can continue his development from a doughy rookie to a low-post force, Phoenix will have problems with the better Eastern Conference teams.

Coaching: One of the enduring images of the playoffs was Paul Westphal's dazzled, almost golly-gee expression whenever the camera trained on him for a reaction to a great Phoenix play. Westphal is not exactly Bobby Knight, but he handles his team pretty shrewdly—by handing out playing time to those who deserve it and withholding it from malingerers. It works. He's assisted by Scotty Robertson and Lionel Hollins.

Analysis: Although the Suns weren't happy to lose in the Finals to Chicago, defeat can be a good teacher. Phoenix must improve its halfcourt game and learn "Eastern style" defense if it wants to win a title. Continued development by Miller could help them in both areas. The Suns could do it this season, but their window of opportunity is small. Barkley is losing interest and Ainge is getting old. If not now, maybe never.

Prediction: First place, Pacific

PORTLAND TRAIL BLAZERS

Home: Memorial Coliseum
Capacity: 12,884
Year Built: 1960

Address
700 N.E. Multnomah St.
Suite 600
Portland, OR 97232
(503) 234-9291

Governor: Paul Allen
V.P./Player Personnel:
Brad Greenberg
Head Coach: Rick Adelman
Assistant Coach: Jack Schalow
Assistant Coach: John Wetzel

Coach Rick Adelman			
	W	L	Pct.
NBA Record	244	119	.672
W/Blazers	244	119	.672
1992-93 Record	51	31	.622

Trail Blazers History

Few teams in sports can boast of fan loyalty the way Portland can. The Blazers have sold out Memorial Coliseum more than 700 consecutive times, believed to be a record for any sport.

Portland was a typical expansion team in the early 1970s, losing far more often than it won and shuttling players and coaches in and out. Early stars included Geoff Petrie, Sidney Wicks, and future Blazers coach Rick Adelman.

Things began to change in 1974 when the Blazers drafted UCLA center Bill Walton. Two years later, Jack Ramsay became coach and led the team to its only NBA title. With Walton serving as a do-everything high-post in Ramsay's motion offense, Portland upset Philadelphia in the 1977 Finals 4-2. Bob Gross, Maurice Lucas, Dave Twardzik, and Lionel Hollins comprised the rest of that starting unit.

The Blazers appeared primed to repeat in 1977-78, but Walton injured his foot and Portland was eliminated by Seattle in the West semifinals. Walton never returned to form, and the Blazers fell behind Los Angeles and Seattle as the top team in the Pacific Division.

In the 1980s, management drafted star guards Clyde Drexler and Terry Porter, and in 1989 Portland traded for rebounding forward Buck Williams. The Blazers had world-championship talent, but they couldn't quite win the big one. Portland fell to Detroit in the 1990 NBA Finals, lost to the Lakers in the 1991 West finals, and fell to Chicago in the 1992 NBA Finals.

Last Seven Years

Season	W	L	Pct.	Place	Playoffs	Coach
1986-87	49	33	.598	Second	L-Round 1	Mike Schuler
1987-88	53	29	.646	Second	L-Round 1	Mike Schuler
1988-89	39	43	.476	Fifth	L-Round 1	M. Schuler/R. Adelman
1989-90	59	23	.720	Second	L-NBA Finals	Rick Adelman
1990-91	63	19	.768	First	L-West Finals	Rick Adelman
1991-92	57	25	.695	First	L-NBA Finals	Rick Adelman
1992-93	51	31	.622	Third	L-Round 1	Rick Adelman

1992-93 Review

The days of championship hopes in Rip City appear to be disintegrating. Portland's first-round dismissal—in four games, no less—by San Antonio revealed a team that had stood pat a year too long. After losses in two of the previous three NBA Finals, the Blazers were just another also-ran in 1992-93.

Following their loss to the Bulls in the '92 Finals, the Blazers realized that a change had to be made yet didn't know how to break up their talented nucleus. Their third-place Pacific Division finish and early playoff exit showed Portland brass that they had better figure a way to rebuild quickly.

On the surface, things looked great in Portland at the season's outset. That solid starting lineup was back, and even though bench bomber Danny Ainge wasn't, the additions of Rod Strickland and Mario Elie appeared to bolster the Blazer reserve unit. There was no reason to think Portland wouldn't challenge Phoenix and Seattle for Pacific primacy.

But nagging injuries and Dream Team fatigue limited high-flying guard Clyde Drexler to only 49 games. And though Drexler's longtime backcourt mate Terry Porter combined with Strickland and Elie to provide some scoring pop, Portland wasn't its usual scoreboard-spinning self. Although the Blazers averaged 108.5 PPG, it was nearly three points less than the previous year's per-game output.

Up front, forward Jerome Kersey's numbers dwindled again, just as they had in the previous four years, and center Kevin Duckworth's myriad weaknesses (immobility, poor rebounding) were magnified. Veteran Buck Williams was again a warrior on the backboards, but his scoring output dropped noticeably.

Cliff Robinson picked up a considerable amount of the frontcourt slack, registering career highs in scoring and rebounding and running away with the NBA's Sixth Man Award. Mark Bryant was again a serviceable back-up center, but rookie Tracy Murray was a bust, shooting only 41.5 percent from the field.

1993-94 Roster

No.	Player	Pos.	Ht.	Wt.	Exp.	College	G	PPG	RPG	APG
							|——1992-93——|			
2	Mark Bryant	F	6'9"	245	5	Seton Hall	80	5.9	4.0	0.5
22	Clyde Drexler	G	6'7"	222	10	Houston	49	19.9	6.3	5.7
—	Chris Dudley	C	6'11"	240	6	Yale	71	3.5	7.2	0.2
—	Harvey Grant	F	6'9"	235	5	Oklahoma	72	18.6	5.7	2.8
4	Dave Johnson	G/F	6'7"	210	1	Syracuse	42	3.7	1.1	0.3
25	Jerome Kersey	F	6'7"	225	9	Longwood	65	10.6	6.2	1.9
31	Tracy Murray	G/F	6'8"	225	1	UCLA	48	5.7	1.7	0.2
30	Terry Porter	G	6'3"	195	8	Wis.-Stevens Pt.	81	18.2	3.9	5.2
3	Cliff Robinson	F	6'10"	225	4	Connecticut	82	19.1	6.6	2.2
—	James Robinson	G	6'2"	180	R	Alabama	—	—	—	—
11	Delaney Rudd	G	6'2"	195	4	Wake Forest	15	1.7	0.6	1.1
54	Reggie Smith	F	6'10"	250	1	Texas Christian	23	1.0	0.9	0.0
1	Rod Strickland	G	6'3"	185	5	DePaul	78	13.7	4.3	7.2
—	Kevin Thompson	F	6'10"	260	R	N. Carolina St.	—	—	—	—
52	Buck Williams	F	6'8"	225	12	Maryland	82	8.3	8.4	0.9
6	Joe Wolf	F/C	6'11"	230	6	North Carolina	23	2.3	2.1	0.2

Portland Trail Blazers
1993-94 Season Preview

Opening Line: By the time the Blazers' new arena is unveiled in late 1995, few of the team's current players will still be on the roster. Pity. For a while there, it looked like Blazermania would infect the whole country. Not so. But there is some hope. Dealing disgruntled center Kevin Duckworth for smooth-scoring forward Harvey Grant injects some new life into a once-decaying front line. The continued emergence of Cliff Robinson could be another booster shot. And rookie guard James "Hollywood" Robinson of Alabama will add backcourt depth.

Guard: When he was healthy last year, Clyde Drexler was Portland's leading scorer and its catalyst. But "The Glide" missed almost half of the season with injuries, and his play—while tops on the team—wasn't up to its usual levels. Drexler must be Drexler for Portland to compete. Point guard Terry Porter will be counted on for more of the same this season—solid scoring, great ability on the break, and plenty of big 3-pointers. No problem there. Back-up Rod Strickland will still make the occasional bonehead play, but he led the Blazers in assists last year and displayed better consistency. Robinson is an explosive scorer but his small size will hold him back. Mario Elie, a solid reserve last year, was traded in July for a future draft pick.

Forward: By the end of last season, Portland's front line—once one of the game's best—had faltered. The addition of Grant adds new life. Grant is an efficient scorer who can also clear the glass. He should start in place of veteran Jerome Kersey, whose numbers fell last year for the fifth consecutive season. Kersey's tough on the break, but he can't shoot. Ancient Buck Williams is starting to show his age, but he's a warrior and will continue to grab boards and play big defense. Second-year shooter Tracy Murray has to learn that the NBA is not a game of H-O-R-S-E.

Center: He may not be the prototypical NBA center, but Cliff Robinson can do several things well, from dominating around the basket offensively to playing some inspired "D" and clearing the boards. Back-up Mark Bryant has limited range, but he bangs inside and excels on the offensive boards.

Coaching: Say good night, Rick. Unless the Blazers re-create their near-championship ways, Adelman could be swept out with many of the players. His calm stewardship served the team well when its solid starting unit was humming, but the starters are struggling and Adelman's approach seems out of touch with the team's current situation. He's assisted by Jack Schalow and John Wetzel.

Analysis: A healthy Drexler and the addition of Grant should keep the Blazers strong, but with Phoenix, Seattle, and even Golden State ascending in the Pacific, Portland doesn't appear to have much of a future. Sure, you'll probably see 45-50 wins in Rip City this season, but don't count on too much success come playoff time.

Prediction: Fourth place, Pacific

SACRAMENTO KINGS

Home: ARCO Arena
Capacity: 17,014
Year Built: 1988

Address
One Sports Parkway
Sacramento, CA 95834
(916) 928-0000

Managing General Partner:
Jim Thomas
General Manager: Jerry Reynolds
Head Coach: Garry St. Jean
Assistant Coach: Mike Schuler
Assistant Coach: Eddie Jordan
Assistant Coach: Mike Bratz

Coach Garry St. Jean			
	W	L	Pct.
NBA Record	25	57	.305
W/Kings	25	57	.305
1992-93 Record	25	57	.305

Kings History

Like the sun rises in the East and sets in the West, so has the Royals/Kings franchise. The Rochester (New York) Royals, a charter member of the NBA, won the franchise's only league title in 1950-51. But cross-country franchise moves, ending in Sacramento, have only led to futility.

That Rochester championship team featured a slick backcourt of Bob Davies, Bobby Wanzer, and Red Holzman, with Arnie Risen in the middle. Rochester advanced to the West finals in 1951-52, but it lost to Minneapolis. The Royals made the playoffs only once from 1956-61, though they featured a potent forecourt of Maurice Stokes, Jack Twyman, and Clyde Lovellette.

The team moved to Cincinnati for the 1957-58 season and added exciting rookie Oscar Robertson in 1960. The Royals advanced to the Eastern finals in 1962-63 and 1963-64, thanks to Robertson, Twyman, and 1963-64 Rookie of the Year Jerry Lucas, but the success was short-lived. The team didn't have a winning season from 1966-67 to 1973-74 and moved again in 1972, splitting time between Kansas City and Omaha as the Kings.

In 1974-75, the team won 44 games and featured brilliant point guard Nate "Tiny" Archibald. The 1980-81 edition lost to Houston in the conference finals. The most recent move came in 1985, when the franchise landed in Sacramento. Aside from a brief playoff appearance that season, the club has been a perennial lottery team ever since.

Last Seven Years

Season	W	L	Pct.	Place	Playoffs	Coach
1986-87	29	53	.354	Fifth	DNQ	Phil Johnson/J. Reynolds
1987-88	24	58	.293	Sixth	DNQ	Bill Russell/J. Reynolds
1988-89	27	55	.329	Sixth	DNQ	Jerry Reynolds
1989-90	23	59	.280	Seventh	DNQ	Jerry Reynolds/D. Motta
1990-91	25	57	.305	Seventh	DNQ	Dick Motta
1991-92	29	53	.347	Seventh	DNQ	Dick Motta/Rex Hughes
1992-93	25	57	.305	Seventh	DNQ	Garry St. Jean

1992-93 Review

No, the Kings are not the unluckiest team in the NBA. It just seems that way. It looked like they were finally building a talented young team when all of a sudden everybody decided to spend half the year on the injured list.

The Kings hit the Pacific floor in 1992-93 with a 25-57 record, spoiling the debut of new coach Garry St. Jean. This time, critics couldn't blame the Kings' putrid finish on a mediocre collection of talent. There were actually some extraneous circumstances.

Shooting guard Mitch Richmond was having a big-time season until a broken right thumb required surgery, sidelining him for much of the season's second half. Do-it-all rookie Walt Williams, who could play either guard spot or small forward, played only 59 games, succumbing to a fractured right hand and a bad left foot. And center Duane Causwell, an imposing defensive presence, missed a third of the season with a stress fracture in his right foot.

The depleted Kings never got a chance to show what they could do. When healthy, Richmond was his usual light-it-up self, one of the league's top gunners, and Williams's versatility was a revelation. Small forward Lionel Simmons had another strong season, racking up points, rebounds, and assists.

The one thing the Kings couldn't do was play defense. Sacramento allowed the second-most points in the league, 111.1, negating their substantial offensive output of 107.9 PPG. Most of the trouble came up front. Wayman Tisdale was forced to play pivot way too much in Causwell's stead, and he was clearly overmatched. Pete Chilcutt was an inadequate force inside as well.

Point guard Spud Webb played well but was slowing down as his achy knees got older. Young lead guard Randy Brown started 34 games and made his mark on defense. Reserve forward Anthony Bonner rebounded well, while swing man Rod Higgins and guard Jim Les popped in the occasional 3-pointer.

1993-94 Roster

No.	Player	Pos.	Ht.	Wt.	Exp.	College	G	PPG	RPG	APG
								1992-93		
24	Anthony Bonner	F	6'8"	225	3	St. Louis	70	8.6	6.5	1.4
3	Randy Brown	G	6'3"	190	2	New Mexico St.	75	7.6	2.8	2.6
—	Evers Burns	F	6'8"	260	R	Maryland	—	—	—	—
31	Duane Causwell	C	7'0"	240	3	Temple	55	8.2	5.5	0.6
32	Pete Chilcutt	F/C	6'10"	232	2	North Carolina	59	6.1	3.3	1.1
25	Marty Conlon	F	6'11"	245	2	Providence	46	4.8	2.7	0.8
21	Rod Higgins	F	6'7"	215	11	Fresno St.	69	8.3	2.8	1.7
—	Alex Holcombe	F/C	6'9"	244	R	Baylor	—	—	—	—
—	Bobby Hurley	G	6'0"	165	R	Duke	—	—	—	—
33	Jim Les	G	5'11"	175	5	Bradley	73	4.5	1.2	2.3
—	Mike Peplowski	C	6'11"	270	R	Michigan St.	—	—	—	—
30	Kurt Rambis	F	6'8"	213	12	Santa Clara	72	2.5	3.2	0.7
2	Mitch Richmond	G	6'5"	215	5	Kansas St.	45	21.9	3.4	4.9
22	Lionel Simmons	F	6'7"	210	3	La Salle	69	17.9	7.2	4.5
23	Wayman Tisdale	F	6'9"	260	8	Oklahoma	76	16.6	6.6	1.4
4	Spud Webb	G	5'7"	135	8	N. Carolina St.	69	14.5	2.8	7.0
42	Walt Williams	G/F	6'8"	230	1	Maryland	59	17.0	4.5	3.0

Sacramento Kings
1993-94 Season Preview

Opening Line: Let's be blunt about it. The addition of Bobby Hurley is not going to transform the Kings from a perennial lottery team to a playoff contender—not in the tough Pacific Division. The 6'0" Blue Devil will help the Kings get better—they need a real point guard—but he's not going to improve the team's miserable defense, particularly up front. Maryland forward Evers Burns, a 6'8", 260-pounder, may take up space, but he's hardly the answer either. While the rest of the Pacific makes real strides, the Kings continue to take baby steps.

Guard: The healthy return of Mitch Richmond (broken right thumb) gives Sacramento a potent two guard. Richmond can fill it up from downtown or take it strong to the hoop. Hurley will need time to adjust to the big show, particularly when shooting the ball. Still, he'll be great in the Kings' up-tempo offense. That relegates Spud Webb to the bench, but there are worse things than having a feisty mini-jet as a back-up point. Webb doesn't shoot it too well, but he leads the break expertly. So, where does that leave Walt Williams? He isn't a point guard, but will he be happy logging minutes behind Richmond? Coach Garry St. Jean will have to find quality P.T. for Williams, a versatile talent who can score from anywhere on the floor. Jim Les will be used as a 3-point specialist.

Forward: Lionel Simmons provides a little of everything at small forward. He scores, passes, rebounds, plays defense, and works his tail off. His shooting percentage could stand a little boost. Wayman Tisdale scores nearly at will underneath and isn't a bad board man, though his defense leaves a lot to be desired. Anthony Bonner doesn't have the best shot in the world, but he is a valuable rebounder. Burns will bang a little but is slow and heavy. Rod Higgins is another 3-point expert.

Center: Duane Causwell will never be mistaken for a scoring machine, but that's not his job. If he stays healthy and avoids foul trouble—neither a guarantee—he'll provide a solid defensive presence for the Kings. His rebounding could stand some improvement, but Causwell isn't all that bad. Pete Chilcutt is a soft reserve.

Coaching: St. Jean employs the same frenetic, up-tempo style of his mentor, Golden State coach Don Nelson, but he doesn't quite have the personnel that Nellie does. St. Jean's style is popular with players (who doesn't like to shoot?) but it won't win him too many titles. He's assisted by Mike Schuler, Eddie Jordan, and Mike Bratz.

Analysis: Sacramento will continue to get its mail delivered to the Pacific basement, no matter how healthy the players remain. Expect to see plenty of 110-plus scoring efforts out of the Kings, but even more of the same from opponents. Sacramento has enough guards and swing men to populate a full team. What it could really use is a major-league power forward and a legitimate back-up center.

Prediction: Seventh place, Pacific

SEATTLE SUPERSONICS

Home: The Coliseum
Capacity: 14,132
Year Built: 1962

Owner: Barry Ackerley
President: Bob Whitsitt
Head Coach: George Karl
Assistant Coach: Bob Kloppenburg
Assistant Coach: Tim Grgurich

Address
190 Queen Anne Ave. N.
Suite 200
Seattle, WA 98109
(206) 281-5800

Coach George Karl			
	W	L	Pct.
NBA Record	201	218	.480
W/Sonics	82	42	.661
1992-93 Record	55	27	.671

SuperSonics History

Though Seattle has been in the league for 26 years, there has been only one Sonic boom. It came in the late 1970s.

Seattle's 1977-78 team featured rookie center Jack Sikma, rebounding machine Paul Silas, and the guard triumvirate of Gus Johnson, Dennis Johnson, and "Downtown" Fred Brown. They fell in seven games to Washington in the NBA Finals. The team was not denied the following season. The Sonics soared to the Pacific Division championship and dispatched Los Angeles and Phoenix in the playoffs. The Sonics won the title in five games over the Bullets.

That two-year period stands in stark contrast to the team's early years. Born in 1967, the team failed to qualify for the playoffs for seven seasons and boasted few stars, other than powerful Bob Rule and highly talented but enigmatic Spencer Haywood. Seattle made it to the Western semifinals in 1974-75 and 1975-76, setting the stage for its runs to the Finals.

After a 56-26 season in 1979-80, the Sonics wallowed through a decade of mediocrity. The 1986-87 season was a stunner, however. Despite finishing with a losing record, the Sonics advanced to the Western finals, thanks to the high-scoring trio of Xavier McDaniel, Dale Ellis, and Tom Chambers. A new cast of characters emerged in the early 1990s, headed by Shawn Kemp and Ricky Pierce and coached by George Karl. They roared to the 1993 Western finals, where they lost to Phoenix in seven games.

Last Seven Years

Season	W	L	Pct.	Place	Playoffs	Coach
1986-87	39	43	.476	Fourth	L-West Finals	Bernie Bickerstaff
1987-88	44	38	.537	Third	L-Round 1	Bernie Bickerstaff
1988-89	47	35	.573	Third	L-West Semis	Bernie Bickerstaff
1989-90	41	41	.500	Fourth	DNQ	Bernie Bickerstaff
1990-91	41	41	.500	Fifth	L-Round 1	K.C. Jones
1991-92	47	35	.573	Fourth	L-West Semis	K.C. Jones/George Karl
1992-93	55	27	.671	Second	L-West Finals	George Karl

1992-93 Review

The SuperSonics packed a lot of excitement into the 1992-93 season. By registering the fourth-best regular-season record in the NBA and extending Phoenix to seven games in an exciting Western Conference final—following an exhilarating seven-game win over Houston in the semis—Seattle proved that its future is indeed bright.

Alas, not too many people noticed. Talk around the NBA focused on the Suns, Bulls, and Knicks—the other three conference finalists. Seattle's anonymity shouldn't last, however. Though tucked into America's upper left-hand corner, the Sonics belong on center stage.

Six different Sonics scored in double figures in 1992-93, and Seattle led the NBA in scoring differential and turnovers forced. Coach George Karl used his deep bench magnificently, blending veterans with young talents.

Mighty man-child Shawn Kemp was again the team's focus. The 6'10", 245-pounder posted career highs in scoring and rebounding and became one of the league's forces down low—all at the tender age of 23. Fellow forward Derrick McKey was another offensive weapon, but he slumbered through several games and was not nearly as imposing on the backboards as he should have been.

Midseason acquisition Sam Perkins cost the Sonics '92 first-round pick Doug Christie and mercurial center Benoit Benjamin, but the veteran's savvy, experience, and diverse skills proved invaluable at playoff time. Another frontcourter, Michael Cage, was again a consistent rebounder and defender.

Backcourt gunner Ricky Pierce led Seattle in scoring for the third straight year. He continued to display the ability to take over stretches of games with his outside shooting. His running mate, point guard Gary Payton, backed up his incessant trash-talking with precise playmaking and outstanding defense.

As always, sweet-shooting Eddie Johnson was potent off the bench, and versatile Nate McMillan provided quality depth at three positions. Dana Barros entered every game firing and led the team in 3-pointers.

1993-94 Roster

No.	Player	Pos.	Ht.	Wt.	Exp.	College	G	1992-93 PPG	RPG	APG
17	Vincent Askew	G/F	6'6"	225	4	Memphis St.	73	5.6	2.2	1.7
3	Dana Barros	G	5'11"	163	4	Boston College	69	7.8	1.6	2.2
44	Michael Cage	C/F	6'9"	230	9	San Diego St.	82	6.1	8.0	0.8
8	Eddie Johnson	F	6'7"	215	12	Illinois	82	14.4	3.3	1.6
50	Ervin Johnson	C	6'11"	242	R	New Orleans	—	—	—	—
30	Adonis Jordan	G	5'11"	170	R	Kansas	—	—	—	—
40	Shawn Kemp	F	6'10"	245	4	None	78	17.8	10.7	2.0
25	Rich King	C	7'2"	265	2	Nebraska	3	2.0	1.6	0.3
31	Derrick McKey	F	6'10"	225	6	Alabama	77	13.4	4.2	2.6
10	Nate McMillan	G/F	6'5"	197	7	N. Carolina St.	73	7.5	4.2	5.3
21	Gerald Paddio	F	6'7"	205	2	UNLV	41	3.9	1.2	0.8
20	Gary Payton	G	6'4"	190	3	Oregon St.	82	13.5	3.4	4.9
14	Sam Perkins	F/C	6'9"	257	9	North Carolina	79	13.1	6.6	2.0
22	Ricky Pierce	G	6'4"	215	11	Rice	77	18.2	2.5	2.9
55	Steve Scheffler	C	6'9"	250	3	Purdue	29	2.3	1.2	0.2

Seattle SuperSonics
1993-94 Season Preview

Opening Line: The Sonics enter 1993-94 with a chance to bury their enigma status for good. Seattle may have the league's deepest collection of talent, and the additions of rookies Ervin Johnson (a center) and Adonis Jordan (a cat-quick guard) give the Sonics canyon-style depth. But any giddy expectations should be tempered with concern. Sure, Seattle is deep, young, and exciting. But the Sonics need to mature if they want to contend for the title.

Guard: Gary Payton's mouth slowed down in 1992-93 and his play at the point improved significantly. Now entering his fourth year, Payton is developing into a strong floor leader who can score and play sticky defense. His mate, veteran Ricky Pierce, continues to light it up, and his experience adds some stability to the volatile mix. Veteran Nate McMillan plays three spots but is primarily a valuable back-up to Payton at the point, while Dana Barros is one of the game's best 3-point specialists. Jordan may be a bit small (5'11") to be a premier NBA point man, but he is quick and has good range.

Forward: Behold the man-child. Shawn Kemp, fresh off a monstrous 1992-93 campaign, has become one of the league's marquee attractions. Though his offensive game is limited primarily to five feet around the hoop, that's enough. Kemp rebounds ferociously, gets to the line plenty, and can play some low-post defense. If only small forward Derrick McKey had so much energy. The talented, 6'10" McKey can be marvelous one minute, clueless the next. Coach George Karl has gotten on his case, and not without reason. Eddie Johnson doesn't have such problems. His job is to shoot, and he does that with the best of them. Vincent Askew is an NBA survivor who does little that stands out.

Center: The Sonics dumped troublesome Benoit Benjamin last year and added Sam Perkins. That's an upgrade. The smooth, silent Perkins is a deft scorer from all over the court and adds a necessary air of leadership. Back-up Michael Cage remains a warrior on the backboards and a willing defender, no matter how restricted his offensive game is. Expect more of the same from rookie Ervin Johnson, a tireless worker, particularly on the offensive boards.

Coaching: Karl may look like an aw-shucks guy you'd meet on a stool at the local taproom, but he can be a tyrant. He'll bench malingerers, yell at underachievers, and shake up the lineup if he's unhappy. He's also done some big winning in Seattle since arriving midway through the 1991-92 campaign. He is assisted by Bob Kloppenburg and Tim Grgurich.

Analysis: A full year of Perkins, the continued development of Kemp and Payton, and the experience of going seven full games in the Western Conference finals should all help the Sonics. But Seattle will have to wait another year to win the West. Key players like Kemp, Payton, and McKey still need a little more maturity.

Prediction: Second place, Pacific

N B A Awards and Records

This section showcases the NBA's champions, award-winners, and record-setters—as well as a history of No. 1 draft picks. Here is a breakdown of what you'll find:

- World Champions
- Most Valuable Players
- Rookies of the Year
- NBA Finals MVPs
- Defensive Players of the Year
- Sixth Man Award winners
- Coaches of the Year

- All-NBA Teams
- All-Rookie Teams
- All-Defensive Teams

- All-Star Game results

- career leaders
- active career leaders
- regular-season records
- game records
- team records—season
- team records—game
- playoff records—career
- playoff records—series
- playoff records—game
- playoff records—team

- history of No. 1 draft picks

WORLD CHAMPIONS

	CHAMPION	FINALIST	RESULT		CHAMPION	FINALIST	RESULT
1946-47	Philadelphia	Chicago	4-0	1970-71	Milwaukee	Baltimore	4-0
1947-48	Baltimore	Philadelphia	4-2	1971-72	Los Angeles	New York	4-1
1948-49	Minneapolis	Washington	4-2	1972-73	New York	Los Angeles	4-1
1949-50	Minneapolis	Syracuse	4-2	1973-74	Boston	Milwaukee	4-3
1950-51	Rochester	New York	4-3	1974-75	Golden State	Washington	4-0
1951-52	Minneapolis	New York	4-3	1975-76	Boston	Phoenix	4-2
1952-53	Minneapolis	New York	4-1	1976-77	Portland	Philadelphia	4-2
1953-54	Minneapolis	Syracuse	4-3	1977-78	Washington	Seattle	4-3
1954-55	Syracuse	Fort Wayne	4-3	1978-79	Seattle	Washington	4-1
1955-56	Philadelphia	Fort Wayne	4-1	1979-80	Los Angeles	Philadelphia	4-2
1956-57	Boston	St. Louis	4-3	1980-81	Boston	Houston	4-2
1957-58	St. Louis	Boston	4-2	1981-82	Los Angeles	Philadelphia	4-2
1958-59	Boston	Minneapolis	4-0	1982-83	Philadelphia	Los Angeles	4-0
1959-60	Boston	St. Louis	4-3	1983-84	Boston	Los Angeles	4-3
1960-61	Boston	St. Louis	4-1	1984-85	L.A. Lakers	Boston	4-2
1961-62	Boston	Los Angeles	4-3	1985-86	Boston	Houston	4-2
1962-63	Boston	Los Angeles	4-2	1986-87	L.A. Lakers	Boston	4-2
1963-64	Boston	San Francisco	4-1	1987-88	L.A. Lakers	Detroit	4-3
1964-65	Boston	Los Angeles	4-1	1988-89	Detroit	L.A. Lakers	4-0
1965-66	Boston	Los Angeles	4-3	1989-90	Detroit	Portland	4-1
1966-67	Philadelphia	San Francisco	4-2	1990-91	Chicago	L.A. Lakers	4-1
1967-68	Boston	Los Angeles	4-2	1991-92	Chicago	Portland	4-2
1968-69	Boston	Los Angeles	4-3	1992-93	Chicago	Phoenix	4-2
1969-70	New York	Los Angeles	4-3				

MOST VALUABLE PLAYERS

	PLAYER	PPG		PLAYER	PPG
1955-56	Bob Pettit, St. Louis	25.7	1974-75	Bob McAdoo, Buffalo	34.5
1956-57	Bob Cousy, Boston	20.6	1975-76	Kareem Abdul-Jabbar, L.A.	27.7
1957-58	Bill Russell, Boston	16.6	1976-77	Kareem Abdul-Jabbar, L.A.	26.2
1958-59	Bob Pettit, St. Louis	29.2	1977-78	Bill Walton, Portland	18.9
1959-60	Wilt Chamberlain, Phil.	37.6	1978-79	Moses Malone, Houston	24.8
1960-61	Bill Russell, Boston	16.9	1979-80	Kareem Abdul-Jabbar, L.A.	24.8
1961-62	Bill Russell, Boston	18.9	1980-81	Julius Erving, Philadelphia	24.6
1962-63	Bill Russell, Boston	16.8	1981-82	Moses Malone, Houston	31.1
1963-64	Oscar Robertson, Cincinnati	31.4	1982-83	Moses Malone, Philadelphia	24.5
1964-65	Bill Russell, Boston	14.1	1983-84	Larry Bird, Boston	24.2
1965-66	Wilt Chamberlain, Phil.	33.5	1984-85	Larry Bird, Boston	28.7
1966-67	Wilt Chamberlain, Phil.	24.1	1985-86	Larry Bird, Boston	25.8
1967-68	Wilt Chamberlain, Phil.	24.3	1986-87	Magic Johnson, L.A. Lakers	23.9
1968-69	Wes Unseld, Baltimore	13.8	1987-88	Michael Jordan, Chicago	35.0
1969-70	Willis Reed, New York	21.7	1988-89	Magic Johnson, L.A. Lakers	22.5
1970-71	Lew Alcindor, Milwaukee	31.7	1989-90	Magic Johnson, L.A. Lakers	22.3
1971-72	Kareem Abdul-Jabbar, Mil.	34.8	1990-91	Michael Jordan, Chicago	31.5
1972-73	Dave Cowens, Boston	20.5	1991-92	Michael Jordan, Chicago	30.1
1973-74	Kareem Abdul-Jabbar, Mil.	27.0	1992-93	Charles Barkley, Phoenix	25.6

ROOKIES OF THE YEAR

1952-53	Don Meineke, Fort Wayne	1972-73	Bob McAdoo, Buffalo
1953-54	Ray Felix, Baltimore	1973-74	Ernie DiGregorio, Buffalo
1954-55	Bob Pettit, Milwaukee	1974-75	Keith Wilkes, Golden State
1955-56	Maurice Stokes, Rochester	1975-76	Alvan Adams, Phoenix
1956-57	Tom Heinsohn, Boston	1976-77	Adrian Dantley, Buffalo
1957-58	Woody Sauldsberry, Philadelphia	1977-78	Walter Davis, Phoenix
1958-59	Elgin Baylor, Minneapolis	1978-79	Phil Ford, Kansas City
1959-60	Wilt Chamberlain, Philadelphia	1979-80	Larry Bird, Boston
1960-61	Oscar Robertson, Cincinnati	1980-81	Darrell Griffith, Utah
1961-62	Walt Bellamy, Chicago	1981-82	Buck Williams, New Jersey
1962-63	Terry Dischinger, Chicago	1982-83	Terry Cummings, San Diego
1963-64	Jerry Lucas, Cincinnati	1983-84	Ralph Sampson, Houston
1964-65	Willis Reed, New York	1984-85	Michael Jordan, Chicago
1965-66	Rick Barry, San Francisco	1985-86	Patrick Ewing, New York
1966-67	Dave Bing, Detroit	1986-87	Chuck Person, Indiana
1967-68	Earl Monroe, Baltimore	1987-88	Mark Jackson, New York
1968-69	Wes Unseld, Baltimore	1988-89	Mitch Richmond, Golden State
1969-70	Lew Alcindor, Milwaukee	1989-90	David Robinson, San Antonio
1970-71	Dave Cowens, Boston	1990-91	Derrick Coleman, New Jersey
	Geoff Petrie, Portland	1991-92	Larry Johnson, Charlotte
1971-72	Sidney Wicks, Portland	1992-93	Shaquille O'Neal, Orlando

MOST IMPROVED PLAYERS

1985-86	Alvin Robertson, San Antonio	1989-90	Rony Seikaly, Miami
1986-87	Dale Ellis, Seattle	1990-91	Scott Skiles, Orlando
1987-88	Kevin Duckworth, Portland	1991-92	Pervis Ellison, Washington
1988-89	Kevin Johnson, Phoenix	1992-93	Chris Jackson, Denver

NBA FINALS MVPS

1969	Jerry West, Los Angeles	1982	Magic Johnson, Los Angeles
1970	Willis Reed, New York	1983	Moses Malone, Philadelphia
1971	Lew Alcindor, Milwaukee	1984	Larry Bird, Boston
1972	Wilt Chamberlain, Los Angeles	1985	Kareem Abdul-Jabbar, L.A. Lakers
1973	Willis Reed, New York	1986	Larry Bird, Boston
1974	John Havlicek, Boston	1987	Magic Johnson, L.A. Lakers
1975	Rick Barry, Golden State	1988	James Worthy, L.A. Lakers
1976	Jo Jo White, Boston	1989	Joe Dumars, Detroit
1977	Bill Walton, Portland	1990	Isiah Thomas, Detroit
1978	Wes Unseld, Washington	1991	Michael Jordan, Chicago
1979	Dennis Johnson, Seattle	1992	Michael Jordan, Chicago
1980	Magic Johnson, Los Angeles	1993	Michael Jordan, Chicago
1981	Cedric Maxwell, Boston		

DEFENSIVE PLAYERS OF THE YEAR

1982-83	Sidney Moncrief, Milwaukee	1988-89	Mark Eaton, Utah
1983-84	Sidney Moncrief, Milwaukee	1989-90	Dennis Rodman, Detroit
1984-85	Mark Eaton, Utah	1990-91	Dennis Rodman, Detroit
1985-86	Alvin Robertson, San Antonio	1991-92	David Robinson, San Antonio
1986-87	Michael Cooper, L.A. Lakers	1992-93	Hakeem Olajuwon, Houston
1987-88	Michael Jordan, Chicago		

SIXTH MAN AWARD WINNERS

1982-83	Bobby Jones, Philadelphia	1988-89	Eddie Johnson, Phoenix
1983-84	Kevin McHale, Boston	1989-90	Ricky Pierce, Milwaukee
1984-85	Kevin McHale, Boston	1990-91	Detlef Schrempf, Indiana
1985-86	Bill Walton, Boston	1991-92	Detlef Schrempf, Indiana
1986-87	Ricky Pierce, Milwaukee	1992-93	Cliff Robinson, Portland
1987-88	Roy Tarpley, Dallas		

COACHES OF THE YEAR

1962-63	Harry Gallatin, St. Louis	1978-79	Cotton Fitzsimmons, Kansas City
1963-64	Alex Hannum, San Francisco	1979-80	Bill Fitch, Boston
1964-65	Red Auerbach, Boston	1980-81	Jack McKinney, Indiana
1965-66	Dolph Schayes, Philadelphia	1981-82	Gene Shue, Washington
1966-67	Johnny Kerr, Chicago	1982-83	Don Nelson, Milwaukee
1967-68	Richie Guerin, St. Louis	1983-84	Frank Layden, Utah
1968-69	Gene Shue, Baltimore	1984-85	Don Nelson, Milwaukee
1969-70	Red Holzman, New York	1985-86	Mike Fratello, Atlanta
1970-71	Dick Motta, Chicago	1986-87	Mike Schuler, Portland
1971-72	Bill Sharman, Los Angeles	1987-88	Doug Moe, Denver
1972-73	Tom Heinsohn, Boston	1988-89	Cotton Fitzsimmons, Phoenix
1973-74	Ray Scott, Detroit	1989-90	Pat Riley, L.A. Lakers
1974-75	Phil Johnson, K.C.-Omaha	1990-91	Don Chaney, Houston
1975-76	Bill Fitch, Cleveland	1991-92	Don Nelson, Golden St.
1976-77	Tom Nissalke, Houston	1992-93	Pat Riley, New York
1977-78	Hubie Brown, Atlanta		

ALL-NBA TEAMS

1946-47
Joe Fulks, PHI
Bob Feerick, WAS
Stan Miasek, DET
Bones McKinney, WAS
Max Zaslofsky, CHI

1947-48
Joe Fulks, PHI
Max Zaslofsky, CHI
Ed Sadowski, BOS
Howie Dallmar, PHI
Bob Feerick, WAS

1948-49
George Mikan, MIN
Joe Fulks, PHI
Bob Davies, ROC
Max Zaslofsky, CHI
Jim Pollard, MIN

1949-50
George Mikan, MIN
Jim Pollard, MIN
Alex Groza, IND
Bob Davies, ROC
Max Zaslofsky, CHI

1950-51
George Mikan, MIN
Alex Groza, IND
Ed Macauley, BOS
Bob Davies, ROC
Ralph Beard, IND

1951-52
George Mikan, MIN
Ed Macauley, BOS
Paul Arizin, PHI
Bob Cousy, BOS
Bob Davies, ROC
Dolph Schayes, SYR

1952-53
George Mikan, MIN
Bob Cousy, BOS
Neil Johnston, PHI
Ed Macauley, BOS
Dolph Schayes, SYR

1953-54
Bob Cousy, BOS
Neil Johnston, PHI

George Mikan, MIN
Dolph Schayes, SYR
Harry Gallatin, NY

1954-55
Neil Johnston, PHI
Bob Cousy, BOS
Dolph Schayes, SYR
Bob Pettit, MIL
Larry Foust, FW

1955-56
Bob Pettit, STL
Paul Arizin, PHI
Neil Johnston, PHI
Bob Cousy, BOS
Bill Sharman, BOS

1956-57
Paul Arizin, PHI
Dolph Schayes, SYR
Bob Pettit, STL
Bob Cousy, BOS
Bill Sharman, BOS

1957-58
Dolph Schayes, SYR
George Yardley, DET
Bob Pettit, STL
Bob Cousy, BOS
Bill Sharman, BOS

1958-59
Bob Pettit, STL
Elgin Baylor, MIN
Bill Russell, BOS
Bob Cousy, BOS
Bill Sharman, BOS

1959-60
Bob Pettit, STL
Elgin Baylor, MIN
Wilt Chamberlain, PHI
Bob Cousy, BOS
Gene Shue, DET

1960-61
Elgin Baylor, LA
Bob Pettit, STL
Wilt Chamberlain, PHI
Bob Cousy, BOS
Oscar Robertson, CIN

1961-62
Bob Pettit, STL
Elgin Baylor, LA
Wilt Chamberlain, PHI
Jerry West, LA
Oscar Robertson, CIN

1962-63
Elgin Baylor, LA
Bob Pettit, STL
Bill Russell, BOS
Oscar Robertson, CIN
Jerry West, LA

1963-64
Bob Pettit, STL
Elgin Baylor, LA
Wilt Chamberlain, SF
Oscar Robertson, CIN
Jerry West, LA

1964-65
Elgin Baylor, LA
Jerry Lucas, CIN
Bill Russell, BOS
Oscar Robertson, CIN
Jerry West, LA

1965-66
Rick Barry, SF
Jerry Lucas, CIN
Wilt Chamberlain, PHI
Oscar Robertson, CIN
Jerry West, LA

1966-67
Rick Barry, SF
Elgin Baylor, LA
Wilt Chamberlain, PHI
Jerry West, LA
Oscar Robertson, CIN

1967-68
Elgin Baylor, LA
Jerry Lucas, CIN
Wilt Chamberlain, PHI
Dave Bing, DET
Oscar Robertson, CIN

1968-69
Billy Cunningham, PHI
Elgin Baylor, LA
Wes Unseld, BAL

Earl Monroe, BAL
Oscar Robertson, CIN

1969-70
Billy Cunningham, PHI
Connie Hawkins, PHO
Willis Reed, NY
Jerry West, LA
Walt Frazier, NY

1970-71
John Havlicek, BOS
Billy Cunningham, PHI
Lew Alcindor, MIL
Jerry West, LA
Dave Bing, DET

1971-72
John Havlicek, BOS
Spencer Haywood, SEA
Kareem Abdul-Jabbar, MIL
Jerry West, LA
Walt Frazier, NY

1972-73
John Havlicek, BOS
Spencer Haywood, SEA
Kareem Abdul-Jabbar, MIL
Nate Archibald, KCO
Jerry West, LA

1973-74
John Havlicek, BOS
Rick Barry, GS
Kareem Abdul-Jabbar, MIL
Walt Frazier, NY
Gail Goodrich, LA

1974-75
Rick Barry, GS
Elvin Hayes, WAS
Bob McAdoo, BUF
Nate Archibald, KCO
Walt Frazier, NY

1975-76
Rick Barry, GS
George McGinnis, PHI
Kareem Abdul-Jabbar, LA
Nate Archibald, KC
Pete Maravich, NO

1976-77
Elvin Hayes, WAS
David Thompson, DEN

Kareem Abdul-Jabbar, LA
Pete Maravich, NO
Paul Westphal, PHO

1977-78
Truck Robinson, NO
Julius Erving, PHI
Bill Walton, POR
George Gervin, SA
David Thompson, DEN

1978-79
Marques Johnson, MIL
Elvin Hayes, WAS
Moses Malone, HOU
George Gervin, SA
Paul Westphal, PHO

1979-80
Julius Erving, PHI
Larry Bird, BOS
Kareem Abdul-Jabbar, LA
George Gervin, SA
Paul Westphal, PHO

1980-81
Julius Erving, PHI
Larry Bird, BOS
Kareem Abdul-Jabbar, LA
George Gervin, SA
Dennis Johnson, PHO

1981-82
Larry Bird, BOS
Julius Erving, PHI
Moses Malone, HOU
George Gervin, SA
Gus Williams, SEA

1982-83
Larry Bird, BOS
Julius Erving, PHI
Moses Malone, PHI
Magic Johnson, LA
Sidney Moncrief, MIL

1983-84
Larry Bird, BOS
Bernard King, NY
Kareem Abdul-Jabbar, LA
Magic Johnson, LA
Isiah Thomas, DET

1984-85
Larry Bird, BOS
Bernard King, NY
Moses Malone, PHI
Magic Johnson, LAL
Isiah Thomas, DET

1985-86
Larry Bird, BOS
Dominique Wilkins, ATL
Kareem Abdul-Jabbar, LAL
Magic Johnson, LAL
Isiah Thomas, DET

1986-87
Larry Bird, BOS
Kevin McHale, BOS
Akeem Olajuwon, HOU
Magic Johnson, LAL
Michael Jordan, CHI

1987-88
Larry Bird, BOS
Charles Barkley, PHI
Akeem Olajuwon, HOU
Michael Jordan, CHI
Magic Johnson, LAL

1988-89
Karl Malone, UTA
Charles Barkley, PHI
Akeem Olajuwon, HOU
Magic Johnson, LAL
Michael Jordan, CHI

1989-90
Karl Malone, UTA
Charles Barkley, PHI
Patrick Ewing, NY
Magic Johnson, LAL
Michael Jordan, CHI

1990-91
Karl Malone, UTA
Charles Barkley, PHI
David Robinson, SA
Michael Jordan, CHI
Magic Johnson, LAL

1991-92
Karl Malone, UTA
Chris Mullin, GS
David Robinson, SA
Michael Jordan, CHI
Clyde Drexler, POR

1992-93

FIRST	SECOND	THIRD
Charles Barkley, PHO	Dominique Wilkins, ATL	Scottie Pippen, CHI
Karl Malone, UTA	Larry Johnson, CHA	Derrick Coleman, NJ
Hakeem Olajuwon, HOU	Patrick Ewing, NY	David Robinson, SA
Michael Jordan, CHI	John Stockton, UTA	Tim Hardaway, GS
Mark Price, CLE	Joe Dumars, DET	Drazen Petrovic, NJ

ALL-ROOKIE TEAMS

1962-63
Terry Dischinger, CHI
Chet Walker, SYR
Zelmo Beaty, STL
John Havlicek, BOS
Dave DeBusschere, DET

1963-64
Jerry Lucas, CIN
Gus Johnson, BAL
Nate Thurmond, SF
Art Heyman, NY
Rod Thorn, BAL

1964-65
Willis Reed, NY
Jim Barnes, NY
Howard Komives, NY
Lucious Jackson, PHI
Wally Jones, BAL
Joe Caldwell, DET

1965-66
Rick Barry, SF
Billy Cunningham, PHI
Tom Van Arsdale, DET
Dick Van Arsdale, NY
Fred Hetzel, SF

1966-67
Lou Hudson, STL
Jack Marin, BAL
Erwin Mueller, CHI
Cazzie Russell, NY
Dave Bing, DET

1967-68
Earl Monroe, BAL
Bob Rule, SEA
Walt Frazier, NY
Al Tucker, SEA
Phil Jackson, NY

1968-69
Wes Unseld, BAL
Elvin Hayes, SD
Bill Hewitt, LA
Art Harris, SEA
Gary Gregor, PHO

1969-70
Lew Alcindor, MIL
Bob Dandridge, MIL
Jo Jo White, BOS
Mike Davis, BAL
Dick Garrett, LA

1970-71
Geoff Petrie, POR
Dave Cowens, BOS
Pete Maravich, ATL
Calvin Murphy, SD
Bob Lanier, DET

1971-72
Elmore Smith, BUF
Sidney Wicks, POR
Austin Carr, CLE
Phil Chenier, BAL
Clifford Ray, CHI

1972-73
Bob McAdoo, BUF
Lloyd Neal, POR
Fred Boyd, PHI
Dwight Davis, CLE
Jim Price, LA

1973-74
Ernie DiGregorio, BUF
Ron Behagen, KCO
Mike Bantom, PHO
John Brown, ATL
Nick Weatherspoon, CAP

1974-75
Keith Wilkes, GS
John Drew, ATL
Scott Wedman, KCO
Tom Burleson, SEA
Brian Winters, LA

1975-76
Alvan Adams, PHO
Gus Williams, GS
Joe Meriweather, HOU
John Shumate, PHO/BUF
Lionel Hollins, POR

1976-77
Adrian Dantley, BUF
Scott May, CHI
Mitch Kupchak, WAS
John Lucas, HOU
Ron Lee, PHO

1977-78
Walter Davis, PHO
Marques Johnson, MIL
Bernard King, NJ
Jack Sikma, SEA
Norm Nixon, LA

1978-79
Phil Ford, KC
Mychal Thompson, POR
Ron Brewer, POR
Reggie Theus, CHI
Terry Tyler, DET

1979-80
Larry Bird, BOS
Magic Johnson, LA
Bill Cartwright, NY
Calvin Natt, POR
David Greenwood, CHI

1980-81
Joe Barry Carroll, GS
Darrell Griffith, UTA
Larry Smith, GS
Kevin McHale, BOS
Kelvin Ransey, POR

1981-82
Kelly Tripucka, DET
Jay Vincent, DAL
Isiah Thomas, DET
Buck Williams, NJ
Jeff Ruland, WAS

1982-83
Terry Cummings, SD
Clark Kellogg, IND
Dominique Wilkins, ATL
James Worthy, LA
Quintin Dailey, CHI

1983-84
Ralph Sampson, HOU
Steve Stipanovich, IND
Byron Scott, LA
Jeff Malone, WAS
Thurl Bailey, UTA
Darrell Walker, NY

1984-85
Michael Jordan, CHI
Akeem Olajuwon, HOU
Sam Bowie, POR

Charles Barkley, PHI
Sam Perkins, DAL

1985-86
Xavier McDaniel, SEA
Patrick Ewing, NY
Karl Malone, UTA
Joe Dumars, DET
Charles Oakley, CHI

1986-87
Brad Daugherty, CLE
Ron Harper, CLE
Chuck Person, IND
Roy Tarpley, DAL
John Williams, CLE

1987-88
Mark Jackson, NY
Armon Gilliam, PHO
Kenny Smith, SAC
Greg Anderson, SA
Derrick McKey, SEA

1988-89
Mitch Richmond, GS
Willie Anderson, SA
Hersey Hawkins, PHI
Rik Smits, IND
Charles Smith, LAC

1989-90
David Robinson, SA
Tim Hardaway, GS

Vlade Divac, LAL
Sherman Douglas, MIA
Pooh Richardson, MIN

1990-91
Derrick Coleman, NJ
Lionel Simmons, SAC
Dee Brown, BOS
Kendall Gill, CHA
Dennis Scott, ORL

1991-92
Larry Johnson, CHA
Dikembe Mutombo, DEN
Billy Owens, GS
Steve Smith, MIA
Stacey Augmon, ATL

1992-93

FIRST
Shaquille O'Neal, ORL
Alonzo Mourning, CHA
Christian Laettner, MIN
Tom Gugliotta, WAS
LaPhonso Ellis, DEN

SECOND
Walt Williams, SAC
Robert Horry, HOU
Latrell Sprewell, GS
Clarence Weatherspoon, PHI
Richard Dumas, PHO

ALL-DEFENSIVE TEAMS

1968-69
Dave DeBusschere, NY
Nate Thurmond, SF
Bill Russell, BOS
Walt Frazier, NY
Jerry Sloan, CHI

1969-70
Dave DeBusschere, NY
Gus Johnson, BAL
Willis Reed, NY
Walt Frazier, NY
Jerry West, LA

1970-71
Dave DeBusschere, NY
Gus Johnson, BAL

Nate Thurmond, SF
Walt Frazier, NY
Jerry West, LA

1971-72
Dave DeBusschere, NY
John Havlicek, BOS
Wilt Chamberlain, LA
Jerry West, LA
Walt Frazier, NY
Jerry Sloan, CHI

1972-73
Dave DeBusschere, NY
John Havlicek, BOS
Wilt Chamberlain, LA

Jerry West, LA
Walt Frazier, NY

1973-74
Dave DeBusschere, NY
John Havlicek, BOS
Kareem Abdul-Jabbar, MIL
Norm Van Lier, CHI
Walt Frazier, NY
Jerry Sloan, CHI

1974-75
John Havlicek, BOS
Paul Silas, BOS
Kareem Abdul-Jabbar, MIL
Jerry Sloan, CHI
Walt Frazier, NY

1975-76
Paul Silas, BOS
John Havlicek, BOS
Dave Cowens, BOS
Norm Van Lier, CHI
Don Watts, SEA

1976-77
Bobby Jones, DEN
E.C. Coleman, NO
Bill Walton, POR
Don Buse, IND
Norm Van Lier, CHI

1977-78
Bobby Jones, DEN
Maurice Lucas, POR
Bill Walton, POR
Lionel Hollins, POR
Don Buse, PHO

1978-79
Bobby Jones, PHi
Bobby Dandridge, WAS
Kareem Abdul-Jabbar, LA
Dennis Johnson, SEA
Don Buse, PHO

1979-80
Bobby Jones, PHI
Dan Roundfield, ATL
Kareem Abdul-Jabbar, LA
Dennis Johnson, SEA
Don Buse, PHO
Micheal Ray Richardson, NY

1980-81
Bobby Jones, PHI
Caldwell Jones, PHI
Kareem Abdul-Jabbar, LA
Dennis Johnson, PHO
Micheal Ray Richardson, NY

1981-82
Bobby Jones, PHI
Dan Roundfield, ATL
Caldwell Jones, PHI

Michael Cooper, LA
Dennis Johnson, PHO

1982-83
Bobby Jones, PHI
Dan Roundfield, ATL
Moses Malone, PHI
Sidney Moncrief, MIL
Dennis Johnson, PHO
Maurice Cheeks, PHI

1983-84
Bobby Jones, PHI
Michael Cooper, LA
Tree Rollins, ATL
Maurice Cheeks, PHI
Sidney Moncrief, MIL

1984-85
Sidney Moncrief, MIL
Paul Pressey, MIL
Mark Eaton, UTA
Michael Cooper, LAL
Maurice Cheeks, PHI

1985-86
Paul Pressey, MIL
Kevin McHale, BOS
Mark Eaton, UTA
Sidney Moncrief, MIL
Maurice Cheeks, PHI

1986-87
Kevin McHale, BOS
Michael Cooper, LAL
Akeem Olajuwon, HOU
Alvin Robertson, SA
Dennis Johnson, BOS

1987-88
Kevin McHale, BOS
Rodney McCray, HOU
Akeem Olajuwon, HOU
Michael Cooper, LAL
Michael Jordan, CHI

1988-89
Dennis Rodman, DET
Larry Nance, CLE
Mark Eaton, UTA
Michael Jordan, CHI
Joe Dumars, DET

1989-90
Dennis Rodman, DET
Buck Williams, POR
Akeem Olajuwon, HOU
Michael Jordan, CHI
Joe Dumars, DET

1990-91
Dennis Rodman, DET
Buck Williams, POR
David Robinson, SA
Michael Jordan, CHI
Alvin Robertson, MIL

1991-92
Dennis Rodman, DET
Scottie Pippen, CHI
David Robinson, SA
Michael Jordan, CHI
Joe Dumars, DET

1992-93
FIRST
Dennis Rodman, DET
Scottie Pippen, CHI
Hakeem Olajuwon, HOU
Michael Jordan, CHI
Joe Dumars, DET

SECOND
Larry Nance, CLE
Horace Grant, CHI
David Robinson, SA
Dan Majerle, PHO
John Starks, NY

ALL-STAR GAMES

	RESULT	SITE	MVP
1950-51	East 111, West 94	Boston	Ed Macauley, Boston
1951-52	East 108, West 91	Boston	Paul Arizin, Philadelphia
1952-53	West 79, East 75	Fort Wayne	George Mikan, Minneapolis
1953-54	East 98, West 93 (OT)	New York	Bob Cousy, Boston
1954-55	East 100, West 91	New York	Bill Sharman, Boston
1955-56	West 108, East 94	Rochester	Bob Pettit, St. Louis
1956-57	East 109, West 97	Boston	Bob Cousy, Boston
1957-58	East 130, West 118	St. Louis	Bob Pettit, St. Louis
1958-59	West 124, East 108	Detroit	E. Baylor, Minn./B. Pettit, St. L.
1959-60	East 125, West 115	Philadelphia	Wilt Chamberlain, Philadelphia
1960-61	West 153, East 131	Syracuse	Oscar Robertson, Cincinnati
1961-62	West 150, East 130	St. Louis	Bob Pettit, St. Louis
1962-63	East 115, West 108	Los Angeles	Bill Russell, Boston
1963-64	East 111, West 107	Boston	Oscar Robertson, Cincinnati
1964-65	East 124, West 123	St. Louis	Jerry Lucas, Cincinnati
1965-66	East 137, West 94	Cincinnati	Adrian Smith, Cincinnati
1966-67	West 135, East 120	San Francisco	Rick Barry, San Francisco
1967-68	East 144, West 124	New York	Hal Greer, Philadelphia
1968-69	East 123, West 112	Baltimore	Oscar Robertson, Cincinnati
1969-70	East 142, West 135	Philadelphia	Willis Reed, New York
1970-71	West 108, East 107	San Diego	Lenny Wilkens, Seattle
1971-72	West 112, East 110	Los Angeles	Jerry West, Los Angeles
1972-73	East 104, West 84	Chicago	Dave Cowens, Boston
1973-74	West 134, East 123	Seattle	Bob Lanier, Detroit
1974-75	East 108, West 102	Phoenix	Walt Frazier, New York
1975-76	East 123, West 109	Philadelphia	Dave Bing, Washington
1976-77	West 125, East 124	Milwaukee	Julius Erving, Philadelphia
1977-78	East 133, West 125	Atlanta	Randy Smith, Buffalo
1978-79	West 134, East 129	Detroit	David Thompson, Denver
1979-80	East 144, West 135 (OT)	Washington	George Gervin, San Antonio
1980-81	East 123, West 120	Cleveland	Nate Archibald, Boston
1981-82	East 120, West 118	E. Rutherford	Larry Bird, Boston
1982-83	East 132, West 123	Los Angeles	Julius Erving, Philadelphia
1983-84	East 154, West 145 (OT)	Denver	Isiah Thomas, Detroit
1984-85	West 140, East 129	Indianapolis	Ralph Sampson, Houston
1985-86	East 139, West 132	Dallas	Isiah Thomas, Detroit
1986-87	West 154, East 149 (OT)	Seattle	Tom Chambers, Seattle
1987-88	East 138, West 133	Chicago	Michael Jordan, Chicago
1988-89	West 143, East 134	Houston	Karl Malone, Utah
1989-90	East 130, West 113	Miami	Magic Johnson, L.A. Lakers
1990-91	East 116, West 114	Charlotte	Charles Barkley, Philadelphia
1991-92	West 153, East 113	Orlando	Magic Johnson, L.A. Lakers
1992-93	West 135, East 132 (OT)	Utah	Karl Malone, Utah/ John Stockton, Utah

CAREER LEADERS

(Players active at the close of 1992-93
are listed in bold)

POINTS
Kareem Abdul-Jabbar	38,387
Wilt Chamberlain	31,419
Elvin Hayes	27,313
Moses Malone	**27,066**
Oscar Robertson	26,710
John Havlicek	26,395
Alex English	25,613
Jerry West	25,192
Adrian Dantley	23,177
Elgin Baylor	23,149
Dominique Wilkins	**22,096**
Larry Bird	21,791
Robert Parish	**21,628**
Hal Greer	21,586
Michael Jordan	**21,541**
Walt Bellamy	20,941
Bob Pettit	20,880
George Gervin	20,708
Bernard King	**19,655**
Walter Davis	19,521

GAMES
Kareem Abdul-Jabbar	1,560
Robert Parish	**1,339**
Elvin Hayes	1,303
John Havlicek	1,270
Moses Malone	**1,257**
Paul Silas	1,254
Alex English	1,193
Hal Greer	1,122
Jack Sikma	1,107
Maurice Cheeks	**1,101**

MINUTES
Kareem Abdul-Jabbar	57,446
Elvin Hayes	50,000
Wilt Chamberlain	47,859
John Havlicek	46,471
Moses Malone	**44,304**
Oscar Robertson	43,886
Robert Parish	**40,873**
Rill Russell	40,726
Hal Greer	39,788
Walt Bellamy	38,940

SCORING AVERAGE
(Minimum 400 Games or 10,000 Points)
Michael Jordan	**32.3**
Wilt Chamberlain	30.1
Elgin Baylor	27.4
Jerry West	27.0
Dominique Wilkins	**26.5**
Bob Pettit	26.4
George Gervin	26.2
Karl Malone	**26.1**
Oscar Robertson	25.7
Kareem Abdul-Jabbar	24.6

REBOUNDS
Wilt Chamberlain	23,924
Bill Russell	21,620
Kareem Abdul-Jabbar	17,440
Elvin Hayes	16,279
Moses Malone	**15,940**
Nate Thurmond	14,464
Walt Bellamy	14,241
Wes Unseld	13,769
Robert Parish	**13,440**
Jerry Lucas	12,942

ASSISTS
Magic Johnson	9,921
Oscar Robertson	9,887
Isiah Thomas	**8,662**
John Stockton	**8,352**
Maurice Cheeks	**7,392**
Lenny Wilkens	7,211
Bob Cousy	6,955
Guy Rodgers	6,917
Nate Archibald	6,476
John Lucas	6,454

STEALS
Maurice Cheeks	**2,310**
Alvin Robertson	**1,946**
John Stockton	**1,832**
Michael Jordan	**1,815**
Isiah Thomas	**1,793**
Magic Johnson	1,698
Gus Williams	1,638
Clyde Drexler	**1,623**
Larry Bird	1,556
Julius Erving	1,508

BLOCKED SHOTS

Kareem Abdul-Jabbar	3,189
Mark Eaton	3,064
Tree Rollins	2,471
Hakeem Olajuwon	2,444
Robert Parish	2,156
George T. Johnson	2,082
Manute Bol	2,061
Larry Nance	1,972
Elvin Hayes	1,771
Patrick Ewing	1,767

PERSONAL FOULS

Kareem Abdul-Jabbar	4,657
Elvin Hayes	4,193
Robert Parish	4,001
Jack Sikma	3,879
Hal Greer	3,855
James Edwards	3,847
Dolph Schayes	3,664
Bill Laimbeer	3,603
Walt Bellamy	3,536
Caldwell Jones	3,527

DISQUALIFICATIONS

Vern Mikkelsen	127
Walter Dukes	121
Charlie Share	105
Paul Arizin	101
Darryl Dawkins	100
James Edwards	95
Tom Gola	94
Tom Sanders	94
Steve Johnson	92
Tree Rollins	91

FIELD GOALS ATTEMPTED

Kareem Abdul-Jabbar	28,307
Elvin Hayes	24,272
John Havlicek	23,930
Wilt Chamberlain	23,497
Alex English	21,036
Elgin Baylor	20,171
Oscar Robertson	19,620
Jerry West	19,032
Moses Malone	18,958
Hal Greer	18,811

FIELD GOALS MADE

Kareem Abdul-Jabbar	15,837
Wilt Chamberlain	12,681
Elvin Hayes	10,976
Alex English	10,659
John Havlicek	10,513

Oscar Robertson	9,508
Moses Malone	9,320
Jerry West	9,016
Robert Parish	8,909
Elgin Baylor	8,693

FIELD GOAL PCT.
(Minimum 2,000 FGM)

Artis Gilmore	.599
Steve Johnson	.572
Darryl Dawkins	.572
James Donaldson	.571
Charles Barkley	.569
Jeff Ruland	.564
Kareem Abdul-Jabbar	.559
Kevin McHale	.554
Otis Thorpe	.554
Buck Williams	.554

FREE THROWS ATTEMPTED

Wilt Chamberlain	11,862
Moses Malone	10,941
Kareem Abdul-Jabbar	9,304
Oscar Robertson	9,185
Jerry West	8,801
Adrian Dantley	8,351
Dolph Schayes	8,273
Bob Pettit	8,119
Walt Bellamy	8,088
Elvin Hayes	7,999

FREE THROWS MADE

Moses Malone	8,419
Oscar Robertson	7,694
Jerry West	7,160
Dolph Schayes	6,979
Adrian Dantley	6,832
Kareem Abdul-Jabbar	6,712
Bob Pettit	6,182
Wilt Chamberlain	6,057
Elgin Baylor	5,763
Lenny Wilkens	5,394

FREE THROW PCT.
(Minimum 1,200 FTM)

Mark Price	.908
Rick Barry	.900
Calvin Murphy	.892
Larry Bird	.886
Bill Sharman	.883
Ricky Pierce	.876
Jeff Malone	.874
Kiki Vandeweghe	.872
Reggie Miller	.872

3-PT. FIELD GOALS ATTEMPTED

Michael Adams	2,544
Danny Ainge	2,193
Dale Ellis	2,188
Reggie Miller	1,860
Derek Harper	1,749
Larry Bird	1,727
Chuck Person	1,662
Terry Porter	1,610
Darrell Griffith	1,596
Vernon Maxwell	1,578

3-PT. FIELD GOALS MADE

Dale Ellis	882
Michael Adams	851
Danny Ainge	844
Reggie Miller	717
Larry Bird	649
Terry Porter	619
Derek Harper	608
Chuck Person	584
Mark Price	581
Trent Tucker	575

3-PT. FIELD GOAL PCT.
(Minimum 100 Made)

Steve Kerr	.455
B.J. Armstrong	.443
Drazen Petrovic	.437
Mark Price	.412
Trent Tucker	.408
Dana Barros	.407
Hersey Hawkins	.406
Mike Iuzzolino	.404
Dale Ellis	.403
Jim Les	.403

MOST VICTORIES, COACH

Red Auerbach	938
Lenny Wilkens	869
Jack Ramsay	864
Dick Motta	856
Bill Fitch	845
Cotton Fitzsimmons	805
Gene Shue	784
Don Nelson	753
John MacLeod	707
Red Holzman	696

ACTIVE CAREER LEADERS

(Includes players active at the close
of the 1992-93 season)

POINTS

Moses Malone	27,066
Dominique Wilkins	22,096
Robert Parish	21,628
Michael Jordan	21,541
Bernard King	19,655
Tom Chambers	18,628
Mark Aguirre	18,045
Isiah Thomas	17,966
Kevin McHale	17,335
Rolando Blackman	17,223

GAMES

Robert Parish	1,339
Moses Malone	1,257
Maurice Cheeks	1,101
James Edwards	1,067
Tree Rollins	1,060
Bill Laimbeer	1,057
Kevin McHale	971
Buck Williams	959
Eddie Johnson	934
Tom Chambers	933

MINUTES

Moses Malone	44,304
Robert Parish	40,873
Maurice Cheeks	34,845
Isiah Thomas	33,766
Bill Laimbeer	33,708
Buck Williams	33,500
Rolando Blackman	31,118
Dominique Wilkins	30,858
Tom Chambers	30,751
Kevin McHale	30,118

SCORING AVERAGE
(Minimum 400 Games or 10,000 Points)

Michael Jordan	32.3
Dominique Wilkins	26.5
Karl Malone	26.1
Charles Barkley	23.8
Patrick Ewing	23.7
Hakeem Olajuwon	23.2
Chris Mullin	22.5
Bernard King	22.3
Moses Malone	21.5
Terry Cummings	21.1

REBOUNDS

Moses Malone	15,940
Robert Parish	13,440
Buck Williams	10,521
Bill Laimbeer	10,344
Hakeem Olajuwon	8,509
Larry Smith	8,125
Charles Barkley	8,007
James Donaldson	7,366
Larry Nance	7,125
Kevin McHale	7,122

ASSISTS

Isiah Thomas	8,662
John Stockton	8,352
Maurice Cheeks	7,392
Sleepy Floyd	4,948
Terry Porter	4,785
Derek Harper	4,692
Doc Rivers	4,504
Clyde Drexler	4,392
Kevin Johnson	4,275
Jay Humphries	4,101

STEALS

Maurice Cheeks	2,310
Alvin Robertson	1,946
John Stockton	1,832
Michael Jordan	1,815
Isiah Thomas	1,793
Clyde Drexler	1,623
Derek Harper	1,414
Doc Rivers	1,400
Hakeem Olajuwon	1,320
Dominique Wilkins	1,182

BLOCKED SHOTS

Mark Eaton	3,064
Tree Rollins	2,471
Hakeem Olajuwon	2,444
Robert Parish	2,156
Manute Bol	2,061
Larry Nance	1,972
Patrick Ewing	1,767
Moses Malone	1,713
Kevin McHale	1,690
Herb Williams	1,468

PERSONAL FOULS

Robert Parish	4,001
James Edwards	3,847
Bill Laimbeer	3,603
Tom Chambers	3,321
Buck Williams	3,290

Tree Rollins	3,259
Rick Mahorn	3,117
Moses Malone	3,009
Larry Smith	2,966
Mark Eaton	2,955

DISQUALIFICATIONS

James Edwards	95
Tree Rollins	91
Robert Parish	83
Rick Mahorn	74
Tom Chambers	72
Alton Lister	72
Hakeem Olajuwon	67
Larry Smith	64
Bill Laimbeer	63
Danny Schayes	60

FIELD GOALS ATTEMPTED

Moses Malone	18,958
Dominique Wilkins	17,747
Robert Parish	16,442
Michael Jordan	15,647
Isiah Thomas	15,141
Bernard King	15,109
Tom Chambers	14,541
Mark Aguirre	14,517
Eddie Johnson	14,268
Terry Cummings	13,804

FIELD GOALS MADE

Moses Malone	9,320
Robert Parish	8,909
Dominique Wilkins	8,322
Michael Jordan	8,079
Bernard King	7,830
Mark Aguirre	7,038
Isiah Thomas	6,876
Tom Chambers	6,845
Kevin McHale	6,830
Eddie Johnson	6,815

FIELD GOAL PCT.
(Minimum 2,000 FGM)

James Donaldson	.571
Charles Barkley	.569
Kevin McHale	.554
Otis Thorpe	.554
Buck Williams	.554
Larry Nance	.548
Robert Parish	.542
Dennis Rodman	.537
Brad Daugherty	.536
David Robinson	.533

FREE THROWS ATTEMPTED

Moses Malone	10,941
Dominique Wilkins	6,184
Karl Malone	6,154
Michael Jordan	6,025
Charles Barkley	5,929
Tom Chambers	5,852
Bernard King	5,444
Robert Parish	5,283
Isiah Thomas	5,058
Buck Williams	5,041

FREE THROWS MADE

Moses Malone	8,419
Michael Jordan	5,096
Dominique Wilkins	5,013
Tom Chambers	4,731
Karl Malone	4,445
Charles Barkley	4,365
Bernard King	3,972
Isiah Thomas	3,855
Robert Parish	3,810
Kevin McHale	3,634

FREE THROW PCT.
(Minimum 1,200 FTM)

Mark Price	.908
Ricky Pierce	.876
Jeff Malone	.874
Reggie Miller	.872
Kiki Vandeweghe	.872
Chris Mullin	.869
Hersey Hawkins	.867
Jeff Hornacek	.856
Michael Adams	.853
Danny Ainge	.850

3-PT. FIELD GOALS ATTEMPTED

Michael Adams	2,544
Danny Ainge	2,193
Dale Ellis	2,188
Reggie Miller	1,860
Derek Harper	1,749

Chuck Person	1,662
Terry Porter	1,610
Vernon Maxwell	1,578
Sleepy Floyd	1,475
Mark Price	1,410

3-PT. FIELD GOALS MADE

Dale Ellis	882
Michael Adams	851
Danny Ainge	844
Reggie Miller	717
Terry Porter	619
Derek Harper	608
Chuck Person	584
Mark Price	581
Trent Tucker	575
Byron Scott	522

3-PT. FIELD GOAL PCT.
(Minimum 100 Made)

Steve Kerr	.455
B.J. Armstrong	.443
Drazen Petrovic	.437
Mark Price	.412
Trent Tucker	.408
Dana Barros	.407
Hersey Hawkins	.406
Mike Iuzzolino	.404
Dale Ellis	.403
Jim Les	.403

MOST VICTORIES, COACH

Lenny Wilkens	869
Don Nelson	753
Pat Riley	644
Chuck Daly	519
Larry Brown	434
Kevin Loughery	415
Jerry Sloan	345
Rick Adelman	244
Phil Jackson	244
Matt Guokas	230

REGULAR-SEASON RECORDS

MINUTES
(First Kept in 1951-52)

3,882	Wilt Chamberlain, PHI	1961-62
3,836	Wilt Chamberlain, PHI	1967-68
3,806	Wilt Chamberlain, SF	1962-63
3,773	Wilt Chamberlain, PHI	1960-61
3,737	Wilt Chamberlain, PHI	1965-66
3,698	John Havlicek, BOS	1971-72
3,689	Wilt Chamberlain, SF	1963-64
3,682	Wilt Chamberlain, PHI	1966-67
3,681	Nate Archibald, KCO	1972-73
3,678	John Havlicek, BOS	1970-71

POINTS

4,029	Wilt Chamberlain, PHI	1961-62
3,586	Wilt Chamberlain, SF	1962-63
3,041	Michael Jordan, CHI	1986-87
3,033	Wilt Chamberlain, PHI	1960-61
2,948	Wilt Chamberlain, SF	1963-64
2,868	Michael Jordan, CHI	1987-88
2,831	Bob McAdoo, BUF	1974-75
2,822	Kareem Abdul-Jabbar, MIL	1971-72
2,775	Rick Barry, SF	1966-67
2,753	Michael Jordan, CHI	1989-90

SCORING AVERAGE
(Minimum 70 Games or 1,400 Points)

50.4	Wilt Chamberlain, PHI	1961-62
44.8	Wilt Chamberlain, SF	1962-63
38.4	Wilt Chamberlain, PHI	1960-61
37.6	Wilt Chamberlain, PHI	1959-60
37.1	Michael Jordan, CHI	1986-87
36.9	Wilt Chamberlain, SF	1963-64
35.6	Rick Barry, SF	1966-67
35.0	Michael Jordan, CHI	1987-88
34.8	Kareem Abdul-Jabbar, MIL	1971-72
34.7	Wilt Chamberlain, SF/PHI	1964-65

REBOUNDS
(First Kept in 1950-51)

2,149	Wilt Chamberlain, PHI	1960-61
2,052	Wilt Chamberlain, PHI	1961-62
1,957	Wilt Chamberlain, PHI	1966-67
1,952	Wilt Chamberlain, PHI	1967-68
1,946	Wilt Chamberlain, SF	1962-63
1,943	Wilt Chamberlain, PHI	1965-66
1,941	Wilt Chamberlain, PHI	1959-60
1,930	Bill Russell, BOS	1963-64
1,878	Bill Russell, BOS	1964-65
1,868	Bill Russell, BOS	1960-61

ASSISTS

1,164	John Stockton, UTA	1990-91
1,134	John Stockton, UTA	1989-90
1,128	John Stockton, UTA	1987-88
1,126	John Stockton, UTA	1991-92
1,123	Isiah Thomas, DET	1984-85
1,118	John Stockton, UTA	1988-89
1,099	Kevin Porter, DET	1978-79
991	Kevin Johnson, PHO	1988-89
989	Magic Johnson, LAL	1990-91
988	Magic Johnson, LAL	1988-89

STEALS
(First Kept in 1973-74)

301	Alvin Robertson, SA	1985-86
281	Don Buse, IND	1976-77
265	Micheal Richardson, NY	1979-80
263	John Stockton, UTA	1988-89
261	Slick Watts, SEA	1975-76
260	Alvin Robertson, SA	1986-87
259	Michael Jordan, CHI	1987-88
246	Alvin Robertson, MIL	1990-91
244	John Stockton, UTA	1991-92
243	Micheal Richardson, NJ	1984-85
243	Alvin Robertson, SA	1987-88

BLOCKED SHOTS
(First Kept in 1973-74)

456	Mark Eaton, UTA	1984-85
397	Manute Bol, WAS	1985-86
393	Elmore Smith, LA	1973-74
376	Akeem Olajuwon, HOU	1989-90
369	Mark Eaton, UTA	1985-86
351	Mark Eaton, UTA	1982-83
345	Manute Bol, GS	1988-89
343	Tree Rollins, ATL	1982-83
342	Hakeem Olajuwon, HOU	1992-93
338	Kareem Abdul-Jabbar, LA	1975-76

PERSONAL FOULS

386	Darryl Dawkins, NJ	1983-84
382	Darryl Dawkins, NJ	1982-83
372	Steve Johnson, KC	1981-82
367	Bill Robinzine, KC	1978-79
366	Bill Bridges, STL	1967-68
363	Lonnie Shelton, NY	1976-77
363	James Edwards, IND	1978-79
361	Kevin Kunnert, HOU	1976-77
358	Dan Roundfield, ATL	1978-79
358	Rick Mahorn, WAS	1983-84

DISQUALIFICATIONS
(First Kept in 1950-51)

26	Don Meineke, FTW	1952-53
25	Steve Johnson, KC	1981-82
23	Darryl Dawkins, NJ	1982-83
22	Walter Dukes, DET	1958-59
22	Darryl Dawkins, NJ	1983-84
21	Joe Meriweather, ATL	1976-77
20	Joe Fulks, PHI	1952-53
20	Vern Mikkelsen, MIN	1957-58
20	Walter Dukes, DET	1959-60
20	Walter Dukes, DET	1961-62
20	George Johnson, NJ	1977-78

FIELD GOALS ATTEMPTED

3,159	Wilt Chamberlain, PHI	1961-62
2,770	Wilt Chamberlain, SF	1962-63
2,457	Wilt Chamberlain, PHI	1960-61
2,311	Wilt Chamberlain, PHI	1959-60
2,298	Wilt Chamberlain, SF	1963-64

2,279	Michael Jordan, CHI	1986-87
2,273	Elgin Baylor, LA	1962-63
2,217	Rick Barry, GS	1974-75
2,215	Elvin Hayes, SD	1970-71
2,166	Elgin Baylor, LA	1960-61

FIELD GOALS MADE

1,597	Wilt Chamberlain, PHI	1961-62
1,463	Wilt Chamberlain, SF	1962-63
1,251	Wilt Chamberlain, PHI	1960-61
1,204	Wilt Chamberlain, SF	1963-64
1,159	Kareem Abdul-Jabbar, MIL	1971-72
1,098	Michael Jordan, CHI	1986-87
1,095	Bob McAdoo, BUF	1974-75
1,074	Wilt Chamberlain, PHI	1965-66
1,069	Michael Jordan, CHI	1987-88
1,065	Wilt Chamberlain, PHI	1959-60

FIELD GOAL PCT.
(Minimum 300 FGM)

.727	Wilt Chamberlain, LA	1972-73
.683	Wilt Chamberlain, PHI	1966-67
.670	Artis Gilmore, CHI	1980-81
.652	Artis Gilmore, CHI	1981-82
.649	Wilt Chamberlain, LA	1971-72
.637	James Donaldson, LAC	1984-85
.632	Steve Johnson, SA	1985-86
.626	Artis Gilmore, SA	1982-83
.625	Mark West, PHO	1989-90
.623	Artis Gilmore, SA	1984-85

FREE THROWS ATTEMPTED

1,363	Wilt Chamberlain, PHI	1961-62
1,113	Wilt Chamberlain, SF	1962-63
1,054	Wilt Chamberlain, PHI	1960-61
1,016	Wilt Chamberlain, SF	1963-64
991	Wilt Chamberlain, SF	1959-60
977	Jerry West, LA	1965-66
976	Wilt Chamberlain, SF	1965-66
972	Michael Jordan, CHI	1986-87
951	Charles Barkley, PHI	1987-88
946	Adrian Dantley, UTA	1983-84

FREE THROWS MADE

840	Jerry West, LA	1965-66
835	Wilt Chamberlain, PHI	1961-62
833	Michael Jordan, CHI	1986-87
813	Adrian Dantley, UTA	1983-84
800	Oscar Robertson, CIN	1963-64
753	Rick Barry, SF	1966-67
742	Oscar Robertson, CIN	1965-66
737	Moses Malone, PHI	1984-85
736	Oscar Robertson, CIN	1966-67
723	Michael Jordan, CHI	1987-88

FREE THROW PCT.
(Minimum 125 FTM)

.958	Calvin Murphy, HOU	1980-81
.948	Mark Price, CLE	1992-93
.947	Mark Price, CLE	1991-92
.947	Rick Barry, HOU	1978-79
.945	Ernie DiGregorio, BUF	1976-77
.935	Chris Jackson, DEN	1992-93
.935	Ricky Sobers, CHI	1980-81
.935	Rick Barry, HOU	1979-80
.932	Bill Sharman, BOS	1958-59
.930	Larry Bird, BOS	1989-90

3-PT. FIELD GOALS ATTEMPTED
(Rule went into effect in 1979-80)

564	Michael Adams, DEN	1990-91
510	Vernon Maxwell, HOU	1990-91
473	Vernon Maxwell, HOU	1991-92
466	Michael Adams, DEN	1988-89
438	Dan Majerle, PHO	1992-93
432	Michael Adams, DEN	1989-90
419	Reggie Miller, IND	1992-93
396	Glen Rice, MIA	1991-92
379	Michael Adams, DEN	1987-88
386	Michael Adams, WAS	1991-92
386	Glen Rice, MIA	1992-93

3-PT. FIELD GOALS MADE

172	Vernon Maxwell, HOU	1990-91
167	Michael Adams, DEN.	1990-91
167	Dan Majerle, PHO.	1992-93
167	Reggie Miller, IND	1992-93
166	Michael Adams, DEN.	1988-89
162	Dale Ellis, SEA	1988-89
162	Vernon Maxwell, HOU	1991-92
158	Michael Adams, DEN.	1989-90
155	Glen Rice, MIA.	1991-92
152	Mark Price, CLE	1989-90

3-PT. FIELD GOAL PCT.
(Minimum 50 Made)

.507	Steve Kerr, CLE	1989-90
.491	Craig Hodges, MIL/PHO	1987-88
.486	Mark Price, CLE	1987-88
.481	Craig Hodges, CHI	1989-90
.478	Dale Ellis, SEA	1988-89
.461	Jim Les, SAC	1990-91
.453	B.J. Armstrong, CHI	1992-93
.451	Chris Mullin, GS	1992-93
.451	Craig Hodges, MIL	1985-86
.449	Drazen Petrovic, NJ	1992-93

GAME RECORDS

POINTS

100...Wilt Chamberlain, PHI vs. NY, March 2, 1962
78.....Wilt Chamberlain, PHI vs. LA, Dec. 8, 1961 (3 OT)
73.....Wilt Chamberlain, PHI vs. CHI, Jan. 13, 1962
73.....Wilt Chamberlain, SF vs. NY, Nov. 6, 1962
73.....David Thompson, DEN vs. DET, April 9, 1978
72.....Wilt Chamberlain, SF vs. LA, Nov. 3, 1962
71.....Elgin Baylor, LA vs. NY, Nov. 15, 1960
70.....Wilt Chamberlain, SF vs. SYR, March 10, 1963
69.....Michael Jordan, CHI vs. CLE, March 28, 1990 (OT)
68.....Wilt Chamberlain, PHI vs. CHI, Dec. 16, 1967
68.....Pete Maravich, NO vs. NY, Feb. 25, 1977

REBOUNDS

55.....Wilt Chamberlain, PHI vs. BOS, Nov. 24, 1960
51.....Bill Russell, BOS vs. SYR, Feb. 5, 1960
49.....Bill Russell, BOS vs. PHI, Nov. 16, 1957
49.....Bill Russell, BOS vs. DET, March 11, 1965
45.....Wilt Chamberlain, PHI vs. SYR, Feb. 6, 1960
45.....Wilt Chamberlain, PHI vs. LA, Jan. 21, 1961

ASSISTS

30.....Scott Skiles, ORL vs. DEN, Dec. 30, 1990
29.....Kevin Porter, NJ vs. HOU, Feb. 24, 1978
28.....Bob Cousy, BOS vs. MIN, Feb., 27, 1959
28.....Guy Rodgers, SF vs. STL, March 14, 1963
28.....John Stockton, UTA vs. SA, Jan. 15, 1991

STEALS

11.....Larry Kenon, SA vs. KC, Dec. 26, 1976
10.....Jerry West, LA vs. SEA, Dec. 7, 1973
10.....Larry Steele, POR vs. L.A., Nov. 16, 1974
10.....Fred Brown, SEA vs. PHI, Dec. 3, 1976
10.....Gus Williams, SEA vs. NJ, Feb. 22, 1978
10.....Eddie Jordan, NJ vs. PHI, March 23, 1979
10.....Johnny Moore, SA vs. IND, March 6, 1985
10.....Fat Lever, DEN vs. IND, March 9, 1985
10.....Clyde Drexler, POR vs. MIL, Jan. 10, 1986
10.....Alvin Robertson, SA vs. PHO, Feb. 18, 1986

10.....Ron Harper, CLE vs. PHI, March 10, 1987
10.....Michael Jordan, CHI vs. NJ, Jan. 29, 1988
10.....Alvin Robertson, SA vs. HOU, Jan. 11, 1989 (OT)
10.....Alvin Robertson, MIL vs. UTA, Nov. 19, 1990

BLOCKED SHOTS

17.....Elmore Smith, LA vs. POR, Oct. 28, 1973
15.....Manute Bol, WAS vs. ATL, Jan. 25, 1986
15.....Manute Bol, WAS vs. IND, Feb. 26, 1987
14.....Elmore Smith, LA vs. DET, Oct. 26, 1973
14.....Elmore Smith, LA vs. HOU, Nov. 4, 1973
14.....Mark Eaton, UTA vs. POR, Jan. 18, 1985
14.....Mark Eaton, UTA vs. SA, Feb. 18, 1989

FIELD GOALS ATTEMPTED

63.....Wilt Chamberlain, PHI vs. NY, March 2, 1962
62.....Wilt Chamberlain, PHI vs. LA, Dec. 8, 1961 (3 OT)
60.....Wilt Chamberlain, SF vs. CIN, Oct. 28, 1962 (OT)
58.....Wilt Chamberlain, SF vs. PHI, Nov. 26, 1964
57.....Wilt Chamberlain, SF vs. SYR, Dec. 11, 1962

FIELD GOALS MADE

36.....Wilt Chamberlain, PHI vs. NY, March 2, 1962
31.....Wilt Chamberlain, PHI vs. LA, Dec. 8, 1961 (3 OT)
30.....Wilt Chamberlain, PHI vs. CHI, Dec. 16, 1967
30.....Rick Barry, GS vs. POR, March 26, 1974
29.....Wilt Chamberlain, PHI vs. CHI, Jan. 13, 1962
29.....Wilt Chamberlain, SF vs. LA, Nov. 3, 1962
29.....Wilt Chamberlain, SF vs. NY, Nov. 16, 1962
29.....Wilt Chamberlain, LA vs. PHO, Feb. 9, 1969

FIELD GOAL PCT.

(Minimum 15 Attempts)
1.000.Wilt Chamberlain, PHI vs. BAL, Feb. 24, 1967 (18/18)
1.000.Wilt Chamberlain, PHI vs. BAL, March 19, 1967 (16/16)
1.000.Wilt Chamberlain, PHI vs. LA, Jan. 20, 1967 (15/15)

947 ...Wilt Chamberlain, SF vs. NY, Nov. 27, 1963 (18/19)
.941 ..Wilt Chamberlain, PHI vs. BAL, Nov. 25, 1966 (16/17)

FREE THROWS ATTEMPTED
34 .....Wilt Chamberlain, PHI vs. STL, Feb. 22, 1962
32 .....Wilt Chamberlain, PHI vs. NY, March 2, 1962
31 .....Adrian Dantley, UTA vs. DEN, Nov. 25, 1983
29 .....Lloyd Free, SD vs. ATL, Jan. 13, 1979
29 .....Adrian Dantley, UTA vs. DAL, Oct. 31, 1980
29 .....Adrian Dantley, UTA vs. HOU, Jan. 4, 1984

FREE THROWS MADE
28 .....Wilt Chamberlain, PHI vs. NY, March 2, 1962
28 .....Adrian Dantley, UTA vs. HOU, Jan. 4, 1984
27 .....Adrian Dantley, UTA vs. DEN, Nov. 25, 1983
26 .....Adrian Dantley, UTA vs. DAL, Oct. 31, 1980
26 .....Michael Jordan, CHI vs. NJ, Feb. 26, 1987

FREE THROW PCT.
(Most with No Misses)
1.000..Dominique Wilkins, ALT vs. CHI, Dec. 8, 1992 (23/23)
1.000..Bob Pettit, STL vs. BOS, Nov. 22, 1961 (19/19)
1.000..Bill Cartwright, NY vs. KC, Nov. 17, 1981 (19/19)
1.000..Adrian Dantley, DET vs. CHI, Dec. 15, 1987 (19/19) (OT)

3-PT. FIELD GOALS ATTEMPTED
20 .....Michael Adams, DEN vs. LAC, April 12, 1991
19 ....Dennis Scott, ORL vs. MIL, April 13, 1993
16 ....Michael Adams, DEN vs. MIL, March 23, 1991 (OT)
15 .....Michael Adams, DEN vs. UTA, March 14, 1988
15 .....John Starks, NY vs. CHI, March 31, 1992
15 .....Brian Shaw, MIA vs. MIL, April 8, 1993

3-PT. FIELD GOALS MADE
10 ....Brian Shaw, MIA vs. MIL, April 8, 1993
9 ....Dale Ellis, SEA vs. LAC, April 20, 1990
9 ....Michael Adams, DEN vs. LAC, April 12, 1991
9 ....Dennis Scott, ORL vs. MIL, April 13, 1993

TEAM RECORDS—SEASON

HIGHEST WINNING PCT.
.841 .....69-13 Los Angeles, 1971-72
.840 ....68-13 Philadelphia, 1966-67
.829 ....68-14 Boston, 1972-73

LOWEST WINNING PCT.
.110 ..... 9-73 Philadelphia, 1972-73
.125 ..... 6-42 Providence, 1947-48
.134 .....11-71 Dallas, 1992-93

HIGHEST WINNING PCT., HOME
.976 .....40-1 Boston, 1985-86
.971 ....33-1 Rochester, 1949-50
.969 ....31-1 Syracuse, 1949-50

HIGHEST WINNING PCT., ROAD
.816 .....31-7 Los Angeles, 1971-72
.800 .....32-8 Boston, 1972-73
.780 .....32-9 Boston, 1974-75

CONSECUTIVE WINS
33 ....Los Angeles, Nov. 5, 1971-Jan. 7, 1972
20 ....Milwaukee, Feb. 6-March 8, 1971
20 ....Washington, March 13-Dec. 4, 1948 (overlapping seasons)

CONSECUTIVE WINS
(Start of Season)
15 ....Washington, Nov. 3-Dec. 4, 1948
14 ....Boston, Oct. 22-Nov. 27, 1957
12 ....Seattle, Oct. 29-Nov. 19, 1982

CONSECUTIVE LOSSES
24 ....Cleveland, March 19-Nov. 5, 1982 (overlapping seasons)
21 ....Detroit, March 7-Oct. 22, 1980 (overlapping seasons)
20 ....Philadelphia, Jan. 9-Feb. 11, 1973

CONSECUTIVE WINS, HOME
38 ....Boston, Dec. 10, 1985-Nov. 28, 1986
         (overlapping seasons)
36 ....Philadelphia, Jan. 14, 1966-Jan. 20,
         1967 (overlapping seasons)
34 ....Portland, March 5, 1977-Feb. 3, 1978
         (overlapping seasons)

CONSECUTIVE WINS, ROAD
16 ....Los Angeles, Nov. 6, 1971-Jan. 7, 1972
12 ....New York, Oct. 14-Dec. 10, 1969
12 ....Los Angeles, Oct. 15-Dec. 20, 1972

HIGHEST SCORING AVERAGE
126.5 ...Denver, 1981-82
125.4 ...Philadelphia, 1961-62
125.2 ...Philadelphia, 1966-67

LOWEST SCORING AVERAGE
(Since 1954-55, first year of the 24-second
clock)
87.4 .....Milwaukee, 1954-55
90.8 .....Rochester, 1954-55
91.1 .....Syracuse, 1954-55

FEWEST POINTS ALLOWED PER GAME
(Since 1954-55, first year of the 24-second
clock)
89.9 .....Syracuse, 1954-55
90.0 .....Ft. Wayne, 1954-55
90.4 .....Milwaukee, 1954-55

MOST POINTS ALLOWED PER GAME
130.8 ...Denver, 1990-91
126.0 ...Denver, 1981-82
125.1 ...Seattle, 1967-68

TEAM RECORDS—GAME

MOST POINTS
186 ......Detroit vs. Denver, Dec. 13, 1983
         (3 OT)
184 ......Denver vs. Detroit, Dec. 13, 1983
         (3 OT)
173 .....Boston vs. Minneapolis, Feb. 27, 1959
173 .....Phoenix vs. Denver, Nov. 10, 1990
171 ......San Antonio vs. Milwaukee, March 6,
         1982 (3 OT)
169 ......Philadelphia vs. New York, March 2,
         1962

FEWEST POINTS
(Since 1954-55, first year of the 24-second
clock)
57 ....Milwaukee vs. Boston, Feb. 27, 1955
59 ....Sacramento vs. Charlotte, Jan. 10, 1991
61 ....New York vs. Detroit, April 12, 1992

MOST POINTS, BOTH TEAMS
370 ...Detroit (186) vs. Denver (184), Dec. 13,
       1983 (3 OT)
337 ...San Antonio (171) vs. Milwaukee (166),
       March 6, 1982 (3 OT)
318 ...Denver (163) vs. San Antonio (155), Jan.
       11, 1984
316 ...Philadelphia (169) vs. New York (147),
       March 2, 1962
316 ...Cincinnati (165) vs. San Diego (151),
       March 12, 1970
316 ...Phoenix (173) vs. Denver (143), Nov. 10,
       1990

FEWEST POINTS, BOTH TEAMS
(Since 1954-55, first year of the 24-second
clock)
119 ...Milwaukee (57) vs. Boston (62), Feb. 27,
       1955
133 ...New York (61) vs. Detroit (72), April 12,
       1992
135 ...Syracuse (66) vs. Ft. Wayne (69), Jan. 25,
       1955

LARGEST MARGIN OF VICTORY
68 .....Cleveland (148) vs. Miami (80), Dec. 17,
       1991
63 .....Los Angeles (162) vs. Golden State (99),
       March 19, 1972
62 .....Syracuse (162) vs. New York (100), Dec.
       25, 1960
59 .....Golden State (150) vs. Indiana (91),
       March 19, 1977
59 .....Milwaukee (143) vs. Detroit (84), Dec. 26,
       1978

PLAYOFF RECORDS—CAREER

POINTS
5,762 ...Kareem Abdul-Jabbar
4,457 ...Jerry West
3,897 ...Larry Bird

SCORING AVERAGE
(Minimum 25 Games)
34.7 .....Michael Jordan
29.1 ......Jerry West
27.6 .....Karl Malone

REBOUNDS
4,104 ...Bill Russell
3,913 ...Wilt Chamberlain
2,481 ...Kareem Abdul-Jabbar

REBOUNDS PER GAME
(Minimum 25 Games)
24.9 .....Bill Russell
24.5 .....Wilt Chamberlain
14.9 .....Wes Unseld

ASSISTS
2,320 ...Magic Johnson
1,062 ...Larry Bird
1,006 ...Dennis Johnson

ASSISTS PER GAME
(Minimum 25 Games)
12.5 .....Magic Johnson
11.4 .....John Stockton
 8.9 ......Isiah Thomas

PLAYOFF RECORDS—SERIES

POINTS
2-Game Series
68 ....Bob McAdoo, NY vs. CLE, 1978

3-Game Series
135 ......Michael Jordan, CHI vs. MIA, 1992

4-Game Series
150 ......Akeem Olajuwon, HOU vs. DAL, 1988

5-Game Series
226 ......Michael Jordan, CHI vs. CLE, 1988

6-Game Series
278 ......Jerry West, LA vs. BAL, 1965

7-Game Series
284 ......Elgin Baylor, LA vs. BOS, 1962

REBOUNDS
2-Game Series
41 ....Moses Malone, HOU vs. ATL, 1979

3-Game Series
84 ....Bill Russell, BOS vs. SYR, 1957

4-Game Series
118 ......Bill Russell, BOS vs. MIN, 1959

5-Game Series
160 ......Wilt Chamberlain, PHI vs. BOS, 1967

6-Game Series
171 ......Wilt Chamberlain, PHI vs. SF, 1967

7-Game Series
220 ......Wilt Chamberlain, PHI vs. BOS, 1965

ASSISTS
2-Game Series
20 ....Frank Johnson, WAS vs. NJ, 1982

3-Game Series
48 ....Magic Johnson, LAL vs. SA, 1986

4-Game Series
57 ....Magic Johnson, LAL vs. PHO, 1989

5-Game Series
85 ....Magic Johnson, LAL vs. POR, 1985

6-Game Series
90 ....Johnny Moore, SA vs. LA, 1983

7-Game Series
115 ......John Stockton, UTA vs. LAL, 1988

PLAYOFF RECORDS—GAME

POINTS
63.....Michael Jordan, CHI vs. BOS, April 20, 1986 (2 OT)
61.....Elgin Baylor, LA vs. BOS, April 14, 1962
56.....Wilt Chamberlain, PHI vs. SYR, March 22, 1962

REBOUNDS
41.....Wilt Chamberlain, PHI vs. BOS, April 5, 1967
40.....Bill Russell, BOS vs. PHI, March 23, 1958
40.....Bill Russell, BOS vs. STL, March 29, 1960
40.....Bill Russell, BOS vs. LA, April 18, 1962 (OT)

ASSISTS
24.....Magic Johnson, LA vs. PHO, May 15, 1984
24.....John Stockton, UTA vs. LAL, May 17, 1988

23.....Magic Johnson, LAL vs. POR, May 3, 1985

STEALS
8.......Rick Barry, GS vs. SEA, April 14, 1975
8.......Lionel Hollins, POR vs. LA, May 8, 1977
8.......Maurice Cheeks, PHI vs. NJ, April 11, 1979
8.......Craig Hodges, MIL vs. PHI, May 9, 1986
8.......Tim Hardaway, GS vs. LAL, May 8, 1991

BLOCKED SHOTS
10.....Mark Eaton, UTA vs. HOU, April 26, 1985
10.....Akeem Olajuwon, HOU vs. LAL, April 29, 1990
9.....Kareem Abdul-Jabbar, LA vs. GS, April 22, 1977
9......Manute Bol, WAS vs. PHI, April 18, 1986

PLAYOFF RECORDS—TEAM

CONSECUTIVE GAMES WON
13.....L.A. Lakers, 1988-89
12.....Detroit, 1989-90
9 .....Los Angeles, 1982

CONSECUTIVE GAMES LOST
11.....Baltimore, 1965-66 and 1969-70
9 .....New York, 1953-55
9 .....Denver, 1988-90 (still active)

CONSECUTIVE SERIES WON
18.....Boston 1959-1967
12.....Chicago, 1991-93
11.....L.A. Lakers 1987-89

MOST POINTS, GAME
157...Boston vs. New York, April 28, 1990
156...Milwaukee vs. Philadelphia, March 30, 1970
153...L.A. Lakers vs. Denver, May 22, 1985
153...Portland vs. Phoenix, May 11, 1992 (2 OT)

FEWEST POINTS, GAME
(Since 1954-55, first year of the 24-second clock)
70.....Golden State vs. Los Angeles, April 21, 1973

70.....Seattle vs. Houston, April 23, 1982
71.....Syracuse vs. Ft. Wayne, April 7, 1955
71.....Houston vs. Boston, May 5, 1981

MOST POINTS, BOTH TEAMS, GAME
304...Portland (153) vs. Phoenix (151), May 11, 1992 (2 OT)
285...San Antonio (152) vs. Denver (133), April 26, 1983
285...Boston (157) vs. New York (128), April 28, 1990

FEWEST POINTS, BOTH TEAMS, GAME
145...Syracuse (71) vs. Ft. Wayne (74), March 24, 1956
157...Kansas City (76) vs. Phoenix (81), April 17, 1981
157...Detroit (78) vs. Boston (79), May 30, 1988

LARGEST MARGIN OF VICTORY, GAME
58.....Minneapolis (133) vs. St. Louis (75), March 19, 1956
56.....Los Angeles (126) vs. Golden State (70), April 21, 1973
50.....Milwaukee (136) vs. San Francisco (86), April 4, 1971

NBA FIRST-ROUND PICKS
(Since 1970)

ATLANTA HAWKS

1993	Doug Edwards, Florida St.
1992	Adam Keefe, Stanford
1991	Stacey Augmon, UNLV
	Anthony Avent, Seton Hall
1990	Rumeal Robinson, Michigan
1989	Roy Marble, Iowa
1988	(no 1st-round pick)
1987	Dallas Comegys, DePaul
1986	Billy Thompson, Louisville
1985	Jon Koncak, Southern Methodist
1984	Kevin Willis, Michigan St.
1983	(no 1st-round pick)
1982	Keith Edmonson, Purdue
1981	Al Wood, N. Carolina
1980	Don Collins, Washington St.
1979	(no 1st-round pick)
1978	Butch Lee, Marquette
	Jack Givens, Kentucky
1977	Tree Rollins, Clemson
1976	Armond Hill, Princeton
1975	David Thompson, N. Carolina St.
	Marvin Webster, Morgan St.
1974	Tom Henderson, Hawaii
	Mike Sojourner, Utah
1973	Dwight Jones, Houston
	John Brown, Missouri
1972	(no 1st-round pick)
1971	George Trapp, Long Beach St.
1970	Pete Maravich, Louisiana St.
	John Vallely, UCLA

BOSTON CELTICS

1993	Acie Earl, Iowa
1992	Jon Barry, Georgia Tech
1991	Rick Fox, N. Carolina
1990	Dee Brown, Jacksonville
1989	Michael Smith, Brigham Young
1988	Brian Shaw, Cal.-Santa Barbara
1987	Reggie Lewis, Northeastern
1986	Len Bias, Maryland
1985	Sam Vincent, Michigan St.
1984	Michael Young, Houston
1983	Greg Kite, Brigham Young
1982	Darren Tillis, Cleveland St.
1981	Charles Bradley, Wyoming
1980	Kevin McHale, Minnesota
1979	(no 1st-round pick)
1978	Larry Bird, Indiana St.
	Freeman Williams, Portland St.
1977	Cedric Maxwell, N.C.-Charlotte
1976	Norm Cook, Kansas
1975	Tom Boswell, S. Carolina
1974	Glenn McDonald, Long Beach St.

1973	Steve Downing, Indiana
1972	Paul Westphal, Southern Cal.
1971	Clarence Glover, Western Kentucky
1970	Dave Cowens, Florida St.

CHARLOTTE HORNETS

1993	Greg Graham, Indiana
	Scott Burrell, Connecticut
1992	Alonzo Mourning, Georgetown
1991	Larry Johnson, UNLV
1990	Kendall Gill, Illinois
1989	J.R. Reid, N. Carolina
1988	Rex Chapman, Kentucky

CHICAGO BULLS

1993	Corie Blount, Cincinnati
1992	Byron Houston, Oklahoma St.
1991	Mark Randall, Kansas
1990	(no 1st-round pick)
1989	Stacey King, Oklahoma
	B.J. Armstrong, Iowa
	Jeff Sanders, Georgia Southern
1988	Will Perdue, Vanderbilt
1987	Olden Polynice, Virginia
	Horace Grant, Clemson
1986	Brad Sellers, Ohio St.
1985	Keith Lee, Memphis St.
1984	Michael Jordan, N. Carolina
1983	Sidney Green, UNLV
1982	Quintin Dailey, San Francisco
1981	Orlando Woolridge, Notre Dame
1980	Kelvin Ransey, Ohio St.
1979	David Greenwood, UCLA
1978	Reggie Theus, UNLV
1977	Tate Armstrong, Duke
1976	Scott May, Indiana
1975	(no 1st-round pick)
1974	Maurice Lucas, Marquette
	Cliff Pondexter, Long Beach St.
1973	Kevin Kunnert, Iowa
1972	Ralph Simpson, Michigan St.
1971	Kennedy McIntosh, E. Michigan
1970	Jimmy Collins, New Mexico St.

CLEVELAND CAVALIERS

1993	Chris Mills, Arizona
1992	(no 1st-round pick)
1991	Terrell Brandon, Oregon
1990	(no 1st-round pick)
1989	John Morton, Seton Hall
1988	Randolph Keys, Southern Miss.
1987	Kevin Johnson, California
1986	Brad Daugherty, N. Carolina
	Ron Harper, Miami (OH)

1985	Charles Oakley, Virginia Union
1984	Tim McCormick, Michigan
1983	Roy Hinson, Rutgers
	Stewart Granger, Villanova
1982	John Bagley, Boston College
1981	(no 1st-round pick)
1980	Chad Kinch, N.C.-Charlotte
1979	(no 1st-round pick)
1978	Mike Mitchell, Auburn
1977	(no 1st-round pick)
1976	Chuckie Williams, Kansas St.
1975	John Lambert, Southern Cal.
1974	Campy Russell, Michigan
1973	Jim Brewer, Minnesota
1972	Dwight Davis, Houston
1971	Austin Carr, Notre Dame
1970	John Johnson, Iowa

DALLAS MAVERICKS

1993	Jamal Mashburn, Kentucky
1992	Jim Jackson, Ohio St.
1991	Doug Smith, Missouri
1990	(no 1st-round pick)
1989	Randy White, Louisiana Tech
1988	(no 1st-round pick)
1987	Jim Farmer, Alabama
1986	Roy Tarpley, Michigan
1985	Detlef Schrempf, Washington
	Bill Wennington, St. John's
	Uwe Blab, Indiana
1984	Sam Perkins, N. Carolina
	Terence Stansbury, Temple
1983	Dale Ellis, Tennessee
	Derek Harper, Illinois
1982	Bill Garnett, Wyoming
1981	Mark Aguirre, DePaul
	Rolando Blackman, Kansas St.
1980	Kiki Vandeweghe, UCLA

DENVER NUGGETS

1993	Rodney Rogers, Wake Forest
1992	LaPhonso Ellis, Notre Dame
	Bryant Stith, Virginia
1991	Dikembe Mutombo, Georgetown
	Mark Macon, Temple
1990	Chris Jackson, Louisiana St.
1989	Todd Lichti, Stanford
1988	Jerome Lane, Pittsburgh
1987	(no 1st-round pick)
1986	Maurice Martin, St. Joseph's
	Mark Alarie, Duke
1985	Blair Rasmussen, Oregon
1984	(no 1st-round pick)
1983	Howard Carter, Louisiana St.
1982	Rob Williams, Houston
1981	(no 1st-round pick)
1980	James Ray, Jacksonville
	Carl Nicks, Indiana St.

1979	(no 1st-round pick)
1978	Rod Griffin, Wake Forest
	Mike Evans, Kansas St.
1977	Tom LaGarde, N. Carolina
	Anthony Roberts, Oral Roberts
1976	(no 1st-round pick)

DETROIT PISTONS

1993	Lindsey Hunter, Jackson St.
	Allan Houston, Tennessee
1992	Don MacLean, UCLA
1991	(no 1st-round pick)
1990	Lance Blanks, Texas
1989	Kenny Battle, Illinois
1988	(no 1st-round pick)
1987	(no 1st-round pick)
1986	John Salley, Georgia Tech
1985	Joe Dumars, McNeese St.
1984	Tony Campbell, Ohio St.
1983	Antoine Carr, Wichita St.
1982	Cliff Levingston, Wichita St.
	Ricky Pierce, Rice
1981	Isiah Thomas, Indiana
	Kelly Tripucka, Notre Dame
1980	Larry Drew, Missouri
1979	Greg Kelser, Michigan St.
	Roy Hamilton, UCLA
	Phil Hubbard, Michigan
1978	(no 1st-round pick)
1977	(no 1st-round pick)
1976	Leon Douglas, Alabama
1975	(no 1st-round pick)
1974	Al Eberhard, Missouri
1973	(no 1st-round pick)
1972	Bob Nash, Hawaii
1971	Curtis Rowe, UCLA
1970	Bob Lanier, St. Bonaventure

GOLDEN ST. WARRIORS

1993	Anfernee Hardaway, Memphis St.
1992	Latrell Sprewell, Alabama
1991	Chris Gatling, Old Dominion
	Victor Alexander, Iowa St.
	Shaun Vandiver, Colorado
1990	Tyrone Hill, Xavier
1989	Tim Hardaway, Texas-El Paso
1988	Mitch Richmond, Kansas St.
1987	Tellis Frank, Western Kentucky
1986	Chris Washburn, N. Carolina St.
1985	Chris Mullin, St. John's
1984	(no 1st-round pick)
1983	Russell Cross, Purdue
1982	Lester Conner, Oregon St.
1981	(no 1st-round pick)
1980	Joe Barry Carroll, Purdue
	Rickey Brown, Mississippi St.
1979	(no 1st-round pick)
1978	Purvis Short, Jackson St.

Raymond Townsend, UCLA
1977 Rickey Green, Michigan
Wesley Cox, Louisville
1976 Robert Parish, Centenary
Sonny Parker, Texas A&M
1975 Joe Bryant, La Salle
1974 Jamaal Wilkes, UCLA
1973 Kevin Joyce, S. Carolina
1972 (no 1st-round pick)
1971 Darnell Hillman, San Jose St.
1970 (no 1st-round pick)

HOUSTON ROCKETS

1993 Sam Cassell, Florida St.
1992 Robert Horry, Alabama
1991 John Turner, Phillips
1990 Alec Kessler, Georgia
1989 (no 1st-round pick)
1988 Derrick Chievous, Missouri
1987 (no 1st-round pick)
1986 Buck Johnson, Alabama
1985 Steve Harris, Tulsa
1984 Akeem Olajuwon, Houston
1983 Ralph Sampson, Virginia
Rodney McCray, Louisville
1982 Terry Teagle, Baylor
1981 (no 1st-round pick)
1980 (no 1st-round pick)
1979 Lee Johnson, E. Texas St.
1978 (no 1st-round pick)
1977 (no 1st-round pick)
1976 John Lucas, Maryland
1975 Joe Meriweather, Southern Illinois
1974 Bobby Jones, N. Carolina
1973 Ed Ratleff, Long Beach St.
1972 (no 1st-round pick)
1971 Cliff Meely, Colorado
1970 Rudy Tomjanovich, Michigan

INDIANA PACERS

1993 Scott Haskin, Oregon St.
1992 Malik Sealy, St. John's
1991 Dale Davis, Clemson
1990 (no 1st-round pick)
1989 George McCloud, Florida St.
1988 Rik Smits, Marist
1987 Reggie Miller, UCLA
1986 Chuck Person, Auburn
1985 Wayman Tisdale, Oklahoma
1984 Vern Flemming, Georgia
1983 Steve Stipanovich, Missouri
Mitchell Wiggins, Florida St.
1982 Clark Kellogg, Ohio St.
1981 Herb Williams, Ohio St.
1980 (no 1st-round pick)
1979 Dudley Bradley, N. Carolina
1978 Rick Robey, Kentucky
1977 (no 1st-round pick)
1976 (no 1st-round pick)

LOS ANGELES CLIPPERS

1993 Terry Dehere, Seton Hall
1992 Randy Woods, La Salle
Elmore Spencer, UNLV
1991 LeRon Ellis, Syracuse
1990 Bo Kimble, Loyola Marymount
Loy Vaught, Michigan
1989 Danny Ferry, Duke
1988 Danny Manning, Kansas
Hersey Hawkins, Bradley
1987 Reggie Williams, Georgetown
Joe Wolf, N. Carolina
Ken Norman, Illinois
1986 (no 1st-round pick)
1985 Benoit Benjamin, Creighton
1984 Lancaster Gordon, Louisville
Michael Cage, San Diego St.
1983 Byron Scott, Arizona St.
1982 Terry Cummings, DePaul
1981 Tom Chambers, Utah
1980 Michael Brooks, La Salle
1979 (no 1st-round pick)
1978 (no 1st-round pick)
1977 (no 1st-round pick)
1976 Adrian Dantley, Notre Dame
1975 (no 1st-round pick)
1974 Tom McMillen, Maryland
1973 Ernie DiGregorio, Providence
1972 Bob McAdoo, N. Carolina
1971 Elmore Smith, Kentucky St.
1970 John Hummer, Princeton

LOS ANGELES LAKERS

1993 George Lynch, North Carolina
1992 Anthony Peeler, Missouri
1991 (no 1st-round pick)
1990 Elden Campbell, Clemson
1989 Vlade Divac, Yugoslavia
1988 David Rivers, Notre Dame
1987 (no 1st-round pick)
1986 Ken Barlow, Notre Dame
1985 A.C. Green, Oregon St.
1984 Earl Jones, District of Columbia
1983 (no 1st-round pick)
1982 James Worthy, N. Carolina
1981 Mike McGee, Michigan
1980 (no 1st-round pick)
1979 Earvin Johnson, Michigan St.
Brad Holland, UCLA
1978 (no 1st-round pick)
1977 Ken Carr, N. Carolina St.
Brad Davis, Maryland
Norm Nixon, Duquesne
1976 (no 1st-round pick)
1975 David Meyers, UCLA
Junior Bridgeman, Louisville
1974 Brian Winters, S. Carolina
1973 Kermit Washington, American

1972	Travis Grant, Kentucky St.
1971	Jim Cleamons, Ohio St.
1970	Jim McMillian, Columbia

MIAMI HEAT

1993	(no 1st-round pick)
1992	Harold Miner, Southern Cal.
1991	Steve Smith, Michigan St.
1990	Willie Burton, Minnesota
	Dave Jamerson, Ohio
1989	Glen Rice, Michigan
1988	Rony Seikaly, Syracuse
	Kevin Edwards, DePaul

MILWAUKEE BUCKS

1993	Vin Baker, Hartford
1992	Todd Day, Arkansas
	Lee Mayberry, Arkansas
1991	Kevin Brooks, S.W. Louisiana
1990	Terry Mills, Michigan
1989	(no 1st-round pick)
1988	Jeff Grayer, Iowa St.
1987	(no 1st-round pick)
1986	Scott Skiles, Michigan St.
1985	Jerry Reynolds, Louisiana St.
1984	Kenny Fields, UCLA
1983	Randy Breuer, Minnesota
1982	Paul Pressey, Tulsa
1981	Alton Lister, Arizona St.
1980	(no 1st-round pick)
1979	Sidney Moncrief, Arkansas
1978	George Johnson, St. John's
1977	Kent Benson, Indiana
	Marques Johnson, UCLA
	Ernie Grunfeld, Tennessee
1976	Quinn Buckner, Indiana
1975	(no 1st-round pick)
1974	Gary Brokaw, Notre Dame
1973	Swen Nater, UCLA
1972	Russell Lee, Marshall
	Julius Erving, Massachusetts
1971	Collis Jones, Notre Dame
1970	Gary Freeman, Oregon St.

MINNESOTA TIMBERWOLVES

1993	Isaiah (J.R.) Rider, UNLV
1992	Christian Laettner, Duke
1991	Luc Longley, New Mexico
1990	Felton Spencer, Louisville
	Gerald Glass, Mississippi
1989	Pooh Richardson, UCLA

NEW JERSEY NETS

1993	Rex Walters, Kansas
1992	(no 1st-round pick)
1991	Kenny Anderson, Georgia Tech
1990	Derrick Coleman, Syracuse

	Tate George, Connecticut
1989	Mookie Blaylock, Oklahoma
1988	Chris Morris, Auburn
1987	Dennis Hopson, Ohio St.
1986	Dwayne Washington, Syracuse
1985	(no 1st-round pick)
1984	Jeff Turner, Vanderbilt
1983	(no 1st-round pick)
1982	Sleepy Floyd, Georgetown
	Eddie Phillips, Alabama
1981	Buck Williams, Maryland
	Albert King, Maryland
	Ray Tolbert, Indiana
1980	Mike O'Koren, N. Carolina
	Mike Gminski, Duke
1979	Calvin Natt, N.E. Louisiana
	Cliff Robinson, Southern Cal.
1978	Winford Boynes, San Francisco
1977	Bernard King, Tennessee
1976	(no 1st-round pick)

NEW YORK KNICKS

1993	(no 1st-round pick)
1992	Hubert Davis, North Carolina
1991	Greg Anthony, UNLV
1990	Jerrod Mustaf, Maryland
1989	(no 1st-round pick)
1988	Rod Strickland, DePaul
1987	Mark Jackson, St. John's
1986	Kenny Walker, Kentucky
1985	Patrick Ewing, Georgetown
1984	(no 1st-round pick)
1983	Darrell Walker, Arkansas
1982	Trent Tucker, Minnesota
1981	(no 1st-round pick)
1980	Mike Woodson, Indiana
1979	Bill Cartwright, San Francisco
	Larry Demic, Arizona
	Sly Williams, Rhode Island
1978	Micheal Ray Richardson, Montana
1977	Ray Williams, Minnesota
1976	(no 1st-round pick)
1975	Eugene Short, Jackson St.
1974	(no 1st-round pick)
1973	Mel Davis, St. John's
1972	Tom Riker, S. Carolina
1971	Dean Meminger, Marquette
1970	Mike Price, Illinois

ORLANDO MAGIC

1993	Chris Webber, Michigan
	Geert Hammink, Louisiana St.
1992	Shaquille O'Neal, Louisiana St.
1991	Brian Williams, Arizona
	Stanley Roberts, Louisiana St.
1990	Dennis Scott, Georgia Tech
1989	Nick Anderson, Illinois

PHILADELPHIA 76ERS

1993	Shawn Bradley, Brigham Young
1992	Clarence Weatherspoon, S. Miss.
1991	(no 1st-round pick)
1990	(no 1st-round pick)
1989	Kenny Payne, Louisville
1988	Charles Smith, Pittsburgh
1987	Chris Welp, Washington
1986	(no 1st-round pick)
1985	Terry Catledge, S. Alabama
1984	Charles Barkley, Auburn
	Leon Wood, Fullerton St.
	Tom Sewell, Lamar
1983	Leo Rautins, Syracuse
1982	Mark McNamara, California
1981	Franklin Edwards, Cleveland St.
1980	Andrew Toney, S.W. Louisiana
	Monti Davis, Tennessee St.
1979	Jim Spanarkel, Duke
1978	(no 1st-round pick)
1977	Glenn Mosley, Seton Hall
1976	Terry Furlow, Michigan St.
1975	Darryl Dawkins, Evans High School
1974	Marvin Barnes, Providence
1973	Doug Collins, Illinois St.
	Raymond Lewis, Los Angeles St.
1972	Fred Boyd, Oregon St.
1971	Dana Lewis, Tulsa
1970	Al Henry, Wisconsin

PHOENIX SUNS

1993	Malcolm Mackey, Georgia Tech
1992	Oliver Miller, Arkansas
1991	(no 1st-round pick)
1990	Jayson Williams, St. John's
1989	Anthony Cook, Arizona
1988	Tim Perry, Temple
	Dan Majerle, Central Michigan
1987	Armon Gilliam, UNLV
1986	William Bedford, Memphis St.
1985	Ed Pinckney, Villanova
1984	Jay Humphries, Colorado
1983	(no 1st-round pick)
1982	David Thirdkill, Bradley
1981	Larry Nance, Clemson
1980	(no 1st-round pick)
1979	Kyle Macy, Kentucky
1978	Marty Byrnes, Syracuse
1977	Walter Davis, N. Carolina
1976	Ron Lee, Oregon
1975	Alvan Adams, Oklahoma
	Ricky Sobers, UNLV
1974	John Shumate, Notre Dame
1973	Mike Bantom, St. Joseph's
1972	Corky Calhoun, Pennsylvania
1971	John Roche, S. Carolina
1970	Greg Howard, New Mexico

PORTLAND TRAIL BLAZERS

1993	James Robinson, Alabama
1992	Dave Johnson, Syracuse
1991	(no 1st-round pick)
1990	Alaa Abdelnaby, Duke
1989	Byron Irvin, Missouri
1988	Mark Bryant, Seton Hall
1987	Ronnie Murphy, Jacksonville
1986	Walter Berry, St. John's
	Arvidas Sabonis, Soviet Union
1985	Terry Porter, Wisc.-Stevens Point
1984	Sam Bowie, Kentucky
	Bernard Thompson, Fresno St.
1983	Clyde Drexler, Houston
1982	Lafayette Lever, Arizona St.
1981	Jeff Lamp, Virginia
	Darnell Valentine, Kansas
1980	Ronnie Lester, Iowa
1979	Jim Paxson, Dayton
1978	Mychal Thompson, Minnesota
	Ron Brewer, Arkansas
1977	Rich Laurel, Hofstra
1976	Wally Walker, Virginia
1975	Lionel Hollins, Arizona St.
1974	Bill Walton, UCLA
1973	Barry Parkhill, Virginia
1972	LaRue Martin, Loyola (IL)
1971	Sidney Wicks, UCLA
1970	Geoff Petrie, Princeton

SACRAMENTO KINGS

1993	Bobby Hurley, Duke
1992	Walt Williams, Maryland
1991	Billy Owens, Syracuse
	Pete Chilcutt, N. Carolina
1990	Lionel Simmons, La Salle
	Travis Mays, Texas
	Duane Causwell, Temple
	Anthony Bonner, St. Louis
1989	Pervis Ellison, Louisville
1988	Ricky Berry, San Jose St.
1987	Kenny Smith, N. Carolina
1986	Harold Pressley, Villanova
1985	Joe Kleine, Arkansas
1984	Otis Thorpe, Providence
1983	Ennis Whatley, Alabama
1982	LaSalle Thompson, Texas
	Brook Steppe, Georgia Tech
1981	Steve Johnson, Oregon St.
	Kevin Loder, Alabama St.
1980	Hawkeye Whitney, N. Carolina St.
1979	Reggie King, Alabama
1978	Phil Ford, N. Carolina
1977	Otis Birdsong, Houston
1976	Richard Washington, UCLA
1975	Bill Robinzine, DePaul
	Bob Bigelow, Pennsylvania

1974	Scott Wedman, Colorado
1973	Ron Behagen, Minnesota
1972	(no 1st-round pick)
1971	Ken Durrett, La Salle
1970	Sam Lacey, New Mexico St.

SAN ANTONIO SPURS

1993	(no 1st-round pick)
1992	Tracy Murray, UCLA
1991	(no 1st-round pick)
1990	Dwayne Schintzius, Florida
1989	Sean Elliott, Arizona
1988	Willie Anderson, Georgia
1987	David Robinson, Navy
	Greg Anderson, Houston
1986	Johnny Dawkins, Duke
1985	Alfredrick Hughes, Loyola (IL)
1984	Alvin Robertson, Arkansas
1983	John Paxson, Notre Dame
1982	(no 1st-round pick)
1981	(no 1st-round pick)
1980	Reggie Johnson, Tennessee
1979	Wiley Peck, Mississippi St.
1978	Frankie Sanders, Southern
1977	(no 1st-round pick)
1976	(no 1st-round pick)

SEATTLE SUPERSONICS

1993	Ervin Johnson, New Orleans
1992	Doug Christie, Pepperdine
1991	Rich King, Nebraska
1990	Gary Payton, Oregon St.
1989	Dana Barros, Boston College
	Shawn Kemp, Trinity J.C.
1988	Gary Grant, Michigan
1987	Scottie Pippen, Central Arkansas
	Derrick McKey, Alabama
1986	(no 1st-round pick)
1985	Xavier McDaniel, Wichita St.
1984	(no 1st-round pick)
1983	Jon Sundvold, Missouri
1982	(no 1st-round pick)
1981	Danny Vranes, Utah
1980	Bill Hanzlik, Notre Dame
1979	James Bailey, Rutgers
	Vinnie Johnson, Baylor
1978	(no 1st-round pick)
1977	Jack Sikma, Illinois Wesleyan
1976	Bob Wilkerson, Indiana
1975	Frank Oleynick, Seattle
1974	Tom Burleson, N. Carolina St.
1973	Mike Green, Louisiana Tech
1972	Bud Stallworth, Kansas
1971	Fred Brown, Iowa
1970	Jim Ard, Cincinnati

UTAH JAZZ

1993	Luther Wright, Seton Hall
1992	(no 1st-round pick)
1991	Eric Murdock, Providence
1990	(no 1st-round pick)
1989	Blue Edwards, E. Carolina
1988	Eric Leckner, Wyoming
1987	Jose Ortiz, Oregon St.
1986	Dell Curry, Virginia Tech
1985	Karl Malone, Louisiana Tech
1984	John Stockton, Gonzaga
1983	Thurl Bailey, N. Carolina St.
1982	Dominique Wilkins, Georgia
1981	Danny Schayes, Syracuse
1980	Darrell Griffith, Louisville
	John Duren, Georgetown
1979	Larry Knight, Loyola (IL)
1978	James Hardy, San Francisco
1977	(no 1st-round pick)
1976	(no 1st-round pick)
1975	Rich Kelley, Stanford
1974	(no 1st-round pick)

WASHINGTON BULLETS

1993	Calbert Cheaney, Indiana
1992	Tom Gugliotta, N. Carolina St.
1991	LaBradford Smith, Louisville
1990	(no 1st-round pick)
1989	Tom Hammonds, Georgia Tech
1988	Harvey Grant, Oklahoma
1987	Muggsy Bogues, Wake Forest
1986	John Williams, Louisiana St.
	Anthony Jones, UNLV
1985	Kenny Green, Wake Forest
1984	Melvin Turpin, Kentucky
1983	Jeff Malone, Mississippi St.
	Randy Wittman, Indiana
1982	(no 1st-round pick)
1981	Frank Johnson, Wake Forest
1980	Wes Matthews, Wisconsin
1979	(no 1st-round pick)
1978	Roger Phegley, Bradley
	Dave Corzine, DePaul
1977	Greg Ballard, Oregon
	Bo Ellis, Marquette
1976	Mitch Kupchak, N. Carolina
	Larry Wright, Grambling
1975	Kevin Grevey, Kentucky
1974	Len Elmore, Maryland
1973	Nick Weatherspoon, Illinois
1972	(no 1st-round pick)
1971	Stan Love, Oregon
1970	George Johnson, Stephen F. Austin

N B A Year-By-Year Results

This section lists the final standings of every NBA season since its inception in 1946-47. Actually, in its first three years of existence, the league was called the BAA (Basketball Association of America), but it is still considered part of NBA history.

This section also includes league leaders in every major category since 1946-47. In its first four years of existence, the league kept track of only four statistics—scoring, assists, field goal percentage, and free throw percentage. In 1950-51, it began keeping track of rebounds. In 1973-74, the league added blocked shots and steals to the stat sheets. In 1979-80, the 3-point shot arrived in the NBA.

Because most statistical categories are based on averages, the NBA has had to establish qualifying criteria (e.g., a player can only qualify for the scoring championship if he appears in at least 70 games). Through the years, the league has frequently changed its qualifying criteria. These are the standards that players have had to meet in order to qualify:

Scoring
1946-47 to 1968-69: Based on total points, not on an average.
1969-70 to 1973-74: Minimum 70 games.
1974-75 to present: Minimum 70 games or 1,400 points.

Rebounds
1950-51 to 1968-69: Based on total rebounds, not on an average.
1969-70 to 1973-74: Minimum 70 games.
1974-75 to present: Minimum 70 games or 800 rebounds.

Assists
1946-47 to 1968-69: Based on total assists, not on an average.
1969-70 to 1973-74: Minimum 70 games.
1974-75 to present: Minimum 70 games or 400 assists.

Steals
1973-74: Minimum 70 games.
1974-75 to present: Minimum 70 games or 125 steals.

Blocked Shots
1973-74: Minimum 70 games.
1974-75 to present: Minimum 70 games or 100 blocks.

Field Goal Pct.
Over the years, the NBA has changed the qualifications for field goal percentage 14 times. Since 1974-75, a player has needed to make 300 field goals in order to qualify.

Free Throw Pct.
Since its inception, the league has changed the qualifications for free throw percentage 13 times. Since 1974-75, a player has needed to make 125 free throws in order to qualify.

3-Point Field Goal Pct.
1979-80 to 1989-90: Minimum 25 3-point field goals made.
1990-91 to present: Minimum 50 3-point field goals made.

Besides standings and statistics, this section contains results of every playoff series of every season. The last year of this section, 1992-93, has been expanded to include more statistical information.

1946-47
FINAL STANDINGS

Eastern Division

	W	L	PCT	GB
Washington	49	11	.817	
Philadelphia	35	25	.583	14
New York	33	27	.550	16
Providence	28	32	.467	21
Toronto	22	38	.367	27
Boston	22	38	.367	27

Western Division

	W	L	PCT	GB
Chicago	39	22	.639	
St. Louis	38	23	.623	1
Cleveland	30	30	.500	8.5
Detroit	20	40	.333	18.5
Pittsburgh	15	45	.250	23.5

POINTS

	AVG	NO.
J. Fulks, PHI	23.2	1389
B. Feerick, WAS	16.3	926
S. Miasek, DET	14.9	895
E. Sadowski, TOR/CLE	16.5	877
M. Zaslofsky, CHI	14.4	877
E. Calverley, PRO	14.3	845
C. Halbert, CHI	12.7	773
J. Logan, STL	12.6	770
L. Mogus, CLE/TOR	13.0	753
C. Gunther, PIT	14.1	734
D. Martin, PRO	12.2	733
F. Scolari, WAS	12.6	728
H. Beenders, PRO	12.3	713
J. Janisch, DET	11.6	697
H. McKinney, WAS	12.0	695
E. Shannon, PRO	12.1	687
M. Riebe, CLE	12.1	663
M. McCarron, TOR	10.8	649
F. Baumholtz, CLE	14.0	631
D. Carlson, CHI	10.7	630
E. Shannon, PRO	1.5	84
L. Mogus, CLE/TOR	1.4	84
J. Logan, STL	1.3	78
B. Feerick, WAS	1.3	69

ASSISTS

	AVG	NO.
E. Calverley, PRO	3.4	202
K. Sailors, CLE	2.3	134
O. Schectman, NY	2.0	109
H. Dallmar, PHI	1.7	104
M. Rottner, CHI	1.7	93
S. Miasek, DET	1.6	93

FIELD GOAL PCT

Bob Feerick, WAS	.401
Ed Sadowski, TOR/CLE	.369
Earl Shannon, PRO	.339
Coulby Gunther, PIT	.336
Max Zaslofsky, CHI	.329
Don Carlson, CHI	.322
Connie Simmons, BOS	.320
John Norlander, WAS	.319
Ken Sailors, CLE	.309
Mel Riebe, CLE	.307

FREE THROW PCT

Fred Scolari, WAS	.811
Tony Kapper, PIT/BOS	.795
Stan Stutz, NY	.782
Bob Feerick, WAS	.762
John Logan, STL	.748
Max Zaslofsky, CHI	.737
Joe Fulks, PHI	.730
Leo Mogus, CLE/TOR	.723
George Mearns, PRO	.720
Tony Jaros, CHI	.707

QUARTERFINALS

Philadelphia 73, St. Louis 68
St. Louis 73, Philadelphia 51
Philadelphia 75, St. Louis 59

Cleveland 77, New York 51
New York 86, Cleveland 74
New York 93, Cleveland 71

SEMIFINALS

Chicago 81, Washington 65
Chicago 69, Washington 53
Chicago 67, Washington 55
Washington 76, Chicago 69
Washington 67, Chicago 55
Chicago 66, Washington 61

Philadelphia 82, New York 70
Philadelphia 72, New York 53

BAA FINALS

Philadelphia 84, Chicago 71
Philadelphia 85, Chicago 74
Philadelphia 75, Chicago 72
Chicago 74, Philadelphia 73
Philadelphia 83, Chicago 80

1947-48
FINAL STANDINGS

Eastern Division	W	L	PCT	GB	Western Division	W	L	PCT	GB
Philadelphia	27	21	.563		St. Louis	29	19	.604	
New York	26	22	.542	1	Baltimore	28	20	.583	1
Boston	20	28	.417	7	Chicago	28	20	.583	1
Providence	6	42	.125	21	Washington	28	20	.583	1

POINTS	AVG	NO.
M. Zaslofsky, CHI	21.0	1007
J. Fulks, PHI	22.1	949
E. Sadowski, BOS	19.4	910
B. Feerick, WAS	16.1	775
S. Miasek, CHI	14.9	716
C. Braun, NY	14.3	671
J. Logan, STL	13.4	644
J. Palmer, NY	13.0	622
R. Rocha, STL	12.7	611
F. Scolari, WAS	12.5	589
H. Dallmar, PHI	12.2	587
K. Hermsen, BAL	12.0	575
E. Calverley, PRO	11.9	559
J. Reiser, BAL	11.5	541
B. Smawley, STL	11.1	535
K. Sailors, PRO	11.9	524
G. Nostrand, PRO	11.6	521
M. Bloom, BAL/BOS	10.6	508
D. Holub, NY	10.5	504
B. Jeannette, BAL	10.7	491

ASSISTS	AVG	NO.
H. Dallmar, PHI	2.5	120
E. Calverley, PRO	2.5	119
J. Seminoff, CHI	1.8	89
C. Gilmur, CHI	1.6	77
A. Phillip, CHI	2.3	74
E. Sadowski, BOS	1.6	74

B. Jeannette, BAL	1.5	70
J. Logan, STL	1.3	62
C. Braun, NY	1.3	61
S. Mariaschin, BOS	1.4	60

FIELD GOAL PCT	
Bob Feerick, WAS	.340
Ed Sadowski, BOS	.323
Carl Braun, NY	.323
Max Zaslofsky, CHI	.323
Chick Reiser, BAL	.322
John Palmer, NY	.315
Red Rocha, STL	.314
Mel Riebe, BOS	.309
Belus Smawley, STL	.308
Stan Miasek, CHI	.303

FREE THROW PCT	
Bob Feerick, WAS	.788
Max Zaslofsky, CHI	.784
Joe Fulks, PHI	.762
Buddy Jeannette, BAL	.758
Howie Dallmar, PHI	.744
John Palmer, NY	.744
John Logan, STL	.743
John Norlander, WAS	.742
Chick Reiser, BAL	.741
Fred Scolari, WAS	.732

QUARTERFINALS

Baltimore 85, New York 81
New York 79, Baltimore 69
Baltimore 84, New York 77

Chicago 79, Boston 72
Boston 81, Chicago 77
Chicago 81, Boston 74

SEMIFINALS

St. Louis 60, Philadelphia 58
Philadelphia 65, St. Louis 64
Philadelphia 84, St. Louis 56
St. Louis 56, Philadelphia 51
St. Louis 69, Philadelphia 62
Philadelphia 84, St. Louis 61
Philadelphia 85, St. Louis 46

Baltimore 73, Chicago 67
Baltimore 89, Chicago 72

BAA FINALS

Philadelphia 71, Baltimore 60
Baltimore 66, Philadelphia 63
Baltimore 72, Philadelphia 70
Baltimore 78, Philadelphia 75
Philadelphia 91, Baltimore 82
Baltimore 88, Philadelphia 73

1948-49
FINAL STANDINGS

Eastern Division

	W	L	PCT	GB
Washington	38	22	.633	
New York	32	28	.533	6
Baltimore	29	31	.483	9
Philadelphia	28	32	.467	10
Boston	25	35	.417	13
Providence	12	48	.200	26

Western Division

	W	L	PCT	GB
Rochester	45	15	.750	
Minneapolis	44	16	.733	1
Chicago	38	22	.633	7
St. Louis	29	31	.483	16
Fort Wayne	22	38	.367	23
Indianapolis	18	42	.300	27

POINTS

	AVG	NO.
G. Mikan, MIN	28.3	1698
J. Fulks, PHI	26.0	1560
M. Zaslofsky, CHI	20.6	1197
A. Risen, ROC	16.6	995
E. Sadowski, PHI	15.3	920
B. Smawley, STL	15.5	914
B. Davies, ROC	15.1	904
K. Sailors, PRO	15.8	899
C. Braun, NY	14.2	810
J. Logan, STL	14.1	803
J. Pollard, MIN	14.8	784
C. Simmons, BAL	13.0	779
R. Lumpp, IND/NY	12.7	777
B. Feerick, WAS	13.0	752
H. Shannon, PRO	13.4	736
H. McKinney, WAS	12.7	723
A. Phillip, CHI	12.0	718
J. Palmer, NY	12.3	714
K. Hermsen, WAS	11.8	708
W. Budko, BAL	11.5	692

ASSISTS

	AVG	NO.
B. Davies, ROC	5.4	321
A. Phillip, CHI	5.3	319
J. Logan, STL	4.8	276
E. Calverley, PRO	4.3	251
G. Senesky, PHI	3.9	233
J. Seminoff, BOS	3.9	229

G. Mikan, MIN	3.6	218
K. Sailors, PRO	3.7	209
B. Feerick, WAS	3.2	188
B. Wanzer, ROC	3.1	186

FIELD GOAL PCT

Arnie Risen, ROC	.423
George Mikan, MIN	.416
Ed Sadowski, PHI	.405
Jim Pollard, MIN	.396
Red Rocha, STL	.389
Bob Wanzer, ROC	.379
Connie Simmons, BAL	.377
Herm Schaefer, MIN	.374
Belus Smawley, STL	.372
Howie Shannon, PRO	.364

FREE THROW PCT

Bob Feerick, WAS	.859
Max Zaslofsky, CHI	.840
Bob Wanzer, ROC	.823
Herm Schaefer, MIN	.817
Howie Shannon, PRO	.804
Harold Tidrick, IND/BAL	.800
John Logan, STL	.791
John Pelkington, FTW/BAL	.790
Walter Budko, BAL	.790
Joe Fulks, PHI	.787

EAST SEMIFINALS

Washington 92, Phil. 70
Washington 80, Phil. 78

Baltimore 82, New York 81
New York 84, Baltimore 74
New York 103, Balt. 99 (OT)

EAST FINALS

Washington 77, New York 71
New York 86, Wash. 84 (OT)
Washington 84, New York 76

WEST SEMIFINALS

Rochester 93, St. Louis 64
Rochester 66, St. Louis 64

Minneapolis 84, Chicago 77
Minneapolis 101, Chicago 85

WEST FINALS

Minneapolis 80, Rochester 79
Minneapolis 67, Rochester 55

BAA FINALS

Minneapolis 88, Washington 84
Minneapolis 76, Washington 62
Minneapolis 94, Washington 74
Washington 83, Minneapolis 71
Washington 74, Minneapolis 65
Minneapolis 77, Washington 56

1949-50
FINAL STANDINGS

Eastern Division

	W	L	PCT	GB
Syracuse	51	13	.797	
New York	40	28	.588	13
Washington	32	36	.471	21
Philadelphia	26	42	.382	27
Baltimore	25	43	.368	28
Boston	22	46	.324	31

Western Division

	W	L	PCT	GB
Indianapolis	39	25	.609	
Anderson	37	27	.578	2
Tri-Cities	29	35	.453	10
Sheboygan	22	40	.355	16
Waterloo	19	43	.306	19
Denver	11	51	.177	27

Central Division

	W	L	PCT	GB
Minneapolis	51	17	.750	
Rochester	51	17	.750	
Fort Wayne	40	28	.588	11
Chicago	40	28	.588	11
St. Louis	26	42	.382	25

POINTS

	AVG	NO.
G. Mikan, MIN	27.4	1865
A. Groza, IND	23.4	1496
F. Brian, AND	17.8	1138
M. Zaslofsky, CHI	16.4	1115
E. Macauley, STL	16.1	1081
D. Schayes, SYR	16.8	1072
C. Braun, NY	15.4	1031
K. Sailors, DEN	17.3	987
J. Pollard, MIN	14.7	973
F. Schaus, FTW	14.3	972
J. Fulks, PHI	14.2	965
R. Beard, IND	14.9	895
B. Davies, ROC	14.0	895
D. Mehen, WAT	14.4	892
J. Nichols, WAS/TC	13.1	879
E. Sadowski, PHI/BAL	12.6	872
P. Hoffman, BAL	14.4	866
F. Scolari, WAS	13.0	860
V. Gardner, PHI	13.5	853
B. Smawley, STL	13.7	834

ASSISTS

	AVG	NO.
D. McGuire, NY	5.7	386
A. Phillip, CHI	5.8	377
B. Davies, ROC	4.6	294
A. Cervi, SYR	4.7	264
G. Senesky, PHI	3.9	264

D. Schayes, SYR	4.0	259
J. Pollard, MIN	3.8	252
J. Seminoff, BOS	3.8	249
C. Braun, NY	3.7	247
J. Logan, STL	3.9	240

FIELD GOAL PCT

Alex Groza, IND	.478
Dick Mehen, WAT	.420
Bob Wanzer, ROC	.414
George Mikan, MIN	.407
John Hargis, AND	.405
Red Rocha, STL	.405
Vern Mikkelsen, MIN	.399
Ed Macauley, STL	.398
Jack Toomay, DEN	.397
Harry Gallatin, NY	.396

FREE THROW PCT

Max Zaslofsky, CHI	.843
Chick Reiser, WAS	.835
Al Cervi, SYR	.829
Belus Smawley, STL	.828
Frank Brian, AND	.824
Fred Scolari, WAS	.822
Fred Schaus, FTW	.818
Leo Kubiak, WAT	.814
Bob Wanzer, ROC	.806
John Logan, STL	.783

EAST SEMIFINALS
Syracuse 2, Philadelphia 0
New York 2, Washington 0

EAST FINALS
Syracuse 2, New York 1

CENTRAL SEMIFINALS
Minneapolis 2, Chicago 0
Fort Wayne 2, Rochester 0

CENTRAL FINALS
Minneapolis 2, Fort Wayne 0

WEST SEMIFINALS
Indianapolis 2, Sheboygan 1
Anderson 2, Tri-Cities 1

WEST FINALS
Anderson 2, Indianapolis 1

NBA SEMIFINALS
Minneapolis 2, Anderson 0

NBA FINALS
Minneapolis 68, Syracuse 66
Syracuse 91, Minneapolis 85
Minneapolis 91, Syracuse 77
Minneapolis 77, Syracuse 69
Syracuse 83, Minneapolis 76
Minneapolis 110, Syracuse 95

1950-51
FINAL STANDINGS

Eastern Division

	W	L	PCT	GB
Philadelphia	40	26	.606	
Boston	39	30	.565	2.5
New York	36	30	.545	4
Syracuse	32	34	.485	8
Baltimore	24	42	.364	16
Washington*	10	25	.286	14.5

*Folded on Jan. 9, 1951

Western Division

	W	L	PCT	GB
Minneapolis	44	24	.647	
Rochester	41	27	.603	3
Fort Wayne	32	36	.471	12
Indianapolis	31	37	.456	13
Tri-Cities	25	43	.368	19

POINTS

	AVG	NO.
G. Mikan, MIN	28.4	1932
A. Groza, IND	21.7	1429
E. Macauley, BOS	20.4	1384
J. Fulks, PHI	18.7	1236
F. Brian, TC	16.8	1144
P. Arizin, PHI	17.2	1121
D. Schayes, SYR	17.0	1121
R. Beard, IND	16.8	1111
B. Cousy, BOS	15.6	1078
A. Risen, ROC	16.3	1077
D. Eddleman, TC	15.3	1040
F. Schaus, FTW	15.1	1028
V. Boryla, NY	14.9	982
B. Davies, ROC	13.5	955
L. Foust, FTW	13.5	915
V. Mikkelsen, MIN	14.1	904
F. Scolari, WAS/SYR	13.4	883
K. Murray, BAL/FTW	12.9	850
G. Ratkovicz, SYR	12.9	849
H. Gallatin, NY	12.8	845

REBOUNDS

	AVG	NO.
D. Schayes, SYR	16.4	1080
G. Mikan, MIN	14.1	958
H. Gallatin, NY	12.1	800
A. Risen, ROC	12.0	795
A. Groza, IND	10.7	709
L. Foust, FTW	10.0	681
V. Mikkelsen, MIN	10.2	655
P. Arizin, PHI	9.8	640
E. Macauley, BOS	9.1	616
J. Coleman, ROC	8.7	584

ASSISTS

	AVG	NO.
A. Phillip, PHI	6.3	414
D. McGuire, NY	6.3	400
G. Senesky, PHI	5.3	342
B. Cousy, BOS	4.9	341
R. Beard, IND	4.8	318
B. Davies, ROC	4.6	287
F. Brian, TC	3.9	266
F. Scolari, WAS/SYR	3.9	255
E. Macauley, BOS	3.7	252
D. Schayes, SYR	3.8	251

FIELD GOAL PCT

Alex Groza, IND	.470
Ed Macauley, BOS	.466
George Mikan, MIN	.428
Jack Coleman, ROC	.421
Harry Gallatin, NY	.416
George Ratkovicz, SYR	.415
Paul Arizin, PHI	.407
Vince Boryla, NY	.406
Vern Mikkelsen, MIN	.402
Robert Wanzer, ROC	.401

FREE THROW PCT

Joe Fulks, PHI	.855
Belus Smawley, SYR/BAL	.850
Bob Wanzer, ROC	.850
Fred Scolari, WAS/SYR	.843
Vince Boryla, NY	.837
Fred Schaus, FTW	.835
Sonny Hertzberg, BOS	.826
Frank Brian, TC	.823

EAST SEMIFINALS

Syracuse 91, Phil. 89 (OT)
Syracuse 90, Philadelphia 78

New York 83, Boston 69
New York 92, Boston 78

EAST FINALS

New York 103, Syracuse 92
Syracuse 102, New York 80
New York 97, Syracuse 75
Syracuse 90, New York 83
New York 83, Syracuse 81

WEST SEMIFINALS

Minneapolis 95, Indian. 81
Indianapolis 108, Minn. 88
Minneapolis 85, Indian. 80

Rochester 110, Fort Wayne 81
Fort Wayne 83, Rochester 78
Rochester 97, Fort Wayne 78

WEST FINALS

Minneapolis 76, Rochester 73
Rochester 70, Minneapolis 66
Rochester 83, Minneapolis 70
Rochester 80, Minneapolis 75

NBA FINALS

Rochester 92, New York 65
Rochester 99, New York 84
Rochester 78, New York 71
New York 79, Rochester 73
New York 92, Rochester 89
New York 80, Rochester 73
Rochester 79, New York 75

1951-52
FINAL STANDINGS

Eastern Division

	W	L	PCT	GB
Syracuse	40	26	.606	
Boston	39	27	.591	1
New York	37	29	.561	3
Philadelphia	33	33	.500	7
Boston	20	46	.303	20

Western Division

	W	L	PCT	GB
Rochester	41	25	.621	
Minneapolis	40	26	.606	1
Indianapolis	34	32	.515	7
Fort Wayne	29	37	.439	12
Milwaukee	17	49	.258	24

POINTS	AVG	NO.
P. Arizin, PHI	25.4	1674
G. Mikan, MIN	23.8	1523
B. Cousy, BOS	21.7	1433
E. Macauley, BOS	19.2	1264
B. Davies, ROC	16.2	1052
F. Brian, FTW	15.9	1051
L. Foust, FTW	15.9	1047
B. Wanzer, ROC	15.7	1033
A. Risen, ROC	15.6	1032
V. Mikkelsen, MIN	15.3	1009
J. Pollard, MIN	15.5	1005
F. Scolari, BAL	14.6	933
M. Zaslofsky, NY	14.1	931
J. Fulks, PHI	15.1	922
J. Graboski, IND	13.7	904
F. Schaus, FTW	14.1	872
D. Schayes, SYR	13.8	868
R. Rocha, SYR	12.9	854
L. Barnhorst, IND	12.4	820
A. Phillip, PHI	12.0	790

REBOUNDS	AVG	NO.
L. Foust, FTW	13.3	880
M. Hutchins, MIL	13.3	880
G. Mikan, MIN	13.5	866
A. Risen, ROC	12.7	841
D. Schayes, SYR	12.3	773
P. Arizin, PHI	11.3	745
N. Clifton, NY	11.8	731
J. Coleman, ROC	10.5	692
V. Mikkelsen, MIN	10.3	681
H. Gallatin, NY	10.0	661

ASSISTS	AVG	NO.
A. Phillip, PHI	8.2	539
B. Cousy, BOS	6.7	441
B. Davies, ROC	6.0	390
D. McGuire, NY	6.1	388
F. Scolari, BAL	4.7	303
G. Senesky, PHI	4.9	280
B. Wanzer, ROC	4.0	262
L. Barnhorst, IND	3.9	255
S. Martin, MIN	3.8	249
F. Schaus, FTW	4.0	247

FIELD GOAL PCT

Paul Arizin, PHI	.448
Harry Gallatin, NY	.442
Ed Macauley, BOS	.432
Bob Wanzer, ROC	.425
Vern Mikkelsen, MIN	.419
Jack Coleman, ROC	.415
George King, SYR	.406
Paul Walther, IND	.401
Red Rocha, SYR	.401
Bob Lavoy, IND	.397

FREE THROW PCT

Bob Wanzer, ROC	.904
Al Cervi, SYR	.883
Bill Sharman, BOS	.859
Frank Brian, FTW	.848
Fred Scolari, BAL	.835
Fred Schaus, FTW	.833
Joe Fulks, PHI	.825
Bill Tosheff, IND	.824

EAST SEMIFINALS

Syracuse 102, Phil. 83
Philadelphia 100, Syrac. 95
Syracuse 84, Phil. 78

Boston 105, New York 94
New York 101, Boston 97
New York 88, Boston 87 (2OT)

EAST FINALS

New York 87, Syracuse 85
Syracuse 102, New York 92
New York 99, Syracuse 92
New York 100, Syracuse 93

WEST SEMIFINALS

Rochester 95, Fort Wayne 78
Rochester 92, Fort Wayne 86

Minneapolis 78, Indian. 70
Minneapolis 94, Indian. 87

WEST FINALS

Rochester 88, Minn. 78
Minneapolis 83, Roch. 78
Minneapolis 77, Roch. 67
Minneapolis 82, Roch. 80

NBA FINALS

Minneapolis 83, N.Y. 79 (OT)
New York 80, Minneapolis 72
Minneapolis 82, New York 77
New York 90, Minn. 89 (OT)
Minneapolis 102, New York 89
New York 76, Minneapolis 68
Minneapolis 82, New York 65

1952-53
FINAL STANDINGS

Eastern Division

	W	L	PCT	GB
New York	47	23	.671	
Syracuse	47	24	.662	.5
Boston	46	25	.648	1.5
Baltimore	16	54	.229	31
Philadelphia	12	57	.174	34.5

Western Division

	W	L	PCT	GB
Minneapolis	48	22	.686	
Rochester	44	26	.629	4
Fort Wayne	36	33	.522	11.5
Indianapolis	28	43	.394	20.5
Milwaukee	27	44	.380	21.5

POINTS

	AVG	NO.
N. Johnston, PHI	22.3	1564
G. Mikan, MIN	20.6	1442
B. Cousy, BOS	19.8	1407
E. Macauley, BOS	20.3	1402
D. Schayes, SYR	17.8	1262
B. Sharman, BOS	16.2	1147
J. Nichols, MIL	15.8	1090
V. Mikkelsen, MIN	15.0	1047
B. Davies, ROC	15.6	1029
B. Wanzer, ROC	14.6	1020
C. Braun, NY	14.0	977
L. Barnhorst, IND	13.6	967
L. Foust, FTW	14.3	958
P. Seymour, SYR	14.2	952
D. Barksdale, BAL	12.8	899
J. Graboski, IND	13.0	894
A. Risen, ROC	13.0	884
H. Gallatin, NY	12.4	865
J. Pollard, MIN	13.0	859
J. Fulks, PHI	11.9	832

REBOUNDS

	AVG	NO.
G. Mikan, MIN	14.4	1007
N. Johnston, PHI	13.9	979
D. Schayes, SYR	13.0	920
H. Gallatin, NY	13.1	916
M. Hutchins, MIL	11.2	793
J. Coleman, ROC	11.1	774
L. Foust, FTW	11.5	769
N. Clifton, NY	10.9	761
A. Risen, ROC	11.0	745
J. Graboski, IND	10.0	687

ASSISTS

	AVG	NO.
B. Cousy, BOS	7.7	547
A. Phillip, PHI/FTW	5.7	397
G. King, SYR	5.1	364
D. McGuire, NY	4.9	296
P. Seymour, SYR	4.4	294
B. Davies, ROC	4.2	280
E. Macauley, BOS	4.1	280
L. Barnhorst, IND	3.9	277
G. Senesky, PHI	3.8	264
B. Wanzer, ROC	3.6	252

FIELD GOAL PCT

Neil Johnston, PHI	.45242
Ed Macauley, BOS	.45236
Harry Gallatin, NY	.444
Bill Sharman, BOS	.436
Vern Mikkelsen, MIN	.435
Ernie Vandeweghe, NY	.435
Jack Coleman, ROC	.420
Slater Martin, MIN	.410
Bob Lavoy, IND	.402
George King, SYR	.402

FREE THROW PCT

Bill Sharman, BOS	.850
Fred Scolari, FTW	.844
Dolph Schayes, SYR	.827
Carl Braun, NY	.825
Fred Schaus, FTW	.821
Odie Spears, ROC	.819
Paul Seymour, SYR	.817
Bob Cousy, BOS	.816

EAST SEMIFINALS

New York 80, Baltimore 62
New York 90, Baltimore 81

Boston 87, Syracuse 81
Boston 111, Syr. 105 (4OT)

EAST FINALS

New York 95, Boston 91
Boston 86, New York 70
New York 101, Boston 82
New York 82, Boston 75

WEST SEMIFINALS

Minneapolis 85, Indian. 69
Minneapolis 81, Indian. 79

Fort Wayne 84, Rochester 77
Rochester 83, Fort Wayne 71
Fort Wayne 67, Rochester 65

WEST FINALS

Minneapolis 83, Fort Wayne 73
Minneapolis 82, Fort Wayne 75
Fort Wayne 98, Minneapolis 95
Fort Wayne 85, Minneapolis 82
Minneapolis 74, Fort Wayne 58

NBA FINALS

New York 96, Minneapolis 88
Minneapolis 73, New York 71
Minneapolis 90, New York 75
Minneapolis 71, New York 69
Minneapolis 91, New York 84

1953-54
FINAL STANDINGS

Eastern Division

	W	L	PCT	GB
New York	44	28	.611	
Boston	42	30	.583	2
Syracuse	42	30	.583	2
Philadelphia	29	43	.403	15
Baltimore	16	56	.222	28

Western Division

	W	L	PCT	GB
Minneapolis	46	26	.639	
Rochester	44	28	.611	2
Fort Wayne	40	32	.556	6
Milwaukee	21	51	.292	25

POINTS

	AVG	NO.
N. Johnston, PHI	24.4	1759
B. Cousy, BOS	19.2	1383
E. Macauley, BOS	18.9	1344
G. Mikan, MIN	18.1	1306
R. Felix, BAL	17.6	1269
D. Schayes, SYR	17.1	1228
B. Sharman, BOS	16.0	1155
L. Foust, FTW	15.1	1090
C. Braun, NY	14.8	1062
B. Wanzer, ROC	13.3	958
H. Gallatin, NY	13.2	949
A. Risen, ROC	13.2	949
J. Graboski, PHI	13.3	944
P. Seymour, SYR	13.1	931
B. Davies, ROC	12.3	887
J. Pollard, MIN	11.7	831
G. King, SYR	11.3	817
M. Zaslofsky, FTW	12.5	811
V. Mikkelsen, MIN	11.1	797
D. Sunderlage, MIL	11.2	760

REBOUNDS

	AVG	NO.
H. Gallatin, NY	15.3	1098
G. Mikan, MIN	14.3	1028
L. Foust, FTW	13.4	967
R. Felix, BAL	13.3	958
D. Schayes, SYR	12.1	870
N. Johnston, PHI	11.1	797
A. Risen, ROC	10.1	728
M. Hutchins, FTW	9.7	695
L. Hitch, MIL	9.6	691
J. Graboski, PHI	9.4	670

ASSISTS

	AVG	NO.
B. Cousy, BOS	7.2	518
A. Phillip, FTW	6.3	449
P. Seymour, SYR	5.1	364
D. McGuire, NY	5.2	354
B. Davies, ROC	4.5	323
J. George, PHI	4.4	312
P. Hoffman, BAL	4.0	285
G. King, SYR	3.8	272
E. Macauley, BOS	3.8	271
D. Finn, PHI	3.9	265

FIELD GOAL PCT

Ed Macauley, BOS	.486
Bill Sharman, BOS	.450
Neil Johnston, PHI	.449
Clyde Lovellette, MIN	.423
Ray Felix, BAL	.411
Larry Foust, FTW	.409
Eddie Miller, BAL	.407
Jack Coleman, ROC	.405
Harry Gallatin, NY	.404
Mel Hutchins, FTW	.401

FREE THROW PCT

Bill Sharman, BOS	.844
Dolph Schayes, SYR	.827
Carl Braun, NY	.825
Paul Seymour, SYR	.813
Bob Zawoluk, PHI	.809
Bob Cousy, BOS	.787
Harry Gallatin, NY	.784
George Mikan, MIN	.777

EAST ROUND ROBIN

Boston 93, New York 71
Syracuse 96, Boston 95 (OT)
Syracuse 75, New York 68
Boston 79, New York 78
Syracuse 103, New York 99
Syracuse 98, Boston 85

EAST FINALS

Syracuse 109, Boston 104
Syracuse 83, Boston 76

WEST ROUND ROBIN

Rochester 82, Fort Wayne 75
Minneapolis 109, Rochester 88
Minneapolis 90, Fort Wayne 85
Minneapolis 78, Fort Wayne 73
Rochester 89, Fort Wayne 71

WEST FINALS

Minneapolis 89, Rochester 76
Rochester 74, Minneapolis 73
Minneapolis 82, Rochester 72

NBA FINALS

Minneapolis 79, Syracuse 68
Syracuse 62, Minneapolis 60
Minneapolis 81, Syracuse 67
Syracuse 80, Minneapolis 69
Minneapolis 84, Syracuse 73
Syracuse 65, Minneapolis 63
Minneapolis 87, Syracuse 80

1954-55
FINAL STANDINGS

Eastern Division

	W	L	PCT	GB
Syracuse	43	29	.597	
New York	38	34	.528	5
Boston	36	36	.500	7
Philadelphia	33	39	.458	10

Western Division

	W	L	PCT	GB
Fort Wayne	43	29	.597	
Minneapolis	40	32	.556	3
Rochester	29	43	.403	14
Milwaukee	26	46	.361	17

POINTS

	AVG	NO.
N. Johnston, PHI	22.7	1631
P. Arizin, PHI	21.0	1512
B. Cousy, BOS	21.2	1504
B. Pettit, MIL	20.4	1466
F. Selvy, BAL/MIL	19.0	1348
D. Schayes, SYR	18.8	1333
V. Mikkelsen, MIN	18.4	1327
C. Lovellette, MIN	18.7	1311
B. Sharman, BOS	18.4	1253
E. Macauley, BOS	17.6	1248
L. Foust, FTW	17.0	1189
C. Braun, NY	15.1	1074
H. Gallatin, NY	14.6	1053
P. Seymour, SYR	14.6	1050
R. Felix, NY	14.4	1038
G. Yardley, FTW	17.3	1036
J. Baechtold, NY	13.9	1003
S. Martin, MIN	13.6	976
J. Graboski, PHI	13.6	954
N. Clifton, NY	13.1	944

REBOUNDS

	AVG	NO.
N. Johnston, PHI	15.1	1085
H. Gallatin, NY	13.8	995
B. Pettit, MIL	13.8	994
D. Schayes, SYR	12.3	887
R. Felix, NY	11.4	818
C. Lovellette, MIN	11.5	802
J. Coleman, ROC	10.1	729
V. Mikkelsen, MIN	10.2	722
A. Risen, ROC	10.2	703
L. Foust, FTW	10.0	700

ASSISTS

	AVG	NO.
B. Cousy, BOS	7.8	557
D. McGuire, NY	7.6	542
A. Phillip, FTW	7.7	491
P. Seymour, SYR	6.7	483
S. Martin, MIN	5.9	427
J. George, PHI	5.3	359
G. King, SYR	4.9	331
B. Sharman, BOS	4.1	280
E. Macauley, BOS	3.9	275
C. Braun, NY	3.9	274

FIELD GOAL PCT

Larry Foust, FTW	.487
Jack Coleman, ROC	.462
Neil Johnston, PHI	.440
Ray Felix, NY	.438
Clyde Lovellette, MIN	.435
Bill Sharman, BOS	.427
Ed Macauley, BOS	.424
Vern Mikkelsen, MIN	.422
John Kerr, SYR	.419
George Yardley, FTW	.418

FREE THROW PCT

Bill Sharman, BOS	.897
Frank Brian, FTW	.851
Dolph Schayes, SYR	.833
Dick Schnittker, MIN	.823
Jim Baechtold, NY	.823
Harry Gallatin, NY	.814
Odie Spears, ROC	.812
Paul Seymour, SYR	.811

EAST SEMIFINALS

Boston 122, New York 101
New York 102, Boston 95
Boston 116, New York 109

EAST FINALS

Syracuse 110, Boston 100
Syracuse 116, Boston 110
Boston 100, Syracuse 97 (OT)
Syracuse 110, Boston 94

WEST SEMIFINALS

Minneapolis 82, Rochester 78
Rochester 94, Minneapolis 92
Minneapolis 119, Roch. 110

WEST FINALS

Fort Wayne 96, Minneapolis 79
Fort Wayne 98, Minn. 97 (OT)
Minneapolis 99, F.W. 91 (OT)
Fort Wayne 105, Minn. 96

NBA FINALS

Syracuse 86, Fort Wayne 82
Syracuse 87, Fort Wayne 84
Fort Wayne 96, Syracuse 89
Fort Wayne 109, Syracuse 102
Fort Wayne 74, Syracuse 71
Syracuse 109, Fort Wayne 104
Syracuse 92, Fort Wayne 91

1955-56
FINAL STANDINGS

Eastern Division

	W	L	PCT	GB
Philadelphia	45	27	.625	
Boston	39	33	.542	6
Syracuse	35	37	.486	10
New York	35	37	.486	10

Western Division

	W	L	PCT	GB
Fort Wayne	37	35	.514	
Minneapolis	33	39	.458	4
St. Louis	33	39	.458	4
Rochester	31	41	.431	6

POINTS

	AVG	NO.
B. Pettit, STL	25.7	1849
P. Arizin, PHI	24.2	1741
N. Johnston, PHI	22.1	1547
C. Lovellette, MIN	21.5	1526
D. Schayes, SYR	20.4	1472
B. Sharman, BOS	19.9	1434
B. Cousy, BOS	18.8	1356
E. Macauley, BOS	17.5	1240
G. Yardley, FTW	17.4	1233
L. Foust, FTW	16.2	1166
M. Stokes, ROC	16.8	1125
C. Braun, NY	15.4	1112
J. Twyman, ROC	14.4	1038
J. Graboski, PHI	14.4	1034
H. Gallatin, NY	13.9	1002
J. George, PHI	13.9	1000
C. Share, STL	13.6	976
V. Mikkelsen, MIN	13.4	962
J. Kerr, SYR	13.3	961
J. Coleman, ROC/STL	12.8	957

REBOUNDS

	AVG	NO.
B. Pettit, STL	16.2	1164
M. Stokes, ROC	16.3	1094
C. Lovellette, MIN	14.0	992
D. Schayes, SYR	12.4	891
N. Johnston, PHI	12.5	872
C. Share, STL	10.8	774
H. Gallatin, NY	10.3	740
J. Coleman, ROC/STL	9.2	688
G. Yardley, FTW	9.7	686
L. Foust, FTW	9.0	648

ASSISTS

	AVG	NO.
B. Cousy, BOS	8.9	642
J. George, PHI	6.3	457
S. Martin, MIN	6.2	445
A. Phillip, FTW	5.9	410
G. King, SYR	5.7	410
T. Gola, PHI	5.9	404
D. McGuire, NY	5.8	362
B. Sharman, BOS	4.7	339
M. Stokes, ROC	4.9	328
C. Braun, NY	4.1	298

FIELD GOAL PCT

Neil Johnston, PHI	.457
Paul Arizin, PHI	.448
Larry Foust, FTW	.447
Ken Sears, NY	.438
Bill Sharman, BOS	.438
Clyde Lovellette, MIN	.434
Charles Share, STL	.430
Bob Houbregs, FTW	.430
Bob Pettit, STL	.429
Mel Hutchins, FTW	.425

FREE THROW PCT

Bill Sharman, BOS	.867
Dolph Schayes, SYR	.858
Dick Schnittker, MIN	.856
Bob Cousy, BOS	.844
Carl Braun, NY	.838
Slater Martin, MIN	.833
Paul Arizin, PHI	.810
Vern Mikkelsen, MIN	.804

EAST SEMIFINALS

Boston 110, Syracuse 93
Syracuse 101, Boston 98
Syracuse 102, Boston 97

EAST FINALS

Philadelphia 109, Syracuse 87
Syracuse 122, Phil. 118
Philadelphia 119, Syracuse 96
Syracuse 108, Phil. 104
Philadelphia 109, Syrac. 104

WEST SEMIFINALS

St. Louis 116, Minneapolis 115
Minneapolis 133, St. Louis 75
St. Louis 116, Minneapolis 115

WEST FINALS

St. Louis 86, Fort Wayne 85
St. Louis 84, Fort Wayne 74
Fort Wayne 107, St. Louis 84
Fort Wayne 93, St. Louis 84
Fort Wayne 102, St. Louis 97

NBA FINALS

Philadelphia 98, Fort Wayne 94
Fort Wayne 84, Philadelphia 83
Philadelphia 100, Fort W. 96
Philadelphia 107, Fort W. 105
Philadelphia 99, Fort Wayne 88

1956-57
FINAL STANDINGS

Eastern Division

	W	L	PCT	GB
Boston	44	28	.611	
Syracuse	38	34	.528	6
Philadelphia	37	35	.514	7
New York	36	36	.500	8

Western Division

	W	L	PCT	GB
St. Louis	34	38	.472	
Minneapolis	34	38	.472	
Fort Wayne	34	38	.472	
Rochester	31	41	.431	3

POINTS

	AVG	NO.
P. Arizin, PHI	25.6	1817
B. Pettit, STL	24.7	1755
D. Schayes, SYR	22.5	1617
N. Johnston, PHI	22.8	1575
G. Yardley, FTW	21.5	1547
C. Lovellette, MIN	20.8	1434
B. Sharman, BOS	21.1	1413
B. Cousy, BOS	20.6	1319
E. Macauley, STL	16.5	1187
D. Garmaker, MIN	16.3	1177
J. Twyman, ROC	16.3	1174
T. Heinsohn, BOS	16.2	1163
M. Stokes, ROC	15.6	1124
H. Gallatin, NY	15.0	1079
K. Sears, NY	14.8	1069
J. Graboski, PHI	14.3	1032
C. Braun, NY	13.9	1001
V. Mikkelsen, MIN	13.7	986
E. Conlin, SYR	13.4	953
J. Kerr, SYR	12.4	891

REBOUNDS

	AVG	NO.
M. Stokes, ROC	17.4	1256
B. Pettit, STL	14.6	1037
D. Schayes, SYR	14.0	1008
B. Russell, BOS	19.6	943
C. Lovellette, MIN	13.5	932
N. Johnston, PHI	12.4	855
J. Kerr, SYR	11.2	807
W. Dukes, MIN	11.2	794
G. Yardley, FTW	10.5	755
J. Loscutoff, BOS	10.4	730

ASSISTS

	AVG	NO.
B. Cousy, BOS	7.5	478
J. McMahon, STL	5.1	367
M. Stokes, ROC	4.6	331
J. George, PHI	4.6	307
S. Martin, NY/STL	4.1	269
C. Braun, NY	3.6	256
G. Shue, FTW	3.3	238
B. Sharman, BOS	3.5	236
L. Costello, PHI	3.3	236
D. Schayes, SYR	3.2	229

FIELD GOAL PCT

Neil Johnston, PHI	.447
Charles Share, STL	.439
Jack Twyman, ROC	.439
Bob Houbregs, FTW	.432
Bill Russell, BOS	.427
Clyde Lovellette, MIN	.426
Paul Arizin, PHI	.422
Ed Macauley, STL	.419
Ken Sears, NY	.418
Ray Felix, NY	.416

FREE THROW PCT

Bill Sharman, BOS	.905
Dolph Schayes, SYR	.904
Dick Garmaker, MIN	.839
Paul Arizin, PHI	.829
Neil Johnston, PHI	.826
Bob Cousy, BOS	.821
Carl Braun, NY	.809
Vern Mikkelsen, MIN	.807

EAST SEMIFINALS

Syracuse 103, Philadelphia 96
Syracuse 91, Philadelphia 80

EAST FINALS

Boston 108, Syracuse 90
Boston 120, Syracuse 105
Boston 83, Syracuse 80

WEST SEMIFINALS

Minneapolis 131, Fort W. 127
Minneapolis 110, Fort W. 108

WEST FINALS

St. Louis 118, Minneapolis 109
St. Louis 106, Minneapolis 104
St. Louis 143, Minn. 135 (2OT)

NBA FINALS

St. Louis 125, Boston 123 (OT)
Boston 119, St. Louis 99
St. Louis 100, Boston 98
Boston 123, St. Louis 118
Boston 124, St. Louis 109
St. Louis 96, Boston 94
Boston 125, St. L. 123 (2OT)

1957-58
FINAL STANDINGS

Eastern Division

	W	L	PCT	GB
Boston	49	23	.681	
Syracuse	41	31	.569	8
Philadelphia	37	35	.514	12
New York	35	37	.486	14

Western Division

	W	L	PCT	GB
St. Louis	41	31	.569	
Detroit	33	39	.458	8
Cincinnati	33	39	.458	8
Minneapolis	19	53	.264	22

POINTS

	AVG	NO.
G. Yardley, DET	27.8	2001
D. Schayes, SYR	24.9	1791
B. Pettit, STL	24.6	1719
C. Lovellette, CIN	23.4	1659
P. Arizin, PHI	20.7	1406
G. King, CIN	20.7	1406
B. Sharman, BOS	22.3	1402
C. Hagan, STL	19.9	1391
N. Johnston, PHI	19.5	1388
K. Sears, NY	18.6	1342
V. Mikkelsen, MIN	17.3	1248
J. Twyman, CIN	17.2	1237
T. Heinsohn, BOS	17.8	1230
W. Naulls, NY	18.1	1228
L. Foust, MIN	16.8	1210
C. Braun, NY	16.5	1173
B. Cousy, BOS	18.0	1167
B. Russell, BOS	16.6	1142
F. Ramsey, BOS	16.5	1137
D. Garmaker, MIN	16.1	1094
J. Kerr, SYR	15.2	1094

REBOUNDS

	AVG	NO.
B. Russell, BOS	22.7	1564
B. Pettit, STL	17.4	1216
M. Stokes, CIN	18.1	1142
D. Schayes, SYR	14.2	1022
J. Kerr, SYR	13.4	963
W. Dukes, DET	13.3	954
L. Foust, MIN	12.2	876
C. Lovellette, CIN	12.1	862
V. Mikkelsen, MIN	11.2	805
W. Naulls, NY	11.8	799

ASSISTS

	AVG	NO.
B. Cousy, BOS	7.1	463
D. McGuire, DET	6.6	454
M. Stokes, CIN	6.4	403
C. Braun, NY	5.5	393
G. King, CIN	5.3	337
J. McMahon, STL	4.6	333
T. Gola, PHI	5.5	327
R. Guerin, NY	5.0	317
L. Costello, SYR	4.4	317
J. George, PHI	3.3	234

FIELD GOAL PCT

Jack Twyman, CIN	.452
Cliff Hagan, STL	.443
Bill Russell, BOS	.442
Ray Felix, NY	.442
Clyde Lovellette, CIN	.441
Ken Sears, NY	.439
Neil Johnston, PHI	.429
Ed Macauley, STL	.428
Larry Costello, SYR	.426
Bill Sharman, BOS	.424

FREE THROW PCT

Dolph Schayes, SYR	.904
Bill Sharman, BOS	.893
Bob Cousy, BOS	.850
Carl Braun, NY	.849
Dick Schnittker, MIN	.848
Larry Costello, SYR	.847
Gene Shue, DET	.844
Willie Naulls, NY	.826

EAST SEMIFINALS

Syracuse 86, Philadelphia 82
Philadelphia 95, Syracuse 93
Philadelphia 101, Syracuse 88

EAST FINALS

Boston 107, Philadelphia 98
Boston 109, Philadelphia 87
Boston 106, Philadelphia 92
Philadelphia 111, Boston 97
Boston 93, Philadelphia 88

WEST SEMIFINALS

Detroit 100, Cincinnati 93
Detroit 124, Cincinnati 104

WEST FINALS

St. Louis 114, Detroit 111
St. Louis 99, Detroit 96
Detroit 109, St. Louis 89
St. Louis 145, Detroit 101
St. Louis 120, Detroit 96

NBA FINALS

St. Louis 104, Boston 102
Boston 136, St. Louis 112
St. Louis 111, Boston 108
Boston 109, St. Louis 98
St. Louis 102, Boston 100
St. Louis 110, Boston 109

1958-59
FINAL STANDINGS

Eastern Division

	W	L	PCT	GB
Boston	52	20	.722	
New York	40	32	.556	12
Syracuse	35	37	.486	17
Philadelphia	32	40	.444	20

Western Division

	W	L	PCT	GB
St. Louis	49	23	.681	
Minneapolis	33	39	.458	16
Detroit	28	44	.389	21
Cincinnati	19	53	.264	30

POINTS

	AVG	NO.
B. Pettit, STL	29.2	2105
J. Twyman, CIN	25.8	1857
P. Arizin, PHI	26.4	1851
E. Baylor, MIN	24.9	1742
C. Hagan, STL	23.7	1707
D. Schayes, SYR	21.3	1534
K. Sears, NY	21.0	1488
B. Sharman, BOS	20.4	1466
B. Cousy, BOS	20.0	1297
R. Guerin, NY	18.2	1291
J. Kerr, SYR	17.8	1285
G. Shue, DET	17.6	1266
T. Heinsohn, BOS	18.8	1242
G. Yardley, DET/SYR	19.8	1209
B. Russell, BOS	16.7	1168
W. Sauldsberry, PHI	15.4	1112
L. Costello, SYR	15.8	1108
F. Ramsey, BOS	15.4	1107
W. Naulls, NY	15.7	1068
J. Graboski, PHI	14.7	1058

REBOUNDS

	AVG	NO.
B. Russell, BOS	23.0	1612
B. Pettit, STL	16.4	1182
E. Baylor, MIN	15.0	1050
J. Kerr, SYR	14.0	1008
D. Schayes, SYR	13.4	962
W. Dukes, DET	13.3	958
W. Sauldsberry, PHI	11.5	826
C. Hagan, STL	10.9	783
J. Graboski, PHI	10.4	751
W. Naulls, NY	10.6	723

ASSISTS

	AVG	NO.
B. Cousy, BOS	8.6	557
D. McGuire, DET	6.2	443
L. Costello, SYR	5.4	379
R. Guerin, NY	5.1	364
C. Braun, NY	4.8	349
S. Martin, STL	4.7	336
J. McMahon, STL	4.1	298
B. Sharman, BOS	4.1	292
E. Baylor, MIN	4.1	287
T. Gola, PHI	4.2	269

FIELD GOAL PCT

Ken Sears, NY	.490
Bill Russell, BOS	.457
Cliff Hagan, STL	.456
Clyde Lovellette, STL	.454
Hal Greer, SYR	.454
John Kerr, SYR	.441
Bob Pettit, STL	.438
Larry Costello, SYR	.437
Sam Jones, BOS	.434
Paul Arizin, PHI	.431

FREE THROW PCT

Bill Sharman, BOS	.932
Dolph Schayes, SYR	.864
Ken Sears, NY	.861
Bob Cousy, BOS	.855
Willie Naulls, NY	.830
Clyde Lovellette, STL	.820
Paul Arizin, PHI	.813
Vern Mikkelsen, MIN	.806

EAST SEMIFINALS

Syracuse 129, New York 123
Syracuse 131, New York 115

EAST FINALS

Boston 131, Syracuse 109
Syracuse 120, Boston 118
Boston 133, Syracuse 111
Syracuse 119, Boston 107
Boston 129, Syracuse 108
Syracuse 133, Boston 121
Boston 130, Syracuse 125

WEST SEMIFINALS

Minneapolis 92, Detroit 89
Detroit 117, Minneapolis 103
Minneapolis 129, Detroit 102

WEST FINALS

St. Louis 124, Minneapolis 90
Minneapolis 106, St. Louis 98
St. Louis 127, Minneapolis 97
Minneapolis 108, St. Louis 98
Minneapolis 98, St. L. 97 (OT)
Minneapolis 106, St. Louis 104

NBA FINALS

Boston 118, Minneapolis 115
Boston 128, Minneapolis 108
Boston 123, Minneapolis 120
Boston 118, Minneapolis 113

1959-60
FINAL STANDINGS

Eastern Division

	W	L	PCT	GB
Boston	59	16	.787	
Philadelphia	49	26	.653	10
Syracuse	45	30	.600	14
New York	27	48	.360	32

Western Division

	W	L	PCT	GB
St. Louis	46	29	.613	
Detroit	30	45	.400	16
Minneapolis	25	50	.333	21
Cincinnati	19	56	.253	27

POINTS	AVG	NO.
W. Chamberlain, PHI	37.6	2707
J. Twyman, CIN	31.2	2338
E. Baylor, MIN	29.6	2074
B. Pettit, STL	26.1	1882
C. Hagan, STL	24.8	1859
G. Shue, DET	22.8	1712
D. Schayes, SYR	22.5	1689
T. Heinsohn, BOS	21.7	1629
R. Guerin, NY	21.8	1615
P. Arizin, PHI	22.3	1606
G. Yardley, SYR	20.2	1473
B. Cousy, BOS	19.4	1455
C. Lovellette, STL	20.8	1416
W. Naulls, NY	21.4	1388
B. Sharman, BOS	19.3	1370
B. Russell, BOS	18.2	1350
B. Howell, DET	17.8	1332
K. Sears, NY	18.5	1187
T. Gola, PHI	15.0	1122
F. Ramsey, BOS	15.3	1117

REBOUNDS	AVG	NO.
W. Chamberlain, PHI	27.0	1941
B. Russell, BOS	24.0	1778
B. Pettit, STL	17.0	1221
E. Baylor, MIN	16.4	1150
D. Schayes, SYR	12.8	959
W. Naulls, NY	14.2	921
J. Kerr, SYR	12.2	913
W. Dukes, DET	13.4	883
K. Sears, NY	13.7	876
C. Hagan, STL	10.7	803

ASSISTS	AVG	NO.
B. Cousy, BOS	9.5	715
G. Rodgers, PHI	7.1	482
R. Guerin, NY	6.3	468
L. Costello, SYR	6.3	449
T. Gola, PHI	5.5	409
D. McGuire, DET	5.3	358
R. Hundley, MIN	4.6	338
S. Martin, STL	5.2	330
J. McCarthy, STL	4.4	328
C. Hagan, STL	4.0	299

FIELD GOAL PCT	
Ken Sears, NY	.477
Hal Greer, SYR	.476
Clyde Lovellette, STL	.468
Bill Russell, BOS	.467
Cliff Hagan, STL	.464
W. Chamberlain, PHI	.461
Bill Sharman, BOS	.456
Bailey Howell, DET	.456
Sam Jones, BOS	.454
George Yardley, SYR	.453

FREE THROW PCT	
Dolph Schayes, SYR	.893
Gene Shue, DET	.872
Ken Sears, NY	.868
Bill Sharman, BOS	.866
Larry Costello, SYR	.862
Willie Naulls, NY	.836
Clyde Lovellette, STL	.821
George Yardley, SYR	.816

EAST SEMIFINALS

Philadelphia 115, Syracuse 92
Syracuse 125, Phil. 119
Philadelphia 132, Syrac. 112

EAST FINALS

Boston 111, Philadelphia 105
Philadelphia 115, Boston 110
Boston 120, Philadelphia 90
Boston 112, Philadelphia 104
Philadelphia 128, Boston 107
Boston 119, Philadelphia 117

WEST SEMIFINALS

Minneapolis 113, Detroit 112
Minneapolis 114, Detroit 99

WEST FINALS

St. Louis 112, Minneapolis 99
Minneapolis 120, St. Louis 113
St. Louis 93, Minneapolis 89
Minneapolis 103, St. Louis 101
Minn. 117, St. L. 110 (OT)
St. Louis 117, Minneapolis 96
St. Louis 97, Minneapolis 86

NBA FINALS

Boston 140, St. Louis 122
St. Louis 113, Boston 103
Boston 102, St. Louis 86
St. Louis 106, Boston 96
Boston 127, St. Louis 102
St. Louis 105, Boston 102
Boston 122, St. Louis 103

1960-61
FINAL STANDINGS

Eastern Division

	W	L	PCT	GB
Boston	57	22	.722	
Philadelphia	46	33	.582	11
Syracuse	38	41	.481	19
New York	21	58	.266	36

Western Division

	W	L	PCT	GB
St. Louis	51	28	.646	
Los Angeles	36	43	.456	15
Detroit	34	45	.430	17
Cincinnati	33	46	.418	18

POINTS

	AVG	NO.
W. Chamberlain, PHI	38.4	3033
E. Baylor, LA	34.8	2538
O. Robertson, CIN	30.5	2165
B. Pettit, STL	27.9	2120
J. Twyman, CIN	25.3	1997
D. Schayes, SYR	23.6	1868
W. Naulls, NY	23.4	1846
P. Arizin, PHI	23.2	1832
B. Howell, DET	23.6	1815
G. Shue, DET	22.6	1765
R. Guerin, NY	21.8	1720
C. Hagan, STL	21.9	1705
T. Heinsohn, BOS	21.3	1579
H. Greer, SYR	19.6	1551
C. Lovellette, STL	22.0	1471
J. West, LA	17.6	1389
B. Cousy, BOS	18.1	1378
B. Russell, BOS	16.9	1322
D. Barnett, SYR	16.9	1320
F. Ramsey, BOS	15.1	1191

REBOUNDS

	AVG	NO.
W. Chamberlain, PHI	27.2	2149
B. Russell, BOS	23.9	1868
B. Pettit, STL	20.3	1540
E. Baylor, LA	19.8	1447
B. Howell, DET	14.4	1111
W. Naulls, NY	13.4	1055
W. Dukes, DET	14.1	1028
D. Schayes, SYR	12.2	960
J. Kerr, SYR	12.0	951
W. Embry, CIN	10.9	864

ASSISTS

	AVG	NO.
O. Robertson, CIN	9.7	690
G. Rodgers, PHI	8.7	677
B. Cousy, BOS	7.7	587
G. Shue, DET	6.8	530
R. Guerin, NY	6.4	503
J. McCarthy, STL	5.4	430
L. Costello, SYR	5.5	413
C. Hagan, STL	4.9	381
E. Baylor, LA	5.1	371
R. Hundley, LA	4.4	350

FIELD GOAL PCT

W. Chamberlain, PHI	.509
Jack Twyman, CIN	.488
Larry Costello, SYR	.482
Oscar Robertson, CIN	.473
Barney Cable, SYR	.472
Bailey Howell, DET	.469
Clyde Lovellette, STL	.453
Dick Barnett, SYR	.452
Wayne Embry, CIN	.451
Hal Greer, SYR	.451

FREE THROW PCT

Bill Sharman, BOS	.921
Dolph Schayes, SYR	.868
Gene Shue, DET	.856
Frank Ramsey, BOS	.833
Paul Arizin, PHI	.833
Dave Gambee, SYR	.831
Clyde Lovellette, STL	.830
Ken Sears, NY	.830

EAST SEMIFINALS

Syracuse 115, Phil. 107
Syracuse 115, Phil. 114
Syracuse 106, Phil. 103

EAST FINALS

Boston 128, Syracuse 115
Syracuse 115, Boston 98
Boston 133, Syracuse 110
Boston 120, Syracuse 107
Boston 123, Syracuse 101

WEST SEMIFINALS

Los Angeles 120, Detroit 102
Los Angeles 120, Detroit 118
Detroit 124, Los Angeles 113
Detroit 123, Los Angeles 114
Los Angeles 137, Detroit 120

WEST FINALS

Los Angeles 122, St. Louis 118
St. Louis 121, Los Angeles 106
Los Angeles 118, St. Louis 112
St. Louis 118, Los Angeles 117
Los Angeles 121, St. Louis 112
St. Louis 114, L.A. 113 (OT)
St. Louis 105, Los Angeles 103

NBA FINALS

Boston 129, St. Louis 95
Boston 116, St. Louis 108
St. Louis 124, Boston 120
Boston 119, St. Louis 104
Boston 121, St. Louis 112

1961-62
FINAL STANDINGS

Eastern Division

	W	L	PCT	GB
Boston	60	20	.750	
Philadelphia	49	31	.613	11
Syracuse	41	39	.513	19
New York	29	51	.363	31

Western Division

	W	L	PCT	GB
Los Angeles	54	26	.675	
Cincinnati	43	37	.538	11
Detroit	37	43	.463	17
St. Louis	29	51	.363	25
Chicago	18	62	.225	36

POINTS	AVG	NO.
W. Chamberlain, PHI	50.4	4029
W. Bellamy, CHI	31.6	2495
O. Robertson, CIN	30.8	2432
B. Pettit, STL	31.1	2429
J. West, LA	30.8	2310
R. Guerin, NY	29.5	2303
W. Naulls, NY	25.0	1877
E. Baylor, LA	38.3	1836
J. Twyman, CIN	22.9	1831
C. Hagan, STL	22.9	1764
T. Heinsohn, BOS	22.1	1742
P. Arizin, PHI	21.9	1706
H. Greer, SYR	22.8	1619
B. Howell, DET	19.9	1576
G. Shue, DET	19.0	1522
W. Embry, CIN	19.8	1484
B. Russell, BOS	18.9	1436
S. Jones, BOS	18.4	1435
R. LaRusso, LA	17.2	1374
D. Gambee, SYR	16.7	1338

REBOUNDS	AVG	NO.
W. Chamberlain, PHI	25.7	2052
B. Russell, BOS	23.6	1790
W. Bellamy, CHI	19.0	1500
B. Pettit, STL	18.7	1459
J. Kerr, SYR	14.7	1176
J. Green, NY	18.4	1066
B. Howell, DET	12.6	996
O. Robertson, CIN	12.5	985
W. Embry, CIN	13.0	977
E. Baylor, LA	18.6	892

ASSISTS	AVG	NO.
O. Robertson, CIN	11.4	899
G. Rodgers, PHI	7.9	663
B. Cousy, BOS	7.8	584
R. Guerin, NY	6.9	539
G. Shue, DET	5.8	465
J. West, LA	5.4	402
F. Selvy, LA	4.8	381
B. Leonard, CHI	5.4	378
C. Hagan, STL	4.8	370
A. Bockhorn, CIN	4.6	366

FIELD GOAL PCT	
Walt Bellamy, CHI	.519
W. Chamberlain, PHI	.506
Jack Twyman, CIN	.479
Oscar Robertson, CIN	.478
Al Attles, PHI	.474
Larry Foust, STL	.471
Clyde Lovellette, STL	.471
Cliff Hagan, STL	.470
Wayne Embry, CIN	.466
Rudy LaRusso, LA	.466

FREE THROW PCT	
Dolph Schayes, SYR	.896
Willie Naulls, NY	.842
Larry Costello, SYR	.837
Frank Ramsey, BOS	.825
Cliff Hagan, STL	.825
Tom Meschery, PHI	.824
Richie Guerin, NY	.820
Hal Greer, SYR	.819

EAST SEMIFINALS

Philadelphia 110, Syrac. 103
Philadelphia 97, Syracuse 82
Syracuse 101, Phil. 100
Syracuse 106, Philadelphia 99
Philadelphia 121, Syrac. 104

EAST FINALS

Boston 117, Philadelphia 89
Philadelphia 113, Boston 106
Boston 129, Philadelphia 114
Philadelphia 110, Boston 106
Boston 119, Philadelphia 104
Philadelphia 109, Boston 99
Boston 109, Philadelphia 107

WEST SEMIFINALS

Detroit 123, Cincinnati 122
Cincinnati 129, Detroit 107
Detroit 118, Cincinnati 107
Detroit 112, Cincinnati 111

WEST FINALS

Los Angeles 132 Detroit 108
Los Angeles 127, Detroit 112
Los Angeles 111, Detroit 106
Detroit 118, Los Angeles 117
Detroit 132, Los Angeles 125
Los Angeles 123, Detroit 117

NBA FINALS

Boston 122, Los Angeles 108
Los Angeles 129, Boston 122
Los Angeles 117, Boston 115
Boston 115, Los Angeles 103
Los Angeles 126, Boston 121
Boston 119, Los Angeles 105
Boston 110, L.A. 107 (OT)

1962-63
FINAL STANDINGS

Eastern Division

	W	L	PCT	GB
Boston	58	22	.725	
Syracuse	48	32	.600	10
Cincinnati	42	38	.525	16
New York	21	59	.263	37

Western Division

	W	L	PCT	GB
Los Angeles	53	27	.663	
St. Louis	48	32	.600	5
Detroit	34	46	.425	19
San Francisco	31	49	.388	22
Chicago	25	55	.313	28

POINTS

	AVG	NO.
W. Chamberlain, SF	44.8	3586
E. Baylor, LA	34.0	2719
O. Robertson, CIN	28.3	2264
B. Pettit, STL	28.4	2241
W. Bellamy, CHI	27.9	2233
B. Howell, DET	22.7	1793
R. Guerin, NY	21.5	1701
J. Twyman, CIN	19.8	1586
H. Greer, SYR	19.5	1562
D. Ohl, DET	19.3	1547
S. Jones, BOS	19.7	1499
J. West, LA	27.1	1489
L. Shaffer, SYR	18.6	1488
T. Dischinger, CHI	25.5	1452
J. Green, NY	18.1	1444
T. Heinsohn, BOS	18.9	1440
D. Barnett, LA	18.0	1437
W. Embry, CIN	18.6	1411
B. Russell, BOS	16.8	1309
J. Kerr, SYR	15.7	1255

REBOUNDS

	AVG	NO.
W. Chamberlain, SF	24.3	1946
B. Russell, BOS	23.0	1843
W. Bellamy, CHI	16.4	1309
B. Pettit, STL	15.1	1191
E. Baylor, LA	14.3	1146
J. Kerr, SYR	13.1	1049
J. Green, NY	12.1	964
W. Embry, CIN	12.3	936
B. Howell, DET	11.5	910
B. Boozer, CIN	11.1	878

ASSISTS

	AVG	NO.
G. Rodgers, SF	10.4	825
O. Robertson, CIN	9.5	758
B. Cousy, BOS	6.8	515
S. Green, CHI	5.8	422
E. Baylor, LA	4.8	386
L. Wilkens, STL	5.1	381
B. Russell, BOS	4.5	348
R. Guerin, NY	4.4	348
L. Costello, SYR	4.3	334
J. Barnhill, STL	4.2	322

FIELD GOAL PCT

W. Chamberlain, SF	.528
Walt Bellamy, CHI	.527
Oscar Robertson, CIN	.518
Bailey Howell, DET	.516
Terry Dischinger, CHI	.512
Dave Budd, NY	.502
Jack Twyman, CIN	.480
Al Attles, SF	.478
Sam Jones, BOS	.476
John Kerr, SYR	.474

FREE THROW PCT

Larry Costello, SYR	.881
Richie Guerin, NY	.848
Elgin Baylor, LA	.837
Tom Heinsohn, BOS	.835
Hal Greer, SYR	.834
Frank Ramsey, BOS	.816
Dick Barnett, LA	.815
Adrian Smith, CIN	.811

EAST SEMIFINALS
Syracuse 123, Cincinnati 120
Cincinnati 133, Syracuse 115
Syracuse 121, Cincinnati 117
Cincinnati 125, Syracuse 118
Cincinnati 131, Syrac. 127 (OT)

EAST FINALS
Cincinnati 135, Boston 132
Boston 125, Cincinnati 102
Cincinnati 121, Boston 116
Boston 128, Cincinnati 110
Boston 125, Cincinnati 120
Cincinnati 109, Boston 99
Boston 142, Cincinnati 131

WEST SEMIFINALS
St. Louis 118, Detroit 99
St. Louis 122, Detroit 108
Detroit 107, St. Louis 103
St. Louis 104, Detroit 100

WEST FINALS
Los Angeles 112, St. Louis 104
Los Angeles 101, St. Louis 99
St. Louis 125, Los Angeles 112
St. Louis 124, Los Angeles 114
Los Angeles 123, St. Louis 100
St. Louis 121, Los Angeles 113
Los Angeles 115, St. Louis 100

NBA FINALS
Boston 117, Los Angeles 114
Boston 113, Los Angeles 106
Los Angeles 119, Boston 99
Boston 108, Los Angeles 105
Los Angeles 126, Boston 119
Boston 112, Los Angeles 109

1963-64
FINAL STANDINGS

Eastern Division

	W	L	PCT	GB
Boston	59	21	.738	
Cincinnati	55	25	.688	4
Philadelphia	34	46	.425	25
New York	22	58	.275	37

Western Division

	W	L	PCT	GB
San Francisco	48	32	.600	
St. Louis	46	34	.575	2
Los Angeles	42	38	.525	6
Baltimore	31	49	.388	17
Detroit	23	57	.288	25

POINTS

	AVG	NO.
W. Chamberlain, SF	.36.9	2948
O. Robertson, CIN	.31.4	2480
B. Pettit, ST	.27.4	2190
W. Bellamy, BAL	.27.0	2159
J. West, LA	.28.7	2064
E. Baylor, LA	.25.4	1983
H. Greer, PHI	.23.3	1865
B. Howell, DET	.21.6	1666
T. Dischinger, BAL	.20.8	1662
J. Havlicek, BOS	.19.9	1595
S. Jones, BOS	.19.4	1473
D. Barnett, LA	.18.4	1433
C. Hagan, STL	.18.4	1413
R. Scott, DET	.17.6	1406
J. Lucas, CIN	.17.7	1400
W. Embry, CIN	.17.3	1383
G. Johnson, BAL	.17.3	1352
L. Chappell, PHI/NY	.17.1	1350
J. Kerr, PHI	.16.8	1340
C. Walker, PHI	.17.3	1314

REBOUNDS

	AVG	NO.
B. Russell, BOS	.24.7	1930
W. Chamberlain, SF	.22.3	1787
J. Lucas, CIN	.17.4	1375
W. Bellamy, BAL	.17.0	1361
B. Pettit, STL	.15.3	1224
R. Scott, DET	.13.5	1078
G. Johnson, BAL	.13.6	1064
J. Kerr, PHI	.12.7	1018
E. Baylor, LA	.12.0	936
W. Embry, CIN	.11.6	925

ASSISTS

	AVG	NO.
O. Robertson, CIN	.11.0	868
G. Rodgers, SF	7.0	556
K. Jones, BOS	5.1	407
J. West, LA	5.6	403
W. Chamberlain, SF.	5.0	403
R. Guerin, NY/STL	.4.7	375
H. Greer, PHI	4.7	374
B. Russell, BOS	4.7	370
L. Wilkens, STL	4.6	359
J. Egan, DET/NY	5.4	358

FIELD GOAL PCT

Jerry Lucas, CIN	.527
W. Chamberlain, SF	.524
Walt Bellamy, BAL	.513
Terry Dischinger, BAL	.496
Bill McGill, NY	.487
Jerry West, LA	.484
Oscar Robertson, CIN	.483
Bailey Howell, DET	.472
John Green, NY	.470
Bob Pettit, STL	.463

FREE THROW PCT

Oscar Robertson, CIN	.853
Jerry West, LA	.832
Hal Greer, PHI	.829
Tom Heinsohn, BOS	.827
Richie Guerin, NY/STL	.818
Cliff Hagan, STL	.813
Bailey Howell, DET	.809
Elgin Baylor, LA	.804

EAST SEMIFINALS

Cincinnati 127, Phil. 102
Philadelphia 122, Cinc. 114
Cincinnati 101, Philadelphia 89
Philadelphia 129, Cinc. 120
Cincinnati 130, Phil. 124

EAST FINALS

Boston 103, Cincinnati 87
Boston 101, Cincinnati 90
Boston 102, Cincinnati 92
Cincinnati 102, Boston 93
Boston 109, Cincinnati 95

WEST SEMIFINALS

St. Louis 115, Los Angeles 104
St. Louis 106, Los Angeles 90
Los Angeles 107, St. Louis 105
Los Angeles 97, St. Louis 88
St. Louis 121, Los Angeles 108

WEST FINALS

St. Louis 116, San Fran. 111
San Francisco 120, St. L. 85
St. Louis 113, San Fran. 109
San Francisco 111, St. L. 109
San Francisco 121, St. L. 97
St. Louis 123, S.F. 95
San Francisco 105, St. L. 95

NBA FINALS

Boston 108, San Francisco 96
Boston 124, San Francisco 101
San Francisco 115, Boston 91
Boston 98, San Francisco 95
Boston 105, San Francisco 99

1964-65
FINAL STANDINGS

Eastern Division

	W	L	PCT	GB
Boston	62	18	.715	
Cincinnati	48	32	.600	14
Philadelphia	40	40	.500	22
New York	31	49	.388	31

Western Division

	W	L	PCT	GB
Los Angeles	49	31	.613	
St. Louis	45	35	.563	4
Baltimore	37	43	.463	12
Detroit	31	49	.388	18
San Francisco	17	63	.213	32

POINTS

	AVG	NO.
W. Chamber., SF/PHI	34.7	2534
J. West, LA	31.0	2292
O. Robertson, CIN	30.4	2279
S. Jones, BOS	25.9	2070
E. Baylor, LA	27.1	2009
W. Bellamy, BAL	24.8	1981
W. Reed, NY	19.5	1560
B. Howell, BAL	19.2	1534
T. Dischinger, DET	18.2	1456
D. Ohl, BAL	18.4	1420
G. Johnson, BAL	18.6	1415
J. Lucas, CIN	21.4	1414
H. Greer, PHI	20.2	1413
J. Havlicek, BOS	18.3	1375
Z. Beaty, STL	16.9	1351
D. DeBusschere, DET	16.7	1322
L. Wilkens, STL	16.5	1284
N. Thurmond, SF	16.5	1273
A. Smith, CIN	15.1	1210
J. Barnes, NY	15.5	1159

REBOUNDS

	AVG	NO.
B. Russell, BOS	24.1	1878
W. Chamber., SF/PHI	22.9	1673
N. Thurmond, SF	18.1	1395
J. Lucas, CIN	20.0	1321
W. Reed, NY	14.7	1175
W. Bellamy, BAL	14.6	1166
G. Johnson, BAL	13.0	988
L. Jackson, PHI	12.9	980
Z. Beaty, STL	12.1	966
E. Baylor, LA	12.8	950

ASSISTS

	AVG	NO.
O. Robertson, CIN	11.5	861
G. Rodgers, SF	7.3	565
K. Jones, BOS	5.6	437
L. Wilkens, STL	5.5	431
B. Russell, BOS	5.3	410
J. West, LA	4.9	364
H. Greer, PHI	4.5	313
K. Loughery, BAL	3.7	296
E. Baylor, LA	3.8	280
L. Costello, PHI	4.3	275

FIELD GOAL PCT

W. Chamber., SF/PHI	.510
Walt Bellamy, BAL	.509
Jerry Lucas, CIN	.498
Jerry West, LA	.497
Bailey Howell, BAL	.495
Terry Dischinger, DET	.493
John Egan, NY	.488
Zelmo Beaty, STL	.482
Oscar Robertson, CIN	.480
Paul Neumann, PHI/SF	.473

FREE THROW PCT

Larry Costello, PHI	.877
Oscar Robertson, CIN	.839
Howard Komives, NY	.835
Adrian Smith, CIN	.830
Jerry West, LA	.821
Sam Jones, BOS	.820
Bob Pettit, STL	.820
Jerry Lucas, CIN	.814

EAST SEMIFINALS

Philadelphia 119, Cinc. 117(OT)
Cincinnati 121, Phil. 120
Philadelphia 108, Cincinnati 94
Philadelphia 119, Cinc. 112

EAST FINALS

Boston 108, Philadelphia 98
Philadelphia 109, Boston 103
Boston 112, Philadelphia 94
Philadelphia 134, Bos. 131 (OT)
Boston 114, Philadelphia 108
Philadelphia 112, Boston 106
Boston 110, Philadelphia 109

WEST SEMIFINALS

Baltimore 108, St. Louis 105
St. Louis 129, Baltimore 105
Baltimore 131, St. Louis 99
Baltimore 109, St. Louis 103

WEST FINALS

Los Angeles 121, Balt. 115
Los Angeles 118, Balt. 115
Baltimore 122, L.A. 115
Baltimore 114, L.A. 112
Los Angeles 120, Balt. 112
Los Angeles 117, Balt. 115

NBA FINALS

Boston 142, Los Angeles 110
Boston 129, Los Angeles 123
Los Angeles 126, Boston 105
Boston 112, Los Angeles 99
Boston 129, Los Angeles 96

1965-66
FINAL STANDINGS

Eastern Division	W	L	PCT	GB
Philadelphia	55	25	.688	
Boston	54	26	.675	1
Cincinnati	45	35	.563	10
New York	30	50	.375	25

Western Division	W	L	PCT	GB
Los Angeles	45	35	.563	
Baltimore	38	42	.475	7
St. Louis	36	44	.450	9
San Francisco	35	45	.438	10
Detroit	22	58	.275	23

POINTS	AVG	NO.
W. Chamberlain, PHI	33.5	2649
J. West, LA	31.3	2476
O. Robertson, CIN	31.3	2378
R. Barry, SF	25.7	2059
W. Bellamy, BAL/NY	22.8	1820
H. Greer, PHI	22.7	1819
D. Barnett, NY	23.1	1729
J. Lucas, CIN	21.5	1697
Z. Beaty, STL	20.7	1656
S. Jones, BOS	23.5	1577
E. Miles, DET	19.6	1566
D. Ohl, BAL	20.6	1502
A. Smith, CIN	18.4	1470
G. Rodgers, SF	18.6	1468
R. Scott, DET	17.9	1411
B. Howell, BAL	17.3	1364
K. Loughery, BAL	18.2	1349
J. Havlicek, BOS	18.8	1334
D. DeBusschere, DET	16.4	1297
L. Wilkens, STL	18.0	1244

REBOUNDS	AVG	NO.
W. Chamberlain, PHI	24.6	1943
B. Russell, BOS	22.8	1779
J. Lucas, CIN	21.1	1668
N. Thurmond, SF	18.0	1312
W. Bellamy, BAL/NY	15.7	1254
Z. Beaty, STL	13.6	1086
B. Bridges, STL	12.2	951
D. DeBusschere, DET	11.6	916
W. Reed, NY	11.6	883
R. Barry, SF	10.6	850

ASSISTS	AVG	NO.
O. Robertson, CIN	11.1	847
G. Rodgers, SF	10.7	846
K. Jones, BOS	6.3	503
J. West, LA	6.1	480
L. Wilkens, STL	6.2	429
H. Kornives, NY	5.3	425
W. Chamberlain, PHI	5.2	414
W. Hazzard, LA	4.9	393
R. Guerin, STL	4.9	388
H. Greer, PHI	4.8	384

FIELD GOAL PCT	
W. Chamberlain, PHI	.540
John Green, NY/BAL	.536
Walt Bellamy, BAL/NY	.506
Al Attles, SF	.503
Happy Hairston, CIN	.489
Bailey Howell, BAL	.488
Bob Boozer, LA	.484
Oscar Robertson, CIN	.475
Zelmo Beaty, STL	.473
Jerry West, LA	.473

FREE THROW PCT	
Larry Siegfried, BOS	.881
Rick Barry, SF	.862
Howard Komives, NY	.861
Jerry West, LA	.860
Adrian Smith, CIN	.850
Oscar Robertson, CIN	.842
Paul Neumann, SF	.836
Kevin Loughery, BAL	.830

EAST SEMIFINALS
Cincinnati 107, Boston 103
Boston 132, Cincinnati 125
Cincinnati 113, Boston 107
Boston 120, Cincinnati 103
Boston 112, Cincinnati 103

EAST FINALS
Boston 115, Philadelphia 96
Boston 114, Philadelphia 93
Philadelphia 111, Boston 105
Boston 114, Phil. 110 (OT)
Boston 120, Philadelphia 112

WEST SEMIFINALS
St. Louis 113, Baltimore 111
St. Louis 105, Baltimore 100
St. Louis 121, Baltimore 112

WEST FINALS
Los Angeles 129, St. Louis 106
Los Angeles 125, St. Louis 116
St. Louis 120, Los Angeles 113
Los Angeles 107, St. Louis 105
St. Louis 112, Los Angeles 100
St. Louis 131, Los Angeles 127
Los Angeles 130, St. Louis 121

NBA FINALS
Los Angeles 133, Bost. 129 (OT)
Boston 129, Los Angeles 109
Boston 120, Los Angeles 106
Boston 122, Los Angeles 117
Los Angeles 121, Boston 117
Los Angeles 123, Boston 115
Boston 95, Los Angeles 93

1966-67
FINAL STANDINGS

Eastern Division

	W	L	PCT	GB
Philadelphia	68	13	.840	
Boston	60	21	.741	8
Cincinnati	39	42	.481	29
New York	36	45	.444	32
Baltimore	20	61	.247	48

Western Division

	W	L	PCT	GB
San Francisco	44	37	.543	
St. Louis	39	42	.481	5
Los Angeles	36	45	.444	8
Chicago	33	48	.407	11
Detroit	30	51	.370	14

POINTS

	AVG	NO.
R. Barry, SF	35.6	2775
O. Robertson, CIN	30.5	2412
W. Chamberlain, PHI	24.1	1956
J. West, LA	28.7	1892
E. Baylor, LA	26.6	1862
H. Greer, PHI	22.1	1765
J. Havlicek, BOS	21.4	1733
W. Reed, NY	20.9	1628
B. Howell, BOS	20.0	1621
D. Bing, DET	20.0	1601
S. Jones, BOS	22.1	1594
C. Walker, PHI	19.3	1567
G. Johnson, BAL	20.7	1511
W. Bellamy, NY	19.0	1499
B. Cunningham, PHI	18.5	1495
L. Hudson, STL	18.4	1471
G. Rodgers, CHI	18.0	1459
J. Lucas, CIN	17.8	1438
B. Boozer, CHI	18.0	1436
E. Miles, DET	17.6	1425

REBOUNDS

	AVG	NO.
W. Chamberlain, PHI	24.2	1957
B. Russell, BOS	21.0	1700
J. Lucas, CIN	19.1	1547
N. Thurmond, SF	21.3	1382
B. Bridges, STL	15.1	1190
W. Reed, NY	14.6	1136
D. Imhoff, LA	13.3	1080
W. Bellamy, NY	13.5	1064
L. Ellis, BAL	12.0	970
D. DeBusschere, DET	11.8	924

ASSISTS

	AVG	NO.
G. Rodgers, CHI	11.2	908
O. Robertson, CIN	10.7	845
W. Chamberlain, PHI	7.8	630
B. Russell, BOS	5.8	472
J. West, LA	6.8	447
L. Wilkens, STL	5.7	442
H. Komives, NY	6.2	401
K. Jones, BOS	5.0	389
R. Guerin, STL	4.4	345
P. Neumann, SF	4.4	342

FIELD GOAL PCT

W. Chamberlain, PHI	.683
Walt Bellamy, NY	.521
Bailey Howell, BOS	.512
Oscar Robertson, CIN	.493
Willis Reed, NY	.490
Chet Walker, PHI	.488
Bob Boozer, CHI	.487
Tom Hawkins, LA	.481
Happy Hairston, CIN	.479
Dick Barnett, NY	.478

FREE THROW PCT

Adrian Smith, CIN	.903
Rick Barry, SF	.884
Jerry West, LA	.878
Oscar Robertson, CIN	.873
Sam Jones, BOS	.857
Larry Siegfried, BOS	.847
Wally Jones, PHI	.838
John Havlicek, BOS	.828

EAST SEMIFINALS
Philadelphia 3, Cincinnati 1
Boston 3, New York 1

EAST FINALS
Philadelphia 127, Boston 113
Philadelphia 107, Boston 102
Philadelphia 115, Boston 104
Boston 121, Philadelphia 117
Philadelphia 140, Boston 116

WEST SEMIFINALS
San Francisco 3, L.A. 0
St. Louis 3, Chicago 0

WEST FINALS
San Francisco 117, St. L. 115
San Francisco 143, St. L. 136
St. Louis 115, S.F. 109
St. Louis 109, S.F. 104
San Francisco 123, St. L. 102
San Francisco 112, St. L. 107

NBA FINALS
Phil. 141, S.F. 135 (OT)
Philadelphia 126, S.F. 95
San Francisco 130, Phil. 124
Philadelphia 122, S.F. 108
San Francisco 117, Phil. 109
Philadelphia 125, S.F. 122

1967-68
FINAL STANDINGS

Eastern Division	W	L	PCT	GB
Philadelphia	62	20	.756	
Boston	54	28	.659	8
New York	43	39	.524	19
Detroit	40	42	.488	22
Cincinnati	39	43	.476	23
Baltimore	36	46	.439	26

Western Division	W	L	PCT	GB
St. Louis	56	26	.683	
Los Angeles	52	30	.634	4
San Francisco	43	39	.524	13
Chicago	29	53	.354	27
Seattle	23	59	.280	33
San Diego	15	67	.183	41

POINTS
	AVG	NO.
D. Bing, DET	27.1	2142
E. Baylor, LA	26.0	2002
W. Chamberlain, PHI	24.3	1992
E. Monroe, BAL	24.3	1991
H. Greer, PHI	24.1	1976
O. Robertson, CIN	29.2	1896
W. Hazzard, SEA	23.9	1894
J. Lucas, CIN	21.4	1760
Z. Beaty, STL	21.1	1733
R. LaRusso, SF	21.8	1726
J. Havlicek, BOS	20.7	1700
W. Reed, NY	20.8	1685
B. Boozer, CHI	21.5	1655
L. Wilkens, STL	20.0	1638
B. Howell, BOS	19.8	1621
A. Clark, LA	19.9	1612
S. Jones, BOS	21.3	1553
J. Mullins, SF	18.9	1493
B. Rule, SEA	18.1	1484
C. Walker, PHI	17.9	1465

REBOUNDS
	AVG	NO.
W. Chamberlain, PHI	23.8	1952
J. Lucas, CIN	19.0	1560
B. Russell, BOS	18.6	1451
C. Lee, SF	13.9	1141
N. Thurmond, SF	22.0	1121
R. Scott, BAL	13.7	1111
B. Bridges, STL	13.4	1102
D. DeBusschere, DET	13.5	1081
W. Reed, NY	13.2	1073
W. Bellamy, NY	11.7	961

ASSISTS
	AVG	NO.
W. Chamberlain, PHI	8.6	702
L. Wilkens, STL	8.3	679
O. Robertson, CIN	9.7	633
D. Bing, DET	6.4	509
W. Hazzard, SEA	6.2	493
A. Williams, SD	4.9	391
A. Attles, SF	5.8	390
J. Havlicek, BOS	4.7	384
G. Rodgers, CHI/CIN	4.8	380
H. Greer, PHI	4.5	372

FIELD GOAL PCT
W. Chamberlain, PHI	.595
Walt Bellamy, NY	.541
Jerry Lucas, CIN	.519
Jerry West, LA	.514
Len Chappell, CIN/DET	.513
Oscar Robertson, CIN	.500
Tom Hawkins, LA	.499
Terry Dischinger, DET	.494
Don Nelson, BOS	.494
Henry Finkel, SD	.492

FREE THROW PCT
Oscar Robertson, CIN	.873
Larry Siegfried, BOS	.868
Dave Gambee, SD	.847
Fred Hetzel, SF	.833
Adrian Smith, CIN	.829
Sam Jones, BOS	.827
Flynn Robinson, CIN/CHI	.821
John Havlicek, BOS	.812

EAST SEMIFINALS
Philadelphia 4, New York 2
Boston 4, Detroit 2

EAST FINALS
Boston 127, Philadelphia 118
Philadelphia 115, Boston 106
Philadelphia 122, Boston 114
Philadelphia 110, Boston 105
Boston 122, Philadelphia 104
Boston 114, Philadelphia 106
Boston 100, Philadelphia 96

WEST SEMIFINALS
San Francisco 4, St. Louis 2
Los Angeles 4, Chicago 1

WEST FINALS
Los Angeles 133, S.F. 105
Los Angeles 115, S.F. 112
Los Angeles 128, S.F. 124
Los Angeles 106, S.F. 100

NBA FINALS
Boston 107, Los Angeles 101
Los Angeles 123, Boston 113
Boston 127, Los Angeles 119
Los Angeles 119, Boston 105
Boston 120, L.A. 117 (OT)
Boston 124, Los Angeles 109

1968-69
FINAL STANDINGS

Eastern Division

	W	L	PCT	GB
Baltimore	57	25	.695	
Philadelphia	55	27	.671	2
New York	54	28	.659	3
Boston	48	34	.585	9
Cincinnati	41	41	.500	16
Detroit	32	50	.390	25
Milwaukee	27	55	.329	30

Western Division

	W	L	PCT	GB
Los Angeles	55	27	.671	
Atlanta	48	34	.585	7
San Francisco	41	41	.500	14
San Diego	37	45	.451	18
Chicago	33	49	.402	22
Seattle	30	52	.366	25
Phoenix	16	66	.195	39

POINTS

	AVG	NO.
E. Hayes, SD	28.4	2327
E. Monroe, BAL	25.8	2065
B. Cunningham, PHI	24.8	2034
B. Rule, SEA	24.0	1965
O. Robertson, CIN	24.7	1955
G. Goodrich, PHO	23.8	1931
H. Greer, PHI	23.1	1896
E. Baylor, LA	24.8	1881
L. Wilkens, SEA	22.4	1835
D. Kojis, SD	22.5	1820
K. Loughery, BAL	22.6	1806
D. Bing, DET	23.4	1800
J. Mullins, SF	22.8	1775
J. Havlicek, BOS	21.6	1771
L. Hudson, ATL	21.9	1770
W. Reed, NY	21.1	1733
B. Boozer, CHI	21.7	1716
D. Van Arsdale, PHO	21.0	1678
W. Chamberlain, LA	20.5	1664
F. Robinson, CHI/MIL	20.0	1662

REBOUNDS

	AVG	NO.
W. Chamberlain, LA	21.1	1712
W. Unseld, BAL	18.2	1491
B. Russell, BOS	19.3	1484
E. Hayes, SD	17.1	1406
N. Thurmond, SF	19.7	1402
J. Lucas, CIN	18.4	1360
W. Reed, NY	14.5	1191
B. Bridges, ATL	14.2	1132
W. Bellamy, NY/DET	12.5	1101
B. Cunningham, PHI	12.8	1050

ASSISTS

	AVG	NO.
O. Robertson, CIN	9.8	772
L. Wilkens, SEA	8.2	674
W. Frazier, NY	7.9	635
G. Rodgers, MIL	6.9	561
D. Bing, DET	7.1	546
A. Williams, SD	6.6	524
G. Goodrich, PHO	6.4	518
W. Hazzard, ATL	5.9	474
J. Havlicek, BOS	5.4	441
J. West, LA	6.9	423

FIELD GOAL PCT

W. Chamberlain, LA	.583
Jerry Lucas, CIN	.551
Willis Reed, NY	.521
Terry Dischinger, DET	.515
Walt Bellamy, NY/DET	.510
Joe Caldwell, ATL	.507
Walt Frazier, NY	.505
Tom Hawkins, LA	.499
Lou Hudson, ATL	.492
Jon McGlocklin, MIL	.487

FREE THROW PCT

Larry Siegfried, BOS	.864
Jeff Mullins, SF	.843
Jon McGlocklin, MIL	.842
Flynn Robinson, CHI/MIL	.839
Oscar Robertson, CIN	.838
Fred Hetzel, MIL/CIN	.838
Jack Marin, BAL	.830
Jerry West, LA	.821

EAST SEMIFINALS
New York 4, Baltimore 0
Boston 4, Philadelphia 1

EAST FINALS
Boston 108, New York 100
Boston 112, New York 97
New York 101, Boston 91
Boston 97, New York 96
New York 112, Boston 104
Boston 106, New York 105

WEST SEMIFINALS
Los Angeles 4, San Fran. 2
Atlanta 4, San Diego 2

WEST FINALS
Los Angeles 95, Atlanta 93
Los Angeles 104, Atlanta 102
Atlanta 99, Los Angeles 86
Los Angeles 100, Atlanta 85
Los Angeles 104, Atlanta 96

NBA FINALS
Los Angeles 120, Boston 118
Los Angeles 118, Boston 112
Boston 111, Los Angeles 105
Boston 89, Los Angeles 88
Los Angeles 117, Boston 104
Boston 99, Los Angeles 90
Boston 108, Los Angeles 106

1969-70
FINAL STANDINGS

Eastern Division	W	L	PCT	GB
New York	60	22	.732	
Milwaukee	56	26	.683	4
Baltimore	50	32	.610	10
Philadelphia	42	40	.512	18
Cincinnati	36	46	.439	24
Boston	34	48	.415	26
Detroit	31	51	.378	29

Western Division	W	L	PCT	GB
Atlanta	48	34	.585	
Los Angeles	46	36	.561	2
Chicago	39	43	.476	9
Phoenix	39	43	.476	9
Seattle	36	46	.439	12
San Francisco	30	52	.366	18
San Diego	27	55	.329	21

SCORING
Jerry West, LA 31.2
Lew Alcindor, MIL 28.8
Elvin Hayes, SD 27.5
Billy Cunningham, PHI 26.1
Lou Hudson, ATL 25.4
Connie Hawkins, PHO 24.6
Bob Rule, SEA 24.6
John Havlicek, BOS 24.2
Earl Monroe, BAL 23.4
Dave Bing, DET 22.9
Tom Van Arsdale, CIN 22.8
Jeff Mullins, SF 22.1
Hal Greer, PHI 22.0
Flynn Robinson, MIL 21.8
Willis Reed, NY 21.7
Chet Walker, CHI 21.5
Dick Van Arsdale, PHO....21.3
Joe Caldwell, ATL............21.1
Bob Love, CHI 21.0
Walt Frazier, NY 20.9

REBOUNDS
Elvin Hayes, SD 16.9
Wes Unseld, BAL 16.7
Lew Alcindor, MIL 14.5
Bill Bridges, ATL 14.4
Gus Johnson, BAL 13.9
Willis Reed, NY 13.9
Billy Cunningham, PHI 13.6
Tom Boerwinkle, CHI 12.5
Paul Silas, PHO 11.7
Clyde Lee, SF 11.3

ASSISTS
Len Wilkens, SEA 9.1
Walt Frazier, NY 8.2
Clem Haskins, CHI 7.6
Jerry West, LA 7.5
Gail Goodrich, PHO........... 7.5
Walt Hazzard, ATL 6.8
John Havlicek, BOS 6.8
Art Williams, SD 6.3
Norm Van Lier, CIN 6.2
Dave Bing, DET 6.0

FIELD GOAL PCT
Johnny Green, CIN............ .559
Darrall Imhoff, PHI .... .540
Lou Hudson, ATL .... .531
Jon McGlocklin, MIL........... .530
Dick Snyder, SEA .... .528
Jim Fox, PHO .... .524
Lew Alcindor, MIL.............. .518
Wes Unseld, BAL .... .518
Walt Frazier, NY .... .518
Dick Van Arsdale, PHO .... .508

FREE THROW PCT
Flynn Robinson, MIL .... .898
Chet Walker, CHI .... .850
Jeff Mullins, SF .... .847
John Havlicek, BOS .... .844
Bob Love, CHI .... .842
Earl Monroe, BAL .... .830
Lou Hudson, ATL .... .824
Jerry West, LA .... .824

EAST SEMIFINALS
New York 4, Baltimore 3
Milwaukee 4, Philadelphia 1

EAST FINALS
New York 110, Milwaukee 102
New York 112, Milwaukee 111
Milwaukee 101, New York 96
New York 117, Milwaukee 105
New York 132, Milwaukee 96

WEST SEMIFINALS
Atlanta 4, Chicago 1
Los Angeles 4, Phoenix 3

WEST FINALS
Los Angeles 119, Atlanta 115
Los Angeles 105, Atlanta 94
Los Angeles 115, Atl. 114 (OT)
Los Angeles 133, Atlanta 114

NBA FINALS
New York 124, L.A. 112
Los Angeles 105, N.Y. 103
New York 111, L.A. 108 (OT)
Los Angeles 121, N.Y. 115 (OT)
New York 107, L.A. 100
Los Angeles 135, N.Y. 113
New York 113, L.A. 99

1970-71
FINAL STANDINGS

Eastern Conference
Atlantic Division

	W	L	PCT	GB
New York	52	30	.634	
Philadelphia	47	35	.573	5
Boston	44	38	.537	8
Buffalo	22	60	.268	30

Central Division

	W	L	PCT	GB
Baltimore	42	40	.512	
Atlanta	36	46	.439	6
Cincinnati	33	49	.402	9
Cleveland	15	67	.183	27

Western Conference
Midwest Division

	W	L	PCT	GB
Milwaukee	66	16	.805	
Chicago	51	31	.622	15
Phoenix	48	34	.585	18
Detroit	45	37	.549	21

Pacific Division

	W	L	PCT	GB
Los Angeles	48	34	.585	
San Francisco	41	41	.500	7
San Diego	40	42	.488	8
Seattle	38	44	.463	10
Portland	29	53	.354	19

SCORING
Lew Alcindor, MIL	31.7
John Havlicek, BOS	28.9
Elvin Hayes, SD	28.7
Dave Bing, DET	27.0
Lou Hudson, ATL	26.8
Bob Love, CHI	25.2
Geoff Petrie, POR	24.8
Pete Maravich, ATL	23.2
Billy Cunningham, PHI	23.0
Tom Van Arsdale, CIN	22.9
Chet Walker, CHI	22.0
Dick Van Arsdale, PHO	21.9
Walt Frazier, NY	21.7
Earl Monroe, BAL	21.4
Jo Jo White, BOS	21.3
Archie Clark, PHI	21.3
Willis Reed, NY	20.9
Connie Hawkins, PHO	20.9
Jeff Mullins, SF	20.8

REBOUNDS
W. Chamberlain, LA	18.2
Wes Unseld, BAL	16.9
Elvin Hayes, SD	16.6
Lew Alcindor, MIL	16.0
Jerry Lucas, SF	15.8
Bill Bridges, ATL	15.0
Dave Cowens, BOS	15.0
Tom Boerwinkle, CHI	13.8
Nate Thurmond, SF	13.8
Willis Reed, NY	13.7

ASSISTS
Norm Van Lier, CIN	10.1
Len Wilkens, SEA	9.2
Oscar Robertson, MIL	8.2
John Havlicek, BOS	7.5
Walt Frazier, NY	6.7
Walt Hazzard, ATL	6.3
Ron Williams, SF	5.9
Nate Archibald, CIN	5.5
Archie Clark, PHI	5.4
Dave Bing, DET	5.0

FIELD GOAL PCT
Johnny Green, CIN	.587
Lew Alcindor, MIL	.577
W. Chamberlain, LA	.545
Jon McGlocklin, MIL	.535
Dick Snyder, SEA	.531
Greg Smith, MIL	.512
Bob Dandridge, MIL	.509
Wes Unseld, BAL	.501
Jerry Lucas, SF	.498

FREE THROW PCT
Chet Walker, CHI	.859
Oscar Robertson, MIL	.850
Ron Williams, SF	.844
Jeff Mullins, SF	.844
Dick Snyder, SEA	.837
Stan McKenzie, POR	.836
Jerry West, LA	.832
Jimmy Walker, DET	.831

EAST SEMIFINALS
New York 4, Atlanta 1
Baltimore 4, Philadelphia 3

EAST FINALS
New York 112, Baltimore 111
New York 107, Baltimore 88
Baltimore 114, New York 88
Baltimore 101, New York 80
New York 89, Baltimore 84
Baltimore 113, New York 96
Baltimore 93, New York 91

WEST SEMIFINALS
Milwaukee 4, San Francisco 1
Los Angeles 4, Chicago 3

WEST FINALS
Milwaukee 106, L.A. 85
Milwaukee 91, Los Angeles 73
Los Angeles 118, Milw. 107
Milwaukee 117, L.A. 94
Milwaukee 116, L.A. 98

NBA FINALS
Milwaukee 98, Baltimore 88
Milwaukee 102, Baltimore 83
Milwaukee 107, Baltimore 99
Milwaukee 118, Baltimore 106

1971-72
FINAL STANDINGS

Eastern Conference
Atlantic Division

	W	L	PCT	GB
Boston	56	26	.683	
New York	48	34	.585	8
Philadelphia	30	52	.366	26
Buffalo	22	60	.268	34

Central Division

	W	L	PCT	GB
Baltimore	38	44	.463	
Atlanta	36	46	.439	2
Cincinnati	30	52	.366	8
Cleveland	23	59	.280	15

Western Conference
Midwest Division

	W	L	PCT	GB
Milwaukee	63	19	.768	
Chicago	57	25	.695	6
Phoenix	49	33	.598	14
Detroit	26	56	.317	37

Pacific Division

	W	L	PCT	GB
Los Angeles	69	13	.841	
Golden State	51	31	.622	18
Seattle	47	35	.573	22
Houston	34	48	.415	35
Portland	18	64	.220	51

SCORING

K. Abdul-Jabbar, MIL	34.8
Nate Archibald, CIN	28.2
John Havlicek, BOS	27.5
Spencer Haywood, SEA	26.2
Gail Goodrich, LA	25.9
Bob Love, CHI	25.8
Jerry West, LA	25.8
Bob Lanier, DET	25.7
Archie Clark, BAL	25.2
Elvin Hayes, HOU	25.2
Lou Hudson, ATL	24.7
Sidney Wicks, POR	24.5
Billy Cunningham, PHI	23.3
Walt Frazier, NY	23.2
Jo Jo White, BOS	23.1
Jack Marin, BAL	22.3
Chet Walker, CHI	22.0
Jeff Mullins, GS	21.5
Nate Thurmond, GS	21.4
Cazzie Russell, GS	21.4

REBOUNDS

W. Chamberlain, LA	19.2
Wes Unseld, BAL	17.6
K. Abdul-Jabbar, MIL	16.6
Nate Thurmond, GS	16.1
Dave Cowens, BOS	15.2
Elmore Smith, BUF	15.2
Elvin Hayes, HOU	14.6
Clyde Lee, GS	14.5
Bob Lanier, DET	14.2

ASSISTS

Jerry West, LA	9.7
Len Wilkens, SEA	9.6
Nate Archibald, CIN	9.2
Archie Clark, BAL	8.0
John Havlicek, BOS	7.5
Norm Van Lier, CIN/CHI	6.9
Billy Cunningham, PHI	5.9
Jeff Mullins, GS	5.9
Walt Frazier, NY	5.8
Walt Hazzard, BUF	5.6

FIELD GOAL PCT

W. Chamberlain, LA	.649
K. Abdul-Jabbar, MIL	.574
Walt Bellamy, ATL	.545
Dick Snyder, SEA	.529
Jerry Lucas, NY	.512
Walt Frazier, NY	.512
Jon McGlocklin, MIL	.510
Chet Walker, CHI	.505
Lucius Allen, MIL	.505

FREE THROW PCT

Jack Marin, BAL	.894
Calvin Murphy, HOU	.890
Gail Goodrich, LA	.850
Chet Walker, CHI	.847
Dick Van Arsdale, PHO	.845
Stu Lantz, HOU	.838
John Havlicek, BOS	.834
Cazzie Russell, GS	.833

EAST SEMIFINALS
Boston 4, Atlanta 2
New York 4, Baltimore 2

EAST FINALS
New York 116, Boston 94
New York 106, Boston 105
Boston 115, New York 109
New York 116, Boston 98
New York 111, Boston 103

WEST SEMIFINALS
Los Angeles 4, Chicago 0
Milwaukee 4, Golden St. 1

WEST FINALS
Milwaukee 93, Los Angeles 72
Los Angeles 135, Milw. 134
Los Angeles 108, Milw. 105
Milwaukee 114, L.A. 88
Los Angeles 115, Milw. 90
Los Angeles 104, Milw. 100

NBA FINALS
New York 114, Los Angeles 92
Los Angeles 106, New York 92
Los Angeles 107, New York 96
Los Angeles 116, N.Y. 111 (OT)
Los Angeles 114, N.Y. 100

1972-73
FINAL STANDINGS

Eastern Conference
Atlantic Division

	W	L	PCT	GB
Boston	68	14	.829	
New York	57	25	.695	11
Buffalo	21	61	.256	47
Philadelphia	9	73	.110	59

Central Division

	W	L	PCT	GB
Baltimore	52	30	.634	
Atlanta	46	36	.561	6
Houston	33	49	.402	19
Cleveland	32	50	.390	20

Western Conference
Midwest Division

	W	L	PCT	GB
Milwaukee	60	22	.732	
Chicago	51	31	.622	9
Detroit	40	42	.488	20
K.C.-Omaha	36	46	.439	24

Pacific Division

	W	L	PCT	GB
Los Angeles	60	22	.732	
Golden State	47	35	.573	13
Phoenix	38	44	.463	22
Seattle	26	56	.317	34
Portland	21	61	.256	39

SCORING

Nate Archibald, KCO	34.0
K. Abdul-Jabbar, MIL	30.2
Spencer Haywood, SEA	29.2
Lou Hudson, ATL	27.1
Pete Maravich, ATL	26.1
Charlie Scott, PHO	25.3
Geoff Petrie, POR	24.9
Gail Goodrich, LA	23.9
Sidney Wicks, POR	23.8
Bob Lanier, DET	23.8
John Havlicek, BOS	23.8
Bob Love, CHI	23.1
Dave Bing, DET	22.4
Rick Barry, GS	22.3
Elvin Hayes, BAL	21.2
Walt Frazier, NY	21.1
Austin Carr, CLE	20.5
Dave Cowens, BOS	20.5
Len Wilkens, CLE	20.5

REBOUNDS

W. Chamberlain, LA	18.6
Nate Thurmond, GS	17.1
Dave Cowens, BOS	16.2
K. Abdul-Jabbar, MIL	16.1
Wes Unseld, BAL	15.9
Bob Lanier, DET	14.9
Elvin Hayes, BAL	14.5
Walt Bellamy, ATL	13.0
Paul Silas, BOS	13.0
Spencer Haywood, SEA	12.9

ASSISTS

Nate Archibald, KCO	11.4
Len Wilkens, CLE	8.4
Dave Bing, DET	7.8
Oscar Robertson, MIL.	7.5
Norm Van Lier, CHI	7.1
Pete Maravich, ATL	6.9
John Havlicek, BOS	6.6
Herm Gilliam, ATL	6.3
Charlie Scott, PHO	6.1
Jo Jo White, BOS	6.1

FIELD GOAL PCT

W. Chamberlain, LA	.727
Matt Guokas, KCO	.570
K. Abdul-Jabbar, MIL.	.554
Curtis Rowe, DET	.519
Jim Fox, SEA	.515
Jerry Lucas, NY	.513
Mike Riordan, BAL	.510
Archie Clark, BAL	.507
Bob Kauffman, BUF	.505

FREE THROW PCT

Rick Barry, GS	.902
Calvin Murphy, HOU	.888
Mike Newlin, HOU	.886
Jimmy Walker, HOU	.884
Bill Bradley, NY	.871
Cazzie Russell, GS	.864
Dick Snyder, SEA	.861
Dick Van Arsdale, PHO	.859

EAST SEMIFINALS

Boston 4, Atlanta 2
New York 4, Baltimore 1

EAST FINALS

Boston 134, New York 108
New York 129, Boston 96
New York 98, Boston 91
New York 117, Bost. 110 (2OT)
Boston 98, New York 97
Boston 110, New York 100
New York 94, Boston 78

WEST SEMIFINALS

Los Angeles 4, Chicago 3
Golden St. 4, Milwaukee 2

WEST FINALS

Los Angeles 101, G.S. 99
Los Angeles 104, G.S. 93
Los Angeles 126, G.S. 70
Golden St. 117, L.A. 109
Los Angeles 128, G.S. 118

NBA FINALS

Los Angeles 115, N.Y. 112
New York 99, Los Angeles 95
New York 87, Los Angeles 83
New York 103, Los Angeles 98
New York 102, Los Angeles 93

1973-74
FINAL STANDINGS

Eastern Conference
Atlantic Division

	W	L	PCT	GB
Boston	56	26	.683	
New York	49	33	.598	7
Buffalo	42	40	.512	14
Philadelphia	25	57	.305	31

Central Division

	W	L	PCT	GB
Capital	47	35	.573	
Atlanta	35	47	.427	12
Houston	32	50	.390	15
Cleveland	29	53	.354	18

Western Conference
Midwest Division

	W	L	PCT	GB
Milwaukee	59	23	.720	
Chicago	54	28	.659	5
Detroit	52	30	.634	7
K.C.-Omaha	33	49	.402	26

Pacific Division

	W	L	PCT	GB
Los Angeles	47	35	.573	
Golden State	44	38	.537	3
Seattle	36	46	.439	11
Phoenix	30	52	.366	17
Portland	27	55	.329	20

SCORING
Bob McAdoo, BUF 30.6
Pete Maravich, ATL 27.7
K. Abdul-Jabbar, MIL 27.0
Gail Goodrich, LA............25.3
Rick Barry, GS 25.1
Rudy Tomjanovich, HOU ..24.5
Geoff Petrie, POR............24.3
Spencer Haywood, SEA ..23.5
John Havlicek, BOS 22.6
Bob Lanier, DET 22.5

REBOUNDS
Elvin Hayes, CAP.............18.1
Dave Cowens, BOS 15.7
Bob McAdoo, BUF 15.1
K. Abdul-Jabbar, MIL 14.5
Happy Hairston, LA..........13.5
Spencer Haywood, SEA ...13.4
Sam Lacey, KCO 13.4
Bob Lanier, DET 13.3
Clifford Ray, CHI 12.2

ASSISTS
Ernie DiGregorio, BUF 8.2
Calvin Murphy, HOU 7.4
Len Wilkens, CLE............. 7.1
Walt Frazier, NY 6.9
Dave Bing, DET................ 6.9
Norm Van Lier, CHI 6.9
Oscar Robertson, MIL. 6.4
Rick Barry, GS.................. 6.1

STEALS
Larry Steele, POR.............2.68
Steve Mix, PHI 2.59
Randy Smith, BUF 2.48
Jerry Sloan, CHI...............2.38
Rick Barry, GS 2.11
Phil Chenier, CAP.............2.04

BLOCKED SHOTS
Elmore Smith, LA..............4.85
K. Abdul-Jabbar, MIL 3.49
Bob McAdoo, BUF 3.32
Bob Lanier, DET 3.04
Elvin Hayes, CAP.............2.96
Garfield Heard, BUF 2.84

FIELD GOAL PCT
Bob McAdoo, BUF............ .547
K. Abdul-Jabbar, MIL........ .539
Rudy Tomjanovich, HOU.. .536
Calvin Murphy, HOU .... .522
Butch Beard, GS .... .512
Clifford Ray, CHI .... .511

FREE THROW PCT
Ernie DiGregorio, BUF ..... .902
Rick Barry, GS.................. .899
Jeff Mullins, GS .... .875
Chet Walker, CHI .... .875
Bill Bradley, NY................ .874
Calvin Murphy, HOU .... .868

EAST SEMIFINALS
Boston 4, Buffalo 2
New York 4, Capital 3

EAST FINALS
Boston 113, New York 88
Boston 111, New York 99
New York 103, Boston 100
Boston 98, New York 91
Boston 105, New York 94

WEST SEMIFINALS
Milwaukee 4, Los Angeles 1
Chicago 4, Detroit 3

WEST FINALS
Milwaukee 101, Chicago 85
Milwaukee 113, Chicago 111
Milwaukee 113, Chicago 90
Milwaukee 115, Chicago 99

NBA FINALS
Boston 98, Milwaukee 83
Milwaukee 105, Bos. 96 (OT)
Boston 95, Milwaukee 83
Milwaukee 97, Boston 89
Boston 96, Milwaukee 87
Milwaukee 102, Bos. 101 (2OT)
Boston 102, Milwaukee 87

1974-75
FINAL STANDINGS

Eastern Conference
Atlantic Division

	W	L	PCT	GB
Boston	60	22	.732	
Buffalo	49	33	.598	11
New York	40	42	.488	20
Philadelphia	34	48	.415	26

Central Division

	W	L	PCT	GB
Washington	60	22	.732	
Houston	41	41	.500	19
Cleveland	40	42	.488	20
Atlanta	31	61	.378	29
New Orleans	23	59	.280	37

Western Conference
Midwest Division

	W	L	PCT	GB
Chicago	47	35	.573	
K.C.-Omaha	44	38	.537	3
Detroit	40	42	.488	7
Milwaukee	38	44	.463	9

Pacific Division

	W	L	PCT	GB
Golden State	48	34	.585	
Seattle	43	39	.524	5
Portland	38	44	.463	10
Phoenix	32	50	.390	16
Los Angeles	30	52	.366	18

SCORING

Bob McAdoo, BUF	34.5
Rick Barry, GS	30.6
K. Abdul-Jabbar, MIL	30.0
Nate Archibald, KCO	26.5
Charlie Scott, PHO	24.3
Bob Lanier, DET	24.0
Elvin Hayes, WAS	23.0
Gail Goodrich, LA	22.6
Spencer Haywood, SEA	22.4
Fred Carter, PHI	21.9

REBOUNDS

Wes Unseld, WAS	14.8
Dave Cowens, BOS	14.7
Sam Lacey, KCO	14.2
Bob McAdoo, BUF	14.1
K. Abdul-Jabbar, MIL	14.0
Happy Hairston, LA	12.8
Paul Silas, BOS	12.5
Elvin Hayes, WAS	12.2
Bob Lanier, DET	12.0

ASSISTS

Kevin Porter, WAS	8.0
Dave Bing, DET	7.7
Nate Archibald, KCO	6.8
Randy Smith, BUF	6.5
Pete Maravich, NO	6.2
Rick Barry, GS	6.2
Slick Watts, SEA	6.1

STEALS

Rick Barry, GS	2.85
Walt Frazier, NY	2.44
Larry Steele, POR	2.41
Slick Watts, SEA	2.32
Fred Brown, SEA	2.31
Phil Chenier, WAS	2.29

BLOCKED SHOTS

K. Abdul-Jabbar, MIL	3.26
Elmore Smith, LA	2.92
Nate Thurmond, CHI	2.44
Elvin Hayes, WAS	2.28
Bob Lanier, DET	2.26
Bob McAdoo, BUF	2.12

FIELD GOAL PCT

Don Nelson, BOS	.539
Butch Beard, GS	.528
Rudy Tomjanovich, HOU	.525
K. Abdul-Jabbar, MIL	.513
Bob McAdoo, BUF	.512
Kevin Kunnert, HOU	.512

FREE THROW PCT

Rick Barry, GS	.904
Calvin Murphy, HOU	.883
Bill Bradley, NY	.873
Nate Archibald, KCO	.872
Jim Price, LAMIL	.871
John Havlicek, BOS	.870

EAST FIRST ROUND
Houston 2, New York 1

EAST SEMIFINALS
Washington 4, Buffalo 3
Boston 4, Houston 1

EAST FINALS
Washington 4, Boston 2

WEST FIRST ROUND
Seattle 2, Detroit 1

WEST SEMIFINALS
Golden St. 4, Seattle 2
Chicago 4, K.C.-Omaha 2

WEST FINALS
Golden St. 4, Chicago 3

NBA FINALS
Golden St. 101, Washington 95
Golden St. 92, Washington 91
Golden St. 109, Wash. 101
Golden St. 96, Washington 95

1975-76
FINAL STANDINGS

Eastern Conference
Atlantic Division

	W	L	PCT	GB
Boston	54	28	.659	
Buffalo	46	36	.561	8
Philadelphia	46	36	.561	8
New York	38	44	.463	16

Central Division

	W	L	PCT	GB
Cleveland	49	33	.598	
Washington	48	34	.585	1
Houston	40	42	.488	9
New Orleans	38	44	.463	11
Atlanta	29	53	.354	20

Western Conference
Midwest Division

	W	L	PCT	GB
Milwaukee	38	44	.463	
Detroit	36	46	.439	2
Kansas City	31	51	.378	7
Chicago	24	58	.293	14

Pacific Division

	W	L	PCT	GB
Golden State	59	23	.720	
Seattle	43	39	.524	16
Phoenix	42	40	.512	17
Los Angeles	40	42	.488	19
Portland	37	45	.451	22

SCORING
Bob McAdoo, BUF	31.1
K. Abdul-Jabbar, LA	27.7
Pete Maravich, NO	25.9
Nate Archibald, KC	24.8
Fred Brown, SEA	23.1
George McGinnis, PHI	23.0
Randy Smith, BUF	21.8
John Drew, ATL	21.6
Bob Dandridge, MIL	21.5
Rick Barry, GS	21.0

REBOUNDS
K. Abdul-Jabbar, LA	16.9
Dave Cowens, BOS	16.0
Wes Unseld, WAS	13.3
Paul Silas, BOS	12.7
Sam Lacey, KC	12.6
George McGinnis, PHI	12.6
Bob McAdoo, BUF	12.4
Elmore Smith, MIL	11.4
Spencer Haywood, NY	11.3

ASSISTS
Slick Watts, SEA	8.1
Nate Archibald, KC	7.9
Calvin Murphy, HOU	7.3
Norm Van Lier, CHI	6.6
Rick Barry, GS	6.1
Dave Bing, WAS	6.0
Randy Smith, BUF	5.9

STEALS
Slick Watts, SEA	3.18
George McGinnis, PHI	2.57
Paul Westphal, PHO	2.56
Rick Barry, GS	2.49
Chris Ford, DET	2.17
Larry Steele, POR	2.10

BLOCKED SHOTS
K. Abdul-Jabbar, LA	4.12
Elmore Smith, MIL	3.05
Elvin Hayes, WAS	2.53
Harvey Catchings, PHI	2.19
George Johnson, GS	2.12
Bob McAdoo, BUF	2.05

FIELD GOAL PCT
Wes Unseld, WAS	.56085
John Shumate, BUF	.56081
Jim McMillian, BUF	.536
Bob Lanier, DET	.532
K. Abdul-Jabbar, LA	.529
Elmore Smith, MIL	.518

FREE THROW PCT
Rick Barry, GS	.923
Calvin Murphy, HOU	.907
Cazzie Russell, LA	.892
Bill Bradley, NY	.878
Fred Brown, SEA	.869
Mike Newlin, HOU	.865

EAST FIRST ROUND
Buffalo 2, Philadelphia 1

EAST SEMIFINALS
Boston 4, Buffalo 2
Cleveland 4, Washington 3

EAST FINALS
Boston 4, Cleveland 2

WEST FIRST ROUND
Detroit 2, Milwaukee 1

WEST SEMIFINALS
Golden St. 4, Detroit 2
Phoenix 4, Seattle 2

WEST FINALS
Phoenix 4, Golden St. 3

NBA FINALS
Boston 98, Phoenix 87
Boston 105, Phoenix 90
Phoenix 105, Boston 98
Phoenix 109, Boston 107
Boston 128, Phoe. 126 (3OT)
Boston 87, Phoenix 80

1976-77
FINAL STANDINGS

Eastern Conference
Atlantic Division

	W	L	PCT	GB
Philadelphia	50	32	.610	
Boston	44	38	.537	6
N.Y. Knicks	40	42	.488	10
Buffalo	30	52	.366	20
N.Y. Nets	22	60	.288	28

Central Division

	W	L	PCT	GB
Houston	49	33	.598	
Washington	48	34	.585	1
San Antonio	44	38	.537	5
Cleveland	43	39	.524	6
New Orleans	35	47	.427	14
Atlanta	31	51	.378	18

Western Conference
Midwest Division

	W	L	PCT	GB
Denver	50	32	.610	
Detroit	44	38	.537	6
Chicago	44	38	.537	6
Kansas City	40	42	.488	10
Indiana	36	46	.439	14
Milwaukee	30	52	.366	20

Pacific Division

	W	L	PCT	GB
Los Angeles	53	29	.646	
Portland	49	33	.598	4
Golden State	46	36	.561	7
Seattle	40	42	.488	13
Phoenix	34	48	.415	19

SCORING
Pete Maravich, NO	31.1
Billy Knight, IND	26.6
K. Abdul-Jabbar, LA	26.2
David Thompson, DEN	25.9
Bob McAdoo, BUF/NYK	25.8
Bob Lanier, DET	25.3
John Drew, ATL	24.2
Elvin Hayes, WAS	23.7
George Gervin, SA	23.1
Dan Issel, DEN	22.3

REBOUNDS
Bill Walton, POR	14.4
K. Abdul-Jabbar, LA	13.3
Moses Malone, BUF/HOU	13.1
Artis Gilmore, CHI	13.0
Bob McAdoo, BUF/NYK	12.9
Elvin Hayes, WAS	12.5
Swen Nater, MIL	12.0
George McGinnis, PHI	11.5

ASSISTS
Don Buse, IND	8.5
Slick Watts, SEA	8.0
Norm Van Lier, CHI	7.8
Kevin Porter, DET	7.3
Tom Henderson, ATL/WAS	6.9
Rick Barry, GS	6.0
Jo Jo White, BOS	6.0

STEALS
Don Buse, IND	3.47
Brian Taylor, KC	2.76
Slick Watts, SEA	2.71
Quinn Buckner, MIL	2.43
Mike Gale, SA	2.33
Bobby Jones, DEN	2.27

BLOCKED SHOTS
Bill Walton, POR	3.25
K. Abdul-Jabbar, LA	3.18
Elvin Hayes, WAS	2.68
Artis Gilmore, CHI	2.48
Caldwell Jones, PHI	2.44
George Johnson, GS/BUF	2.27

FIELD GOAL PCT
K. Abdul-Jabbar, LA	.579
Mitch Kupchak, WAS	.572
Bobby Jones, DEN	.570
George Gervin, SA	.544
Bob Lanier, DET	.534
Bob Gross, POR	.529

FREE THROW PCT
Ernie DiGregorio, BUF	.945
Rick Barry, GS	.916
Calvin Murphy, HOU	.886
Mike Newlin, HOU	.885
Fred Brown, SEA	.884

EAST FIRST ROUND
Washington 2, Cleveland 1
Boston 2, San Antonio 0

EAST SEMIFINALS
Philadelphia 4, Boston 3
Houston 4, Washington 2

EAST FINALS
Philadelphia 4, Houston 2

WEST FIRST ROUND
Portland 2, Chicago 1
Golden St. 2, Detroit 1

WEST SEMIFINALS
Los Angeles 4, Golden St. 3
Portland 4, Denver 2

WEST FINALS
Portland 4, Los Angeles 0

NBA FINALS
Philadelphia 107, Portland 101
Philadelphia 107, Portland 89
Portland 129, Philadelphia 107
Portland 130, Philadelphia 98
Portland 110, Philadelphia 104
Portland 109, Philadelphia 107

1977-78
FINAL STANDINGS

Eastern Conference
Atlantic Division

	W	L	PCT	GB
Philadelphia	55	27	.671	
New York	43	39	.524	12
Boston	32	50	.390	23
Buffalo	27	55	.329	28
New Jersey	24	58	.293	31

Central Division

	W	L	PCT	GB
San Antonio	52	30	.634	
Washington	44	38	.537	8
Cleveland	43	39	.524	9
Atlanta	41	41	.500	11
New Orleans	39	43	.476	13
Houston	28	54	.341	24

Western Conference
Midwest Division

	W	L	PCT	GB
Denver	48	34	.585	
Milwaukee	44	38	.537	4
Chicago	40	42	.488	8
Detroit	38	44	.463	10
Indiana	31	51	.378	17
Kansas City	31	51	.378	17

Pacific Division

	W	L	PCT	GB
Portland	58	24	.707	
Phoenix	49	33	.598	9
Seattle	47	35	.573	11
Los Angeles	45	37	.549	13
Golden State	43	39	.524	15

SCORING
George Gervin, SA...........27.22
David Thompson, DEN 27.15
Bob McAdoo, NY 26.5
K. Abdul-Jabbar, LA 25.8
Calvin Murphy, HOU 25.6
Paul Westphal, PHO 25.2
Randy Smith, BUF 24.6
Bob Lanier, DET 24.5
Walter Davis, PHO............24.2
Bernard King, NJ...............24.2

REBOUNDS
Truck Robinson, NO 15.7
Moses Malone, HOU.........15.0
Dave Cowens, BOS..........14.0
Elvin Hayes, WAS.............13.3
Swen Nater, BUF..............13.2
Artis Gilmore, CHI.............13.1
K. Abdul-Jabbar, LA 12.9
Bob McAdoo, NY 12.8

ASSISTS
Kevin Porter, DET/NJ...........10.2
John Lucas, HOU 9.4
Ricky Sobers, IND 7.4
Norm Nixon, LA 6.8
Norm Van Lier, CHI 6.8
Henry Bibby, PHI................5.7

STEALS
Ron Lee, PHO...................2.74
Gus Williams, SEA............2.34
Quinn Buckner, MIL...........2.29
Mike Gale, SA...................2.27
Don Buse, PHO 2.26
Foots Walker, CLE...........2.17

BLOCKED SHOTS
George Johnson, NJ.........3.38
K. Abdul-Jabbar, LA 2.98
Tree Rollins, ATL...............2.73
Bill Walton, POR 2.52
Billy Paultz, SA..................2.43
Artis Gilmore, CHI 2.21

FIELD GOAL PCT
Bobby Jones, DEN .... .578
Darryl Dawkins, PHI .... .575
Artis Gilmore, CHI .... .559
K. Abdul-Jabbar, LA .... .550
Alex English, MIL.............. .542

FREE THROW PCT
Rick Barry, GS................. .924
Calvin Murphy, HOU .... .918
Fred Brown, SEA.............. .898
Mike Newlin, HOU .... .874
Scott Wedman, KC........... .870

EAST FIRST ROUND
Washington 2, Atlanta 0
New York 2, Cleveland 0

EAST SEMIFINALS
Philadelphia 4, New York 0
Washington 4, San Antonio 2

EAST FINALS
Washington 4, Philadelphia 2

WEST FIRST ROUND
Seattle 2, Los Angeles 1
Milwaukee 2, Phoenix 0

WEST SEMIFINALS
Seattle 4, Portland 2
Denver 4, Milwaukee 3

WEST FINALS
Seattle 4, Denver 2

NBA FINALS
Seattle 106, Washington 102
Washington 106, Seattle 98
Seattle 93, Washington 92
Washington 120, Seat. 116(OT)
Seattle 98, Washington 94
Washington 117, Seattle 82
Washington 105, Seattle 99

1978-79
FINAL STANDINGS

Eastern Conference
Atlantic Division

	W	L	PCT	GB
Washington	54	28	.659	
Philadelphia	47	35	.573	7
New Jersey	37	45	.451	17
New York	31	51	.378	23
Boston	29	53	.354	25

Central Division

	W	L	PCT	GB
San Antonio	48	34	.585	
Houston	47	35	.573	1
Atlanta	46	36	.561	2
Cleveland	30	52	.366	18
Detroit	30	52	.366	18
New Orleans	26	56	.317	22

Western Conference
Midwest Division

	W	L	PCT	GB
Kansas City	48	34	.585	
Denver	47	35	.573	1
Indiana	38	44	.463	10
Milwaukee	38	44	.463	10
Chicago	31	51	.378	17

Pacific Division

	W	L	PCT	GB
Seattle	52	30	.634	
Phoenix	50	32	.610	2
Los Angeles	47	35	.573	5
Portland	45	37	.549	7
San Diego	43	39	.524	9
Golden State	38	44	.463	14

SCORING

George Gervin, SA	29.6
Lloyd Free, SD	28.8
Marques Johnson, MIL	25.6
Bob McAdoo, NY/BOS	24.8
Moses Malone, HOU	24.8
David Thompson, DEN	24.0
Paul Westphal, PHO	24.0
K. Abdul-Jabbar, LA	23.8
Artis Gilmore, CHI	23.7
Walter Davis, PHO	23.6

REBOUNDS

Moses Malone, HOU	17.6
Rich Kelley, NO	12.8
K. Abdul-Jabbar, LA	12.8
Artis Gilmore, CHI	12.7
Jack Sikma, SEA	12.4
Elvin Hayes, WAS	12.1
Robert Parish, GS	12.1

ASSISTS

Kevin Porter, DET	13.4
John Lucas, GS	9.3
Norm Nixon, LA	9.0
Phil Ford, KC	8.6
Paul Westphal, PHO	6.5
Rick Barry, HOU	6.3

STEALS

M.L. Carr, DET	2.46
Ed Jordan, NJ	2.45
Norm Nixon, LA	2.45
Foots Walker, CLE	2.36
Phil Ford, KC	2.20
Randy Smith, SD	2.16

BLOCKED SHOTS

K. Abdul-Jabbar, LA	3.95
George Johnson, NJ	3.24
Tree Rollins, ATL	3.14
Robert Parish, GS	2.86
Terry Tyler, DET	2.45

FIELD GOAL PCT

Cedric Maxwell, BOS	.584
K. Abdul-Jabbar, LA	.577
Wes Unseld, WAS	.577
Artis Gilmore, CHI	.575
Swen Nater, SD	.569

FREE THROW PCT

Rick Barry, HOU	.947
Calvin Murphy, HOU	.928
Fred Brown, SEA	.888
Robert Smith, DEN	.883
Ricky Sobers, IND	.882

EAST FIRST ROUND
Philadelphia 2, New Jersey 0
Atlanta 2, Houston 0

EAST SEMIFINALS
Washington 4, Atlanta 3
San Antonio 4, Philadelphia 3

EAST FINALS
Washington 4, San Antonio 3

WEST FIRST ROUND
Phoenix 2, Portland 1
Los Angeles 2, Denver 1

WEST SEMIFINALS
Seattle 4, Los Angeles 1
Phoenix 4, Kansas City 1

WEST FINALS
Seattle 4, Phoenix 3

NBA FINALS
Washington 99, Seattle 97
Seattle 92, Washington 82
Seattle 105, Washington 95
Seattle 114, Wash. 112 (OT)
Seattle 97, Washington 93

1979-80
FINAL STANDINGS

Eastern Conference
Atlantic Division

	W	L	PCT	GB
Boston	61	21	.744	
Philadelphia	59	23	.720	2
Washington	39	43	.476	22
New York	39	43	.476	22
New Jersey	34	48	.415	27

Central Division

	W	L	PCT	GB
Atlanta	50	32	.610	
Houston	41	41	.500	9
San Antonio	41	41	.500	9
Indiana	37	45	.451	13
Cleveland	37	45	.451	13
Detroit	16	66	.195	34

Western Conference
Midwest Division

	W	L	PCT	GB
Milwaukee	49	33	.598	
Kansas City	47	35	.573	2
Denver	30	52	.366	19
Chicago	30	52	.366	19
Utah	24	58	.293	25

Pacific Division

	W	L	PCT	GB
Los Angeles	60	22	.732	
Seattle	56	26	.683	4
Phoenix	55	27	.671	5
Portland	38	44	.463	22
San Diego	35	47	.427	25
Golden State	24	58	.293	36

SCORING
George Gervin, SA	33.1
Lloyd Free, SD	30.2
Adrian Dantley, UTA	28.0
Julius Erving, PHI	26.9
Moses Malone, HOU	25.8
K. Abdul-Jabbar, LA	24.8
Dan Issel, DEN	23.8
Elvin Hayes, WAS	23.0
Otis Birdsong, KC	22.7
Mike Mitchell, CLE	22.2

REBOUNDS
Swen Nater, SD	15.0
Moses Malone, HOU	14.5
Wes Unseld, WAS	13.3
Caldwell Jones, PHI	11.9
Jack Sikma, SEA	11.1

ASSISTS
Micheal Richardson, NY	10.1
Nate Archibald, BOS	8.4
Foots Walker, CLE	8.0
Norm Nixon, LA	7.8
John Lucas, GS	7.5

STEALS
Micheal Richardson, NY	3.23
Ed Jordan, NJ	2.72
Dudley Bradley, IND	2.57
Gus Williams, SEA	2.44
Magic Johnson, LA	2.43

BLOCKED SHOTS
K. Abdul-Jabbar, LA	3.41
George Johnson, NJ	3.19
Tree Rollins, ATL	2.98
Terry Tyler, DET	2.68
Elvin Hayes, WAS	2.33

FIELD GOAL PCT
Cedric Maxwell, BOS	.609
K. Abdul-Jabbar, LA	.604
Artis Gilmore, CHI	.595
Adrian Dantley, UTA	.576
Tom Boswell, DEN/UTA	.564

FREE THROW PCT
Rick Barry, HOU	.935
Calvin Murphy, HOU	.897
Ron Boone, UTA	.893
Paul Silas, SA	.887

3-PT. FIELD GOAL PCT
Fred Brown, SEA	.443
Chris Ford, BOS	.427
Larry Bird, BOS	.406
John Roche, DEN	.380

EAST FIRST ROUND
Philadelphia 2, Washington 0
Houston 2, San Antonio 1

EAST SEMIFINALS
Boston 4, Houston 0
Philadelphia 4, Atlanta 1

EAST FINALS
Philadelphia 4, Boston 1

WEST FIRST ROUND
Seattle 2, Portland 1
Phoenix 2, Kansas City 1

WEST SEMIFINALS
Los Angeles 4, Phoenix 1
Seattle 4, Milwaukee 3

WEST FINALS
Los Angeles 4, Seattle 1

NBA FINALS
Los Angeles 109, Phil. 102
Philadelphia 107, L.A. 104
Los Angeles 111, Phil. 101
Philadelphia 105, L.A. 102
Los Angeles 108, Phil. 103
Los Angeles 123, Phil. 107

1980-81
FINAL STANDINGS

Eastern Conference
Atlantic Division

	W	L	PCT	GB
Boston	62	20	.756	
Philadelphia	62	20	.756	
New York	50	32	.610	12
Washington	39	43	.476	23
New Jersey	24	58	.293	38

Central Division

	W	L	PCT	GB
Milwaukee	60	22	.732	
Chicago	45	37	.549	15
Indiana	44	38	.537	16
Atlanta	31	51	.378	29
Cleveland	28	54	.341	32
Detroit	21	61	.256	39

Western Conference
Midwest Division

	W	L	PCT	GB
San Antonio	52	30	.634	
Kansas City	40	42	.488	12
Houston	40	42	.488	12
Denver	37	45	.451	15
Utah	28	54	.341	24
Dallas	15	67	.183	37

Pacific Division

	W	L	PCT	GB
Phoenix	57	25	.695	
Los Angeles	54	28	.659	3
Portland	45	37	.549	12
Golden State	39	43	.476	18
San Diego	36	46	.439	21
Seattle	34	48	.415	23

SCORING
Adrian Dantley, UTA 30.7
Moses Malone, HOU........27.8
George Gervin, SA............27.1
K. Abdul-Jabbar, LA........26.2
David Thompson, DEN 25.5
Otis Birdsong, KC 24.6
Julius Erving, PHI............24.6
Mike Mitchell, CLE............24.5
Lloyd Free, GS.................24.1
Alex English, DEN.............23.8

REBOUNDS
Moses Malone, HOU........14.8
Swen Nater, SD 12.4
Larry Smith, GS 12.1
Larry Bird, BOS.................10.9
Jack Sikma, SEA 10.4

ASSISTS
Kevin Porter, WAS 9.1
Norm Nixon, LA 8.8
Phil Ford, KC 8.8
Micheal Richardson, NY 7.9
Nate Archibald, BOS 7.7

STEALS
Magic Johnson, LA 3.43
Micheal Richardson, NY ...2.94

Quinn Buckner, MIL 2.40
Maurice Cheeks, PHI 2.38
Ray Williams, NY 2.34

BLOCKED SHOTS
George Johnson, SA........3.39
Tree Rollins, ATL 2.93
K. Abdul-Jabbar, LA.........2.85
Robert Parish, BOS 2.61
Artis Gilmore, CHI 2.41

FIELD GOAL PCT
Artis Gilmore, CHI .... .670
Darryl Dawkins, PHI .... .607
Cedric Maxwell, BOS .... .588
Bernard King, GS .... .588
K. Abdul-Jabbar, LA .... .574

FREE THROW PCT
Calvin Murphy, HOU .... .958
Ricky Sobers, CHI .... .935
Mike Newlin, NJ................ .888
Jim Spanarkel, DAL......... .887

3-PT. FIELD GOAL PCT
Brian Taylor, SD .... .383
Freeman Williams, SD...... .340
Joe Hassett, DAL/GS........ .340
Mike Bratz, CLE .... .337

EAST FIRST ROUND
Philadelphia 2, Indiana 0
Chicago 2, New York 0

EAST SEMIFINALS
Boston 4, Chicago 0
Philadelphia 4, Milwaukee 3

EAST FINALS
Boston 4, Philadelphia 3

WEST FIRST ROUND
Houston 2, Los Angeles 1
Kansas City 2, Portland 1

WEST SEMIFINALS
Kansas City 4, Phoenix 3
Houston 4, San Antonio 3

WEST FINALS
Houston 4, Kansas City 1

NBA FINALS
Boston 98, Houston 95
Houston 92, Boston 90
Boston 94, Houston 71
Houston 91, Boston 86
Boston 109, Houston 80
Boston 102, Houston 91

1981-82
FINAL STANDINGS

Eastern Conference
Atlantic Division

	W	L	PCT	GB
Boston	63	19	.768	
Philadelphia	58	24	.707	5
New Jersey	44	38	.537	19
Washington	43	39	.524	20
New York	33	49	.402	30

Central Division

	W	L	PCT	GB
Milwaukee	55	27	.671	
Atlanta	42	40	.512	13
Detroit	39	43	.476	16
Indiana	35	47	.427	20
Chicago	34	48	.415	21
Cleveland	15	67	.183	40

Western Conference
Midwest Division

	W	L	PCT	GB
San Antonio	48	34	.585	
Denver	46	36	.561	2
Houston	46	36	.561	2
Kansas City	30	52	.366	18
Dallas	28	54	.341	20
Utah	25	57	.305	23

Pacific Division

	W	L	PCT	GB
Los Angeles	57	25	.695	
Seattle	52	30	.634	5
Phoenix	46	36	.561	11
Golden State	45	37	.549	12
Portland	42	40	.512	15
San Diego	17	65	.207	40

SCORING
George Gervin, SA............32.3
Moses Malone, HOU.........31.1
Adrian Dantley, UTA.........30.3
Alex English, DEN.............25.4
Julius Erving, PHI..............24.4
K. Abdul-Jabbar, LA.........23.9
Gus Williams, SEA............23.4
Bernard King, GS.............23.2
World B. Free, GS.............22.9
Larry Bird, BOS................22.9

REBOUNDS
Moses Malone, HOU........14.7
Jack Sikma, SEA 12.7
Buck Williams, NJ 12.3
Mychal Thompson, POR....11.7
Maurice Lucas, NY............11.3

ASSISTS
Johnny Moore, SA............. 9.6
Magic Johnson, LA............ 9.5
Maurice Cheeks, PHI 8.4
Nate Archibald, BOS 8.0
Norm Nixon, LA 8.0

STEALS
Magic Johnson, LA 2.67
Maurice Cheeks, PHI........2.65

Micheal Richardson, NY ...2.60
Quinn Buckner, MIL 2.49
Ray Williams, NJ...............2.43

BLOCKED SHOTS
George Johnson, SA........3.12
Tree Rollins, ATL 2.84
K. Abdul-Jabbar, LA..........2.72
Artis Gilmore, CHI 2.70
Robert Parish, BOS 2.40

FIELD GOAL PCT
Artis Gilmore, CHI .... .652
Steve Johnson, KC............ .613
Buck Williams, NJ.............. .582
K. Abdul-Jabbar, LA .... .579
Calvin Natt, POR .... .576

FREE THROW PCT
Kyle Macy, PHO .... .899
Charlie Criss, SD .... .887
John Long, DET .... .865
George Gervin, SA .... .864

3-PT. FIELD GOAL PCT
Campy Russell, NY 439
Andrew Toney, PHI 424
Kyle Macy, PHO 390
Brian Winters, MIL.............387

EAST FIRST ROUND
Philadelphia 2, Atlanta 0
Washington 2, New Jersey 0

EAST SEMIFINALS
Boston 4, Washington 1
Philadelphia 4, Milwaukee 2

EAST FINALS
Philadelphia 4, Boston 3

WEST FIRST ROUND
Seattle 2, Houston 1
Phoenix 2, Denver 1

WEST SEMIFINALS
Los Angeles 4, Phoenix 0
San Antonio 4, Seattle 1

WEST FINALS
Los Angeles 4, San Antonio 0

NBA FINALS
Los Angeles 124, Phil. 117
Philadelphia 110, L.A. 94
Los Angeles 129, Phil. 108
Los Angeles 111, Phil. 101
Philadelphia 135, L.A. 102
Los Angeles 114, Phil. 104

1982-83
FINAL STANDINGS

Eastern Conference
Atlantic Division

	W	L	PCT	GB
Philadelphia	65	17	.793	
Boston	56	26	.683	9
New Jersey	49	33	.598	16
New York	44	38	.537	21
Washington	42	40	.512	23

Central Division

	W	L	PCT	GB
Milwaukee	51	31	.622	
Atlanta	43	39	.524	8
Detroit	37	45	.451	14
Chicago	28	54	.341	23
Cleveland	23	59	.280	28
Indiana	20	62	.244	31

Western Conference
Midwest Division

	W	L	PCT	GB
San Antonio	53	29	.646	
Denver	45	37	.549	8
Kansas City	45	37	.549	8
Dallas	38	44	.463	15
Utah	30	52	.366	23
Houston	14	68	.171	39

Pacific Division

	W	L	PCT	GB
Los Angeles	58	24	.707	
Phoenix	53	29	.646	5
Seattle	48	34	.585	10
Portland	46	36	.561	12
Golden State	30	52	.366	28
San Diego	25	57	.305	33

SCORING
Alex English, DEN............28.4
Kiki Vandeweghe, DEN.....26.7
Kelly Tripucka, DET 26.5
George Gervin, SA............26.2
Moses Malone, PHI..........24.5
Mark Aguirre, DAL 24.4
Joe Barry Carroll, GS........24.1
World B. Free, GS/CLE.......23.9
Reggie Theus, CHI 23.8
Terry Cummings, SD 23.7

REBOUNDS
Moses Malone, PHI...........15.3
Buck Williams, NJ 12.5
Bill Laimbeer, DET 12.1
Artis Gilmore, SA 12.0
Jack Sikma, SEA 11.4

ASSISTS
Magic Johnson, LA 10.5
Johnny Moore, SA 9.8
Rickey Green, UTA 8.9
Larry Drew, KC.................. 8.1
Frank Johnson, WAS 8.1

STEALS
Micheal Richardson, GS/NJ....2.84
Rickey Green, UTA 2.82

Johnny Moore, SA 2.52
Isiah Thomas, DET 2.46
Darwin Cook, NJ...............2.37

BLOCKED SHOTS
Tree Rollins, ATL 4.29
Bill Walton, POR 3.61
Mark Eaton, UTA 3.40
Larry Nance, PHO.............2.65
Artis Gilmore, CHI 2.34

FIELD GOAL PCT
Artis Gilmore, SA............... .626
Steve Johnson, KC............ .624
Darryl Dawkins, NJ............ .599
K. Abdul-Jabbar, LA .... .588
Buck Williams, NJ............. .588

FREE THROW PCT
Calvin Murphy, HOU .... .920
Kiki Vandeweghe, DEN .... .875
Kyle Macy, PHO .... .872
George Gervin, SA .... .853

3-PT. FIELD GOAL PCT
Mike Dunleavy, SA .... .345
Isiah Thomas, DET........... .288
Darrell Griffith, UTA .... .288
Allen Leavell, HOU .... .240

EAST FIRST ROUND
Boston 2, Atlanta 1
New York 2, New Jersey 0

EAST SEMIFINALS
Philadelphia 4, New York 0
Milwaukee 4, Boston 0

EAST FINALS
Philadelphia 4, Milwaukee 1

WEST FIRST ROUND
Denver 2, Phoenix 1
Portland 2, Seattle 0

WEST SEMIFINALS
Los Angeles 4, Portland 1
San Antonio 4, Denver 1

WEST FINALS
Los Angeles 4, San Antonio 2

NBA FINALS
Philadelphia 113, L.A. 107
Philadelphia 103, L.A. 93
Philadelphia 111, L.A. 94
Philadelphia 115, L.A. 108

1983-84
FINAL STANDINGS

Eastern Conference
Atlantic Division

	W	L	PCT	GB
Boston	62	20	.756	
Philadelphia	52	30	.634	10
New York	47	35	.573	15
New Jersey	45	37	.549	17
Washington	35	47	.427	27

Central Division

	W	L	PCT	GB
Milwaukee	50	32	.610	
Detroit	49	33	.598	1
Atlanta	40	42	.488	10
Cleveland	28	54	.341	22
Chicago	27	55	.329	23
Indiana	26	56	.317	24

Western Conference
Midwest Division

	W	L	PCT	GB
Utah	45	37	.549	
Dallas	43	39	.524	2
Denver	38	44	.463	7
Kansas City	38	44	.463	7
San Antonio	37	45	.451	8
Houston	29	53	.354	16

Pacific Division

	W	L	PCT	GB
Los Angeles	54	28	.659	
Portland	48	34	.585	6
Seattle	42	40	.512	12
Phoenix	41	41	.500	13
Golden State	37	45	.451	17
San Diego	30	52	.366	24

SCORING
Adrian Dantley, UTA 30.6
Mark Aguirre, DAL 29.5
Kiki Vandeweghe, DEN....29.4
Alex English, DEN.............26.4
Bernard King, NY 26.3
George Gervin, SA............25.9
Larry Bird, BOS 24.2
Mike Mitchell, SA 23.3
Terry Cummings, SD 22.9
Purvis Short, GS 22.8

REBOUNDS
Moses Malone, PHI...........13.4
Buck Williams, NJ 12.3
Jeff Ruland, WAS...............12.3
Bill Laimbeer, DET 12.2
Ralph Sampson, HOU 11.1

ASSISTS
Magic Johnson, LA 13.1
Norm Nixon, SD 11.1
Isiah Thomas, DET 11.1
John Lucas, SA..................10.7
Johnny Moore, SA............. 9.6

STEALS
Rickey Green, UTA............2.65
Isiah Thomas, DET 2.49

Gus Williams, SEA............2.36
Maurice Cheeks, PHI 2.28
Magic Johnson, LA 2.24

BLOCKED SHOTS
Mark Eaton, UTA 4.28
Tree Rollins, ATL 3.60
Ralph Sampson, HOU 2.40
Larry Nance, PHO.............2.11
Artis Gilmore, SA 2.06

FIELD GOAL PCT
Artis Gilmore, SA...............631
James Donaldson, SD...... .596
Mike McGee, LA.................594
Darryl Dawkins, NJ............593
Calvin Natt, POR................583

FREE THROW PCT
Larry Bird, BOS .... .888
John Long, DET .... .884
Bill Laimbeer, DET .... .866
Walter Davis, PHO .... .863

3-PT. FIELD GOAL PCT
Darrell Griffith, UTA .... .361
Mike Evans, DEN .... .360
Johnny Moore, SA............. .322
Michael Cooper, LA.......... .314

EAST FIRST ROUND
Boston 3, Washington 1
Milwaukee 3, Atlanta 2
New Jersey 3 Philadelphia 2
New York 3, Detroit 2
EAST SEMIFINALS
Boston 4, New York 3
Milwaukee 4, New Jersey 2
EAST FINALS
Boston 4, Milwaukee 1
WEST FIRST ROUND
Los Angeles 3, Kansas City 0
Utah 3, Denver 2
Phoenix 3, Portland 2
Dallas 3, Seattle 2
WEST SEMIFINALS
Los Angeles 4, Dallas 1
Phoenix 4, Utah 2
WEST FINALS
Los Angeles 4, Phoenix 2
NBA FINALS
Los Angeles 115, Boston 109
Boston 124, L.A. 121 (OT)
Los Angeles 137, Boston 104
Boston 129, L.A. 125 (OT)
Boston 121, Los Angeles 103
Los Angeles 119, Boston 108
Boston 111, Los Angeles 102

1984-85
FINAL STANDINGS

Eastern Conference
Atlantic Division

	W	L	PCT	GB
Boston	63	19	.768	
Philadelphia	58	24	.707	5
New Jersey	42	40	.512	21
Washington	40	42	.488	23
New York	24	58	.293	39

Central Division

	W	L	PCT	GB
Milwaukee	59	23	.720	
Detroit	46	36	.561	13
Chicago	38	44	.463	21
Cleveland	36	46	.439	23
Atlanta	34	48	.415	25
Indiana	22	60	.268	37

Western Conference
Midwest Division

	W	L	PCT	GB
Denver	52	30	.634	
Houston	48	34	.585	4
Dallas	44	38	.537	8
San Antonio	41	41	.500	11
Utah	41	41	.500	11
Kansas City	31	51	.378	21

Pacific Division

	W	L	PCT	GB
L.A. Lakers	62	20	.756	
Portland	42	40	.512	20
Phoenix	36	46	.439	26
L.A. Clippers	31	51	.378	31
Seattle	31	51	.378	31
Golden State	22	60	.268	40

SCORING

Bernard King, NY 32.9
Larry Bird, BOS.................28.7
Michael Jordan, CHI 28.2
Purvis Short, GS 28.0
Alex English, DEN..............27.9
Dominique Wilkins, ATL....27.4
Adrian Dantley, UTA 26.6
Mark Aguirre, DAL 25.7
Moses Malone, PHI............24.6
Terry Cummings, MIL 23.6

REBOUNDS

Moses Malone, PHI............13.1
Bill Laimbeer, DET 12.4
Buck Williams, NJ 12.3
Akeem Olajuwon, HOU.....11.9
Mark Eaton, UTA 11.3

ASSISTS

Isiah Thomas, DET 13.9
Magic Johnson, LAL 12.6
Johnny Moore, SA 10.0
Norm Nixon, LAC 8.8
John Bagley, CLE................8.6

STEALS

Micheal Richardson, NJ 2.96
Johnny Moore, SA 2.79

Lafayette Lever, DEN.........2.46
Michael Jordan, CHI 2.39
Doc Rivers, ATL.................2.36

BLOCKED SHOTS

Mark Eaton, UTA 5.56
Akeem Olajuwon, HOU.....2.68
Sam Bowie, POR...............2.67
Wayne Cooper, DEN 2.46
Tree Rollins, ATL 2.39

FIELD GOAL PCT

James Donaldson, LAC.... .637
Artis Gilmore, SA...............623
Otis Thorpe, KC.................600
K. Abdul-Jabbar, LAL 599
Larry Nance, PHO 587

FREE THROW PCT

Kyle Macy, PHO 907
Kiki Vandeweghe, POR......896
Brad Davis, DAL.................888
Kelly Tripucka, DET............885

3-PT. FIELD GOAL PCT

Byron Scott, LAL 433
Larry Bird, BOS 427
Brad Davis, DAL.................409
Trent Tucker, NY 403

EAST FIRST ROUND

Boston 3, Cleveland 1
Milwaukee 3, Chicago 1
Philadelphia 3, Washington 1
Detroit 3, New Jersey 0

EAST SEMIFINALS

Boston 4, Detroit 2
Philadelphia 4, Milwaukee 0

EAST FINALS

Boston 4, Philadelphia 1

WEST FIRST ROUND

L.A. Lakers 3, Phoenix 0
Denver 3, San Antonio 2
Utah 3, Houston 2
Portland 3, Dallas 1

WEST SEMIFINALS

L.A. Lakers 4, Portland 1
Denver 4, Utah 1

WEST FINALS

L.A. Lakers 4, Denver 1

NBA FINALS

Boston 148, L.A. Lakers 114
L.A. Lakers 109, Boston 102
L.A. Lakers 136, Boston 111
Boston 107, L.A. Lakers 105
L.A. Lakers 120, Boston 111
L.A. Lakers 111, Boston 100

1985-86
FINAL STANDINGS

Eastern Conference
Atlantic Division

	W	L	PCT	GB
Boston	67	15	.817	
Philadelphia	54	28	.659	13
Washington	39	43	.476	28
New Jersey	39	43	.476	28
New York	23	59	.280	44

Central Division

	W	L	PCT	GB
Milwaukee	57	25	.695	
Atlanta	50	32	.610	7
Detroit	46	36	.561	11
Chicago	30	52	.366	27
Cleveland	29	53	.354	28
Indiana	26	56	.317	31

Western Conference
Midwest Division

	W	L	PCT	GB
Houston	51	31	.622	
Denver	47	35	.573	4
Dallas	44	38	.537	7
Utah	42	40	.512	9
Sacramento	37	45	.451	14
San Antonio	35	47	.427	16

Pacific Division

	W	L	PCT	GB
L.A. Lakers	62	20	.756	
Portland	40	42	.488	22
L.A. Clippers	32	50	.390	30
Phoenix	32	50	.390	30
Seattle	31	51	.378	31
Golden State	30	52	.366	32

SCORING
Dominique Wilkins, ATL....30.3
Adrian Dantley, UTA 29.8
Alex English, DEN.............29.8
Larry Bird, BOS.................25.8
Purvis Short, GS 25.5
Kiki Vandeweghe, POR 24.8
Moses Malone, PHI...........23.8
Akeem Olajuwon, HOU 23.5
Mike Mitchell, SA 23.4
World B. Free, CLE............23.4

REBOUNDS
Bill Laimbeer, DET 13.1
Charles Barkley, PHI........12.8
Buck Williams, NJ 12.0
Moses Malone, PHI...........11.8
Ralph Sampson, HOU 11.1

ASSISTS
Magic Johnson, LAL 12.6
Isiah Thomas, DET 10.8
Reggie Theus, SAC............ 9.6
John Bagley, CLE.............. 9.4
Maurice Cheeks, PHI 9.2

STEALS
Alvin Robertson, SA..........3.67
Micheal Richardson, NJ 2.66

Clyde Drexler, POR 2.63
Maurice Cheeks, PHI 2.52
Lafayette Lever, DEN........2.28

BLOCKED SHOTS
Manute Bol, WAS..............4.96
Mark Eaton, UTA 4.61
Akeem Olajuwon, HOU 3.40
Wayne Cooper, DEN 2.91
Benoit Benjamin, LAC.......2.61

FIELD GOAL PCT
Steve Johnson, SA .... .632
Artis Gilmore, SA .... .618
Larry Nance, PHO............. .581
James Worthy, LAL........... .579
Kevin McHale, BOS .... .574

FREE THROW PCT
Larry Bird, BOS............... .8963
Chris Mullin, GS .... .8957
Mike Gminski, NJ .... .893
Jim Paxson, POR............. .889

3-PT. FIELD GOAL PCT
Craig Hodges, MIL............ .4506
Trent Tucker, NY............. .4505
Ernie Grunfeld, NY .... .426
Larry Bird, BOS................ .423

EAST FIRST ROUND
Boston 3, Chicago 0
Milwaukee 3, New Jersey 0
Philadelphia 3, Washington 2
Atlanta 3, Detroit 1

EAST SEMIFINALS
Boston 4, Atlanta 1
Milwaukee 4, Philadelphia 3

EAST FINALS
Boston 4, Milwaukee 0

WEST FIRST ROUND
L.A. Lakers 3, San Antonio 0
Houston 3, Sacramento 0
Denver 3, Portland 1
Dallas 3, Utah 1

WEST SEMIFINALS
L.A. Lakers 4, Dallas 2
Houston 4, Denver 2

WEST FINALS
Houston 4, L.A. Lakers 1

NBA FINALS
Boston 112, Houston 100
Boston 117, Houston 95
Houston 106, Boston 104
Boston 106, Houston 103
Houston 111, Boston 96
Boston 114, Houston 97

1986-87
FINAL STANDINGS

Eastern Conference
Atlantic Division

	W	L	PCT	GB
Boston	59	23	.720	
Philadelphia	45	37	.549	14
Washington	42	40	.512	17
New Jersey	24	58	.293	35
New York	24	58	.293	35

Central Division

	W	L	PCT	GB
Atlanta	57	25	.695	
Detroit	52	30	.634	5
Milwaukee	50	32	.610	7
Indiana	41	41	.500	16
Chicago	40	42	.488	17
Cleveland	31	51	.378	26

Western Conference
Midwest Division

	W	L	PCT	GB
Dallas	55	27	.671	
Utah	44	38	.537	11
Houston	42	40	.512	13
Denver	37	45	.451	18
Sacramento	29	53	.354	26
San Antonio	28	54	.341	27

Pacific Division

	W	L	PCT	GB
L.A. Lakers	65	17	.793	
Portland	49	33	.598	16
Golden State	42	40	.512	23
Seattle	39	43	.476	26
Phoenix	36	46	.439	29
L.A. Clippers	12	70	.146	53

SCORING
Michael Jordan, CHI 37.1
Dominique Wilkins, ATL....29.0
Alex English, DEN............28.6
Larry Bird, BOS................28.1
Kiki Vandeweghe, POR ...26.9
Kevin McHale, BOS 26.1
Mark Aguirre, DAL 25.7
Dale Ellis, SEA................24.9
Moses Malone, WAS 24.1
Magic Johnson, LAL 23.9

REBOUNDS
Charles Barkley, PHI........14.6
Charles Oakley, CHI 13.1
Buck Williams, NJ 12.5
James Donaldson, DAL ...11.9
Bill Laimbeer, DET 11.6

ASSISTS
Magic Johnson, LAL 12.2
Sleepy Floyd, GS 10.3
Isiah Thomas, DET 10.0
Doc Rivers, ATL................10.0
Terry Porter, POR 8.9

STEALS
Alvin Robertson, SA.........3.21
Michael Jordan, CHI 2.88

Maurice Cheeks, PHI.......2.65
Ron Harper, CLE 2.55
Clyde Drexler, POR 2.49

BLOCKED SHOTS
Mark Eaton, UTA 4.06
Manute Bol, WAS.............3.68
Akeem Olajuwon, HOU....3.39
Benoit Benjamin, LAC......2.60
Alton Lister, SEA..............2.40

FIELD GOAL PCT
Kevin McHale, BOS.......... .604
Artis Gilmore, SA.............. .597
Charles Barkley, PHI........ .594
James Donaldson, DAL.... .586
K. Abdul-Jabbar, LAL .... .564

FREE THROW PCT
Larry Bird, BOS .... .910
Danny Ainge, BOS .... .897
Bill Laimbeer, DET .... .894
Byron Scott, LAL .... .892

3-PT. FIELD GOAL PCT
Kiki Vandeweghe, POR.... .481
Detlef Schrempf, DAL....... .478
Danny Ainge, BOS .... .443
Byron Scott, LAL .... .436

EAST FIRST ROUND
Boston 3, Chicago 0
Atlanta 3, Indiana 0
Detroit 3, Washington 0
Milwaukee 3, Philadelphia 2

EAST SEMIFINALS
Boston 4, Milwaukee 3
Detroit 4, Atlanta 1

EAST FINALS
Boston 4, Detroit 3

WEST FIRST ROUND
L.A. Lakers 3, Denver 0
Seattle 3, Dallas 1
Houston 3, Portland 1
Golden St. 3, Utah 2

WEST SEMIFINALS
L.A. Lakers 4, Golden St. 1
Seattle 4, Houston 2

WEST FINALS
L.A. Lakers 4, Seattle 0

NBA FINALS
L.A. Lakers 126, Boston 113
L.A. Lakers 141, Boston 122
Boston 109, L.A. Lakers 103
L.A. Lakers 107, Boston 106
Boston 123, L.A. Lakers 108
L.A. Lakers 106, Boston 93

1987-88 FINAL STANDINGS

Eastern Conference
Atlantic Division

	W	L	PCT	GB
Boston	57	25	.695	
Washington	38	44	.463	19
New York	38	44	.463	19
Philadelphia	36	46	.439	21
New Jersey	19	63	.232	38

Central Division

	W	L	PCT	GB
Detroit	54	28	.659	
Atlanta	50	32	.610	4
Chicago	50	32	.610	4
Cleveland	42	40	.512	12
Milwaukee	42	40	.512	12
Indiana	38	44	.463	16

Western Conference
Midwest Division

	W	L	PCT	GB
Denver	54	28	.659	
Dallas	53	29	.646	1
Utah	47	35	.573	7
Houston	46	36	.561	8
San Antonio	31	51	.378	23
Sacramento	24	58	.293	30

Pacific Division

	W	L	PCT	GB
L.A. Lakers	62	20	.756	
Portland	53	29	.646	9
Seattle	44	38	.537	18
Phoenix	28	54	.341	34
Golden State	20	62	.244	42
L.A. Clippers	17	65	.207	45

SCORING
Michael Jordan, CHI 35.0
Dominique Wilkins, ATL...30.7
Larry Bird, BOS................29.9
Charles Barkley, PHI........28.3
Karl Malone, UTA..............27.7
Clyde Drexler, POR 27.0
Dale Ellis, SEA.................25.8
Mark Aguirre, DAL 25.1
Alex English, DEN............25.0
Akeem Olajuwon, HOU.....22.8

REBOUNDS
Michael Cage, LAC 13.03
Charles Oakley, CHI 13.00
Akeem Olajuwon, HOU....12.1
Karl Malone, UTA.............12.0
Buck Williams, NJ 11.9

ASSISTS
John Stockton, UTA..........13.8
Magic Johnson, LAL 11.9
Mark Jackson, NY.............10.6
Terry Porter, POR 10.1
Doc Rivers, ATL 9.3

STEALS
Michael Jordan, CHI 3.16
Alvin Robertson, SA..........2.96

John Stockton, UTA..........2.95
Lafayette Lever, DEN........2.72
Clyde Drexler, POR 2.51

BLOCKED SHOTS
Mark Eaton, UTA 3.71
Benoit Benjamin, LAC......3.41
Patrick Ewing, NY 2.99
Akeem Olajuwon, HOU....2.71
Manute Bol, WAS.............2.70

FIELD GOAL PCT
Kevin McHale, BOS........... .604
Robert Parish, BOS.......... .589
Charles Barkley, PHI .... .587
John Stockton, UTA .... .574
Walter Berry, SA............... .563

FREE THROW PCT
Jack Sikma, MIL................ .922
Larry Bird, BOS .... .916
John Long, IND .... .907
Mike Gminski, NJ/PHI .... .906

3-PT. FIELD GOAL PCT
Craig Hodges, MIL/PHO. ..... .491
Mark Price, CLE .... .486
John Long, IND .... .442
G. Henderson, NY/PHI .... .423

EAST FIRST ROUND
Boston 3, New York 1
Detroit 3, Washington 2
Atlanta 3, Milwaukee 2
Chicago 3, Cleveland 2

EAST SEMIFINALS
Boston 4, Atlanta 3
Detroit 4, Chicago 1

EAST FINALS
Detroit 4, Boston 2

WEST FIRST ROUND
L.A. Lakers 3, San Antonio 0
Denver 3, Seattle 2
Utah 3, Portland 1
Dallas 3, Houston 1

WEST SEMIFINALS
L.A. Lakers 4, Utah 3
Dallas 4, Denver 2

WEST FINALS
L.A. Lakers 4, Dallas 3

NBA FINALS
Detroit 105, L.A. Lakers 93
L.A. Lakers 108, Detroit 96
L.A. Lakers 99, Detroit 86
Detroit 111, L.A. Lakers 86
Detroit 104, L.A. Lakers 94
L.A. Lakers 103, Detroit 102
L.A. Lakers 108, Detroit 105

1988-89 FINAL STANDINGS

Eastern Conference
Atlantic Division

	W	L	PCT	GB
New York	52	30	.634	
Philadelphia	46	36	.561	6
Boston	42	40	.512	10
Washington	40	42	.488	12
New Jersey	26	56	.317	26
Charlotte	20	62	.244	32

Central Division

	W	L	PCT	GB
Detroit	63	19	.768	
Cleveland	57	25	.695	6
Atlanta	52	30	.634	11
Milwaukee	49	33	.598	14
Chicago	47	35	.573	16
Indiana	28	54	.341	35

Western Conference
Midwest Division

	W	L	PCT	GB
Utah	51	31	.622	
Houston	45	37	.549	6
Denver	44	38	.537	7
Dallas	38	44	.463	13
San Antonio	21	61	.256	30
Miami	15	67	.183	36

Pacific Division

	W	L	PCT	GB
L.A. Lakers	57	25	.695	
Phoenix	55	27	.671	2
Seattle	47	35	.573	10
Golden State	43	39	.524	14
Portland	39	43	.476	18
Sacramento	27	55	.329	30
L.A. Clippers	21	61	.256	36

SCORING
Michael Jordan, CHI 32.5
Karl Malone, UTA..............29.1
Dale Ellis, SEA..................27.5
Clyde Drexler, POR 27.2
Chris Mullin, GS................26.5
Alex English, DEN..............26.5
Dominique Wilkins, ATL...26.2
Charles Barkley, PHI..........25.8
Tom Chambers, PHO.........25.7
Akeem Olajuwon, HOU.....24.8

REBOUNDS
Akeem Olajuwon, HOU....13.5
Charles Barkley, PHI.........12.5
Robert Parish, BOS 12.5
Moses Malone, ATL..........11.8
Karl Malone, UTA..............10.7

ASSISTS
John Stockton, UTA 13.6
Magic Johnson, LAL 12.8
Kevin Johnson, PHO..........12.2
Terry Porter, POR 9.5
Nate McMillan, SEA 9.3

STEALS
John Stockton, UTA..........3.21
Alvin Robertson, SA..........3.03

Michael Jordan, CHI 2.89
Lafayette Lever, DEN........2.75
Clyde Drexler, POR 2.73

BLOCKED SHOTS
Manute Bol, GS.................4.31
Mark Eaton, UTA...............3.84
Patrick Ewing, NY 3.51
Akeem Olajuwon, HOU.....3.44
Larry Nance, CLE 2.82

FIELD GOAL PCT
Dennis Rodman, DET ...... .595
Charles Barkley, PHI.......... .579
Robert Parish, BOS........... .570
Patrick Ewing, NY............. .567
James Worthy, LAL........... .548

FREE THROW PCT
Magic Johnson, LAL........... .911
Jack Sikma, MIL .... .905
Scott Skiles, IND .... .903
Mark Price, CLE .... .901

3-PT. FIELD GOAL PCT
Jon Sundvold, MIA .... .522
Dale Ellis, SEA .... .478
Mark Price, CLE .... .441
Hersey Hawkins, PHI .... .428

EAST FIRST ROUND
Detroit 3, Boston 0
New York 3, Philadelphia 0
Chicago 3, Cleveland 2
Milwaukee 3, Atlanta 2

EAST SEMIFINALS
Detroit 4, Milwaukee 0
Chicago 4, New York 2

EAST FINALS
Detroit 4, Chicago 2

WEST FIRST ROUND
L.A. Lakers 3, Portland 0
Golden St. 3, Utah 0
Phoenix 3, Denver 0
Seattle 3, Houston 1

WEST SEMIFINALS
L.A. Lakers 4, Seattle 0
Phoenix 4, Golden St. 1

WEST FINALS
L.A. Lakers 4, Phoenix 0

NBA FINALS
Detroit 109, L.A. Lakers 97
Detroit 108, L.A. Lakers 105
Detroit 114, L.A. Lakers 110
Detroit 105, L.A. Lakers 97

1989-90 FINAL STANDINGS

Eastern Conference

Atlantic Division

	W	L	PCT	GB
Philadelphia	53	29	.646	
Boston	52	30	.634	1
New York	45	37	.549	8
Washington	31	51	.378	22
Miami	18	64	.220	35
New Jersey	17	65	.207	36

Central Division

	W	L	PCT	GB
Detroit	59	23	.720	
Chicago	55	27	.671	4
Milwaukee	44	38	.537	15
Cleveland	42	40	.512	17
Indiana	42	40	.512	17
Atlanta	41	41	.500	18
Orlando	18	64	.220	41

Western Conference

Midwest Division

	W	L	PCT	GB
San Antonio	56	26	.683	
Utah	55	27	.671	1
Dallas	47	35	.573	9
Denver	43	39	.524	13
Houston	41	41	.500	15
Minnesota	22	60	.268	34
Charlotte	19	63	.232	37

Pacific Division

	W	L	PCT	GB
L.A. Lakers	63	19	.768	
Portland	59	23	.720	4
Phoenix	54	28	.659	9
Seattle	41	41	.500	22
Golden State	37	45	.451	26
L.A. Clippers	30	52	.366	33
Sacramento	23	59	.280	40

SCORING

Michael Jordan, CHI 33.6
Karl Malone, UTA.............31.0
Patrick Ewing, NY 28.6
Tom Chambers, PHO 27.2
Dominique Wilkins, ATL...26.7
Charles Barkley, PHI........25.2
Chris Mullin, GS 25.1
Reggie Miller, IND............24.6
Akeem Olajuwon, HOU....24.3
David Robinson, SA..........24.3

REBOUNDS

Akeem Olajuwon, HOU....14.0
David Robinson, SA..........12.0
Charles Barkley, PHI.......11.5
Karl Malone, UTA.............11.1
Patrick Ewing, NY 10.9

ASSISTS

John Stockton, UTA..........14.5
Magic Johnson, LAL 11.5
Kevin Johnson, PHO.........11.4
Tyrone Bogues, CHA 10.7

STEALS

Michael Jordan, CHI 2.77
John Stockton, UTA...........2.65

Scottie Pippen, CHI...........2.57
Alvin Robertson, MIL.........2.56
Derek Harper, DAL 2.28

BLOCKED SHOTS

Akeem Olajuwon, HOU.....4.59
Patrick Ewing, NY 3.99
David Robinson, SA...........3.89
Manute Bol, GS.................3.17
Benoit Benjamin, LAC.......2.63

FIELD GOAL PCT

Mark West, PHO .... .625
Charles Barkley, PHI......... .600
Robert Parish, BOS........... .580
Karl Malone, UTA............. .562

FREE THROW PCT

Larry Bird, BOS .... .930
Eddie Johnson, DEN........ .917
Walter Davis, DEN .... .912
Joe Dumars, DET............. .900

3-PT. FIELD GOAL PCT

Steve Kerr, CLE .... .507
Craig Hodges, CHI .... .481
Drazen Petrovic, POR...... .459
Jon Sundvold, MIA .... .440

EAST FIRST ROUND

Detroit 3, Indiana 0
Philadelphia 3, Cleveland 2
Chicago 3, Milwaukee 1
New York 3, Boston 2

EAST SEMIFINALS

Detroit 4, New York 1
Chicago 4, Philadelphia 1

EAST FINALS

Detroit 4, Chicago 3

WEST FIRST ROUND

L.A. Lakers 3, Houston 1
San Antonio 3, Denver 0
Portland 3, Dallas 0
Phoenix 3, Utah 2

WEST SEMIFINALS

Phoenix 4, L.A. Lakers 1
Portland 4, San Antonio 3

WEST FINALS

Portland 4, Phoenix 2

NBA FINALS

Detroit 105, Portland 99
Portland 106, Detroit 105 (OT)
Detroit 121, Portland 106
Detroit 112, Portland 109
Detroit 92, Portland 90

1990-91 FINAL STANDINGS

Eastern Conference
Atlantic Division

	W	L	PCT	GB
Boston	56	26	.683	
Philadelphia	44	38	.537	12
New York	39	43	.476	17
Washington	30	52	.366	26
New Jersey	26	56	.317	30
Miami	24	58	.293	32

Central Division

	W	L	PCT	GB
Chicago	61	21	.744	
Detroit	50	32	.610	11
Milwaukee	48	34	.585	13
Atlanta	43	39	.524	18
Indiana	41	41	.500	20
Cleveland	33	49	.402	28
Charlotte	26	56	.317	35

Western Conference
Midwest Division

	W	L	PCT	GB
San Antonio	55	27	.671	
Utah	54	28	.659	1
Houston	52	30	.634	3
Orlando	31	51	.378	24
Minnesota	29	53	.354	26
Dallas	28	54	.341	27
Denver	20	62	.244	35

Pacific Division

	W	L	PCT	GB
Portland	63	19	.768	
L.A. Lakers	58	24	.707	5
Phoenix	55	27	.671	8
Golden State	44	38	.537	19
Seattle	41	41	.500	22
L.A. Clippers	31	51	.378	32
Sacramento	25	57	.305	38

SCORING
Michael Jordan, CHI..........31.5
Karl Malone, UTA..........29.0
Bernard King, WAS 28.4
Charles Barkley, PHI..........27.6
Patrick Ewing, NY..........26.6
Michael Adams, DEN..........26.5
Dominique Wilkins, ATL...25.9
Chris Mullin, GS..............25.7
David Robinson, SA 25.6
Mitch Richmond, GS 23.9

REBOUNDS
David Robinson, SA 13.0
Dennis Rodman, DET 12.5
Charles Oakley, NY..........12.1
Karl Malone, UTA..............11.8
Patrick Ewing, NY..............11.2

ASSISTS
John Stockton, UTA 14.2
Magic Johnson, LAL..........12.5
Michael Adams, DEN.........10.5
Kevin Johnson, PHO.........10.1

STEALS
Alvin Robertson, MIL..........3.04
John Stockton, UTA 2.85

Michael Jordan, CHI..........2.72
Tim Hardaway, GS 2.61
Scottie Pippen, CHI...........2.35

BLOCKED SHOTS
Hakeem Olajuwon, HOU ...3.95
David Robinson, SA 3.90
Patrick Ewing, NY..............3.19
Manute Bol, PHI 3.01
Chris Dudley, NJ 2.51

FIELD GOAL PCT
Buck Williams, POR 602
Robert Parish, BOS...........598
Kevin Gamble, BOS 587
Charles Barkley, PHI........570

FREE THROW PCT
Reggie Miller, IND 918
Jeff Malone, UTA...............917
Ricky Pierce, MIL/SEA..........913
Kelly Tripucka, CHA 910

3-PT. FIELD GOAL PCT
Jim Les, SAC....................461
Trent Tucker, NY 418
Jeff Hornacek, PHO 418
Terry Porter, POR 415

EAST FIRST ROUND
Chicago 3, New York 0
Boston 3, Indiana 2
Detroit 3, Atlanta 2
Philadelphia 3, Milwaukee 0

EAST SEMIFINALS
Chicago 4, Philadelphia 1
Detroit 4, Boston 2

EAST FINALS
Chicago 4, Detroit 0

WEST FIRST ROUND
Portland 3, Seattle 2
Golden St. 3, San Antonio 1
L.A. Lakers 3, Houston 0
Utah 3, Phoenix 1

WEST SEMIFINALS
Portland 4, Utah 1
L.A. Lakers 4, Golden St. 1

WEST FINALS
L.A. Lakers 4, Portland 2

NBA FINALS
L.A. Lakers 93, Chicago 91
Chicago 107, L.A. Lakers 86
Chicago 104, L.A. 96 (OT)
Chicago 97, L.A. Lakers 82
Chicago 108, L.A. Lakers 101

1991-92 FINAL STANDINGS

Eastern Conference
Atlantic Division

	W	L	PCT	GB
Boston	51	31	.622	
New York	51	31	.622	
New Jersey	40	42	.488	11
Miami	38	44	.463	13
Philadelphia	35	47	.427	16
Washington	25	57	.305	26
Orlando	21	61	.256	30

Central Division

	W	L	PCT	GB
Chicago	67	15	.817	
Cleveland	57	25	.695	10
Detroit	48	34	.585	19
Indiana	40	42	.488	27
Atlanta	38	44	.463	29
Charlotte	31	51	.378	36
Milwaukee	31	51	.378	36

Western Conference
Midwest Division

	W	L	PCT	GB
Utah	55	27	.671	
San Antonio	47	35	.573	8
Houston	42	40	.512	13
Denver	24	58	.293	31
Dallas	22	60	.268	33
Minnesota	15	67	.183	40

Pacific Division

	W	L	PCT	GB
Portland	57	25	.695	
Golden State	55	27	.671	2
Phoenix	53	29	.646	4
Seattle	47	35	.573	10
L.A. Clippers	45	37	.549	12
L.A. Lakers	43	39	.524	14
Sacramento	29	53	.347	28

SCORING
Michael Jordan, CHI 30.1
Karl Malone, UTA 28.0
Chris Mullin, GS...............25.6
Clyde Drexler, POR 25.0
Patrick Ewing, NY.............24.0
Tim Hardaway, GS 23.4
David Robinson, SA 23.2
Charles Barkley, PHI 23.1
Mitch Richmond, SAC.......22.5
Glen Rice, MIA 22.3

REBOUNDS
Dennis Rodman, DET.......18.7
Kevin Willis, ATL...............15.5
Dikembe Mutombo, DEN ..12.3
David Robinson, SA 12.2
Hakeem Olajuwon, HOU ..12.1

ASSISTS
John Stockton, UTA 13.7
Kevin Johnson, PHO 10.7
Tim Hardaway, GS 10.0
Muggsy Bogues, CHA 9.1

STEALS
John Stockton, UTA 2.98
Micheal Williams, IND.......2.95

Alvin Robertson, MIL ..2.56
Mookie Blaylock, NJ ...2.36
David Robinson, SA 2.32

BLOCKED SHOTS
David Robinson, SA 4.49
Hakeem Olajuwon, HOU ..4.34
Larry Nance, CLE 3.00
Patrick Ewing, NY 2.99
Dikembe Mutombo, DEN ..2.96

FIELD GOAL PCT
Buck Williams, POR......... .604
Otis Thorpe, HOU .... .592
Horace Grant, CHI........... .578
Brad Daugherty, CLE ...... .570

FREE THROW PCT
Mark Price, CLE .... .947
Larry Bird, BOS................ .926
Ricky Pierce, SEA............ .916
Rolando Blackman, DAL... .898

3-PT. FIELD GOAL PCT
Dana Barros, SEA .... .446
Drazen Petrovic, NJ......... .444
Jeff Hornacek, PHO......... .439
Mike Iuzzolino, DAL......... .434

EAST FIRST ROUND
Chicago 3, Miami 0
Boston 3, Indiana 1
Cleveland 3, New Jersey 1
New York 3, Detroit 2

EAST SEMIFINALS
Chicago 4, New York 3
Cleveland 4, Boston 3

EAST FINALS
Chicago 4, Cleveland 2

WEST FIRST ROUND
Portland 3, L.A. Lakers 1
Utah 3, L.A. Clippers 2
Seattle 3, Golden St. 1
Phoenix 3, San Antonio 0

WEST SEMIFINALS
Portland 4, Phoenix 1
Utah 4, Seattle 1

WEST FINALS
Portland 4, Utah 2

NBA FINALS
Chicago 122, Portland 89
Portland 115, Chi. 104 (OT)
Chicago 94, Portland 84
Portland 93, Chicago 88
Chicago 119, Portland 106
Chicago 97, Portland 93

1992-93 FINAL STANDINGS

Eastern Conference
Atlantic Division

	W	L	PCT	GB
New York	60	22	.732	
Boston	48	34	.585	12
New Jersey	43	39	.524	17
Orlando	41	41	.500	19
Miami	36	46	.439	24
Philadelphia	26	56	.317	34
Washington	22	60	.268	38

Central Division

	W	L	PCT	GB
Chicago	57	25	.695	
Cleveland	54	28	.659	3
Charlotte	44	38	.537	13
Atlanta	43	39	.524	14
Indiana	41	41	.500	16
Detroit	40	42	.488	17
Milwaukee	28	54	.341	29

Western Conference
Midwest Division

	W	L	PCT	GB
Houston	55	27	.671	
San Antonio	49	33	.598	6
Utah	47	35	.573	8
Denver	36	46	.439	19
Minnesota	19	63	.232	36
Dallas	11	71	.134	44

Pacific Division

	W	L	PCT	GB
Phoenix	62	20	.756	
Seattle	55	27	.671	7
Portland	51	31	.622	11
L.A. Clippers	41	41	.500	21
L.A. Lakers	39	43	.476	23
Golden State	34	48	.415	28
Sacramento	25	57	.305	37

SCORING
Michael Jordan, CHI	32.6
Dominique Wilkins, ATL	29.9
Karl Malone, UTA	27.0
Hakeem Olajuwon, HOU	26.1
Charles Barkley, PHO	25.6
Patrick Ewing, NY	24.2
Joe Dumars, DET	23.5
Shaquille O'Neal, ORL	23.4
David Robinson, SA	23.4
Danny Manning, LAC	22.8
Drazen Petrovic, NJ	22.3
Larry Johnson, CHA	22.1
Tim Hardaway, GS	21.5
Reggie Miller, IND	21.2
Alonzo Mourning, CHA	21.0
Reggie Lewis, BOS	20.8
Derrick Coleman, NJ	20.7
Hersey Hawkins, PHI	20.3

REBOUNDS
Dennis Rodman, DET	18.3
Shaquille O'Neal, ORL	13.9
Dikembe Mutombo, DEN	13.0
Hakeem Olajuwon, HOU	13.0
Kevin Willis, ATL	12.9
Charles Barkley, PHO	12.2
Patrick Ewing, NY	12.1
Rony Seikaly, MIA	11.8

ASSISTS
John Stockton, UTA	12.0
Tim Hardaway, GS	10.6
Scott Skiles, ORL	9.4
Mark Jackson, LAC	8.8
Muggsy Bogues, CHA	8.8
Micheal Williams, MIN	8.7
Isiah Thomas, DET	8.5
Mookie Blaylock, ATL	8.4

STEALS
Michael Jordan, CHI	2.83
Mookie Blaylock, ATL	2.54
John Stockton, UTA	2.43
Nate McMillan, SEA	2.37
Alvin Robertson, MIL/DET	2.25
Ron Harper, LAC	2.21
Eric Murdock, MIL	2.20
Micheal Williams, MIN	2.17

BLOCKED SHOTS
Hakeem Olajuwon, HOU	4.17
Shaquille O'Neal, ORL	3.53
Dikembe Mutombo, DEN	3.50
Alonzo Mourning, CHA	3.47
David Robinson, SA	3.22
Larry Nance, CLE	2.57
Pervis Ellison, WAS	2.20
Manute Bol, PHI	2.05

FIELD GOAL PCT
Cedric Ceballos, PHO	.576
Brad Daugherty, CLE	.571
Dale Davis, IND	.568
Shaquille O'Neal, ORL	.562
Otis Thorpe, HOU	.558
Karl Malone, UTA	.552
Larry Nance, CLE	.549
Frank Brickowski, MIL	.545

FREE THROW PCT
Mark Price, CLE	.948
Chris Jackson, DEN	.935
Eddie Johnson, SEA	.911
Micheal Williams, MIN	.907
Scott Skiles, ORL	.892
Ricky Pierce, SEA	.889
Reggie Miller, IND	.880
Kenny Smith, HOU	.878

3-PT. FIELD GOAL PCT
B.J. Armstrong, CHI	.453
Chris Mullin, GS	.451
Drazen Petrovic, NJ	.449
Kenny Smith, HOU	.438
Jim Les, SAC	.429
Mark Price, CLE	.416
Terry Porter, POR	.414
Danny Ainge, PHO	.403

1992-93 HOME-AWAY RECORDS

	HOME	ROAD	TOTAL		HOME	ROAD	TOTAL
New York	37-4	23-18	60-22	Orlando	27-14	14-27	41-41
Phoenix	35-6	27-14	62-20	New Jersey	26-15	17-24	43-39
Cleveland	35-6	19-22	54-28	Miami	26-15	10-31	36-46
Seattle	33-8	22-19	55-27	Atlanta	25-16	18-23	43-39
Chicago	31-10	26-15	57-25	Charlotte	22-19	22-19	44-38
Houston	31-10	24-17	55-27	L.A. Lakers	20-21	19-22	39-43
San Antonio	31-10	18-23	49-33	Golden State	19-22	15-26	34-48
Portland	30-11	21-20	51-31	Milwaukee	18-23	10-31	28-54
Boston	28-13	20-21	48-34	Sacramento	16-25	9-32	25-57
Utah	28-13	19-22	47-35	Philadelphia	15-26	11-30	26-56
Detroit	28-13	12-29	40-42	Washington	15-26	7-34	22-60
Denver	28-13	8-33	36-46	Minnesota	11-30	8-33	19-63
Indiana	27-14	14-27	41-41	Dallas	7-34	4-37	11-71
L.A. Clippers	27-14	14-27	41-41				

1992-93 PLAYOFFS

EAST FIRST ROUND
New York 107, Indiana 104
New York 101, Indiana 91
Indiana 116, New York 93
New York 109, Ind. 100 (OT)

Chicago 114, Atlanta 90
Chicago 117, Atlanta 102
Chicago 98, Atlanta 88

Cleveland 114, New Jersey 98
New Jersey 101, Cleveland 99
Cleveland 93, New Jersey 84
New Jersey 96, Cleveland 79
Cleveland 99, New Jersey 89

Boston 112, Charlotte 101
Charlotte 99, Bost. 98 (2OT)
Charlotte 119, Boston 89
Charlotte 104, Boston 103

EAST SEMIFINALS
New York 111, Charlotte 95
New York 105, Char. 101 (OT)
Charlotte 110, N.Y. 106 (2OT)
New York 94, Charlotte 92
New York 105, Charlotte 101

Chicago 91, Cleveland 84
Chicago 104, Cleveland 85
Chicago 96, Cleveland 90
Chicago 103, Cleveland 101

EAST FINALS
New York 98, Chicago 90
New York 96, Chicago 91
Chicago 103, New York 83
Chicago 105, New York 95
Chicago 97, New York 94
Chicago 96, New York 88

WEST FIRST ROUND
L.A. Lakers 107, Phoenix 103
L.A. Lakers 86, Phoenix 81
Phoenix 107, L.A. Lakers 102
Phoenix 101, L.A. Lakers 86
Phoenix 112, L.A. 104 (OT)

Houston 117, L.A. Clippers 94
L.A. Clippers 95, Houston 83
Houston 111, L.A. Clippers 99
L.A. Clippers 93, Houston 90
Houston 84, L.A. Clippers 80

Seattle 99, Utah 85
Utah 89, Seattle 85
Utah 90, Seattle 80
Seattle 93, Utah 80
Seattle 100, Utah 92

San Antonio 87, Portland 86
Portland 105, San Antonio 96
San Antonio 107, Port. 101
San Antonio 100, Port. 97 (OT)

WEST SEMIFINALS
Seattle 99, Houston 90
Seattle 111, Houston 100
Houston 97, Seattle 79
Houston 103, Seattle 92
Seattle 120, Houston 95
Houston 103, Seattle 90
Seattle 103, Hous. 100 (OT)

Phoenix 98, San Antonio 89
Phoenix 109, San Antonio 103
San Antonio 111, Phoenix 96
San Antonio 117, Phoenix 103
Phoenix 109, San Antonio 97
Phoenix 102, San Antonio 100

WEST FINALS
Phoenix 105, Seattle 91
Seattle 103, Phoenix 99
Phoenix 104, Seattle 97
Seattle 120, Phoenix 101
Phoenix 120, Seattle 114
Seattle 118, Phoenix 102
Phoenix 123, Seattle 110

NBA FINALS
Chicago 100, Phoenix 92
Chicago 111, Phoenix 108
Phoenix 129, Chic. 121 (3OT)
Chicago 111, Phoenix 105
Phoenix 108, Chicago 98
Chicago 99, Phoenix 98

1992-93 OFFENSIVE TEAM STATISTICS

TEAM	FIELD GOALS			FREE THROWS			REBOUNDS			MISCELLANEOUS						SCORING	
	ATT	FGs	PCT	ATT	FTs	PCT	OFF	DEF	TOT	AST	PFs	DQ	STL	TO	BLK	PTS	AVG
Phoenix	7093	3494	.493	2539	1912	.753	1141	2510	3651	2087	1739	10	752	1359	455	9298	113.4
Charlotte	7210	3474	.481	2374	1831	.771	1095	2508	3603	2161	1790	15	639	1325	473	9030	110.1
Golden State	7212	3474	.482	2465	1768	.717	1219	2384	3603	2010	2056	29	693	1451	383	9014	109.9
Portland	7343	3361	.458	2551	1901	.745	1226	2507	3733	1969	1892	14	770	1215	425	8898	108.5
Seattle	7140	3473	.486	2259	1720	.761	1222	2254	3476	1906	1971	27	944	1267	409	8884	108.3
Sacramento	7264	3360	.463	2447	1865	.762	1137	2281	3418	2075	2085	35	768	1364	348	8847	107.9
Indiana	7022	3371	.480	2399	1837	.766	1220	2455	3675	2144	2045	17	615	1256	403	8836	107.8
Cleveland	6887	3425	.497	2119	1699	.802	929	2496	3425	2349	1580	10	615	1120	536	8832	107.7
Atlanta	7272	3392	.466	2221	1648	.742	1290	2344	3634	2084	1807	12	806	1339	278	8814	107.5
L.A. Clippers	7329	3544	.484	2177	1562	.718	1183	2360	3543	2242	1920	30	847	1338	491	8783	107.1
Utah	6828	3336	.489	2491	1907	.766	1041	2463	3504	2177	1965	15	746	1270	344	8709	106.2
San Antonio	6762	3311	.490	2346	1794	.765	919	2542	3461	2012	1844	17	582	1227	514	8652	105.5
Orlando	6708	3257	.486	2495	1821	.730	1040	2566	3606	1952	1925	30	542	1429	467	8652	105.5
Denver	7282	3352	.460	2360	1784	.756	1266	2564	3830	1735	2039	25	651	1413	565	8626	105.2
Chicago	7205	3475	.482	1952	1431	.733	1290	2283	3573	2133	1804	13	783	1103	410	8625	105.2
Philadelphia	7075	3225	.456	2259	1776	.786	1031	2431	3462	2038	1604	9	672	1362	566	8556	104.3
L.A. Lakers	6994	3309	.473	2304	1741	.756	1103	2288	3391	2013	1778	9	782	1266	431	8546	104.2
Houston	6744	3280	.486	2090	1584	.758	985	2532	3517	2115	1699	11	682	1295	543	8531	104.0
Boston	7093	3453	.487	1912	1486	.777	1076	2436	3512	1999	1862	13	647	1174	458	8502	103.7
Miami	6850	3127	.456	2476	1908	.771	1134	2384	3518	1688	2011	37	609	1287	350	8495	103.6
New Jersey	7046	3272	.462	2258	1732	.767	1291	2506	3797	1872	1892	19	693	1355	526	8431	102.8
Milwaukee	6924	3268	.472	2081	1544	.742	1050	2113	3163	2084	1978	15	863	1363	393	8392	102.3
Washington	7065	3302	.467	2107	1575	.748	1031	2317	3348	2110	1795	10	673	1323	359	8353	101.9
New York	6898	3209	.465	2316	1717	.741	1150	2660	3810	2125	2111	20	680	1296	372	8328	101.6
Detroit	7211	3267	.453	1957	1426	.729	1293	2315	3608	1941	1747	16	580	1152	249	8252	100.6
Dallas	7271	3164	.435	2171	1530	.705	1234	2265	3499	1683	2302	38	649	1459	355	8141	99.3
Minnesota	6529	3043	.466	2247	1794	.798	940	2204	3144	2001	2028	32	649	1422	455	8046	98.1

1992-93 DEFENSIVE TEAM STATISTICS

TEAM	FIELD GOALS			FREE THROWS			REBOUNDS			MISCELLANEOUS						SCORING		
	ATT	FGs	PCT	ATT	FTs	PCT	OFF	DEF	TOT	AST	PFs	DQ	STL	TO	BLK	PTS	AVG	DIF
New York	6621	2822	.426	2582	1949	.755	1031	2325	3356	1658	2010	26	657	1360	384	7823	95.4	+6.2
Chicago	6622	3139	.474	2033	1584	.779	1039	2265	3304	1918	1731	15	595	1372	357	8109	98.9	+6.3
Houston	7129	3255	.457	1877	1432	.763	1167	2295	3462	1965	1793	22	717	1228	327	8184	99.8	+4.2
Cleveland	7229	3370	.466	1742	1334	.766	1115	2379	3494	2109	1828	19	610	1203	365	8303	101.3	+6.5
Seattle	6707	3143	.469	2299	1746	.759	1075	2220	3295	1835	1853	19	655	1516	406	8304	101.3	+7.1
New Jersey	6945	3231	.465	2248	1665	.741	1102	2345	3447	1786	1881	16	780	1304	416	8328	101.6	+1.3
Detroit	6906	3321	.481	1987	1463	.736	1099	2442	3541	2048	1804	16	623	1219	363	8366	102.0	-1.4
Boston	6980	3232	.463	2269	1749	.771	1094	2378	3472	1971	1676	14	637	1181	386	8429	102.8	+0.9
San Antonio	7177	3290	.458	2051	1583	.772	1082	2388	3470	1905	1998	33	655	1131	373	8433	102.8	+2.7
Utah	6970	3258	.467	2343	1743	.744	1120	2314	3434	1928	1970	20	648	1291	468	8531	104.0	+2.2
Orlando	7255	3307	.456	2306	1682	.729	1166	2271	3437	2091	1975	27	715	1119	401	8544	104.2	+1.3
Miami	6791	3232	.476	2416	1860	.770	1032	2424	3456	1965	2053	20	656	1304	426	8589	104.7	-1.1
Portland	7125	3357	.468	2226	1692	.760	1022	2527	3549	2059	2089	24	649	1404	452	8643	105.4	+3.1
L.A. Lakers	7116	3438	.483	2050	1529	.746	1158	2411	3569	2130	1872	12	686	1304	384	8650	105.5	-1.3
Minnesota	6814	3323	.488	2413	1830	.758	1122	2331	3453	2144	1875	20	734	1231	494	8684	105.9	-7.8
Indiana	6955	3262	.469	2635	1957	.743	1189	2345	3534	1987	1979	28	693	1178	387	8697	106.1	+1.7
Milwaukee	6843	3303	.483	2437	1823	.748	1269	2398	3667	2087	1810	14	773	1476	456	8698	106.1	-3.7
Phoenix	7307	3500	.479	2078	1502	.723	1118	2316	3434	2107	2041	24	708	1328	512	8752	106.7	+6.7
L.A. Clippers	7051	3311	.470	2434	1857	.763	1179	2437	3616	1970	1772	12	765	1445	453	8754	106.8	+0.4
Denver	7214	3324	.461	2517	1899	.754	1039	2505	3664	1890	1983	20	750	1340	503	8769	106.9	-1.7
Atlanta	7074	3509	.496	2092	1586	.758	1080	2413	3493	2189	1881	16	735	1363	363	8885	108.4	-0.9
Washington	7214	3557	.493	2106	1577	.749	1135	2555	3690	2062	1818	14	718	1279	425	8930	108.9	-7.0
Philadelphia	7548	3666	.486	1878	1417	.755	1258	2634	3892	2406	1730	13	781	1290	491	9029	110.1	-5.8
Charlotte	7698	3634	.472	2080	1548	.744	1350	2403	3753	2277	1923	26	599	1245	438	9050	110.4	-0.2
Golden State	7197	3471	.482	2492	1881	.755	1174	2345	3519	2098	1993	23	824	1350	457	9095	110.9	-1.0
Sacramento	7024	3420	.487	2711	2054	.758	1138	2562	3700	2073	2010	22	767	1466	551	9107	111.1	-3.2
Dallas	6783	3401	.501	3071	2351	.766	1063	2740	3803	2047	1861	8	802	1273	520	9387	114.5	-15.2

1993 NBA FINALS COMPOSITE BOX

Chicago	AVG MIN	FGs FG-ATT	PCT	FTs FT-ATT	PCT	REB	AST	STL	BLK	PF	TOT PTS	AVG PTS
Michael Jordan	45.7	101-199	.508	34-49	.694	51	38	10	4	20	246	41.0
Scottie Pippen	44.3	54-123	.439	19-35	.543	55	46	12	6	19	127	21.2
B.J. Armstrong	41.8	32-63	.508	7-7	1.00	11	30	5	1	21	81	13.5
Horace Grant	38.8	28-53	.528	11-19	.579	62	14	9	9	24	67	11.2
John Paxson	16.0	13-21	.619	0-0	.000	9	5	3	1	10	35	5.8
Scott Williams	26.5	13-32	.406	2-7	.286	38	10	3	9	19	28	4.7
Bill Cartwright	21.3	12-30	.400	2-4	.500	19	10	3	1	15	26	4.3
Trent Tucker	6.8	7-10	.700	0-0	.000	2	4	1	0	5	17	2.8
Stacey King	8.2	3-11	.273	7-8	.876	8	3	2	1	6	13	2.2
Darrell Walker	1.7	0-0	.000	0-1	.000	0	1	0	0	0	0	0.0
Rodney McCray	4.0	0-0	.000	0-0	.000	1	0	0	0	0	0	0.0
Will Perdue	9.0	0-2	.000	0-0	.000	3	0	0	0	2	0	0.0
Totals	50.5	263-544	.483	82-130	.631	321	161	48	32	141	640	106.7

3-PT FG—32-69, .464 (Jordan 10-25, Armstrong 10-19, Paxson 9-14, Tucker 3-5, Pippen 0-6).

Phoenix	AVG MIN	FGs FG-ATT	PCT	FTs FT-ATT	PCT	REB	AST	STL	BLK	PF	TOT PTS	AVG PTS
Charles Barkley	46.2	60-126	.476	42-56	.750	78	33	7	3	20	164	27.3
Kevin Johnson	43.3	40-95	.421	23-25	.920	18	39	8	2	19	103	17.2
Dan Majerle	46.8	35-79	.443	16-20	.800	49	22	8	13	8	103	17.2
Richard Dumas	26.7	44-77	.571	7-9	.778	26	6	8	6	15	92	15.8
Danny Ainge	27.0	19-40	.475	7-9	.778	18	15	2	0	12	53	8.8
Tom Chambers	15.3	14-39	.359	12-15	.800	18	3	1	3	12	40	6.7
Mark West	21.7	13-21	.619	8-15	.533	26	4	0	7	21	34	5.7
Oliver Miller	17.8	12-27	.444	6-8	.750	25	8	4	12	20	30	5.0
Frank Johnson	7.3	7-17	.418	4-4	1.00	2	5	3	0	6	18	3.0
Jerrod Mustaf	1.0	0-0	.000	0-0	.000	0	0	0	0	0	0	0.0
Totals	50.5	244-521	.468	125-161	.776	321	135	41	46	133	640	106.7

3-PT FG—27-62, .435 (Majerle 17-39, Ainge 8-12, Barkley 2-8, K. Johnson 0-2, Miller 0-1).

1992-93 MOST VALUABLE PLAYER VOTING

	1st/2nd/3rd/4th/5th	Tot.		1st/2nd/3rd/4th/5th	Tot.
C. Barkley, PHO	59 27 10 2 0	835	Mark Price, CLE	0 0 0 0 10	10
H. Olajuwon, HOU	22 42 19 12 2	647	Karl Malone, UTA	0 0 0 1 7	10
Michael Jordan, CHI	13 21 50 12 2	565	Brad Daugherty, CLE	0 0 0 0 1	1
Patrick Ewing, NY	4 8 18 55 8	359	Clyde Drexler, POR	0 0 0 0 1	1
D. Wilkins, ATL	0 0 0 10 24	54	Joe Dumars, DET	0 0 0 0 1	1
David Robinson, SA	0 0 0 2 27	33	Shawn Kemp, SEA	0 0 0 0 1	1
S. O'Neal, ORL	0 0 1 4 13	30	John Stockton, UTA	0 0 0 0 1	1

ROOKIE OF THE YEAR
Shaquille O'Neal, ORL......96
Alonzo Mourning, CHA 2

SIXTH MAN AWARD
Cliff Robinson, POR..........89
Danny Ainge, PHO 3
Anthony Mason, NY 3
Dell Curry, CHA 2
Tom Chambers, PHO 1

DEFENSIVE PLAYER OF THE YEAR
Hakeem Olajuwon, HOU ..73
Michael Jordan, CHI 9
David Robinson, SA............9
Dennis Rodman, DET........3
Dan Majerle, PHO...............1
Patrick Ewing, NY 1
John Starks, NY 1
Charles Oakley, NY 1

COACH OF THE YEAR
Pat Riley, NY 32
Rudy Tomjanovich, HOU ..31
George Karl, SEA 10
Paul Westphal, PHO...........9
Chuck Daly, NJ 7
John Lucas, SA..................6
Chris Ford, BOS 2
Lenny Wilkens, CLE 1

1993-94 NBA Schedule

Below is the NBA schedule for the 1993-94 season. All game times listed are local. TNT telecasts are denoted by a "•", while NBC games are signified by a "#". The symbol "@" indicates more games that NBC may telecast; the network will make its decision at a later date.

Fri Nov 5
NY at Bos, 7:30
Was at Phi, 7:30
Orl at Mia, 8:00
•Chi at Cha, 8:00
Ind at Atl, 7:30
Mil at Cle, 7:30
Min at Det, 8:00
NJ at Hou, 7:30
GS at SA, 7:30
Dal at Uta, 7:00
Por at LAC, 7:30
•Pho at LAL, 7:30
Den at Sac, 7:30

Sat Nov 6
Bos at Was, 7:30
Phi at Orl, 7:30
Det at Ind, 7:30
Mia at Chi, 7:30
Cha at Mil, 8:00
Uta at Min, 7:00
GS at Dal, 7:30
LAL at Sea, 7:00

Sun Nov 7
NY at Cle, 7:00
NJ at SA, 7:30
LAC at Den, 7:00
Sac at Pho, 7:00
Hou at Por, 7:30

Mon Nov 8
Mil at Bos, 7:30
Atl at Chi, 7:30
Sea at Uta, 7:00

Tue Nov 9
Phi at NY, 7:30
Ind at Orl, 7:30
Cha at Cle, 7:30
Was at Det, 7:30
NJ at Dal, 7:30
Min at SA, 7:30
Pho at LAC, 7:30

Por at LAL, 7:30
Hou at GS, 7:30
Den at Sea, 7:00

Wed Nov 10
•Bos at Phi, 8:00
NY at Was, 7:30
Chi at Mil, 7:30
Atl at Uta, 7:00
SA at Pho, 7:00
LAL at Sac, 7:30

Thu Nov 11
Ind at NJ, 7:30
Mil at Mia, 7:30
Orl at Cha, 7:30
Min at Hou, 7:30
Det at LAC, 7:30
Cle at Sea, 7:00

Fri Nov 12
Cha at Bos, 7:30
Phi at Was, 7:30
Mia at Orl, 7:30
•NY at Ind, 8:00
Dal at Min, 7:00
Det at Uta, 7:00
Den at LAL, 7:30
Cle at GS, 7:30
•SA at Sac, 7:30
Atl at Por, 7:30

Sat Nov 13
Mil at NY, 7:30
Phi at NJ, 7:30
Bos at Chi, 7:30
Uta at Dal, 7:30
Pho at Hou, 7:30
GS at Den, 7:00
SA at LAC, 7:30
Atl at Sea, 7:00

Sun Nov 14
Sac at NJ, 7:00
Cle at LAL, 7:30
Det at Por, 5:00

Mon Nov 15
Hou at Phi, 7:30

Tue Nov 16
Hou at NJ, 7:30
Uta at Orl, 7:30
Sac at Atl, 7:30
Cha at Ind, 7:30
Min at Mil, 7:30
NY at Dal, 7:30
SA at Den, 7:00
LAC at LAL, 7:30
Pho at GS, 7:30
Cle at Por, 7:30
•Chi at Sea, 5:00

Wed Nov 17
NJ at Bos, 7:30
Atl at Phi, 7:30
Mil at Was, 7:30
Uta at Mia, 7:30
Sac at Cha, 7:30
Orl at Det, 7:30
NY at SA, 7:30

Thu Nov 18
Hou at Ind, 7:30
Cle at Den, 7:00
Dal at LAC, 7:30
LAL at GS, 7:30
Chi at Por, 7:30

Fri Nov 19
Orl at Bos, 7:30
Uta at Phi, 7:30
Atl at Mia, 7:30
•Was at Cha, 8:00
SA at Det, 8:00
Sac at Min, 7:00
Por at Pho, 7:00

Chi at LAL, 7:30
Dal at Sea, 7:00

Sat Nov 20
Uta at NY, 8:30
Orl at NJ, 7:30
Mia vs Was (Balt), 7:30
Cha at Atl, 7:30
Bos at Ind, 7:30
SA at Mil, 8:00
Den at Min, 7:00
LAC at Hou, 7:30
Cle at Pho, 7:00
Sea at GS, 7:30

Sun Nov 21
LAL at NJ, 7:00
Phi at Det, 7:30
Chi at Sac, 6:00
Dal at Por, 7:30

Mon Nov 22
Ind vs Bos (Hart), 7:30
Mia at NY, 7:30
LAC at SA, 7:30

Tue Nov 23
Cha at Was, 7:30
•GS at Orl, 8:00
LAL at Atl, 7:30
LAC at Dal, 7:30
Chi at Hou, 7:30
Den at Por, 7:30

Wed Nov 24
GS at Mia, 7:30
LAL at Cha, 7:30
Was at Cle, 7:30
Bos at Det, 7:30
Phi at Ind, 7:30
Atl at Mil, 7:30
NJ at Min, 7:00
Chi at SA, 7:30

Hou at Uta, 7:00
Den at Pho, 7:00
Sea at Sac, 7:30

Fri Nov 26
Mia at Bos, 7:30
GS at Phi, 7:30
Mil at Cha, 7:30
Was at Atl, 7:30
LAL at Ind, 7:30
Sea at Min, 7:30
Chi at Dal, 7:30
Por at Den, 7:00
NJ at Uta, 7:00
Hou at Sac, 7:30

Sat Nov 27
Det at NY, 1:00
Orl at Was, 7:30
Cha at Mia, 7:30
Phi at Atl, 7:30
Sea at Cle, 7:30
Bos at Mil, 8:00
LAL at Min, 7:00
Dal at SA, 7:30
NJ at Den, 7:00
Uta at Pho, 7:00
Hou at LAC, 7:30

Sun Nov 28
GS at Det, 7:00
Sac at Por, 7:30

Mon Nov 29
Mil at SA, 7:30
NJ at LAC, 7:30
Ind at Sac, 7:30

Tue Nov 30
Sea at Phi, 7:30
Por at Mia, 7:30
Bos at Atl, 7:30
Det at Cle, 7:30
●Pho at Chi, 7:00
Mil at Hou, 7:30
Den at Uta, 7:00
Dal at GS, 7:30

Wed Dec 1
Was at Bos, 7:30
Cle at NJ, 7:30
Por at Orl, 7:30
SA at Cha, 7:30
Ind at LAC, 7:30

Dal at LAL, 7:30
Min at Sac, 7:30

Thu Dec 2
Hou at NY, 7:30
Sea at Was, 7:30
Pho at Det, 7:30
Ind at Uta, 7:00
Min at GS, 7:30

Fri Dec 3
Por at Bos, 7:30
Pho at NJ, 7:30
●SA at Orl, 8:00
Chi at Mia, 7:30
Hou at Atl, 7:30
Mil at Dal, 7:30
●Cha at Den, 8:30

Sat Dec 4
Sac at NY, 1:00
SA at Phi, 7:30
Por at Was, 7:30
Orl at Cle, 7:30
Cha at Uta, 7:00
LAL at LAC, 7:30
Ind at GS, 7:30
Min at Sea, 7:00

Sun Dec 5
Hou at Cle, 7:00
Pho at Mil, 7:30
Dal at Den, 7:00
Min at LAL, 7:30

Mon Dec 6
NY at Uta, 7:00
Was at Sea, 7:00

Tue Dec 7
●Bos at NJ, 8:00
Det at Orl, 7:30
Por at Cle, 7:30
Sac at Ind, 7:30
LAC at Chi, 7:30
Mia at Dal, 7:30
Cha at Hou, 7:30
NY at LAL, 7:30
Den at GS, 7:30

Wed Dec 8
Sac at Bos, 7:30
Chi at Phi, 7:30
Atl at Det, 7:30
LAC at Mil, 7:30

Por at Min, 7:00
Sea at SA, 7:30
Was at Uta, 7:00

Thu Dec 9
Cle at Cha, 7:30
SA at Atl, 7:30
Orl at Ind, 7:30
Sea at Dal, 7:30
Mia at Hou, 7:30
Was at Pho, 7:00
NY at GS, 7:30

Fri Dec 10
Chi at NJ, 7:30
Sac at Phi, 7:30
Bos at Orl, 7:30
●Mil at Det, 8:00
LAC at Min, 7:00
Uta at Den, 7:00
LAL at Por, 7:30

Sat Dec 11
Ind at NY, 7:30
Atl vs Was (Balt),
  7:30
Bos at Mia, 7:30
NJ at Cha, 7:30
Cle at Chi, 7:30
Phi at Mil, 8:00
Det at Min, 7:00
Pho at Dal, 7:30
Sea at Hou, 7:30
Den at SA, 7:30
Uta at GS, 7:30

Sun Dec 12
GS at LAL, 7:30
LAC at Sac, 6:00
Orl at Por, 5:00

Mon Dec 13
Phi at Bos, 7:30
Mia at NJ, 7:30
SA at Uta, 7:00
Mil at Pho, 7:00

Tue Dec 14
Den at NY, 7:30
Hou at Mia, 7:30
Min at Cha, 7:30
Atl at Cle, 7:30
LAL at Det, 7:30
Was at Ind, 7:30

●Por at Dal, 7:00
Orl at Sea, 7:00

Wed Dec 15
Chi at Bos, 7:30
Den at Phi, 7:30
Uta at Min, 7:00
Por at SA, 7:30
GS at Pho, 7:30
Orl at LAC, 7:30
Mil at Sac, 7:30

Thu Dec 16
LAL at NY, 7:30
Cha at NJ, 7:30
Det at Was, 7:30
Cle at Mia, 7:30
Ind at Atl, 7:30
SA at Dal, 7:30

Fri Dec 17
Uta at Bos, 7:30
LAL at Phi, 7:30
Den at Cha, 7:30
●NY at Chi, 7:30
●Orl at Pho, 8:30
Min at LAC, 7:30
GS at Sac, 7:30
Mil at Sea, 7:00

Sat Dec 18
Uta at Was, 7:30
Phi at Mia, 7:30
Den at Atl, 7:30
Cle at Det, 7:30
NJ at Ind, 7:30
SA at Chi, 7:30
Dal at Hou, 7:30
LAC at Pho, 7:00
Min at Por, 7:30
GS at Sea, 7:00

Sun Dec 19
LAL at Cle, 7:30
Orl at Sac, 6:00
Mil at Por, 7:30

Mon Dec 20
Dal at NY, 7:30
Det at Phi, 7:30
Cha at Chi, 7:30
Was at Min, 7:00
Ind at Pho, 7:00
Mil at LAC, 7:30

Tue Dec 21
NY at NJ, 7:30
LAL at Orl, 7:30
Uta at Cle, 7:30
Cha at Det, 7:30
Hou at SA, 7:30
Pho at Den, 7:00
●Por at GS, 6:00
Ind at Sea, 7:00

Wed Dec 22
Atl at Bos, 7:30
Mia at Phi, 7:30
Min at Chi, 7:30
Dal at Mil, 7:30
Was at LAC, 7:30

Thu Dec 23
Atl at NY, 7:30
NJ at Orl, 7:30
LAL at Mia, 7:30
Bos at Cha, 7:30
Mil at Cle, 7:30
Chi at Det, 7:30
Dal at Min, 7:00
Den at Hou, 7:30
Uta at SA, 7:30
LAC at GS, 7:30
Was at Sac, 7:30
Ind at Por, 7:30
Pho at Sea, 7:00

Sat Dec 25
#Orl at Chi, 7:30
#Hou at Pho, 12:30

Sun Dec 26
Atl at NJ, 6:00
Sac at Mia, 7:30
Ind at Cle, 1:00
Bos at SA, 7:30
Min at Den, 7:00
Hou at LAL, 7:30
GS at Por, 5:00

Mon Dec 27
Sac at Orl, 7:30
Det at Cha, 7:30
Was at Mil, 7:30
Min at Uta, 7:00
Bos at Pho, 7:00
Phi at LAC, 7:30

Tue Dec 28
NJ at NY, 7:30

SA at Mia, 7:30
Det at Atl, 7:30
Cha at Cle, 7:30
Den at Dal, 7:30
Phi at GS, 7:30
Hou at Sea, 7:00

Wed Dec 29
Sac at Was, 7:30
Atl at Orl, 7:30
NJ at Chi, 7:30
Bos at Uta, 7:00
Sea at LAL, 7:30
LAC at Por, 7:30

Thu Dec 30
Was at NY, 7:30
Orl at Mia, 7:30
Chi at Cha, 7:30
Sac at Det, 7:30
SA at Ind, 7:30
Cle at Mil, 7:30
Hou at Min, 7:00
GS at Den, 7:00
Phi at Pho, 7:00
Bos at LAC, 7:30

Sat Jan 2
NJ at Bos, 7:00
Cha at NY, 6:00
Mia at Det, 7:00
LAL at SA, 7:30
Phi at Den, 7:00
Dal at Sac, 6:00
Uta at Por, 5:00

Mon Jan 3
Dal at Uta, 7:00

Tue Jan 4
Orl at NY, 7:30
NJ at Mia, 7:30
Cha at Atl, 7:30
Cle at Ind, 7:30
Det at Chi, 7:30
Por at Hou, 7:30
Phi at SA, 7:30
LAL at Den, 7:00
●Sea at Pho, 7:00
Sac at GS, 7:30

Wed Jan 5
Mil at NJ, 7:30
Ind at Was, 7:30
●Chi at Orl, 8:00

Bos at Cle, 7:30
Den at Min, 7:00
Hou at Dal, 7:30
Pho at Uta, 7:00
Sea at LAC, 7:30
LAL at Sac, 7:30

Thu Jan 6
Por at Cha, 7:30
NY at Mil, 7:30
SA at GS, 7:30

Fri Jan 7
Cle at Bos, 7:30
Chi at Was, 7:30
Por at Atl, 7:30
●Pho at Min, 7:00
Phi at Dal, 7:30
SA at Den, 7:00
Mia at Uta, 7:00
LAC at LAL, 7:30
Sac at Sea, 7:00

Sat Jan 8
Was at Orl, 7:30
NY at Cha, 7:30
Cle at Atl, 7:30
Ind at Det, 7:30
Dal at Chi, 7:30
NJ at Mil, 8:00
Bos at Min, 7:00
Phi at Hou, 7:30
Sac at Den, 7:00
Mia at LAC, 8:00
Uta at Sea, 7:00

Sun Jan 9
Por at NY, 6:00
●GS at Pho, 6:00
SA at LAL, 7:30

Mon Jan 10
Bos at Phi, 7:30
●Hou at Orl, 8:00

Tue Jan 11
LAC at NY, 7:30
Was at NJ, 7:30
Den at Det, 7:30
Ind at Mil, 7:30
Min at SA, 7:30
Cha at Pho, 7:00
GS at LAL, 7:30
Mia at Sac, 7:30
Sea at Por, 7:30

Wed Jan 12
Hou at Bos, 7:30
LAC at Phi, 7:30
Cle at Orl, 7:30
Chi at Atl, 7:30
Den at Ind, 7:30
Min at Dal, 7:30
Mia at GS, 7:30

Thu Jan 13
Hou at Was, 7:30
NJ at Cle, 7:30
NY at Det, 7:30
Uta at Mil, 7:30
Pho at SA, 7:30
Cha at Sac, 7:30

Fri Jan 14
●LAC at Bos, 8:00
Den at NJ, 7:30
Ind at Phi, 7:30
Dal at Atl, 7:30
Uta at Chi, 7:30
Orl at Min, 7:00
Cha at LAL, 7:30
Sea at GS, 7:30
Mia at Por, 7:30

Sat Jan 15
Det at NY, 1:00
LAC at Was, 7:30
Phi at Cle, 7:30
Atl at Ind, 7:30
Hou at Chi, 7:30
Orl at Mil, 8:00
SA at Dal, 7:30
Pho at Sac, 7:30
Mia at Sea, 7:00

Sun Jan 16
Den at Bos, 7:00
Uta at NJ, 6:00
Cha at Por, 5:00

Mon Jan 17
Min at NY, 1:00
SA at Was, 1:00
Mil at Atl, 3:30
Orl at Cle, 6:00
Uta at Det, 7:30
Phi at Chi, 2:30
Sac at LAL, 1:30
●Pho at GS, 5:00

Tue Jan 18
LAC at Mia, 7:30
Det at Mil, 7:30
Bos at Hou, 7:30
Por at Den, 7:00
Dal at Pho, 7:00
LAL at Sea, 7:00

Wed Jan 19
SA at NY, 7:30
Min at NJ, 7:30
LAC at Orl, 7:30
Phi at Cha, 8:30
GS at Atl, 7:30
Mia at Ind, 7:30
Was at Chi, 7:30
Bos at Dal, 7:30
Cle at Uta, 7:00
Sea at Sac, 7:30

Thu Jan 20
SA at Min, 7:00
Hou at Den, 7:00
Pho at LAL, 7:30

Fri Jan 21
GS at Bos, 7:30
●NY at Orl, 8:00
Det at Mia, 7:30
NJ at Atl, 7:30
Ind at Chi, 7:30
Cha at Mil, 8:00
Sea at Dal, 7:30
Sac at Uta, 7:00
Cle at LAC, 7:30
LAL at Por, 7:30

Sat Jan 22
GS at NJ, 7:30
Orl at Phi, 7:30
Det vs Was
  (Balt), 7:30
Mil at Cha, 7:30
Chi at Ind, 7:30
Atl at Min, 7:00
Uta at Hou, 7:30
Dal at SA, 7:30
Sea at Den, 7:00
Por at Pho, 7:00
Cle at Sac, 7:30

Sun Jan 23
Phi at NY, 6:00
Was at Mia, 7:30

Mon Jan 24
Dal at Bos, 7:30
Chi at Det, 7:30
Mil at Ind, 7:30
Sea at Uta, 7:30

Tue Jan 25
●Pho at NY, 8:00
Was at Orl, 7:30
Cha at Mia, 7:30
Atl at Mil, 7:30
Cle at Hou, 7:30
Sac at SA, 7:30
NJ at Por, 7:30
LAC at Sea, 7:00

Wed Jan 26
Mia at Bos, 7:30
Dal at Phi, 7:30
Orl at Cha, 7:30
Pho at Atl, 7:30
Uta at Min, 7:00
Ind at LAL, 7:30
Det at GS, 7:30

Thu Jan 27
Dal at Was, 7:30
Chi at Cle, 7:30
Sac at Hou, 7:30
Ind at Den, 7:00
NY at LAC, 7:30
NJ at Sea, 7:00

Fri Jan 28
Pho at Phi, 7:30
Mia at Orl, 7:30
Atl at Cha, 7:30
Mil at Chi, 7:30
●GS at Uta, 6:00
Det at LAL, 7:30
Min at Por, 7:30

Sat Jan 29
Mil at Phi, 7:30
Orl at Was, 7:30
Mia at Cle, 7:30
Sac at Dal, 7:30
Ind at Hou, 7:30
Atl at SA, 7:30
Det at Den, 7:00
Min at LAC, 7:30
NJ at GS, 7:30
NY at Sea, 7:00

Sun Jan 30
#Pho at Bos, 12:30
NY at Por, 7:30

Mon Jan 31
●Cle at Det, 8:00
Atl at Dal, 7:30
GS at LAC, 7:30

Tue Feb 1
Bos at NY, 7:30
Sea at NJ, 7:30
Was at Ind, 7:30
Mia at Mil, 7:30
LAL at SA, 7:30
Chi at Den, 7:00
Hou at Uta, 7:00
LAC at Pho, 7:00
Por at Sac, 7:30

Wed Feb 2
Sea at Bos, 7:30
Cle at Phi, 7:30
NY at Was, 7:30
Ind at Cha, 7:30
Orl at Atl, 7:30
Mil at Det, 7:30
Dal at Min, 7:00
Den at GS, 7:30

Thu Feb 3
SA at Cle, 7:30
LAL at Hou, 7:30
Chi at Uta, 7:00
Pho at Por, 7:30

Fri Feb 4
SA at Bos, 7:30
Was at Phi, 7:30
Mil at Orl, 7:30
Mia at Cha, 7:30
●NY at Atl, 8:00
Sea at Det, 8:00
Min at Ind, 7:30
LAL at Dal, 7:30
Chi at GS, 7:30
Den at Sac, 7:30

Sat Feb 5
Phi at Mia, 7:30
Atl at Cle, 7:30
NJ at Det, 7:30
Cha at Ind, 7:30
Sea at Mil, 8:00

Por at Uta, 7:00
Sac at LAC, 7:30

Sun Feb 6
#Orl at NY, 1:00
SA at NJ, 6:00
GS at Was, 1:00
Min at Hou, 5:00
Dal at Den, 7:00
#Chi at Pho, 1:30
Uta at LAL, 7:30

Mon Feb 7
Cha at Phi, 7:30
●NY at Mia, 8:00
Det at at, 7:30
GS at Ind, 7:30

Tue Feb 8
NJ at Cle, 7:30
Hou at Mil, 7:30
Min at Dal, 7:30
Was at SA, 7:30
Uta at Den, 7:00
Chi at LAC, 7:30
Pho at LAL, 7:30
Sac at Por, 7:30

Wed Feb 9
Det at Bos, 7:30
Cle at NJ, 7:30
NY at Phi, 7:30
Atl at Orl, 7:30
Ind at Mia, 7:30
●GS at Cha, 8:00
LAL at Uta, 7:00
Min at Pho, 7:30
LAC at Sac, 7:30
Por at Sea, 7:00

Thu Feb 10
GS at NY, 7:30
Mia at Atl, 7:30
Hou at Det, 7:30
Chi at Mil, 7:30
Was at Dal, 7:30
Den at SA, 7:30

Sun Feb 13
#All-Star Game
  (Min), 5:30

Tue Feb 15
NY at NJ, 7:30

Bos at Orl, 7:30
Den at Cle, 7:30
Was at Det, 7:30
Mil at Min, 7:00
Por at Dal, 7:30
Atl at Hou, 7:30
Ind at SA, 7:30
LAC at LAL, 7:30
Sac at GS, 7:30
Phi at Sea, 7:00

Wed Feb 16
Hou at Cha, 7:30
Mia at Chi, 7:30
Den at Mil, 7:30
Por at Pho, 7:00
Uta at LAC, 7:30
Phi at Sac, 7:30

Thu Feb 17
NJ vs Bos (Hart), 7:30
Min at Was, 7:30
Sea at Mia, 7:30
NY at Cle, 7:30
Ind at Dal, 7:30
Det at SA, 7:30
Atl at GS, 7:30

Fri Feb 18
NJ vs Was (Balt), 7:30
●Sea at Orl, 8:00
Mil at Cha, 7:30
Den at Chi, 7:30
Cle at Min, 7:00
LAL at Pho, 7:00
Atl at LAC, 7:30
Uta at Sac, 7:30
Phi at Por, 7:30

Sat Feb 19
Det at Dal, 7:30
Pho at Hou, 7:30
Mia at SA, 7:30
LAC at Uta, 7:00
Bos at GS, 7:30

Sun Feb 20
#Chi at NY, 1:00
Was at Mil, 3:30
Cle at Cha, 4:00
Sea at Ind, 3:30
Orl at Mil, 2:30

Atl at Den, 7:00
Phi at LAL, 7:30
Bos at Por, 7:30

Mon Feb 21
Was at Mia, 7:30
Dal at Det, 7:30
Cha at Chi, 2:30
SA at Min, 2:00
Phi at Uta, 7:00
Sac at Pho, 7:00

Tue Feb 22
Sea at NY, 7:30
Mia at NJ, 7:30
Min at Cle, 7:30
Dal at Ind, 7:30
GS at Mil, 7:30
Den at Hou, 7:30
Bos at Sac, 7:30
LAC at Por, 7:30

Wed Feb 23
NJ at Phi, 7:30
Cle at Was, 7:30
Ind at Orl, 7:30
Sea at Atl, 7:30
GS at Chi, 7:30
Bos at Den, 7:00
SA at Uta, 7:00
Por at LAC, 7:30

Thu Feb 24
Dal at Cha, 7:30
Pho at Min, 7:30
●NY at Hou, 7:00
LAL at Sac, 7:30

Fri Feb 25
Mia at Phi, 7:30
Chi at Was, 7:30
NJ at Orl, 7:30
Mil at Atl, 7:30
GS at Cle, 7:30
Det at Ind, 7:30
NY at Den, 7:00
Pho at Uta, 7:00
Sac at LAC, 7:30
SA at LAL, 7:30
Bos at Sea, 7:00

Sat Feb 26
Atl at Phi, 7:30
Dal at Cle, 7:30

Mia at Det, 7:30
Ind at Mil, 8:00
Was at Mil, 8:00
Uta at Hou, 7:30
SA at Por, 7:30

Sun Feb 27
Dal at NJ, 6:00
#Cha at Orl, 12:30
GS at Min, 2:00
#NY at Pho, 3:30
Sea at LAC, 6:00
Bos at LAL, 7:30
Den at Por, 7:30

Mon Feb 28
●Cle at Chi, 7:00
Hou at Uta, 7:00

Tue Mar 1
Det at NJ, 7:30
Was at Phi, 7:30
Min at Atl, 7:30
Por at Ind, 7:30
Mia at Mil, 7:30
Orl at Hou, 7:30
LAC at GS, 7:30
NY at Sac, 7:30
Cha at Sea, 7:00

Wed Mar 2
Cle at Bos, 7:30
Por at Det, 7:30
LAL at Chi, 7:30
Mia at Min, 7:00
Uta at SA, 7:30
Cha at LAC, 7:30

Thu Mar 3
NJ at NY, 7:30
Atl at Was, 7:30
Phi at Cle, 7:30
Orl at Dal, 7:30
●Pho at GS, 6:00

Fri Mar 4
●LAL at Bos, 8:00
NJ at Ind, 7:30
Por at Chi, 7:30
LAC at SA, 7:30
Orl at Den, 7:00
Min at Pho, 7:00

Sat Mar 5
LAL at Was, 7:30
Phi at Mia, 7:30
Ind at Atl, 7:30
Det at Mil, 8:00
Uta at Dal, 7:30
LAC at Hou, 7:30
Cha at GS, 7:30
Sac at Sea, 7:00

Sun Mar 6
Phi at NJ, 6:00
#Chi at Cle, 1:00
#Orl at SA, 2:30
Min at Den, 7:00
Uta at Pho, 7:00
Sea at Sac, 6:00

Mon Mar 7
Bos at Mia, 7:30
NY at Det, 7:30
LAL at Mil, 7:30
GS at Por, 7:30

Tue Mar 8
Den at Orl, 7:30
Pho at Cha, 7:30
Sac at Cle, 7:30
Atl at Chi, 7:30
LAC at Dal, 7:30
Hou at SA, 7:30
Min at Uta, 7:00
GS at Sea, 7:00

Wed Mar 9
Orl at Phi, 7:30
Pho at Was, 7:30
Den at Mia, 7:30
NY at Atl, 7:30
NJ at Det, 7:30
Ind at Mil, 7:30
Sac at Min, 7:00
Uta at Por, 7:30

Thu Mar 10
●Sea at Hou, 7:00
Dal at LAL, 7:30
Por at GS, 7:30

Fri Mar 11
NY at Bos, 7:30
Ind at NJ, 7:30
Den at Was, 7:30
Phi at Orl, 7:30

Pho at Mia, 7:30
Chi at Atl, 7:30
Cle at Det, 8:00
Sac at Mil, 8:00
Cha at Min, 7:00
Sea at SA, 7:30
Dal at LAC, 7:30

Sat Mar 12
Cle at NY, 8:30
Cha at NJ, 7:30
Atl at Det, 7:30
Mil at Ind, 7:30
Sac at Chi, 7:30
SA at Hou, 7:30

Sun Mar 13
Mia at Was, 7:00
Phi at Was, 1:00
#Pho at Orl, 12:00
LAL at Min, 2:00
Hou at Dal, 7:00
GS at LAC, 6:00
Por at Sea, 7:00

Mon Mar 14
Bos at Cha, 7:30
SA at Den, 7:00
●LAL at Uta, 7:00
Det at Sac, 7:30

Tue Mar 15
Ind at NY, 7:30
Mil at Mia, 7:30
Pho at Cle, 7:30
●Orl at Chi, 7:00
Phi at Min, 7:00
Por at Hou, 7:30
Uta at LAC, 7:30
Was at GS, 7:30
Det at Sea, 7:00

Wed Mar 16
Chi at Bos, 7:30
Dal at Orl, 7:30
Atl at Cha, 7:30
Pho at Ind, 7:30
Por at SA, 7:30
Was at LAL, 7:30
NJ at Sac, 7:30

Thu Mar 17
Mil at NY, 7:30
Dal at Mia, 7:30

Sea at Min, 7:00
GS at Hou, 7:30
Den at LAC, 7:30

Fri Mar 18
Min at Phi, 7:30
Cle at Orl, 7:30
Uta at Cha, 7:30
Atl at Ind, 7:30
Sea at Chi, 7:30
Sac at Den, 7:00
Det at Pho, 7:00
NJ at LAL, 7:30
Was at Por, 7:30

Sat Mar 19
Bos at NY, 1:00
Cle at Mia, 7:30
Uta at Ind, 7:30
GS at Dal, 7:30
Det at Hou, 7:30
Sac at SA, 7:30
NJ at Pho, 7:00

Sun Mar 20
@Atl at Bos, 12:00
@Sea at Cha, 12:00
Phi at Mil, 1:30
Chi at Min, 2:00
Was at Den, 7:00
Por at LAC, 6:00
Orl at LAL, 7:30

Mon Mar 21
Uta at Atl, 7:30
Was at Hou, 7:30
Mia at LAL, 7:30

Tue Mar 22
●Chi at NY, 8:00
LAC at NJ, 7:30
Phi at Cha, 7:30
Ind at Cle, 7:30
Hou at Min, 7:00
Mil at Den, 7:00
Mia at Pho, 7:30
Orl at GS, 7:30
Por at Sac, 7:30
SA at Sea, 7:00

Wed Mar 23
Chi at Phi, 7:30
Cha at Atl, 7:30
LAC at Det, 7:30

Cle at Ind, 7:30
LAL at Dal, 7:30
Orl at Uta, 7:00

Thu Mar 24
Bos at Was, 7:30
NY at Min, 7:00
LAL at Hou, 7:30
Mia at Den, 7:00
Mil at GS, 7:30
SA at Sac, 7:30
Pho at Sea, 7:00

Fri Mar 25
Chi at NJ, 7:30
Cle at Phi, 7:30
LAC at Atl, 7:30
Cha at Det, 8:00
NY at Ind, 7:30
Mil at Uta, 7:00
Dal at Pho, 7:00
Sac at Por, 7:30

Sat Mar 26
NJ at Was, 7:30
LAC at Cha, 7:30
Mia at Atl, 7:30
Ind at Chi, 7:30
Uta at Hou, 7:30
Dal at Den, 7:00
SA at GS, 7:30
Min at Sea, 7:00

Sun Mar 27
Phi vs Bos
   (Hart), 2:30
#NY at Orl, 12:00
Det at Cle, 7:00
●Hou at Pho, 5:00
Mil at LAL, 7:30
SA at Por, 7:30

Mon Mar 28
LAC at Ind, 7:30
Den at Sea, 7:00

Tue Mar 29
●Cha at NY, 8:00
Was at Orl, 7:30
Det at Mia, 7:30
NJ at Atl, 7:30
LAC at Cle, 7:30
Phi at Chi, 7:30
Bos at Mil, 7:30

SA at Dal, 7:30
GS at Uta, 7:00
Min at LAL, 7:30
Hou at Sac, 7:30
Sea at Por, 7:30

Wed Mar 30
Ind at Bos, 7:30
Mia at NJ, 7:30
Hou at GS, 7:30

Thu Mar 31
Por at Mil, 7:30
●Cle at SA, 7:00
Pho at LAC, 7:30
Atl at Sac, 7:30
LAL at Sea, 7:00

Fri Apr 1
Was at Bos, 7:30
Orl at NJ, 7:30
Por at Phi, 7:30
Ind at Mia, 7:30
●Det at Chi, 7:00
Cha at Dal, 7:30
Atl at Pho, 7:00
Hou at LAL, 7:30
Min at GS, 7:30

Sat Apr 2
Mia at NY, 8:30
Mil at Was, 7:30
Orl at Ind, 7:30
Cle at Dal, 7:30
Cha at SA, 7:30
Den at Uta, 7:00
Min at Sac, 7:30
GS at Sea, 7:00

Sun Apr 3
Por at NJ, 4:00
Bos at Phi, 7:30
#Chi at Det, 1:30
Den at Pho, 7:00
Hou at LAC, 3:00
Atl at LAL, 7:30

Tue Apr 5
Bos at NJ, 7:30
Mil at Orl, 7:30
NY at Mia, 7:30
Cha at Cle, 7:30
Det at Ind, 7:30
Was at Chi, 7:30

GS at SA, 7:30
LAC at Den, 7:00
Dal at Sac, 7:30
Pho at Por, 7:30
Uta at Sea, 7:00

Wed Apr 6
Mil at Phi, 7:30
Mia at Was, 7:30
Ind at Cha, 7:30
Bos at Atl, 7:30
LAC at Min, 7:00
SA at Pho, 7:00
Sac at LAL, 7:30

Thu Apr 7
Cle at NY, 7:30
Atl at NJ, 7:30
•GS at Hou, 7:00
Sea at Den, 7:00
Dal at Uta, 7:00

Fri Apr 8
Min at Bos, 7:30
NY at Phi, 7:30
Cle at Was, 7:30
Det at Orl, 7:30
NJ at Cha, 7:30
Chi at Ind, 7:30
Den at LAL, 7:30
Pho at Sac, 7:30
Dal at Sea, 7:00

Sat Apr 9
Cha at Phi, 7:30
Orl at Mia, 7:30
Was at Atl, 7:30
Mil at Chi, 7:30
GS at Min, 7:00
@SA at Hou, 2:30
@LAC at Uta, 1:30
LAL at Por, 7:30

Sun Apr 10
@NY at NJ, 1:00
@Bos at Det, 1:00
Hou at Den, 7:00
#Pho at Sea, 12:30

Mon Apr 11
•Orl at NY, 8:00
Mia at Cha, 7:30
Bos at Ind, 7:30
Min at SA, 7:30
Dal at GS, 7:30
LAC at Sac, 7:30

Tue Apr 12
Mil at Cle, 7:30
Phi at Det, 7:30
NJ at Chi, 7:30
Min at Hou, 7:30
Pho at Den, 7:00
Sac at Uta, 7:00
Sea at LAC, 7:30
GS at LAL, 7:30
Dal at Por, 7:30

Wed Apr 13
Det at Bos, 7:30
Ind at Phi, 7:30
Chi at Mia, 7:30
Cle at Atl, 7:30
NJ at Mil, 7:30
Den at SA, 7:30
LAL at Pho, 7:00

Thu Apr 14
NY at Was, 7:30
•Cha at Orl, 8:00
Sac at Hou, 7:30
SA at Uta, 7:00
Por at GS, 7:30
LAC at Sea, 7:00

Fri Apr 15
Orl at Bos, 7:30
Was at NY, 7:30
Det at NJ, 7:30

•Chi at Cha, 8:00
Mia at Cle, 7:30
Atl at Mil, 8:00
Ind at Min, 7:00
Den at Dal, 7:30
Por at LAL, 7:30

Sat Apr 16
Phi at Atl, 7:30
Cle at Mil, 8:00
Sac at Dal, 7:30
@Pho at SA, 2:30
LAL at LAC, 7:30
Uta at GS, 7:30
@Hou at Sea, 12:30

Sun Apr 17
Bos at Was, 12:30
#Chi at Orl, 5:30
NJ at Mia, 4:00
#NY at Cha, 3:00
Ind at Det, 12:30
Den at Min, 2:00
Hou at Por, 7:30

Mon Apr 18
Atl at Chi, 7:30
Pho at Dal, 7:30
GS at LAC, 7:30

Tue Apr 19
Mil at Bos, 7:30
Atl at NY, 7:30
NJ at Phi, 7:30
Ind at Was, 7:30
Min at Mia, 7:30
Orl at Det, 7:30
•Hou at SA, 7:00
LAL at Den, 7:00
Sea at Pho, 7:00
Uta at Sac, 7:30

Wed Apr 20
Min at Orl, 7:30
Was at Cha, 7:30
Cle at Ind, 7:30

Det at Mil, 7:30
Den at LAC, 7:30
Sea at LAL, 7:30

Thu Apr 21
Cha at Bos, 7:30
Phi at NY, 7:30
Atl at Mia, 7:30
Dal at Hou, 7:30
Por at Uta, 7:00
Sac at GS, 7:30

Fri Apr 22
Was at Cle, 7:30
Phi at Ind, 7:30
Bos at Chi, 7:30
NY at Mil, 8:00
Por at Min, 7:00
Hou at Dal, 7:30
Uta at Den, 7:00
LAC at Pho, 7:00
SA at Sea, 7:30

Sat Apr 23
Mil at NJ, 7:30
@Det at Cha, 3:30
Orl at Atl, 7:30
Mia at Ind, 7:30
Sac at Pho, 7:00
@LAL at GS, 12:30

Sun Apr 24
Det at Phi, 1:00
Cha at Was, 1:00
NJ at Orl, 7:30
@Bos at Cle, 3:30
#NY at Chi, 12:00
Min at Dal, 7:00
@Den at Hou, 2:30
@SA at LAC, 12:30
@Uta at LAL, 12:30
GS at Sac, 6:00
@Sea at Por, 12:30

BASKETBALL HALL OF FAME

This section honors the 195 people—and four teams—that are enshrined in the Naismith Memorial Basketball Hall of Fame in Springfield, Massachusetts.

Like the Hall of Fame, this section is divided into five categories: "players," "coaches," "contributors," "referees," and "teams." The section includes bios on each member of the Hall. At the end of each bio is a date in parentheses; this is the year the member was enshrined into the Hall.

Abbreviations include BAA (Basketball Association of America), NBL (National Basketball League), ABA (American Basketball Association), and AAU (American Athletic Union). Others include NAIA (National Association of Intercollegiate Athletics), NIT (National Invitational Tournament), NABC (National Association of Basketball Coaches), and USBWA (United States Basketball Writers Association).

PLAYERS

NATE ARCHIBALD
Guard: Small in stature at 6'1", "Tiny" Archibald was a giant on the court. After starring at Texas-El Paso, he began his pro career in Cincinnati in 1970-71. In 1972-73, he led the NBA in assists (11.4) and scoring (34.0). In 1980-81, he helped the Celtics win the NBA title. Archibald played in six All-Star Games and was league MVP in 1981. (1991)

PAUL ARIZIN
Forward: A star at Villanova, where he was college Player of the Year in 1950, the sharp-shooting Arizin averaged better than 22 PPG over his ten-year NBA career in Philadelphia. Known for his deadly jump shot, Arizin led the league in scoring in 1952 and '57 and led the Warriors to the NBA title in 1956. He retired with 16,266 points and ten All-Star Game appearances. (1977)

TOM BARLOW
Forward: In the early years of this century, when the Eastern League was popular, "Babe" Barlow was among the game's most exciting players. A pro at age 16, Babe enjoyed 20 seasons of roundball (from 1912-32). Barlow was known as much for his defensive skills as for his scoring. (1980)

RICK BARRY
Forward: One of the game's most accurate shooters, Barry starred at Miami of Florida. In 1965, Rick led the NCAA with an average of 37.4 PPG. As a pro, he played in both the ABA and NBA and is the only player to lead both leagues in scoring. His career NBA free throw pct. was .900, a record that held until 1992-93. In 1975, he led the Golden State Warriors to the NBA title. (1986)

ELGIN BAYLOR
Forward: Baylor was considered the most devastating, artistic forward of his era. After a spectacular college career in which he led Seattle to the NCAA finals in 1958, Baylor debuted in the NBA in 1958-59. He averaged 24.9 PPG as a rookie for Minneapolis and won Rookie of the Year honors. Over his 14-year career, he netted 23,149 points, averaging 27.4 per game. (1976)

JOHNNY BECKMAN

Forward: From 1910 until the 1940s, "Becky" Beckman was often referred to as the Babe Ruth of basketball. A star in the Interstate, New York State, and Eastern Leagues, Beckman eventually joined the Original Celtics. As their captain, he led them to some of their greatest years. In 1935, he was selected by Nat Holman as "Basketball's Finest Competitive Athlete." (1972)

WALT BELLAMY

Center: After playing for Indiana University and the 1960 gold-medal-winning Olympic team, Bellamy became NBA Rookie of the Year with the 1962 Chicago Packers, averaging 31.6 PPG and 19.0 RPG. He played 14 NBA seasons with six different teams, averaging 20.1 PPG and 13.7 RPG. Bellamy scored 20,941 points in his NBA career. (1993)

SERGEI BELOV

Guard: Belov was considered a basketball magician who could score at will. The 6'3" guard led the Russian national team to four European and two world championships. In the Olympics, he helped the Soviet national team to one gold medal (1972) and three bronze medals. (1992)

BENNIE BORGMANN

Guard: Though only 5'8", Borgmann was one of the most popular touring pros on the East Coast in the early years. His pro career spanned over 2,500 games in various Eastern leagues. It wasn't unusual for Borgmann to score half of his team's points during any given game. He later coached both at the college and professional level. (1961)

BILL BRADLEY

Forward: "Dollar Bill" Bradley was an intelligent player with a graceful, deadly shooting touch. As a three-time All-American at Princeton, he averaged 30 PPG and was the 1965 college Player of the Year. In 1964, he helped the U.S. win the Olympic gold medal. A Rhodes Scholar, Bradley played ten seasons with the New York Knicks, amassing 9,217 points, 2,533 assists, and two NBA championship rings. He is currently a U.S. senator in New Jersey. (1982)

JOE BRENNAN

Forward: "Poison Joe" Brennan enjoyed a 17-year pro career, starting at age 19 when he joined the Brooklyn Visitation and led them to their greatest years. In 1950, the New York Basketball Old-Timers voted Brennan second only to Johnny Beckman as the greatest player of his era. (1974)

AL CERVI

Guard: An outstanding clutch performer, Cervi was an immediate star with the NBL's Buffalo Bisons. His pro career was interrupted by a five-year stint in World War II, but he resumed his career in 1945, playing for the Rochester Royals. In 1948, he became a player/coach for the Syracuse Nats. He was named Coach of the Year five times in the next eight seasons. (1984)

WILT CHAMBERLAIN

Center: At 7'1", Wilt "The Stilt" Chamberlain was an awesome, dominant figure on the court. After two All-America years at Kansas, Wilt spent a year with the Harlem Globetrotters before entering the NBA in 1959. In just his first year, he was named the NBA's MVP. During 14 years, he was the league MVP four times (1960, 1966-68). He still holds NBA records for career rebounds (23,924), season scoring average (50.4 in 1961-62), and most points in a game (100). He won world titles with Philadelphia (1967) and Los Angeles ('72). (1978)

CHARLES COOPER

Center: In his day, "Tarzan" Cooper was a giant among men. The 6'4", 214-pound Cooper was a consistent winner for 20 years of pro basketball. In 11 years with the New York Renaissance, his teams compiled a record of 1,303-203. In 1932-33, the club won 88 straight games. He has been called the greatest center of his day. (1976)

BOB COUSY

Guard: At 6'1", Cousy made his name as the most sensational passer the game had ever known. After three All-America years at Holy Cross, "Mr. Basketball" joined the Boston Celtics in 1950. Eventually, he led them to six NBA titles, including five in a row (1959-63). He led the league in assists for eight straight years (1953-60) and played in 13 consecutive All-Star Games. (1970)

DAVE COWENS

Center: Cowens was a tough, physical player. "The Redhead" starred at Florida State, where he averaged 19 points and 17 rebounds per game. In his first NBA season with Boston, he was Co-Rookie of the Year. In ten seasons with the Celtics, he won two championships (1974 and '76) and was player/coach for a year. In his career, Cowens averaged 17.6 PPG and collected 10,444 rebounds. (1991)

BILLY CUNNINGHAM

Guard: A scrappy playmaker at North Carolina, Cunningham debuted in the NBA with the Philadelphia 76ers in 1965. In 11 pro seasons (including two with the ABA Carolina Cougars), Cunningham made the All-NBA first team three times and was named ABA MVP in 1973. In 770 pro games, he averaged 21.8 PPG. He became the 76ers' coach in 1978, bringing them a 454-196 record over eight seasons, including a league title in 1983. (1985)

BOB DAVIES

Guard: Davies has been called the "first superstar of modern pro basketball." A two-time All-American at Seton Hall, Davies turned pro in 1945 with Rochester. In ten BAA and NBA seasons, he was all-league seven times. He led the Royals to league titles in 1946, '47, and '51. His patented behind-the-back dribble made him popular with fans. (1969)

FORREST DEBERNARDI

Forward/Guard/Center: DeBernardi's career revolved around AAU tournaments. He was an AAU All-American in 1921, '22, and '23 and won four AAU titles. In 11 AAU tournaments, "De" was all-tournament seven times. He starred at three different positions. (1961)

DAVE DEBUSSCHERE

Forward: DeBusschere was one of the game's great defensive forwards. After three All-America years at the University of Detroit, DeBusschere debuted with his hometown Pistons in 1962. Two years later at age 24, he became the Pistons' player/coach. He was traded to the Knicks in 1969 and helped them to two championships (1970 and '73). In 875 games, he amassed 14,053 points and 9,618 rebounds. (1982)

DUTCH DEHNERT

Guard: Without Henry "Dutch" Dehnert, there might never have been a three-second rule in basketball. Back in the 1920s, playing for the powerful Celtics, Dehnert inadvertently invented pivot play when he routinely stationed himself at the foul line to relay passes back and forth to weaving teammates. Though he didn't play either high school or college ball, Dehnert honed his skills in Eastern pro leagues. He joined the Celts at age 22. (1968)

PAUL ENDACOTT

Guard: Endacott attended Kansas, where he achieved status as "the greatest player ever coached" by Kansas' Phog Allen. Endacott was selected as Player of the Year in 1923. In 1969, he received the Sportsmen's World Award in basketball, because his "exemplary personal conduct has made him an outstanding inspiration for youth to emulate." (1971)

JULIUS ERVING

Forward: An extraordinary leaper, the spectacular Dr. J. had the ability to change directions mid-air. The Massachusetts alum brought attention to the ABA, where he averaged 28.7 PPG and 12.1 RPG in five seasons. With the NBA's 76ers, he made 11 All-Star Games, averaged 22.0 PPG, and led his 1983 team to the world title. He's one of three ABA/NBA players to reach 30,000 points. (1993)

BUD FOSTER

Guard: Harold "Bud" Foster, a star player in college, also excelled as a coach. As a senior at Wisconsin in 1930, he earned All-America honors. Foster played briefly as a pro before embarking on a glorious 25-year career as a coach. He guided Wisconsin to three Big Ten titles (1935, '41, and '47) and the NCAA championship (1941). (1964)

WALT FRAZIER

Guard: A smooth backcourt specialist known for sleek passing and laser-accurate shooting, "Clyde" Frazier played 13 seasons in the NBA, including ten with the New York Knicks. Frazier helped the Knicks to league titles in 1970 and 1973, played in seven All-Star Games, was a celebrated defensive wizard, and finished his career with an average of 18.9 PPG. (1986)

MARTY FRIEDMAN

Guard: A turn-of-the-century hero, Max "Marty" Friedman was one of a pair of hoops stars known as the "Heavenly Twins" (his counterpart was longtime buddy Barney Sedran). Friedman was one of the great defensive players of his era. He played in six Eastern leagues and, in 1915, helped Carbondale win 35 straight games. He later won accolades as well as championships as a coach. (1971)

JOE FULKS

Forward: "Jumping Joe" Fulks was one of the first scoring superstars of the BAA and NBA. An ambidextrous jump-shot artist, Fulks shocked the BAA in 1946-47 by scoring 23.2 points per game for Philadelphia. Two years later, he averaged 26.0 PPG and was named *The Sporting News* Athlete of the Year for 1949. (1977)

LADDIE GALE

Forward: Lauren "Laddie" Gale's excellence on the court helped bring recognition to the basketball programs in the Pacific Northwest. Gale was an All-American at Oregon, and in 1939 he led his school to the NCAA title. Gale played professionally and was also a successful coach. (1976)

HARRY GALLATIN

Center: A large center for his time (6'6"), Harry "The Horse" Gallatin was the centerpiece of the New York Knicks for nine years. Gallatin established a consecutive-games-played record (746) that included regular-season, playoff, All-Star, and exhibition contests. In 1953-54, he led the NBA in rebounds (1,098). He later went on to a successful coaching career at the pro and college levels. (1991)

WILLIAM GATES

Guard: "Pop" Gates went from a championship high school team to a champion pro team in consecutive seasons. In 1938, he led Benjamin Franklin (New York) to a high school title. In 1939, he helped the New York Renaissance to 68 straight victories and a World Professional Championship. Throughout his 12-year career, he played for many outstanding teams, including the Harlem Globetrotters, where he was a player/coach from 1950-55. (1988)

TOM GOLA

Forward: Gola combined outstanding scoring prowess with defensive wizardry to become one of the most respected all-around players in the game. At La Salle in the mid-1950s, Gola was a four-year All-American, averaging 21 points and 20 rebounds per game. He played ten years professionally with Philadelphia, San Francisco, and New York, scoring 7,871 points. He was often high in assists and rebounds. (1975)

HAL GREER

Guard: Greer was the first black scholarship athlete to attend Marshall (1955-59) and earned All-America status in 1958. He played five years with the Syracuse Nationals before joining the powerful Philadelphia 76ers for another ten seasons. He recorded 21,586 career points, was named to ten All-Star Games, and won a world title in 1967. (1981)

ROBERT GRUENIG

Center: A 6'8" center with a shooter's touch, "Ace" Gruenig was a brilliant AAU performer. He shined in the AAU from 1931 until he retired in the late 1940s. From 1937-48, he was the annual choice as first-team all-tournament center. In 1943, he received the Los Angeles Sports Award Medallion as the nation's greatest player. (1963)

CLIFF HAGAN

Forward: At Kentucky, Hagan was a two-time All-American (1952 and '54) who led his Wildcats to an NCAA title in 1951 and a perfect 25-0 record in 1954. During ten years in the NBA with the St. Louis Hawks, he scored 13,447 points, relying heavily on his amazingly accurate hook shot. He appeared in four All-Star Games and helped the Hawks win the league title in 1958. He also played three years in the ABA, serving as player/coach for the Dallas Chaparrals. (1977)

VICTOR HANSON

Guard: Hanson starred at Syracuse in basketball, football, and baseball. He was a three-time All-American in hoops (1925-27), winning a national championship in 1926. In his senior campaign, Hanson was the college Player of the Year. He later played pro ball with the Cleveland Rosenblums, and he also played minor-league baseball in the New York Yankees farm system. (1960)

LUSIA HARRIS

Center: During her career at Delta State, the 6'3" Harris became one of women's basketball's early superstars. She finished her career with 2,981 points (25.9 PPG) and 1,662 rebounds (14.4 RPG). Harris was a three-time All-American and won three national titles (1975-77). She also played on the 1976 Olympic team. (1992)

JOHN HAVLICEK

Forward: After leading Ohio State to three NCAA finals and one championship, "Hondo" Havlicek embarked on a 16-year NBA career with Boston. Havlicek began as the Celts' sixth man, ultimately earned a starting spot, and was later named team captain. In his career, he scored 26,395 points, appeared in 13 All-Star Games, and was an eight-time member of the NBA All-Defensive Team. (1983)

CONNIE HAWKINS

Forward: Hawkins, similar in style to Julius Erving, left Iowa during his freshman year and played two years with the Harlem Globetrotters (1964-66). In the ABA's inaugural season, he was named league MVP after leading Pittsburgh to the title. Hawkins played seven NBA seasons with Phoenix, Los Angeles, and Atlanta, averaging 16.5 PPG and 7.9 RPG. (1992)

ELVIN HAYES

Forward: The 6'9" Hayes used strength, speed, and grace to achieve amazing results. At Houston, "The Big E." was a three-time All-American and 1968 college Player of the Year. Hayes led the NBA in scoring as a rookie and went on to play 16 years with San Diego, the Bullets, and Houston. In 1977-78, he led the Bullets to the NBA title. He played exactly 50,000 NBA minutes—second most in league history. He scored 27,313 points in his career. (1989)

TOMMY HEINSOHN

Forward: A two-time All-American at Holy Cross, Heinsohn became the NBA Rookie of the Year for Boston in 1957 and started for the champion Celtics for the next eight seasons. Heinsohn, who was named to six All-Star Games, averaged 18.6 PPG over his career. In 1970, he took over as coach. He guided Boston to a 427-263 record and two NBA titles, in 1974 and '76. (1985)

NAT HOLMAN

Guard: Holman, who gained fame as coach of the City College of New York Beavers, was also a player of note from 1916-33. Holman joined the Original Celtics in 1920, stayed nine seasons, and was one of their greatest players, exploiting his skills as a passer, shooter, and strategist. In 1933, he retired from playing to concentrate on coaching. In 1950, his Beavers won both the NIT and NCAA titles, which no team had ever done before. Holman retired from coaching in 1960. (1964)

BOB HOUBREGS

Center: A superb collegian, Houbregs was an All-American with Washington in 1953, leading the Huskies to a third-place finish in the '53 NCAA Tournament. Houbregs held the second-highest scoring average in NCAA Tournament history (34.8 PPG) before being drafted by Milwaukee. He played five years in the NBA and later served as G.M. of the Seattle SuperSonics from 1970-73. (1986)

CHUCK HYATT

Forward: One of the finest amateur players of the century, Hyatt starred at the University of Pittsburgh from 1927-30 and was a three-time All-American. He was the top scorer in the nation in 1930. The Panthers were 60-7 during Hyatt's career, winning national titles in 1928 and '30. He later joined the Phillips 66 Oilers and became a legend of the AAU circuit, earning All-America honors nine times. (1959)

DAN ISSEL

Forward: After averaging 25.8 PPG in college at Kentucky, Issel continued to smoke the nets in the ABA (six years, 25.6 PPG) and the NBA (nine years, all with Denver, 20.4 PPG). Though a solid rebounder, Issel will forever be known for his scoring, as he tallied 27,482 points in his pro career. He became coach of the Nuggets in 1992-93. (1993)

WILLIAM JOHNSON

Center: Tall and lanky, "Skinny" Johnson was a dominant center for Kansas from 1930-33, earning All-America honors in his senior year. He guided his squad to a record of 42-11 and three Big Six championships. In 1934, as an AAU star, he was the top scorer in the Missouri Valley. In 1975, he was named an All-Time Great in Oklahoma, his home state. (1976)

NEIL JOHNSTON

Center: After two years at Ohio State, the 6'8" Johnston tried his luck as a pitcher, signing a pro baseball contract. A sore arm turned him back to basketball, where he joined the Philadelphia Warriors in 1951. In eight seasons, he led the NBA in scoring and field goal percentage three times, led in rebounding once, and helped the Warriors win the title in 1956. A knee injury ended his playing career, but he stayed in the game as a coach, a scout, and an athletic director. (1989)

K.C. JONES

Guard: After starring in college at San Francisco, Jones joined the Boston Celtics in 1958 and stayed for nine years, where he was a dependable guard on their championship teams. As a coach, Jones won more than 500 NBA games, including 308 with the Celts. He was involved in 11 titles in Boston—eight as a player, one as an assistant coach, and two more as head coach (1984 and '86). (1988)

SAM JONES

Guard: After playing brilliantly at tiny North Carolina College, Jones cracked the Celtics lineup in 1958 and became part of ten championship teams. He led the club in scoring three times and averaged 25.9 PPG in 1964-65. His patented jump shot off the glass, his most effective weapon, was feared around the NBA. (1983)

EDWARD KRAUSE

Center: A star at Notre Dame in the early 1930s, Krause was a three-time All-American in two sports—basketball and football. At 6'3", 215 pounds, he was considered the first "agile" center, setting many scoring records for the Irish. "Moose" later played professionally in the Midwest and New England before returning to the college scene as a coach and athletic director. (1975)

BOB KURLAND

Center: The first of the truly great seven-foot centers, Kurland carved out one of the most impressive amateur careers ever. At Oklahoma State, he led his squad to NCAA titles in 1945 and '46, leading the nation in scoring the latter year. He later played six seasons of AAU ball with the Phillips 66 Oilers, where he was All-AAU each year and an Olympian in 1948 and '52. (1961)

BOB LANIER

Center: A two-time All-American at St. Bonaventure, Lanier debuted with the Detroit Pistons in 1970. A strong, no-nonsense center, Lanier played in eight All-Star Games and tallied 19,248 points and 9,698 rebounds in his career. In each of Lanier's five seasons in Milwaukee, the Bucks won the Central Division title. (1992)

JOE LAPCHICK

Center: The son of poor, immigrant parents, Lapchick began playing professional basketball at age 17 without a high school education. The 6'5" center played in several leagues and centered the Original Celtics from 1923-27. Later, he became a great coach, leading St. John's to four NIT titles. He also coached the New York Knicks for nine seasons. (1966)

CLYDE LOVELLETTE

Center: Lovellette was a winner wherever he played. As a college star at Kansas, he was a three-time All-American (1950-52) and the Big Seven scoring champion each year. In 1952, he led the nation in scoring and guided the Jayhawks to the NCAA title. He played for the 1952 gold-medal Olympic team before starting an 11-year NBA career. He played with the champion Minneapolis Lakers in 1954 and later won titles with the 1963 and '64 Boston Celtics. (1987)

JERRY LUCAS

Forward: A fine shooter, passer, and defensive ace, Lucas was a two-time college Player of the Year at Ohio State, where his team captured one NCAA title and three Big Ten titles. He also helped the U.S. win the gold in the 1960 Olympics. In 1963-64 with Cincinnati, Lucas was the NBA's Rookie of the Year. He went on to play in seven All-Star Games and was part of the New York Knicks' 1973 championship team. He finished his career with 14,053 points and 12,942 rebounds. (1979)

HANK LUISETTI

Forward: Luisetti was a revolutionary who broke old standards by developing a one-handed shot. In three seasons at Stanford, Hank led his squad to succes-sive Pacific Coast Conference titles. An All-American in 1937 and '38, Luisetti was the first college player ever to score 50 points in a game. He later starred on the AAU scene, twice more earning All-America honors. (1959)

ED MACAULEY

Forward: "Easy Ed" Macauley was a four-time All-American at St. Louis (1946-49). In 1947, he led the nation with a .524 shooting percentage, and was MVP of the NIT the following year. Professionally, Macauley played ten NBA seasons, earning seven All-Star Game appear-ances and netting 11,234 career points. (1960)

PETE MARAVICH

Forward: Maravich, one of the great gunners in basketball history, shattered many NCAA records, including highest career scoring average (44.2). Maravich starred at Louisiana State, earning three All-America berths and college Player of the Year honors in 1970. "Pistol Pete" played NBA ball with Atlanta, the Jazz, and Boston. In 658 NBA games, he averaged 24.2 PPG. In 1976-77, he led the league in scoring with a 31.1 average. (1986)

SLATER MARTIN

Guard: At 5'10", "Dugie" Martin was the first "small superstar" of the NBA, playing throughout the 1950s. After three outstanding years at Texas, Martin joined the NBA. He played for four league championship teams in Minneapolis before moving to St. Louis, where he helped the Hawks win the 1958 title. In 11 seasons, he tallied 7,337 points and 3,160 assists and earned a reputation as a defensive genius. (1981)

BRANCH McCRACKEN

Forward: One of Indiana's great amateurs, McCracken starred for three years at Indiana University, winning the conference MVP Award in 1928. During his career, he scored nearly one-third of all the points recorded by the Hoosiers. He later had great success as a coach, winning four Big Ten and two NCAA titles at Indiana. (1960)

JACK McCRACKEN

Center: A two-time All-American at N.W. Missouri State (1931-32), McCracken was known for his outstanding passing and domination of the backboards. As a star of the AAU circuit, he was an eight-time All-American between 1932 and 1945 and won two AAU championships. (1962)

BOBBY McDERMOTT

Forward: McDermott turned pro after his freshman year of high school and played for 17 years. According to coaches and managers of the NBL in 1945, McDermott was "the greatest professional basketball player of all time." He was a seven-time NBL All-Star, won five straight MVP Awards, and led the league twice in scoring. He was a champion with Brooklyn, Fort Wayne, Chicago, and the Original Celtics. (1987)

DICK McGUIRE

Guard: McGuire, an All-American at St. John's, helped the New York Knicks to three straight NBA Finals (1951-53). Though he averaged just 8.0 PPG in 11 NBA seasons with New York and Detroit, McGuire made seven All-Star Games thanks to his strong point-guard skills. (1993)

ANN MEYERS

Guard: Meyers, of UCLA, was women's basketball's first four-time All-American. She also helped the 1976 Olympic team to a silver medal. In 1979, Meyers became the first and only woman to sign with an NBA club (Indiana Pacers), although she didn't make the team. (1993)

GEORGE MIKAN

Center: The game's first dominating big man, the 6'10" Mikan was a three-time NBA scoring leader and played in the first four NBA All-Star Games. Previously, he was a three-time All-American at DePaul and twice was named college Player of the Year (1945 and '46), leading the nation in scoring in both of those years. Mikan played on five NBA title teams in Minneapolis. (1959)

EARL MONROE

Guard: Earl "The Pearl" Monroe's slick ball-handling and dead-eye shooting made him a prolific scorer and crowd-pleaser. A two-time All-American at Winston-Salem State, he was drafted by Baltimore and was the NBA Rookie of the Year in 1968. He spent 13 years in the NBA and helped the New York Knicks win the 1973 league title. An amazing clutch player, Monroe set an NBA record for most points (13) in a single overtime period. (1989)

CALVIN MURPHY

Guard: The 5'9" Murphy was a brilliant free throw shooter, canning 78 straight with Houston in 1980-81, the year he shot a record .958 overall. The mighty mite averaged 33.1 PPG as a three-time All-American at Niagara. He scored 17.9 per game in his 13 NBA seasons, all with the Rockets. (1993)

STRETCH MURPHY

Center: "Stretch" Murphy was one of the most feared big men of his time, as he helped Purdue to a Big Ten championship in 1928. A two-time All-American, Murphy set a Western Conference and Big Ten scoring mark when he netted 143 points in 1929. In his senior year, 1930, he captained Purdue to an undefeated record. (1960)

PAT PAGE

Forward: An outstanding defensive player and a star in three sports, Page led his University of Chicago squad to Western Conference titles in 1907, 1909 (when they were undefeated), and 1910. In 1910, Page was named college Player of the Year. He later coached at Chicago, Butler, and the College of Idaho. (1962)

BOB PETTIT

Forward: A three-time All-American at Louisiana State (1952-54), Pettit played ten NBA seasons with the St. Louis Hawks. He was named NBA Rookie of the Year in 1955 and league MVP in 1956 and '59. He led the Hawks to the league title in 1958. He finished as the greatest scorer in league history with 20,880 points. (1970)

ANDY PHILLIP

Guard: One of the stars of the University of Illinois "Whiz Kids," Phillip set Big Ten scoring marks in 1942 and '43 and once scored 40 points in a game. Phillip's college career was disrupted by three years in World War II. However, he returned to Illinois and enjoyed an All-America year in 1947. He later played in the BAA and NBA for more than a decade. (1961)

JIM POLLARD

Forward: After earning All-America status at Stanford, Pollard entered the military, where he was a Service All-Star. He led Stanford to an NCAA championship in 1942 and later starred in the AAU circuit, winning MVP honors in 1947 and '48. He joined the Minneapolis Lakers in 1949 and helped them to five league championships. (1977)

FRANK RAMSEY

Guard: A two-time All-American while playing at Kentucky (1952 and '54), Ramsey joined the Boston Celtics and revolutionized the game by "inventing" the sixth-man position. Ramsey won seven titles in nine NBA seasons. He was called "the most versatile player in the NBA" by his longtime coach, Red Auerbach. (1981)

WILLIS REED

Center: One of the most intense competitors of his time, Reed began as a two-time All-American at Grambling. In ten pro seasons with the New York Knicks, he won two NBA titles (1970 and '73), was Rookie of the Year (1964-65), and played in seven All-Star Games. He averaged 18.7 PPG in his career and grabbed 8,414 boards. (1981)

OSCAR ROBERTSON

Guard: One of the greatest all-around players ever, "The Big O," starred at the University of Cincinnati, where he was a two-time college Player of the Year and a three-time scoring leader among major-college players. As a pro for Cincinnati, he was league MVP in 1964. Later, he led the Milwaukee Bucks to the 1971 NBA title. He finished his career with 26,710 points (25.7 PPG) and set an NBA record with 9,887 assists. (1979)

JOHN ROOSMA

Forward: Roosma made his mark on the game as a member of the U.S. Army squad. In his Army career, he scored more than 1,000 points, including 354 in one season. Roosma, whose Army team went 70-3 during his tenure, served in the military for 30 years and retired as an Army colonel in 1956. (1961)

BILL RUSSELL

Center: Russell reigns as one of the great winners and rebounders of all time. As a collegian, he was Player of the Year in 1956 for San Francisco and also led his school to two NCAA titles. He then led the U.S. to gold in the 1956 Olympic Games. As a pro, he helped the Celtics to eight straight NBA crowns (1959-66) and 11 in 13 years. He collected 21,620 rebounds, averaged 15.1 PPG, and was league MVP five times. As player/coach, he led the Celts to titles in 1968 and '69. (1974)

HONEY RUSSELL

Guard: A great defensive player, John "Honey" Russell played against the best players in virtually every professional league during his 28-year career. He led the Cleveland Rosenblums to five straight titles (1925-29) and later coached his alma mater, Seton Hall, to nearly 300 victories, including a string of 44 straight. In 1946-47, he became the first coach of the NBA Boston Celtics. (1964)

DOLPH SCHAYES

Forward: Schayes played his college ball at New York University, where he was an All-American in 1948. In 15 seasons with the Syracuse Nationals, he was one of the game's great scorers, chalking up 19,249 points (18.2 per game). From February 1952 to December 1961, he played in a record 765 straight games. Later, he was named Coach of the Year in 1966 when he guided the Philadelphia 76ers to a division title. His son Danny plays for the Milwaukee Bucks. (1972)

ERNEST SCHMIDT

Forward: Schmidt was known as "One Grand Schmidt" after scoring 1,000 career points in his Kansas State Teachers College days. He was a four-time conference all-star in the early 1930s and was widely recognized as the greatest player ever to come out of the Missouri Valley. Later, he suited up for three seasons on the AAU circuit, playing for Denver and Reno. (1973)

JOHN SCHOMMER

Center: A star in basketball, football, baseball, and track, Schommer led the Chicago Maroon basketball squad to three straight Big Ten titles (1907-09) and was the conference scoring leader all three years. He also enjoyed a 47-year career as athletic director, coach, and teacher at Illinois Institute of Technology. In 1949, the Helms Foundation named him a center on its All-Time All-America Team. (1959)

BARNEY SEDRAN

Guard: At 5'4", Sedran proved that size truly wasn't everything. Despite being banished from high school basketball, Sedran starred at City College of New York and was his team's leading scorer three years in a row. Upon his graduation in 1911, he embarked on a 15-year pro career that included ten championships.

He helped Carbondale to 35 straight victories in 1914-15 and later was a coach for another 20 years. (1962)

JULIANA SEMENOVA

Center: The Soviet seven-footer dominated her international opponents, winning two Olympic gold medals (1976 and 1980) and three World Championship golds. Semenova never lost a game in 18 years of international competition. (1993)

BILL SHARMAN

Guard: After two All-America years at Southern California, the sharp-shooting Sharman enjoyed an 11-year stint in the NBA, where he played on four championship Boston Celtics teams in the 1950s and early 1960s. Sharman's secret weapon was free throw shooting. His career 88-percent mark is among the best ever. After retiring with 12,665 points, he won titles as a coach in the ABA and NBA. (1975)

CHRISTIAN STEINMETZ

Guard: The "father of Wisconsin basketball," Christian Steinmetz turned basketball into a recognized sport at the University of Wisconsin. As a senior in 1905, he set school scoring records (some of which would stand for the next 50 years) including: most points in a game (50), most free throws in a game (26), and most points in a season (462). (1961)

JOHN THOMPSON

Guard: A star at Montana State, John "Cat" Thompson was selected to All-Rocky Mountain Conference teams for four years in a row. In 1929, they were the Helms national champions and the Cat was named Player of the Year. Thompson eventually became a coach, where he remained for 14 years. (1962)

NATE THURMOND

Center: An All-American at Bowling Green, Thurmond was a defensive genius with strong shooting skills. In his 14-year NBA career, he averaged 15 points and 15 rebounds per game. In a 1974 game, he became the first to record a "quadruple-double." Playing for several NBA teams, Thurmond was named to seven All-Star Games and finished his career with 14,464 boards. (1984)

JACK TWYMAN

Forward: An All-American at Cincinnati, Jack Twyman joined the Rochester Royals in 1955-56. In 11 NBA seasons, he scored 15,840 points. A durable forward with precision shooting skills, Twyman played 823 games (including a stretch of 609 consecutively) and averaged 19.2 PPG. He also played on six All-Star teams. (1982)

WES UNSELD

Center: After an explosive career at Louisville, where he was an All-American in 1967 and '68, Unseld entered the NBA with an equally loud bang in 1968-69, when he was the NBA's MVP for the Baltimore Bullets. Unseld led the Bullets to an NBA title in 1978. In his career, he averaged 14 boards a game and played in five All-Star Games. He's currently coach of the Washington Bullets. (1987)

FUZZY VANDIVIER

Guard: Robert "Fuzzy" Vandivier was a high school superstar who became one of the greatest players in the history of Indiana basketball. He took his perennial-champion Franklin High School team directly to Franklin College in 1922 and helped establish a legendary squad. He is a member of the All-Time All-Star Five of Indiana. (1974)

ED WACHTER

Center: As a turn-of-the-century player, Wachter starred on nearly every team in the Eastern circuit. He was an annual scoring champion and a member of more title-winning clubs than anyone else of his time. Later, as a coach at Harvard, he founded the New England Basketball Association and struggled to gain national uniformity of rules and regulations. (1961)

BILL WALTON

Center: The big redhead carried UCLA to an 86-4 record and two NCAA titles (1972-73), earning college Player of the Year awards from 1972-74. Though he sat out four different NBA seasons because of injuries, he helped both Portland (1977) and Boston (1986) to NBA titles. Walton was named league MVP in 1977-78 with Portland. (1993)

BOBBY WANZER

Guard: An All-American at Seton Hall in 1946, Wanzer played professionally for ten seasons with the Rochester Royals, appearing in five All-Star Games. He was the NBA's MVP in 1952-53, two years after helping the Royals win the 1951 NBA title. An outstanding shooter, Wanzer led the league in free throw accuracy (90 percent) in 1951-52. Later, he coached the Royals for three years. (1986)

JERRY WEST

Guard: One of the greatest high-pressure performers of all time, Jerry West earned his nickname "Mr. Clutch" during 14 seasons with the Los Angeles Lakers. A former two-time All-American while at West Virginia, and a gold medalist at the 1960 Olympic Games, West averaged 27.0 PPG in the NBA. He was also named to 14 All-Star Games and helped the Lakers win the 1972 NBA title. (1979)

NERA WHITE

Center: The 6'1" White was one of the most complete female players of all time. From 1955-69, she led a team sponsored by Nashville Business College to ten AAU national championships. She was named the AAU tournament's MVP ten times and an AAU All-American 15 years in a row. In 1957-58, White led the U.S. to the World Basketball championship. (1992)

LENNY WILKENS

Guard: A leader and a winner, Lenny Wilkens enjoyed success at every level of the game. As an All-American at Providence College, he was the 1960 NIT MVP. Wilkens, a 6'1" guard, went on to play 15 seasons in the NBA, averaging 16.5 PPG and making nine All-Star teams. He later coached the Seattle SuperSonics, one of his former teams, to the 1979 NBA championship. As an NBA coach, he has won 869 games. (1988)

JOHN WOODEN

Forward: Before becoming one of basketball's greatest coaches, Wooden was an outstanding player in his own right. A three-time All-American at Purdue (1930-32) and college Player of the Year (1932), he set a Big Ten scoring record in his senior year and led his team to the national title. Wooden later starred as a pro for Indianapolis' Kautsky Grocers, where he once hit 138 straight free throws. (1960)

COACHES

PHOG ALLEN

Forrest "Phog" Allen was one of the game's greatest coaches. In nearly 40 years of coaching, much of it at his alma mater (Kansas), Allen's teams won 31 championships, three national titles, and 746 games. He co-founded the National Association of Basketball Coaches in 1927, and in 1950 was given the NABC/MIBA/NIT Award in recognition of his basketball excellence. (1959)

HAROLD ANDERSON

Anderson was a star athlete in college, earning 11 letters in three sports before turning to coaching at age 23. After nine successful years coaching high school ball, he moved to the University of Toledo in 1934. There, he went 142-41. In more than 20 years at Bowling Green, he made several trips to NCAA Tournaments and NITs. His college coaching record was 504-226. (1984)

RED AUERBACH

Called by many "the greatest coach in the history of the NBA," Red Auerbach is the only coach ever to win more than 1,000 games in pro basketball. A player at George Washington, Auerbach joined the burgeoning NBA as a coach in 1946. He took the job at Boston in 1950 and led the Celtics to nine NBA titles, including eight straight from 1959-66. He has been a part of the Celtic front office ever since. (1968)

SAM BARRY

A graduate of Wisconsin, Justin "Sam" Barry coached at Iowa for seven years, where he won the Big Ten title in 1923 and shared it in 1926. His greatest years came when he moved to Southern California, where he coached for 17 years. There, he won three conference championships and seven division titles. (1978)

ERNEST BLOOD

Blood enjoyed a high school coaching career that was simply mind-boggling. From 1906-15, his Potsdam (New York) High School squad never lost a game. From 1915-24 at Passaic (New Jersey) High School, his team won 200 games, lost just once, and claimed seven state titles. He later coached at St. Benedict's Prep, winning another five state crowns. He also coached at West Point and Clarkson. (1960)

HOWARD CANN

A three-sport athlete while at New York University, Cann led NYU to the 1920 AAU title. He was a shot-putter on the 1920 Olympic team before becoming a coach at NYU for 35 years. His record was 409-232, which included an undefeated season in 1933-34. (1967)

H. CLIFFORD CARLSON

Two years after earning a medical degree, Dr. Carlson began coaching the University of Pittsburgh and remained a coach for more than 30 years. He led Pitt to a pair of national championships (1928 and '30) and is credited with inventing the "Figure Eight" offense. A founder of the National Association of Basketball Coaches, he was given the NABC/MIBA/NIT Award in 1948. (1959)

LOU CARNESECCA

Carnesecca took every one of his St. John's teams to a postseason tournament (18 NCAAs, six NITs). Carnesecca, who won his 500th collegiate game in 1991, earned national Coach of the Year honors in both 1983 and '85. His 1985 Redmen appeared in the Final Four. Carnesecca also coached the ABA's New York Nets from 1970-73. (1992)

BEN CARNEVALE

A graduate of New York University, Bernard Carnevale became a great teacher and coach. He earned his greatest honors during a 20-year stay with the U.S. Naval Academy, where he coached the Middies to 257 wins between 1946 and 1966. He also managed the 1968 U.S. Olympic team in Mexico City. (1969)

EVERETT CASE

A graduate of Wisconsin, Case enjoyed a 40-year coaching career. In 21 years of high school coaching, he won 467 games and four Indiana state championships (1925, '29, '36, and '39). He later went to coach at North Carolina State (1946-65), where he won 377 games and six straight Southern Conference titles. He finished his career with 844 wins and 258 losses. (1981)

EVERETT DEAN

An All-American at Indiana in 1921, Dean went to Carleton College after graduation and coached his way to a 48-4 record. He returned to Indiana and won 163 games over the next 14 years, tying for three Big Ten titles. He joined Stanford as a coach in 1938 and led the school to the 1942 NCAA title. He retired from coaching in 1955. (1966)

ED DIDDLE

A Kentucky product, Diddle was a successful high school coach before joining Western Kentucky in 1922. He stayed at WKU for the next 42 years, guiding the famous "fastbreak" Hilltoppers to 32 conference titles. He also took them to three NCAA Tournaments and eight NITs. Diddle was the first man ever to coach 1,000 games at the same school. (1971)

BRUCE DRAKE

An accomplished college athlete while attending Oklahoma, Drake later coached the Sooners, starting in 1939. In 17 years, his club won 200 games and captured six

Big Six or Big Seven titles. Drake also served as chairman of the National Rules Committee and president of the NABC. (1972)

CLARENCE GAINES

In 1947, "Big House" Gaines was named athletic director and head coach of all sports at Winston-Salem State College. Five decades later, he was still at Winston-Salem and had become only the second college basketball coach to win 800 games. In 1967, his Rams, led by future NBA superstar Earl Monroe, won the NCAA College Division title with a 30-2 record. (1981)

JACK GARDNER

James "Jack" Gardner is the only college coach to lead two different universities to the Final Four twice apiece. At Kansas State, he won three Big Seven titles and made it to the Final Four in 1948 and 1951. At Utah, Gardner guided his ballclub to the 1961 and 1966 Final Four. In 36 years of coaching, he posted a 70-percent winning mark and 649 victories. (1983)

SLATS GILL

An All-American at Oregon State, Amory "Slats" Gill eventually coached his alma mater for 35 years, until 1964. His Beavers won 599 games, five Pacific Coast Conference titles, nine Northern Division titles, and eight straight Far West Classics. Under Gill, the Beavers were ranked in the top five nationally in 1947, '49, and '55. (1967)

MARV HARSHMAN

An outstanding all-around athlete, Harshman captured 13 letters at Pacific Lutheran and was a two-time All-American in basketball. He began his coaching career in the mid-1940s at Lutheran, then coached at Washington State and Washington during the next

four decades. His teams won a total of 642 games. (1984)

EDDIE HICKEY

Besides being a prolific writer and researcher, Hickey was a successful coach. He enjoyed success at three universities—Creighton, St. Louis (where he won the 1948 NIT title), and Marquette (where he was named USBWA Coach of the Year in 1959). Over 35 years, his teams won 436 games and were participants in countless NCAA Tournaments and NITs. (1978)

HOWARD HOBSON

Hobson was the first coach to win major championships on the West Coast *and* the East Coast. "Hobby" took Oregon to three conference titles (1937-39) and the first NCAA crown (1939), and he later guided Yale to five Big Three titles. His basketball teams won 400 games during his 28-year tenure. With an advanced degree in education, Hobson used his vast intellect to advance the game strategically and tactically. (1965)

RED HOLZMAN

Holzman was a collegiate star at the City College of New York, where he was a two-time All-American. Later, during his eight years as a player with NBL Rochester, he guided the club to the 1951 league title. He coached the New York Knicks for 14 years, winning NBA titles in 1970 and '73. He was the NBA's Coach of the Year in 1970. In 1981, Holzman became the first man to receive the NBA Coaches Achievement Award. (1985)

HENRY IBA

Iba was a fine player and an even better coach. He took over at Oklahoma State in 1934 and led the Aggies to 14 Missouri Valley championships, the 1965 Big Eight crown, and the 1945 and '46 NCAA titles. Iba also coached the U.S. Olympic team to gold medals in 1964 and 1968. He won 767 Division I games—third on the all-time list. (1968)

DOGGIE JULIAN

An accomplished athlete who played pro baseball and football, Alvin "Doggie" Julian won ten letters as a college star. He then became a solid coach for 41 years. His basketball teams won 381 games and made several trips to NCAA Tournaments and NITs. In 1947, his Holy Cross club won the NCAA crown. At Dartmouth, his squad was a three-time Ivy League champ (1956, '58, and '59). He received the NABC/MIBA/NIT Award in 1967. (1967)

FRANK KEANEY

Keaney was instrumental in changing the face of basketball at the University of Rhode Island. Named athletic director at the school in 1920, Keaney instituted the fastbreak, "point-per-minute" offense that eventually led his teams to four National Invitation Tournaments and 403 victories over 27 seasons. (1960)

GEORGE KEOGAN

Keogan took over as coach of Notre Dame in 1923 and led the Fighting Irish to 327 wins in the next two decades. During one stretch, his team lost only five of 61 games. His greatest claim to fame was creating a shifting man-to-man defense. After his death at the age of 52, he was posthumously bestowed the NABC/MIBA/NIT Award in 1943. (1961)

BOB KNIGHT

His practices may come under fire, but no one has ever questioned Knight's ability to get the most from his players. He has coached 21 years at Indiana, where he has won three NCAA championships (1976, '81, and '87) and has never had a losing season. Knight also coached successfully at Army, where he led the Cadets to a 102-52 record over six years. He is a three-time USBWA Coach of the Year. (1991)

WARD LAMBERT

A trained chemist, Ward "Piggy" Lambert also coached at Purdue, where he won 11 Big Ten titles and 371 games over 30 years. Among his more famous players were Charlie Murphy and John Wooden, both of whom executed Lambert's fastbreak style to near perfection. Lambert was bestowed the NABC/MIBA/NIT Award in 1954. (1960)

HARRY LITWACK

Though rarely blessed with great talent, Litwack coached 21 years at Temple, his alma mater. At Temple, Litwack earned the reputation for "doing more with less than any coach in basketball history." Litwack's Owls won 373 games (losing 193) and went to 13 postseason tournaments. In 1969, they captured the NIT title. (1975)

KENNETH LOEFFLER

Loeffler played and coached the game and also earned a degree in law. He led La Salle to the 1952 NIT title and the 1954 NCAA crown. He also guided the NBA St. Louis Bombers to a 1948 division title. Loeffler also coached at Yale and Texas A&M and served as a representative of the U.S. State Department and the Armed Services. (1964)

DUTCH LONBORG

A star at Kansas, Arthur "Dutch" Lonborg took to coaching in 1922. Dutch won 323 games at McPherson College, Washburn, and Northwestern. Later, he served as chairman of the NCAA Tournament committee and the U.S. Olympic basketball committee, and was manager of the 1960 U.S. Olympic basketball team. (1972)

ARAD McCUTCHAN

A graduate of Evansville College, McCutchan returned to his alma mater in 1946 and began a remarkable coaching career. He won five NCAA College Division championships and 514 games. In 1964 and '65, Arad was NCAA College Division Coach of the Year. McCutchan is one of only two college basketball coaches to win at least five NCAA titles. (1980)

AL McGUIRE

In his last game as a coach, McGuire led Marquette to the 1977 NCAA championship. It capped off a 13-year career at Marquette that saw him go 295-80. McGuire won the 1970 NIT championship and went 28-1 in 1970-71. He won Coach of the Year honors in both 1971 and '74. (1992)

FRANK McGUIRE

McGuire is the only coach to win at least 100 games at three different colleges: St. John's (103), North Carolina (164), and South Carolina (283). He also is the only coach to reach the NCAA finals at two schools, winning it all with the 32-0 North Carolina Tar Heels in 1957, and losing it with St. John's in '52. McGuire also coached a season in the NBA, leading the 1962 Philadelphia Warriors to 49 wins. At the time of his induction into the Hall of Fame, McGuire had 675 career wins. (1976)

JOHN McLENDON

McLendon began his long coaching career while still a student at Kansas. He coached high school, college, AAU, and pro basketball, winning 522 total games. He was the first coach to win three straight national titles, as he led Tennessee State to NAIA crowns in 1957-59. He also coached the Denver Rockets of the fledgling ABA and received the NABC/MIBA/NIT Award in 1976. (1978)

WALTER MEANWELL

A doctor of public health medicine, Dr. Meanwell coached basketball at Wisconsin for two decades and also coached Missouri for a couple years. During that time, he won 290 games and six conference titles. He later authored a book (with Knute Rockne) on training, conditioning, and injury care. Meanwell received the NABC/MIBA/NIT Award in 1953. (1959)

RAY MEYER

A coaching legend at DePaul, Meyer started out as captain of the Notre Dame basketball team. He eventually spent 42 years as leader of the Blue Demons (1943-84), guiding them to 724 victories and 22 NCAA and National Invitation Tournaments. His Demons captured the NIT title in 1945. With his 724 victories, Meyer is sixth on the all-time Division I win list. (1978)

RALPH MILLER

A star player under Phog Allen at Kansas, "Cappy" Miller began a 38-year college coaching career in 1951. He coached at Wichita State (13 years), Iowa (six years), and Oregon State (19 years). He enjoyed 33 winning seasons and was the USBWA Coach of the Year in 1981 and '82. In all, his teams won 657 games. (1987)

PETE NEWELL

A 1939 graduate of Loyola, Newell coached at the University of San Francisco, Michigan State, and Cal.-Berkeley. As a coach, Newell won the 1949 NIT title with USF, the 1959 NCAA crown with Cal.-Berkeley, and the 1960 Olympic gold medal. In 1960, he was elected USBWA Coach of the Year. Newell's instructional programs have helped develop countless NBA stars. He received the NABC/MIBA/NIT Award in 1968. (1978)

JACK RAMSAY

Not only did Ramsay win 864 NBA games (third most in history), but he also won 234 college games at St. Joseph's (PA). Ramsay's NBA stops included Philadelphia, Buffalo, Portland, and Indiana. During his Portland years, the Trail Blazers made the playoffs nine times in ten years and won the 1977 NBA title. (1992)

ADOLPH RUPP

After a championship career at Kansas, Rupp coached Kentucky from 1931-72 and became the winningest coach in college history. Along the way, he won 875 games. His teams advanced to 24 Southeast Conference titles, won four NCAA crowns, and nabbed one NIT championship. He was co-coach of the 1948 gold-medal Olympic team, and he received the NABC/MIBA/NIT Award in 1966. (1968)

LEONARD SACHS

When he was 19 years old, Sachs was the star of the Illinois A.C., which won the national AAU championship in 1917. Sachs became the coach at Loyola of Chicago in 1924. Over the next 19 years, his teams won 224 games. His use of the 2-2-1 zone defense, in which the center was used as a blocker, was responsible for a growing trend toward big men in the game. (1961)

EVERETT SHELTON

A coach and clinician, Shelton won 850 games in his 46-year career. Shelton coached two national title-winning teams—the AAU Denver Safeways in 1937 and the NCAA champion Wyoming team in 1943. He was a successful teaching coach in high school, college, and amateur basketball, and was recognized for his contributions by receiving the NABC/MIBA/NIT Award in 1969. (1979)

DEAN SMITH

A successful player in Phog Allen's program at Kansas, Smith became coach of North Carolina in 1962. He's still there. Smith has won 774 games, has a winning percentage of .776, and has appeared in an all-time record 22 NCAA Tournaments. He won the NCAA championship in 1982 and 1993 and copped a gold medal in the 1976 Olympics. (1982)

FRED TAYLOR

The Ohio-born Taylor starred on Ohio State's 1950 Big Ten championship team. After a brief pro baseball career in the Washington Senators system, Taylor eventually became head coach of Ohio State in 1959. Over the next 18 years, the Buckeyes won 297 games, took the 1960 NCAA title, and were runners-up in 1961 and '62. He was named the USBWA Coach of the Year in both 1961 and '62. (1985)

MARGARET WADE

Wade coached girls high school basketball in Mississippi, going 453-89 over 19 years. She returned to her alma mater, Delta State, in 1973 and led it to three straight national championships. Wade retired in 1979 with a career record of 633-117. (1984)

STANLEY WATTS

A graduate of Brigham Young, Watts became coach of the BYU varsity in 1949. During his 23 years in that post, the Cougars won 433 games and two NIT crowns (1951 and '66). In 1970, he was given the NABC/MIBA/NIT Award. Two years later, he left coaching to become BYU's athletic director. (1985)

JOHN WOODEN

One of the greatest coaches of all time, Wooden coached 13 years of ball in high schools and at Indiana State before arriving at UCLA in 1948. From 1964-75,

UCLA won ten NCAA titles, including seven straight from 1967-73. He was UPI Coach of the Year six times and twice (1970 and 1972) swept all four Coach of the Year polls (NABC, USBWA, A.P., and UPI). Wooden is the only person to be voted into the Hall of Fame twice—as both a player and a coach. (1972)

PHIL WOOLPERT

Woolpert made his mark in the mid-1950s. His University of San Francisco team, led by Bill Russell and K.C. Jones, won national titles in 1955 and '56, winning 60 games in a row. Woolpert won UPI Coach of the Year honors both years. In 1955, he became the youngest coach ever to win an NCAA title. (1992)

CONTRIBUTORS

SENDA ABBOTT

The "mother of women's basketball," Senda Berenson Abbott read of the "invention" of basketball by Dr. James Naismith, contacted him, and subsequently adapted a set of rules for women. Abbott's guidelines remained in effect for 75 years. (1984)

CLAIR BEE

A coach for 29 years, Bee's Long Island University teams (1931-51) won an astonishing 95 percent of their games. In 1939, they won the NIT championship. Bee later coached Baltimore in the NBA (1952-54) and was the inventor of the 1-3-1 zone defense. Bee wrote more than 20 instructional and non-fiction sports books. (1967)

WALTER BROWN

In 1946, Brown spearheaded the movement to organize the BAA. As president of the Boston Garden Arena Corporation, he was able to house one of the first BAA franchises—the Celtics. From 1961-64, Brown served as chairman of the Basketball Hall of Fame's board of trustees. (1965)

JOHN BUNN

An all-around athlete at Kansas, Bunn coached 25 years at Stanford, Springfield, and Colorado State, winning 321 games in his career. Bunn wrote several textbooks on basketball and, in 1961, received the NABC/MIBA/NIT Award. (1964)

BOB DOUGLAS

Douglas organized the famous all-black Renaissance Five in 1922. A road club facing racism and discrimination wherever they went, the Rens won 2,318 games in 22 years, including 88 straight in 1933, another 128 total in 1934, and the World Professional Championship in 1939. (1971)

AL DUER

Duer helped establish and develop the NAIA, formerly the National Association of Intercollegiate Basketball. He served as its executive secretary from 1949-1971. He supervised the 1955 tournament, which was the first national basketball tourney to include black institutions. (1981)

CLIFFORD FAGAN

A tireless administrator, Fagan became executive director of the National Federation of High School Athletic Associations in 1959. He held the post for 18 years and expanded the organization to include all 50 states. He also was co-editor of *Basketball Rules Simplified*. (1983)

HARRY FISHER

Fisher led Columbia in scoring four years straight and guided them to undefeated seasons in 1904 and '05. He also coached for 11 years at Columbia. Later, Fisher was hand-picked by General Douglas MacArthur to guide the U.S. Military Academy. He led the Academy to a 46-5 record. (1973)

LARRY FLEISHER

Fleisher founded and led the National Basketball Players Association from 1962-88. Schooled at Harvard Law, Fleisher introduced collective bargaining to pro sports. Through his negotiations, players obtained benefits such as pension plans and minimum-salary levels. Fleisher also helped establish free agency in sports. (1991)

EDDIE GOTTLIEB

A Russian-born immigrant and an adroit promoter, Gottlieb helped organize the BAA in 1946. He coached the Philadelphia Warriors team that won the first BAA title (1947). Gottlieb served as chairman of the NBA Rules Committee for 25 years. (1971)

LUTHER GULICK

As physical training chairman at Springfield College, Dr. Gulick asked James Naismith to create "an indoor game." The game Naismith created, of course, was basketball. Gulick helped create the Public School League of New York City, the Camp Fire Girls, and the Boy Scouts of America. (1959)

LESTER HARRISON

As owner of the Rochester Royals for 13 years, Harrison won an NBL title in 1946 and an NBA crown in 1951. Harrison was a proponent of the time clock and many other game innovations. (1979)

FERENC HEPP

The "father of basketball in Hungary," Dr. Hepp was the first director of Hungary's National School of Physical Education and Sports. Hepp was associated with basketball in Hungary from the 1930s on, and he wrote an important multi-language dictionary of basketball terminology. (1980)

EDWARD HICKOX

Hickox spent four decades as a coach and was the first executive secretary of the NABC. He served as president from 1944-46. Hickox also was a resident historian for two decades. (1959)

TONY HINKLE

Paul "Tony" Hinkle coached Butler University in his native Indiana, where he won 560 games and a national title in 1929. He became known as the "dean of Indiana coaches;" at one point, 55 of his charges held coaching positions in Indiana. He received the NABC/MIBA/NIT Award in 1962. (1965)

NED IRISH

Irish was a master promoter who, as basketball director at Madison Square Garden, instituted college doubleheaders. In 1946, he helped organize the BAA and also formed the New York Knickerbockers. Irish received the first NABC/MIBA/NIT Award, in 1942. (1964)

R. WILLIAM JONES

Jones was a British subject born and educated in Rome, Italy. In 1929, he brought basketball to Switzerland, and three years later he co-founded the International Amateur Basketball Federation. Ultimately, Jones helped spread the game of basketball to 130 countries. (1964)

J. WALTER KENNEDY

Kennedy was a scorekeeper, coach, referee, and publicity director for the NBA. More importantly, he served as NBA commissioner from 1963-75. Under Kennedy's caring and watchful leadership, the NBA boomed in TV revenue, in attendance, and in the number of teams competing. (1980)

EMIL LISTON

Besides coaching Baker University for 25 years, Liston organized the National Association of Intercollegiate Basketball and became its executive director in 1940. It has since grown to 500 members and is now known as the National Association of Intercollegiate Athletics (NAIA). (1974)

BILL MOKRAY

A superstar among basketball publicists, Mokray spent 21 years with the Boston Celtics. He compiled statistics for the *Converse Basketball Yearbook*, wrote a basketball history for the 1957 *Encyclopedia Britannica*, and edited an award-winning basketball encyclopedia in 1963. (1965)

RALPH MORGAN

As a student at Pennsylvania, Morgan called for the formation of the Collegiate Basketball Rules Committee. He remained an active member of the committee for more than a quarter-century. In 1910, at age 26, he formed the Eastern Intercollegiate Basketball League, currently known as the Ivy League. (1959)

FRANK MORGENWECK

"Pop" Morgenweck began his pro basketball career in 1901 as a 26-year-old manager in the NBL. In 1925, his Kingston (New York) squad played a six-game championship series with the New York Celtics, splitting it 3-3. From 1912 to his retirement in 1931, Morgenweck won various championship titles. (1962)

JAMES NAISMITH

Naismith is universally recognized as the "father of basketball." While serving as an instructor at the Springfield YMCA in 1891, Prof. Naismith searched for an indoor game that his boys could enjoy during the winter. He asked a custodian to nail two peach baskets to the gymnasium balcony, and the rest is history. (1959)

JOHN O'BRIEN

Besides playing pro basketball and serving as a referee, O'Brien formed the Metropolitan Basketball League in 1921. He served as president and treasurer of the MBL for seven years. He then reorganized the American Basketball League and served as president until 1953. (1961)

LARRY O'BRIEN

O'Brien spent many years in politics as advisor to Presidents John Kennedy and Lyndon Johnson. He was named commissioner of the NBA in 1975. During his nine-year tenure, a collective-bargaining agreement was reached and the league expanded to 23 teams. (1991)

HAROLD OLSEN

Olsen coached for 23 years at Ohio State, winning five conference titles. Later, as chairman of the National Rules Committee, he helped pass the adoption of the ten-second rule. In 1938-39, he chaired the NABC study of an NCAA Tournament, which eventually became a huge national event. (1959)

MAURICE PODOLOFF

Born in Russia, Podoloff assumed the leadership of the BAA in June 1946. Through his sensitivity and high standards, he was able to lead a merger between the BAA and the NBL, thus creating the NBA in 1949. He served as NBA president and, in 1954, secured the league's first TV contract. Podoloff retired in 1963. (1973)

HENRY PORTER

Porter invented the "molded" basketball, the fan-shaped backboard, and the 29½-inch ball. He also served on the National Rules Committee for three decades. Later, he wrote a handbook and developed the use of instructional films. (1960)

WILLIAM REID

A 1918 graduate of Colgate, Reid later coached his alma mater to 151 wins. He also served as manager and athletic director at Colgate for 36 years. Reid headed the Eastern Collegiate Athletic Conference (1944-45) and was vice-president of the NCAA (1942-46). (1963)

ELMER RIPLEY

A star pro player in the 1910s, Ripley later coached at Wagner, Yale, Georgetown, Columbia, Notre Dame, John Carroll, West Point, and Regis, accumulating nearly 300 victories. He also guided the Harlem Globetrotters (1953-56) and the 1960 Canadian Olympic team. (1972)

LYNN ST. JOHN

A star athlete in four sports and a successful college coach in Ohio, St. John served as Ohio State's athletic director from 1915-47. He was chairman of the NCAA Rules Committee for 18 years, and he helped form the National Basketball Committee of United States and Canada. (1962)

ABE SAPERSTEIN

The "father of the Harlem Globetrotters," Saperstein originally was asked to coach the Negro American Legion Team in 1926. It was from this team that the famous Globetrotters were born. Saperstein served the team as owner, manager, coach, and sometimes player. (1970)

ARTHUR SCHABINGER

A four-sport college star, Schabinger coached two decades and won 80 percent of his games at Ottawa University, Emporia State, and Creighton. Schabinger helped conceive the NABC and wrote its bylaws. He won the NABC/MIBA/NIT Award in 1955. (1961)

AMOS ALONZO STAGG

Besides becoming a great college football coach, Stagg played in the first public basketball game, held on March 11, 1892. Stagg also led the University of Chicago's first basketball team, back in 1896. (1959)

EDWARD STEITZ

Steitz coached Springfield College and also served as the school's athletic director. Steitz wrote more than 300 articles and 60 books and conducted hundreds of rules clinics around the world. In 1974, he received the NABC/MIBA/NIT Award. (1983)

CHUCK TAYLOR

Following an 11-year pro career, Charles Taylor became well known for several other basketball achievements. He produced the first *Converse Basketball Yearbook* and, in 1931, designed the famous Converse Chuck Taylor basketball sneaker. (1968)

BERTHA TEAGUE

Teague coached girls basketball at Cairo (Oklahoma) High School in 1926, then moved to Byng High and stayed for 42 years (1927-69). Her teams won 38 conference titles and eight state championships, winning 1,152 games while losing 115. (1984)

OSWALD TOWER

Tower remained in basketball for more than 60 years. As a member of the Rules Committee (1910-1959), he edited the *Official Guide* from 1915-59 and was official rules interpreter during the same period. He was given the NABC/MIBA/NIT Award in 1944. (1959)

ARTHUR TRESTER

Trester was brought in to save the struggling Indiana High School Athletic Association in 1913. Over time, he helped the IHSAA stabilize and grow. In the meantime, he built Indiana's annual basketball tournament, which became known as a model of efficiency. (1961)

CLIFFORD WELLS

A 1920 graduate of Indiana University, Wells won 617 games during 29 years of high school coaching in Indiana. In 1945, he became head coach at Tulane, where he stayed for 18 years. Wells conducted more than 100 clinics worldwide and received the NABC/MIBA/NIT Award in 1963. (1971)

LOU WILKE

In three years as coach of the Phillips 66 Oilers, Wilke won two AAU titles. He later served as president of the National AAU, and he chaired the AAU Basketball Committee for seven terms. Wilke was manager of the 1948 U.S. Olympic basketball team. (1982)

REFEREES

JIM ENRIGHT

During his 24-year career, Enright was a respected referee in the Big Ten, Big Eight, and Missouri Valley. He was also a clinician and a sports writer and served as president of the USBWA in 1967. (1978)

GEORGE HEPBRON

A friend of Dr. James Naismith, Hepbron was a pioneer of basketball rules. Hepbron helped draft the first guide book on how to play the game. He also refereed the first AAU tournament at Bay Ridge Athletic Club. (1960)

GEORGE HOYT

An early pioneer of the game, Hoyt traveled the Northeast introducing the principles of officiating to coaches and referees. He coached many teams and refereed many games during the first half of this century. (1961)

PAT KENNEDY

The colorful Kennedy officiated for 18 years at the high school, college, and pro levels. He was the NBA's supervisor of officials from 1946-50, and he also toured with the Harlem Globetrotters for seven years. (1959)

LLOYD LEITH

Leith began a coaching career in 1927 and won 207 games at three California high schools. For 25 years, he was the top referee in the Pacific Coast Conference. He officiated in numerous NCAA Tournaments. (1982)

RED MIHALIK

Mihalik began refereeing in the mid-1930s, and by 1951 he was voted the "best referee in the United States." An official at the amateur, collegiate, and professional levels, Mihalik also refereed at the 1964 and '68 Olympic Games. (1985)

JOHN NUCATOLA

Nucatola played ten years of pro basketball before starting his officiating career. Over the years, he called more than 2,000 games, including games in the NCAA Tournament. He worked the NBA as well. (1977)

ERNEST QUIGLEY

Quigley, a four-sport star at Kansas at the turn of the century, became a multi-sport official too. For three decades, he was a National League umpire, a football official, and a respected basketball referee. (1961)

J. DALLAS SHIRLEY

Shirley presented countless papers and clinics worldwide addressing development and improvement of rules interpretation. Shirley spent 32 years as an official in various college conferences and interna-

tional tournaments—including the 1960 Olympics. (1979)

DAVID TOBEY

After a successful pro career as a player, Tobey turned to coaching, winning 367 high school games and 348 college games. From 1918-25, he refereed all vital pro games and was considered one of the best. (1961)

DAVID WALSH

Walsh enjoyed a 45-year career as a teacher, coach, and official in high school, college, and pro basketball. Walsh went on to conduct many clinics and rules-interpretation conferences to create uniformity in rules. (1961)

TEAMS

FIRST TEAM

Under the direction of James Naismith, the first game was played in 1891 at the Springfield (Massachusetts) YMCA Training School. The game was played with a peach basket and a soccer ball, and legend has it that only one basket was scored in the contest. (1959)

ORIGINAL CELTICS

Founded by promoters Jim and Tom Furey after World War I, the Original Celtics were a sensational barnstorming team. The Celts were known for their innovative strategies and brilliant passing. Johnny Beckman and Joe Lapchick were among the stars. (1959)

BUFFALO GERMANS

The Germans were a touring team from Buffalo that played from 1895-1929. The Germans played against amateurs and pros and compiled an all-time record of 792-86. At one point, they won 111 straight games. (1961)

NEW YORK RENS

Founded by Bob Douglas in 1922, the all-black Renaissance Five was a brilliant barnstorming club. Though they often encountered racism, the Rens won 2,318 games in 22 years, including 88 straight in 1933. Charles "Tarzan" Cooper starred in the middle. (1963)

On September 22, 1992, the Knicks, Clippers, and Magic pulled off an elaborate three-team deal. The Knicks received Doc Rivers, Charles Smith, and Bo Kimble from the Clippers; the Clippers received Stanley Roberts from the Magic and Mark Jackson and a 1995 2nd-round pick from the Knicks; and the Magic received a 1993 1st-round pick from the Knicks and a 1993 or 1994 1st-round pick from the Clippers.

100 Top College Stars & 64 Top College Teams

The following two sections evaluate the top players and teams in college basketball. Of the thousands of players in the college ranks, you'll read about the 100 that are expected to make the biggest impact in 1993-94. You'll also find season previews of the top 64 teams in the country.

Each player's scouting report begins with his vital stats, such as school, position, and height. Next comes a four-part evaluation of the player. "Background" reviews the player's career, starting with high school and continuing up through the 1992-93 season. "Strengths" examines his best assets, and "weaknesses" pinpoints his significant flaws. "Analysis" tries to put the player's whole game into perspective.

For a quick run-down on each player, you'll find a "player summary" box. You'll also get the player's career statistics. The stats include games (G), field goal percentage (FGP), free throw percentage (FTP), rebounds per game (RPG), assists per game (APG), and points per game (PPG).

Each of the 64 teams receives a one-page season preview. It begins with the basics, including 1992-93 overall record (this record includes NCAA or NIT games). It also lists the team's record in 1993 tournament play ("NCAAs: 2-1" means the team won two NCAA Tournament games and then lost the third). The coach's career Division I record is also listed.

Each season preview begins with an "opening line," which discusses the players it lost and the newcomers that are coming in. The preview then rates the team at each position—guard, forward, and center. "Analysis" evaluates the team's strengths and weaknesses and puts it all into perspective.

Finally, each season preview contains the team's 1993-94 roster, which includes the team's top 12 players. The roster lists each player's 1992-93 statistics. The stats include field goal percentage (FGP), free throw percentage (FTP), 3-point field goals/attempts (3-PT), rebounds per game (RPG), assists per game (APG), and points per game (PPG).

CORY ALEXANDER

School: Virginia
Year: Junior
Position: Guard
Height: 6'1" **Weight:** 176
Birthdate: June 22, 1973
Birthplace: Waynesboro, VA

PLAYER SUMMARY	
Will	distribute the ball
Can't	block shots
Expect	more scoring
Don't Expect	many turnovers

Background: This workhorse honed his game at Oak Hill Academy, where he averaged 15.9 PPG and 9.4 APG as a senior. The All-American was viewed as the best point guard in his class. Alexander suffered with his shot selection as a freshman, but he improved markedly last year.

Strengths: Alexander is comfortable with the ball in his hands, and it shows. He knows how to feed the post, and no one is more appreciative than Junior Burrough. Effective in either an up-tempo or slower pace, Alexander can score off the drive or from the outside. He can also force turnovers with his quick hands.

Weaknesses: Alexander is not a pure shooter, although he made strides with the jump shot last year. On occasion, his penchant for the flashy pass will get him into trouble.

Analysis: Alexander was one of the ACC's most improved players in 1992-93, and the growth chart should spiral higher. He's one of the fastest players in the country with the basketball and is more confident in his skills than he was a season ago. Alexander was the prime reason that Virginia reached the NCAA's Sweet 16.

COLLEGE STATISTICS

	G	FGP	FTP	RPG	APG	PPG
91-92 VA	33	.376	.686	3.2	4.4	11.2
92-93 VA	31	.453	.705	3.5	4.6	18.9
Totals	64	.421	.696	3.3	4.5	14.9

JEROME ALLEN

School: Pennsylvania
Year: Junior
Position: Guard
Height: 6'4" **Weight:** 175
Birthdate: January 28, 1973
Birthplace: Philadelphia, PA

PLAYER SUMMARY	
Will	slash to the basket
Can't	bury long jumpers
Expect	fine leadership
Don't Expect	national acclaim

Background: After a fine schoolboy career at Episcopal Academy, Allen received offers from larger basketball programs, but this splendid student preferred Penn. He became one of the Ivy League's top players as a freshman, finishing second to Princeton's Rick Hielscher in Freshman of the Year balloting.

Strengths: Allen blends exceptional quickness with shot-making and passing skills. The unquestioned floor leader for Penn, he'll take the big shot or set up backcourt partner Matt Maloney for a 3. At the defensive end, he can pick a foe's pocket and his understanding of the game rarely leaves him vulnerable.

Weaknesses: As a freshman, Allen had trouble deciding which shots were acceptable within the offensive structure and which shots weren't. He improved in that area as a sophomore. He is not a great shooter.

Analysis: Penn thrived in 1992-93, winning the Ivy League crown and nearly upending Massachusetts in the first round of the NCAA Tournament. Its guards, Allen and Maloney, led the way. Allen makes the Quakers go and he is the odds-on choice to be Ivy Player of the Year.

COLLEGE STATISTICS

	G	FGP	FTP	RPG	APG	PPG
91-92 PENN	26	.411	.684	3.6	3.2	12.2
92-93 PENN	27	.423	.667	4.7	4.9	13.1
Totals	53	.417	.677	4.2	4.1	12.7

DERRICK ALSTON

School: Duquesne
Year: Senior
Position: Center/Forward
Height: 6'11" **Weight:** 230
Birthdate: August 20, 1972
Birthplace: Hoboken, NJ

PLAYER SUMMARY	
Will	score facing the basket
Can't	be a classic center
Expect	many double-teams
Don't Expect	dominance

Background: As a prep player in Hoboken, New Jersey, Alston boasted great skills but was razor thin at 6'8". He has since grown three inches and bulked up. As a sophomore, Alston earned second-team All-Atlantic 10 honors.

Strengths: There aren't many 6'11" types who run the floor as well as Alston does. Duquesne plays at a frenzied pace and Alston scores from a variety of spots on the floor. He's quick and knows how to use that to his advantage against opposing centers. Contact is not a problem for him, and he has a nose for the ball off the backboard.

Weaknesses: Though he's nearly 7'0", Alston sometimes appears reluctant to use his size inside. He's also an abysmal free throw shooter.

Analysis: Alston is listed as a center but prefers playing facing the basket. He would be greatly aided if coach John Carroll were able to find a post player to free him of that burden. All of the tools are in place here, and what Carroll seeks now from Alston are intangibles—leadership, confidence, and improved free throw shooting. None seem out of reach.

COLLEGE STATISTICS

		G	FGP	FTP	RPG	APG	PPG
90-91	DUQ	28	.536	.598	6.3	1.3	11.3
91-92	DUQ	28	.556	.526	8.0	1.5	13.9
92-93	DUQ	28	.563	.574	9.3	1.1	19.9
Totals		84	.554	.563	7.9	1.3	15.1

ADRIAN AUTRY

School: Syracuse
Year: Senior
Position: Guard
Height: 6'4" **Weight:** 195
Birthdate: February 28, 1972
Birthplace: Monroe, NC

PLAYER SUMMARY	
Will	create in open floor
Can't	loft a pretty jumper
Expect	plenty of passes
Don't Expect	textbook play

Background: This former *Parade* All-American teamed with North Carolina's Brian Reese on a powerful Tolentine High School squad in New York City. Autry enjoyed a promising freshman season with the Orange, struggled some as a sophomore, and then closed with a flurry in 1993.

Strengths: There is a lot of schoolyard in Autry's game. He is capable of creating his own shot off the dribble or setting up his teammates if defenders converge upon him. The Syracuse staff has worked long and hard on Autry's shooting motion and there have been signs of progress, if not outright success.

Weaknesses: In his effort to make the great play, Autry will often make a silly one—he led the Big East in turnovers per game last season. Though he is adept at creating plays, he hasn't always finished well.

Analysis: This is Autry's chance to shuck the inconsistency label. He was more assertive and confident late in 1992-93, and coach Jim Boeheim hopes that carries over to the new year. A huge season could mean big dollars a year from now, as Autry has a pro body and ball-handling skills.

COLLEGE STATISTICS

		G	FGP	FTP	RPG	APG	PPG
90-91	SYR	31	.402	.705	2.5	5.3	9.7
91-92	SYR	31	.367	.703	4.1	4.0	11.0
92-93	SYR	29	.432	.798	3.7	5.6	13.7
Totals		91	.401	.734	3.4	4.9	11.4

DAMON BAILEY

School: Indiana
Year: Senior
Position: Guard
Height: 6'3" **Weight:** 195
Birthdate: October 21, 1971
Birthplace: Heltonville, IN

PLAYER SUMMARY	
Will	find the open man
Can't	depend on speed
Expect	excellent FT shooting
Don't Expect	selfish play

Background: Bailey, the leading scorer in Indiana high school history, made first-team all-state four times and was named prep Player of the Decade by *USA Today*. Bailey was the Big Ten's Freshman of the Year in 1991 and has been a solid though somewhat disappointing contributor since.

Strengths: Bailey is the typical product of the Indiana high school system—smart, tough, and sound fundamentally, though not gifted with great physical tools. A sound ball-handler, he is an unselfish passer with a knack for threading the needle. Although he slumped early in 1992-93, he is a solid jump-shooter who can nail the 3.

Weaknesses: Though hardworking, Bailey has physical limitations that inhibit him. Quick guards pose particular problems. He must also be willing to shoulder more of the scoring burden this season and not pass up sound 3-point chances.

Analysis: With numerous freshmen on the roster, Bailey will be asked to provide both points and leadership. He figures to be up to that task. The senior can direct the team from the point or play without the ball, and he'll probably do both this season.

COLLEGE STATISTICS

	G	FGP	FTP	RPG	APG	PPG
90-91	IND	33	.506	.692	2.9	2.9	11.4
91-92	IND	34	.497	.765	3.6	3.1	12.4
92-93	IND	35	.459	.728	3.3	4.1	10.1
Totals		102	.487	.727	3.3	3.4	11.3

ANTHONY BEANE

School: Kansas St.
Year: Senior
Position: Guard
Height: 5'10" **Weight:** 170
Birthdate: February 7, 1972
Birthplace: Dexter, MO

PLAYER SUMMARY	
Will	fly past defenders
Can't	block shots
Expect	clutch playmaking
Don't Expect	bushels of points

Background: This point guard led Three Rivers (Missouri) J.C. to the 1992 national juco championship, clinching the title with a 3-pointer. That penchant for nailing big shots followed him to KSU, where he beat Iowa State and Cal.-Santa Barbara with shots and made numerous other large plays at crunch time.

Strengths: The unquestioned on-court leader for KSU, Beane is extremely quick. He led the Wildcats in assists and became known as "Federal Express" for delivering in the clutch. Beane has the courage to attack the basket and lives by an intense work ethic.

Weaknesses: Beane is not a great pure shooter. He shies away from taking medium-range jumpers in favor of setting up teammates. At the defensive end, he hustles but lacks the physique to handle powerful guards.

Analysis: Coach Dana Altman is blessed to have a gritty leader like Beane, and he knows it. This guy is a superb floor general who loves the lonely moments. He'll make KSU a major factor in the Big Eight and should garner a few more headlines for himself in the process.

COLLEGE STATISTICS

	G	FGP	FTP	RPG	APG	PPG
92-93	KSU	30	.412	.714	2.9	4.6	10.1
Totals		30	.412	.714	2.9	4.6	10.1

TRAVIS BEST

School: Georgia Tech
Year: Junior
Position: Guard
Height: 5'11" **Weight:** 180
Birthdate: July 12, 1972
Birthplace: Springfield, MA

PLAYER SUMMARY	
Will	direct traffic
Can't	be ignored on perimeter
Expect	terrific defense
Don't Expect	much rest

Background: Best led Central High School in Springfield to a 69-4 mark in three years and once scored 81 points in a game. A first-team *Parade* All-American, he chose Georgia Tech over Connecticut, Virginia, and Kentucky. Bobby Cremins handed him Tech's offense to run as a freshman and Best has been in charge ever since.

Strengths: By trade a shooting guard, Best has admirably learned how to handle a college offense. He is an excellent long-range bomber and also has the quickness to take it to the goal. A large pair of hands makes him a fine passer and ball-handler. His one-on-one defensive skills are excellent.

Weaknesses: Cremins rarely removes Best from the game, and the burden sometimes shows in the form of turnovers and poor choices in the latter stages of the second half. He needs to fight through screens better on defense.

Analysis: Best has quietly emerged as one of the fine point guards in the ACC. He has immense offensive talent and has slowly added the intangibles that define quality point-guard play. Best will contribute heavily at both ends of the floor for a team that should be a constant in the top 25.

COLLEGE STATISTICS

	G	FGP	FTP	RPG	APG	PPG
91-92	GT	35	.449	.735	2.5	5.7	12.3
92-93	GT	30	.472	.752	3.1	5.9	16.3
Totals		65	.461	.744	2.8	5.8	14.1

BERNARD BLUNT

School: St. Joseph's
Year: Senior
Position: Guard
Height: 6'3" **Weight:** 210
Birthdate: November 21, 1971
Birthplace: Syracuse, NY

PLAYER SUMMARY	
Will	shoot early and often
Can't	force turnovers
Expect	lots of points
Don't Expect	intense defense

Background: At Jamesville-DeWitt High School, Blunt became the third-leading scorer in New York State history. He moved immediately into the lineup for the Hawks and was named a first-team Freshman All-American by *Basketball Times*. He was a first-team Atlantic 10 choice last year and is on track to become the all-time leading scorer at St. Joseph's.

Strengths: In a word, Blunt is a scorer. Even though he is not a pure shooter, he finds ways to get to the goal and finish in traffic. Blunt uses his size to overpower smaller defenders. Bigger foes must cope with his explosiveness.

Weaknesses: Not the most intense defender, Blunt tends to let his concentration wander on nights when his offense isn't in high gear. He has also been guilty of trying to do too much on occasion.

Analysis: Blunt possesses a skill that NBA general managers will tell you can't be taught—the ability to create a shot and score. That talent has served him well on the collegiate level and, if he can upgrade the rest of his game, he may have a future in the pro ranks.

COLLEGE STATISTICS

	G	FGP	FTP	RPG	APG	PPG
90-91	STJ	30	.418	.708	6.5	2.6	18.8
91-92	STJ	28	.452	.685	7.0	3.1	19.7
92-93	STJ	29	.371	.725	5.7	2.1	18.0
Totals		87	.413	.706	6.4	2.6	18.8

MELVIN BOOKER

School: Missouri
Year: Senior
Position: Guard
Height: 6'1" **Weight:** 176
Birthdate: August 20, 1972
Birthplace: Moss Point, MS

PLAYER SUMMARY	
Will	steal the ball
Can't	grab offensive rebounds
Expect	an All-Big Eight pick
Don't Expect	bad passes

Background: Despite an excellent high school career in Mississippi, Booker was not listed among the nation's top prep point guards. At Missouri, he has started since his sophomore season. Last year, he led the Big Eight in minutes and was named first-team all-conference.

Strengths: The cornerstone of Missouri's offense, Booker sees to it that the proper people get the ball where they can score. A superb ball-handler, he is comfortable in either an open- or halfcourt setting. He has proven to be a clutch free throw shooter.

Weaknesses: As 1992-93 wore on, Booker's heavy workload took a toll. This was reflected in a shooting percentage that, after early improvement, slipped. During a seven-game losing streak, Booker shot only 34 percent.

Analysis: After Anthony Peeler left, many expected the Tigers to struggle. That they reached the NCAA Tournament with a great finish is a credit to this man, who kept Mizzou under control at all times and added to his point production. If Booker gets enough rest, he'll lead Mizzou back to the Big Dance.

COLLEGE STATISTICS

		G	FGP	FTP	RPG	APG	PPG
90-91	MO	30	.434	.671	2.2	3.5	8.3
91-92	MO	30	.475	.768	3.8	3.9	11.6
92-93	MO	33	.439	.817	4.3	3.7	15.8
Totals		93	.449	.772	3.5	3.7	12.0

DONNIE BOYCE

School: Colorado
Year: Junior
Position: Guard/Forward
Height: 6'5" **Weight:** 195
Birthdate: September 2, 1973
Birthplace: Chicago, IL

PLAYER SUMMARY	
Will	score reliably
Can't	allow defense to suffer
Expect	All-Big Eight votes
Don't Expect	much notoriety

Background: A force at Chicago's Proviso East High School, Boyce wasted no time making an impact at the collegiate level. He was a fifth-team All-American selection by *Basketball Weekly* and led the Buffaloes in scoring. As a sophomore, he was a member of the first-team All-Big Eight squad.

Strengths: Isiah Thomas once noted the difficulty in shooting the basketball as a youngster in the Windy City, and so it is that many of Chicago's products are scorers, not pure shooters. Boyce fits that profile to a "T." He is athletic and unselfish and has no qualms about handling the basketball in tense moments.

Weaknesses: The Buffaloes didn't always defend well in 1992-93 and Boyce had a hand in that. Also, improvement at the free throw line would probably add several points to his scoring average.

Analysis: The Buffaloes were the only Big Eight team not to receive a postseason invitation last year. Until that is changed, Boyce will remain something of an afterthought on the national scene. However, he is a quality player—one who can score with the best the Big Eight has to offer.

COLLEGE STATISTICS

		G	FGP	FTP	RPG	APG	PPG
91-92	COLO	28	.419	.564	4.8	3.1	14.9
92-93	COLO	26	.481	.639	6.2	3.6	19.1
Totals		54	.449	.610	5.5	3.4	16.9

JAMIE BRANDON

School: Louisiana St.
Year: Senior
Position: Guard/Forward
Height: 6'4" **Weight:** 205
Birthdate: April 28, 1971
Birthplace: Chicago, IL

PLAYER SUMMARY	
Will	slash to the basket
Can't	let effort wane
Expect	more consistency
Don't Expect	great ball skills

Background: As a senior at Martin Luther King High School in Chicago, Brandon was named Illinois' Mr. Basketball. He initially committed to Illinois but wound up at LSU, where he was forced to sit out his freshman season because of academic reasons. Inconsistency marred both his sophomore and junior seasons.

Strengths: A natural scoring guard, Brandon has spent much of his career at LSU out of position at point guard. Midway through the 1992-93 campaign, however, he found his niche as part of Dale Brown's three-guard offense. This system allows him to create shots off the dribble. He also has excellent strength for his size and can finish plays.

Weaknesses: Brandon has been woefully inconsistent. At times, he's been in the doghouse; at other times, he's looked unstoppable. He's not a great defender.

Analysis: No one questions his gift for taking the ball to the basket or draining a jumper with a defender draped upon him. Maturity has been the issue, and in the latter stages of last season, Brandon looked to have made the adjustment. If that holds true, he'll be a scoring force.

COLLEGE STATISTICS

		G	FGP	FTP	RPG	APG	PPG
91-92	LSU	29	.454	.733	2.5	3.6	10.5
92-93	LSU	26	.487	.697	4.9	1.2	11.8
Totals		55	.470	.715	3.6	2.4	11.1

JOEY BROWN

School: Georgetown
Year: Senior
Position: Guard
Height: 5'10" **Weight:** 180
Birthplace: Morgan City, LA

PLAYER SUMMARY	
Will	defend tenaciously
Can't	shoot pure jumpers
Expect	savvy leadership
Don't Expect	him to back down

Background: Brown, one of many Georgetown recruits from Louisiana, took over the reins of the Hoya offense as a freshman and didn't disappoint. In the years since, he has developed into the undeniable Hoya captain. He was second in the Big East in both steals and assists last winter.

Strengths: There are few guards in the country more adept at stopping the basketball than this senior. Brown is not afraid of contact, and he has the strength and the quickness to impede a foe's progress. Offensively, he's the Hoyas' unquestioned floor general.

Weaknesses: Brown's at his best driving to the basket, but because defenders don't respect his shaky jump shot, they lay off. That puts more pressure on the Hoyas' interior players.

Analysis: Brown is a favorite of John Thompson's, an understandable development given Joey's work ethic and mental toughness. Although he doesn't have the flash others bring to the proceedings, this veteran is a blue-collar leader who understands the game. He'll push himself and the Hoyas back into NCAA Tournament play.

COLLEGE STATISTICS

		G	FGP	FTP	RPG	APG	PPG
90-91	GEOR	32	.350	.721	4.2	3.6	9.1
91-92	GEOR	31	.351	.807	4.1	5.4	9.9
92-93	GEOR	32	.416	.750	4.1	6.2	10.7
Totals		95	.373	.763	4.1	5.1	9.9

JUNIOR BURROUGH

School: Virginia
Year: Junior
Position: Forward
Height: 6'8" **Weight:** 235
Birthdate: January 18, 1973
Birthplace: Charlotte, NC

PLAYER SUMMARY	
Will	take it to the goal
Can't	pass very well
Expect	continued improvement
Don't Expect	flashy play

Background: As a senior at the prestigious Oak Hill Academy, Burrough emerged as one of the nation's top power forwards. As a freshman at Virginia, he averaged 30 minutes a game. Last year, he was the go-to guy as the Cavaliers advanced to the Sweet 16 of the NCAA Tournament.

Strengths: Burrough has never shied away from contact and is excellent in the painted area. He catches the ball well and takes it to the goal with force. He improved both as a rebounder and a passer in 1993. At the defensive end, Burrough uses his bulk to force opponents out of position.

Weaknesses: Like many big men, Burrough still must upgrade his passing game from the low post—especially since he's often double-teamed. Also, he sometimes allows his concentration to ebb on defense.

Analysis: After making strides in 1992-93, Burrough is prepared to take another step forward, this time toward national prominence. He's not flashy and doesn't have the size to overwhelm people, but he is explosive around the goal and isn't afraid to use his strength. Look for him to continue his steady progression.

COLLEGE STATISTICS

	G	FGP	FTP	RPG	APG	PPG
91-92	VA	33	.446	.695	5.8	0.2	13.2
92-93	VA	31	.438	.638	7.2	0.6	14.6
Totals		64	.442	.667	6.5	0.4	13.9

RANDOLPH CHILDRESS

School: Wake Forest
Year: Junior
Position: Guard
Height: 6'2" **Weight:** 175
Birthdate: September 21, 1972
Birthplace: Clinton, MD

PLAYER SUMMARY	
Will	score in bunches
Can't	thrive inside
Expect	20 PPG
Don't Expect	many rebounds

Background: One of the top point guards in the nation at Flint Hill High School, Childress excelled as a Wake Forest freshman in the role of sixth man. His 1991-92 campaign was wiped out by a torn anterior cruciate ligament, but he returned last year and averaged 19.7 PPG.

Strengths: It is no coincidence that Wake Forest underachieved during the season in which Childress was injured. That it rose to national prominence last year upon his return underscores Childress's talent. He is a natural leader who can shoot the 3-point shot or score in transition.

Weaknesses: Major knee surgery often can create both mental and physical hurdles, and Childress enured both. He has lost some mobility but he didn't shy away from contact and appeared more comfortable as 1992-93 progressed.

Analysis: Many experts believe it takes two years to fully recover from a traumatic injury like the one Childress suffered. If that's so, then Childress appears headed toward a banner campaign. He's a gifted shooter who's also a proven winner. This season, watch for him to play a larger role now that Rodney Rogers is gone.

COLLEGE STATISTICS

	G	FGP	FTP	RPG	APG	PPG
90-91	WF	29	.449	.772	2.1	2.2	14.0
92-93	WF	30	.484	.810	2.8	4.2	19.7
Totals		59	.469	.794	2.5	3.2	16.9

CHARLES CLAXTON

School: Georgia
Year: Junior
Position: Center
Height: 7'0" **Weight:** 265
Birthdate: December 13, 1970
Birthplace: St. Thomas, Virgin Islands

PLAYER SUMMARY	
Will	discourage lane drives
Can't	be pushed around
Expect	more consistency
Don't Expect	high FT pct.

Background: The native of St. Thomas spent his prep career at Miami Carol City High School, where he averaged 18 points and 11 rebounds as a senior. He enrolled at Georgia and hit the weight room during a redshirt year. He was on the SEC's All-Freshman team in 1992 and added several points to his scoring average last year.

Strengths: Very agile for a man his size, Claxton has a fine shooting touch around the basket. He is a presence at the defensive end, blocking shots and altering many more. Contact does not offend him and he plays particularly well against prime-time competition.

Weaknesses: The adjective that best describes Claxton is "raw." One night he looks like a superstar; the next night he's barely visible. He often commits ill-advised fouls, and his free throw shooting is far below par.

Analysis: A preseason first-team All-SEC choice last year, Claxton didn't quite live up to that billing. There were many flashes of brilliance but there were also "off" nights. Claxton, though, is a gifted performer. With more experience, he should become a huge factor for the Bulldogs.

COLLEGE STATISTICS

	G	FGP	FTP	RPG	APG	PPG
91-92 GEOR	29	.524	.532	6.6	0.3	9.4
92-93 GEOR	29	.564	.482	6.6	0.4	11.5
Totals	58	.545	.506	6.6	0.3	10.5

JEVON CRUDUP

School: Missouri
Year: Senior
Position: Forward
Height: 6'9" **Weight:** 240
Birthdate: April 27, 1972
Birthplace: Kansas City, MO

PLAYER SUMMARY	
Will	clean the glass
Can't	sink his FTs
Expect	high-percentage shots
Don't Expect	fancy passing

Background: The Missouri Player of the Year as a senior, Crudup sparked Raytown South High School to the state championship. As a college freshman, he tutored at the knee of Tiger star Doug Smith and made progress, despite missing 15 games due to injury. He has led Mizzou in rebounding in each of the last two seasons.

Strengths: An impressive physique allows Crudup to thrive in the paint. He is tenacious and pursues the ball well off the glass. He is on target to finish as one of the top ten rebounders in school history. On defense, he can leave his own man to block a shot.

Weaknesses: Crudup barely crept past the 50 percent mark from the free throw line last winter and that probably cost him two to three points a game. Passing is not his forte, and too often he is careless with the basketball.

Analysis: Many thought Crudup would blossom into a star last year, but that never really happened. Poor free throw shooting played a role. He shot 68 percent from the line two years ago, so the ability is there. With that aspect of his game in gear, Crudup would be a major force on the plains.

COLLEGE STATISTICS

	G	FGP	FTP	RPG	APG	PPG
90-91 MO	15	.526	.571	7.1	1.3	12.0
91-92 MO	30	.507	.676	8.2	1.8	15.3
92-93 MO	33	.501	.504	8.3	1.2	13.6
Totals	78	.508	.589	8.0	1.4	14.0

BILL CURLEY

School: Boston College
Year: Senior
Position: Forward/Center
Height: 6'9" **Weight:** 220
Birthdate: May 29, 1972
Birthplace: Boston, MA

PLAYER SUMMARY	
Will	score in the paint
Can't	shoot the 3
Expect	a strange-looking shot
Don't Expect	great strength

Background: Curley was Massachusetts' top prep player as a senior at Duxbury High School, and the raves continued when he reached Chestnut Hill. As a freshman, he was named Big East Rookie of the Year. Last year, he made that league's first-team squad.

Strengths: Long and lanky, Curley has a variety of unorthodox post moves and fakes that make defending him difficult. He displays a soft touch and is effective shooting the ball facing the basket. He has a quirky-looking shot, but it usually falls.

Weaknesses: Curley's body is not the stuff of your typical power forward. He's rather thin and he can't match muscle with some of the classic low-post threats. Yet Curley does have a big heart, and that helps overcome some of those shortcomings.

Analysis: Curley grew up watching Larry Bird, and there are some similarities in their styles. This Bostonian can't shoot like Bird could from the perimeter, but he displays the same heart and toughness. Curley is poised to lead B.C. to the Big Dance in his farewell campaign.

COLLEGE STATISTICS

		G	FGP	FTP	RPG	APG	PPG
90-91	BOST	30	.542	.691	6.9	1.3	12.6
91-92	BOST	31	.577	.774	8.1	0.9	17.8
92-93	BOST	31	.580	.849	7.6	1.2	15.8
Totals		92	.568	.774	7.5	1.1	15.4

YINKA DARE

School: George Washington
Year: Sophomore
Position: Center
Height: 7'1". **Weight:** 265
Birthdate: October 10, 1972
Birthplace: Kabba, Nigeria

PLAYER SUMMARY	
Will	dominate inside
Can't	shoot the 3
Expect	terrific shot-blocking
Don't Expect	polish—yet

Background: Dare played for the Nigeria national team before emigrating to the U.S. He prepped at Milford Academy in Connecticut for a year, where asthma limited him to three minutes of action at a time. Medication remedied the situation and Dare became a *Basketball Times* first-team Freshman All-American.

Strengths: Dare possesses great size, strength, and raw skills. His frame conjures up images of Shaquille O'Neal, and he's a diligent worker who improved steadily throughout his freshman season. An excellent athlete, Dare can run the floor and swat away shots.

Weaknesses: A latecomer to the game, Dare has yet to master the intricacies of low-post offense. His lack of experience occasionally gets him into foul trouble. He must understand when to go for the block and when to back off.

Analysis: Don't let Dare's zero-point performance against Michigan in the NCAA Tournament fool you. This youngster might be the nation's next great pivot. He overpowers people inside and, as he learns the subtle tricks of the interior trade, his scoring will increase. He could someday be the No. 1 pick in the NBA draft.

COLLEGE STATISTICS

		G	FGP	FTP	RPG	APG	PPG
92-93	GW	30	.551	.473	10.3	0.1	12.2
Totals		30	.551	.473	10.3	0.1	12.2

TYUS EDNEY

School: UCLA
Year: Junior
Position: Guard
Height: 5'10" **Weight:** 145
Birthdate: February 14, 1973
Birthplace: Gardena, CA

PLAYER SUMMARY	
Will	create open shots
Can't	outmuscle anyone
Expect	an All-Pac-10 year
Don't Expect	foolish shots

Background: Edney, from Long Beach Poly High School, unseated four-year starter Darrick Martin as UCLA's starting point guard late in his freshman campaign. He earned third-team Freshman All-America kudos from *Basketball Weekly*, and last year he garnered first-team All-Pac-10 honors.

Strengths: Few players in the nation can match Edney's quickness and court vision. Yet unlike many speedy guards, Tyus is seldom out of control. He is adept at finding his mates with passes after drawing defenders to him. He can also finish drives to the basket and is a competent perimeter shooter.

Weaknesses: Edney's lack of size can create trouble for him at the defensive end, as taller guards can post him. He must rely on anticipation and quickness. Fullcourt traps can impair his vision too.

Analysis: Though much has been made of Jason Kidd as the heir to Bobby Hurley's point-guard pedestal, do not overlook this man's point-guard qualifications. His incredible quickness causes foes (whom last year included Hurley) fits. Edney's national profile should expand greatly in 1993-94.

COLLEGE STATISTICS

	G	FGP	FTP	RPG	APG	PPG
91-92 UCLA	32	.472	.797	2.1	2.8	5.6
92-93 UCLA	33	.483	.841	3.5	5.6	13.6
Totals	65	.480	.829	2.8	4.2	9.7

DAVID EDWARDS

School: Texas A&M
Year: Senior
Position: Guard
Height: 5'10" **Weight:** 170
Birthdate: December 2, 1971
Birthplace: Richmond, VA

PLAYER SUMMARY	
Will	play strong defense
Can't	turn program around
Expect	first-team All-SWC
Don't Expect	3-point accuracy

Background: As a senior at New York's Andrew Jackson High School, Edwards averaged 41 PPG. He selected Georgetown, where he played regularly as a freshman and helped the Hoyas to a 24-7 record. In 1990-91, he sat out after transferring to Texas A&M. He has been the Aggies' starting lead guard ever since.

Strengths: Toughness is an attribute John Thompson covets at Georgetown, and this former Hoya fits the mold. Edwards is asked to carry a heavy load for a program attempting to rebuild. He is an excellent defensive player and can score on slashes to the basket.

Weaknesses: Edwards is not a dead-eye jump-shooter. He is at his best in the open floor, and defenses can lay off him on the perimeter in the halfcourt. Edwards is not especially good at setting up his teammates.

Analysis: Edwards is one of the best defensive guards in the nation, but much of his work now goes unnoticed because of a weak supporting cast. His pressure on the basketball is superb, and his quick hands force turnovers. He should be one of the SWC's premier players this year.

COLLEGE STATISTICS

	G	FGP	FTP	RPG	APG	PPG
89-90 GEOR	31	.353	.675	2.3	4.8	5.4
91-92 TA&M	28	.391	.752	4.0	5.7	13.8
92-93 TA&M	27	.372	.677	5.1	6.6	13.3
Totals	86	.376	.703	3.8	5.7	10.6

STEVE EDWARDS

School: Miami (FL)
Year: Sophomore
Position: Guard
Height: 6'6" **Weight:** 195
Birthdate: March 1, 1973
Birthplace: Miami, FL

PLAYER SUMMARY	
Will	pile up the points
Can't	avoid turnovers
Expect	impressive dunks
Don't Expect	safe play

Background: Three years younger than his brother, former Florida State All-American Doug Edwards, this youngster chose to become Leonard Hamilton's pioneer recruit. An honorable-mention prep All-American by *Basketball Times,* Edwards emerged as a force in his debut season, leading the Hurricanes in scoring.

Strengths: A map to the hoop has never been necessary for this young player. Edwards uses an array of fakes and excellent athletic skills to take his man off the dribble. He is especially effective in the open court, where he can finish plays with thunderclap dunks. Edwards can even man the point if asked.

Weaknesses: At times, Edwards's desire to make a big play leads to turnovers. He needs to value the basketball more and be careful about taking too many risks, despite the fact that he averaged 2.1 SPG last year.

Analysis: Doug Edwards was one of the nation's top players as a senior and there's no reason his younger sibling can't follow in those footsteps. Steve is a fine perimeter shooter who'll take it to the hole as well. Look for him to challenge for the Big East scoring championship.

COLLEGE STATISTICS

	G	FGP	FTP	RPG	APG	PPG
92-93 MIA	27	.418	.693	3.4	3.9	15.9
Totals	27	.418	.693	3.4	3.9	15.9

HOWARD EISLEY

School: Boston College
Year: Senior
Position: Guard
Height: 6'3" **Weight:** 180
Birthdate: December 4, 1972
Birthplace: Detroit, MI

PLAYER SUMMARY	
Will	make smart decisions
Can't	get much rest
Expect	3-point accuracy
Don't Expect	showmanship

Background: Long respected for his leadership skills, Eisley captained the 1989-90 Detroit Southwestern High School squad that was ranked second nationally by *USA Today.* He has started every game that he's played at B.C. and was second in the conference in free throw shooting last year.

Strengths: A quiet sort, Eisley boasts none of the flash that high school mate Jalen Rose does. However, he is an excellent long-range shooter who has learned how to use screens to free himself for jumpers. He is also an able penetrator and willing defender.

Weaknesses: Though a competent passer, Eisley lacks creativity. That keeps turnovers down but fails to provide the kind of show-stopping dunk that can really turn the crowd on. Eisley also has a heavy workload and might benefit from fewer minutes.

Analysis: Few outside Boston appreciate Eisley's gifts. That's because A) B.C. hasn't been to the NCAA Tournament in his career and B) he doesn't draw attention to himself. Eisley, though, is an excellent floor leader who forces opponents to acknowledge his superb long-range shooting skills.

COLLEGE STATISTICS

	G	FGP	FTP	RPG	APG	PPG
90-91 BOST	30	.360	.750	2.6	3.3	9.9
91-92 BOST	31	.488	.746	3.6	4.4	11.6
92-93 BOST	31	.443	.834	3.5	4.9	13.7
Totals	92	.429	.782	3.2	4.2	11.8

MICHAEL FINLEY

School: Wisconsin
Year: Junior
Position: Forward/Guard
Height: 6'7" **Weight:** 167
Birthdate: March 6, 1973
Birthplace: Melrose Park, IL

PLAYER SUMMARY	
Will ....flourish in open floor
Can't...................overpower people
Expect.......continued development
Don't Expect.........more anonymity

Background: This lithe swing man enjoyed a fine schoolboy career at Proviso East High School in the Chicago area, playing alongside future Colorado star Donnie Boyce. He started all but three games as a freshmen with the Badgers and was a major factor as a sophomore, earning a first-team All-Big Ten nod.

Strengths: While people focused their attention on teammate Tracy Webster, it was Finley who stepped forward. Michael is a fine rebounder who can handle the basketball when necessary. He'll shoot the 3 or knife to the goal to score. He's also a willing passer.

Weaknesses: Upper-body strength is the only item Finley lacks. His ball-handling is adequate for a small forward but it could use improvement if he is to spend the majority of his minutes at off guard, where quick-handed thieves might pose problems.

Analysis: A smooth athlete, Finley plays with grace and skill. Though somewhat unheralded, he has gradually emerged as one of the Big Ten's finest players. He'll likely keep NBA scouts glued to press row at the Wisconsin Fieldhouse over the next two seasons.

COLLEGE STATISTICS

	G	FGP	FTP	RPG	APG	PPG
91-92 WISC	31	.453	.742	4.9	2.7	12.3
92-93 WISC	28	.467	.771	5.8	3.1	22.1
Totals	59	.461	.757	5.3	2.9	17.0

TRAVIS FORD

School: Kentucky
Year: Senior
Position: Guard
Height: 5'9" **Weight:** 160
Birthdate: December 29, 1969
Birthplace: Murray, KY

PLAYER SUMMARY	
Will...........................nail the trifecta
Can't ....win many footraces
Expect ....sound leadership
Don't Expect ....turnovers

Background: A first-team all-state performer in high school, Ford enrolled at Missouri and was chosen to UPI's Big Eight All-Freshman team. He transferred to Kentucky the following year and was slowed by a broken left kneecap in 1991-92. He gained a starting spot last season.

Strengths: That John Stockton is Ford's favorite player is not a shock. Like Stockton, Ford has an excellent feel for the game. His passes are sharp and he understands when to push the ball up the floor and when to wait for assistance. Defenders must stay close because he is a superb 3-point shooter.

Weaknesses: Though determined, Ford is limited defensively by his size. Larger guards can post him up and smaller ones can use their quickness to accelerate past him.

Analysis: In terms of athletic gifts, Ford is not a great one. But he is an excellent fundamental player with a dead-eye jumper and the guts to take it. He also beats people off the dribble in spite of his lack of foot speed. A shrewd senior, Ford should be the heart of the 1993-94 'Cats and one of the SEC's best players.

COLLEGE STATISTICS

	G	FGP	FTP	RPG	APG	PPG
89-90 MO	30	.394	.896	1.8	3.5	6.4
91-92 KEN	33	.350	.800	1.1	2.1	3.5
92-93 KEN	34	.527	.881	2.1	4.9	13.6
Totals	97	.457	.871	1.6	3.5	7.9

JAMES FORREST

School: Georgia Tech
Year: Junior
Position: Forward
Height: 6'8" **Weight:** 240
Birthdate: August 13, 1972
Birthplace: Macon, GA

PLAYER SUMMARY	
Will	crash the boards
Can't	bury multiple 3's
Expect	All-ACC honors
Don't Expect	many blocks

Background: Forrest graduated from Southside High School, where he was one of the most decorated prep athletes in Atlanta history. Bobby Cremins placed him in the lineup immediately. After learning to adjust to small forward, Forrest became a first-team Freshman All-America selection of *Basketball Weekly*.

Strengths: This man possesses a rare blend of power and finesse. His chiseled frame allows him to punish the opposition inside, while a soft shooting touch permits him to drain medium-range jumpers. He's quick and extremely athletic.

Weaknesses: Forrest carried excess weight early in his career, causing his perimeter defense to suffer. He has slimmed down, though, and that has made him more effective. Forrest is not much of a shot-blocker.

Analysis: Forrest was left off the All-ACC team last season, which turned out to be a major oversight. After the regular season, he became a virtually unguardable force and led Tech to the ACC title—in the process handing North Carolina its final loss of the campaign. A gutty performer who has hit huge shots in his career, Forrest appears ready to emerge as an All-American.

COLLEGE STATISTICS

	G	FGP	FTP	RPG	APG	PPG
91-92 GT	35	.509	.708	6.4	1.8	13.3
92-93 GT	30	.542	.687	7.5	1.4	19.5
Totals	65	.527	.696	6.9	1.6	16.2

LAWRENCE FUNDERBURKE

School: Ohio St.
Year: Senior
Position: Forward
Height: 6'9" **Weight:** 225
Birthdate: December 15, 1970
Birthplace: Columbus, OH

PLAYER SUMMARY	
Will	create interior offense
Can't	find consistency
Expect	better patience
Don't Expect	a one-man show

Background: Funderburke signed on with Indiana after a stellar career at Columbus' Wehrle High School, saying he needed the discipline. However, Funderburke lasted only one semester before seeking a transfer. He enrolled at OSU, where he has become an impact performer.

Strengths: Funderburke is a muscular type with good touch around the basket. When he receives the ball in the paint, he explodes to the goal. This fine athlete runs the floor well and can connect on medium-range jump shots.

Weaknesses: Funderburke was inconsistent last year, although his teammates could be blamed for some of his failings. The Buckeyes were very young and he faced constant double- and triple-teaming. As a result, he often forced scoring chances that weren't there.

Analysis: Last year was tough for Funderburke, as he was forced to shoulder too heavy of a burden. Toward the end of the season, however, young players like Greg Simpson and Derek Anderson came on. If they take some heat off Funderburke, he'll be an All-Big Ten choice.

COLLEGE STATISTICS

	G	FGP	FTP	RPG	APG	PPG
89-90 IND	6	.491	.519	6.7	1.3	11.7
91-92 OSU	23	.548	.654	6.2	0.8	12.2
92-93 OSU	28	.533	.622	6.8	1.2	16.3
Totals	57	.534	.621	6.6	1.1	14.2

BRIAN GRANT

School: Xavier
Year: Senior
Position: Forward/Center
Height: 6'8" **Weight:** 245
Birthdate: March 5, 1972
Birthplace: Columbus, OH

PLAYER SUMMARY	
Will	attack the glass
Can't	leap through the roof
Expect	MCC's top player
Don't Expect	lazy play

Background: Grant grew three inches as a senior at Georgetown (Ohio) High School, giving him the size to operate on the interior in college. Grant became an instant factor at Xavier, earning second-team All-MCC honors as a freshman and sophomore. In 1992-93, he was that league's Player of the Year.

Strengths: Superior rebounding generally reflects a strong work ethic, and Grant has that in abundance. Along with good size and strength, he has a nose for the basketball. He receives the ball well on offense and features a strong low-post game. He rarely takes bad shots.

Weaknesses: Grant's game is restricted to the shadow of the basket. To move to the next level, he will have to extend the range on his face-up jumper.

Analysis: Coach Pete Gillen has a history of developing under-recruited big men, and Grant is the latest. He's more polished offensively than former X.U. standout Tyrone Hill was at this stage. A third-team All-American nod is not out of the question, as Grant will be the centerpiece of another strong Xavier squad.

COLLEGE STATISTICS

	G	FGP	FTP	RPG	APG	PPG
90-91 XAV	32	.572	.694	8.5	0.6	11.6
91-92 XAV	26	.576	.583	9.1	0.9	11.8
92-93 XAV	30	.654	.692	9.4	1.5	18.5
Totals	88	.609	.660	9.0	1.0	14.0

RASHARD GRIFFITH

School: Wisconsin
Year: Freshman
Position: Center
Height: 7'1" **Weight:** 265
Birthdate: October 8, 1974
Birthplace: Chicago, IL

PLAYER SUMMARY	
Will	flex his muscles
Can't	miss as a future star
Expect	sudden impact
Don't Expect	outside scoring

Background: The latest in a long line of prep stars at Martin Luther King High School, Griffith was encouraged by his mother, Elaine, to play basketball to keep out of harm's way. As a junior, Griffith was an all-state selection. He closed his career by leading King to a state championship and the No. 2 ranking in the United States.

Strengths: Griffith has an NBA body right now. It's naturally strong and he isn't reluctant to take advantage of that frame. Once he catches the ball in the key, there's not much a single defender can do to impede him. He doesn't force shots and can pass out of the post. At the defensive end, he challenges shots and boxes out well beneath the backboards.

Weaknesses: Stamina could be an early problem because Griffith got plenty of rest for a King team that boasted another giant, Thomas Hamilton, in its lineup. Earlier this year, Griffith was fighting to attain the proper test score to attain freshman eligibility.

Analysis: If this youngster had been available in the 1993 NBA draft, he would have been a lottery pick. Griffith is a classic low-post center who possesses some fine interior moves. There's room for improvement, of course, but the bottom line is that he will make Wisconsin a top-25 threat the first night he steps onto the court.

OTHELLA HARRINGTON

School: Georgetown
Year: Sophomore
Position: Center
Height: 6'10" **Weight:** 236
Birthplace: Jackson, MS

PLAYER SUMMARY	
Will	score inside
Can't	be stopped by one man
Expect	lots of rebounds
Don't Expect	bad shots

Background: Harrington was the most coveted prep prospect in the country as a senior at Murrah (Mississippi) High School. An immediate starter last year, Harrington was fourth in the Big East in scoring and second in rebounding—totals that earned him Freshman of the Year honors from *Basketball Times*.

Strengths: Few possess the knack for rebounding that Harrington has. He's tireless on the glass and is a willing worker on defense. On offense, he is blessed with a soft shooting touch and a fine turnaround post jumper. He's also a willing passer.

Weaknesses: Occasionally too unselfish, Harrington needs to better grasp when to kick the ball back out and when to take it strong to the basket. Though blessed with more offensive skills than some of his Hoya post predecessors, he is not the shot-blocking presence Ewing, Mutombo, or Mourning were.

Analysis: Opposing defenses learned early last year that Harrington demands attention. He's a legitimate preseason All-American choice this year and, if he receives a little more help from his friends entrusted with shooting perimeter jumpers, the possibilities are endless.

COLLEGE STATISTICS

	G	FGP	FTP	RPG	APG	PPG
92-93 GEOR	33	.573	.746	8.8	1.0	16.8
Totals	33	.573	.746	8.8	1.0	16.8

ALAN HENDERSON

School: Indiana
Year: Junior
Position: Forward
Height: 6'9" **Weight:** 214
Birthdate: December 12, 1972
Birthplace: Carmel, IN

PLAYER SUMMARY	
Will	explode to the hoop
Can't	seem to bulk up
Expect	points, rebounds
Don't Expect	bad grades

Background: As a high school senior, Henderson challenged Glenn Robinson for Mr. Basketball honors in the state of Indiana. After joining the Hoosiers, he was named third-team Freshman All-American by *Basketball Weekly*. Henderson enjoyed a superb campaign last year until succumbing to a knee injury.

Strengths: In the transition game, few power forwards are more explosive than this guy. He also displays a wonderfully soft touch and is an eager rebounder. Henderson is a terrific student and a heady player.

Weaknesses: Despite attempts to bulk up, Henderson is not as muscular as he could be. There are some stars who can move him around inside. A dose of assertiveness wouldn't hurt, and no one knows how much psychological damage the knee injury has caused.

Analysis: The consensus was that Henderson's injury kept the Hoosiers from reaching the Final Four. Assuming the prognosis on the knee remains good, Henderson should replace Calbert Cheaney as the Hoosiers' main man. He is a superb offensive talent, and coach Bob Knight is likely to turn him loose offensively.

COLLEGE STATISTICS

	G	FGP	FTP	RPG	APG	PPG
91-92 IND	33	.508	.661	7.2	0.5	11.6
92-93 IND	30	.487	.637	8.1	0.9	11.1
Totals	63	.498	.650	7.6	0.7	11.4

RONNIE HENDERSON

School: Louisiana St.
Year: Freshman
Position: Guard
Height: 6'4" **Weight:** 190
Birthdate: March 29, 1974
Birthplace: Jackson, MS

PLAYER SUMMARY	
Will	shoot the lights out
Can't	assume it'll be easy
Expect	awesome dunks
Don't Expect	boring play

Background: Mississippi has produced several terrific collegians in recent years—including Othella Harrington, Clarence Weatherspoon, and Henderson's cousin Chris Jackson—but experts think Henderson might be the best ever. In his varsity debut at Murrah High School, he scored 36 points and averaged around 30 as a junior. A separated shoulder short-circuited his senior season.

Strengths: First and foremost, Henderson is a superb shooter. His range is extraordinary and he will be an immediate 3-point concern for LSU's foes. He is also blessed with athletic gifts that make him dangerous in the open floor. Finishing drives to the goal is one of his specialties.

Weaknesses: Like most freshmen, Henderson needs to learn the nuances of defense. He also could use a good weight program to improve his upper-body strength and stamina in the wake of an injury-racked senior year at Murrah.

Analysis: This is one of the finest shooters to enter college ball in recent years. Much has been made of Henderson's backcourt partner Randy Livingston (and Livingston is terrific) and the shoulder injury caused some to forget about this newcomer in 1993. But Henderson will remind everyone of his gifts in 1993-94 and will be a viable contender for national freshman-of-the-year honors.

GRANT HILL

School: Duke
Year: Senior
Position: Guard/Forward
Height: 6'8" **Weight:** 225
Birthdate: November 5, 1972
Birthplace: Reston, VA

PLAYER SUMMARY	
Will	take it to the hole
Can't	shoot 3-pointers
Expect	All-America status
Don't Expect	lax defense

Background: Hill earned McDonald's All-America honors as a prep star in suburban Washington, D.C. Grant, the son of former Dallas Cowboy Calvin Hill, helped lead Duke to national titles in his freshman and sophomore years. Last season, he was selected the nation's Defensive Player of the Year by the NABC.

Strengths: NBA scouts love Hill's versatility and tools. He can score facing the basket or in traffic. A quality ball-handler, Hill can—and will—run the Duke offense. His passes are crisp, his vision impressive. He is also an effective rebounder and a noted ball thief at the defensive end.

Weaknesses: In each of the last two seasons, Hill has missed significant action in February with injuries, causing some to doubt his durability. Others think he is too passive at times when Duke needs him to step forward.

Analysis: With Christian Laettner and Bobby Hurley gone, Hill is now the main man. He'll see a great deal of action at point guard. Expect him to thrive. It would be a major shock if he is not one of the first five players selected in the 1994 NBA draft.

COLLEGE STATISTICS

	G	FGP	FTP	RPG	APG	PPG
90-91 DUKE	36	.516	.609	5.1	2.2	11.2
91-92 DUKE	33	.611	.733	5.7	4.1	14.0
92-93 DUKE	26	.578	.746	6.4	2.8	18.0
Totals	95	.568	.695	5.6	3.0	14.0

JUWAN HOWARD

School: Michigan
Year: Junior
Position: Center
Height: 6'9" **Weight:** 242
Birthdate: February 7, 1973
Birthplace: Chicago, IL

PLAYER SUMMARY	
Will	drop in short jumpers
Can't	dribble in transition
Expect	many more headlines
Don't Expect	him to back down

Background: A consensus prep All-American at Chicago's Vocational High School, Howard was the first of the fabled Fab Five to sign with Michigan. He pushed past veteran Eric Riley to start early in his freshman season and helped lead Michigan to its first of two NCAA title games. Last year, he was a *Basketball Times* All-Mideast pick.

Strengths: This pure center is a throwback. He surrenders ground in the post grudgingly and doesn't shy away from contact. Quick feet give him an edge on offense, and he's deadly with his turnaround jumper. He's also an outstanding interior passer. What coach Steve Fisher likes most, though, is his heart.

Weaknesses: Howard's great competitive spirit can occasionally lead to silly fouls, and he sometimes has trouble controlling his temper. Turnovers can occur when he is asked to handle the ball in the open floor.

Analysis: The 1993-94 season looms as Howard's breakout year. The one-time prep All-American will be the Wolverines' prime weapon in the paint—now that Chris Webber is gone—and that means more shot and rebound opportunities. He's an All-American waiting to happen.

COLLEGE STATISTICS

	G	FGP	FTP	RPG	APG	PPG
91-92 MICH	34	.450	.688	6.2	1.8	11.1
92-93 MICH	36	.506	.700	7.4	1.9	14.6
Totals	70	.481	.695	6.8	1.9	12.9

ASKIA JONES

School: Kansas St.
Year: Senior
Position: Guard/Forward
Height: 6'5" **Weight:** 205
Birthdate: December 3, 1971
Birthplace: Philadelphia, PA

PLAYER SUMMARY	
Will	upgrade his shooting
Can't	beat you off the dribble
Expect	3-point bombs
Don't Expect	great defense

Background: Askia, the son of former Philadelphia 76er Wali Jones, was a prep star at San Antonio's Marshall High School, where he averaged 33 PPG. In the KSU record book, he ranks 11th in career scoring, seventh in career assists, and third in career steals and triples.

Strengths: A quality scorer, he can drive to the basket or excel on the perimeter. His size and willingness to work allow him to play a meaningful rebounding role also. He takes excellent care of the basketball, posting KSU's best assist-to-turnover ratio.

Weaknesses: After enjoying a strong sophomore campaign, he struggled with his shot from beyond the 3-point line in 1992-93. Jones also needs to be more consistent on defense.

Analysis: The numbers suggest that Jones had an "off" year in 1992-93, which is true to some degree. But Jones also received more help than he had in the past and some of his contributions weren't measured on the stat sheet. The seasoned veteran sets the tone for KSU and has the skills to improve upon last winter.

COLLEGE STATISTICS

	G	FGP	FTP	RPG	APG	PPG
89-90 KSU	31	.412	.648	2.8	1.5	7.9
91-92 KSU	30	.445	.800	4.3	2.3	15.5
92-93 KSU	30	.417	.750	4.1	2.9	13.2
Totals	91	.426	.746	3.7	2.3	12.1

DANA JONES
School: Pepperdine
Year: Senior
Position: Forward
Height: 6'6" **Weight:** 190
Birthdate: April 16, 1972
Birthplace: Los Angeles, CA

PLAYER SUMMARY	
Will	blow by defenders
Can't	make FTs regularly
Expect	athleticism and hustle
Don't Expect	silly decisions

Background: Though he starred at North Hollywood High School, Jones was not considered more than a local phenomenon. After spurning California, Jones chose Pepperdine. In 1990-91, he was Freshman of the Year in the West Coast Conference, and last winter he became that league's Player of the Year.

Strengths: Early in his career, Jones made his mark on defense. He's an athletic big man with a nose for the ball. Foes must pay particular attention to him on the offensive glass. Jones is also effective taking defenders off the dribble, thanks to explosive quickness.

Weaknesses: Pure perimeter shooting is not Jones's top attribute, although he has upgraded that part of his game significantly. He struggles at the free throw line.

Analysis: After making steady progress, Jones seems poised for a big finish. The senior has a tremendous feel for the game and the tools to make an impact. He's the best player in the WCC and belongs in a category with the other standouts of the region—Ed O'Bannon, Jason Kidd, Tyus Edney, and the rest.

COLLEGE STATISTICS

		G	FGP	FTP	RPG	APG	PPG
90-91	PEPP	30	.578	.532	8.2	2.4	10.0
91-92	PEPP	30	.583	.582	7.1	2.4	11.4
92-93	PEPP	31	.620	.614	9.1	1.4	15.6
Totals		91	.594	.584	8.1	2.0	12.4

EDDIE JONES
School: Temple
Year: Senior
Position: Forward/Guard
Height: 6'6" **Weight:** 175
Birthdate: October 20, 1971
Birthplace: Pompano Beach, FL

PLAYER SUMMARY	
Will	score off the drive
Can't	can his FTs
Expect	smooth moves
Don't Expect	impatience

Background: A product of Ely High School in Florida, Jones averaged 26 points and ten rebounds as a senior. Although an academic casualty as a freshman, he scored in double figures off the bench in 1991-92. Jones started as a junior, helping Temple reach the Final Eight.

Strengths: When people talk about Temple, the conversation usually centers on its slow scoring pace and match-up zone. The implication is that the Owls aren't athletic. Well, Jones disproves that theory. He is extremely quick, is a smooth ball-handler, and would approach 20 PPG in a higher-octane system.

Weaknesses: At his best shooting on the move, Jones is not a great stand-still jumpshooter. That is particularly true at the free throw line, where he often struggles. An upgrade there would be an enormous benefit.

Analysis: Though unheralded, Jones is a marvelous performer. He is a versatile athlete who excels on the wings of coach John Chaney's patient offense. Jones doesn't rush his shots and he lofts few ill-timed attempts. Look for him to be a major factor in the Atlantic 10 in his farewell campaign.

COLLEGE STATISTICS

		G	FGP	FTP	RPG	APG	PPG
91-92	TEMP	29	.437	.547	4.2	1.0	11.5
92-93	TEMP	32	.458	.604	7.0	1.8	17.0
Totals		61	.450	.581	5.7	1.4	14.3

ARTURAS KARNISHOVAS

School: Seton Hall
Year: Senior
Position: Forward
Height: 6'8" **Weight:** 210
Birthdate: April 27, 1971
Birthplace: Vilnius, Lithuania

PLAYER SUMMARY	
Will	connect on treys
Can't	bang inside
Expect	FT accuracy
Don't Expect	hang time

Background: Karnishovas learned basketball in the former Soviet Union and played for that country's junior national team. Fellow Lithuanian Sarunas Marciulionis recommended Karnishovas to Seton Hall coach P.J. Carlesimo. He cracked the lineup immediately. He also played for Lithuania in the '92 Olympics.

Strengths: Like many other foreign players, Karnishovas is a skilled perimeter shooter. He is effective at finding holes in the defense and exploiting them. A very good athlete, Karnishovas is also a quality defender. His combination of size and agility makes it difficult for opposing wing players to shake free from him.

Weaknesses: Karnishovas lacks the strength needed to be effective on the inside. Rebounding is not his domain and he can't elevate to alter many shots.

Analysis: The departed Terry Dehere had been Seton Hall's top scoring threat, so Karnishovas's scoring stats have not been overwhelming. That won't be the case in 1993-94. Arturas will be the go-to guy in the Hall's offense, and he should challenge for a spot on the All-Big East team.

COLLEGE STATISTICS

		G	FGP	FTP	RPG	APG	PPG
90-91	SH	33	.414	.844	4.6	1.2	7.3
91-92	SH	26	.434	.729	4.2	1.2	8.5
92-93	SH	34	.508	.832	6.6	1.7	14.6
Totals		93	.465	.808	5.2	1.4	10.3

DAMON KEY

School: Marquette
Year: Senior
Position: Forward/Center
Height: 6'8" **Weight:** 245
Birthdate: December 17, 1971
Birthplace: Milwaukee, WI

PLAYER SUMMARY	
Will	drop in soft jumpers
Can't	block shots
Expect	a hard worker
Don't Expect	tons of boards

Background: A two-time all-stater in Wisconsin, Key chose to play college ball locally at Marquette. He became the first freshman to lead Marquette in scoring since 1951-52. He again topped the club in scoring as a sophomore, and last year he helped bring Marquette back to the NCAA Tournament after a ten-year absence.

Strengths: With his soft shooting touch, Key can effectively shoot the medium-range jumper. He is particularly capable from the foul line area in a high-post set. Key can also use his powerful frame to create openings for himself in the paint.

Weaknesses: Weight may always be an issue with Key. He's prone to large weight gains that can affect his stamina. Key is not a shot-blocker nor a particularly potent rebounder for a man of his stature.

Analysis: Because of the slower tempo at which Marquette usually plays, Key will not post enormous scoring numbers. But he is a quality player with a sound work ethic and leadership skills. He'll be the focal point up front for a Warrior team that will be this school's best since the glory days of Al McGuire.

COLLEGE STATISTICS

		G	FGP	FTP	RPG	APG	PPG
90-91	MARQ	29	.514	.816	5.7	1.5	13.2
91-92	MARQ	28	.577	.756	5.7	0.8	13.6
92-93	MARQ	27	.515	.869	5.7	1.1	13.6
Totals		84	.534	.812	5.7	1.2	13.4

JASON KIDD

School: California
Year: Sophomore
Position: Guard
Height: 6'4" **Weight:** 205
Birthdate: March 23, 1973
Birthplace: San Francisco, CA

PLAYER SUMMARY	
Will ....make breathtaking passes	
Can't............................drain the trey	
Expect ....great floor leadership	
Don't Expect ....boredom	

Background: Kidd starred at St. Joseph of Notre Dame High School in Alameda, California, and was named *USA Today's* national prep Player of the Year as a senior. He was the Pac-10's Freshman of the Year last season and became only the fifth rookie to earn a spot on the first-team All-Pac-10 squad.

Strengths: Kidd has a superb notion of when to push the ball up the floor and when to back off. As a pure passer, few are better. Fans in the Bay Area speak of Kidd's passes in the way they do Joe Montana's. Kidd's great hands and hustle resulted in 3.8 SPG last year—tops in the country.

Weaknesses: Kidd has the hands of a thief, but that also can leave him out of position at times. For all the spectacular plays he creates on offense, he is not a first-rate shooter from long range.

Analysis: A dark cloud hovered over Cal after coach Lou Campanelli was fired in midseason, but the Golden Bears—led by Kidd—came back to upset Duke in the NCAA Tournament. The victory proved that Kidd is a prime-time player whose star is on the rise. This year, he'll be one of the nation's premier point guards and a highlight-reel regular.

COLLEGE STATISTICS

		G	FGP	FTP	RPG	APG	PPG
92-93	CAL	29	.463	.657	4.9	7.7	13.0
Totals		29	.463	.657	4.9	7.7	13.0

JIMMY KING

School: Michigan
Year: Junior
Position: Guard
Height: 6'5" **Weight:** 201
Birthdate: February 9, 1973
Birthplace: Plano, TX

PLAYER SUMMARY	
Will...........................increase scoring	
Can't ....hit 3's like he should	
Expect ....superb defense	
Don't Expect .....underachievement	

Background: A former McDonald's All-American, King averaged more than 25 PPG at Plano High School before joining the Fab Five. As a freshman, he earned a starting spot early in the year and he has never relinquished that post. King has displayed a knack for making big plays at crunch time.

Strengths: When the Wolverines are running, King is at his best. He is a terrific leaper who is an excellent finisher in transition. Unselfish, King sometimes looks to pass too often. The Texan is a tenacious defender capable of shutting down smaller guards or larger ones.

Weaknesses: After leading the Wolverines in 3-point percentage as a freshman, King seemed to lose confidence in his perimeter game in 1992-93. He passed up a number of open 3's in the NCAA Tournament, often choosing to force shots on the run.

Analysis: The Wolverines' inconsistency from the perimeter hurt them last year, and King is the key to insuring that it doesn't happen again. A talented marksman, King must develop the scorer's mentality to go with it. Michigan will need King to step up now that Chris Webber is gone.

COLLEGE STATISTICS

		G	FGP	FTP	RPG	APG	PPG
91-92	MICH	34	.496	.736	3.3	2.3	9.9
92-93	MICH	36	.509	.648	4.4	3.1	10.8
Totals		70	.503	.688	3.9	2.7	10.4

TOM KLEINSCHMIDT

School: DePaul
Year: Junior
Position: Guard/Forward
Height: 6'5" **Weight:** 210
Birthdate: February 21, 1973
Birthplace: Chicago, IL

PLAYER SUMMARY	
Will	find the open man
Can't	control his emotions
Expect	points inside and out
Don't Expect	quick feet

Background: In 1990-91, Kleinschmidt finished runner-up as Illinois' Mr. Basketball. Among those honoring him were *USA Today, Basketball Weekly,* and *Parade.* An inconsistent freshman year at DePaul was forgotten during the 1992-93 season, as Kleinschmidt earned first-team All-Great Midwest honors.

Strengths: Kleinschmidt is one of the lucky players who have a great feel for the game. At 6'5", he can see over most other guards and find the open man. A fine long-distance shooter, he can also put the ball on the floor and drive the lane.

Weaknesses: Kleinschmidt does not have quick feet, which can hurt him on defense. Immaturity was a large problem during his freshman year and, though he has made great strides, he still allows incidents to affect him at times.

Analysis: Kleinschmidt rebounded successfully from a disappointing freshman campaign. The local product settled into the spot vacated by David Booth and made it his own. With additional help, he could lift the Blue Demons back to the postseason after they sat home last year for the first time since 1977.

COLLEGE STATISTICS

		G	FGP	FTP	RPG	APG	PPG
91-92	DeP	28	.396	.714	2.8	2.1	5.6
92-93	DeP	31	.465	.755	5.4	3.0	17.9
Totals		59	.447	.746	4.1	2.6	12.0

VOSHON LENARD

School: Minnesota
Year: Junior
Position: Guard
Height: 6'4" **Weight:** 195
Birthdate: May 14, 1973
Birthplace: Detroit, MI

PLAYER SUMMARY	
Will	break down defenses
Can't	avoid turnovers
Expect	scoring and leadership
Don't Expect	him to slide back

Background: Lenard, with Jalen Rose and Howard Eisley, helped Detroit Southwestern to two state high school titles. At Minnesota, he was named third-team Freshman All-American by *Basketball Weekly.* Last winter, he helped Minnesota win the National Invitation Tournament.

Strengths: Lenard is the key figure on one of the Big Ten's rising teams. He attacks the basket and finishes plays with authority. An excellent outside shooter, he has the courage to take big shots and the touch to make them. Opponents beware: Lenard will swipe the basketball if you're not careful.

Weaknesses: In his first two college seasons, Lenard wasn't as consistent as he should have been. Turnovers were a problem too. He needs to be more under control in the open floor, although he should improve with more experience.

Analysis: This is a big-time talent who is on the verge of stepping forward into the upper echelon of the Big Ten. He is already a terrific defender and scorer, and the mission now is to do it on a more consistent basis. Lenard was a spark for the Golden Gophers in the postseason and will be again in 1993-94.

COLLEGE STATISTICS

		G	FGP	FTP	RPG	APG	PPG
91-92	MINN	32	.421	.812	3.7	2.7	12.8
92-93	MINN	31	.481	.802	3.6	2.6	17.1
Totals		63	.454	.807	3.7	2.7	15.0

ORLANDO LIGHTFOOT

School: Idaho
Year: Senior
Position: Forward
Height: 6'7" **Weight:** 235
Birthdate: December 4, 1970
Birthplace: Chattanooga, TN

PLAYER SUMMARY	
Will......................pile up the points	
Can't......pass out of double-teams	
Expect.....him to dominate Big Sky	
Don't Expect..................much hype	

Background: A high school star in Chattanooga, Tennessee, Lightfoot first signed with Oklahoma but instead started out at Hiwassee Junior College. His impact at Idaho has been immense. As a sophomore, he was the Big Sky's Newcomer of the Year. Last year, he was the league's Player of the Year.

Strengths: This well-built man is equipped with a marvelous set of basketball skills. A soft touch allows him to shoot well from 3-point land, yet he can also grapple with the big bodies inside. He works hard on the glass and isn't afraid to bump his man.

Weaknesses: Lightfoot is not a pure passer from the post, which makes him susceptible to turnovers when the opposition double-teams him in the paint. He sometimes lacks concentration on defense.

Analysis: Lightfoot was one of the top 100 players in his class as a prep senior, so his collegiate success is not a total shock. Orlando should take home another Big Sky Player of the Year Award, and he gives Idaho a chance to return to the NCAA Tournament. Unfortunately, not many people will pay much attention.

COLLEGE STATISTICS

		G	FGP	FTP	RPG	APG	PPG
91-92	IDA	31	.481	.738	8.9	0.6	21.8
92-93	IDA	32	.495	.713	8.6	0.7	22.3
Totals		63	.488	.725	8.8	0.6	22.1

DONYELL MARSHALL

School: Connecticut
Year: Junior
Position: Forward
Height: 6'9" **Weight:** 200
Birthdate: May 18, 1973
Birthplace: Reading, PA

PLAYER SUMMARY	
Will...................convert in transition	
Can't..............................play center	
Expect................improved scoring	
Don't Expect..............him to slump	

Background: At Reading High School in Pennsylvania, Marshall was one of the nation's most coveted schoolboys. As a freshman at Connecticut, the lanky forward made a splash with several important blocks and solid scoring. Last year, he finished third in the Big East in scoring.

Strengths: The UConn coaching staff has likened Marshall to Connie Hawkins, and the comparison has merit. An incredible athlete, Marshall has long arms that allow him to swoop past opponents in the lane. He can pull up for short jumpers or take the ball to the goal. His timing on shot blocks is outstanding.

Weaknesses: UConn lost center Toraino Walker early last season and was forced to play Marshall in the middle. That is not his best defensive position because of his slight build. On offense, he needs to be more consistent with his perimeter shooting.

Analysis: The Huskies didn't make the Big Dance last year, but not because of Marshall's work. He gave a valiant effort, never complaining when he was asked to play out of position. A return to a forward post should allow him to become one of the East's top performers.

COLLEGE STATISTICS

		G	FGP	FTP	RPG	APG	PPG
91-92	CONN	30	.424	.742	6.1	1.5	11.1
92-93	CONN	27	.500	.829	7.8	1.1	17.0
Totals		57	.464	.793	6.9	1.3	13.9

BILLY McCAFFREY

School: Vanderbilt
Year: Senior
Position: Guard
Height: 6'4" **Weight:** 181
Birthdate: May 30, 1971
Birthplace: Waynesboro, VA

PLAYER SUMMARY	
Will	drill the trey
Can't	be ignored
Expect	All-America status
Don't Expect	turnovers

Background: This McDonald's All-American was widely second-guessed when he chose to transfer from Duke to Vanderbilt after 1991. McCaffrey, though, proved his point, leading Vanderbilt to a spot in last year's Sweet 16. He was a second-team *Basketball Weekly* All-American.

Strengths: McCaffrey is a superb marksman from long range, hitting better than 52 percent of his trey attempts last year. He has also became more of a ball-handler, and his assist-to-turnover ratio is strong. McCaffrey, an excellent free throw shooter, also plays sound fundamental defense.

Weaknesses: McCaffrey really worked well for Eddie Fogler, but some wonder what type of adjustments he'll need to make for new coach Jan van Breda Kolff. For his size, McCaffrey is not much of a rebounder.

Analysis: The decision to move to Nashville has worked out well. McCaffrey wanted to display his point-guard skills for pro scouts and understood that could never happen while playing alongside Bobby Hurley at Duke. At Vandy, he has proven to be a floor general as well as a shooter. He'll be in the hunt for All-America votes again this winter.

COLLEGE STATISTICS

	G	FGP	FTP	RPG	APG	PPG
89-90 DUKE	38	.450	.793	0.7	0.9	6.6
90-91 DUKE	38	.481	.832	1.8	1.9	11.6
92-93 VAND	34	.553	.870	2.6	3.6	20.6
Totals	110	.507	.839	1.7	2.1	12.6

JERRY McCULLOUGH

School: Pittsburgh
Year: Junior
Position: Guard
Height: 5'11" **Weight:** 175
Birthdate: November 26, 1973
Birthplace: New York, NY

PLAYER SUMMARY	
Will	push the ball
Can't	exhibit patience
Expect	an armful of assists
Don't Expect	to be bored

Background: This native of Harlem first caught scouts' eyes as a member of New York's famed Gauchos AAU squad. He prepped at Manhattan's St. Ignatius Rice High School before signing with the Panthers. As a sophomore, he made the statement he belonged, earning *Basketball Times* All-East honors.

Strengths: UCLA's Tyus Edney notwithstanding, McCullough is perhaps the quickest collegiate guard in America. He turns the corner on most foes and is a passer capable of reaching most any teammate at any time. He'll also step out and knock down a jumper if the defenders back off.

Weaknesses: Patience is not McCullough's strong suit. He didn't like sitting on the bench as a freshman, and on the floor he'll sometimes force the action. Defensively, he has trouble with bigger, stronger guards.

Analysis: In spite of dismal forecasts, Pitt reached the NCAA Tournament last year and McCullough had a large hand in it. He directs the Pitt offense and is at his best in the open court. A touch of experience should help him reduce his turnovers. If that happens, he'll be the Big East's most exciting floor general.

COLLEGE STATISTICS

	G	FGP	FTP	RPG	APG	PPG
91-92 PITT	33	.386	.629	1.6	2.7	7.4
92-93 PITT	27	.389	.774	3.7	5.6	15.7
Totals	60	.388	.715	2.6	4.0	11.1

AARON McKIE

School: Temple
Year: Senior
Position: Guard
Height: 6'5" **Weight:** 209
Birthdate: October 2, 1972
Birthplace: Philadelphia, PA

PLAYER SUMMARY	
Will ....light up the scoreboard
Can't................handle the ball well
Expect ....explosive drives
Don't Expect ....lots of rest

Background: At Simon Gratz High School, McKie averaged 19 PPG and led Gratz to the Philadelphia Public League title. Academics kept him on the sidelines as a freshman at Temple, but as a sophomore he earned third-team All-Atlantic 10 honors. Last year, he was A-10 Player of the Year.

Strengths: McKie has terrific size for a shooting guard and superb athletic ability. Explosive, he can cut to the basket with a vengeance. On the perimeter, he has upgraded his shot selection. He's a willing passer with great court vision, and he'll battle for rebounds too.

Weaknesses: While strong on forays to the basket, McKie is not a first-rate ball-handler. Stamina is another area that needs to be improved. McKie sometimes wore down in John Chaney's system, which doesn't rely heavily on reserves.

Analysis: McKie's performance in last year's NCAA Tournament turned a number of heads. He's athletic, quick, and an efficient scorer. At the defensive end, he contributes on the boards and knows his role in Chaney's match-up zone. Temple has the look of a top-ten team and McKie will be its leader.

COLLEGE STATISTICS

	G	FGP	FTP	RPG	APG	PPG
91-92 TEMP	28	.433	.754	6.0	3.4	13.9
92-93 TEMP	33	.432	.789	5.9	3.3	20.6
Totals	61	.433	.774	5.9	3.3	17.5

SAM MITCHELL

School: Cleveland St.
Year: Senior
Position: Forward
Height: 6'9" **Weight:** 240
Birthdate: January 11, 1971
Birthplace: Buchanan, MI

PLAYER SUMMARY	
Will ....intimidate foes
Can't.....................sky to the rafters
Expect ....quality shot selection
Don't Expect ....TV exposure

Background: A native of the Kalamazoo area, Mitchell spent his final year of prep eligibility at Brewster Academy in New Hampshire, where he averaged 24 PPG and 16 RPG. Signed by Michigan, he started eight times as a freshman. But then the Fab Five arrived and Mitchell decided to transfer to Cleveland State, where he became the Mid-Continent Conference's Newcomer of the Year.

Strengths: Mitchell's strength allowed him to compete in the Big Ten. In the Mid-Continent, it allows him to dominate. At 6'9", he has excellent ball skills and strong hands. He's not shy about getting his hands dirty, particularly on the backboards.

Weaknesses: Because he is not a great leaper, Mitchell isn't a great shot-blocker. Improvement at the free throw line is a must, especially since he gets there so often.

Analysis: Mitchell is an intimidating presence with tremendous scoring skills. His forte is work on the interior but he can also nail the occasional 3. The media won't follow his every move, but Mitchell is a strong player who will allow Mike Boyd to continue the rebirth of Viking basketball.

COLLEGE STATISTICS

	G	FGP	FTP	RPG	APG	PPG
90-91 MICH	29	.410	.641	3.6	0.6	4.9
91-92 MICH	4	.357	.400	2.8	0.8	3.0
92-93 CSU	27	.540	.586	8.0	1.9	16.8
Totals	60	.444	.591	5.5	1.2	10.1

ERIC MONTROSS

School: North Carolina
Year: Senior
Position: Center
Height: 7'0" **Weight:** 270
Birthdate: September 23, 1971
Birthplace: Indianapolis, IN

PLAYER SUMMARY	
Will	overpower most centers
Can't	be budged
Expect	Player of Year votes
Don't Expect	on-court antics

Background: This hunting and fishing enthusiast has travelled to Alaska, Africa, and Cuba in search of adventures. On the court, he led Lawrence North High School to the Indiana state championship in 1989. After spurning Michigan and Indiana, Montross signed with North Carolina and has been to two Final Fours, winning one NCAA title.

Strengths: Not only does Montross have a wonderfully huge body, but he knows how to use it. He seals off defenders and receives the ball well. Once he catches the ball, he is virtually indefensible thanks to a soft touch and superior hands.

Weaknesses: Eric's bulk can often be a negative. He's slow, and agile pivots who can take him away from the shadow of the basket can cause him trouble.

Analysis: After two quiet seasons, Montross lived up to his billing last year by carrying the Tar Heels to the national title. One of Montross's greatest gifts is his understanding of his strengths and weaknesses. He realizes what he can and cannot do and seldom makes foolish mistakes. That makes him the best pure center in the country.

COLLEGE STATISTICS

		G	FGP	FTP	RPG	APG	PPG
90-91	NC	35	.587	.612	4.2	0.3	5.8
91-92	NC	31	.574	.624	7.0	0.6	11.2
92-93	NC	38	.615	.684	7.6	0.7	15.8
Totals		104	.596	.656	6.3	0.5	11.1

HARRY MOORE

School: St. Bonaventure
Year: Senior
Position: Forward
Height: 6'8" **Weight:** 215
Birthdate: May 22, 1971
Birthplace: Philadelphia, PA

PLAYER SUMMARY	
Will	lead Bonnies in scoring
Can't	light it up from 3
Expect	first-team A-10
Don't Expect	great ball skills

Background: Moore missed 14 games during his senior year at Simon Gratz High School after falling victim to a drive-by shooting. Many recruiters backed off, and he signed with St. Bonaventure. Though forced to sit out as a freshman, Moore enjoyed a superior sophomore year and was first-team All-Atlantic 10 last season.

Strengths: The Bonnies' top offensive threat is quick off his feet. He creates space for himself inside and has the soft shot needed to convert. A solid rebounder, Moore can toss an outlet pass or trail the play and drop a mid-range jumper.

Weaknesses: Moore is not a good 3-point shooter, nor is he at home at the free throw line. His passes are sometimes forced and his assist-to-turnover ratio could stand improvement.

Analysis: One of the top players in the Atlantic 10 last winter, Moore was largely overlooked because the Bonnies finished last in the conference. An effective inside scorer, Moore can score at a 20-PPG clip. Had he not suffered the bullet wound, it's quite likely that Moore would be thriving closer to the spotlight.

COLLEGE STATISTICS

		G	FGP	FTP	RPG	APG	PPG
91-92	STB	28	.457	.648	6.0	0.9	15.7
92-93	STB	27	.481	.619	8.2	1.3	19.0
Totals		55	.470	.633	7.0	1.1	17.3

MARTICE MOORE
School: Georgia Tech
Year: Sophomore
Position: Guard/Forward
Height: 6'8" **Weight:** 212
Birthdate: November 30, 1974
Birthplace: Atlanta, GA

PLAYER SUMMARY	
Will	leap through the roof
Can't	push people around
Expect	nice scoring touch
Don't Expect	fiery intensity

Background: Moore played at Atlanta's North Fulton High School and Virginia's Oak Hill Academy. Bob Gibbons's *All-Star Sports* listed Moore as one of its "Super Six" seniors for 1992. An instant starter at Georgia Tech, Moore captured ACC Rookie of the Year honors.

Strengths: On a team that boasted power in James Forrest and Malcolm Mackey, Moore was the picture of finesse. He is an effortless athlete who can score from medium range or post up smaller guards. A good ball-handler for his size, Moore uses that talent to free himself for scores. He's also adroit at finding the open man.

Weaknesses: The knock on Moore at Oak Hill Academy was that he wasn't very aggressive, and he indeed lacked the killer instinct as a freshman. Tougher ACC types pushed Moore around; he needs to add more muscle.

Analysis: Moore had an outstanding first year, and now his mission is to add to his game. This versatile athlete must get stronger and improve his stamina. The rest of the package is already in place. He'll score in the mid-teens and continue to move up the ladder into the elite group of ACC players.

COLLEGE STATISTICS
	G	FGP	FTP	RPG	APG	PPG
92-93	GT	28	.451	.763	4.6	2.2	10.5
Totals		28	.451	.763	4.6	2.2	10.5

DWAYNE MORTON
School: Louisville
Year: Senior
Position: Forward
Height: 6'6" **Weight:** 190
Birthdate: August 8, 1971
Birthplace: Louisville, KY

PLAYER SUMMARY	
Will	drop in 3-pointers
Can't	avoid needless fouls
Expect	explosiveness
Don't Expect	poor work habits

Background: Morton was Kentucky's Mr. Basketball and the object of an intense recruiting war between Kentucky and Louisville. He sat out as a freshman for academic reasons but finished second on the Cardinals in scoring as a sophomore. Last season, he was a first-team All-Metro Conference selection.

Strengths: Morton provides Denny Crum with a dimension he previously lacked—effective long-range shooting. What's more, he operates effectively in Crum's transition game. A great athlete, Morton explodes to the bucket in a manner that the old Doctors of Dunk would appreciate.

Weaknesses: The great work ethic Morton brings to the gym occasionally results in silly fouls and a spot on the bench. Morton must know when to surrender a battle so that he may win the war. He could also use more upper-body strength.

Analysis: Similar in style to Calbert Cheaney, Morton can lead Louisville back to national prominence. His first step is excellent and his perimeter shot—though not much to look at—is very effective. This is the best forward Louisville has featured since Pervis Ellison.

COLLEGE STATISTICS
	G	FGP	FTP	RPG	APG	PPG
91-92	LOU	30	.578	.672	3.7	1.2	13.6
92-93	LOU	31	.531	.738	4.7	2.2	16.1
Totals		61	.552	.705	4.2	1.7	14.9

LAWRENCE MOTEN

School: Syracuse
Year: Junior
Position: Forward
Height: 6'5" **Weight:** 185
Birthdate: March 25, 1972
Birthplace: Washington, DC

PLAYER SUMMARY	
Will	convert tough chances
Can't	be stopped by one man
Expect	versatility
Don't Expect	fear

Background: Moten was an excellent wide receiver and safety at Archbishop Carroll High School. After high school, he spent a year at New Hampton Prep in New Hampshire. He splashed onto the scene at Syracuse, where he won national Freshman of the Year honors in 1991-92. Last season, he led Syracuse in scoring and was named All-Big East.

Strengths: With socks pulled over the calf, Moten challenges foes off the dribble. He's quick and smooth and can finish a play when contested. Moten uses his size to his advantage on the interior, posting up on offense and rebounding on defense.

Weaknesses: Moten doesn't specialize in the 3, although his 33-percent accuracy somehow placed him eighth in the Big East last year. Also, Moten can be a little reckless with the ball at times.

Analysis: If the Big East is to reverse its downward slide, it will need a huge year from Moten. He is quite capable. A brave competitor, Moten toils diligently and is one of the game's great natural scorers. If he can be a bit more consistent on the perimeter, he'll challenge for Big East Player of the Year honors.

COLLEGE STATISTICS

	G	FGP	FTP	RPG	APG	PPG
91-92 SYR	32	.497	.752	6.0	2.0	18.2
92-93 SYR	29	.473	.652	4.8	2.7	17.9
Totals	61	.485	.711	5.4	2.3	18.0

KENYON MURRAY

School: Iowa
Year: Sophomore
Position: Forward/Guard
Height: 6'5" **Weight:** 190
Birthdate: December 18, 1973
Birthplace: Battle Creek, MI

PLAYER SUMMARY	
Will	force turnovers
Can't	be slowed in transition
Expect	increased scoring
Don't Expect	shoddy defense

Background: Michigan's Mr. Basketball in 1992, Murray also received an award for being the top student at the McDonald's All-America Game. Murray was a top-25 recruit according to *FutureStars*. As a collegiate frosh last year, he made ten starts for the Hawkeyes.

Strengths: This fine athlete is well-suited to the trapping and pressing attack favored by coach Tom Davis. Murray uses his athletic frame to cut off passing angles and is speedy enough to get back into position once the press is broken. Though he didn't get to show it much as a rookie, Murray is a pure shooter who can't be ignored. He's a quick leaper who contributes on the backboards.

Weaknesses: The adjustment to college basketball was not without its pitfalls. Murray struggled to adapt to Davis's system, which favored frequent substitution. Sometimes he was overanxious to make up for lost time.

Analysis: Murray is sure to get more P.T. this season. He'll be asked to double his scoring average, and that's an attainable goal. This noted pickpocket could lead the Big Ten in steals and should be one of the league's most entertaining athletes.

COLLEGE STATISTICS

	G	FGP	FTP	RPG	APG	PPG
92-93 IOWA	32	.423	.579	4.1	1.1	6.7
Totals	32	.423	.579	4.1	1.1	6.7

LAMOND MURRAY

School: California
Year: Junior
Position: Forward
Height: 6'7" **Weight:** 220
Birthdate: April 20, 1973
Birthplace: Pasadena, CA

PLAYER SUMMARY	
Will	find ways to score
Can't	take things for granted
Expect	acrobatic dunks
Don't Expect	selfish play

Background: As a high school senior in the Bay Area, Murray wowed fans with 30 PPG and about 15 RPG. After choosing Cal, he was cited as a member of the Pac-10 All-Freshman team. Last season, he was a first-team All-Pac-10 selection and an integral part of the Golden Bears' march to the Sweet 16.

Strengths: It's hard to match Murray's collection of on-court skills. He has the shooting touch to score on face-up jumpers and can sink the occasional 3. In transition, he finishes plays with an exclamation point. Unlike his cousin Tracy Murray, Lamond is not shy about using his size inside.

Weaknesses: Murray's rebounding has not been as good as it should. With Brian Hendrick no longer around, Murray will have to pay more attention to the defensive glass. That may cut down on some transition opportunities but it will enhance his overall game.

Analysis: If Jason Kidd is Cal's Joe Montana, then Murray is its Jerry Rice. He'll be on the finishing end of many Kidd passes. This junior means as much to Cal as Tracy Murray once did to UCLA. Lamond might join his cousin in the NBA one day.

COLLEGE STATISTICS

	G	FGP	FTP	RPG	APG	PPG
91-92 CAL	28	.474	.710	6.1	2.0	13.8
92-93 CAL	30	.517	.628	6.3	1.4	19.1
Totals	58	.499	.664	6.2	1.7	16.5

ED O'BANNON

School: UCLA
Year: Junior
Position: Forward
Height: 6'8" **Weight:** 215
Birthdate: August 14, 1972
Birthplace: Los Angeles, CA

PLAYER SUMMARY	
Will	slash to the goal
Can't	be left alone
Expect	excitement
Don't Expect	laziness

Background: O'Bannon was *Basketball Times'* prep Player of the Year as a senior at Artesia (California) High School. A torn anterior cruciate ligament in his left knee ruined his first college season, and as a redshirt freshman he shook off considerable rust. Last season, he was an All-Pac-10 first-team selection. He'll be joined this year by his brother Charles, a heralded freshman.

Strengths: Sometimes likened to a young James Worthy, O'Bannon is explosive to the goal. His first step is quicker than most and he uses the dribble effectively. He's got a nice shooting touch to 17 feet and is excellent in the transition game.

Weaknesses: In the halfcourt game, O'Bannon can still get lost. This was evident in the NCAA Tournament against Michigan. He opened with 14 points in the first ten minutes, but once the Wolverines slowed the pace, he struggled to make an impact.

Analysis: Physically, O'Bannon seems like his old self; now he needs to add some diversity to his game. With a bit more range on his shot and a greater awareness of how to cope with double-teams, he would become one of the nation's elite players.

COLLEGE STATISTICS

	G	FGP	FTP	RPG	APG	PPG
91-92 UCLA	23	.416	.630	3.0	0.5	3.6
92-93 UCLA	33	.539	.707	7.0	1.7	16.7
Totals	56	.518	.696	5.4	1.2	11.3

CHEROKEE PARKS

School: Duke
Year: Junior
Position: Center
Height: 6'11" **Weight:** 235
Birthdate: October 11, 1972
Birthplace: Huntington Beach, CA

PLAYER SUMMARY	
Will	take good shots
Can't	rely on quickness
Expect	strong post play
Don't Expect	3-point bombs

Background: A consensus All-American in high school, Parks averaged 29 PPG and 14 RPG as a senior. Duke fans dubbed him the heir to the Danny Ferry/Christian Laettner legacy. Although Parks struggled with those burdens as a freshman, he blossomed as a sophomore.

Strengths: A traditional center, Parks establishes himself well on the blocks and presents a good target for the guards to hit. He catches the ball well and takes it strong to the glass. The turnaround jumper serves him well. Defensively, he's an able shot-blocker.

Weaknesses: It was Parks's misfortune to follow one of the college game's all-time best in Laettner. Parks is not the perimeter player Laettner was, nor does he possess Laettner's versatility. Parks could still use a little more bulk.

Analysis: Parks was only fourth on his team in scoring last year. However, he emerged as an inside presence who could find the open man when opponents brought a second or third defender. When Duke was eliminated by California, it was no coincidence that its starting center was on the bench with a sprained ankle.

COLLEGE STATISTICS

	G	FGP	FTP	RPG	APG	PPG
91-92 DUKE	34	.571	.725	2.4	0.4	5.0
92-93 DUKE	32	.652	.720	6.9	0.4	12.3
Totals	66	.628	.722	4.6	0.4	8.5

WESLEY PERSON

School: Auburn
Year: Senior
Position: Guard/Forward
Height: 6'4" **Weight:** 180
Birthdate: March 28, 1971
Birthplace: Crenshaw, AL

PLAYER SUMMARY	
Will	tickle the twines
Can't	push people around
Expect	All-SEC votes
Don't Expect	power moves

Background: While at Brantley High School in Alabama, Person re-wrote the record books, pushing aside older brother Chuck (now with the Minnesota Timberwolves) in the process. Wesley has led Auburn in both scoring and rebounding in each of the last two seasons and was fifth in the SEC in scoring last year.

Strengths: Exceptionally smooth, Person accomplishes much with an effortless style. He runs the floor exceptionally well and his shooting stroke is sweet. Though not blessed with great size, he understands where rebounds will carom and works hard to be in a position to retrieve them.

Weaknesses: Despite attempts, Person never has been able to add the bulk that would allow him to operate more effectively on the interior. He can also be pushed around by stronger opponents at the defensive end.

Analysis: This Alabaman is a quiet force, a man capable of dominating a game with seemingly very little sweat expended. He'll be a factor in SEC Player of the Year balloting, and he should lead the Tide to the NCAA Tournament.

COLLEGE STATISTICS

	G	FGP	FTP	RPG	APG	PPG
90-91 AUB	26	.471	.765	5.7	1.8	15.4
91-92 AUB	27	.506	.726	6.8	2.0	19.9
92-93 AUB	27	.556	.772	7.1	3.8	18.8
Totals	80	.512	.755	6.5	2.6	18.1

DERRICK PHELPS

School: North Carolina
Year: Senior
Position: Guard
Height: 6'4" **Weight:** 180
Birthdate: July 31, 1972
Birthplace: Queens, NY

PLAYER SUMMARY	
Will	strip foes clean
Can't	drain the 3
Expect	great playmaking
Don't Expect	super scoring

Background: This left-hander once made a hole-in-one to win a prep golf tournament. On the hardwood at Christ the King High School, he was rated one of the East's top prospects. Phelps selected North Carolina and earned a starting assignment as a sophomore. Last season, he quarterbacked UNC to the national title.

Strengths: When the Tar Heels must get into their offense, they look to Phelps. He's a creative passer who knows when to feed the post. Few guards pressure the basketball as well as this one does, and he's a tough competitor who'll play through pain.

Weaknesses: The one area that cries out for improvement is Phelps's jump shot. He rarely looks at the basket when beyond the 3-point line, which allows teams to sag off him. This makes his passing chores that much more difficult.

Analysis: To a man, the Tar Heels will tell you that Phelps is the catalyst that drives them. He sets the tone defensively with his pressure on the opposing guard and runs the offense in expert fashion. Don't judge this guy by the stat sheet alone, for his intangibles are what help make Carolina great.

COLLEGE STATISTICS

		G	FGP	FTP	RPG	APG	PPG
90-91	NC	30	.490	.762	1.1	1.9	2.3
91-92	NC	33	.400	.712	3.5	6.3	9.2
92-93	NC	36	.457	.675	4.4	5.4	8.1
Totals		99	.433	.702	3.1	4.7	6.7

ERIC PIATKOWSKI

School: Nebraska
Year: Senior
Position: Forward/Guard
Height: 6'7" **Weight:** 215
Birthdate: September 30, 1970
Birthplace: Steubenville, OH

PLAYER SUMMARY	
Will	rifle home 3's
Can't	create his own offense
Expect	leadership
Don't Expect	shoddy passing

Background: South Dakota's Mr. Basketball in 1989, Piatkowski spent his first season at Nebraska as a redshirt. He became an effective role-player in 1990-91 and led the Cornhuskers in scoring in 1991-92. Last year, he was named to the first-team All-Big Eight squad.

Strengths: First and foremost, Piatkowski is a deadly gunner from long range. He has also become a fine rebounder, and he passes the ball well from either the small-forward or second-guard spot. He has the ball-handling skills to occasionally fill in at the point.

Weaknesses: Though he is Nebraska's clear leader, Piatkowski does not possess the traits that can free a star for points—namely athleticism or explosiveness. Consequently, he can never allow his concentration to lapse.

Analysis: Piatkowski's father, Walt Piatkowski, toiled for a couple years in the ABA, and Eric has a chance to play professionally too. First, though, he would like to end Nebraska's NCAA Tournament hex—they've been eliminated in the first round each of the last three seasons.

COLLEGE STATISTICS

		G	FGP	FTP	RPG	APG	PPG
90-91	NEBR	34	.465	.837	3.7	2.0	10.9
91-92	NEBR	33	.426	.725	6.3	3.3	14.3
92-93	NEBR	29	.476	.760	5.8	2.5	16.3
Totals		92	.455	.769	5.2	2.6	13.7

KEVIN RANKIN

School: Northwestern
Year: Senior
Position: Center/Forward
Height: 6'11" **Weight:** 245
Birthdate: August 26, 1971
Birthplace: De Pere, WI

PLAYER SUMMARY	
Will	give maximum effort
Can't	leap to the rafters
Expect	durability
Don't Expect	much notoriety

Background: Rankin has contributed from Day One in Evanston. He has never failed to average double figures in scoring and has received his share of honors, including a spot at the 1991 Olympic Festival and an invitation to the USA international teams trials this past summer.

Strengths: Rankin has a shooting touch that would be the envy of some perimeter players. He can step out to 15 feet and drop jumpers or work with his back to the basket. An unselfish type, he'll spot the open man. He's also a tremendous free throw shooter.

Weaknesses: Quicker interior players like Glenn Robinson torment the slower Rankin. He fouled out 12 times as a freshman and can still get into difficulty in that area. More upper-body strength could help as well.

Analysis: Rankin's play has been virtually ignored due to Northwestern's lowly status. It's not likely the Wildcats will reverse their fortunes under their new coach (Ricky Byrdsong) and that's going to keep Rankin's game far from public view. He's a strong player, though, and one with a chance of making an impact on the Big Ten.

COLLEGE STATISTICS

		G	FGP	FTP	RPG	APG	PPG
90-91	NW	28	.505	.756	7.4	2.4	11.4
91-92	NW	28	.465	.831	7.6	1.7	14.3
92-93	NW	27	.523	.730	8.4	2.1	15.3
Totals		83	.497	.773	7.8	2.0	13.6

BRIAN REESE

School: North Carolina
Year: Senior
Position: Forward
Height: 6'6" **Weight:** 215
Birthdate: July 2, 1971
Birthplace: New York, NY

PLAYER SUMMARY	
Will	swoop to the basket
Can't	shoot treys
Expect	spectacular plays
Don't Expect	great endurance

Background: Reese made headlines at Tolentine High School in New York and also toiled for the famed Riverside Church AAU team. He saw spot duty for the Tar Heels as a freshman and emerged as a starter in 1991-92. Last season, he played a pivotal role in UNC's national championship.

Strengths: Reese is a player who makes things happen. He has long strides and is at his best on drives to the basket in traffic. Changing direction in mid-air is one of his specialties. Defensively, he is capable of closing down the other team's best perimeter scorer.

Weaknesses: Reese committed major blunders in last year's NCAA tourney. He missed a last-second dunk against Cincinnati that forced the game into overtime. Against Michigan in the title game, he stepped out of bounds with under a minute to go.

Analysis: Though at his best in the open floor, Reese is more comfortable in the half-court setting than he was previously and his defense is much improved. An asthma condition can slow him at times, but he's a key cog in the Tar Heels' engine.

COLLEGE STATISTICS

		G	FGP	FTP	RPG	APG	PPG
90-91	NC	33	.533	.545	1.6	0.5	4.0
91-92	NC	32	.490	.776	3.9	2.2	9.8
92-93	NC	35	.507	.692	3.6	2.4	11.4
Totals		100	.505	.700	3.0	1.7	8.5

BRYANT REEVES

School: Oklahoma St.
Year: Junior
Position: Center
Height: 7'0" **Weight:** 285
Birthdate: June 8, 1973
Birthplace: Fort Smith, AR

PLAYER SUMMARY	
Will	occupy space
Can't	fly down the floor
Expect	interior power
Don't Expect	regression

Background: "Big Country" hails from a tiny Oklahoma town, where he averaged 32 points and 19 rebounds as a high school senior. As a freshman, Reeves emerged as a starter on OSU's Sweet 16 squad thanks to incredible improvement. Last season, he was the Big Eight's Player of the Year.

Strengths: Obviously, Reeves's enormous frame is a major plus. But in a short period of time, he has learned how to use that bulk to his advantage. He's got soft hands, receives the ball well, and uses a variety of short hooks and face-up shots to score. Those big hands help him on the backboards too.

Weaknesses: Not the most agile guy, Reeves can have difficulty defensively against quicker foes. He also needs to become a better passer from the low post and recognize double-teams more quickly.

Analysis: The late coaching icon Henry Iba said he had never before seen a player make as much progress as Reeves had in such a short period of time. This soft-spoken giant is one of the top centers in the nation and a crowd favorite. He can lead OSU back to the NCAAs, and a pro career now looks probable.

COLLEGE STATISTICS

	G	FGP	FTP	RPG	APG	PPG
91-92 OSU	36	.521	.633	5.1	0.7	8.1
92-93 OSU	29	.621	.650	10.0	1.2	19.5
Totals	65	.583	.645	7.3	0.9	13.2

KHALID REEVES

School: Arizona
Year: Senior
Position: Guard
Height: 6'1" **Weight:** 197
Birthdate: July 15, 1972
Birthplace: Queens, NY

PLAYER SUMMARY	
Will	thrive in transition
Can't	live up to billing
Expect	first-team All-Pac-10
Don't Expect	fiery showmanship

Background: Everyone's schoolboy All-American, Reeves was pursued by major programs across the land as a prepster at Christ the King High School in New York. He picked Arizona and has contributed in a large way since his arrival, failing to average in double figures in scoring only as a freshman.

Strengths: Reeves loves to handle the basketball in the open court and generally makes the proper decision on the fastbreak. He's very quick, has good strength, and breaks down defenders off the dribble. His long-range shooting eye is excellent, making him a double threat.

Weaknesses: Reeves has yet to become the assertive leader so many of the prep experts believed he would be. In addition, he is sometimes lax on the defensive end.

Analysis: In some quarters, Reeves has been viewed as a disappointment, particularly in light of Arizona's first-round pratfalls in the NCAA Tournament. Truth is, Reeves has enjoyed a solid career and has improved each year. If that continues, he'll turn some heads and, more importantly, reverse the Wildcats' tournament trend.

COLLEGE STATISTICS

	G	FGP	FTP	RPG	APG	PPG
90-91 ARIZ	35	.454	.690	2.3	2.9	9.1
91-92 ARIZ	30	.476	.788	3.2	3.7	13.9
92-93 ARIZ	28	.498	.727	3.5	2.9	12.2
Totals	93	.476	.733	2.9	3.2	11.6

TERRENCE RENCHER

School: Texas
Year: Junior
Position: Guard
Height: 6'3" **Weight:** 170
Birthdate: February 19, 1973
Birthplace: Bronx, NY

PLAYER SUMMARY	
Will	force the action
Can't	bully people
Expect	All-SWC honors
Don't Expect	more setbacks

Background: Tom Penders reached back to New York City, where he coached at Columbia and Fordham, to land Rencher, who became an immediate hit in Austin. He poured in nearly 20 PPG, and Dick Vitale named him national Freshman of the Year. Injuries ruined his sophomore season.

Strengths: Rencher grew up in the city and his game bears New York's trademark. He's tough and excels in the open floor. On the break, Rencher can pull up for jumpers or take the ball effectively to the basket. His knowledge of the game is excellent and his passing decisions are usually proper.

Weaknesses: On defense, the smallish Rencher can be overpowered by larger guards. Though a great point producer, Rencher is not a pure jump-shooter. He is much better off the dribble than he is catching the ball and firing.

Analysis: Rencher was plagued by injuries—both his and those of his teammates—in a difficult sophomore season. Penders, however, believes the extra burdens Rencher was forced to shoulder helped him. He became a better ball-handler and defender. Now he's poised to become the SWC's marquee attraction.

COLLEGE STATISTICS

	G	FGP	FTP	RPG	APG	PPG
91-92 TEX	34	.463	.706	4.3	3.6	19.1
92-93 TEX	24	.381	.713	5.1	3.5	19.6
Totals	58	.426	.709	4.6	3.5	19.3

SHAWN RESPERT

School: Michigan St.
Year: Junior
Position: Guard
Height: 6'3" **Weight:** 175
Birthdate: February 6, 1972
Birthplace: Detroit, MI

PLAYER SUMMARY	
Will	fire when ready
Can't	direct the offense
Expect	scores in transition
Don't Expect	many rebounds

Background: A knee injury sidelined Respert when he arrived at MSU, but he has been making up for the lost time ever since. He was named second-team Freshman All-American by *Basketball Weekly* after leading the Spartans in scoring. He did the same as a sophomore and became a *Basketball Times* All-Mideast selection.

Strengths: Respert's greatest weapon is his scoring. Defenders can never rest, as Respert can hit the long straight-up jumper or score off the dribble. He thrives in the open court and isn't shaken when he misses a few shots.

Weaknesses: The Spartans were desperate for backcourt leadership last season, but Respert wasn't the type who could handle anything other than the off-guard position. He needs help getting open shots in the halfcourt game, and sometimes he loses his patience and forces bad attempts.

Analysis: As it is, Respert is a quality Big Ten player, one capable of changing the course of a game. With a little more emphasis on getting to the basket and the free throw line, Respert could find himself grouped with the nation's classiest guards.

COLLEGE STATISTICS

	G	FGP	FTP	RPG	APG	PPG
90-91 MSU	1	—	—	—	—	—
91-92 MSU	30	.503	.872	2.1	2.1	15.8
92-93 MSU	28	.481	.856	4.0	2.6	20.1
Totals	59	.490	.862	3.0	2.3	17.6

JOHNNY RHODES

School: Maryland
Year: Sophomore
Position: Guard/Forward
Height: 6'4" **Weight:** 170
Birthdate: September 13, 1973
Birthplace: Washington, DC

PLAYER SUMMARY	
Will	see the floor
Can't	add enough strength
Expect	tons of minutes
Don't Expect	limited results

Background: One of Washington, D.C.'s top players in 1991, Rhodes was forced to attend prep school for a year when he couldn't get the proper test score to enter Maryland. He spent that time at Maine Central Institute, got the score, and stepped forward as one of the ACC's top rookies in 1992-93.

Strengths: Rhodes offers an extremely well-rounded game. His first step is explosive, and not many defenders can cope with his quickness. He's a quality shooter who is comfortable pulling up from the perimeter or attacking the basket. Few 6'4" players handle the basketball as well as this sophomore, and he has a knack for being around the ball.

Weaknesses: As a freshman, Rhodes played often and stamina was an issue. He needs to develop more consistency and must learn how to conserve energy. More time in the weight room is imperative.

Analysis: Martice Moore was last season's ACC Freshman of the Year, but this man wasn't far behind. Rhodes has terrific skills and a real sense for the game. As the Terps mature, Rhodes will become a household name. He's a real threat to become an All-ACC choice this winter.

COLLEGE STATISTICS

		G	FGP	FTP	RPG	APG	PPG
92-93	MD	28	.420	.530	5.2	3.3	14.0
Totals		28	.420	.530	5.2	3.3	14.0

RODRICK RHODES

School: Kentucky
Year: Sophomore
Position: Forward
Height: 6'6" **Weight:** 200
Birthdate: September 24, 1973
Birthplace: Jersey City, NJ

PLAYER SUMMARY	
Will	run the court
Can't	miss as a future star
Expect	great improvement
Don't Expect	more inconsistency

Background: Rhodes is one of only two freshmen ever to start at famed St. Anthony's High School in Jersey City and was a consensus All-American as a senior. Seton Hall was greatly disappointed when he spurned the Pirates to sign with Kentucky. As a rookie, Rhodes had a great December and finished fourth on a Final Four team in scoring.

Strengths: The greatest feature Rhodes offers is his tremendous versatility. He is a superb scorer in the open court and can slash to the goal in a halfcourt set too. He can also knock down the 3. Defensively, he is fundamentally sound and willing to work.

Weaknesses: A case of the freshman blues plagued Rhodes in the second half of last year. He lost his starting assignment to Jared Prickett as Rick Pitino grew weary of his inconsistency. The bouts of immaturity substantially reduced his playing time, and that needs to be corrected.

Analysis: Dick Vitale dubbed this man the crown prince to Jamal Mashburn's King of the Bluegrass early in 1992-93, but some of the luster wore off as the campaign moved along. Rhodes just needs more maturity and more consistency. The skills are there for greatness.

COLLEGE STATISTICS

		G	FGP	FTP	RPG	APG	PPG
92-93	KEN	33	.451	.693	2.4	1.8	9.1
Totals		33	.451	.693	2.4	1.8	9.1

GLENN ROBINSON

School: Purdue
Year: Junior
Position: Forward
Height: 6'8" **Weight:** 215
Birthdate: January 10, 1973
Birthplace: Gary, IN

PLAYER SUMMARY	
Will	become NBA's top choice
Can't	find perimeter help
Expect	one more college year
Don't Expect	to be bored

Background: As a senior, Robinson led Roosevelt High School to a 30-1 record and was a *Basketball Weekly* first-team All-American. He came to Purdue as the best recruit of the Gene Keady era, although academics sidelined him as a freshman. Last year, he became a one-man show for Purdue and earned first-team All-America honors from *Basketball Times*.

Strengths: Robinson does pretty much what he wants on the court. He's athletic, strong, and gifted with great shooting and passing skills. His first step is extraordinary for a big man and he possesses a jump shot with range to 15 feet. He's a superb rebounder who also swats shots.

Weaknesses: Robinson occasionally makes poor passes, but that goes with the territory when you're swarmed at all times.

Analysis: Last year, Robinson was somewhat overshadowed by fellow Big Ten forwards Chris Webber and Calbert Cheaney—stars with bigger reputations who played on better teams. But Robinson was just as outstanding, and he now ranks as the best player in college basketball. Moreover, he'll likely be the No. 1 man taken in the 1994 NBA draft.

COLLEGE STATISTICS

	G	FGP	FTP	RPG	APG	PPG
92-93 PURD	28	.474	.741	9.2	1.8	24.1
Totals	28	.474	.741	9.2	1.8	24.1

LOU ROE

School: Massachusetts
Year: Junior
Position: Forward
Height: 6'7" **Weight:** 210
Birthdate: July 14, 1972
Birthplace: Atlantic City, NJ

PLAYER SUMMARY	
Will	keep UMass strong
Can't	pass very well
Expect	enhanced scoring
Don't Expect	temerity

Background: This Atlantic City High School star was named his state's Player of the Year. He chose UMass largely because of its exciting young coach, John Calipari. As a freshman, Roe became an important role-player off the bench for a squad that reached the Sweet 16. Last year, he became a key starter and the team's best rebounder.

Strengths: Soft hands and a nose for the ball make Roe a terror in the paint. He can score either from a post-up or wing position. Underneath the basket, Roe carves good position for himself. His excellent quickness allows him to defend on the perimeter and his strength allows him to handle larger men.

Weaknesses: Calipari often tells Roe that if he were relentless, he would be an All-American. Calipari needs him to be a team leader this year. Roe also needs to improve his passing skills.

Analysis: Larger schools overlooked Roe early in the recruiting process, but now they're kicking themselves. This is a terrific talent who so far has played a fine supporting role. With Harper Williams now gone, UMass becomes Roe's team. He'll be up to the challenge.

COLLEGE STATISTICS

	G	FGP	FTP	RPG	APG	PPG
91-92 MASS	34	.529	.672	6.4	0.9	7.8
92-93 MASS	31	.564	.725	9.2	1.3	13.8
Totals	65	.551	.702	7.8	1.1	10.7

CARLOS ROGERS

School: Tennessee St.
Year: Senior
Position: Center
Height: 6'11" **Weight:** 210
Birthdate: February 6, 1971
Birthplace: Detroit, MI

PLAYER SUMMARY	
Will	collect rebounds
Can't	shoot the 3
Expect	OVC Player of Year
Don't Expect	any hoopla

Background: This Detroiter was not even listed among Tennessee State's most influential newcomers last fall, but he stepped forward in a big way. Rogers, a transfer from Arkansas-Little Rock, led TSU in scoring and was voted Ohio Valley Player of the Year and Newcomer of the Year.

Strengths: Outstanding shot-blockers are rare in the OVC, but Rogers is that. He combines height with timing and savvy to become a force at the defensive end. He does so without leaving himself out of position for rebounding. When Tennessee State has the ball, he makes his presence known in the middle thanks to a nice touch.

Weaknesses: Two areas on offense could use some work. For starters, he is a mediocre free throw shooter; teams would rather foul Rogers than see him convert easy scores. Then there is his range, which is somewhat limited.

Analysis: Tennessee State won a surprising 19 games last winter, largely due to Rogers's arrival. He was the dominant performer in the OVC and one of the nation's hidden treasures. Continued improvement will result in a professional career.

COLLEGE STATISTICS

		G	FGP	FTP	RPG	APG	PPG
90-91	ALR	19	.508	.554	6.9	1.2	8.4
92-93	TSU	29	.621	.624	11.7	1.0	20.3
Totals		48	.593	.607	9.8	1.1	15.6

JALEN ROSE

School: Michigan
Year: Junior
Position: Guard
Height: 6'8" **Weight:** 186
Birthdate: January 30, 1973
Birthplace: Detroit, MI

PLAYER SUMMARY	
Will	exude confidence
Can't	avoid the spotlight
Expect	improved shooting
Don't Expect	jitters

Background: The axis of Detroit Southwestern High School's state championship club as a prep senior, Rose has filled the same role for the Wolverines. He took the reins from Michael Talley early in his freshman season and has directed the Wolverines to two NCAA title games. He was a *Basketball Times* All-Mideast selection in 1992-93.

Strengths: A 6'8" point guard, Rose can see the floor with unusual clarity. He finds the open man off drives to the basket better than anyone in the college game. His size also allows him to post up smaller guards and chip in with rebounds, and he can harass foes when the spirit strikes.

Weaknesses: Rose lost a bit of confidence in his perimeter shot as a sophomore. This allowed defenders to sag on teammates Juwan Howard and Chris Webber. He can be a superb defender, but too often he wanders and loses track of his man.

Analysis: Rose led the Wolverines to a second national title game, but he heard more criticism than he did as a precocious frosh. However, Rose is an excellent athlete with a wide array of skills. Look for him to respond with a standout campaign.

COLLEGE STATISTICS

		G	FGP	FTP	RPG	APG	PPG
91-92	MICH	34	.486	.756	4.3	4.0	17.6
92-93	MICH	36	.446	.720	4.2	3.9	15.4
Totals		70	.465	.740	4.2	3.9	16.5

CLIFFORD ROZIER

School: Louisville
Year: Junior
Position: Center
Height: 6'9" **Weight:** 235
Birthdate: October 31, 1972
Birthplace: Bradenton, FL

PLAYER SUMMARY	
Will	post up foes
Can't	maintain concentration
Expect	glass cleaning
Don't Expect	low FG pct.

Background: At Bradenton High School, Rozier was rated one of the top power forwards in the nation. He signed with North Carolina and was a member of the playing rotation as a freshman, but he transferred to Louisville and sat out the 1991-92 season. Last year, he was chosen Metro Conference Player of the Year.

Strengths: In the lane, Rozier can be unstoppable. He has strong hands and is very smooth for someone so tall. When he receives the ball, he goes up strong and can change direction in traffic. On the backboards, he uses his muscle and size to great advantage. His timing on shot blocks is also first-rate.

Weaknesses: Rozier sometimes lacks focus. He doesn't always demand the basketball in the post, and on defense he isn't as intense as he should be. His foul shooting could use some work.

Analysis: Tar Heel fans groaned when Rozier left Chapel Hill, but North Carolina has rebounded from the divorce and so has Rozier. He provides the Cards with an inside dimension that was sorely lacking earlier in this decade. Louisville will be a top-ten team and Rozier its center of attention.

COLLEGE STATISTICS

	G	FGP	FTP	RPG	APG	PPG
90-91 NC	34	.471	.565	3.0	0.5	4.9
92-93 LOU	31	.561	.568	10.9	2.0	15.7
Totals	65	.536	.567	6.8	1.2	10.1

JERVAUGHN SCALES

School: Southern
Year: Senior
Position: Center
Height: 6'7" **Weight:** 223
Birthdate: August 11, 1971
Birthplace: Bronx, NY

PLAYER SUMMARY	
Will	clean the windows
Can't	dribble out of trouble
Expect	SWAC honors
Don't Expect	name recognition

Background: Scales spent his prep years at Dayton (Ohio) Colonel White High School, where he averaged 23 PPG and 12 RGP as a senior. After sitting out his freshman season at Southern for academic reasons, Scales emerged as the Jaguars' starting center as a sophomore. As a junior last year, he finished second in the country in rebounding.

Strengths: Scales plays a lot like his idol, Charles Barkley. He creates a nice target in the low post and is adept at getting putbacks off the offensive glass. On defense, Scales puts a body on people and seals off second-chance opportunities.

Weaknesses: An aggressive player, Scales can be drawn into early foul trouble. He also turns the ball over too often. Scales gets to the free throw line but doesn't connect like he should.

Analysis: The Southwestern Athletic Conference doesn't usually feature many players of national renown, but this is a worthy candidate. Scales pounds the backboards relentlessly and piles up tons of rebounds. If he can add an exterior dimension to his game, he might find a niche at the next level.

COLLEGE STATISTICS

	G	FGP	FTP	RPG	APG	PPG
91-92 SOU	29	.541	.556	10.7	1.3	16.0
92-93 SOU	31	.523	.563	12.7	1.6	18.7
Totals	60	.530	.559	11.7	1.5	17.4

RICHARD SCOTT

School: Kansas
Year: Senior
Position: Forward
Height: 6'7" **Weight:** 215
Birthdate: July 12, 1971
Birthplace: Little Rock, AR

PLAYER SUMMARY	
Will	establish inside position
Can't	shoot the trey
Expect	strong defense
Don't Expect	lack of effort

Background: As a senior at Little Rock Central High School, Scott averaged 21 points and 12 rebounds per contest. He became an immediate contributor to the 1990-91 Jayhawk squad that reached the NCAA title game. He also boasts one of the top field goal shooting percentages in school history.

Strengths: There are limitations to Scott's game and he understands them as well as anyone. You won't see this senior wander outside and take bad shots. He concentrates on rebounding and scoring inside and, consequently, does both with style. The hardworking Scott plays strong defense too.

Weaknesses: If Scott is to take his game up a notch, he will have to improve at the line. He is such a liability there that he can't be on the floor when the Jayhawks are trying to protect a lead late in the contest.

Analysis: If Dick Vitale had an "All-Blue-Collar Team," Scott would be on it. He's got fine skills and can power his way to the hole. He is one of the reasons for coach Roy Williams's success at Kansas, and he'll be a large factor for the Jayhawks in 1993-94.

COLLEGE STATISTICS

		G	FGP	FTP	RPG	APG	PPG
90-91	KAN	35	.563	.407	2.6	0.4	5.9
91-92	KAN	32	.639	.390	4.7	0.9	10.1
92-93	KAN	36	.608	.507	5.3	0.9	10.6
Totals		103	.608	.441	4.2	0.7	8.8

ORLANDO SMART

School: San Francisco
Year: Senior
Position: Guard
Height: 6'0" **Weight:** 165
Birthdate: June 19, 1971
Birthplace: Kansas City, MO

PLAYER SUMMARY	
Will	press pedal to the metal
Can't	swish long jumpers
Expect	assist marks to fall
Don't Expect	much muscle

Background: As a freshman, Smart set an NCAA standard for assists by a rookie. He also was tabbed a Freshman All-American by *Basketball Times*. In his three seasons, he has become USF's all-time assists leader, and he has a chance to reach Bobby Hurley's all-time NCAA mark.

Strengths: Playing at a frantic pace, Smart finds the open man. He moves swiftly with the basketball and weaves through holes in the manner of a Barry Sanders. His great quickness also helps him on defense, where he often forces steals.

Weaknesses: While Smart flourishes in the open floor, he is much more defensible in the halfcourt setting because he does not possess a great jump shot. Opponents can lay off him. He sometimes makes showy passes that result in turnovers.

Analysis: One of the NCAA's best-kept secrets, Smart has been a whirling dervish for the Dons for three seasons. He has entertained Bay Area fans and helped USF gain respectability. A trip to a postseason tournament would cap a career that has already assured him a prominent spot in the NCAA record book.

COLLEGE STATISTICS

		G	FGP	FTP	RPG	APG	PPG
90-91	SF	29	.420	.733	2.5	8.2	10.3
91-92	SF	29	.442	.775	1.9	8.3	12.1
92-93	SF	31	.525	.810	3.1	7.1	14.6
Totals		89	.467	.775	2.5	7.8	12.4

MICHAEL SMITH

School: Providence
Year: Senior
Position: Forward
Height: 6'8" **Weight:** 230
Birthdate: March 28, 1972
Birthplace: Washington, DC

PLAYER SUMMARY	
Will	rebound with verve
Can't	shoot the 3
Expect	good shots
Don't Expect	ball-handling

Background: This power forward was listed as the "East's Best Defensive Rebounder" by *Eastern Basketball* as a senior at Dunbar High School. He sat out his freshman year because of academics but became P.C.'s top rebounder in 1991-92. Last season, he was the ninth-leading rebounder in the nation.

Strengths: "Relentless" is the word that best describes Smith on the boards. He has a superb feel for where a missed shot will carom and he understands how to use his muscle to get in position. When he corrals an offensive rebound, he puts it back with authority and a decent touch.

Weaknesses: For one who spends much time earning free throws, Smith converts at a low rate. He has limited range on his shot and his assist-to-turnover ratio needs to be upgraded.

Analysis: While he is a competent offensive player, Smith's strength is his work on the glass. He gives Providence a distinct edge in a rugged league and he's not the type to back down from a confrontation. P.C. enjoyed a marvelous late-season surge last year and this man was a major contributor.

COLLEGE STATISTICS

	G	FGP	FTP	RPG	APG	PPG
91-92 PROV	31	.495	.579	10.3	1.3	10.7
92-93 PROV	33	.556	.546	11.4	1.2	11.8
Totals	64	.527	.562	10.8	1.2	11.3

STEVIN SMITH

School: Arizona St.
Year: Senior
Position: Guard
Height: 6'2" **Weight:** 205
Birthdate: January 24, 1972
Birthplace: Dallas, TX

PLAYER SUMMARY	
Will	apply pressure
Can't	slow down
Expect	physical basketball
Don't Expect	high FG pct.

Background: *The Sporting News* rated Smith the eighth-best point-guard prospect when he was attending Spruce High School. Nicknamed "Hedake" by his mother because he had a hard head as a toddler, Smith made four starts as a freshman at Arizona State. In 1992-93, he made the All-Pac-10 team.

Strengths: Similar to Rumeal Robinson, Smith is an explosive athlete who attacks the basket from the wing on the break. He thrives in coach Bill Frieder's "shoot first, ask questions later" offense, as he was second in America last year with 113 3-pointers. He's a noted ball thief on defense.

Weaknesses: The run-and-gun approach can lead to ill-advised shots, and Smith delivers his share of those. Like Robinson, he doesn't set others up nearly as well as he does himself.

Analysis: The Sun Devils were forced to the wide-open style by a series of injuries, and Smith responded well to the new look. He's quick, forceful, and must be accounted for at all times by the defensive unit. Expect him to rack up a 20-PPG average and constantly be in motion.

COLLEGE STATISTICS

	G	FGP	FTP	RPG	APG	PPG
90-91 ASU	30	.407	.650	2.0	2.7	8.2
91-92 ASU	30	.374	.874	2.4	3.1	12.3
92-93 ASU	27	.422	.780	2.8	3.7	20.0
Totals	87	.403	.772	2.4	3.1	13.3

DUANE SPENCER

School: Georgetown
Year: Sophomore
Position: Forward
Height: 6'10" **Weight:** 205
Birthplace: New Orleans, LA

PLAYER SUMMARY	
Will	drain soft jumpers
Can't	intimidate inside
Expect	continued development
Don't Expect	weak defense

Background: Spencer has been a winner at every level at which he has played. At Cohen High School, his teams won two state championships, and the 1992-93 Georgetown edition came within two points of an NIT title. The two-time *Parade* All-American was a second-team All-Freshman pick by *Eastern Basketball*.

Strengths: Spencer is one of the most agile big men in the country. He is an excellent ball-handler who can free himself for open shots. His jump shot is excellent and his size allows him to shoot over most defenders. Effective rebounding is another attractive facet of his game.

Weaknesses: This is not a classic, blood-and-guts warrior. Spencer is more comfortable on the perimeter facing the basket than he is in traffic. Pro scouts project him as a small-forward type, yet Spencer could use more upper-body strength. He would help himself by adding a few low-post moves.

Analysis: The focus at Georgetown is on Spencer's classmate, Othella Harrington, but Spencer is a potent Hoya weapon too. His outside shooting is a must if the Hoyas are to realize the potential they displayed in their march to the NIT final.

COLLEGE STATISTICS

	G	FGP	FTP	RPG	APG	PPG
92-93 GEOR	33	.386	.643	7.1	1.6	8.7
Totals	33	.386	.643	7.1	1.6	8.7

JERRY STACKHOUSE

School: North Carolina
Year: Freshman
Position: Forward
Height: 6'7" **Weight:** 220
Birthdate: November 5, 1974
Birthplace: Kinston, NC

PLAYER SUMMARY	
Will	score from the wing
Can't	be the go-to guy yet
Expect	thundering dunks
Don't Expect	tons of P.T.

Background: Labeled the best basketball prospect in North Carolina since Michael Jordan, Stackhouse sparked Kinston to the finals of the state tournament as a junior. In 1992, he chose to attend Oak Hill Academy in Virginia, a move bemoaned in North Carolina. However, Stackhouse redeemed himself in his home state by signing with the Tar Heels.

Strengths: Viewed by some as this year's top freshman prospect, Stackhouse combines raw power with great skills. He is very quick and can muscle his way to the goal or pull up for a soft jumper. Few forwards can challenge him on the boards, and he has good hands. He'll also surrender the basketball when a teammate is open.

Weaknesses: Stackhouse was "the man" throughout his prep career, but Dean Smith's system puts great emphasis on upperclassmen. In other words, Stackhouse will have to cope with limited minutes, which he may find difficult.

Analysis: The prep gurus compare Stackhouse to one-time Duke star Gene Banks, though they believe his shooting range is better than Banks's was. Had he joined virtually any other team besides the loaded Tar Heels, Stackhouse would have become a full-time starter and a go-to guy. Stackhouse will sit a lot with North Carolina this year, but he's still one of the game's great freshmen.

DAMON STOUDAMIRE

School: Arizona
Year: Junior
Position: Guard
Height: 5'10" **Weight:** 150
Birthdate: September 9, 1973
Birthplace: Portland, OR

PLAYER SUMMARY	
Will	dash to the hole
Can't	pound the glass
Expect	All-Pac-10 honors
Don't Expect	blocked shots

Background: Stoudamire was Oregon's Player of the Year in 1991. His father played at Portland State and a cousin, Antoine, completed a fine career at Oregon last season. Damon spelled Matt Othick effectively as a freshman and then became Arizona's starting point guard in 1992-93. He was voted to the All-Pac-10 team.

Strengths: In recent years, the Wildcats have emphasized the running game—much to Stoudamire's delight. This junior flourishes in the open court. He is extremely quick off the dribble and turns the corner exceptionally well. Pinpoint passes are commonplace.

Weaknesses: Arizona has failed at NCAA Tournament time, and that casts a cloud over each Wildcat. Stoudamire will be the team's co-leader with backcourt partner Khalid Reeves, and the two must ensure that another collapse does not occur.

Analysis: Stoudamire makes sound decisions and can make teams pay when they leave him alone on the perimeter. His extraordinary quickness sets the pace for Arizona, and he'll probably score a bit more than he has in the past. He and Reeves will form one of America's best backcourts.

COLLEGE STATISTICS

	G	FGP	FTP	RPG	APG	PPG
91-92 ARIZ	30	.455	.771	2.2	2.5	7.2
92-93 ARIZ	28	.438	.791	4.1	5.7	11.0
Totals	58	.445	.784	3.1	4.1	9.1

BOB SURA

School: Florida St.
Year: Junior
Position: Forward/Guard
Height: 6'5" **Weight:** 200
Birthdate: March 25, 1973
Birthplace: Wilkes-Barre, PA

PLAYER SUMMARY	
Will	launch shots
Can't	play under control
Expect	great scoring
Don't Expect	wise decisions

Background: Sura was Pennsylvania's small-school Player of the Year as a senior at GAR Memorial High School. He scored a school-record 2,468 points and once tallied 68 in a single game. He was voted ACC Freshman of the Year in 1991-92 and finished second in the league in scoring last winter.

Strengths: This is one of the most durable players in the ACC. Sura is not afraid of risking life and limb on drives to the goal, and the Seminole faithful love him for it. He is a first-rate scorer and loves to slash to the basket. He can bury the 3-pointer and is a tenacious defender.

Weaknesses: Sura's assist-to-turnover ratio is poor. Too often he attempts to make a great pass when a simple one would suffice. He's frequently out of control on the fastbreak, and that leads to silly fouls.

Analysis: Sura has exceeded expectations since coming out of high school. Few expected him to be the dominant scorer that he is. Although impatient at times, he fits well into Pat Kennedy's up-tempo system. Above all, he is one of the most watchable players in the college game because he's always making something happen.

COLLEGE STATISTICS

	G	FGP	FTP	RPG	APG	PPG
91-92 FSU	31	.461	.627	3.5	2.5	12.3
92-93 FSU	34	.452	.638	6.1	2.7	19.9
Totals	65	.455	.633	4.9	2.6	16.2

SHON TARVER

School: UCLA
Year: Senior
Position: Forward/Guard
Height: 6'6" **Weight:** 198
Birthdate: December 21, 1972
Birthplace: Norfolk, MA

PLAYER SUMMARY

Will ....find good shots
Can't..............rely solely on jumper
Expect...................athletic brilliance
Don't Expect..............lack of hustle

Background: Tarver's father, John, spent four years as a running back in the NFL. In high school, Shon was a coveted recruit who gave a verbal commitment to UNLV before that program's probation steered him to UCLA. He played a key role as a freshman reserve and began starting in 1991-92.

Strengths: When the ball is being pushed up and down the court, Tarver is at his best. He runs the floor well and is especially effective converting from the wing on passes from Tyus Edney. Slashing to the basket is another strength, and he'll shoot the 3-pointer effectively too.

Weaknesses: Too frequently, Tarver concerns himself with scoring and neglects the defensive end—even though he has the skills to be a fine defender. Offensively, he needs to work on freeing himself if the game slows to a halfcourt pace.

Analysis: UCLA needed Tarver to step up on offense last winter, and he did so. Tarver and Ed O'Bannon form a one-two punch that most foes have a tough time contending with. This is a versatile open-court player who will be a major part of UCLA's push for the Pac-10 title.

COLLEGE STATISTICS

		G	FGP	FTP	RPG	APG	PPG
90-91	UCLA	32	.507	.526	3.0	2.1	9.0
91-92	UCLA	33	.523	.585	3.1	1.8	10.6
92-93	UCLA	32	.524	.641	4.3	2.9	17.2
Totals		97	.519	.595	3.5	2.3	12.2

DEDAN THOMAS

School: UNLV
Year: Senior
Position: Guard
Height: 6'0" **Weight:** 170
Birthdate: January 21, 1971
Birthplace: Woodland Hills, CA

PLAYER SUMMARY

Will ....involve teammates
Can't......................challenge giants
Expect. ....steals aplenty
Don't Expect ....3-point assaults

Background: Thomas began his collegiate career at Antelope Junior College in California, where he averaged nearly ten APG in a season there. He enrolled at UNLV, sat out a year, and became a competent reserve as a sophomore. Last year, he assumed control of the Runnin' Rebels fast-break offense, leading the club in assists.

Strengths: This point guard understands who among his teammates can score and where they need the ball. Thomas set up J.R. Rider often. He doesn't make mistakes when pressured and gets UNLV into its offense. He's a pest on defense.

Weaknesses: Thomas is not the type of guard who can assault a team with 3-point bombs. Generally, teams would rather take their chances with Thomas shooting than with some of his pals.

Analysis: The kudos and glory went to Dexter Boney and Rider last year, but Thomas was an irreplaceable cog in Rollie Massimino's scheme. He kept an offense that could have played fast and loose under control without stifling imagination. That's an unusual gift; now we'll have to see how Thomas reacts without the proven scorers to feed.

COLLEGE STATISTICS

		G	FGP	FTP	RPG	APG	PPG
91-92	UNLV	28	.415	.537	2.3	3.4	2.5
92-93	UNLV	29	.546	.547	4.1	8.6	7.5
Totals		57	.518	.542	3.2	6.0	5.0

DEON THOMAS

School: Illinois
Year: Senior
Position: Forward/Center
Height: 6'9" **Weight:** 232
Birthdate: February 24, 1971
Birthplace: Chicago, IL

PLAYER SUMMARY	
Will	reject shots
Can't	launch bombs
Expect	active defense
Don't Expect	poor shot choices

Background: Thomas was Illinois' Mr. Basketball as a high school senior, but his career was shaken in 1989 when an Iowa assistant coach produced a tape on which Thomas was said to have implicated Illinois in recruiting violations. The investigation forced him to redshirt in 1989-90, but he has led the Illini in scoring each of the past two seasons.

Strengths: There aren't many areas in which Thomas struggles. Few big men can match his quickness off the floor or his first step. He has powerful hands and understands the nuances of rebounding. At the defensive end, opponents must respect his shot-blocking ability.

Weaknesses: Earlier in his career, stamina was a major problem. At this stage, that can still get him into trouble, especially on defense. Foul trouble can also be an issue.

Analysis: In his first two seasons, Thomas battled tirelessly against defenses stacked against him. With more assistance last year, he carried the Illini to their first NCAA Tournament appearance since the investigation of 1990. He's a superb talent and quite resilient too.

COLLEGE STATISTICS

		G	FGP	FTP	RPG	APG	PPG
90-91	ILL	30	.577	.643	6.8	0.6	15.1
91-92	ILL	28	.585	.661	6.9	0.7	19.4
92-93	ILL	32	.606	.646	8.0	1.2	18.3
Totals		90	.591	.651	7.2	0.8	17.6

SCOTTY THURMAN

School: Arkansas
Year: Sophomore
Position: Forward
Height: 6'5" **Weight:** 190
Birthdate: November 10, 1974
Birthplace: Ruston, LA

PLAYER SUMMARY	
Will	hit area-code "J's"
Can't	overpower people
Expect	a superb career
Don't Expect	poor work habits

Background: Thurman was rated as one of the top two seniors in Louisiana at Ruston High School, where he scored a school-record 2,475 points. Only 17 when he enrolled at Arkansas, he became one of the nation's top first-year players, earning first-team Freshman All-America honors from *Basketball Times.*

Strengths: Arkansas needed someone to replace Todd Day, and Thurman fits the bill. He has incredible range on his jump shot and is not shy about launching it. He's also adept at pulling up for the short jumper on the break. Like Day, he has long arms and might grow to be 6'7".

Weaknesses: After a great start, Thurman's pace was slowed during the season's second half. He needs to adjust to defenses that react to his every move. He must stop forcing off-balance shots. Coach Nolan Richardson hopes to see him add some upper-body strength.

Analysis: Thurman's athletic style is well-suited to Richardson's "40 minutes of hell" approach, and he displayed the willingness to take on a heavy dose of responsibility. A strong recruiting class means Arkansas should be a viable top-ten team, and Thurman will be one of its most potent weapons.

COLLEGE STATISTICS

		G	FGP	FTP	RPG	APG	PPG
92-93	ARK	31	.465	.800	4.4	2.2	17.4
Totals		31	.465	.800	4.4	2.2	17.4

TONY TOLBERT

School: Detroit Mercy
Year: Senior
Position: Guard
Height: 6'4" **Weight:** 190
Birthdate: April 9, 1971
Birthplace: Detroit, MI

PLAYER SUMMARY	
Will	force defenses to extend
Can't	stop shooting
Expect	lots of scoring
Don't Expect	great defense

Background: Tolbert was a two-time all-state choice at Detroit's St. Martin DePorres, averaging 40 PPG as a senior. At Michigan, he showed promise as a freshman and sophomore, but he chose to transfer to Detroit. Last season, his first with UDM, Tolbert was named first-team All-MCC.

Strengths: This is a pure outside shooter, one who can fill it up consistently from beyond the 3-point arc. He is also very effective in taking the ball to the basket in fast-break situations. Tolbert isn't afraid to take the big shots.

Weaknesses: Tolbert has never been regarded as an outstanding defender since most of his thoughts are directed toward scoring. He's not particularly physical and would rather try to outscore his opposite number than shut him down. Bad shots are a little too common.

Analysis: Detroit Mercy improved to 15 wins last season, its first winning effort since 1985-86. Much of the credit is owed to Tolbert. He provides the Titans with a go-to guy, an answer man who can take and make big shots. This quick swing man will pile up the points for the Titans again.

COLLEGE STATISTICS

	G	FGP	FTP	RPG	APG	PPG
89-90 MICH	18	.429	.730	1.8	1.1	6.3
90-91 MICH	23	.460	.652	1.5	0.6	6.0
92-93 UDM	27	.443	.684	4.0	2.1	20.4
Totals	68	.443	.688	2.5	1.3	11.8

KAREEM TOWNES

School: La Salle
Year: Junior
Position: Guard
Height: 6'3" **Weight:** 175
Birthdate: February 9, 1973
Birthplace: Philadelphia, PA

PLAYER SUMMARY	
Will	shoot from all angles
Can't	turn down a shot
Expect	huge scoring nights
Don't Expect	high FG pct.

Background: Townes averaged 41 PPG as a senior at Southern High School. That effort was the Philadelphia Public League's second-best season output ever, surpassed only by Wilt Chamberlain's 47-PPG campaign in 1954-55. Townes signed with La Salle and sat out a year due to Proposition 48. In his debut, he became a first-team All-MCC pick.

Strengths: When La Salle needs a bucket, they call on Townes. He is a marvelous scorer, possessing the quickness to create his own shots and the skill to make them. He boasts exceptional range and is a constant 3-point threat. He's not a bad passer.

Weaknesses: Townes often fires up bad shots. Among all Division I players who topped 20 PPG last year, Townes had the lowest field goal percentage. La Salle coach Speedy Morris is working hard to teach Townes defense.

Analysis: The Explorers were a young team last year and relied solely on Townes for offense. As his younger peers grow into their roles, this junior should find more open shots. When that happens, his point production will likely rise. It would not be a shock if Townes made a run at the NCAA scoring crown.

COLLEGE STATISTICS

	G	FGP	FTP	RPG	APG	PPG
92-93 LaS	27	.369	.698	3.5	1.8	22.5
Totals	27	.369	.698	3.5	1.8	22.5

DAVID VAUGHN

School: Memphis St.
Year: Sophomore
Position: Forward/Center
Height: 6'9" **Weight:** 225
Birthdate: March 23, 1973
Birthplace: Whites Creek, TN

PLAYER SUMMARY	
Will	display great touch
Can't	avoid bad fouls
Expect	return to prominence
Don't Expect	ball-handling

Background: Memphis State coach Larry Finch had little trouble recruiting Vaughn, his nephew. Tennessee's Mr. Basketball did not endure a difficult transition period, as he was a first-team Freshman All-America pick by *Basketball Times*. Vaughn was redshirted last year after going down with a knee injury in MSU's opener at Arkansas.

Strengths: Vaughn is a superb shooter facing the basket. A hand in his face won't be enough to deter or alter the trajectory. The range on his shot extends to 17 feet. He's a fine free throw shooter and he also swats shots.

Weaknesses: When pressured, Vaughn will give up the basketball—he's not a great ball-handler. His post defense needs to be upgraded too, and he must stay away from silly fouls.

Analysis: Memphis State's dreams of advancing to the Final Four effectively ended when Vaughn went down last December. We'll never know what he and Anfernee Hardaway might have accomplished now that Hardaway's a pro. Nonetheless, Vaughn's presence makes MSU a viable threat to take the Great Midwest Conference. He's smooth and tough.

COLLEGE STATISTICS

	G	FGP	FTP	RPG	APG	PPG
91-92 MSU	34	.513	.761	8.3	0.7	13.4
92-93 MSU	1	.364	—	8.0	2.0	10.0
Totals	35	.508	.761	8.3	0.8	13.3

RASHEED WALLACE

School: North Carolina
Year: Freshman
Position: Center
Height: 7'0" **Weight:** 230
Birthdate: September 17, 1974
Birthplace: Philadelphia, PA

PLAYER SUMMARY	
Will	become a dominant force
Can't	control temper
Expect	athletic moves
Don't Expect	overnight stardom

Background: Despite playing little more than 20 minutes a game, Wallace averaged 16.3 PPG and 14.3 RPG for Philadelphia Simon Gratz, *USA Today's* top high school team in the country. Wallace was one of *the* top prospects in the nation, and North Carolina won a spirited recruiting tussle that included Villanova, Temple, and Georgetown.

Strengths: Enormously gifted, Wallace is much more David Robinson than he is Shaquille O'Neal. He has great hands and he moves with speed and grace. In an open-court attack, he is a superb trailer, capable of pulling up for a 15-foot jumper or finishing with a slam dunk. At the defensive end, he can block shots and isn't afraid to mix it up underneath.

Weaknesses: This is an intense competitor whose temper sometimes gets the better of him. He has been known to lose his focus after disagreeing with an official's call.

Analysis: The most anticipated hoop announcement of the spring was Wallace's selection of North Carolina. It was a wise choice. Dean Smith offers a structured program that can develop his post skills and do it without instant pressure. His freshman numbers won't be big—Eric Montross is still on campus—but Wallace will contribute to the top team in the nation, especially on defense. He'll explode as a sophomore.

CHARLIE WARD

School: Florida St.
Year: Senior
Position: Guard
Height: 6'1" **Weight:** 190
Birthdate: October 12, 1970
Birthplace: Thomasville, GA

PLAYER SUMMARY	
Will	play football first
Can't	play hoops till January
Expect	great leadership
Don't Expect	poor decisions

Background: Ward quarterbacked both the football and basketball teams at Thomasville Central High School and has done the same at FSU. He led the ACC in steals per game as a sophomore despite not joining the team until January. On the gridiron, he has developed into a Heisman Trophy candidate.

Strengths: Ward is a natural leader. His teammates admire his cool-headedness under pressure and the fact that he rarely makes mistakes in coach Pat Kennedy's frenetic offense. Most passes are crisp and he has a firm understanding of how the game should be played.

Weaknesses: One has to wonder if the stress of playing two major college sports isn't having an effect on Ward. He has been plagued by shoulder injuries in each of the last two basketball campaigns.

Analysis: Kennedy can only imagine how much better FSU and Ward would be if he stuck exclusively to basketball. Ward is a first-class leader, a calm director in an up-tempo system. He's a respectable shooter and superb passer. Ward's basketball season won't begin until January, but to Kennedy it's worth the wait.

COLLEGE STATISTICS

	G	FGP	FTP	RPG	APG	PPG
90-91 FSU	30	.455	.713	3.0	3.4	8.0
91-92 FSU	28	.497	.530	3.2	4.4	7.2
92-93 FSU	17	.462	.667	2.6	5.5	7.8
Totals	75	.471	.639	3.0	4.2	7.6

KENDRICK WARREN

School: Virginia Commonwealth
Year: Senior
Position: Forward
Height: 6'8" **Weight:** 225
Birthdate: May 27, 1971
Birthplace: Richmond, VA

PLAYER SUMMARY	
Will	score inside
Can't	square up for 3's
Expect	Barkley comparisons
Don't Expect	high FT pct.

Background: In each of his first three seasons, Warren has been chosen first-team all-conference (VCU was in the Sun Belt during Warren's freshman season and is now in the Metro). His bid for wider recognition was derailed last year, as an injury ended his season prematurely.

Strengths: VCU's Sonny Smith, who once coached Charles Barkley and Chuck Person, sees similarities between his past stars and Warren. Kendrick isn't the perimeter shooter Person is, nor does he have Barkley's complete game. However, he does have powerful low-post moves and the work ethic to accomplish things in the paint.

Weaknesses: Free throw shooting has never been a Warren strong suit—a troublesome sign for someone with professional aspirations. His face-up jumper could be smoother too.

Analysis: One of the great secrets of the college game is back for one last hurrah. Warren is a skilled athlete who capitalizes on nifty moves and has the determination to pile up points and rebounds. If he adds some other dimensions to the package, he'll get a long look from NBA G.M.'s.

COLLEGE STATISTICS

	G	FGP	FTP	RPG	APG	PPG
90-91 VCU	31	.541	.506	8.5	1.6	15.7
91-92 VCU	29	.543	.508	9.5	2.1	19.0
92-93 VCU	19	.502	.522	9.1	1.9	17.6
Totals	79	.531	.510	9.0	1.9	17.4

JEFF WEBSTER

School: Oklahoma
Year: Senior
Position: Forward
Height: 6'8" **Weight:** 220
Birthdate: February 19, 1971
Birthplace: Pine Bluff, AR

PLAYER SUMMARY	
Will	stroke sweet "J's"
Can't	harass other forwards
Expect	high scoring
Don't Expect	much leadership

Background: At Carl Albert High School, Webster was the most ballyhooed Oklahoman since Wayman Tisdale. As an O.U. frosh, Webster was sidelined for the season by a stress fracture in his foot. He received a medical redshirt and stepped forward as the Big Eight's Newcomer of the Year in 1990-91.

Strengths: Those who watch Webster regularly rave about his pure shooting stroke. He has good range on his jumper and is at his best facing the basket. He has added some weight during his career, which helps him on defense.

Weaknesses: Don't ask Webster to beat people off the dribble. He needs someone to create the shot for him. Defensively, he's a step slow and isn't fond of crashing the backboards. He is not a leader.

Analysis: Webster disappeared too frequently last year—one of the main reasons O.U. missed the NCAA tourney. Webster is steadily moving up the Oklahoma career scoring list, but his impact in Soonerland hasn't been as strong as it would have been had he added more to his game.

COLLEGE STATISTICS

	G	FGP	FTP	RPG	APG	PPG
89-90 OKLA	3	.571	.333	2.7	—	5.7
90-91 OKLA	35	.565	.802	5.5	0.2	18.3
91-92 OKLA	30	.521	.798	6.2	0.6	14.4
92-93 OKLA	32	.491	.740	5.8	0.5	16.5
Totals	**100**	**.527**	**.776**	**5.7**	**0.4**	**16.2**

TRACY WEBSTER

School: Wisconsin
Year: Senior
Position: Guard
Height: 5'11" **Weight:** 178
Birthdate: April 7, 1971
Birthplace: Harvey, IL

PLAYER SUMMARY	
Will	pick defenses apart
Can't	get sufficient rest
Expect	high-octane offense
Don't Expect	shaky defense

Background: As a senior at Thornton Township High School near Chicago, Webster averaged 18 points and 14 assists per contest. Proposition 48 sidelined him as a freshman, but he was a second-team All-Big Ten choice as a sophomore. Last year, he was a *Basketball Times* honorable-mention All-Midwest choice.

Strengths: Webster is most comfortable with the ball in his hands—and so is his coach, Stu Jackson. He sets the pace for the Badgers with excellent penetration skills. Away from the goal, he is a legitimate 3-point threat. He finds the open man and, on defense, applies strong pressure.

Weaknesses: Wisconsin lacks depth and that results in too many minutes for Webster. Jackson needs him on the floor, but at times fatigue causes him to make bad decisions.

Analysis: There are few point guards in the Big Ten who can match Webster's acceleration or scoring touch. He and Michael Finley provided a one-two punch that nearly got Wisconsin into the NCAA Tournament a season ago. Webster has the guile to steer Wisconsin to that promised land this time around.

COLLEGE STATISTICS

	G	FGP	FTP	RPG	APG	PPG
91-92 WISC	31	.444	.783	3.7	4.9	17.3
92-93 WISC	28	.393	.809	3.4	6.4	14.1
Totals	**59**	**.420**	**.794**	**3.6**	**5.6**	**15.8**

DONALD WILLIAMS

School: North Carolina
Year: Junior
Position: Guard
Height: 6'2" **Weight:** 183
Birthdate: February 24, 1973
Birthplace: Raleigh, NC

PLAYER SUMMARY	
Will	fire home treys
Can't	run the offense
Expect	further improvement
Don't Expect	flashy passes

Background: "The Donald" was North Carolina's Player of the Year as a senior at Garner High School. As a college freshman, Williams was forced to learn an unfamiliar position—point guard—and struggled at times. Last year, he returned to his natural shooting-guard spot and was named MVP of the 1993 Final Four.

Strengths: Williams has an effortless stroke, and Carolina uses a series of screens to free him for the long-range bomb. In the NCAA Tournament, he displayed an ability to take the ball strongly to the basket on the dribble. Williams has the athletic tools to halt other scoring guards in their tracks.

Weaknesses: Prior to the NCAAs, Williams was a bit too reliant on that sweet jumper. If it wasn't dropping, he could vanish from the offense. He must continue to take people off the dribble and finish plays around the basket.

Analysis: No player saw his stock rise in New Orleans more than Williams. This is a very important man in Chapel Hill, for he gives the Tar Heels a perimeter shooting threat to complement the inside heroics of Eric Montross. UNC's NCAA title hopes may again hinge on Williams's jumper.

COLLEGE STATISTICS

		G	FGP	FTP	RPG	APG	PPG
91-92	NC	29	.377	.571	0.7	0.6	2.2
92-93	NC	37	.458	.829	1.9	1.2	14.3
Totals		66	.445	.815	1.4	1.0	9.0

MONTY WILLIAMS

School: Notre Dame
Year: Senior
Position: Forward
Height: 6'8" **Weight:** 207
Birthdate: October 8, 1971
Birthplace: Fredericksburg, VA

PLAYER SUMMARY	
Will	score in the flow
Can't	get enough support
Expect	no rust
Don't Expect	any limitations

Background: After helping Potomac High School to the Maryland Class AAA title as a senior, Williams enjoyed a terrific freshman campaign for Notre Dame. However, a heart condition forced him to the sidelines for two lonely seasons. Last winter, he became the Irish's leading scorer.

Strengths: Williams is a silky-smooth forward who can effectively operate in the interior or on the perimeter. He is a quality jump-shooter and his quickness allows him to beat many forwards off the dribble. The two-year layoff gave him a zest for the game that is a joy to watch.

Weaknesses: A measure of rust had accumulated on Williams's game that had to slowly be peeled off. By year's end, it was. Williams is frequently double-teamed, which can force him into turnovers.

Analysis: In one of the nicer stories of 1992-93, Williams returned to the game he loves to become a force again. John MacLeod showed no reluctance in giving Williams a heavy workload once the physicians gave him clearance to play, and he responded with a superb effort. This smooth operator has an NBA body and the skills to match.

COLLEGE STATISTICS

		G	FGP	FTP	RPG	APG	PPG
89-90	ND	29	.483	.740	3.7	1.1	7.7
92-93	ND	27	.461	.791	9.3	1.4	18.5
Totals		56	.468	.774	6.4	1.3	12.9

CORLISS WILLIAMSON

School: Arkansas
Year: Sophomore
Position: Forward
Height: 6'7" **Weight:** 245
Birthdate: December 4, 1973
Birthplace: Russellville, AR

PLAYER SUMMARY	
Will	score around the basket
Can't	bury his FTs
Expect	consistency
Don't Expect	a weakling

Background: Billed as the best prep player in Arkansas history, Williamson first attracted attention when he shattered a backboard in the eighth grade. He became a consensus All-American as a high school senior on the strength of 27 PPG. A fractured bone in his foot caused him to miss 13 games as a freshman last year, but he was the Razorbacks' second-leading scorer behind fellow frosh Scotty Thurman.

Strengths: He has been likened to Larry Johnson, and that's due to muscle and great quickness. Williamson understands how to establish himself in the paint and knife his way to the goal. He is also a key operative in the Razorbacks' fastbreak. Williamson uses his bulk on the backboards.

Weaknesses: There is still some refinement needed in Williamson's post game. His free throw shooting must improve, and he needs to pass better out of the double-team.

Analysis: Williamson's foot injury seriously hampered his freshman campaign. However, he did demonstrate a variety of skills that suggests he'll be a force in the SEC—particularly now that he'll be working alongside a natural center in freshman Darnell Robinson.

COLLEGE STATISTICS

	G	FGP	FTP	RPG	APG	PPG
92-93 ARK	18	.574	.622	5.1	1.7	14.6
Totals	18	.574	.622	5.1	1.7	14.6

DONTONIO WINGFIELD

School: Cincinnati
Year: Freshman
Position: Forward
Height: 6'9" **Weight:** 235
Birthplace: Albany, GA

PLAYER SUMMARY	
Will	create excitement
Can't	afford to slack off
Expect	flashy dunks
Don't Expect	great quotes

Background: The soft-spoken Georgian led Westover High School to four consecutive state titles and was twice named his state's Mr. Basketball. A *Parade* and McDonald's All-American, Wingfield averaged 22 points, 14 rebounds, four steals, and five assists per game last season. He signed with Cincinnati in the early signing period.

Strengths: The new-age power forward, as embodied by Seattle SuperSonic Shawn Kemp, features an unusual blend of strength and grace. Wingfield fits the bill. He's mobile and quick with a tremendous first step. On the break, few opponents will be brave enough to take a charge from this man. In a halfcourt set, he's smooth enough to drain mid-range jumpers and even the occasional 3-pointer.

Weaknesses: Wingfield's choice of Cincinnati should prove interesting. The only criticism of Wingfield's game has been that he tends to coast at times, and that's not something U.C. coach Bob Huggins will tolerate.

Analysis: So far, Cincinnati has succeeded with a collection of unheralded, "last chance" players. This is the biggest recruit the school has landed in decades. No one doubts that Wingfield will make a major impact on a team that needs help up front. The interesting question is, How will he respond to Huggins's tough love?

STEVE WOODBERRY

School: Kansas
Year: Senior
Position: Guard/Forward
Height: 6'4" **Weight:** 180
Birthdate: October 9, 1971
Birthplace: Wichita, KS

PLAYER SUMMARY	
Will	make clutch shots
Can't	block shots
Expect	improved scoring
Don't Expect	sixth-man role

Background: Woodberry was Kansas' Player of the Year as a senior at Wichita South High School. After knee surgery in the fall of his freshman year, he came back and contributed at three different positions. In the last two seasons, he has been rated among the nation's finest sixth men.

Strengths: Wonderfully versatile, Woodberry can play point guard, off guard, and small forward. He is a fine ball-handler who can score on the drive or off pull-up jumpers. He's a classy defensive player who will take on the opponent's top scorer.

Weaknesses: Woodberry has made spectacular plays and scored well, but he has never had to do it with defenses focusing their attention on him. He will meet that challenge this year and it remains to be seen how he'll fare.

Analysis: Kansas has made two trips to the Final Four in Woodberry's career and, though he has rarely started, he has played an important role. When the going gets tough, he is at his best, meaning he should be able to face the larger challenge that will present itself in 1993-94.

COLLEGE STATISTICS

	G	FGP	FTP	RPG	APG	PPG
90-91 KAN	35	.507	.784	1.9	1.5	3.0
91-92 KAN	32	.476	.685	3.2	2.3	7.2
92-93 KAN	36	.512	.879	4.2	2.8	10.1
Totals	103	.499	.794	3.1	2.2	6.8

SHARONE WRIGHT

School: Clemson
Year: Junior
Position: Center
Height: 6'10" **Weight:** 250
Birthdate: January 30, 1973
Birthplace: Macon, GA

PLAYER SUMMARY	
Will	swat shots
Can't	rack up assists
Expect	an NBA future
Don't Expect	FT success

Background: Wright was viewed as a quality recruit but not a program-changer when he arrived at Clemson. He has altered that perception in the days since. As a frosh, his per-game rebound average was the sixth best ever by an ACC rookie. Last year, he was the second-best shot-blocker in America with 4.1 BPG.

Strengths: Wright is the backbone of Clemson's defense, as his exquisite timing makes him an extraordinary shot-blocker. His blocked shots often start Tiger fastbreaks. Offensively, he has a deft shooting touch and a strong work ethic that results in rebounds.

Weaknesses: Clemson has had its share of poor free throw shooters over the years and Wright won't set the world afire on the line either. Improved accuracy might add four to five points to his average.

Analysis: Clemson coach Cliff Ellis made an unusual move this off-season, subtracting a year from his contract in an effort to save his position for 1993-94. There's no doubt that Wright's presence played a big role in Ellis's decision. Should Sharone get a little help, the Tigers could move back into the NCAA Tournament picture.

COLLEGE STATISTICS

	G	FGP	FTP	RPG	APG	PPG
91-92 CLEM	28	.498	.563	8.1	0.4	12.0
92-93 CLEM	30	.567	.669	10.5	0.9	15.0
Totals	58	.535	.622	9.3	0.6	13.6

ALABAMA

Conference: Southeastern
1992-93: 16-13, 4th SEC West

1992-93 NIT: 0-1
Coach: David Hobbs (16-13)

Opening Line: Following four straight 20-plus victory seasons under Wimp Sanderson (1988-92), the Tide slumped to 16-13 last winter under the direction of new coach David Hobbs. A miserable road team all season long, Alabama's season ended at home in an opening-round NIT loss to UAB. While the loss of leading scorer James Robinson will be difficult to overcome, Alabama does boast several proven players and a terrific recruiting class.

Guard: Even without Robinson (20.6 PPG), the Tide returns a fairly formidable backcourt of Marvin Orange, Bryan Passink, Anthony Brown, and Walter Pitts. Although still a bit shy on experience, Orange will likely man the point. Juco transfer Terrance Bethel figures to push him. Fellow transfer Artie Griffin is Passink's main competition at shooting guard.

Forward: Underrated Jason Caffey (14.5 PPG, 8.7 RPG) will no doubt log most of the minutes at big forward. Shon Peck-Love will either be switched to big guard or relegated to bench duty in order to make room for Arizona State transfer Jamal Faulkner and heralded frosh Antonio McDyess. Faulkner, the 1991 Pac-10 Freshman of the Year, is a rising star who has endured a few personal setbacks.

Center: Roy Rogers will never be mistaken for a scorer, but he does dig in defensively and battle for rebounds. Cedric Moore, a player similar to Rogers, has left school, meaning Hobbs might play three of his four fine forwards at the same time.

Analysis: Without Robinson, Alabama's new go-to guy figures to be either Caffey or Faulkner (the leading candidate for SEC Newcomer of the Year honors). Orange or Bethel must take charge at the point, while someone must become a bona fide perimeter-shooting threat—perhaps Griffin. If the recruits come around in a hurry, this promises to be a very fine club. If not, Hobbs will have to settle for another NIT invite.

1993-94 ROSTER

	POS	HT	YR	FGP	FTP	3-PT	RPG	APG	PPG
Jason Caffey	F	6'8"	Jr.	.52	.62	3/11	8.7	1.3	14.5
Shon Peck-Love	G/F	6'5"	Sr.	.48	.68	14/45	2.9	0.8	6.6
Anthony Brown	G/F	6'5"	So.	.48	.77	10/24	1.0	0.5	4.9
Walter Pitts	G	6'1"	Sr.	.51	.56	4/14	2.4	0.7	4.8
Marvin Orange	G	6'0"	So.	.38	.52	20/61	0.9	1.5	4.3
Bryan Passink	G	6'3"	So.	.40	.50	25/67	1.2	0.8	3.8
Roy Rogers	C	6'9"	So.	.52	.50	0/1	2.3	0.3	2.5
Terrance Bethel	G	6'0"	Jr.	—	—	—	—	—	—
Jamal Faulkner	F	6'7"	Jr.	—	—	—	—	—	—
Artie Griffin	G/F	6'4"	Jr.	—	—	—	—	—	—
Antonio McDyess	F	6'9"	Fr.	—	—	—	—	—	—
Eric Washington	G	6'4"	Fr.	—	—	—	—	—	—

ARIZONA

Conference: Pac-10
1992-93: 24-4, 1st Pac-10

1992-93 NCAAs: 0-1
Coach: Lute Olson (429-173)

Opening Line: After East Tennessee State shocked Arizona in the first round of the 1992 NCAA tourney, lightning struck again in 1993, as Santa Clara upended the No. 2-seeded Wildcats. The premature loss ruined Arizona's 19-game midseason winning streak and glittering 17-1 league mark. Although All-America forward Chris Mills and center Ed Stokes have departed, three starters and four key reserves are back.

Guard: All-league point guard Damon Stoudamire and veteran Khalid Reeves can hold their own with any backcourt in the nation. Stoudamire's quickness sparks the Wildcats' offense, while the multi-talented Reeves can play either guard spot. Defensive specialist Reggie Geary, an outstanding leaper, gives the 'Cats a very strong three-guard rotation.

Forward: Mills's departure means Ray Owes becomes the frontcourt go-to guy. Although still a bit inconsistent, Owes displays all-league potential. Joseph Blair, better than expected last winter as a freshman, should have little trouble holding down the big-forward position for the next three seasons. He's the strongest player on the squad. Youngsters Corey Williams and Jarvis Kelley should help in time.

Center: While Stokes never did live up to his lofty advance billing, his dozen points, eight rebounds, and 1.5 blocks per game last year will be missed. Etdrick Bohannon was expected to replace Stokes, but he decided to transfer. Coach Lute Olson will have to go to a three-forward lineup.

Analysis: Olson will be under the gun this year. First, Arizona fans will expect him to approach last year's sensational regular-season record. Then in March, critics will wonder aloud whether the 'Cats will pull another first-round choke job. Olson, though, does have the talent. The guard play is top-notch, while Owes appears to be on the verge of greatness up front.

1993-94 ROSTER

	POS	HT	YR	FGP	FTP	3-PT	RPG	APG	PPG
Khalid Reeves	G	6'1"	Sr.	.50	.73	26/79	3.5	2.9	12.2
Damon Stoudamire	G	5'10"	Jr.	.44	.79	39/102	4.1	5.7	11.0
Ray Owes	F	6'7"	Jr.	.54	.53	1/8	5.1	0.4	7.6
Joseph Blair	F/C	6'8"	So.	.65	.60	—	3.8	0.4	7.1
Joe McLean	G	6'5"	So.	.40	.65	11/28	1.8	1.1	4.6
Reggie Geary	G	6'1"	So.	.42	.46	7/31	1.9	3.4	4.2
Corey Williams	F	6'5"	So.	.46	.80	1/8	2.0	0.8	2.6
Kevin Flanagan	F	6'9"	Sr.	.35	.25	—	1.5	0.1	1.1
Jarvis Kelley	F	6'8"	Fr.	—	—	—	—	—	—
Dylan Rigdon	G	6'3"	Sr.	—	—	—	—	—	—

ARIZONA STATE

Conference: Pac-10   **1992-93 NIT:** 0-1
1992-93: 18-10, T-3rd Pac-10   **Coach:** Bill Frieder (263-137)

Opening Line: Picked to finish last in the Pac-10 following numerous preseason injuries and dismissals, the overachieving Sun Devils had the last laugh last year when they tied UCLA for third place. With 6'6" Lester Neal the tallest regular on the team, ASU made it to the NIT, where it lost in the first round to Georgetown. Four starters return to the nation's top 3-point shooting club, as does star forward Mario Bennett.

Guard: Shooting guard Stevin Smith canned an NCAA-high 113 3-pointers last winter. The NBA scouts love his stroke. He's joined by ASU's single-season assist leader, Marcell Capers (7.1 APG last year). Depth could be a problem because Tes Whitlock, the first guard off the bench last year, has transferred. Quincy Brewer, a prep All-American two years ago, returns following a medical redshirt year (kneecap).

Forward: While no one can be sure how well Bennett will perform after sitting out all of last year with an injured knee, he was the Sun Devils' best all-around player in 1991-92. He'll no doubt push Dwayne Fontana and Ron Riley for a starting job. Fontana is a bullish rebounder who takes the ball to the basket with authority. Jimmy Kolyszko is back after missing last year with an injured shoulder.

Center: Neal, the leading rebounder in the Pac-10 last year, will be missed. It'll be up to respectable reserve Robert Conlisk to take over with help from inexperienced James Bacon. Forwards Bennett, Fontana, and Riley could end up spending a lot of time on the floor together.

Analysis: Maybe one of these years Bill Frieder—always a super recruiter—will receive the credit he rightfully deserves as a bench coach. His club is in much better shape this year, thanks to veterans like Smith, Capers, Fontana, and Bennett. The Devils won't fire as many 3's this season, but they will wind up in the NCAA tourney.

1993-94 ROSTER

	POS	HT	YR	FGP	FTP	3-PT	RPG	APG	PPG
Stevin Smith	G	6'2"	Sr.	.42	.78	113/300	2.8	3.7	20.0
Dwayne Fontana	F	6'5"	Sr.	.56	.50	—	7.1	0.8	14.5
Ron Riley	F	6'4"	So.	.36	.66	66/217	3.5	1.8	13.0
Marcell Capers	G	6'2"	Sr.	.39	.66	26/55	2.5	7.1	9.7
Robert Conlisk	C	6'11"	Sr.	.55	.61	—	2.5	—	3.2
James Bacon	C	6'9"	Jr.	.41	.67	—	2.9	0.4	2.2
Mario Bennett	F	6'9"	So.	—	—	—	—	—	—
Quincy Brewer	G	6'3"	Fr.	—	—	—	—	—	—
Isaac Burton	G	6'4"	Jr.	—	—	—	—	—	—
Jay Knollmiller	C	6'10"	Fr.	—	—	—	—	—	—
Jimmy Kolyszko	F	6'7"	So.	—	—	—	—	—	—

ARKANSAS

Conference: Southeastern   **1992-93 NCAAs:** 2-1
1992-93: 22-9, 1st SEC West   **Coach:** Nolan Richardson (308-109)

Opening Line: Return three starters and the first four reserves off the bench from one of the best young teams in the nation and you've got a potential powerhouse. Throw in one of the top three high school centers in America and the expectations become even higher. With the exception of forward Darrell Hawkins and guard Robert Shepherd, this is virtually the same cast that knocked off Holy Cross and St. John's in the 1992 NCAA tourney before falling to eventual champion North Carolina.

Guard: A starter throughout the first half of 1992-93, Corey Beck returns after splitting minutes with Shepherd. Beck led last year's team in assists and is recognized as one of the best defensive guards in the SEC. Shooting guards Roger Crawford and Clint McDaniel combined to average more than 14 PPG last winter. Crawford's the better 3-point shooter.

Forward: Scotty Thurman burst onto the national scene last season as one of the five best freshmen in America. He led the Razorbacks in scoring and minutes played. Although he missed half of the year with a foot injury, fellow frosh Corliss Williamson was just as impressive down the stretch. Elmer Martin, Ray Biggers, and Ken Biley supply a wealth of experienced depth.

Center: California native Darnell Robinson attracted as much interest from college recruiters as any high school senior in the country. Incredibly mobile for his size, he could make the same kind of sudden impact that Thurman did last year. Dwight Stewart started 21 games in the pivot last season.

Analysis: The best is yet to come for what could eventually shape up as the country's premier frontcourt trio in Thurman, Williamson, and Robinson. Beck and the rest of the guards thrive in coach Nolan Richardson's back-and-forth pressure attack. Anything less than a Sweet 16 finish would be disappointing. A national title will be a realistic goal in 1994-95.

1993-94 ROSTER

	POS	HT	YR	FGP	FTP	3-PT	RPG	APG	PPG
Scotty Thurman	F	6'5"	So.	.47	.80	80/181	4.4	2.2	17.4
Corliss Williamson	F	6'7"	So.	.57	.62	—	5.1	1.7	14.6
Clint McDaniel	G	6'3"	Jr.	.43	.68	21/73	1.9	1.6	7.5
Corey Beck	G	6'2"	Jr.	.50	.67	0/2	3.8	3.6	7.0
Roger Crawford	G	6'4"	Sr.	.54	.65	20/48	1.4	2.2	6.9
Dwight Stewart	C	6'9"	Jr.	.54	.56	8/17	3.6	0.7	6.9
Ken Biley	F	6'6"	Sr.	.42	.54	—	2.5	0.6	2.4
Reggie Merritt	G	6'1"	So.	.50	.60	2/4	0.3	0.3	2.1
Elmer Martin	F	6'8"	Jr.	.43	.40	1/2	1.4	0.8	1.9
Davor Rimac	G	6'7"	Jr.	.36	.88	2/17	0.8	0.6	1.8
Ray Biggers	F	6'8"	Jr.	.44	—	1/2	1.5	0.4	1.3
Darnell Robinson	F/C	6'11"	Fr.	—	—	—	—	—	—

AUBURN

Conference: Southeastern   **1992-93 NIT:** 0-1
1992-93: 15-12, 3rd SEC West   **Coach:** Tommy Joe Eagles (140-101)

Opening Line: The Tigers made it to the postseason last year for the first time since 1988, and although they lost to Clemson in the first round of the NIT, it was a step in the right direction. Led by star forward Wesley Person, they finished the regular season on a high note by winning four of their final five games. While the frontcourt returns intact, suitable replacements must be found in a hurry for graduated guards Ronnie Battle and Reggie Gallon. A solid recruiting haul produced a half-dozen players.

Guard: Strip any team of 24.9 PPG and 7.6 APG and there's obvious reason for concern. But not only do the Tigers lose the points and assists Battle and Gallon produced, they also lose their veteran leadership. Heralded juco transfer Antonio Dixon and freshman Wesley Flanigan will battle for the starting point-guard job, while reserve Lance Weems will swing between both backcourt positions. Person may play some big guard too.

Forward: Person's 18.8 PPG ranked him among the SEC leaders last year. He's one of the most complete players in the nation. He'll be joined by consistent Aubrey Wiley and enigmatic Mark Hutton. Hutton failed to live up to his press clippings last year following a brilliant junior college career. Newcomers Willie Jones and Leroy Davis supply immediate depth.

Center: Although only 6'5", Aaron Swinson started 23 games in the pivot last winter and quietly had a productive year. Not only did he lead the Tigers in rebounding (7.7), but he topped the SEC in field goal percentage (.600). Juco recruit Jim Costner is a seven-footer.

Analysis: If underrated coach Tommy Joe Eagles can come up with a dependable point guard, the Tigers might claw themselves into the NCAAs. While Person understandably hogs most of the headlines, Swinson and Hutton will also play key roles. Hutton's a far better player than he showed last year.

1993-94 ROSTER

	POS	HT	YR	FGP	FTP	3-PT	RPG	APG	PPG
Wesley Person	F/G	6'6"	Sr.	.56	.77	58/125	7.1	3.8	18.8
Aaron Swinson	F/C	6'5"	Sr.	.60	.59	0/1	7.7	1.0	15.6
Aubrey Wiley	F	6'6"	Sr.	.55	.67	10/26	5.1	0.6	9.4
Mark Hutton	F/C	6'8"	Sr.	.42	.48	16/42	5.0	0.7	6.0
Lance Weems	G	6'2"	So.	.36	.75	9/26	1.0	1.0	1.7
Shawn Stuart	G	6'2"	Sr.	.33	.40	—	1.0	0.7	0.6
Pat Burke	C	6'9"	Fr.	—	—	—	—	—	—
Jim Costner	C	7'0"	Jr.	—	—	—	—	—	—
Leroy Davis	F	6'5"	Fr.	—	—	—	—	—	—
Antonio Dixon	G	6'2"	Jr.	—	—	—	—	—	—
Wesley Flanigan	G	6'1"	Fr.	—	—	—	—	—	—
Willie Jones	F	6'6"	Jr.	—	—	—	—	—	—

BOSTON COLLEGE

Conference: Big East   **1992-93 NIT:** 2-1
1992-93: 18-13, T-4th Big East   **Coach:** Jim O'Brien (162-167)

Opening Line: Providence turned out to be the thorn in B.C.'s side last year. Not only did the Friars knock off the Eagles twice during the regular season, but they also tripped 'em up in the NIT quarterfinals. The Eagles still managed to post their most victories since 1987-88. With the team's top seven scorers returning, an NCAA Tournament berth should be a lock. Providence, and the rest of the Big East, better beware.

Guard: In Howard Eisley, Malcolm Huckaby, and Gerrod Abram, Eagle coach Jim O'Brien boasts one of the premier backcourt trios in the East. The multi-talented Eisley led last year's squad in assists and ranked second in scoring. Huckaby is a capable long-range threat, as is steady reserve Marc Molinsky. When the game's on the line, Abram is at his best. Freshman Keenan Jourdan, a lanky shooting guard, could help in a hurry.

Forward: Although David Hinton's veteran leadership will be missed, he scored fewer than five points per game last year. Kevin Hrobowski and Paul Grant will see plenty of frontcourt action. They combined to average nearly 12 points and seven boards per game last year. Hrobowski's the more complete defender. Reserve Robert Blackwell's minutes are expected to increase.

Center: Bill Curley is the star of this team. While the Eagles technically list him as a forward in the club's three-guard, two-forward set, he's always assigned to the opposing team's top big man. Curley is a capable scorer and rebounder, but his uncanny passing separates him from the rest.

Analysis: If O'Brien can't contend for a top-three Big East finish with this veteran cast, he had better update his resume. The Eagles appear every bit as talented as the Michael Adams-led 1984-85 squad that advanced to the NCAA's Sweet 16. Curley possesses the necessary skills to develop into an All-American, while a deep backcourt is almost as special.

1993-94 ROSTER

	POS	HT	YR	FGP	FTP	3-PT	RPG	APG	PPG
Bill Curley	F/C	6'9"	Sr.	.58	.85	—	7.6	1.2	15.8
Howard Eisley	G	6'3"	Sr.	.44	.83	43/104	3.5	4.9	13.7
Malcolm Huckaby	G	6'4"	Sr.	.43	.58	61/147	4.0	3.8	11.5
Gerrod Abram	G	6'1"	Sr.	.43	.67	36/88	2.7	1.5	9.6
Kevin Hrobowski	F	6'6"	Jr.	.55	.66	4/11	3.3	0.9	6.5
Marc Molinsky	G	6'5"	Jr.	.41	.88	35/95	1.1	0.9	5.1
Paul Grant	F	6'10"	So.	.50	.68	—	3.5	0.3	5.0
Robert Blackwell	F	6'8"	So.	.50	.60	0/3	0.8	0.2	2.0
Derek Jackson	G	6'3"	Jr.	.62	.88	0/1	0.8	0.7	1.7
Joseph Giacona	G	6'0"	So.	—	—	0/2	0.3	0.5	—
Danya Abrams	F	6'7"	Fr.	—	—	—	—	—	—
Keenan Jourdan	G	6'7"	Fr.	—	—	—	—	—	—

BRIGHAM YOUNG

Conference: Western Athletic   **1992-93 NCAAs:** 1-1
1992-93: 25-9, T-1st WAC   **Coach:** Roger Reid (92-38)

Opening Line: Cougar coach Roger Reid must still be in shock over losing 7'6" All-America candidate Shawn Bradley to the NBA following his two-year Mormon mission in Australia. Reid will now turn to his son to help replace four seniors who played instrumental roles in last year's 15-3 league record and NCAA tourney win over SMU. Talented guard Ryan Cuff has transferred to Arizona State, but three players return from missions.

Guard: With a little help from Dad, Randy Reid established himself as one of the WAC's premier floor generals last winter. Statistics simply don't do justice to this scrappy, young playmaker. Reid will be flanked by promising juco transfer Craig Wilcox and veteran Kurt Christensen in a backcourt that lacks depth and quickness. All three play solid defense.

Forward: Mark Durrant and Shane Knight both started 14 ballgames last season. Durrant, a superb passer and wing defender, was particularly effective late in the year. Knight (4.5 PPG) will be expected to score more, due to the departure of Kevin Nixon and Jared Miller. Kenneth Roberts and Jeff Campbell, who are back from missions, will supply much-needed bench support.

Center: Not only is Bradley gone, but so is two-time All-WAC honoree Gary Trost. Forward Russell Larson will likely be moved to the pivot. Larson is a brilliant shooter (63 percent) and the only returning double-digit scorer. Newcomer Jay Thompson possesses loads of raw ability.

Analysis: With Bradley in the middle, BYU would have undoubtedly become a top-ten team nationally. Without him, the Coogs still remain the team to beat in the WAC. The sooner they're mentally able to cope with Bradley's absence, the better off they'll be. Roger Reid is too good a coach and Randy Reid's too good a player for anything less than a 20-win season.

1993-94 ROSTER

	POS	HT	YR	FGP	FTP	3-PT	RPG	APG	PPG
Russell Larson	F	6'10"	Jr.	.63	.73	0/2	4.4	1.0	10.8
Randy Reid	G	6'2"	So.	.38	.86	23/65	2.2	4.1	6.2
Shane Knight	F	6'9"	Jr.	.48	.51	11/31	2.3	0.8	4.5
Mark Durrant	F	6'7"	Jr.	.51	.75	1/5	3.4	1.9	4.3
Kurt Christensen	G	6'0"	Sr.	.57	.80	4/12	1.0	1.1	3.8
John Fish	F/C	6'9"	Sr.	.40	.57	—	1.5	0.3	1.5
Grant Berges	F	6'8"	Fr.	—	—	—	—	—	—
Jeff Campbell	F	6'9"	So.	—	—	—	—	—	—
Bret Jepsen	C	6'10"	Fr.	—	—	—	—	—	—
Kenneth Roberts	F	6'8"	So.	—	—	—	—	—	—
Jay Thompson	C	6'8"	Jr.	—	—	—	—	—	—
Craig Wilcox	G/F	6'5"	Jr.	—	—	—	—	—	—

CALIFORNIA

Conference: Pac-10
1992-93: 21-9, 2nd Pac-10

1992-93 NCAAs: 2-1
Coach: Todd Bozeman (11-2)

Opening Line: In a highly successful but bizarre 1992-93 season, the Golden Bears said hello to the great Jason Kidd and goodbye to coach Lou Campanelli. With Kidd and interim coach Todd Bozeman leading the way, the team closed out the regular season at 9-1 and climbed to second place in the Pac-10—Cal's highest finish in league play since 1960. Impressive NCAA tourney wins over LSU and Duke followed, as the interim label was deleted from Bozeman's title.

Guard: It took Kidd only a handful of games to establish himself as one of the game's rising young superstars. He led the nation in steals and was sixth in the country in assists. While some insiders feared he might leave school early for the NBA, it was actually starting backcourt mate Jerod Haase who split—he left school unexpectedly and later enrolled at Kansas. Swing man Monty Buckley takes over for Haase at shooting guard, while K.J. Roberts and Akili Jones provide veteran depth.

Forward: All-league performer Lamond Murray (19 PPG and six RPG) combines a strong inside game with a soft shooting stroke and impressive athleticism. He's one of the premier small forwards in the country. Much-improved big forward Alfred Grigsby is an animal in the paint. Sophomore Stevie Johnson provides the only proven bench support.

Center: The Bears will surely miss Brian Hendrick, a force on the boards and a veteran leader. He'll be replaced by muscular Ryan Jamison, who will get plenty of help from heralded frosh Michael Stewart (6'10").

Analysis: The up-tempo Golden Bears shape up as the Pac-10's finest collection of talent. California has its Jordan (Kidd), its Pippen (Murray), and its Grant (Grigsby), as well as an adequate supporting cast. If the Bears can avoid major injuries to the Big Three, then another Sweet 16 appearance would be a realistic goal.

1993-94 ROSTER

	POS	HT	YR	FGP	FTP	3-PT	RPG	APG	PPG
Lamond Murray	F	6'7"	Jr.	.52	.63	36/99	6.3	1.4	19.1
Jason Kidd	G	6'4"	So.	.46	.66	24/84	4.9	7.7	13.0
Alfred Grigsby	F	6'9"	Jr.	.60	.65	0/2	5.8	0.6	10.0
K.J. Roberts	G	5'11"	Jr.	.36	.60	21/72	1.4	1.8	5.1
Monty Buckley	G/F	6'6"	Jr.	.49	.71	12/37	1.3	0.8	4.0
Stevie Johnson	F/C	6'9"	So.	.39	.71	—	3.0	0.4	3.9
Akili Jones	G	6'0"	Sr.	.43	.74	6/31	1.0	0.7	3.8
Ryan Jamison	C	6'11"	Jr.	.45	.52	—	2.7	0.6	3.2
George Ashley	G	6'1"	So.	.50	.50	—	0.3	—	0.8
Okwi Anuluoha	F	6'4"	Jr.	.40	.50	—	—	—	0.6
Sean Marks	C	6'10"	Fr.	—	—	—	—	—	—
Michael Stewart	C	6'10"	Fr.	—	—	—	—	—	—

CINCINNATI

Conference: Great Midwest
1992-93: 27-5, 1st GMC

1992-93 NCAAs: 3-1
Coach: Bob Huggins (191-82)

Opening Line: You won't recognize many names on this year's Bearcat club, as all five starters have departed. Yet, coach Bob Huggins has excelled in the past with a collection of no-names, thanks to unique defenses that force turnovers at an alarming rate. Last year's squad—led by Nick Van Exel and Corie Blount—executed Huggins's game plan to perfection in three postseason wins before falling in the East Regional final to North Carolina in O.T. Three of Huggins's six recruits are 6'9" or taller.

Guard: Minus Van Exel (18-plus PPG and nearly five APG), perimeter shooting threat LaZelle Durden must rise to the occasion. He started two games last winter. Frosh point guard Marko Wright has the ability to start from Day One. He makes things happen at both ends. Reserves David Evans and Jerome Gray will have to be worked into the rotation slowly.

Forward: If you've never seen 6'9", 235-pound Dontonio Wingfield play, you're in for a real treat. A big-time banger underneath who can step outside and bury the jumper, he'll make Bearcat fans forget about Blount and Erik Martin in no time. Hard-working Curtis Bostic, a 21-game starter in 1992-93, gets the call at small forward. Keith Gregor is a consummate team player, while Mike Harris runs the floor quite well.

Center: Juco transfer Arthur Long possesses plenty of pure talent and an intense work ethic. His size (6'10") alone will help the 'Cats compete against bigger teams. John Jacobs, 6'7" and growing, is a capable reserve.

Analysis: In due time, Huggins could mold any five athletes into winners. Although Bostic and Durden are the premier returnees, Wingfield's the youngster to watch. His presence, as well as that of spunky lead guard Wright, should help immediately. While it'll take time for so many newcomers to familiarize themselves with one other, remember that the tournament is not until March.

1993-94 ROSTER

	POS	HT	YR	FGP	FTP	3-PT	RPG	APG	PPG
Curtis Bostic	F	6'5"	Jr.	.60	.74	0/3	3.7	0.6	8.9
LaZelle Durden	G	6'2"	Jr.	.38	.87	31/92	1.0	0.3	5.3
Keith Gregor	F	6'5"	So.	.41	.63	0/15	2.0	0.3	3.1
Mike Harris	F	6'6"	Sr.	.50	.53	—	2.2	0.3	2.1
John Jacobs	F	6'7"	So.	.48	.30	0/1	1.1	0.3	1.6
David Evans	G	6'2"	So.	.36	.88	2/6	0.2	0.3	1.3
Jerome Gray	G	6'4"	Jr.	.44	—	0/2	0.3	0.1	0.7
Darnell Burton	G	6'4"	Fr.	—	—	—	—	—	—
Jackson Julson	F	6'9"	Fr.	—	—	—	—	—	—
Arthur Long	C	6'10"	Jr.	—	—	—	—	—	—
Dontonio Wingfield	F	6'9"	Fr.	—	—	—	—	—	—
Marko Wright	G	6'1"	Fr.	—	—	—	—	—	—

CONNECTICUT

Conference: Big East   **1992-93 NIT:** 0-1
1992-93: 15-13, T-4th Big East   **Coach:** Jim Calhoun (383-223)

Opening Line: Despite a strong finish last year, the Huskies made it only to the NIT, where they lost in the first round to Jackson State. Nine players return to this year's squad, including four starters. The only significant loss was four-year starter Scott Burrell, one of the nation's premier small forwards. Junior forward Donyell Marshall is compiling All-America credentials.

Guard: While Kevin Ollie and Brian Fair experienced a few problems at times, they eventually settled in as one of the East's most productive backcourts. Ollie, the only Husky to start every game last winter, sports nearly a 3-to-1 assist-to-turnover ratio. Fair can score in bunches when given the green light. Depth will likely be a problem. Jeff Calhoun, the coach's son, has minimal experience and the other back-ups are freshmen.

Forward: A first-team All-Big East performer last season, Marshall paced UConn in scoring, rebounding, and blocked shots. Once he gets the ball inside, it's lights out. He was the only Big East player listed on the 1993 Team USA roster. Donny Marshall (not Donyell) is a multi-talented small forward who gets the job done night in and night out. Eric Hayward, Rudy Johnson, and heralded frosh Kirkland King would start for many clubs.

Center: While sophomore Travis Knight and junior Nantambu Willingham would make ideal back-ups, one will likely have to start. Knight had the superior reputation coming out of high school, but Willingham's strength and impressive moves to the basket give him the edge.

Analysis: The 1993-94 season promises to be a far better year for UConn. Donyell Marshall's continued improvement could eventually carry this bunch, while most coaches would be ecstatic with an Ollie-Fair backcourt. If either Knight or Willingham emerges as a legitimate center, then the Huskies will really be in business.

1993-94 ROSTER

	POS	HT	YR	FGP	FTP	3-PT	RPG	APG	PPG
Donyell Marshall	F	6'9"	Jr.	.50	.83	20/54	7.8	1.1	17.0
Brian Fair	G	6'3"	Jr.	.42	.65	64/166	3.6	1.3	13.7
Kevin Ollie	G	6'3"	Jr.	.39	.74	1/9	2.3	5.6	7.9
Donny Marshall	F	6'6"	Jr.	.47	.76	1/3	4.2	1.1	7.8
Eric Hayward	F	6'7"	So.	.61	.53	—	2.6	0.3	3.7
Travis Knight	C	7'0"	So.	.46	.41	0/5	2.5	0.4	2.9
Rudy Johnson	F	6'6"	So.	.39	.43	4/17	2.1	0.6	2.7
Nantambu Willingham	C	6'10"	Jr.	.33	.41	—	2.1	0.2	1.4
Jeff Calhoun	G	6'2"	So.	.18	—	2/9	0.1	0.2	0.5
Ray Allen	G	6'5"	Fr.	—	—	—	—	—	—
Ruslan Inyatkin	G/F	6'6"	Fr.	—	—	—	—	—	—
Kirkland King	F	6'7"	Fr.	—	—	—	—	—	—

DePAUL

Conference: Great Midwest
1992-93: 16-15, 5th GMC

1992-93 NCAAs: Not invited
Coach: Joey Meyer (184-94)

Opening Line: Why the Blue Demons failed to receive an NIT invite following the 1992-93 season was one of the year's great mysteries—particularly when you consider that UAB got a bid despite losing to DePaul three times. However, it was hardly a vintage Blue Demon team, anyway. They won fewer games than they had in any single season since 1976-77. Added experience, solid coaching, and a decent recruiting class will put DePaul back in the tourney hunt.

Guard: Although he can play four positions, Tom Kleinschmidt (17.7 PPG) will start the year at big guard. He's the team's best all-around player by far. Brandon Cole is a very talented playmaker who must refrain from always forcing the action. Peter Patton, a pleasant surprise last winter, displays unusual maturity. Lead guards Dwayne Austin (freshman) and Belefia Parks want Cole's job.

Forward: Muscular Kris Hill is a proven rebounder (8.3 RPG), but he needs to refine his offensive game. Former prep phenom Will Macon arrives at DePaul with two years of eligibility. A big-time scorer, he'll be tough to keep out of the lineup at small forward. Brian Currie still needs polish. Heavily recruited frosh Marcus Singer will see time at guard and forward.

Center: The pro scouts haven't exactly formed a line to watch senior Michael Ravizee and sophomore Bryant Bowden; but when these two manage to stay out of foul trouble, they can make a difference at the defensive end. Ravizee is a tenacious rebounder who spent the off-season playing regularly in the famed Chicago summer leagues.

Analysis: The Blue Demons will face terrific competition game after game in the Great Midwest, but—with good health and a few breaks—they should approach the 20-win plateau. While Kleinschmidt is a proven commodity, Cole and Ravizee are the two players who must lift their respective games to the next level. Macon is a special recruit.

1993-94 ROSTER

	POS	HT	YR	FGP	FTP	3-PT	RPG	APG	PPG
Tom Kleinschmidt	G	6'5"	Jr.	.47	.76	27/90	5.4	3.0	17.7
Brandon Cole	G	6'0"	Jr.	.46	.76	54/152	3.0	4.4	13.7
Kris Hill	F	6'8"	Sr.	.60	.69	1/1	8.3	1.1	9.5
Bryant Bowden	F/C	6'8"	So.	.52	.63	0/2	3.5	0.2	4.8
Michael Ravizee	C	6'9"	Sr.	.48	.64	—	4.5	0.4	4.3
Brian Currie	F	6'7"	So.	.53	.52	—	2.1	0.4	3.3
Peter Patton	G	6'1"	So.	.27	.76	21/72	1.8	2.5	3.2
Malik Murray	F	6'8"	So.	.80	.40	0/1	0.4	0.1	0.8
Dwayne Austin	G	6'1"	Fr.	—	—	—	—	—	—
Will Macon	F	6'7"	Jr.	—	—	—	—	—	—
Belefia Parks	G	6'1"	Jr.	—	—	—	—	—	—
Marcus Singer	G/F	6'6"	Fr.	—	—	—	—	—	—

DUKE

Conference: Atlantic Coast   **1992-93** NCAAs: 1-1
1992-93: 24-8, T-3rd ACC   **Coach:** Mike Krzyzewski (394-184)

Opening Line: After making the Final Four six times in seven years and winning consecutive national championships, the Blue Devils were conspicuous by their absence in New Orleans last April. Does that mean the program has hit the skids? Hardly. Grant Hill may be the country's best player and Mike Krzyzewski ranks as the premier coach. A heralded recruiting class will shore up any holes, especially up front.

Guard: There's no replacing Bobby Hurley, who ranks as one of the best point guards ever to grace the college game. But Chris Collins, son of former NBA star Doug Collins, showed enough last year to make the ACC's All-Freshman team. Marty Clark has plenty of experience and Kenny Blakeney provides good defense. The athletic and versatile Grant can dominate from either guard spot or forward. Freshman Jeff Capel should make an immediate impact.

Forward: Hill will once again be teamed with 6'8" Antonio Lang, who is an inside threat at both ends of the court. Clark can also play forward. A couple of 6'11" prep studs, Greg Newton and Joey Beard, will add size and depth to a team that got outrebounded in ACC play last year. Tony Moore showed promise before being sidelined midway through his freshman season.

Center: Cherokee Parks has quietly done an admirable job in the shadow of Christian Laettner. His injury vs. California in the NCAA tourney (a game Duke lost) shows what he means to the team. Erik Meek will never dominate, but he fills in adequately.

Analysis: The Blue Devils don't rebuild, they reload. While Hurley and Thomas Hill will be sorely missed, Duke should have better depth in 1993-94 than last season. What it will no longer have is the NCAA's most prolific playmaker, meaning Grant Hill and Parks will have to work harder for their points. A trip to nearby Charlotte in early April would surprise no one.

1993-94 ROSTER

	POS	HT	YR	FGP	FTP	3-PT	RPG	APG	PPG
Grant Hill	F/G	6'8"	Sr.	.58	.75	4/14	6.4	2.8	18.0
Cherokee Parks	C	6'11"	Jr.	.65	.72	—	6.9	0.4	12.3
Marty Clark	G/F	6'6"	Sr.	.51	.87	17/40	2.3	1.4	7.3
Antonio Lang	F	6'8"	Sr.	.52	.66	0/1	5.5	0.8	6.9
Chris Collins	G	6'3"	So.	.40	.63	37/85	1.1	1.2	5.8
Erik Meek	C	6'10"	Jr.	.59	.57	—	2.9	0.2	3.5
Tony Moore	F	6'8"	So.	.59	1.00	—	2.0	0.3	2.9
Kenny Blakeney	G	6'4"	Sr.	.42	.66	4/17	1.5	0.7	2.9
Joey Beard	C/F	6'11"	Fr.	—	—	—	—	—	—
Jeff Capel	G	6'4"	Fr.	—	—	—	—	—	—
Greg Newton	C/F	6'11"	Fr.	—	—	—	—	—	—
Carmen Wallace	G/F	6'7"	Fr.	—	—	—	—	—	—

FLORIDA

Conference: Southeastern
1992-93: 16-12, 3rd SEC East

1992-93 NIT: 0-1
Coach: Lon Kruger (179-148)

Opening Line: The last two years, Lon Kruger's teams were big flirts during the regular season yet were not asked to the Big Dance. Actually, both clubs came up lame in the stretch run of the regular season and were subsequently banished to the NIT. The Gators are more experienced this year, especially in the backcourt, and thus should avoid any late-season pitfalls.

Guard: Craig Brown boasts a solid stroke from 3-point land and will be counted on to score more this season. His ball-handling skills are better than those of most shooting guards. Dan Cross can play both guard spots but is needed most at the point. He must improve upon last season's meager output of 1.8 assists per game. Look for sophomore Jason Anderson and freshman Greg Williams to be in the regular rotation.

Forward: There's a huge void with the departures of 1992-93 starters Stacey Poole and Hosie Grimsley. Heralded transfer Ben Davis, a tenacious rebounder, should step into Poole's power-forward post. He played well and contributed as a freshman at powerhouse Kansas two seasons ago. Sophomore swing man Brian Thompson, one of the nation's best preps two years ago, should start living up to his billing. Finland native Martti Kuisma has good shooting range for his size.

Center: Andrew DeClercq has been a starter since arriving on campus and has improved steadily as a result of his tremendous work ethic. Reserve Jermaine Carlton transferred earlier this year, meaning Svein Dyrkolbotn or John Griffiths could find unexpected playing time.

Analysis: Florida was supposed to make its move last year, but the club didn't deal well with the expectations and regressed a bit. A year older and wiser, the Gators have the experience at guard and center and the talent at forward to finally make the NCAA Tournament. Either Brown or DeClercq has to emerge as the go-to man.

1993-94 ROSTER

	POS	HT	YR	FGP	FTP	3-PT	RPG	APG	PPG
Craig Brown	G	6'3"	Sr.	.43	.68	51/118	3.2	2.4	10.9
Andrew DeClercq	C	6'10"	Jr.	.57	.58	—	7.1	0.5	10.5
Martti Kuisma	F	6'11"	Sr.	.44	.55	50/123	3.4	0.7	8.2
Dan Cross	G	6'3"	Jr.	.57	.64	6/15	2.3	1.8	5.2
Jason Anderson	G/F	6'4"	So.	.32	.44	7/23	1.1	0.6	2.2
Brian Thompson	F	6'6"	So.	.35	.78	0/1	1.2	0.4	2.1
Dametri Hill	F	6'7"	So.	.33	.64	—	0.6	0.2	1.1
Svein Dyrkolbotn	C	6'8"	Jr.	.55	.50	—	0.9	0.2	1.0
Ben Davis	F	6'9"	Jr.	—	—	—	—	—	—
John Griffiths	C	6'0"	Fr.	—	—	—	—	—	—
Tony Mickens	F	6'5"	Jr.	—	—	—	—	—	—
Greg Williams	G	6'3"	Fr.	—	—	—	—	—	—

FLORIDA STATE

Conference: Atlantic Coast   **1992-93 NCAAs:** 3-1
1992-93: 25-10, 2nd ACC   **Coach:** Pat Kennedy (268-136)

Opening Line: Florida State proved that 1991-92 wasn't beginner's luck after all. During their inaugural ACC season that year, the Seminoles went 22-10, finished second in the nation's premier conference, and advanced to the Sweet 16 for the first time in 20 years. Despite numerous injuries last season, FSU once again finished second in the ACC while making it a round further in the NCAA Tournament. This season, the Seminoles must replace standout performers Sam Cassell, Doug Edwards, and Rodney Dobard.

Guard: Charlie Ward took a pounding as the football team's starting quarterback last year, and he carried shoulder and foot problems into the basketball season. Coach Pat Kennedy can ill-afford to have Ward less than 100 percent this time around. It's doubtful that Chuck Graham will be as explosive as he was before suffering a season-ending knee injury in the 1992-93 opener.

Forward: Scintillating swing man Bob Sura, who finished second in the ACC in scoring last season, will likely spend most of his time in the frontcourt to fill the void left by Edwards and Dobard. Derrick Carroll and Maurice Robinson both gained valuable experience as freshmen last year. Stephen Gruhl and freshmen David Grabuloff and Kirk Luckman will provide much-needed height.

Center: Seven-footer Andre Reid returns after missing most of last season with a broken hand. In addition to assuming a good chunk of the rebounding load, Reid will have to become more offensive-minded. If nothing else, Jonathan Kerner supplies good size as a back-up.

Analysis: The Seminoles will probably struggle until Ward joins the team in January. The erratic Sura holds the key to season-long success. He must keep the mental lapses to a minimum. FSU still has the athletes to get up and down the court with the best of them, but rebounding is a huge question mark minus Edwards and Dobard.

1993-94 ROSTER

	POS	HT	YR	FGP	FTP	3-PT	RPG	APG	PPG
Bob Sura	F	6'5"	Jr.	.45	.64	73/220	6.1	2.7	19.9
Charlie Ward	G	6'1"	Sr.	.46	.67	16/50	2.6	5.5	7.8
Derrick Carroll	F	6'6"	So.	.40	.70	26/79	2.6	1.0	5.4
Maurice Robinson	F	6'6"	So.	.57	.57	—	2.0	0.1	3.5
Andre Reid	C	7'0"	Jr.	.50	.50	—	4.2	0.4	3.4
Stephen Gruhl	F	6'8"	Jr.	.67	.33	—	0.2	—	1.8
Scott Shepherd	G	5'11"	So.	.25	.73	1/7	0.3	0.5	1.5
Jonathan Kerner	C	6'11"	So.	.60	.75	—	1.2	0.1	0.9
Chuck Graham	G	6'3"	Sr.	—	—	—	1.0	—	—
James Collins	G	6'4"	Fr.	—	—	—	—	—	—
David Grabuloff	F	6'7"	Fr.	—	—	—	—	—	—
Kirk Luckman	F/C	6'10"	Fr.	—	—	—	—	—	—

GEORGETOWN

Conference: Big East
1992-93: 20-13, 8th Big East

1992-93 NIT: 4-1
Coach: John Thompson (484-178)

Opening Line: Eleven scholarship players return to a Hoya squad that fell to Minnesota, 62-61, in last year's NIT title game. Largely due to an 8-10 league record, 1992-93 marked the first time since 1978 that Georgetown failed to advance to the NCAA Tournament. All eyes will be on sophomore All-America candidate Othella Harrington at center and veteran playmaker Joey Brown.

Guard: Brown's the quarterback who controls nearly everything on the floor. He makes up for a few too many bad decisions with tremendous quickness and an improved shooting touch. Brown will be supported by Eric Micoud and John Jacques at big guard. Micoud is a solid perimeter scorer, while Jacques can distribute the ball as well as he shoots it. Lamont Morgan provides in-your-face defense off the bench.

Forward: Robert Churchwell has quietly emerged as one of the Big East's most dependable small forwards—at both ends of the floor. He moves as well without the ball as anyone on the Hoya team. Duane Spencer (6'10") has the tools to play inside or out. Like Harrington, he didn't miss a start as a true freshman in 1992-93. Back-up Lonnie Harrell left school, meaning swing man Kevin Millen will have to bear a heavier load.

Center: Step aside, Mr. Ewing, Mr. Mutombo, and Mr. Mourning—a young stud named Harrington is the new sheriff in town. Harrington combines relentless rebounding with a soft shooting touch, and his outlet passing is a thing of beauty. Don Reid contributes solid minutes when needed.

Analysis: The time is now for a Hoya team with the perfect blend of experience and youth. It's not often a coach as talented as John Thompson has the luxury of welcoming back virtually an entire roster. If Micoud and Jacques can improve their perimeter strokes, it will free up the big fellas inside. If that happens, Georgetown will become a major player on the national scene.

1993-94 ROSTER

	POS	HT	YR	FGP	FTP	3-PT	RPG	APG	PPG
Othella Harrington	C	6'10"	So.	.57	.75	—	8.8	1.0	16.8
Robert Churchwell	F	6'6"	Sr.	.45	.73	17/46	6.1	1.8	11.5
Joey Brown	G	5'10"	Sr.	.42	.75	28/82	4.1	6.2	10.7
Duane Spencer	F	6'10"	So.	.39	.64	0/2	7.1	1.6	8.7
Eric Micoud	G	6'1"	So.	.36	.83	24/78	1.3	1.0	6.0
John Jacques	G	6'3"	Jr.	.39	.69	18/47	1.5	0.9	5.0
Kevin Millen	G/F	6'6"	Jr.	.42	.55	8/22	1.5	0.2	2.4
Irvin Church	G	6'1"	Jr.	.25	.50	10/47	0.7	0.1	2.2
Lamont Morgan	G	6'3"	Sr.	.52	.53	2/10	0.8	0.3	1.7
Don Reid	C/F	6'8"	Jr.	.42	.45	—	2.1	0.1	1.6
Vladimir Bosanac	F	6'9"	Sr.	.25	—	0/2	0.8	—	0.5
Cheikh Dia	F/C	6'8"	Fr.	—	—	—	—	—	—

GEORGE WASHINGTON

Conference: Atlantic 10
1992-93: 21-9, T-2nd A-10

1992-93 NCAAs: 2-1
Coach: Mike Jarvis (157-84)

Opening Line: Last year was truly a dream season for a G.W. team that made its first NCAA Tournament appearance since 1961 and its first-ever Sweet 16 showing. After knocking off New Mexico and Southern in NCAA tourney play, the Colonials fell in the next round to Michigan. The team loses three of its top four scorers, but six key contributors return, including last year's freshman phenom, Yinka Dare.

Guard: Shifty Alvin Pearsall enters his fourth season as the Colonials' starting point guard. He's only five assists away from becoming the school's all-time leader. Kwame Evans, instant offense off the bench last winter as a frosh, will take over for Dirkk Surles (14.5 PPG). Key reserve Omo Moses can play either backcourt position, while swing man Marcus Ford excels on defense.

Forward: The graduation of last year's starting forwards, Sonni Holland and Bill Brigham, costs G.W. 21.5 PPG and 10.3 RPG. Pure shooter Nimbo Hammons and young but talented Vaughn Jones will be their likely replacements, along with Ford. Jones's many contributions don't always show up in the boxscore. True frosh Ferdinand Williams was one of the premier high school players in New Jersey last season.

Center: Dare, 7'1" and 265 pounds, put G.W. on the basketball map with more than ten rebounds, three blocks, and a dozen points per game last winter. While Dare hails from Nigeria, back-ups Rene Harry and Adama Kah are natives of the West Indies and Gambia, respectively.

Analysis: The incredibly athletic Dare, seemingly a Hakeem Olajuwon clone, made a good Colonial team great in 1992-93. Although his supporting cast won't be quite as experienced this time around, he'll still have a field day with most Atlantic 10 centers. With Dare in the pivot and heralded coach Mike Jarvis on the sidelines, G.W. will be in the A-10 title hunt from start to finish.

1993-94 ROSTER

	POS	HT	YR	FGP	FTP	3-PT	RPG	APG	PPG
Yinka Dare	C	7'1"	So.	.55	.47	—	10.3	0.1	12.2
Nimbo Hammons	F	6'6"	Jr.	.43	.58	37/83	3.0	1.0	5.8
Kwame Evans	G	6'6"	So.	.40	.74	23/54	1.7	0.5	5.6
Alvin Pearsall	G	5'11"	Sr.	.36	.71	13/39	2.7	3.1	5.6
Vaughn Jones	F	6'6"	So.	.37	.67	3/14	2.8	1.6	5.4
Omo Moses	G	6'2"	Jr.	.37	.70	15/39	2.4	1.9	5.4
Antoine Hart	F	6'8"	Jr.	.46	.52	—	1.4	0.1	1.9
Marcus Ford	G/F	6'7"	Sr.	.16	1.00	2/13	0.5	0.4	0.6
Anthony Wise	C	6'10"	Jr.	—	.50	—	0.7	—	0.1
Adama Kah	C	6'9"	Sr.	.50	—	—	0.1	—	0.1
Rene Harry	C	6'11"	Fr.	—	—	—	—	—	—
Ferdinand Williams	F	6'9"	Fr.	—	—	—	—	—	—

GEORGIA

Conference: Southeastern   **1992-93 NIT:** 0-1
1992-93: 15-14, 4th SEC East   **Coach:** Hugh Durham (496-285)

Opening Line: Despite lofty expectations at this time last year, the Bulldogs could do no better than 15-14. They advanced to the NIT after a strong finish, but they promptly fell to West Virginia in the first round. With part-time starter Kendall Rhine the only significant loss, the forecast for 1993-94 is quite bright. Coach Hugh Durham is expecting great things from his much-ballyhooed 1992 recruiting class now that they're more experienced as sophomores.

Guard: Senior Bernard Davis is more than adequate at the point. Lightning quick on the break, he's also a defensive stopper. Ty Wilson is a solid two guard with nice range who didn't miss a start last winter. He'll share time with multi-talented Cleveland Jackson (11 PPG) and fundamentally sound Steve Jones. Five other guards are also on the roster.

Forward: Carlos Strong was the most highly regarded of Georgia's 1992 recruiting haul and he didn't disappoint. His tremendous athletic ability and brute strength make him a force in the paint. Fellow sophomore Shandon Anderson played well in a reserve role last year and deserves a chance to start—but so does super-smooth Dathon Brown. Freshman Melvin Drake, a prep All-American, can play every position except center.

Center: Although frequent double-teams and collapsing defenses give seven-footer Charles Claxton fits, he'll be the next Bulldog in the pros. Despite his inconsistent play, he's expected to emerge as one of the South's most dominant big men. Sophomore Terrell Bell was declared academically ineligible.

Analysis: With so many new faces on last year's squad, the Bulldogs' inability to win the close ones wasn't all that surprising. That won't be tolerated this time around, though. With Claxton, Strong, and Jackson leading the way, anything less than an NCAA tourney invite will be viewed as a disappointment.

1993-94 ROSTER

	POS	HT	YR	FGP	FTP	3-PT	RPG	APG	PPG
Charles Claxton	C	7'0"	Jr.	.56	.48	—	6.6	0.4	11.5
Cleveland Jackson	G	6'5"	Sr.	.47	.66	35/91	2.9	1.5	11.0
Shandon Anderson	F/G	6'6"	So.	.49	.61	9/26	3.6	1.5	9.4
Carlos Strong	F	6'8"	So.	.48	.51	—	5.7	1.1	9.2
Bernard Davis	G	5'11"	Sr.	.40	.74	55/135	2.0	4.0	9.0
Ty Wilson	G	6'3"	Jr.	.39	.78	43/116	2.8	2.1	8.5
Dathon Brown	F	6'5"	Jr.	.39	.78	2/3	2.8	0.3	3.8
Steve Jones	G/F	6'6"	So.	.67	.67	0/2	0.9	0.1	1.7
Pertha Robinson	G	6'0"	So.	.44	.47	3/7	0.8	1.5	1.3
Brian Peterson	G	6'4"	Jr.	.40	—	0/1	0.3	0.3	1.0
Chris Tiger	F	6'8"	Fr.	—	—	—	1.0	—	—
Melvin Drake	F/G	6'6"	Fr.	—	—	—	—	—	—

GEORGIA TECH

Conference: Atlantic Coast   **1992-93 NCAAs:** 0-1
1992-93: 19-11, 6th ACC   **Coach:** Bobby Cremins (340-205)

Opening Line: Coach Bobby Cremins had everyone scratching their heads last spring, as he accepted the head-coaching job at South Carolina on March 24 but then changed his mind three days later. This came shortly after Georgia Tech's upset victory in the ACC championship game and its upset loss to Southern in Round 1 of the NCAA tourney. The Yellow Jackets lose Malcolm Mackey to graduation, but four starters return.

Guard: Sharp-shooting point guard Travis Best provides excellent floor leadership. He shot nearly 46 percent from 3-point range last winter and ranked fourth in the ACC in assists. Big guard Drew Barry, a starter throughout the second half of the 1992-93 season, is also a long-range scoring threat and a superb ball-handler. Little-used Rod Balanis and Todd Harlicka supply shaky backcourt depth.

Forward: Solidly built James Forrest has emerged as one of the nation's premier big forwards after ranking among last year's ACC leaders in scoring, rebounding, and field goal percentage. He was the ACC tourney MVP. Multi-talented Martice Moore, the 1993 ACC Rookie of the Year, is the perfect complement to Forrest up front. He can also swing to big guard. Veteran Darryl Barnes and Tech's lone recruit, promising 6'10" Eddie Elisma, will help off the bench.

Center: Ivano Newbill, the Yellow Jackets' top frontcourt reserve for the past two seasons, appears more than ready to take over for Mackey in the low post. He's not as tenacious a rebounder as Mackey was, but Newbill does throw his weight around on defense.

Analysis: This group was incredibly inconsistent a year ago, but added experience should do wonders, especially for youngsters like Barry and Moore. Still, while Cremins's first five players can match up with any five in the ACC, there's barely any depth. The starters will have to play a ton of minutes and, more importantly, stay healthy.

1993-94 ROSTER

	POS	HT	YR	FGP	FTP	3-PT	RPG	APG	PPG
James Forrest	F	6'8"	Jr.	.54	.69	2/4	7.5	1.4	19.5
Travis Best	G	5'11"	Jr.	.47	.75	80/175	3.1	5.9	16.3
Martice Moore	G/F	6'8"	So.	.45	.76	24/72	4.6	2.2	10.5
Drew Barry	G	6'5"	So.	.47	.81	25/78	3.4	5.5	7.3
Ivano Newbill	C	6'10"	Sr.	.51	.56	0/1	3.8	0.8	2.8
John Kelly	G	5'11"	Jr.	.50	.50	2/4	0.6	0.4	1.6
Rod Balanis	G	6'3"	Sr.	.44	1.00	0/3	0.8	—	1.5
Darryl Barnes	F	6'9"	Sr.	.54	.50	—	1.4	0.2	1.4
Todd Harlicka	G	6'2"	Jr.	.25	—	1/4	0.3	0.4	0.7
Eddie Elisma	F	6'10"	Fr.	—	—	—	—	—	—
Fred Vinson	G	6'4"	Sr.	—	—	—	—	—	—

ILLINOIS

Conference: Big Ten
1992-93: 19-13, T-3rd Big Ten

1992-93 NCAAs: 1-1
Coach: Lou Henson (609-295)

Opening Line: Illinois hasn't managed to win 20 games in either of the last two seasons, which come after a stretch of nine straight 20-win campaigns. Is this a program on the decline? Hardly. After a two-year absence from the NCAA Tournament, Illinois made it back to the Big Dance last year thanks to a third-place finish in the Big Ten. With most everyone returning, Lou Henson's club will again be one of the league's top teams.

Guard: Unsung Rennie Clemons is the best point guard most people have never heard of. He's an excellent penetrator and distributor and has improved the range on his jumper. After experimenting at the point, heralded frosh Richard Keene found his niche at shooting guard last season. He's deadly from 3-point land. Senior T.J. Wheeler is a dependable reserve.

Forward: Andy Kaufmann, the school's fourth-leading all-time scorer, is gone, but the Illini certainly don't lack experience with the return of fifth-year senior Tom Michael and junior Robert Bennett. Michael can light it up from downtown, while Bennett is pretty efficient close to the basket. Transfer Shelly Clark, a junior college All-American, should provide what the Illini starved for last season—physical play.

Center: Deon Thomas, a fifth-year senior, has emerged as one of the best centers in the country. Despite off-court problems early in his career, he is now focused and playing well consistently. Expect 20 points and ten rebounds per game from the big guy.

Analysis: Kaufmann's departure may be a blessing in disguise. His on-court tendencies to hog the ball and turn it over (a team-high 112 in 1992-93) and his well-chronicled class-attendance problems disrupted the team's cohesiveness. Thomas, along with Keene, should give the Illini a potent inside-outside combination. Twenty wins is certainly a reachable goal.

1993-94 ROSTER

	POS	HT	YR	FGP	FTP	3-PT	RPG	APG	PPG
Deon Thomas	C/F	6'9"	Sr.	.61	.65	—	8.0	1.2	18.3
Rennie Clemons	G	6'0"	Sr.	.48	.63	6/16	3.1	4.2	9.9
Richard Keene	G	6'6"	So.	.41	.74	57/145	2.2	2.3	8.3
T.J. Wheeler	G	6'4"	Sr.	.46	.87	27/78	3.4	2.3	8.0
Robert Bennett	F	6'6"	Jr.	.54	.54	0/1	6.8	0.5	7.6
Tom Michael	F	6'8"	Sr.	.42	.70	26/65	2.2	0.6	4.1
Steve Roth	C	6'10"	Jr.	.67	—	—	0.3	—	0.3
Matt Griswold	G	6'4"	So.	—	—	—	0.4	—	—
Shelly Clark	C/F	6'9"	Jr.	—	—	—	—	—	—
Kiwane Garris	G	6'2"	Fr.	—	—	—	—	—	—
Jerry Hester	F	6'6"	Fr.	—	—	—	—	—	—
Brett Robisch	F	6'10"	Fr.	—	—	—	—	—	—

INDIANA

Conference: Big Ten
1992-93: 31-4, 1st Big Ten

1992-93 NCAAs: 3-1
Coach: Bob Knight (619-214)

Opening Line: If any coach can survive the loss of three starters, including national Player of the Year Calbert Cheaney, Bob Knight's the guy. It doesn't hurt to have the likes of Damon Bailey, Alan Henderson, and one of the top three recruiting classes in America at your disposal. Led by Cheaney (22.4 PPG), the Hoosiers went 17-1 in the Big Ten last year and were ranked No. 1, but they fell in the Midwest Regional final to Kansas.

Guard: When the ball's in Bailey's hands, good things usually happen. His court savvy and veteran leadership will help this young club, as will his ability to put the ball in the basket. Designated shooter Todd Leary seems best suited to coming off the bench. Knight may move Pat Graham from small forward to big guard or give freshmen Sherron Wilkerson or Robert Foster a chance. Wilkerson has all the tools to be a special player.

Forward: The $64,000 question centers around Henderson's injured knee, which hampered him from February on last year. If healthy, he'll push for a league rebounding title and All-Big Ten honors. Hard-nosed Brian Evans was a pleasant surprise last season. Knight raves about him every chance he gets. Graham, Wilkerson, and fellow frosh Robbie Eggers figure to see plenty of minutes.

Center: As sparkling as Richard Mandeville's high school press clippings may be, replacing Matt Nover is going to take time. Nover was a true blue-collar performer. Todd Lindeman may be in over his head at this level.

Analysis: Despite the losses of Cheaney, Greg Graham, and Nover, Knight returns several quality veterans and complements them with three highly regarded recruits: Wilkerson, Eggers, and Mandeville. While it may take them a couple of months (or longer) to feel comfortable in the I.U. system, the Hoosiers again will be a team no one wants to draw in the postseason.

1993-94 ROSTER

	POS	HT	YR	FGP	FTP	3-PT	RPG	APG	PPG
Alan Henderson	F	6'9"	Jr.	.49	.64	1/6	8.1	0.9	11.1
Damon Bailey	G	6'3"	Sr.	.46	.73	38/91	3.3	4.1	10.1
Pat Graham	G/F	6'5"	Sr.	.51	.72	9/21	1.3	1.4	6.5
Brian Evans	F	6'8"	So.	.43	.69	23/65	3.9	1.3	5.3
Todd Leary	G	6'3"	Sr.	.47	.89	22/57	1.0	1.2	4.8
Pat Knight	G	6'6"	Jr.	.47	.45	—	0.5	0.8	1.0
Robbie Eggers	F	6'10"	Fr.	—	—	—	—	—	—
Robert Foster	G	6'4"	Fr.	—	—	—	—	—	—
Steve Hart	G	6'2"	Fr.	—	—	—	—	—	—
Todd Lindeman	C	7'0"	So.	—	—	—	—	—	—
Richard Mandeville	C	7'0"	Fr.	—	—	—	—	—	—
Sherron Wilkerson	G/F	6'4"	Fr.	—	—	—	—	—	—

IOWA

Conference: Big Ten
1992-93: 23-9, T-3rd Big Ten

1992-93 NCAAs: 1-1
Coach: Tom Davis (426-222)

Opening Line: No team suffered through more adversity last year than Iowa. The death of workhorse forward Chris Street devastated the team. There were also four key seniors on the roster who will be tough to replace, three of whom were starters. Optimism in Iowa City centers around two of the Big Ten's premier sophomores, as well as a pair of touted freshmen. James Winters and Kevin Smith must provide senior leadership.

Guard: Coach Tom Davis will try to replace the 3-point shooting of Val Barnes with that of Chris Kingsbury, a hot-shot recruit who can fill it up. At the point, Smith is cat-quick and can handle the ball, although consistency is a question. Mon'ter Glasper is a steady back-up. Fred Brown Jr., son of the NBA's "Downtown" Freddie Brown, sat out last year as a redshirt freshman and then decided to transfer.

Forward: Winters is tough on the glass and a big reason Iowa led the nation in rebounding margin last year. Ditto for sophomore banger Russ Millard. Fellow soph Kenyon Murray excels in the open court, meaning he fits right in with Davis's style of play. Junior Jim Bartels pitches in at both guard and forward. The most help among the newcomers will likely be supplied by Jess Settles, Iowa's Mr. Basketball.

Center: The Hawkeyes will have to make do without Acie Earl, one of the game's premier shot-blockers. Millard and junior college transfer John Carter will be asked to pick up the slack, but neither has Earl's height or advanced skills at both ends of the court.

Analysis: There's enough gas in the tank to reach the NCAA Tournament, where Davis-coached teams never lose in the first round. However, it's unlikely the Hawkeyes will make any noise after Round 1. Davis's liberal substitution patterns will be hindered by a lack of experience and depth. Moreover, no one on the roster is a proven scorer.

1993-94 ROSTER

	POS	HT	YR	FGP	FTP	3-PT	RPG	APG	PPG
James Winters	F	6'5"	Sr.	.52	.61	0/2	5.5	1.1	8.6
Kenyon Murray	F	6'5"	So.	.42	.58	6/31	4.1	1.1	6.7
Russ Millard	F/C	6'8"	So.	.45	.67	3/8	3.8	0.5	5.2
Kevin Smith	G	5'11"	Sr.	.39	.63	8/30	2.0	3.9	5.0
Jim Bartels	G/F	6'5"	Jr.	.38	.76	13/46	1.6	0.8	3.2
Kevin Skillett	G	6'3"	Jr.	.65	.64	3/6	0.8	0.3	2.0
Mon'ter Glasper	G	6'2"	So.	.41	.66	4/10	1.7	1.8	1.9
John Carter	F/C	6'9"	Jr.	—	—	—	—	—	—
Chris Kingsbury	G	6'5"	Fr.	—	—	—	—	—	—
Jess Settles	F	6'7"	Fr.	—	—	—	—	—	—

IOWA STATE

Conference: Big Eight
1992-93: 20-11, T-2nd Big Eight

1992-93 NCAAs: 0-1
Coach: Johnny Orr (452-333)

Opening Line: Last spring's NCAA tourney journey was short-lived, as Johnny Orr's Cyclones shot 36 percent from the field and lost the opener to UCLA. Minus the finest all-around backcourt tandem in school history in Justus Thigpen and Ron Bayless, Orr is hoping that some of his 1993 recruits can contribute immediately. Wishful thinking? You never know. A veteran frontcourt does return intact. ISU boasted a perfect record at home last year.

Guard: All-league performers Thigpen and Bayless combined for more than 30 PPG last season. Diminutive freshmen Jason Kimbrough and Jacy Holloway will battle for the starting point job, while fellow frosh Derek Hayes will get a long look at shooting guard. Kimbrough, a passing whiz, displays the most potential of the three. Count on plenty of freshman mistakes.

Forward: Julius Michalik (12.0 PPG) and swing man Fred Hoiberg are back as the Cyclones' leading returning scorers. Michalik played for the Czechoslovakian Olympic team in 1992. Although he's seven inches shorter than Michalik, Hoiberg led the team in rebounding last year. Always hustling, Hoiberg also tops ISU in skinned elbows and knees. Bradley transfer James Hamilton and returnees Hurl Beechum and Fred Brown offer above-average depth.

Center: Besides maybe Kimbrough, no other Cyclone player will be scrutinized more closely than 6'11" junior Loren Meyer. One of the most improved players in the Big Eight in 1992-93, Meyer must continue to mature. His intense work ethic certainly helps.

Analysis: With one of the Big Eight's top two backcourts suddenly ranking among the least experienced in the nation, ISU will likely struggle in the early going. The continued development of Meyer, along with that of the newcomers, will ultimately determine the team's fate. The Cyclones could post another 20-win season if—and only if—Kimbrough and Hayes live up to their advance billing.

1993-94 ROSTER

	POS	HT	YR	FGP	FTP	3-PT	RPG	APG	PPG
Julius Michalik	F	6'11"	Jr.	.52	.89	21/59	4.3	3.1	12.0
Fred Hoiberg	F/G	6'4"	Jr.	.55	.82	22/60	6.3	3.0	11.6
Loren Meyer	C	6'11"	Jr.	.54	.71	0/3	4.9	1.3	9.8
Hurl Beechum	F	6'5"	Jr.	.40	.73	18/53	1.6	0.6	3.0
Fred Brown	F	6'4"	Sr.	.35	.66	1/7	1.0	0.5	2.6
Donnell Bivens	F	6'5"	Sr.	.45	.70	0/3	1.0	0.3	1.8
James Hamilton	F	6'7"	Jr.	—	—	—	—	—	—
Derek Hayes	G	6'4"	Fr.	—	—	—	—	—	—
Jacy Holloway	G	6'0"	Fr.	—	—	—	—	—	—
Saun Jackson	F	6'5"	Jr.	—	—	—	—	—	—
Jason Kimbrough	G	5'11"	Fr.	—	—	—	—	—	—
Joe Modderman	F/G	6'8"	Fr.	—	—	—	—	—	—

KANSAS

Conference: Big Eight
1992-93: 29-7, 1st Big Eight

1992-93 NCAAs: 4-1
Coach: Roy Williams (132-37)

Opening Line: The Jayhawks' level of play was as high as their lofty reputation last year. They reached the Final Four for the third time in six years, beating Indiana in the Midwest Regional before falling to North Carolina. While the graduation of standout guards Rex Walters and Adonis Jordan and center Eric Pauley creates quite a predicament, coach Roy Williams did corral one of the country's top recruiting classes.

Guard: Losing perhaps the No. 1 starting backcourt in the country (Walters and Jordan) is bound to take its toll. Nonetheless, it doesn't sting as much when the premier high school playmaker, Jacque Vaughn, and college basketball's top sixth man, Steve Woodberry, are the replacements. Vaughn, a 4.0 student, and super-quick Calvin Rayford will share time at the point, while Sean Pearson and Greg Gurley will spell Woodberry.

Forward: Kansas suffered another blow when starter Darrin Hancock was declared ineligible for 1993-94. He was the best athlete on the squad. Richard Scott, who's coming off an outstanding postseason, will contend for all-league recognition. Swing man Patrick Richey and heralded frosh B.J. Williams will fill the void left by Hancock. Richey's a deadly perimeter shooter.

Center: Improved Greg Ostertag and recruits Scot Pollard (7'0") and Nick Proud (6'10") should be able to equal Pauley's output of a year ago (12 PPG, five RPG). While Ostertag has always been a fine shot-blocker, he emerged offensively in last year's NCAAs.

Analysis: If any team can survive the loss of the nation's best backcourt and two other starters, it's K.U. The coaching staff will continue to rely on offensive precision, relentless defense, and an abundance of depth. It's the Kansas way. The perimeter shooting, point-guard play, and Ostertag's maturity will determine how far Kansas will go in the NCAA tourney.

1993-94 ROSTER

	POS	HT	YR	FGP	FTP	3-PT	RPG	APG	PPG
Richard Scott	F	6'7"	Sr.	.61	.51	—	5.3	0.9	10.6
Steve Woodberry	G/F	6'4"	Sr.	.51	.88	25/58	4.2	2.8	10.1
Patrick Richey	G/F	6'8"	Sr.	.54	.79	10/24	3.4	1.0	6.7
Greg Ostertag	C	7'2"	Jr.	.52	.60	—	4.1	0.4	5.3
Sean Pearson	G/F	6'4"	So.	.44	.50	17/57	1.2	0.4	3.4
Greg Gurley	G	6'5"	Jr.	.49	.59	12/31	0.9	0.5	2.1
Calvin Rayford	G	5'6"	Jr.	.39	.60	2/8	0.6	1.6	1.4
T.J. Whatley	G	6'4"	So.	.44	.40	1/2	—	0.1	1.4
Scot Pollard	F/C	7'0"	Fr.	—	—	—	—	—	—
Nick Proud	C	6'10"	Fr.	—	—	—	—	—	—
Jacque Vaughn	G	6'0"	Fr.	—	—	—	—	—	—
B.J. Williams	F	6'8"	Fr.	—	—	—	—	—	—

KANSAS STATE

Conference: Big Eight
1992-93: 19-11, T-5th Big Eight

1992-93 NCAAs: 0-1
Coach: Dana Altman (63-53)

Opening Line: Despite numerous skeptics who said KSU was too small, had little depth, and couldn't shoot straight, coach Dana Altman's "Cardiac 'Cats" clawed and scratched their way to another NCAA Tournament last spring. It marked KSU's fifth trip to the Big Dance in the past seven seasons. Despite falling to Tulane by two points in the opening round, the Wildcats had made their mark with conference tourney wins over Nebraska and Kansas. Three starters and the team's top two reserves return.

Guard: No individual player keyed KSU's surge in 1992-93 any more than lightning-quick point guard Anthony Beane, the Big Eight Newcomer of the Year. He specializes in nailing game-winning shots. Backcourt mate Askia Jones led the 'Cats in scoring during league play. Reserve Brian Henson, whose brother Steve plays for the Atlanta Hawks, is a long-range scorer and pesky defender. Newcomer Belvis Noland was a juco All-American.

Forward: The graduation of starters Vincent Jackson and Aaron Collier means Altman is missing nearly 23 PPG and 11 RPG. Dependable sub Ron Lucas will have first crack at the small-forward job, while junior college transfers Demond Davis and Stanley Hamilton are expected to contribute in a hurry.

Center: Deryl Cunningham averages nearly double figures in points and rebounds. Altman would prefer to move him to his more natural big-forward post if frosh Kevin Lewis—a top-100 recruit—is ready to man the pivot. He averaged five blocks per game in high school.

Analysis: Although the 'Cats aren't a very pretty team, their tenacious defense and good ball movement on offense keeps them in nearly every game they play. If a couple of the newcomers can blend their talents with Beane, Jones, and Cunningham, they will continue their trend of exciting, surprising play.

1993-94 ROSTER

	POS	HT	YR	FGP	FTP	3-PT	RPG	APG	PPG
Askia Jones	G	6'5"	Sr.	.42	.75	45/135	4.1	2.9	13.2
Anthony Beane	G	5'10"	Sr.	.41	.71	42/110	2.9	4.6	10.1
Deryl Cunningham	F/C	6'7"	Sr.	.48	.60	—	8.3	1.8	9.3
Brian Henson	G	6'1"	Jr.	.35	.67	48/149	2.3	1.1	7.3
Ron Lucas	F	6'7"	Sr.	.49	.69	0/1	3.1	0.8	4.7
George Hill	C	6'8"	So.	.60	.27	—	0.6	—	1.4
Brian Gavin	G	6'1"	So.	.40	.75	4/7	0.8	1.3	1.4
Hamilton Strickland	C	6'9"	Jr.	.33	—	—	0.9	0.1	0.5
Demond Davis	G/F	6'4"	Jr.	—	—	—	—	—	—
Stanley Hamilton	F	6'6"	Jr.	—	—	—	—	—	—
Kevin Lewis	C	6'10"	Fr.	—	—	—	—	—	—
Belvis Noland	G/F	6'4"	Jr.	—	—	—	—	—	—

KENTUCKY

Conference: Southeastern
1992-93: 30-4, 2nd SEC East

1992-93 NCAAs: 4-1
Coach: Rick Pitino (228-105)

Opening Line: Last year's appearance in the Final Four brought Kentucky basketball all the way back from the dark days of the late 1980s. Now, the future of Big Blue hoops looks like the old days—glorious. Do you think Rick Pitino would have turned down all those NBA offers if he didn't see a possible national championship in the near future? All-America forward Jamal Mashburn will be missed, but there is no shortage of talent in Lexington.

Guard: Diminutive Travis Ford (5'9") is a crafty playmaker who is deadly from 3-point range. He just might be the best point guard in college basketball. He'll get ample backcourt scoring support from long-range bombers Jeff Brassow, Tony Delk, and freshman Jeff Sheppard. Brassow will join Ford and center Gimel Martinez as the Wildcats' co-captains. Sheppard shot 53 percent from 3-point land as a high school senior.

Forward: Rodrick Rhodes has shown flashes of the brilliance that made him one of the nation's top preps in 1991-92. Now he needs to concentrate on being more consistent. Jared Prickett really came on at the end of his freshman season, and Pitino has called him a "bigger, more skilled version of (former Wildcat) Deron Feldhaus." Andre Riddick's forte is blocking shots; his nemesis is free throw shooting. Walter McCarty (6'9"), a top-40 prep who sat out last year as a Prop 48, should contribute immediately.

Center: The steady combo of Rodney Dent and Martinez brings a lot of poise and experience to this position. Kentucky won't win many games from the pivot, but it won't lose many either.

Analysis: Ford is the little engine that can drive the Wildcats back to the Final Four. His decision-making and long-distance shooting will be the foundation for the season. There are enough of the quick, athletic types in the supporting cast to make this team a legitimate NCAA title contender.

1993-94 ROSTER

	POS	HT	YR	FGP	FTP	3-PT	RPG	APG	PPG
Travis Ford	G	5'9"	Sr.	.53	.88	101/191	2.1	4.9	13.6
Rodrick Rhodes	F	6'6"	So.	.45	.69	27/70	2.4	1.8	9.1
Rodney Dent	C	6'10"	Sr.	.58	.53	—	5.1	0.5	6.4
Gimel Martinez	C	6'8"	Sr.	.49	.71	17/34	3.0	1.3	6.2
Jared Prickett	F	6'9"	So.	.49	.68	2/17	4.6	1.6	5.5
Tony Delk	G	6'1"	So.	.45	.73	18/51	1.9	0.7	4.5
Andre Riddick	F/C	6'9"	Jr.	.60	.46	—	3.1	0.2	4.5
Jeff Brassow	G	6'5"	Sr.	.44	.69	23/68	1.9	1.2	4.1
Chris Harrison	G	6'1"	Jr.	.27	.67	2/12	0.4	1.0	1.5
Anthony Epps	G	6'2"	Fr.	—	—	—	—	—	—
Walter McCarty	C	6'9"	So.	—	—	—	—	—	—
Jeff Sheppard	G	6'4"	Fr.	—	—	—	—	—	—

LOUISIANA STATE

Conference: Southeastern   **1992-93 NCAAs:** 0-1
1992-93: 22-11, 2nd SEC West   **Coach:** Dale Brown (403-223)

Opening Line: In case you haven't heard, there are a couple of newcomers in Baton Rouge. And word is they're pretty good. Actually, there are four incoming recruits at LSU, but two of them were penciled in as starters the day they signed. The tailor-made backcourt of Randy Livingston and Ronnie Henderson won't make fans forget Chris Jackson and Shaquille O'Neal just yet, but there's no denying that their impact will be substantial.

Guard: *Basketball Weekly* united Livingston and Henderson last spring when the magazine released its five-man prep All-America first team. Henderson is a leaper with a soft shooting touch, while Livingston is a one-man band at the point-guard spot. Hot-shooting Jamie Brandon and versatile Andre Owens won't relinquish the backcourt without a fight. Brandon was the team's second-leading scorer last year.

Forward: Clarence Ceasar has made some clutch baskets in his day. He can stick the outside jumper and has a knack for robbing opponents of the ball on defense. Sean Gipson emerged as a steady performer last year after transferring in from Hiwassee Junior College in Tennessee. Lenear Burns and swing man Doug Annison offer capable relief. Brandon can also play forward.

Center: For the second straight year, the Tigers have to replace a pivot man who was their leading scorer. This time it's Geert Hammink. Dale Brown might have to rely heavily on newcomers Glover Jackson and James Bristow.

Analysis: Brown followed his trend of "less is more" last year by guiding the Shaq-less Tigers into the NCAA Tournament. This time around, he'll have some real blue-chippers on the roster, which belies his underdog preference. There's a major question mark in the middle, but Livingston, Henderson, Ceasar, and Brandon are enough to the lead the team to the Big Dance.

1993-94 ROSTER

	POS	HT	YR	FGP	FTP	3-PT	RPG	APG	PPG
Jamie Brandon	G	6'4"	Sr.	.49	.70	27/53	4.9	1.2	11.8
Clarence Ceasar	F	6'7"	Jr.	.38	.58	38/112	6.2	1.7	9.8
Sean Gipson	F	6'6"	Sr.	.44	.73	0/1	4.9	1.7	9.2
Andre Owens	G	6'5"	Sr.	.45	.67	18/59	1.9	2.7	8.1
Doug Annison	G/F	6'6"	So.	.41	.68	6/28	1.7	0.6	4.2
Lenear Burns	F	6'7"	Sr.	.53	.53	2/5	2.5	0.4	4.0
Roman Roubtchenko	F	6'8"	So.	.43	1.00	0/3	0.9	0.1	0.6
James Bristow	C/F	6'9"	Fr.	—	—	—	—	—	—
Ronnie Henderson	G	6'5"	Fr.	—	—	—	—	—	—
Glover Jackson	C	6'10"	Jr.	—	—	—	—	—	—
Randy Livingston	G	6'4"	Fr.	—	—	—	—	—	—

LOUISVILLE

Conference: Metro   **1992-93 NCAAs:** 2-1
1992-93: 22-9, 1st Metro   **Coach:** Denny Crum (518-192)

Opening Line: Last season, the Louisville program regained some of its old luster with its best conference record since 1982-83 and its first Sweet 16 appearance since Pervis Ellison was a senior. The team does lose two starters, but hometown prep hero Jason Osborne joins the fray. Denny Crum seems to be coaching with renewed enthusiasm, no doubt fueled by the fact that his roster is full of thoroughbreds.

Guard: Greg Minor is a rock at the two-guard position. Last year, he canned 53 percent of his field goals and 43 percent of his 3-pointers. The Cards suffered a blow over the summer when Keith LeGree, last year's starter at lead guard, announced he was transferring. Sophomore shooter Tick Rogers will see his minutes rise. Osborne, a 6'8" swing man, may spend time in the backcourt.

Forward: All Dwayne Morton did in 1992-93 was shoot 53.1 percent from 3-point range—nearly the best mark in the country. With a lethal first step and a good inside game to boot, Morton will make a bid for All-America honors. Osborne and Beau Zach Smith were both among the country's top 75 prep players last winter, according to *Basketball Weekly*. Osborne, ranked No. 10 by the publication, offers both power and finesse. Reserve Brian Kiser can help bust a zone with his outside shot.

Center: Clifford Rozier, a transfer from North Carolina, has become a devastating inside force. He's among the top half-dozen players at his position in the country. Brian Hopgood, a part-timer last year, has transferred.

Analysis: The unexpected loss of LeGree certainly weakens the backcourt, and the team still needs to improve its free throw shooting. However, the Cards are as athletic as ever and sport four prime-time players in Rozier, Morton, Minor, and Osborne—all of whom are at least 6'6". The Cardinals will likely improve upon last year's success.

1993-94 ROSTER

	POS	HT	YR	FGP	FTP	3-PT	RPG	APG	PPG
Dwayne Morton	F	6'6"	Sr.	.53	.74	51/96	4.7	2.2	16.1
Cliff Rozier	C	6'9"	Jr.	.56	.57	0/2	10.9	2.0	15.7
Greg Minor	G	6'6"	Sr.	.53	.75	42/97	5.5	2.8	14.1
Brian Kiser	F	6'7"	So.	.34	.50	11/30	1.1	0.4	2.2
Tick Rogers	G	6'5"	So.	.46	.50	9/18	1.0	0.9	1.9
Robby Wine	G	6'4"	So.	.25	—	—	—	0.3	0.5
Doug Calhoun	F	6'4"	Sr.	—	.50	—	0.3	—	0.3
Jason Osborne	F/G	6'8"	Fr.	—	—	—	—	—	—
Matt Simons	C	6'11"	Fr.	—	—	—	—	—	—
Beau Zach Smith	F	6'8"	Fr.	—	—	—	—	—	—
DeJuan Wheat	G	6'0"	Fr.	—	—	—	—	—	—
Alvin Sims	G/F	6'4"	Fr.	—	—	—	—	—	—

MARQUETTE

Conference: Great Midwest   **1992-93 NCAAs:** 0-1
1992-93: 20-8, 3rd GMC   **Coach:** Kevin O'Neill (62-53)

Opening Line: Kevin O'Neill is bringing the Marquette program back to the prosperity it enjoyed during the Al McGuire era (and the years shortly thereafter). Last year, with a squad that returned all of its scholarship players from the previous season, Marquette made its first appearance in the NCAA Tournament in ten years. It also made it into the A.P. poll for the first time in 14 years. A strong nucleus returns, but standout forward Ron Curry has departed.

Guard: Diminutive Tony Miller has blossomed into the player most believed him to be when he arrived in Milwaukee two years ago—someone who could make the Warriors a national power. Miller is both the offensive and defensive catalyst, and the only chink in his armor is his free throw shooting. Robb Logterman and defensive ace William Gates are both experienced performers, while newcomer Anthony Pieper was a scoring machine in high school.

Forward: A starter at center last season, Damon Key will probably fill Curry's spot at power forward, where he has also seen significant time throughout his career. With Key and sophomore swing man Roney Eford, the Warriors could have one of the best shooting tandems in the country at the two forward slots. Sophomore Dwaine Streater needs to bulk up to effectively bang down low. Three freshmen forwards are also available.

Center: Shot-blocker Jim McIlvaine is back to patrol the paint. While he has improved his offensive game, McIlvaine still needs to get a better feel for things in the paint, especially dealing with double-teams.

Analysis: O'Neill's intensity mirrors that of conference rival Bob Huggins at Cincinnati. With his fiery demeanor, and with a host of quality players returning, the Warriors are sure to meet the success they achieved last season. Eford's primed for a big scoring year, as he's sure to benefit from Miller's creativity.

1993-94 ROSTER

	POS	HT	YR	FGP	FTP	3-PT	RPG	APG	PPG
Damon Key	F/C	6'8"	Sr.	.52	.87	2/6	5.7	1.1	13.6
Jim McIlvaine	C	7'1"	Sr.	.58	.71	—	4.8	0.8	11.0
Roney Eford	G/F	6'8"	So.	.46	.80	29/68	4.2	1.7	11.0
Tony Miller	G	5'11"	Jr.	.42	.67	46/98	4.1	7.6	8.8
Robb Logterman	G	6'3"	Sr.	.37	.82	46/124	1.9	2.2	7.1
William Gates	G	6'0"	Jr.	.46	.44	1/3	2.3	1.6	3.4
Dwaine Streater	F/C	6'9"	So.	.25	.80	—	1.4	0.1	0.8
Faisal Abraham	F	6'7"	Fr.	—	—	—	—	—	—
Chris Crawford	F	6'8"	Fr.	—	—	—	—	—	—
Abel Joseph	F	6'8"	Fr.	—	—	—	—	—	—
Amal McCaskill	C/F	6'9"	So.	—	—	—	—	—	—
Anthony Pieper	G	6'4"	Fr.	—	—	—	—	—	—

MASSACHUSETTS

Conference: Atlantic 10
1992-93: 24-7, 1st A-10

1992-93 NCAAs: 1-1
Coach: John Calipari (101-57)

Opening Line: Although 1991-92 was the greatest season in school history record-wise (30-5), last year's performance was just as admirable. Able to stay in the top 25 for most of the season despite the loss of three starters from the 1991-92 team, John Calipari showed that the program he created in five short years had arrived to stay. Calipari's strength—recruiting—makes UMass a perennial player on the national scene.

Guard: Steady Derek Kellogg improved nicely as the 1992-93 campaign progressed, and he returns to quarterback the club. Athletic Mike Williams was supposed to take over at the point last season, but he was hampered by injuries. Williams is best suited to the role of scorer off the bench. Jerome Malloy, a double-digit scorer last season, decided to transfer.

Forward: Lou Roe and Donta Bright, Calipari's two biggest recruiting prizes thus far at UMass, comprise a formidable duo. A Prop 42 casualty last season, Bright should have no trouble stepping in for the departed Tony Barbee. Swing man Dana Dingle will also help out. Tough and talented, Roe has already distinguished himself as the A-10's best power forward.

Center: Harper Williams, the team's cornerstone the last two years, has departed, and little is left in the cupboard. Look for help to come from Marcus Camby, a 6'11" freshman, as well as borderline talents Jeff Meyer (7'2") and Ted Cottrell. Tyrone Weeks, an undersized workhorse who fits the mold of Harper Williams, was ruled academically ineligible.

Analysis: Calipari's style has been to rely on a solid backcourt and a quick and aggressive front line. With Harper Williams standing at 6'7", it was essentially a three-forward look for the starting lineup, which is likely to continue. Roe could slide over to the pivot at times and easily hold his own. Wherever he plays, the Minutemen's attack will be structured around him.

1993-94 ROSTER

	POS	HT	YR	FGP	FTP	3-PT	RPG	APG	PPG
Lou Roe	F	6'7"	Jr.	.56	.73	—	9.2	1.3	13.8
Mike Williams	G	6'2"	Jr.	.42	.70	30/100	2.7	1.9	11.6
Derek Kellogg	G	6'3"	Jr.	.37	.81	19/57	2.8	5.2	5.0
Dana Dingle	F	6'6"	So.	.43	.60	3/13	3.7	1.1	4.9
Craig Berry	G	6'1"	Sr.	.43	.75	1/1	0.6	0.4	2.0
Jeff Meyer	C	7'2"	Jr.	.29	.53	—	1.5	0.2	1.8
Ted Cottrell	C/F	6'9"	So.	.39	.78	—	1.5	0.1	1.1
Chris Robinson	G	6'2"	Sr.	.29	.39	1/4	0.6	0.7	0.7
Donta Bright	F	6'6"	So.	—	—	—	—	—	—
Marcus Camby	C/F	6'11"	Fr.	—	—	—	—	—	—
Carmelo Travieso	G	6'3"	Fr.	—	—	—	—	—	—

MEMPHIS STATE

Conference: Great Midwest   **1992-93 NCAAs:** 0-1
1992-93: 20-12, 2nd GMC   **Coach:** Larry Finch (145-81)

Opening Line: Don't feel too bad for Tiger coach Larry Finch following the departure of four starters, including All-American Anfernee Hardaway. With the return of David Vaughn following knee surgery, three top reserves, an important starter, two highly regarded prep recruits, and five additional newcomers, Finch's cupboard is hardly bare. MSU frequently underachieved last year and lost to Western Kentucky in the first round of the NCAA tourney.

Guard: Freshman Sylvester "Deuce" Ford may eventually make fans forget about Hardaway and shooting guard Billy Smith (15.9 PPG). Ford handles the ball well and displays solid range. He'll start from Day One. Either returning regular Sidney Coles or capable back-up Marcus Nolan will start alongside Ford. Coles, whose brother Bimbo plays for the Miami Heat, can swing between both guard positions.

Forward: If Vaughn can sufficiently recover from knee surgery, he should help comprise a pretty formidable front line along with sophomore Rodney Newsom and much-ballyhooed freshman Cedric Henderson. Vaughn will eventually join Hardaway in the NBA, while Newsom is a solid scorer who doesn't mind mixing it up inside. Henderson's a quick leaper who finishes well and plays great defense.

Center: While Jerrell Horne's a decent jumper, shot-blocker, and rebounder, he's no Anthony Douglas (11.8 PPG, 8.3 RPG). He lacks Douglas's stamina and nasty demeanor. Unless Horne's game suddenly explodes, Finch will likely move Vaughn (his nephew) to the pivot.

Analysis: Though long on potential, MSU is one of the most difficult teams in the country to access accurately. Vaughn's health is an unknown, as are flashy recruits Ford and Henderson (both McDonald's All-Americans). If this trio does play up to par, they'll have sufficient help from a handful of dependable role-players to make the year exciting.

1993-94 ROSTER

	POS	HT	YR	FGP	FTP	3-PT	RPG	APG	PPG
David Vaughn	F	6'9"	So.	.36	—	2/2	8.0	2.0	10.0
Rodney Newsom	F/G	6'6"	So.	.39	.66	27/90	2.1	0.9	6.3
Jerrell Horne	C/F	6'8"	Sr.	.49	.59	—	2.7	0.2	3.9
Leon Mitchell	G	6'3"	Jr.	.49	.72	4/17	1.6	2.4	3.3
Marcus Nolan	G	6'2"	Jr.	.45	.55	8/21	0.7	1.2	2.9
Sidney Coles	G	6'4"	So.	.35	.70	4/16	1.4	1.9	2.0
Rob Forrest	G	5'11"	So.	.50	—	0/2	0.3	0.2	1.0
Deuce Ford	G/F	6'6"	Fr.	—	—	—	—	—	—
Chris Garner	G	5'10"	Fr.	—	—	—	—	—	—
Cedric Henderson	F	6'7"	Fr.	—	—	—	—	—	—
Johnny Miller	G	6'4"	Fr.	—	—	—	—	—	—
Justin Wimmer	F/G	6'8"	Jr.	—	—	—	—	—	—

MICHIGAN

Conference: Big Ten
1992-93: 31-5, 2nd Big Ten

1992-93 NCAAs: 5-1
Coach: Steve Fisher (99-37)

Opening Line: The Wolverines have become a victim of their own success. With such a young starting lineup advancing to the NCAA title game the past two seasons, blue-chip recruits got scared off because potential playing time seemed limited. Now, the Fab Five is broken up with Chris Webber's early departure to the NBA. Also, the team's top four reserves—Eric Riley, Rob Pelinka, James Voskuil, and Michael Talley—have graduated. That leaves only ten players on the roster and a lot of questions about depth, especially up front.

Guard: This will be Michigan's strength, as Jalen Rose and Jimmy King return as starters and heralded freshman Bobby Crawford joins the fray. Plus, sophomore point guard Dugan Fife seems ready to contribute. King, a leaper with a good jump shot, could emerge as a star. Rose didn't show much improvement after a spectacular freshman season.

Forward: Other than defensive stopper Ray Jackson, the cupboard is bare. Jackson was perhaps the most improved player on the team last year, and he'll be counted on for more offense and help on the boards. Olivier Saint Jean is a promising swing-type player from France, but he'll need time to adjust to American basketball. Leon Derricks, little used as a freshman, is rail-thin. Expect frequent use of a three-guard lineup.

Center: Juwan Howard had better stay out of foul trouble, as he's the sole inside presence on the team. With tremendous determination and a soft shooting touch, he'll control the middle when he's on the floor. Derricks must get stronger to provide relief.

Analysis: The Beatles managed to do pretty well as a Fab Four, but Michigan won't be so lucky. If Webber had returned, they'd be talking national championship in Ann Arbor. As it stands, the Wolverines consist of four top-line returning starters and supporting players that have scored a combined 59 points in their college careers. It'll be a good year for Michigan, but not fab.

1993-94 ROSTER

	POS	HT	YR	FGP	FTP	3-PT	RPG	APG	PPG
Jalen Rose	G	6'8"	Jr.	.45	.72	33/103	4.2	3.9	15.4
Juwan Howard	C	6'9"	Jr.	.51	.70	0/2	7.4	1.9	14.6
Jimmy King	G	6'5"	Jr.	.51	.65	37/92	4.1	3.1	10.8
Ray Jackson	F	6'6"	Jr.	.49	.63	2/13	4.4	2.2	9.0
Jason Bossard	G	6'4"	Sr.	.37	—	1/10	0.3	—	1.5
Leon Derricks	F/C	6'9"	So.	.29	.43	0/1	1.3	0.2	0.8
Dugan Fife	G	6'2"	So.	—	.59	0/4	0.9	0.7	0.5
Bobby Crawford	G	6'3"	Fr.	—	—	—	—	—	—
Chris Fields	F	6'5"	So.	—	—	—	—	—	—
Olivier Saint Jean	F	6'7"	Fr.	—	—	—	—	—	—

MICHIGAN STATE

Conference: Big Ten   **1992-93 NIT:** 0-1
1992-93: 15-13, T-8th Big Ten   **Coach:** Jud Heathcote (378-255)

Opening Line: Last year was a litany of frustration for MSU, as it habitually choked during the Big Ten season. With rumors flying, Jud Heathcote decided in the off-season to coach the club one more year, possibly two, and assistant Tom Izzo has been designated as his successor. This should prove to be beneficial for the Spartans because it will eliminate distracting in-season speculation.

Guard: Junior shooting guard Shawn Respert, who has led the team in scoring the past two seasons, is the best in the Big Ten at his position. He'll be one of the school's all-time greats by the time he's finished. Point guard Eric Snow's pathetic free throw shooting (.234 career percentage) has made him a major liability down the stretch of close games.

Forward: Sweet-shooting swing man Kris Weshinskey is more of a guard than a small forward, but he can be deadly from the wing opposite Respert. There's a glut of talent with sophomores Daimon Beathea, Quinton Brooks, and Jamie Feick, as well as incoming freshman Jon Garavaglia. One of them must bulk up and be willing to do the dirty work that departed Dwayne Stephens did the last three years.

Center: Big Mike Peplowski is gone, leaving the pivot duties to senior Anthony Miller. "Pig" is a natural power forward who's an effective scorer close to the basket and a workhorse on the glass. Miller's stamina has yet to be tested with starter's minutes, however. There's little depth, if any, behind him.

Analysis: MSU will definitely be an undersized team, but Heathcote knows how to get the most out of an unconventional lineup. This year, he'll need to implement an up-tempo attack with Respert, who thrives in transition, as the centerpiece. Weshinskey must play well consistently, as his performance fluctuated too often last season. Snow must somehow become a respectable free throw shooter.

1993-94 ROSTER

	POS	HT	YR	FGP	FTP	3-PT	RPG	APG	PPG
Shawn Respert	G	6'3"	Jr.	.48	.86	60/140	4.0	2.6	20.1
Kris Weshinskey	F/G	6'4"	Sr.	.42	.71	37/108	3.4	2.4	10.4
Anthony Miller	C/F	6'9"	Sr.	.61	.54	1/1	5.2	0.5	6.6
Eric Snow	G	6'3"	Jr.	.55	.27	0/5	2.6	5.2	4.3
Quinton Brooks	F	6'7"	So.	.58	.58	0/1	2.7	0.2	4.2
Daimon Beathea	F	6'7"	So.	.45	.43	0/2	1.4	0.1	2.2
Steve Nicodemus	G	6'4"	So.	.56	.43	1/7	0.5	0.3	1.1
Jamie Feick	F	6'8"	So.	.13	.25	0/1	1.4	0.1	0.4
David Hart	G	6'4"	So.	.60	—	—	0.3	0.6	0.3
Mark Bluem	F	6'6"	Jr.	—	—	0/1	0.2	—	—
Jon Garavaglia	F	6'9"	Fr.	—	—	—	—	—	—
Steve Polonowski	F	6'9"	Fr.	—	—	—	—	—	—

MINNESOTA

Conference: Big Ten
1992-93: 22-10, T-5th Big Ten

1992-93 NIT: 5-0
Coach: Clem Haskins (212-173)

Opening Line: After catching fire in March and capturing the first NIT crown in school history, the Golden Gophers are more determined—and more qualified—than ever to make their first NCAA tourney visit since 1990. All five starters and the team's No. 1 reserve are back, thereby putting the pressure on Clem Haskins to coach the Gophers into legitimate Big Ten title contention.

Guard: Arriel McDonald and future pro Voshon Lenard have quietly emerged as the Big Ten's best all-around backcourt. While Lenard (17.1 PPG) seemingly was born to score points, McDonald is a superb passer who displays great court awareness. Lenard thrives in pressure situations, as he showed throughout the NIT. Townsend Orr and Ryan Wolf both can do damage from long range.

Forward: Jayson Walton, an exceptional inside-outside player, improved as much as any starter in the Big Ten last winter. He ranked No. 2 on the team in scoring and rebounding. Leading rebounder Randy Carter is a big, physical youngster with good hands and a soft shooting touch. Versatile reserves David Washington and Kevin Baker—as well as muscular freshman John Thomas—will enable Walton and Carter to catch their breath from time to time.

Center: Chad Kolander is no star, but he gets the job done in the middle. He's an aggressive rebounder and defender who has yet to really develop his offensive game. The coaching staff is still waiting for enigmatic Ernest Nzigamasabo to realize his potential.

Analysis: Haskins has bellyached about the Gophers not receiving the credit they rightfully deserve for the past two seasons. Now it's time to put up or shut up, as his club has accumulated plenty of proven talent. How many teams return 74 points of offense? If relatively injury free, Minnesota should contend for its first league title in a dozen years.

1993-94 ROSTER

	POS	HT	YR	FGP	FTP	3-PT	RPG	APG	PPG
Voshon Lenard	G	6'4"	Jr.	.48	.80	58/158	3.6	2.6	17.1
Jayson Walton	F/G	6'6"	Jr.	.49	.71	1/2	6.3	2.0	11.9
Randy Carter	F	6'8"	Sr.	.55	.59	0/2	6.9	1.0	11.4
Arriel McDonald	G	6'2"	Sr.	.47	.74	24/63	2.8	4.4	11.0
Townsend Orr	G	6'1"	Sr.	.37	.75	28/88	2.6	2.8	6.6
Chad Kolander	C/F	6'9"	Jr.	.60	.51	—	4.3	1.2	5.9
Ryan Wolf	G	6'3"	Jr.	.36	.56	16/44	0.6	0.4	3.2
Ernest Nzigamasabo	F/C	6'9"	Sr.	.52	.69	—	2.1	0.5	3.1
David Washington	F/C	6'10"	Jr.	.50	.17	—	1.8	0.3	2.0
David Grim	F	6'7"	So.	.19	.44	2/9	0.9	0.7	1.3
Kevin Baker	F	6'6"	So.	.44	—	—	0.6	0.3	0.7
John Thomas	F	6'9"	Fr.	—	—	—	—	—	—

MISSOURI

Conference: Big Eight
1992-93: 19-14, 7th Big Eight

1992-93 NCAAs: 0-1
Coach: Norm Stewart (612-306)

Opening Line: Four starters and as many prominent reserves return to a Tiger team that rode a roller-coaster last season. The Tigers lost seven straight games in February, rebounded to win the Big Eight Tournament, then lost in the first round of the NCAAs to Temple. Although Mizzou doesn't shoot particularly well and has tended to lose the close games, things still look pretty bright for 1993-94.

Guard: Melvin Booker (15.8 PPG) came into his own last year as a do-it-all lead guard, earning first-team all-league honors. He still may be guilty of thinking shot before pass on occasion. Reggie Smith is extremely quick and a great leaper, while Mark Atkins (the team's top 3-point threat) gives the club an offensive spark off the bench. Frosh Jason Sutherland has glowing credentials.

Forward: The graduation of multi-talented starter Jeff Warren opens up a small-forward job for Lamont Frazier or Marlo Finner. Frazier was hobbled for a portion of 1992-93 with an injured ankle, while Finner (a UTEP transfer the year before last) has had trouble with stiffness in his knee. Power forward Jevon Crudup is the best all-around performer on the Tiger team. He definitely makes his presence felt in the paint at both ends of the floor.

Center: No longer just a tall, skinny kid who showed occasional glimpses of potential, Chris Heller made a name for himself last season. He's blessed with impressive offensive skills and runs the floor well for a big man. Heller was named MVP of the Big Eight Tournament.

Analysis: Led by Booker, Crudup, and Heller, the Tigers will likely battle Oklahoma State and Kansas for top honors in the Big Eight. Long-time coach Norm Stewart is a little concerned about Booker's ability to handle the ball in pressure and Crudup's tendency to get into foul trouble. However, most college coaches have bigger worries.

1993-94 ROSTER

	POS	HT	YR	FGP	FTP	3-PT	RPG	APG	PPG
Melvin Booker	G	6'2"	Sr.	.44	.82	51/141	4.3	3.7	15.8
Jevon Crudup	F	6'9"	Sr.	.50	.50	3/3	8.3	1.2	13.6
Mark Atkins	G	6'5"	Sr.	.40	.67	81/212	3.5	1.2	12.2
Chris Heller	C	6'10"	Sr.	.42	.52	—	5.9	1.2	7.7
Lamont Frazier	G/F	6'4"	Sr.	.53	.70	2/6	4.0	2.8	7.5
Reggie Smith	G	6'2"	Sr.	.35	.65	4/27	2.4	3.9	4.5
Marlo Finner	F	6'6"	Jr.	.51	.34	3/9	3.4	0.4	3.7
Jed Frost	G	6'1"	Sr.	.37	.75	8/22	0.5	1.5	2.0
Derrick Johnson	G	6'1"	So.	.36	.78	0/2	0.7	0.7	1.9
Jason Sutherland	G	6'1"	Fr.	—	—	—	—	—	—
Kelly Thames	G/F	6'7"	Fr.	—	—	—	—	—	—
Julian Winfield	G/F	6'5"	So.	—	—	—	—	—	—

NEBRASKA

Conference: Big Eight
1992-93: 20-11, T-2nd Big Eight

1992-93 NCAAs: 0-1
Coach: Danny Nee (233-160)

Opening Line: Last season, Nebraska went to the NCAA Tournament for the third straight year—the longest such streak in school history. The 'Huskers were again knocked off in the first round, this time by New Mexico State, but it was still a fine year for the young squad as it tied for second place in the Big Eight. Center Derrick Chandler (11 PPG, eight RPG) is the only graduation loss, although back-up center Amos Gregory has transferred.

Guard: Senior playmaker Jamar Johnson is the driving force behind Nebraska's offensive attack. A consummate point guard, he does a superb job of establishing tempo. Backcourt mate Eric Piatkowski is Nebraska's leading scorer. A first-team All-Big Eight pick, he's a deadly outside shooter who also enjoys drawing contact inside. Nebraska has good guard depth, as Jaron Boone and Erick Strickland (1992-93 Big Eight Freshman of the Year) come off the bench. Andre Woolridge transferred to Iowa.

Forward: Veteran starter Bruce Chubick is a heady, hard-working player who does all the little things coaches love, while Terrance Badgett has the potential to become one of the Big Eight's premier frontcourters. A standout freshman last season, Badgett is the team's most athletic player. Tom Best is the only regular contributor off the bench.

Center: The loss of Gregory over the summer has dimmed some of the hopes in Nebraska. However, sturdy Melvin Brooks was a junior college standout last year and could be a pleasant surprise.

Analysis: As three talented sophomores continue to play with greater confidence, this team is sure to improve. Nee's teams are always well-schooled in the fundamentals and this group is no exception. The senior leadership is superb, led by Johnson and Piatkowski. There has never been this much individual talent on a Nebraska team, meaning March could actually be an enjoyable month for a change.

1993-94 ROSTER

	POS	HT	YR	FGP	FTP	3-PT	RPG	APG	PPG
Eric Piatkowski	G	6'7"	Sr.	.49	.76	48/129	5.7	2.5	16.7
Jamar Johnson	G	6'0"	Sr.	.43	.74	28/92	2.9	3.3	9.8
Bruce Chubick	F	6'7"	Sr.	.52	.68	3/12	5.7	1.0	8.4
Erick Strickland	G	6'3"	So.	.45	.73	32/88	2.0	2.1	7.8
Jaron Boone	G	6'6"	So.	.41	.82	17/57	2.3	2.8	6.9
Terrance Badgett	F	6'6"	So.	.50	.66	10/28	3.5	1.1	6.7
Tom Best	F	6'8"	Sr.	.45	.47	8/22	4.8	1.3	4.7
Melvin Brooks	C	6'8"	Jr.	—	—	—	—	—	—
Jason Glock	G/F	6'5"	So.	—	—	—	—	—	—
Clinton Moore	C	6'10"	Fr.	—	—	—	—	—	—

NEVADA-LAS VEGAS

Conference: Big West   **1992-93 NIT:** 0-1
1992-93: 21-8, 2nd Big West   **Coach:** Rollie Massimino (378-249)

Opening Line: A late-season collapse sabotaged what looked to be a glorious first year for Rollie Massimino; UNLV had raced out to a 13-1 start in 1992-93. The Rebels finished in second place in the Big West's regular season, then were upset in the Big West Tournament in the second round. Despite finishing the season 25th in the A.P. poll, UNLV was bypassed for the NCAA tourney. Needless to say, fans in Vegas are anxious for a return to the Big Dance after the school went to consecutive Final Fours in 1990 and '91.

Guard: Distributor deluxe Dedan Thomas (8.6 APG) returns to quarterback the offense. Not only is Thomas a tremendous asset directing the Rebels' high-octane attack, but he does an excellent job on the defensive end. Reggie Manuel, who can play both guard posts, will see most of his time at shooting guard. Ken Gibson and Lawrence Thomas supply quality depth.

Forward: The top-notch trio of J.R. Rider (29.1 PPG), Dexter Boney (17.0 PPG), and Evric Gray (16.2 PPG)—70 percent of last season's scoring—is gone, leaving the Rebels with marked inexperience here. Junior college transfers Patrick Savoy and Clayton Johnson will provide immediate help. Both boast tremendous athleticism and should fit right in.

Center: Essentially, UNLV will have a three-forward look to its lineup, much like last season. Height comes from senior Fred Haygood, redshirt freshman Kebu Stewart, and incoming frosh Brian Hocevar. Stewart should see the most time.

Analysis: Minus a suspended Rider, the Rebels were trounced in the first round of last year's NIT by USC, 90-74, their worst loss ever at the Thomas and Mack Center. Massimino is certainly hoping that wasn't a harbinger of things to come. With the backcourt being by far the strongest part of his team, Rollie's Rebels will indeed be a runnin' bunch in 1993-94.

1993-94 ROSTER

	POS	HT	YR	FGP	FTP	3-PT	RPG	APG	PPG
Reggie Manuel	G	6'3"	Jr.	.46	.73	22/67	4.3	1.3	8.5
Dedan Thomas	G	6'0"	Sr.	.55	.55	4/19	4.1	8.6	7.5
Ken Gibson	G	6'3"	Sr.	.47	.79	55/120	1.5	0.9	7.3
Lawrence Thomas	G	6'1"	So.	.48	.64	10/25	1.0	1.3	4.4
Damian Smith	G	6'2"	So.	.47	.83	2/5	0.3	—	1.5
Fred Haygood	F	6'8"	Sr.	.45	.44	—	1.6	0.1	1.0
Brian Hocevar	F	6'8"	Fr.	—	—	—	—	—	—
Clayton Johnson	F	6'5"	Jr.	—	—	—	—	—	—
Seth Meyers	G	6'6"	Fr.	—	—	—	—	—	—
Patrick Savoy	F	6'8"	Jr.	—	—	—	—	—	—
Jermaine Smith	G	6'2"	Fr.	—	—	—	—	—	—
Kebu Stewart	F	6'8"	Fr.	—	—	—	—	—	—

NEW ORLEANS

Conference: Sun Belt
1992-93: 26-4, 1st Sun Belt

1992-93 NCAAs: 0-1
Coach: Tim Floyd (141-74)

Opening Line: After missing postseason play in 1991-92 for the first time in Tim Floyd's tenure at New Orleans, the Privateers rebounded with a vengeance last year. They blasted through the Sun Belt with an 18-0 mark and were Division I's only unbeaten team on the road (9-0). Three starters and two key reserves return from last season's NCAA Tournament club, but late-bloomer Ervin Johnson, an All-American honoree last year, is gone.

Guard: UNO has lots of backcourt experience. Starters Gerald Williams and Reni Mason are back, as is back-up Tony Madison. Williams and Mason are both natural point guards whose primary duty in 1992-93 was to dump it inside to Johnson. This year, the Privateers will undoubtedly need more scoring punch from the backcourt, which means Madison's minutes will increase. He has great range on his shot, although he's inconsistent.

Forward: Senior Melvin Simon, Floyd's biggest recruit at UNO, has yet to live up to his advance billing, partly because of a sophomore slump and partly due to Johnson's emergence. Statistically, Simon did improve slightly last season. More importantly, he demonstrated much better work habits. Starter Reggie Garrett transferred over the summer, meaning Andrej Zelenbaba or one of four incoming forwards will have to step up.

Center: Like Johnson, probable starter Michael McDonald didn't play high school basketball. He's a gifted runner and jumper who can be a disruptive defensive force (1.6 BPG last year). However, he's not going to supply the offense Johnson (18.4 PPG) did last season.

Analysis: This is Simon's year to display the skills that made him Louisiana's top prep prospect in 1989-90. He'll need some scoring help from the backcourt and a little rebounding assistance from McDonald. The Privateers won't duplicate last season's record, but they're still the best in the Sun Belt.

1993-94 ROSTER

	POS	HT	YR	FGP	FTP	3-PT	RPG	APG	PPG
Melvin Simon	F	6'8"	Sr.	.48	.60	0/1	7.5	1.9	12.5
Gerald Williams	G	5'9"	Sr.	.40	.79	12/22	2.0	3.4	9.5
Reni Mason	G	5'9"	Sr.	.45	.78	10/24	2.4	4.0	7.3
Tony Madison	G	6'4"	Sr.	.36	.68	46/127	1.6	1.1	6.5
Dedric Willoughby	G	6'2"	Fr.	.29	.56	7/22	2.6	2.4	5.2
Michael McDonald	C/F	6'10"	Sr.	.66	.65	—	2.5	0.1	4.2
Andrej Zelenbaba	F	6'8"	Jr.	.31	.70	3/11	1.4	0.2	2.4
Eric Matthews	G	6'3"	Sr.	.35	.50	8/26	0.7	0.7	2.1
Junior Conerly	F	6'6"	Jr.	—	—	—	—	—	—
Steve Jiles	F	6'5"	Fr.	—	—	—	—	—	—
Kevin Johnson	F	6'7"	Jr.	—	—	—	—	—	—
David Kornel	F	6'8"	Fr.	—	—	—	—	—	—

NORTH CAROLINA

Conference: Atlantic Coast
1992-93: 34-4, 1st ACC

1992-93 NCAAs: 6-0
Coach: Dean Smith (774-223)

Opening Line: The NCAA championship trophy doesn't seem to want to leave Tobacco Road, and it might not have to in the near future. UNC looks to have just as good a chance at repeating its national title as nearby Duke did in 1992. With the best freshman class in the country and George Lynch the only major loss, the Tar Heels enter 1993-94 as No. 1 on most preseason lists. Whether Dean Smith likes it or not, expectations will be sky-high.

Guard: The backcourt is loaded. Donald Williams simply took over the Final Four last April with his deadly outside shooting. When he gets hot, there is virtually nothing a team can do to stop him. Left-handed Derrick Phelps is probably the best defensive guard in the country, and a nifty playmaker to boot. He'll be backed up at the point by freshman Jeff McInnis, a second-team prep All-American last year according to *Basketball Weekly*.

Forward: McInnis's high school teammate—Jerry Stackhouse, a *B.W.* first-team All-American—joins a unit that isn't as distinguished as the Tar Heel guards or centers, but one that won't lose a lot of match-ups. Senior Brian Reese is an athletic player best noted for his defense, but his offense has steadily improved every year. Gym rat Pat Sullivan is a solid role-player.

Center: Rasheed Wallace, another *B.W.* first-team prep All-American, gets a year of valuable tutelage under the best pure center in the college game, Eric Montross. Seven-footer Kevin Salvadori, who also plays forward, is tough to shoot over.

Analysis: Carolina's success is usually linked to strong senior leadership, so much will depend on how well Montross, Phelps, Reese, and Sullivan wear that mantle. The Tar Heels have a dominant force in the middle (Montross), but someone must replace Lynch's relentless board work. No team in the country looks better on paper.

1993-94 ROSTER

	POS	HT	YR	FGP	FTP	3-PT	RPG	APG	PPG
Eric Montross	C	7'0"	Sr.	.62	.68	—	7.6	0.7	15.8
Donald Williams	G	6'3"	Jr.	.46	.83	83/199	1.9	1.2	14.3
Brian Reese	F/G	6'6"	Sr.	.51	.69	22/60	3.6	2.4	11.4
Derrick Phelps	G	6'4"	Sr.	.46	.68	15/48	4.4	5.4	8.1
Pat Sullivan	F	6'8"	Sr.	.52	.79	9/30	2.4	1.3	6.4
Kevin Salvadori	C/F	7'0"	Sr.	.46	.70	—	3.6	0.3	4.5
Larry Davis	G	6'3"	So.	.35	.61	2/9	0.8	0.2	2.1
Ed Geth	F	6'9"	So.	.64	.71	—	1.3	—	2.1
Dante Calabria	G	6'4"	So.	.46	.78	9/23	0.8	0.8	1.8
Jeff McInnis	G	6'4"	Fr.	—	—	—	—	—	—
Jerry Stackhouse	F	6'6"	Fr.	—	—	—	—	—	—
Rasheed Wallace	C	6'11"	Fr.	—	—	—	—	—	—

OHIO STATE

Conference: Big Ten
1992-93: 15-13, 7th Big Ten

1992-93 NIT: 0-1
Coach: Randy Ayers (85-36)

Opening Line: After a pair of Big Ten titles, the Buckeyes sunk to NIT level last year in an expected rebuilding season. They should be NCAA Tournament caliber in 1993-94, though the loss of star recruit Damon Flint dims some of the expectations. Last May, the NCAA ruled the 6'5" swing man ineligible to play at OSU after citing 17 rules violations in his recruitment.

Guard: The Buckeyes' top-five recruiting class of 1992 has now had a season of quality playing time, and that should pay the biggest dividends in the backcourt. Sophomore Greg Simpson earned Big Ten Freshman of the Year honors last year, while soph Derek Anderson, a swing man, will be a superstar if he adds muscle. Senior Jamie Skelton is a streak shooter who loves to launch from downtown, while Doug Etzler provides good depth at the point.

Forward: Lawrence Funderburke is an outstanding talent who led the team in scoring and rebounding last season. Still, he's often a victim of inconsistency, which may be explained by his relative inexperience despite his age. Rickey Dudley is a proven commodity on the boards, while Charles Macon should begin to live up to his advance hype. More will be expected of Nate Wilbourne and Jimmy Ratliff.

Center: Antonio Watson will be the guy coach Randy Ayers counts on to shore up the pivot. While Funderburke plays like a center to help out the inside game, Dudley and the 6'11" duo of Wilbourne and redshirt frosh Gerald Eaker might be able to ease some of that burden. Watson and Eaker need to bulk up.

Analysis: Don't expect the Buckeyes to rejoin the nation's elite after a year's sabbatical. However, Ohio State will be an upper-division Big Ten team if A) Funderburke shows more maturity, B) someone helps him out on the glass, and C) there is better overall team defense. Once again, the Buckeyes will be a guard-oriented ballclub.

1993-94 ROSTER

	POS	HT	YR	FGP	FTP	3-PT	RPG	APG	PPG
Lawrence Funderburke	F	6'9"	Sr.	.53	.62	1/3	6.8	1.2	16.3
Jamie Skelton	G	6'2"	Sr.	.40	.73	55/164	3.0	2.8	14.2
Derek Anderson	G/F	6'6"	So.	.46	.81	9/35	3.3	2.7	10.2
Greg Simpson	G	6'1"	So.	.44	.77	28/74	2.2	2.6	9.6
Rickey Dudley	F/C	6'7"	Jr.	.55	.61	—	4.8	0.8	5.1
Antonio Watson	C	6'9"	Jr.	.45	.69	—	2.3	0.4	2.9
Doug Etzler	G	6'0"	Jr.	.41	.90	12/25	1.0	1.8	2.9
Charles Macon	F	6'6"	So.	.46	.56	0/1	1.9	0.2	2.2
Jimmy Ratliff	F	6'9"	Sr.	.32	.57	0/3	1.6	0.4	1.6
Nate Wilbourne	C/F	6'11"	So.	.43	.50	—	0.4	0.1	0.6
Gerald Eaker	C	6'11"	Fr.	—	—	—	—	—	—

OKLAHOMA STATE

Conference: Big Eight
1992-93: 20-9, T-2nd Big Eight

1992-93 NCAAs: 1-1
Coach: Eddie Sutton (502-189)

Opening Line: Last season was supposed to be a rebuilding year for OSU. However, overnight sensation Bryant "Big Country" Reeves became one of the nation's top centers, and newcomers Brooks Thompson and Randy Rutherford solidified a shaky backcourt. While Reeves was magnificent in an NCAA tourney win over Marquette, Louisville put an end to the Cowboys' surprising season two days later.

Guard: Thompson and Rutherford combined to average 28 points, eight rebounds, eight assists, and three steals per game last season. Thompson is a natural two guard who played out of position at the point and flourished. Rutherford's tremendous quickness helps him create a lot of shots. Scott Sutton, the coach's son, can run his father's system with his eyes closed.

Forward: The Cowboys must replace starter Milton Brown and sixth man Von Bennett. Returning starter Fred Burley can be counted on for a dozen points and a half-dozen rebounds a game. Transfer Scott Pierce is a solid inside player who made 16 starts for Illinois in 1991-92. Junior college catch Ian Phillip displays uncanny athletic ability for a player his size (6'10", 245). All three dig in defensively.

Center: A virtual unknown at this time last year, Reeves emerged as the Big Eight Player of the Year, topping the league in scoring, rebounding, and field goal percentage. His agility, soft hands, and defensive presence make him extra special. Seven-footer Ben Baum was the top schoolboy in Colorado last winter.

Analysis: With Reeves and Burley inside and Thompson and Rutherford outside, it's hard to find many weaknesses. The low-post defense can hold its own with any team in the country, particularly with the addition of Phillip and Baum. With a good start, OSU should reside in the top ten nationally and draw at least a No. 3 seed come NCAA Tournament time.

1993-94 ROSTER

	POS	HT	YR	FGP	FTP	3-PT	RPG	APG	PPG
Bryant Reeves	C	7'0"	Jr.	.62	.65	1/2	10.0	1.2	19.5
Brooks Thompson	G	6'4"	Sr.	.46	.76	60/161	3.9	5.0	14.6
Randy Rutherford	G	6'3"	Jr.	.46	.80	55/126	4.0	2.9	13.3
Fred Burley	F	6'6"	Sr.	.51	.76	—	3.9	1.4	10.7
Bryndon Manzer	G	6'1"	Sr.	.46	.53	4/11	0.6	0.6	2.1
Terry Collins	F	6'6"	Jr.	.40	.32	3/12	1.8	1.6	2.0
Scott Sutton	G	6'5"	Sr.	.33	.46	6/22	1.3	2.1	1.4
Chad Alexander	G	6'3"	Fr.	—	—	—	—	—	—
Ben Baum	C	7'0"	Fr.	—	—	—	—	—	—
Ian Phillip	F	6'10"	Jr.	—	—	—	—	—	—
Scott Pierce	F	6'8"	Jr.	—	—	—	—	—	—
Chianti Roberts	G/F	6'6"	Fr.	—	—	—	—	—	—

OLD DOMINION

Conference: Colonial Athletic   **1992-93 NIT:** 1-1
1992-93: 21-8, T-1st CAA   **Coach:** Oliver Purnell (80-65)

Opening Line: Old Dominion was locked out of last year's NCAA Tournament after losing to Cinderella East Carolina in the conference tourney. Nevertheless, it was a splendid second year for coach Oliver Purnell, who guided the Monarchs to a share of the regular-season Colonial crown and their second straight postseason appearance. Fortified by 1992's outstanding recruiting class, ODU could put a stranglehold on the CAA title for the next several years.

Guard: Keith Jackson (16.8 PPG) and Donald Anderson (4.9 APG) are the biggest losses to absorb, but the Monarchs don't hurt for experience with seniors Kevin Swann and Kevin Larkin. Swann, a transfer from Central Connecticut State, was a part-time starter last season, while Larkin was a solid role-player off the bench. Incoming freshmen Mark Johnson, Corey Robinson, and E.J. Sherod should all figure into the fray.

Forward: There's not much worry here, as junior Petey Sessoms and sophomore Mario Mullen are back. Both started every game last season. With his shooting stroke from 3-point land (.438), Sessoms has no problem getting going offensively. Mullen, who was selected to the CAA All-Rookie team in 1992-93, is tough on the boards.

Center: Odell Hodge, the two-time Virginia AA Player of the Year, took the conference by storm last season as he was named the CAA's Freshman of the Year. The team's leading rebounder in 1992-93, Hodge is also capable of going on big scoring binges. He's the perfect complement to Sessoms.

Analysis: Purnell likes to get everyone involved in his running and pressing attack; four players averaged in double figures in scoring last season. It may take some time to integrate some of the new parts, but come February, watch out. The frontcourt can hold its own with anybody. Count on another postseason appearance.

1993-94 ROSTER

	POS	HT	YR	FGP	FTP	3-PT	RPG	APG	PPG
Petey Sessoms	F	6'7"	Jr.	.43	.82	69/160	5.9	1.2	16.9
Odell Hodge	C	6'9"	So.	.56	.76	—	9.1	0.7	14.7
Mario Mullen	F	6'6"	So.	.52	.72	2/11	7.3	1.4	10.8
Kevin Swann	G	6'2"	Sr.	.44	.85	11/26	2.0	3.0	5.7
Mike Jones	F	6'5"	Jr.	.40	.78	14/35	0.8	0.5	4.5
Kevin Larkin	G	6'4"	Sr.	.53	.70	12/25	1.2	2.1	3.2
David Harvey	F	6'8"	Jr.	.63	.49	—	2.0	0.3	2.6
Allon Wright	C	6'10"	Sr.	.50	.50	—	1.6	0.2	1.6
Derrick Parker	C	6'9"	So.	.47	.14	—	1.2	0.1	1.3
Mark Johnson	G	6'2"	Fr.	—	—	—	—	—	—
Corey Robinson	G	6'2"	Fr.	—	—	—	—	—	—
E.J. Sherod	G	6'4"	Fr.	—	—	—	—	—	—

PENNSYLVANIA

Conference: Ivy League
1992-93: 22-5, 1st Ivy

1992-93 NCAAs: 0-1
Coach: Fran Dunphy (59-46)

Opening Line: For the first time in five seasons, someone other than Princeton won the Ivy League. And the Quakers did it in grand fashion too, with a perfect 14-0 record in 1992-93. It was Penn's first 20-win season since 1980-81. Vanderbilt transfer Matt Maloney and Jerome Allen comprised the first-team All-Ivy backcourt, while forward Barry Pierce was a second-team all-league choice. Amazingly, underrated coach Fran Dunphy hasn't lost a single player from last year's team.

Guard: The Maloney-Allen combination would likely hold its own in even a marquee conference. Maloney, a *Basketball Weekly* All-Transfer team honoree, led the Quakers in scoring, steals, free throws, and 3-point percentage last year. Allen, Co-Ivy Player of the Year, is best known for his slashing moves to the basket and tenacious defense. Scott Kegler is good for about 15 minutes per game off the bench.

Forward: Pierce, a deadly baseline jump-shooter, thrives in the open court. Although overshadowed somewhat by Maloney and Allen, he plays every bit as important a role. Tim Krug, Andy Baratta, and hot-shooting Shawn Trice will all see time at big forward. Baratta, most effective with his back to the basket, also plays a lot of center.

Center: Eric Moore, a fundamentally sound performer, was the only Penn player other than Maloney to start every game in 1992-93. One of the league's best rebounders, Moore is also a shot-blocking threat—as is Krug.

Analysis: It would be interesting to see how this club would fare in a more competitive conference. The Quakers' strong man-to-man defense and terrific 3-point shooting would seemingly give them a chance versus bigger and quicker teams. The Ivy League should be a cakewalk. The real question is, Can they win a tournament game?

1993-94 ROSTER

	POS	HT	YR	FGP	FTP	3-PT	RPG	APG	PPG
Matt Maloney	G	6'3"	Jr.	.41	.78	91/205	3.3	3.6	16.3
Barry Pierce	F/G	6'3"	Sr.	.49	.72	22/61	5.5	2.1	14.5
Jerome Allen	G	6'4"	Jr.	.42	.67	50/127	4.7	4.9	13.1
Eric Moore	F/C	6'6"	Jr.	.49	.59	5/18	6.6	0.9	6.9
Shawn Trice	F	6'7"	Jr.	.49	.68	0/1	4.6	0.9	6.1
Tim Krug	F/C	6'9"	So.	.43	.60	8/26	3.0	0.5	5.2
Andy Baratta	C/F	6'8"	Sr.	.49	.53	0/1	3.2	0.6	4.5
Scott Kegler	G	6'5"	Jr.	.39	.68	19/45	1.6	0.8	3.6
Donald Moxley	G	6'2"	So.	.19	.60	0/1	0.8	0.2	1.1
Ken Hans	F	6'6"	Sr.	.33	.50	1/3	0.5	0.3	0.9
Nathaniel Graham	C	6'7"	Fr.	—	—	—	—	—	—
James Lyren	G	6'2"	Fr.	—	—	—	—	—	—

PEPPERDINE

Conference: West Coast
1992-93: 23-8, 1st WCC

1992-93 NIT: 1-1
Coach: Tom Asbury (106-48)

Opening Line: It was business as usual for last year's Waves, as they chalked up their third straight West Coast championship. The fun ended quickly, though, as Pepperdine lost to trey-shooting Santa Clara in the WCC title game. The Waves settled for the NIT, where they knocked off Cal.-Santa Barbara before falling to Southern California. Four starters return, including WCC Player of the Year Dana Jones.

Guard: Despite missing three weeks with a broken hand, diminutive Damin Lopez turned in another fine season in 1992-93 with 14 points and four assists per game. He shot a blistering 43 percent from 3-point territory. Bryan Parker is a great passer (6.5 APG) who offers sound offensive skills and aggressive defense. Super sixth man Steve Guild was a jack-of-all-trades who'll be missed.

Forward: The silky-smooth Jones has caught the eye of more than one NBA scout. He's a smart player who does an exceptional job of catching the ball in traffic. He shot better from the floor (62 percent) than the line (61 percent) last year. LeRoi O'Brien is expected to replace Byron Jenson at the other forward spot, unless junior college transfer Clark James or heralded frosh Bryan Hill have other ideas.

Center: The presence of 6'8" starter Derek Noether, 6'11" reserve Gavin Vanderputten, and 7'1" Jamar Holcomb gives the Waves one of the most formidable pivot trios on the West Coast. The improvement Noether showed last winter should continue. Holcomb may be redshirted.

Analysis: Unlike last year when the Waves were trying to adjust to life without superstar Doug Christie, the core of the 1992-93 squad returns. While Jones will continue to be the club's go-to guy, it's important for players like Parker and Noether to expand their respective roles. A fifth postseason tourney appearance in six seasons is a virtual lock.

1993-94 ROSTER

	POS	HT	YR	FGP	FTP	3-PT	RPG	APG	PPG
Dana Jones	F	6'6"	Sr.	.62	.61	—	9.1	1.4	15.6
Damin Lopez	G	5'8"	Sr.	.45	.82	63/147	2.3	3.9	14.0
Derek Noether	C	6'8"	Sr.	.55	.58	—	6.1	1.1	11.7
Bryan Parker	G	6'2"	Sr.	.40	.70	29/77	3.4	6.5	7.2
LeRoi O'Brien	F	6'7"	Jr.	.51	.59	—	1.9	0.2	3.8
Steve Clover	G	6'4"	Sr.	.30	.63	10/32	0.6	0.1	1.7
Gavin Vanderputten	C	6'11"	So.	.39	.50	—	1.4	0.1	1.3
Gerald Brown	G	6'3"	Fr.	—	—	—	—	—	—
Kirk Goehring	F	6'5"	So.	—	—	—	—	—	—
Bryan Hill	F	6'7"	Fr.	—	—	—	—	—	—
Jamar Holcomb	C	7'1"	Fr.	—	—	—	—	—	—
Clark James	F	6'5"	Jr.	—	—	—	—	—	—

PROVIDENCE

Conference: Big East   **1992-93 NIT:** 3-2
1992-93: 20-13, T-4th Big East   **Coach:** Rick Barnes (108-76)

Opening Line: Just 1-6 one month into league play last year, Providence's 8-3 finish ranks as one of the greatest comebacks in Big East history. The Friars posted their first 20-win season in six years and made a trip to the NIT's Final Four. Tony Turner and Trent Forbes started a combined 25 games in 1992-93, but they've graduated. The three-man recruiting class includes Jason Murdock, the younger brother of former Friar star Eric Murdock.

Guard: Freshman Michael Brown took over the point from Abdul Abdullah in late January and never relinquished the job. Brown helped key the club's late-season run. Shooting guard Franklin Western is a tough defender whose scoring average hovers around eight PPG. He'll be expected to score more from the perimeter, as will reserves Abdullah and Murdock.

Forward: Michael Smith led the Friars in both rebounding (11.4 RPG) and scoring (11.8 PPG) last year. He's an NBA prospect. Dependable Rob Phelps, a part-time starter in 1992-93, takes over for Turner at small forward. He'll fire up the 3-pointer. Reserves Troy Brown and Eric Williams (a recruit) both know a thing or two about crashing the boards.

Center: Super-athletic senior Dickey Simpkins came into his own last season with nearly 11 points and seven caroms per night. If he can cut down on the silly fouls and continue to improve defensively, he'll warrant mention among the premier big men in the East.

Analysis: Coach Rick Barnes's veteran squad must avoid a repeat of last season's abysmal start if the Friars are going to be a factor in the Big East race. While Smith and Simpkins will no doubt push for all-league mention, the likes of Michael Brown, Western, and Phelps are the players to watch. Their play may mean the difference between the NCAA Tournament and another NIT invite.

1993-94 ROSTER

	POS	HT	YR	FGP	FTP	3-PT	RPG	APG	PPG
Michael Smith	F	6'8"	Sr.	.56	.55	—	11.4	1.2	11.8
Dickey Simpkins	C	6'9"	Sr.	.45	.60	1/3	6.5	1.2	10.6
Franklin Western	G/F	6'7"	Sr.	.53	.70	0/4	2.5	0.6	8.4
Michael Brown	G	6'1"	So.	.41	.82	24/56	2.2	2.4	7.3
Rob Phelps	F/G	6'5"	Sr.	.37	.71	28/89	1.9	1.5	6.8
Troy Brown	F/C	6'8"	Sr.	.40	.70	0/2	3.8	0.3	4.5
Maciej Zielinski	F	6'7"	Jr.	.39	.71	7/20	1.4	0.6	2.7
Abdul Abdullah	G	5'10"	Sr.	.24	.47	4/23	1.7	5.7	2.2
Austin Croshere	F	6'9"	Fr.	—	—	—	—	—	—
Jason Murdock	G	6'3"	Fr.	—	—	—	—	—	—
Piotr Szibilski	C	6'10"	Fr.	—	—	—	—	—	—
Eric Williams	F	6'8"	Jr.	—	—	—	—	—	—

PURDUE

Conference: Big Ten   **1992-93 NCAAs:** 0-1
1992-93: 18-10, T-5th Big Ten   **Coach:** Gene Keady (306-149)

Opening Line: As long as national Player of the Year candidate Glenn Robinson sticks around, this is going to be a competitive basketball team. Last season, Robinson became the first first-year player in 21 years to pace the Big Ten in scoring (24.1 PPG). Guard Matt Painter is the only graduation loss. This year's recruiting class includes a 7'2" project.

Guard: Painter's graduation leaves gutsy Matt Waddell as the likely lead guard, with help from sophomore Porter Roberts. While Waddell has far more experience, Roberts's quickness and defensive prowess can't be overlooked. Heady Linc Darner is a gym rat who can play big guard or small forward. While he came off the bench last year, he did start 25 games from 1990-92. Herb Dove is a steady, young back-up.

Forward: Robinson is a threat from anywhere on the floor. A dazzling dunker with incredible athleticism, he led Purdue in rebounds, steals, and blocks and ranked third in assists. His spirited 36-point performance vs. Rhode Island in the NCAA tourney was a sight to behold. Much-improved Cuonzo Martin—coach Gene Keady's youngest team captain ever—is the team's No. 2 scoring option. He'll also see action at big guard.

Center: Although Ian Stanback's natural position is big forward, he'll again play the pivot while Cornelius McNary continues to develop. Stanback plays taller than his 6'7" size thanks to hard work and superb defensive positioning. Matt ten Dam (7'2", 305 pounds), a native of Holland, could help in time.

Analysis: Combine a stud like Robinson with decent players like Waddell, Martin, and Stanback and you get a team that could be a postseason sleeper. The only time this club gets in trouble is when the players stand around and marvel at Robinson. One must admit, he is fun to watch.

1993-94 ROSTER

	POS	HT	YR	FGP	FTP	3-PT	RPG	APG	PPG
Glenn Robinson	F	6'8"	Jr.	.47	.74	32/80	9.2	1.8	24.1
Cuonzo Martin	F/G	6'6"	Jr.	.52	.81	0/6	3.7	2.4	11.9
Matt Waddell	G	6'4"	Jr.	.44	.80	19/44	2.9	2.6	7.1
Ian Stanback	F/C	6'7"	Sr.	.56	.67	—	4.6	0.8	6.8
Porter Roberts	G	6'3"	So.	.36	.62	16/41	2.0	1.6	3.6
Kenny Williams	F/C	6'9"	Sr.	.57	.56	—	1.1	0.1	2.4
Herb Dove	G	6'4"	So.	.59	.56	—	0.8	0.4	2.0
Linc Darner	G/F	6'4"	Sr.	.33	.47	13/36	0.8	0.9	2.0
Cornelius McNary	C	6'9"	Sr.	.50	.68	—	1.4	0.1	1.6
Brandon Brantley	F	6'8"	So.	—	—	—	—	—	—
Paul Gilvydis	F	6'8"	Fr.	—	—	—	—	—	—
Matt ten Dam	C	7'2"	Fr.	—	—	—	—	—	—

ST. JOHN'S

Conference: Big East   **1992-93 NCAAs:** 1-1
1992-93: 19-11, 2nd Big East   **Coach:** Brian Mahoney (19-11)

Opening Line: The Johnnies came within one game of making Brian Mahoney the first coach in school history to win 20 games in his inaugural season. The graduation of key starters David Cain (All-Big East) and Lamont Middleton strips the Redmen of more than 23 points, ten rebounds, and eight assists per game. Standout recruit Roshown McLeod played at famed St. Anthony's in New Jersey.

Guard: Cain's ability to skillfully run the show and break the press won't be duplicated any time soon by Derek Brown, Lee Green, or Maurice Brown. While all three can handle the rock, Derek Brown's perimeter shooting is more suited for the two-guard position, where he started last year. Sergio Luyk is a good 3-point shooter when healthy, which isn't often. The presence of Carl Beckett and sweet-shooting juco transfer James Scott gives the backcourt depth galore.

Forward: With Middleton and consistent reserve Mitchell Foster no longer around, sophomores Fred Lyson (25-game starter) and Charles Minlend must pick up the slack. Lyson is a terrific perimeter shooter, while Minlend works as hard as anyone on the St. John's roster. McLeod, who's as capable with his left hand as he is his right, should pay immediate dividends.

Center: Shawnelle Scott is a tremendous talent when he wants to be. He topped the Redmen last season in scoring and rebounding and ranked No. 2 in steals. He continues to improve upon his offensive moves, while taking full advantage of his great strength on the defensive boards.

Analysis: Thanks to tenacious defense and rebounding, the Redmen should continue to keep almost every game they play close. While Scott is on the verge of stardom and there appears to be a plethora of depth, Mahoney is concerned about the point-guard play and perimeter shooting. Thus, Derek Brown and Luyk will largely determine just how much success the Johnnies enjoy.

1993-94 ROSTER

	POS	HT	YR	FGP	FTP	3-PT	RPG	APG	PPG
Shawnelle Scott	F	6'11"	Sr.	.59	.52	0/2	7.8	1.1	13.7
Derek Brown	G	6'3"	Jr.	.41	.76	27/88	3.7	3.0	11.0
Charlie Minlend	F	6'6"	So.	.54	.72	3/6	3.9	0.7	7.8
Sergio Luyk	F/G	6'8"	Jr.	.45	.46	19/49	1.7	0.5	6.0
Fred Lyson	F/G	6'6"	So.	.41	.80	19/54	1.6	0.8	4.6
Carl Beckett	G	6'4"	Sr.	.58	.80	2/7	1.3	0.2	3.5
Rowan Barrett	G/F	6'5"	So.	.43	.37	3/10	1.0	0.3	2.8
Lee Green	G	6'3"	Sr.	.42	.26	4/10	0.4	0.4	2.2
Maurice Brown	G	5'9"	So.	.44	.75	2/6	0.2	0.6	1.4
Tom Bayne	C	6'9"	So.	—	—	—	—	—	—
Roshown McLeod	F	6'8"	Fr.	—	—	—	—	—	—
James Scott	F/G	6'6"	Jr.	—	—	—	—	—	—

ST. JOSEPH'S

Conference: Atlantic 10
1992-93: 18-11, T-2nd A-10

1992-93 NIT: 0-1
Coach: John Griffin (114-87)

Opening Line: With a healthy Rap Curry back at the point last year, the Hawks flew back into postseason play for the first time since 1986, although they lost in the first round of the NIT to S.W. Missouri State. This year's team returns all five starters, four of whom averaged double-figure PPG in 1992-93. Few backcourts in America house a twosome as experienced and talented as seniors Curry and Bernard Blunt.

Guard: In an effort to get the top five players on the court together, coach John Griffin has had a lot of success with a three-guard offense. Curry's a cool customer at the point, Blunt's a relentless scorer, and 5'9" Mark Bass bombs away as soon as he gets past halfcourt. While Blunt's shooting touch makes him an appealing NBA prospect, Bass is a bona fide pest on defense.

Forward: Bernard Jones is a hard worker who made a lot of progress in all phases of his game last winter, particularly his perimeter skills. He'll share time with promising Demetrius Poles, a fine passer who lacks Jones's consistency. Freshman Dmitri Domani, a native of Moscow, Russia, has received rave reviews.

Center: With nine caroms per game, Carlin Warley has emerged as one of the premier 6'7" rebounders in the game today. The keys to his play are his versatility and outstanding instincts. No pushover at the offensive end either, he ranked No. 3 on last year's squad in scoring (12.0 PPG). Improved Reggie Townsend plays aggressive defense.

Analysis: Scoring from the perimeter and defending the perimeter are the major components of the Hawks' success. Big, methodical teams that are able to pound the ball inside give this bunch fits. While the three-guard rotation of Blunt, Curry, and Bass is certainly top notch, it may not be enough since Warley is left to go solo inside. If Warley holds up, then St. Joe's should shine.

1993-94 ROSTER

	POS	HT	YR	FGP	FTP	3-PT	RPG	APG	PPG
Bernard Blunt	G	6'3"	Sr.	.37	.73	45/138	5.7	2.1	18.0
Rap Curry	G	6'3"	Sr.	.37	.71	50/156	4.2	5.1	12.4
Carlin Warley	C/F	6'7"	Sr.	.50	.65	3/12	9.0	1.9	12.0
Bernard Jones	F	6'5"	Jr.	.52	.77	6/20	6.5	0.5	11.6
Mark Bass	G	5'9"	So.	.37	.87	41/122	2.4	2.1	9.8
Demetrius Poles	F	6'8"	Jr.	.44	.63	0/6	4.4	0.4	4.2
Kevin Connor	G	6'5"	So.	.41	.53	—	1.0	0.2	1.6
Reggie Townsend	F/C	6'7"	So.	.48	.42	—	1.0	0.1	1.4
Alex Compton	G	6'0"	So.	.42	.83	4/11	0.3	0.2	1.3
Chris DiMascio	G	6'6"	Fr.	—	—	—	—	—	—
Dmitri Domani	F	6'7"	Fr.	—	—	—	—	—	—
Terrell Myers	G	6'1"	Fr.	—	—	—	—	—	—

ST. LOUIS

Conference: Great Midwest   **1992-93 NCAAs:** Not invited
1992-93: 12-17, 6th GMC   **Coach:** Charlie Spoonhour (209-98)

Opening Line: After finishing last in the Great Midwest in 1992-93, second-year coach Charlie Spoonhour is ready to make his move. Thanks to Spoonhour's tutelage, the return of three high-scoring regulars, and the addition of five talented transfers (including four jucos), the necessary ingredients are in place for the Billikens to become one of the nation's most improved teams. Impressive late-season wins over DePaul and Marquette served as huge confidence boosts.

Guard: Not only did shake-and-bake lead guard Erwin Claggett pace the Billikens in assists, but he also finished tops in scoring (19.7 PPG). Backcourt mate Scott Highmark, like Claggett a feared 3-point threat, averaged 16.0 PPG. Unselfish Carlos McCauley didn't miss a start last winter as a result of St. Louis' three-guard set, but UNLV transfer H Waldman is bound to work his way into the lineup with superior defense. The competition for minutes should be fierce.

Forward: Muscular Donnie Dobbs, a high school teammate of NBA star Jimmy Jackson, gives the Billikens plenty of offense (17.3 PPG) and strong rebounding. Only 6'3", he holds his own with players who are often at least six inches taller. Veteran reserve Eric Jones will have to compete for a job with proven juco talents like Corey Grays, Donnie Campbell, and David Robinson. Grays displays the most potential of the three.

Center: Though not a scorer, Evan Pedersen provides strong defense and plenty of much-needed leadership. Back-up Eric Bickel displays some offensive potential.

Analysis: Although most will pick St. Louis to finish no higher than fourth or fifth in league play, don't be surprised if it's one of the nation's "sleeper teams." The addition of proven players like Waldman and Grays should do wonders for Claggett, Highmark, and Dobbs. The new-look Billikens appear NCAA tourney-bound for the first time in 37 seasons.

1993-94 ROSTER

	POS	HT	YR	FGP	FTP	3-PT	RPG	APG	PPG
Erwin Claggett	G	6'1"	Jr.	.45	.83	71/158	3.8	3.8	19.7
Donnie Dobbs	F	6'3"	Sr.	.56	.71	6/18	6.5	2.5	17.3
Scott Highmark	G	6'4"	Jr.	.47	.78	58/153	4.2	2.4	16.0
Evan Pedersen	F/C	6'8"	Sr.	.46	.71	1/2	4.4	0.9	5.8
Carlos McCauley	G	5'11"	So.	.34	.67	3/17	2.0	2.9	3.0
Eric Bickel	C	6'10"	Jr.	.57	.73	0/1	1.5	0.3	2.1
Eric Jones	F	6'5"	Jr.	.35	.60	0/1	1.3	0.2	1.0
Donnie Campbell	F	6'6"	Jr.	—	—	—	—	—	—
Corey Grays	F	6'5"	Jr.	—	—	—	—	—	—
David Robinson	F	6'6"	Jr.	—	—	—	—	—	—
Carl Turner	G	5'11"	Jr.	—	—	—	—	—	—
H Waldman	G	6'3"	Jr.	—	—	—	—	—	—

SANTA CLARA

Conference: West Coast
1992-93: 19-12, 3rd WCC

1992-93 NCAAs: 1-1
Coach: Dick Davey (19-12)

Opening Line: Not only did the Broncos surprise their own conference last year by upsetting Pepperdine in the WCC tourney and advancing to the NCAA Tournament, but they shocked the world by knocking off No. 2-seeded Arizona once they got there. Temple finally ended their Cinderella season with a 68-57 victory. Starting guard Mark Schmitz, a 3-point specialist, is the only Bronco not returning from the team's eight-man rotation.

Guard: Lead guard John Woolery (5.2 APG) is an effective penetrator who excels at pushing the ball up the court. He started 27 games last winter. Steve Nash, a *Basketball Weekly* Freshman All-American, will replace Schmitz. Nash can turn a game around in a hurry with his perimeter shooting. Heralded frosh Marlon Garnett averaged 26 PPG as a high school senior in Los Angeles.

Forward: Pete Eisenrich and DeWayne Lewis comprise one of the best forward tandems on the West Coast. They each earned first-team all-league honors last year, combining for 27 PPG. Eisenrich is a solid mid-range jump-shooter, while Lewis is a very quick, explosive scorer. Kevin Dunne and Jason Sedlock contributed quality minutes as freshmen last year.

Center: Kevin Fitzwilson is the starting center for a team that relies almost exclusively on perimeter shooting. The Broncos rarely go inside to him, as his 2.0 PPG would attest. California transfer Brendan Graves (6'10", 235) is far more refined at both ends of the court.

Analysis: It's likely that the Broncos will only go as far as their 3-point shooting will take them. When their shots are falling, they can beat the Arizonas and Pepperdines of the world. When they're not, St. Mary's and San Diego can pose problems. With the addition of Graves and the presence of Eisenrich and Lewis, there's seemingly enough firepower for the Broncos to become more diversified.

1993-94 ROSTER

	POS	HT	YR	FGP	FTP	3-PT	RPG	APG	PPG
Pete Eisenrich	F	6'9"	Sr.	.47	.79	39/109	6.4	1.1	14.4
DeWayne Lewis	F	6'5"	Sr.	.44	.84	19/68	5.3	1.9	12.9
Steve Nash	G	6'2"	So.	.42	.83	49/120	2.6	2.2	8.1
John Woolery	G	6'1"	Sr.	.43	.63	15/44	2.4	5.2	8.0
Kevin Dunne	F	6'6"	So.	.51	.45	5/17	3.2	0.8	4.8
Jason Sedlock	F	6'7"	So.	.30	.58	1/14	1.8	0.4	2.2
Kevin Fitzwilson	C/F	6'8"	Sr.	.33	.68	1/1	2.3	0.3	2.0
Phil Von Buchwaldt	C	6'11"	So.	.31	.67	—	1.7	0.1	1.7
Adam Anderson	G/F	6'5"	So.	.42	.55	1/6	1.0	0.3	1.4
Marlon Garnett	G	6'2"	Fr.	—	—	—	—	—	—
Brendan Graves	C	6'10"	Jr.	—	—	—	—	—	—
Jacobi Thompson	G/F	6'5"	Fr.	—	—	—	—	—	—

SETON HALL

Conference: Big East
1992-93: 28-7, 1st Big East

1992-93 NCAAs: 1-1
Coach: P.J. Carlesimo (195-153)

Opening Line: Coach P.J. Carlesimo loses arguably the premier player in Pirate history in Terry Dehere (22.0 PPG), the hardest working player in Jerry Walker (12.2 PPG), and the biggest player in 7'2", 270-pound Luther Wright (7.5 RPG). Wright's decision to leave school a year early caught everyone off guard. All-America candidate Arturas Karnishovas is the only player returning who started more than 18 games last season.

Guard: The backcourt should do just fine under the direction of capable playmakers Danny Hurley and Bryan Caver. While both are solid penetrators who see the floor well, one will likely be moved to shooting guard. That is, unless heralded juco transfer Dwight Brown moves into Dehere's two-guard slot. Hurley's probably the best pure shooter of the group.

Forward: Karnishovas has quietly taken his place among the top forwards in the East. His defense is outstanding, as are his shooting range and post passing. Another hard-working defender who will fire up a few 3's is excitable John Leahy. Following a fine all-around frosh season, defensive ace Adrian Griffin will likely round out the starting frontcourt. Small forward Tchaka Shipp reportedly showed a lot of improvement over the summer.

Center: Not only did Wright bolt for the pros, but career back-up Jim Dickinson (7'1") also declared himself eligible for the NBA draft. No one can figure out why. With no one on the roster taller than 6'8", the Pirates will basically play with two guards and three forwards.

Analysis: While this club doesn't boast the manpower Seton Hall fans have grown accustomed to, there's still loads of talent. This shapes up as a balanced, team-oriented group that will rely on Carlesimo's coaching to get them through the rough times. Led by Karnishovas and Hurley, the Hall is destined to play its best basketball in March.

1993-94 ROSTER

	POS	HT	YR	FGP	FTP	3-PT	RPG	APG	PPG
Arturas Karnishovas	F	6'8"	Sr.	.51	.83	48/107	6.6	1.7	14.6
Danny Hurley	G	6'2"	Jr.	.39	.73	22/53	1.8	3.4	6.1
John Leahy	F	6'7"	Jr.	.46	.90	31/84	2.5	1.7	5.8
Bryan Caver	G	6'4"	Sr.	.43	.69	4/19	1.8	3.0	4.2
Adrian Griffin	F	6'5"	So.	.51	.59	0/2	3.5	0.8	3.4
Tchaka Shipp	F	6'7"	So.	.33	.50	—	1.4	0.1	1.4
Chris Davis	F	6'7"	Jr.	.47	.50	0/1	0.9	0.1	1.4
Andre Brown	G	6'3"	Fr.	—	—	—	—	—	—
Dwight Brown	G	6'4"	Jr.	—	—	—	—	—	—
Darrell Mims	F	6'8"	Sr.	—	—	—	—	—	—
Donnell Williams	F	6'8"	Fr.	—	—	—	—	—	—

SYRACUSE

Conference: Big East
1992-93: 20-9, 3rd Big East

1992-93 NCAAs: Not eligible
Coach: Jim Boeheim (411-133)

Opening Line: Forced to sit home last March due to NCAA sanctions, the Orangemen are hungrier than ever for an NCAA Tournament bid. Although they fell to Seton Hall in the finals of the Big East tourney, the Orange reached 20 wins for the 16th time in coach Jim Boeheim's 17 seasons. Two starters—center Conrad McRae and forward Mike Hopkins—have graduated. Back-up forward Glenn Sekunda transferred to Penn State.

Guard: In Lawrence "Poetry In" Moten and Adrian Autry, the Orange house one of the finest backcourt tandems in America. They ranked one-two on the team in scoring last year. Autry came into his own last winter, taking full advantage of his size, court vision, and penetrating ability. Moten, a smooth shooter with great poise, is expected to vie for All-America honors. Lazarus Sims saw limited action in 20 games last year. Heralded recruit Todd Burgan has been ruled academically ineligible.

Forward: John Wallace made a sudden impact last season with more than 11 points and nearly eight caroms per game. He's a bull on the inside. Lucious Jackson and hard-nosed Scott McCorkle figure to share time at small forward, while wide-body Otis Hill will spell Wallace. Moten can also take a turn at the three spot if needed.

Center: The club's only two centers are Jim Hayes, a 6'9" walk-on who was redshirted last season, and J.B. Reafsnyder, who appeared in only seven games last year. Hill, who's built like a tight end, will get a long look.

Analysis: While the Moten-Autry combination can carry this club a long way, someone will eventually have to help Wallace clean the glass. Hill and Gelatt are the most likely candidates. Versatility will help, as several players on this team can contribute from more than one position. Playing half of your games in the deafening Carrier Dome helps too. Multiple injuries could cause a major problem, since there are only nine players on the roster.

1993-94 ROSTER

	POS	HT	YR	FGP	FTP	3-PT	RPG	APG	PPG
Lawrence Moten	F/G	6'5"	Jr.	.47	.65	44/131	4.8	2.7	17.9
Adrian Autry	G	6'4"	Sr.	.43	.80	33/109	3.7	5.6	13.7
John Wallace	F	6'7"	So.	.53	.72	0/1	7.6	1.3	11.1
Lucious Jackson	F	6'6"	Jr.	.46	.53	16/56	2.0	0.8	4.9
J.B. Reafsnyder	C	6'10"	So.	.54	.78	—	1.9	0.1	3.0
Scott McCorkle	F/G	6'5"	Sr.	.44	.75	4/11	1.4	0.4	2.5
Lazarus Sims	G	6'4"	So.	.35	.33	0/7	0.6	1.2	1.1
Jim Hayes	C/F	6'9"	Fr.	—	—	—	—	—	—
Otis Hill	F	6'7"	Fr.	—	—	—	—	—	—

TEMPLE

Conference: Atlantic 10
1992-93: 20-13, T-2nd A-10

1992-93 NCAAs: 3-1
Coach: John Chaney (253-97)

Opening Line: After disposing of Missouri, Santa Clara, and Vanderbilt in NCAA tourney play last year, Bill Cosby's favorite club fell to Michigan by a scant five points. The 13 losses were largely a result of coach John Chaney scheduling highly regarded non-conference foes like Florida State, Cincinnati, and Wake Forest. All five starters return, led by Atlantic 10 Player of the Year Aaron McKie. Two freshmen, Keon Clark and Huey Futch, have been ruled academically ineligible, trimming the roster to ten.

Guard: McKie will chase All-America honors this year. He led last year's squad in scoring (20.6 PPG) and steals, while ranking No. 2 in rebounds and assists. Since taking over for injured Vic Carstarphen early last year, Rick Brunson has quietly emerged as one of the nation's most efficient lead guards. Junior Chris Ozment will help off the bench.

Forward: Like McKie, silky-smooth Eddie Jones will also be in the hunt for postseason accolades. The Owls' leading rebounder, he can strike from inside or out. His running mate, sophomore Derrick Battie, plays sound defense and gets a lot of easy put-back buckets underneath. Back-up Jason Ivey is a fundamentally sound player with an intimidating presence, while Julian King is a perimeter scoring threat.

Center: With some off-court problems now behind him, 6'11" William Cunningham has turned his full attention to basketball. Still, he needs to improve his paltry rebounding and shot-blocking numbers. Despite great talent, he can sometimes totally disappear.

Analysis: With McKie, Jones, Brunson, and Battie each averaging more than 33.5 minutes per game, Chaney didn't need much bench support last season. He may be pushing his luck if he again relies so heavily on his starters. While the defense should be superb, free throw shooting and bench strength loom as the primary pitfalls.

1993-94 ROSTER

	POS	HT	YR	FGP	FTP	3-PT	RPG	APG	PPG
Aaron McKie	G	6'5"	Sr.	.43	.79	77/196	5.9	3.3	20.6
Eddie Jones	F/G	6'6"	Sr.	.46	.60	49/141	7.0	1.8	17.0
Rick Brunson	G	6'3"	Jr.	.40	.66	57/177	3.0	4.5	14.0
Derrick Battie	F	6'9"	So.	.50	.56	—	5.8	0.2	7.3
William Cunningham	C	6'11"	So.	.58	.56	—	3.9	—	3.8
Jason Ivey	F	6'6"	So.	.46	.56	—	3.0	0.2	2.5
Chris Ozment	G	6'4"	Jr.	.39	.42	2/11	1.3	0.3	1.5
Julian King	F/G	6'5"	So.	.20	.43	0/1	0.4	0.1	0.6
William Rice	F/G	6'6"	So.	.29	.25	0/3	0.5	—	0.6
Marco Van Velsen	F	6'9"	So.	—	—	—	0.2	—	—

TEXAS

Conference: Southwest
1992-93: 11-17, 7th SWC

1992-93 NCAAs: Not invited
Coach: Tom Penders (322-247)

Opening Line: After a disastrous 1992-93 season, the Longhorns suffered another blow in August when star guard B.J. Tyler withdrew from school, checking himself into a drug and alcohol rehab program. This comes after a season filled with injuries, suspensions, and dismissals. The 1993-94 season was supposed to be a comeback year for Texas, but the loss of Tyler dims the hopes. Also, last year's leading scorer, Michael Richardson, has graduated.

Guard: Tyler missed half of last year with a broken wrist, but he still averaged 18.1 PPG and led the team in APG—so you can see why he'll be missed. Terrence Rencher does return. Despite 38-percent shooting, he averaged 19.6 PPG last year. Veteran Tony Watson, a potent 3-point weapon, will likely win a starting spot. Guards Tommy Penders, Lamont Hill, and Al Coleman all have experience, but their shooting percentages last year were woeful.

Forward: Well-built Gerrald Houston is as physical as they come, although he's not much of an offensive threat. He started 23 games last winter. Until Al Segova returns from a severe knee injury, Houston will likely be joined by Louisville transfer Tremaine Wingfield or New York City standout frosh Reggie Freeman. Like Houston, Wingfield thrives on contact inside.

Center: Albert Burditt was averaging 14.1 RPG last year before being shelved by academics in January. It's likely he'll retain eligibility for this season. Raw talent Sheldon Quarles and Michigan transfer Rich McIver are the alternatives.

Analysis: Before the loss of Tyler, the Longhorns were looking to double last year's victory total of 11. With B.J., they would have been favored to win the Southwest Conference. Nevertheless, Texas still has a star in the backcourt in Rencher, while a successful return by Burditt would be a huge boost. Texas is still a contender in the mediocre SWC.

1993-94 ROSTER

	POS	HT	YR	FGP	FTP	3-PT	RPG	APG	PPG
Terrence Rencher	G	6'3"	Jr.	.38	.71	26/99	5.1	3.5	19.6
Albert Burditt	C/F	6'8"	Sr.	.54	.61	—	14.1	1.4	14.9
Tony Watson	G	6'3"	Sr.	.42	.62	46/129	4.5	1.2	11.3
Gerrald Houston	F/C	6'8"	Sr.	.41	.54	1/4	5.0	0.4	5.1
Tommy Penders	G	6'2"	Jr.	.32	.79	8/41	1.3	2.1	4.8
Lamont Hill	G	6'1"	Jr.	.35	.59	12/38	1.6	0.4	4.2
Sheldon Quarles	C/F	6'10"	So.	.37	.74	—	3.3	0.2	2.6
Al Coleman	G	6'1"	So.	.26	1.00	9/36	0.6	0.5	2.3
Jesse Sandstad	F	6'7"	So.	.39	.50	0/1	1.9	0.2	0.6
Reggie Freeman	G/F	6'5"	Fr.	—	—	—	—	—	—
Rich McIver	C/F	6'9"	Jr.	—	—	—	—	—	—
Tremaine Wingfield	F	6'6"	Jr.	—	—	—	—	—	—

TEXAS TECH

Conference: Southwest
1992-93: 18-12, 5th SWC

1992-93 NCAAs: 0-1
Coach: James Dickey (33-26)

Opening Line: Led by star center Will Flemons (20.2 PPG, 10.8 RPG), the Red Raiders made their first NCAA Tournament appearance in seven seasons last year as a result of their surprising SWC Tournament victory. Although Flemons has graduated, his four fellow starters are back, led by standout shooting guard Lance Hughes. Six newcomers were inked to letters of intent, including a trio of juco transfers.

Guard: Hughes scored 16.2 PPG last season, while also improving all other facets of his game. A tremendous all-around athlete, his 25 slam dunks ranked tops on the team. Lead guard Lenny Holly was named the premier frosh in the SWC last season. He's a superb playmaker whose maturity level is beyond his years. Chad Collins returns after starting half of 1992-93 at the point prior to Holly's emergence. Sophomore Koy Smith is deadly from 3-point range.

Forward: It didn't take long for freshman Jason Sasser to work his way into the starting lineup. His all-around game sparkled down the stretch. Hard-working Brad Dale was the only player besides Flemons to start every game, and his tenacious defense often rubbed off on his frontcourt mates. Junior college transfers Darvin Ham and Mark Davis will supply some needed depth.

Center: Tech's postseason chance may hinge on the play of Bernard Lloyd, a highly regarded juco recruit who must prove himself on the Division I level. True frosh Gionet Cooper needs work.

Analysis: Minus Flemons, Hughes will have to emerge as the Red Raiders' go-to guy in the clutch. He appears more than ready to meet the challenge. Coach James Dickey's "James Gang" (consisting of 1992-93 recruits Holly, Sasser, and Smith) are sure to benefit from last year's experience. All three will improve. The fact that this is a down year for the SWC will help Tech's cause.

1993-94 ROSTER

	POS	HT	YR	FGP	FTP	3-PT	RPG	APG	PPG
Lance Hughes	G	6'4"	Jr.	.56	.67	31/65	4.0	2.2	16.2
Koy Smith	G	6'5"	So.	.44	.68	63/152	3.2	1.8	11.4
Jason Sasser	F	6'7"	So.	.43	.63	17/54	5.1	1.6	10.6
Lenny Holly	G	6'4"	So.	.37	.70	34/102	3.0	5.0	8.8
Chad Collins	G	6'0"	Jr.	.31	.50	10/28	0.8	1.8	1.9
Guy Clayton	G	6'2"	Jr.	.43	.25	—	0.4	0.4	1.0
Brock Barnes	G	6'5"	Fr.	—	—	—	—	—	—
Gionet Cooper	F/C	6'8"	Fr.	—	—	—	—	—	—
Mark Davis	F	6'7"	Jr.	—	—	—	—	—	—
Darvin Ham	F	6'7"	Jr.	—	—	—	—	—	—
Jason Hamm	F/G	6'6"	Fr.	—	—	—	—	—	—
Bernard Lloyd	C	6'9"	Jr.	—	—	—	—	—	—

TOLEDO

Conference: Mid-American
1992-93: 12-16, 5th MAC

1992-93 NCAAs: Not invited
Coach: Larry Gipson (19-36)

Opening Line: Following a slow start in 1992-93, second-year coach Larry Gipson's Rockets improved steadily as the season progressed. With five returning starters (including *Basketball Weekly* All-Juco Transfer honoree Tim Schirra) joining forces with a collection of talented newcomers, Toledo just might claim its first MAC title since 1980-81.

Guard: What 5'10" Sam Brown and 5'11" Archie Fuller lack in size, they make up for with ability. Not only do they put the ball in the hole, particularly from long range, but they terrorize opponents with their fullcourt pressure defense. Returning starter Craig Thames (6'0") is a superb all-around athlete who'll likely be relegated to bench duty due to the recruitment of six players 6'5" or taller. James Heck offers proven backcourt depth.

Forward: Darell Sizemore, a solid passer with good shooting range, started 24 games last winter as a true frosh. The other forward post has become crowded with the addition of Dayton transfer Sean Scrutchins, UNC-Asheville transfer John Jacoby, and juco transfers Scoop Williams and Kalvin White.

Center: Last year, Schirra posted solid numbers in his first season at the Division I level. He relies on quickness and agility for many of his defensive boards. Although lacking polish, frosh Casey Shaw (6'10") is the tallest player on the Toledo team.

Analysis: Taking advantage of the contacts he made during a nine-year coaching career at Northeastern Oklahoma A&M (a junior college), Gipson has stocked the Rockets' roster with talent not often seen in the MAC. If Brown, Fuller, and Schirra alone can match last year's numbers, Toledo should soar past perennial front-runners Miami of Ohio and Ball State. If newcomers like Scrutchins and Jacoby are as good as advertised, an NCAA tourney victory isn't out of the question.

1993-94 ROSTER

	POS	HT	YR	FGP	FTP	3-PT	RPG	APG	PPG
Archie Fuller	G	5'11"	Sr.	.38	.65	58/162	3.1	2.2	14.4
Craig Thames	G	6'0"	So.	.54	.73	17/44	4.8	1.4	12.2
Tim Schirra	C	6'8"	Sr.	.50	.67	—	8.4	1.2	11.9
Sam Brown	G	5'10"	Sr.	.45	.67	68/141	2.1	2.7	11.8
Darell Sizemore	F	6'9"	So.	.48	.64	—	3.3	0.7	4.5
James Heck	G	5'10"	Sr.	.32	.71	16/41	0.6	1.0	2.8
John Defoe	F	6'5"	Jr.	—	—	—	—	—	—
John Jacoby	F	6'6"	Jr.	—	—	—	—	—	—
Sean Scrutchins	G/F	6'5"	Jr.	—	—	—	—	—	—
Casey Shaw	C	6'10"	Fr.	—	—	—	—	—	—
Kalvin White	F	6'5"	Jr.	—	—	—	—	—	—
Scoop Williams	F	6'5"	Jr.	—	—	—	—	—	—

TULANE

Conference: Metro   **1992-93 NCAAs:** 1-1
1992-93: 22-9, 2nd Metro   **Coach:** Perry Clark (63-55)

Opening Line: Before Green Wave fans panic over the loss of four starters, they should be reminded that they still have plenty to be thankful for. In the fold are dazzling point guard Pointer Williams, a healthy Kim Lewis, last year's top three reserves (who often played more minutes than the starters), and one of the best high school recruits in the country in Jerald Honeycutt.

Guard: No point guard in America gets the ball up the floor any faster than Williams. He also ranked among the national leaders in steals last year with 2.9 per game. Lewis, sidelined for all but two games last winter after breaking his leg, should supply the perimeter shooting this team badly needed last year. Multi-talented LeVeldro Simmons, Lewis's replacement, will likely shift between big guard and small forward.

Forward: No one's going to take the power-forward job from Honeycutt, who's seemingly a clone of Anthony Reed (the school's all-time leading scorer). Honeycutt, a *Parade* and McDonald's All-American who was born to rebound, was expected to attend either LSU or Arkansas. Fellow freshmen Rayshard Allen and Correy Childs ranked among the top 50 high school prospects in the country. However, the starting small-forward spot will likely go to Carlin Hartman, a long-time reserve.

Center: Makeba Perry came off the bench last year, but he actually played more minutes than the starter. Perry's a strong defender, but unless he picks up the pace a bit on offense, don't be surprised to see Honeycutt moved inside.

Analysis: It won't be as easy for Tulane to advance to the second round of the NCAA Tournament as it was last year, but plenty of proven talent does return to this squad. And that doesn't even include one of the top recruiting classes in the country. If the youngsters can eventually blend in with the veterans, Bourbon Street will be jumping.

1993-94 ROSTER

	POS	HT	YR	FGP	FTP	3-PT	RPG	APG	PPG
Carlin Hartman	F	6'7"	Sr.	.53	.64	0/5	5.4	1.4	11.8
Pointer Williams	G	6'0"	Jr.	.38	.68	25/84	2.9	5.4	9.7
Kim Lewis	G	6'4"	Jr.	.56	.83	2/4	4.0	3.5	8.5
LeVeldro Simmons	G/F	6'4"	So.	.41	.60	26/83	2.2	1.5	8.4
Makeba Perry	C	6'10"	Sr.	.35	.65	—	3.4	0.4	3.1
Antonio Jackson	G	6'2"	Jr.	.40	.25	1/5	0.5	0.7	1.3
Pete Rasche	C	6'11"	Sr.	.39	.33	—	1.0	0.1	1.0
Rayshard Allen	F	6'7"	Fr.	—	—	—	—	—	—
Chris Cameron	G	6'4"	Fr.	—	—	—	—	—	—
Correy Childs	F	6'6"	Fr.	—	—	—	—	—	—
Jerald Honeycutt	F	6'9"	Fr.	—	—	—	—	—	—
David McLeod	C	6'11"	Fr.	—	—	—	—	—	—

UCLA

Conference: Pac-10
1992-93: 22-11, T-3rd Pac-10

1992-93 NCAAs: 1-1
Coach: Jim Harrick (283-143)

Opening Line: A disputed Michigan basket with 1.5 seconds left in overtime stood between the Bruins and the Sweet 16 last spring. After defeating Iowa State, they blew a 19-point lead against the Wolverines. Starters Mitchell Butler (9.5 PPG) and Richard Petruska (11.8 PPG) are key graduation losses. Heralded freshmen Charles O'Bannon and Cameron Dollar are key additions.

Guard: Super-quick Tyus Edney has developed into an outstanding playmaker and an even better defender, while NBA hopeful Shon Tarver is a big-time scorer (team-high 17.2 PPG). With a little better perimeter shooting and more defensive intensity from Tarver, this dynamic duo will rank among the top backcourt tandems in the country. Improved Marquis Burns and Dollar figure to see plenty of reserve action.

Forward: The O'Bannon brothers, Ed and Charles, have been reunited in the Bruins' frontcourt. Ed, an All-Pac-10 selection last winter, overcame major knee surgery to establish himself as one of the premier sophomores in the country last season, while Charles was the best high school player on the West Coast. Multi-talented Kevin Dempsey, a fine perimeter shooter, will likely start ahead of Charles until the latter gains more experience.

Center: Rodney Zimmerman, who averaged 14 minutes per game last year, will see twice as much action this season. He led UCLA in field goal percentage last year and ranked second in blocks. Jiri Zidek, whose father coaches the Czech national team, is progressing slower than expected.

Analysis: Thanks to Edney and Tarver, the Bruins should again be a deadly transition team with sufficient talent to rack up yet another 20-plus win season. The perimeter shooting does need improving and there's hardly a surplus of depth. It'll be interesting to see how the O'Bannon boys play together. Expect big things out of Tarver in his final collegiate season.

1993-94 ROSTER

	POS	HT	YR	FGP	FTP	3-PT	RPG	APG	PPG
Shon Tarver	G	6'5"	Sr.	.52	.64	21/79	4.3	2.9	17.2
Ed O'Bannon	F	6'8"	Jr.	.54	.71	18/40	7.0	1.7	16.7
Tyus Edney	G	5'10"	Jr.	.48	.84	34/82	3.5	5.6	13.6
Kevin Dempsey	F	6'6"	So.	.42	.61	28/65	2.2	1.5	4.5
Rodney Zimmerman	C	6'9"	Sr.	.58	.54	—	3.1	0.5	3.3
Jiri Zidek	C	7'0"	Jr.	.42	.76	—	1.7	0.3	2.4
Marquis Burns	G	6'4"	So.	.35	.50	6/13	1.0	0.6	1.1
David Boyle	F	6'5"	Sr.	.40	.25	1/2	0.6	—	0.8
Ike Nwankwo	C	6'11"	So.	—	—	0/1	3.0	—	—
Cameron Dollar	G	6'1"	Fr.	—	—	—	—	—	—
Charles O'Bannon	F	6'7"	Fr.	—	—	—	—	—	—

VANDERBILT

Conference: Southeastern
1992-93: 28-6, 1st SEC East

1992-93 NCAAs: 2-1
Coach: Jan van Breda Kolff (23-29)

Opening Line: Vandy, which finished ahead of Kentucky in the SEC East last year, has lost Eddie Fogler, the 1992-93 *Basketball Weekly* Coach of the Year. He resigned to take the lucrative South Carolina head job after guiding the Commodores to NCAA tourney wins over Boise State and Illinois. Enter Jan van Breda Kolff, the former Vandy star who most recently coached at Cornell. Standout forwards Kevin Anglin and Bruce Elder will be missed.

Guard: Billy McCaffrey, the celebrated transfer from Duke, earned All-America honors last year after leading his team in scoring (20.6 PPG) and assists. Underrated Ronnie McMahan started every game last year at big guard. Frosh Howard Pride is the team's point guard of the future, while Frank Seckar averaged 18 minutes per game off the bench. McCaffrey, McMahan, and Seckar are lethal from 3-point land.

Forward: Dan Hall and Bryan Milburn, frequently used subs a year ago, replace Anglin and Elder (both second-team all-league selections) in the Vandy frontcourt. Hall led the 1991-92 team in rebounding, while Milburn's a high-percentage shooter. Freshman Austin Bates should play by default due to a lack of proven depth.

Center: Beefy Chris Lawson enjoyed a fine 1992-93 campaign after transferring from Indiana. He ranked second on the team in scoring and rebounding. Back-up Chris Woods is a space eater who can be effective in short spurts.

Analysis: Minus Anglin and Elder, van Breda Kolff shouldn't be expected to achieve what Fogler did last year. The Commodores are one of the least athletic teams in the SEC, and no one besides McCaffrey is all that impressive. Nevertheless, Vandy (or "van-dy") will win its share of games because of its fundamentally sound players.

1993-94 ROSTER

	POS	HT	YR	FGP	FTP	3-PT	RPG	APG	PPG
Billy McCaffrey	G	6'4"	Sr.	.55	.87	83/162	2.6	3.6	20.6
Chris Lawson	C	6'9"	Sr.	.52	.65	5/16	5.5	1.4	11.5
Ronnie McMahan	G	6'4"	Jr.	.47	.66	73/167	2.4	2.3	11.1
Dan Hall	F	6'8"	Sr.	.56	.63	—	4.4	1.1	6.0
Frank Seckar	G	6'1"	So.	.40	.73	30/70	1.6	1.6	4.5
Bryan Milburn	F	6'7"	Jr.	.57	.74	—	3.6	0.6	3.7
Aaron Beth	G	5'10"	Sr.	.50	.83	5/8	1.0	0.9	2.5
Chris Woods	C	6'10"	Jr.	.42	.64	—	1.6	0.1	2.2
Chad Sheron	F	6'7"	So.	.33	.50	6/17	0.7	0.5	2.0
Austin Bates	F	6'9"	Fr.	—	—	—	—	—	—
Malik Evans	F	6'8"	So.	—	—	—	—	—	—
Howard Pride	G	6'3"	Fr.	—	—	—	—	—	—

VIRGINIA

Conference: Atlantic Coast
1992-93: 21-10, 5th ACC

1992-93 NCAAs: 2-1
Coach: Jeff Jones (62-35)

Opening Line: Coach Jeff Jones's Cavs advanced to the Sweet 16 last year with impressive wins over Manhattan and Massachusetts. Virginia's smothering man-to-man defense and inside strength made the difference, as did the play of superstar-in-the-making Cory Alexander. Center Ted Jeffries is the only significant loss, as Alexander and three other starters return. None of the team's four recruits appears to be an immediate factor.

Guard: The ACC's leading scoring point guard, Alexander now deserves mention with the premier guards in the country. He did a much better job of distributing the basketball during the second half of 1992-93. Defensive standout Cornel Parker is the ACC's top rebounding guard. Also a capable scorer, he excels in the open court. Chris Havlicek is expected to see more playing time.

Forward: Neither Junior Burrough nor Jason Williford missed a start last winter. They work well together, as Burrough provides plenty of inside scoring and rebounding punch, while Williford is a jack-of-all-trades type who does the little things that often go unnoticed. Chris Alexander and Shawn Wilson possess basketball bodies but lack ability.

Center: It just won't seem like a Virginia team without Jeffries, a four-year starter, in the middle. Dependable Yuri Barnes spelled both Jeffries at center and Burrough at big forward last season. After adding some muscle in the off-season, he's ticketed to become the starter with back-up help from untested newcomer Mark Bogosh.

Analysis: Coach Jones has that unique ability to push all the right buttons when it matters most. The Cavaliers will battle you all game long at the defensive end and rely on either Cory Alexander or Burrough to get the hot hand offensively. Virginia's not a real pretty team, but it get results.

1993-94 ROSTER

	POS	HT	YR	FGP	FTP	3-PT	RPG	APG	PPG
Cory Alexander	G	6'1"	Jr.	.45	.71	64/174	3.5	4.6	18.8
Junior Burrough	F	6'8"	Jr.	.44	.64	0/4	7.2	0.6	14.6
Cornel Parker	G/F	6'7"	Sr.	.42	.66	22/78	6.9	3.2	11.0
Jason Williford	F	6'5"	Jr.	.38	.77	10/40	4.7	1.6	6.1
Yuri Barnes	F/C	6'8"	Jr.	.48	.62	—	4.0	0.1	5.5
Shawn Wilson	F/C	6'11"	Sr.	.71	.50	—	0.8	—	0.8
Chris Havlicek	G	6'5"	Sr.	.24	.50	0/5	0.8	0.6	0.6
Chris Alexander	F	6'8"	So.	.50	.21	—	1.0	0.2	0.5
Mark Bogosh	C	7'1"	Jr.	—	—	—	—	—	—
Harold Deane	G	6'2"	Fr.	—	—	—	—	—	—
Mike Powell	G	6'3"	Fr.	—	—	—	—	—	—
Jamal Robinson	G	6'6"	Fr.	—	—	—	—	—	—

VIRGINIA COMMONWEALTH

Conference: Metro
1992-93: 20-10, 3rd Metro

1992-93 NIT: 0-1
Coach: Sonny Smith (262-236)

Opening Line: Despite losing All-America candidate Kendrick Warren with a broken foot in the middle of last season, the Rams rallied to win seven of their final ten ballgames before falling to Old Dominion in the opening round of the NIT. Guided by Metro Conference Coach of the Year Sonny Smith, VCU made its first postseason appearance since 1988. Most everyone is back to battle Louisville and Tulane in the Metro, including a healthy Warren. Gone are starting forward Sherron Mills and reserve guard Chris Brower.

Guard: Kenny Harris, a transfer from North Carolina, was superb while starting every game at the point. He led the Metro in assists and ranked fourth in 3-point field goal percentage. Terrence Gibson returns as the starting off guard. A former juco standout, he's a streak shooter whose defense draws rave reviews. Freshman Keith Davis should get an early look. Rich Mount decided to forgo his senior season to become a state trooper in Indiana.

Forward: Nearly impossible to defend, Warren enters his final season as the finest player in school history. Arguably the college game's most underrated player, he's sure to be a first-round NBA draft choice. Tyron McCoy, a solid producer at both ends, exploded to average more than 16 PPG during the final 11 games of the 1992-93 season. Kareem Washington is the top reserve.

Center: String-bean Eugene Kissourine averaged 6.8 PPG and 6.0 RPG in his 22 starts in the pivot last winter. Standout recruit Marc Jackson (6'9", 275 pounds) is expected to eventually take Kissourine's job.

Analysis: Considering how well the Rams played late last season without their star player, Warren's return is sure to transform VCU into a top-flight contender. The inside-outside duo of Warren and Harris—combined with plenty of additional size, speed, and depth—is sure to make Smith's fifth season with the Rams his best yet.

1993-94 ROSTER

	POS	HT	YR	FGP	FTP	3-PT	RPG	APG	PPG
Kendrick Warren	F	6'8"	Sr.	.50	.52	3/15	9.1	1.9	17.6
Tyron McCoy	F	6'5"	Jr.	.53	.60	42/97	4.9	1.9	14.2
Kenny Harris	G	6'1"	Sr.	.42	.66	60/155	2.9	6.3	11.3
Terrence Gibson	G	6'3"	Sr.	.42	.67	33/85	3.5	3.2	7.5
Eugene Kissourine	C/F	6'9"	Jr.	.47	.52	9/28	5.7	1.2	6.0
Kareem Washington	F/G	6'5"	Jr.	.48	.63	1/1	1.3	0.4	2.4
Rodney Ashby	F	6'7"	Sr.	.48	.25	—	2.0	0.3	1.3
James Barnes	G	6'3"	So.	1.00	—	—	0.3	—	1.0
Alvin Mobley	F	6'9"	Sr.	.17	.75	0/1	1.1	0.4	0.7
George Byrd	F/C	6'7"	Fr.	—	—	—	—	—	—
Keith Davis	G	6'4"	Fr.	—	—	—	—	—	—
Marc Jackson	F/C	6'9"	Fr.	—	—	—	—	—	—

WAKE FOREST

Conference: Atlantic Coast
1992-93: 21-9, T-3rd ACC

1992-93 NCAAs: 2-1
Coach: Dave Odom (107-90)

Opening Line: Oh, what might have been.... Had Rodney Rogers not elected to turn pro a year early, the Demon Deacons would have returned 91 percent of their offensive production from an outstanding 1992-93 team. Even without his All-America forward, coach Dave Odom has to feel good about his team's experience factor this time around.

Guard: Despite sitting out the 1991-92 season with a knee injury, Randolph Childress didn't skip a beat last year. He finished third in the ACC in scoring last season, and his outside shooting is a key to Wake's success. Transfer Charlie Harrison, who played two guard at Georgetown, struggled early last year but eventually took command of the point. Three-point marksman Marc Blucas has emerged as an important reserve.

Forward: Trelonnie Owens, king of the Deacon weight room, stepped up his game last year after a promotion from sixth man to starting forward. Opposite him in Rogers's vacated position will likely be junior Travis Banks, the team's top frontcourt reserve in 1992-93. This past summer, a cloud of controversy surrounded Wake's recruitment of Makhtar Ndiaye.

Center: The board work of graduated Derrick Hicks (nine RPG) will be sorely missed. Seven-footer Stan King hasn't made much of an impact in three years, so redshirt frosh Marc Schoone (from Holland) and true frosh Tim Duncan (from the Virgin Islands) should get shots at playing time.

Analysis: The Deacons are too light up front, especially at center, to contend for the ACC title. Still, the trio of Childress, Harrison, and Owens will ensure that Wake wins its share of games. Odom has built a solid program, the only one in the country that can claim a victory over the eventual national champion in each of the past three seasons. It would have been a great one had Rogers stayed one more year.

1993-94 ROSTER

	POS	HT	YR	FGP	FTP	3-PT	RPG	APG	PPG
Randolph Childress	G	6'2"	Jr.	.48	.81	96/217	2.8	4.2	19.7
Trelonnie Owens	F	6'8"	Sr.	.50	.69	5/18	5.9	2.0	11.1
Charlie Harrison	G	6'1"	Sr.	.36	.78	13/51	1.6	3.7	6.1
Travis Banks	F	6'6"	Jr.	.56	.71	1/2	2.7	1.1	5.3
Marc Blucas	G	6'3"	Sr.	.56	.61	29/56	1.6	1.1	4.3
Stacey Castle	G	6'1"	So.	.52	.50	0/1	0.1	0.7	1.5
Rusty Larue	G	6'2"	So.	.429	.800	5/10	0.5	0.1	1.4
Bobby Fitzgibbons	F	6'8"	So.	.12	.70	0/2	0.9	0.1	0.8
Stan King	C	7'0"	Sr.	.20	.46	—	0.7	—	0.5
Tim Duncan	C/F	6'10"	Fr.	—	—	—	—	—	—
Makhtar Ndiaye	F/C	6'9"	Fr.	—	—	—	—	—	—
Marc Schoone	C	6'11"	Fr.	—	—	—	—	—	—

WEST VIRGINIA

Conference: Atlantic 10   **1992-93 NIT:** 1-1
1992-93: 17-12, 6th A-10   **Coach:** Gale Catlett (429-201)

Opening Line: West Virginia's up-and-down 1992-93 season was highlighted by late-season victories over UMass and Temple and an NIT triumph over Georgia. Small forward Pervires Greene, a dunking machine, played like a man possessed during the final month of the season. With the exception of part-time starters Tracy Shelton (14 games) and Jeremy Bodkin (ten), everyone's back. Juco transfers Kymar Barron, Zain Shaw, and Chet Loudermilk are capable of contributing immediately.

Guard: Marsalis Basey, a tireless little floor general, handed out more than five assists per contest last year. He also poured in 13.2 PPG. Although 6'1" Mike Boyd lacks the size and shooting range most coaches look for in an off guard, he's a fearless penetrator and a gritty defender. Loudermilk will push for playing time, as will well-schooled Yugoslav Nenad Grmusa.

Forward: Greene blossomed from a solid athlete into a solid basketball player last winter. The Mountaineers' leading scorer, he shoots particularly well in traffic. Although overshadowed somewhat by Greene, Ricky Robinson is probably the best all-around player on the WVU squad. A ferocious rebounder, Robinson's a pro prospect in coach Gale Catlett's eyes.

Center: An excellent defender and shot-blocker, Phil Wilson took over in the middle last season when Bodkin was injured. He more than held his own, as evidenced by an 11-rebound performance vs. St. Joseph's. Barron displays quickness and a soft shooting stroke.

Analysis: The next time someone boasts about quality Atlantic 10 teams like Massachusetts, Temple, and George Washington, remind them of the Mountaineers. While not loaded with individual stars, WVU is a well-coached, disciplined team that never gives less than 100 percent. This year's veteran cast (five senior starters) realizes that it won't get another chance.

1993-94 ROSTER

	POS	HT	YR	FGP	FTP	3-PT	RPG	APG	PPG
Pervires Greene	F	6'8"	Sr.	.44	.67	0/9	5.5	1.7	15.1
Ricky Robinson	F	6'8"	Sr.	.52	.61	0/1	7.7	1.5	13.8
Marsalis Basey	G	5'8"	Sr.	.40	.75	54/145	4.4	5.5	13.2
Mike Boyd	G	6'1"	Sr.	.60	.70	3/11	2.9	3.2	11.4
Phil Wilson	C	6'10"	Sr.	.53	.40	—	4.5	0.7	3.1
Peca Arsic	F	6'9"	So.	.44	.71	0/5	1.1	0.2	1.7
Nenad Grmusa	G	6'4"	Sr.	.29	.59	4/18	1.3	0.6	1.5
Kymar Barron	C	6'10"	Jr.	—	—	—	—	—	—
Sheldon Jefferson	G	6'3"	Fr.	—	—	—	—	—	—
David Ligouri	G	6'4"	Fr.	—	—	—	—	—	—
Chet Loudermilk	G	6'4"	Jr.	—	—	—	—	—	—
Zain Shaw	F	6'6"	Jr.	—	—	—	—	—	—

WISCONSIN

Conference: Big Ten
1992-93: 14-14, T-8th Big Ten

1992-93 NIT: 0-1
Coach: Stu Jackson (14-14)

Opening Line: Last year, Stu Jackson posted the best first-year record by a Badger coach in 58 seasons, leading the Badgers to the NIT. Everyone, except centers Louis Ely and Damon Harrell, returns. All-Big Ten forward Michael Finley is sure to contend for All-America honors, while Rashard Griffith and Jalil Roberts rank as two of the finest frosh recruits in the country.

Guard: Whether he's penetrating, finding an open teammate, or pulling up and nailing an open jumper, Tracy Webster is the main man in the Badger backcourt. A third-team all-league pick, he set school single-season records for assists and steals last winter. Big guard Andy Kilbride nails 3-pointers and plays relentless defense. Freshman Darnell Hoskins will back up Webster, while much-improved Jason Johnsen will share time with Kilbride.

Forward: A legitimate candidate for Big Ten Player of the Year in 1993-94, Finley topped last season's team in scoring (22.1 PPG), rebounding, and 3-point field goals, while ranking second in assists and steals. He makes the game look incredibly easy. Brian Kelley's a big, tough kid who may have a difficult time holding onto his job following Roberts's arrival. Roberts, who'll also play some big guard, is a far more accomplished scorer.

Center: Though 7'0" Grant Johnson has experience, Griffith will wrestle the starting job away from him. One of the top two high school big men in the nation last season, Griffith is a major-league rebounder and shot-blocker whose offensive game is also quite refined.

Analysis: While it has been 47 years since the Badgers made an NCAA Tournament appearance, the wait is finally over. Thanks largely to Finley and Webster, Wisconsin has the potential to hang right in there for Big Ten bragging rights with the likes of Indiana, Minnesota, Illinois, and Michigan. The development of Griffith and Roberts should be the telling tale.

1993-94 ROSTER

	POS	HT	YR	FGP	FTP	3-PT	RPG	APG	PPG
Michael Finley	F	6'7"	Jr.	.47	.77	63/173	5.8	3.1	22.1
Tracy Webster	G	5'11"	Sr.	.39	.81	45/134	3.4	6.4	14.1
Jason Johnsen	G	6'2"	Sr.	.38	.27	49/126	1.4	0.7	6.7
Andy Kilbride	G	6'3"	Jr.	.42	.80	49/107	1.3	1.4	6.7
Jeff Petersen	C/F	6'10"	Sr.	.62	.69	—	1.6	—	5.3
Brian Kelley	F	6'7"	Jr.	.42	.69	0/2	4.1	0.9	5.0
Carlton McGee	F	6'6"	Sr.	.48	.50	—	3.1	0.6	3.3
Otto McDuffie	F	6'5"	So.	.42	.36	—	1.4	0.1	1.4
Grant Johnson	C	7'0"	Sr.	.35	.63	—	1.5	0.1	0.9
Rashard Griffith	C	7'0"	Fr.	—	—	—	—	—	—
Darnell Hoskins	G	6'0"	Fr.	—	—	—	—	—	—
Jalil Roberts	G/F	6'5"	Fr.	—	—	—	—	—	—

XAVIER

Conference: Midwestern Collegiate   **1992-93 NCAAs:** 1-1
1992-93: 24-6, T-1st MCC   **Coach:** Pete Gillen (180-67)

Opening Line: Last year was the Musketeers' seventh trip to the NCAA Tournament in eight seasons under Pete Gillen, who has brought the program unprecedented recognition. Still, over the last two years, Xavier has been relegated to second banana in its own town, due to Bob Huggins's Cincinnati Bearcats. While it'll be tough to match Cincinnati's recent prowess, the Musketeers should stay on the tournament track in 1993-94.

Guard: Michael Hawkins and Steve Gentry will try to offset the loss of three-time All-MCC selection Jamie Gladden. A left-hander, Gentry is steady at the point on offense and spectacular on defense. Hawkins is an athletic talent, but he must become more offensive-minded this season. Gillen scored a major coup by signing Jeff Massey, a scoring machine in the juco ranks.

Forward: If Massey's as good as advertised, Hawkins could see a lot of time at small forward, where he started 21 games last season. However, explosive swing man Tyrice Walker might receive the most minutes at the position if he continues to improve at the same pace as last season. As Xavier's most physical big man, Larry Sykes is the likely replacement for shot-blocker Aaron Williams at power forward. Juco transfer Pete Sears should be an immediate contributor.

Center: Brian Grant was named the MCC's Player of the Year last season after doing the job on the low blocks to the tune of 18.5 points and 9.4 rebounds per game. His play reminds fans of former Xavier star Tyrone Hill.

Analysis: Despite losing two standouts in Gladden and Williams, Gillen has the right components for a very successful season. There are enough interchangeable parts in the backcourt and on the wing to maintain an up-tempo, frenetic style. At the same time, the Musketeers have in Grant that dominating physical presence to thrive in a halfcourt game.

1993-94 ROSTER

	POS	HT	YR	FGP	FTP	3-PT	RPG	APG	PPG
Brian Grant	C	6'8"	Sr.	.65	.69	—	9.4	1.5	18.5
Tyrice Walker	G/F	6'4"	Sr.	.53	.57	—	3.7	1.6	8.2
Michael Hawkins	G/F	6'0"	Jr.	.46	.78	36/88	2.5	3.7	8.1
Steve Gentry	G	5'11"	Sr.	.37	.72	21/68	2.8	3.7	7.1
Larry Sykes	F/C	6'9"	Jr.	.51	.41	—	2.8	0.8	2.3
Erik Edwards	F	6'8"	Sr.	.41	.67	5/12	1.1	0.2	1.7
DeWaun Rose	F	6'7"	Jr.	.62	.67	—	0.5	0.3	1.1
Sherwin Anderson	G	5'11"	Fr.	—	—	—	—	—	—
Ken Harvey	G	6'2"	Fr.	—	—	—	—	—	—
Jeff Massey	G	6'1"	Jr.	—	—	—	—	—	—
Pete Sears	G/F	6'5"	Jr.	—	—	—	—	—	—
Andre Smith	F	6'6"	Fr.	—	—	—	—	—	—

College Basketball Review

The final section in the book reviews the 1992-93 college basketball season and lists important historical information.

First, you'll find the final 1992-93 standings of 32 conferences in Division I. Their conference records include regular-season conference games only. Their overall records include all postseason tournament games, including conference tournaments, the NCAA, and the NIT. The standings indicate the teams that made the NCAA Tourney (*), those that won their conference tournaments (#), and those that were ineligible for postseason play (@).

The recap of the 1992-93 season also includes the following:

- final A.P. poll and A.P. All-Americans
- Division I statistical leaders
- NCAA Tournament game-by-game results
- Final Four box scores
- NIT results
- women's NCAA tourney results
- women's final A.P. poll

Finally, you'll find Division I historical information, including the following:

- national champions (1901-93)
- Final Four results (1939-93)
- Division I career leaders
- Division I season records
- Division I game records
- winningest Division I teams

The NCAA Tournament didn't begin until 1939. Prior to that, there were no official national champions. However, the Helms Foundation selected national champs retroactively for the years 1901-38. These are the teams that are listed in the national champions chart.

DIVISION I FINAL STANDINGS, 1992-93

Atlantic Coast

	Conference			Overall		
	W	L	PCT.	W	L	PCT.
*North Carolina	14	2	.875	34	4	.895
*Florida St.	12	4	.750	25	10	.714
*Duke	10	6	.625	24	8	.750
*Wake Forest	10	6	.625	21	9	.700
*Virginia	9	7	.563	21	10	.677
*#Georgia Tech	8	8	.500	19	11	.633
Clemson	5	11	.313	17	13	.567
Maryland	2	14	.125	12	16	.429
N. Carolina St.	2	14	.125	8	19	.296

Atlantic 10

	Conference			Overall		
	W	L	PCT.	W	L	PCT.
*#Massachusetts	11	3	.786	24	7	.774
*George Washin.	8	6	.571	21	9	.700
*Rhode Island	8	6	.571	19	11	.633
St. Joseph's	8	6	.571	18	11	.621
*Temple	8	6	.571	20	13	.606
West Virginia	7	7	.500	17	12	.586
Rutgers	6	8	.429	13	15	.464
St. Bonaventure	0	14	.000	10	17	.370

Big East

	Conference			Overall		
	W	L	PCT.	W	L	PCT.
*#Seton Hall	14	4	.778	28	7	.800
*St. John's	12	6	.667	19	11	.633
@Syracuse	10	8	.556	20	9	.690
*Pittsburgh	9	9	.500	17	11	.607
Providence	9	9	.500	20	13	.606
Boston College	9	9	.500	18	13	.581
Connecticut	9	9	.500	15	13	.536
Georgetown	8	10	.444	20	13	.606
Miami (FL)	7	11	.389	10	17	.370
Villanova	3	15	.167	8	19	.296

Big Eight

	Conference			Overall		
	W	L	PCT.	W	L	PCT.
*Kansas	11	3	.786	29	7	.806
*Oklahoma St.	8	6	.571	20	9	.690
*Iowa St.	8	6	.571	20	11	.645
*Nebraska	8	6	.571	20	11	.645
*Kansas St.	7	7	.500	19	11	.633
Oklahoma	7	7	.500	20	12	.625
*#Missouri	5	9	.357	19	14	.576
Colorado	2	12	.143	10	17	.370

Big Sky

	Conference			Overall		
	W	L	PCT.	W	L	PCT.
Idaho	11	3	.786	24	8	.750
*#Boise St.	10	4	.714	21	8	.724
Weber St.	10	4	.714	20	8	.714
Montana	8	6	.571	17	11	.607
Idaho St.	5	9	.357	10	18	.357
Montana St.	5	9	.357	9	18	.333
Northern Arizona	4	10	.286	10	16	.385
E. Washington	3	11	.214	6	20	.231

Big South

	Conference			Overall		
	W	L	PCT.	W	L	PCT.
Towson St.	14	2	.875	18	9	.667
*#Coastal Carol.	12	4	.750	22	10	.688
Campbell	10	6	.625	12	15	.444
Liberty	9	7	.563	16	14	.533
Radford	8	8	.500	15	16	.484
Maryl.-Bal. County	7	9	.438	12	16	.429
Winthrop	5	11	.313	14	16	.467
Charleston South.	5	11	.313	9	18	.333
N.C.-Asheville	2	14	.125	4	23	.148

Big Ten

	Conference			Overall		
	W	L	PCT.	W	L	PCT.
*Indiana	17	1	.944	31	4	.886
*Michigan	15	3	.833	31	5	.861
*Iowa	11	7	.611	23	9	.719
*Illinois	11	7	.611	19	13	.594
Minnesota	9	9	.500	22	10	.688
*Purdue	9	9	.500	18	10	.643
Ohio St.	8	10	.444	15	13	.536
Michigan St.	7	11	.389	15	13	.536
Wisconsin	7	11	.389	14	14	.500
Northwestern	3	15	.167	8	19	.296
Penn St.	2	16	.111	7	20	.259

Big West

	Conference			Overall		
	W	L	PCT.	W	L	PCT.
*New Mexico St.	15	3	.833	26	8	.765
UNLV	13	5	.722	21	8	.724
Pacific	12	6	.667	16	11	.593
*#Long Beach St.	11	7	.611	22	10	.688
Cal.-Santa Barb.	10	8	.556	18	11	.621
Fullerton St.	10	8	.556	15	12	.556
Utah St.	7	11	.389	10	17	.370
Nevada	4	14	.222	9	17	.346
San Jose St.	4	14	.222	7	19	.269
Cal.-Irvine	4	14	.222	6	21	.222

Colonial Athletic

	Conference			Overall		
	W	L	PCT.	W	L	PCT.
Old Dominion	11	3	.786	21	8	.724
James Madison	11	3	.786	21	9	.700
Richmond	10	4	.714	15	12	.556
N.C.-Wilmington	6	8	.429	17	11	.607
William & Mary	6	8	.429	14	13	.519
American	6	8	.429	11	17	.393
*#East Carolina	4	10	.286	13	17	.433
George Mason	2	12	.143	7	21	.250

Great Midwest

	Conference			Overall		
	W	L	PCT.	W	L	PCT.
*#Cincinnati	8	2	.800	27	5	.844
*Memphis St.	7	3	.700	20	12	.625
*Marquette	6	4	.600	20	8	.714
Alabama-Birm.	5	5	.500	21	14	.600

	W	L	PCT.	W	L	PCT.
DePaul	3	7	.300	16	15	.516
St. Louis	1	9	.100	12	17	.414

Ivy League

	Conference			Overall		
	W	L	PCT.	W	L	PCT.
*Pennsylvania	14	0	1.00	22	5	.815
Cornell	10	4	.714	16	10	.615
Columbia	9	5	.643	16	10	.615
Princeton	7	7	.500	15	11	.577
Yale	6	8	.429	10	16	.385
Dartmouth	5	9	.357	11	15	.423
Harvard	3	11	.214	6	20	.231
Brown	2	12	.143	7	19	.269

Metro

	Conference			Overall		
	W	L	PCT.	W	L	PCT.
*#Louisville	11	1	.917	22	9	.710
*Tulane	9	3	.750	22	9	.710
Virginia Common.	7	5	.583	20	10	.667
N.C.-Charlotte	6	6	.500	15	13	.536
S. Mississippi	6	6	.500	10	17	.370
South Florida	2	10	.167	8	19	.296
Virginia Tech	1	11	.083	10	18	.357

Metro Atlantic Athletic

	Conference			Overall		
	W	L	PCT.	W	L	PCT.
*#Manhattan	12	2	.857	23	7	.767
Niagara	11	3	.786	23	7	.767
Iona	9	5	.643	16	11	.593
Siena	8	6	.571	16	13	.552
Fairfield	7	7	.500	14	13	.519
Canisius	5	9	.357	10	18	.357
St. Peter's	3	11	.214	9	18	.333
Loyola (MD)	1	13	.071	2	25	.074

Mid-American

	Conference			Overall		
	W	L	PCT.	W	L	PCT.
*#Ball St.	14	4	.778	26	8	.765
Miami (OH)	14	4	.778	22	9	.710
West. Michigan	12	6	.667	17	12	.586
Ohio	11	7	.611	14	13	.519
Toledo	9	9	.500	12	16	.429
Eastern Michigan	8	10	.444	13	17	.433
Bowling Green	8	10	.444	11	16	.407
Kent St.	7	11	.389	10	17	.370
Central Michigan	4	14	.222	8	18	.308
Akron	3	15	.167	8	18	.308

Mid-Continent

	Conference			Overall		
	W	L	PCT.	W	L	PCT.
Cleveland St.	15	1	.938	22	6	.786
*#Wright St.	10	6	.625	20	10	.667
Northern Illinois	10	6	.625	15	12	.556
Illinois-Chicago	9	7	.563	17	15	.531
Wis.-Green Bay	9	7	.563	13	14	.481
Valparaiso	7	9	.438	12	16	.429
Eastern Illinois	7	9	.438	10	17	.370
Western Illinois	4	12	.250	7	20	.259
Youngstown St.	1	15	.063	3	23	.115

Mid-Eastern Athletic

	Conference			Overall		
	W	L	PCT.	W	L	PCT.
*#Coppin St.	16	0	1.00	22	8	.733
S. Carolina St.	9	7	.563	16	13	.552
N. Carolina A&T	9	7	.563	14	13	.519
Morgan St.	9	7	.563	9	17	.346
Florida A&M	8	8	.500	10	18	.357
Maryland-E. Shore	7	9	.438	12	15	.444
Delaware St.	6	10	.375	13	16	.448
Howard	6	10	.375	10	18	.357
Bethune-Cookman	2	14	.125	3	24	.111

Midwestern Collegiate

	Conference			Overall		
	W	L	PCT.	W	L	PCT.
*Xavier (OH)	12	2	.857	24	6	.800
*#Evansville	12	2	.857	20	7	.767
La Salle	9	5	.643	14	13	.519
Detroit Mercy	7	7	.500	15	12	.556
Duquesne	5	9	.357	13	15	.464
Butler	5	9	.357	11	17	.393
Loyola (IL)	3	11	.214	7	20	.259
Dayton	3	11	.214	4	26	.133

Missouri Valley

	Conference			Overall		
	W	L	PCT.	W	L	PCT.
Illinois St.	13	5	.722	19	10	.655
*#South. Illinois	12	6	.667	23	10	.697
S.W. Missou. St.	11	7	.611	20	11	.645
@Tulsa	10	8	.556	15	14	.517
Drake	9	9	.500	14	14	.500
Northern Iowa	8	10	.444	12	15	.444
Bradley	7	11	.389	11	16	.407
Indiana St.	7	11	.389	11	17	.393
Wichita St.	7	11	.389	10	17	.370
Creighton	6	12	.333	8	18	.308

North Atlantic

	Conference			Overall		
	W	L	PCT.	W	L	PCT.
Drexel	12	2	.857	22	7	.759
Northeastern	12	2	.857	20	8	.714
*#Delaware	10	4	.714	22	8	.733
Hartford	7	7	.500	14	14	.500
Maine	4	10	.286	10	17	.370
Vermont	4	10	.286	10	17	.370
New Hampshire	4	10	.286	6	21	.222
Boston	3	11	.214	6	21	.222

Northeast

	Conference			Overall		
	W	L	PCT.	W	L	PCT.
*#Rider	14	4	.778	19	11	.633
Wagner	12	6	.667	18	12	.600
Marist	10	8	.556	14	16	.467
Mount St. Mary's	10	8	.556	13	15	.464
Fairleigh Dickin.	8	10	.444	11	17	.393
St. Francis (NY)	8	10	.444	9	18	.333
Long Island	7	11	.389	11	17	.393
Monmouth	7	11	.389	11	17	.393
Robert Morris	7	11	.389	9	18	.333
St. Francis (PA)	7	11	.389	9	18	.333

Ohio Valley

	Conference			Overall		
	W	L	PCT.	W	L	PCT.
*#Tennessee St.	13	3	.813	19	10	.655
Murray St.	11	5	.688	18	12	.600
Eastern Kentucky	11	5	.688	15	12	.556
S.E. Missouri St.	9	7	.563	16	11	.593
Tennessee Tech	9	7	.563	15	13	.536
@Middle Tenn. St.	6	10	.375	6	21	.222
Morehead St.	5	11	.313	10	16	.385
Tenn.-Martin	4	12	.250	7	19	.269
Austin Peay	4	12	.250	7	20	.259

Pacific-10

	Conference			Overall		
	W	L	PCT.	W	L	PCT.
*Arizona	17	1	.944	24	4	.857
*California	12	6	.667	21	9	.700
*UCLA	11	7	.611	22	11	.667
Arizona St.	11	7	.611	18	10	.643
Southern Cal.	9	9	.500	18	12	.600
Washington St.	9	9	.500	15	12	.556
Oregon St.	9	9	.500	13	14	.481
Washington	7	11	.389	13	14	.481
Oregon	3	15	.167	10	20	.333
Stanford	2	16	.111	7	23	.233

Patriot League

	Conference			Overall		
	W	L	PCT.	W	L	PCT.
Bucknell	13	1	.929	23	6	.793
*#Holy Cross	12	2	.857	23	7	.767
Colgate	9	5	.643	18	10	.643
Fordham	9	5	.643	15	16	.484
Navy	5	9	.357	8	19	.296
Lafayette	4	10	.286	7	20	.259
Army	2	12	.143	4	22	.154
Lehigh	2	12	.143	4	23	.148

Southeastern
East

	Conference			Overall		
	W	L	PCT.	W	L	PCT.
*Vanderbilt	14	2	.875	28	6	.824
*#Kentucky	13	3	.813	30	4	.882
Florida	9	7	.563	16	12	.571
Georgia	8	8	.500	15	14	.517
South Carolina	5	11	.313	9	18	.333
Tennessee	4	12	.250	13	17	.433

West

	Conference			Overall		
	W	L	PCT.	W	L	PCT.
*Arkansas	10	6	.625	22	9	.710
*Louisiana St.	9	7	.563	22	11	.667
Auburn	8	8	.500	15	12	.556
Alabama	7	9	.438	16	13	.552
Mississippi St.	5	11	.313	13	16	.448
Mississippi	4	12	.250	10	18	.357

Southern

	Conference			Overall		
	W	L	PCT.	W	L	PCT.
*#Tenn.-Chattan.	16	2	.889	26	7	.788
Georgia Southern	12	6	.667	19	9	.679
E. Tenn. St.	12	6	.667	19	10	.655
Marshall	11	7	.611	16	11	.593
Davidson	10	8	.556	14	14	.500
Appalachian St.	8	10	.444	13	15	.464
Furman	8	10	.444	11	17	.393
Citadel	8	10	.444	10	17	.370
Virginia Military	3	15	.167	5	22	.185
Western Carolina	2	16	.111	6	21	.222

Southland

	Conference			Overall		
	W	L	PCT.	W	L	PCT.
*#N.E. Louisiana	17	1	.944	26	5	.839
Nicholls St.	11	7	.611	14	12	.538
Texas-Arlington	10	8	.556	16	12	.571
Texas-San Ant.	10	8	.556	15	14	.517
S.W. Texas St.	9	9	.500	14	13	.519
McNeese St.	9	9	.500	12	16	.429
Stephen Austin	8	10	.444	12	14	.462
N.W. Louisiana	7	11	.389	13	13	.500
North Texas	5	13	.278	5	21	.192
Sam Houston St.	4	14	.222	6	19	.240

Southwest

	Conference			Overall		
	W	L	PCT.	W	L	PCT.
*SMU	12	2	.857	20	8	.714
Rice	11	3	.786	18	10	.643
Houston	9	5	.643	21	9	.700
Baylor	7	7	.500	16	11	.593
*#Texas Tech	6	8	.429	18	12	.600
Texas A&M	5	9	.357	10	17	.370
Texas	4	10	.286	11	17	.393
Texas Christian	2	12	.143	6	22	.214

Southwestern Athletic

	Conference			Overall		
	W	L	PCT.	W	L	PCT.
Jackson St.	13	1	.929	25	9	.735
*#Southern-B.R.	9	5	.643	21	10	.677
Alabama St.	9	5	.643	14	13	.519
Texas Southern	8	6	.571	12	15	.444
Missi. Valley St.	7	7	.500	13	15	.464
Grambling St.	5	9	.357	13	14	.481
Alcorn St.	5	9	.357	7	20	.259
Prairie View	0	14	.000	1	26	.037

Sun Belt

	Conference			Overall		
	W	L	PCT.	W	L	PCT.
*New Orleans	18	0	1.00	26	4	.867
*#West. Kentucky	14	4	.778	26	6	.813
Arkansas St.	11	7	.611	16	12	.571
S.W. Louisiana	11	7	.611	17	13	.567
Arkan.-Little Rock	10	8	.556	15	12	.556
Lamar	9	9	.500	15	12	.556
South Alabama	9	9	.500	15	13	.536
Louisiana Tech	3	15	.167	7	21	.250

	Conference			Overall		
	W	L	PCT.	W	L	PCT.
Jacksonville	3	15	.167	5	22	.185
Texas-Pan Am.	2	16	.111	2	20	.091

Trans America Athletic

	Conference			Overall		
	W	L	PCT.	W	L	PCT.
Florida Intl.	9	3	.750	20	10	.667
Samford	7	5	.583	17	10	.630
Mercer	7	5	.583	13	14	.481
Stetson	6	6	.500	13	14	.481
Georgia St.	5	7	.417	13	14	.481
S.E. Louisiana	4	8	.333	12	15	.444
Centenary	4	8	.333	9	18	.333

West Coast

	Conference			Overall		
	W	L	PCT.	W	L	PCT.
Pepperdine	11	3	.786	23	8	.742
Gonzaga	10	4	.714	19	9	.679
*#Santa Clara	9	5	.643	19	12	.613
San Francisco	8	6	.571	19	12	.613
San Diego	7	7	.500	13	14	.481
St. Mary's	6	8	.429	11	16	.407
Portland	3	11	.214	9	18	.333
Loyola Marymount	2	12	.143	7	20	.259

Western Athletic

	Conference			Overall		
	W	L	PCT.	W	L	PCT.
*Utah	15	3	.833	24	7	.774
*Brigham Young	15	3	.833	25	9	.735
*#New Mexico	13	5	.722	24	7	.774
Texas-El Paso	10	8	.556	21	13	.618
Colorado St.	9	9	.500	17	12	.586
Fresno St.	8	10	.444	13	15	.464
Wyoming	7	11	.389	13	15	.464
Hawaii	7	11	.389	12	16	.429
Air Force	3	15	.167	9	19	.321
San Diego St.	3	15	.167	8	21	.276

Division I Independents

	Overall		
	W	L	PCT
Wisconsin-Milwaukee	23	4	.852
College of Charleston	19	8	.704
Missouri-Kansas City	15	12	.556
Southern Utah St.	14	13	.519
N.E. Illinois	11	16	.407
Cal. St.-Northridge	10	17	.370
Central Florida	10	17	.370
@N.C.-Greensboro	10	17	.370
Hofstra	9	18	.333
Notre Dame	9	18	.333
Central Connecticut St.	8	19	.296
Buffalo	5	22	.185
Chicago St.	4	23	.148
Sacramento St.	3	24	.111

* Selected to the NCAA Tournament.

\# Won postseason conference tournament. The Big Ten, Ivy League, and Pacific-10 did not hold tournaments.

@ Ineligible for both the NCAA Tournament and the NIT.

FINAL A.P. POLL, 1992-93

	W-L	Points
1) Indiana (39)	28-3	1,580
2) Kentucky (9)	26-3	1,518
3) Michigan (9)	26-4	1,504
4) North Carolina (7)	28-4	1,488
5) Arizona	24-3	1,328
6) Seton Hall (1)	27-6	1,325
7) Cincinnati	24-4	1,193
8) Vanderbilt	26-5	1,143
9) Kansas	25-6	1,073
10) Duke	23-7	1,052
11) Florida St.	22-9	.895
12) Arkansas	20-8	.758
13) Iowa	22-8	.757
14) Massachusetts	23-6	.748
15) Louisville	20-8	.724
16) Wake Forest	19-8	.640
17) New Orleans	26-3	.464
18) Georgia Tech	19-10	.447
19) Utah	23-6	.425
20) Western Kentucky	24-5	.312
21) New Mexico	24-6	.306
22) Purdue	18-9	.218
23) Oklahoma St.	19-8	.175
24) New Mexico St.	25-7	.120
25) UNLV	21-7	.107

A.P. ALL-AMERICA TEAM

First Team
*Calbert Cheaney, Indiana
Jamal Mashburn, Kentucky
Chris Webber, Michigan
Bobby Hurley, Duke
Anfernee Hardaway, Memphis St.

Second Team
Rodney Rogers, Wake Forest
Glenn Robinson, Purdue
Eric Montross, North Carolina
J.R. Rider, UNLV
Terry Dehere, Seton Hall

* Winner of the Naismith Award, Wooden Award, and Rupp Trophy, which recognize the national Player of the Year.

Poll taken prior to the NCAA Tournament and the NIT. Won-loss records reflect performances at the time the poll was taken. First-place votes in parentheses.

DIVISION I LEADERS, 1992-93

SCORING

Greg Guy, Texas-Pan American 29.3
J.R. Rider, Nevada-Las Vegas 29.1
John Best, Tennessee Tech 28.5
Vin Baker, Hartford 28.3
Lindsey Hunter, Jackson St. 26.7
Alphonso Ford, Mississippi Valley St. 26.0
Bill Edwards, Wright St. 25.2
Billy Ross, Appalachian St. 24.4
Glenn Robinson, Purdue 24.1
Kenneth Sykes, Grambling 23.9

REBOUNDS

Warren Kidd, Middle Tennessee St. 14.8
Jervaughn Scales, Southern-B.R. 12.7
Reggie Jackson, Nicholls St. 12.5
Spencer Dunkley, Delaware 12.2
Dan Callahan, Northeastern 12.1
Ervin Johnson, New Orleans 11.9
Carlos Rogers, Tennessee St. 11.7
Malik Rose, Drexel 11.4
Michael Smith, Providence 11.4
Darren Brown, Colgate 11.3

ASSISTS

Sam Crawford, New Mexico St. 9.1
Dedan Thomas, Nevada-Las Vegas 8.6
Mark Woods, Wright St. 8.4
Bobby Hurley, Duke 8.2
Chuck Evans, Mississippi St. 8.1
Jason Kidd, California 7.7
Tony Miller, Marquette 7.6
Nelson Haggerty, Baylor 7.3
Atiim Browne, Lamar 7.2
Marcell Capers, Arizona St. 7.1

STEALS

Jason Kidd, California 3.8
Jay Goodman, Utah St. 3.8
Mark Woods, Wright St. 3.6
Mike Bright, Bucknell 3.2
Darnell Mee, Western Kentucky 3.1
Jeff Myers, St. Francis (NY) 3.1
Marcus Woods, Charleston........................3.1
Dana Johnson, Canisius 3.0
Russell Peyton, Bucknell 3.0
Terry Evans, Oklahoma 3.0

BLOCKED SHOTS

Theo Ratliff, Wyoming...............................4.4
Sharone Wright, Clemson..........................4.1
Bo Outlaw, Houston 3.8
Carlos Rogers, Tennessee St. 3.2
Theron Wilson, Eastern Michigan 3.2
Spencer Dunkley, Delaware 3.2
Rodney Dobard, Florida St. 3.2
Constantin Popa, Miami (FL) 3.1
Harry Hart, Iona 3.1
Shelby Thurman, Western Illinois 3.1

FIELD GOAL PCT.

Bo Outlaw, Houston 65.8
Brian Grant, Xavier 65.4
Harry Hart, Iona 65.4
Cherokee Parks, Duke 65.2
Gary Trent, Ohio 65.1
Mike Nahar, Wright St. 64.2
Mike Peplowski, Michigan St. 63.9
Jimmy Lunsford, Alabama St. 63.7
Warren Kidd, Middle Tennessee St. 63.0
Eddie Gay, Winthrop 62.8

FREE THROW PCT.

Josh Grant, Utah.....................................92.0
Roger Breslin, Holy Cross.........................90.1
Jeremy Lake, Montana 89.9
Casey Schmidt, Valparaiso 89.7
Scott Hartzell, N.C.-Greensboro 88.9
Greg Holman, Kent 88.5
Travis Ford, Kentucky 88.1
Pat Baldwin, Northwestern........................88.0
Don Burgess, Radford 87.9
Allan Houston, Tennessee.........................87.8

3-PT. FIELD GOAL PCT.

Jeff Anderson, Kent 53.7
Roosevelt Moore, Sam Houston 53.3
Dwayne Morton, Louisville........................53.1
Travis Ford, Kentucky 52.9
Pat Graham, Indiana 51.4
Bill McCaffrey, Vanderbilt.........................51.2
Brad Divine, Eastern Kentucky 50.6
Sean Wightman, Western Michigan.............48.8
Chris Mills, Arizona 48.3
Sam Brown, Toledo 48.2

SCORING OFFENSE, TEAM

Southern-B.R. 97.1
Northwestern Louisiana 90.7
Nevada-Las Vegas 89.4
Wright St. 89.1
Oklahoma 89.1
Lamar 88.3
Alabama St. 88.1
Kentucky 87.5
Northeast Louisiana 87.2
Tennessee Tech 87.1

SCORING DEFENSE, TEAM

Princeton...54.7
Yale..55.5
Miami (OH) 57.3
Cincinnati 58.5
S.W. Missouri St. 58.5
Charleston..60.4
Marquette..60.4
New Orleans 61.2
Bradley..61.3
Montana...61.5

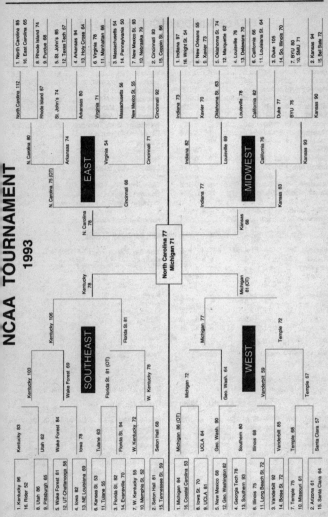

FINAL FOUR BOX SCORES, 1992-93

NCAA SEMIFINAL: North Carolina 78, Kansas 68

N. Carol.	MIN	FG-A	FT-A	REB	AST	PF	PTS
Reese	22	3-5	1-2	4	6	0	7
Lynch	33	5-12	4-6	10	0	3	14
Montross	26	9-14	5-8	4	1	4	23
Phelps	30	1-3	1-2	5	6	2	3
Williams	28	7-11	6-6	3	0	1	25
Sullivan	17	0-2	0-0	1	1	1	0
Rodl	20	0-0	0-0	0	2	2	0
Salvadori	17	3-5	0-0	3	1	0	6
Calabria	1	0-0	0-0	0	0	0	0
Cherry	2	0-0	0-0	2	0	0	0
Davis	1	0-0	0-0	0	0	0	0
Stephenson	1	0-0	0-0	0	0	0	0
Geth	1	0-0	0-0	0	0	0	0
Wenstrom	1	0-0	0-0	0	0	0	0
Totals	200	28-52	17-24	32	17	13	78

FGP—.538. FTP—.708. 3-PT FGP—5-7, .714 (Williams 5-7). Technical fouls—none.

Kansas	MIN	FG-A	FT-A	REB	AST	PF	PTS
Hancock	23	2-5	2-2	5	1	1	6
Scott	23	3-5	2-2	1	1	5	8
Pauley	27	2-5	1-1	9	2	3	5
Walters	32	7-15	0-0	0	5	2	19
Jordan	35	7-13	0-0	1	4	1	19
Rayford	5	0-0	0-0	0	0	0	0
Woodberry	20	2-5	0-0	2	2	4	4
Richey	17	1-4	0-0	2	0	1	2
Ostertag	12	0-2	2-2	2	0	3	2
Gurley	5	1-2	0-0	0	0	0	3
Pearson	1	0-1	0-0	0	0	0	0
Totals	200	25-57	7-7	22	15	20	68

FGP—.439. FTP—1.00. 3-PT FGP—11-20, .550 (Jordan 5-7, Walters 5-9, Gurley 1-1, Pearson 0-1, Woodberry 0-2). Technical fouls—none.

Halftime—North Carolina 40, Kansas 36.

NCAA SEMIFINAL: Michigan 81, Kentucky 78 (OT)

Michigan	MIN	FG-A	FT-A	REB	AST	PF	PTS
Webber	39	10-17	7-9	13	0	3	27
Jackson	33	4-7	3-5	8	1	4	11
Howard	40	6-12	5-7	3	3	4	17
Rose	42	6-16	6-7	6	1	3	18
King	33	1-3	0-0	3	3	5	2
Riley	12	2-4	0-0	4	1	2	4
Pelinka	23	0-1	2-2	1	0	3	2
Voskuil	3	0-1	0-0	0	0	0	0
Totals	225	29-61	23-30	38	9	24	81

FGP—.475. FTP—.767. 3-PT FGP—0-4, .000 (Webber 0-1, Pelinka 0-1, Rose 0-2). Technical fouls—none.

Halftime—Michigan 40, Kentucky 35
Regulation—Michigan 71, Kentucky 71.

Kentucky	MIN	FG-A	FT-A	REB	AST	PF	PTS
Mashburn	41	10-18	5-9	6	2	5	26
Prickett	27	1-6	7-7	7	2	5	9
Dent	27	2-6	2-2	3	1	4	6
Ford	45	3-10	4-4	5	6	2	12
Brown	27	6-10	0-0	1	1	2	16
Rhodes	14	0-1	1-2	1	0	4	1
Riddick	16	2-4	0-0	2	1	2	4
Martinez	6	0-3	0-0	1	0	3	0
Brassow	3	0-0	0-0	0	0	0	0
Delk	18	1-3	2-2	3	0	0	4
Braddy	1	0-0	0-0	0	0	0	0
Totals	225	25-61	21-26	29	13	27	78

FGP—.410. FTP—.808. 3-PT FGP—7-21, .333 (Brown 4-6, Ford 2-6, Mashburn 1-3, Prickett 0-1, Rhodes 0-1, Martinez 0-2, Delk 0-2). Tec. fouls—none.

NCAA FINAL: North Carolina 77, Michigan 71

N. Carol.	MIN	FG-A	FT-A	REB	AST	PF	PTS
Reese	27	2-7	4-4	5	3	1	8
Lynch	28	6-12	0-0	10	1	3	12
Montross	31	5-11	6-9	5	0	2	16
Phelps	36	4-6	1-2	3	6	0	9
Williams	31	8-12	4-4	1	1	1	25
Sullivan	14	1-2	1-2	1	1	2	3
Salvadori	18	0-0	2-2	4	1	1	2
Rodl	11	1-4	0-0	0	0	0	2
Calabria	1	0-0	0-0	0	0	0	0
Wenstrom	2	0-1	0-0	0	0	0	0
Cherry	1	0-0	0-0	0	0	0	0
Totals	200	27-55	18-23	29	13	10	77

FGP—.491. FTP—.783. 3-PT FGP—5-11, .455 (Williams 5-7, Reese 0-1, Phelps 0-1, Rodl 0-2). Technical fouls—none.

Michigan	MIN	FG-A	FT-A	REB	AST	PF	PTS
Webber	33	11-18	1-2	11	1	2	23
Jackson	20	2-3	2-2	1	1	5	6
Howard	34	3-8	1-1	7	3	3	7
Rose	40	5-12	0-0	1	4	3	12
King	34	6-13	2-2	6	4	2	15
Riley	14	1-3	0-0	3	1	1	2
Pelinka	17	2-4	0-0	2	1	1	6
Talley	4	0-0	0-0	0	1	1	0
Voskuil	4	0-1	0-0	0	1	0	0
Totals	200	30-62	6-7	31	17	18	71

FGP—.484. FTP—.857. 3-PT FGP—5-15, .333 (Pelinka 2-3, Rose 2-6, King 1-5, Webber 0-1). Technical fouls—Webber.

Halftime—North Carolina 42, Michigan 36.

NIT RESULTS

First Round
Minnesota 74, Florida 66
Oklahoma 88, Michigan St. 86
Southern Cal. 90, UNLV 74
Miami (OH) 56, Ohio St. 53
Rice 77, Wisconsin 73
West Virginia 95, Georgia 84
S.W. Missouri St. 56, St. Joseph's 34
Alabama-Birmingham 58, Alabama 56
Providence 73, James Madison 61
Clemson 84, Auburn 72
Boston College 87, Niagara 83
Georgetown 78, Arizona St. 68
Old Dominion 74, Virginia Commonwealth 68
Jackson St. 90, Connecticut 88
Pepperdine 53, Cal.-Santa Barbara 50
Texas-El Paso 67, Houston 61

Second Round
Providence 68, West Virginia 67

Boston College 101, Rice 68
Minnesota 86, Oklahoma 72
Miami (OH) 60, Old Dominion 58
Alabama-Birmingham 65, Clemson 64
S.W. Missouri St. 70, Jackson St. 52
Southern Cal. 71, Pepperdine 59
Georgetown 71, Texas-El Paso 44

Third Round
Providence 75, Boston College 58
Minnesota 76, Southern Cal. 58
Alabama-Birmingham 61, S.W. Missouri St. 52
Georgetown 66, Miami (OH) 53

Semifinals
Georgetown 45, Alabama-Birmingham 41
Minnesota 76, Providence 70

Finals
Minnesota 62, Georgetown 61

1992-93 WOMEN'S NCAA TOURNAMENT

First Round
Alabama 102, Georgia Southern 70
California 62, Kansas 47
Cal.-Santa Barbara 88, Brigham Young 79
Clemson 70, Xavier 64
Florida 69, Bowling Green 67
Georgetown 76, Northern Illinois 74
Georgia 85, San Diego St. 68
Louisiana Tech 70, DePaul 59
Louisville 74, Connecticut 71
Miami (FL) 61, St. Peter's 44
Nebraska 81, San Diego 58
Northwestern 90, Georgia Tech 62
Old Dominion 77, Tennessee Tech 60
Rutgers 80, Vermont 74
S.W. Missouri St. 86, Oklahoma St. 71
Washington 80, Montana St. 51

Second Round
Auburn 66, Louisville 61
Colorado 81, Cal.-Santa Barbara 54
Georgetown 68, Penn St. 67
Iowa 82, Old Dominion 56
Louisiana Tech 82, Texas 78
North Carolina 74, Alabama 73 (OT)
Ohio St. 91, Rutgers 60
Southern Cal. 78, Nebraska 60
S.W. Missouri St. 86, Maryland 82
Stanford 93, Georgia 60
Stephen F. Austin 89, Clemson 78
Tennessee 89, Northwestern 66
Texas Tech 70, Washington 64
Vanderbilt 82, California 63
Virginia 69, Florida 55
Western Kentucky 78, Miami (FL) 63

Regional Finals
Colorado 80, Stanford 67
Iowa 63, Auburn 50
Louisiana Tech 59, S.W. Missouri St. 43

Ohio St. 86, Western Kentucky 73
Tennessee 74, North Carolina 54
Texas Tech 87, Southern Cal. 67
Vanderbilt 59, Stephen F. Austin 56
Virginia 77, Georgetown 57

Regional Championships
Iowa 72, Tennessee 56
Ohio St. 75, Virginia 73
Texas Tech 79, Colorado 54
Vanderbilt 58, Louisiana Tech 53

National Semifinals
Ohio St. 73, Iowa 72 (OT)
Texas Tech 60, Vanderbilt 46

National Championship
Texas Tech 84, Ohio St. 82

FINAL A.P. POLL, 1992-93

1) Vanderbilt (55)	27-2	1,677
2) Tennessee (13)	27-2	1,639
3) Ohio St.	24-3	1,559
4) Iowa	24-3	1,424
5) Texas Tech	26-3	1,383
6) Stanford	25-5	1,336
7) Auburn	24-3	1,286
8) Penn St.	22-5	1,223
9) Virginia	24-5	1,160
10) Colorado	25-3	1,124
11) Maryland	22-7	940
12) Stephen F. Austin	27-4	904
13) Western Kentucky	23-6	872
14) Louisiana Tech	23-5	808
15) Southern Cal.	21-6	701
16) Texas	22-7	699
17) North Carolina	22-6	582
18) Vermont	28-0	566
19) Bowling Green	25-4	370
20) Miami (FL)	23-6	295

NATIONAL CHAMPIONS

YEAR	CHAMPION	RECORD	COACH	YEAR	CHAMPION	RECORD	COACH
1901	Yale	10-4	No coach	1948	Kentucky	36-3	Adolph Rupp
1902	Minnesota	11-0	Louis Cooke	1949	Kentucky	32-2	Adolph Rupp
1903	Yale	15-1	W.H. Murphy	1950	CCNY	24-5	Nat Holman
1904	Columbia	17-1	No coach	1951	Kentucky	32-2	Adolph Rupp
1905	Columbia	19-1	No coach	1952	Kansas	28-3	Phog Allen
1906	Dartmouth	16-2	No coach	1953	Indiana	23-3	Branch McCracken
1907	Chicago	22-2	Joseph Raycroft	1954	La Salle	26-4	Ken Loeffler
1908	Chicago	21-2	Joseph Raycroft	1955	San Francisco	28-1	Phil Woolpert
1909	Chicago	12-0	Joseph Raycroft	1956	San Francisco	29-0	Phil Woolpert
1910	Columbia	11-1	Harry Fisher	1957	North Carolina	32-0	Frank McGuire
1911	St. John's	14-0	Claude Allen	1958	Kentucky	23-6	Adolph Rupp
1912	Wisconsin	15-0	Doc Meanwell	1959	California	25-4	Pete Newell
1913	Navy	9-0	Louis Wenzell	1960	Ohio St.	25-3	Fred Taylor
1914	Wisconsin	15-0	Doc Meanwell	1961	Cincinnati	27-3	Edwin Jucker
1915	Illinois	16-0	Ralph Jones	1962	Cincinnati	29-2	Edwin Jucker
1916	Wisconsin	20-1	Doc Meanwell	1963	Loyola (IL)	29-2	George Ireland
1917	Washington St.	25-1	Doc Bohler	1964	UCLA	30-0	John Wooden
1918	Syracuse	16-1	Edmund Dollard	1965	UCLA	28-2	John Wooden
1919	Minnesota	13-0	Louis Cooke	1966	Texas Western	28-1	Don Haskins
1920	Pennsylvania	22-1	Lon Jourdet	1967	UCLA	30-0	John Wooden
1921	Pennsylvania	21-2	Edward McNichol	1968	UCLA	29-1	John Wooden
1922	Kansas	16-2	Phog Allen	1969	UCLA	29-1	John Wooden
1923	Kansas	17-1	Phog Allen	1970	UCLA	28-2	John Wooden
1924	North Carolina	25-0	Bo Shepard	1971	UCLA	29-1	John Wooden
1925	Princeton	21-2	Al Wittmer	1972	UCLA	30-0	John Wooden
1926	Syracuse	19-1	Lew Andreas	1973	UCLA	30-0	John Wooden
1927	Notre Dame	19-1	George Keogan	1974	N. Carol. St.	30-1	Norm Sloan
1928	Pittsburgh	21-0	Doc Carlson	1975	UCLA	28-3	John Wooden
1929	Montana St.	36-2	Shubert Dyche	1976	Indiana	32-0	Bobby Knight
1930	Pittsburgh	23-2	Doc Carlson	1977	Marquette	25-7	Al McGuire
1931	Northwestern	16-1	Dutch Lonborg	1978	Kentucky	30-2	Joe B. Hall
1932	Purdue	17-1	Piggy Lambert	1979	Michigan St.	26-6	Jud Heathcote
1933	Kentucky	20-3	Adolph Rupp	1980	Louisville	33-3	Denny Crum
1934	Wyoming	26-3	Dutch Witte	1981	Indiana	26-9	Bobby Knight
1935	New York	18-1	Howard Cann	1982	North Carolina	32-2	Dean Smith
1936	Notre Dame	22-2-1	George Keogan	1983	N. Carol. St.	28-8	Jim Valvano
1937	Stanford	25-2	John Bunn	1984	Georgetown	34-3	John Thompson
1938	Temple	23-2	James Usilton	1985	Villanova	25-10	Rollie Massimino
1939	Oregon	29-5	Howard Hobson	1986	Louisville	32-7	Denny Crum
1940	Indiana	20-3	Branch McCracken	1987	Indiana	30-4	Bobby Knight
1941	Wisconsin	20-3	Bud Foster	1988	Kansas	27-11	Larry Brown
1942	Stanford	28-4	Everett Dean	1989	Michigan	30-7	Steve Fisher
1943	Wyoming	31-2	Everett Shelton	1990	UNLV	35-5	Jerry Tarkanian
1944	Utah	22-4	Vadal Peterson	1991	Duke	32-7	Mike Krzyzewski
1945	Oklahoma A&M	27-4	Hank Iba	1992	Duke	34-2	Mike Krzyzewski
1946	Oklahoma A&M	31-2	Hank Iba	1993	North Carolina	34-4	Dean Smith
1947	Holy Cross	27-3	Doggie Julian				

FINAL FOUR RESULTS

YEAR	CHAMPION	FINALS OPP.	SCORE	RUNNER-UP	RUNNER-UP
1939	Oregon	Ohio St.	46-33	Oklahoma	Villanova
1940	Indiana	Kansas	60-42	Duquesne	Southern Cal.
1941	Wisconsin	Washington St.	39-34	Arkansas	Pittsburgh
1942	Stanford	Dartmouth	53-38	Colorado	Kentucky
1943	Wyoming	Georgetown	46-34	DePaul	Texas
1944	Utah	Dartmouth	42-40 (OT)	Iowa St.	Ohio St.
1945	Oklahoma A&M	New York	49-45	Arkansas	Ohio St.
1946	Oklahoma A&M	North Carolina	43-40	Ohio St.	California
1947	Holy Cross	Oklahoma	58-47	Texas	CCNY
1948	Kentucky	Baylor	58-42	Holy Cross	Kansas St.
1949	Kentucky	Oklahoma A&M	46-36	Illinois	Oregon St.
1950	CCNY	Bradley	71-68	N. Carol. St.	Baylor
1951	Kentucky	Kansas St.	68-58	Illinois	Oklahoma A&M
1952	Kansas	St. John's	80-63	Illinois	Santa Clara
1953	Indiana	Kansas	69-68	Washington	Louisiana St.
1954	La Salle	Bradley	92-76	Penn St.	Southern Cal.
1955	San Francisco	La Salle	77-63	Colorado	Iowa
1956	San Francisco	Iowa	83-71	Temple	SMU
1957	North Carolina	Kansas	54-53 (3 OT)	San Francisco	Michigan St.
1958	Kentucky	Seattle	84-72	Temple	Kansas St.
1959	California	West Virginia	71-70	Cincinnati	Louisville
1960	Ohio St.	California	75-55	Cincinnati	New York
1961	Cincinnati	Ohio St.	70-65 (OT)	St. Joe's (PA)	Utah
1962	Cincinnati	Ohio St.	71-59	Wake Forest	UCLA
1963	Loyola (IL)	Cincinnati	60-58 (OT)	Duke	Oregon St.
1964	UCLA	Duke	98-83	Michigan	Kansas St.
1965	UCLA	Michigan	91-80	Princeton	Wichita St.
1966	Texas Western	Kentucky	72-65	Duke	Utah
1967	UCLA	Dayton	79-64	Houston	North Carolina
1968	UCLA	North Carolina	78-55	Ohio St.	Houston
1969	UCLA	Purdue	92-72	Drake	North Carolina
1970	UCLA	Jacksonville	80-69	New Mexico St.	St. Bonaventure
1971	UCLA	Villanova	68-62	W. Kentucky	Kansas
1972	UCLA	Florida St.	81-76	North Carolina	Louisville
1973	UCLA	Memphis St.	87-66	Indiana	Providence
1974	N. Carol. St.	Marquette	76-64	UCLA	Kansas
1975	UCLA	Kentucky	92-85	Louisville	Syracuse
1976	Indiana	Michigan	86-68	UCLA	Rutgers
1977	Marquette	North Carolina	67-59	UNLV	N.C.-Charlotte
1978	Kentucky	Duke	94-88	Arkansas	Notre Dame
1979	Michigan St.	Indiana St.	75-64	DePaul	Pennsylvania
1980	Louisville	UCLA	59-54	Purdue	Iowa
1981	Indiana	North Carolina	63-50	Virginia	Louisiana St.
1982	North Carolina	Georgetown	63-62	Houston	Louisville
1983	N. Carol. St.	Houston	54-52	Georgia	Louisville
1984	Georgetown	Houston	84-75	Kentucky	Virginia
1985	Villanova	Georgetown	66-64	Memphis St.	St. John's
1986	Louisville	Duke	72-69	Kansas	Louisiana St.
1987	Indiana	Syracuse	74-73	Providence	UNLV
1988	Kansas	Oklahoma	83-79	Arizona	Duke
1989	Michigan	Seton Hall	80-79 (OT)	Duke	Illinois
1990	UNLV	Duke	103-73	Arkansas	Georgia Tech
1991	Duke	Kansas	72-65	North Carolina	UNLV
1992	Duke	Michigan	71-51	Indiana	Cincinnati
1993	North Carolina	Michigan	77-71	Kansas	Kentucky

DIVISION I CAREER LEADERS

POINTS

3,667	Pete Maravich, Louisiana St.
3,249	Freeman Williams, Portland St.
3,217	Lionel Simmons, La Salle
3,165	Alphonso Ford, Miss. Valley St.
3,066	Harry Kelly, Texas Southern
3,008	Hersey Hawkins, Bradley
2,973	Oscar Robertson, Cincinnati
2,951	Danny Manning, Kansas
2,914	Alfredrick Hughes, Loyola (IL)
2,884	Elvin Hayes, Houston

SCORING AVERAGE

44.2	Pete Maravich, Louisiana St.
34.6	Austin Carr, Notre Dame
33.8	Oscar Robertson, Cincinnati
33.1	Calvin Murphy, Niagara
32.7	Dwight Lamar, S.W. Louisiana
32.5	Frank Selvy, Furman
32.3	Rick Mount, Purdue
32.1	Darrell Floyd, Furman
32.0	Nick Werkman, Seton Hall
31.5	Willie Humes, Idaho St.

REBOUNDS

2,201	Tom Gola, La Salle
2,030	Joe Holup, George Washington
1,916	Charlie Slack, Marshall
1,884	Ed Conlin, Fordham
1,802	Dickie Hemric, Wake Forest
1,751	Paul Silas, Creighton
1,716	Art Quimby, Connecticut
1,688	Jerry Harper, Alabama
1,679	Jeff Cohen, William & Mary
1,675	Steve Hamilton, Morehead St.

ASSISTS

1,076	Bobby Hurley, Duke
1,038	Chris Corchiani, N. Carolina St.
983	Keith Jennings, E. Tennessee St.
960	Sherman Douglas, Syracuse
950	Greg Anthony, Portland & UNLV
938	Gary Payton, Oregon St.
894	Andre LaFleur, Northeastern
884	Jim Les, Bradley
883	Frank Smith, Old Dominion
877	Taurence Chisholm, Delaware

STEALS

376	Eric Murdock, Providence
341	Michael Anderson, Drexel
341	Ken Robertson, New Mex. & Clev. St.
334	Keith Jennings, E. Tennessee St.
329	Greg Anthony, Portland & UNLV
328	Chris Corchiani, N. Carolina St.
321	Gary Payton, Oregon St.
314	Mark Woods, Wright St.
310	Scott Burrell, Connecticut
304	Elliot Perry, Memphis St.

BLOCKED SHOTS

453	Alonzo Mourning, Georgetown
419	Rodney Blake, St. Joseph's (PA)
412	Shaquille O'Neal, Louisiana St.
409	Kevin Roberson, Vermont
392	Tim Perry, Temple
374	Pervis Ellison, Louisville
365	Acie Earl, Iowa
354	Dikembe Mutombo, Georgetown
351	David Robinson, Navy
346	Charles Smith, Pittsburgh

FIELD GOAL PCT.

68.5	Steve Scheffler, Purdue
67.8	Steve Johnson, Oregon St.
66.8	Murray Brown, Florida St.
66.5	Lee Campbell, S.W. Missouri St.
66.4	Warren Kidd, Middle Tenn. St.
66.2	Joe Senser, West Chester
65.6	Kevin Magee, California-Irvine
65.4	Orlando Phillips, Pepperdine
65.1	Bill Walton, UCLA
64.8	William Herndon, Massachusetts

FREE THROW PCT.

90.9	Greg Starrick, Kentucky & S. Illinois
90.1	Jack Moore, Nebraska
90.0	Steve Henson, Kansas St.
89.8	Steve Alford, Indiana
89.8	Bob Lloyd, Rutgers
89.5	Jim Barton, Dartmouth
89.2	Tommy Boyer, Arkansas
88.8	Rob Robbins, New Mexico
88.5	Sean Miller, Pittsburgh
88.5	Ron Perry, Holy Cross

3-PT FIELD GOAL PCT.

49.7	Tony Bennett, Wisc.-Green Bay
49.3	Keith Jennings, E. Tennessee St.
47.5	Kirk Manns, Michigan St.
47.2	Tim Locum, Wisconsin
46.6	David Olson, Eastern Illinois
46.0	Sean Jackson, Ohio & Princeton
46.0	Barry Booker, Vanderbilt
45.9	Kevin Booth, Mt. St. Mary's
45.9	Dave Calloway, Monmouth (NJ)
45.8	Tony Ross, San Diego St.

MOST VICTORIES, COACH

875	Adolph Rupp
774	Dean Smith
767	Hank Iba
759	Ed Diddle
746	Phog Allen
724	Ray Meyer
664	John Wooden
657	Ralph Miller
642	Marv Harshman
627	Don Haskins
627	Norm Sloan

DIVISION I SEASON RECORDS

POINTS

1,381	Pete Maravich, Louisiana St.	1970
1,214	Elvin Hayes, Houston	1968
1,209	Frank Selvy, Furman	1954
1,148	Pete Maravich, Louisiana St.	1969
1,138	Pete Maravich, Louisiana St.	1968
1,131	Bo Kimble, Loyola Marymount	1990
1,125	Hersey Hawkins, Bradley	1988
1,106	Austin Carr, Notre Dame	1970
1,101	Austin Carr, Notre Dame	1971
1,090	Otis Birdsong, Houston	1977

SCORING AVERAGE

44.5	Pete Maravich, Louisiana St.	1970
44.2	Pete Maravich, Louisiana St.	1969
43.8	Pete Maravich, Louisiana St.	1968
41.7	Frank Selvy, Furman	1954
40.1	Johnny Neumann, Mississippi	1971
38.8	Freeman Williams, Portland St.	1977
38.8	Billy McGill, Utah	1962
38.2	Calvin Murphy, Niagara	1968
38.1	Austin Carr, Notre Dame	1970
38.0	Austin Carr, Notre Dame	1971

REBOUNDS

734	Walter Dukes, Seton Hall	1953
652	Leroy Wright, Pacific	1959
652	Tom Gola, La Salle	1954
645	Charlie Tyra, Louisville	1956
631	Paul Silas, Creighton	1964
624	Elvin Hayes, Houston	1968
621	Artis Gilmore, Jacksonville	1970
618	Tom Gola, La Salle	1955
612	Ed Conlin, Fordham	1953
611	Art Quimby, Connecticut	1955

ASSISTS

406	Mark Wade, Nevada-Las Vegas	1987
399	Avery Johnson, Southern	1988
373	Anthony Manuel, Bradley	1988
333	Avery Johnson, Southern	1987
328	Mark Jackson, St. John's	1986
326	Sherman Douglas, Syracuse	1989
310	Greg Anthony, Nevada-Las Vegas	1991
309	Reid Gettys, Houston	1984
305	Carl Golston, Loyola (IL)	1985
310	Sam Crawford, New Mexico St.	1993

STEALS

150	Mookie Blaylock, Oklahoma	1988
142	Aldwin Ware, Florida A&M	1988
139	Darron Brittman, Chicago St.	1986
138	Nadav Henefeld, Connecticut	1990
131	Mookie Blaylock, Oklahoma	1989

130	Ronn McMahon, Eastern Washington	1990
124	Marty Johnson, Towson St.	1988
120	Jim Paguaga, St. Francis (NY)	1986
114	Tony Fairley, Charleston So.	1987
112	Scott Burrell, Connecticut	1991

BLOCKED SHOTS

207	David Robinson, Navy	1986
177	Shawn Bradley, Brigham Young	1991
169	Alonzo Mourning, Georgetown	1989
160	Alonzo Mourning, Georgetown	1992
157	Shaquille O'Neal, Louisiana St.	1992
151	Dikembe Mutombo, Georgetown	1991
144	David Robinson, Navy	1987
143	Cedric Lewis, Maryland	1991
140	Shaquille O'Neal, Louisiana St.	1991
139	Kevin Roberson, Vermont	1992

FIELD GOAL PCT.

74.6	Steve Johnson, Oregon St.	1981
72.2	Dwayne Davis, Florida	1989
71.3	Keith Walker, Utica	1985
71.0	Steve Johnson, Oregon St.	1980
70.4	Oliver Miller, Arkansas	1991
70.3	Alan Williams, Princeton	1987
70.2	Mark McNamara, California	1982
70.0	Warren Kidd, Middle Tenn. St.	1991
70.0	Pete Freeman, Akron	1991
69.9	Joe Senser, West Chester	1977

FREE THROW PCT.

95.9	Craig Collins, Penn St.	1985
95.0	Rod Foster, UCLA	1982
94.4	Carlos Gibson, Marshall	1978
94.2	Jim Barton, Dartmouth	1986
93.9	Jack Moore, Nebraska	1982
93.5	Rob Robbins, New Mexico	1990
93.3	Tommy Boyer, Arkansas	1962
93.1	Damon Goodwin, Dayton	1986
92.9	Brian Magid, George Washington	1980
92.9	Mike Joseph, Bucknell	1990

3-PT FIELD GOAL PCT.

63.4	Glenn Tropf, Holy Cross	1988
63.2	Sean Wightman, Western Michigan	1992
59.2	Keith Jennings, E. Tenn. St.	1991
58.5	Dave Calloway, Monmouth	1989
57.3	Steve Kerr, Arizona	1988
57.1	Reginald Jones, Prairie View	1987
56.3	Joel Tribelhorn, Colorado St.	1989
56.0	Mike Joseph, Bucknell	1988
55.7	Christian Laettner, Duke	1992
54.8	Reginald Jones, Prairie View	1988

DIVISION I GAME RECORDS

POINTS

72	Kevin Bradshaw, U.S. Intl. vs. Loyola Mary.	1991
69	Pete Maravich, Louisiana St. vs. Alabama	1970
68	Calvin Murphy, Niagara vs. Syracuse	1968
66	Jay Handlan, Washington & Lee vs. Furman	1951
66	Pete Maravich, Louisiana St. vs. Tulane	1969
66	Anthony Roberts, Oral Rob. vs. N.C. A&T	1977
65	Anthony Roberts, Oral Roberts vs. Oregon	1977
65	Scott Haffner, Evansville vs. Dayton	1989
64	Pete Maravich, Louisiana St. vs. Kentucky	1970
63	Johnny Neumann, Mississippi St. vs. LSU	1971
63	Hersey Hawkins, Bradley vs. Detroit	1988
21	Anthony Manuel, Bradley vs. Cal.-Irvine	1987
21	Avery Johnson, Southern vs. Alabama St.	1988

REBOUNDS

51	Bill Chambers, William & Mary vs. Virginia	1953
43	Charlie Slack, Marshall vs. Morris Harvey	1954
42	Tom Heinsohn, Holy Cross vs. Boston Coll.	1955
40	Art Quimby, Connecticut vs. Boston U.	1955
39	Maurice Stokes, St. Fran. (PA) vs. J. Carroll	1955
39	Dave DeBusschere, Detroit vs. C. Michigan	1960
39	Keith Swagerty, Pacific vs. Cal.-Santa Barb.	1965

ASSISTS

22	Tony Fairley, Charleston So. vs. Arms. St.	1987
22	Avery Johnson, Southern vs. Texas South.	1988
22	Sherman Douglas, Syracuse vs. Providence	1989
21	Mark Wade, Nevada-Las Vegas vs. Navy	1986
21	Kelvin Scarborough, New Mexico vs. Hawaii	1987

STEALS

13	Mookie Blaylock, Oklahoma vs. Centenary	1987
13	Mookie Blaylock, Oklahoma vs. Loyola Mary.	1988
12	Kenny Robertson, Cleveland St. vs. Wagner	1988
12	Terry Evans, Oklahoma vs. Florida A&M	1993
11	Darron Brittman, Chicago St. vs. McKendree	1986
11	Darron Brittman, Chicago St. vs. St. Xavier	1986
11	Marty Johnson, Towson St. vs. Bucknell	1988
11	Aldwin Ware, Florida A&M vs. Tuskegee	1988
11	Mark Macon, Temple vs. Notre Dame	1989
11	Carl Thomas, E. Michigan vs. Chicago St.	1991
11	Ron Arnold, St. Fran. (NY) vs. Mt. St. Mary's	1993

BLOCKED SHOTS

14	David Robinson, Navy vs. N.C.-Wilmington	1986
14	Shawn Bradley, BYU vs. E. Kentucky	1990
13	Kevin Roberson, Vermont vs. New Hamp.	1992
12	David Robinson, Navy vs. James Madison	1986
12	Derrick Lewis, Maryland vs. James Madison	1987
12	Rodney Blake, St. Joseph's (PA) vs. Cle. St.	1987
12	Walter Palmer, Dartmouth vs. Harvard	1988
12	Alan Ogg, Alabama-Birm. vs. Florida A&M	1988
12	Dikembe Mutombo, Georget. vs. St. John's	1989
12	Shaquille O'Neal, LSU vs. Loyola Mary.	1990
12	Cedric Lewis, Maryland vs. South Florida	1991

DIVISION I WINNINGEST TEAMS

ALL-TIME WINS

	YRS	WINS
North Carolina	83	1,570
Kentucky	90	1,560
Kansas	95	1,515
St. John's	86	1,482
Duke	88	1,435
Oregon St.	92	1,415
Temple	97	1,393
Notre Dame	88	1,362
Pennsylvania	92	1,362
Syracuse	92	1,360
Indiana	93	1,329
Washington	91	1,318
UCLA	74	1,294
Western Kentucky	74	1,284
Princeton	93	1,279
Fordham	90	1,275
West Virginia	84	1,262
Purdue	95	1,257
North Carolina St.	81	1,254
Utah	85	1,248

ALL-TIME WINNING PCT.

	W	L	T	PCT
Nevada-Las Vegas	747	227	0	.767
Kentucky	1,560	506	1	.755
North Carolina	1,570	564	0	.736
St. John's	1,482	635	0	.700
UCLA	1,294	577	0	.692
Kansas	1,515	689	0	.687
Western Kentucky	1,284	605	0	.680
Syracuse	1,360	644	0	.679
Duke	1,435	703	0	.671
DePaul	1,134	557	0	.671
Notre Dame	1,362	701	1	.660
Louisville	1,229	654	0	.653
La Salle	1,045	559	0	.651
Indiana	1,329	711	0	.651
Houston	867	467	0	.650
Arkansas	1,141	623	0	.647
Temple	1,393	761	0	.647
Weber St.	564	309	0	.646
Illinois	1,245	690	0	.643
North Carolina St.	1,254	698	0	.642